March 9–12, 2011
Dallas, Texas, USA

Association for
Computing Machinery

Advancing Computing as a Science & Profession

SIGCSE'11

Proceedings of the 42nd ACM Technical Symposium on
Computer Science Education

Sponsored by:

ACM SIGCSE

Editors:

Thomas J. Cortina, Carnegie Mellon University
Ellen L. Walker, Hiram College
Laurie Smith King, College of the Holy Cross
David R. Musicant, Carleton College
Lester I. McCann, The University of Arizona

Association for
Computing Machinery

Advancing Computing as a Science & Profession

The Association for Computing Machinery
2 Penn Plaza, Suite 701
New York, New York 10121-0701

ISBN: 978-1-4503-0500-6

Additional copies may be ordered prepaid from:

ACM Order Department
PO Box 11405
New York, NY 10286-1405

Phone: 1-800-342-6626 (USA and Canada)
+1-212-626-0500 (all other countries)
Fax: +1-212-944-1318
E-mail: acmhelp@acm.org

ACM Order Number: 457110

Printed in the USA

Message from the SIGCSE Chair

Welcome to the greatest computer science education show on Earth! If this is your first SIGCSE Technical Symposium, you will soon know what I'm talking about. If you are a regular attendee, well, of course you already know this! There are several good computing education conferences. SIGCSE sponsors the top three, and of the three, this meeting offers the most diverse program to the largest audience.

I attended my first symposium in 1987 and have attended every one since 1992. Over the years, the symposium has grown from a small conference held in conjunction with other ACM conferences, to an international meeting attended by more than 1100 CS educators. Its program has evolved to contain many varied educational sessions: workshops, papers, panels, posters, special sessions, exhibits, vendor sessions, birds-of-a-feather sessions, keynote addresses, the annual SIGCSE business meeting, and the annual UPE meeting and award ceremony. This symposium is the place to hear meaningful keynote addresses, to learn about cutting-edge technology, resources and pedagogy, to renew friendships, to meet future collaborators, and to have fun and learn lots while you are doing it.

How can we pack so much into three days? It takes a lot of work by many people. The ring masters of this, the 42nd SIGCSE Technical Symposium, are Thomas Cortina, Carnegie Mellon University, and Ellen Walker, Hiram College. Both have worked for more than two years on all aspects of this conference. They have assembled the team required to make everything happen – a committee of 26 CS educators and SIGCSE members. On behalf of the SIGCSE Board and membership, I thank Tom, Ellen and each member of the 42nd SIGCSE organizational committee for this fabulous event. Last but not least, the perennial committee members, on whom the SIGCSE board and the conference chairs depend year in and year out to handle conference registration (Lynn Degler, Cary Laxer, and Larry Merkle), to manage the conference database (Henry Walker and John Dooley) and to coordinate with exhibitors (Susan Rodger). We thank all of you for your tireless efforts.

I encourage you, the reader, to consider becoming more involved in the SIGCSE community and the workings of the SIGCSE organization. Being here gives you a great opportunity to do that. Try to talk to new people, make new friends, and start new collaborations.

Finally, make sure you attend the annual SIGCSE business meeting. In this 45-minute meeting, your SIGCSE Board members will present the "state of the organization" and invite your comments. This meeting will be held Friday, March 11, from 5:10 - 5:55 pm in Lonestar A4. We sincerely hope to see you there.

Enjoy the show!

Renée McCauley
College of Charleston
SIGCSE Chair, 2010-2013

Message from the Symposium and Program Chairs

Welcome to the proceedings of the 42nd ACM Technical Symposium on Computer Science Education, or SIGCSE 2011, where you will find the archival record of over one hundred papers as well as multiple other session formats that document the latest in computer science education: research, tool building, teaching, curriculum and philosophy. This year, a number of sessions address the symposium theme of "reaching out". We need to reach out to colleagues in other fields, to develop interdisciplinary courses and research projects that integrate computer science and other fields, enriching both. We need to reach out to create programs that attract and educate the next generation of computer scientists, especially currently underserved populations. We need to reach out to policy makers, educating them on the importance and promise of our discipline. Finally, we need to reach out to each other, as always, to share our best ideas and experiences.

We are pleased to announce the winners of the two annual SIGCSE awards. Trustee Professor Matthias Felleisen of Northeastern University will receive the SIGCSE award for Outstanding Contribution to CS Education, and will provide the opening keynote address. Gordon Davies of the Open University will accept the SIGCSE Award for Lifetime Service to the CS Education Community and speak at our First Timer's Lunch. In addition, we've invited two keynote speakers to highlight our "reaching out" theme. Susan Landau, fellow at the Radcliffe Institute for Advanced Study at Harvard University, will give Friday's address on "*A Computer Scientist Goes to Washington: How to be Effective in a World Where Facts are 10% of the Equation.*" Luis von Ahn, professor at Carnegie Mellon University and researcher at Google, will address Saturday's luncheon with "*Three Human Computation Projects.*"

Symposium statistics are presented below. Many thanks to the authors, reviewers, and Program Committee members whose enormous and vital service generated this program. This year's program includes the usual wide selection of events, including the First-Timer's Lunch and Evening Reception on Thursday and the SIGCSE luncheon on Saturday. Our exhibit hall features a number of exhibitors showcasing the latest in hardware, software tools, textbooks and educational programs and research. We continue to increase accessibility at SIGCSE 2011 for the deaf and hard of hearing.

Proposal type	*Accepted*	*Received*	*Acceptance Rate*
Paper	107	315	34 %
Panel/Special Session	22	38	58 %
Workshop	35	78	45 %
Poster	48	66	73 %
Birds of a Feather	36	48	75 %
Video	7	10	70 %

We are offering our traditional Wednesday preconference workshops for department chairs and new educators, and we are excited about our additional Wednesday pre-symposium events on: Program By Design - Bootstrap, TeachScheme, ReachJava, and Beyond, the CSTA Source Web Repository Cataloging Workshop, Programming with Alice 2.2 and 3, Microsoft Research's Hawaii Project, Innovative Approaches to Introducing Computer Science, Managing the Academic Career for Women Faculty in Undergraduate Computing Programs, SIGCAS Open Meeting, Teaching Professional Ethics in Computer Science, and the 3rd Annual Humanitarian FOSS Symposium. On Friday during the lunch period, the UPE will present their annual Abacus Award to Donald Knuth, with a special talk by the awardee. On Saturday, top undergraduate and graduate students will present their work at the ACM SIGCSE Student Research Competition, managed by Ann Sobel.

Our sincere thanks go out to the people who made this Symposium extraordinary. First, our symposium committee: Ruth Anderson, Stacey Armstrong, Tim Bell, Dennis Bouvier, Tzu-Yi Chen, Pam Cutter, Adrienne Decker, Lynn Degler, John Dooley, Mary Ann Egan, Kurt Eiselt, Scott Grissom, Michael T. Helmick, Judy Hromcik, Deborah Hwang, Cary Laxer, Lester I. McCann, Larry Merkle, Brianna Morrison, Kristine Nagel, Susan Rodger, RoxAnn Stalvey, Kimberly Voll, Henry Walker, and Jian Zhang. Additional thanks go to our Associate Program Chairs who provided meta-reviews for papers: John Barr, Tracy Camp, Boots Cassell, Steve Edwards, Mike Goldweber, Chuck Leska, Sara Miner More, Sam Rebelsky, and Ingrid Russell. In honor of our host city, Dallas, we are running a new event this year: the Robot Hoedown and Rodeo, with special thanks to the trail bosses, Jennifer Kay and Tom Lauwers. We'd also like to thank all of our student volunteers who help us with all of the small details.

In difficult economic times, we extend a *very* grateful thank you to our supporters, vendors, exhibitors and in-kind donors whose participation literally made the symposium possible. We especially thank platinum plus supporter Microsoft, platinum supporters Intel and Google, and gold supporters IBM and Amazon. Special thanks go to Dorothea Heck and her team at D. Lawrence Planners for coordinating an outstanding exhibition and to Susan Rodger, our amazing supporter/exhibitor liaison for the last three years.

We received support and guidance from SIGCSE Symposium Site Coordinators Bob Beck and Scott Grissom, SIGCSE President Renee McCauley, former SIGCSE President Barbara Boucher Owens, and the entire SIGCSE Board, as well as from Ashley Cozzi of ACM. Lisa Tolles of Sheridan Printing Company brought all materials together. The City of Dallas provided valuable information and prizes through their excellent Convention and Visitor's Bureau, with special thanks to Heather Lovato. We were supported at the Sheraton Dallas by Mark Story, Victor Aguilar, Jerry Balousek and Jeffrey Webb.

Special thanks to our home institutions for providing needed resources: Carnegie Mellon University, Hiram College, College of the Holy Cross and Carleton College. We genuinely hope you enjoy the Symposium and find the SIGCSE 2011 Proceedings of use for your work now and your future projects and activities.

Symposium Chairs
Thomas J. Cortina, *Carnegie Mellon University*
Ellen L. Walker, *Hiram College*

Program Chairs
Laurie Smith King, *College of the Holy Cross*
David R. Musicant, *Carleton College*

Table of Contents

Session 11: Teaching Programming: Non-Traditional Approaches

Session Chair: Khadija Stewart *(DePauw University)*

Session 12: Assessing and Reviewing

Session Chair: David Ranum *(Luther College)*

Session 13: Algorithms

Session Chair: Delvin Defoe *(Rose-Hulman Institute of Technology)*

Session 14: Software Engineering

Session Chair: Rowena Turner *(Intel Corporation)*

Session 15: Panel

Session Moderator: Henry M. Walker *(Grinnell University)*

Session 16: Panel

Session Moderator: Mehran Sahami *(Stanford University)*

Keynote Address 2

Session Chairs: Laurie Smith King *(College of the Holy Cross)*, David R. Musicant *(Carleton College)*

Session 22: Panel

Session Moderator: Jacob D. Furst *(DePaul University)*

Session 23: Special Session

Session Chair: Sue Fitzgerald *(Metropolitan State University)*

Session 24: Special Session

Session Chair: J. Philip East *(University of Northern Iowa)*

Session 25: Computational Thinking

Session Chair: Jill Pala *(Girls Preparatory School)*

Session 26: Discrete Mathematics

Session Chair: Sara Miner More *(McDaniel College)*

Session 27: Operating Systems and Databases

Session Chair: Ingrid Russell *(University of Hartford)*

Session 46: Communication Skills

Session Chair: Daniel Stevenson *(University of Wisconsin - Eau Claire)*

Session 47: Teacher Endorsement and Preparation

Session Chair: Sherri Goings *(Carleton College)*

Session 48: Expanding the Community

Session Chair: Chun Liew *(Lafayette College)*

Session 49: Mobile Computing

Session Chair: Kent Lee *(Luther College)*

SIGCSE 2011 Symposium Committee

Thomas J. Cortina, Symposium Co-Chair
Carnegie Mellon University

Laurie Smith King, Program Co-Chair
College of the Holy Cross

John Barr, Associate Program Chair
Ithaca College

Boots Cassel, Associate Program Chair
Villanova

Mike Goldweber, Associate Program Chair
Xavier University

Sara Miner More, Associate Program Chair
McDaniel College

Ingrid Russell, Associate Program Chair
University of Hartford

Ruth E. Anderson, Workshops
University of Washington

Lester I. McCann, Publications
The University of Arizona

Larry Merkle, Registration
Wright State University

Tzu-Yi Chen, Posters
Pomona College

Dennis Bouvier, Videos
Southern Illinois University - Edwardsville

Brianna Morrison, Student Volunteers and Activities
Southern Polytechnic State University

Henry Walker, Database Administrator
Grinnell College

Michael T. Helmick, Webmaster
Google

Kimberly Voll, Kid's Camp Coordinator
University of British Columbia

Susan Rodger, Supporter/Exhibitor Liaison
Duke University

Stacey Armstrong, K-12 Liaison
Cypress Woods High School

Kristine Nagel, Pre-Conference Event Liaison
Georgia Gwinnett College

Jennifer Kay, Robot Hoedown Head Wrangler
Rowan University

Ann Sobel, Student Research Competition
Miami University (Ohio)

Ellen L. Walker, Symposium Co-Chair
Hiram College

David R. Musicant, Program Co-Chair
Carleton College

Tracy Camp, Associate Program Chair
Colorado School of Mines

Steve Edwards, Associate Program Chair
Virginia Tech

Chuck Leska, Associate Program Chair
Randolph-Macon College

Sam Rebelsky, Associate Program Chair
Grinnell College

Pam Cutter, Panels and Special Sessions
Kalamazoo College

Adrienne Decker, Workshops
University at Buffalo (SUNY)

Cary Laxer, Registration
Rose-Hulman Institute of Technology

Lynn Degler, Registration
Rose-Hulman Institute of Technology

Deborah Hwang, Birds-of-a-Feather
University of Evansville

Scott Grissom, Treasurer
Grand Valley State University

Mary Anne Egan, Student Volunteers and Activities
Siena College

John Dooley, Database Administrator
Knox College

Kurt Eiselt, Evaluations
University of British Columbia

RoxAnn Stalvey, Kid's Camp Coordinator
College of Charleston

Tim Bell, International Liaison
University of Canterbury

Judy Hromcik, K-12 Liaison
Arlington High School

Jian Zhang, Local Arrangements
Texas Women's University

Tom Lauwers, Robot Hoedown Head Wrangler
Carnegie Mellon University

The SIGCSE 2011 logo was designed by Tom Cortina and Beatrice Anghelache (Carnegie Mellon University)

SIGCSE 2011 Board-Sponsored Pre-Symposium Events

New Educators Roundtable

Julie Zelenski, *Stanford University*; David Reed, *Creighton University*

New to teaching? Seeking advice and mentorship? Join us at the New Educators Roundtable (NER), a half-day workshop designed to mentor college and university faculty who are new to teaching. We welcome participants from across the entire teaching spectrum: tenure-track faculty at institutions where teaching is central, teaching-track faculty and lecturers, and graduate students who currently teach or are looking forward to an academic career. Come with your questions and concerns, learn from the experiences and best practices of sage elders, and build an international support group for your career. The roundtable will be held from 1:00 – 5:00 pm on Wednesday, March 9, 2011, before the SIGCSE Symposium.

Department Chairs' Pre-Symposium Workshop

Sandra J. DeLoatch, *Norfolk State University*; Frank Friedman, *Temple University*;
C. Dianne Martin, *George Washington University*

The Pre-Symposium Workshop for Department Chairs is an opportunity for all department chairs (experienced and inexperienced) to improve their understanding of their duties and their ability to perform them. Participants should also include those interested in becoming department chairs. Three experienced former department chairs will serve as resources for the group as the participants review and discuss the duties of the department chair and explore ways that chairs can do their jobs efficiently and effectively. Some specific discussion topics will include leadership styles, time management, legal issues, academic program assessment, and faculty promotion and tenure.

Upcoming Events

ITiCSE 2011

Technische Universität Darmstadt
Darmstadt, Germany
June 27–29, 2011
http://www.sigcse.org/iticse2011

Conference Chair
Guido Rößling - *TU Darmstadt*

ICER 2011

Providence, Rhode Island, USA
August 8–9, 2011
http://icer-conference.org/

General Chair
Kate Sanders, *Rhode Island College*

SIGCSE 2012

Raleigh, North Carolina, USA
February 29–March 3, 2012
http://sigcse.org/sigcse2012/

Symposium Co-Chairs
Laurie Smith King,
College of the Holy Cross
Dave Musicant, *Carleton College*

CALL FOR PARTICIPATION

SIGCSE 2012: Teaching, Learning, and Collaborating The 43rd ACM Technical Symposium on Computer Science Education

February 29 - March 3, 2012, Raleigh, North Carolina, USA

http://www.sigcse.org/sigcse2012

SIGCSE 2012 continues our long tradition of bringing together colleagues from around the world to present papers, panels, posters, special sessions, and workshops, and to discuss computer science education in birds-of-a-feather sessions and informal settings. The SIGCSE Technical Symposium addresses problems common among educators working to develop, implement and/or evaluate computing programs, curricula, and courses. The symposium provides a forum for sharing new ideas for syllabi, laboratories, and other elements of teaching and pedagogy, at all levels of instruction.

Our three-sided conference theme, "Teaching, Learning, and Collaborating," commemorates North Carolina's renowned "Research Triangle" where SIGCSE 2012 will be held. Teaching, learning, and collaborating occur inside and outside of the classroom, among various combinations of students, academics, industry professionals, and others.

PAPERS

Papers describe an educational research project, classroom experience, teaching technique, curricular initiative, or pedagogical tool. Two versions of a submission are required: a full version having author names and affiliations and an anonymous version for use in reviewing. Papers will undergo a blind reviewing process and must not exceed six pages. Authors will have approximately 25 minutes for their presentations, including questions and answers. At least one author of each accepted paper must register and attend the conference to present.

PANELS

Panels present multiple perspectives on a specific topic. To allow each panelist sufficient time to present his or her perspective and still enable audience participation, a panel will normally have at most four panelists, including one moderator. Panel submissions should include a list of the panelists, their affiliations, and a description of the topic, with brief position statements from panelists. Proposals with more than four panelists must provide a statement connecting the extra panelist to the effectiveness of the panel and must convincingly show that each panelist will be able to speak, and the audience able to respond, within the session time. Panel abstracts must not exceed two pages. A panel session is approximately 75 minutes long.

SPECIAL SESSIONS

Special sessions are your opportunity to customize and experiment with the SIGCSE conference format. Possible special sessions include a seminar on a new topic, a committee report, or a forum on curriculum issues. More generally, they must be 75 minutes in length, held in standard conference spaces, and justifiably distinct from the panel, paper, and poster tracks. Within those constraints, the form is yours to design. Special session abstracts must not exceed two pages.

WORKSHOPS

Workshops provide introductory and advanced topics to help make participants more effective teachers and scholars. Workshop proposals (including abstract) must not exceed two pages. Submissions must specify equipment needs (e.g., participant laptops or projector required) and any limitation on the number of participants. Workshops are scheduled for a three-hour session and are offered separately from the technical track session times.

BIRDS OF A FEATHER SESSIONS

Birds of a Feather (BOF) sessions provide an environment for colleagues with similar interests to meet for informal discussions. A maximum one-page description (including abstract) is requested to describe the informal discussion topic. A/V equipment will not be provided for these sessions. Approximately 45 minutes are allocated to each BOF topic.

POSTERS

Posters describe computer science education materials or research, particularly works in progress. Proposals (including abstract) are limited to two pages. Poster demonstrations are scheduled to permit one-on-one discussion with conference attendees, typically during session breaks. Prepared handouts are encouraged in order to share your work.

Association for Computing Machinery
Advancing Computing as a Science & Profession

SIGCSE
ACM Special Interest Group on Computer Science Education

IMPORTANT DUE DATES

Friday, September 2, 2011: *Paper, Panel, Special Session, and Workshop submissions*

Monday, October 24, 2011: *Birds of a Feather and Poster submissions*

PROGRAM COMMITTEE

Symposium Chairs

Laurie Smith King
College of the Holy Cross
lking@holycross.edu

Dave Musicant
Carleton College
dmusican@carleton.edu

Program Chairs

Tracy Camp
Colorado School of Mines
tcamp@mines.edu

Paul Tymann
Rochester Institute of Technology
ptt@cs.rit.edu

Panels and Special Sessions

Chuck Leska
Randolph Macon College
cleska@rmc.edu

Workshops

Adrienne Decker
University at Buffalo, SUNY
adrienne@buffalo.edu

Lester I. McCann
The University of Arizona
mccann@cs.arizona.edu

Publications

Brad Miller
Luther College
bmiller@luther.edu

Database Administrators

Henry Walker
Grinnell College
walker@cs.grinnell.edu

John Dooley
Knox College
jdooley@knox.edu

Registration

Cary Laxer
Rose-Hulman Institute of Technology

Lynn Degler
Rose-Hulman Institute of Technology

Larry Merkle
Wright State University

sigcse2012@csse.rose-hulman.edu

Posters

Kris Nagel
Georgia Gwinnett College
knagel@ggc.edu

Birds of a Feather

Olaf Hall-Holt
St. Olaf College
olaf@stolaf.edu

Student Volunteers and Student Activities

Mary Anne Egan
Siena College
maegan@siena.edu

Steven Huss-Lederman
Beloit College
huss@beloit.edu

Webmaster

Michael T. Helmick
Google
mike.helmick@gmail.com

Treasurer

Scott McElfresh
Wake Forest University
ScottMcElfresh@acm.org

Evaluations

Carl Alphonce
University at Buffalo, SUNY
alphonce@buffalo.edu

Kids Camp

Susan Fox
Macalester Collage
fox@macalester.edu

Sarah Monisha Pulimood
The College of New Jersey
pulimood@tcnj.edu

Support/Exhibitor Liaison

Susan Rodger
Duke University
rodger@cs.duke.edu

Pre-Conference Events Liaison

Briana Morrison
Southern Polytechnic State University
bmorriso@spsu.edu

K-12 Liaison

John Harrison
Princess Anne High School
Virginia Beach, VA
jharrison64@cox.net

International Liaison

Raymond Lister
University of Technology, Sydney
Raymond.Lister@uts.edu.au

Local Arrangements

Sarah Heckman
North Carolina State University
sarah_heckman@ncsu.edu

Student Research Competition

Ann Sobel
Miami University (Ohio)
sobelae@muohio.edu

Association for Computing Machinery
Advancing Computing as a Science & Profession

SIGCSE
ACM Special Interest Group on Computer Science Education

Recipients of the SIGCSE Award for Outstanding Contributions to Computer Science Education

1981 **William F. Atchison**, *University of Maryland*

1982 **Alan Perlis**, *Yale University*

1983 **Karl V. Karlstrom**, *Prentice-Hall*

1985 **Elliot I. Organick**, *University of Utah*

1986 **Donald Knuth**, *Stanford University*

1987 **Niklaus Wirth**, *ETH, Zurich*

1988 **Grace Murray Hopper**, *Rear Admiral, USN, Digital Equipment Corp.*

1989 **Edsger W. Dijkstra**, *The University of Texas at Austin*

1990 **Curriculum '68 Committee**:
William F. Atchison, Samuel D. Conte, John Hamblen, Thomas E. Hull, Thomas A. Keenan, William B. Kehl, Edward J. McClusey, Silvio O. Navarro, Werner Rheinboldt, Earl J. Schweppe, William Viavant, David M. Young, Jr.

1991 **David Gries**, *Cornell University*

1992 **Daniel D. McCraken**, *City College, City University of New York*

1993 **Alan C. Kay**, *Apple Computer*

1994 **Norman E. Gibbs**, *Software Engineering Institute*

1995 **Robert M. Aiken**, *Temple University*

1996 **Nell B. Dale**, *The University of Texas at Austin*

1997 **Andrew Tannenbaum**, *Vrije University*

1998 **William A. Wulf**, *University of Virginia and National Academy of Engineering*

1999 **Peter J. Denning**, *George Mason University*

2000 **Andries Van Dam**, *Brown University*

2001 **Allen B. Tucker**, *Bowdoin College*

2002 **Elliot Soloway**, *University of Michigan*

2003 **Eric Roberts**, *Stanford University*

2004 **Mordechai Ben-Ari**, *Weizmann Institute of Science*

2005 **Kim Bruce**, *Williams College*

2006 **Richard Pattis**, *Carnegie Mellon University*

2007 **Judith Gal-Ezer**, *Open University of Israel* and **John Hughes**, *University of Technology, Sydney*

2008 **Randy Pausch,** *Carnegie Mellon University*

2009 **Elliot B. Koffman,** *Temple University*

2010 **Sally Fincher,** *University of Kent, Canterbury*

2011 **Matthias Felleisen,** *Northeastern University*

Recipients of the SIGCSE Lifetime Service Award

1997 **Richard Austing**, *University of Maryland*
1998 **Della Bonnette**, *University of Southwestern Louisiana*
1999 **Robert Aiken**, *Temple University*
2000 **James E. Miller**, *University of Southern Mississippi*
2001 **Lillian N. (Boots) Cassel**, *Villanova University*
2002 **Joe Turner**, *Clemson University and Zayed University*
2003 **Harriet Taylor**, *National Science Foundation and Louisiana State University*
2004 **Bruce Klein**, *Grand Valley State University*
2005 **Andrew McGettrick**, *University of Strathclyde*
2006 **Joyce Currie Little**, *Towson State University*
2007 **John Impagliazzo**, *Hofstra University*
2008 **Dennis Frailey**, *Raytheon Corporation*
2009 **Michael J. Clancy**, *University of California, Berkeley*
2010 **Peter Denning**, *Naval Postgraduate School*
2011 **Gordon Davies**, *Open University*

SIGCSE 2011 Reviewers

Adel Abunawass, *University of West Georgia*
Ernest Ackermann, *University of Mary Washington*
Donald Acton, *University of British Columbia*
Raman Adaikkalavan, *Indiana University South Bend*
Victor Adamchik, *Carnegie Mellon University*
Elizabeth S. Adams, *James Madison University*
Evans Adams, *Fort Lewis College*
Joel Adams, *Calvin College*
Robert Adams, *Grand Valley State University*
Paul Addison, *Ivy Tech Community College*
Iwan Adhicandra, *University of Pisa*
Rajeev Agrawal, *North Carolina A&T State University*
Shakil Akhtar, *Clayton State University*
Paul Albee, *Central Michigan University*
Vicki Almstrum, *Univ. of Texas at Austin*
Carl Alphonce, *University at Buffalo, The State University of New York*
Jamal Alsabbagh, *Grand Valley State University*
Ruth Anderson, *University of Washington*
Stefan Andrei, *Lamar University*
Peter Andrews, *Eastern Illinois University*
Steven K. Andrianoff, *St. Bonaventure University*
Karen Anewalt, *University of Mary Washington*
Barbara Anthony, *Southwestern University*
Antonio Araujo, *Faculdade de Engenharia da Universidade do Porto*
Michal Armoni, *Weizmann Institute of Science*
David Arnow, *Brooklyn College*
Charles Ashbacher, *Charles Ashbacher Technologies*
Owen Astrachan, *Duke University*
Stephanie August, *Loyola Marymount University*
John Aycock, *University of Calgary*
Pavel Azalov, *Penn State*
Shiri Azenkot, *University of Washington*
Laura Baker, *St. Edward's University*
Doug Baldwin, *SUNY Geneseo*
Jie Bao, *University of Minnesota*
Catherine Bareiss, *Olivet Nazarene University*
Ian Barland, *Radford University*
David Barnes, *University of Kent*
Tiffany Barnes, *University of North Carolina at Charlotte*
Lewis Barnett, *University of Richmond*
N. Dwight Barnette, *Virginia Tech*
John Barr, *Ithaca College*
Valerie Barr, *Union College*
Joao Barros, *Instituto Politecnico de Beja - ESTIG*
Phillip Barry, *University of Minnesota*
Rebecca Bates, *Minnesota State University Mankato*
Michael Bauer, *University of Hawaii - Leeward Community College*
Robert Beck, *Villanova University*
Byron Weber Becker, *University of Waterloo*
Andrew Begel, *Microsoft Research*
John Beidler, *University of Scranton*
Tim Bell, *University of Canterbury*
Mordechai Ben-Ari, *Weizmann Institute of Science*
Jens Bennedsen, *Aarhus School of Engineering*
Chris Bennett, *University of Maine Farmington*
Susan Bergin, *National University of Ireland, Maynooth*
Seth Bergmann, *Rowan University*
Mikael Berndtsson, *University of Skovde*
Sanjukta Bhowmick, *University of Nebraska at Omaha*
Devi Prasad Bhukya, *Osmania University*
Robert Biddle, *Carleton University*
William Birmingham, *Grove City College*
M. Brian Blake, *Georgetown University*
Michael Blumenstein, *Griffith University*
Esmail Bonakdarian, *Franklin University*
William Booth, *Baylor University*
Matthew Boutell, *Rose-Hulman Institute of Technology*
Dennis Bouvier, *Southern Illinois University-Edwardsville*
Roger Boyle, *University of Leeds*
Stefan Brandle, *Taylor University*
Anna Bretscher, *University of Toronto at Scarborough*
Josef Breutzmann, *Wartburg College*
Monica Brockmeyer, *Wayne State University*
Kim Bruce, *Pomona College*
Renee Bryce, *Utah State University*
Dennis Brylow, *Marquette University*
Joel Brynielsson, *Royal Institute of Technology*
Suzanne Buchele, *Southwestern University*
Duane Buck, *Otterbein University*
Everett Bull, *Pomona College*
David Bunde, *Knox College*
Barry Burd, *Drew University*
Darci Burdge, *Nassau Community College*
Kevin Burger, *Arizona State University*
Gerald Burgess, *Western New Mexico University*
Vicky Bush, *University of Gloucestershire*
Caldeira Caldeira, *University of Evora*
Mary Elaine Califf, *Illinois State University*
Andre Paul Calitz, *Nelson Mandela Metropolitan University*
Debra Calliss, *Arizona State University*
Johan Calu, *KHBO*
Mario Camilleri, *University of Malta*
Tracy Camp, *Colorado School of Mines*
Daniel Canas, *Wake Forest University*
Angela Carbone, *Monash University*
James Caristi, *Valparaiso University*
Stephen Carl, *Sewanee: The University of the South*
Martin Carlisle, *US Air Force Academy*
Janet Carter, *University of Kent at Canterbury*
Lori Carter, *Point Loma Nazarene University*
Jeffrey Carver, *University of Alabama*
Lori Case, *University of Waterloo*
Steven Case, *University of the Virgin Islands*
Lillian N. Cassel, *Villanova University*
Mano Chad, *Utah State University*
Tim Chamillard, *University of Colorado at Colorado Springs*
Tat Chan, *Methodist University*
Maiga Chang, *Athabasca University*
Mahesh Chaudhari, *Arizona State University*
Ranjan Chaudhuri, *Eastern Michigan University*
Tom Cheatham, *Middle Tennessee State University*
Tzu-Yi Chen, *Pomona College*
Wei Kian Chen, *Champlain College*
Jimmy Chen, *Salt Lake Community College*
Peng-Wen Chen, *Oriental Institute of Technology*
Ping Chen, *University of Houston-Downtown*
Li-hsiang Cheo, *William Paterson University of New Jersey*
Chia-Chu Chiang, *University of Arkansas at Little Rock*
Donald Chinn, *University of Washington, Tacoma*

Jayan Kurian Chirayath, *Royal Melbourne Institute of Technology*
Radhouane Chouchane, *Columbus State University*
Vincent Cicirello, *Richard Stockton College*
John Cigas, *Park University*
Dawn Cizmar, *University of Texas at Austin*
Michael Clancy, *University of California, Berkeley*
Peter Clarke, *Florida International University*
Tony Clear, *Auckland University of Technology*
Daniel Cliburn, *University of the Pacific*
Joe Clifton, *University of Wisconsin, Platteville*
Curt Clifton, *Rose-Hulman Inst. of Technology*
Osvaldo Clua, *Universidad de Buenos Aires*
Marge Coahran, *Dickinson College*
Avi Cohen, *Ministry of Education*
Ben Coleman, *Moravian College*
Robert Cook, *Georgia Southern University*
Stephen Cooper, *Stanford University*
Peter Cooper, *Sam Houston State University*
Jean F. Coppola, *Pace University*
David Cordes, *University of Alabama*
Jose L. Cordova, *University of Louisiana at Monroe*
Marc Corliss, *Hobart & William Smith Colleges*
Lee Cornell, *Minnesota State University, Mankato*
Jill Courte, *Miami University Hamilton Campus*
Mary Courtney, *Pace University*
Michelle Craig, *University of Toronto*
Al Cripps, *Middle Tennessee State University*
James Cross, *Auburn University*
Mark Crouch, *Angelo State University*
Joyce Blair Crowell, *Belmont University*
Jose Cunha, *New University of Lisbon*
Steve Cunningham, *Brown Cunningham Associates*
Edwin P. Curran, *University of Ulster*
Jorge Filipe Custodio, *Universidade Nova Lisboa*
Robert Cutler, *Tutor Crossing*
Quintin Cutts, *University of Glasgow*
Lawrence D'Antonio, *Ramapo College of New Jersey*
Mohammad Dadfar, *Bowling Green State University*
Roy Daigle, *University of South Alabama*
Nell Dale, *University of Texas at Austin*
Andrew Dalton, *Western Carolina University*
Mats Daniels, *Uppsala University*
Douglas Dankel, *University of Florida*
Wanda Dann, *Ithaca College*
Andrew Danner, *Swarthmore College*
Andrea Danyluk, *Williams College*
Stephen Davies, *University of Mary Washington*
Janet Davis, *Grinnell College*
Renzo Davoli, *University of Bologna*
Susan Dean, *UMUC - Europe*
Hannah Mary Dee, *Grenoble Institute of Technology*
Katherine Deibel, *University of Washington - Seattle*
Rafael del Vado, *Universidad Complutense de Madrid*
William Denny, *McNeese State University*
Peter DePasquale, *The College of New Jersey*
Dorothy Deremer, *Montclair State University*
Molisa Derk, *Dickinson State University*
Yogesh Deshpande, *University of Western Sydney*
Lucia Dettori, *DePaul University*
Kamyar Dezhgosha, *University of Illinois at Springfield*
Michele Di Santo, *University of Sannio*
Paloma Diaz, *Universidad Carlos III de Madrid*
Martin Dick, *RMIT University*
Suzanne W. Dietrich, *Arizona State University*
Wei Ding, *University of Massachusetts-Boston*
Junhua Ding, *East Carolina University*
Adair Dingle, *Seattle University*
William Doane, *Bennington College*
Zachary Dodds, *Harvey Mudd College*
Michael Doherty, *University of the Pacific*
John Dooley, *Knox College*
Brian Dorn, *University of Hartford*
John Dougherty, *Haverford College*
Maureen Doyle, *Northern Kentucky University*
Peter Drexel, *Plymouth State University*
Deborah Dunn, *Stephen F. Austin State University*
Robert Duvall, *Duke University*
Shannon Duvall, *Elon University*
James Early, *SUNY Oswego*
J. Philip East, *University of Northern Iowa*
Jeffrey Edgington, *University of Denver*
Stephen Edwards, *Virginia Tech*
Roger Eggen, *University of North Florida*
Kurt Eiselt, *University of British Columbia*
Joseph Ekstrom, *Brigham Young University*
Hala ElAarag, *Stetson University*
Heidi J. C. Ellis, *Western New England College*
Stephanie Elzer, *Millersville University*
Richard Enbody, *Michigan State University*
Alec Engebretson, *Doane College*
Gerald Engel, *University of Connecticut, Stamford*
Eileen B. Entin, *Aptima, Inc.*
Ed C. Epp, *Intel Corp.*
Barbara Ericson, *Georgia Tech*
Daniel Ernst, *The University of Wisconsin - Eau Claire*
John Estell, *Ohio Northern University*
Yadran Eterovic, *Pontificia Universidad Catolica de Chile*
Henry Etlinger, *Rochester Institute of Technology*
Barry Fagin, *US Air Force Academy*
Ali Farahani, *National University*
Homma Farian, *SUNY Geneseo*
David Farrell, *Glasgow Caledonian University*
Yvon Feaster, *Clemson University*
Dave Feinberg, *Carnegie Mellon University*
Alan Fekete, *University of Sydney*
Maria Feldgen, *Universidad de Buenos Aires*
John Fendrich, *Bradley University*
Ernest Ferguson, *Northwest Missouri State University*
Roger Ferguson, *Grand Valley State University*
Joao Miguel Fernandes, *Universidade do Minho*
Francesc J. Ferri, *Universitat de Valencia*
Sue Fitzgerald, *Metropolitan State University*
Robin Flatland, *Siena College*
Rudolf Fleischer, *Fudan University, Shanghai*
William Fleischman, *Villanova University*
Samantha Foley, *Oak Ridge National Laboratory*
Jeffrey Forbes, *Duke University*
Davide Fossati, *Carnegie Mellon University*
Timothy Fossum, *SUNY College at Potsdam*
Kent Foster, *Winthrop University*
Edward Fox, *Virginia Tech*
Charles Frank, *Northern Kentucky University*
Robert Franks, *Central College*
Karen Fraser, *University of Ulster*
Andre Freire, *University of York*
Bill Freitas, *The Lawrenceville School*
Ines Friss de Kereki, *ORT Uruguay University*
S. Jane Fritz, *St. Joseph's College*
Daniel Frost, *University of California, Irvine*
Jacob Furst, *DePaul University*
Stephen Fyfe, *Central College*

Angel Garcia-Beltran, *Universidad Politecnica de Madrid*
Charlie Garrod, *Carnegie Mellon University*
Alessio Gaspar, *University of South Florida Polytechnic*
Dick Gayler, *Kennesaw State University*
Rick Gee, *Okanagan College*
Edward M. Gellenbeck, *Central Washington University*
Carlisle E. George, *Middlesex University, London*
Jill Gerhardt, *Richard Stockton College of New Jersey*
Judith Gersting, *Indiana University Purdue University at Indianapolis*
Paul Gestwicki, *Ball State University*
Ahmad Ghafarian, *North Georgia College & State University*
Lila Ghemri, *Texas Southern University*
J. Paul Gibson, *T&M Sud Paris*
Mark Goadrich, *Centenary College of Louisiana*
Don Goelman, *Villanova University*
Michael Goldweber, *Xavier University*
Evan Golub, *University of Maryland*
Mercedes Gomez-Albarran, *Dep. Ingenieria del Software e Inteligencia Artificial*
Marco Antonio Gomez-Martin, *Universidad Complutense de Madrid*
Pedro Pablo Gomez-Martin, *Universidad Complutense*
Aaron Gordon, *Fort Lewis College*
Jean Goulet, *Universite de Sherbrooke*
Mary Granger, *George Washington University*
Larry Griffith, *Westfield State College*
Mario Guimaraes, *Kennesaw State Univ.*
Jiang Guo, *California State University Los Angeles*
Mark Guzdial, *Georgia Institute of Technology*
Max Hailperin, *Gustavus Adolphus College*
Olaf Hall-Holt, *St. Olaf College*
Susan Haller, *SUNY Potsdam*
Ranette Halverson, *Midwestern State University*
John Hamer, *University of Auckland*
Nadeem Hamid, *Berry College*
Brian Hanks, *Amazon.com*
Stuart Hansen, *University of Wisconsin - Parkside*
Mindy Hart, *Purdue University*
Thanos Hatziapostolou, *City College - International Faculty of University of Sheffield*
Jessen Havill, *Denison University*
Christopher Haynes, *Indiana University*
Carol Hazlewood, *Texas State University*
Orit Hazzan, *Technion — Israel Institute of Technology*
Sarah Heckman, *North Carolina State University*
Phillip Heeler, *Northwest Missouri State University*
Cecily Heiner, *University of Utah*
Rachelle Heller, *George Washington University*
Michael Helmick, *Amazon.com*
David Hemmendinger, *Union College*
Dean Hendrix, *Auburn University*
Tyson Henry, *California State University, Chico*
Katherine Herbert, *Montclair State University*
Matthew Hertz, *Canisius College*
Curtis Hill, *Valley City State University*
Gregory Hislop, *Drexel University*
Lewis Hitchner, *Cal Poly State University, San Luis Obispo*
William Hochstettler, *Franklin University*
Jesper Holck, *Copenhagen Business School*
Mark A. Holliday, *Western Carolina University*
Joe Hollingsworth, *Indiana University*
William Hooper, *Belmont University*
Charles Hoot, *Oklahoma City University*
Cay Horstmann, *San Jose State University*
Hoda Hosny, *The American University in Cairo*
Shahadat Hossain, *University of Lethbridge*
Mahmood Hossain, *Fairmont State University*
Dwight House, *Fayetteville State University*
David Hovemeyer, *York College of Pennsylvania*
Brian Howard, *DePauw University*
Trudy Howles, *Rochester Institute of Technology*
Michelle Hribar, *OHSU*
Wen-Jung Hsin, *Park University*
Chenglie Hu, *Carroll University*
Meriel Huggard, *Trinity College, Dublin*
James Huggins, *Kettering University*
Janet Hughes, *University of Dundee*
Richard Hull, *Lenoir-Rhyne University*
Dalton R. Hunkins, *St. Bonaventure Univ.*
Frances Hunt, *Educational Testing Service*
Kenny Hunt, *University of Wisconsin - La Crosse*
Steven Huss-Lederman, *Beloit College*
Michelle Hutton, *The Girls' Middle School/CSTA*
Deborah Hwang, *University of Evansville*
Jorge Eduardo Ibarra-Esquer, *Universidad Autonoma de Baja California*
Lubomir Ivanov, *Iona College*
Sridhar Iyer, *Indian Institute of Technology, Bombay*
Jana Jackova, *University of Zilina*
Matthew Jadud, *Allegheny College*
Mark Jaeger, *Baker College*
David Janzen, *California Polytechnic State University, San Luis Obispo*
Ciera Jaspan, *Carnegie Mellon University*
Giti Javidi, *Virginia State University*
Jam Jenkins, *Georgia Gwinnett College*
Kuodi Jian, *Metropolitan State University*
Mike Jipping, *Hope College*
David John, *Wake Forest University*
Mark Johnson, *Central College*
Colin Johnson, *University of Kent at Canterbury*
Julie Johnson, *Vanderbilt University*
Lawrence G. Jones, *Carnegie Mellon University*
Jose R. Hilera, *University of Alcala*
Anthony Joseph, *Pace University*
Mike Joy, *University of Warwick*
Daniel Joyce, *Villanova University*
Maria Jump, *King's College*
Edward Jung, *Southern Polytechnic State University*
Mark Kampe, *Hitachi Data Systems*
Pankaj Kamthan, *Concordia University*
Debbie Kaneko, *Old Dominion University*
Evangelos Kanidis, *University of Athens / Ministry of Education*
Ville Karavirta, *Aalto University*
Elizabeth Katz, *Millersville University*
David Kauchak, *Pomona College*
David G. Kay, *Univ. of California, Irvine*
Jennifer Kay, *Rowan University*
Charles Kelemen, *Swarthmore College*
Thomas Kelliher, *Goucher College*
Andreas Kerren, *Linnaeus University*
Mark Kerstetter, *Western Michigan University*
Sami Khuri, *San Jose State University*
K. N. King, *Georgia State University*
Nancy Kinnersley, *University of Kansas*
Myungsook Klassen, *California Lutheran University*
Frank Klassner, *Villanova University*
Carsten Kleiner, *University of Applied Sciences & Arts Hannover*
Peter J. Knoke, *University of Alaska Fairbanks*
Jane Kochanov, *Pennsylvania State University - Capital College*
Elliot Koffman, *Temple University*
Michael Kölling, *University of Kent*
April Kontostathis, *Ursinus College*
Yana Kortsarts, *Widener University, Chester*
Janet Kourik, *Webster University*
Nicholas Kraft, *The University of Alabama*
Joan Krone, *Denison University*

Jan Kruger, *Unisa School for Business Leadership*
Marja Kuittinen, *University of Joensuu*
Amruth Kumar, *Ramapo College of New Jersey*
Benjamin Kuperman, *Oberlin College*
Stan Kurkovsky, *Central Connecticut State University*
Zachary Kurmas, *Grand Valley State Univ.*
Brian Ladd, *SUNY Potsdam*
Lynn Lambert, *Christopher Newport University*
H. Chad Lane, *University of Southern California*
Catherine Lang, *Swinburne University of Technology*
Mathew Lang, *Moravian College*
Joan Langdon, *Bowie State University*
Yedidyah Langsam, *Brooklyn College of CUNY*
Mick Lantis, *Purdue University North Central*
David Largent, *Ball State University*
Eric Larson, *Seattle University*
Patricia Lasserre, *UBC Okanagan*
Mary Last, *Self-Employed*
Robert Law, *Glasgow Caledonian University*
Deirdre Lawless, *Dublin Institute of Technology*
Barry Lawson, *University of Richmond*
Lucas Layman, *Fraunhofer USA*
Alina Lazar, *Youngstown State University*
Christopher League, *Long Island University*
Cathie LeBlanc, *Plymouth State College*
Mark LeBlanc, *Wheaton College*
Byong Lee, *Bennett College*
Tony Lee, *The Boeing Company*
Gilliean Lee, *Lander University*
Arthur Lee, *Claremont McKenna College*
Rob LeGrand, *Angelo State University*
Jeffrey Lehman, *Huntington University*
Noel LeJeune, *Metropolitan State College of Denver*
Chuck Leska, *Randolph-Macon College*
Scott Leutenegger, *University of Denver*
David Levine, *St. Bonaventure University*
Anany Levitin, *Villanova University*
Roy Levow, *Florida Atlantic University*
Lon Levy, *Bergen County Academies*
Gary Lewandowski, *Xavier University*
John Lewis, *Virginia Tech*
Weidong Liao, *Shepherd University*
Billy Lim, *Illinois State University*
Hong Lin, *University of Houston-Downtown*
Janne Lindqvist, *Carnegie Mellon University*
Raymond Lister, *University of Technology, Sydney*
Joyce Currie Little, *Towson University*
Jigang Liu, *Metropolitan State University*
Jiang-Jiang Liu, *Lamar University*
Peter Liu, *Seneca College*
William S. Lloyd, *Univ. of West Georgia*
Kate Lockwood, *California State University, Monterey Bay*
Antonio M. Lopez, *Retired*
Salvador Lopez-Mendoza, *Universidad Nacional Autonoma de Mexico*
Joao Lourenco, *Dep. Informatica -- FCT / Universidade Nova de Lisboa*
Susan Loveland, *Adams State College*
Joan Lucas, *State University of New York, College at Brockport*
Stephanie Ludi, *Rochester Institute of Technology*
Geoffrey Lund, *University of Abertay Dundee*
Andrew Luxton-Reilly, *The University of Auckland*
William Lyle, *Murray State University*
Ian Macdonald, *Victoria University*
Bonnie MacKellar, *St John's University*
Peter Macpherson, *Rogers State University*
Joaquim Madeira, *University of Aveiro*
Michael Main, *University of Colorado at Boulder*
David Malan, *Harvard University*
Bill Manaris, *College of Charleston*
Maynard Mansfield, *Indiana-Purdue Fort Wayne*
Bill Marion, *Valparaiso University*
Kenneth Martin, *Univ. of North Florida*
Manuel Martins Barata, *ISEL - Instituto Superior de Engenharia de Lisboa*
Bruce R. Maxim, *University of Michigan-Dearborn*
Bruce Maxwell, *Colby College*
Lester I. McCann, *The Univ. of Arizona*
Robert McCloskey, *University of Scranton*
O. William McClung, *Nebraska Wesleyan University*
Jeffrey McConnell, *Canisius College*
Frank McCown, *Harding University*
W. Michael McCracken, *Georgia Institute of Technology*
Sean McCulloch, *Ohio Wesleyan University*
Chris McDonald, *The University of Western Australia*
Charlie McDowell, *University of California Santa Cruz*
Scott McElfresh, *Wake Forest University*
Ryan McFall, *Hope College*
James McGuffee, *St. Edward's University*
Hugh McGuire, *Grand Valley State Univ.*
Tim McGuire, *Sam Houston State Univ.*
Michael McMillan, *Pulaski Technical College*
Pedro Medeiros, *Universidade Nova de Lisboa - Dep. Informatica*
Lisa Meeden, *Swarthmore College*
Gloria Melara, *California State University, Northridge*
Antonio Jose Mendes, *University of Coimbra*
Susan Mengel, *Texas Tech University*
Suzanne Menzel, *Indiana University*
Jose Carlos Metrolho, *Polytechnic Institute of Castelo Branco*
Timothy Meyer, *Edinboro University of Pennsylvania*
Gail Miles, *Lenoir-Rhyne College*
James Miller, *Bradley University*
James Miller, *University of Alberta*
Bradley Miller, *Luther College*
Keith Miller, *University of Illinois at Springfield*
Joe Miro, *Universitat de les Illes Balears*
Susan Mitchell, *University of Maryland, Baltimore County*
Sriram Mohan, *Rose-Hulman Institute of Technology*
Sara Miner More, *McDaniel College*
Nelma Moreira, *University of Porto*
Ralph Morelli, *Trinity College*
Patricia Morreale, *Kean University*
Briana Morrison, *Southern Polytechnic State University*
Michael Murphy, *Concordia University Texas*
Laurie Murphy, *Pacific Lutheran University*
Keitha Murray, *Iona College*
Ani Nahapetian, *UCLA*
Krish Narayanan, *Eastern Michigan University*
Pavol Navrat, *Slovak University of Technology*
Rance Necaise, *Washington and Lee University*
Robert Neufeld, *McPherson College - Emeritus*
Tia Newhall, *Swarthmore College*
Lijun Ni, *Georgia Institute of Technology*
Delmer Nicholson, *University of Cincinnati*
Jaime Nino, *University of New Orleans*
Daniel Nohl, *Benedictine University*
Robert Noonan, *College of William and Mary*
Cindy Norris, *Appalachian State University*
Linda Null, *Penn State University*
William Oblitey, *Indiana University of Pennsylvania*
Rainer Oechsle, *University of Applied Sciences, Trier*
Chris Okasaki, *USMA*
Amos Olagunju, *St. Cloud State University*

Joseph Oldham, *Centre College*
Richard Ord, *University of California, San Diego*
Mary Jo Orzech, *The College at Brockport*
Lawrence Osborne, *Lamar University*
Youwen Ouyang, *California State University at San Marcos*
Barbara Owens, *Southwestern University*
Alex Pagan-Ortiz, *Anne Arundel Community College*
Jill Pala, *Girls Preparatory School*
Edward K Palmer, *Goshen College*
Katherine Panciera, *University of Minnesota*
Greta Pangborn, *Saint Michael's College*
Iraklis Paraskakis, *City College, Intern. Faculty of the University of Sheffield*
Abelardo Pardo, *Carlos III Univ. of Madrid*
Young Park, *Bradley University*
Brenda C. Parker, *Middle Tennessee State University*
David Parker, *Salisbury University*
June Parsons, *MediaTechnics*
James Paterson, *Glasgow Caledonian University*
Laurie Patterson, *University of North Carolina Wilmington*
Richard E. Pattis, *Univ. of California, Irvine*
Anand Paul, *National Cheng Kung University*
Thaddeus Pawlicki, *University of Rochester Computer Science*
Lisa Peairs, *Pomona College*
Arnold Pears, *Uppsala University*
Ramanee Peiris, *University of Dundee*
Bin Peng, *Southwestern College*
Manuel A. Perez-Quinones, *Virginia Tech*
Teresa Peterman, *Grand Valley State University*
Chrisila C. Pettey, *Middle Tennessee State University*
Charles Pheatt, *Emporia State University*
Vreda Pieterse, *University of Pretoria*
Paul Piwowarski, *University of Kentucky*
Jennifer Polack-Wahl, *University of Mary Washington*
Wayne Pollock, *Hillsborough Community College*
Irene Polycarpou, *Colorado School of Mines*
Elvira Popescu, *University of Craiova*
Jeffrey Popyack, *Drexel University*
Lori Postner, *Nassau Community College*
George J. Pothering, *College of Charleston*
Annu Prabhakar, *University of Cincinnati*
John-Paul Pretti, *University of Waterloo*
Roger Priebe, *Texas State University - San Marcos*
Philip Prins, *Seattle Pacific University*
William Pugh, *University of Maryland*
Sarah Monisha Pulimood, *The College of New Jersey*
Tarsem Purewal, *University of Tennessee at Chattanooga*
John Rager, *Amherst College*
Noa Ragonis, *Beit Berl College, Technion*
Rajendra Raj, *Rochester Institute of Technology*
Muthu Ramachandran, *Leeds Metropolitan University*
Bina Ramamurthy, *University at Buffalo, SUNY*
Eliseo Reategui, *Universidade Federal do Rio Grande do Sul*
Samuel Rebelsky, *Grinnell College*
Michael Redmond, *La Salle University*
David Reed, *Creighton University*
Donna Reese, *Mississippi State University*
Stuart Reges, *University of Washington*
Karen Reid, *University of Toronto*
Dan Resler, *Virginia Commonwealth University*
Eugene K. Ressler, *United States Military Academy*
Loren Rhodes, *Juniata College*
Catherine Ricardo, *Iona College*
Brad Richards, *University of Puget Sound*
Michael Rieck, *Drake University*
Charles Riedesel, *University of Nebraska - Lincoln*
Suzanne Rivoire, *Sonoma State University*
Steven Robbins, *University of Texas at San Antonio*
Christian Roberson, *Plymouth State University*
Eric Roberts, *Stanford University*
Don Roberts, *University of Evansville*
Stefan Robila, *Montclair State University*
Paolo Rocchi, *IBM*
Timothy Roden, *Angelo State University*
Susan H. Rodger, *Duke University*
Ken Rodham, *Brigham Young University*
Guido Roessling, *Technische Universitaet Darmstadt*
John Ross, *Indiana University Kokomo*
Jerry Roth, *Vanderbilt University*
Constantine Roussos, *Lynchburg College*
Martin Ruckert, *Munich University of Applied Sciences*
Anthony Ruocco, *Roger Williams University*
Paulo Rupino da Cunha, *University of Coimbra*
Ingrid Russell, *University of Hartford*
Adrian Rusu, *Rowan University*
Amalia Rusu, *Fairfield University*
Rebecca Rutherfoord, *Southern Polytechnic State University*
Roberta Evans Sabin, *Loyola College*
Mihaela Sabin, *University of New Hampshire*
Shazia Sadiq, *The University of Queensland*
Mehran Sahami, *Stanford University*
Richard Salter, *Oberlin College*
Samuel Sambasivam, *Azusa Pacific University*
Ian Sanders, *University of the Witwatersrand*
William Sanders, *University of Hartford*
Donald Sanderson, *East Tennessee State University*
Vijayalakshmi Saravanan, *VIT University*
Amit Sawant, *NetApp*
Suzanne Schaefer, *University of California, Los Angeles*
Christelle Scharff, *Pace University*
Diane Schwartz, *California State University Northridge*
Leslie Schwartzman, *UIS*
Dino Schweitzer, *United States Air Force Academy*
Otto Seppala, *Helsinki University of Technology*
Sirkemaa Seppo, *Turku School of Economics and Business Administration, Pori*
Behrooz Seyed-Abbassi, *University of North Florida*
Cliff Shaffer, *Virginia Tech*
Victor R.L. Shen, *National Taipei University*
Ching-Kuang Shene, *Michigan Technological University*
Linda Sherrell, *University of Memphis*
Mark Sherriff, *University of Virginia*
Yasuto Shirai, *Shizuoka University*
Keith Shomper, *Cedarville University*
Charles Shub, *University of Colorado at Colorado Springs*
Scott Sigman, *Drury University*
Gavin Sim, *University of Central Lancashire*
Simple Simon, *University of Newcastle, Australia*
Oberta Slotterbeck, *Hiram College*
William Slough, *Eastern Illinois University*
Peter Smith, *California State University - Channel Islands*
Robert Snapp, *University of Vermont*
Leen-Kiat Soh, *University of Nebraska*
Takako Soma, *Illinois College*
Joel Sommers, *Colgate University*
Sara Sood, *Pomona College*
Raja Sooriamurthi, *Carnegie Mellon University*
Vijayasree Sooriamurthi, *Carnegie Mellon University*
Jonathan Sorenson, *Butler University*
Barry Soroka, *Cal Poly Pomona*

Jaime Spacco, *Knox College*
Greg Speegle, *Baylor University*
David Spooner, *Rensselaer Polytechnic Institute*
Carol Spradling, *Northwest Missouri State University*
Denbigh Starkey, *Montana State University*
Mark Stehlik, *Carnegie Mellon University*
Josh Steinhurst, *Bucknell University*
Daniel Stevenson, *University of Wisconsin - Eau Claire*
Khadija Stewart, *DePauw University*
Evelyn Stiller, *Plymouth State University*
Vojislav Stojkovic, *Morgan State Univ.*
Jeffrey Stone, *Pennsylvania State University*
Christopher Stone, *Harvey Mudd College*
Fred Strickland, *South University*
Catherine Stringfellow, *Midwestern State University*
Lena Stromback, *Linkoping University*
Deborah Sturm, *College of Staten Island CUNY*
Dario Suarez Gracia, *Universidad de Zaragoza*
Jose Such, *Technical University of Valencia*
Leigh Ann Sudol, *Carnegie Mellon University*
Wayne Summers, *Columbus State University*
Ken Surendran, *Southeast Missouri State University*
Hengky Susanto, *University of Massachusetts Lowell*
Jerry Talton, *Stanford University*
Joo Tan, *Kutztown University*
Yonglei Tao, *Grand Valley State University*
Blair Taylor, *Towson University*
Carol Taylor, *Eastern Washington University*
James Teresco, *Siena College*
Allison Elliott Tew, *Georgia Institute of Technology*
William Thacker, *Winthrop University*
Soe Than, *Virginia Military Institute*
Rebecca Thomas, *Bard College*
Megan Thomas, *California State University Stanislaus*
Stan Thomas, *Wake Forest University*
Alfred Thompson, *Microsoft*
Jodi Tims, *Baldwin-Wallace College*
Fergus Toolan, *University College Dublin*
Gloria Childress Townsend, *DePauw University*
Christian Trefftz, *Grand Valley State University*
Deborah Trytten, *University of Oklahoma*
George Tsiknis, *University of British Columbia*
Shengru Tu, *University of New Orleans*
David S. Tucker, *Midwestern State University*
William Turner, *Wabash College*
Guenter Tusch, *Grand Valley State University*
Sharon M. Tuttle, *Humboldt State University*
Hakan Tuzun, *Hacettepe University*
Paul Tymann, *Rochester Institute of Technology*
Suleyman Uludag, *The University of Michigan - Flint*
Susan D. Urban, *Texas Tech University*
Timothy Urness, *Drake University*
Jaime Urquiza-Fuentes, *Rey Juan Carlos University*
Ian Utting, *University of Kent at Canterbury*
Jan Vahrenhold, *Technische Universitat Dortmund*
Ignatios Vakalis, *California Polytechnic and State University*
David Valentine, *Slippery Rock University*
Robert Van Camp, *Marietta College*
Tammy VanDeGrift, *University of Portland*
Jorge Vasconcelos, *Johns Hopkins University*
Troy Vasiga, *University of Waterloo*
Steven Vegdahl, *University of Portland*
J. Angel Velazquez-Iturbide, *Universidad Rey Juan Carlos*
Gabriela Vilanova, *National Patagonia Austral University*
Tamar Vilner, *The Open University of Israel*
Kimberly Voll, *Univ. of British Columbia*
Ken Vollmar, *Missouri State University*
David Voorhees, *Le Moyne College*
Paul Wagner, *University of Wisconsin - Eau Claire*
Sally Wahba, *Clemson University*
Gursimran Walia, *North Dakota State University*
Henry Walker, *Grinnell College*
Xinli Wang, *Michigan Technological University*
Yi Wang, *City University of Hong Kong*
Stan Warford, *Pepperdine University*
Richard Wasniowski, *California State University Channel Islands*
Thomas Way, *Villanova University*
Scott Weiss, *Mt. St. Mary's University*
Emily Wenk, *Penn State York*
Linda Werner, *University of California, Santa Cruz*
Roger West, *University of Illinois at Springfield*
Suzanne Westbrook, *The University of Arizona*
Curt White, *DePaul University*
Laurie White, *Mercer University*
Elizabeth White, *George Mason University*
Howard Whitston, *University of South Alabama*
Paul Wiedemeier, *The University of Louisiana at Monroe*
Sheila Wiggins, *Morgan State University*
Linda Wilkens, *Providence College*
Judith Williams, *William Penn University*
Craig Wills, *Worcester Polytechnic Institute*
Linda Wilson, *Texas Lutheran University*
Brent Wilson, *George Fox University*
Michael Wirth, *University of Guelph*
Lee Wittenberg, *GW Software*
Walter Wolf, *Rochester Institute of Technology*
Rosalee Wolfe, *DePaul University*
Christine Wolfe, *Ohio University*
David Wolff, *Pacific Lutheran University*
Greg Wolffe, *Grand Valley State University*
Steven Wolfman, *University of British Columbia*
Ursula Wolz, *The College of New Jersey*
Gary Ka Wai Wong, *The Community College at Lingnan University*
David Wonnacott, *Haverford College*
Karl Wurst, *Worcester State University*
T. Andrew Yang, *University of Houston - Clear Lake*
Arthur Yanushka, *Christian Brothers University*
Ken Yasuhara, *University of Washington*
Dowming Yeh, *National Kaohsiung Normal University*
Juang Yih-Ruey, *Jinwen University of Science & Technology*
Duane Yoder, *University of West Georgia*
Alison Young, *Christchurch Polytechnic Institute of Technology*
Benjamin Yu, *UBC*
Kwok-Bun Yue, *University of Houston – Clear Lake*
Timothy Yuen, *UTSA*
Marsha Zaidman, *University of Mary Washington*
Carol Zander, *University of Washington, Bothell*
Alan Zaring, *Ohio Wesleyan University*
Julie Zelenski, *Stanford University*
Dean Zeller, *Art Institute of Jacksonville*
Jinghua Zhang, *Winston-Salem State Univ.*
Uta Ziegler, *Western Kentucky University*
Jill Zimmerman, *Goucher College*
Guy Zimmerman, *Bowling Green State University*
Daniel Zingaro, *University of Toronto*
Fani Zlatarova, *Elizabethtown College*

Keynote Talk

TeachScheme!

Matthias Felleisen
College of Computer and Information Science
Northeastern University
matthias@ccs.neu.edu

Abstract

In 1995, my research team and I decided to create TeachScheme!, an educational outreach project, with the hope that our work on programming languages could effect a dramatic change in K-12 computer science. Specifically, we envisioned a virtuous cycle of two mutually reinforcing ideas. On the one hand, we would create a design-oriented curriculum path from middle school through college. On the other hand, our approach would help kids with learning school mathematics. Hence a course on programming would benefit every student, not just those who end up choosing computer science as a college major. At this point, we have a new design-oriented curriculum; a pedagogic program development environment to make it fun; and a series of matching programming languages. After focusing at the overlap between high schools and colleges at first, we now use after-school programs to move upstream, and we are working on two major downstream courses for the second semester in college: one on object-oriented design and another on logic in program design.

My talk will focus on just one aspect of the project: the design-oriented curriculum and its smooth path from middle school to college. I will first demonstrate how to teach an intellectually interesting and fun course on programming with something that looks like plain school mathematics. For the rest of the talk, I will sketch the path from there through college.

Categories & Subject Descriptors: K.3.2 [Computers and Education]: Computer and Information Science Education – computer science education

General Terms: Human Factors, Languages

Bio

Matthias Felleisen obtained his PhD ('87) from Daniel P. Friedman who also pointed him in the direction of a professorial career. He then spent the next 15 years at Rice University in Houston, including long and short sabbaticals at Carnegie Mellon University (Pittsburgh) and Ecole Normale Superieure (Paris). In 2001, he took on a position at Northeastern University in Boston and moved his entire team there. Felleisen and his distributed PLT team conduct research on all aspects of programming languages: design, implementations, and applications. On the side, they also run TeachScheme!, an educational outreach project. Over his 25-year career, Felleisen co-authored six books. As a PhD student, he revised his adviser's "Little LISPer" (MIT Press), which is still in print in its 35th year of existence. The two of them also wrote "A Little Java, A Few Patterns". With some of his own PhD students, Felleisen produced "How to Design Programs" (MITP, 2001) and "Semantics Engineering" (MITP, 2009).

SIGCSE'11, March 9–12, 2011, Dallas, Texas, USA.
ACM 978-1-4503-0500-6/11/03.

Starting a Computational Science Program

James Caristi (Moderator)
Valparaiso University
James.Caristi@valpo.edu

Joe Sloan
Wofford College
SloanJD@wofford.edu

Valerie Barr
Union College
barrv@union.edu

Eric Stahlberg
Wittenberg University
EStahlberg@wittenberg.edu

Summary

It is evident from the recent discussions about computational thinking and the number of papers, panels and birds-of-a-feather sessions at the 2010 SIGCSE Symposium that there is not only a deep connection between computer science and many other disciplines, especially in the sciences, but also a desire to think of computation as an equal partner with experimentation and theory in the solution of science problems. As David Hemmendinger said in a thought piece that appeared recently in *ACM Inroads*: "Teaching computational thinking [to students in disciplines other than computer science] ... is to teach them how to think like an economist, a physicist, an artist, and to understand how to use computation to solve their problems, to create, and to discover new questions that can be fruitfully explored." [1].

As a consequence of this way to think about a proper role for computational thinking, what is emerging is a new discipline, computational science, that brings to bear the knowledge and tools of mathematics, statistics and computer science to solve problems in the sciences and engineering. This multidisciplinary approach is also leading to the creation of new scientific knowledge.

In the past few years computational science programs, both at the undergraduate and the graduate level, have been springing up at a number of colleges and universities. This panel is designed to explore this relatively new phenomenon. Each of the panelists has been a leader at her/his institution in the development of such programs. And, each will present what led them to take on this task, how they went about building a program, some of the features of each program and some of the successes and failures.

Categories and Subject Descriptors

K.3.2 [Computer and Information Science Education]: Curriculum

General Terms: Standardization

Keywords

Computational Science, Computational Thinking, Computer Science, Engineering, Programs: Minor, Major, Graduate Sciences

SIGCSE'11, March 9–12, 2011, Dallas, Texas, USA.
ACM 978-1-4503-0500-6/11/03.

POSITION STATEMENTS

2.1 James Caristi

At Valparaiso University, faculty from the College of Arts and Sciences and the College of Engineering have developed a 4+1 BS/MS program in Computational Science. Science and engineering majors with strong computational skills or computer science, mathematics and meteorology majors who are well-versed in at least one area of science will be able to obtain a BS in Astronomy, Biology, Chemistry, Computer Science, Engineering, Mathematics, Meteorology or Physics plus a MS in Computational Science in a new five-year program. Consideration will also be given to students with a BS degree from another university in one of the above fields provided they have the requisite mathematics, statistics and computer science courses.

As a member of the University's Strategic Planning Committee, Bill Marion was a strong advocate for putting in place a computational science program. He was also a member of the Task Force exploring the creation of just such a program. Bill passed away at about the time when the program was given final approval. We will discuss many of the relevant issues surrounding the development of the program: attracting qualified students, developing an appropriate curriculum, especially at the graduate level, and building through hiring or retraining a well-trained faculty.

2.2 Joe Sloan

Computation Science at Wofford College is taught as an Emphasis, an approach that works well for a smaller school. Students majoring in Biology, Chemistry, Mathematics, Physics, or Psychology may complete the emphasis by taking five additional courses and completing a summer internship involving computation in the sciences. These five courses include Calculus I, our introductory programming and data structures sequence, and two courses created specifically for the emphasis, Data and Visualization, and Modeling and Simulation.

Angela Shiflet, who is currently on professional development leave, created the Emphasis. Angela and George Shiflet have authored the book *Introduction to Computational Science*; Angela is a member of the SIAM subcommittee that developed a report on "Undergraduate Computational Science and Engineering Education" and is a member of the Education Board for SIURO, SIAM Undergraduate Research Online.

As Acting Department Chair, I am currently administering the program in her absence. With the exception of Calculus I, I have taught all of the courses in the Emphasis on multiple occasions. I will describe the history of the emphasis, how it has been fine-tuned over the years, and it current place in Wofford's curriculum.

2.3 Eric Stahlberg

Wittenberg University has an established and growing minor in computational science. The program has been in place formally since 2004 as an interdisciplinary minor, introducing computational thinking and approaches to students primarily majoring in biology, biochemistry-molecular biology, chemistry, economics, physics, geology, mathematics and computer science. Starting with only a small numbers of minors, our most recent graduating class had ten students complete their Wittenberg education with the computational science minor, with realistic projections for even larger numbers in the future.

Upon joining Wittenberg University in 2007 following several years of commercial experience in high-performance computing and applications, it has been my responsibility to build the program and expand opportunities. Geographical location, timing, funding opportunities and previous industry relationships have combined to build a successful computational science minor and interest in the broader application of computational thinking. Further efforts have also proven successful, finding unique opportunities to introduce computational thinking and interest in several non-traditional disciplines including art, psychology and international studies. I will discuss the several efforts undertaken and lessons learned in creating a successful computational science minor with interest extending well beyond the computer science department.

2.4 Valerie Barr

The Union College CS department is engaged in the development of a campus-wide computation initiative. One element of this is a computational methods minor. A student can complete the minor by taking three CS courses and three additional courses that have a computational component. The minor requires that the student take one of our six theme-based conceptually equivalent introductory CS courses. This is followed by two intermediate level CS courses, drawn from a set that includes Natural Language Processing, Web Programming, Modeling Simulation, and The Computer Science of Computer Games (in 2011-2012 we will add a course on visualization). Outside the CS department a student can take three of an increasing number of courses which have an added computational component. For example, a Biology major might take CS courses Taming Big Data (intro), Modeling & Simulation, and Visualization, along with Plant Ecology, Introduction to Cellular Neurosciences, and Introduction to Bioinformatics. An Economics major might take the same set of CS courses, followed by Contemporary Issues in Macroeconomics, Quantitative Economics, and Social Data Analysis (note courses taken for the minor within the major department are in addition to those that satisfy the major requirements).

The computational methods minor has support among a core group of non-CS faculty who have been infusing computation into their courses. A major focus of the CS department during 2010-2011 will be to 1) increase support an interest among a wider group of faculty and 2) improve strategies for directly informing key student populations about the minor.

REFERENCES

[1] Hemmendinger, D. "A Plea for Modesty," Inroads (ACM SIGCSE Bulletin), 1, 2, (June 2010), 4-7.

SIGCSE Special Project Showcase

Doug Baldwin
SUNY Geneseo
Geneseo, NY 14454
baldwin@geneseo.edu

Peter Sanderson
Otterbein University
Westerville, OH 43081
psanderson@otterbein.edu

Robert McCartney
University of Connecticut
Storrs, CT 06269
robert@engr.uconn.edu

Stephanie Ludi
Rochester Institute of Technology
Rochester, NY 14623
salvse@rit.edu

Narayanan T. Ramachandran
Middle East College of Information Technology
Muscat, Sultanate of Oman
narayanan@mecit.edu.om

Carol Taylor
Eastern Washington University
Cheney, WA 99004-2493
ctaylor4214@comcast.net

ABSTRACT

SIGCSE's special projects grant program provides small grants to SIGCSE members to carry out computing education projects whose results generalize to the whole computing education community. This session is a "showcase" for five recent grant projects: a MIPS simulator extended into FPGA hardware, a study of informal learning of computing, software engineering learning modules for the visually impaired, a study of student projects in computing, and curriculum resources for computer security.

Categories and Subject Descriptors

K.3.2 [**Computers and Education**]: Computer and Information Science Education—*computer science education, information systems education*

General Terms

Design, Experimentation, Human Factors

Keywords

SIGCSE special projects, MIPS, informal learning, visually impaired students, student projects, security

1. INTRODUCTION

SIGCSE's special projects grant program provides small grants (up to US$5000) to SIGCSE members who wish to carry out a project in computing education whose results generalize to the larger computing education community. Recipients are required to report on their projects in a "special projects showcase" at the annual SIGCSE symposium, or via a paper or poster at the ITiCSE conference. This special session constitutes the 2011 SIGCSE Symposium special projects showcase.

Five grant recipients are ready to present at SIGCSE 2011, as summarized below. The session will therefore consist of five minutes of introductory remarks by the moderator (Baldwin), followed by presentations by each grant recipient. These presentations will include 10 to 12 minutes of description of a project and its main results, followed by 2 to 4 minutes for questions from the audience. Given the short time, presentations will be designed to start conversations with interested listeners, conversations that will continue later in the Symposium and electronically afterwards.

The projects to be presented in this session are as follows:

2. EXTENDING A MIPS SIMULATOR FOR FPGA SUPPORT

Peter Sanderson and **Ken Vollmar**. This project enriches computer organization education by providing another avenue for execution of MIPS code. The initial and existing avenue is the MARS simulator for MIPS code, a well-established open source product for educational environments, in use at universities and colleges worldwide (http://www.cs.missouristate.edu/MARS). The new avenue is a special adaptation of MIPS circuitry on a Field Programmable Gate Array (FPGA) platform. FPGAs such as the Altera DE2 are very attractive in an educational environment because of their flexibility, re-use, and low cost. The FPGA MIPS circuit includes VGA graphical output for real-time display of the MIPS machine state, including registers, memory, etc. Students write MIPS code and compare its behavior and performance in the two environments of the MARS simulator and the FPGA MIPS hardware.

3. INFORMAL LEARNING OF COMPUTING BY COMPUTING STUDENTS

Robert McCartney. To keep up, computer scientists need to keep learning. Some of this learning takes place in formal settings—college courses, short courses, and professional development—but much of it takes place informally. Both students and professionals need to learn things that are too new to be included in formal courses, that aren't covered in any course available to them, or that are specialized to their individual goals. In those situations, informal learning is the method of choice.

This SIGCSE special project is an exploratory investigation into computing students' informal learning: what, how, and why they choose to learn on their own. It is a multi-institutional, multinational study, with data from three institutions in the US, three in Sweden, and one in Wales. In the presentation, we will provide some overall perspective by discussing the variety of research areas that fall under the general description "informal learning." We then will discuss preliminary findings that concern what the students learn, what resources they bring to bear, what strategies they employ, and how they evaluate their progress. These results identify one frequent type of informal learning of computing, in which students learn specific technologies, both motivated and evaluated

SIGCSE'11, March 9-12, 2011, Dallas, Texas, USA.
ACM 978-1-4503-0500-6/11/03.

by project work. Our findings further show, however, that students learn informally in a large variety of ways dependent on both context and individual preferences.

The researchers associated with this project are Jonas Boustedt (University of Gävle, Sweden), Anna Eckerdal (Uppsala University, Sweden), Robert McCartney, (University of Connecticut), Jan Erik Moström (Umeå University, Sweden), Kate Sanders (Rhode Island College), Lynda Thomas (Aberystwyth University, Wales), and Carol Zander (University of Washington, Bothell).

4. ACCESSIBLE SOFTWARE ENGINEERING FOR THE VISUALLY IMPAIRED (ASE-VI)

Stephanie Ludi. Broadening participation in computer science has taken many forms in the last few years, reaching a diverse population of (prospective) students. As an underrepresented group, students who are visually impaired often struggle with computer science courses. Attitudinal factors and access to resources are contributing factors. Educational materials often reflect visual information, which is difficult for the students to interpret. Students with visual impairments need support for participation in computing. The project goal is to increase the instructional opportunities for visually impaired students through:

> The development of software engineering learning modules for use in courses to increase the preparation of students with visual impairments.
>
> The development of an accessible web-based resource where computing educators can access course modules and participate in an online community.

The special project presentation will demonstrate a sample of the learning modules and the website itself. In addition, the assessment of the modules will be presented in terms of the content and accessibility to students who are visually impaired.

5. TOWARDS DEVELOPING A RESOURCE GUIDE FOR STUDENT PROJECTS

Narayanan T. Ramachandran and **Abdul Huq**.
Projects form an important component in the academic programmes offered by higher education institutions (HEIs). Students face several challenges while carrying out their project. Some of them are generic and others are context specific. Identifying these issues and resolving them will help students and staff across similar institutions. They will also be better equipped to identify the relative strengths and opportunities for improvement in their approach to enhancing student experiences through projects. From a global perspective, projects invite special attention on account of the variations in the academic systems and quality assurance framework in which HEIs operate and policies and practices followed in the development, design and delivery of academic programmes.

This SIGCSE special project is an attempt to study the perception of students and academic staff in the context of projects in the Diploma and Undergraduate programmes in IT and related subject areas. The study explores common issues faced by students and their supervisors for the successful completion of the project with data collected from a sample survey of students and academic staff in the HEIs in the Sultanate of Oman. Our findings show that students recognise the role of project and its importance in academic programme. Supervisors as well as students are keen on doing a relatively *strong project* and look forward to *standards* across the institutions for projects. Furthermore, both recognise supervisor as a major reason for success of the project.

In the presentation, we propose to outline the context, its implications to projects in the curriculum, and also provide an overview of the results. We shall discuss some important results relating to orientation for the project, manuals, culturally sensitive issues, marking methods, resources, English language skills, and other project management issues and their implications to projects. We shall describe how open source such as *moodle* may be used to provide useful resources, online support and feedback to students and, facilitate students to maintain the progress of their project in *Ediaries*. Some efforts in this direction, the benefits realized, and how all these can be incorporated into a resource guide will be discussed

6. CURRICULUM RESOURCE REPOSITORY FOR TEACHING COMPUTER SECURITY

Carol Taylor. The purpose of this project is to create a web-based repository for curriculum related to computer security. There currently is no existing site that offers instructors access to resources for teaching computer security. The proposed curriculum repository would offer course materials from NSA certified academic institutions that have curriculum standards in accordance with government training requirements. In addition to course materials, instructor training materials and links to further education in computer security will be aggregated on this site. The creation of a site offering free, easily accessible computer security curriculum and training will provide a valuable teaching aid for both experienced and inexperienced instructors.

Computing and Music: A Spectrum of Sound

Robert E. Beck
Villanova University
Villanova, PA 19085
+1.610.519.7352
Robert.beck@villanova.edu

Jennifer Burg
Wake Forest University
Winston-Salem, NC 27106
+1.336.758.4465
Burg@wfu.edu

Jesse M. Heines
University of Massachusetts Lowell
Lowell, MA 01854
+1.978.934.3634
Jesse_Heines@uml.edu

Bill Manaris
College of Charleston
Charleston, SC 29424
+1.843.953.8159
Manarisb@cofc.edu

SUMMARY

This special session implements the first goal of the SIGCSE Committee on Computing and Music. It provides a venue in which the committee conveners can present their work to SIGCSE attendees and in return acquire information from others who are using music to promote learning of deep computing concepts. By describing four diverse approaches, the audience will understand the breadth of the topic and will be inspired to contribute to the effort.

Categories and Subject Descriptors

H.5.5 Sound and Music Computing; K.3.2 Computer and Information Science Education

General Terms

Algorithms, Design, Experimentation, Languages.

Keywords

Computing and music, music algorithms, computational analysis of music, music programming

1. OVERALL OBJECTIVE

The Computing and Music Committee of SIGCSE was established in May 2010 with the overarching purpose of exploring the synergy between music and computer science and investigating ways in which this relationship can be used to enhance computer science education through music applications. The rationale for this purpose is that music applications are inherently interesting to students, and there are many computational issues involved in these applications for illustrating computing concepts.

The special session will allow the committee to describe examples of courses that were the foundation for its establishment. More importantly, it will also provide a venue in which the audience can suggest other examples.

SIGCSE'11, March 9–12, 2011, Dallas, Texas, USA.
ACM 978-1-4503-0500-6/11/03.

The committee set as an initial goal the cataloging of the breadth of music and computing courses across colleges and universities. This catalog is to become the basis for the music portion of the Computing and the Arts curriculum document, a supplement to the proposed Curriculum 2012 document that will focus on courses for the major.

2. OUTLINE OF SESSION

The four presenters will describe the courses they have developed, which combine computing and music, and related pedagogic endeavors. The presentations will highlight the distinctive approaches that have been used to demonstrate the strong connections between the two disciplines. The approaches include:

a) connecting concepts of music theory and programming language structure through the use of ChucK to make concrete the ideas from theory. For example, one can write a ChucK function that plays the major fifth above a given note;

b) describing the nature of sound and music and algorithms for their analysis and manipulation in digital representations; creating curriculum material that moves through levels of abstraction and links basic concepts, practice, and mathematical and algorithmic underpinnings;

c) inventing notations for music played on found instruments and writing programs to process the notations;

d) analyzing songs to identify their melodic and rhythmic patterns for the purpose of modifying the order and properties of those patterns through computer programs to create new compositions;

e) writing computer programs to play both pre-recorded and MIDI music with multiple parts in real time, addressing the synchronization issues involved in doing so;

f) connecting sensor-enabled devices to computer programs to create new musical instruments;

g) treating the computer itself as one's instrument to play music in real time through "live coding"; and intertwining the teaching of computational thinking with music making, and developing a B.A. degree program combining CS and music (among other arts areas).

3. EXPECTATIONS

By leaving about 20 minutes of session time for audience participation, the committee expects a lively discussion of the approaches it has presented and short descriptions of courses others have developed. The opportunity for exchange of ideas and networking among those interested in computing and music is an essential aspect of this session.

4. SUITABILITY

The conveners of the special session have used Birds of a Feather sessions at the last two SIGCSE Symposia to judge interest in the topic. After the meeting in Milwaukee, they proposed and received approval for establishing a SIGCSE Committee. Discussing the Committee's work and goals in a special session brings more formality and broader recognition to the importance of the topic. The special session format is particularly appropriate given the focused topic and the ability to use the time to present and discuss ideas.

5. ACKNOWLEDGMENTS

Some of the speakers' materials are based upon work supported by the National Science Foundation under Grant Nos. 0722161, 0717743, and 0722276. Any opinions, findings, and conclusions or recommendations expressed by the authors do not necessarily reflect the views of the National Science Foundation.

Science Fiction Prototyping and Security Education: Cultivating Contextual and Societal Thinking in Computer Security Education and Beyond

Tadayoshi Kohno
Computer Science and Engineering
University of Washington
yoshi@cs.washington.edu

Brian David Johnson
Future Casting, Interactions and Experience Research
Intel Corporation
brian.david.johnson@intel.com

ABSTRACT

Computer security courses typically cover a breadth of technical topics, including threat modeling, applied cryptography, software security, and Web security. The technical artifacts of computer systems – and their associated computer security risks and defenses – do not exist in isolation, however; rather, these systems interact intimately with the needs, beliefs, and values of people. This is especially true as computers become more pervasive, embedding themselves not only into laptops, desktops, and the Web, but also into our cars, medical devices, and toys. Therefore, in addition to the standard technical material, we argue that students would benefit from developing a mindset focused on the broader societal and contextual issues surrounding computer security systems and risks. We used *science fiction (SF) prototyping* to facilitate such societal and contextual thinking in a recent undergraduate computer security course. We report on our approach and experiences here, as well as our recommendations for future computer security and other computer science courses.

Categories and Subject Descriptors

K.3.2 [**Computer and Information Science Education**]: Computer Science Education

General Terms

Security, Human Factors.

Keywords

Computer science, computer security, prototyping, science fiction, science fiction prototyping, security mindset.

1. INTRODUCTION

Computer security is the subfield of computer science dedicated to the design and analysis of computer systems in the presence of adversaries. These adversaries – a.k.a. "attackers" or "hackers" – are people seeking to maliciously compromise computing systems. Unfortunately, hackers do exist and they can cause serious damage. Today's threats of phishing, identity theft, and spam are well known, and new threats will emerge as computers embed themselves more intimately into our environments and daily lives. Consider, for example, the teenager who recently hacked a train control system and caused 12 people to be injured in the resulting accident [16], or the recent discovery of security vulnerabilities in modern automotive computers [15] and wireless implantable medical devices [10].

There have been numerous explorations of methods for helping students learn the technical skills necessary to protect computer systems against attackers, including both early works, e.g., [17], [22] and more recent works, e.g., [1]. Outside the classroom there have also emerged undergraduate and graduate cyber-security competitions in which students apply and expand their knowledge *in situ*. While these are great advances, three key challenges remain. First, because technology is evolving at a very rapid rate, any technical skills taught today may become dated and thus less applicable in the future. Second, because of the field's breadth, any single course or short sequence of courses must undoubtedly omit some information about technical computer security defenses – but it could be that the omitted information is exactly what a student might later need to protect his or her system against certain attacks. And third, even if a student learns all the relevant technical materials, simply knowing *how* to protect against a computer security threat *after* the threat has been identified and deemed important does not mean that one necessarily knows to look for threats in the first place, how significant those threats are once identified, what new threats might manifest in the future as the technology or its deployment environment evolve, when to apply the relevant defenses, whether there might be negative consequences to applying those defenses, and so on. Laced over this entire discussion is the fact that computer security risks do not just apply to laptops, desktops, and the Web, but can also apply to any product with an embedded computer.

A key goal of the undergraduate computer security course at the University of Washington is to help students learn how to *think* about the real world and broader societal contexts surrounding computers and computer security. Doing so directly addresses the third challenge above. Such thinking skills empower students with the ability to answer questions like those that we posed earlier. We believe that if students can learn to think critically and deeply not just about the technologies themselves, but about the interactions between technologies and society, then they will be well equipped to identify potential computer security risks when they design and deploy new computer systems – risks that they might not have otherwise identified. This applies both to traditional computing systems, like desktops and the Web, and to emerging technologies. Such a skill also makes the first two challenges above less relevant. As long as students will, after their graduation, be able to identify and reason about the potential security risks with their systems, they will be able to work with more current technical experts to overcome those risks; on the other hand, an inability to identify potential computer security risks is almost a guarantee that those risks will not be guarded against in the resulting system. Additionally, some security defenses can be invasive to people's lives or have unexpected consequences, and the designer of security systems must be cognizant of those possibilities. Our initial approach to helping students cultivate this broader contextual thinking required students to (1) regularly review current events related to computer security and (2) analyze the security of newly announcements products; we describe this approach in a recent book [7].

This past year we embarked on a new approach for helping students develop broader contextual thinking around computer security. Our new approach is based on the budding field of *SF prototyping* [12]. Originally targeted towards engineers, SF prototyping is a process through which the creators of new technologies use science fiction storytelling to help them envision their technologies in the context of future society, understand the nuances of their potential future uses, and – informed by their increased understanding of how those technologies might interact with people in the future – revise their designs accordingly. We adopted SF prototyping to our course. The principal goal was to use SF prototyping to help students develop a mindset for thinking deeply about the security of computing technologies in the context of future users and society. An additional expected benefit was to provide students the opportunity to exercise their communications and creative thinking skills in a computer science course. We describe our experiences below, as well as lessons for future courses in computer security and other areas.

2. COURSE CONTEXT AND GOALS

CSE 484, Computer Security, is an optional senior-level course for Computer Science and Computer Engineering students at the University of Washington. Prior to taking CSE 484, students will have taken two introductory programming courses, a data structures course, and a computer architecture course. Many – though not all – students will have taken operating systems or computer networks. Students are therefore familiar with multiple technical aspects of computers.

The course covers a standard range of technical computer security material at the depth commensurate with a 10-week quarter, including applied cryptography, network security, Web security, software security, and usable security. Lectures provide a high-level description of these technical aspects, and homework and software laboratories provide students with an opportunity to dive more deeply into the technical materials. A key fact stressed throughout the course is that computer security issues may arise anywhere there are computers. For example, attackers can affect the brake control computer within a car and forcibly engage or disengage a car's brakes [15], and attackers can compromise a child's wireless toy robot, drive it around, and spy on the occupants of a home [4].

Our use of SF prototyping is aimed at fulfilling the following non-technical course goal: to help students develop a deeper understanding of the broader contextual issues surrounding computers and computer security, as well as an ability to reason about those broader contextual issues. The vision is that, by empowering students with an understanding of and appreciation for the broader context surrounding computer security, students will be better positioned to identify (and therefore address) potential computer security risks with computer systems that they develop, work with, or manage later in their careers, and that their resulting solutions will acceptable to users.

3. SF PROTOTYPING AND CONTEXTUAL EXPLORATIONS

SF prototyping began as a tool to help engineers design technologies that are sensitive to the needs of future users and society [13]. Engineers charged with designing a particular technology would use the science fiction writing process to help them dive deeply into, explore, and understand the future implications of those technologies and possible future derivatives. By placing the technology in a realistic future environment with realistic characters, engineers can develop an informed and thoughtful understanding of how that technology might interact with people in the future. We conjectured that students in any computer science course – including our computer security course – could similarly benefit from the SF prototyping process. Namely, the process of preparing a realistic story set in the future about a chosen technology would force students to think deeply about the interactions between that technology and society. Moreover, the SF prototyping process would also help students develop an intuition for thinking about potential adversaries against future technologies.

Because the greatest learning arises during the *planning* of a story – the development of the characters, the setting, the plot, and the interactions between the technology and the surrounding ecosystem – and *not* the *writing* of a story, and because our course already had significant other requirements, we did not ask our students to write complete stories in prose. Instead, we culminated the assignment with two key deliverables: (1) complete outlines for short stories, and (2) detailed write-ups reflecting upon the lessons the students learned about the technologies when developing the stories.

Those familiar with computer security might ask how this process compares to traditional threat modeling. Threat modeling is the practice of rigorously identifying the adversaries against a system and how those adversaries might try to attack the system. SF prototyping is complementary to, not a replacement for, rigorous threat modeling. The first few lectures of our course – and some of our assignments – are focused specifically on threat modeling. Threat modeling is however only effective if one knows to apply it – i.e., if one knows that there might be a need for computer security, which is not always the case. Our SF prototyping efforts are designed to help students develop a predisposition for evaluating technologies in the context of future users, which would thereby give students a better intuition for when and where security is needed. Additionally, traditional threat modeling alone may not identify all the complex – and potentially important – interactions between technologies and society. For example, threat modeling may find that tattooing passwords on patients' bodies may be a good solution for securing wireless implantable medical devices because the patients will never be without the tattoo; however, threat modeling may not uncover the fact that such tattoos may also negatively remind patients of WWII concentration camps [2]. In short, SF prototyping is a vehicle to help students develop a habit of not evaluating technologies in isolation, but to instead realize that there are multiple layers of complexities with these technologies, to challenge assumptions, and to think deeply about the interactions between technologies and people and the associated potential computer security risks.

We elaborate on the SF prototyping process that we used in our course below. We also note that the creation of SF prototypes for didactical purposes is different from, though complementary to, supported learning through reflection on existing science fiction, e.g., [20].

4. TOPIC SELECTION

We asked students to form groups of up to three people. The first task was to select a technology on which to focus. We gave students three key criteria for selecting their technology to study. Different groups were allowed to pick different technologies.

First, the technology had to be emerging and forward-looking. We wanted to empower students with an opportunity to think outside the box, with innovative new emerging technologies, and creatively envision future implications of these technologies. So emerging technologies like robots or "app stores" for cars were preferred over contemporary and well-understood technologies like Web browsers (unless students could identify some emerging and as-of-yet understudied aspects of such contemporary technologies).

Second, the chosen technology had to interact with other technologies, people, and society in non-trivial ways. An example might be a future wireless continuous glucose monitor for children with diabetes. Parents can monitor the child's glucose levels constantly over the Internet, and call their children or the school's nurse if a child's glucose levels get too low or too high. Such interactions are non-trivial; for example, such a technology could affect the relationship between the parent, the child, and the school. What if the parent was abusive or over-controlling? What if there was a bug in the software that made a parent think that the child was in danger when in fact the child was safe? What if the child wanted to hide his condition from his friends, or wanted to sneak a cookie without his parents finding out?

Third, because this was a computer security course, the chosen technology had to have some relationship to computer security. We explicitly told students that we would be very liberal in our definition of computer security. Any technology would qualify as long as there could conceivably be an attacker who might wish to compromise some desirable property of that technology. Students could therefore pick emerging technologies that might have computer security risks, or emerging technologies that are designed to mitigate security risks.

We encouraged students to explore numerous venues for finding a technology to study. They were highly encouraged to look for potential candidate technologies while reading the news – such as Slashdot or other media sites. This recommendation was aimed at helping students develop a habit of thinking about computer security risks – and broader contextual issues – outside the classroom and throughout their daily activities. For example, suppose a student saw an ad for a new game system. They might ask themselves: would there be interesting computer security issues and/or societal issues with the game system that would make a nice story? Even if they decided not to use this technology in their story, the process of rejecting this technology would have forced students to practice their deep, context-focused thinking about the broader issues surrounding technology.

We also encouraged students to familiarize themselves with emerging technologies presented at both research and industry conferences. For example, we pointed students to the HRI, Ubicomp, and CHI research conferences, as well as the industry CES conference. We encouraged students to consider computer security risks that are not present with today's versions of these technologies, but that might be present in future embodiments. Having students peruse the proceedings of academic conferences had a secondary benefit of helping students develop a better appreciation for the breadth of computer science.

Finally, we provided students with pointers to known information in the computer security research community about potential risks with emerging technologies. The risks are complex enough not to have clear solutions, and hence the known candidate solutions raise complex societal questions like how to appropriately balance security with safety, cost, and device lifetime, or whether it's appropriate for users to change their behavior to increase security (e.g., as an extreme example, patients might receive password tattoos [2], [21]). Examples of such security research abound, though we focused on examples with which we were already familiar, including implantable neural devices [3], other wireless implantable medical devices [10], wireless robots [4], and automobiles with wireless interfaces [15]. We also provided pointers to emerging security systems, like anonymity systems [5] and self-destructing data systems [9] that, if they become more feasible and widespread, could affect the way people interact with technologies.

5. MECHANICS: THE STORY

The key educational aspects of our SF prototyping process are in the *thinking* about the chosen technology in the context of a future society. The resulting story is the driver for this thinking. The story provides a framework for students to evaluate their technologies in realistic settings. We describe the process of developing a complete story outline below.

5.1 The Idea and the Plot

Since our class was targeted at senior-level computer science students – not writing students – we began with a brief introduction to the structure of stories. We stressed that the structural purpose of the outline is the capture the *idea* behind the story and put it into a *plot*. We provided students with the following quote from Alan Moore, comic book writer and creator of *The Watchmen*, *V for Vendetta*, and the *Sandman* series. This quote describes the distinction between the *idea* and the *plot* as follows [18]:

> The idea is what is the story is about; not the plot of the story, or the unfolding of the events within the story, but what the story is essentially about. As an example from my own work (not because it's a particularly good example but because I can speak about the work with more authority about it than I can the work of other people) I would cite issue #40 of *Swamp Thing*, "The Curse."
>
> The story was about the difficulties endured by women in masculine societies; using the common taboo of menstruation as a central motif. This was not the plot of the story – the plot concerned a young married woman moving into a new home built upon the site of an old Indian lodge and finding herself possessed by the dominating spirit that still resided there, turning her into a form of a werewolf.

The *idea* for the students' stories therefore come from the technology that they chose to study. The *plot* of the story is what is explored in the outline and is what allows the students to explore the broader contextual issues surrounding the technology.

We provided students with one more example to help crystallize the difference between the idea and the plot. In the story *Nebulous Mechanisms* [11], the idea of the story comes from a scientific paper [6] exploring the benefits of building irrationality into the artificial intelligence of domestic robots to improve their ability to adapt to complex environments. The plot of the story revolves around a character's investigation of why the robots from the Ceres mine have started going to church on Sundays.

In *Nebulous Mechanisms*, the *idea* is why the story is being told; the idea is what is being worked out in the fiction. The *plot* is what actually happens in the narrative. It is a linear set of events involving characters, locations, and situations where we can explore the implications of the idea. The SF prototyping process therefore involves putting the idea (technology) into a real world setting and seeing how the story plays out in order to develop a better understanding of the idea's affect on and interaction with both the characters and the locations.

5.2 Exploring the Technology: Planning

In planning their stories, students were instructed to consider future versions of the technologies they selected to explore. Students began by asking themselves some basic (and entertaining) questions, including:

- What are the implications of the mass adoption of the technology?
- What is the worst thing that could go wrong and how would it affect the people and locations in the story?
- What is the best thing that could happen and how would it better the lives of the people and locations of the story?
- If this technology were in an average home how would it actually work?

As with the choice of technologies to study, because this was a computer security course, we required an element of computer security in (at least some of) the questions that the students explored. But, as noted before, we explicitly told students that we would take a fairly broad and liberal definition of security.

After gaining some initial insights from these questions, students began to brainstorm about one or more potential broader contextual issues raised by their chosen technology. We stressed that it was important for students to remember that they were placing their topic (idea) in a real world. Even though the goal was a science fiction story, and the real world might be in the future, the world must feel real. It is still governed by the laws and logic of science, for example. We also stressed that real people will still populate this world. These real people will have real problems that have nothing to do with the students' chosen technologies. For example, in the future people will still not want to go to a boring job. In the future people will still fall in love and some will have their hearts broken. In the future we still will feel too lazy to take out the trash.

We suggested that students pick a setting in the "near" future. A near-future setting, rather than a far-future setting, would make it easier for students to place their technologies in a realistic environment. To help students understand the challenges with creating a plausible near-future setting, we provided students with the following passage from a book on writing science fiction [14]:

> Because most science fiction takes place in the future, the backgrounds are largely products of the writers' imaginations. The future can be researched only to a limited extent, for when it comes to saying exactly what the years ahead hold for us, even the most well-informed scientists can offer only conjecture. The SF (science fiction) writer's vision of the future must be detailed and believable, or ultimately the reader will not believe *anything* about the story – not the characters, the motivation, or the plot.
>
> The *near future*. Structuring a story background of near future – twenty, thirty, or forty years from now – is in some way more difficult than creating an entire alien planet in some impossibly distant age, for the near-future background cannot be *wholly* a product of the imagination. The writer must conduct extensive research to discover what engineer and scientists project for every aspect of future life. From that data, the author then *extrapolates* a possible world of tomorrow, one which might logically rise out of the base of the future which we are building today.

This passage also helped to solidify for students that the writing of science fiction requires a deep understanding of the interactions between technology and science / engineering – which is exactly what motivated us to use SF prototyping in our course.

5.3 Exploring the Technology: The Outline

Students culminated their stories with complete outlines. An outline provides a step-by-step description of what happens in the story – "a linear arrangement of related incidents, episodes or events leading to a dramatic resolution [8]." We informed students that brief descriptions would be sufficient to describe event in their outlines. We also provided students with a simple outline structure for their stories, adopted from Field [8]. The plot is broken down into five parts:

- **Act I:** Act I is where one sets up the world of the story and introduces the reader to the people and locations. Act I answers very simple questions like: who are the main characters, where will the action take place, and what is this future society like? Act I also begins to explore an explanation of the students' chosen technology – what is the technology, what is it designed to do, how does it work, and so on.
- **Plot Point I:** A *plot point* is "an incident or event that 'hooks' into the action and spins it around into another direction. It moves the story forward [8]." For our course, the plot point is the implication of the chosen technology on the world within the story. For a typical science fiction story, this is how the science affects the people and locations in the story in a way that is unexpected or surprising. There might be an unexpected risk, possibility, or reaction to the technology, for example.
- **Act II:** Act II is where students explore the implications of Plot Point I on their story's world. What affect does the technology have? How does it change people lives? Does it

create a new danger? What needs to be done to fix the problem?

- **Plot Point II:** Plot Point II describes lessons learned from seeing the chosen technology placed in the real world. What needed to happen to fix the problem? Does the technology need to be modified? Is there a new area for experimentation or research?
- **Act III:** Act III explores the possible implications and areas for exploration from Plot Point II.

For clarity, we provided students with an example outline for the previously mentioned story *Nebulous Mechanisms* [11]. The example outline is also included in a new text [12].

Stepping Back. The outline development process directly facilitates broader thinking about technologies. Students must envision realistic future scenarios for deploying their chosen technologies (Act I), think about how the technologies will be used and uncover potentially unexpected properties (Plot Point I), explore the implications of those unexpected properties (Act II), draw lessons from those implications (Plot Point II), and reflect upon those latter lessons (Act III). Additionally, most students would not simply write one outline from start to finish. Rather, most students would iteratively revise their plots and produce new outlines as they progressively thought more deeply about their chosen technologies – and each level of iteration provides additional learning opportunities and greater insights into the broader contextual issues surrounding the chosen technology.

6. DELIVERABLES

Students completed their SF prototyping projects in two phases. The first deadline was several weeks after the announcement of the project, and the second deadline was several weeks after that.

The first deadline required each group to submit: a short description (at most one paragraph) of the technology that they planned to explore (including background references); a short (at most one paragraph) description of the broader contextual issues that the students anticipated encountering; and a short (at most one paragraph) synopsis of the envisioned story, including key plot points and other story artifacts. We carefully read each of these reports to gauge progress and spot unforeseen obstacles. We also provided feedback to students, including suggested questions that the students might ask themselves in order to more deeply explore the broader contextual issues surrounding the technologies and to help them continue to shape their the stories.

The final deadline required students to submit a short description of the technology that the students explored (in case the choice of technology changed between the first and second deadlines) and a story outline as described in Section 5.3.

The final step in the SF prototyping process is to reflect on what one has learned from taking the chosen technology through the story development process. Therefore, we also required students to submit a short (two- to three-page) reflection on the broader contextual and societal issues surrounding their chosen technology. Given the focus of this course, we asked students to primarily focus their reflection on the computer security issues surrounding their chosen technologies. We asked students to discuss how their understanding of the relevant computer security issues evolved through the SF prototyping process. For example, did this process expand their understanding of the risks or potential defenses and, if so, how? What issues were raised that the students did not foresee? We also asked students to reflect upon how they would design future technologies to address the issues that they uncovered.

Finally, to facilitate cooperative learning and the sharing of lessons, we encouraged students to post their outlines and reflections to the online class forum. We also encouraged students to discuss others' outlines and reflections on the forum.

7. REFLECTIONS AND NEXT STEPS

We found numerous benefits to the use of SF prototyping in our computer security course. As evidenced both from student feedback, and our subjective observations of student progress, the SF prototyping process successfully catalyzed broader thinking about the contextual and societal issues and computer security risks associated with emerging technologies. This broader contextual thinking complemented the more traditional technical components of our course, such as threat modeling, cryptography, software security, Web security, and usable security.

Many students also enjoyed this project, as evidenced by feedback like "The process of developing our science fiction prototype was very informative, in addition to being fun and rewarding" and "It was great to do an assignment in a computer science class that actually got an alternate stream of imagination and creativity flowing, and I hope this prototyping assignment is given in future iterations of this class." Our experience suggests that because of the fun, non-traditional nature of this project, many students were more motivated to think about it outside the traditional classroom and lab setting, thereby further aiding in its educational impact.

There were however some students who were surprised to find such a strong creative writing component in a senior-level computer science course. We briefly discussed this project at the beginning of the term, but did not officially assign the project or provide full details until after the course's drop date. Some students might prefer computer science courses with less creative writing components, and hence might have preferred to drop the course. We therefore suggest clearly describing this project, and its scope and purpose, at the beginning of the term to minimize any misalignment in expectations.

A second downside with our approach is that the final science fiction outline can only reasonably explore one or two broader contextual issues in depth (the plot points). Some students might have explored numerous other broader contextual issues in depth before finalizing on the ones for their stories, but other students might not have. Informed by our successes with SF prototyping, but cognizant of this concern, we anticipate exploring the use of vignettes in lieu of or in addition to SF prototypes in future courses. The use of vignettes, similar to their use in "value scenarios" for system design [19], would allow students to create multiple short scenes to explore particular issues about emerging technologies, rather than full stories around only a few issues.

Our experience with SF prototyping in a senior-level computer security course makes us even more enthusiastic about its potential impact and utility in other courses. A first year undergraduate computer science course on SF prototyping, especially if cross-listed with another department, could appeal to a larger audience than a traditional computer science course. Students in our computer security course explored topics ranging from ubiquitous embedded digital cameras to prosthetics, autonomous vehicles, nanotechnologies, and future uses of biometrics. We expect similarly broad technology coverage in a first-year undergraduate course. Covering such a wide range of technologies will likely help broaden these students' understanding of what constitutes computer science, e.g., students new to computer science would learn that computer science is much broader than just laptop, desktop, and Web computing. This awakening could attract new students to the field. Additionally, the broader contextual thinking established in this first-year undergraduate course would help future majors develop a predisposition for thinking about the broader world in which technologies may be deployed. We believe that this perspective would prove valuable to students throughout their careers.

8. CONCLUSIONS

Computers do not exist in isolation, but rather interact intimately with people and society. This is particularly true as computers become more pervasive and begin to embed themselves throughout our environments and daily lives. Given this trend, we argue that it is important for students in computer security courses to develop a mindset for thinking about computers, computer security risks, and their defenses in the context of people and society. Further, we argue that the ability to think rationally about computer security risks can be useful to students throughout their careers, whereas knowledge of today's latest and greatest security weaknesses and defenses may prove ephemeral as technologies evolve. Therefore, and in addition to covering standard technical materials, we introduce a non-standard component into our undergraduate computer security course: SF prototyping.

Our experiences suggest that SF prototyping can be a valuable facilitator for broader contextual and societal thinking about computers, computer security risks, and security defenses. Our experiences also suggest natural next steps for the evaluation of this effort, such as the use of vignettes instead of or in addition to complete stories in upper-division courses. Our experiences also suggest that SF prototyping could serve as a valuable, entertaining, and enjoyable bridge for exposing lower-division students in other disciplines to the breadth of computer science. We plan to explore these latter observations as future work.

9. ACKNOWLEDGMENTS

We thank all the students in CSE 484 for their participation and feedback, as well as the other instructional staff: Slava Chernyak, Alexei Czeskis, and Miro Enev. This work was supported in part by NSF Award CNS-0846065.

10. REFERENCES

[1] S. Bratus, A. Shubina, and M. E. Locasto. Teaching the principles of the hacker curriculum to undergraduates. In *SIGCSE*, 2010.

[2] T. Denning, A. Borning, B. Friedman, B. T. Gill, T. Kohno, and W. H. Maisel. Patients, pacemakers, and implantable defibrillators: Human values and security for wireless implantable medical devices. In *CHI*, 2010.

[3] T. Denning, Y. Matsuoka, and T. Kohno. Neurosecurity: Security and privacy for neural devices. *Neurosurgical Focus*, 27, July 2009.

[4] T. Denning, C. Matuszek, K. Koscher, J. R. Smith, and T. Kohno. A spotlight on security and privacy risks with future household robots: Attacks and lessons. In *Ubicomp*, 2009.

[5] R. Dingledine, N. Mathewson, and P. Syverson. Tor: The second-generation onion router. In *USENIX Security*, 2004.

[6] S. Egerton, V. Callaghan, and G. Clarke. Using multiple personas in service robots to improve exploration strategies when mapping new environments. In *Intelligent Environments*, 2008.

[7] N. Ferguson, B. Schneier, and T. Kohno. *Cryptography Engineering: Design Principles and Practical Applications*. Wiley Publishing, Inc., 2010.

[8] S. Field. *Screenplay: The Foundations of Screenwriting*. Dell, 1979.

[9] R. Geambasu, T. Kohno, A. A. Levy, and H. M. Levy. Vanish: Increasing data privacy with self-destructing data. In *USENIX Security*, 2009.

[10] D. Halperin, T. S. Heydt-Benjamin, B. Ransford, S. S. Clark, B. Defend, W. Morgan, K. Fu, T. Kohno, and W. H. Maisel. Pacemakers and implantable cardiac defibrillators: Software radio attacks and zero-power defenses. In *IEEE Symposium on Security and Privacy*, 2008.

[11] B. D. Johnson. Nebulous Mechanisms. In *Intelligent Environments*, 2009.

[12] B.D. Johnson. *Science Fiction Prototyping: A Framework for Design*. Morgan and Claypool, 2010.

[13] B.D. Johnson. Science Fiction Prototypes Or: How I Learned to Stop Worrying about the Future and Love Science Fiction. In *Intelligent Environments*, 2009.

[14] D. Koontz. *How to Write Best Selling Fiction*. Writers Digest Books, 1981.

[15] K. Koscher, A. Czeskis, F. Roesner, S. Patel, T. Kohno, S. Checkoway, D. McCoy, B. Kantor, D. Anderson, H. Shacham, and S. Savage. Experimental security analysis of a modern automobile. In *IEEE Symposium on Security and Privacy*, 2010.

[16] J. Leyden. Polish teen derails tram after hacking train network, 2008. http://www.theregister.co.uk/2008/01/11/tram_hack/.

[17] P. Mateti. A laboratory-based course on Internet security. In *SIGCSE*, 2003.

[18] A. Moore. *Alan Moore's Writing for Comics*. Avatar Press, 2008.

[19] L. P. Nathan, B. Friedman, P. Klasnja, S. K. Kane, and J. K. Miller. Envisioning systemic effects on persons and society throughout interactive system design. In *Designing Interactive Systems*, 2008.

[20] D. Sanderson. Using Science Fiction to Teach Computer Science. In *WWW@10*, 2004.

[21] S. Schechter. Security that is meant to be skin deep: Using ultraviolet micropigmentation to store emergency-access keys for implantable medical devices. In *USENIX Workshop on Health Security and Privacy*, 2010.

[22] G. White and G. Nordstrom. Security across the curriculum: Using computer security to teach computer science principles. In *National Information Systems Security Conference*, 1996.

Security in Computer Literacy- A Model for Design, Dissemination, and Assessment

Claude F. Turner
Department of Computer Science
Bowie State University
(301) 860-3965
cturner@bowiestate.edu

Blair Taylor
Department of Computer and Information Sciences
Towson University
(410) 704-4560
btaylor@towson.edu

Siddharth Kaza
Department of Computer and Information Sciences
Towson University
(410) 704-6310
skaza@towson.edu

ABSTRACT

While many colleges offer specialized security courses and tracks for students in computing majors, there are few offerings in information security for the non-computing majors. Information security is becoming increasingly critical in many fields, yet most computer literacy courses insufficiently address the security challenges faced by our graduates. This paper discusses the development and impact of a set of modules designed to integrate security into computer literacy across two universities and several community colleges in the state of Maryland. Results from our comparative analyses based on pre- and post- test analysis show significant improvements in post-test results.

Categories and Subject Descriptors

K3.2 [**Computers and Education**]: Computer and Information Science Education - *computer science education, curriculum, information systems education.*

General Terms: Security

Keywords: Security Education, Computer Science Curriculum, Information Security Curriculum Development.

1. INTRODUCTION

Computer literacy is offered as a required course by a variety of universities and colleges, where it aims to provide students with current knowledge and understanding of computers and their uses. For many college instructors, the computer literacy course is the bane of their teaching load – often the first course they teach and the first course they drop from their schedule. The disadvantages of teaching this course include: a new textbook every few years; lecture notes that quickly become obsolete; a variable, often ill-defined list of topics [4]; and large classes full of non-majors looking for an easy 'A'. Additionally, the class seems to afford few research or publishing opportunities; since 2000, less than a dozen papers have been written on computer literacy [4].

SIGCSE'11, March 9–12, 2011, Dallas, Texas, USA.

Epperson [4] provides an excellent history of computer literacy, starting with the coinage of the term in 1972, as well as its future direction. Shelly [11] informs us that the requirements that determine computer literacy evolve as technology changes. In recent years, to help people adapt to these rapid changes, become effective users quickly, and prepare for lifelong learning, there has begun a reexamination of the general structure of computer literacy. A National Research Council (NRC) report titled, *Being Fluent with Information Technology* [10], has proposed a variety of recommendations, including a new term that would replace computer literacy—*fluency with information technology* (FIT)—or as put more succinctly by Snyder, *fluency* [13]. FIT is described as "a package of skills, concepts, and capabilities wrapped into a project-oriented learning approach that ensures that the content is fully integrated" [13]. Other authors including Bartholomew [2], Hoffman & Blake [6] and Sloan & Halaris [12] have discussed this subject and have provided their recommendations on providing a breadth of IT knowledge to non-computing majors.

We believe that in addition to other important topics, non-computing majors need to be exposed to security topics. Information security has become increasingly critical to many other fields, business and health for example, and college graduates from all majors will encounter information security issues in their personal and professional lives. Even so, many books on literacy and fluency often have only a chapter or section on security, and lack the active learning component that would help students internalize the concepts.

To address this issue, we added the computer literacy course to the Security Injections project [8,14,18,19] currently underway at Towson University, Bowie State University, and several other community colleges in Maryland. The objective of the project is to integrate security throughout computing curricula using a minimally invasive thread based approach [14,18,19]. The project began with a focus on the core computer science classes, but the addition of the computer literacy course had many unforeseen advantages. With apologies to Dr. Seuss, "Maybe the Computer Literacy class...perhaps...means a little bit more!" Consider the following, which holds true at many institutions, including Towson and Bowie State University:

- The computer literacy class reaches more students than any other class in our department.
- The computer literacy class reaches students in computing majors, non-computing majors and students who have not yet decided on a major.

- The computer literacy class includes more female and minority students than any other class in our department.
- The computer literacy class allows some flexibility to add interesting and relevant topics.

This work reports on our efforts to integrate security into the computer literacy [1,3,7] course using modules that encourage active learning. We have developed, deployed, and assessed a set of three modules (called security injections) for computer literacy based on the general structure proposed by Taylor et al. [18]. The modules cover the topics of phishing, passwords and cryptography and are designed to provide students with the experiential learning in computer security. In this paper, we present and discuss the collaborative process involving two and four year institutions to design, disseminate, and assess the modules. We describe the general structure of the modules and provide a specific example. We also report on our experience in deploying modules and our assessment results.

2. PROJECT OVERVIEW

2.1 Security across the Curriculum

In fall 2006, we initiated a plan to integrate security throughout the computing curriculum. The goal was to complement our security track and introduce security principles to computing majors early and often. Early efforts targeted select sections of the core computing required courses, CS0 and CS1 [18]. Using a common set of learning objectives to link the materials across the classes, we created a set of security related laboratory modules that focused on the major secure coding issues of integer overflow, buffer overflow, and input validation. In 2008, the project expanded to include five additional courses: CS2, Computer Literacy, Database, Web Programming, and Networking; and to encompass five institutions: Towson, Bowie State, and three partnering community colleges: Anne Arundel Community College, the Community Colleges of Baltimore County, and Harford Community College.

2.2 The Model

Our collaborative approach to implementing curriculum change across varying institutions is based on a model with a set of well-defined goals and repeats a process of: develop materials, pilot across institutions, evaluate, revise, and disseminate [15]. Formal evaluation includes materials review from a technical expert in security, qualitative and quantitative feedback from experienced teachers at our partnering institutions, results from ongoing pilot programs, and quantitative results from security surveys and code checks. This model and assessment results for CS0, CS1, CS2 have been reported in previous publications [8,15,16].

2.3 Security Modules

Security modules were created with the objectives of *maximizing the learning experience* and *minimizing the burden on the instructor*. To increase the effectiveness of the module, we designed it with active learning in mind [9]. The "active" components include security related exercises and a security checklist, described below. Additionally, we formalized the module structure to promote critical thinking and reflection [17]. In contrast to the traditional computer laboratory exercise which is a loosely structured set of problems or exercises that inadequately address synthetic and analytical thinking [17, 18], the security lab modules in this project are patterned after the structured labs in physics and biology. Each module contains the following components:

- **Background** - The module begins with background information, including a concise description of the topic, the risk involved, and real-life examples that include links to articles describing actual occurrences of security vulnerabilities. The purpose of this section is to set the stage for the active learning process that follows.
- **Laboratory Assignments** – There are several hands-on lab exercises related to the specific security concept. Hands-on exercises that present meaningful concepts in an engaging manner increase motivation and enhance learning. Research shows that in a "learning by doing" environment, students learn more, retain the information longer, can apply learned material in more contexts, and the environment of the classroom is more enjoyable [9].
- **Security Checklists**. A key component to each module is the security checklist. A security checklist is a well-defined set of procedures for identifying potential security concerns. Checklists have many relevant applications, including aviation, software assurance, and have recently been shown to reduce errors in emergency rooms [5]. A well-developed checklist can reduce human error, serve as a reminder list, and help ensure consistency and completeness. Additionally, checklists can reinforce security principles and help students quantify and internalize important security principles. The checklists in our modules, initially designed to find potential vulnerabilities in software, proved to be readily adaptable for passwords, phishing, and cryptography.
- **Discussion questions** require students to reflect upon the process, the results, and the security implications of the new concept.

Minimally invasive. Finally, each module was designed towards ease of use by the instructor. Using feedback from faculty and students, each module has been streamlined and formatted to allow simple insertion within a lab or for stand-alone use. Estimated completion time for most modules is 20-30 minutes. We encourage instructors to use or adapt the modules to accommodate instructional needs. We also recommend that instructors allow students to work in pairs to encourage collaborative learning. The intention of each lab is that it can be completed without class instruction and with minimal help from the instructor.

3. Computer Literacy Modules

3.1 Module Design

Developing security modules for computer literacy is a challenging activity. Many of the students are freshmen and often lack the necessary prerequisites to understand computer security principles. In our case, this is further compounded by the fact that our modules are targeted to different communities of students, ranging from community colleges, minority serving institutions, to comprehensive universities. To address these challenges, we designed the modules to be self-contained and targeted to a freshman audience. We also hold workshops at participating institutions to help train and prepare faculty who teach using the modules.

The topics for the modules were determined through discussions in workshops attended by faculty from all partner institutions. We found the computer literacy instructors, some of whom are graduate students and adjunct instructors, to be very receptive to our approach and full of ideas for future modules. We sought to identify essential issues in information security that were topical and cut across various communities of students. Although a variety of important topics were considered, phishing, passwords and cryptography emerged at the top of the list. A module that encompassed the basic definition of security—illustrating the challenge and significance of meeting the triangular concepts of confidentiality, integrity and availability (CIA), as well as the concept of risk analysis—was also deemed very important.

3.2 Using the Security Injection Modules in your Classroom

Currently, our project includes the following three modules for Computer Literacy: (1) Passwords, (2) Phishing, and (3) Cryptography. Modules are located at: http://triton.towson.edu/~cssecinj. A compressed form of the Phishing module is shown in Table 1. These modules are currently being used at Bowie State University, Towson University, Anne Arundel Community College, Community College of Baltimore County, and Harford Community College. The procedure for using the modules, described in the 'Faculty Access' section of the website is as follows:

1. Administer Security Survey
2. Introduce Security Injections in Class
3. Administer Security Survey after introducing Security Injections
4. Complete Faculty Survey.

4. ASSESSMENT DESIGN AND RESULTS

The primary goals for this project are: increasing students' general security awareness, improving students' knowledge on the content of specific security modules, increasing faculty security awareness, and increasing the number of security-skilled students. Each of these objectives is assessed using various instruments including surveys, qualitative inputs from faculty, and institutional data. In this paper, we present the student survey design and results on student awareness and learning from the use of modules in the computer literacy courses.

4.1 Pre and Post Surveys

Each class that used our modules was given a pre-survey at the beginning of the class and a post-survey at the end of the class. An independent evaluator has reviewed all assessment materials, including pre-surveys and post-surveys. The student surveys contain demographic questions (including questions on the interest in security), and two sets of multiple choice questions – one section targets general security awareness and the other focuses on specific knowledge gained through the modules (a list of sample questions is shown in Table 2). We used parts of this survey in CS0, CS1, and CS2 previously and it was well accepted by students [8].

Table 2. Sample survey questions

General Security Awareness
What are the possible consequences of insufficient computer security?
A set of related programs, usually located at a network gateway server, that protects the resources of a private network from other networks, is known as a …
Module specific
Who is it safe to tell your password to?
Phishing is …
The following are characteristics of suspicious email:
Encryption is a special technique employed only by agencies with highly sensitive data such as the FBI or CIA.
Consider the following email: (followed by an phishing email that the students had to identify)
Using letters from a memorable phrase is a recommended way to construct a password.(T or F)
Never give out personal information upon an email request (T or F)
Encrypting your personal files requires purchasing special software. (T or F)
The conversion of data into a ciphertext that cannot be easily understood by unauthorized people is known as …

Based on the pre and post survey, a set of two hypotheses were proposed to test student learning.

H1: The post-survey scores will be significantly higher than pre-survey scores.

H2: The post-survey scores in specific module topics will be significantly higher than pre-survey scores.

4.2 Basic Statistics and Demographics

A total of 384 survey responses from four institutions were received with 357 responses from sections that used the modules. After data cleaning, 300 valid survey responses were analyzed. Figure 1 presents the demographics of students who took the survey.

As can be seen, the classes had a fairly even distribution between gender and ethnicity. The classes also had a majority of freshman as was expected in a literacy course. Also as expected, the classes showed a skewed distribution among majors. A large majority of students were non-computing majors – this provides us with an opportunity to spread security concepts among students in other disciplines who are not exposed to security issues that they are almost certain to face in their professional and personal lives. In addition, the even spread in gender and ethnicity offers an excellent platform to introduce exciting computer science concepts and attract women and URMs to the field.

Table 1. An abbreviated version of the Phishing module (see complete module at http://triton.towson.edu/~csseciŋj)

Phishing – "A scam to steal private information"

Summary - Phishing is a type of social engineering technique in which an attacker sends an e-mail or displays a Web announcement that falsely claims to be from a legitimate organization. The intention of the messenger is to trick the user into surrendering private information.

Description - A more specific definition is offered by the Anti-phishing Working Group (APWG): "Phishing is a criminal mechanism employing both social engineering and technical subterfuge to steal consumers' personal identity data and financial account credentials." The victim in a phishing attack is asked to respond to an e-mail or is directed to a Web site to update personal information, such as passwords, credit card numbers, Social Security numbers, bank account numbers, or other information for which the legitimate organization already has a record. However, the site is actually a fraudulent Web site designed to steal the user's information.

Risk - Phishing can and usually leads to online identity theft. By capturing a user's personal information, an attacker can gain access to the user's account on a legitimate Web site, and can engage in a number of activities resulting in substantial financial loss to the user, denial of access to e-mail, and other problems.

Example of occurrence - On the weekend of January 3, 2009, several users on the social network Web site, Twitter, became victims of a phishing attack. The users were deceived into giving away their passwords when they received an e-mail similar to one that they would receive from Twitter with a link that read, "hey, check out this funny blog about you…". The link redirects to a site masquerading as the real Twitter site. Any personal information entered by the user on the fake site is then captured by the attacker.

Anti-Phishing Training - Training users to identify a 'phish' is an important component in the fight against phishing. Training has taken two forms: the first is simply to provide anti-phishing information to users through e-mail and other media. The second is to give firsthand experience to users through games, simulated phish, cartoons, etc. Recent studies seem to indicate that the latter—giving firsthand experience to users—might be more effective. The game, Anti-Phishing Phil http://wombatsecurity.com/antiphishingphil, which teaches people how to identify suspicious Web site addresses while providing the experience of being captured by a phisher, is such an example. PhishGuru in the previous section is another example. It delivers cartoon-based, anti-phishing information after a user has been deceived by simulated phishing messages.

Anti-Phishing Technologies - Although user ability to identify phish is an important component in the battle against phishing, combining it with technology yields better results. One of the techniques used to automatically identify phish is **filtering**. The objective of filtering is to identify (or flag) phishing attempts in e-mail or on Web pages. Filters are usually integrated into browsers or e-mail software. When a Web address is encountered the software compares it with a so-called "blacklist" of known phishing Web sites. It then takes appropriate actions, which usually include informing the user. The blacklist is updated periodically (for example, every 30 minutes) as new phishing sites become available. As with any blacklist, there is also a "whitelist" of known legitimate sites.

Lab questions - Consider the PayPal e-mail in the figure (an email is provided to the students, please see website for the complete module) . The Web address in the box, http//211.248.156/Paypal/cgi-bin/webscrcmd_login.php, appears when the user mouse-over the "Click here to verify your account" link.

1. Complete the following checklist for this e-mail.

2. List any sentence, phrase or word that makes the e-mail a suspected phish.

Security Checklist	
Vulnerability: Phishing **Course:** Computer Literacy	
Task – Read the e-mail carefully; answer yes/no in the space provided	**Yes/No**
1. Were there suspicious words, phrases or sentences	
2. Were there suspicious links?	
3. Are there grammatical or spelling errors in the e-mail?	
4. Does the e-mail start with a generic greeting?	
5. Does the e-mail contain any pop-up boxes or attachments?	
6. Does the e-mail contain an air of urgency or a need to respond immediately?	
7. Does the email ask you for personal information such as passwords and social security number?	
If you answered yes to any of the above questions, then the e-mail is a suspected phishing mail.	

Discussion questions

1. Play at least two games of Anti-Phishing Phil at http://wombatsecurity.com/antiphishingphil. Create a "blacklist" of the phishing Web site addresses you encountered, and a "whitelist" of the legitimate Web sites. (Hint: see the section on Anti-phishing Technologies.) Describe how the Anti-Phising Phil experience has helped you to better recognize phishing Web sites. What are your likes and dislikes about the game? Are there any suggestion(s) that you would like to provide so as to improve it? If so, explain.

2. Take the "SonicWall Phishing and Spam IQ Test" a couple of times (http://www.sonicwall.com/phishing/). What was your maximum score? Look at the test result sheet, and give the name that appears in the "Subject" column for three of the questions. For each of the subjects, click on the "Why?" link that appears under the "Explain Answer Column." The e-mail you viewed for that question should re-appear—this time with explanations. Copy one of the given explanations for each of the e-mails.

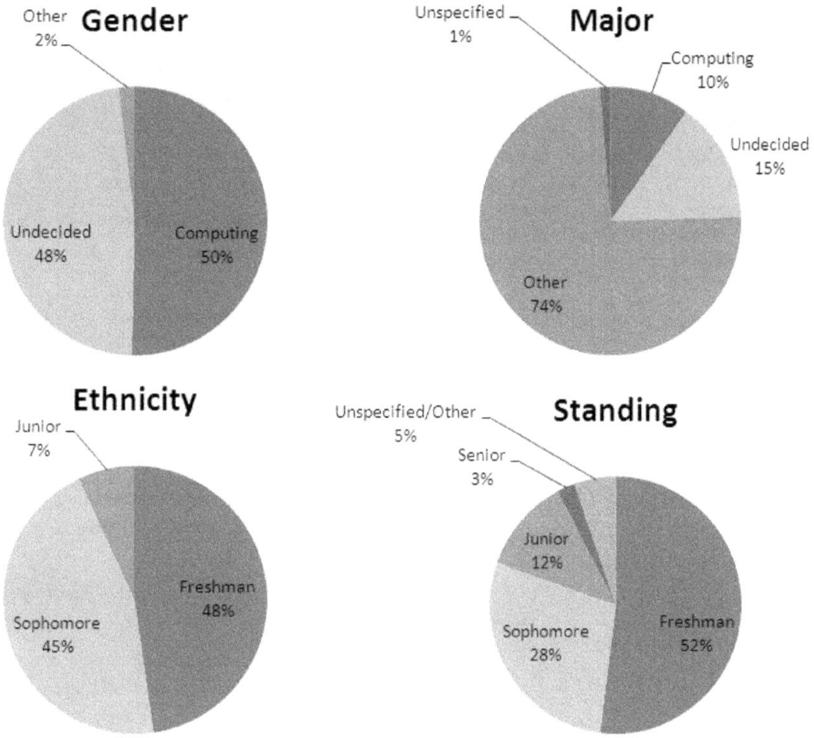

Figure 1. Demographics of survey respondents

4.3 Survey Results

This assessment involved class sections in five institutions and we found that it was difficult to get a similar response rate for both the pre-surveys and the post-surveys. There were 300 survey responses with 86 in the pre-survey and 214 in the post-survey. In line with our Institutional Review Board requirements, the survey did not contain any information that could identify the student or pair the responses between the pre and post tests. Each question in the survey was a multiple choice question with three or more options (the T/F questions had a unsure option) and one correct option. The score of each survey was calculated by counting the number of correct answers from a total of 14 questions (including general security and module specific questions). We picked the Mann-Whitney non-parametric test to compare the mean rank of the scores in the two groups (pre and post). This was done because of two primary reasons – 1) the n for the groups is different and 2) the Kolmogorov-Smirnov and Shapiro-Wilk test showed that the scores were not normally distributed. Figure 2 summarizes the results. The average score obtained in the pre-surveys was 9.09 and the average score in the post-surveys was 10.67. It was found that this was a statistically significant increase ($p < 0.001$). These results look promising and support H1.

For individual modules, it was found that there was a statistically significant increase ($p < 0.001$) in the scores obtained in the questions targeted at each of the modules with a 34.71% increase in knowledge related to the phishing module, 25.82% increase in the cryptography module, and 9.14% increase in the password module. This supports H2.

Deeper analysis on the data showed that the significant increase in overall scores persisted across gender and ethnicity. Additionally, we found that women started significantly lower than men, yet, caught up in the post-test; and at the end of the semester there was no significant difference in their scores. Further analysis of this data is in progress.

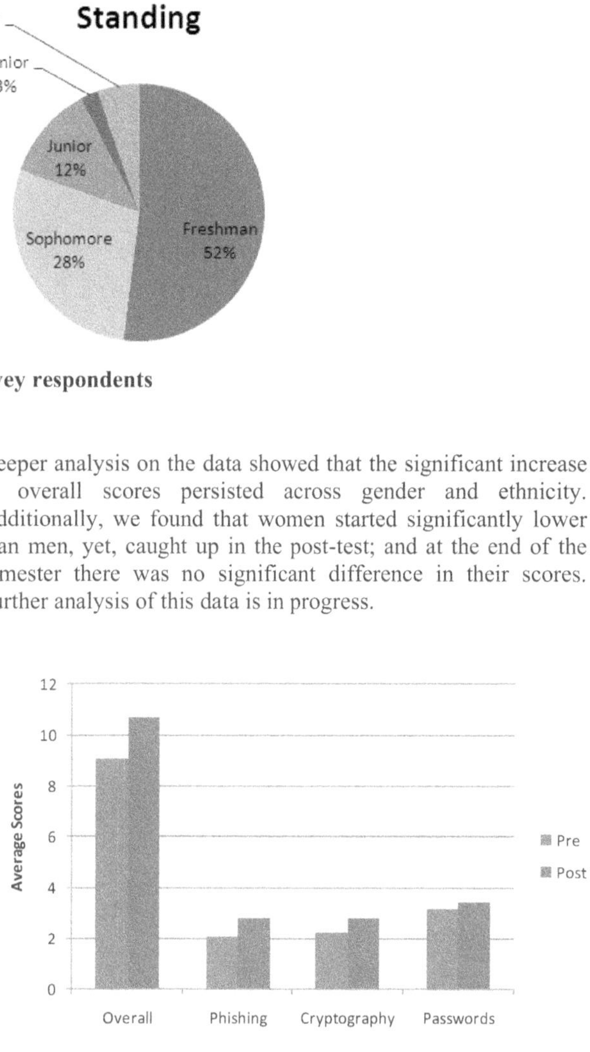

Figure 2. Survey results for pre and post surveys

5. Conclusion

Many colleges offer specialized security courses and tracks for students in computing majors since computer security is recognized as an essential topic for computer scientists. For the non-computing majors, there are few offerings in information security. Increasingly, information security is becoming critical in many fields and the current computer literacy courses insufficiently address the security challenges faced by our graduates. This paper discussed the development and impact of a set of modules designed to integrate security into computer literacy across two universities and several community colleges in the state of Maryland. Results from our comparative analyses based on pre and post test results showed statistically significant improvements in the post-tests. Overall scores improved 17.37%; phishing module related scores increased 34.71%; cryptography related scores increased 25.82%, and password related scores increased 9.14%. Also of interest, females, who scored lower on the pre-tests, caught up with males on the post-tests.

6. ACKNOWLEDGMENTS

This project is partially supported by the NSF Course Curriculum and Laboratory Improvement (CLLI) grant number DUE-0817267. We greatly appreciate our colleagues and partners at Bowie State University, Harford County Community College, Community College of Baltimore County, and Anne Arundel Community College. In particular, we are grateful to Harry Hochheiser, Mike O'Leary, Shiva Azadegan, AC Chaplin, Patricia Gregory, Jack McLaughlin for their contributions.

7. REFERENCES

[1] Bacon, T. and Tikekar, R. Experiences with developing a computer security information assurance curriculum. *Journal of Computing Sciences in Colleges 18*, 4 (2003), 254 - 267.

[2] Bartholomew, K.W. Computer literacy: is the emperor still exposed after all these years? *Journal of Computing Sciences in Colleges 20*, 1 (2004), 323.

[3] Bogolea, B. and Wijekumar, K. Information security curriculum creation: a case study. *Information Security Curriculum Development*, ACM (2004), 59-65.

[4] Epperson, A. Computer literacy revisited: a comprehensive investigation of computer literacy. *ACM Inroads 1*, 2 (2010), 30-33.

[5] Gawande, A. *The checklist manifesto: how to get things right*. Metropolitan Books, 2009.

[6] Hoffman, M., Blake, J., McKeon, J., Leone, S., and Schorr, M. A critical computer literacy course. *Journal of Computing Sciences in Colleges 20*, 5 (2005), 163.

[7] Irvine, C. and Chin, S. Integrating security into the curriculum. *IEEE Computer 31*, 12 (1998), 25-30.

[8] Kaza, S., Taylor, B., Hochheiser, H., Azadegan, S., O□Leary, M., and Turner, C.F. Injecting Security in the Curriculum – Experiences in Effective Dissemination and Assessment Design. *The Colloquium for Information Systems Security Education (CISSE)*, (2010).

[9] McConnell, J. Active Learning and its use in computer science. *Proceeds of the 1st conference on Integrating Technology into computer science education*, (1996), 52-54.

[10] Multiple. Being Fluent with Information Technology. 1999, 128. http://www.amazon.com/Fluent-Information-Technology-Committee-Literacy/dp/030906399X.

[11] Shelly, G.B. *Computer Concepts - Discovering Computers: Living in a Digital World, Fundamentals*. Course Technology, 2010.

[12] Sloan, L. and Halaris, A. Towards a definition of computing literacy for the liberal arts environment. *Technical Symposium on Computer Science Education*, (1985), 320.

[13] Snyder, L. *Fluency with Information Technology: Skills, Concepts, and Capabilities*. Pearson, 2011.

[14] Taylor, B., Hochheiser, H., Azadegan, S., and O'Leary, M. Cross-site Security Integration: Preliminary Experiences across Curricula. *13th Colloquium for Information Systems Security Education (CISSE)*, (2009), 158-165.

[15] Taylor, B., Hochheiser, H., Azadegan, S., and O'Leary, M. Cross-site Security Integration: Preliminary Experiences across Curricula. *13th Colloquium for Information Systems Security Education (CISSE)*, (2009), 158-165.

[16] Taylor, B. and Azadegan, S. Using Security Checklists and Scorecards in CS Curriculum. *National Colloquium for Information Systems Security Education*, (2007), 4-9.

[17] Taylor, B. and Azadegan, S. Teaching Security through Active Learning. *Proceedings of Frontiers in Education: Computer Science and Engineering, Las Vegas*, (2007).

[18] Taylor, B. and Azadegan, S. Moving beyond security tracks: integrating security in CS0 and CS1. *SIG Computer Science Education (SIGCSE)*, ACM (2008).

[19] Turner, C., Hochheiser, H., Feng, J., Taylor, B., and Lazar, J. Cooperative Information Assurance Capacity Building. *13th Colloquium for Information Systems Security Education (CISSE)*, (2009), 44-50.

Training Students to Steal: A Practical Assignment in Computer Security Education

Trajce Dimkov, Wolter Pieters, Pieter Hartel
Distributed and Embedded Security Group
University of Twente, The Netherlands
{trajce.dimkov, wolter.pieters, pieter.hartel}@utwente.nl

ABSTRACT

Practical courses in information security provide students with first-hand knowledge of technical security mechanisms and their weaknesses. However, teaching students only the technical side of information security leads to a generation of students that emphasize digital solutions, but ignore the physical and the social aspects of security. In the last two years we devised a course where students were given a practical assignment which includes a combination of physical security, social engineering and digital penetration testing. As part of the course, the students stole laptops using social engineering from unaware employees throughout the university campus. The assignment provided the students with a practical overview of security and increased their awareness of the strengths and weaknesses of security mechanisms. In this paper we present the design of the practical assignment and the observations from the execution.

Categories and Subject Descriptors: K.3.2 [Computer and Information Science Education]: Computer science education;

General Terms: computer crime, computer science education.

Keywords: computer security education, laptop theft, penetration testing, physical security, social engineering.

1. INTRODUCTION

Educational institutes are starting to offer specialized CSIA (Computer Security and Information Assurance) courses, designed to train students in assessing and improving the security of digital systems. Computer security focuses on the protection of data from theft and corruption by using a combination of physical, digital and social mechanisms. Physical mechanisms focus on restricting and detecting physical access to the data, such as locks, CCTV, infrared sensors and heat sensors. Digital mechanisms focus on digital detection and protection of the data. Common digital mechanisms are firewalls, intrusion detection systems and encryption. Finally, social mechanisms focus on increasing the security awareness of the employees and reducing mistakes from human factors. Examples of social mechanisms that improve security are lectures on social engineering and clearly defined policies.

Graduate courses in computer security often provide a narrow view on security and focus mostly on the digital aspects (Figure 1, dashed line). Such a focus provides an unrealistic view of the security requirements of an organization and leads to students assuming that digital means ensure secured data. A recent study by the Threat Assessment Center [1] shows that 87% of the attacks performed by insiders required no technical knowledge and 26% of the insiders used physical means or the account of another employee as part of the attack. In the literature there are numerous examples where an adversary uses social engineering and physical access to obtain data [2, 3, 4]. Thus, it is important to get the students acquainted with attacks in which the hacker uses also physical and social means to compromise the data (Figure 1, solid line).

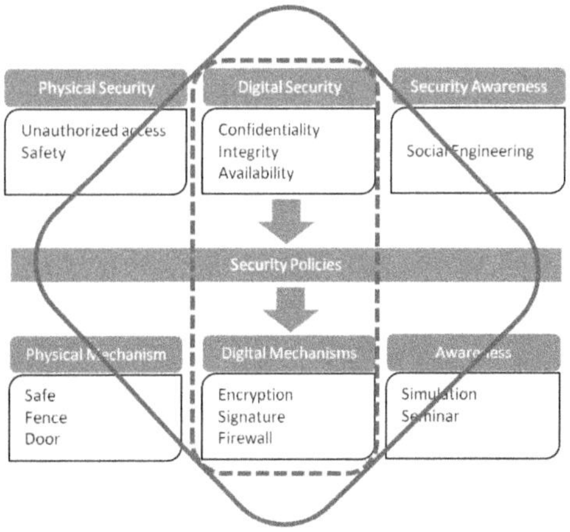

Figure 1: Computer security in context

Practical assignments clarify and support the theory students learn. In practical assignments students use the same methods and tools that hackers with malicious intent use to gain access to information. The usage of practical assignments in computer security is performed as part of many computer security courses, such as in forensics [5], in education on spam [6] and in social engineering [7]. We believe that students need to understand the hacking mentality and see how an adversary would attack also in the physical and the social domain of information security. That can be done by giving students first hand experience of the effectiveness

SIGCSE'11, March 9–12, 2011, Dallas, Texas, USA.

of the physical and social security mechanisms, exploring which attack vectors are more likely to succeed than others.

In this paper we present the practical assignment of an introductory graduate course in computer security. The goal of the course is to give a broad overview of security to the students and to increase their interest in the field. As part of the course, the students steal laptops from unaware employees, mount offline attacks on the laptop and attack a vulnerable server using the data from the laptop.

In section 2 we present the course and give a description of the practical assignment as well as observations from the execution of the assignment. In section 3 we present in greater detail the practical and ethical implications of the physical penetration test from the assignment. In section 4 we summarize our experience.

2. COURSE DESCRIPTION

Since 2008 we have taught a class on introduction to computer security to graduate students. The duration of the course is eight weeks, in which the students need to write a scientific paper and take part in a practical assignment which can be either suggested by them or by the lecturer. The course is part of a master track in computer security, and introduces the students to all concepts in security. The rest of the courses in the security track provides in-depth knowledge in different aspects of information security. The goal of the introductory course is threefold:

1. Describe important concepts in computer security from the perspective of physical, digital and social security.
2. Prepare the students to place security mechanisms in an overall security context; for example, design a system or analyze a situation and determine what the different physical, digital and social mechanisms could achieve in a given scenario or what techniques could be applied to reach a given goal.
3. Provide students with a first-hand experience with the strengths and weaknesses of security mechanisms from the physical, digital and social domain.

As part of the class, we provide a practical assignment where the students take the point of view of an adversary.

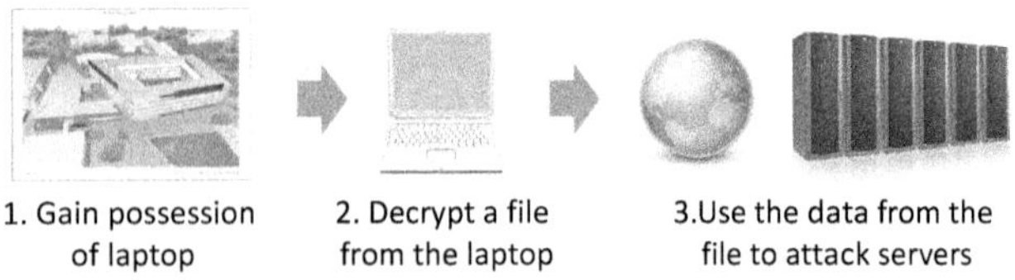

Figure 2: The steps in the practical assignment

The practical assignment is divided in three exercises, (1) physical penetration exercise using social engineering, (2) offline attacks on a laptop and (3) online attacks on a vulnerable server (Figure 2).

The goal of the physical penetration exercise (1), which follows the methodology described in [8] is to make the students aware of the social engineering and physical activities an attacker can use to get sensitive data, by stealing a laptop. After this exercise the students should have knowledge of social engineering and physical security, and know the threats that arise from them.

During the digital penetration testing exercise, the students need to get access to encrypted data residing in a laptop (2) and use the data as an attack vector in online attack on a vulnerable server (3). The goal of the exercise is to give the students an overview of the current offline and online techniques in compromising a system. After the exercise, the students should to be able to use the common tools used in penetration testing, and know their capabilities. In 2008 we performed a pilot study using practical assignment with nine students divided in three groups. After positive feedback and applying the lessons learned in the pilot study, we gave the practical assignment to all students in the class of 2009, eleven groups of three students.

2.1 Design of the practical assignment

To set up the environment for the practical assignment, we used 11 marked laptops and deployed 11 servers in which we introduced a few vulnerabilities. On each of the laptops we put two copies of a file containing the IP address of one vulnerable server. One copy was encrypted with WinZip[1] and the other with TrueCrypt[2].

We distributed the laptops to 11 unaware employees in nine buildings. The employees were recruited through snowball sampling [9]. As a cover story, we told the employees we were performing a usability study of laptops, and needed to record the results using web-cameras. Telling the employees about the real nature of the assignment would have made them overprotective of the laptops. Each employee signed an informed consent, upon which we gave them a laptop, a Kensington lock and a web-camera.

Each laptop was protected with at least three layers of access control: the entrance of the building, the entrance to the office of the employee and a Kensington lock.

After setting up the environment, we gave each of the teams the location of a single laptop they should obtain. First, each team scouted their location and collected as much information as possible about the employee and the security mechanisms in place. Then, each team proposed a list of attack scenarios they wanted to conduct. Each scenarios was approved by us and the security management. The students had two weeks to gain possession of the laptop.

The actions of the teams were logged using the web-cameras we positioned in the offices of the employees and through recording devices carried by the students, such as mobile phones. We used such comprehensive recordings to be sure the employees were treated with respect by the penetration testers. After each successful or failed attempt, the teams provided an attack trace listing which mechanisms they circumvented and, in case of failed attempts, which mechanism caused the attack to fail.

In the second exercise from the assignment, the students used offline attacks, such as the coldboot attack [10] and/or password cracking tools such as John the Ripper[3] and Hydra[4] to obtain the IP address from the encrypted file. In the last exercise the students used Backtrack[5] to attack the vulnerable server and obtain a protected file.

In this paper we focus only on the first exercise of the assignment, the physical penetration test. The second and

[1] www.winzip.com
[2] www.truecrypt.org
[3] www.openwall.com/john
[4] freeworld.thc.org/thc-hydra
[5] www.backtrack-linux.org

third exercise can be considered as a reproduction of exercises reported by other authors [5, 11, 12].

2.2 Results from the physical penetration tests

In both academic years, all groups managed to gain possession of the laptop. Besides the 3 successful attempts in 2008 and the 11 successful attempts in 2009, there were 11 unsuccessful attempts. During the tests, students took on roles as course assistant, help desk worker, PhD or graduate student or even a film crew in their social engineering attacks. The main targets of the social engineering were the employees who possessed the laptop and the support staff such as the secretaries, janitors and people from the cleaning service.

Figure 3: The student (left) went to the janitor (right) with a spoofed email stating that they need to pick up a laptop. The janitor unlocked the office with the laptop and helped the students find the key of the Kensington lock.

In nine cases the employees gave the laptop either after being showing a spoofed email or being promised they would get the laptop back in a few hours. However, in five cases the students were not able to social engineer the employee directly and were forced to look for alternative approaches, such as social engineering the janitor (Figure 3) or an employee from the cleaning service (Figure 4). The complete results from the penetration tests are presented in [13].

2.3 Observations

Running the practical assignment is challenging. We had difficulties in attracting employees to participate in a study where they are not told what the exact goal is. Recruiting employees becomes even harder the following years, when more people know about the exercise, and therefore are not eligible as participants. This makes the exercise more suitable for larger universities, which have more employees.

Another problem we encountered is positioning the web-cameras. A web-camera requires all employees in the office to agree with its presence, a desktop to store the data, and administrative rights on the desktop. Only a few employees had a desktop, and even fewer had administrative rights.

Another concern we had was debriefing the employees after the exercise. During the debriefing we explained the benefits of the exercise and the reason why we could not inform them in advance. At the end of the debriefing all employees were given small presents. Although the employees were pleased with the exercise, we expect that this will not always be the case.

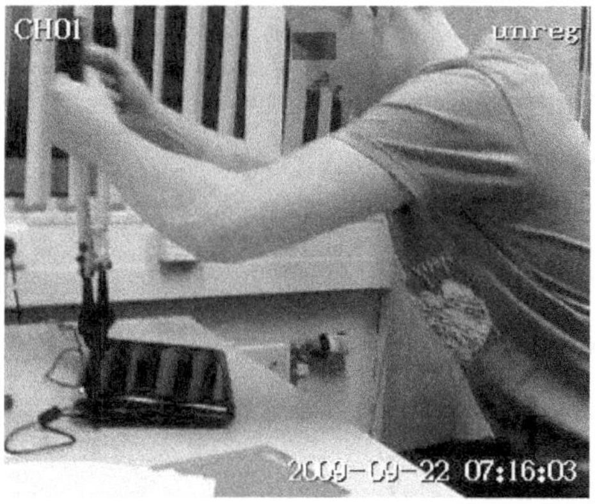

Figure 4: A student cutting a lock with a bolt cutter. The student came to the building at 7am and claimed to the employee from the cleaning service he forgot the key of his office. After the employee from the cleaning service gave the student a spare key, the student went inside the office, cut the Kensington lock with a bolt cutter and obtained the laptop.

During the assignment, we obtained a realistic picture of the physical security of the university and the security awareness of the employees. The security management discovered weaknesses in their CCTV monitoring and in the adherence to policies by security personnel.

3. IMPLICATIONS

During the design of the course, we had four major concerns. First, the execution of the assignment might violate the law. Second, the assignment is executed in an environment where the outcome cannot be controlled. Thirdly, the assignment teaches students to steal and lie. Finally, the assignment includes deceiving employees. In the rest of this section we explore the implications.

3.1 Legal implications

To ensure that we were operating within the law, before deploying the assignment we consulted the legal department of the university. Following the advice from the legal department, we forbade all scenarios that included (1) theft of any object besides the laptop, (2) searching through the belonging of the employees and (3) impersonation of officials of the university, police, fire department, etc.

3.2 Reducing unexpected outcomes

The assignment was executed on the campus of the university. This is a semi-controlled environment, where we could neither fully control the behavior of the students nor the behavior of the employees and the security personnel. We applied the following principles to the design of the exercise:

1. *Limit the scope of the activity.* The students were not allowed to use intimidation, violence nor to put the employees or themselves at risk. They were also forbidden to cause any physical damage, except for cutting the Kensington locks. The laptops were clearly marked and the students were allowed to gain possession only of a specific laptop. All students signed the rules of engagement before the scouting phase.
2. *Control the risk.* All attack scenarios were approved in advance by us, and only minor deviations in the ex-

ecution were allowed. The web-cameras and the students recorded with video/audio of all their activities. The recordings allowed us to see if the employees were treated with respect or were put at risk. Finally, all students were given a lecture on the ethical aspects of social engineering and theft.

3. *Reduce the impact of the exercise.* Just after the execution of the task, the students reported to us. When the laptops were stolen without knowledge of the employees, we tried to inform the employees before they found the laptop gone. The employees were briefed from the beginning not to store any sensitive, private nor critical information on the laptops, and to use them only for gaming and surfing. At the end of the assignment, we properly debriefed all the employees, and provided small gifts for the participation.
4. *Introduce escape clauses.* The employees and the students participated voluntarily in the study. Both groups were aware, and signed an informed consent stating they can stop with the activity at any time. All students were given "get out of jail" cards in case they are caught by the security guards. The cards contained phone numbers of the security management and the lecturers. The security management had information about all the target employees and all the students who participated in the exercise.

3.3 Ethical implications for the students

During the design of the first part of the assignment, the physical penetration tests, we were concerned (1) whether the students would feel comfortable with the activity and (2) whether we were training a future generation of criminals.

Benefits:
1. Practical in-depth overview of all aspects of security.
2. Awareness of the strengths and weaknesses of security mechanisms.
Risks:
1. Reduced comfort level of the students.
2. Misuse of the knowledge.

Figure 5: Risks and benefits from the assignment to the students

3.3.1 Comfort level of the students

Before the start of the assignments, all the students were given the opportunity to perform an experiment of their choice instead of participating in the assignment. The only limitation was that the experiment should have the same workload as the assignment. All the students decided to join the assignment.

Survey among the students

To evaluate their level of comfort we devised two questionnaires, one before the exercise and one after the exercise. We had 31 respondents (94%) for each of the questionnaires. The students graded on a scale of 1 (strongly disagree) to 5 (strongly agree) how much they agree with a statement.

The majority of students felt comfortable during the assignment. The number increased from 65% before the execution of the exercise, to 77% after the exercise. Most students thought the assignment would be fun, but the percentage

Question	Av.	SD
Before the exercise:		
The exercise will be fun	4.6	0.7
The exercise is useful	4.1	0.8
I feel fine about the exercise in general	3.8	1.1
I feel fine about the ethical implications of the exercise	3.5	1.2
After the exercise		
The exercise was fun	4.5	0.7
The exercise was useful	4.1	0.9
I feel fine about the exercise in general	4.1	1.0
I feel fine about the ethical implications of the exercise	3.6	1.2
I would do the exercise again	3.9	1.2
I am now more aware of physical and social security	3.9	0.9

Figure 6: Results from the students before and after the first part of the assignment

dropped from 71% to 65% after conducting it. At the beginning students felt less comfortable because they were not sure what kind of attacks they would perform. After we approved only the low risk scenarios, the comfort level increased, but the fun part of the activity decreased. 68% said they would repeat the assignment if they were again given the chance. The results are summarized in Figure 6.

Year:	2008	2009
Respondents:	40 (100%)	28 (90%)
1. The course was well organized	7.4	8.6
2. My attendance was above 80%	7.3	8.9
3. I liked the practical assignment	5.6	8.2
4. Overall grade of the course	6.8	7.8

Figure 7: Results from the students after passing the course

The students filled out another questionnaire after finishing the course, as part of the standard quantitative evaluation of courses in the university. The results show the satisfaction of the students increased as well as their attendance in class compared to the previous year (Figure 7). The grade of the course increased a whole point, from 6.8 in 2008 to 7.8 in 2009, thanks to the enthusiasm of the students for the practical assignment. The average grade of the rest of the courses were 7.2, both in 2008 and 2009.

3.3.2 Risks of teaching students to steal

Checking if we are teaching the next generation of criminals is a more subtle issue. The benefit of educating students in the adversarial aspect of security is widely discussed and implemented in many security courses. Pashel [14] and Logan and Clarkson [15] discuss the ethical implications of teaching students to hack and the possibility of misusing the acquired knowledge. We show that the arguments in favor of teaching digital penetration testing also hold for the physical domain, by establishing an analogy between digital and physical penetration testing.

Analogy to teaching digital penetration testing

According to Pashel [14] and Logan and Clarkson [15], teaching hacking to students is mostly justified, because to provide the best security defense, a system administrator

Question	Average	SD
1: Deceiving the subject	3.5	1.2
2.1: Physical damage - Discomfort	2.3	1.1
2.2: Physical damage - Injury	1.3	0.8
2.3: Physical damage - Death	1.0	0.0
3.1: Material damage - Emotional	2.4	1.2
3.2: Material damage - Financial	2.8	1.3
3.3: Material damage - Production loss	2.1	1.4
4.1: Psychological damage - Threats	2.1	1.0
4.2: Psychological damage - Deception	4.2	0.8
5.1: Privacy - Assume identity	4.0	1.0
5.2: Privacy - Access sensitive informa.	3.6	1.3
5.3: Privacy - Destroy information	2.3	1.1
5.4: Privacy - Theft of information	3.2	1.3

Figure 8: Ethical acceptability of damage according to students

must possess the same skills as the attacker. We consider this to be the *Locksmith Argument*. For any locksmith to be able to create decent locks they also need to have the ability to break locks (or at least have extensive knowledge on the techniques of a lock picker). The same argument can be applied to teaching physical penetration testing. The only way a student is able to secure physical objects is to have extensive knowledge on how attackers penetrate organizations, buildings and so forth. Letting them gain experience from an attacker's point of view will positively affect this knowledge.

Another argument in favor of teaching students digital penetration testing is that these skills are useful in discovering weaknesses in the security of a system [15]. The same argument can be applied to physical penetration testing. For example, an insurance company needs to review the physical security (such as cameras and security guards) and digital security (the network infrastructure that controls the cameras, the locks and the alarms) of a museum before determining the insurance premium.

Survey among the students

In the questionnaires we gave to the students, we also asked for their opinion on ethical issues. The students were told to assume there were no rules in the assignment, the only objective was to obtain the laptop.

We asked what type of damage the students are willing to inflict on the employee or the surroundings: physical, material, psychological damage and invasion of privacy. Each type of damage consists of some subtypes that contain examples of such damage, varying from light to severe (in our perception). In this way, we could identify the ethical sensitivity of types of damage, in the perception of the students.

The results from this survey are shown in Figure 8. The scale is from 1 (uncomfortable / I will never do that) to 5 (comfortable / I have no problem doing that). The questionere was filled out by 28 students(85%).

Physical damage is a sensitive matter. Even light physical damage or emotional damage was rated only around 2. The roots for this rating can be found in the basic ethics of society e.g. "do not hurt people" and "respect your fellow human beings". The students are less concerned with material damage than physical damage. Ratings are rather spread with this type of damage: some students do not care about material damage at all while other students do feel very uncomfortable causing material damage. It is surprising to see that the students feel uncomfortable with causing production loss.

Furthermore, threats and intimidation are again sensitive according to the students: The rating averages around 2. Deception however does not seem to be such a big problem, most students have no difficulty in feeling comfortable with deceiving the employee. It is also surprising to see that privacy issues do not make the students feel very uncomfortable. Destroying information does rate as very uncomfortable, but other types of privacy issues tend to rate toward comfortable.

3.4 Ethical implications for the employees

Baumrind [16] considers deception of subjects in testing as unethical. The National Commission for the Protection of Human Subjects of Biomedical and Behavioral Research, also clearly states this in their first rule of ethical principles: "Respect for persons" [17].

Benefits:
1. Increased awareness of the employees.
2. Checks the security mechanisms in the university.
Risks:
1. Employees are deceived.
2. Employees or their data might be put at risk.

Figure 9: Risks and benefits from the assignment to the employees

However, in some studies deception of the participants cannot be avoided. Finn [18] defines four conditions that need to be met to make deception acceptable: (1) The assessment cannot be performed without the use of deception. (2) The knowledge obtained from the assessment has important value. (3) The test involves no more than minimal risk and does not violate the rights and the welfare of the individual. Minimal risk is defined as: "the probability and magnitude of physical or psychological harm that is normally encountered in the daily lives" [19]. (4) Where appropriate, the subjects are provided with relevant information about the assessment after participating in the test.

Physical penetration testing using social engineering can never be completely respectful because it is based on deception. However, the deception used in the assignment presented in this paper is justifiable.

The first two conditions are general for penetration testing and its benefits, and have been discussed earlier in the literature (for example, Barrett [2]). The third condition states that the risk induced by the test should be no greater than the risks we face in daily lives. Students cannot physically harm the employee because of the rules of engagement, thus only psychological harm is possible. If the employees help the student voluntarily, the risk of psychological harm is minimal. The logging equipment assures the interaction can be audited in case of dispute. The only case when the risk is above minimal for the employee is if the student gains possession of the asset without knowledge of the employee. When the employee finds the asset missing, her stress level might increase. Therefore it is crucial for the lecturers to debrief the employee before the employee learns about the theft. The fourth condition states that all employees should be debriefed after the assignment. All employees signed an informed consent and are debriefed after the assignment.

Survey among the employees

Nine employees (82%) from which the students obtained the laptop filled a questionnaire after the debriefing. They answered multiple questions, on a scale of 1 (I strongly disagree) to 5 (I strongly agree) and yes/no questions. The results are summarized in Figure 10.

About 60% of the employees said that the university should continue letting graduate students perform these assignments and most of them, 89%, also agreed that these kinds of assignments can improve the security awareness, both that of the students and of the university employees.

Question	Av.	SD
1. I found the exercise interesting	3.2	0.9
2. The exercise increased my awareness	2.5	1.4
3. The exercise should be done more often	3.0	1.0
4. During the exercise I found myself stressed	1.0	0.8
5. I find the assignment ethical	3.0	1.1
6. These exercises are harmful	1.0	0.4
7. These exercises will benefit students	1.8	0.5
8. The security awareness of students and employees can be improved through such exercises?	4.5	1.5

Figure 10: The view of the employees

4. CONCLUSION

To make students aware of physical and social aspects of security, these aspects need to be included in security courses, both from a theoretical and a practical point of view. We presented a practical assignment consisting of three steps. First, the students needed to steal a laptop from an unaware employee, then decrypt a document from the laptop, and finally use the information from the document to attack vulnerable servers.

The students enjoyed the assignment and their awareness of the physical and social aspects of security increased. During the course they learned the strengths and weaknesses of common physical, digital and social mechanisms used to secure sensitive information. Such experience is essential for the future security architects and chief security officers. Furthermore, the practical assignment increased the overall attendance in the course and improved the course grade.

However, the assignment is challenging to administer and draws ethical and legal implications. The students might feel uncomfortable to execute the attacks or the employees might not be treated with respect. The students might also abuse the new skills in illegal actions.

Surveys among students and employees indicate that the risks can be managed. Employees who participated in the exercise did not feel stressed nor considered the exercise harmful. Moreover, the arguments used in favor of digital penetration testing also apply for physical penetration testing. Therefore, we believe the benefits of the practical assignment outweigh the mentioned risks. This assignment can be used by other universities in introducing computer security to graduate students.

References

[1] M.R. Randazzo, M. Keeney, E. Kowalski, D. Cappelli, and A. Moore. Insider threat study: Illicit cyber activity in the banking and finance sector. *U.S. Secret Service and CERT Coordination Center Software Engineering Institute*, pages 1–25, 2004.

[2] N. Barrett. Penetration testing and social engineering hacking the weakest link. *Information Security Technical Report*, 8(4):56–64, 2003.

[3] K.D. Mitnick and W.L. Simon. *The Art of Deception: Controlling the Human Element of Security.* Wiley, 2002.

[4] W. Allsopp. *Unauthorised Access: Physical Penetration Testing For IT Security Teams.* Wiley, 2009.

[5] L.L. DeLooze. Counter hack: Creating a context for a cyber forensics course. In *FIE'08: Frontiers in Education Conference*, pages 1–6, New York, 2008. IEEE.

[6] J. Sommers. Educating the next generation of spammers. In *SIGCSE'10: Special Interest Group on Computer Science Education*, pages 117–121, Wisconsin, USA, 2010. ACM.

[7] B. Endicott-Popovski and D.L. Lockwood. A Social Engineering Project in a Computer Security Course. *Academy of Information and Management Sciences Journal*, 9(1):37–44, 2006.

[8] T. Dimkov, A. Cleef van, W. Pieters, and P. Hartel. Two methodologies for physical penetration testing using social engineering. In *ACSAC'10*, Chicago, USA, 2010. ACM.

[9] B.L.A. Goodman. Snowball sampling. *The Annals of Mathematical Statistics*, 32(1):148–170, 1961.

[10] J.A. Halderman, S.D. Schoen, N. Heninger, W. Clarkson, W. Paul, J.A. Calandrino, A.J. Feldman, J. Appelbaum, and E.W. Felten. Lest we remember: Cold boot attacks on encryption keys. *USENIX Security*, pages 45–60, 2008.

[11] A.M. Minkley. Cyberattacks: a lab-based introduction to computer security. In *SIGITE '06: Proceedings of the 7th conference on Information technology education*, pages 39–46. ACM, 2006.

[12] J. R. Aman, J. E. Conway, and C. Harr. A capstone exercise for a cybersecurity course. *Journal in Computing in Small Colleges*, 25(5):207–212, 2010.

[13] T. Dimkov, W. Pieters, and P. Hartel. Effectiveness of physical, social and digital mechanisms against laptop theft in open organizations. In *IEEE/ACM International Conference on Cyber, Physical and Social Computing.* IEEE, 2010.

[14] B.A. Pashel. Teaching students to hack: ethical implications in teaching students to hack at the university level. In *InfoSecCD '06: Proceedings of the 3rd annual conference on Information security curriculum development*, pages 197–200, NY, USA, 2006. ACM.

[15] P.Y. Logan and A. Clarkson. Teaching students to hack: curriculum issues in information security. In *SIGCSE'05: Special Interest Group on Computer Science Education*, pages 157–161, Missouri, USA, 2005. ACM.

[16] D. Baumrind. Research using intentional deception. Ethical issues revisited. *The American psychologist*, 40(2):165–174, 1985.

[17] National Commission for the Protection of Human Subjects of Biomedical and Behavioral Research. The Belmont report: Ethical principles and guidelines for the protection of human subjects of research. pages 1–18, 1978.

[18] P.R. Finn. *Research Ethics: Cases and Materials*, chapter The ethics of deception in research, pages 87–118. Indiana University Press, 1995.

[19] Code of Federal Regulations. Title 45: Public welfare department of health and human services. part 46: Protection of human subjects. pages 1–12. 2005.

A Cluster for CS Education in the Manycore Era*

Joel Adams, Kathy Hoogeboom, Jon Walz
Calvin College
Department of Computer Science
1-616-526-8666
{adams, kmh23, jmw26}@calvin.edu

ABSTRACT
Traditional Beowulf clusters have been homogeneous platforms for distributed-memory MIMD parallelism. However, the shift to multicore architectures has made shared-memory MIMD parallelism increasingly important, and inexpensive manycore GPGPUs have revived SIMD parallelism. This paper presents a case study in designing and building a heterogeneous cluster as a learning platform for tera-scale distributed- and shared-memory MIMD parallelism, and GPGPU parallelism.

Categories and Subject Descriptors
C.4 [**Computer Systems Organization**]: Performance of Systems – *design studies, measurement techniques*

General Terms
Design, Experimentation, Performance.

Keywords
Beowulf, cluster, CUDA, GPGPU, Infiniband, OpenCL, manycore, MIMD, multicore, parallel, shared-memory, SIMD, tera-scale.

1. INTRODUCTION
We live in exciting times. In just a few short years:

(A) Microprocessor architectures have shifted from 1-core to multi-core processors. Personal laptop and desktop computers can now benefit from shared-memory parallel processing, for which servers offer 16, 32, and more cores.

(B) Inexpensive graphics cards, coupled with the release of libraries like Nvidia's *Compute Unified Device Architecture (CUDA)* [11] and Apple's *Open Computing Language (OpenCL)* [4], now provide programmers with direct access to hundreds of SIMD-like cores on a general purpose graphics processing unit (GPGPU) to solve data-parallel problems.

(C) High-end clusters have pushed sustained double-precision floating point performance from the billions of operations (giga-scale) through the trillions of operations (tera-scale). The state of the art is quadrillions of operations (peta-scale).

These changes in hardware platforms bring a major challenge to the computer science education community:

> *How do we prepare young computer scientists to design and write software for these systems?*

Others have begun to address the curricular changes that are needed to answer this challenge [5][7][8], and there is general agreement that *experiential learning* – in which students receive hands-on experiences using a system – is pedagogically preferable to a hands-off, theoretical approach. However, hardware is needed to provide those hands-on experiences.

The SIGCSE literature includes some discussions of hardware for cluster computing [1][2][6], but these are homogeneous clusters, focused solely on distributed-memory parallelism. Intel's 32-core *Manycore Testing Lab* (www.intel.com/software/academic) is focused on shared-memory parallelism.

In this paper, we present a case study of how one small CS department designed and built a heterogeneous cluster to provide (A) shared-memory, (B) GPGPU, and (C) distributed-memory systems for student learning. Section 2 of the paper presents different factors we considered in designing our system. Section 3 presents the implementation of our design. Section 4 discusses some of the uses we make of the system, and concludes the paper.

2. DESIGN CONSIDERATIONS
Since hardware costs money, designing a system consists of trying to maximize the system's features and performance while minimizing its cost. This is an exercise in tradeoff analysis, answering numerous questions such as *"What kind of processors can we afford?" How much memory can we afford?" How much network bandwidth can we afford?"* and so on.

2.1 Funding
We were fortunate enough to procure a grant from the National Science Foundation's Office of Cyber Infrastructure's Major Research Instrumentation (NSF-OCI-MRI) program to fund our project. The first author of this paper was the principal investigator (PI), and the project budget was about $206,000 over three years.

As its name implies, the primary purpose of the MRI program is *research* instrumentation. The key to our proposal's success was assembling a group of co-PIs from different departments (Chemistry, CS, Engineering, Physics), and proposing to build a system to support interdisciplinary research and CS education.

Over six months elapsed between the submission of our proposal and its being funded. During this interval, new processor models, changes in memory prices, etc., made it necessary to completely revise our proposal's design.

At this time, there are only a few peta-scale supercomputers in the world, and they cost millions of dollars. As a small school with a modest research agenda, our goal was to build a tera-scale cluster.

* This work made possible by NSF grant OCI-0722819.

SIGCSE'11, March 9–12, 2011, Dallas, Texas, USA.

2.2 Nodes With Roles

An N-node cluster commonly has N-1 compute nodes, to which the tasks of distributed computations are launched, and a single "head" node, from which computations are launched. Different nodes thus commonly have different roles.

Our design takes this idea a step further. The general idea is to design a cluster containing nodes to provide students with hands-on experience on systems of type (A), (B), and (C), namely:

- For (A), a *shared-memory node* with lots of cores and abundant memory to run shared-memory parallel applications.
- For (B), a *GPGPU node* containing a high-end graphics card to run data-parallel applications.
- For (C), sufficiently many *compute nodes* to run distributed-memory parallel applications at tera-scale performance.
- Two identical *file-server nodes* (primary and backup), with the backup acting as another compute node when not serving files.

Figure 1 is a simple sketch of our initial design:

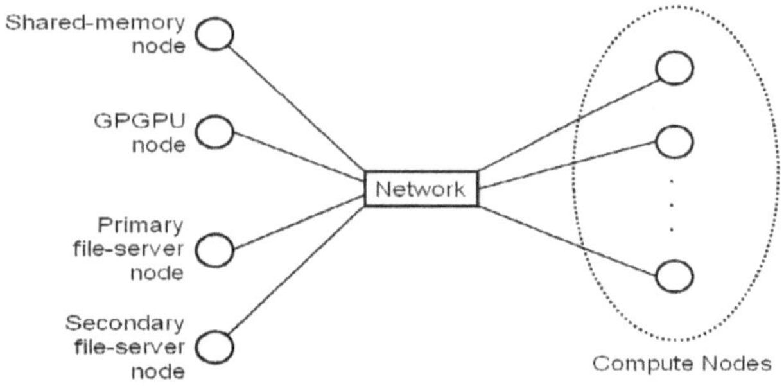

Figure 1. Initial Design Sketch

2.3 Balancing The System

According to Amdahl's rule of thumb for *balanced* computing systems [3], the hertz of *processing speed*, the bytes of *main memory*, and the bits per second of I/O *bandwidth* (including the network) should all match. Otherwise, the design will be imbalanced and computations will be bound by the lowest factor. For example, a cluster that has a powerful processor and a fast network but low memory will be *memory bound*; a cluster with a powerful processor and abundant memory but a slow network will be *network bound*; and a cluster with abundant memory and a fast network but underpowered processors will be *processor bound*. An ideal system design seeks to balance these three parameters to the extent possible within the project's budget constraints.

2.3.1 Processor Speed And Memory

In a balanced system, the memory is equal to the number of cores times their clock speed. For example, a system with two quad-core 2.5 GHz processors has a total of 2 x 4 x 2.5 = 20 GHz and so should have 20 GB of RAM to be balanced.

However, achieving exact processor-memory balance can be difficult due to clock speeds like 2.81 GHz vs RAM stick sizes, the need to pair identical RAM sticks, etc. We therefore chose quad-core processors running at 2.4 or 2.5 GHz, and gave each node 2 GB of RAM per core. The resulting system is very slightly memory bound. As it was, our cluster's 784 GB of RAM weighed over 55 pounds (25 kg), leading our vendor to joke, *"I've never ordered memory by the pound before!"*

2.3.2 Processor Speed And Network Bandwidth

Balancing processor speed and bandwidth can be a challenge, even though most current server motherboards are equipped with two Gigabit Ethernet (GigE) adaptors. The reason is that these same server boards have sockets for two quad (or more) core processors, which can more than saturate two GigE connections. That is, the two GigE adaptors provide a total of 2 gigabits per second (Gbps) of network bandwidth; two quad core processors running at 2.5 GHz provide a total of 2 x 4 x 2.5 = 20 GHz worth of processing load, leading to a cluster that is network bound by a factor of ten. Distributed computations whose tasks communicate frequently will perform poorly on such a network-bound cluster.

One way to achieve the desired balance is *Infiniband* (IB) [10], a high-speed, low-latency communications fabric for high performance clusters. IB's base signaling rate is 2.5 Gbps; double data rate (DDR) IB doubles this rate to 5 Gbps; and 4X DDR IB aggregates 4 DDR links in a single channel. A single 4X DDR IB adaptor thus provides 4 x 2 x 2.5 = 20 Gbps of raw bandwidth. (IB's data bandwidth is 4/5 its raw bandwidth.)

At least as importantly, the end-to-end latency of IB is between 1 and 2 microseconds, compared to roughly 120 microseconds for GigE. With its higher bandwidth and lower latency, IB is much, much faster than GigE. It is also much more expensive than GigE. Given that the alternative is a network-bound cluster, we added a 4X DDR IB switch to our design and adjusted our budget.

Pure Infiniband does not support TCP/IP protocols, such as the Network File System (NFS), whereas GigE does. Since each of our servers came with GigE adaptors, and GigE switches are comparatively inexpensive (see below), we decided to also add a GigE network to our design. By using GigE to carry the cluster's administrative traffic, we could dedicate our IB network to data traffic among the nodes, as shown in Figure 2:

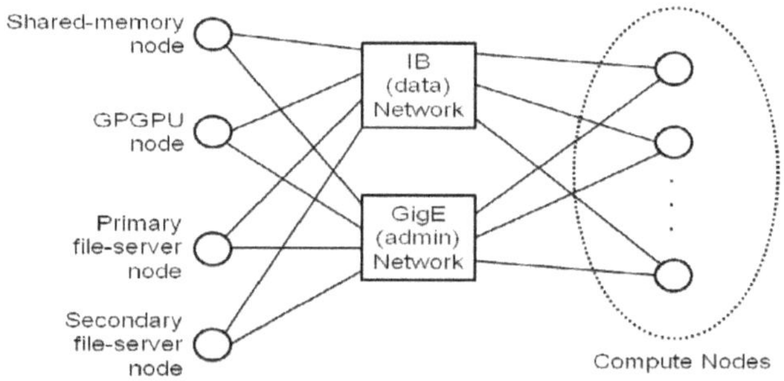

Figure 2. A Two-Network Cluster

2.4 Other Design Decisions

In addition to the actual computing hardware and network fabric, there are other design decisions that do not directly affect a cluster's performance, but can be beneficial to its operation.

One decision is whether or not to use a keyboard-video-mouse (KVM) switch, which lets one control multiple computer systems with a single mouse, keyboard, and display. For example, a 16-port KVM switch can control 16 different nodes, and by daisy-chaining such switches, 32, 48, 64, or more nodes can all be controlled with one mouse, keyboard, and display. A KVM can thus greatly simplify a cluster's configuration and maintenance.

Another decision is whether or not to use rack-mounting hardware. Traditional 'tower' cases are inexpensive, but as a cluster grows in size, the space it requires becomes prohibitive. Rack-mounted nodes are more expensive, but can be quite space-efficient: we were able to fit 42 compute nodes, a shared-memory node, two file-server nodes, a 48-port IB switch, a 48-port GigE switch, and three 16-port KVM switches, in *one* rack.

A related decision is choosing where a cluster will reside, which has three aspects:

- *Space.* There must be space for all of the cluster's nodes. Rack-mounted solutions generally consume the least space.
- *Power.* The more nodes a cluster has, the more power it requires. We had to add electrical circuits to our facility.
- *Climate Control.* High heat and humidity can greatly reduce the life of computing systems, and a cluster produces a lot of heat. We had to upgrade our facility's air conditioning unit.

A final decision is whether or not to power the cluster using an uninterruptible power supply (UPS). A good UPS includes a battery system and "power conditioning" circuitry to filter out voltage spikes and drops. In our climate, summer thunderstorms and winter ice storms are common, making power interruptions a frequent problem. Since some of our co-PIs' computations could run for weeks at a time, an interruption could cause much work to be lost. We therefore chose a reconditioned Liebert AP362 UPS to power our cluster *and* air conditioning system.

3. BUILDING THE DESIGN

Choosing the components for our project involved getting quotes from vendors, plugging those numbers into a spreadsheet, and adjusting the models and quantities to fit our budget.

3.1 The Shared-Memory Node

For (A), our goal was to have a node where students could experience the benefits of shared-memory parallelism by manipulating large matrices (e.g., double precision, 2048x2048 and larger). For this node, we chose a SuperMicro 8025C-3RB server, equipped with four 2.4 GHz quad-core Xeon CPUs, 64 GB of RAM, and an 80 GB disk. This system does not include an IB adaptor, so we added a Mellanox MHGS18-XTC IB adaptor.

3.2 The GPGPU Node: CUDA Or OpenCL?

For (B), we had to make a decision about the GPGPU node: did we want to teach students to use Nvidia's CUDA library, or Apple's OpenCL library? Some of the tradeoffs include:

- CUDA is the older of the two technologies, so there are more tutorials and example programs available for it.
- OpenCL is vendor-independent; CUDA is Nvidia-specific.
- OpenCL threads can run on both the CPU cores and the GPGPU cores; CUDA threads are limited to the GPGPU cores.

After much deliberation, we decided that the vender-independence of OpenCL was a strong reason to choose it for teaching students, since at least some of our graduates would find themselves using machines containing non-Nvidia devices.

Apple's MacOS 10.6 and later operating systems include a stable version of OpenCL, so we chose a MacPro workstation equipped with two 2.4 GHz quad-core Xeon processors, 16 GB of RAM, 1 TB of disk, and an ATI Radeon HD 5870 1GB graphics card.

3.3 The Compute Nodes

For (C), we chose the SuperMicro 6015T-INF as our compute nodes. Each 1U 6015T box actually holds 2 nodes side-by-side, so 21 of these boxes can store 42 nodes. We equipped each node with two 2.5 GHz quad-core Xeon CPUs, 16 GB of RAM, and an 80 GB disk. Our budget was sufficient to purchase 42 compute nodes, providing a combined 336 cores, 672 GB of RAM, and 3.36 TFLOPS of double-precision peak (R_{PEAK}) performance.

3.4 The File-Server Nodes

A file server node's primary responsibility is providing space for home directories. So far, we are using the Network File System (NFS) to provide system-wide reliable access to these files. Since some of our co-PIs had datasets that were (literally) astronomical, we needed ample disk space on each file server.

For these servers, we chose Intel S5000PSL systems, each equipped with two 2.5 GHz quad-core Xeon processors, 16 GB of RAM, and 10 TB of disk space in a RAID-5 configuration. Since these servers do not include an on-board IB adaptor, we added a Mellanox MHGS18-XTC IB adaptor to each.

As mentioned previously, one of these systems is the primary file server; the other normally acts as a 43rd compute node. This effectively brings the number of compute node cores to 344, their total RAM to 688, and their R_{PEAK} to 3.44 TFLOPS.

3.5 The Networks

At the time of this writing, a single 4X DDR IB adaptor costs $475, and a 48-port 4X DDR IB switch (a QLogic 9040 chassis with 4 leaves) cost over $31,000. Thankfully, each SuperMicro 6015T-INF server has an on-board 4X DDR IB adaptor, sparing us the cost of 42 IB adaptors for our compute nodes.

A 6015T server also has two GigE ports, so we purchased a 48-port GigE switch (SMC 8648), and configured our systems to isolate administrative (TCP) traffic on the GigE network, leaving the IB network dedicated to data communication.

3.6 Project Summary

Table 1 summarizes our cluster's performance.

Table 1. System Performance Summary

Node	# Nodes	CPU Cores	RAM (GB)	CPU R_{PEAK} (GFLOPS)
shared-mem.	1	16	64	153.6
GPGPU	1	8	16	76.8
compute	42	336	672	3,360
file-server	2	16	32	160
Total	**46**	**376**	**784**	**3,751**

Note that the R_{PEAK} values in Table 1 are double-precision TFLOPS from CPUs only. For data-parallel problems, the HD 5870 graphics card on our GPGPU node provides an additional 540 GFLOPS (double precision) or 2.7 TFLOPS (single precision).

Table 2 provides an in-depth look at our hardware expenses:

Table 2. Project Cost Summary

Node	shared-mem.	GPGPU	compute	file-server	Node Total
Cost	$13,419	$4,282	$97,696	$14,308	$129,705
IB	switch	adaptors	cables		IB Total
Cost	$31,304	$1,425	$6,287		$39,016
GigE	switch	adaptors	cables		GigE Total
Cost	$1,465	$87	$480		$2,032
Control	Display	KVMs	Cables		Control Total
Cost	$972	$684	$360		$2,016
Misc	Rack	UPS	Other		Misc Total
Cost	$1,139	$18,900	$500		$20,539
Total					**$193,308**

The rest of our budget went toward commercial software licenses (see below).

Figure 2 (to the right) is a picture of our cluster. Since it was intended to be used extensively for simulation, we named it *Dahl* in honor of Ole Johan Dahl, the Norwegian computer scientist who co-invented the Simula programming language.

4. SOFTWARE

We initially configured Dahl using the *Rocks* cluster management software (www.rocksclusters.org). However, we have recently encountered several issues with its version of Linux (CentOS), so we are currently switching to *Ubuntu Linux* (www.ubuntu.com).

4.1 Software for Computer Science Education

For parallel programming on distributed-memory systems, the *message-passing interface (MPI)* is the industry standard. Our course *High Performance Computing* includes extensive coverage of MPI, so we installed OpenMPI (www.open-mpi.org) on each of Dahl's nodes. By doing so, any node may be used to launch a distributed computation (i.e., as a head node). We are also installing *Hadoop* (hadoop.apache.org) so that we can use Dahl to introduce our students to MapReduce [6].

For parallel programming on shared-memory systems, *OpenMP* (openmp.org) is a library that makes it relatively easy to write multithreaded C, C++, or Fortran programs. The GNU compiler suite has supported OpenMP since gcc 4.2. We use OpenMP to introduce our students to multithreading in CS2, and build on this foundation in subsequent courses like *Operating Systems* and *High Performance Computing*. Since each of our nodes has at least 8 cores, we installed gcc 4.3 on each node in our cluster, allowing multithreading to be used anywhere. Having both OpenMP and MPI installed on the cluster allows us to write single programs that are both distributed across multiple nodes and multithreaded on the individual nodes.

Figure 2. The Dahl Cluster

We also installed MPI and OpenMP on each workstation in our Linux lab, so that students can develop, test, and debug their programs away from the cluster. When their program seems to be correct, they copy it across the network to Dahl, compile it, and run it several times, varying the number of nodes, cores, or threads and recording its execution times. This lets them compute their program's speedup and efficiency, and assess its scalability.

4.2 Software for STEM Education

In keeping with the SIGCSE 2011 theme of "reaching out", we have installed software packages for other departments who are incorporating more computing in their courses. To get instructor buy-in, we installed the packages they requested, including:

- The *Absoft* compilers (www.absoft.com) and *IMSL* numerical libraries (www.vni.com), for our physicists.
- *Gaussian* (www.gaussian.com) computational chemistry software and its WebMO (www.webmo.net) browser interface, for our chemists.
- *Mathematica*'s *Parallel Computing Toolkit* (www.wolfram.com), for our engineers and physicists.
- *Python* (www.python.org), *R* (www.r-project.org) and *Sage* (www.sagemath.org), for our astronomers, mathematicians, physicists, and others.

To illustrate, our chemists now have a first-year lab exercise in which their students conduct virtual reactions on Dahl, using it to visualize the structure and properties of the resulting molecules. Serving faculty members in other departments this way helps their students see how computing is important to their major. In our experience, this has not produced new CS majors, but it has led some of their students to take our introductory CS courses.

5. RESULTS & CONCLUSIONS

Our students have greatly enjoyed using Dahl. Student evaluations in our *High Performance Computing* course were very positive, as a dedicated cluster let them conduct timing studies that accurately reflected the performance of their programs. The diversity of experiences (shared-memory, distributed-memory, etc.) kept even the strongest students from being bored. Having a heterogeneous cluster let students directly experience the different kinds of parallelism.

For distributed-memory exercises, we configured MPI to allocate 1 process per compute node. Since each node has eight cores, this let eight students simultaneously allocate 1- 43 processes without conflict. By scheduling student access, a student can allocate 1-344 processes, and so gain experience in tera-scale computing.

With just one shared-memory node and one GPGPU node, we must schedule student access to these nodes for those exercises. We have just acquired our GPGPU node, and so are still designing the OpenCL exercises our students will complete. We hope to make them the subject of a future report.

For shared-memory exercises, our students conduct OpenMP experiments using 1-32 threads on our Linux lab's quad-core workstations and then repeat the experiments using Dahl's 16-core shared-memory node. The difference in results provides students with experiential learning in the different hardware limits of 4-core vs 16-core shared-memory systems. Variations on these exercises provide students with experiential learning for Amdahl's and Gustavson's Laws [9].

Dahl has also helped us build bridges to students and colleagues in other departments, as they learn how high performance computing can enhance their practice of science.

Our project has been a success, but it has not been without snags. Unlike GigE, Infiniband is a sufficiently new technology that different vendors are implementing the standard differently, leading to incompatibilities when their products are mixed. Our advice: avoid mixing IB hardware from different vendors.

We gratefully acknowledge the support of the NSF-OCI-MRI program, which funded this project. This program understands the critical importance of parallel software design for our future, and is willing to help colleges and universities acquire the infrastructure needed for parallel education, provided the primary use of the infrastructure is research. We encourage the readers of this report to write grant proposals that mix multidisciplinary research with computer science education. By doing so, they can acquire the tera-scale hardware needed to educate computer science students for the systems of today and tomorrow.

6. REFERENCES

[1] J. Adams and D. Vos. Small College Supercomputing: Building a Beowulf Cluster at a Comprehensive College. *Proc. of the 33rd SIGCSE Technical Symposium*, Covington, KY, March 2002, 411-415.

[2] J. Adams and T. Brom. Microwulf: A Beowulf Cluster for Every Desk. *Proc. of the 39th SIGCSE Technical Symposium*, Portland, OR, March 2008, 121-125.

[3] G. Amdahl. Storage and I/O Parameters and Systems Potential. *Proc. of the IEEE International Computer Group Conference (Memories, Terminals, and Peripherals)*, Washington, D. C., June 1970, 371-372.

[4] Apple Computer. 2010. OpenCL. Retrieved Aug 15, 2010 from http://developer.apple.com/technologies/mac/snowleopard/opencl.html.

[5] R. Brown, E. Shoop, J. Adams, C. Clifton, M, Gardner, M. Haupt, and P. Hinsbeek. Strategies for Preparing Computer Science Students for the Multicore World. *Proc. of 15th ITiCSE Conference*, Ankara, Turkey, June 2010, to appear.

[6] R. Brown. Hadoop at Home: Large-Scale Computing at a Small College. *Proc. of the 40th SIGCSE Technical Symposium*, Chattanooga, TN, March 2009, 106-110.

[7] D. Ernst and D. Stevenson. Concurrent CS: Preparing Students for a Multicore World. *Proc. of 13th Annual Conference on Innovation and Technology in Computer Science Education*, Madrid, Spain, June 2008, 230-234.

[8] D. Ernst, B. Wittman, B. Harvey, T, Murphy, M. Wrinn. Preparing Students for Ubiquitous Parallelism. *Proc. of the 40th SIGCSE Technical Symposium*, Chattanooga, TN, March 2009, 136-137.

[9] J. Gustavson. Reevaluating Amdahl's Law. *Communications of the ACM*, (31) 5, May 1988, 532-533.

[10] Infiniband Trade Association. 2010. Retrieved Aug 15, 2010 from http://www.infinibandta.org/.

[11] Nvidia, CUDA Zone, 2010. Retrieved Aug 15, 2010 from http://www.nvidia.com/object/cuda_home_new.html.

Games as Motivation in Computer Design Courses: I/O is the Key

Erik Brunvand
School of Computing
University of Utah
elb@cs.utah.edu

ABSTRACT

The design of computer games can be a powerful motivator as students learn about computer architecture and design. Students in classes where computer designs are developed and implemented (usually on Field Programmable Gate Arrays (FPGAs)) seem much more highly motivated if their computer design can be used for something visual and interactive when the project is complete. However, ensuring that the student teams can have a working game by the end of a semester requires careful planning of how their computer designs will interact with the world. Keyboard inputs and VGA outputs are a relatively simple set of I/O interfaces that open up significant new potential for development of game applications on the student's own computer designs. In this paper we describe the curriculum of a computer design course that uses game design as a "carrot" to encourage active student exploration and deeper understanding of computer architecture, I/O subsystems, and computer implementation.

Categories and Subject Descriptors:
K.3.2 [**Computer and Information Science Eduction**], C.5.3 [**Microcomputers**]

General Terms: Design

Keywords: Games, Computer Design, FPGA

1. INTRODUCTION

Good motivation for learning is a powerful part of any successful curriculum. Especially in project courses where students design and build an artifact, the time spent working on the project, and the depth of knowledge that comes out of the project, are dramatically increased if there is some strong internal motivation to go beyond the basics and delve into the project details [3, 7]. In particular we focus on a course where students learn about computer design by designing and building a computer from scratch on a Field Programmable Gate Array (FPGA). We believe, as do others [8], that the best way to learn about computer design is to design a computer. For many students the opportunity to develop interactive games on a computer they designed is a strong motivator. Without some form of graphical I/O, however, computer design projects are often limited to an interface where programs are loaded into memory, programs are run, and memory is uploaded to see if the correct answer is in the correct memory location. While computing Fibonacci numbers into a correct memory location may be interesting to some students, interactive games with colorful graphics are a much more exciting demonstration application. Exotic I/O devices are not necessary, but something beyond switches and seven segment LEDs is definitely required. Relatively simple interfaces such as PS/2 keyboard input and VGA output are standard I/O systems that dramatically increase the potential for students to design visually interesting games. However, success in using these I/O systems with student-designed processors requires that the details of these systems and the infrastructure to support them be carefully planned.

Designing a computer processor on an FPGA in a computer design course is certainly not novel. A number of papers have described interesting variations on this curriculum (e. g. [9, 4, 1, 11, 12]). Likewise, using games as motivators in CS software classes is also a well-studied area (e.g. [14, 15, 2, 10, 16]). What we argue in this paper is that games can also be a strong motivator in a hardware-centric computer design course, but that to facilitate games the curriculum should include specific information about I/O interfaces that support game development.

A focus on interactive games as a driving application for computer design courses has a significant positive side effect of forcing the students to pay careful attention to details of the I/O system that are too frequently overlooked in system design projects. Designing a computer that can use VGA outputs to display an interactive game requires that students understand not only the VGA controller itself, but also how game information relates to screen (frame buffer) locations, how to organize the frame buffer into a reasonable set of memory requirements, how to use pre-designed glyphs which may be stored in a separate memory, how time, clock cycles, and memory are shared between the processor and the VGA controller, and other issues that contribute to a much deeper understanding of the computer system as a whole.

It's also interesting that the increased complexity of the computer design projects to support games is largely student-driven. That is, the goal of the class has not changed (build a computer and demonstrate it), but there has been a signifi-

SIGCSE'11, March 9–12, 2011, Dallas, Texas, USA.

cant jump in complexity of the projects when games become the preferred demonstration application. The teams that target games also tend to increase their own software support more than other teams by developing assemblers and other support systems for their own code development. The results are reasonably complex and realistic 16-bit computer systems demonstrating interactive games though standard keyboard and VGA interfaces. These are all the more impressive as they are the result of only the second course in digital design in our curriculum.

In this paper we discuss the curriculum of the junior-level Computer Design Lab course at the University of Utah (CS/ECE 3710) that uses game design as a motivator for computer design and implementation projects. We also highlight the projects from three student teams. The games that have been implemented on these student-designed 16-bit computers will not put Playstation or Xbox out of business any time soon, but they are visually interesting, run on completely student-designed hardware, and motivate the students to have a much richer experience in their computer design course.

2. CURRICULUM

The course described in this paper is an undergraduate semester-long project-based computer design course. It is typically taken in the Fall semester of a student's junior year. It is essentially a second semester of digital system design, but with a computer design as the focus. The prerequisites are:

Digital System Design I: This course is a semester-long lab-based course that covers the fundamental concepts of digital system theory and design. The course covers digital logic, Boolean algebra, binary number representation, design of combinational and sequential circuits, arithmetic circuits, finite state machines, the Verilog hardware description language, and includes labs where students build, test, and demonstrate circuits on an FPGA board.

Computer Organization: This course is a semester-long course in computer architecture where students examine the design of modern computers with an emphasis on understanding computer performance. Topics include RISC instruction sets, number systems, CPU design, pipelining, memory and caches, and multicore issues. Labs in this course currently involve assembly language programming and the MARS simulator [18].

Based on these prerequisites we can assume that the students have an understanding of computer architecture, specifically as it relates to executing an instruction set architecture. They also have a working knowledge of a hardware description language such as Verilog. Students who have their earlier class in VHDL find that although it seems daunting, it takes only a short time to make the switch to a different HDL. The main activity in the computer design class described in this paper is to take the architecture knowledge and the circuit knowledge from previous classes, and combine them together in a semester-long project to design and implement (on an FPGA) a fully-functioning computer processor. Computer Design Lab is an elective course for Computer Science and for Electrical Engineering majors, and a required course for Computer Engineering majors.

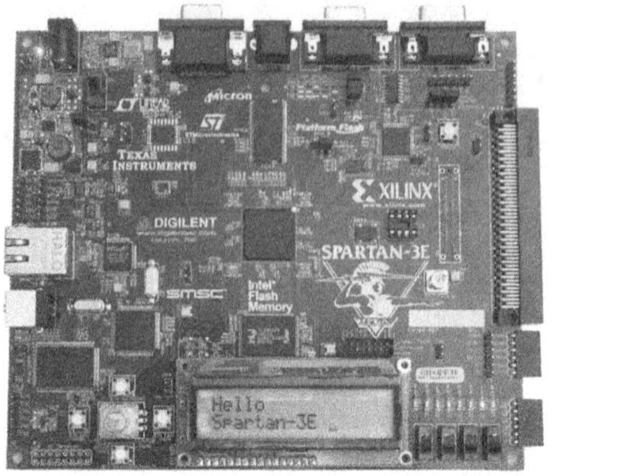

Figure 1: Spartan3e FPGA Prototyping Board

The course proceeds with lectures and individual assignments for the first five weeks of the semester. Teams of 3-4 students are then formed to work on designing and building their project computer for the rest of the semester. The class culminates with an open-house where the students demonstrate their processors and applications.

Currently we use FPGA boards from Xilinx [20] that use a Xilinx Spartan3 FPGA, and a variety of ancillary circuits including SDRAM, flash memory, LEDs, a variety of switches, PS/2 and VGA connectors, and a 2-line 16-character LCD display. The board is shown in Figure 1. It is important to note that the I/O connectors on the board are just that, connectors. Any circuits that interface to those connectors must be designed by the students and mapped onto the FPGA. We use the free ISEWebpack tools, also from Xilinx, for system design, simulation, and mapping to the FPGA board.

The main lecture topics in the first part of the course are:

Digital design review	Finite state machines Arithmetic/logic circuits RTL descriptions
Verilog language review	FSM examples Arithmetic code examples
Processor design overview	Simple MIPS architecture Class baseline ISA and memory map
I/O systems	Memory mapped I/O PS/2 and VGA Serial communications: RS232, SPI
Programming support	Assembler basics

This curriculum is a fairly standard lead-in to a computer design project, but includes a focus on I/O that is specifically intended to lead to a games-capable computer design. The labs done by individuals prior to forming teams are:

Lab1 - Finite State Machine: In this lab the students design a simple finite state machine that takes inputs from the buttons on the FPGA board and produces output on the LEDs on the FPGA board. This lab refreshes the students' understanding about FSMs and Verilog, and introduces them to the design tools and the specifics of the FPGA board we use.

Lab2 - MIPS architecture: In this lab students are given a complete Verilog description of a small MIPS-inspired processor. We use the 8-bit mini-MIPS from the VLSI text of Harris and Weste [19]. The task is to add a new instruction to this machine, ADDI (Add Immediate), include memory mapped I/O to the switches and LEDs on the FPGA board, and then write the dreaded Fibonacci program using that new instruction. The program is required to compute the first 14 Fibonacci numbers and store them in consecutive memory locations starting at location 128 (the mini-MIPS has only an 8-bit address space so this is the high half of the accessible memory). It should then enter a loop where it reads the value on the switches on the FPGA board, and uses that as an address to the memory. The program should display the value stored in that memory location. That is, by changing the switches once the program has entered the loop phase, the corresponding Fibonacci number will be displayed on the LEDs.

This lab is essentially a tiny version of the project in a nutshell. The students will see a complete (albeit tiny) processor, understand it well enough to modify the code to add new features, learn how to use the internal memory on the FPGA, how to map that memory into the processor's address space, and to write and run a small assembly language program on that processor.

Lab3 - VGA: In this lab every student in the class implements a simple VGA controller. Students implement a control and timing circuit for a 640x480 VGA output circuit. They demonstrate that they can paint the entire screen in a different color based on reading the switches on the FPGA board (our board allows only one bit each of R, G, and B so there are eight colors possible without designing a new VGA output circuit). They also take the state machine from Lab1 and drive regions of the VGA screen to correspond to the LEDs that lit up in Lab 1. This lab uses the same state machine from Lab 1, but maps its output to the VGA screen instead of to the LEDs on the FPGA board.

This lab is a response to experience in the course related to the VGA controller. We have found that teams that get VGA working earlier in the semester have a much higher chance of finishing and polishing their project. With this lab, every student in the class will have designed and built a simple VGA interface before the team project starts which will give all students a running start on the main project's I/O requirements.

The project portion of this course is defined rather loosely as "design and implement a computer system and demonstrate it doing something interesting." Unless the students have a specific alternative project in mind, the "something interesting" is defined to be an interactive game running on the computer and displaying on a VGA display. Students are given a baseline instruction set architecture (ISA) for a 16-bit computer architecture. To this baseline ISA the students add extra instructions as desired, and I/O interfaces. The teams usually also develop assemblers for their customized versions of the baseline ISA and write their game applications in assembly language. Some groups have gone even further and written simple compilers for their machines but this is certainly not required.

ADD, ADDI	Addition
SUB, SUBI	Subtraction
CMP, CMPI	Compare Subtract with no writeback to RF
AND, ANDI	Logical AND
OR, ORI	Logical OR
XOR, XORI	Logical XOR
MOV, MOVI	Move data
LSH, LSHI	Logical shift by one Direction is in extended opcode
LUI	Load and 8-bit left shift
LOAD, STOR	Memory load and store
Bcond	Branch to PC-relative signed displacement (16 conditions)
Jcond	Jump to address in Rtarget (16 conditions)
JAL	Jump and save PC in link register

Figure 2: Baseline ISA

In the project phase of the course there are no further lectures unless specific topics come up that the whole class would benefit from hearing. Instead the teams each meet with the instructor and the TA once a week to discuss the project, describe their current state, and make goals for the following week. The general plan is to demonstrate a series of checkpoints (that may not occur in the same order for each team). The checkpoints are:

- Functioning register file and ALU
- Complete datapath including a connection to the block RAM on the FPGA
- Memory map including the I/O mappings
- Instruction decoding and interactions with the datapath
- I/O system demonstration
- Full system demonstration

The final report consists of written documentation in the form of a conference-style paper, a collection design documents including Verilog code, schematics, etc., and a user guide to the group's processor and programming environment.

2.1 Baseline Architecture

For our baseline we have developed an ISA based on the National Semiconductor CR-16 microcontroller [6]. Our version of this ISA has a subset of the full CR-16 instruction set, and simplified instruction encoding, but it retains the flavor of a "real" microcontroller rather than an overly-simplified pedagogical architecture. The instruction set is a basic two-address load-store format with the result being written to the same register as one of the arguments. That is, `ADD R1 R2` performs the function `R1` ← `R1 + R2`. Instructions are encoded in single 16-bit words, and memory is accessed in a word-aligned way. ALU operations (ADD, SUB, CMP) set the conditions in the condition code register (FLCNZ flags). Instructions ending with "I" are immediate and use the eight least-significant bits of the instruction as data (sign-extended or zero-extended to 16 bits). The baseline instruction set is shown in Figure 2.

There are unused opcodes (up to 28 depending on how instructions are grouped) that allow the student groups to

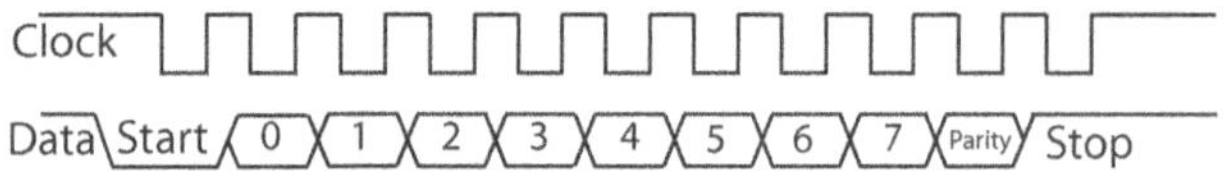

Figure 3: PS/2 keyboard interface serial protocol

add additional instructions to this baseline instruction set. Typical additions included arithmetic shift, unsigned arithmetic, multiple precision arithmetic (add with carry, for example), multiplication, multiply-accumulate, and instructions to support interrupt processing. The baseline architecture uses a 16-bit PC which allows an address space of 128k bytes (word-aligned), and 16 16-bit registers. The memory map is defined by the students but a starting point is to use the top two address bits to define I/O space so that 1/4 of the address space is usable for memory mapped I/O such as a frame buffer. This ISA serves as a good generic baseline from which the students can branch out and explore enhancements to the basic architecture.

3. I/O INTERFACES

The main distinction in this course's curriculum is a specific focus on I/O in the computer architecture. Our argument is that by spending time talking about I/O we create an environment where the students pursue the project with extra enthusiasm because the final result is visually interesting. We spend time making sure that the students have been exposed not only to the I/O protocols themselves, but also how those I/O devices are typically mapped into the computer's memory space. The two main I/O systems that we cover are PS/2 (keyboards) and VGA (graphic output).

3.1 PS/2 Interface

A PS/2 interface allows the students to use a standard keyboard as an input device. There is a PS/2 socket on the FPGA board, but no built-in controller so the interface circuit is designed by students. The low-level PS/2 protocol is a relatively simple serial interface: Codes are sent serially using two wires: a *Clock* and a *Data* wire as seen in Figure 3 (see [13] for more information). Data changes when the clock is high and is valid when the clock is low. Frames are always 11 bits long and begin with a start bit followed by eight data bits, an odd parity bit, and one stop bit. The key-mapping protocol is more complex than simple ASCII with one or two bytes being sent then the key is pressed (called the *make code*), and two or three bytes sent when the key is released (called the *break code*). Teams typically implement this interface by mapping the PS/2 data registers to a memory location which can be read by their processor for decoding.

3.2 VGA Interface

Game outputs are all about graphics. Augmenting the processor with a VGA output interface is critical to making the processor usable for games. A VGA interface can seem daunting to a student at first, but once understood it can be fairly easily added to the processor design. The main point is that the monitor is always moving the electron beam across and down the screen at some rate. The VGA interface keeps track of where the beam is on the screen and provides intensity data on the R, G, and B signals that correspond to the pixel color at that spot on the screen (see [17, 5] for details). What the VGA interface really controls is when the beam stops tracing and moves back (*retraces*) to the starting point. To cause the beam to stop tracing a row and retrace back to start tracing the next row the VGA interface sends a low-going pulse on the *Hsync* wire. To cause the beam to stop moving down the screen and move back to the top the VGA interface sends a low-going pulse on the *Vsync* wire.

The VGA timing interface is essentially just a pair of counters that keep track of the horizontal and vertical position of the beam and generate the required retrace timing signals. The timing for these signals is straightforward, and as seen in Figure 4, there are "official" timings, and there are relaxed timings that students can use with fewer pixels on the screen. The on-screen graphics happen between the retrace signals when the circuit sends signals to the display to make colors on the screen. This leads to essentially three different modes of generating an image on the screen:

Bitmap mode: In this mode a color value is stored for every pixel on the screen. The VGA controller reads the colors from that memory (the frame buffer) as it traverses the screen. This is the most flexible approach, and the most memory-intensive.

Glyph mode: In this mode the screen is broken up into multiple pixel chunks (8x8 pixels for example), and for each chunk a pointer is stored instead of a color. The pointer references a glyph which is stored in a separate memory. If there are (for example) 256 glyphs, then an 8-bit pointer is stored for every 8x8 chunk on the screen. Character maps are often stored as glyphs.

Direct mode: In direct mode the drawing circuit checks the horizontal and vertical counters directly and decides when to change the beam color. This mode is useful for drawing backgrounds or other static structures on the screen. It is also the mode most likely to be used in the VGA lab described in Section 2.

4. EXAMPLE SYSTEMS

The following examples demonstrate what the students teams can achieve in the semester-long class. These are admittedly among the better projects that students have done in the recent offerings of the course, but most groups achieve similar, if slightly less polished, results. These examples all use the same baseline 16-bit ISA described in Section 2.1. Each group has extended the baseline ISA in some way, and integrated memory-mapped I/O suitable for their project. Screen shots and pictures of these example projects are seen in Figure 5.

4.1 Slalom/Chicken

This group targeted a 512x480 VGA screen with 64 colors using a 25MHz VGA clock. They created an 8x16 pixel character set which was stored in the flash memory on the FPGA board. This allowed them to fit 64x30 characters on the screen which could include text characters as well as glyphs used for their game applications. By shrinking the logical frame buffer to only 64x30 locations where each location contains a pointer to an 8x16 character glyph they were easily able to map that frame buffer (under 2k bytes) into their main memory map.

Horizontal Timing	640x480	128x256
A = Scanline time	31.77 us	30 us
B = Hsync pulse	3.77 us	2.0 us
C = Back porch	1.89 us	10.7 us
D = Bright time	25.17 us	12.8 us
E = Front porch	0.94 us	4.5 us
Pixel clock frequency	24.4 MHz	10 MHz

Vertical Timing	640x480	128x256
A = Frame time	16.68 ms	16.68 ms
B = Vsync pulse	0.06 ms	0.09 ms
C = Back porch	1.02 ms	4.86 ms
D = Bright time	15.25 ms	7.65 ms
E = Front porch	0.35 ms	4.08 ms
Vertical Frequency	60 Hz	60 Hz

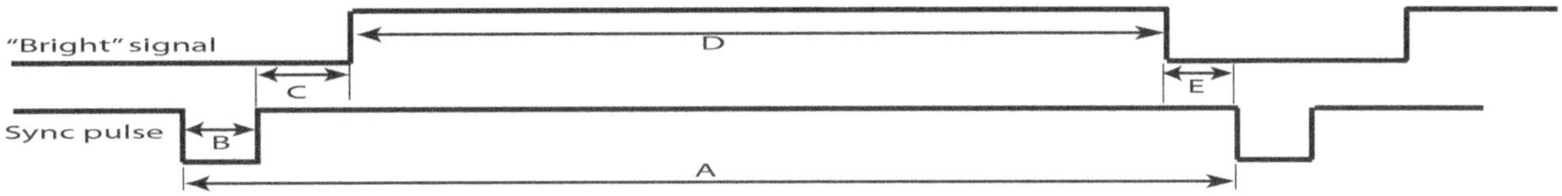

Figure 4: VGA interface signal timing

In addition to an assembler for their ISA, this group also built a character editor web application so that the task of designing characters and game glyphs could be shared by all group members. Because they focused on getting their VGA controller working early in the project, they actually used their VGA output to help debug their code as the project progressed by writing diagnostic data to the screen in their assembly programs. This group wrote three different games for their system which involved approximately 2000 lines of assembly code:

Giant Slalom: The skier tries to make it down a course without hitting trees or other obstacles.

Chicken: a two-player game based on the arcade classic Frogger. Each player tries to get their chicken across the road without being hit by any of the cars.

Tron: based on the classic arcade classic Tron. Players move around a playing field leaving trails.

4.2 Pong/Breakout

This group emulated classic video games Pong and Breakout by taking a different approach to their VGA output. They used 128x96 pixel resolution where these pixels are expanded on the screen such that the 128x96 pixels took up the entire screen space. In order to save frame buffer space each 16-bit location in their frame buffer memory held four 4-bit pixel color values. They implemented a library of assembly language graphics functions including painting single pixels, drawing a line from point to point using Bresenham's line drawing algorithm, drawing a box, and drawing characters on a screen using a simple font map stored in a separate area of memory.

4.3 Dance Dance Revolution

This group used dance pads from a home version of this popular arcade game as inputs, and used a combination of splash screens stored in flash memory and glyph-based VGA to control the moving arrows during game play. They synchronized the movement of the arrows to a song playing on an attached mp3 player. The mp3 player's controls were mapped into the processor's I/O space so that the start and stop of the music could be controlled by the program along with the graphics. This game was by far the most popular during the class open house at the end of the semester.

5. CONCLUSIONS

We have presented some details of a semester-long project-based course on computer design from the University of Utah. In this course the ability to design interactive games on student-designed computer hardware has greatly increased student excitement about their projects, and also increased the depth of student learning related to computer design and implementation. In order to target games as an application area important, but often overlooked, project features such as I/O must be dealt with in a strong way. While we did not do detailed assessment, it was clear to us from the final project reports that the game teams ended with a deeper understanding of many core computer design issues than non-game teams. The infrastructure required to add this dimension to project courses is not overwhelming, and the payoff is large. Not only do the students learn more about computer design, architecture, and implementation, but they have more fun doing it and they are much more likely to keep their projects to show off to friends, family, and prospective employers.

6. ACKNOWLEDGMENTS

I thank my students in the Computer Design Lab course over the years who have risen to the challenge and designed great projects. In particular I thank the students who designed the projects described in this paper. For Slalom / Chicken / Tron: Ryan Anderson, Whit Johnson, Brad Macdonald, and Adam Walker. For Pong/Breakout: Mike Green, Derik Jolley, Vic Lopez, Erik Nordstrom, and Vinh Pham. For DDR Colby Litnak, Paul Willoughby, Jacob Johns, and Jason Hansen.

7. REFERENCES

[1] J. Amaral, P. Berube, and P. Mehta. Teaching digital design to computing science students in a single academic term. *IEEE Transactions on Education*, 48(1), feb. 2005.

[2] T. Barnes, H. Richter, E. Powell, A. Chaffin, and A. Godwin. Game2learn: building CS1 learning games for retention. In *SIGSCE conference on ITi '07*, Dundee, Scotland, 2007.

[3] J. Brophy. *Motivating Students to Learn*. Lawrence Erlbaum Associates, 2nd edition, 2004.

[4] N. Calazans and F. Moraes. Integrating the teaching of computer organization and architecture with digital

Figure 5: Images from the interactive games developed by students. From left to right on top: Slalom Super-G, Chicken, and Breakout. On the bottom from left to right: Dance Dance revolution — dance pads, splash screen, and game.

hardware design early in undergraduate courses. *IEEE Transactions on Education*, 44(2), may. 2001.

[5] P. Chu. *FPGA Prototyping by Verilog Examples: Xilinx Spartan-3 Version.* Wiley Interscience, 2008.

[6] National semiconductor CR16 microcontroller http://www.national.com/appinfo/cr16.

[7] K. Eble. *The Craft of Teaching: A Guide to Mastering the Professor's Art.* Jossey-Bass, 2nd edition, 1994.

[8] D. Harris. The microprocessor as a microcosm: a hands-on approach to VLSI design education. In *Frontiers in Education Conf.*, Boston, MA, Nov 2002.

[9] M. Holland, J. Harris, and S. Hauck. Harnessing FPGAs for computer architecture education. In *Microelectronic Systems Education, 2003.*, jun. 2003.

[10] S. Leutenegger and J. Edgington. A games first approach to teaching introductory programming. *SIGCSE Bull.*, 39(1):115–118, 2007.

[11] R. Paharsingh and J. Skobla. A novel approach to teaching microprocessor design using FPGA and hierarchical structure. In *Microelectronic Systems Education, 2009.*, jul. 2009.

[12] M. Pearson, D. Armstrong, and T. McGregor. Design of a processor to support the teaching of computer systems. In *Electronic Design, Test and Applications, 2002.*, 2002.

[13] PS/2 protocol description. http://www.computer-engineering.org/ps2protocol/.

[14] S. Shabanah, J. Chen, H. Wechsler, D. Carr, and E. Wegman. Designing computer games to teach algorithms. In *Information Technology: New Generations (ITNG), 2010*, apr. 2010.

[15] K. Sung. Computer games and traditional CS courses. *Commun. ACM*, 52(12):74–78, 2009.

[16] E. Sweedyk, M. deLaet, M. C. Slattery, and J. Kuffner. Computer games and CS education: why and how. In *SIGCSE '05*, St. Louis, Missouri, USA, 2005.

[17] VGA timing description. http://www.epanorama.net/documents/pc/vga_timing.html.

[18] K. Vollmar and P. Sanderson. MARS: an education-oriented mips assembly language simulator. *SIGCSE Bull.*, 38(1):239–243, 2006.

[19] N. Weste and D. Harris. *CMOS VLSI Design: A Circuits and Systems Perspective.* Pearson Education, 3 edition, 2006.

[20] Xilinx corporation web page. http://www.xilinx.com.

VIREOS: An Integrated, Bottom-Up, Educational Operating Systems Project with FPGA Support

Marc L. Corliss
Hobart and William Smith Colleges
Dept. of Mathematics and Computer Science
Geneva, NY
corliss@hws.edu

Marcela Melara
Hobart and William Smith Colleges
Dept. of Mathematics and Computer Science
Geneva, NY
marcela.melara@hws.edu

ABSTRACT

In this paper, we present the VIREOS project, a new operating system designed specifically for the classroom. VIREOS is a simple, Unix-like, operating system, which runs on the Larc educational architecture. A VIREOS/Larc system can either be simulated or run on a pre-configured FPGA. The VIREOS project is well integrated with an introductory computer architecture course using Larc and the assignments are structured in a similar fashion: using a bottom-up approach. We have several resources available on the Web, which help reduce the overhead of adopting VIREOS. Finally, VIREOS has been used in one operating systems course already, and the feedback from students was generally favorable.

Categories and Subject Descriptors

D.4.7 [**Operating Systems**]: Organization and Design; K.3.2 [**Computer and Information Science Education**]: Computer Science Education

General Terms

Design

Keywords

VIREOS, operating systems, education

1. INTRODUCTION

The operating system (OS) is a core component in modern computers and naturally an important area of study for undergraduate computer science students. Obviously, operating systems are ubiquitous in modern computers, and thus, students should know something about them. Moreover, perhaps more than any other course in computer science, an operating systems course ties together all aspects of computer system design. After all, it is the responsibility of the OS to manage application software running on the computer as well as to provide that software with an abstract view of the hardware.

SIGCSE'11, March 9–12, 2011, Dallas, Texas, USA.

Naturally, the best way for a student to learn how the operating system works is to build one. Of course, a student cannot be expected to build a commercial-caliber OS such as Linux from scratch. The student must be either given a substantial amount of starting code or the OS must be simple enough that it can be completed in a single semester. In this paper, we explore the latter approach; we introduce and describe a new operating system designed specifically for the classroom.

The operating system, which we call VIREOS (a Vanilla, Introductory, but Realistic, Educational Operating System), is a simple, Unix-like OS written entirely in C. VIREOS is implemented on top of the Larc classroom architecture [5], which has a much simpler instruction set architecture (ISA), input/output (I/O) interface, and memory management hardware support (among other things) than most commercial architectures. VIREOS was used in an operating systems course in fall 2009 at Hobart and William Smith Colleges, and overall, it was well received by the students.

VIREOS has several virtues that make it well suited for the classroom. First, although it was designed for simplicity, VIREOS includes many important features of modern operating systems such as a Unix-like file system (using i-nodes) and virtual memory via paging. Second, though a VIREOS/Larc system is often simulated, we also provide support for running it on a pre-configured FPGA. Third, VIREOS can be integrated with a course on computer architecture (especially one using Larc). The VIREOS assignments are structured in a bottom-up fashion so that students are always implementing new components on top of components they have already built and understand. Finally, we have several resources including comprehensive documentation and code available on the Web at *http://math.hws.edu/vireos*.

In the remainder of this paper, we describe the VIREOS project in more detail. In Section 2, we discuss related work. In Section 3, we enumerate our goals in designing the VIREOS project. In Section 4, we give an overview of the VIREOS project. In Section 5, we share our experiences using the VIREOS project in the classroom. Finally, in Section 6, we present future work.

2. RELATED WORK

There are many existing educational operating system projects (too many to cite them all), but there are three main approaches. One approach is to have students modify an existing, commercial operating system rather than write one from scratch [6, 9, 13]. Obviously, the advantage of this approach is that the student works with a commercial OS. They can also potentially look more deeply into issues of performance and security. But the disadvantage is that the student misses out on implementing some aspects of the OS. As a result, the student may leave the class with an incomplete view of some parts of the OS.

A second approach is to have students build a complete OS for a commercial machine [2, 3, 8, 11, 12, 18]. The OS, itself, may also have commercial uses, which is the case for Minix [18]. For Minix though, we believe some students may find the software infrastructure daunting. Even with a simpler infrastructure, using a commercial machine, while certainly appealing, has some drawbacks. In particular, many aspects of a commercial machine, such as interrupt handling, I/O, and memory management, are complicated and can make the job of the student more challenging. Some of this complexity can be traded off for features in the operating system such as paging and more complex file systems. But, in this case, as with modifying an existing OS, the student may have gaps in their understanding of some parts of the OS.

A third approach, which is taken in the VIREOS project, is to build an operating system for a simpler, non-commercial machine; one that is designed specifically for the classroom. Nachos [4] and OS 161 [7] are two prominent examples that fall into this category. With this approach some complexity is naturally avoided (with regards to the underlying machine) at the expense of some loss of realism. We address this deficiency in the VIREOS project to some extent by configuring an FPGA to run as a VIREOS system. Although it is probably not practical for use in assignments, it can be used to demonstrate to the student that their operating system will be a part of a complete, working system. In fact, this use of hardware in the VIREOS project is similar in many educational OS projects, even those running on commercial hardware. During OS implementation and testing, emulation or simulation is often used.

One aspect of VIREOS that is different from many educational operating systems projects is the potential for integration with other computer science courses. In particular, the machine that VIREOS runs on top of, Larc [5], was designed specifically for an introductory computer architecture class (sometimes called computer organization). The approach in both projects works similarly: each new assignment builds on top of previous work done by the student. Therefore, operating systems instructors can leverage student's knowledge and experience gained in the architecture course. In the future, we plan on exploring connections with other courses such as an advanced computer architecture course.

Embedded XINU [3] is a recent project similar to VIREOS in terms of its integration with other computer science courses. But Embedded XINU differs from VIREOS in that it targets embedded systems and runs on top of a Linksys wireless router. On the one hand, Embedded XINU has the virtue that the operating system runs on real hardware. But at the same time, this hardware must be installed and maintained by the instructor, which adds some overhead to its adoption. With VIREOS, the use of hardware (*i.e.*, FPGAs) is optional.

3. GOALS

We had several goals in mind when designing the VIREOS project. Here we list each goal along with a description of how it was met.

- **From scratch.** First, we want students to write the operating system basically from scratch (with just a little auxiliary starting code). Of course, the OS and/or machine must be simple for the student to complete the OS in a single semester. To achieve this goal, we use an education-based architecture (Larc [5]). We also primarily do not use any interrupts (except in a single case). We have found that these two simplifications are enough to ensure that the OS is doable in a single semester without sacrificing some other important and interesting aspects of the OS (*e.g.*, file system functionality and memory management).

- **Good coverage.** Although the machine and OS are simplified in some ways, we still want the OS to contain as many features as possible. For instance, VIREOS has a Unix-like file system (using i-nodes), multi-processing, and virtual memory. We have found from experience in teaching operating systems that some students have trouble fully understanding these aspects of the OS unless they have actually implemented them.

- **Realistic.** Even though we use an educational architecture, we still want students to feel that they are building a "realistic" operating system. We have configured an FPGA to run the VIREOS system so that instructors can demonstrate VIREOS running on real hardware. In addition, we modeled parts of VIREOS after *nix operating systems, which students at our institution use when doing their computer science work. In particular, each VIREOS system call is similar to a corresponding call in Unix/Linux and the file system is implemented using i-nodes.

- **Well integrated.** One very important goal for us was integrating the operating systems course with our introductory course in computer architecture. For the student, the study of operating systems is a natural extension from their study of computer architecture. Consequently, we implemented VIREOS to run on the Larc classroom architecture [5], which we use in our architecture course. It should be pointed out, however, that VIREOS can be used at institutions where Larc is not adopted in the architecture course.

- **Bottom-up.** Another important goal for us was to use a bottom-up approach in structuring the assignments. Each assignment should build off of the previous assignment; the student should never work with code that they do not yet understand. In the first VIREOS project assignment (minus a preliminary assignment where the student builds a shell), the student builds a basic trap and I/O handler, and then in later assignments adds additional functionality (a file system, process manager, and memory manager).

- **Well documented and supported.** Finally, we want to provide thorough documentation and support to lower overhead for instructors to adopt the project and for students to use it. We have written a lab manual, which includes in-depth descriptions of both the OS and the hardware, as well as a detailed write-up for each assignment. The manual is freely available off the Web at *http://math.hws.edu/vireos* along with the API for all the assignments. The solution code can also be requested by instructors (and instructors only – see the VIREOS web page for details). The instructor can also obtain Verilog files for configuring an FPGA (the Altera DE1 [1]) to run the VIREOS/Larc system.

4. VIREOS PROJECT

This section describes the VIREOS project in more detail. Section 4.1 describes the VIREOS system and Section 4.2 describes the assignments and the available resources for both students and instructors.

4.1 VIREOS System

General. VIREOS is a *nix-like (Unix/Linux) operating system (although greatly simplified). VIREOS has support for a file system, time sharing, and virtual memory via paging. The file system support includes both files and directories although it does not include links. Unlike a *nix system, however, VIREOS does not have support for multiple users. It also mostly does not provide security (*e.g.*, the user can read/write any file) although it does include some safety measures to prevent an errant program from corrupting the system.

The VIREOS system calls enable user programs to work with files and directories, as well as manage processes. Each of these system calls is similar to a corresponding *nix system call. VIREOS also has support for communicating directly with I/O devices such as the disk. Although this is not ideal from a safety/security standpoint (*e.g.*, an errant application could corrupt the disk), it makes it much easier for students to test their operating system implementation. (Note: these system calls could be disabled in a working version of VIREOS.)

Source language. VIREOS is written entirely in a C-like language called C--, which was first developed by Jim Lenz [10], although it has been significantly extended for the VIREOS project. In the future we plan on implementing VIREOS in full ANSI C, but in order to get the project up-and-running faster, we opted to initially use a simple, easily extendable compiler. Moreover, the C-- compiler adds some OS-specific features such as providing an array for saving and restoring registers at the source language level. Because of these features, the OS can be written entirely in C-- (no extra assembly code is required).

C-- is missing some features from C including multi-dimensional arrays, unions, nested functions/structs, typedefs, switch statements, do/while loops, function pointers, and primitives besides int and char (among other things). But C-- retains most of the features of C and in practice the programming experience is much the same.

Target machine. VIREOS runs on the Larc architecture [5]. Larc is a simple, 16-bit, MIPS-like architecture designed specifically for the classroom. It can support most text-based (non-graphical) systems such as those that use a command-line interface (*i.e.*, a shell) for entering commands and running programs. A Larc machine is primarily simulated although we have configured a Larc processor on an FPGA (discussed below).

Larc has ISA support for four I/O devices: a keyboard, a text-based monitor, a disk (the block size is 1/2 KB), and a real-time clock. To simplify the OS, polling is used to communicate with I/O devices. The only supported interrupt is a timer for implementing time sharing. In the future, we will explore adding support for interrupt-driven I/O.

Each I/O device includes a set of registers for communication between the CPU and that device. These are programmed via memory-mapped I/O. There are also a set of memory-mapped registers for managing the CPU.

Larc has support for two memory management techniques: virtual memory via paging as well as a simple sandboxing technique (using a base and limit register) [17].

Run environment. The VIREOS/Larc system can be run in one of two ways. First, it can be run in a Larc simulator, which is written in C and compiled to run on most Linux machines. It can also be run on a pre-configured Altera DE1 FPGA [1] (other FPGAs could potentially be used by modifying our provided configuration files). When students are implementing VIREOS, it probably makes more sense for them to use the simulator as there is no hardware overhead. But the FPGA can be used to demonstrate a "real" VIREOS/Larc system. There is also the potential for integrating this project with a course on microarchitecture.

Note: we are currently in the process of adding paging support to the FPGA but we expect to have this completed by the time of publication. All other OS features are supported, and as a result, the FPGA can still be used for demonstration purposes as well as for the non-paging course assignments.

Code organization. VIREOS consists of five components: a trap handler, an I/O handler, a file system manager, a process manager, and a memory manager. Each component is contained in a separate C module. Students implement each of these components over the course of the semester.

In addition to these components, there are also a couple of modules for performing auxiliary functionality such as manipulating strings or converting between data types. These modules are provided to students.

4.2 Assignments and Resources

Assignments. Table 1 lists each of the assignments students undertake in the VIREOS project. There are 5 total assignments. the first 2 are shorter two-week assignments and the last 3 are longer three-week assignments. Students start by implementing an interactive shell (a two-week assignment) with support for redirection, piping, and background processing. The shell serves as the core application in a VIREOS system and it is important that students understand how an application like the shell works. This assignment also gives students a better understanding of the OS functionality, particularly with regards to process management, which they may not have fully understood prior to completing the assignment.

In the remainder of the assignments students implement the various components of the VIREOS kernel. As much as possible, these assignments are ordered in a bottom-up fashion; students build each component on top of components built in previous assignments.

Assignment	Component	Length	Details
0	Interactive Shell	2 weeks	Supports redirection, background processing, and piping
1	Trap and I/O handler	2 weeks	Uses polling
2	File system manager	3 weeks	Uses i-nodes, supports files (for base credit) and directories (for extra credit)
3	Process manager	3 weeks	Uses round-robin scheduling, supports fork, exec, wait
4	Memory manager	3 weeks	Uses paging

Table 1: VIREOS project assignments.

At the start of each assignment, the student is given a precompiled, working version of the components implemented in earlier assignments. In some cases, these must be slightly augmented to work with the new component. However, these augmentations are generally small.

At the end of each assignment, the student has a working kernel although it may not include some functionality, which will be implemented in a later assignment. The student is given a set of test programs, which they can use to test their implementation of the new component(s). The student is also given a compiled, reference operating system to see how the test programs should behave with a working OS.

In the first kernel assignment, a two-week assignment, students build a trap and I/O handler. This kernel will support applications that directly communicate with I/O devices, several of which the student is provided with. Of course, this kernel will not support applications that make use of the file system or create processes.

In the second kernel assignment, a three-week assignment, students build a file system on top of their trap and I/O handler. For base credit, the student must support all the file-related (and not directory-related) system calls. The directory-related system calls are saved for extra credit. The student is given several test programs that manipulate files (and potentially directories) as well as stress test the file system. Of course, none of these test programs include multiprocessing.

In the third kernel assignment, a three-week assignment, students build a process manager with a simple round-robin scheduler. With the process manager, VIREOS has support for the fork, exec, and wait system calls (among others) and time sharing. However, the kernel is highly inefficient. Because paging is unimplemented and so each process can use the entire user space, the kernel saves and restores the entire address space on a context switch. In this assignment, the student is given a working shell along with several shell utilities (*e.g.*, **ls**, **mkdir**). The student is also given a program for stress testing the process manager.

In the final kernel assignment, a three-week assignment, students implement paging. Although this adds no additional functionality to the OS, it significantly improves its efficiency. Because the address space is small and the clock speed is slow, the entire page table can be stored in a translation lookaside buffer (TLB), which greatly simplifies the operating system. To test their implementation of paging, the student can use the same test programs from the process manager assignment along with one new test program for stress testing the memory manager.

Student/instructor resources. We have several, freely-available resources for both students and instructors using VIREOS. These can be attained off of the VIREOS web page at *http://math.hws.edu/vireos*. First, we have a comprehensive student manual (a PDF file), documenting all aspects of the VIREOS project. It includes informational sections on the Larc ISA, VIREOS code layout, and C-- language, as well as detailed write-ups for each assignment. Although this manual does not cover operating systems theory, it is intended to be used alongside a traditional operating systems textbook [14, 15, 17].

We also have the API for each assignment available on the web page. It is generated from comments in the source code using the tool doxygen [19], which works similarly to javadoc [16].

We also provide instructors and students with the incomplete toolset, which the student must complete over the course of the semester. Instructors (and instructors only) can get the solution code for the assignments. Instructors can also get the Larc simulator source code as well as the Verilog code used to configure the FPGA. Details are available on the web page for requesting this restricted code, although instructors should expect some delay as each request must be validated.

5. EXPERIENCES

The VIREOS project was used in the fall 2009 offering of Operating Systems at Hobart and William Smith Colleges (HWS). We had not yet configured an FPGA to run VIREOS, but all other aspects of the project were fully implemented and tested in the class.

The class was taught by the first author of this paper. The class consisted of a lecture (3 hours per week) and a lab (1 and 1/2 hours per week). The lab period gave students a chance to get help from the instructor on the programming assignments. The course was taught using the textbook by Tanenbaum [17], which was supplemented with the VIREOS documentation.

The size of the class was small with only 8 students in total. Interestingly, 3 of the 8 students were exchange students from a European university. The 5 HWS students had used Larc before while the 3 exchange students had not.

None of the students had any significant experience programming in C (which VIREOS is written in) although the 3 exchange students had some experience programming in C++ (the HWS students did not). As a result, the students were given a week-long primer on C in the beginning of the course along with a short, 1-week programming assignment designed to familiarize them with C. Students were also given a second 1-week assignment at the beginning of the course on using the interactive shell and its advanced features (*e.g.*, piping) prior to building their own. Note: these preliminary assigments would be lifted for students with more C and/or shell experience.

Overall, the VIREOS project was well received by the students in the class. At the end of each assignment, the students were asked whether they found the assignment challenging and interesting, whether they had a better understanding of how operating systems work, and whether the time allotted was reasonable (as well as a call for any other comments). All of the students in the class generally found each assignment challenging and interesting. The students also found that each assignment gave them a better understanding of how operating systems work. For example, one student commented on the file system assignment:

> This [assignment] was definitely challenging, but it really helped me get a grasp on the file system concepts we talked about in class. I found the translation from file system theory to implementation pretty interesting–it took a lot of work to make sure the underlying theory was working correctly.

A second student commented on the process manager assignment:

> I learned a lot about implementing a process manager and all the complications that make it challenging. Working on this project really did help me to understand how operating systems manage multiple processes.

There were other similar comments across the various assignments. In addition to this OS-specific feedback, several students also felt that the assignments made them much better C programmers (a relatively new language for them) as well as code testers. One student mentioned on the file system assignment:

> I also am beginning to feel pretty comfortable with C since so much of its ins and outs is used to program the file system.

At the end of the semester, we also asked the 5 HWS students, who had taken both the operating systems and introductory architecture courses at HWS, if they found the integration between the two courses helpful in their overall understanding of computer systems. All of the students agreed that it was beneficial using Larc in both courses. One student wrote:

> I think the integration of the courses was immensely helpful in giving me a better understanding of computer systems. The hands on design and coding experience was a very valuable part of learning the course material, and using Larc ... across the board made it easier to jump into each new project.

There were also some negative comments. Many students found errors or omissions in the write-up, which have subsequently been fixed. Some students commented that the assignments had a significant learning curve and it was hard to get started. We have modified the assignment write-ups with this in mind.

In addition, some students felt that it was hard to complete the assignments in the time allotted. However, often these same students commented that they started the assignment too late. On average, students reported working 7-9 hours outside of class (for all the course work), which we thought was reasonable. Furthermore, for each project, nearly all the students submitted working code albeit with some minor bugs.

Finally, many students commented that testing was difficult. Most of these comments were made on the process management assignment. One student states:

> This is a difficult project to get fully working because it can be very hard to debug given the nature of the assignment. At the same time, I think it is a valuable assignment because it does a very good job of reinforcing the course material and it is interesting to try and implement. The problem is that it is so hard to get every detail working properly.

In the future, we plan to explore ways to make the debugging process easier for students, either by adding better test programs or by adding new debugging tools to the infrastructure. Other students commented that testing was slow, particularly for the process management assignment (which probably added to the difficulty in testing). In this assignment, memory is not paged (paging is added in the next assignment), and so, the processor manager is inefficient. We are looking for ways to address this in the future such as requiring, for this assignment, all concurrently-running programs to reside in memory in order to avoid expensive disk operations. This requirement would limit the size of the test programs (since they would all need to simultaneously fit in memory) but would make for faster testing.

We hope to address these negative comments in a future version of VIREOS. In general though, we are happy with the initial feedback we received from students.

6. FUTURE WORK

We plan to explore several directions of future work. First, we want to look at incorporating interrupt-driven I/O into the project. As this will represent more complexity and work for the student, we will give instructors the option of choosing between interrupt-driven I/O and polling.

We also want to look at incorporating new I/O devices such as a graphical monitor and a mouse. The closer the VIREOS system is to a commercial machine, the more appealing it will be to the student. But as with interrupt-driven I/O, we plan to make these I/O devices optional, and give instructors more flexibility in tailoring the project to their own class.

We also want to incorporate some security into VIREOS and potentially move from a single-user system to a multi-user system. Students would implement mechanisms for authenticating users and for protecting system resources (*e.g.*, files), among other things.

We also plan on migrating VIREOS from C-- to ANSI C. Although the programming experience is similar for the two languages, there are some differences, which can make it difficult when programming in C--.

In addition, we plan on adding a set of tools to ease the difficult debugging process. For instance, we hope to add a graphical debugger to the toolset to allow students to step through their operating system code. We will also look for other tools and resources to make debugging VIREOS easier for the student.

Finally, we plan to add applications to the VIREOS/Larc system to make it more usable and appealing to the student.

It currently includes only a shell, some basic shell utilities, and few simple (text-based) games.

7. CONCLUSIONS

The VIREOS project is a new, simple, Unix-like, classroom operating system running on the Larc educational architecture. The VIREOS project uses a bottom-up structure for assignments and can be well-integrated with a course on introductory architecture, which also uses Larc. The VIREOS project has many resources available on the Web, including the project API, solution code, and configuration files for running VIREOS on an FPGA. In fall 2009, we used VIREOS in the classroom and the feedback from students was generally favorable.

8. ACKNOWLEDGMENTS

Professor John Vaughn at Hobart and William Smith Colleges gave valuable input and advice on this work. Marcela Melara was supported by a generous grant from the Office of the Provost at Hobart and William Smith Colleges. Finally, the anonymous reviewers provided helpful feedback.

9. REFERENCES

[1] Altera Coorporation. *DE1 Development and Education Board – User Manual*, 2006.

[2] M. D. Black. Build an operating system from scratch: a project for an introductory operating systems course. In *SIGCSE '09: Proc. of the 40th ACM tech. symp. on computer science education*, pages 448–452, 2009.

[3] D. Brylow. An experimental laboratory environment for teaching embedded operating systems. In *SIGCSE '08: Proc. of the 39th SIGCSE tech. symp. on computer science education*, pages 192–196, 2008.

[4] W. A. Christopher, S. J. Procter, and T. E. Anderson. The Nachos instructional operating system. Technical report, 1993.

[5] M. L. Corliss and R. Hendry. Larc: A little architecture for the classroom. *Journal of Computing Sciences in Small Colleges*, 24(6):15–20, 2009.

[6] R. Hess and P. Paulson. Linux kernel projects for an undergraduate operating systems course. In *SIGCSE '10: Proc. of the 41st ACM tech. symp. on computer science education*, pages 485–489, 2010.

[7] D. A. Holland, A. T. Lim, and M. I. Seltzer. A new instructional operating system. In *SIGCSE '02: Proc. of the 33rd SIGCSE tech. symp. on computer science education*, pages 111–115, 2002.

[8] D. Hovemeyer, J. K. Hollingsworth, and B. Bhattacharjee. Running on the bare metal with GeekOS. In *SIGCSE '04: Proc. of the 35th SIGCSE tech. symp. on computer science education*, pages 315–319, 2004.

[9] O. Laadan, J. Nieh, and N. Viennot. Teaching operating systems using virtual appliances and distributed version control. In *SIGCSE '10: Proc. of the 41st ACM tech. symp. on computer science education*, pages 480–484, 2010.

[10] J. Lenz. Wisc C-- compiler. URL: *http://pages.cs.wisc.edu/~lenz/compiler.html*, 2003.

[11] H. Liu, X. Chen, and Y. Gong. BabyOS: a fresh start. In *SIGCSE '07: Proc. of the 38th SIGCSE tech. symp. on computer science education*, pages 566–570, 2007.

[12] B. Pfaff, A. Romano, and G. Back. The Pintos instructional operating system kernel. In *SIGCSE '09: Proc. of the 40th ACM tech. symp. on computer science education*, pages 453–457, 2009.

[13] A. Schmidt, A. Polze, and D. Probert. Teaching operating systems: windows kernel projects. In *SIGCSE '10: Proc. of the 41st ACM tech. symp. on computer science education*, pages 490–494, 2010.

[14] A. Silberschatz, P. B. Galvin, and G. Gagne. *Operating System Concepts*. John Wiley & Sons, Inc., 8th edition, 2008.

[15] W. Stallings. *Computer Organization and Architecture: Designing for Performance*. Prentice Hall, 7th edition, 2005.

[16] Sun Microsystems, Inc. *javadoc - The Java API Documentation Generator*, 2002. URL: *http://java.sun.com/j2se/1.5.0/docs/tooldocs /solaris/javadoc.html*.

[17] A. S. Tanenbaum. *Modern Operating Systems*. Pearson Prentice Hall, 3rd edition, 2008.

[18] A. S. Tanenbaum and A. S. Woodhull. *Operating Systems: Design and Implementation*. Pearson Prentice Hall, 3rd edition, 2006.

[19] D. van Heesch. *Doxygen Manual*, 2010. URL: *http://www.doxygen.org/manual.html*.

Revising Computer Science Learning Objects from Learner Interaction Data

L.D. Miller, Leen-Kiat Soh, Beth Neilsen, Erica Lam, Ashok Samal
Department of Computer Science and Engineering
University of Nebraska
Lincoln, NE 68588
1-402-472-3200
{lmille, lksoh, bneilsen, elam, samal}@cse.unl.edu

Kevin Kupzyk, Gwen Nugent
Center for Research on Youth, Family and Schools
University of Nebraska
Lincoln, NE 68588-0342
1-402-472-2448
{kkupzyk2, gnugent1}@unl.edu

ABSTRACT
Learning objects (LO) have previously been used to help deliver introductory computer science (CS) courses to students. Students in such introductory CS courses have diverse backgrounds and characteristics requiring revision to LO content and assessment to promote learning in all students. However, revising LOs in an ad hoc manner could make student learning harder for subsequent deployments. To address this problem, we present a systematic revision process for LOs (LOSRP) using proven techniques from educational research including Bloom's Taxonomy levels, item-total correlation, and Cronbach's Alpha. LOSRP uses these validation methods to answer seven questions in order to diagnose what needs to be revised in the LO. Then, LOSRP provides guidelines on revising LOs for each of the seven questions. As an example, we discuss how LOSRP was used to revise the content and assessment for 16 LOs deployed to over 400 students in introductory CS courses in 2009. Lastly, although initially designed for LO revision, we briefly discuss how LOSRP could be used for assessment revision in intelligent tutoring systems.

Categories and Subject Descriptors
K.3.2. [**Computer and Education**]: Computer and Information Science Education.

General Terms
Experimentation

Keywords
learning objects, intelligent tutoring system, systematic revision process

1. INTRODUCTION
LOs have previously been used successfully to teach introductory computer science courses to students [3][7][8][9]. For example, students who used the LOs achieved significantly higher scores than students in the control group [9] and rated the LOs highly in terms of usefulness and appropriateness [8]. However, such introductory courses contain students with a wide variety of backgrounds. For example, at our university, students in introductory computer science (CS) courses run the gamut from non-majors taking a single, required CS course to CS and computer engineering majors to honors students in a hybrid CS and business program. These students have also been shown [8][10] to have very diverse characteristics in terms of motivation, self-efficacy, and programming background. This diversity makes it difficult to create LOs that are appropriate for all prospective students. Content and assessment for LOs may be easy for students with some backgrounds but difficult for other students. A question so difficult that students cannot choose the correct answer from the distracters does not promote learning. The same is true for questions that are so easy that the distracters are completely obvious. Thus, it is often necessary to evaluate and revise the LO content and assessment. However, unlike existing Science, Technology, Education, and Math (STEM courses), "computer science courses do not yet have a similar set of validated assessment tools" [12]. This can make it extremely difficult for content developers who try to revise the LOs. Doing this in an ad hoc manner runs the risk of accidently making them worse.

We present a systematic revision process for LOs (LOSRP) using the assessment data collected from actual deployment data. This process was developed after extensive collaboration with educational experts. LOSRP uses proven assessment validation tools from educational research including item-total correlation [13], Cronbach's Alpha statistic [6], and Bloom's Taxonomy [4] levels. These methods are used to provide the answers for seven separate questions that diagnose what part of the LO requires revisions: (1) Does the assessment use multiple mark questions instead of true/false or multiple-choice? (2) Is the item-total correlation on the assessment questions below a threshold? (3) Are specific distracters in the questions not being chosen? (4) Are specific distracters chosen more often than the correct answer? (5) Is the Cronbach's Alpha statistic for the assessment below a threshold? (6) Do the questions fail to cover all the Bloom's Taxonomy levels? (7) Are objectives of the content and the questions inconsistent? All these questions are commonly used for assessment validation in the educational field [2]. To the best of our knowledge, this is the first use of such questions for CS LO revision. Second, LOSRP provides guidelines for revising the LO to address each question listed above. An extensive example of using this systematic revision process on LOs deployed to introductory CS students is also presented in this paper.

Note that the systematic process described here has broader application than just to LOs. Using the same principles, this process can also be used for content and assessment revision in Intelligent Tu-

SIGCSE'11, March 9-12, 2011, Dallas, Texas, USA.

toring Systems. We see two possible applications. First, intelligent tutoring systems (ITS) could use our process to improve the assessment by selecting appropriate distracters for questions and appropriate questions for the assessment. Second, the ITS could also use this process to diagnose whether students are struggling with the content learning objectives or the assessments questions.

The remainder of this paper is organized as follows: Section 2 provides related work on assessment revision in current computer science and education research and background on the education methods used to answer the questions. Section 3 discusses the design and deployment of the LOs. Section 4 discusses the guidelines for addressing the questions in more detail and provides examples of LO content and assessment revision. Finally, we provide conclusions and discuss future work on improving the LO revision process.

Note that in this paper we focus primarily on the assessment revision for the LOs. The statistics used in LOSRP consider only the assessment data. For Question (7), the consistency between the content objectives and assessment questions is measured only qualitatively. The LOSRP is by no means complete or optimal. However, this is the first step towards a systematic revision process for CS LOs. Also, LOSRP could make an impact in automating this process for intelligent tutoring systems as noted above. The LO revision process should also include revision of the tutorial and exercises of the LOs in addition to the assessment. For example, factors such as empirical usage behavior that captures the interactive sessions (e.g., questions that are too long or too time consuming and inconsistent correlation between time spent on tutorial concepts and the corresponding questions) can be used to revise content from time and learner attention viewpoints. To illustrate, if the average view time spent on a concept in the tutorial is much longer than the average time spent on viewing the set of questions associated with that particular concept, then perhaps there should be more questions for that concept or the discussions on that concept should be shortened. We will consider this in more detail in the future work.

2. RELATED WORK AND BACKGROUND

This section first discusses assessment revision in current CS and education research. Then, it provides background on the educational methods used in the LOSRP.

2.1 Assessment Revision

Previous work on assessment revision in CS education research has considered many of the questions used in LOSRP. This includes using multiple-choice questions (MCQ), revising the question distracters, using Bloom's Taxonomy to create the questions, and making sure that the questions cover the learning objectives. However, none of this previous work takes an integrated view in which all these approaches are used together. Further, none of this previous work involves revising LOs for CS. Instead, previous work focuses on ITS or developing the curriculum for CS courses. We provide summaries on such previous work below. Table 1 categorizes current CS education research on assessment revision based on our seven questions.

Tew and Guzdial [12] claim that CS lacks strong assessment validation found in STEM courses. Such assessment validation is a necessary step in creating reliable assessments. The authors give a language independent assessment for introductory CS courses. This assessment is based on content commonly presented in textbooks. It contains MCQs developed using experts in CS educations. The authors emphasize using distracters and content objectives coverage for revising the initial questions. However, no pilot study has yet been conducted to evaluate this assessment. LOSRP also considers well-defined statistical measures such as item-total correlation and the Bloom's Taxonomy when revising the questions.

Burge & Leach [5] provide a tool for evaluating how well students understand the learning objectives for introductory CS courses. This tool consists of an Excel spreadsheet that maps learning objectives to assessment questions and evaluates the average score. It was used as part of the ABET accreditation process for the CS program. This tool only considers the raw averages for assessment scores. Our LOSRP uses validation methods such as item-total correlation and Cronbach's Alpha to provide more detailed information on the assessment questions.

Starr et al. [11] use Bloom's Taxonomy (BT) to categorize all the concepts in introductory CS courses. In a case study, the learning objectives and assessment were revised to cover multiple BT levels. In particular, the questions required certain levels of expertise to complete. The authors also determine whether content objectives and assessment questions are consistent through comparing their BT levels. At this time, LOSRP focuses more on assessment than content revision. We use BT levels and several methods to evaluate the assessment questions.

Agarwal et al. [1] use the NetCoach ITS to present introduction to testing concepts to CS2 students. This content is organized in a series of linked hypermedia pages. NetCoach provides recommendations by varying color of the links between the pages (e.g., red link means prerequisites for content are not satisfied). However, students can ignore this advice and visit the page. After students are done navigating through the content NetCoach gives an assessment using MCQs. The authors revised the assessment questions based on an analysis using BT and item-total correlation. LOSRP also considers the distracters in the questions and Cronbach's Alpha when analyzing the scores.

2.2 Educational Statistics

Item-total correlation [13] is used to compare the scores on individual questions in the assessment. Item-total correlation measures the degree of consistency between the score for a single item (i.e., question) with that for the other questions. It uses the correlation between the scores of an individual item and the sum of the scores of the remaining items. For example, if high-scoring students tend to score worse on a particular question than low-scoring students, then the item-total correlation for that particular question would be low. Item-total correlation of 0.30 or higher is generally acceptable in educational research [13].

Cronbach's Alpha [6] is used to estimate the internal consistency of the assessment questions. It increases with the inter-correlation between scores on the assessment questions—similar questions should elicit similar responses. Thus, it can be used to measure the reliability of the assessment questions as a single latent construct (i.e., how closely related the questions are). A Cronbach's Alpha value of 0.70 or higher is necessary for an assessment to be considered valid [6].

Blooms Taxonomy provides a categorization on question difficulty based on the learning objectives [4]. For cognitive learning objectives this includes six ordered processes from easiest to hardest: Knowledge, Comprehension, Application, Analysis, Synthesis, and Evaluation. Knowledge questions are generally easy requiring only the memorization of facts. Comprehension questions usually require students to describe or explain certain concepts or demonstrate their understanding, while Application questions usually require students to apply what they understand in a situation or to a problem where its solution is not apparent. Answering Analysis questions often involve analysis, categorization, comparison, and differentiation of different solutions or options. Synthesis and Evaluation questions require an explanation about responses (e.g., why or why not?) making them less suitable for online systems such as LOs. Thus, when revising assessment questions for LOs it is important to include questions covering the first four levels of the Bloom's Taxonomy: Knowledge to Analysis.

Table 1: Assessment Revision in Recent CSE Research. MCQ stands for multiple-choice questions, IT for item-total correlation, ND for distracter not chosen, DC for distracter chosen often, CA for Cronbach's Alpha, BT for Bloom's Taxonomy, and O for learning objectives.

Paper	MCQ	IT	ND	DC	CA	BT	O
Tew & Guzdial [12]	✓		✓	✓			✓
Burge & Leach [5]							✓
Starr et al. [11]						✓	✓
Agarwal et al. [1]	✓	✓				✓	
LOSRP	✓	✓	✓	✓	✓	✓	✓

3. LO DESCRIPTIONS

Sixteen LOs were created to cover a wide range of concepts in introductory CS courses. This includes a range of concepts (see Table 2) from basic concepts on arrays and numeric data to more advanced concepts on sorting and recursion. Each of these LOs follows the same general format. First, the LO contains a tutorial with a list of learning objectives followed by a set of pages explaining the concept using text and figures. Each page of the LO covers a succinct section on the concept equivalent to several pages in a traditional textbook. Second, it contains a set of 1-4 interactive exercises for the students to practice. These exercises require several steps to complete and students receive feedback on their progress at each step. In particular, students are given hints if they become stuck in an exercise. Students are able to repeat each exercise as often as desired. Finally, the assessment consists of between 4-14 questions depending on the amount of content in the tutorial. These questions are designed to measure whether students have learned the content in the tutorial and exercises that was specified by the learning objectives. Originally, assessments included true/false, multiple-choice and multiple mark questions.

In 2009, the LOs were used in five offerings of introductory CS courses at the University of Nebraska, Lincoln. The courses contained over 400 students allowing us to collect a considerable amount of data resulting in more reliable results for the assessment validation methods used in LOSRP. This data also allows us to support additional research on active learning [9], elaborative feedback [8], and automatic metadata generation [8][10]. Interested readers in the details of the software design and research should consult those papers.

All the LOs are built in compliance with the Sharable Content Object Reference Model (SCORM) standard for web-based e-learning. This makes the LOs usable on any SCORM-complaint learning management systems (LMS) such as Blackboard and Moodle. This greatly simplifies the deployment of the LOs.

The downside to SCORM is that the LMS generally tracks only the student's final score on the assessment. This makes it impossible to evaluate distracters or to use validation methods such as item-total correlation that require data on the answers to the individual assessment questions. Thus, to provide the required assessment data, we have modified each LO to include additional software called the ***LO Wrapper***. It employs a modification of the Easy SCO Adapter [http://www.ostyn.com] to record student assessment data using the SCORM API. The wrapper also records student interactions with the LO (e.g., page navigation, clicks on a page, etc.). It transmits all recorded data (i.e., assessment and interactions) using JavaScript to our remote server.

We have also developed a remote application for our project called the ***MetaGen***. MetaGen runs offline on our server and handles all the data logging, data extraction and data analysis for our project using separate modules. The *data logging module* uses PHP to store the student interactions received from the wrapper in a MySQL database. The *data extraction module* queries the database and processes the data into our dataset. The *data analysis module* computes all the assessment validation methods used to answer the LOSRP questions and also runs data mining techniques (such as feature selection and association rule mining) to support automatic metadata generation [8][10].

4. LO REVISION PROCESS

As previously discussed, LOSRP uses seven questions to diagnose whether LO content or assessment needs revision. In this section, we explain the seven diagnosis questions in more detail. We also provide the LOSRP guidelines on revising LOs for each question. Throughout, as a comprehensive example, we discuss how LOSRP was used to revise our LOs after the 2009 deployment. This includes examples of actual LO content and assessment questions where appropriate. The revisions done to the LOs are summarized in Table 2. Finally, we provide general guidelines on revising both the LO content and assessments.

4.1 Multiple Mark Questions

Multiple mark questions have multiple correct answers and all of them must be selected in order to get the question correct. The problem with these questions is that students can choose a subset of the correct answers and still get the question wrong. Consequently, multiple mark questions in the LOs were either removed or replaced with MCQs. The easiest way to change the multiple mark questions into MCQs is to retain all the multiple mark answer choices, labeling them using numerals, and then offering answer choices that are differing groups of numeral answers. For example, the following multiple mark question in the Arrays LO was converted into the MCQ shown below:

Original: Multiple Mark Question
Which of the following are true of arrays? (Select all that apply)

A. Arrays and loops can be used together to simplify code. (correct)
B. Arrays help avoid the problems associated with memory garbage.
C. Arrays can make it easier to keep track of variable names. (correct)
D. Arrays can help group related variables together. (correct)

Revised: Multiple Choice Question
Which of the following are true of arrays?

1. Arrays and loops can be used together to simplify code.
2. Arrays help avoid the problems associated with memory garbage.
3. Arrays can make it easier to keep track of variable names.
4. Arrays can help group related variables together.
   A. 1 and 2
   B. 2 and 3
   C. 1, 2, and 3
   D. 1, 3, and 4 (correct)
   E. 2, 3, and 4

Table 2. Summary of Revisions to the 2009 Deployment LOs. Entry gives number of questions revised for each LO.

LO Name	Multiple Mark	Low item-total correlation	Not chosen Distracters	Distracters chosen too often	New Questions Added	Total
Advanced Logic	3	0	0	0	4	**7**
Advanced Recursion	0	1	0	1	5	**7**
Algorithms	0	6	1	2	4	**10**
Arrays	0	0	0	0	4	**7**
Conditionals	2	2	0	2	4	**8**
Debugging	0	2	1	1	5	**7**
Functions	3	6	2	1	0	**8**
Logic	2	0	0	0	2	**4**
Looping	3	0	0	0	5	**8**
Non-OO Prob Analysis	0	5	1	2	3	**8**
Numeric Data	1	7	1	2	3	**10**
OO Problem Analysis	0	0	1	0	5	**6**
Recursion	1	2	1	0	4	**7**
Searching	2	1	2	0	0	**3**
Sorting	1	3	0	0	0	**3**
Variables & Constants	0	2	2	2	4	**8**
Total	18 16%	37 33%	12 10%	13 11%	52 46%	**111**

4.2 Low Item-Total Correlation

Item-total correlation is a measurement of the correlation between the scores of an individual item and the sum of the scores of the remaining items [13]. The item-total correlation on a question is low when high-scoring students get the question wrong more frequently than low-scoring students. *An item-total correlation below 0.3 is considered low.* Generally, this occurs when either the question or the related content are ambiguous to the students. It could also be caused by ambiguity in the answers as discussed later (see Section 4.4). To address this issue, we revised the questions (see example below) and related content (see Section 4.7) to make sure that the wording was clear and unambiguous. For example, the wording in this Numeric Data question was clarified:

Original: Low Item-Total Correlation
The four integer data types are essentially the same.
A. TRUE (correct)
B. FALSE

Revised: Clarified Question
*The four integer data types are essentially the same, **and there are not reasons to choose one type over another type.***
C. TRUE (correct)
D. FALSE

4.3 Distracters Not Being Chosen

Distracters not being chosen by any student are indicators that they are not pertinent to the question so students do not consider them as possible answers [13]. If a distracter was not chosen by any student, it needs to be changed or replaced. If every student got the question correct and none of the distracters were chosen, the question should be removed or made more challenging because it is not providing any valuable information regarding students' abilities. For example, the distracter in this Debugging question was never chosen so we replaced it with a distracter more relevant to the specific question being asked.

Original: Distracter Not Chosen
What is the purpose of a debugger's breakpoint?
A. It generates a list of variables containing their value
B. It stops execution of a program at the breakpoint (not chosen)
C. It pauses the program at the breakpoint (correct)
D. It skips execution of the statement at the breakpoint

Revised: New Distracter Added
What is the purpose of a debugger's breakpoint?
A. It generates a list of variables containing their values
B. It causes the program to exit at the breakpoint (new)
C. It pauses the program at the breakpoint (correct)
D. It skips execution of the statement at the breakpoint

4.4 Distracters Being Chosen Too Often

Distracters being chosen too often are indicators that the question is either unclear or the answer choices are ambiguous. Ideally, all distracters should be chosen in equal proportions. A distracter that is chosen too often should be compared with the correct answer. If the two answers are similar, one or both should be elaborated upon to distinguish them. For example, in this Variables & Constants question, point-biserial correlation [13] (.059) indicated that one distracter was often chosen by high-scoring students so we revised the answers to make the correct answer unambiguous.

Original: Distracters Chosen Too Often
Which of the following constant declarations is <u>incorrect</u>?
A. final double KS_TAXRATE
B. int MAX_MILES = 100000
C. final double PI = 3.14159 (chosen too often)
D. A and B (correct)
E. A, B, and C

Revised: Question Answers Reworded
Which of the following constant declarations is <u>incorrect</u>?
1. final double KS_TAXRATE
2. final int MAX_MILES = 100000
3. final double PI = 3.14159
4. int METERS_IN_MILE = 1600
   A. 1 & 2
   B. 1 & 4 (correct)
   C. 1 & 3
   D. 2, 3, and 4
   E. All are correct

4.5 Cronbach's Alpha

Cronbach's Alpha [6] is a statistical measure of internal consistency or reliability of the set of items contained in the LO. *Any value above 0.7 is considered an acceptable consistency.* Unfortunately, several LOs had Cronbach's Alpha values below 0.7. This was most likely due to the limited number of questions in each LO. In an attempt to increase the Cronbach's Alpha value, it was decided that each LO should have at least ten questions to increase the reliability of the assessment questions as a single latent construct [6]. For every LO that had fewer than ten questions, new questions were added to the LOs assessment. The number of questions added to each LO is given in Table 2.

4.6 Bloom's Taxonomy Coverage

LO assessment questions were categorized into the first four levels of BT: Knowledge, Comprehension, Application, and Analysis. This categorization was performed independently by two researchers and was then compared to ensure accuracy. Table 3 gives the BT Levels for questions in the 2009 deployment. We analyzed the BT coverage for each LO to determine which categories the new questions should fit in to. As stated earlier, it was decided that each LO should have at least ten questions, so we strived to write the new questions such that the ten questions would be equally spread across the first four levels of BT. However, because the LOs are intended for introductory CS courses we focused on adding knowledge and comprehension questions because they better assess the student learning necessary for an introductory course. Additionally, given the number of LOs that needed revision, we prioritized the LOs with the most "need" based on the insufficient number of questions, Cronbach's Alpha, and item-total correlation values.

Table 3. BT Coverage for Assessment Questions in 2009 Deployment Before and After Revision. KN: knowledge, CO: comprehension, AP: application, AN: analysis. A single entry indicates that no additional questions were added.

LO Name	KN	CO	AP	AN
Advanced Logic	0/2	0/1	3	3/4
Advanced Recursion	0/2	1/3	3	1/2
Algorithms	2/4	3	0/2	1
Arrays	2/3	2	1/3	1/2
Conditionals	0/3	2/3	3	1
Debugging	2/6	0/1	0	3
Functions	10	0	1	3
Logic	2/4	0	2	1
Looping	0/2	3/4	0/1	2/3
Non OO Problem Analysis	1/2	2/4	3	0
Numeric Data	3	1/2	3	0/2
OO Problem Analysis	1/4	0/1	2/3	1
Recursion	1/2	2/4	2	1/2
Searching	2	5	0	4
Sorting	4	2	2	2
Variables & Constants	2/3	2/3	2	0/2

4.7 Learning Objectives Coverage

Several learning objectives are listed at the beginning of each tutorial to describe what students should learn by the end of the LO. Similar to the BT categorization, the assessment questions were also categorized by which learning objective they fulfilled. For the LOs that did not have at least ten questions, we strived to write the new questions so that the questions are equally spread across the learning objectives. In some cases, there were already questions that did not fit the learning objectives so new content was added to align the content and the assessment. For example, in the Non OO Problem Analysis LO, additional content on the divide-and-conquer approach was added.

Original: No Tutorial Coverage for Question

The principle of this divide-and-conquer approach to problem analysis is to divide a large problem into smaller problems and handle each smaller problem with its own

A. TRUE (correct)

B. FALSE

Revised: Added Tutorial Content

As you can see, there are 6 specific tasks that must occur when the submit button is clicked, and each one can be handled by its own separate module (divide-and-conquer), instead of trying to lump everything together within the body of the "button clicked" function. This is useful for several reasons:

1. You can focus on implementing each small sub-problem individually instead of trying to work on the entire problem at once.
2. When other programmers look at your code, they will clearly be able to tell what part of the code handles which sub- problem.
3. If you come across errors when testing your program, it will be easier for you to isolate where the problem occurs if each step of the big problem clearly has its own module.

4.8 How to Examine and Write Questions

Here we provide general guidelines on revising LO questions. It is important to make sure that the assessment questions and the tutorial content use the same vocabulary and are consistent throughout. If this is not the case, the question or the tutorial content should be adjusted to preserve consistency. Next, the question itself should be examined. It is important to have multiple people look at each question and provide feedback about the clarity and fairness of a question. Finally, examine each of the answer choices for a question. If any of the incorrect answer choices are similar to the correct answer or if any of them do not have a specific reason why they are incorrect, either the correct answer choice should be clarified to make it the only correct answer or the incorrect answer should be changed to emphasize how it is incorrect.

There are several ways to handle the questions after they are examined. These include removing the question, changing the answer choices, clarifying the question, or determining that the question is acceptable as written. If a question is examined and more than one reviewer deems a question incorrect or inappropriate it might be reasonable to remove the question entirely from the LO assessment. Before removing a question, however, it is important to consider the purpose of a question and what objective it is based on. If a question is removed, another question based on the same objective should be added.

When determining what new questions to write, the writer should analyze both BT and learning objective coverage. Ideally the assessment questions for each LO will cover the first four level of BT and every learning objective, which should be representative of the material covered in the LO. A good principle to follow is evenly spread the assessment questions across the first four levels of BT and cover all the learning objectives for each LO. In the revision process, we strived to write questions that specifically fulfilled a BT level and correspond to a specific learning objective that needed more questions. However, revising BT coverage is less important on LOs with (1) sufficient number of questions, (2) high value of Cronbach's Alpha, and (3) high item-total correlation values.

5. CONCLUSIONS & FUTURE WORK

In this paper we present a systematic revision process called LOSRP for LOs that uses assessment validation methods from educational research including Bloom's Taxonomy [4], item-total correlation [13] and Cronbach's Alpha [6]. These validation methods are used to answer seven questions in order to diagnose what needs to be revised in the LO. LOSRP also provides guidelines on revising LO content and assessment for each diagnosis question. For all diagnosis questions that elicit a "yes" response, the appropriate guidelines (➡) should be used to revise the LO content or assessment.

Does the assessment use multiple mark questions instead of true/false or multiple choice?

➡ Change multi mark questions to multiple-choice questions.

Is the item-total correlation on the assessment questions below a threshold of 0.3?

➡ Add additional content to clarify what the questions are asking.

Are specific distracters in the questions not being chosen? Are specific distracters chosen more often than the correct answer?

➡ Replace the distracters that are not chosen. Change the wording for distracters chosen to differentiate them from the correct answer.

Is the Cronbach's Alpha statistic for the assessment below a threshold of 0.7?

➡ Add additional questions to better evaluate student understanding of the content.

Do the questions fail to cover the first four Bloom's Taxonomy levels?

➡ Add additional questions with different BT levels to promote student learning.

Are objectives of the content and the assessment questions inconsistent?

➡ Add additional questions based on the learning objectives, add additional content covering the learning objectives, or change the learning objectives.

We used LOSRP on sixteen LOs deployed in 2009 to introductory CS courses. Overall, we found that many of our LOs needed to be revised because they did not have enough assessment questions. We rigorously applied all LOSRP guidelines to the revision of the LOs for the 2010 deployment (see Table 2 and 3). The LOs are currently being deployed to 403 students in five introductory CS courses. In the future, we will compare the results on the same LOs from the 2009 and 2010 deployments. We expect to see improvements on all assessment validation methods used not just in the assessment scores for the LOs.

LOSRP currently focuses on assessment revision rather than content revision. Even the best assessment questions ever written would not be effective when the content cannot convey the concepts and learning objectives to the students. Currently, LOSRP only gives qualitative guidelines on revising LO content. This is not complete, but it provides the first step towards a systematic revision process for LOs. In the future, we will add to LOSRP the capability to quantitatively diagnose between problems with the content and the assessment questions. This will involve combining assessment validation methods and natural language processing on student interactions and assessment responses to identify "disconnects" between the LO content/questions.

We would also like to apply LOSRP to ITS. An ITS would gain even more benefit from LOSRP than LOs because it could dynamically revise the assessments rather than waiting an entire year between LO deployments. Additionally, an ITS could use the LOSRP to diagnosis in real-time whether students are struggling with the learning objectives or the assessment questions.

6. ACKNOWLEDGMENTS

This material is based upon work supported by the National Science Foundation under Grants No. 0632642 and 0829647.

7. REFERENCES

[1] Agarwal, R., Edwards, S.H. et al. 2006. Designing an adaptive learning module to teach software testing. *SIGCSE* (2006), 259-263.

[2] Association, A.P. 1986. *Standards for Educational and Psychological Testing*. Amer Psychological Assn.

[3] Balci, B. and Inceoglu, M. 2006. Reusable Learning Objects (RLOs) for Computer Science Students. *Computer Science and Its Applications*. 373-382.

[4] Bloom, B.S. 1956. *Taxonomy of Educational Objectives, Handbook 1: Cognitive Domain.* Addison Wesley Publishing Company.

[5] Burge, L.L. and Leach, R.J. 2010. An Advanced Assessment Tool and Process. *SIGCSE* (2010), 451-454.

[6] Cronbach, L. 1951. Coefficient Apha and the Internal Structure of Tests. *Psychometrika*. 16, 3 (1951), 297-334.

[7] Mundy, D.P. 2006. Using Learning Objects to Support Introductory Computer Architecture Education. *IASTED* (2006), 305-310.

[8] Nugent, G., Kupzyk, K. et al. 2009. Empirical Usage Metadata in Learning Objects. *FIE* (2009), 1285-1290.

[9] Nugent, G., Soh, L. et al. 2005. Design, development, and validation of a learning object for CS1. *SIGCSE* (2005), 370-370.

[10] Riley, S., Miller, L.D. et al. 2009. Intelligent Learning Object Guide (iLOG): A Framework for Automatic Empirically-Based Metadata Generation. *AIED* (2009), 515-522.

[11] Starr, C.W., Manaris, B. et al. 2008. Bloom's Taxonomy Revisited: Specifying Assessable Learning Objectives in Computer Science. *SIGCSE* (2008), 261-265.

[12] Tew, A.E. and Guzdial, M. 2010. Developing a Validated Assessment of Fundamental CS1Concepts. *SIGCSE* (2010), 97-101.

[13] Thorndike, R. 1982. *Applied Psychometrics*. Boston: Houghton Mifflin.

The Impact of Problem-Oriented Animated Learning Modules in a CS1-Style Course

Jeffrey A. Stone
Pennsylvania State University
200 University Drive
Schuylkill Haven, PA 17972
+1-570-385-6267
stonej@psu.edu

Tricia K. Clark
Pennsylvania State University
Tulpehocken Road, P.O. Box 7009
Reading, PA 19610
+1-610-396-6349
tkc3@psu.edu

ABSTRACT
CS educators face many challenges in teaching basic computer programming to first-year students. As a result, faculty must find new and interesting ways to engage students and to provide opportunities for student success. This paper reports on a two-year study involving the Problem-Oriented Animated Learning Modules for Introductory Computer Science (PALMS for CS1) project. PALMS for CS1 is a set of animated learning modules designed to enhance student engagement, success, and retention through the use of computer animation, video, audio, and storytelling. The results of this study indicate that PALMS for CS1 has been successful in engaging introductory students but more work remains to improve student success and retention. Marked improvement in student success and retention was seen during the second year of the study, though success and retention are still a challenge for traditionally underrepresented groups.

Categories and Subject Descriptors
K.3.2 **[Computers and Education]**: Computer and Information Science Education – Computer Science Education.

General Terms
Human Factors.

Keywords
CS1, Non-Majors, Animation, PALMS.

1. INTRODUCTION
Computer Science (CS) educators face many challenges in teaching basic computer programming to first-year students. Increasingly these students are non-majors who likely have a low interest level in the course content. Research suggests that introductory course failure rates climb for non-majors, many of whom are often overwhelmed by the complexity and time commitment of the course [1]. As a result, faculty must find new and interesting ways to maintain student interest and to provide an equitable opportunity for all students to succeed. Compounding the challenges facing CS faculty is the increasing heterogeneity of student experiences and backgrounds. Faculty are often challenged to make their discipline relevant to a generation of skeptical students. Because of the ubiquity of technology in today's world, students now enter college or university life with high levels of confidence in their information and communication technology skills. However, research suggests that the reality of their skills may not match their confidence level (e.g. [6], [10]). Research also suggests that CS is not necessarily seen as relevant to students' everyday world or as existing in a social context [2].

Despite an increasing pool of students who have grown up with technology, CS enrollments still do not appear to be meeting workforce needs [8]. One reason might be that the traditional methods of instruction in introductory CS courses no longer attract and retain the interest of the majority of students. A large body of research suggests that multimedia and animation can assist in student engagement and enhance learning of basic concepts (e.g. [4], [5], [11]). While not a silver bullet, such techniques can assist in relating CS to the technological landscape to which many young students have been exposed.

This paper will report on a two-year study involving the use of problem-oriented animated learning modules in six sections of a CS1-style course. The goals of this project were to create a set of learning tools which would improve both student engagement and retention while fostering the development of problem-solving skills. The challenges and outcomes associated with these custom-built tools will be discussed. This research aligns with other works which discuss the use of animation to engage and retain students in CS and other science majors (e.g. [7], [9]).

2. THE PALMS FOR CS1 PROJECT
The Problem-Oriented Animated Learning Modules for Introductory Computer Science (PALMS for CS1) project is a set of animated learning modules designed to enhance the ability of first-year students to succeed in introductory computer programming, specifically the content featured in CS1 courses. The PALMS for CS1 modules are intended to address three primary objectives. First, the use of animation, video, audio, and storytelling is expected to more fully engage the student and get them both interested and excited about the course and the material which follows, assisting in student retention. Second, the animated modules were expected to enhance the problem-solving skills of introductory students and thereby increase the success rate of students. Third, the animated modules are constructed in such a way as to illustrate the wider applicability of CS concepts. Examples from different disciplinary domains were used to

engage the non-major population. The natural science disciplines are prominently featured.

The PALMS for CS1 modules function as an introduction to programming concepts with a focus on problem-solving. Each of the PALMS modules includes specific learning objectives, assignments from multiple problem domains, progress indicators/benchmarks (frequent quizzes and lab evaluations to allow students to chart their progress) and custom animations for learning module content (audio-enhanced) and for demonstrating project topics. PALMS for CS1 uses a variety of technologies to create and deliver multimedia presentations, integrated quizzing mechanisms, and problem-solving demonstrations that appeal to a range of learning modes and reinforce concepts in multiple ways.

2.1 Module 1: Problem-Solving & Algorithms

The first PALMS module, entitled "Problem-Solving and Algorithms", is used during the first four weeks of a CS1-style course. The goal of Module 1 is to provide students with a gentle introduction to CS1 programming concepts by focusing on algorithms and how to solve computer-based problems. By introducing these concepts and vocabulary absent of any specific syntax quirks, PALMS Module 1 builds a foundation for students to use in the traditional, programming language–specific part of the course.

The primary component of Module 1 is an online multimedia presentation with embedded flash animations and review questions. This multimedia presentation functions as an electronic textbook and includes the following main topics:

- *Problems and Their Solutions*: This topic introduces basic vocabulary and concepts central to algorithmic problem-solving.
- *How Does a Computer Solve Problems?*: This topic introduces the discrete nature of computation problem-solving as well as the different types of errors encountered in programs.
- *Algorithms and Input/Output:* This topic focuses on more complex algorithms as well as restrictions, conditions, and formatting involved with input and output.
- *Variables, Arithmetic, and Assignment*: This topic focuses on assignment, expressions, operators, and arithmetic evaluation.
- *Control Structures:* This topic focuses on the concepts of conditional selection and conditional repetition.

Each of these topics can be explored at the student's leisure outside of class and build on the in-class activities. Each topic includes multiple, detailed algorithmic examples, flash animations describing particular concepts (e.g. assignment, desk-checking) and electronic quizzing mechanisms at the end of the topic's content. All content is narrated in audio form by one of the authors. A transcript of the audio is also available inline with the presentation starting in Year 2 (but must be explicitly activated by the student). Figures 1-2 are example screenshots from Module 1.

Other components of Module 1 include a set of graded lab exercises and in-class quizzes. The graded lab assignments ask students to use what they have learned in Module 1 to create both English-like algorithms and simple flowcharts to solve a given problem. The flowcharts are created using the RAPTOR tool developed by Carlisle et al (see [3]). The use of RAPTOR aids student verification of their algorithms as well as providing an additional visual component to the learning experience. Embedded animations are also included in several of the lab assignments to provide a visual reference for the problem domain.

Once this four-week introduction is complete, the remaining 11 weeks of the course function as a traditional CS1 course. At the Penn State Schuylkill campus, this involves the use of structured C++ as the implementation language. The use of PALMS Module 1 was expected to provide a foundation upon which the basics of C++ – or any structured programming language – could be more easily absorbed.

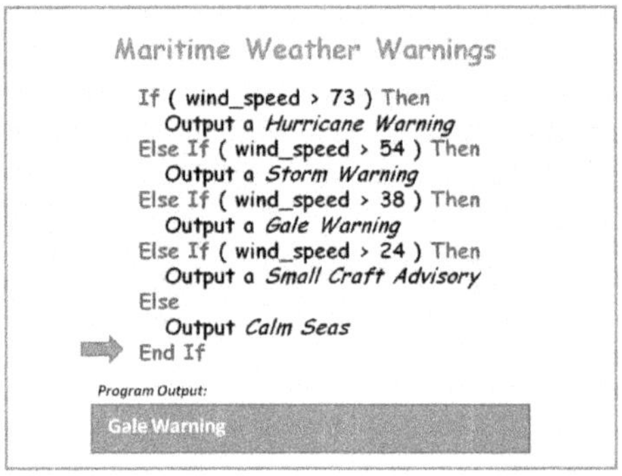

Figure 1. Sample PALMS Module 1 Animated Example.

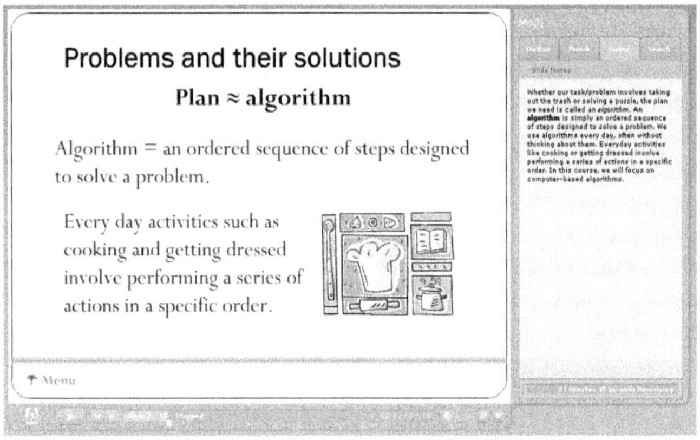

Figure 2. Sample PALMS Module 1 Presentation Slide.

2.2 Module 2: Basics of C++

The second PALMS Module, entitled "Basics of C++", involves a series of brief, animated flash-based presentations describing a particular C++ component (e.g. data types). An initial set of PALMS Module 2 presentations were introduced during the second year of this study. The goal of Module 2 is to provide students with a simple introduction to C++ syntax while reinforcing the concepts discussed in PALMS Module 1.

The style of the Module 2 presentations is similar to the Module 1 content but smaller in scope, focusing on a single C++ topic (e.g. while loops, one-dimensional arrays). These animated podcast-style presentations utilize audio narration and can be explored at the student's leisure outside of class. Figure 3 depicts a sample screenshot of a Module 2 presentation. A transcript of the audio is available inline with the presentation. The smaller, more focused approach of PALMS Module 2 was utilized due to the abundance of C++ resources available to students via the class textbook, the Internet, and other outlets.

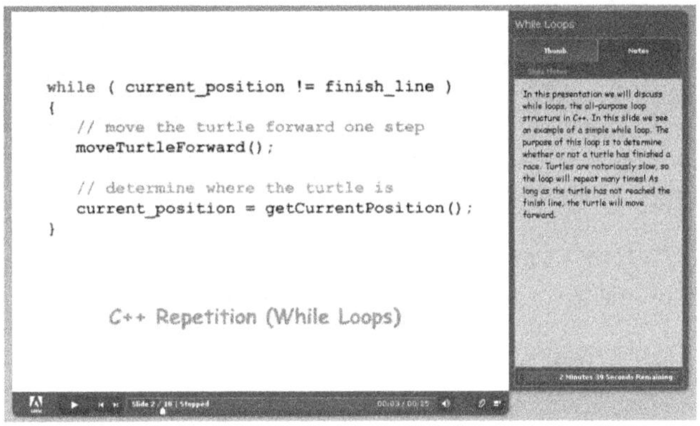

Figure 3. Sample PALMS Module 2 Presentation Slide.

3. STUDY DESIGN

A multi-year, non-experimental study was undertaken to determine if the PALMS for CS1 tools were effective in achieving three outcomes related to our CS1-style course: student engagement, course retention, and student success. The following sections describe the study methods, procedures, and instruments.

3.1 Methods and Procedures

The PALMS for CS1 content was utilized in six sections of a CS1-style course over two academic years (2008-2010). Four sections of this course were general education (CS101) and two sections of this course were intended specifically for CS and Engineering majors (CS121). Despite the difference in populations, the content of the two courses was virtually identical. Due to the limited number of students enrolled in these courses, the use of a control group was deemed infeasible.

PALMS Module 1 was employed for the first four weeks of each course section over the two study years. The remainder of the course was a traditional, structured programming CS1 course using C++. Two sections of CS101 and one section of CS121 participated in the first year. During the second year of the study an introductory set of PALMS Module 2 presentations were introduced during the C++ portion of the course. Two sections of CS101 and one section of CS121 participated in the second year.

Student outcomes related to this study were assessed using both survey and grade data. The survey aspect of the study has two initial components. First, a pre-test survey was given to all students at the beginning of the course. This survey was designed to measure students' experience with computer technology, their demography, and their academic backgrounds. Second, a post-test survey was administered to the students at the end of the PALMS Module 1 portion of the course. The survey included questions designed to measure attitudes towards PALMS Module 1 as well as students' comfort level entering the C++ portion of the course.

Two changes were made to the survey instruments for Year 2. First, additional questions were added to the pre- and post-test surveys to measure students' comfort levels with abstract thinking and solving word problems. Second, another post-test survey was added to the end of the course. This "final" survey was designed to measure student attitudes about PALMS for CS1 as well as their comfort level with abstract thinking and solving word problems after the C++ portion of the course (i.e. PALMS Module 2). These changes were made based on the experiences and feedback from the first year. At the end of each semester the survey data was collected and analyzed using SPSS. The results were compared against the grade information for those students who consented to be included in the study.

3.2 Profile of Participants

The study yielded 90 consenting participants (54 in Year 1, 36 in Year 2), or approximately 76.90% of the total enrollment (117 students total). A total of 81 of the 90 participants provided survey responses. The 81 responses included 13 females (16.0%) and 68 males (84.0%). The vast majority of participating students (79, or 97.5%) were in the 18-30 year age range. The course was fairly diverse in terms of race and ethnicity; 51.9% reported themselves as white/Caucasian, 34.6% were African-American/Black, 4.9% were Asian-American/Asian, 4.9% were Latino/Hispanic, and 3.7% reported themselves as "other".

The majority of students self-reported themselves as Science, Technology, Engineering, or Mathematics (STEM) majors (55.6%). The course was being used as a major requirement by most of the students (90.1%). The CS121 course is a requirement for Computer Science and most Engineering majors at Penn State University, while the CS101 course serves a variety of majors (e.g. IST, Criminal Justice, and Physics). For a majority of the students, the most recent math course taken was college-level algebra/trigonometry (39.5%) or introductory calculus (38.3%).

4. RESULTS

4.1 Year 1 Results

4.1.1 Pre-Module 1 Survey Results

Participating students in Year 1 reported high levels of confidence in their computing ability. Students primarily rated themselves as "Good", "Very Good", or "Expert" (82.2%, N=45) in their ability to use Office-style programs. Similar results were reported for students' ability to search the Internet, with 56.5% (N=46) self-reporting themselves as having "Expert" knowledge. Students also rated themselves as "Very Good" (39.1%, N=46) or "Expert" (37.0%) in their ability to install and remove programs on their own computer. In terms of programming ability, 86.9% (N=46) rated themselves as "Beginner" or as having "No Knowledge".

4.1.2 Post-Module 1 Survey Results

The post-PALMS Module 1 survey results were very positive. 67.4% of respondents (N=46) reported that the PALMS Module 1 animated presentations were helpful or very helpful in preparing them for the course quizzes, projects, and lab assignments. When asked to rate their level of agreement that viewing the PALMS Module 1 animated presentations improved their understanding of programming concepts, a large majority of students agreed or strongly agreed with the statement (71.8%, N=46). Only 6.5% disagreed with the statement.

Students reported the built-in review questions as the most helpful PALMS Module 1 presentation component (37.8%, N=45) followed by the audio narration (33.3%) and the embedded flash animations (15.6%). The majority of students also reported that having access to more PALMS Module 1-style animated presentations would have no effect on their in-class attendance (58.7%, N=46) or make them more likely to attend class (19.6%). A majority of students (73.3%, N=45) also indicated they would be likely to view or would definitely view more such animated presentations if they were made available.

Student comments about their PALMS Module 1 experience were very positive. The comments predominantly noted the visual nature of the material (e.g. "The animated modules helped me because it gave a visual and audio view of the content we were learning"; "It thoroughly explained the concepts with audio and with visual context") as well as the 24/7 accessibility of PALMS and the ability to access the content repeatedly (e.g. "I could reference [PALMS] as many times as I wanted to from home"; "Basically it was like having a class I could repeatedly attend as many times as necessary until the information was learned.") The comparatively few negative comments seemed to indicate some students' aversion to the CS1 material (e.g. "not interested in that"), feelings of being overwhelmed (e.g. "It was just too much information to take in all at one time") or a belief that the PALMS Module 1 content did not correlate with the given quizzes.

4.1.3 Student Retention and Success Results

An examination of the final student retention and grade results suggested that the initial enthusiasm for the PALMS Module 1 content did not translate into desirable student success rates. The mean course average for the three participating sections was 65.4% (N=36). For the PALMS Module 1 content only, the mean score was 66.98%. Only 30.8% of consenting students received a "C" or better in the course (N=52); 36.5% received a "D" or "F" and 32.7% withdrew from the course. In terms of two of the desired outcomes of the study – student success and retention – the first year of the study was not successful.

One-way ANOVA found significant differences in course grade distribution between the three participating sections ($F=3.89$, $df=2$, $p < 0.05$). Post-hoc Scheffe analysis found that the first participating section of CS101 (Fall 2008) had a significantly higher course average than the second section of CS101 (Spring 2009), with a mean difference of 23.3%. Significant differences between the sections were also found for the distribution of PALMS Module 1 grades ($F=5.279$, $df=2$, $p < 0.01$). Scheffe analysis found that the averages for the first CS101 section were significantly different than the other two participating sections. The mean difference between the Fall 2008 CS101 section and the Spring 2009 CS101 section was 17.8%. The mean difference between the Fall 2008 CS101 section and the Spring 2009 CS121 section was 15.9%. The results suggest that the first course section was the most successful of the three participating sections.

4.2 Year 2 Results

The second year of this study involved some additional PALMS materials designed to help correct the student retention and grade deficiencies of Year 1. Student attitudes were observed to wane after the transition from PALMS Module 1 to the C++ portion of the course during Year 1. The enthusiasm generated by the Module 1 animated content appeared to be dampened by the lecture-based, textbook-enhanced traditional nature of the C++ material. This decline in engagement, combined with the low student success and retention rates, encouraged researchers to make changes to the course by continuing development of PALMS Module 2.

The PALMS Module 2 presentations were introduced in Year 2 to augment the C++ portion of the course. These small podcast-style presentations focused on introductory C++ topics (e.g. program structure, data types, while loops, one-dimensional arrays) and well as more complex programmatic ideas (e.g. functions and parameters). It was expected that these "familiar" tools would help students transition into C++.

4.2.1 Pre-Module 1 Survey Results

Participating students in Year 2 once again were highly confident in their computing ability. Students primarily rated themselves as "Good", "Very Good", or "Expert" (91.4%, N=35) in their ability to use Office-style programs. Similar results were reported for students' ability to search the Internet, with 52.8% (N=35) self-reporting themselves as having "Expert" knowledge. Students also rated themselves as "Good", "Very Good", or "Expert" (82.4%, N=34) in their ability to install and remove programs on their own computer. When asked about their programming ability, 82.4% (N=34) rated themselves as "Beginner" or as having "No Knowledge". A vast majority of students were confident in their ability to solve word problems (71.4%, N=35) but fewer students reported being comfortable with abstract thinking (51.4%, N=35).

4.2.2 Post-Module 1 Survey Results

As seen in Year 1, the post-PALMS Module 1 survey results were very positive. 71.4% of respondents (N=28) reported that the PALMS Module 1 animated presentations were helpful or very helpful in preparing them for the course quizzes, projects, and lab assignments (see Figure 4 for combined Year 1 & 2 results). When asked to rate their level of agreement that viewing the PALMS Module 1 animated presentations improved their understanding of programming concepts, a large majority of students agreed or strongly agreed with the statement (82.8%, N=29). No respondents disagreed with the statement, though 17.2% were undecided.

Year 2 Students reported the embedded flash animations as the most helpful PALMS Module 1 presentation component (27.6%, N=29) followed by the built-in review questions (24.1%), audio narration (13.8%) and the text content (13.8%). The majority of students also reported that having access to more PALMS Module 1-style animated presentations would have no effect on their in-class attendance (67.9%, N=28) or make them more likely to attend class (21.4%). A majority of students (75.8%, N=29) also indicated they would be likely to view or would definitely view more such animated presentations if they were made available.

A greater percentage of students were confident in their ability to solve word problems at the end of PALMS Module 1 (82.7%, N=29) and in their comfort with thinking in an abstract manner (75.8%, N=29). Paired samples t-Test analysis showed significant differences between the pre-PALMS Module 1 survey results and the post-PALMS Module 1 survey results ($t = -0.321$, $df=27$, $p \leq 0.01$) for these questions.

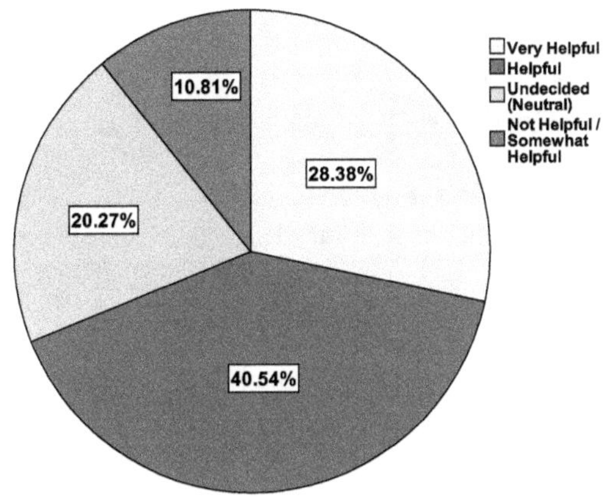

Figure 4. Helpfulness of PALMS in Preparing Students for Course Assignments and Quizzes (Combined Years 1 & 2).

Student comments about their PALMS Module 1 experience were again very positive. The visual nature of the material was again prominently mentioned, but the student comments seemed to mostly laud the structure of the Module 1 content (e.g. "It displayed the material in an organized manner and explained the material step by step in detail when necessary"; "It brought together groups of ideas into small lessons that were easy to absorb"). As with Year 1 there were comparatively few negative student comments. These comments indicated a mismatch between PALMS and some students' preferred learning style (e.g. "I need someone to do the problems right in front of me") though other comments indicated a desire for more interactivity (e.g. "I believe the PALMS material could be enhanced with more hands-on work inside the modules"). The Module 1 content for Year 2 was unchanged from Year 1.

4.2.3 Post-Module 2 Survey Results

The post-PALMS Module 2 survey results suggested that the positive feelings reported at the end of PALMS Module 1 carried through the rest of the course. 75.0% of respondents (N=20) reported that the PALMS for CS1 materials were helpful or very helpful in preparing them for the C++ portion of the course. When asked to rate their level of agreement that the PALMS for CS1 materials improved their understanding of programming concepts, a large majority of students agreed or strongly agreed with the statement (85.0%, N=20).

Students were once again asked about their confidence in solving word problems and thinking abstractly. A smaller percentage of students reported confidence in their ability to solve word problems than at the end of PALMS Module 1 (75.0%, N=20) but a higher percentage reported comfort with abstract thinking (80.0%, N=20). Paired samples t-Test analysis found no significant differences between the post-PALMS Module 1 results and the post-PALMS Module 2 results for these questions.

4.2.4 Course Retention and Student Success Results

The final course retention and grade results for Year 2 were more positive than for Year 1. The mean course average for the three participating sections was 73.7% (N=29). For the PALMS Module 1 content only, the mean score was 79.3%. The PALMS Module 1 averages were found to be significantly different between Years 1 and 2 ($t=-4.053$, $df=81$, $p < 0.01$). Figure 5 depicts the pass/fail/withdraw distributions for Years 1 & 2. In terms of letter grades, 57.1% of consenting students received a "C" or better in the course (N=35); 25.7% received a "D" or "F" and 17.1% withdrew from the course. These results indicate an improvement in retention and success rates from Year 1, though neither the success rate nor the retention rate can be considered optimal. One-way ANOVA found no significant differences in course grade distribution between the three participating sections. No significant differences between the sections were found for the distribution of PALMS Module 1 grades.

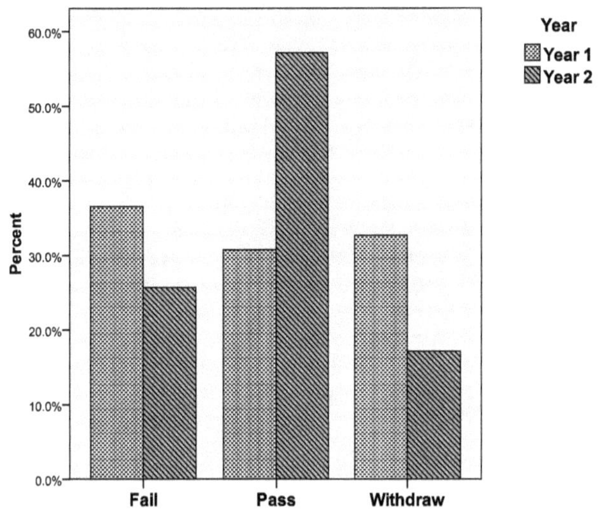

Figure 5. Course Retention and Success Rates (Years 1 & 2).

4.3 Demographic Relationships

Demographic data was analyzed for both Year 1 and Year 2 to ascertain the impact of PALMS for CS1 on success and retention rates for different gender and racial/ethnic groups. Race/ethnicity was found to have a significant relationship with student success and retention. Whites were significantly more likely to pass the class than non-whites ($X^2=17.031$, $df=1$, $\gamma=0.746$, $p < 0.01$) and non-whites were significantly more likely to withdraw from the class ($X^2=4.980$, $df=1$, $\gamma=0.525$, $p < 0.05$). Non-Whites also had a significantly lower mean course average than whites ($\bar{x}=61.70\%$ vs. $\bar{x}=75.4\%$; $t=2.652$, $df=63$, $p \leq 0.01$).

Gender also had a significant relationship with student success, though the limited number of female students tempers this result. Males were significantly more likely to pass the class than females ($X^2=4.561$, $df=1$, $\gamma=0.667$, $p < 0.05$). No significant relationships were found between gender and the likelihood of withdrawal or between gender and overall course average. Student major, math background, and perceptions of computing abilities were not significantly related to overall course average or the likelihood of passing or withdrawal. These demographic results suggest that PALMS for CS1 has thus far been challenged in promoting positive student retention and success rates for traditionally underrepresented groups.

5. DISCUSSION

The results of the PALMS for CS1 experiment are a mixed bag. The PALMS Module 1 materials were successful in engaging the interest of students, though this interest did not translate into improved retention and success rates in Year 1. The transition from the more visual Module 1 content to the traditional, syntax-intensive C++ portion of the course proved to be a challenge for many students. The greater student engagement, retention, and success rates experienced during Year 2 coincided with the introduction of PALMS Module 2 animated presentations. The small, animated, "podcast"-style presentations of PALMS Module 2 were designed to provide a familiar and comfortable mechanism by which C++ could be more easily absorbed by students. The Year 2 results also indicated that PALMS had a positive, significant effect on students' confidence and comfort level with abstract thinking and solving word problems. This is an especially positive outcome, given that poor problem-solving skills have been cited as a key factor in CS1 retention and success [1].

Despite the marked improvement in student retention and success rates in Year 2, these rates are by no means optimal. The marked improvement in student success and retention for Year 2 is also tempered by the significant relationship between failure rates and traditionally underrepresented groups, as well as the limited sample size. However, the fact that students' choice of major was not a significant factor in success and retention is a positive outcome. Given the diverse nature of the students enrolled in our course, a great deal of effort was taken to make the course appealing to students with different academic interests.

6. FUTURE DIRECTIONS

The PALMS for CS1 tools are currently being revised for version 2.0. The PALMS Module 2 materials are being expanded to include additional podcasts and an integrated set of lab exercises. It is expected that these changes will allow us to build on the promise shown during the second year of the study. Investigation into building interactivity into PALMS is also currently ongoing. Many of the PALMS for CS1 materials have been made available on the project Web site (http://sl-community.sl.psu.edu/PALMS/).

Additional assessment work (quantitative and qualitative) is being performed to assess how students use the PALMS for CS1 materials. It is expected that this information will allow us to refine the materials for more effective and widespread use. Especially important to this research is learning how to better engage and retain students from traditionally underrepresented groups; these students are expected to make up a larger percentage of our student population in the coming years.

7. CONCLUSION

The PALMS for CS1 online modules are designed to enhance the ability of first-year students to succeed in CS1-style courses. These modules are designed to aid student comprehension and problem-solving skills via a mix of animation, video, audio, and storytelling. The results of the study described here indicate that the PALMS materials have been successful in engaging introductory students but more work remains to improve student success and retention, especially in traditionally underrepresented groups. The more positive success and retention rates for the second year of the study indicates that further development and integration of PALMS content throughout the course may be beneficial to student success and retention.

8. ACKNOWLEDGMENTS

The authors would like to acknowledge the funding support of the Penn State Schuylkill Advisory Board. The authors would also like to thank the many faculty and undergraduate students who provided feedback and valuable assistance in this project.

[1] Beaubouef, T. and Mason, J. 2005. Why the high attrition rate for computer science students: some thoughts and observations. *SIGCSE Bull.* 37, 2 (Jun. 2005), 103-106.

[2] Biggers, M., Brauer, A., and Yilmaz, T. 2008. Student perceptions of computer science: a retention study comparing graduating seniors with cs leavers. In *Proceedings of the 39th SIGCSE Technical Symposium on Computer Science Education* (Portland, OR, USA, March 12 - 15, 2008). SIGCSE '08. ACM, New York, NY, 402-406.

[3] Carlisle, M. C. 2009. Raptor: a visual programming environment for teaching object-oriented programming. *J. Comput. Small Coll.* 24, 4 (Apr. 2009), 275-281.

[4] Dougherty, J. P. 2007. Concept visualization in CS0 using *ALICE. J. Comput. Small Coll.* 22, 3 (Jan. 2007), 145-152.

[5] Franceschi, H. 2005. Use of animation director movies to teach CS1 programming concepts. *J. Comput. Small Coll.* 20, 3 (Feb. 2005), 19-27.

[6] Hilberg, J. S. and Meiselwitz, G. 2008. Undergraduate fluency with information and communication technology: perceptions and reality. In *Proceedings of the 9th ACM SIGITE Conference on information Technology Education* (Cincinnati, OH, USA, October 16 - 18, 2008). SIGITE '08. ACM, New York, NY, 5-10.

[7] Matthews, R., Hin, H. S., and Choo, K. A. 2009. Multimedia learning object to build cognitive understanding in learning introductory programming. In *Proceedings of the 7th international Conference on Advances in Mobile Computing and Multimedia* (Kuala Lumpur, Malaysia, December 14 - 16, 2009). MoMM '09. ACM, New York, NY, 396-400.

[8] Rosenberger, J. 2010. U.S.'s Bright CS Job Forecast. *Commun. ACM* 53, 7 (July 2010), 20.

[9] Stelzer, T., Brookes, D., Gladding, G., & Mestre, J. 2010. Impact of multimedia learning modules on an introductory course on electricity and magnetism. *American Journal of Physics* 78, 7 (July 2010), 755-759.

[10] Stone, J. A. and Madigan, E. 2007. Inconsistencies and Disconnects. *Commun. ACM* 50, 4 (Apr. 2007), 76-79.

[11] Villalobos, J. A., Calderon, N. A., and Jiménez, C. H. 2009. Developing programming skills by using interactive learning objects. In *Proceedings of the 14th Annual ACM SIGCSE Conference on innovation and Technology in Computer Science Education* (Paris, France, July 06 - 09, 2009). ITiCSE '09. ACM, New York, NY, 151-155.

Evaluating the Use of Learning Objects in CS1

L.D. Miller, Leen-Kiat Soh, Ashok Samal
Department of Computer Science and Engineering
University of Nebraska
Lincoln, NE 68588
1-402-472-3200
{lmille, lksoh, samal}@cse.unl.edu

Gwen Nugent, Kevin Kupzyk,
Leyla Masmaliyeva
Center for Research on Youth, Family and Schools
University of Nebraska
Lincoln, NE 68588-0342
1-402-472-2448
{gnugent1, kkupzyk2}@unl.edu
leylamasmaliyeva@yahoo.com

ABSTRACT
Learning objects (LOs) have been previously used in computer science education. However, analyses in previous studies have been limited to surveys with limited numbers of LOs and students. The lack of copious quantitative data on how LOs impact student learning makes detailed analysis of LO usefulness problematic. Using an empirical approach, we have studied a suite of LOs, comprehensive in both the content covered and the range of difficulty, deployed to CS1 courses from 2007-2010. We review previous work on predictors of achievement and impact of active learning and feedback. We also provide a high-level overview of our LO deployment. Finally, based on our analysis of student interaction data, we found that (1) students using LOs have significantly higher assessment scores than the control group, (2) several student attributes are significant predictors of learning, (3) active learning has a significant effect on student assessment scores, and (4) feedback does not have a significant effect, but there are variables with significant moderating effects.

Categories and Subject Descriptors
K.3.2. [**Computer and Education**]: Computer and Information Science Education.

General Terms
Experimentation

Keywords
learning objects, self-efficacy, motivation, active learning, feedback

1. INTRODUCTION
Learning objects (LOs) have been used in computer science education as part of e-learning or supplements to traditional classroom lectures and labs. Their usefulness has been investigated but most studies employed pre- and post-treatment knowledge tests or surveys [17]. In-depth analyses have been scarce due to the limited nature of their deployment, both in number of LOs and the number of students involved [19]. Therefore, there is a need (1) to better understand how the use of LOs can impact student learning under different instructional and pedagogical situations, (2) to gain insights to facilitate e-learning in CS education in particular, and (3) to help address the heterogeneity of educational activities in general.

Our research takes an empirical approach to address these issues. The strength of our empirical approach is three-fold: First, we deployed a suite of 16 LOs on computer science concepts to CS1 courses involving more than 1100 students. This suite of LOs is comprehensive in terms of both the content covered and the range of difficulty. The large number of students minimizes variance on our analysis of active learning and feedback in the LOs. On the other hand, LOs on different topics allow more general predictors of student achievement. Second, we use a software tool to automatically collect and store all student interaction data, from mouse clicks to time spent on each page. This allows for a higher resolution analysis on student learning than using only results from the assessment questions or survey. In particular, this allows for the identification of significant moderating effects between the learning interaction data collected and the feedback. Finally, we use statistical methods to analyze the collected data, guided by rigorously validated instructional theories and pedagogies. In particular, we use hierarchical linear modeling to measure variability in LO performance simultaneously at both the student and LO levels.

These three aspects of our approach help us in answering four fundamental questions on using LOs for computer science education: (1) Do students learn from learning objects? (2) What attributes of the students and LOs are predictive of learning? (3) What is the effect of active learning, when a student can interact and determine the flow of the content? (4) What is the effect of feedback?

These questions are important to understanding how LOs impact student learning. The need for the first question is obvious. Identifying attributes that are predictive of learning allows revision of LOs and informs instructors of student behaviors linked to learning or lack of learning. In active learning, students actively interact with the LOs rather than passively reading the content. Previous work has shown that active learning generally enhances the learning process [1][9]. However, this has not been previously verified specifically for LOs on computer science. In feedback, students are given explanations immediately after they complete exercises in the LO. Varying the amount of feedback may have an impact on the learning process [13][21].

The remainder of this paper is organized as follows: Section 2 provides background on the instructional strategies and achievement variables used in the research. Section 3 discusses the LOs and our research project in more detail and discusses how the student interaction data is collected. Section 4 discusses the results and

SIGCSE'11, March 9-12, 2011, Dallas, Texas, USA.

lessons learned from our research. Finally, we provide high level conclusions and future work for this project.

2. RELATED WORK

This section discusses previous work related to the questions addressed by our analysis.

2.1 Learning from LOs

Research has shown that students' use of learning objects increases achievement and promotes success [8][14][26]. While establishing the learning value of LOs is critical, it is important to go beyond this broad generalization and examine what specific characteristics of the students and LOs are predictive of learning, as well as to determine the effectiveness of LO-based instructional strategies such as active learning and feedback.

2.2 Predictors of Achievement

Here we review studies examining factors that are believed to function as indicators of achievement in an introductory computer science course. Comfort level, math background, and previous programming experience appear to be the primary factors under investigation across several studies [5][10][29][30]. Other factors include age, gender, intended major, self-efficacy, and motivation.

Some researchers have found comfort level to be the best predictor of success as measured by midterm course grade in a computer science class [30]. Comfort level refers to the set of physical or psychological circumstances in which students feel most at ease while asking questions in class, low level of anxiety while working on computer assignments, students' perceived difficulty of the course, completing assignments and understanding of the course concepts [30]. Students who perceived the course material as not difficult tend to perform better than their peers who consider the course difficult [24].

Math background has been shown to be important in predicting success [24][30]. Research findings suggest a statistically significant correlation between previous academic experience in mathematics and science to achievement as measured by continuous assessment and final grade [5]. However, other studies have found that the number of math courses a student took in high school did not affect achievement, and effort (as measured by percent of lab usage) and comfort level measures were more important predictors than SAT math scores [27].

Examination of previous programming experience has revealed mixed results. While some of the studies suggest that previous programming experience significantly influences achievement [30], others found no effect of previous programming experience on achievement [5][10][24]. Previous programming experience was found, however, to influence students' pre-self-efficacy [29].

Self-efficacy, or students' perceived judgment of their capabilities, appears to become more accurate over the course of a semester, and therefore, the timing of the measurement is important. Some students underestimate or overestimate their ability to perform. Their perception becomes more accurate as students learn to evaluate their abilities based on the direct interaction with the task [29].

Motivation is found to impact student achievement as well. Students with high intrinsic motivation perform significantly better in a computer science course than students with low intrinsic motivation [4][6].

Gender, age, and intended major did not have significant impact on achievement in a computer science class [3][5][27].

While it is important to keep in mind that the results are dependent on the settings, instructional materials used and the subjects, there are certain factors that seem to be more accurate in predicting successful performance in a computer science class and require further investigation. The results of our study confirm this. Student achievement was significantly correlated with average LO completion percentage (r=.56). Baseline self-efficacy was also significantly correlated with achievement (r=.30).

2.3 Effect of Active Learning

Here we review learning theory and research on enhancing learning by actively engaging students in the learning process [1][9]. Research has confirmed this principle with computer science undergraduate classes, showing that students gain greater mastery of the material and retain more information when active learning strategies are employed [1]. Active learning environments in computer science also impact student note taking, studying, and reading the textbook [12]. Other research has shown that the use of active learning techniques leads to better student attitudes and improvements in students' thinking [22].

Technology is a tool that can encourage active learning; computer-based multimedia instruction prompts students to become actively engaged with the material, making choices and actively manipulating objects and models on the computer screen. The term *interactive* is often used to reflect such computer-based active learning strategies. Our use of interactive learning techniques within our LOs was a critical instructional design consideration, and one aspect of our research focused on examining the effectiveness of this instructional strategy.

2.4 Effect of Feedback

Here we also review studies on the role of feedback in interactive exercises. Studies that report positive effect of feedback on achievement differentiate between various levels of feedback, such as verification (correct/incorrect), knowledge of correct response (correct answer) and elaborative feedback (addresses the answer and errors, provides explanation, example or/and guidance) [11][13][20][21]. Research on the effect of feedback on learning has generated inconclusive results. A meta-analysis of 250 studies conducted by Bangert-Drowns et al. [2] found weak effects of feedback on achievement.

Overall, researchers appear to be in agreement that elaborative feedback yields the highest scores [2][16][21]. More specifically, it was found that elaborative feedback produced the highest scores for low ability students, while verification feedback (correct/incorrect) produced the highest scores for high ability students [13].

Some studies indicate that elaborated feedback is significantly more effective on retention task than corrective feedback or general advice [16][20][28]. There is also evidence that elaborative feedback is more effective on a transfer task, since students that received elaborative feedback did better on post-test as compared to the pre-test [16][21].

3. DEPLOYMENT OF LOs

Our LOs follow the Sharable Content Object Reference Model (SCORM) standard for web-based e-learning so they are usable on any SCORM-compliant learning management system (e.g., Blackboard, Moodle, etc.). Each of our LOs contains (1) a tutorial, (2) a set of flash/applet interactive exercises, and (3) an assessment.

The tutorial starts with a page that lists the objective of the LO, followed by a set of pages that explains the content using text and graphics. The amount of information in each tutorial component is a succinct section on a particular topic—about several pages of a traditional textbook. The tutorial concludes with a summary and hints for reflections. Each LO also has a set of 1-4 exercises on the content covered in the tutorial. Exercises generally require several steps to arrive at the correct answer. Students can repeat exercises as many times as desired. The assessment consists of a set of 7-15 questions depending on the length of the tutorial. All the questions are either multiple choice or true/false. These questions are used to measure whether students understand the content presented in the tutorial and exercises.

We have developed LOs for all the introductory computer science concepts in the ABET approved syllabus for CS1 [25]. The LOs cover a comprehensive range of content ranging from basic concepts as arrays, numeric data, and logic to advanced concepts such as searching, sorting, and recursion. The LOs also cover a range of difficulty measured using both subjective and objective means. The subjective difficulty was determined using the vote of five content experts on a scale from 1-7 with 7 being the most difficult. The objective difficulty was computed using average student assessment scores. Table 1 shows all the LOs provided along with the subjective/objective difficulty.

Table 1. LO Content and Difficulty Rating.

LO Content	Subj. Difficulty	Obj. Difficulty
Advanced Logic	4.33	77.25
Advanced Recursion	5.33	71.14
Algorithms	3.66	77.74
Arrays	5.00	65.93
Conditionals	3.66	54.74
Debugging	4.33	75.27
Functions	3.66	80.78
Logic	2.33	85.59
Looping	4.33	63.06
Non OO Problem Analysis	5.33	74.73
Numeric Data	2.33	73.94
OO Problem Analysis	4.00	83.29
Recursion	4.66	68.01
Searching	4.00	85.74
Sorting	4.33	75.39
Variables & Constants	3.00	58.45

Active learning in our LOs is provided in the exercises. Exercises use a variety of response methods including drag-and-drop, fill-in-the-blank, etc. Students use multiple response methods to complete each exercise. We also provide a version of the exercises with no active learning. This "passive" version contains a video of the exercise being completed successfully.

Feedback in our LOs is also implemented in the exercises. Students receive feedback at each step during the exercise not just at the end. We provide two separate versions for the exercises with either verification or elaborative feedback. The verification feedback version informs the student when the step taken is incorrect and when the problem has been completed. The elaborative feedback version provides detailed explanations on why the student response was incorrect and also clarifies when the response was correct. For example, a verification feedback exercise on the Functions LO tells students that the parameters entered are incorrect (e.g., For the Arg2 box your entry of MakeLemonade is incorrect) whereas the elaborative version explains why the parameters are incorrect and provides hints on choosing the correct parameters (e.g., Arguments to functions are normally things, not actions. MakeLemonade is more likely to be the name of a function, etc.).

To collect the student interaction data, we make use of a software tool called Intelligent Learning Object Guide (iLOG) [18][23]. First, each LO contains a ***Wrapper*** that tracks all student interactions with the LO and uploads them in real-time to an external database. The wrapper tracks not only scores on assessment questions, but also the time students spend on specific content, the steps taken on the practice exercises, etc. This provides data on whether students are struggling with the content that shows up later in the lecture. Second, the iLOG automatically administers surveys (as part of the LOs) to measure student demographic, motivation, and self-efficacy information. The survey results are used to generate individual student models used to improve analysis of the student interactions. The student interaction data collected using iLOG is summarized in Table 2. This includes static data collected from the surveys and interaction data collected from the wrapper. Finally, iLOG uses a ***MetaGen*** system to automatically "crunch" the data collected from the LO wrapper and student models. MetaGen provides details to the instructor on exactly what is causing students to struggle with the content. Such details are given as empirical usage metadata on what student interactions are linked with success or failure to understand the content.

The iLOG has been deployed at the University of Nebraska, Lincoln from 2007-2010. By the end of 2010, our LOs will have been used in 16 offerings of introductory CS courses involving over 1100 students. Table 3 shows the deployment details for our study. In all courses, the LOs were part of a student's course grade. All the LOs together counted for between 3-5% of the total course grade based on instructor preference. This was done to ensure students had some motivation to take the LOs. The deployment schedule of the LOs varied between the courses to make sure students had the opportunity to take the LOs before the lecture/labs on the same topic. This was done to ensure student assessment scores reflected understanding of the LO content and not other sources (e.g., lecture on same content). As mentioned previously, all courses cover the same introductory computer science concepts. However, because of the different programming languages used (e.g., MATLAB, C, and Java) some revision of the LO content was required to accommodate underlying differences in the languages (e.g., Arrays in MATLAB are 1-indexed instead of 0-indexed). Also, the students in these courses included non-majors, CS majors, CS honors students as well as honors students in a special CS-business program. This required carefully balancing the difficulty of the assessment questions to accommodate students with varying aptitude.

Table 2. Student Interaction Data Collected using iLOG.

Static Student Data	Static LO Data	Interaction Data
Baseline motivation	Topic	Assessment scores
Baseline self-efficacy	Length	Avg. time per assessment question
Gender	Difficulty	Total time on exercises
Major	Feedback type	Min time spent on a tutorial page
GPA	Bloom's taxonomy for assessment	Avg. clicks on exercises
SAT/ACT score	...	Feedback received on exercises
...		...

Table 3. iLOG Deployment Details.

Deployment	# of LOs	# of Courses	# of Students
Fall 2007	3	1	~30
Fall 2008	8	4	271
Fall 2009	16	5	360
Spring 2010	5	1	48
Fall 2010	16	5	403
Totals	48	16	1112

4. RESULTS & LESSONS LEARNED

This section uses the empirical analysis on student interaction data to address four questions on LOs.

4.1 Question 1: Do LOs impact learning?

Our previous research has confirmed the learning value of LOs in computer science. First, Nugent et al. [19] compared achievement results for students using LOs to laboratory activities. We found that the LOs were an effective substitute for face-to-face laboratory activities and students rated them highly in terms of design, usefulness and appropriateness. Second, In a randomized experiment Nugent et al. [18] compared learning of students in introductory computer science courses who viewed LOs versus those that did not have access to these online resources (control condition). Results showed the LO condition resulted in significantly higher assessment scores than did the control condition. This previous work begins to show the efficacy for using LOs in CS education. However, we still need to determine (1) the specific student and learning object attributes that are predictive of learning (2) whether active learning and feedback has a significant impact on student performance. Both are addressed later—Sections 4.3 and 4.4—in this paper.

4.2 Question 2: What Attributes Are Predictive of Learning?

Our early projects showed that certain attributes of the student —collected from the student interaction data—were more useful in understanding and diagnosing student success or failure. A major research component of our project has been identifying which of the many possible parameters are most useful to predict learning and learning progress. Regression analysis provides a way to evaluate the attributes of students and LOs that are significant predictors of individual performance in the assessment component of the LOs. Ordinary least squares regression assumes outcome scores are independent cases. However, students could have provided data for up to 16 LOs. Outcome scores that are from different LOs (but the same person) may be correlated due to clustering within students. Therefore, hierarchical linear modeling (HLM) was used to account for the clustered nature of the data (i.e. LOs within students). HLM accounts for this by estimating a variance component, in addition to the normal residual variance, that captures the variability in average outcome scores across students (i.e. compound symmetry model). In fact, a significant amount of the variability in LO performance was found at the student level. The HLM framework allows for predictors of LO performance to be assessed at the LO level (level 1; e.g. LO difficulty) as well as the student level (level 2; e.g. student gender). Due to the possibility that predictor variables may be correlated (i.e., multicollinearity), independent models were run for each predictor. Table 4 shows several of the variables that have been identified as significant ($p<.05$) or marginal ($p<.10$) predictors of learning.

Table 4. Significant Predictors of Learning.

Student Attributes/Baseline Questions	B (*p*-value)
GPA	8.25 (<.001)
ACT Score	2.19 (<.001)
Number of Programming Courses Taken	4.42 (<.001)
Computer Science Placement Exam	2.02 (<.001)
Baseline Student Motivation	1.01 (.003)
Baseline Student Self Efficacy	1.52 (<.001)
LO Attributes/Evaluation Questions	
LO Difficulty	-1.04 (.083)
Assessment Total Seconds	-.01 (.001)
Assessment Total Clicks	.10 (.013)
"The learning object was easy to use."	5.93 (<.001)
"Was any part of this learning object confusing?"	-9.20 (<.001)
"Overall how would you rate this learning object?"	3.42 (<.001)

Entries in the second column of Table 4 are regression coefficients (**B**) and their associated *p*-values. The regression coefficients can be interpreted as the expected increase in percent correct for a one unit increase in the predictor variable. For example, a one unit increase in GPA (e.g. 2.0 to 3.0) leads to an expected increase of 8.25 percentage points on the LO assessment. Several LO- and student-level variables were significant predictors of student learning. The LO evaluation question: "the learning object was easy to use" is one of many LO evaluation questions that predicted student performance. Increased LO difficulty, increased time spent on the assessment, and reports of confusing LOs are also negatively associated with student learning and potentially negatively impact student learning. Student gender was not found to be a significant predictor.

4.3 Question 3: What Is the Impact of Active Learning?

Our research [18] has explored the impact of active versus passive engagement with the LO. In the active condition students manipulated graphical objects on the screen; in the passive condition a predetermined sequence of responses was demonstrated with no opportunity for students to interact with the material. Scores on the LO assessments were significantly higher for students in the active versus passive learning condition $F(1,390 = 4.62, p = .032)$. Supporting this result is our current finding that when students interact more with the LOs (measured by the amount of mouse clicks within an LO), their scores on the assessment are significantly higher ($B=.093, p=.019$).

4.4 Question 4: What is the Effect of Feedback on Student Learning?

Our research on feedback focused on two levels: (1) low level feedback as represented by simple knowledge of results, and (2) elaborative feedback, as represented by extensive explanations and models. Although the main effects for feedback were non-significant, there were several significant moderating effects [15].

Several variables were found to significantly or marginally moderate the effect of elaborative feedback, as shown in Table 5.

Table 5. Significant Moderators of the Effect of Feedback.

Student Attributes/Baseline Questions	B (*p*-value)
"I am confident in my computer science knowledge and abilities."	2.171 (.051)
"Compared to other students in this class I expect to do well."	2.224 (.068)
"After completing this course I expect to take more computer science courses."	2.064 (.038)
Total Self Efficacy	.421 (.100)
"The learning object helped me understand more about this topic."	2.266 (.050)
"I will use the same learning object again in the future if I have questions about this topic."	2.205 (.048)
"Overall how would you rate this learning object?"	1.870 (.060)
Number of Programming Courses Taken	1.929 (.089)

Elaborative feedback had a positive effect on scores among students with high ratings on a few of the motivation and self-efficacy questions. This is likely due to the fact that students were not forced to attend to the feedback. Those that were more confident and motivated may have been more likely to seek out feedback. Several LO evaluation questions also moderated the effect of elaborative feedback. Positive effects of elaborative feedback were found when students gave positive ratings to the LOs (e.g. it helped them understand the topic).

Instructional supports will not promote learning if students do not attend to them. Students spent an average of just under three minutes on the LO exercise sessions, which includes time spent reading feedback. The amount of time spent looking at feedback should be an important predictor of the effectiveness of elaborative feedback, but this was not tracked explicitly. The feedback was provided in a small window embedded low in the screen. In fact, students had the ability to skip the feedback completely, making it difficult to establish causal validity in the effect of elaborative feedback and is likely the reason that the main effect of elaborative feedback was not significant.

5. CONCLUSIONS & FUTURE WORK

Learning objects have been previously used in CS education either to support e-learning or supplement traditional classroom lectures. Previous studies focused only on assessment/survey results from a limited number of LOs. This made it difficult to understand how LOs impact student learning. We provide an empirical approach that addresses these issues by (1) deploying a comprehensive suite of LOs, (2) using a software tool to collect and store student interaction data, and (3) using statistical methods and instructional theories to analyze the collected data. This analysis provides the main contribution of this paper: key steps in answering four fundamental questions on using LOs for computer science education.

Do students learn from learning objects? We found that students using LOs had significantly higher assessment scores than the control group and that students rated the LOs highly in terms of usefulness and appropriateness. This supports our claim that LOs facilitate e-learning in CS education.

What attributes of the students and LOs are predictive of learning? We found that attributes significantly related to the assessment scores varied between the LOs. However, we found that several LO and student attributes were significant predictors of learning. Positive predictors included GPA, motivation, and self-efficacy. Negative predictors included LO difficulty and time spent on the assessment. Overall, such results indicate that struggling students learned less from LOs than high aptitude students. For our next study, we have revised our LOs to be more tightly coupled between each pair of components (tutorial, exercises, and assessment) to better link the content to improve student learning [7], with the hope that poor-performing students will be motivated to view the materials. We will also add a qualitative component to our study—an educational psychologist observing a sample set of students one-on-one on how he or she completes their LO assignments and interviewing them on their cognitive process—to identify why struggling students are benefiting less from the LOs.

What is the effect of active learning? We found that scores on LO assessments were significantly higher for students who had active participation with exercises in the LO compared to students who simply watched the exercises. Our results support the use of exercises with active learning in LOs on CS education. We now exclusively use exercises with active learning for our LOs.

What is the effect of feedback? We found in our initial study that the main effects of feedback were not significant. However, there were several variables with significant moderating effects. In particular, elaborative feedback had a positive effect on students with high motivation and self-efficacy. After our study, we discovered that students were not attending to the feedback on many exercises. In our next study we have made feedback more salient by requiring the student to at least scroll through the feedback before moving on to the assessment. The feedback will be presented in a new active window, allowing us to more accurately assess the amount of time spent reading the elaborative feedback as well.

ACKNOWLEDGEMENTS

This material is based upon work supported by the National Science Foundation under Grant No. 0632642 and an NSF GAANN fellowship.

REFERENCES

[1] Astrachan, O., Duvall, R. et al. 2002. Active Learning in Small to Large Courses. *Frontiers in Education, Annual* (Los Alamitos, CA, USA, 2002), T2A16-20.

[2] Bangert-Drowns, R., Kulik, C. et al. 1991. The Instructional Effect of Feedback in Test-Like Events. *Review of Educational Research*. 61, 2 (Jan. 1991), 213-238.

[3] Bennedsen, J. and Caspersen, M.E. 2005. An Investigation of Potential Success Factors for an Introductory Model-driven Programming Course. *Proceedings of the first international workshop on Computing education research* (Seattle, WA, USA, 2005), 155-163.

[4] Bergin, S. and Riley, R. 2005. The Influence of Motivation and Comfort-level on Learning to Program. (2005), 293-304.

[5] Bergin, S. and Reilly, R. 2005. Programming: Factors that Influence Success. *SIGCSE Bull.* 37, 1 (2005), 411-415.

[6] Bergin, S., Reilly, R. et al. 2005. Examining the Role of Self-Regulated Learning on Introductory Programming Performance. *Proceedings of the first international workshop on Computing education research* (Seattle, WA, USA, 2005), 81-86.

[7] Boettcher, J.V. 2003. Designing for Learning: The Pursuit of Well-Structured Content. *Syllabus*. 16, 6 (2003).

[8] Bradley, C. and Boyle, T. 2004. The Design, Development, and Use of Multimedia Learning Objects. *Journal of Educational Multimedia and Hypermedia*. 13, 4, 371-389.

[9] Bransford, J.D. and Schwartz, D.L. 1999. Rethinking Transfer: A Simple Proposal with Multiple Implications. *Review of Research in Education*. 24, (1999), 61-100.

[10] Chen, C.S. 2002. Self-regulated Learning Strategies and Achievement in an Introduction to Information Systems Course. *Information Technology, Learning and Performance Journal*. 20, (2002), 11-23.

[11] Clark, K.A. 1993. The Effects of Feedback on the Problem Solving Ability of Academically At-Risk Students.

[12] Cordes, D. and Parrish, A. 2002. Active Learning in Computer Science: Impacting Student Behavior. *Frontiers in Education, Annual* (Los Alamitos, CA, USA, 2002), T2A1-5.

[13] Hanna, G.S. 1976. Effects of Total and Partial Feedback in Multiple-Choice Testing upon Learning. *The Journal of Educational Research*. 69, 5 (Jan. 1976), 202-205.

[14] Herrmann, N., Popyack, J.L. et al. 2004. Assessment of a Course Redesign: Introductory Computer Programming using Online Modules. *Proceedings of the 35th SIGCSE technical symposium on Computer science education* (Norfolk, Virginia, USA, 2004), 66-70.

[15] Kluger, A.N. and Denisi, A. 1996. The effects of feedback interventions on performance: A historical review, a meta-analysis, and a preliminary feedback intervention theory. *Psychological Bulletin*. 119, 2 (1996), 254-284.

[16] Moreno, R. 2004. Decreasing Cognitive Load for Novice Students: Effects of Explanatory versus Corrective Feedback in Discovery-Based Multimedia. *Instructional Science*. 32, 1/2 (2004), 99-113.

[17] Mundy, D.P. 2006. Using Learning Objects to Support Introductory Computer Architecture Education. *Proceedings of the 5th IASTED international conference on Web-based education* (Puerto Vallarta, Mexico, 2006), 305-310.

[18] Nugent, G., Kupzyk, K. et al. 2009. Empirical Usage Metadata in Learning Objects. *Proceedings of the 39th IEEE international conference on Frontiers in education conference* (San Antonio, Texas, USA, 2009), 1285-1290.

[19] Nugent, G., Soh, L. et al. 2005. Design, development, and validation of a learning object for CS1. *SIGCSE Bull.* 37, 3 (2005), 370-370.

[20] Phye, G.D. and Sanders, C.E. 1994. Advice and Feedback: Elements of Practice for Problem Solving. *Contemporary Educational Psychology*. 19, 3 (Jul. 1994), 286-301.

[21] Pridemore, D.R. and Klein, J.D. 1991. Control of Feedback in Computer-Assisted Instruction. *Educational Technology Research and Development*. 39, 4 (1991), 27-32.

[22] Prince, M. 2004. Does Active Learning Work? A Review of the Research. *Journal of Engineering Education*. 223-231.

[23] Riley, S., Miller, L.D. et al. 2009. Intelligent Learning Object Guide (iLOG): A Framework for Automatic Empirically-Based Metadata Generation. *Artificial Intelligence in Education* (2009), 515-522.

[24] Rountree, N., Rountree, J. et al. 2002. Predictors of success and failure in a CS1 course. *SIGCSE Bull.* 34, 4 (2002), 121-124.

[25] Soh, L., Samal, A. et al. 2009. Renaissance Computing: an Initiative for Promoting Student Participation in Computing. *Proceedings of the 40th ACM technical symposium on Computer science education* (Chattanooga, TN, USA, 2009), 59-63.

[26] Van Zele, E., Vandaele, P. et al. 2003. Implementation and Evaluation of a Course Concept Based on Reusable Learning Objects. *Journal of Educational Computing Research*. 28, 4 (2003), 355-372.

[27] Ventura, P.R. 2005. Identifying Predictors of Success for an Objects-First CS1. *Computer Science Education*. 15, 3 (2005), 223-243.

[28] Whyte, M., Karolick, M. et al. 1995. Cognitive Styles and Feedback in Computer-Assisted Instruction. *Journal of Educational Computing Research*. 12, 2 (1995), 195-203.

[29] Wiedenbeck, S., Labelle, D. et al. 2004. Factors Affecting Course Outcomes in Introductory Programming. *16th Workshop of the Psychology of Programming Interest Group*. (2004), 97-109.

[30] Wilson, B.C. and Shrock, S. 2001. Contributing to Success in an Introductory Computer Science Course: a Study of Twelve Factors. *SIGCSE Bull.* 33, 1 (2001), 184-188.

Early Participation of CS Students in Research

Rahman Tashakkori, Barry L. Kurtz, Dolores A. Parks, James B. Fenwick Jr., Alice A. McRae
Appalachian State University
Boone, NC 28608
001-828-262-2370
{rt, blk, dap, jbf, aam}@cs.appstate.edu

ABSTRACT

Research experiences are widely available to upper-division computer science students during the academic year and during summer. Co-op and internship opportunities are available to this group as well. Due to the fact that freshman and sophomore students do not have sufficient background, they are often left behind and are not involved in research activities. This paper shares some experiences with a program that was put in place through an NSF STEP grant that provides research opportunities to freshman, sophomore, and first year transfer students. The paper presents examples of projects in which computer science scholars were involved. We have learned that lower-division computer science students are excited about the opportunity to participate in research. Early participation in research helps build a strong community among the freshman and sophomore students, keeps these students engaged, and results in a higher retention rate.

Categories and Subject Descriptors

K.8.m [Computing Milieux], Computers and Society, Miscellaneous

General Terms

Experimentation

Keywords

Undergraduate research, STEP, collaborative research and learning

1. INTRODUCTION

In recent years, undergraduate research experience has been valued highly [2,5,8] and has been promoted and reasonably funded by various state and federal agencies. A majority of the programs supporting undergraduate research target upper-division students as a way to encourage these students to pursue graduate studies [1,3]. The few programs that involve lower-division students often benefit from these students performing administrative tasks as contrasted with research. The main reasons lower-division students are not involved in research are lack of sufficient experience and skills and not being mentored by a faculty member. This paper provides a summary of the importance of early involvement of computer science students in research and provides some background information about the NSF program that sponsors undergraduate research activities in our department. Following this we provide some examples of the projects in which our students have been involved. We conclude with student evaluations of their participation in research clusters.

1.1 Importance of Participation in Research by Lower-Division Students

There are several reasons for undergraduate students to participate in research: financial rewards, course credit, personal interest, and/or building connections [10]. In some fields, especially in natural sciences, a large number of pre-professional students participate in research voluntarily in preparation for admission into their target fields. This may not necessarily apply to undergraduate students in computer science. Regardless of the reason for participation, upper-division undergraduate students are targeted more widely and are more likely to have an opportunity to participate in research; hence they seem to have a clear advantage over the lower-division students.

Early participation of undergraduate students in research has many benefits. Below is a list of some of these benefits:

Sense of Belonging and Gaining Greater Confidence – By participating in research early on, freshman and sophomore students join a team of faculty and students to work on a common project. For students just graduating from high school, being a member of an intellectual community whose members share similar interests is valuable and builds self-confidence.

Positive Relationship with Peer Mentors and Faculty Mentors – Despite the fact that lower-division students may not have the skills to carry out complex projects to their completion, they are often energetic and look up to their peer mentors and faculty mentors as role models. The positive relationships that are established between the students and their mentors motivate students to participate more actively. Of particular importance in building this positive relationship are clear guidelines and instructions to these students and meeting with them regularly as a way to monitor their progress.

Higher Retention Rate – As stated in [3] students who are engaged early in research are less likely to leave school. In particular, when these students are part of a larger mentoring community [9], they enjoy a support system that results in higher retention.

Improves Problem Solving Using a Scientific Approach – By participating in research, students solve problems on a regular basis. Despite the complexity of these problems, students learn to approach them with scientific reasoning and work with their teams to come up with solutions. Faculty mentors are vital in this process as they can provide direction to lead students to the solution without solving the problem for them.

1.2 Our STEP NSF Project

The Science, Technology, Engineering, and Mathematics Talent Expansion Program (STEP) seeks to increase the number of students (U.S. citizens or permanent residents) receiving associate or baccalaureate degrees in established or emerging fields within science, technology, engineering, and mathematics (STEM).

The program on our campus provides scholarships to freshman, sophomore, and entering transfer students from Chemistry, Computer Science, Geology, Mathematics, and Physics and Astronomy to establish research clusters within their disciplines or across multiple disciplines. These clusters consist of four college students and possibly one high school intern working together for two semesters on a discipline specific or an interdisciplinary project. In the past two years Computer Science has maintained, on average, 5 research clusters per year. Some of the research clusters in their second year consisted of a mix of freshman and sophomore students. The program has several components to actively engage students and build a community:

Scholarships – Students participating in the research clusters receive $350 per semester in their first year and, upon satisfactory performance, $500 per semester in their second year. This scholarship amount is not substantial and we have learned that this by itself is not a prime motivating factor to students. We have a mechanism in place that encourages students to do better in their courses and earn additional funding. For example, computer science students in their second year with a GPA of 3.0 or higher can apply to serve as peer mentors to either assist with research in one of the research clusters or serve as tutors in one of the computer labs. Students who work as tutors earn wages on an hourly basis and the peer-mentors in research clusters earn an additional $250 toward their scholarship funding.

Research Clusters – All students are required to participate in research for 2-3 hours per week to work on their projects. Each research cluster is led by a faculty mentor and the cluster receives $750 per year for purchasing necessary instruments or software for their research project. Research teams share their findings with their peers twice per year: once at the end of Fall semester and again at the end of Spring. The research clusters provide an excellent medium where students learn new things about computer science. For lower-level computer science students this is a unique opportunity and has increased their excitement about a discipline that may appear boring in early years. Several examples of the projects are presented in section 2. Research clusters consisting of all freshmen, mixture of freshman and sophomore students, or all sophomore students work on projects with various levels of complexity. In general, students participate in more advanced projects in year two as explained in the ClockIt example.

Residential Learning Community (RLC) – All incoming freshmen and transfer students who are admitted to our program are given a chance to live in the program's RLC. Having students with the same interests live together helps build a community that works together in various activities that may include fun, sports and social activities, service, and/or academics. The Housing Department on our campus coordinates various activities that cover the first three. The program reserves a study room on the first floor of the RLC and if necessary sets up laptops for students to work together on their class assignments.

Study Halls and Study Groups – The program sponsors supervised study halls in computer science as well as in other disciplines. Students in computer science meet once per week for two hours in a computer lab to work on programming assignments from their classes. These study halls are supervised by peer-mentors who have done well in their courses and have had some training to assist their peers. Although students spend the majority of their time working on problems in computer science, they may discuss problems in other subjects. If a student needs additional assistance either with computer science or other math or science subjects, she/he can make a request to join a study group for that subject or to have tutoring hours. In addition to our own tutoring sessions in a variety of math and science subjects, we coordinate with the Tutoring Center on our campus to provide additional tutoring hours.

Summer Bridge – The program sponsors a summer bridge program that involves students who are under-prepared in mathematics. We expect that a freshman computer science major should be calculus-ready and have strong problem solving skills. During the summer bridge program, students participate in a five-week summer session where they earn four credit hours in pre-calculus math and three credits in a required freshman seminar on problem solving. The program provides study halls in pre-calculus twice per day. The goal is to make sure students are never behind in their assignments and are always ready to take an exam the next day. In the past two years we have had 11 computer science students participate in the Summer Bridge Program. As part of the activities in the Problem Solving course, students participate in an all-day outdoor program on all Saturdays. The theme of these activities is problem solving during which students work together to come up with better strategies to complete a task or to find solutions to possible problems they face.

1.3 Student Recruitment, Selection, and Team Building

Some students are recruited from local and nearby high schools, some at Family Day and Open House events, and some from freshman level courses on campus. To be considered, candidates complete an online application form. The form includes questions about their research interests and the math and science courses they have taken. All applications are screened by the program director and those that meet the requirements are grouped by major for review by the departmental coordinators. The faculty coordinators select some number of these applicants depending on the availability of resources, such as lab space and availability of faculty. It is obvious that it may not be possible to accommodate all interests, thus students are given a chance to select a cluster closest to their interest or withdraw their applications. Upon selection, a time is set that works for all members of the team to begin working on their research.

It is worth nothing that the diversity of faculty mentors is important in students' active participation. Our institution is fortunate to have a gender-diverse group of faculty in computer science. Two out of five faculty mentors participating are women which provides significant role models to the program.

2. EXAMPLES OF THE PROJECTS

In this section, we will present several examples of the projects from our research clusters in computer science.

2.1 Smart Phone Software Development

In Spring 2009 Kurtz's cluster elected to work on iPhone software development. Despite providing students sole access to a machine for development, no significant progress was made by the end of the semester beyond getting some programs taken directly from reference books up and running. His Spring 2010 research cluster, a different group of four freshmen students, elected to do Android development. They made significant progress by the end of the semester, as described below. In Fall 2010 this group moved to iPad software development after their experience using Android. They have been much more successful than the original group noted above and have developed three different two person games that can be played using Bluetooth connectivity. Kurtz believes that the Android experience may have eased the learning curve for development using the iPhone/iPad.

The 3D tic-tac-toe game consists of three boards stacked one on top of the other. There are 27 potential positions for making a move, but the center square on the middle board is so powerful that the player is not allowed to select that square. The human player competes against the computer; the human player goes first and uses the X marker. Figure 1 shows a mid-game position. X can win in a couple of moves by selecting the upper left corner on the top board. The graphics provided some challenge but the most difficult task was getting the computer to play with at least some intelligence. The computer tended to use a very defensive strategy.

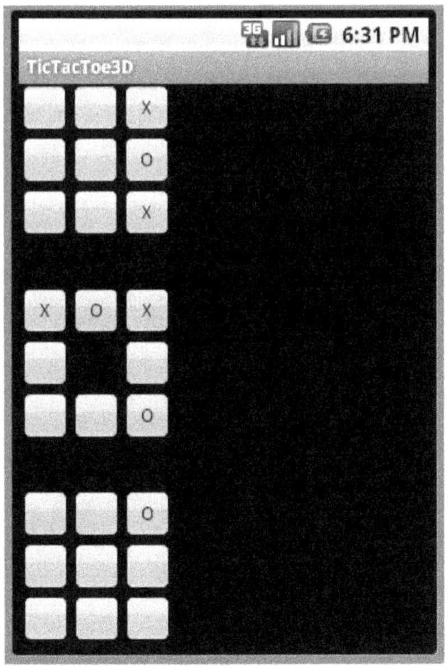

Figure 1: 3D Tic Tac Toe

The final program the students developed queries the U.S. Geological Survey earthquake web service (http://earthquake.usgs.gov/) to find any large earthquakes in the world in the last 24 hours. The results are displayed using Google Maps; in Figure 2 the students zoomed into California to look for any earthquakes in that region. The user can click on any one of the bubbles and get detailed information on that particular quake, as shown in Figure 3. It is worth noting that these were freshman students who at the time were completing their CS2 course but they were already learning to consume web services.

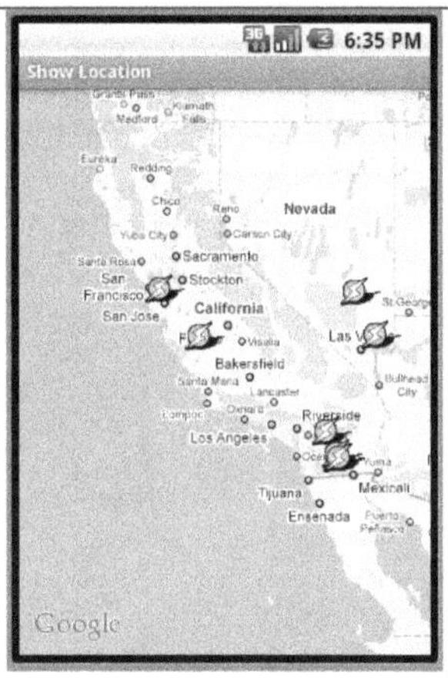

Figure 2: CA Earthquakes

Figure 3: Detailed Information

2.2 Joe the Robot Project

In Fall 2009 and Spring 2010, Tashakkori mentored a team of students who were interested in robotics. This team consisted of four freshmen, one high school intern, and a second year peer-mentor. The team used a BIOLOID Comprehensive Kit in their project as seen in Figure 4. They started by building simple robots from the instruction manual and by uploading and executing the corresponding programs to control these robots. As they built various modules, they learned about the motions of individual parts and how the program controls each of the components. Students expanded their learning by adding light and sound sensors to their robot and then modifying their programs. By the end of Fall 2009, their robot reacted to sound signals such as hand claps and would recognize obstacles such as walls. Students were able to program the robot to respond to these obstacles or loud noises.

Figure 4: One of our freshmen running the robot simulator

In the Spring 2010 students added their own movements and functionalities to the program and added a remote sensor to their robot to control its movements remotely. This stage of the work presented several challenges for establishing two-way communications. The team members improved their problem-solving by working together to meet these challenges. During the Spring semester they built a human-like robot, called Joe, that received commands from either the computer or the remote, as seen in Figure 5. The team was able to make Joe perform the YMCA dance with clap of hands. The next goal of the team is to have Joe react to a simple music pieces such as the YMCA music and perform different movements. Another goal is to set up two robots that mimic each other's movements.

Figure 5: One of the peer-mentors assisting the freshman participant solve a hardware problem

2.3 Genetic Algorithms in Intractable Problems

McRae mentored a team of two sophomore and two freshman students starting Fall 2009. During the Fall semester, students learned about various concepts related to the logic behind games and puzzles. In Spring 2010, her cluster studied genetic algorithms as an approach to attacking intractable problems. The students wrote a genetic algorithm program to make progress on an open problem in Ramsey theory.

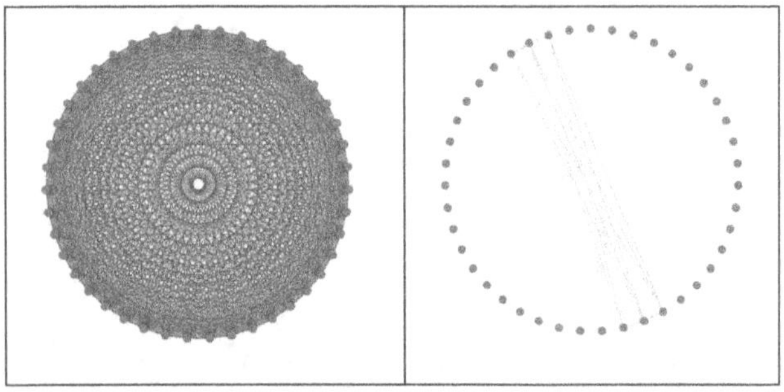

Figure 6: A red-blue coloring of K_{43} with two blue 5 cliques

The students tried to find a way to two-color the edges of a complete graph on 43 vertices so that in the subgraphs induced by every group of six vertices there would be at least one edge of each color. Since there are 903 edges in the complete graph of 43 vertices and 2^{903} different ways to color the edges, a brute force approach is impractical.

So far, no such coloring has been found; in fact, it is possible that no such coloring exists. Although the students did not find the desired coloring, they did find a graph that has only two groups of six vertices that have all edges of the same color (and those two groups share three vertices in common). This result was found after students seeded their genetic algorithm with a known solution for the complete graph on 42 vertices. Students in this team ended the semester discussing possible enhancements to their algorithm, and believing that there does exist a coloring that has the desired property.

2.5 ClockIt Project

Fenwick is co-PI on an NSF funded grant that is developing a system that continually and unobtrusively collects usage data from an IDE while student programmers are working. The project has been successful with several prominent conference publications [4, 7]. Of course, useful software incurs change requests and this system is no different. Fenwick requested a STEP Academy of Science research cluster composed of more mature CS students. While this decreased some peer-to-peer mentoring, it enabled an early REU-like experience for some of the program's better students. The ClockIt cluster was composed of 4 sophomore students: three highly qualified students and one active but somewhat struggling student. The group contained one female. Two additional students were hired by the ClockIt project to work with these four students.

The ClockIt project is concerned with gathering data on how introductory students learn to program. The BlueJ and Eclipse IDEs have been instrumented to collect programming event information, such as compilations, and log this data. Logged data is transmitted to a central database for offline analysis. Fenwick isolated three projects for the cluster. The first was a major refactoring of the code base to encapsulate the IDE's reported events. Previously events were simply logged as text in a file. Another project was to subdivide the database web service that received reported events. Previously a single service was employed with various parameters indicating appropriate internal behavior selections, as seen in Figure 7, which was part of the students' Academy's Conference presentation. A third project was to upgrade the ClockIt website with more dynamic content.

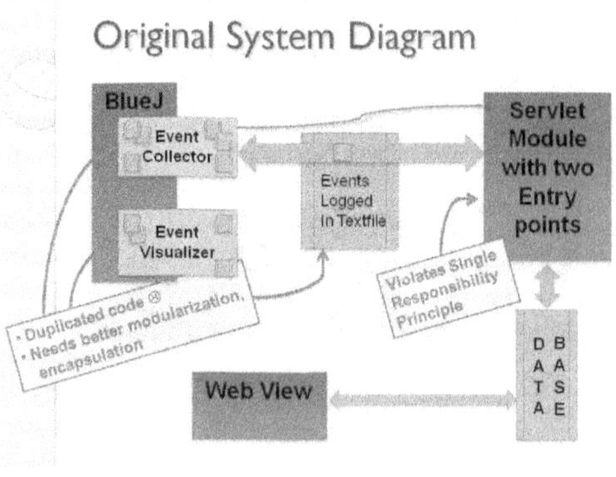

Figure 7: The original system diagram

The students and the faculty mentor met weekly for a 3-hour work session. Occasionally students would also do some work outside of this session. Sessions were enjoyable and fun but most certainly working sessions. Students were exposed to a real project, to collaborative team organizations, and to some new engineering tools including source code control. The ClockIt project benefitted immensely because not only did some of these desired but just-can't-find-the-time-to-do changes finally get done but a cadre of potential future project employees was also developed. A diagram of the new system is shown in Figure 8. The students know the system now and can perhaps contribute at a high level at a later time (for example, during a summer).

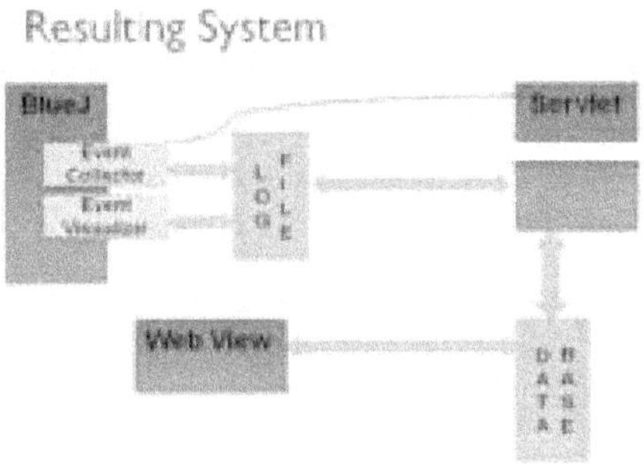

Figure 8: The new system diagram

2.4 Video Game Exploration

Parks mentored a team of four freshmen starting Fall 2009. All the students wanted to work on video game development. During the first semester, the four freshmen used Greenfoot to create an original game called Fireland, as shown in Figure 9. In Fireland, the player uses a helicopter to put out forest fires. The students designed the game, created the artwork, developed the game play, and programmed the game in Java. The work was divided up differently each week depending on what needed to be done next. For example, one week two students worked on getting the fire to spread "naturally", one student worked on placing trees randomly for each game, and one student worked on controlling the helicopter. Greenfoot [6] provided an excellent platform for these beginning students since they were using BlueJ in their CS1 course and both IDEs were created by the same team.

Figure 9: Fireland Game

In the second semester the students were joined by an upper-level peer-mentor. Because of his knowledge of the Quake 3 game engine, the team decided to switch to this platform to experience a realistic video game development environment. One student created a game level, as seen in Figure 10, while the others modified or created new weapons. Having the peer-mentor as part of the cluster greatly enhanced the experience both for the freshmen and faculty mentor. However, students found the C++ code used in the Quake 3 engine quite challenging. This year the team is returning to Java and will again create original games.

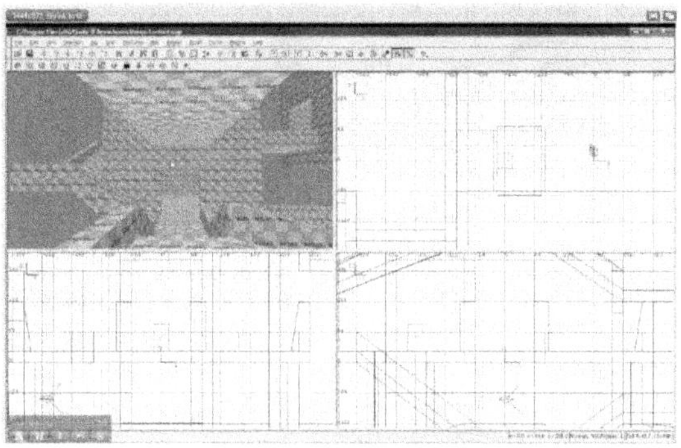

Figure 10: Level for Quake 3

3.0 RESULTS

Since the Fall 2008 semester we have had 19 research clusters in computer science with the distribution shown in Table 1.

Table 1 – CS Research clusters science since Fall 2008

Semester	Number of Research Clusters	No of Students involved
Fall 08	2: MATLAB and Socket Programming	8 (all cs)
Spring 09	2: Robots and Web Programming	11 (10 cs & 1 high school intern)
Fall 09	5: Game and Puzzles, Robots, Mobile Programming, ClockIt, and Game Boys	20 (19 cs & 1 high school intern)
Spring 10	5: Graph theory, Robots, Mobile Programming, ClickIt, and Game Boys	22 (21 cs and 1 high school intern)
Fall 10	5: iPhone programming, Android Programming, Game Boys, and Concepts behind games	23 (21 cs and 2 high school interns)

Eight of the computer science students who joined the program in the first two years have successfully graduated from the program and are continuing their computer science studies. Two high-school interns have participated in the program and both have joined our department for their undergraduate studies. Two students who joined the program have changed their major to CIS, and two were put on probation due to poor GPA.

In Spring 2010, 18 computer science students in the program completed a survey containing various questions about the program activities. In one of the questions, students were asked How helpful participation in research clusters has been in general? As shown in Figure 11, 61% indicated Very Helpful, 17% Helpful, and 22% Little Helpful.

Also, in the same survey students were asked How helpful working with peers in the clusters has been? On this question, 44.4% have indicated Very Helpful, 33.3% Helpful, and 22.2% Little Helpful (see Figure 12).

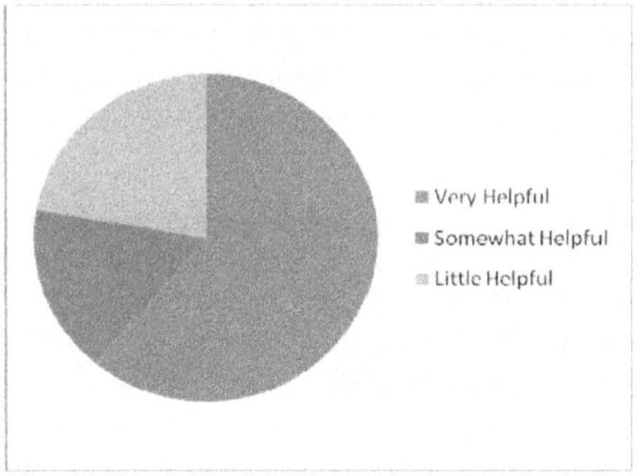

Figure 11: Helpfulness of research clusters

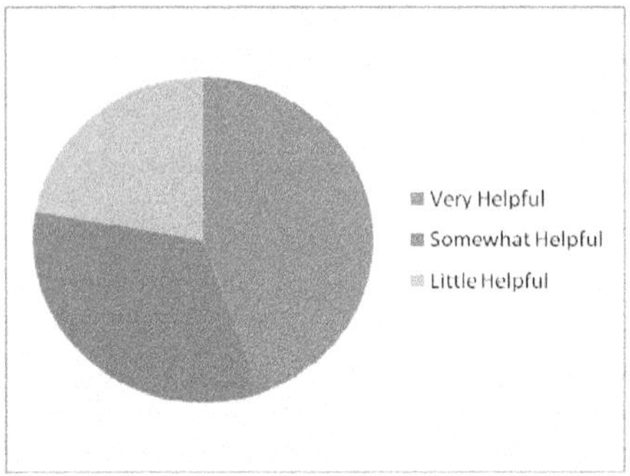

Figure 12: Helpfulness of peer-mentors in research clusters

On a question regarding how enjoyable participation in research clusters has been, 72% answered Very Helful and 22% Somewhat Helful (see Figure 13).

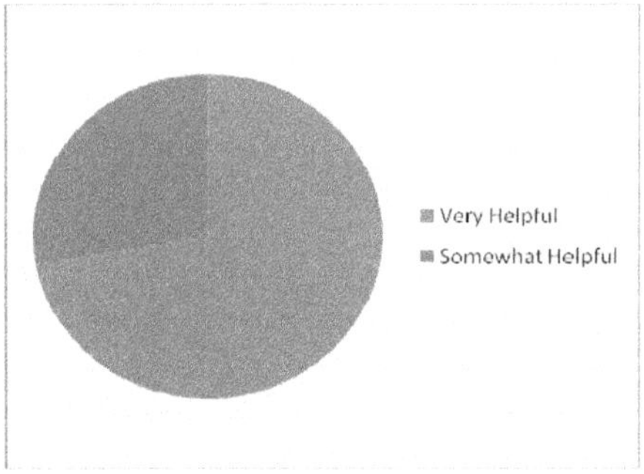

Figure 13: Enjoyable participation in research clusters

Our experience indicates that all students who participated in research early on through this program are well connected and are engaged with different activities that are going on in the department. We believe that even strong students would not be at this level of engagement in the department if the research opportunity had not been provided to them in their first year.

Each of the research clusters in the program has presented their research work at the end of each semester. Several teams have presented their research at the Student Research Day which is a local event to promote student research.

In summary, students who participated in the program are engaged, excited about the work they do outside the classroom setting, and are part of a community with whom they conduct research or study on regular basis.

ACKNOWLEDGMENTS

The activities presented in this paper were supported by a NSF (0756928) entitled *Appalachian Undergraduate Academy of Science* funded as a Phase 1 Science, Technology, Engineering, and Mathematics Talent Program (STEP) proposal. The funding level is $1,000,000 for five years commencing May 2013.

The authors wish to thank Clinton Freeman, Luke Rice, Ryan Belt, Brian Pratt, Dale Henries, and Shawn Waldon who have served the computer science research clusters as peer-mentors. We also wish to thank the Department of Computer Science on our Campus for providing computer labs to all our clusters.

REFERENCES

[1] BARKER, **L.**, Student and Faculty Perceptions of Undergraduate Research Experiences in Computing, ACM Transactions on Computing Education, Vol. 9, No. 1, Article 5, March 2009.

[2] Dannelly, R.S. and C.W. Steidley. 2002. "A National Science Foundation Supported Undergraduate CSMET Research Project," *Journal of Computing Sciences in Colleges*, Volume 17, No. 5 (April 2002) 13-17.

[3] Dahlberg, Teresa , Tiffany Barnes, Audrey Rorrer, Eve Powell Improving Retention and Graduate Recruitment through Immersive Research Experiences for Undergraduates, SIGCSE' 08, March 12-15, 2008, Portland, Oregon.

[4] Fenwick Jr., James B., Norris, Cindy, Barry, Frank, Spicer, Cole, Rountree, Josh, Cheek, Scott, "Another Look at the Behaviors of Novice Programmers," Proceedings of the 40th SIGCSE Technical Symposium on Computer Science Education (SIGCSE '09), Chattanooga, Tennessee, USA, March 2009.

[5] Gates, A.Q. P.J. Teller, A. Bernat, N. Delgado and C.K. Della-Piana. 1999. "Expanding Participation in Undergraduate Research Using the Affinity Group Model," *Journal of Engineering Education*, October, 1999, 88:4, 409-414.

[6] Kolling, Michael, Introduction to Programming with Java, Prentice Hall, August 2009.

[7] Norris, Cindy, Barry, Frank, Fenwick Jr., James B., Reid, Kathryn, Rountree, Josh, "ClockIt: Collecting Quantitative Data on How Beginning Software Developers Really Work," Proceedings of the 13th Conference on Innovation and Technology in Computer Science Education (ITiCSE '08), Madrid, Spain, July 2008.

[8] Polack-Wahl, J.A. and P.N. Squire. 2003. "Overcoming Obstacles to Undergraduate Research at a Small Institution," *Journal of Computing Sciences in Colleges*, Vol. 18, No. 5 (May 2003) 128-135.

[9] Tashakkori, Rahman, Wilkes, James, Norris, Cindy, *Success with CSEMS*,. The ACM SouthEast 2007 Conference, ACMSE 2007 - March 23-24, 2007, Winston Salem, NC.

[10] Ward, Karen, Research with Undergraduates: A Survey of best Practices, *Journal of Computing Sciences in Colleges*, Vol. 21, No. 1 (May 2005) 169-176.

Incorporating Social Issues of Computing in a Small, Liberal Arts College: A Case Study

Janet Davis
Department of Computer Science
Grinnell College
Grinnell, IA 50112
+1 641-269-4306
davisjan@cs.grinnell.edu

Henry M. Walker
Department of Computer Science
Grinnell College
Grinnell, IA 50112
+1 641-269-4208
walker@cs.grinnell.edu

ABSTRACT
CC2001[1] and CC2008[5] recommend that an undergraduate computing curriculum include 16 hours related to social and professional issues. An ITiCSE 2010 Working Group discussed approaches for incorporating this material in the curriculum and outlined seven contrasting implementation cases [8]. Also, Baldwin *et al* discuss the implementation of computing curricula at five different liberal arts colleges [4]. However, none of these provides specific implementation details for addressing social issues in a liberal arts computing curriculum. This paper identifies successful strategies from one college and begins a general discussion of teaching social issues of computing in a liberal arts setting.

Categories and Subject Descriptors
K.3.2 [**Computers and Education**]: Computer and Information Science Education – *computer science education, curriculum*

General Terms
Design, Economics, Human Factors, Theory.

Keywords
Liberal arts, social issues, ethics, teaching methods.

1. INTRODUCTION
National curricular guidelines consistently identify the need for undergraduate computing curricula to address social issues. For example, CC 2008 [5] quotes CC 2001 [1] in stating

> Students … need to develop the ability to ask serious questions about the social impact of computing and to evaluate proposed answers to those questions. Future practitioners must be able to anticipate the impact of introducing a given product into a given environment. Will that product enhance or degrade the quality of life? What will the impact be upon individuals, groups, and institutions? [5, p. 92.]

In particular, CC 2008 specifies 16 hours devoted to social and ethical issues [5, pp. 92-96].

SIGCSE'11, March 9–12, 2011, Dallas, Texas, USA.

Similarly, the first curricular goal in the 2007 Model Curriculum for a Liberal Arts Degree in Computer Science is "To enable understanding the capabilities, limitations, and ramifications (technical, ethical, and social)." The Model Curriculum continues, "In particular, students in the type of program described here should … Recognize the importance of social and ethical issues of computing" [9, sec. 3].

But even when faculty have strong motivation and fine intentions, challenges arise when incorporating social issues into already crowded curricula. An ITiCSE 2010 Working Group addressed such implementation issues; discussions highlighted that diverse educational settings may require different pedagogies. The subsequent report [8] provides seven distinct, high-level implementation cases that outline possible approaches for incorporating social issues within curricula. Due to space limitations, each case was less than one page—enough to compare approaches, but too short to provide extensive guidance for any one approach. These Working Group discussions also highlighted that assumptions, opportunities, and challenges for liberal arts colleges may differ from those encountered in other types of schools [8].

In parallel work, the Liberal Arts Computer Science Consortium compiled five case studies describing computing programs in liberal arts settings. While providing a fine review of approaches for technical materials, space considerations limited discussion of the inclusion of social issues [4].

This paper describes in some detail how social issues can be incorporated in a liberal arts computing curriculum, and in particular, considers ways to build on traditional strengths of the liberal arts environment. Although this paper focuses on a specific environment, presenting these practices can be useful to others in at least two ways:

- the liberal arts environment is an integral part of hundreds of colleges in the United States and elsewhere;
- many of the ideas discussed here may apply in other settings as well.

Of course, each department and school will need to consider what approaches work locally. We hope this discussion can promote brainstorming and provide pragmatic suggestions for many colleges and universities.

The remainder of this paper focuses on challenges and opportunities of the liberal arts setting, and down-to-earth strategies that experience has shown to work—at least in some settings. Section 2 describes the small, liberal arts college setting, and Section 3 considers how computing fits within this context.

As these sections indicate, assumptions and emphases may be different for liberal arts programs than for more technically-oriented curricula; these differences both impose limitations and enable possible synergies.

Section 4 focuses on courses for non-majors, both to promote computer fluency among future citizens and as an opportunity to recruit additional majors. Section 5 provides a parallel discussion for potential majors. Although this paper reports on a successful program, opportunities for refinement and expanded assessment remain; likely next steps are described in Section 6. Section 7 concludes the paper with an invitation to continue the discussion.

2. THE SMALL, LIBERAL ARTS COLLEGE

A liberal arts college fosters breadth of education and interdisciplinary connections, and students typically earn a Bachelor of Arts degree. Students usually have a choice of major, but depth of study in one field is balanced by developing broader interests in the humanities, social studies, and sciences. Thus, in a typical liberal arts program, students devote about 40% of their course work to their major and related subjects (e.g., computer science and supporting mathematics) and the remainder in outside areas. In contrast, a typical Bachelor of Science or Bachelor of Engineering program requires that students devote 60% or more of their course work to the major [9, 13].

Many students are drawn to a liberal arts college because they have a variety of interests. Even a student who wants to pursue a science major, for example, may have serious interests in fine arts, foreign languages, social studies, or other areas. Thus, the vast majority of students in a liberal arts setting feel comfortable studying social issues. For example, Grinnell's *Catalog* identifies the following six "Elements of a Liberal Education" [2009, pp. 13-15:

1. Communication skills: the ability to read, analyze, write, and speak effectively
2. "Study of a language other than one's own"
3. Lab-based science (particularly the scientific method in the natural sciences)
4. Quantitative reasoning
5. The study of human behavior and society
6. "Study of creating expression" and work in the humanities

Within this framework, social and ethical issues are core topics for all students (element 5 in the list, with elements of 1, 2, and 6).

Often, the greater challenge is to encourage students to study computing (or science more generally). This orientation may be different from what is found in many technical programs, where students focus on computing or science and may not have as strong an affinity to social issues.

2.1 Breadth in a Liberal Arts Program

Typical of many liberal arts colleges, the Mission Statement of Grinnell College states that the college seeks to educate students "for the different professions and for the honorable discharge of the duties of life." Those professions include the fine arts, literature, philosophy, social studies, mathematics, physical and life sciences, and even computer science. After undergraduate work, those professions expand to include law, medicine, engineering, social service, politics, teaching, and many others.

Liberal arts institutions employ various strategies to help students achieve a broad program of study. One common approach involves a core curriculum or distribution requirements; students must take courses in different departments or subject ares to meet these requirements. At one extreme, a college may specify one-third or even one-half of an undergraduate degree program. If an introductory computing course satisfies a requirement, then students have an incentive to try it out, and instructors have the chance to excite these students about the discipline. However, this approach also has the disadvantage that students may lack motivation—they may take courses only to complete requirements, with little real interest or commitment.

Grinnell College represents the other extreme, in which advisers are charged to work with students to achieve breadth. Grinnell's only requirements for graduation are completion of a First-Year Tutorial (a writing-intensive course discussed further in Section 5.2), a major (8 primary courses plus a few supporting courses), and 124 credits (no more than 48 in a department, 92 in a division□) with a GPA of 2.0 or higher. Under such a system, advisers bear the primary responsibility for enforcing a breadth of education for each student. Since specific courses are not required (outside the major), students usually are highly motivated for each course—after all, they could have chosen something else. But, without requirements, it can be a challenge to entice students to take courses in unfamiliar fields.

In addition to formal course work, many liberal arts colleges encourage independent projects and close student-teacher relationships. For example, at Grinnell, the Mentored Advanced Project (MAP) program provides an opportunity for students to conduct research or undertake other advanced, student-driven work. MAP students work alone or in small groups under the close supervision of a faculty member, typically in their major or an interdisciplinary concentration.

2.2 Typical Teaching Methods

A small school typically touts small classes, close student-faculty interactions, and personal attention. In this environment, large lectures are rare—at the very least, lectures have relatively few students. Instead, classes of 30 are considered large, and pedagogy often emphasizes active learning. Some examples from computing courses at Grinnell College typify this general environment.

- Only two courses in the entire computing curriculum (algorithms and theory of computation) meet in a traditional classroom; all other courses meet exclusively in a lab setting.
- Pedagogy typically changes class-by-class, according to the topic at hand. Activities may include computer-based lab exercises, small group activities, student presentations, class discussions comparing algorithms or addressing students' questions, problem solving on paper or on a whiteboard, etc.
- Even within a class session, activities may blend fluidly together. A class session might start with a 3-minute introductory talk and then move to a lab exercise. As questions arise, the class might reconvene for clarification or brainstorming, after which the lab activity might resume.
- Introductory computing courses emphasize collaboration and hands-on problem solving. A typical CS1 course might involve 45 lab sessions; one author estimates he lectures only about 4 hours per month when teaching CS1.

A common theme involves the engagement of students in the topic at hand. At Grinnell, it is often said that "students don't learn about science; rather students *do* science." In addressing social issues, faculty seek ways to involve students in discussion. Students should not be passive listeners, but rather active participants.

3. COMPUTING IN A SMALL, LIBERAL ARTS COLLEGE SETTING

At a liberal arts college, faculty across all disciplines understand the importance of social and ethical issues. Thus, the campus culture likely accepts the relevance of discussions of social and ethical issues of computing. At such schools, the more common issue is how computing fits into an overall education.

3.1 Where Computing Fits

At many liberal arts colleges, the computing faculty make the case that computer science fits within core areas, such as those listed earlier, by focusing on multiple approaches to problem solving, emphasizing underlying principles and underlying concepts, articulating precision of exposition (by writing in a precise [programming] language), addressing social and scientific problems raised in other disciplines, and demonstrating intellectual challenge and depth.

Further, computer science curricular recommendations (e.g., [1, 5, 9]) highlight theory, logical rigor, foundations, experimentation, analysis, and other intellectual skills that resonate in an academic community. At some schools, faculty must argue that computer science is different from vocational training, such as required for nursing, plumbing, or auto maintenance. Increasingly, however, colleges understand that computing connects well with the liberal arts; discussions such as that put forth by Walker and Keleman [13] can help educate any skeptics. Overall, in the liberal arts setting, faculty are comfortable discussing social and ethical issues of computing, once they agree that computing itself is worthy of study.

For a more extensive treatment of computing within the framework of a liberal arts institution, see [13].

3.2 Challenges

The small, liberal arts college setting poses some challenges for teaching computer science in general and for the inclusion of social issues in particular. Some challenges arise from institutional and departmental constraints:

- Majors are limited in the number of courses required, and so can require few specialized courses (e.g., on social issues).
- Schools expect students to graduate in four years, so required courses must be offered regularly.
- Faculties are small, so faculty scheduling must often focus on required courses.
- Offering courses in alternate years can provide options, but scheduling is delicate if such courses are required.

Although such constraints yield many consequences, one result is that very few computing departments in liberal arts colleges offer a separate course on "Social issues in computing." None are listed in [4], although courses on technology in society might be offered in a social studies or philosophy department.

Another challenge is to attract non-majors to computing courses. Liberal arts students typically have broad interests, but even students interested in science often have little or no knowledge of computer science. Schools with general education requirements may use them to channel non-majors into computing courses [4, 8]. At other schools, such as Grinnell, faculty must enhance the appeal of courses for non-majors, and advertise them to students and advisers. A discussion of social issues can provide one type of general appeal to this audience.

3.3 Opportunities

Within a small, liberal-arts setting, both faculty and students typically have a broad range of interests. Further, departments are small, and inter-departmental connections flourish. This framework provides numerous opportunities.

Many students who matriculate at liberal arts colleges wish to explore a wide range of disciplines before deciding on a major. Indeed, less than half of Grinnell's computer science majors entered Grinnell thinking they would major in computer science. The others try an introductory computing course and fall in love with the subject. With this breadth, liberal arts students often welcome discussions of social and ethical issues, and they bring knowledge and methods of inquiry from other disciplines. This greatly enhances discussions for all computing students.

Faculty, too, often have a broad range of interests and form close connections with colleagues in other disciplines. Interdisciplinary collaborations are not uncommon, and courses outside computing (e.g., in philosophy, sociology, or psychology) may build on these collaborations to discuss social and ethical issues of computing.

Since active learning techniques and discussion pervade many courses, both faculty and students are used to engaged discussion regarding both technical and social issues. In small classes, even more reserved students are drawn into discussions.

Moreover, faculty at small colleges often have a keen interest in teaching and may work together to develop their skills. For example, at Grinnell College, faculty from all science departments engage in a Science Teaching and Learning Group that has met biweekly for over a decade. This and other forums encourage exploration of creative pedagogy.

Finally, the atmosphere of many small, liberal arts colleges favor the consideration of social and ethical issues in all contexts. Recall Grinnell's mission to prepare students "for the honorable discharge of the duties of life." Grinnell, as one example, is noted for its commitment to social justice, and this commitment is expressed not only in students' extracurricular activities but also in courses across the college's entire curriculum. When social and technical topics are woven together through the careful selection of examples [8], faculty are more likely to be supported than censured by their colleagues for making this choice.

4. ENGAGING NON-MAJORS

As is typical at many liberal arts colleges, students at Grinnell do not have to declare their majors until their fourth semester. Thus, many first- and second-year students in introductory-level courses can be considered as potential majors. If students become excited about the subject, they might take more courses in the field and possibly declare a major. Thus, Grinnell's normal first course in computing emphasizes (functional) problem solving with applications to image processing. The course serves non-majors, but also helps recruit students to the major.

In addition, Grinnell's computer science department offers two courses that serve the general population: *The Digital Age* and sections of the First-Year Tutorial.

4.1 The Digital Age

Open to all students, *The Digital Age* provides background and insights for future citizens. In the early 2000s, the content of the course was strongly influenced by the 1999 report, "Being Fluent with Information Technology" [6]. This report identifies intellectual capacities, concepts, and skills that are vital to citizens in today's society. Over the years, the content and framing of the course has evolved, but the aim is to provide a fundamental background for future citizens. Social issues are addressed regularly (roughly weekly), alongside computer literacy topics. Instructors' approaches to addressing social issues have varied.

In his offerings of *The Digital Age*, Henry Walker connects topics in computing with common questions regarding technology, its applications, and consequences of its use. In many cases, social and ethical questions can motivate discussions of computing principles, algorithms, and perspectives. For example, Web pages may refer to the user's town or city, and e-commerce sites may suggest related items after the user makes a purchase. These experiences raise important technical questions, such as, "How does the Web server know where I am?" and "How did the e-commerce site remember that I had made that purchase?" Walker notes that this question/answer approach is the basis for his book, *The Tao of Computing* [12], which he has used as an assigned textbook. This style of course naturally integrates technical material with discussions of social and ethical issues.

Marge Coahran and Jerod Weinman have used topical readings, discussions, and short essays to address social issues. In one offering, Coahran allowed students to choose topics from Sara Baase's computer ethics textbook, *A Gift of Fire* [3]; similarly, Weinman has assigned readings from Michael J. Quinn's *Ethics for the Information Age* [10]. Coahran has also selected accessible articles from the *Communications of the ACM* on perennial topics such as malware and privacy, less familiar topics such as e-waste and artifact preservation through 3D modeling, and timely topics such as the role of social media in Iran's recent election riots. Students are required to read selections before class and write one-page reflection papers. The instructor poses discussion questions either when the reading is assigned or at the beginning of class; students consider these questions in small groups.

Coahran also has assigned "tech news" presentations. Each week, a different team of 2-3 students chooses a current event in computing technology and presents this news to the class. Although discussions are not as in depth as for the assigned readings, this activity gives students a broad sense of the computing industry and its role in society.

4.2 Tutorial

Incoming students at Grinnell College are required to take a First-Year Tutorial. First instituted in 1971 to replace the writing and composition course formerly offered by the English Department, the First-Year Tutorial is now offered by faculty in each academic department. Although the subject matter may be anything of interest to the instructor, the course must include writing, oral presentations, and library research. Some recent titles offered by computing faculty include "Computers: Facts, Misconceptions, and Ethical Issues" (taught by Walker), "Virtue in Animal and Machine" (Weinman), "Technology and Place" (Janet Davis), "Owning the Intangible: Possession, theft, and (Mis)Appropriation of Ideas" (Samuel Rebelsky), "Free software, free culture" (John David Stone), and "Outward from the middle of the maze: Selected plays of Tom Stoppard" (Stone).

"Computers: Facts, Misconceptions, and Ethical Issues" was the most recent iteration of a tutorial that Walker has taught over a number of years. This course has faced several challenges.

- Incoming students have had increasing contact with computers, but most have had little formal study of computing. They usually accept viewpoints about computing from the popular press (often wrong), and they have little systematic foundation to discuss social and ethical issues.
- For years, incoming students have heard high-level ethical principles, such as "love your neighbor" and "do not steal". Walker notes that even fourth-graders are good at articulating moral imperatives and giving expected responses about good behavior. By the time they enter college, students are often quite adept at repeating platitudes. However, they often do not consider what those principles might mean in practice.
- Initial attempts to integrate isolated articles into the Tutorial readings met with mixed success. Students could read and discuss, but the readings did not seem to capture students' attention and interest.

The most recent iteration of this Tutorial addressed these issues directly in at least three ways:

- Quinn's textbook, *Ethics for the Information Age*, presents multiple ethical philosophies, and these viewpoints are then applied to a range of situations [10]. This textbook provided both a foundation for discussions of ethics and an organization for later class activities.
- Many classes were devoted to student-led discussions. At first, each student presented one ethical perspective from Quinn's textbook [10]. Later they led discussions of chapters, articles, and news stories. All of this helped students take ownership of the material and formulate their own responses.
- Over the semester, each student was asked to present two news reports that suggested something of popular image of computing (what computer science is, what computing professionals do, or how computers are used). Each presentation was to describe the basic facts of a story, but then also suggest 2-4 questions to guide student discussions.

While this Tutorial continues to evolve, the new format seemed significantly more successful than past formats regarding discussions of social and ethical issues. The textbook provided a foundation, student-led discussions encouraged ownership of ideas, and student selection of news stories ensured students were talking about topics they were interested in.

One possible shortcoming of a computing-focused Tutorial is limited appeal to students who are culturally distanced from computing, notably women. Topics that include computing as one topic among many, such as "Virtue in Animal and Machine," "Technology and Place," and "Owning the Intangible," seem to attract more gender-balanced groups of students.

4.3 Assessment

Both *The Digital Age* and the First-Year Tutorial are stand-alone courses; they do not serve as prerequisites for later courses. Assessment, therefore, is self-contained within the course.

Further, both courses emphasize oral and written communication skills; students are expected to participate in discussions, present to the class, and write papers based on class readings and outside research. In each course, students must delve into new topics, synthesize ideas, formulate hypotheses, and justify their conclusions. Since *The Digital Age* and some Tutorial sections explore social issues, evaluation of oral presentations and written work allows assessment of the development of ideas about social and ethical issues. However, neither course utilizes in-class tests, so a strict quantitative assessment is not expected.

5. ENGAGING MAJORS

Majors in liberal arts programs can require relatively few courses for a computer science major: usually just 8-12 CS courses plus 2-4 mathematics courses, and rarely more than 12-14 major-related courses in total. Consequently, none of the programs discussed in [4] has a computer science course dedicated to social and ethical issues, and only Calvin College has an explicit requirement for the CS major regarding social issues [4]. Rather, social and ethical issues typically are discussed in other contexts.

- Computing may be addressed in courses outside of the computer science department, e.g., in a Philosophy of Science or a Technology Studies course.
- Themes or modules may be part of computing courses.
- Informal discussions may arise in a variety of settings.
- Advanced projects may include consideration of the work's social impact, or social issues may frame the overall project.

5.1 Regularly-Offered Courses

A typical approach for incorporating topics into existing courses is to construct a module or sequence of discussions on a specified topic. For example, Davis has students in *Computer Networks* read about the architectural principles that drove the design of the Internet forty years ago. In class, students consider the evolving uses of the internet, and technical implications of supporting (or thwarting) these uses.

Another approach is to inject questions about social and ethical issues as they arise. For example, in the context of *Computer Networks*, Rebelsky might ask his students, "What does it mean that we can gather this data?" or "Hmmm...we can forge email *this easily*. What implications does that have?" Walker finds that social and ethical issues arise naturally in *Databases and Web Application Design, Artificial Intelligence,* and the *Theory of Computation.* For example, in Web applications, it is natural to ask what consequences there might be to gather certain types of data, how that data might be stored (plain text, encrypted), what access there should be for that data, and what consequences might arise if the data were accidentally released. In *AI*, many techniques involve statistics or heuristics, and Walker asks students to consider possible procedures, legal responsibilities, and social impacts when results might be wrong for an individual. In the *Theory of Computation*, the Halting Problem demonstrates that some problems are unsolvable, and it is natural to ask about possible consequences for government policies and managerial decision making.

Faculty may also require students to do independent research on a socio-technical issue and present their findings to the class. For example, in *Software Design*, Rebelsky focuses on the potential impacts of the code one writes, particularly the danger of hidden bugs. In some offerings, he has had the students pick an incident (such as the THERAC-25 incident) and present it to the class. In *Computer Networks*, Davis has had students read and present research papers on network protocols designed to accomplish socially significant ends, such as onion routing, designed to provide anonymity to Internet users [11].

One course in particular is intimately related to the questions regarding quality of life and impacts on individuals and society posed by CC 2008 [5] and CC 2001 [1]: *Human-Computer Interaction.* Topics of special social relevance have included accessibility for people with disabilities, groupware, computers as social actors, persuasive technology, and ubiquitous computing. A focus on methodologies such as User-Centered Design, Value Sensitive Design, and Participatory Design lets students see how researchers and designers systematically consider stakeholders in the design of new technology. The course includes a project component involving system design and evaluation; to be successful, students must interact with stakeholders and consider the real-world use of the system they are working with. Moreover, students must consider ethical treatment of user study participants through through writing a proposal for work with human subjects and gaining approval from the Institutional Review Board.

Several computing faculty argue that social issues may arise in any course. Stone reports that he tries to teach by example, infusing throughout his courses his philosophy on social issues in computing, particularly with respect to intellectual freedom. Rebelsky writes, "I try to at least mention social issues in all of my courses; I think that considering social issues is an important part of the discipline."

5.2 Reading Groups and Informal Learning

Small-group study and informal settings also can be important in raising social issues of computing. For example, in Fall 2005, Walker collaborated with a faculty member in education to organize an independent project to explore the literature on women in computing. In Fall 2007, three computing faculty responded to student concerns about the status of women in computing by organizing a weekly guided reading course. This fall, Davis is offering a course on *Socio-Technical Issues in Computer Networks*, similarly in response to student interest. The latter two courses were offered in the context of our informal "CS Table" lunchtime discussions, to which all students are welcome, regardless of whether they are enrolled in the course or even computer science majors. CS Table often touches on social issues even when there is not a special topic offering.

A small school can take advantage of its size and close interpersonal relationships by organizing such small group and community-building activities. This often requires some faculty time beyond officially recognized teaching duties. However, with relatively modest effort, social issues can be an ongoing theme both inside and out of the computing program.

5.3 Experiential Learning/Mentored Advanced Projects (MAPs)

Computer science students often undertake a range of independent projects under the supervision of a faculty member. In many cases, these projects provide excellent opportunities to raise social and ethical issues—not as abstract concepts but as points that have direct application to the work at hand. For example, Walker has led selected teams in developing software projects for record keeping for Grinnell's recruiting of student athletes, for Grinnell's local food cooperative, for an interactive campus map, and for placing incoming students in computer science, math, and statistics courses. For each of these projects, the development team met periodically with clients to learn needs, to present prototype systems, to receive feedback, and to understand user priorities. Since each system was to support clients, discussions within the team regularly considered social and ethical issues, such as social impact, privacy, security, and authentication. In each case, social and ethical considerations had a significant impact upon software design and implementation.

Also through the Grinnell's program of Mentored Advanced Projects (MAPs), Davis has involved students in her research on applying participatory design methods to the development of persuasive technology: computing systems intended to change attitudes or behaviors. Persuasive technology raises a number of ethical issues relating to the intentions of the designer/persuader, the means of persuasion, and the desirability of outcomes, while participatory design is intended to help address these issues by involving potential users in deciding what behaviors the system will target and how the system will interact with users. Students contributed to developing and implementing participatory design approaches, and to considering the social and ethical implications of the resulting systems.

5.4Assessment

Although this section has identified many ways that social issues can be addressed in courses, readings, and projects, formal assessment poses a challenge. Each individual course focuses on specific technical topics (e.g., operating systems, algorithms, networks), and formal evaluation (e.g., exams) typically focuses on those main topics. Framing an exam question related to social issues can seem awkward. Anecdotally, faculty can observe that students in one course are raising issues of privacy, security, intellectual property, etc. that have been raised in other courses, but assessment of these topics within individual courses is a challenge at best.

6. FUTURE WORK

The discipline of computing continues to develop at a rapid pace, and computing curricula and individual courses evolve quickly to keep up. Part of this evolution involves ongoing efforts to find creative ways to include social issues within courses and discussions. This paper has identified several approaches that work within a liberal arts framework, but the efforts will need to continue as both the discipline and society progress.

One particular area for future work involves assessment. This paper has documented problems in determining the effectiveness of individual courses, in which social issues form a background-level, on-going theme. However, one way to approach effectiveness might be to survey or interview graduating seniors and alumni regarding their exposure to social and ethical issues through the Grinnell computer science curriculum, their attitudes towards such issues, and their perceived ability to address such issues in their work and everyday life.

7. CONCLUSION

This paper has described the environment of the small, liberal-arts college and presented a range of approaches for introducing social and ethical issues of computing. These approaches largely entail readings and discussions that fit into study of traditional topics, but also include opportunities for study and discussion beyond the regular curriculum.

All of this work, however, is meant to provide a foundation. The comments here can provide a starting point for discussion and experimentation. The authors hope that this base leads to new conversations, as the start of expanded collaborations.

8. ACKNOWLEDGMENTS

This paper builds upon numerous conversations and activities of colleagues throughout the computing community. Many thanks to our colleagues, John David Stone, Samuel Rebelsky, and Jerod Weinman, for their on-going contributions in developing Grinnell's program. We also thank Marge Coahran, now at Dickinson College, for her insights, particularly in helping to develop *The Digital Age.* Beyond Grinnell, we gratefully acknowledge the many contributions made over the years by members of the Liberal Arts Computer Science Consortium. We also want to extend our appreciation to Donald Joyce, Unitec, for proposing the ITiCSE 2010 Working Group on social issues, and to the members of that group for their encouragement and insights.

REFERENCES

[1] ACM/IEEE Joint Task Force 2001. *Computing Curricula 2001: Computer Science.*

[2] Alt, A, Astrachan, O., Forbes, J., Lucic, R., and Rodger, S. 2006. Social Networks Generate Interest in Computer Science, *SIGCSE 2006 Proceedings*, pp. 438-442.

[3] Baase, S. 2008. *Ethical Issues for Computing and the Internet Second Edition.* Prentice-Hall.

[4] Baldwin, D., Brady, A., Danyluk, A., Adams, J., and Lawrence, A. 2010. Case studies of liberal arts computer science programs, *ACM Transactions on Computing Education (TOCE□)*, Vol. 10, Issue 1 (March 2010), Article 4.

[5] Cassel, L., et al 2008, *Computer science curriculum 2008: An interim revision of CS 2001. Report from the interim review task force.*

[6] Computer Science Telecommunications Board 1999. *Being fluent with Information Technology*, National Research Council.

[7] Guzdial, M. and Erickson, B. 2010. *Introduction to Computing and Programming in Python: A Multimedia Approach*, Second Edition, Addison-Wesley / Prentice Hall.

[8] ITiCSE 2010 Working Group 8 2010. *Enhancing the Social Issues Components in our Computing Curriculum: Computing for the Social Good,* Report in preparation.

[9] Liberal Arts Computer Science Consortium 2007. A 2007 model curriculum for a liberal arts degree in computer science, *Journal on Educational Resources in Computing (JERIC)*, Vol. 7, Issue 2 (June 2007), Article 2.

[10] Quinn, M. J. 2009. *Ethics for the Information Age, Third Edition,* Pearson / Addison-Wesley.

[11] Reed, M. G., Syverson, P. F., and Goldschlag, D. M. 1998.Anonymous connections and onion routing. *IEEE Journal on Selected Areas in Communications,* Vol. 16, Issue 4, May 1998, pp. 482-494

[12] Walker, H. M. 2005. *The Tao of Computing,* Jones and Bartlett.

[13] Walker, H. M. and Kelemen, C. 2010. Computer science and the liberal arts, *ACM Transactions on Computing Education (TOCE)*, Vol. 10, Issue 1 (March 2010), Article 2.

Using Undergraduate Teaching Assistants in a Small College Environment

Paul E. Dickson
Hampshire College
School of Cognitive Science
893 West St.
Amherst, MA 01002, USA
pdickson@hampshire.edu

ABSTRACT

The use of undergraduate teaching assistants in computer science courses is not new but is primarily thought of as a way to help with large classes in universities and rarely for small classes in small colleges. In this paper we discuss the success we have had over the past 2 years using undergraduate students as teaching assistants for a number of small computer science classes. Our experience has shown that having undergraduates as teaching assistants helps to engage students with the material, creates a more relaxed classroom environment in which students feel more free to ask questions, improves the effectiveness of class time, and improves class quality. We believe that our experiences using undergraduate teaching assistants can be beneficial not only to small colleges but also to large universities.

Categories and Subject Descriptors

K.3.2 [**Computers and Education**]: Computer and Information Science EducationComputer Science Education

General Terms

Management, Human Factors

Keywords

Undergraduate Teaching Assistants, Computer Science Education

1. INTRODUCTION

The best way to understand our undergraduate teaching assistant (UTA) program and its organization is to learn about the environment in which we use UTAs. Hampshire College is a small liberal arts college (approximately 1350 students) with few computer science majors and a student body with a tendency toward the arts. All students are required to fulfill 2 advanced learning activities before they graduate and one of those activities can be serving as a UTA for a course. Hampshire College also has a large number of students who pursue independent studies, which makes the idea of a student acting as a TA not that unusual. It is within this fertile environment that we began experimenting with the use of UTAs.

We first used a UTA in an introductory computer science course on web development. The UTA was a student who volunteered because he needed an advanced learning activity. The experience was so successful that we have used UTAs in 4 of the 7 courses we have taught since then; 2 of those courses have been introductory level and 2 upper level. Of the 3 courses without UTAs, 2 were new courses for which no student was qualified to to be a UTA and the third was a seminar with 12 students for which a TA was not appropriate. The benefit to each course varied from marginal improvement to raging success, with the difference in benefit relating more to the effectiveness of how the UTA was used than to anything else.

In this paper we will discuss how our use of UTAs compares with that at other institutions before discussing details of how we have used UTAs. We will describe the use of UTAs for specific courses, discuss what did and did not work, and then discuss the most effective ways of using UTAs. Finally we will describe the benefits to the UTAs and summarize the UTA program's effectiveness.

2. RELATED WORK

For more than 20 years, undergraduates have functioned as teaching assistants (TAs) for courses and in many institutions UTA programs seem to have been started as a cost-cutting measure. The basic idea was that it would be far less expensive to use UTAs for 100+ person introductory computer science courses than to pay for graduate TAs. While many universities have done this, Reges et al. at Stanford University [6] were some of the first to write about their experience. They found that undergraduate students where quite often willing to be TAs for credit, at least initially. The UTAs would attend lectures, hold their own discussion sections, hold office hours, and grade and discuss those grades with students. What they discovered was that not only was it less expensive to use UTAs but also that they did a better job than graduate TAs because they were more familiar with how Stanford courses were taught. Plus, the UTAs tended to be very motivated and this had a positive effect on the students who were infected by their energy and tended to put in greater effort because of it. We have also noticed this effect and it is noted in many of the papers listed below.

Stanford continued this program and over the years streamlined their system and quantitated results [7]. They found that the system not only benefited the students but also the UTAs, helping the UTAs' understanding of the material. They found that the rapport between the UTAs and students in the course was beneficial and the UTAs often acted as role models for the students in the class, which is especially beneficial when you consider that over 25% of the UTAs were women. The course with the UTAs also consistently gets among the best ratings on campus for quality of teaching. One concern was having undergraduates grade undergraduates, but they got around this by grading assignments using a qualitative method that was based more on overall functioning of programs then on specifics of code. One real benefit was that they were able to staff an area to help students with the introductory course and to staff it approximately 70 hours per week except during high-demand times when hours were extended. They believe this program to be a real success.

When Reges moved from Stanford to the University of Arizona, he brought the idea of a UTA program with him [5]. The same positive results were found despite a very different student body. Especially of interest is that this program helped foster a sense of community among undergraduates that was not present before the program and that the interpersonal skills that the UTAs developed impressed employers after the students graduated. Reges's work implies that while benefits vary by institution, the inclusion of a UTA program would likely benefit any institution that has one. The UTA programs at both Arizona and Stanford are very structured, with weekly meetings and structured UTA training time, though they do encourage UTAs to find their own teaching style.

Paxton at Montana State University implemented an undergraduate consultant program that functioned similar to UTAs in a lab environment [3] and without lecture duties. These upper-level students got credit to assist in closed and open lab environments and they and the students in the courses were surveyed to determine the effectiveness of the program. The consultants overwhelmingly believed that the program benefited their understanding of material, communication skills, and understanding of professional responsibilities. The students found the consultants to be effective at answering questions and helping them within the environment.

Appalachian State University developed a peer mentoring program [9] with undergraduate mentors who attend lab sessions and who meet one-on-one with students outside of formal class time. These are essentially the same as UTAs who would attend class and hold office hours. This program benefited the learning of both the mentors and the students. Also, the students who were mentored put forth an increased level of effort.

The University at Buffalo, SUNY changed from graduate TAs to UTAs specifically to improve the level of teaching [1]. There had been many bad experiences with graduate TAs who did not relate to students nor understand how the program at Buffalo worked and therefore the university shifted to UTAs who have an understanding of the curriculum. Using UTAs and giving them a lot of leeway paid off as the UTAs made suggestions about assignments, changed discussion sections to lab sessions, and gave extra review sessions. The authors report that UTAs took responsibility for the course and course material and improved the quality of the course. As a result of this, student satisfaction with the UTAs was far higher than what it had been with graduate student TAs. UTAs were found to be extremely beneficial to their program and to the students involved.

The use of UTAs for large introductory classes has become common enough that their use was mentioned in passing by professors at the University of Washington [8], University of California Irvine [2], and University of Rhode Island [4] when describing courses in various publications.

What all of these programs have in common is that they were implemented in large schools where the courses required some type of TA in order to function. In many of these cases, without some type of TA to grade the professor never would have been able to handle the course. While each paper describes the successes of using UTAs, it is always in the context of providing required additional help for the professor. What none of these papers describes is the situation we have at Hampshire College, which is more common to small colleges: a TA is not required for a course to succeed but does provide enormous benefit if one can be found. In a small college the UTA is supplemental help for the students and professor instead of a required component.

3. UTA EXPERIENCES

The 5 courses for which UTAs were used were taught over the course of 4 semesters and are described in terms of the semester in which they occurred. This chronological presentation shows the progression of ideas behind UTA involvement in courses. The Hampshire College computer science courses discussed here all have between 15 and 20 students and meet for 80 minutes, twice a week, in a computer lab.

3.1 Fall 2008

Our first experience with a UTA was when a student volunteered to be one for an introductory web development course that we were introducing. As this was a first for us, we decided that his duties would be to attend every lecture, take half the grading, put class examples up on the web, and hold evening lab hours twice a week. This workload doubled when we added a second section of the course and had him attend every lecture of both sections. We thought that we were getting some help grading and adding someone to move around the room helping out when in-class examples were given. In actuality, we got a great addition to the course.

The UTA did everything that was asked and more. During class he added details to topics that we had not realized had not been covered sufficiently. He also updated our knowledge of some recent web design tools that he was familiar with because of a side job in web design. As many of our UTAs have done since, he responded to student questions and met with students outside of lab hours on a fairly regular basis. What might be his greatest addition was his contribution to the class environment. Many students find themselves loath to ask questions in a computer science course because they feel out of their depth and small class sizes do not necessarily help enough to overcome this. Having a UTA who is one of their peers sitting in the classroom, sighing loudly, and correcting the professor by stating that this specific piece of code has not been used by any self-respecting web designer in 4 years and is obsolete does a lot to relax students and make them more likely to ask a question. Unlike when a graduate TA asks a question in class or makes a correction, students view a UTA as their peer and when they see the professor react well to a UTA's question/correction/heckling feel more comfortable verbally participating in class themselves.

3.2 Spring 2009

Our second experience with a UTA was for an upper-level computer graphics course that was being taught for the first time. We enlisted the UTA to hold lab hours so that students could get help with coding issues since most of the class was new to the programming language being used for the course. While the UTA generally attended class, he was never invested in the course. He did his best to try to help students when they had questions with the material but his role was really just as programming support. While his participation as a UTA for the course definitely helped students, his overall benefit was limited as a result of a lack of investment caused by poor planning on our part.

3.3 Fall 2009

When we taught the introductory web development course again we decided to actively look for another UTA for the course based on our previous success. The UTA we ended up bringing in had taken the course the previous fall and had shown considerable interest in the subject material though not the highest level of skill. He was a student whom many of his professors would describe as being flaky. He arrived at college intending to be a film major before gaining interest in computer science thanks to the introductory web development course. We note this information about the UTA because the responsibility of being the TA for this course noticeably improved his work as a student in general. On the last day of the semester, each of the 2 sections of the course gave the UTA an ovation for the outstanding job he had done helping them throughout the semester. This was despite the fact that he had initially seemed like a weak UTA prospect.

The specific tasks for the UTA were the same as for the previous year: to attend all lectures, do half the grading, put class examples up on the web, and hold evening lab hours for students. As with the previous TA for this course, he also made himself available for additional help at odd hours when the students needed it, going above and beyond what was required. It was fairly common to walk into the computer lab where classes and lab hours were held and find his explanations of concepts and problem solving on the whiteboards, left from when he had helped students the previous night. Like the previous UTA for the course, he dramatically lowered our workload by fielding a portion of the questions and grading half the assignments but again this turned out to be more of a side benefit.

Our UTA's biggest benefit to the course was the effect on student moral, attitude, and motivation. Every faculty member finds that by the end of the semester, classes tend to run smoother since students have learned what a specific professor's priorities and teaching style are and know how to best work within that system. By having a UTA who knew that system from day one, students were able to pick up both more quickly. We do not know exactly what our UTA told students about us outside of class, but the students definitely got into the swing of things weeks sooner than they normally do. A specific example of this is that we like to run an informal classroom because we find that it makes students more likely to ask questions. On the first day of class, about 20 minutes after being introduced as the UTA for the course, our UTA heckled part of the lecture saying something like "Paul, I think you gave that explanation better last year". As we explained to the class how the obvious reason for having a UTA was to have their undivided loyalty and respect, students began to visibly relax. The exchange showed them more about our priorities and lecture style in 2 minutes than they would otherwise have picked up in weeks of class.

3.4 Spring 2010

Based on our continuing success with UTAs, we decided to expand their use to two new courses we were offering, an introductory programming course in C and C++ and an advanced web design course. In both cases we had qualified students to be UTAs.

The introductory programming course had 3 UTAs who had been hand-picked for this course. One was a first-year student with a lot of self-taught programming experience but none in C or C++. We encouraged him to TA the course instead of taking it because he would have found the course boring to take but would prove a valuable reference as a UTA. A second year student who had taken 2 courses with us and who is double majoring with theatre brought with her a different perspective that helped many of the diverse students in an introductory course. As a woman she also was a little more approachable for the women in the course. The final UTA was a third-year student who had taken 4 courses with us and is one of the students found on every campus who understands how things work on that campus and can and did help new students acquire that knowledge. Thus we had 4 instructors in the class and a ratio of 1 instructor for every 5 students.

This course had 2 assignments per week and the UTAs were responsible for grading one of them, a task that they rotated through on a schedule of their own devising. The UTAs also were responsible for holding lab hours 3 evenings per week, attending class, and answering student questions by e-mail. How the semester worked out with the 3 UTAs was informative and influenced how we believe UTAs should be used.

All 3 UTAs were competent and determined their schedules and work distribution among themselves. Although they did not grade equal numbers of assignments, they were happy with the distribution and therefore we were as well. They decided that each would hold lab hours on a different day of the week but kept all the scheduled hours open in their own schedules so that if the one holding hours got swamped, the others were available to go to the lab to help so that every student could get personal attention during lab hours.

The real beauty of the 3 of them was their work in class and as student mentors. In this course students follow along with in-class examples, typing them into their own computers. Quite often they have bugs in their code while doing this. In a typical class with no TAs, the professor either needs to stop the entire class to help a student fix a bug or leave that student behind. With the 3 UTAs, when a bug occurred a student could just call out for a UTA for immediate help so that they could go on with the example. This helped both in keeping them up with class but also with finding bugs in code or unclear points. The UTAs were in a great position to see if the same problems kept showing up for multiple people or if the code was right and a compiler error was occurring. In each case the UTAs would interrupt lecture to get it addressed or to fill in details the instructor had missed. The UTAs were able to float around the room keeping track of what problems were occurring and were able to funnel information back when it was needed. They also enabled in-class exercises to be done more often as 4 of us walking around a room made it easy to quickly address all student questions that came up in such exercises.

The other benefit the UTAs had was that they acted as mentors for some of the students in the course. Many of the students found that there was one of the UTAs who could explain things in a way that made the most sense to them specifically and started asking questions mostly of that UTA. By the end of the semester, each UTA had a couple of students whom they had taken under their wings and given extra help. This course had a number of students who were taking it because of distribution requirements and who came from artistic backgrounds antithetical to programming. They might have passed the class without the UTAs. As it was, these students were able to get extra help from the UTAs and in a couple of cases many extra hours of help. Not only did these students pass the class but in almost all cases they finished it as a good solid beginning programmers, something they never believed possible at the beginning of the semester.

At the end of the semester the students in the course felt that the UTAs had been one of the best parts of how the course was taught.

The final course for which we used UTAs was an advanced web development course. The UTA for the course was the same one as for the introductory web development course the semester before and so more than half the class was used to having him as a TA. The UTA had limited grading responsibility for this course but was an active participant without whom the course could not have been taught. Our background in web design comes mainly from picking it up to teach courses in it based on student demand. Our UTA was genuinely interested in the subject and trying to actively acquire more skills in the area. The UTA built the Linux server for the course and got all of the appropriate modules working so that we could do server-side development. This meant that when something went wrong or a student in the course needed something done to the machine late at night, the UTA could do it since he was the sysadmin for the course server.

This course was based around a large-group final project. Each group decided on the website they wished to build and by the end of the semester some of the lectures were written purely to fill in information gaps needed by one group or another. For some of these areas we gave the UTA the assignment of researching the topics and giving 30-minute lectures on them. This was only partially successful because while the UTA learned the material and has a lot of one-on-one teaching experience, he did not have lecture experience and his talks were not quite up to the standard of lecture we would have preferred. This suggested that it might be best to in general leave lecturing to the faculty member and let the UTAs stick to individual instruction if the UTA is not going to have regular lecture duties. As before, the UTA handled office hours and put up class examples on the web. Every student in the course had high praise for the UTA and the help they received from him.

4. EFFECTIVE USE OF UTAS

We believe that the most effective way to use UTAs in a small college environment is to have them attend all lectures, hold lab hours, get class example on the web, keep the lecturer informed on student understanding, and help with some of the grading.

The most important aspect is to have the UTAs present in class. Especially in introductory programming courses, UTAs can be extremely effective in circulating around a room helping students debug code during lecture and as the semester goes on acting as mentors for the students. Most students in introductory computer science courses have recently entered college and how the UTAs act around professors and handle college in general does a lot to inform the new students of how college works and how to handle it. The UTAs also can clarify points that the lecturer may have glossed over and call for the lecturer to slow down or add an extra day of class on a subject if they see that the material is just going over the students' heads. The UTAs have the confidence to state that things are going too fast even when the students do not. By having this power the UTAs start to take responsibility for the course and find themselves equally invested in its outcome and the learning of the students. When they are invested, they put in the extra effort to make sure that the lecturer does a good job and that the students do well.

Having the UTAs in class also does a lot to set the tone for a course. A good UTA will ask questions and interact with the lecturer creating a good dialogue, which pulls the course away from the "sage on the stage" format common to most introductory computer science courses. We have found this to be a very successful way to make students more comfortable about talking in class and asking questions.

Lab hours are also essential because they give the students another time to get help. At Hampshire College few students are willing to wake up for morning office hours and few have time in the afternoon to attend office hours because of course schedules. By having lab hours in the evening, UTAs provide answers to questions at night when students actually need help. Also, if a bad assignment makes it through or is unclear, a UTA can decide during lab hours that it is too flawed to be counted and tell students not to worry about it instead of having them stay up all night trying to figure it out while hoping that the lecturer will respond to an e-mail after 9 pm.

Another good use for UTAs is to have them keep class examples up to date on the web. Instead of the lecturer putting a class example up online after class, a TA who is in class can post examples to the web in real time. This cuts down on the professor's workload and helps students who have poor written notes.

The final area for UTA help is in grading. While the ethics of having undergraduate students grade fellow undergraduate students is open to debate, there is some grading that they can be given in good conscience. Specifically, we have found that giving lots of small assignments in an introductory course is useful because it causes students to engage with the material more often, but to do this effectively all of those assignments need to be graded and no professor has the time to grade multiple assignments per week. As long as the grading for these assignments is more qualitative and in the range of whether or not the student did the assignment, it is reasonable to have a UTA do some of the grading. The professor's time then can be used more effectively on writing better comments on students' code.

UTAs generally have a good grasp of what is useful when learning computer science material as they generally have been introduced to it far more recently than the professor has been. This means that they can easily remember what made the material clear to them; we have found it useful to listen when a UTA says that the explanation is not clear or that a specific method of going over material will not work. Also, UTAs quite often have more time invested in the specific course material than the professor as they often have a passion in the subject area. If encouraged correctly this can lead to more agile course development as the UTA can be asked to update material that the professor may not have had time to update or in some cases even realize is out of date.

5. BENEFITS TO THE UTA

A UTA program not only benefits the professors who make use of UTAs but also the UTAs themselves. Going over material with another student has the obvious advantage to the UTA that you learn something best when you teach it. At the same time UTAs must be able to talk to the students in the course regardless of background differences and this helps to improve the UTAs' communications skills while also building their confidence. We have seen that many of our UTAs who are a little nervous at the start of a semester show great personal gain by the end and have the confidence to speak up more because of having done so successfully for a semester.

The other major benefit to UTAs is that the experience helps develop their sense and understanding of professional responsibilities as was also noted by Paxton [3]. We have a great example of this as one of our UTAs was known for skipping many of his classes and not being the most dedicated of students. He realized that as the UTA he needed to show up because others were counting him and therefore he did. Not only did he show up to all class meetings and lab hours but he also saw the effect that skipping class had on students in it and realized the disservice he had been doing himself by skipping classes. When students who had set up special meeting with him did not show up, it really brought home how one's attendance and keeping of schedules can affect others. Being a UTA matured this particular student in a way that drastically improved his undergraduate career.

A small side benefit to being a UTA was that it has in each case created a situation of more one-on-one faculty-student mentoring because a UTA needs to work closely with a faculty member for the course to function smoothly. This generally leads to more faculty involvement in the student's academic life and to greater student contact with faculty research. Three of our 6 UTAs have gone on to do undergraduate research and 2 of the 3 are working on projects with us.

6. CONCLUSIONS

We have shown how UTAs can benefit courses even in a small college environment. A UTA program can be run without the level of organization used at a Stanford [6, 7] or Arizona [5] and still be effective. Being a UTA has benefit for the UTA and therefore it is reasonable to give students credit for their efforts. Having a UTA in a course can cut down on professor workload and enable greater numbers of assignments to be given in introductory courses, improving student performance. Although UTAs are not required in order to teach a good quality course at a small college, they can certainly make the task easier and improve the quality of the course. We have every intention of continuing to use UTAs in our future computer science courses. Despite a lack of specific organization or set structure, the system continues to grow and prosper with strong students volunteering to be UTAs without being asked.

7. REFERENCES

[1] Adrienne Decker, Phil Ventura, and Christopher Egert. Through the looking glass: reflections on using undergraduate teaching assistants in cs1. *SIGCSE Bull.*, 38(1):46–50, 2006.

[2] David G. Kay. Large introductory computer science classes: strategies for effective course management. In *SIGCSE '98: Proceedings of the twenty-ninth SIGCSE technical symposium on Computer science education*, pages 131–134, New York, NY, USA, 1998. ACM.

[3] John Paxton. Undergraduate consultation: opportunities and challenges. *J. Comput. Small Coll.*, 21(1):231–238, 2005.

[4] Joan Peckham, Lisa DiPippo, James Reynolds, Jake Paris, Phil Monte, and Peter Constantinidis. A first course in computer science: the discipline is more than programming. In *CCSC '00: Proceedings of the fifth annual CCSC northeastern conference on The journal of computing in small colleges*, pages 220–227, , USA, 2000. Consortium for Computing Sciences in Colleges.

[5] Stuart Reges. Using undergraduates as teaching assistants at a state university. In *SIGCSE '03: Proceedings of the 34th SIGCSE technical symposium on Computer science education*, pages 103–107, New York, NY, USA, 2003. ACM.

[6] Stuart Reges, John McGrory, and Jeff Smith. The effective use of undergraduates to staff large introductory cs courses. *SIGCSE Bull.*, 20(1):22–25, 1988.

[7] Eric Roberts, John Lilly, and Bryan Rollins. Using undergraduates as teaching assistants in introductory programming courses: an update on the stanford experience. In *SIGCSE '95: Proceedings of the twenty-sixth SIGCSE technical symposium on Computer science education*, pages 48–52, New York, NY, USA, 1995. ACM.

[8] Marty Stepp, Jessica Miller, and Victoria Kirst. A "cs 1.5" introduction to web programming. In *SIGCSE '09: Proceedings of the 40th ACM technical symposium on Computer science education*, pages 121–125, New York, NY, USA, 2009. ACM.

[9] Rahman Tashakkori, James T. Wilkes, and Edward G. Pekarek. A systemic mentoring model in computer science. In *ACM-SE 43: Proceedings of the 43rd annual Southeast regional conference*, pages 371–375, New York, NY, USA, 2005. ACM.

Educational Advances in Artificial Intelligence

Mehran Sahami (moderator)
Stanford University
Computer Science Department
sahami@cs.stanford.edu

Marie desJardins
University of Maryland, Baltimore County
Dept. of Computer Science and Electrical Engineering
mariedj@cs.umbc.edu

Zachary Dodds
Harvey Mudd College
Computer Science Department
dodds@cs.hmc.edu

Todd Neller
Gettysburg College
Department of Computer Science
tneller@gettysburg.edu

SUMMARY

In 2010 a new annual symposium on Educational Advances in Artificial Intelligence (EAAI) was launched as part of the AAAI annual meeting. The event was held in cooperation with ACM SIGCSE and has many similar goals related to broadening and disseminating work in computer science education. EAAI has a particular focus, however, as the event is specific to educational work in Artificial Intelligence and collocated with a major research conference (AAAI) to promote more interaction between researchers and educators in that domain. This panel seeks to introduce participants to EAAI as a way of fostering more interaction between educational communities in computing. Specifically, the panel will discuss the goals of EAAI, provide an overview of the kinds of work presented at the symposium, and identify potential synergies between that EAAI and SIGCSE as a way of better linking the two communities going forward.

Categories and Subject Descriptors

K.3.2 [**Computers and Education**]: Computer and Information Science Education; I.2.0 [**Artificial Intelligence**]: General.

General Terms

Algorithms, Experimentation, Theory.

Keywords

Artificial Intelligence Education, Model AI Assignments.

1. INTRODUCTION

This past summer marked the inauguration of a new educationally focused annual symposium with the launch of the First Symposium on Educational Advances in Artificial Intelligence (EAAI-2010). EAAI is sponsored by the Association for the Advancement of Artificial Intelligence (AAAI), and seeks to advance AAAI's goal of improving the teaching and training of Artificial Intelligence (AI) researchers, educators, and practitioners. The symposium provides a venue for researchers and educators to discuss pedagogical issues and share resources related to teaching AI and using AI in education across a variety of curricular levels (K-12 through postgraduate training), with a natural emphasis on undergraduate and graduate teaching and learning.

Organized as an independent program within the annual AAAI National Conference, EAAI is also held in cooperation with ACM SIGCSE, reflecting the aligned goal of improving computer science education. Given the SIGCSE 2011 theme of "reaching out", this panel seeks to inform the SIGCSE community of this new event and discuss opportunities for further working together in the future.

Indeed, beyond the obvious issue of how to specifically improve AI education, there are several new thrusts of work involving AI in computer science education. There has recently been a great deal of interest in the use of robotics as a platform for teaching introductory computing [1, 3] as well as encouraging greater participation in computing from underrepresented groups [4, 9]. Several introductory programming courses now use problems in AI as motivating examples [6, 8], and AI has been used as a topic to interest non-majors in computing [2]. Moreover, the use of AI in games [6, 10, 11] has also been advanced as a way of attracting more students into computing.

In support of the shared goal of improving computer science education, EAAI incorporates a number of components including a technical program of high-quality refereed papers, special sessions of peer-reviewed *Model AI Assignments*, a workshop for mentoring new faculty/graduate students on teaching, and coordination with a track on Educational Robotics. These activities are described below, and will be discussed in further detail at the panel as a means for identifying more synergistic activities with the SIGCSE community. We believe the panel will be of interest to AI educators as well as anyone with an interest in using topics/platforms from AI to motivate greater participation in computing at the K-12, undergraduate, or graduate level. The panel includes the general chair of EAAI-2010, the in-coming general chair of EAAI-2011, and the chairs of the Model AI Assignments and Educational Robotics tracks, respectively.

2. TECHNICAL PROGRAM (SAHAMI)

EAAI includes a program of refereed technical papers spanning multiple topics in AI education. One clear focus of the program is

SIGCSE'11, March 9–12, 2011, Dallas, Texas, USA.
ACM 978-1-4503-0500-6/11/03.

the improvement of introductory AI and AI-related courses. Papers on this topic tended to focus on engaging software projects that incorporate multiple themes from AI into a working artifact. In this way, students are motivated to see AI as a technology that is integrated into real systems, rather than simply being a set of somewhat disjoint topics whose commonality is that they appear in the same textbook. Moreover, AI is discussed as a topic that can be integrated into computing courses at multiple levels, including K-12.

Another major focus of the EAAI technical program is the use of robotics in education. Again this work spanned multiple levels. For example, there was coverage of using simple robots as a means for interesting middle and high school students in computing all the way to the development of robotics infrastructure to teach graduate courses in this area at a more accelerated level.

The breadth of coverage in the EAAI technical program reflects the diversity of ways that AI can be used to address many of the same educational issues that are often grappled with at SIGCSE. Thus, we believe there are many opportunities to share and align work by the two communities.

3. MODEL AI ASSIGNMENTS (NELLER)

Another highlight of EAAI-10 is the *Model AI Assignments* program, which presents a number of innovative, ready-to-adopt course assignments that were used successfully in a variety of AI courses. The program is modeled on the popular *Nifty Assignments* [7] session at SIGCSE, but with a focus on AI-related assignments rather than projects directly aimed at CS1/2. This program not only includes presentations on the assignments, but also provides an online repository [5] where educators may download pedagogical materials. In this way, the program helps to promote the sharing of ideas and best pedagogical practices among AI educators. Indeed, in developing this program there were discussions with the original creators of *Nifty Assignments*.

4. TEACHER MENTORING WORKSHOP (DESJARDINES)

In additional to sharing experiences, research, and assignments in AI education, EAAI also seeks to help develop the next generation of AI educators. To this end, the symposium includes a mentoring program aimed at sharing experiences and materials with new faculty and graduate students in AI. The workshop held at EAAI-10 was very successful, and interestingly included many topics in improving pedagogy that were not AI-specific.

While SIGCSE has recently introduced the New Educators Roundtable in a similar vein, the structure of the EAAI teaching mentoring workshop was, in fact, quite different. Rather than focusing on sharing experiences with seasoned educators, the EAAI workshop focused on the theme of active learning, providing a presentation of research in this area as well as concrete examples of how active learning can be used in the classroom generally. Participants in the workshop then engaged in a hands-on session aimed at producing actionable examples of active learning to teach various concrete topics in an introductory AI course. The workshop concluded with a more traditional panel discussion from experienced educators sharing their thoughts on various questions from the audience.

5. EDUCATIONAL ROBOTICS (DODDS)

Highlighting the growing interest in robotics as an education platform, EAAI is also held in coordination with the Educational Robotics track from the AAAI Robotics Exhibition. The Educational Robotics track provides the opportunity for pre-college, undergraduate, or early graduate student teams to exhibit an autonomous robotic system or curricular project.

By sharing participants and presentations with this longstanding exhibition, EAAI taps an established community of regular AAAI attendees already committed to advancing educational practices in the field. It also contributes to the education-track exhibition by offering a focused paper session on novel approaches to robotics education and education with robots.

6. REFERENCES

[1] Blank, D. and Kumar, D. 2010. Assessing the Impact of using Robots in Education, or: How we learned to Stop Worrying and Love the Chaos. *Educational Robotics and Beyond: Design and Evaluation*, AAAI Press, 3-7.

[2] Danyluk, A. 2004. Using Robotics to Motivate Learning in an AI Course Aimed at Non-majors. *Proceedings of AAAI Spring Symposium: Accessible Hands-on Artificial Intelligence and Robotics Education*, AAAI Press, 93-96.

[3] Imberman, S. P., Klibaner, R., and Zelikovitz, S. 2007. Student Feedback on Robotics in CS1. *Proceedings of AAAI Spring Symposium: Robots and Robot Venues: Resources for AI Education*, AAAI Press, 65-68.

[4] Lauwers, T., Hamner, E., and Nourbakhsh, I. 2010. A strategy for collaborative outreach: lessons from the CSbots project. *Proceedings of SIGCSE 2010*, ACM, 315-319.

[5] http://modelai.gettysburg.edu

[6] Neller, T. W., Presser, C. G., Russell, I., and Markov, Z. 2006. Pedagogical possibilities for the dice game pig. *J. Comput. Small Coll.* 21, 6 (Jun. 2006), 149-161.

[7] Parlante, N., Zelenski, J, et al. 2010. Nifty assignments, *Proceedings of SIGCSE 2010*, ACM, 478-479.

[8] Touretzky, D. S. 2010. Preparing computer science students for the robotics revolution. *Communications of the ACM*, 53(8), 27-29.

[9] Williams, A. B. and O'Banner, W. 2008. SpelBots: Using Autonomous Robotics to Inspire Women to Participate in Computer Science. *Proceedings of AAAI Spring Symposium: Using AI to Motivate Greater Participation in Computer Science*, AAAI Press, 108-109.

[10] Wong, D., Zink, R., and Koenig, S. 2010. Teaching Artificial Intelligence and Robotics via Games. *Proceedings of EAAI 2010*, AAAI Press.

[11] Zyda, M. and Koenig, S. 2008. Teaching Artificial Intelligence Playfully. *Proceedings of the AAAI-08 Education Colloquium*, AAAI Press, 90-95.

Learning Through Open Source Participation

Heidi J. C. Ellis
Western New England College
1215 Wilbraham Road
Springfield, MA 01119
hellis@wnec.edu

Mel Chua
Red Hat
1801 Varsity Drive
Raleigh, North Carolina 27606
mel@redhat.com

Matthew C. Jadud
Allegheny College
520 N. Main St.
Meadville, PA 16335
matthew.c@jadud.com

Gregory W. Hislop
(Moderator)
Drexel University
3141 Chestnut St.
Philadelphia, PA 19104
hislop@drexel.edu

Categories and Subject Descriptors

K.3.2 [**Computers and Education**]: Computer and Information Science Education – *Computer Science Education*

General Terms

Human Factors

Keywords

Open source software, faculty development, education

1. SUMMARY

There are many mature free open source software (FOSS) and documentation projects that provide excellent learning opportunities for students. In the context of active learning, communities that surround open source projects are particularly interesting as they are transparent meritocracies that allow students to observe, study, and, best of all, contribute as part of their learning. In exploring the learning opportunities that come from students engaging in open source projects, educators also believe that these projects are intrinsically motivating. They provide an opportunity for ongoing self-regulated learning in the context of working on large-scale projects, to interact with experienced developers and content creators, and to see meaningful, real-world outcomes as a result of their efforts.

This panel will present four different perspectives on student involvement in FOSS projects. Matt Jadud will present a variety of different ways that students can contribute to FOSS projects beyond code including writing, communicating, bug fixing, and more. Mel Chua will present the industry perspective on student involvement in FOSS projects including motivation for the FOSS community to be open to students as well as the challenges presented by student involvement. Heidi Ellis will discuss how Humanitarian FOSS can provide a welcoming environment for student learning including identifying some of the characteristics of more approachable FOSS projects. Greg Hislop will present the viewpoint of faculty involving the students in FOSS including a discussion of barriers to faculty involvement and how such barriers can be overcome.

2. HEIDI ELLIS – HUMANITARIAN FOSS

FOSS projects with a humanitarian nature, Humanitarian FOSS or HFOSS, have been shown to motivate students in pursuing computing degrees while providing them with the opportunity to better the human condition in some fashion. Students across all levels of computing experience find participating in an HFOSS project motivating and students with less computing background indicate that participating in an HFOSS project has caused them to consider computing as a major or at least taking further computing courses. However, the ease of involving students in HFOSS projects varies across communities.

Heidi will discuss the factors that impact the ease or difficulty with which students become involved in an HFOSS project. She will report on experiences of students in a senior-level Software Engineering course at Western New England College. Students are working on Caribou which is a GNOME Accessibility project. Caribou is an onscreen keyboard that is accessible to users needing to interact with the computer using a pointing device. Students are involved in the GNOME Accessibility community and are investigating ways to make the application more robust. As part of the course, students in the Software Engineering course will introduce freshman Computer Science and Information Technology majors to HFOSS and hopefully generate excitement in computing in our new majors.

In addition to the Software Engineering class working on the Caribou project, there are several Western New England College students who are participating in other HFOSS projects as part of independent study courses. These students are both CS and IT majors and are exploring ways that both groups can contribute to HFOSS projects. Heidi will report on the experiences of these students with joining and interacting with their respective HFOSS communities.

SIGCSE'11, March 9–12, 2011, Dallas, Texas, USA.
ACM 978-1-4503-0500-6/11/03.

3. MATT JADUD – BEYOND COMPUTING

Large, open projects provide opportunities for what Jean Lave and Etienne Wenger describe as *legitimate peripheral participation*. This means that it is possible for a classroom full of students studying computing (or literature or psychology) to contribute meaningfully to a project with hundreds or even thousands of contributors by beginning their work on the edge of a community (perhaps by fixing typos in a wiki page or reporting bugs), and if they continue contributing, they can grow naturally into increasingly central roles within the project. There is great power in immersing a class in a decentralized community of contributors, and it is our responsibility as computing educators to introduce students to the world of open collaboration.

In computing, open projects force students to communicate and collaborate in ways that traditional pedagogic approaches eschew: we get teamwork for free, and that matters. In the context of robotics and embedded systems work at Allegheny College, students have contributed to open software and documentation projects (like the work done on the Flying Gator UAV and a Creative Commons licensed text regarding parallel programming for for embedded systems). For example, in our course regarding human-centered design, students work directly with open communities to improve the end-user's experience of living, shipping software[1]. Students can write documentation, conduct interviews, design logos, all while using mailing lists, wikis, and IRC to collaborate with open source communities.

4. MEL CHUA – FOSS COMMUNITY

Red Hat, Fedora, and other open communities have worked on "on-ramping" student into FOSS participation using projects like the POSSE workshop for professors[2], summer camps for high school students, undergraduate co-op mentorships, and more. Through working with the professors in the Teaching Open Source community, we've come to recognize some commmon elements of successful engagements for bridging the FOSS and academic worlds.

First, a successful engagement must focus on helping students become independent do-ers. Students need to learn not just how to use tools, but how to join a community of toolmakers. FOSS communities are full of self-sufficient and intrinsically motivated makers, and the artifacts they create as they learn (chat logs, blog posts, code and code reviews) are openly licensed and freely available so students can "learn to do" from (and alongside) role models beyond their campus context, with professors alongside to help them analyze and reflect on the experiences they're encountering. In the FOSS world, we call this being *productively lost*.

Second, the engagement must immerse students in whole-project thinking, seeing where their individual contributions fit into a large and complex system. Open source projects operate in the real world, where large projects with distributed and diverse teams rely on many types of people—project management, design, marketing, testing, support, translation, documentation, and so forth—in order to get a software product to make a difference in the lives of its users. Each of these roles is one that students can step into from day one. As they do so, the community helps guide them through the process of negotiating technical and social interfaces with other groups on the project that fill diverse roles and may work in dramatically different contexts.

Third, the people involved in the engagement need to make sure that learning and insight flows in both directions. The academic world can benefit from the authentic learning experiences and transparency of open source communities, but open source contributors also have a tremendous amount to learn from students and professors, such as how to reflect on their own growth as learners. FOSS projects, with their "sink or swim" mentality, are notoriously bad at helping newcomers participate. The diversity and retention rates of our communities could be much improved by thinking critically about the participatory scaffolding we build. This is exactly what educators do year after year, getting students established as self-sufficient new contributors to a discipline that may initially be unfamiliar to them.

5. GREG HISLOP – FACULTY ADOPTION

It is generally easy to convince faculty that student participation in FOSS offers excellent learning opportunities. However, faculty belief in the potential value of FOSS participation will not necessarily cause them to incorporate FOSS activities into their courses. There are a variety of issues and obstacles that may hinder adoption.

To begin, FOSS participation may require that faculty master new material. Most likely, the faculty member will need to learn about the FOSS project. They may also need to learn about development processes and tools used by the FOSS project. Even if faculty are comfortable with commercial software development, they may not be familiar with the particular approaches used in FOSS projects. The total amount to learn can be considerable, and faculty time for professional development is scarce.

Second, FOSS participation requires interacting with a FOSS project community. These communities are often globally distributed, and consist of a mix of full-time professionals and part-time, volunteer participants. In addition to taking time, community dependence and interaction introduces uncertainty into the course that may make faculty uncomfortable. It also requires mutual adjustment in schedule and expectations as participants figure out how to map a fixed length term to a FOSS project schedule.

Third, the students in a particular class section represent a varied workforce. Knowledge, skill, and ability to learn and self-direct typically vary greatly across a set of students. In addition, student interest and motivation for a particular course can also impact results. Faculty members need to not only grade student results, but most likely will need to manage student contribution to the FOSS project to ensure that contribution quality is sufficient.

6. ACKNOWLEDGMENTS

This material is based on work supported by the National Science Foundation under Grant Nos. DUE-0736874, DUE-0722137, DUE-0940925, and DUE-0940893 Any opinions, findings and conclusions or recommendations expressed in this material are those of the author(s) and do not necessarily reflect the views of the National Science Foundation (NSF).

[1] `http://rockalypse.org/courses/cmpsc303f10/`
[2] `http://teachingopensource.org/index.php/POSSE`

The CS10K Project: Mobilizing the Community to Transform High School Computing

Owen Astrachan
Duke University
Durham, NC
ola@cs.duke.edu

Jan Cuny
National Science Foundation
Arlington, VA
jcuny@nsf.gov

Chris Stephenson
Executive Director, CSTA
New York, NY
cstephenson@csta.acm.org

Cameron Wilson
Director of Public Policy, ACM
Washington DC
cameron.wilson@acm.org

Categories and Subject Descriptors

K.3.2 [**Computers and Education**]: Computer and Information Science Education – *computer science education*

General Terms

Measurement, Experimentation, Standardization .

Keywords

Computer Science Education, K-12 Curriculum, CS Principles, Computational Thinking.

1. SUMMARY

The CS10K project is a large-scale, collaborative project bringing together stakeholders from wide-ranging constituencies with the goal of systematically changing the scale, curriculum, and pedagogy of teaching computer science at all levels, but focusing in particular on computer science in U.S. high schools as well as introductory computing at the college level. As part of the systemic changes in teaching computer science the CS10K project aims to have 10,000 teachers in 10,000 high schools teaching a new curriculum by 2015.

The CS10K project will require building substantial collaborations between a consortium of partners – including academia at all levels, government agencies, industry, and private foundations – to assist in all aspects of the effort. In this special session, suitable for teachers and educators from all levels, we will report on the goals of the CS10K project, the motivation for the project, its scope, and progress to date of the project. This builds on work reported on in [1][2] and provides an overarching view of the CS10K project with an appeal to the broad computing community to be involved with the project.

Computer Science and computing education is our field of endeavor. We all work to ensure that our field is vibrant, growing, and successful. If computing is to be part of both the academic and future workforce leading to innovation, there is no stage in the academic pipeline more crucial than high school. Students do begin to lose interest in computing much earlier, but engagement programs for K-8 will not be effective if students who become engaged before high school lose that engagement and interest during their high school years. Likewise, revitalized computing programs cannot have a significant impact if too few students take our courses and use our methods.

SIGCSE'11, March 9–12, 2011, Dallas, Texas, USA.
ACM 978-1-4503-0500-6/11/03.

2. Objectives and Organization

We will report on the CS10K project from four perspectives represented by each of the participants. The goal of the session is to help the computing education community understand the scope and potential of the CS10K project and to appeal to the community to help the project succeed. We will be encouraging feedback and active involvement both as part of the session and in ongoing roles for those interested in participating in the CS10K project.

3. Motivation (Chris Stephenson)

There are several projects aimed at making changes in high school computer science. Many of these are referenced and accessible from the CSTA web site [3]. For example, the *Exploring Computer Science* project based on work by Margolis *et al* [6,7,8] is transforming Computer Science education in the Los Angeles Unified School District. Elsewhere the *Georgia Computes!* [9] Project is having a broad impact in Georgia. The framework provided by the ACM K-12 Model Curriculum [3] guides these projects, but their scope is statewide rather than national. The CS Principles project, a component of the CS10K initiative, is national in scope and leverages College Board's Advanced Placement courses to facilitate widespread changes in high school curricula at a national level. These changes must be accompanied by corresponding changes at the college/university level for reasons outlined in [4]. At this session we will talk about how important it is for the entire community to be involved in this initiative, why the CS10K project is a national (if not international) imperative, and how the different stakeholders are working together.

As the executive director of CSTA, Chris Stephenson is spearheading the active involvement of high school teachers and policy makers at both state and national levels in supporting the CS10K project.

4. CS Principles (Owen Astrachan)

The CS Principles course is the national lever by which we hope to move high school computing. This is a national project, with an advisory board of roughly thirty scientists and educators who are developing a new, rigorous introduction to computer science. The process guiding the development and implementation of the CS Principles course has been reported previously [1][2] and documents about the course and its 2010-2011 pilots are available from [5]. This proposed course is being developed at the post secondary level before it is taught in high schools, but the development and delivery are being done with tight coordination of high school policy makers and teachers.

At this session we will report on the curriculum framework developed for the CS Principles course using a process designated by the College Board as the method by which Advanced Placement courses are modified, designed, and re-designed. We will be looking to chairs of computer science departments to endorse this effort as part of beginning the second phase of piloting the course. This endorsement will be a prerequisite for the widespread dissemination of the CS Principles course and an effort we hope to actively engage the community in as part of this special session.

As the PI of the CS Principles course, Owen Astrachan is helping to coordinate the group of educators who are developing curricula and tests for a new, national course.

5. 10,000 Teachers in 10,000 Schools (Jan Cuny)

Curriculum, however, is not the biggest challenge. The biggest challenge will be scaling teacher training to reach 10,000 teachers. Many of the current high school computing courses teach only basic literacy and few of our current high school teachers have a formal CS background. We will launch an unprecedented preparation program, working with in-service as well as pre-service teachers in both traditional and alternative certification programs. We will pair face-to-face training with extensive, state-of-the-art online support that includes curricula, materials, and social networking. We will provide high-quality, ongoing professional development. To accomplish this, we will need to call on the resources of university faculty, undergraduate and graduate students in service learning programs, and IT professionals serving as citizen scientists.

Here we will report on the status of the effort to get the proposed new AP course into 10,000 schools by 2015 (which is the earliest date that a new AP course could be available). We will report on efforts supported by the National Science Foundation, as well as possible alignment with programs of other government agencies and foundations. We will also issue a "call to action," presenting ways for members of our computing community and their students can become involved.

In her role at NSF Jan Cuny is leading the development of the CS10K project and is the principle architect of the initiatives we will report on here.

6. Policy Concerns (Cameron Wilson)

The CS10K project is one aspect of several national and statewide initiatives aimed at increasing the role of computing and computer science in STEM education as well as increasing the number of students from under-represented groups studying computer science. Coordination and understanding of the different initiatives is an important aspect in ensuring the potential for success of the CS10K project. In this session we will report on the synergies between this project and initiatives including the Computing in the Core Coalition, the CS Education Act recently introduced in Congress, and several statewide initiatives built around computing and computer science.

As Director of ACM's Office of Public Policy, Cameron Wilson coordinates and provides guidance on state and national policy aspects relating to the CS10K project.

7. Intended Audience

This special session is a call-for-participation to all computing and computer science educators to help ensure the success of the CS10K project. Educators at every level will be asked to help with the project and will be interested in the different aspects of the project reported in this special session.

8. REFERENCES

[1] Re-Imagining the First Year of Computing, Astrachan, Haynie, Stephenson, Diaz, Briggs, Proceedings of SIGCSE 2010, 329-330

[2] Advanced Placement Computer Science: The Future of Tracking the First Year of Computing. Astrachan, Walker, Stephenson, Diaz, Cuny. Proceedings of SIGCSE 2009.

[3] http://csta.acm.org

[4] NRC, *Learning and Understanding: Improving Advanced Study of Mathematics and Science in U.S. High Schools,* 2002 http://www.nap.edu/openbook.php?record_id=10129

[5] CS Principles Web Site: http://www.csprinciples.org

[6] Exploring Computer Science, Margolis, Goode, Chapman http://intotheloop.gseis.ucla.edu/exploring.html

[7] Jane Margolis, Rachel Estrella, Joanna Goode, Jennifer Jellison Holme, Kimberly Nao. Stuck in the Shallow End. MIT Press, 2008.

[8] Jane Margolis and Allan Fisher. Unlocking the Clubhouse: Women in Computing. MIT Press, 2003.

[9] Georgia Computes! http://gacomputes.cc.gatech.edu

Minimally Invasive Programming Courses – Learning OOP With(out) Instruction

Marc Berges
Technische Universität München
Fakultät für Informatik
Boltzmannstr. 3
D-85748 Garching, Germany
+49 (89) 289 17353
Berges@tum.de

Peter Hubwieser
Technische Universität München
Fakultät für Informatik
Boltzmannstr. 3
D-85748 Garching, Germany
+49 (89) 289 17350
Peter.Hubwieser@tum.de

ABSTRACT

In this paper, we describe a research project that investigates how far freshmen at the University (without any programming background) are able to learn object-oriented programming with as little (human) instruction as possible. We designed specific tasks for programming assignments and supporting worksheets that contained the only information input that the students received during the courses. We examined the program code the students produced in order to assess the quality of their products. The surprising result was that most of the students were able to write quite satisfying programs. Additionally, a cluster analysis of the results showed that there are two different types of students: the ones that accept and apply the object-oriented concepts quite willingly, while the others prefer to program in a more traditional, procedural style.

Categories and Subject Descriptors

K.3.2 [Computer and Information Science Education] Computer science education

General Terms

Algorithms, Human Factors, Languages, Experimentation

Keywords

Programming projects, higher education, programming novices, self-conducted learning, object-oriented programming

1. INTRODUCTION

In order to investigate the limitations of self-learning in the context of object-oriented programming, we invited the freshmen of our Faculty of Informatics to participate in small programming courses that took place before the start of the regular courses of their first semester. The basic idea was that there should be no direct human instruction at all. The only information the students would receive would be written on three worksheets.

Every year, our Faculty welcomes about 300 freshmen that start their computer science studies. Unfortunately, most of them don't have any previous experience in programming. Obviously, this causes many serious problems during the first year's courses. On the one hand, these students often have problems following the more theoretical lessons, because they don't have any idea how to apply all the theory. On the other hand, there isn't enough time left to practice programming in order to improve their skills. Much too often, they end up dropping out of the studies. Due to this situation, many freshmen welcome our invitation to the programming courses.

Our projects started shortly before the academic year 2008/09. Preceding the academic year 2009/10, we organized a second generation of introductory programming courses (called "pre-projects"). Altogether about 300 students or 50% of all freshmen participated in these courses. Additionally, we offered similarly organized courses with more challenging tasks to the students after their first semester ("post-projects"). This second type of projects will be described in another publication.

The program code written by the students helps us to investigate the learning processes of programming novices. Additionally, we will conduct a longitudinal research study by comparing the results of the projects over several years. This might show how the programming skills of our novices will vary over several generations of students. Particularly interesting will be the result of the academic year 2011/12, because at that time we will welcome the first student generation that has attended the new compulsory subject of computer science at the secondary schools of our state, whose curriculum was designed mainly by our working group [5].

In this paper, we describe the design of the pre-projects and present the first "ad-hoc"-results in order to show how successful the students have worked. Additionally, we show some possible research questions that might be answered by more closely investigating the programs of the students.

2. RELATED WORK

In the last few years the engagement of the students in the introductory courses was a central topic for many CS instructors. After the improvement of the lectures, the focus was shifted to programming issues. In 2009, Hansen and his colleagues analyzed a student survey about the engagement and frustration in programming projects that attended their CS introductory courses. They tried to find out, which of their assignments are considered to be engaging. [8]

Another major discussion that is fundamental for our work is the question about the role of programming in introductory computing courses. Henry Walker emphasizes the need of programming skills as an "essential vehicle" to achieve the problem-solving skills [9]. This is one of the central ideas behind our courses.

We are trying to figure out how much instruction is necessary to understand and use OOP. One of the first projects dealing with "minimal invasive" instruction was the "Hole-in-the-Wall"-project of Sugata Mitra. In [10] he introduced a model on how children acquire computing skills without supervision. We transferred this idea to programming skills.

The working group around Jürgen Börstler evaluated OO Example Programs for CS1 [11]. The evaluation of the program code that the students produced is one of the future goals of our work.

3. THE DESIGN OF OUR COURSES

The students were divided into small groups of 10-12 individuals that shared a room and a tutor, but still each student worked individually on his/her own assignments. Unlike the problems encountered by novice pair programmers, described in [12], we wanted to investigate the limitations of self-guided learning in OOP.

Each group was coached by a tutor, usually an experienced student of the 5th or higher semester. The coaches were advised to help the students with practical tips or by explaining the worksheets or the IDE, but were strictly told not to give any instructions beyond this. Besides the tutor, the students had access to instructional sites on the internet. Forced by organizational circumstances, we had to limit the working time of each student group to two and a half days. During this very short period, every student had to complete his/her own small program. Due to the requirements of the curriculum of our faculty, we had to use *Java* as the programming language. Following didactical guidelines, we suggested to use the *BlueJ*-IDE to develop and test the first classes. After the first steps, the students had the choice to continue their project work using *Eclipse*.

The courses took place four weeks before the regular semester started. At the time of registration for their projects, the students had to self-assess their programming skills. They were asked to assess their programming experience in one of three levels: (1) "I have no experience at all", (2) "I have already written programs", and (3) "I have already written object-oriented programs". The working groups were composed homogenously in line with these levels, as we had designed a specific type of assignment for each level. The groups of level 1 were asked to program a "Mastermind" game, while the groups of level 2 were required to write a tool for managing game results, e.g. within a football league. The groups of level 3 were given the task of creating the dice game "Yahzee".

This paper is focused on the results of the students of level 1 ("Mastermind"), because this group represents the most interesting type of participants for us: the "absolute beginners". For this group, the preconditions are very clear. The students of the other two levels had written some programs before and thus had already worked with various programming languages. Therefore, their prior knowledge is very difficult to assess. The "Mastermind"-task was formulated as follows:

```
One of two players sets a four-digit number.
The other player tries to find out which four
digits from zero to nine are building the
number. Therefore, she/he places a four-digit
number as a guess. After each guess, the first
player responds (1) how many digits are
correct and (2) how many digits are correct
and additionally in the correct position. The
goal of the game is to guess the right number
as fast as possible, but at least in twelve
steps.
```

4. THE WORKSHEETS

The main idea of the pre-projects is the absence of any instruction by a teaching assistant, because we wanted to figure out the limitations to self-guided learning on the topic of object-oriented programming. We also did not want to interfere with the theoretical introductory courses of the regular curriculum of our faculty. Despite this, we had to give the freshmen just sufficient information to enable them to complete their projects. Therefore, we created three worksheets [13], which contained all relevant information they required for this purpose.

In their paper [2] Schulte and Ehlert compared the "objects-first" and the "objects-later" strategies and defined a list of object-oriented concepts, that form a typical teaching sequence leading to the ability of object-oriented programming: Classes and objects – Attributes (incl. data types) – Methods (incl. control statements) – Inheritance – Association. We designed our worksheets following this sequence. The items "Inheritance" and "Association" were omitted, because we did not expect the students to understand them without instruction.

The first worksheet gives a short introduction to the basic concepts of object-orientation: objects, classes, attributes and methods. Furthermore, it presents the classification of objects and the representation of classes in UML. One of the most important issues of the first worksheet is encapsulation or rather information hiding in object orientation. This is one of the central principles, which the freshmen should internalize as soon as possible.

The second sheet presents the implementation of the basic concepts of object orientation in Java, which are described textually, as well as by syntax diagrams, as shown in [1] (see Figure 1). It explains the concepts of classes, constructor methods, attribute declaration and initialization, method declaration with or without parameters, data types and value assignments. The explanation of declaration, initialization and the usage of arrays are the most important issues of the worksheet. Schulte and Ehlert argue in [2], that arrays are one of the most difficult concepts of programming in general.

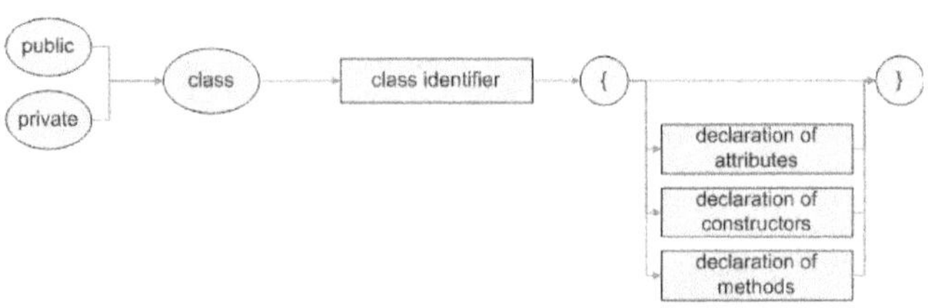

Figure 1: Syntax diagram of Java class structure

The third worksheet presents the concept of algorithms and their control structures (sequential and conditional processing, repetition) as well as their implementation in Java. Additionally, the call of methods and the creation of instances of objects were explained. Finally, the application of a "main"- method and the standard input and output mechanisms in Java were described. For the implementation of user input we offered a specific framework to the students. .

Due to the very short time the students had left to learn programming we had to focus on the most important concepts of object-oriented programming in Java. That was the main purpose of our worksheets. If we had presented a textbook to the students, as it is practiced in the regular introductory course in the first term, the students would hardly have been able to figure out what information is relevant for their projects. Using the worksheets, we could define exactly what information the students would receive.

5. GATHERING OF DATA

The first and most obvious question was, whether the absolute beginners would be able to write a "really working" Java program at all during the very short time of two and a half days. The students were asked to fill out a questionnaire in order to get their personal variables.

5.1 Drawing the sample

The complete population of the second generation of the courses contained the code of 93 programs. As we wanted to compare the code of programs from students with similar prerequisite knowledge, we restricted our investigation to a sample of 37 projects by the following three criteria.

The first criterion was the supposed previous subject domain knowledge in computer science (beyond pure programming skills), which turned out to be very heterogeneous. To ensure that all members of the sample had similar previous knowledge, we restricted the sample to all freshmen that had stated that they had not attended any prior courses in computer science or informatics at school and that graduated from a school within our state, where computer science or informatics was not mandatory for the students that graduated (or will graduate) before 2011. This way we assured that all members of the sample had the same prior school education in computer science (namely none). Indeed, this was the majority of our population.

The second restriction was formed by the self-assessed experience in programming. We restricted the sample to all students that classified themselves to the programming experience level 1 ("I have no experience at all", see above), as the previous programming knowledge of the students of level 2 and 3 was very different, e.g. concerning the different programming languages and styles they had already used. The restriction to the (most interesting) "absolute beginners" made the sample quite homogeneous.

One of the problems encountered in the first generation of the projects in 2008 was the assignment of the prerequisite knowledge of a certain student to its program. Without knowing the prior knowledge it is hardly possible to evaluate the results the students produced.

This problem was solved in the second generation of the projects in 2009 by numbering the questionnaires and inserting this number in each class file as a comment. By using this method it was possible to match the program code to the answers on the questionnaires and thus to the corresponding prerequisite knowledge without sacrificing anonymity.

5.2 The questionnaire

The personal questionnaire was composed of four sections, where the second section contained three subsections. For this paper, only the first section with the personal data and the third section with the self-assessment of the students are relevant. The second section asks for the opinion about the organization and the fourth section is open for individual comments and critical remarks.

We collected the following personal data: gender, age, prior studies, previous knowledge, prior school education, and state or country of origin.

In the self-assessment section, we asked the following three questions:

SA1) "How much did you learn in the pre-projects?"

SA2) "How do you estimate your Java knowledge after the pre-projects?"

SA3) "Did you understand the concept of object-orientation?"

6. EVALUATION OF THE PROGRAMS

After drawing our sample described above, we inspected the program code of the corresponding 37 Java projects.

6.1 Syntactical Correctness

The first aspect we investigated was the syntactical correctness of the programs. For this purpose, the programs of each student were compiled as *Eclipse*-projects, including all necessary libraries.

32 of the 37 examined programs could be successfully compiled after importing them into *Eclipse*. Two programs were missing the corresponding class for the input framework. After inserting this class, these two programs were also compiled successfully. One program even contained a first attempt to implement a graphical user interface. For this purpose a class from a *BlueJ* example project was used. After importing this class into *Eclipse*, this program was also compiled without any problems. Two programs could not be compiled: one because of a small syntax error, the other because it was just fragmental code without making sense.

Although the time for programming was very short and there was a complete lack of instruction by a teacher, all but two programs from our sample could be compiled, some with minor modifications to the code. Nevertheless, we have to take into account, that modern code editors like Eclipse offer many hints that allowed the students to solve syntactical problems following a "trial and error" strategy.

6.2 Fulfillment of the specifications

The fact that nearly all programs could be compiled is only a very weak indicator for the success of the pre-projects. Another more convincing argument could arise from the correctness of the "Mastermind" programs.

Therefore, we tested the program code with two exemplary inputs, one with a special case of four identical digits, e.g. "1111", the second with a quite general form of user input (four different figures to guess, e.g. 3456). A big challenge for the programmers was the calculation of the number of right positions in the special case. If the user guesses only one of the four (equal) digits in the number, the program has to return correctly only one right digit position. The rest of the digits are still not guessed correctly. Only 18 out of the 37 programs could handle numbers with identical digits. In some programs, numbers with two or more equal digits were not accepted at all. In the programs where the computer generated the input, mostly equal digits were not accepted.

The second, more general input example was 3456, which was correctly processed by 26 out of the 37 programs. These programs returned the correct amount of digits and positions. Eleven programs did not accept this input at all. One had a problem with the computer-generated number. Another one had only one user input at the beginning and continued without any further user input. A third one could perform only one guessing action. The other projects did not calculate the correct number of positions or digits.

Half of the programs took the number to be guessed from user input, while the other 19 generated the number by random. For this purpose, the students had to find out how to apply the random function of the *Math* package in Java.

In summary, regarding compilation and functionality, about 50% of the tested projects worked absolutely correct, both with the input "1111" and "3456".

6.3 Implementation of programming concepts

Another very interesting question was which of the concepts that were explained on the three worksheets would be applied by the students in their programs. We extracted the concepts from the worksheets, ordered them in a list by their appearance on the sheets and investigated, which of them were applied by the students. The list looked as follows:

C1) **Order of attributes, constructors and methods in class definitions:** On the second sheet we presented a code sample that showed the correct order of attributes, constructors and methods in a class definition.

C2) **Initialization of attributes with default values in the constructor:** All attributes are set to a default value; arrays are initialized.

C3) **Constructors with parameters:** In the section about constructors on the worksheet the possibility of overloading a constructor was shown.

C4) **Initialization of attributes with default values:** We stressed the initialization of all attributes before they are used.

C5) **Return values of methods:** Did the students use the "return" statement to pass values from methods or did they only operate on global variables?

C6) **Parameters of methods:** Did the students use input parameters or operate on global variables or attributes?

C7) **Access modifiers of methods:** Not all methods have to be public. Did the students mark some of them as private?

C8) **Arrays:** Did the students use arrays?

C9) **Self reference by "this":** Using the same name for attributes and parameters in methods can improve the readability of the code. Did the students use "this" in constructors or methods?

C10) **Main-method:** At the beginning of the pre-projects, the students used *BlueJ*. This IDE allows the direct interactive call of methods without implementing a "main" method. At the end of their work, the students were asked to execute their programs without the usage of *BlueJ*, so they had to implement a "main"-method.

C11) **Conditional statement** The students should use the "if"-construct with "else" if necessary (instead of two separated "if"-constructs).

C12) **"While-Do" repetition:** "While-Do" was the first form of repetition that was explained on the worksheets.

C13) **"Do-While" repetition:** The "Do-While" repetition was presented on the worksheets after "While-Do".

C14) **"For" repetition:** The "For"-repetition was the last form of repetition on the worksheet. The students should use this type if the total amount of repeats is known already before the first one starts.

Figure 2 shows how many of the 37 inspected projects used the concepts C1 – C14, ordered by the frequency of usage. Obviously, some of the concepts are used very rarely, e.g. C3 (constructor method with parameters), which was implemented by only one student. Several other concepts were also not applied very often: C6 (parameters of methods), C13 (do-while), C9 (this), C7 (access modifiers of methods), and C5 (return values).

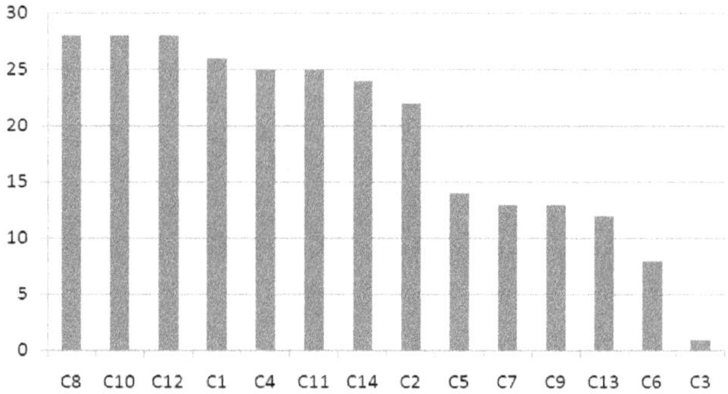

Figure 2: Frequency of the Implementation

On the contrary, the concepts C8 (arrays), C10 (main method) and C12 (while do) have been applied in most of the programs. Thus, these seem to be relatively easy to understand.

The interpretation of the remaining concepts is left to the next section, where conceptions of object orientation will be discussed.

In order to identify different types of students concerning their attitude towards object orientation, we performed a cluster-analysis on the matrix of dichotomous data that is formed by the criteria C1–C14 as columns and the programs as rows (1 in the cell with index ki means that criterion k is applied in project i). The cluster analysis was carried out by the Gnu R software [7]. To make the interpretation of the results more convenient, we rearrange our criteria C1–C14 in three different groups (see Table 1): (A) Algorithmic concepts and their implementation in Java, (F) Functional concepts, (OO) object oriented concepts.

Table1: Renaming and Reordering for the Clusteranalysis

Name	A1	A2	A3	A4	-	F1	F2
Concept	C11	C12	C14	C8	C13	C4	C5
Name	F3	OO1	OO2	OO3	OO4	OO5	-
Concept	C6	C1	C2	C7	C10	C9	C3

The concept C3 was omitted for the cluster analysis, because there was only one student who applied it. We also omitted C13, because the "do-while" repetition was not suitable to the regarded "Mastermind" programs.

As can be seen in Figure 3, the cluster analysis resulted in two groups. The y-axis represents the probability that the concepts on the x-axis are applied in a project that belongs to cluster 1 or cluster 2 respectively. Cluster 1 contains eleven projects (30%), cluster 2 26 projects (70%). It is evident that concept OO4 (C10: main-method) is differently applied than the other OO-concepts. This might result from its ambivalent character between object-oriented (as a "starter" for the creation of the objects) and procedural programming (C programs need main methods, too). Thus, it is applied similarly often by both clusters.

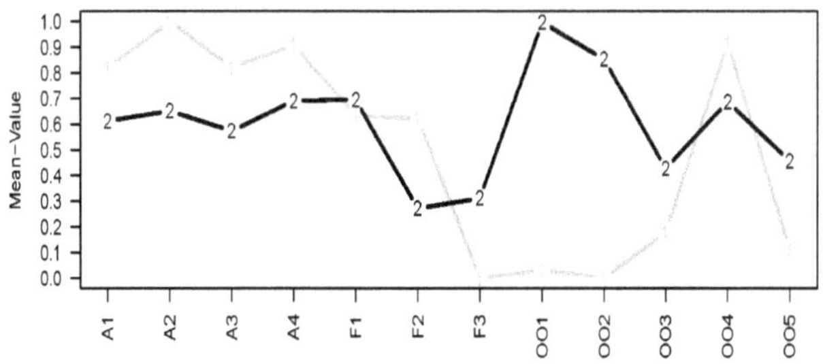

Figure 3: Cluster analysis over the applied concepts

Concerning the other concepts we received a quite interesting result: The students, whose projects belong to cluster 1 seem to have more problems in applying the object-oriented concepts OO1, OO2, OO3 and OO5, but are relatively strong in some of the functional and in all the algorithmic principles. The students of cluster 2 applied most of the concepts quite frequently, except for the functional F2 and F3. The distinction between the two clusters is mainly caused by the concepts OO1 (order in class definitions) and OO2 (initializing attributes in constructors).

Both clusters have nearly the same gender proportion as the total population of students (62% male, 38% female).

6.4 Characteristics of "Object Orientation"

The main purpose of our pre-projects is to investigate the learning process of object-oriented programming (OOP), see [6]. But what is OOP? Unfortunately, many different definitions of OO can be found in literature. Because there is no common definition, it is very hard to state which features a program should have in order to be regarded as "object oriented". Nevertheless, we looked for a set of criteria that allows us to compare programs regarding their "degree of object orientation". At first, we give a short definition of an "object":

"An object is, in simple terms, composed of two types of information, the data and logic information components. An object does not have to have both types of information simultaneously, and can contain data and logic or just logic. The object must contain logic, because, as we shall see, the data component cannot be accessed except via the logic component. The data component is optional." [4, p.42].

Unfortunately, for a comprehensive view on our programs this simple definition does not suffice. Thomas and Sanders gave a summary of concepts and misconceptions regarding OOP in [3]. Most of the misconceptions discussed by them are irrelevant for small projects like ours. Nevertheless, we picked five of their concepts that are relevant even for programs of the scale of our pre-projects:

(O1) Constructors are defined and used

(O2) Methods other than constructors are defined and used

(O3) Methods' return value are used

(O4) The attributes are encapsulated

(O5) At least one instance of a class is created

In figure 4, we give an overview how far these five concepts were implemented in our programs. As you can see, nearly all students applied O1 and O2. In most programs, a constructor was defined, but as we stated in section 6.3 only one student wrote a constructor with parameters. The concept that was used the least was O3. Only a few students used return values for their methods. Most of them worked with global variables instead. At this point, there seem to be difficulties in the understanding of the concept of methods. O4 and O5 deal with information hiding and instantiating. Therefore, they are one of the central concepts of OOP. More than 60% of our students implemented these concepts.

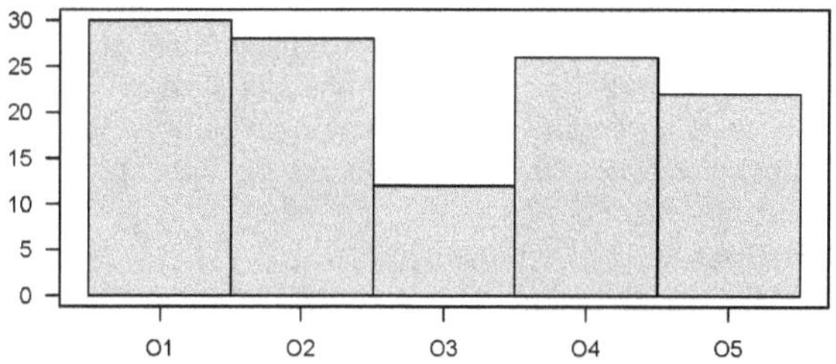

Figure 4: Implementation of the OO concepts

According to the five OO-concepts above, we tried to perform a grading of the degree of "object orientation" of the programs. We simply counted how many of these 5 concepts where implemented in each program and graded the program from "very poor" (0 concepts applied) to "perfect" (all 5 concepts applied). As shown in figure 5, three programs have applied all five concepts. In summary, we found 1 very poor, 6 poor, 18 average, 9 good and 3 perfect programs, concerning their degree of object orientation.

The large number of average programs correlates to the self-assessment of the students concerning the knowledge in Java programming they gained during the pre-projects.

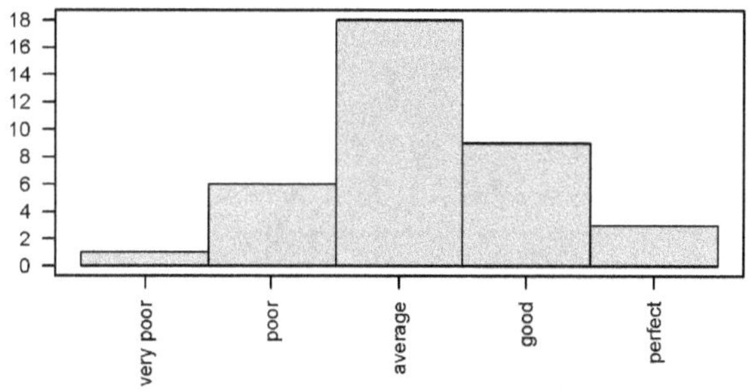

Figure 5: Grading of the projects

6.5 Self-assessment of the students

To get an idea how the students assessed their programming abilities after the courses, we asked them three questions which are listed in 5.2.

Each question could be answered on a scale from one to five. We calculated the mean values for the whole sample as well as for each of the two clusters. The results are shown in table 2.

The question SA1 could be answered from 1 "learned a lot" to 5 "learned only a few things". As can be seen in table 2, the results (average of 2.2) were the same for the whole sample as for both of the clusters.

Table 2: Mean-Value of the Self-Assessment

	Sample	Cluster1	Cluster2
SA1	2.2	2.2	2.2
SA2	2.1	1.7	2.2
SA3	2.4	2.3	2.4

In question SA2 the difference between the clusters and the whole sample is much clearer. The possible answers started from 1 "can program on my own" to 5 "no Java knowledge present". The self-estimation of the Java-knowledge in cluster 1 is significantly better than that of cluster 2. The members of cluster 1 think they have understood more of the programming concepts. It might be that the stronger algorithmic skills of the students of this cluster led to a better functionality of their programs, which resulted in a higher satisfaction of the programmers.

Question SA3 that could be answered from 1 "understood OO" to 5 "did not understand OO" also shows the result of the cluster-analysis. Cluster 1 rated their understanding of the OO-concepts a bit lower than the members of cluster 2. This is quite surprising regarding the different application of object-oriented concepts in the two clusters.

In the next step of our studies, we will have to prove that there is a real correlation between the self-assessment of the students and the analysis of the results of their work.

7. CONCLUSIONS AND FUTURE WORK

Although the tutors were advised quite strictly not to instruct the students, their contribution to the students' products is still very difficult to assess. One of the most interesting questions which has to be answered in future work is how much help is to be given by them really. Therefore, we are going to match the tutors to the questionnaires. To avoid a lack of anonymity we will assign a color to each tutor. With this matching we will find out if there is a correlation between the cluster the student belongs to and the tutors that helped him/her. The questions the tutors are asked by the students will also be gathered in the next semester.

After evaluating more than 300 questionnaires of the participating students we can state that most of the students appreciated the pre-projects and suggested that they had learned something essential (about 90% in the first run). Most students were really surprised that they were able to learn programming in only two and a half days. Nearly all students developed a syntactical correct and more or less "working" and object-oriented program. One of the goals was to reduce the shyness from programming. This goal was apparently reached quite well.

Our next study will investigate how the pre-projects have influenced the scores of the students during their first year at the university. The results we gathered during our project will be validated in the context of a regular CS1-course. Therefore, we have to partly give up the anonymity in order to get a correlation with the results of the CS1-exams.

Another large study will cover the structure of the learning processes that are reflected by the object-orientated programs of the students.

8. REFERENCES

[1] Müller, H. and Weichert F. 2005. Vorkurs Informatik – Der Einstieg ins Informatikstudium. B.G. Teubner Verlag. Wiesbaden.

[2] Schulte, C. and Ehlert, A. 2009. Empirical Comparison of Objects-First and Objects-Later. In Proceedings of the ICER 2009. ACM Press, New York 2009

[3] Thomas, L. and Sanders, K. 2007 Checklists for Grading Object-Oriented CS1 Programs: concepts and misconceptions. In Proceedings for the ITiCSE 2007. ACM Press, New York 2007

[4] Hares, J.S. and Smart, J.D. 1994 Object orientation: technology, techniques, management and migration. John Wiley & Sons Ltd, Chichester 1994

[5] Hubwieser P. 2006. Functions, Objects and States: Teaching Informatics in Secondary Schools. In Mittermeir S. (Ed.): 2nd International Conference ISSEP. Springer, Berlin. pp 104 – 116

[6] Hubwieser P. 2008. Analysis of Learning Objectives in Object Oriented Programming. In: Mittermeir R.T., Syslo M. M.: (eds.): Informatics Education - Supporting Computational Thinking. ISSEP. Springer, Berlin. pp 142-150

[7] Fraley, C. and Raftery, A.E. MCLUST version 3 for R: Normal mixture modeling and model-based clustering. Technical Report 504, Department of Statistics University of Washington, Seattle, WA 98195-4322, USA, 2007.

[8] Hansen, S. 2009. Analyzing Programming Projects. In Proceedings of the SIGCSE 2009. ACM Press, New York 2009.

[9] Walker, H.M. 2010. The Role of Programming in Introductory Computing Courses. In ACM Inroads 2010. Vol.1 – No2

[10] Mitra, S., Dangwal, R., Jha, S. and Chatterjee, S. 2006. A Model of How Children Acquire Computing Skills from Hole-in-the-Wall Computers in Public Places. In Information Technologies and International Development – Volume2, Number 4, The Massachusetts Institute of Technology. Summer 2005

[11] Börstler, J. et al. 2008. Evaluation OO Example Programs for CS1. In Proceedings of the ITiCSE 2008.

[12] Hanks, B. 2007. Problems Encountered by Novice Pair Programmers. In Proceedings of the ICER 2007. ACM Press, New York, 2007

[13] Berges M. and Hubwieser P. 2008. Worksheets for the pre-projects. http://vmhub1.informatik.tu-muenchen.de/publikationen/material/preprojects.pdf

Extreme Apprenticeship Method in Teaching Programming for Beginners

Arto Vihavainen, Matti Paksula and Matti Luukkainen
University of Helsinki
Department of Computer Science
P.O. Box 68 (Gustaf Hällströmin katu 2b)
Fi-00014 University of Helsinki
{ avihavai, paksula, mluukkai }@cs.helsinki.fi

ABSTRACT

Learning a craft like programming is efficient when novices learn from people who already master the craft. In this paper we define *Extreme Apprenticeship*, an extension to the cognitive apprenticeship model. Our model is based on a set of values and practices that emphasize *learning by doing* together with *continuous feedback* as the most efficient means for learning. We show how the method was applied to a CS I programming course. Application of the method resulted in a significant decrease in the dropout rates in comparison with the previous traditionally conducted course instances.

Categories and Subject Descriptors

K.3.2 [**Computers and Education**]: Computer and Information Science Education *Computer Science Education*

General Terms

Design, Human Factors

Keywords

cognitive apprenticeship, course material, continuous feedback, instructional design, programming education, motivation, best practices, learning by doing

1. INTRODUCTION

Teaching programming is hard. Lots of research from many different perspectives has been devoted to the topic during the past couple of decades (see eg. [23, 21]), but there is still no consensus on what is the most effective way to teach programming. Most universities are still using a traditional format in the introductory programming courses (CS I courses). The traditional format consists of lectures, take-home assignments and perhaps also demo sessions where model solutions to the exercises are shown (see eg. [7, 24]). Lectures tend to be structured according to the language constructs, rather than the more general application strategies. This approach is used despite various research results [31, 23, 25] indicating that the problem is not to learn the syntax or semantics of individual language constructs, but to master the process on how to combine constructs to meaningful programs.

The language constructs introduced in lectures are typically applied in programming exercises. With very little support to the programming process, doing exercises is hard for part of the student population [7, 24], to those who in the literature are characterized as stoppers [22] or ineffective novices [23]. Many of these end up dropping the course due to not being able to solve problems and therefore feeling inadequate. Another problem of take-home exercises is that students may learn bad work habits from solving the problems by themselves.

The context in which students do exercises themselves can be regarded as a minimally guided environment. It is well known in educational psychology (see e. g. [20]) that, due to the nature of human cognitive architecture, a minimally guided approach is not optimal for novices learning a cognitively challenging task, such as programming.

In this paper we will describe a variation of *Cognitive Apprenticeship* called *Extreme Apprenticeship* that has a strong emphasis on guided programming exercises. We also report the experiences from its first application at the University of Helsinki Department of Computer Science.

2. PEDAGOGICAL BACKGROUND

The dropout rates of introductory programming courses tend to be high[1], so it is quite evident that the traditional approach shoud be improved.

One of the most interesting approaches in programming instruction is Cognitive Apprenticeship Model [9, 10], where the focus is on the process rather than just on the end products. Cognitive Apprenticeship also puts a heavy emphasis on optimizing coaching and guidance available to the students.

Numerous studies have shown that both the motivation and the comfort level of students have a remarkable effect on learning [5]. Cognitive Apprenticeship already has many ingredients to boost both, but also the role of programming exercises is remarkable.

[1]E.g. in University of Helsinki the long term average dropout rate has been c.a. 45 %.

SIGCSE'11, March 9–12, 2011, Dallas, Texas, USA.

2.1 Cognitive Apprenticeship

The Cognitive Apprenticeship Model has recently had many applications in teaching programming with positive results (see e. g. [1, 6, 8, 16]). The model is based on the ancient model of apprenticeship education where a profession is learned while working under the guidance of a senior master. Traditionally the apprenticeship model has been mostly applied in context of learning professions that require physical skills such as shoe making. In Cognitive Apprenticeship the emphasis is more on acquiring cognitive skills.

The key observation in Cognitive Apprenticeship is that when teaching novices, masters of a skill do not usually take into account the complex process that leads to end products [9, 10]. As stated previously this is far too common also in teaching programming.

Cognitive Apprenticeship divides instruction into three stages: modeling, scaffolding and fading. In the *modeling* stage the teacher gives students a conceptual model of the process, with which an expert performs the task under study. One effective way of modeling is to base the lectures on *worked examples* [8] instead of concentrating on language structures. A worked example shows e.g. completion of a programming task from start to finish. While completing the task, the teacher is thinking aloud all the time, explaining the decisions made during the process.

After the modeling stage, students move to the *scaffolding* stage. Typically this means that the students are exposed to exercises that are made under the guidance of an experienced instructor. Scaffolding refers to the way support is given to the students. The key idea is that students are not given straight answers, but rather just enough hints to be able to discover the answers to their questions themselves. Scaffolding is based on Vygotsky's idea that learning is most efficient when a student is given just enough information that is enough to boost the student's ability to finish the task [27].

When the student starts to master a task by himself, the scaffolding should be dismantled. This is the *fading* stage of apprenticeship learning.

The Apprenticeship-based approach to learning programming seems to be advocated also by the Agile and Software Craftsmanship people in the industry, such as Robert Martin who has stated that *"Software is a craft that takes years to learn, and more years to master. The only way to properly learn the craft is to be taught at the side of a master"* [19]. Martin calls for apprenticeship-type mentoring to the software industry, where the recently graduated apprentices would work in a software project context with constant interactive guidance by journeymen and masters.

2.2 The roles of programming exercises

Somewhat surprisingly the applications of Cognitive Apprenticeship to programming instruction have not had much emphasis on the role of programming assignments. It seems evident that the exercises are crucial in learning programming, and there also exists empirical data to support this fact [12].

The *Active Learning* [14]-based methods (eg. [28, 11]) do raise the programming activity of students to a big role, but seem to still stress collaborative aspects more than individual effort.

Programming exercises can have an even more important role than just applying the theory taught in lectures, as Roumani [24] stated *"we think of them (assignments) as teaching instruments that complement lectures by teaching the same material but in an exploratory fashion"*.

In addition to being an important learning instrument, programming exercises have a huge impact on the motivation of the students. It is well known that the level of motivation correlates positively to success in learning [15, 18]. Empirical evidence for this exists also from the field of programming instruction [5].

It has especially been shown that students who are performing activities for the activities themselves, i.e., intrinsically motivated students perform better than those who seek extrinsic rewards [17]. Giving too difficult programming assignments is a certain way to kill the motivation of weaker students, but suitably challenging and relevant exercises with short-term goals that students can achieve are known to raise intrinsic motivation [17, 26, 18].

The way students get instructional feedback also has an effect on their motivation. Talking with students about their solutions and problem solving strategies while giving them hints on how to improve them is known to have a positive impact on student motivation [18], so from the motivation point of view, the type of programming exercises and the guidance available when solving exercises are crucial for the effectiveness of the scaffolding phase in the apprenticeship type of instruction.

Besides motivation, the *comfort level* of a student has been shown to have a remarkable impact on learning (see eg. [5, 30, 29]. Their comfort level incorporates students orientation to themselves (self-esteem) and judgement of their capabilities to execute the required tasks (self-efficiency) [2, 5]. According to Bandura [2], the most important source of self-efficiency is the student's evaluation of the outcomes of his attempts to perform activities. Thus, suitable exercises with proper guidance and feedback are an essential tool for building students' comfort levels.

3. EXTREME APPRENTICESHIP METHOD

One of the ideas in *Extreme Programming* [4] is to take a group of software development best practices and take those to the extreme levels. For example, in order to improve the quality of written code, development teams should have code reviews. In Extreme Programming this practice becomes integrated as a technique called pair programming where the practice is taken to an extreme level: code is written under constant reviewing.

We took a similar approach in teaching of programming where we constructed our method on top of the Cognitive Apprenticeship model. Especially the scaffolding stage of the model is stressed.

Extreme Apprenticeship Method

The following values are stressed during all the course activities:

- **Learning by doing**. The craft will only be mastered by actually practicing it.
- **Continuous feedback**. Continous feedback must be implemented in both directions. The student receives multi-level feedback from his progress and instructors, and the instructor receives feedback by monitoring the students progress and challenges.

- **No compromise**. The skills to be learned are practiced as long as it takes for each individual.
- **An apprentice becomes a master**. The ultimate goal of instruction should be that the student will eventually become the master.

The values above induce a set of the following practices that are applied in actual course implementation:

- **Avoiding tons of preaching**. Since the effectiveness of lectures in teaching programming is questionable, the lecturing should cover only the bare minimum to get started with exercises.
- **Relevant examples**. Topics covered in the lectures have to be relevant for the exercises.
- **Start early**. Exercises start right after the first lecture of the course. During the first weeks of the course all the students are already solving an extensive amount of simple exercises. This gives all the students a strong routine of code writing and a motivation boost right at the start of the course.
- **Help available**. Exercises are completed in a lab in the presence of instructors who are offering the scaffolding style of guidance.
- **Small goals**. Exercises are split into small parts with clearly set intermediate goals.

  These small intermediate steps guarantee that students feel that they are learning and making progress all the time.
- **Exercises are mandatory**. Since the exercises are the main instrument in learning, the majority of the exercises are mandatory for all the students.
- **Train the routine**. The amount of exercises should be high and to some extent repetitive in their nature.
- **Clean guidelines**. Exercises have to provide clear starting points and structures on how to start solving the task.
- **Encourage to look for information**. While doing the exercises students are also required to find out things that are not covered during the lectures.

4. APPLYING THE METHOD

The method was applied in introductory programming courses at the Department of Computer Science at the University of Helsinki. For administrative purposes the one semester CS I introductory Java programming course is given in two separate parts. The courses *Introduction to Programming* and *Advanced Programming* are taught as separate units where Advanced programming further deepens the knowledge built during the Introduction to programming course. Both parts last 6 weeks, totalling the length of one semester.

Introduction to programming covers assignment, expressions, terminal input and output, basic control structures, classes, objects, methods, arrays and strings. Advanced programming concentrates on advanced object oriented features such as inheritance, interfaces and polymorphism, and familiarizes students with the most essential features of Java API, exceptions and file I/O.

4.1 Study material and lectures

The study material and lectures play a key role in the modeling phase in teaching the skills to be learned. On the other hand, as programming is a craft, it requires plenty of practice.

In order to avoid tons of preaching we reduced the number of lectures from the usual 5 hours per week to just 2 hours. Lectures and the supporting material did not even try to cover every detail of the language. Rather only the required overview for the exercises was given and students were supported and encouraged to look for information themselves.

All the material shown in the lectures was available to students on-line. The material was a web page, written in book-like format. The material followed the structure of exercises, allowing students to read the material as they proceeded with the exercises, providing scaffolding for the actual process of learning by doing.

In the material and lectures all the constructs were always presented with relevant examples from the point of view of exercise solving. This allowed students to remember that the programming tasks in exercises were often just variations of the examples shown in the lectures.

In addition to knowing a collection of language constructs, problem-solving skills are needed in programming. In the material and the lectures the main idea was to give worked examples, not just to show working code or show direct answers, but to demonstrate step by step how a solution could be devised for a problem. This approach helped students to identify good ways of solving programming problems already during the lectures.

4.2 Exercises

It is expected that students use most of the time they devote to the course in active solving of programming exercises. This trains the routine and gives a constant feeling of success by achieving small goals. The exercises especially in the beginning of the course were aimed to build up programming routines and confidence, partly motivated by the Software Craftsmanship community's idea of *Code Katas*, which are small exercises which help programmers to improve their skills through practice and repetition. As Corey Heines puts it *"practising the solution to a Kata until the steps and keystrokes became like second nature, and you could do them without thinking. In this way, you can internalize the process/technique you are practicing until it is under your fingers"* [13].

For each week we introduced a set of new exercises, an amount ranging from 15 to almost 40. Most of the initial exercises were small, like "output numbers from 1 to 99". Sequentially done small exercises combined as bigger programs. This approach in composing bigger programs showed students how to split a big task to smaller sub-tasks – a vital skill in programming.

The exercise difficulty was worked out to be incremental. The first ones of the weekly exercises were used to "warm up" students, providing the first small goals to get started and keeping students in their comfort level.

Each task had a short textual description of the expected behavior of the program. Two additional implementations of technical scaffolding were also introduced: Output- and Main-driven Programming. These two techniques provided additional support for the student.

Output-driven Programming

Similarly to *Test-driven Development* [3] where the unit test for the code is implemented first, our exercises showed the output of the program that the student was supposed to match with his implementation. A typical exercise looked like this:

```
"Write a program that asks user's name and then
 outputs it"

Give your name: Matti

Hello, Matti!
```

This allowed students to understand the textual description of the task better. The expected output also allowed students to verify that their program is working correctly and the small goal is achieved.

The expected output can also provide additional hints for structuring the program. An example of this is shown in the next example.

```
"Write a program that reads a number from the user.
 The program checks if the range of the number is
 between 0 and 100."

Give a number: -2
Please give a number between 0 and 100!

Give a number: 102
Please give a number between 0 and 100!

Give a number: 2
Thank you!
```

From the above output it is possible to determine required parts and their behaviors, providing a starting point for the implementation: the output suggests that there is some kind of loop in the program code combined with reading and conditions.

Main-driven Programming

Later when the tasks became more complicated *Main-driven Programming*, an extension of Output-driven Programming, was introduced. We gave a small testing program that could be inserted into the main method of a Java program.

In the next example the task is to design a `TravelCard`-class, which would have an owner and balance.

```
Copy this to your main-method:

  TravelCard artosCard = new TravelCard("Arto");
  System.out.println(artosCard);

Expected output:

  Owner Arto, balance 0.0 euros
```

To complete this task the student has to create a new class named `TravelCard` and figure out how to implement a `toString()`-method and required attributes for the class. This ensures on some level that the structure in the final program will be good.

4.3 Exercise Sessions

Exercise sessions were organized in computer labs where students worked to solve the exercises. Help was continuously available during the exercise sessions in the form of teachers and teaching assistants, e.g. the instructors. Anyone could enter the class without having to reserve a specific slot. Every week had 8 hours of exercise sessions, and students could attend as many sessions as needed.

An important principle in our approach was that the programming started as early as possible. The first exercise session was right after the starting lecture of the course. For the first week the students already had 30 small exercises. Due to the guidance available in exercise sessions even those with no previous experience of programming managed well with the start early approach: 88% of the students finished over 25 exercises during the first week. The quick and encouraging start raised the self-confidence and comfort level of students, and also had an immense effect on their motivation.

In order to enforce good programming habits, students had to have their finished solutions accepted by the instructors. If an instructor noticed a flaw in the approach (bad naming or indentation, too complex solution logic for the problem, etc.), he pointed it out, and the student had to redo parts of the exercise. In general we allowed no compromises in the solutions of students. This way, each student refined their solutions to the point where the solutions could be passed as "model answers".

4.4 Continuous Feedback

During the course we implemented continuous feedback to provide fast evaluation and a continuous feeling of progress for the students. During the exercise sessions students received positive reinforcement in the form of instructors that were aiding them forward.

If a student did not have specific questions during the exercise session, the instructors still actively engaged with him to make sure he was working towards the right direction. If something to correct was noticed, the instructor nudged the student to the right direction by questioning the approach or by providing constructive feedback. This was the key continuous feedback as the hints received during the learning process are essential for acquiring good programming and problem-solving habits. Instructors were not allowed to give direct solutions to the exercises, and the key idea was to support the students so that they could figure out the solutions themselves.

In addition to instructor feedback, students had their completed exercises marked down to a check-list, allowing them to see the check-list filling with marked exercises. We feel that the list played an important role in feedback; every check was a small victory. Check-lists were also updated to the course web-page at the end of every day, allowing students to see the progress of other students as well.

In addition to evaluation during exercises, students were evaluated with 3 small biweekly exams done with the computer and a final traditional exam. Small exams provided valuable feedback for students and also to instructors throughout the courses.

The final exam was constructed to be as similar as possible to the usual programming exams conducted at our university to provide meaningful comparison of the course results. The exam was a paper exam consisting mostly of programming on paper. It was not allowed to use any material in the exam. A student had to get 50 % of the total maximum score in order to pass the course.

5. COURSE RESULTS

The introductory programming courses at the Department of Computer Science at the University of Helsinki are taught during both fall and spring semesters. Fall semesters consist mostly of students who are majoring in computer science, while spring semesters have mostly students who have computer science as a minor subject. Some of the students minoring in computer science participate only in the Introduction to programming course and do not proceed to Advanced programming.

Until spring 2010 the introductory programming courses have followed the traditional lecture and take-home exercise model. The first course implementation following Extreme Apprenticeship was during the spring semester 2010.

Next we will compare the outcome of the Extreme Apprenticeship-based course to the previous course instances from past 8 years in terms of percentage of passed students. The results are reported separately in the tables below for Introduction to programming and Advanced programming. The Extreme Apprenticeship-based implementation in spring 2010 is highlighted using bold face. The column titled n denotes the number of total participants.

As stated in the previous section, the paper exam in the spring 2010 implementation was similar to the ones that had been used in the course for years already. Because it has always been a requirement to get 50% of the exam score to pass the course, the numbers should be comparable for all the course implementations.

Introduction to Programming

	n	passed
s02	92	38.0 %
f02	332	53.6 %
s03	98	39.8 %
f03	261	64.0 %
s04	84	61.9 %
f04	211	59.2 %
s05	112	46.4 %
f05	146	54.1 %
s06	105	41.9 %
f06	182	65.4 %
s07	84	53.6 %
f07	162	53.0 %
s08	72	58.3 %
f08	164	56.1 %
s09	53	47.7 %
f09	140	64.3 %
s10	**67**	**70.1 %**

Advanced Programming

	n	passed
s02	88	26.1 %
f02	249	56.2 %
s03	65	30.8 %
f03	228	59.2 %
s04	66	43.9 %
f04	177	66.1 %
s05	70	57.1 %
f05	125	56.0 %
s06	52	44.2 %
f06	147	67.3 %
s07	53	58.5 %
f07	136	59.6 %
s08	29	51.7 %
f08	147	56.5 %
s09	22	50.0 %
f09	121	60.3 %
s10	**44**	**86.4 %**

Let us first analyze data from Introduction to programming. The long-term average (excluding spring 2010) for passed students in fall semesters is 58.5 % and in spring semesters 43.7 %. One of the reasons for the higher dropout rate in spring courses might be the student population. In spring terms most of the participants are minoring in computer science, and quite likely have weaker backgrounds for programming. As can be seen, the percentage of passed students in spring 2010 was higher than it has previously been, 70.1 % of the students starting the course passing it, the second highest pass-rate being 65.4 %. Extreme Apprenticeship seemed to bring clear benefits, especially in comparison to normal spring term results.

The trend in the Advanced programming course is similar: the average passing percentage in fall terms is 60.1 % and in spring 45.3 %, both being marginally higher than the acceptance percentages for the introductory course. This is most likely due to the fact that most of the students that fail the Introductory course do not take part in Advanced programming. The acceptance percentage in spring 2010 was 86.4 %, an all-time high in the department with a clear margin. The most natural explanation for the remarkably high passing rate is that the programming routine built during normal course implementations has been quite fragile for an average or below average student. In the Extreme Apprenticeship-based course those students who survived from the initial shock of Introduction to Programming seem to have been getting better and better all the time. With a strong routine built during the introductory course the challenging new concepts encountered in the advanced course have been rather easy to master.

6. CONCLUSIONS

The Extreme Apprenticeship presented in this paper provides a good structure for teaching skills that require building routine and learning best practices from the masters. Emphasizing scaffolding in combination with the set of values and practices yields very promising results as seen in the initial implementations with 67 and 44 students, the most important result being the significant decrease in dropout rates.

We believe that the Extreme Apprenticeship method's idea of taking continuous feedback and scaffolding to an extreme level provides enough support to also help some of the inefficient novices, who usually drop programming courses, to learn programming.

The role of relevant exercises for making learning by doing a reality is a key factor in this approach. The amount of work that a student puts into exercises can have a negative impact on motivation if the exercises do not support his learning process in a meaningful way.

The majority of the anonymous student feedback indicated that learning by doing was considered motivating and rewarding. A quote from an anonymous feedback summarizes the positive outcome of this approach: *"The best thing on the course was the amount of exercises and exercise groups and the availability of teachers. It was very rewarding to be on a course where you could understand the course content by simply working diligently. Making mistakes also helped to learn things."*

The outcome of our initial experiment was so encouraging that the same approach is currently being applied to the fall semester course with almost 200 participants.

7. ACKNOWLEDGMENTS

We thank The Head of Studies, PhD Jaakko "Gandhi" Kurhila for his support and inspiration.

8. REFERENCES

[1] O. Astrachan and D. Reed. AAA and CS 1: the applied apprenticeship approach to CS 1. In *SIGCSE '95: Proceedings of the twenty-sixth SIGCSE technical*

symposium on Computer science education, pages 1–5. ACM, 1995.

[2] A. Bandura. *Social foundations of though and action: a social cognitive theory*. Prentice-Hall, 1986.

[3] K. Beck. *Test Driven Development: By Example*. Addison-Wesley, 2002.

[4] K. Beck and C. Andres. *Extreme Programming Explained: Embrace Change (2nd Edition)*. Addison-Wesley Professional, 2004.

[5] S. Bergin and R. Reilly. The influence of motivation and comfort-level on learning to program. In *Sroceedings of the 17th Workshop on Psychology of Programming, PPIG'05,*, 2005.

[6] T. R. Black. Helping novice programming students succeed. *J. Comput. Small Coll.*, 22(2):109–114, 2006.

[7] R. E. Bruhn and P. J. Burton. An approach to teaching java using computers. *SIGCSE Bull.*, 35(4):94–99, 2003.

[8] M. E. Caspersen and J. Bennedsen. Instructional design of a programming course: a learning theoretic approach. In *ICER '07: Proceedings of the third international workshop on Computing education research*, pages 111–122. ACM, 2007.

[9] A. Collins, J. Brown, and S. Newman. Cognitive apprenticeship: Teaching the craft of reading, writing and mathematics. In *Knowing, Learning and Instruction: Essays in honor of Robert Glaser*. Hillside, 1989.

[10] A. Collins, J. S. Brown, and A. Holum. Cognitive apprenticeship: making thinking visible. *American Educator*, 6:38–46, 1991.

[11] S. Grissom and M. J. Van Gorp. A practical approach to integrating active and collaborative learning into the introductory computer science curriculum. In *Proceedings of the seventh annual consortium on Computing in small colleges midwestern conference*, pages 95–100, USA, 2000. Consortium for Computing Sciences in Colleges.

[12] M. Hassinen and H. Mäyrä. Learning programming by programming: a case study. In *Baltic Sea '06: Proceedings of the 6th Baltic Sea conference on Computing education research: Koli Calling 2006*, pages 117–119. ACM, 2006.

[13] C. Heines. http://katas.softwarecraftsmanship.org/.

[14] K. Huffman and M. Vernoy. *Psychology in Action*. Wiley, 2003.

[15] T. Jenkins. The motivation of students of programming. In *ITiCSE '01: Proceedings of the 6th annual conference on Innovation and technology in computer science education*, pages 53–56. ACM, 2001.

[16] M. Kölling and D. J. Barnes. Enhancing apprentice-based learning of java. In *SIGCSE '04: Proceedings of the 35th SIGCSE technical symposium on Computer science education*, pages 286–290. ACM, 2004.

[17] M. R. Lepper. Motivational considerations in the study of instruction. *Cognition and Instruction*, 5(4):289–309, 1988.

[18] L. Lumsden. *Motivation, Cultivating a Love of Learning*. ERIC Clearinghouse on Educational Management, University of Oregon, 1999.

[19] R. Martin. Review of the Pete McBreen's book Software Craftmanship, http://www.mcbreen.ab.ca/SoftwareCraftsmanship/.

[20] R. E. C. Paul A. Kirschner, John Sweller. Why minimal guidance during instruction does not work: An analysis of the failure of constructivist, problem-based, experiental, and inquiry-based teaching. *Educational Psychologist*, 41(2):75–86, 2006.

[21] A. Pears, S. Seidman, L. Malmi, L. Mannila, E. Adams, J. Bennedsen, M. Devlin, and J. Paterson. A survey of literature on the teaching of introductory programming. In *ITiCSE-WGR '07: Working group reports on ITiCSE on Innovation and technology in computer science education*, pages 204–223. ACM, 2007.

[22] D. Perkins, C. Hancock, R. Hobbins, F. Marsin, and R.Simmons. Conditions of learning in novice programmers. In *Studying the novice programmer*, pages 261–279. Lawrence Erlbaum, 1989.

[23] A. Robins, J. Rountree, and N. Rountree. Learning and teaching programming: A review and discussion. *Computer Science Education*, 13:137–172, 2003.

[24] H. Roumani. Design guidelines for the lab component of objects-first cs1. In *SIGCSE '02: Proceedings of the 33rd SIGCSE technical symposium on Computer science education*, pages 222–226. ACM, 2002.

[25] J. C. Spohrer and E. Soloway. Novice mistakes: are the folk wisdoms correct? *Commun. ACM*, 29(7):624–632, 1986.

[26] D. Stipek. *Motivation to Learn: From theory to practice*. Prentice Hall, 1988.

[27] L. S. Vygotsky. *Mind in Society: The Development of Higher Psychological Processes*. Harvard University Press, Cambridge, MA, 1978.

[28] K. J. Whittington. Infusing active learning into introductory programming courses. *J. Comput. Small Coll.*, 19(5):249–259, 2004.

[29] S. Wiedenbeck, D. LaBelle, and V. Kain. Factors affecting course outcomes in introductory programming. In *Workshop on Psychology of Programming, PPIG'04*, pages 97–109, 2004.

[30] B. C. Wilson and S. Shrock. Contributing to success in an introductory computer science course: a study of twelve factors. In *SIGCSE '01: Proceedings of the thirty-second SIGCSE technical symposium on Computer Science Education*, pages 184–188. ACM, 2001.

[31] L. Winslow. Programming psychology - a psychological overview. *SIGCSE Bulletin*, 27:17–22, 1996.

Expressing Computer Science Concepts Through Kodu Game Lab

Kathryn T. Stolee*
Department of Computer Science and Engineering
University of Nebraska–Lincoln
Lincoln, NE, U.S.A.
kstolee@cse.unl.edu

Teale Fristoe*
Expressive Intelligence Studio
University of California, Santa Cruz
Santa Cruz, CA, U.S.A.
teale@soe.ucsc.edu

ABSTRACT

Educational programming environments such as Microsoft Research's Kodu Game Lab are often used to introduce novices to computer science concepts and programming. Unlike many other educational languages that rely on scripting and Java-like syntax, the Kodu language is entirely event-driven and programming takes the form of 'when – do' clauses. Despite this simplistic programing model, many computer science concepts can be expressed using Kodu. We identify and measure the frequency of these concepts in 346 Kodu programs created by users, and find that most programs exhibit sophistication through the use of complex control flow and boolean logic. Through Kodu's non-traditional language, we show that users express and explore fundamental computer science concepts.

Categories and Subject Descriptors

K.3.2 [**Computers and Education**]: Computer and Information Science Education; D.3.3 [**Programming Languages**]: Language Constructs and Features

General Terms

Languages, Experimentation

Keywords

Educational programming languages, Kodu

1. INTRODUCTION

Since the development of high level programming languages, researchers and educators have embraced domain specific languages designed to introduce children to programming from a young age [10]. While ease of use has always been a concern with these languages, often attractiveness to children is a top priority, with the rationale that students should enjoy their experiences to gain the most from them. For this reason, these languages often target media creation, such as art, animations, or games. However, rarely are the actual educational benefits of the languages the focus of scrutiny, resulting in a stark lack of understanding of the skills these languages provide for their users.

Microsoft Research's Kodu Game Lab [4] is a recent addition to this tradition of educational programming environments. Since its release in the summer of 2009, it has been installed over 50,000 times in over 120 countries. Kodu allows users to create their own video games by designing the world, deciding which characters will appear in it, and programming the characters using an easy-to-understand visual programming language. It takes the unique perspective that children should be both producers and consumers of games. Like many similar programming environments, Kodu has been shown to be enjoyable for users, and clubs have formed worldwide to teach Kodu (e.g., [1, 2, 5]), but its educational benefits have not been explored in any rigorous fashion.

In this work, we begin to identify which computer science concepts users can express through Kodu, and then explore which concepts actual users have utilized in Kodu. We aim to address the following research questions:

RQ1: Which computer science concepts can be expressed through the Kodu Language?

RQ2: How much time do end users spend designing and programming during a Kodu session?

RQ3: How often does each computer science concept appear in the programs created by the Kodu community?

To this end, we look at several language features available in Kodu, connecting them to fundamental computer science concepts. We empirically investigate what users of Kodu are actually learning, first by determining what percentage of their time is spent programming and configuring their program as opposed to playing or exploring, and then by performing a frequency analysis on 346 end user programs, measuring how often each computer science concept appears.

The rest of this paper is structured as follows. Section 2 presents related work in educational programming languages and Section 3 gives some background on Kodu Game Lab and the Kodu language. Section 4 presents the computer science concepts that can be learned in Kodu (*RQ1*), Section 5 shows how users spend their time during a Kodu session (*RQ2*), and Section 6 addresses *RQ3* by exploring how often each concept is present in the games created by the community. Section 7 presents the threats to validity, and Section 8 presents future work and conclusions.

*Work completed while at Microsoft FUSE Labs.

SIGCSE'11, March 9–12, 2011, Dallas, Texas, USA.

Rule	→	Condition Action
Condition	→	Sensor FilterSet
Action	→	Actuator ModifierSet Selector
FilterSet	→	Filter FilterSet | Filter
ModifierSet	→	Modifier ModifierSet | Modifier
Sensor	→	see | bump
Filter	→	apple | red | ϵ
Actuator	→	move | eat
Modifier	→	toward | away | ϵ
Selector	→	it | me | ϵ

Figure 1: Grammar Sketch for a Rule

2. RELATED WORK

Released in 1967, Logo [10] pioneered the development of educational programming environments, and has been very influential on the development of subsequent languages in the domain [3, 6, 13, 15]. While there have been countless educational programming environments since Logo, Alice [6], Greenfoot [3], and Scratch [13] are commonly explored by the research community and have many similarities to Kodu. Like Kodu, all are visual programming languages that allow users to create their own animations, games, and simulations. Scratch also has extensive community features that facilitate sharing of programs and collaboration [13]. Unlike Kodu, the languages of Alice, Greenfoot, and Scratch follow the Java-like syntax of many mainstream programming languages, whereas the Kodu language is entirely event-driven (see Section 3.1 for language details).

In terms of evaluation, educational programming environments have been measured primarily using qualitative and anecdotal evidence [15, 17]. A more recent trend has been toward the inclusion of quantitative data in the evaluation, though sample sizes generally remain small. Kelleher has analyzed user habits by tracking time spent programming versus other activities, such as designing in Alice [9]; we perform a similar analysis with Kodu. Pre- and post-tests have also been used to evaluate what users learn by using Alice and Scratch, and are generally accompanied by qualitative support [11, 12, 14]. Researchers are only beginning to examine artifacts written in Alice and Scratch to determine what the authors of the systems may be learning, a technique we continue in this work [7, 11, 16, 19].

3. ABOUT KODU

At its core, Kodu is an environment that allows users to create and play their own video games. It is available for download for the Xbox and also on the PC. Developed by Microsoft Research, the vision of the tool is to help users learn computer science concepts through game creation.

3.1 Kodu Language

Kodu is a high-level, visual, and interpreted language that can be represented as a context-free grammar [18]. Users can program each character (e.g., a fish, cycle, apple, tree) individually, and the programming defines how it interacts with the world, much like an intelligent agent. The programming takes place on pages, which define different states for the character. A character may contain up to 12 pages of programming, and can maintain its state and control flow by switching between pages. Each page contains a set of rules, where a rule is analogous to a statement in typical programming languages. Each rule is in the form of a condition and an action, which form a *when – do* clause, that is, *when condition, do action.* If the condition is satisfied, then the action is performed. All the rules on a page are evaluated in a single frame, from top to bottom. There are over 500 tiles that can be used to compose rules in the Kodu Language. In Figure 1, we give a grammar sketch for a rule in Kodu, and limit the alphabet to 10 tiles. Each capitalized word (e.g., *Rule, Condition*) represents a non-terminal symbol and appears on the LHS of a production rule. Each lowercased word (e.g., *see, apple*) represents a terminal symbol that maps to one tile in the Kodu language.

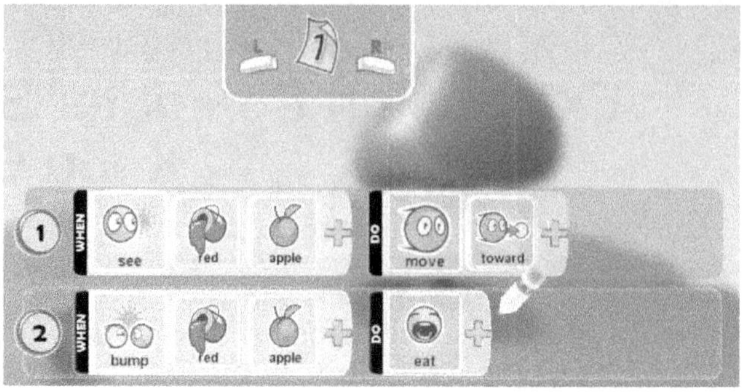

Figure 2: Programming Interface in Kodu

3.2 Programming in Kodu

Programming in Kodu involves the placement of programming tiles in a meaningful order to form the condition and action on each rule. We show an example of the programming user interface in Figure 2, where the program shown was generated using the grammar shown in Figure 1. In the example, there are two rules, one per line. The condition of each rule is on the left, and the action on the right, as is defined by the grammar rule, *Rule → Condition Action.*

For the first rule, the condition is, when *see red apple*, and the action is, *move toward.* In the condition, *see* is the sensor and *red* and *apple* are filters. The action defines the behavior of this particular character when it sees a red apple, that is, it *moves toward.* Here, *move* is the actuator, *toward* is the modifier, and *it* is the default selector, since the condition identifies a target object (i.e., the red apple). The second rule has a similar condition with a different sensor, *bump.* The action, *eat,* indicates that the character should eat any red apple it bumps. The programming in Figure 2 applies to the first page in this character's programming, as indicated by the number "1" at the top of the screen.

4. COMPUTER SCIENCE CONCEPTS IN KODU

While the Kodu language is unlike most mainstream programming languages, it allows its users to explore many fundamental concepts in computer science. In this section, we explore each of these concepts and how they can be expressed and used in the Kodu language (*RQ1*).

4.1 Variables and Scope

Simply, a variable is a symbol that holds a value. In Kodu as in other languages, variables can have a local or global scope. Here, we describe how global, local, and random variables are expressed and used in Kodu.

Global Scope

Global variables in Kodu can be read from or written to by any character. In Kodu, the scores, which hold integer values, act as global variables. There are 37 global scores that can be maintained by any program, one for each letter of the English alphabet and color supported by Kodu.

Local Scope

Characters have four local properties that are analogous to local variables. These are color, glow, expression, and health. Color, glow, and expression each hold an enumerated value (e.g., orange, happy), and health holds an integer value. A character can read and write all properties for itself and some of the properties of other characters. For example, *kodu*[1] can be programmed to *change* the health property of a *cycle*, but it cannot *check* the health of the *cycle*.

Random

A common way to introduce nondeterminism in programming is through random variables, and Kodu has adopted this practice. There are three random variable tiles that can be used, one for time, one for score, and one for color. These can be used as filters or modifiers to trigger behavior or set a property or value at random.

4.2 Boolean Logic

The Kodu language allows users to express logical negation, conjunction, and disjunction in their programs, hence exposing the user to these fundamental concepts.

Negation

The concept of negation is perhaps the most obvious among the boolean logic constructs that can be explored through the Kodu language. A specific tile, called the *not* tile, can be applied to any condition in any rule. Consider the following block of code (where A is a condition and B is an action):

```
(1) When not A do B
```

Here, when condition A is met, then nothing happens. However, if A is not met, then B executes.

A byproduct of the logical negation is the ability to express *if – then – else* statements. All rules in Kodu represent conditional statements of the form *if – then*, but the *not* title can introduce an *else* clause. Consider the following code:

```
(1) When A do B
(2) When not A do C
```

Here, when condition A is met, then action B executes. However, if A is not met, then C executes. In other words, we have *if A, then B, else C.*

Conjunction

The ability to indent rules in the Kodu language creates a logical conjunction in the program structure. Indented rules will be evaluated when the condition on the parent rule is met. Consider the following block of code:

```
(1) When A do B
(2)     When C do D
(3)     When always do E
```

If condition A is not met, then lines (2) and (3) will never be evaluated. However, when condition A, then the conditions on line (2) and (3) are also checked (the *always* condition in line (3) evaluates to true, always). This logical structure forms an implication, where $A \Rightarrow B$, $A \wedge C \Rightarrow D$, and $A \wedge 1 \Rightarrow E$. And so, we have a logical conjunction of actions $B \wedge E$ when $A = true$ and a logical conjunction of conditions $A \wedge C$ to perform action D.

Disjunction

Kodu users can achieve logical disjunction by using two or more rules with different conditions and the same action. Consider the following block of code:

```
(1) When A do B
(2) When C do B
```

Here, we have two implications, $A \Rightarrow B$ and $C \Rightarrow B$, which can be simplified into $A \vee C \Rightarrow B$, representing a logical disjunction in the program. One side effect of the disjunction here is that B will get executed twice in the case that A and C both evaluate to true.

4.3 Objects

In object-oriented programming, objects are data structures that encapsulate fields and methods in a single package. Each character in Kodu is an object, and each has locally scoped variables, discussed previously. When programming, a user can *create* new characters, *delete* characters, and *clone* characters, and characters can also be created and removed during runtime. In most cases, a clone performs a deep copy including programming and properties. However, if the character has been declared to be *creatable*, then a clone will create a new object that references the original and mimics its behavior, forming a rudimentary class system. When a creatable character is modified, the changes to its programming impact all clones.

4.4 Control Flow

Kodu users can introduce non-linear program flow through the use of multiple pages of code and transitions between the pages. As each page represents a state for a character, pages map to nodes in a control flow graph, where each graph's start node is labeled *s*. The edges between nodes are labeled with the condition on which page switch is made, with the exception of the outgoing edge from the start state, which is always taken. Figure 3 shows a program fragment with four pages, which represents the behavior of a character from a program gathered for our study (selection criteria described in Section 6), and the generated control flow graph.

```
--------------------------------------------------
|          Page 1         |         Page 2         |
| (1) When A do Switch 2 | (1) When C do Switch 3 |
| (2) When B do Switch 4 |                         |
--------------------------------------------------
|          Page 3         |         Page 4         |
| (1) When D do Switch 2 | (1) When F do Switch 3 |
| (2) When E do Switch 4 |                         |
--------------------------------------------------
```

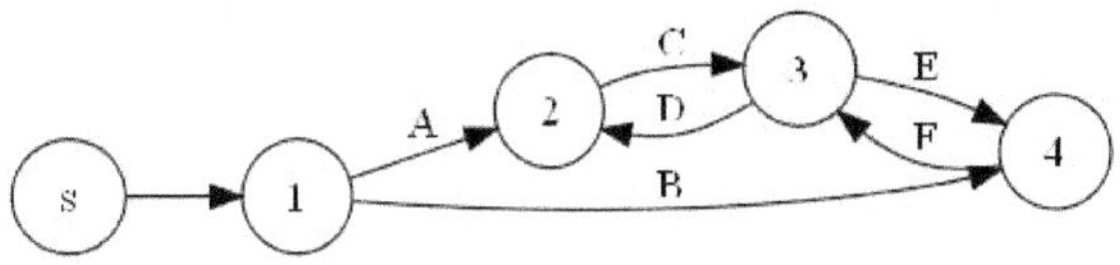

Figure 3: Example Object Control Flow

[1]The *kodu* is a character that can be programmed, like the *cycle* or the *fish*. It is typically the main character in a Kodu game.

While several analyses are possible on the control flow graph, we can determine certain characteristics of the character behavior that are related to computer science concepts by detecting cycles and calculating the maximum *fan-in* and *fan-out*. A control flow graph that contains a cycle, like $2 \rightarrow 3 \rightarrow 2$ in our example, represents the introduction of iteration, as the character can cycle through those states. Nodes that have a high fan-out value (e.g., nodes 1 and 3 have fan-out = 2) are indicative of conditional control flow, where the same state can transition to one of many different states. A high fan-in value (e.g., nodes 2 and 4 have fan-in = 2) is an indication of lightweight code reuse, since that code can be called from many different locations.

5. INSTRUMENTATION

We have shown that many computer science concepts can be expressed through the Kodu language, but unless users are taking advantage of their ability to configure, modify, and program their world, these benefits of Kodu are lost. To address *RQ2*, we have instrumented Kodu so it logs the amount of time spent in each area of the tool. The instrumentation was deployed with Kodu v1.0.65 released on July 1, 2010 for the PC Kodu users only. We collected instrumentation data for 38 days from July 1, 2010 - August 8, 2010. This resulted in data for 4,229 sessions originating from 1,580 installations, for an average of 2.7 sessions per install. (We use installations as a proxy for users. Since Kodu does not require a login ID, we do not know the number of actual users covered by this data.)

We instrumented Kodu using timers that measure the amount of time spent in each of several areas of the user interface. Table 1 shows the average (*avg*), minimum (*min*), 25th percentile (*q1*), median (*med*), 75th percentile (*q3*), and maximum (*max*) percentages of time spent per session in each of five areas of the Kodu Game Lab: *Menu* includes time spent on the main menu, home menu, save menu, and searching for games to load; *Prog.* includes time spent in the programming UI (shown in Figure 2); *Add, Scan* refers to time spent adding characters and exploring the world without changes; *Edit* refers to time spent editing the terrain, editing character properties (e.g., creatables, speed), and editing world properties (e.g., lighting, score visibility); *Play* refers to time spent actually running the game. The final column, *Time*, shows the time spent per session in minutes. The average active time per session was over 25 minutes, with a median of over 14 minutes.

Table 1 shows that an average of 14.6% of each session's time was spent in the programming UI, and 15.6% of each session's time was spent editing the characters and world. In total, this means that an average of 30.2%, or nearly one-third, of the time spent per session involved programming or tweaking parameters in the world (compared to an average of 22.9% of the time spent playing the game). Further, while we did not segment time spent adding characters versus exploring the world, it can be argued that part of the *Add, Scan* time involves program design, as this is when characters are added to the world. Additionally, among the 4,229 sessions, 2,578 (60.9%) entered the programming UI (the interface shown in Figure 2), and 3,308 (78.2%) used one of the edit tools for the world, characters, or terrain. Among those sessions that entered the programming UI, users viewed or edited their code an average of 12.7 times per session and played their game an average of 13.7 times, illustrating that users likely swap between programming and playing as they tweak and test their programs. This rapid switching between developing and testing has been shown to be a successful problem solving technique for students learning how to program [8].

Table 1: Percent of Time Spent in Kodu (Time column shown in minutes)

	Menu	Prog.	Add, Scan	Edit	Play	Time
avg	16.1%	14.6%	30.9%	15.6%	22.9%	25.36
min	0.1%	0.0%	0.2%	0.0%	0.1%	0.16
q1	4.7%	0.0%	18.9%	0.1%	10.0%	5.31
med	10.7%	9.2%	28.4%	9.6%	18.7%	14.30
q3	22.1%	25.8%	40.5%	24.5%	30.9%	36.32
max	98.0%	94.8%	97.1%	92.1%	96.2%	335.32

6. ANALYSIS OF KODU PROGRAMS

Section 4 describes many basic yet important computer science concepts that can be expressed using the Kodu language, and Section 5 shows that end users are regularly using the programming interface while interacting with Kodu. Here, we explore how often each computer science concept is employed in Kodu programs created in the wild (*RQ3*).

To achieve this goal, we obtained 346 Kodu programs created by Xbox users and shared through the Xbox Live community between June 20, 2009 and July 30, 2010. In the Xbox community, users can upload their programs to any of three locations; we collected all the programs from one of those repositories (often users upload to all three). We do not have any demographic information about these users.

6.1 Variables

Table 2 shows the frequency within the population of programs of each type of variable defined in Section 4.1, *Global Variables*, *Local Variables*, and *Random Variables*. The *CS Concept* column indicates the computer science concept being evaluated, *# Games* indicates how often the concept appears in the population, *% Games* shows the percentage of the population, and *% Rules* indicates the average percentage of rules per program that exhibit the concept.

Over half of the programs use global variables in some capacity, and the average number of global variables used per program is 4.1. Within those programs, an average of 23.9% of the total rules interact with a global variable in some capacity. Approximately two-thirds (67%) of these programs perform more reads than writes on the global variables; 29% perform more writes than reads, and 4% perform equal numbers of writes and reads per variable. The average number of reads per variable is 4.0, and the average number of writes is 2.3. This indicates that in the general case, the scores are used to check and maintain program state, as they are read nearly twice as often as they are written, on average.

We found that 81.2% of the games have characters that read the local variables of other characters, whereas only 64.5% perform a write on the local variables. Additionally, among the games that read local variables, 31.8% of the rules perform a read; among the games that write to the local variables, only 17.9% are involved with a write. These numbers indicate that local variables are used to trigger other actions more often than they are modified.

Random variables are present in over one-third of the games, and impact nearly 10% of the rules in those games.

Table 2: Variables and Boolean Logic in Population

CS Concept	# Games	% Games	% Rules
Global Variables	196	56.6%	23.9%
Local Variables – Read	281	81.2%	31.8%
Local Variables – Write	223	64.5%	17.9%
Random Variables	126	36.3%	9.7%
Logical *Not*	61	17.6%	4.4%
If-Then-Else Statements	29	8.4%	8.1%
Logical *And* Condition[2]	17	20.9%	18.5%
Logical *And* Action[2]	13	16.0%	15.6%
Logical *Or*	208	59.9%	16.6%

In general, users put random variables in the condition (62%) rather than the action (38%). A random variable in the condition indicates that the user desires a controlled action to occur at some non-deterministic condition.

6.2 Boolean Logic

The last five rows of Table 2 show the frequency of games and rules within the population that utilize the boolean logic constructs described in Section 4.2. The logical *not* is only present in 17.6% of the games we studied, and among those games, 47.5% of them use the *not* tile to form an *if - then - else* statement. The creation of these predicates maps very naturally to the use of conditionals in traditional programming languages.

The presence of the logical *and* is dependent on the use of indentation in the programming rules[2]. Among the games for which this feature was available, only 22.2% used this feature, but among those games, 28.7% of the rules were indented. And so, even a smaller percentage of the games utilize logical *and* in the condition and in the action. Among the indented rules, we found that 63.6% used the logical *and* in the condition, and 36.4% used the logical *and* in the action. The *and* in the condition implies that a complex state is needed in order to trigger the action, while the *and* in the action binds multiple actions to the same condition.

Duplicating the condition among multiple rules on a page with disparate actions is another way to bind multiple actions to the same condition. Among the population, this was observed in 286 (82.4%) of the games, and within those games, 35.0% of the rules had a condition identical to another condition on its page. If we control for the *when always* condition, then duplicate conditions exist in 207 (59.7%) of the games, and within those games, 17.8% of the rules had a condition identical to another on the page. Among the population for which the indentation was available, 76.5% of the games contain duplicated conditions, and this number only drops to 65.4% if we control for *when always*. These instances can be seen as missed opportunities for usage of the indention feature, which is a more explicit representation of the logical *and*. Further, indentation can remove some code duplication that is exhibited through duplicate conditions and promote reuse.

The logical *or* is the most common among the boolean logic structure, and represents the same action tied to disparate conditions. The high frequency may be the result of multiple similar conditions in which the user does not know which actually triggers the event, but further study is needed to validate that conjecture.

[2]The indentation feature needed for the logical *and* was introduced on March 19, 2010. These values consider only the 81 (23.4%) games published after that date.

Table 3: Object and Control Flow in Population

CS Concept	# Games	% Games	% Objects
Programmed Characters	338	97.7%	74.7%
2+ States	202	58.4%	40.0%
Cycles	166	47.9%	29.3%
Fan-in > 1	174	50.3%	47.5%
Fan-out > 1	123	35.5%	52.0%

6.3 Objects

Within the population of programs, 342 (98.8%) of the games contain characters (e.g., kodus, cycles, rocks), with an average of 28.3 characters per game. While some characters have no behavior, nearly three-fourths of the characters per game contain some programming, as shown in the *Programmed Characters* row of Table 3. The *CS Concept*, *# Games*, and *% Games* columns are similar to Table 2, and *% Objects* indicates the average percentage of characters per game that utilize the concept. Overall, 97.7% of the games contain programmed characters. Games also contain an average of 5.7 distinct character types (median is 5), indicating that if the author included one character of a particular type (e.g., tree, kodu, rock), they included many of that type.

On average, most of the characters (60.0%) included in a world have programming of some kind. For any world, an average of 25.2% of the characters contain no programming. Conversely, the remaining 74.8% of of the characters have programmed behavior, and the average number of rules per character is 5.14, which indicates that users are not only taking time to give characters behavior, but that the programs likely contain complex logic. In terms of creatables, 175 (50.6%) of the games contain programming to generate a creatable character during runtime.

6.4 Control Flow

In the control flow analysis, we analyze the structure of the control flow graphs that represent characters behavior, generated as described in Section 4.4. Table 3 shows the frequency of games that contain at least one character with a certain property, where *2+ States* indicates that an character uses multiple pages, *Cycles* indicates that an character's control flow graph contains a cycle, and *Fan-in > 1* and *Fan-out > 1* indicate that at least one node in at least one character's control flow graph has a fan-in or fan-out value greater than one, respectively.

Most programs (58.4%) have used the page system and have at least one character with two or more states. Additionally, 166 of the programs (47.9%) have an character with a cycle, and in fact 29.3% of the characters in those programs contain cycles. Among the characters with two or more states, 45.8% contain a cycle. About half of the programs have a node with a fan-in greater than one, with the average max fan-in among all programs being 2.8. Additionally, over one-third of the programs have a fan-out greater than one, with the average max fan-out among all programs being 1.7. The higher average max fan-in value may indicate that the characters typically have a "hub" node, or page, that contains default behavior, but further analysis is needed to validate that conjecture.

7. THREATS TO VALIDITY

There are two threats to validity that warrant discussion in this paper. The first is an internal threat concerning the connection between expressing computer science concepts and learning those same concepts, and the second is an external threat concerning artifact selection.

First, we have mapped the Kodu language onto computer science concepts and shown how these concepts can be expressed through Kodu. However, we cannot guarantee that just because a concept is expressed that it is necessarily learned. An empirical user study with pre- and post-tests would be necessary to evaluate the actual user learning.

The second threat is that the programs we analyzed come from those self-selected by the users in the Xbox community as being good enough to share, so they may represent an upper-bound in complexity. Additionally, since we cannot determine the provenance of any single Kodu program, we do not know how much of the program complexity is the product of the author versus how much resulted from an existing program that was modified by the author. However, since these programs come from the Xbox community and were created in an unsupervised environment, and since they were self-selected for sharing, we conjecture that the programming is mostly original.

8. CONCLUSIONS

In this work, we have shown that the Kodu language can be used to represent computer science concepts by pairing language constructs with fundamental concepts in computer science, but further analysis is needed to verify that users are actually grasping these concepts through Kodu. We found that users spend more time programming and configuring their programs than they do playing them, which indicates that the Kodu has reached its goal of making programming accessible to all users. Additionally, through an evaluation of 346 Kodu programs created by the user community, we found the programs to be large, complex, and exhibit many fundamental computer science concepts, which indicates that Kodu may be useful not just as a beginning programming language, but as a launching point from which users can smoothly transition to more mainstream programming languages.

Acknowledgments

We would like to give special thanks to the Kodu team and the FUSE Labs, especially Stephen Coy, Will Portnoy, Matt MacLaurin, Eric Anderson, Brad Gibson, and Rachel Schiff, for their valuable feedback and support of this work.

9. REFERENCES

[1] The impact of web 2.0 technologies in the classroom. State of Victoria: Department of Education and Early Childhood Development, December 2009.

[2] Explorer kodu club. http://koduclub.org/default.aspx, Retrieved August 1, 2010.

[3] Greenfoot. http://www.greenfoot.org/, Retrieved September 1, 2010.

[4] Kodu game lab. http://research.microsoft.com/en-us/projects/kodu/, Retrieved August 1, 2010.

[5] Kodudes – the write buzz. http://sites.google.com/site/koduxperts/, Retrieved August 1, 2010.

[6] S. Cooper, W. Dann, and R. Pausch. Alice: a 3-d tool for introductory programming concepts. In *Northeastern conference on The journal of computing in small colleges*, pages 107–116, 2000.

[7] A. Dahotre, Y. Zhang, and C. Scaffidi. A qualitative study of animation programming in the wild. In *ESEM '08: Symposium on Empirical software engineering and measurement*, 2010. to appear.

[8] B. Hanks and M. Brandt. Successful and unsuccessful problem solving approaches of novice programmers. In *Symposium on Computer science education*, pages 24–28, New York, NY, USA, 2009. ACM.

[9] C. Kelleher. *Motivating programming: using storytelling to make computer programming attractive to middle school girls*. PhD thesis, Pittsburgh, PA, USA, 2006. Adviser-Pausch, Randy.

[10] C. Kelleher and R. Pausch. Lowering the barriers to programming: A taxonomy of programming environments and languages for novice programmers. *ACM Comput. Surv.*, 37(2):83–137, 2005.

[11] C. Kelleher, R. Pausch, and S. Kiesler. Storytelling alice motivates middle school girls to learn computer programming. In *Conference on Human factors in computing systems*, pages 1455–1464, 2007.

[12] C. M. Lewis. How programming environment shapes perception, learning and goals: logo vs. scratch. In *Symposium on Computer science education*, pages 346–350, New York, NY, USA, 2010. ACM.

[13] J. Maloney, L. Burd, Y. Kafai, N. Rusk, B. Silverman, and M. Resnick. Scratch: A sneak preview. In *C5 '04: Conference on Creating, Connecting and Collaborating through Computing*, pages 104–109, 2004.

[14] O. Meerbaum-Salant, M. Armoni, and M. M. Ben-Ari. Learning computer science concepts with scratch. In *ICER '10:Workshop on Computing education research*, pages 69–76, 2010.

[15] S. Papert. *Mindstorms: children, computers, and powerful ideas*. Basic Books, Inc., New York, NY, USA, 1980.

[16] D. Parsons and P. Haden. Programming osmosis: Knowledge transfer from imperative to visual programming environments. In *Conference of the National Advisory Committee on Computing Qualifications*. Citeseer, 2007.

[17] M. Resnick. *Turtles, termites, and traffic jams: explorations in massively parallel microworlds*. MIT Press, Cambridge, MA, USA, 1994.

[18] K. T. Stolee. Kodu language and grammar specification. Microsoft Research whitepaper, Retrieved September 1, 2010.

[19] L. Werner, J. Denner, M. Bliesner, and P. Rex. Can middle-schoolers use storytelling alice to make games?: results of a pilot study. In *Conference on Foundations of Digital Games*, pages 207–214, 2009.

Can Graduating Students Design: Revisited

Chris Loftus
Department of Computer Science
Aberystwyth University
Aberystwyth, Wales, UK
cwl@aber.ac.uk

Lynda Thomas
Department of Computer Science
Aberystwyth University
Aberystwyth, Wales, UK
ltt@aber.ac.uk

Carol Zander
Computing and Software Systems
University of Washington Bothell
Bothell, WA, USA
zander@u.washington.edu

ABSTRACT

In this paper we revisit previous research to elaborate on the question: "Can graduating students design software systems?" The work concluded that the answer was "not really". We wished to determine if this was true currently at our institution and also to look at whether students were able to design software in groups, and evaluate others' designs. In summary, it appears that our students, just as in the original experiment, struggle with doing design, even in a group situation. The representation of behavioural design was particularly lacking. That said, students were able to recognize weaknesses when evaluating other group designs. Based on our findings, we provide several pedagogic recommendations.

Categories and Subject Descriptors

K.3.2 [**Computers and Education**]: Computers and Information Science Education - *Computer Science Education.*

General Terms

Measurement, Experimentation. Design

Keywords

Design, Software Engineering, Student Performance.

1. INTRODUCTION

In this paper we revisit research that started in 2003-2004 as part of the 'Scaffolding' experiment [11]. This was a multi-national, multi-institutional study that analysed software designs collected from different populations of students and educators.

One aspect of the analysis resulted in a paper published in 2006 [6], hereafter called the 'Graduating Design paper', that specifically asked the question "Can graduating students design software systems?" The authors of the paper looked at 149 designs produced by students nearing graduation, and concluded that "the majority of graduating students cannot design a software system."

To reach this conclusion they placed each design into one of six categories, slightly abbreviated in Figure 1, which also shows the results. The conclusions, showing that over 60% contributed little progress towards a design, were clearly sobering for educators.

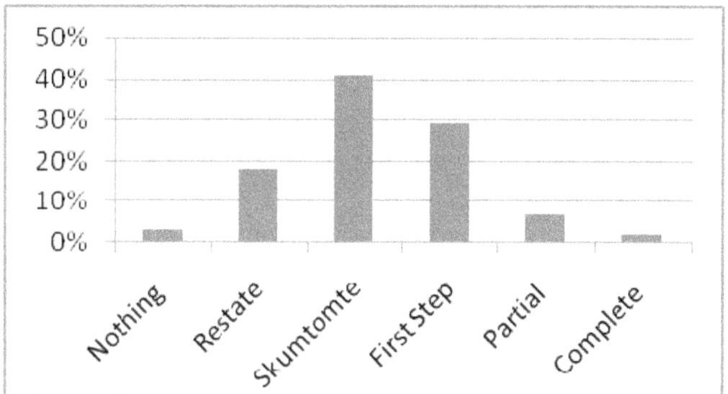

Nothing This category has designs with little or no intelligible content. Tend to be very short, typically an unlabeled diagram.

Restatement These are designs that merely restate requirements from the task description. A typical example is a list of functions corresponding to the items in the description.

Skumtomte Named after a Swedish marshmallow treat, these designs add a small amount to restating the task. Some subjects added a little information in text, or a drawing, or some unimportant implementation details. There is no overall system view, nor any significant work on any of the modules.

First step Designs in this category include some significant work beyond the description: either a partial overview of the system (identifying the parts, but generally not identifying how they are related) or the design of one component.

Partial design A partial design provides an understandable description of each of the parts and an overview of the system that illustrates the relationships between the parts. The descriptions of the parts may be incomplete or superficial.

Complete design These designs show a well-developed solution, including an understandable overview, part descriptions that include responsibilities, and explicit communication. A typical example uses multiple formal notations (e.g., UML, Use cases, CRC cards) as well as text.

Figure 1: The categories of design and the results, from [6]

In Semester one of 2009-2010, we reconsidered the experiment and extended it at Aberystwyth University. This was in a final year compulsory course that consolidates students' design knowledge in the context of studying Agile Methodologies. This paper describes what we did and what we discovered.

The overarching research question was slightly different from the original: "Can graduating students design software systems in groups?" A subsidiary question was also investigated in this local context: "Are students able to evaluate others' designs, and recognise good and bad designs?"

Section 2 examines the relevant literature and looks further at the design categories in Figure 1. Section 3 describes the data collection and analysis. In Section 4 we look at the results, and Section 5 presents conclusions and pedagogical implications.

2. BACKGROUND

It is evident that we must enable our students to acquire the skills to undertake modelling using the appropriate notations and methodologies, and at the right level of abstraction so they can understand and communicate software problems and their solutions. We usually do this with fairly simple designs built from scratch. We note that most real-life problems involve maintaining existing large and complex systems, and it is even more difficult to teach students how to solve these "wicked" problems [5]. In this paper, as in the Graduating Design paper [6], we restrict ourselves to the simpler case (see Figure 2).

The categories of design achieved in the Graduating Design paper were correlated with the number of computer science courses completed. Those who had a 'complete design' had taken on average 17 CS courses. Moreover, students generally producing better designs took longer (students were allowed to spend as long as they liked). Complete and partial designs averaged 60-65 minutes; first step designs, 42 minutes; and the other categories less time [6].

The Graduating Design paper [6] followed Soloway [10] in advocating the following five phases in developing a design: understanding the problem specification, decomposing the problem into programmable goals and objects, selecting and composing plans to solve the problem, implementing plans in language constructs, and reflecting and evaluating the final artefact and process. The paper noted that the first phase can be mapped directly to the Restatement and Skumtomte categories. More information on the category relationships is found in [7].

Another approach is to consider what aspects of design are typically needed, and what artefacts those aspects lead to. All software development methodologies stipulate the analysis and design artefacts that should be produced and when. For example, the IBM Rational Unified Process (UP) [9] takes a use-case driven approach where UML use cases are initially expressed in their diagram and textual form, but individual use cases are then realized as activity diagrams, class diagrams and others. The UP captures analysis, behavioural and static structural information, and both for detailed and architectural views of a system.

Although agile methodologies place more emphasis on code and less on analysis and design artefacts, they still employ such artefacts [4]. For example, Agile Modeling [1] uses the full range of UML diagrams, as well as other kinds of diagram, e.g. GUI story boards. Much less emphasis is placed on software tools and more on using whiteboards and paper. Diagrams are only drawn to help one understand and solve a problem or to communicate with others, but not drawn for their own sake. Even Extreme Programming [2] advocates the use of CRC (Class, Responsibilities and Collaborations) [3] sessions involving brainstorming activities where class and communication diagrams are used, but also in a lightweight fashion.

What is clear from all these methodologies is that modelling using diagrams is required to represent the functional and non-functional analysis of a system (use cases or similar), the behaviour and structure of a system, and at both an architectural and detailed level. Furthermore, most methodologies explicitly encourage linkage between artefacts, and many are iterative and incrementally add to earlier models during the course of a project.

Getting People to Sleep

Your brief is to design a "super alarm clock" for University students to help them to manage their own sleep patterns, and also to provide data to support a research project into the extent of sleep problems in this community. You may assume that, for the prototype, each student will have a Pocket PC (or similar device) which is permanently connected to a network.

Your system will need to:

- Allow a student to set an alarm to wake themselves up.
- Allow a student to set an alarm to remind themselves to sleep.
- Record when a student tells the system they are about to sleep.
- Record when a student tells the system that they have woken up, and whether it is due to an alarm or not.
- Make recommendations as to when a student needs to go to sleep. This should include "yellow alerts" when the student will need sleep soon, and "red alerts" when they need to sleep now.
- Store the collected data in a server or database for later analysis.
- The server/database system (which will also trigger the yellow/red alerts) will be designed and implemented by another team. You should, however, indicate in your design the behaviour you expect from the back-end system.
- Report students who are becoming dangerously sleep-deprived to someone who cares about them (their mother?).

Figure 2: Scaffolding Design brief, abbreviated, based on [6]

3. DATA COLLECTION AND ANALYSIS

Data was collected from students who were taking a compulsory final year, semester one course entitled 'agile methodologies'. All of the students had taken a curriculum of at least a year and a half of full-time computing including courses on Java programming, software design, database and data structures. Some students had also had a year-long internship experience. In their first year, the students had been introduced to UML through use cases, class and instance diagrams in their first course, and sequence diagrams in their second course. In addition, they had looked at object-oriented design patterns in their second year and were being introduced to refactoring and anti-patterns in the Agile methodologies course.

3.1 Group Design – part 1

In the first part of the experiment, in week nine of the semester, students were organised into six groups, each of which contained about 10 final year students. Each group then had about 50 minutes to produce a solution to the same exercise that was used in the Graduating Design paper, outlined in Figure 2. The students were told (as in the original experiment):

"In doing this you should (1) produce an initial solution that someone (not necessarily you) could work from (2) divide your solution into not less than two and not more than ten parts, giving each a name and adding a short description of what it is and what it does – in short, why it is a part. If important to your design, you may indicate an order to the parts, or add some additional detail as to how the parts fit together."

The designs were produced on flip chart paper, collected and photographed.

In the original experiment the time was not fixed and complete designs took on average 60 minutes, but this was not achievable within the constraints of our course. We note that in our experiment the groups all finished before the time was up. We also note that not all members of each group contributed to the same degree and that credit was given just for attending the session, although on the whole participation was quite active.

3.2 Evaluation of Designs – part 2

As an individual exercise, the students were then presented with the designs from the 'other' groups. They were asked to evaluate each design and determine which was the best design and why. As one of these 'other' designs, the authors included a design that we produced ourselves, based on a solution shared by the authors of the Graduating Design paper. The students were not aware of which group produced which design, or of the extra design. Evaluations of the designs were obtained from 47 students.

3.3 Analysis

The authors looked at the seven group designs and categorised them using a modified version of the criteria in [7] and rooted in the discussion in Section 2. The categorisation shown in Table 1 is based on an attempt to answer the question: if a system architect was presented with a design for a system that the architect was about to maintain or build, then what information would s/he hope to find in the perfect design document?

Table 1 summarises the artefacts as marking criteria used to assess a design, providing relative weights for each design area. The artefacts shown are possibilities rather than absolutes. We considered other artefacts so long as they conveyed useful information for a given design area.

Although not shown in Table 1, each design area has a discrete set of nominal marks (0, 0.25, 0.5, 0.75, 1) used when evaluating a design. The 'real mark' awarded for a design area is the nominal mark multiplied by the weighting. The total real mark awarded for a design will range from 0 to 10. The six categories of Figure 1, from the original Graduating Design paper, are mapped to real marks in Table 2.

Our motivation for using the marking criteria of Table 1 and then mapping to categories was to find an objective way to evaluate designs, and to find a scheme that could be applied to very different kinds of design. By using weightings, we are able to tune marking criteria based on context. For example, a small system should place less emphasis on architectural design than a large system comprised of many subsystems. The emphasis on behavioural versus structural design also depends on the nature of the system being constructed.

The *Getting People to Sleep* problem places particular emphasis on message passing behaviour, whereas its static structure is relatively simple. The relative importance persistence or user interface plays in the design will also depend on the nature of the problem. Likewise, the security design area will vary in importance (here, we gave it a weighting of zero as it was not mentioned in the problem statement). These weightings also recognise that if software engineers are provided with limited time to undertake a design exercise then they should focus on the key design areas for the given problem.

Table 1. Marking criteria for the group designs with weightings that reflect the Getting People to Sleep problem

Design area	Possible artefacts	Weight (total = 10)
A: Problem analysis	Use case diagrams with actors linked. Use case descriptions. Stories with stakeholders and business value identified. Interaction scenarios. Functional and non-functional requirements.	2
B: Design		
B1 Architecture		
B1a: Behaviour	Sequence, communication, activity diagrams or similar showing major flows of control through system.	1.5
B1b: Structural	Component diagrams with associations or similar showing major parts of system.	1
B2: Detailed		
B2a: Behaviour	Key algorithms (code, pseudo-code, data flow or activity diagrams...). More detailed sequence diagrams or communication diagrams for more significant object interactions. State diagrams.	1
B2b: Structural	Detailed class diagrams (classes and associations) exploding components from architecture. Identification of boundary, control, entity classes.	0.5
B3: Database	Kind of database: relational, XML, non-SQL. Design of structures: tables, ER diagrams.	1.5
B4: GUI	Mock-ups. Storyboards	0.5
B5: Security	Relevant discussion of authentication, authorisation, confidentiality, data integrity, security auditing, XSS, XSRF, SQL injection.	0
C: Linkage of artefacts	Linkage by placement, words or lines between: analysis and design artefacts; architectural and detailed design artefacts; GUI and other design artefacts; database and other design artefacts; structural and behavioural design artefacts.	2

Table 2. Mapping of real marks to original categories

Real mark range	Category
0	Nothing
>0, <2	Restatement
≥2, <4	Skumtomte
≥4, <6	First step
≥6, <8	Partial design
≥8, ≤10	Complete design

Development methodology may also affect weightings. An agile methodology will discourage overly detailed requirements analysis or big design up-front [2], but rather take an iterative and evolutionary approach to finding both requirements and design.

Many methodologies also place less emphasis on documenting the design [1, 4]. In these methodologies the customer is expected to remain an integral part of the development process providing revised requirements as understanding improves. An architect joining such a project would expect to see fewer detailed UML diagrams, partial capture of requirements reflecting the current iteration cycle, and more emphasis on customer-level and developer-level tests. In contrast, a traditional, phased-based waterfall-style methodology will tend to produce large amounts of documentation of all types.

The above factors should therefore be taken into account when applying the marking criteria to any design weightings. For the *Getting People to Sleep* problem we assume a fairly traditional methodology, but one where time is limited.

4. RESULTS

In this section we look at our analysis of the student groups' designs and also their analysis of each other's (and our) designs.

4.1 Group Designs

The categorisation of the group designs, based on the marking criteria in Table 1 is shown in Table 3 (marks of zero omitted).

Two of the authors independently analysed and categorised the six groups and the authors' design. The marks awarded were compared and found to be similar. One author missed some static detailed design information for Group E. After correction, the authors' categories for each group were the same.

As possible with just six designs to compare, our groups did as badly as those in the original experiment. That said, the way groups were categorised was different and the time allocated to our students was fixed at 50 minutes (it took 60 minutes on average for complete designs in the original study.)

The worst design (Group C) had two sheets that largely restated the problem and one (Figure 3) with an unconventional use case diagram for part of the problem. The mark correctly suggests that the focus is **restatement**. While some designs included vague class diagrams at best (Figure 4), most included none.

The two designs that had the highest marks (Group F and ours) were complete in more areas, and were the only designs with any linkage between parts (Figure 5).

Table 3. Results for group designs

Artifacts	Real Mark
Group A, 6 pages, Category: Skumtomte	
A: Restatement, one use case for single actor	1
B2a: Sequence fragment	0.25
B2b: Class/ER diagram. Another class diagram…	0.375
B3: Mentioned, some implied primary keys	0.375
Total	**2**
Group B, 2 pages, Category: Skumtomte	
A: Good use case diagram	2
B1b: Weak MVC component-like diagram; a few methods	0.5
B2b: Some boundary /control classes	0.125
Total	**2.625**
Group C, 3 pages, Category: Restatement	
A: Some restatement. Unconventional use case	0.5
B1a: Minor reference to interactions with server.	0.375
Total	**0.875**
Group D, 2 pages, Category: Skumtomte	
A: Use case diagram	2
B1a: List of flows of control at an abstract level	0.75
B1b: Small ref. as part of use case diagram	0.25
Total	**3**
Group E, 4 pages, Category: First step	
A: Use cases; unconventional	1
B1a: Some behaviour between actors and system	0.75
B1b: Component-like diagram with textual description	1
B2b: List of classes.	0.25
Total	**3**
Group F, 7 pages, Category: Partial design	
A: Textual. Good use case diagrams.	2
B1a: Hints in one use case	0.375
B1b: List of identifying key components	0.5
B2a: Flow diagrams: operation of alerts	1
B2b: Class diagram: some inheritance	0.5
B3: Textual analysis; some table design	0.75
B4: Textual discussion of features.	0.25
C: Alarm classes with textual linkage to requirements. Also in database design.	1
Total	**6.375**
Ours (design G), 3 pages, Category: Complete design	
A: Detailed use case diagram with relevant actors.	2
B1a: Top level sequence diagram between core components.	1.5
B1b: Major components identified	0.5
B2a: Detailed sequence diagram to show interaction with database.	1
B3: Some design, but not table design.	1.125
C: Elements of different diagrams are linked using numbers.	2
Total	**8.125**

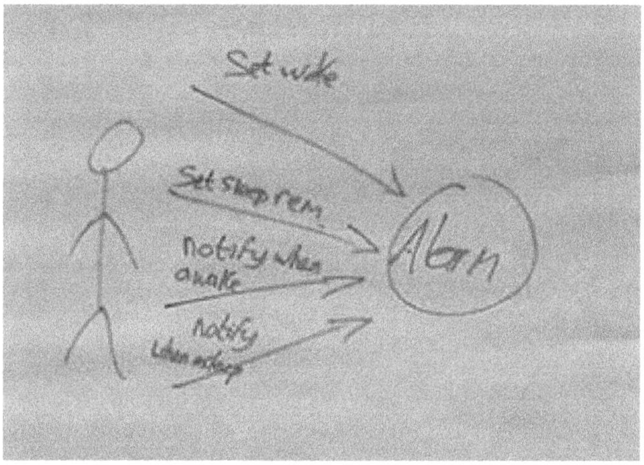

Figure 3: Group C design, showing the only diagram (A)

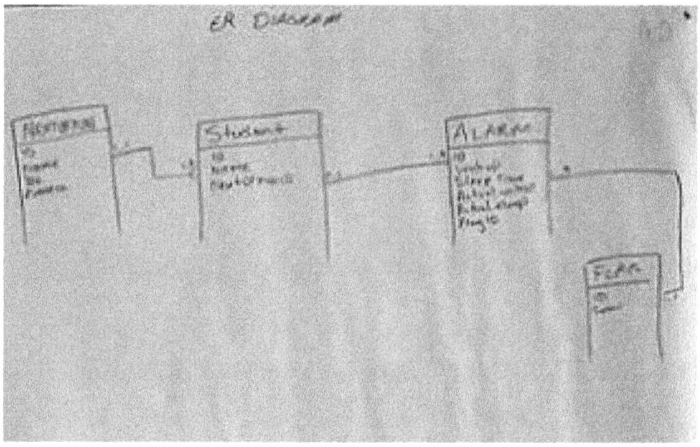

Figure 4: Group A design, showing an ER diagram (B2b)

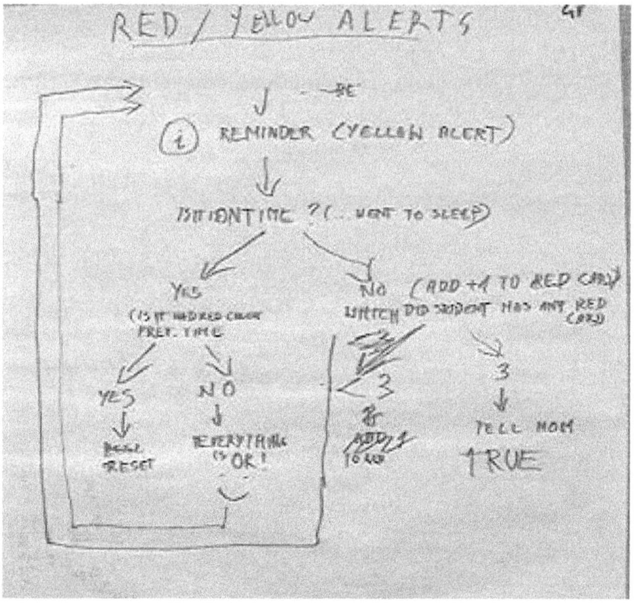

Figure 5: Group F design, showing alert behavior (B2a)

Overall, the groups were strongest at analyzing the problem and providing use case diagrams. Despite the fact that class diagrams are an important part of the design curriculum starting in their first year, two groups (C and D) had nothing resembling a class diagram and other groups had only sketchy ones – mainly names but no detail or relationships.

Structural design was stronger than behavioural design, the latter being mainly absent in all but group F's and the authors' submissions. Having identified the main use cases, groups did not pursue them into answering the question 'how would our system do that?'

4.2 Evaluation of Designs

Table 4 shows the results of the evaluation exercise – students who said that either of 2 (or 3) designs was 'the best' were counted as .5 (or .33). No favourite was chosen by 6 students.

Table 4. Students evaluate designs

Best design to implement from	Number of students	Total
A	2+1*.33	2.33
B	0+2*.5	1
C	0	0
D	1+1*.33	1.33
E	2+1*.5	2.5
F	16 +3*.5+2*.33	18.16
G (authors)	13 +4*.5+2*.33	15.66
None identified	6	

We note that the design which we evaluated as 'restatement' received no support and that the two designs we considered to be reasonable designs were indeed rated best by the students. Design F was seen as the best by the most students (it was also the longest and had the most arrows which may have had an effect). A disproportionate number of the students who chose design G as best were in group F so not able to choose their own.

Students' discussions of the designs varied between very superficial:

> S10 on design F: *"This design was the most in-depth and had nice pictures."*

and quite thoughtful and perceptive:

> S12 on design G: *"...the group has expanded to designing the database schema and including sequence diagrams to explain the relationship between system functionality and database design."*

Some students implied a use case diagram fully describes problem behaviour:

> S15 on design D: *"A good use case diagram that covers the major behaviour in the brief*

Students recognized the weakness of design C, even using similar terminology to ours:

> S21 on design C: *"There is a very simple use-case diagram and another image that just re-iterates some of the points given to us in the brief."*

On the other hand, some students seemed to be confused about what a design was for:

> S31 on design C: *"Design C sets out clearly what the critical levels of alert are .... [but] more design artifacts should be used to tell the programmer or system architect how to build such a system."*

5. DISCUSSION

What did we learn or contribute from this exercise? The first thing is that our experiment confirmed the results of the Graduating Design paper. It appears that many graduating students cannot design software systems. This was very depressing for the authors. We learned that our current crop of students did not do as well as we expected in the design exercise, even when working in groups. Only one student group produced what we considered to be a reasonable design. We note that the original experiment took volunteer students from each institution who may be of a higher caliber on the whole, whereas we used a complete cross section of student abilities. Another threat to the validity of this experiment is that no consideration was taken of group structure or dynamics. We had hoped that working in a group would lead to better solutions, but it may have hindered the design process as opposed to helped it.

Second, our marking criteria elaborates the simpler categorisation of the Graduating Design paper and is useful for assessing designs developed under different software engineering methodologies.

Finally, our analysis has implications for teaching and learning. The main thing that was lacking in the student designs was any attempt to describe behaviour of the system under consideration, leading to our first teaching recommendation (TR):

TR1 More emphasis on behaviour when teaching design.

While the student groups did seem to be able to construct use-case diagrams, they did not relate them to further artefacts in the design. There is a danger when using use-case diagrams that they become simply restatements of the problem, and that is particularly likely if they are not linked to something else in the design – probably a sequence diagram:

TR2: Stress that use-case diagrams need to be linked with other artefacts.

On a positive note, students did seem, on the whole to be able to recognize better designs. We now feel that this exercise should be introduced much earlier into the curriculum. Did the students in group C think what they did was a good design at the time, and what would they think once they had seen other designs? This fits in with the literature on peer-marking: that students contribute to the learning of other students [8]:

TR3: Give students examples of other students' designs so that they can see how they are doing and 'up their game'.

6. ACKNOWLEDGMENTS

Thanks to our students for allowing us to use their work and to the authors of the Graduating Design paper for advice and support.

7. REFERENCES

[1] Ambler, S.W. 2002. Agile Modeling, John Wiley and Sons.

[2] Beck, K. 2004. Extreme Programming Explained, Addison Wesley.

[3] Bellin, D.,Simone, S.S. 1997. The CRC Card Book, Addison Wesley.

[4] Boehm, B. 2002. Get ready for agile methods, with care. IEEE Computer, Vol. 53, 1, 64-69.

[5] Budgen, D. 2003. Software Design, Addison Wesley.

[6] Eckerdal, A., McCartney, R., Moström, J. E., Ratcliffe, M., and Zander, C. 2006. Can graduating students design software systems? In Proceedings of the 37th SIGCSE Technical Symposium on Computer Science Education, SIGCSE '06. ACM, New York, NY, 403-407.

[7] Eckerdal, A., McCartney, R., Moström, J. E., Ratcliffe, M., and Zander, C. 2006. Categorizing student software designs: Methods, results, and implications, Computer Science Education, Vol. 16, 3, 197-209.

[8] Hamer, J., Cutts, Q., Jackova, J., Luxton-Reilly, A., McCartney, R., Purchase, H., Riedesel, C., Saeli, M., Sanders, K., and Sheard, J. 2008. Contributing student pedagogy. SIGCSE Bull. 40, 4, 194-212.

[9] Kruchten, P. 2003. The Rational Unified Process, An Introduction, Addison Wesley.

[10] Soloway, E., Spohrer, J., and D. Littman, D. 1988. E unum pluribus: Generating alternative designs. In R. E. Mayer, editor, Teaching and Learning Computer Programming, Lawrence Erlbaum Associates,, 137-152.

[11] Tenenberg, J., Fincher, S., et al., 2005. Students designing software: a multi-national, multi-institutional study, Informatics in Education, 4(1):143-162.

The FCS1: A Language Independent Assessment of CS1 Knowledge

Allison Elliott Tew
Department of Computer Science
University of British Columbia
Vancouver, BC V6T 1Z4
aetew@cs.ubc.ca

Mark Guzdial
School of Interactive Computing
Georgia Institute of Technology
Atlanta, GA 30332-0760
guzdial@cc.gatech.edu

ABSTRACT

A primary goal of many CS education projects is to determine the extent to which a given intervention has had an impact on student learning. However, computing lacks valid assessments for pedagogical or research purposes. Without such valid assessments, it is difficult to accurately measure student learning or establish a relationship between the instructional setting and learning outcomes.

We developed the Foundational CS1 (FCS1) Assessment instrument, the first assessment instrument for introductory computer science concepts that is applicable across a variety of current pedagogies and programming languages. We applied methods from educational and psychological test development, adapting them as necessary to fit the disciplinary context. We conducted a large scale empirical study to demonstrate that pseudo-code was an appropriate mechanism for achieving programming language independence. Finally, we established the validity of the assessment using a multi-faceted argument, combining interview data, statistical analysis of results on the assessment, and CS1 exam scores.

Categories and Subject Descriptors

K.3.2 [**Computers and Education**]: Computer and Information Science Education—*computer science education, curriculum*

General Terms

Experimentation, measurement

Keywords

Assessment, CS1, programming, validity

1. INTRODUCTION

Measuring student learning is fundamental to any educational endeavor. A primary goal of many computer science education projects is to determine the extent to which a given instructional intervention has had an impact on student learning. However, the field of computing lacks valid and reliable assessment instruments for pedagogical or research purposes. Without such valid assessments, it is difficult to accurately measure student learning or establish a relationship between the instructional setting and learning outcomes. The goal of assessment research in computer science is to have valid ways of measuring student conceptions of fundamental topics, which will enable both research into how understanding of knowledge in the domain develops as well as enable curricular innovation and reform grounded in this knowledge.

Many science, technology, engineering and mathematics (STEM) disciplines have standard validated assessment tools that allow educators and researchers to accurately measure student learning and evaluate curricular innovations (e.g., [6, 9]). However, computer science does not have a similar set of validated assessment tools. There are four existing validated exams of computer science conceptual knowledge. Two, the CS Advanced Placement (AP) exam and the Advanced Level General Certificate of Education (A-level) in Computing, focus on the introductory sequence in computing. These exams, written in the Java programming language, are controlled and administered by specific educational testing boards and thus are not widely applicable and available to educators and researchers for general use. The remaining two exams, the Major Field Test for Computer Science and the GRE Computer Science Subject Test, cover a wide range of material as they are designed to evaluate end of degree program learning objectives.

The CS education community has shown growing interest in assessment research, and two related projects are underway. In dissertation work, Decker [3] designed an assessment for an introductory sequence of programming courses (CS1 and CS2) in Java. The instrument was developed and tested at a single institution, and therefore its validity claims cannot be generalized beyond that context. Craig Zilles and colleagues have received funding to develop a set of concept inventories for computing, in discrete math, digital logic design, and programming fundamentals. The researchers have elicited a set of troublesome concepts from educational experts [4] and are conducting think-aloud interviews to capture student misconceptions [7]. The work is preliminary and instruments are still being developed.

Our work differs from these efforts in that we created a rigorously validated exam that could be widely adopted and used in any introductory CS course. The goal was to create

SIGCSE'11, March 9–12, 2011, Dallas, Texas, USA.

an exam to measure understanding of fundamental computing concepts, independent of programming language, that would not be overly biased by any particular pedagogical paradigm. We focused on three questions regarding assessment of introductory concepts in computer science. How can existing test development methods be applied and adapted to create a valid assessment instrument for CS1 conceptual knowledge? To what extent can pseudo-code be used as the mechanism for achieving programming language independence in an assessment instrument? And to what extent does the language independent instrument provide a valid measure of CS1 conceptual knowledge?

This paper begins with an overview of the method used to develop the first assessment instrument for introductory computer science concepts that is applicable across a variety of current pedagogies and programming languages.

2. METHOD FOR DEVELOPING A VALIDATED CS1 ASSESSMENT

The fields of education and psychology have developed a rich history in developing and validating measurement instruments for a variety of purposes [1]. We applied these established methods and practices for developing valid measures, summarized below, adapting them where necessary for the field of computer science.

The first step in test development is to establish the purpose and definition of the test — what is to be measured and what the scores mean. The test specification includes the definition of the conceptual content, or constructs, that is to be measured, the format of the questions, and the scoring procedures. The test specification should be reviewed by a panel of experts to provide content validity evidence and ensure that all constructs are adequately represented and extraneous constructs are not included.

After the test specification has been developed and verified, a test bank of questions should be developed to cover all constructs identified in the specification. Piloting of the questions then takes place. Pilot tests examine the suitability of the questions, allowing necessary revisions to be made prior to the selection of the final candidate questions. The last stages of test development are empirical studies of individual responses to establish validity and reliability. Validity testing ensures that the test is measuring the intended constructs, and reliability testing verifies that the results are consistent over repeated examinations, and thus are dependable.

To create the FCS1 Assessment, two adaptations were required. The first methodological change centered around creating an exam focused on concepts not programming language syntax, so the assessment can be as widely applicable as possible. The method required the addition of a step to verify the programming language independence of the exam. To achieve language independence for a CS1 exam, we utilized a verbose pseudo-code as the exam programming language. We evaluated the effectiveness of this approach using a combination of think aloud and empirical studies[1]. These studies were required to ensure students are able to appropriately transfer understanding from their programming language of instruction to pseudo-code and to ensure that students are able to demonstrate their understanding adequately in the new language independent exam.

The second change is required because the standard methods for validating the instrument against existing valid measures did not apply to this exam, which is the first of its kind in the field of computing. So a validity argument was crafted using a combination of think aloud interviews and statistical analysis techniques.

The first three steps in this process have previously been described in [13]. Section 3 contains the results of our empirical study investigating the use of pseudo-code as the mechanism to achieve language independence, and the process used to validate the exam is explained in Section 4. The data collected will allow preliminary analysis of the internal reliability of the exam. However, full-scale reliability testing is left for future work.

3. FCS1 ASSESSMENT STUDY

We conducted a large scale empirical study comparing student performance on the FCS1 Assessment[2] to a comparable version of the assessment instrument written in the students' CS1 programming language. Participants were selected at the end of CS1 courses taught in Java, Matlab, or Python, and statistical analysis was used to look for correlations in student performance between the two exams.

3.1 Study Design

We recruited participants from four different introductory courses taught at two universities by four separate faculty members, so that the definition and understanding of CS1 knowledge was not tied to a particular faculty member or institution. There were a total of 952 participants who were enrolled in a CS1 course in Java ($n = 80$), Matlab ($n = 520$), or Python ($n = 352$).

The study consisted of two assessment exams given, one week apart, under testing conditions — no questions were permitted and collaboration was not allowed. Participants completed the FCS1 Assessment and a comparable version of the FCS1 rewritten in the programming language used in their introductory CS course. The comparable version was created using the alternate questions for each concept in the test bank. A counterbalanced quasi-experimental design was used to reduce bias from ordering effect.

3.2 Data Analysis Results

Before data analysis could begin, outliers from the data set that would bias or skew the results were removed. An external researcher verified the rules for exclusion and independently reviewed all of the exams that were removed from the data set to confirm that they met one or more of the exclusionary criteria.

3.2.1 *Scoring the FCS1*

The pseudo-code and CS1 language versions of the FCS1 were graded, awarding a 1 for a correct answer and a 0 for an incorrect answer. (Any question left blank was not scored.) Student participants answered an average of 8.82 (33.78%, $\sigma = 3.649$) questions correctly on the pseudo-code version

[1]Due to space constraints, we limit our discussion here to the empirical study. See [12] for more details.

[2]Unfortunately for the validity and reliability of the assessment instrument, exam questions must remain private and cannot be published. This prevents potentially biasing participants involved in validation studies.

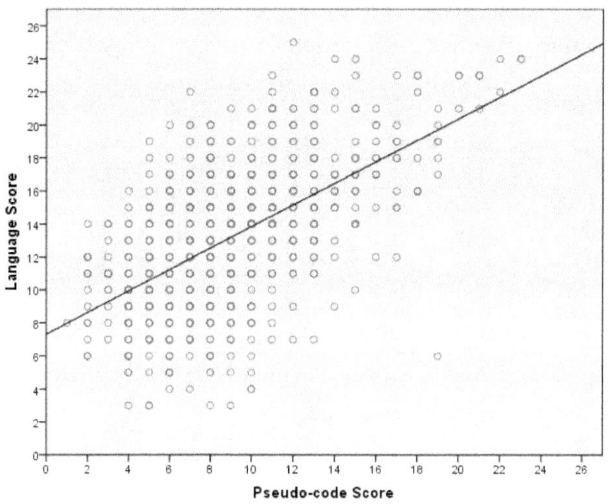

Figure 1: Scatterplot of Scores for Correlation of Pseudo-code and Language Versions of FCS1

of the FCS1. The maximum score was a 23, and the minimum score was a 1. Students were more successful answering questions on the CS1 language specific exam. An average of 13.13 (48.61%, $\sigma = 4.195$) questions were answered correctly, and the minimum and maximum score both increased by two points to 3 and 25, respectively. While the overall scores were higher on this version of this exam, similar concepts appear among those identified as least and most difficult across the populations.

Questions about math operators and *if* statements were among the most commonly answered correctly. The programming constructs related to function parameters, function return values, and recursion were the most difficult questions on both the pseudo-code and the language specific version of the FCS1.

3.2.2 *Correlation with CS1 Language Version*

We investigated the effectiveness of pseudo-code as the mechanism to achieve programming language independence by examining whether students were able to transfer their understanding of fundamental computing concepts from their CS1 programming language to pseudo-code. A correlation analysis was conducted to look for evidence of a positive correlation between the overall scores, i.e. the number of questions answered correctly, for each participant on both versions of the FCS1 Assessment.

A Pearson product-moment correlation coefficient was computed to assess the relationship between the score on the pseudo-code version and the score on the language specific version of the assessment instrument. There was a strong, positive correlation between the two variables, Pearson's $r(850) = .572$, $p <= 0.001$. A scatterplot summarizes the results in Figure 1.

Having found a positive correlation, which meets the guidelines for large effect size ($r >= .37$) in the social sciences [2], subsequent analyses focused on correlating exam scores for each CS1 programming language sub-population. Were students from each of the CS1 programming languages examined – Java, Matlab, and Python – able to transfer their understanding to pseudo-code? Or is the syntax of the pseudo-code too distinct from what the participants have learned to facilitate the expression of conceptual understanding in a new programming language?

Pearson product-moment correlation coefficients were computed to assess the relationship between the score on the pseudo-code version and the score on the language specific version of the assessment for each programming language participant group (see Table 1). There was a strong, positive correlation between the scores on the pseudo-code and language versions of the assessment for each of the programming languages studied. Participants from the CS1 taught in Java had the strongest correlation, Pearson's $r(74) = .665$, $p <= 0.001$. Although the pseudo-code syntax had more elements in common with Python than the other programming languages studied, the Python participant group had the lowest correlation coefficient, Pearson's $r(285) = .415$, $p <= 0.001$. The Python population was comprised of students, normally students from STEM majors, enrolled in an introductory computing course as well as students who were enrolled in a non-traditional media computation course designed for liberal arts students. A Pearson's correlation coefficient was also computed for each of these subpopulations of the Python participant group. There was a strong positive correlation, (Pearson's $r(43) = .615$, $p <= 0.001$), for students enrolled in the CS-based python CS1 course that was similar to the strength of the correlation found in the Java and Matlab populations. While the effect size for the media-based Python course was smaller, $r = .372$, it met guidelines to be classified as a strong, positive correlation.

Overall the results demonstrate that there was a strong, positive correlation between the scores on the pseudo-code and CS1 language versions of the FCS1 for both traditional and non-traditional pedagogical approaches to CS1.

4. ESTABLISHING VALIDITY

After the FCS1 Assessment was piloted, the final step in the development process was to establish the validity of the exam. In general, there are two classes of evidence used to support validity claims. *Content* related evidence ensures that the assessment's content appropriately operationalizes the constructs it is intended to measure. Content validity for the FCS1 was previously established by expert panel review. *Construct* related evidence provides the second set of support for validity and is the focus of the discussion here. Together, content and construct validity enable a test developer to provide evidence that the instrument is measuring student knowledge as intended.

Given the position of this exam as the first of its kind in the field, the standard correlation methods for establishing validity do not apply. Since construct validation is dependent on inferences drawn from a variety of data [8, 10], we proposed a three-pronged approach to establishing the validity of the assessment instrument. The validity evidence is three-fold: think aloud interview data, student responses to the FCS1, and student CS1 exam scores.

4.1 Qualitative Analysis of Student Interviews

Qualitative analysis of transcripts from think aloud interviews with students provides evidence whether students were answering questions based on their knowledge of the conceptual content. The goal of the analysis was to determine whether students were using knowledge about the intended construct to answer the question. Alternatively,

Table 1: Significant Pearson Correlations of FCS1 Assessment‡

Population	Version	Language	Midterm 1	Midterm 2	Midterm 3	Final
Total	Pseudo	.572	.111	.149	.309	.499
	Language	*	.120	.128	.491	.542
Java	Pseudo	.665	.408	.446	—	.511
	Language	*	.406	.582	—	.680
Matlab	Pseudo	.547	.500	.527	.443	.438
	Language	*	.531	.536	.488	.505
Python	Pseudo	.415	.200	.216	*n.s.*	.453
	Language	*	.424	.429	.392	.539
CS-Python	Pseudo	.615	.719	.685	.625	.679
	Language	*	.525	.445†	.429†	.437†
Media-Python	Pseudo	.372	.246	.220	.305	.262
	Language	*	.456	.453	.542	.601

‡ All correlations, unless otherwise noted, are significant at the $p <= 0.001$ level.
† Correlation is significant at the $p <= 0.01$ level.
* Language-Language self comparison omitted.
— No midterm 3 measure was analyzed because only two midterms were administered in the course.

additional information could be required to correctly answer the question or other cues could be enabling correct responses without knowledge of the concept.

Thirteen student participants, of varying ability levels, were recruited from introductory courses taught in three different programming languages (Java, Matlab, and Python). Students were asked to participate in a think aloud interview conducted while they were completing the pseudo-code version of the FCS1. The interview data was transcribed and content analysis was used to analyze the participant responses. Specifically, responses were coded for correctness, errors made, and evidence of reasoning using the new pseudo-code language syntax.

Valid responses demonstrated evidence of student reasoning about the question's intended construct and reaching a correct or incorrect response based upon the level of understanding. That is, if a student held misconceptions about a topic, they selected an incorrect answer. Otherwise, they answered correctly. A majority (83.07%) of the responses analyzed were categorized as valid. The multiple-choice testing format allowed a few correct responses (5.92%) despite students' misunderstanding about the questions conceptual content. Further, there were a small number of responses (4.44%) where student misconceptions about another topic prevented them from answering the question correctly. However, there were no instances where students reasoning about another construct enabled a correct response to a question without knowledge of the concept.

Overall, the interview evidence provides a qualitative argument that students are able to read and reason with the pseudo-code syntax. Further, they are using their knowledge about the intended construct to answer the question.

4.2 Quantitative Analysis using IRT

The FCS1 Assessment study data and analysis provides a quantitative argument towards construct validity. The Pearson correlation analysis demonstrated that students have a comparable knowledge to that measured in a language specific version of the exam. If the questions are representative measures of knowledge in students' CS1 programming language, then validity of the exam is contingent upon the questions themselves. Item response theory (IRT) is the statistical analysis technique employed to make this validity claim. If the questions are shown to be "good" questions (i.e., of appropriate difficulty and discrimination) and students demonstrate comparable knowledge to a language specific exam, then the argument is made that this is an accurate representation of students' understanding of the topics.

Using a three-parameter logistic model (3PL) [5], IRT was used to analyze the FCS1 participant responses to discern the strength and weakness of each item in the test. Overall, most (24 of 27) questions displayed strong item discrimination, adequate difficulty, and low guessing probability. Two questions, Q12 and Q13, were too difficult. That is $b_i > 3.0$, which implies that less than 10% of the examinees had a 50% probability of answering the question correctly. Overall, the items on the exam showed adequate levels of discrimination. However due to the overall high level of difficulty of the exam, the test shows better discrimination among student participants of higher ability than those with lower ability.

Question 2 displayed a guessing probability that exceeded recommended limits. The guessing item parameter, $c_i = 0.442$, a probability of a low ability participant guessing the question correctly over 40% of the time. Two other questions, Q21 and Q25, had guessing parameter values that were elevated but were within one standard deviation of the expected value of c_i =0.20 for a 5 item multiple-choice question.

Overall, IRT analysis identified only four questions, Q2, Q12, Q13, and, Q25 that need to be revised or dropped from the exam. Question 2 has a high guessing probability, questions 12 and 13 are too difficult, and question 25 has a relatively high guessing probability and provides relatively little additional information about an examinees's ability level.

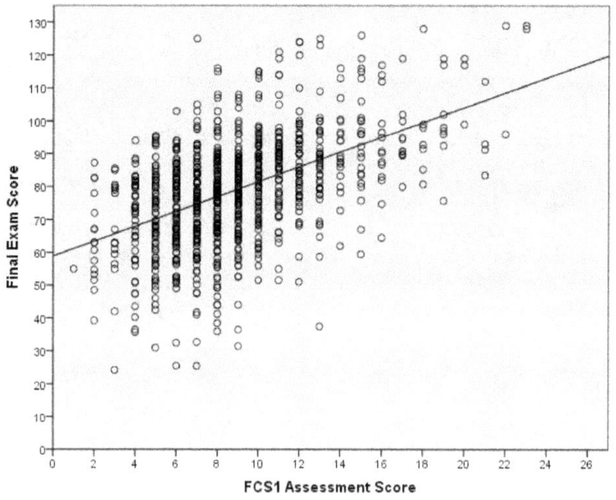

Figure 2: Scatterplot of Scores for Correlation of FCS1 Assessment Score and CS1 Final Exam Score

4.3 Correlation with External Measures of CS1 Knowledge

Student exam scores, as an external definition and measure of CS1 knowledge, provide the final piece of evidence for construct validity. Pearson's correlation analysis was used to investigate whether student scores on the FCS1 can be positively correlated with their scores on CS1 exams.

A Pearson product-moment correlation coefficient was computed to assess the relationship between the score on the FCS1 Assessment and the score on the final exam in CS1. There was a strong, positive correlation between the two variables, Pearson's $r(931) = .499$, $p <= 0.001$. A scatterplot summarizes the results (Figure 2). Further there were significant, yet weaker, correlations between scores on the assessment and scores on individual midterm exams (see Table 1).

Having found a strong positive correlation, subsequent analyses focused on correlating exam scores with each CS1 programming language population. Pearson product-moment correlation coefficients were computed to assess the relationship between the score on the pseudo-code version of the assessment and the final exam score for each programming language participant group (see Table 1). There was a strong, positive correlation between the scores on the assessment and the final exam for each of the programming languages studied. Participants from the CS1 taught in Java had the strongest correlation with final exam score, Pearson's $r(79) = .511$, $p <= 0.001$. The Python population was again comprised of students in CS and media computation versions of CS1. A Pearson's correlation coefficient was computed for each of these subpopulations of the Python participant group. There was the strongest positive correlation, (Pearson's $r(69) = .679$, $p <= 0.001$), for students enrolled in the CS-based python CS1 course. The effect size for the media-based Python course was smaller, $r = .262$, yet there was still a significant positive correlation with medium effect size.

Pearson correlation coefficients were also computed for each midterm score for each programming language participant group (see Table 1). There was a strong, positive correlation between the scores on the assessment and midterm exam scores for all CS1 courses in Java, Matlab, or Python except the non-traditional media computation approach. Participants from the CS-based Python course had the strongest correlations with each midterm exam score. The strongest correlation coefficient was for midterm 1, Pearson's $r(69) = .719$, $p <= 0.001$. The correlation between assessment score and midterm exam scores for the media-based Python course showed significant correlations with medium effect size.

Overall the results demonstrate that there was a strong, positive correlation between the scores on the FCS1 Assessment and final exam scores for both traditional and non-traditional pedagogical approaches to CS1. In addition there was a strong positive correlation with individual midterm exam scores for traditional approaches to CS1 taught in Java, Matlab, and Python.

4.4 Validity Argument

Two issues are central to construct validation of an assessment instrument: *construct under-representation* and *construct-irrelevant variance* [10]. These issues are explored by the following questions: (1) Does the assessment adequately operationalize the intended construct? and (2) Is performance on the assessment influenced by factors that are ancillary to the construct?

The matter of construct under-representation was resolved by the panel of expert reviewers confirming an adequate definition of fundamental CS1 concepts included in the test specification. Further, item response theory analysis indicated that a majority (24 out of 27) of the items on the assessment provide adequate information about student participant ability. Thus, overall the definition and measurement of the constructs specified are appropriate for the FCS1.

A variety of metrics were used to identify potential sources of construct-irrelevant variance, with almost all measures providing evidence to the contrary. Think aloud interviews with participants revealed that students were able to provide valid answers about the intended construct on over 85% of the questions. Scores on the pseudo-code version of the assessment had a strong positive correlation with scores on the CS1 language specific version of the exam. When combined with IRT results that demonstrate that 85.18% of the questions were of appropriate difficulty and discrimination, it is appropriate to infer that the FCS1 is a reasonable measure of CS1 knowledge.

Overall the validity studies provide evidence that students are reading and reasoning with the pseudo-code to answer questions in the manner intended. In addition, there is empirical evidence of the quality of the questions used to measure understanding that further correlates with external faculty definitions and measures of CS1 knowledge. Therefore, the FCS1 does provide a valid measure of introductory computing concepts for procedurally-based introductory computing courses taught in Java, Matlab, or Python at the university level.

5. CONCLUSION AND FUTURE WORK

Research and development on the FCS1 Assessment is continuing along a number of paths. This research has focused on establishing the validity of the exam for a limited number of constructs with a focused population of university students studying common introductory CS1 programming languages. Natural extensions of this work include adding additional concepts, establishing the reliability of the exam, and implementing the test on-line to reduce the resources required for data collection and test administration. We are also exploring the applicability and validity of using the FCS1 for measuring student knowledge across different pedagogical paradigms and programming languages, such as graphical or functional approaches.

The availability of a valid assessment instrument to measure student understanding of CS1 concepts enables a variety of directions for CS education research involving the FCS1. As an example, a programming language independent assessment instrument permits the comparison of pedagogical approaches in ways that were not previously available. In particular, it is now possible to investigate whether there are identifiable and persistent differences in student understanding of fundamental computer science concepts based upon the pedagogical approach or programming language used in the first course. When combined with other research methods, it would be possible to begin to identify which of the many factors in a CS1 learning environment (e.g., the instructor, programming language, integrated development environment (IDE), pedagogical approach, student motivation) are the levers that drive student mastery of computing concepts.

Assessment is an important piece of the computer science education research agenda. But as assessment practices "shape people's understanding about what is important to learn" [11, p. 111] it is vital that the field continues to expand the scope and availability of validated assessment tools.

6. ACKNOWLEDGMENTS

This material is based upon work supported by the National Science Foundation under Grant Nos. 0512213 and 0634629. Any opinions findings, and conclusions or recommendations expressed in this material are those of the author(s) and do not necessarily reflect the views of the National Science Foundation.

7. REFERENCES

[1] American Educational Research Association, American Psychological Association, and National Council on Measurement in Education. *Standards for educational and psychological testing.* American Educational Research Association, Washington, DC, 1999.

[2] J. Cohen. *Statistical Power Analysis for the Behavioral Sciences.* Lawrence Erlbaum Associates, Hillsdale, NJ, 2nd edition, 1988.

[3] A. M. Decker. *How Students Measure Up: An Assessment Instrument for Introductory Computer Science.* PhD thesis, University at Buffalo (SUNY), Buffalo, NY, 2007.

[4] K. Goldman, P. Gross, C. Heeren, G. Herman, L. Kaczmarczyk, M. C. Loui, and C. Zilles. Identifying important and difficult concepts in introductory computing courses using a Delphi process. In *SIGCSE '08: Proceedings of the 39th ACM Technical Symposium on Computer Science Education*, pages 256–260, 2008.

[5] R. K. Hambleton, H. Swaminathan, and H. J. Rogers. *Fundamentals of item response theory.* Sage Publications, Newbury Park, CA, 1991.

[6] D. Hestenes, M. Wells, and G. Swackhamer. Force concept inventory. *The Physics Teacher*, 30:141–158, March 1992.

[7] L. C. Kaczmarczyk, E. R. Petrick, J. P. East, and G. L. Herman. Identifying student misconceptions of programming. In *SIGCSE '10: Proceedings of the 41st ACM Technical Symposium on Computer Science Education*, pages 107–111, 2010.

[8] M. T. Kane. Validation. In R. L. Brennen, editor, *Educational Measurement*, pages 17–64. American Council on Education/Praeger Publishers, Westport, CT, 4th edition, 2006.

[9] J. C. Libarkin and S. Anderson. Assessment of learning in entry-level geoscience courses: Results from the geoscience concept inventory. *Journal of Geoscience Education*, 53:394–401, 2005.

[10] M. D. Miller, R. L. Linn, and N. E. Gronlund. Validity. In *Measurement and assessment in teaching*, pages 80–99. Pearson Education, Upper Saddle River, NJ, 10th edition, 2009.

[11] P. A. Moss, B. J. Girard, and L. C. Haniford. Validity in Educational Assessment. *Review of Research in Education*, 30(1):109–162, 2006.

[12] A. E. Tew. *Assessing fundamental introductory computing concept knowledge in a language independent manner.* PhD thesis, Georgia Institute of Technology, Atlanta, GA, 2010.

[13] A. E. Tew and M. Guzdial. Developing a validated assessment of fundamental CS1 concepts. In *SIGCSE '10: Proceedings of the 41st ACM Technical Symposium on Computer Science education*, pages 97–101, 2010.

Online vs. Face-to-Face Pedagogical Code Reviews: An Empirical Comparison

Christopher Hundhausen*, Pawan Agarwal*, and Michael Trevisan†
Human-centered Environments for Learning and Programming (HELP) Lab
*School of Electrical Engineering and Computer Science
†College of Education
Washington State University
Pullman, WA 99164
+1 509-335-4590
hundhaus@wsu.edu, pagarwal@eecs.wsu.edu, trevisan@wsu.edu

ABSTRACT

Given the increased importance of communication, teamwork, and critical thinking skills in the computing profession, we have been exploring *studio-based* instructional methods, in which students develop solutions and iteratively refine them through critical review by their peers and instructor. We have developed an adaptation of studio-based instruction for computing education called the *pedagogical code review* (PCR), which is modeled after the code inspection process used in the software industry. Unfortunately, PCRs are time-intensive, making them difficult to implement within a typical computing course. To address this issue, we have developed an online environment that allows PCRs to take place asynchronously outside of class. We conducted an empirical study that compared a CS 1 course with online PCRs against a CS 1 course with face-to-face PCRs. Our study had three key results: (a) in the course with face-to-face PCRs, student attitudes with respect to self-efficacy and peer learning were significantly higher; (b) in the course with face-to-face PCRs, students identified more substantive issues in their reviews; and (c) in the course with face-to-face PCRs, students were generally more positive about the value of PCRs. In light of our findings, we recommend specific ways online PCRs can be better designed.

Categories and Subject Descriptors

K.3.2 [**Computer and Information Science Education**]: *Computer science education, Curriculum.*

General Terms

Design, Experimentation, Human Factors.

Keywords

Studio-based learning and instruction, pedagogical code review, code inspection, peer review, CS1

1. INTRODUCTION

Computer science instruction has traditionally emphasized individual problem solving and programming skills, especially at the introductory level. We believe that this traditional approach may not adequately prepare students for jobs in the computing profession, which, in addition to technical programming skills, are increasingly requiring so-called "soft" skills, including communication, teamwork, and critical thinking skills.

SIGCSE '11, March 9–12, 2011, Dallas, Texas, USA.

We have been exploring *studio-based instruction* as a means of providing students with increased opportunities to learn "soft" skills in core computing courses [8]. Adapted from architectural and fine arts education, our iterative studio-based approach includes four key steps:

1. Students are given complex and meaningful problems for which they have to construct computational solutions.
2. Students present their solutions to peers and instructors for discussion and feedback.
3. Their peers and instructors critique the solutions and provide comments.
4. Students are given the opportunity to respond to comments and criticisms, and modify their solutions appropriately.

Based upon the formal code inspection process used in industry (see, e.g., [6]), we have developed the *pedagogical code review (PCR)* as an adaptation of the studio-based approach for lower-division computing courses [7]. In a PCR, students come together in teams to identify, discuss and log issues with each other's code. Students are then given the opportunity to resubmit their code solutions based on the feedback they receive in the reviews. In addition to implementing the four key steps of our studio-based approach, the PCR process provides students with opportunities to develop a variety of skills that are important in the computing profession—most importantly, the ability to critically review and discuss code and to improve code solutions based upon feedback.

In previous work [7,9], we studied face-to-face PCRs, in which teams of four to five students, led by a trained moderator (an upper-division undergraduate or graduate student), reviewed each other's code during 170-minute laboratory sessions. In those studies, we gathered empirical evidence that PCRs can positively influence the quality of students' code solutions [7], engage students in meaningful discussions about code [7], and promote positive attitudes with regard to peer learning [9]. However, given the reality that many computing instructors are unable to sacrifice the large amounts of laboratory or lecture time required for face-to-face PCRs, we posed the following research question:

RQ1:	*How can we design an online environment to enable PCRs be conducted asynchronously outside of class?*

This led to the following question regarding the potential effectiveness of online PCRs:

RQ2:	*Can PCRs conducted online promote the same benefits as PCRs conducted face-to-face?*

In this paper, we address these questions by presenting (a) an updated version of the Online Studio-Based Learning Environment (OSBLE) [10] designed specifically to support completely online PCRs, and (b) an empirical study that compares a CS 1 course that implemented online PCRs using this version of OSBLE against an identical CS 1 course that implemented face-to-face PCRs using our previous version of OSBLE. Our study had three key results: (a) in the course with face-to-face PCRs, student attitudes with respect to self-efficacy and peer learning were significantly higher; (b) in the course with face-to-face PCRs, students identified more substantive issues in their code reviews; and (c) students in the course with face-to-face PCRs were generally more positive about the educational value of PCRs. In light of these findings, we recommend ways online PCRs can be better designed so that they promote the kinds of benefits that have been observed in face-to-face PCRs.

2. BACKGROUND AND RELATED WORK

Studio-based instructional approaches can be traced to the master-apprentice educational system of the Middle Ages [1]. Educators in architecture and the fine arts adapted this approach in the form of the *design studio*: a shared space where students work iteratively on design projects, periodically presenting their work to their peers and instructor for critical review in so-called *design crits* (design critiques).

Studio-based approaches have been successfully integrated into science and math instruction (e.g., [4]). Computing educators have explored studio-based learning in their courses, with a particular interest in human-computer interaction courses, whose focus on design makes them particularly well-suited to the approach (e.g., [15]). There are even entire computing degree programs built upon the studio model (see, e.g., [3]).

The *pedagogical code review* (PCR) evolved out of our prior work to adapt studio-based instruction for lower-division computing courses [7]. PCRs can be seen as a form of *peer review*, a learning activity that has been embraced by several computing educators in both introductory (e.g., [18]) and upper-division (e.g., [2]) computing courses.

We present in this paper a new version of OSBLE designed to support completely online PCRs. This environment differs slightly from an earlier version of OSBLE [10] that was designed to support face-to-face PCRs. Several other web-based systems have been developed to support online peer reviews in computing education. These include RRAS [17], Peer Grader [5] and, most recently, an environment presented by Reilly et al. [14]. OSBLE has much in common with these existing environments—most importantly, its support for the online submission and review of programming assignments. However, whereas these existing environments have students perform reviews by filling in predefined rubrics, OSBLE is tailored specifically to support line-by-line code reviews. As such, OSBLE allows reviewers to fill out structured review log entries and anchor those entries to specific lines or line ranges of code, thus supporting a form of "artifact-centered discourse" [16].

Many computing educators have gathered anecdotal evidence of the effectiveness of their studio-based approaches; however, few have evaluated their approaches empirically. Only a few studies of which we are aware actually compare the outcomes of students who participate in studio-based learning against students who do not (e.g., [9,14]). The study presented here contributes to this line of research by presenting an empirical comparison of online and face-to-face studio-based learning activities, thus also contributing to the rich legacy of empirical research that compares online and face-to-face learning (see, e.g., [12]).

3. USING OSBLE FOR ONLINE PCRS

In order to address RQ1, we redesigned OSBLE [10] so that it supports completely online PCRs. Below we present a high-level walkthrough of how the new version of OSBLE can be used to facilitate completely online PCRs.

Step 1: Instructor creates assignment and assigns review teams. From OSBLE's instructor dashboard, an instructor clicks on "Create New Assignment," and specifies several important pieces of information through the Create New Assignment page: (a) the number and types of files to be handed in; (b) the due date of the initial submission, (c) the due date for performing the online code review; (d) the due date of the required resubmission of the assignment; and (e) the structure of the line-by-line issue log form. In addition, the instructor must create review teams; OSBLE provides a convenient interface that allows one to construct teams of a specified size using four different assignment methods: *manual*, *random*, *matched-ability*, and *mixed-ability*.

Step 2: Students submit assignment through OSBLE. By the due date, students submit their code solution through OSBLE as one or more code files.

Step 3: Student review teams review each other's solutions. Once the due date for the assignment passes, the review period commences. Students perform line-by-line reviews of their team members' code through the interface presented in Figure 1. Note that the reviews are *not* anonymous; students can see the names of the other members of their review team. However, students are unable to see the issues logged by other team members until *after* the review period is over, thus ensuring that their reviews are independent.

Step 4. Students resubmit code solutions based on feedback from the code review. After the review period is over, students revise their code solutions based upon the feedback they received from their team members. Through OSBLE, students specify whether each issue logged on their code was helpful to them, and whether they intend to address it in their resubmission. Finally, students resubmit their solutions through OSBLE by the specified due date.

4. EMPIRICAL COMPARISON

In order to rigorously compare the educational effectiveness of online PCRs to that of face-to-face PCRs (RQ2), we conducted a between-subjects empirical study with two treatments: *Face-to-Face (FTF)* and *Online*. These treatments corresponded to the spring 2009 and fall 2009 offerings of the CS 1 course at

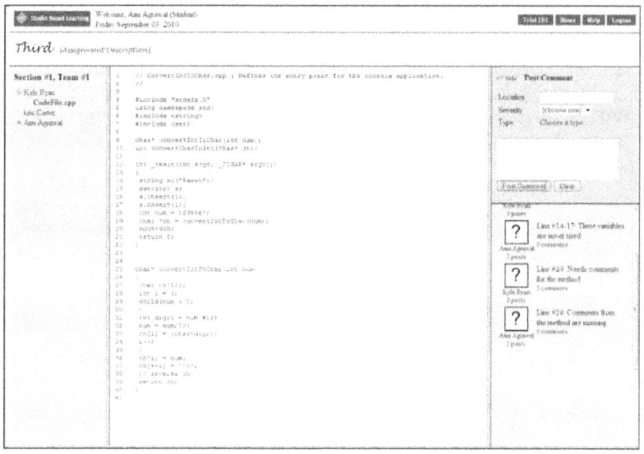

Figure 1. Snapshot of OSBLE's Code Review Interface

Washington State University. These two course offerings were identical in many important ways. Focusing on the C programming language, both had three 50-minute lectures and one 170-minute lab period per week. The spring 2009 (FTF) course was taught by an instructor not involved with this research; the fall 2009 (Online) course was taught by the first author.

The two treatments were defined by the differing ways in which they implemented PCRs. In the FTF treatment, students participated in PCRs of three of the eight course programming assignments. The PCRs were held during the regular lab period in weeks 8, 11, and 13 of the fifteen-week semester. In contrast, in the Online treatment, students participated in completely online PCRs of five of the eight course programming assignments.

Participants' learning outcomes were measured using pre-test to post-test improvement on a test of target programming knowledge. Participants' attitudinal changes were measured using pre-survey to post-survey differences. We used software logs to collect quantitative data regarding the number and types of issues logged in the PCRs of each treatment. Finally, we used exit questionnaires and exit interviews to gather data on students' perceptions of the course and the PCRs.

4.1 Participants

The spring, 2009 course (the FTF treatment) enrolled 87 students, whereas the fall, 2009 course (the Online treatment) enrolled 95 students. In both treatments, the PCRs, pre-test, post-test, and exit questionnaires were required course activities. In contrast, the pre- and post-attitude surveys, along with the exit interviews, were optional. By signing an informed consent form, students could choose to participate in these activities, and to release to this study their data from the required course activities. Those who consented to participate received one percent course extra credit. Because not all students consented to participate, because not all consenting students actually completed the surveys and questionnaires, and because we interviewed only a small number of consenting students, our sample sizes within each treatment differed across study measures (see Table 1).

In addition to the students who participated in this study, we hired six computer science upper-division undergraduate and graduate students to serve as moderators for the PCR teams in the FTF treatment. We required the moderators to attend a one hour training session prior to the first PCR. We paid moderators $40

Table 1. Sample sizes of the two treatments by measure

Measure	FTF	Online
Pre-/Post-Test	63	51
Pre-/Post-Survey	19	48
Exit Questionnaire	65	49
Exit Interview	4	6

for each PCR lab in which they worked. No such moderators were involved in the Online treatment.

4.2 Materials and Procedure

The course that defined each treatment took place during a fifteen-week semester. In the first and last week of the semester, study participants took an online survey that included a subset of the Motivated Strategies for Learning Questionnaire (MSLQ) [13] and the Sense of Community Questionnaire (SCQ) [11]. Participants were given one week to complete the survey, which was designed to get at students' attitudes regarding their own learning, motivation, and sense of community.

Likewise, during the first week of the course, and again as part of the course final exam, students were required to complete a 30-question test of the programming knowledge covered in the course. The test included (a) 20 multiple-choice questions that required students to trace and identify the elements of code snippets of at most 20 lines; and (b) 10 short-answer questions that required students to trace code snippets and write short pieces of code. Students were given up to 45 minutes to answer the pre-test questions, and two hours to complete the comprehensive final exam in which the same post-test questions were embedded.

Students filled out exit questionnaires either after each PCR (FTF treatment) or once during the final week of the course (Online treatment). The exit questionnaires consisted of a mix of Likert-style scale and open-ended questions designed to elicit students' impressions of the PCRs. In addition, during the final week of both courses, we interviewed a small sample of students in each course. To select students to interview, we partitioned the consenting study participants in each course into three groups (low, medium, and high) based on their course performance. We then randomly chose one to two students from each group for a 15 minute interview. Interviews consisted of 16 open-ended questions that focused on three broad issues: (a) students' sense of community and the extent to which they interacted with others in the course; (b) the perceived impact of various course features, including the PCRs, on students' learning; and (c) students' intention to persist in computer science.

Recall that the two treatments were defined by the method they used to implement PCRs. In the FTF treatment, face-to-face PCRs were substituted for the regular labs in weeks 8, 11, and 13 of the semester. The PCRs focused on three of the eight course assignments. The first assignment required students to perform computations on a file of numbers, and to solve equations in different forms; its solution required roughly 150 lines of code. The second assignment, the longest and most complex (over 500 lines of code), had students implement the game of battleship. The final assignment required students to implement a nine-function string library; it required roughly 250 lines of code.

In the lab period following the due date of each assignment that was reviewed, students in the FTF treatment participated in face-to-face PCRs, in which teams of four to five students, led by a trained moderator, used a previous version of OSBLE [10] to review team members' code against an established checklist of best coding practices [19] augmented with a list of requirements for the specific programming solution being reviewed. The checklists included questions in seven general categories, including "structure and design," "loops and branches," and "defensive programming." Each individual code review was limited to 30 minutes, and followed a well-defined procedure we have detailed elsewhere [7]. Students were not required to resubmit their solutions following the review.

In contrast, in the Online treatment, teams of four to five students performed online, asynchronous PCRs of five of the eight course assignments. Three of these assignments were the same as the three assignments on which students in the FTF treatment performed PCRs. The other two assignments, which each required roughly 100 lines of code, had students process student records and characters from input files.

As described in Section 3, students in the Online treatment engaged in online PCRs using OSBLE. After each assignment was due, students had five days to perform independent reviews of team members' code. They were provided with an 11-page tutorial that provided guidelines on the process, which involved examining team members' code line-by-line, checking the code against the same checklist [19] used in the FTF treatment, and logging issues. Following the review period, students had five days to resubmit their assignments based on the feedback they received in their reviews. In addition, they were required, through OSBLE, to rate the helpfulness of each issue logged on their code, and to specify whether they implemented the change suggested by the issue. Students' original submissions were worth 70 percent of their assignment grades; their resubmissions were worth 30 percent.

4.3 Results

We organize the presentation of our results around the study's four dependent measures: attitude surveys, programming knowledge tests, PCR issue logs, and exit interviews and questionnaires.

4.3.1 Attitude Survey Results

Items on the MSLQ [13] were scored using a seven point Likert-style scale, with 1 being "not at all true of me" and 7 being "very true of me." The MSLQ defined seven scales used by our study: *intrinsic motivation*, *extrinsic motivation*, *self efficacy*, *critical thinking*, *self-regulation*, and *peer learning*. In contrast, items on the SCQ [11] were scored on a five point Likert-style scale, with 1 being "strongly agree" and 5 being "strongly disagree." Thus, the scale of the SCQ was the opposite of that of the MSLQ.

Table 2 presents the pre- and post-survey means by treatment. We used a repeated measures analysis of variance (ANOVA) to assess differences in levels of the seven scales from pre- to post-survey by treatment. Given the field-based nature of our study and its use of weak quasi-experimental design, we set the alpha level at 0.10. In order to correct for Type I error, we divided it by 7, giving us a threshold *p*-value of 0.014. We found one statistically significant within-subjects difference: self-efficacy decreased significantly in the Online treatment ($df = 1$, $F = 21.79$, $p < 0.0001$); the effect size was large, $r^2 = 0.85$. No significant decrease was found in the FTF treatment ($df = 1$, $F = 0.72$, $p = 0.4065$).

To measure differences in survey gains between FTF and Online

Table 2. Pre- and post-survey means by treatment (standard deviations in parentheses)

	FTF ($n = 19$)		Online ($n = 47$)	
Scale	**Pre**	**Post**	**Pre**	**Post**
Intrinsic Motivation	4.96 (0.98)	4.65 (1.10)	5.62 (0.91)	5.04 (1.11)
Extrinsic Motivation	5.15 (1.16)	5.10 (0.86)	5.12 (1.10)	5.14 (1.08)
Self Efficacy	5.42 (1.11)	5.19 (1.25)	5.59 (1.17)	4.92 (1.29)
Critical Thinking	3.84 (0.91)	3.88 (1.10)	4.67 (1.05)	4.29 (1.39)
Self Regulation	4.21 (0.68)	4.13 (0.80)	4.53 (0.76)	4.32 (0.85)
Peer Learning	3.08 (1.16)	3.64 (1.28)	3.79 (1.24)	3.54 (1.32)
Sense of Community	2.92 (0.55)	2.95 (0.73)	2.80 (0.45)	2.85 (0.75)

treatments, we employed a between-subjects ANOVA, Again, to correct for Type I error, we divided the alpha level by 7 to obtain a threshold *p*-value of 0.014. Although we were unable to detect any significant between-subjects differences, we made one notable observation: Students in the FTF treatment made a gain in peer learning, as compared to students in Online treatment, that approached significance ($df = 1$, $F = 3.86$, $p = 0.053$).

4.3.2 Programming Knowledge Test Results

A total of 68 points were possible on the programming knowledge test. Table 3 presents the mean pre- and post-test scores by treatment. Both treatments experienced a significant gain in test performance from pre-test to post-test (FTF: $df = 1$; $F = 613.83$; $p < 0.0001$; Online: $df = 1$, $F = 437.98$, $p < 0.0001$). However, there was no significant difference in the pre-test- to post-test improvement of the two treatments ($df = 1$, $F = 0.03$, $p = 0.875$).

4.3.3 PCR Issue Log Results

Table 4 presents the number of issues of each type logged in the PCRs carried out in the FTF and Online treatments. In the FTF treatment, the counts and percentages reflect the issues logged by the two *teams* (of size 3 and 5) in which all team members consented to participate in this study, and which stayed intact throughout all three face-to-face PCRs. In contrast, in the Online treatment, the counts and percentages reflect the issues logged by the 19 *individuals* who actually logged issues in all five online PCRs. This difference in units of analysis (team vs. individual) is a consequence of the differing nature of the PCR process in each treatment: Whereas teams *collaboratively* logged issues in the FTF treatment, individual students *independently* logged issues in the Online treatment. While this comparison should be interpreted with caution, the comparison does point out substantial differences in the types of issues logged in the FTF and Online reviews. Indeed, according to a chi-squared test of homogeneity, there existed a significant difference in the distribution of issue types between the two treatments, $\chi^2(6, N = 1138) = 116.0$, p = < 0.0001. Upon closer inspection, we can note two key categorical differences. First, students in the Online treatment were far more concerned with issues of documentation and code formatting than students in the FTF treatment (32.6% vs. 7.4%). Second, issues logged in the FTF treatment focused more frequently on defensive

Table 3. Pretest, posttest, and pre- to post-test improvement means by treatment (68 pts possible; std. dev. in parentheses)

Treatment	Pre	Post	Improvement
FTF (*n* = 63)	9.9 (7.6)	35.8 (7.9)	26.1 (8.4)
Online (*n* = 51)	16.5 (10.0)	42.8 (7.8)	26.3 (9.1)

Table 4. Categorical breakdown of issues logged by treatment

#	Issue Category	FTF (*n* = 2 teams)	Online (*n* = 19 individuals)
1	Meets assignment requirements	19 (20.2%)	363 (29.2%)
2	Structure and design	25 (26.5%)	297 (23.8%)
3	Documentation, standards & formatting	7 (7.4%)	406 (32.6%)
4	Variables & constants	18 (19.1%)	119 (9.6%)
5	Arithmetic operations	1 (1.1%)	9 (0.7%)
6	Loops & branches	6 (6.4%)	25 (2.0%)
7	Defensive programming	18 (19.1%)	25 (2.0%)

programming (19.1%) and variables (19.1%) than in the Online treatment (9.6% and 2.0% respectively). These differences suggest that the PCRs in the FTF treatment tended to focus on more substantive issues than the PCRs in the Online treatment.

4.3.4 Exit Interview and Questionnaire Results

The exit interviews revealed many notable similarities in students' impressions regarding the value of various learning resources in the CS 1 course in which they enrolled. In both treatments, students were overwhelmingly enthusiastic about the value of the programming assignments. As one interviewee in the Online treatment put it, "the programming assignments were hard but [they] helped a lot, because you make a lot of mistakes and [in so doing] you learn a lot." Likewise, student interviewees in both treatments said they had received helpful feedback on their assignments. Whereas students in the FTF treatment singled out PCR moderators, students in the Online treatment most often cited teaching assistants as having provided helpful feedback.

With regard to the PCRs that took place, all students noted that they became comfortable with giving and receiving feedback through the PCR process. However, students in the FTF treatment were more enthusiastic about the PCRs in which they had engaged: whereas all four student interviewees in the FTF treatment said that they had received helpful feedback in the PCRs, just three of the six student interviewees in the Online treatment said they had received helpful feedback. One student in the Online treatment observed that "most students didn't put much effort into the online reviews, so I didn't find them helpful." As another Online participant noted, "I got a lot of opinionated stuff regarding [code] formatting—not too helpful."

The exit questionnaires completed by participants in both treatments provide further insight into their differing perceptions of PCRs. In the FTF condition, 85 percent of respondents found the PCRs helpful or somewhat helpful, in stark contrast to just 31 percent of the respondents in the Online treatment. Based on a reading of respondents' written comments, these differing perceptions appear to relate to two key factors:

Collaborative vs. individual reviews. In the FTF treatment, students appreciated that they sat down as a team to inspect code collaboratively; questionnaire responses tended to underscore the perceived value of this collaborative process. For example, as one respondent in the FTF treatment stated, "This process is very helpful. You are able to get input to make your program better, plus you get to look at others' programs and see different ways a program could be [written]." In contrast, respondents in the Online treatment tended to regard the PCRs as an opportunity to obtain feedback from *individuals*. Further, their perception of these individuals as reviewers tended not to be positive. As one Online respondent put it, "Most reviewers are just as inexperienced as I am and can't see the more serious problems..in [computer code]." Another stated that "not enough students took the reviews seriously and most students didn't know what they were talking about." A third said, "the criticisms" I received often made me feel [resentful] towards other members of my group."

Presence of skilled moderators. In the FTF treatment, student respondents especially noted the value of the expert moderators in the PCR process. In contrast, in the Online treatment, student respondents longed to have received reviews from more expert reviewers. As one FTF respondent bluntly stated, "Even though it would be more difficult to do, I think it would help students more if the [teaching assistants] did the code reviews."

5. DISCUSSION AND IMPLICATIONS

While our study failed to detect any significant learning outcomes differences between the two treatment groups, our study did identify several notable differences with respect to student attitudes and issue logging behavior:

- Unlike students in the FTF treatment, students in the Online treatment experienced a significant decrease in self efficacy.
- Whereas students in the Online treatment experienced a decrease in peer learning from pre-survey to post-survey, students in the FTF treatment experienced an increase. This difference between the two treatments approached significance.
- The categorical distribution of issues logged in the PCRs of each treatment differed significantly, with the Online treatment logging significantly more issues related to documentation and formatting, and the FTF treatment logging more substantive issues related to variables and defensive programming.
- In exit interviews, students in the FTF treatment were more enthusiastic about PCRs than students in the Online treatment.

We question the extent to which these differences were due to our study's independent variable (PCR medium). We believe two key procedural differences in the PCRs may have confounded our results, overshadowing any effects due to PCR medium. First, in the FTF treatment, PCRs were a *collaborative* process: Student teams worked together to identify issues and provide helpful suggestions. In contrast, in the Online treatment, team members performed PCRs *independently*. There was no attempt among team members to coordinate logged issues and arrive at a consensus. Our choice to require team members to work independently in the Online treatment stemmed from an interest in assessing each individual students' ability to critically review code. While many computing instructors certainly share such an interest in individual assessment, it is arguably somewhat at odds with the spirit of the studio-based learning model. Moreover, requiring students in the Online treatment perform reviews independently may have had unintended consequences unrelated to the fact that students performed the PCRs online. First, it may have diminished the depth of the overall reviews; indeed, issues of documentation and formatting dominated the online PCRs. Second, it may have decreased students' perceptions of their own programming skills (lower self efficacy), and their willingness to learn from each other (lower peer learning).

A second key procedural difference in the PCR process was that, whereas skilled moderators guided the PCR process in the FTF condition, they were not used at all in the Online condition. As we learned in exit interviews in the Online treatment, students longed for feedback from more expert reviewers, who would have been able to provide more substantive feedback and guidance. Moreover, as suggested by past research into online learning [12], we suspect that having an expert moderator oversee and guide the online PCRs of each team would have increased students' motivation and engagement, leading to more positive attitudes about peer learning and more substantive reviews.

We believe our findings have two key implications for computing instructors who cannot spare the time required to implement face-to-face PCRs, and instead would like to implement online PCRs in their courses. First, we recommend that, rather than being concerned with assessing individual reviewing skills, instructors allow teams to perform PCRs *collaboratively*. As our study found, the collaborative process used by teams in the FTF treatment of our study, which was modeled after the successful code inspection process used in industry [19], appeared to promote better student attitudes and also to uncover more substantive coding issues. A more collaborative online PCR process might involve team members being allowed to view issues *as they are logged*. While this could cause team members to slack off, we speculate it might also lead to team members interacting with each other more extensively. As issues are logged, threaded discussions of the issues could take place in an attempt to arrive at a consensus and fine-tune the recommendations. Instructors could provide teams with explicit instructions for engaging in such a process, much as we provided FTF teams with explicit instructions for performing PCRs collaboratively.

Second, based on our findings, we believe it is essential that instructors assign a skilled moderator to each online PCR team. Moderators could be the instructors themselves, volunteer upper-division undergraduate students, or graduate teaching assistants. Whoever they are, moderators should be responsible for keeping the PCR process on track by (a) encouraging discussion around issues that are logged, (b) asking focusing questions, and (c) prompting students to look for deeper (non-superficial) issues. While enlisting skilled moderators in the PCR process will require extra effort on the part of instructors—not to mention a new reviewing interface in OSBLE—we believe our study's results suggest that skilled moderation is so important that it can make or break the success of PCRs conducted online.

6. ACKNOWLEDGMENTS

We thank the instructor who allowed us to run this study in his course. Parts of Section 3 were excerpted from [9], whose study design was similar to the one reported here. This project is funded by the National Science Foundation under grant nos. CNS-0721927 and CNS-093017. Contributions to this work by other members of the research team—N. Hari Narayanan, Dean Hendrix, Martha Crosby, Margaret Ross, and Rita Vick—are gratefully acknowledged.

7. REFERENCES

[1] A History of the Studio-based Learning Model. *http://www.edi.msstate.edu/studio.htm.*

[2] Anewalt, K. 2005. Using peer review as a vehicle for communication skill development and active learning. *J. Computing Sciences in Colleges*. 21, 2 (2005), 148-155.

[3] Docherty, M. et al. 2001. An innovative design and studio-based CS degree. *Proc.32nd SIGCSE Tech. Symposium*. ACM, New York, 233-237.

[4] Faro, S. and Swan, K. 2006. An investigation of the efficacy of the studio model at the high school level. *J. Educational Computing Research*. 35, 1 (2006), 45-59.

[5] Gehringer, E. 2001. Electronic peer review and peer grading in computer science courses. *Proc. 32nd SIGCSE Tech Symposium*. ACM Press, New York. 139-143.

[6] Gilb, T. and Graham, D. 1993. *Software Inspection*. Addison-Wesley.

[7] Hundhausen, C. et al. 2009. Integrating pedagogical code reviews into a CS 1 course: an empirical study. *Proc. 40th SIGCSE Tech Symposium*. ACM, New York 291-295.

[8] Hundhausen, C. et al. 2008. Exploring studio-based instructional models for computing education. *Proc. 39th SIGCSE Tech. Symp.* ACM Press, New York, 392-396.

[9] Hundhausen, C. et al. 2010. Does studio-based instruction work in CS 1? an empirical comparison with a traditional approach. *Proc. 41st SIGCSE Tech. Symposium. mputer* ACM, New York, 500-504.

[10] Hundhausen, C. et al. 2010. The design of an online environment to support pedagogical code reviews. *Proc. 41st SIGCSE Tech. Sympos.* ACM, New York, 182-186.

[11] McKinney, J. et al. The college classroom as a community: Impact on student attitudes and learning. *College Teaching*. 54, 281-284.

[12] Means, B. et al. 2009. *Evaluation of evidence-based practices in online learning: A meta-analysis and review of online learning studies*. U.S. Department of Education, Office of Planning, Evaluation, and Policy Development.

[13] Pintrich, D. et al. 1991. *A manual for the use of the motivated strategies for learning questionnaire*. Technical Report #NCRIPTAL-91-B-004. Nat. Center for Research to Improve Postsecondary Teaching and Learning.

[14] Reily, K. et al. 2009. Two peers are better than one: aggregating peer reviews for computing assignments is surprisingly accurate. *Proc. 2009 ACM GROUP* (Sanibel Island, Florida, USA, 2009), 115-124.

[15] Reimer, Y. and Douglas, S. 2003. Teaching HCI design with the studio approach. *Computer Science Education*. 13, 3 (2003), 191-205.

[16] Suthers, D. and Xu, J. 2002. Kukakuka: an online environment for artifact-centered discourse. *Proc. Eleventh World Wide Web Conference*. WWW2002. 472-480.

[17] Trivedi, A. et al. 2003. Automatic assignment management and peer evaluation. *J. Computing Sciences in Colleges*. 18, 4 (2003), 30-37.

[18] Trytten, D. 2005. A design for team peer code review. *Proc. 36th SIGCSE Tech. Symp.* ACM Press. New York, 455-459.

[19] Wiegers, K. 1995. Improving quality with software inspections. *Software Development*. 3, 4 (1995), 55-64.

Sorting Algorithms as Special Cases of a Priority Queue Sort

Tim Bell
University of Canterbury
Christchurch, New Zealand
+64 3 364-2987
tim.bell@canterbury.ac.nz

Bengt Aspvall
Blekinge Institute of Technology
Karlskrona, Sweden
+46 455-385003
bengt.aspvall@bth.se

ABSTRACT
This paper offers an exercise for revisiting the main sorting algorithms after they have been taught to students. This is done in a way that emphasizes the relationships between them, and shows how considering abstraction and extreme cases can lead to the generation of new algorithms. A number of authors (including textbook authors) have noted particular relationships between algorithms, such as an uneven split in merge sort being equivalent to insertion sort. In this paper we use a flexible priority queue, the d-heap, to derive three common sorting algorithms. We combine this with using a BST as a priority queue, plus prior observations in the literature, to show strong relationships between the main sorting algorithms that appear in textbooks. In the process students are able to revisit a number of algorithms and data structures and explore elegant relationships between them. This approach can also lead to exercises and exam questions that go beyond desk-checking to evaluate students' understanding of these algorithms.

Categories and Subject Descriptors
K.3.2 [**Computer and Education**]: Computer and Information Science Education – *computer science education.*

General Terms
Algorithms, Performance.

Keywords
Sorting algorithms, priority queue, d-heap.

1. INTRODUCTION
Sorting algorithms are a staple of algorithms courses, providing an excellent range of opportunities to illustrate analysis, best/average/worst case considerations, complexity bounds, and design techniques. Teaching each algorithm in isolation can lead to students being faced with a confusing catalogue of names and techniques to remember, and it can be helpful to use relationships between algorithms to help students distinguish them, and also explore which properties they have in common.

SIGCSE'11, March 9–12, 2011, Dallas, Texas, USA.

Textbooks often categorize sorting algorithms as either quadratic or $n \log n$ (for example, [1], [12]), and sometimes other features are used to relate algorithms, such as Merrit and Lau's "easy split" vs. "easy join" for mergesort and quicksort [11], used by Wood [16].

In this paper we introduce a way to relate sorting methods based on priority queue sorting, which can be combined with previously noted links to enable us to derive all the common introductory sorting algorithms from each other primarily by substituting related data structures. A priority queue (PQ) is an abstract data type that can return items in "priority" order based on their key value, so a PQ-based sorting method simply needs to insert all values in a PQ, and then have them returned in increasing (or decreasing) order. We will use a variety of priority queue structures to generate a number of algorithms; the structures include sorted and unsorted lists, heaps, the d-heap (a heap with a branch factor of d), and the binary search tree (which can be used as a priority queue). This data structure-driven approach uncovers all sorts of interesting relationships and shows how algorithms can be derived and not just plucked out of thin air. It also gives opportunities to revisit each algorithm rather than just teach it once, and it relates the analysis of various algorithms to each other, which reinforces the connections between different approaches.

The approach that we propose has been used successfully with algorithms classes, and is a joy to teach because each time a number of students are inspired by the beauty of these relationships. Only simple mathematical concepts are needed to understand the links, which makes it accessible to junior students. Because the ideas are relatively simple but lead to students uncovering powerful concepts for themselves, the approach is particularly suited to a constructivist approach to teaching — students can discover these elegant relationships for themselves with only a little guidance.

Being data-structure driven, it also illustrates the close relationship between data structures and algorithms, and it reinforces the value of abstraction, particularly using the priority queue abstract data type, rather than focusing on a particular implementation.

Several taxonomies have been used for sorting algorithms:

- Knuth's classic "bottom-up" approach, where the three categories are insertion (leading to Shellsort), exchange (leading to quicksort) and selection (leading to heapsort), with mergesort as another case [8] (a similar taxonomy is used by Dromey [5], who derives algorithms by creating invariants from the specification of the output);

- Merritt's "inverted taxonomy" [10], where algorithms are divided into "split by value" (quick, selection and bubble sort) and "split by position" (merge and insertion sort); and
- Merritt and Lau's "logical inverted taxonomy" [11] which introduces "split by partial value" to include radix and distribution sort.

Each of these taxonomies partitions the algorithms into distinct families; this paper shows close relationships between the families in addition to the relationships noted by previous authors within families.

The main sorting algorithms that we consider here are selection sort, insertion sort, quicksort, merge sort and heap sort. Most other sorting algorithms have obvious relationships to these; for example, Shellsort is an optimization of insertion sort [11], as is binary insertion sort. Bubblesort can be regarded as combining the worst features of selection sort and insertion sort, and is perhaps best not mentioned anyway [2]! We will assume the common introductory form of quicksort, where the first (or last) item is used as the pivot; this is sufficient to characterize the algorithm, and keeps descriptions simple, although in practice improvements such as median-of-three would be used. For brevity we haven't included these obviously related methods in our discussion below, although we will introduce some other algorithms that are equivalent to the main five; while these other algorithms aren't of practical importance, they provide an important link between the well-known sorting algorithms. Also, we focus only on comparison-based sorting methods; Merrit and Lau [11] link key-based sorting (radix and distribution sorts) to comparison-based methods, and these connections can be used if key-based algorithms are included in the curriculum.

The five chosen algorithms are commonly presented in introductory computer science texts and courses in a reasonably independent manner, with the occasional relationships between pairs of algorithms noted, such as the worst case of quicksort being equivalent to selection sort [16], and quicksort's relationship with tree insertion sort [8]. This paper provides a more systematic view of the relationships between sorting algorithms, largely based on deriving them from a priority queue (PQ) sort. Rather than the hierarchical views described above, we combine the PQ relationships with those previously identified by Merritt and Lau [11] to show close relationships between all the commonly taught sorting algorithms. We advocate this not as a top-down teaching tool, but as a retrospective review of sorting algorithms that places them all in perspective, relates them to data structures, introduces ideas about algorithm design, and encourages students to think about extreme cases.

The main tool we use to link sorting algorithms is the d-heap, which is a heap priority queue with a branch factor of d. (The name "d-heap" appears to be the most common in current use, although the structure was originally referred to as a beta-heap [7] and has other names such as d-ary heap [3].) The d-heap is explained in section 2, and in section 3 we explore its use in PQ-based sorting algorithms. Section 4 extends this view of sorting to expose many relationships between what might appear to be quite distinct algorithms. We conclude in Section 5 with a summary of all these relationships.

Before continuing, we will note that there is a duality between min- and max-based algorithms, and a similar duality between min- and max- priority queues, and ascending and descending sorted lists. For example, selection sort is often presented as minimum-selection (for example, [1]), but sometimes as maximum-selection (for example, [9]), or both [16]. Heap sort is almost always presented using a max-heap (i.e. based on the delete-max operation) as this leads to a natural in-place sort, although Weiss [14] introduces it using a min-heap, and later points out that a max-heap can be used to avoid reverse-sorting the list for in-place sorting. An in-place min-heap sort is possible, but it is not particularly elegant! In this paper we regard the min- and the max- version of an algorithm as essentially the same since any algorithms that are based on a max-first approach can be converted to a min-first one, and vice versa, without changing the complexity or fundamental concept of the algorithm. Many texts use minimum selection sort but maximum heap sort. Teaching maximum selection sort leads more naturally to heap sort, although authors may have reasons for using minimum selection sort, such as relating it more closely to insertion sort. Because the analysis for min- and max- sorting are the same, we will use whichever is most convenient for our explanations at each stage.

2. THE d-HEAP

A heap [15] is a tree structure where (in the case of a max-heap) the value of every child node is not greater than that of its parent. It is commonly used as a Priority Queue (PQ) because the maximum value is easy to find (at the root), and updates on a heap are easily done in $O(\log n)$ time. The heap data structure is usually presented as a *binary* heap, which is a complete tree with a two-way branch factor (e.g. [1, 8, 12, 16]), such as the max-heap shown in Figure 1(a). By using a *complete* tree, a binary heap it is easily mapped onto an array, and can be navigated by multiplying and dividing the array index by 2, rather than using any explicit child/parent links. Some textbooks index the array from 0, in which case the children of node i are at $2i+1$ and $2i+2$; others index it from 1, in which case the children are at $2i$ and $2i+1$. The array storing the heap can be viewed as a partially ordered list, and its $O(\log n)$ time for both insert and delete-max is an excellent compromise between a PQ using a sorted array ($O(n)$ insert time) and an unsorted array ($O(n)$ delete-max time). In this paper we will refer to both max-heaps (as above), and min-heaps (where the ordering is reversed and the minimum value is easy to find).

A d-heap is a heap with a branch factor of d [7]. These are generally used as a priority queue for graph algorithms, but in this paper we show that they provide a useful teaching tool for enabling students to see the relationship between diverse sorting algorithms.

We would normally use a constructivist approach with students to introduce d-heaps, and will outline this approach to introduce the concept here. First, have the students consider what a 3-way (ternary) heap would be like (one is shown in Figure 1(b)). A good exercise is to work out where the children of a node are (multiply the index by 3 instead of 2) and its parents (divide by 3 instead of 2). Getting the exact formula is a good exercise to test their understanding of heaps. Then the students can analyze a delete-max operation on the 3-heap; again, it is a good exercise to realize that the depth is now $\log_3 n$, but there are 3 comparisons at each level, giving a delete-max time of $3\log_3 n \approx 1.89\log_2 n$ (which is slightly better than the $2\log_2 n$ required for a binary heap).

This raises the question of whether a 4-heap would be even better; a quick analysis shows that $4\log_4 n = 2\log_2 n$ comparisons are required for a delete-max, so it is the same as a 2-heap, and it would appear that 3-heaps are optimal. (In fact, it is sometimes noted that 2- or 4-heaps might be faster than a 3-heap because the multiplications are just shift operations. Interestingly, the optimal value for the branch factor is $e \approx 2.71828$, which raises other interesting questions! Calculating the minimum of $d\log_d n$ is a simple and instructive math exercise.)

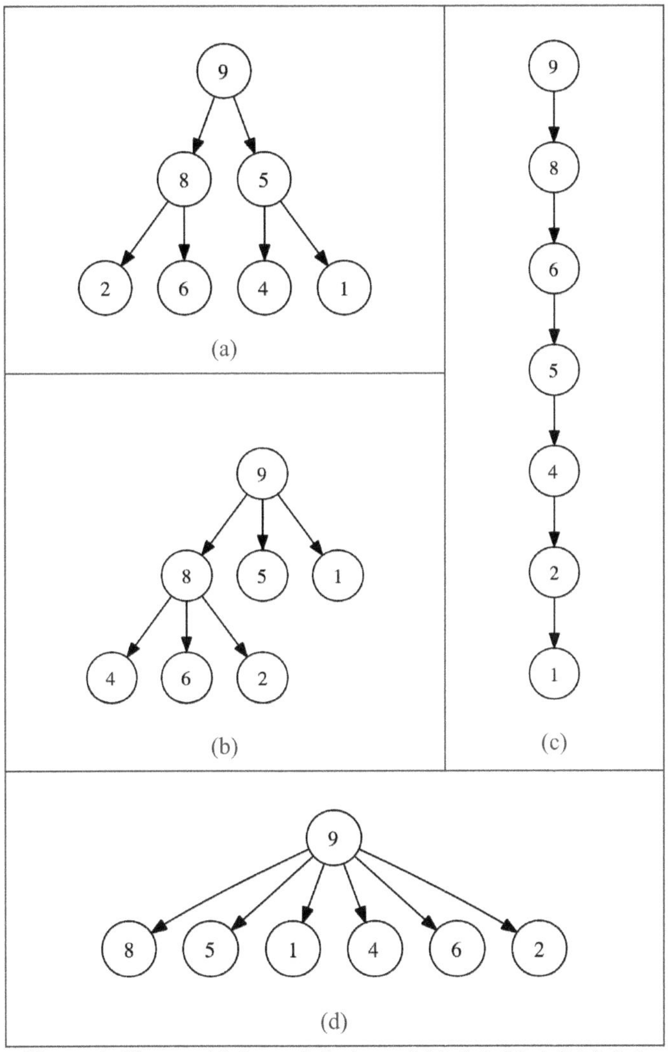

Figure 1: Heaps with branch factors of (a) *d*=2 (b) *d*=3 (c) *d*=1 (d) *d*=*n*

Because the value d can be tuned to change the performance of the heap, a d-heap with a higher value of d is useful for algorithms where there are significantly more insertions than delete-max operations (since insert takes $\log_d n$ time, and becomes faster as d increases). Tuning the value of d can be used where the expected ratio of inserts to deletes can be predicted based on the input data, such as in applications on dense vs. sparse graphs.

The next step for students is to get them to consider extreme values of d (exploring extreme cases is a good habit for computer scientists to have!) The lowest value usually considered for d is 2, and this yields a standard binary heap where both insert and delete-max operations take $O(\log n)$ time. However, considering $d=1$ leads to a structure that is essentially a sorted linked list (Figure 1(c)), with $O(n)$ average time for insert, but $O(1)$ time for delete-max. If $d=n$ (more precisely, $d \geq n-1$), the structure is an unsorted list where the maximum has been pre-selected (Figure 1(d)), giving $O(1)$ time for insertion and $O(n)$ time for delete-max. Thus the d-heap is essentially a flexible data structure that can be tuned from an un-ordered list to an ordered list, with various types of partially-ordered heaps in between.

Getting computer science students to consider the d-heap and extreme cases such as $d=1$ and $d=n$ is a good reminder of the value of looking for general cases and extreme cases. Of course these extreme values are primarily a thought experiment, and are not intended as a practical implementation. We note that Java has a "DHeap" class that provides this functionality, but requires that $d \geq 2$.

3. PQ BASED SORTING WITH A d-HEAP

The idea of using a priority queue (PQ) to introduce sorting algorithms is not new; for example, Knuth uses this approach, describing heap sort as a more efficient way to do selection sort [8]. Thorup [13] explores the relationship between priority queues and sorting, but focuses on general complexity bounds rather than using them for teaching the actual algorithms.

The idea of a PQ-based sort can be illustrated to students as follows. Suppose we are handed a sequence of n (comparable) items one at a time. The items should later be output in sorted (non-decreasing) order. How the sorting should be performed is not specified at this point; we can imagine that it is done in a "black box", which is effectively implementing a priority queue. Each data item is put into the black box, and then each is removed from it in ascending order using the delete-min operation repeatedly. We now investigate how the choice of data structure for the black box will lead to various well-known sorting algorithms.

The black box needs some way of organizing the items as they are handed to it. It could, of course, just record each new item, deferring all work until later. Alternatively, it could do some processing when handed a new item, using one of the following example approaches:

1. "put high effort into maintaining order": compare the new item to all previously received items,
2. "medium effort": compare it to some of the previously received items, or
3. "be lazy, postponing work": compare it to only one of the previously received items.

The d-heap is able to implement all of these possibilities. The three scenarios above correspond to d=1, 2, and n–1, respectively. Thus we may claim that the three approaches are all special cases of d-heap based sorting algorithms, and in turn, PQ based sorting.

In the first scenario, each new item is inserted into its correct place in the partial list obtained by appending it to the end of the 1-heap (linked list), and then sifting it up to its correct position. After inserting all items we will have a sorted list that is trivial to output. The 1-heap PQ sort shares the best and worst cases of insertion sort: for a min-heap, if a new item is the largest so far then it is compared only with the bottom (last) item in the 1-heap; if it is the smallest so far then it will be compared with all the previous values. This gives a best case sorting complexity of $O(n)$, and corresponds to the input being a sorted list; the $O(n^2)$ worst case is caused by the input being a reverse sorted list, which for the 1-heap involves sifting each new value up through the entire heap. This is doing exactly the same processing as a standard insertion sort.

For d=2 we get the normal heap sort algorithm. After inserting all items we have a heap-ordered representation of the data. To get the sorted list we output the root item and rearrange so as to maintain heap order for the remaining items. The picture is the same if we choose a constant branching factor other than two; if the branch factor is d then we have n insertions each taking time no more than $O(\log_d n)$, followed by n delete-mins each requiring no more than $O(d\log_d n)$ time. Overall this gives us a bound of $O(dn\log_d n)$ independent of the order of the input, which means that it is an $O(n\log n)$ algorithm.

Finally, let's consider d=n–1 (or larger). The root of the min-heap will hold the smallest item seen so far. A new item is compared with the current root item. If smaller, it replaces the root item which will be stored in a new leaf node in the (single) level under the root; if larger, the new item itself will be stored in a new leaf. Only one comparison is made for each new item. This initial heap construction, which takes n–1 comparisons, is very closely related to the first pass of selection sort.

Once all n items have been inserted using the n–1 comparisons, the smallest item is now at the root ready to be output, after which we have to re-establish heap order. This will require finding the smallest of the items in the leaves and moving it to the root, taking n–2 comparisons, then n–3, and so on. Repeatedly outputting the items this way will essentially carry out a selection sort. The time complexity is $O(n^2)$ independent of the order of the input.

In the descriptions above we have seen that the use of a d-heap as the data structure for the "black box" leads to the well-known insertion sort, heap sort and selection sort algorithms, depending on the branching factor d. Let's continue exploring the interplay between the choice of data structure and the resulting algorithm.

In general, a d-heap maintains a partial order of the items in the form of a rooted tree. For d=1, the order is total (a degenerate tree of sorted values with no branching), and for d=n–1 it's not much of an order at all! Another tree data structure that maintains "order" is a binary search tree (BST). We note that although a BST would normally be used to implement a dictionary abstract data type, it can be used as a priority queue. A BST with the same values as those in the heaps in Figure 1 is shown in Figure 2. Working out how to perform a delete-min and delete-max on a BST is a good student exercise (for example, the minimum is found by taking left branches until there are no more, which is an $O(\log n)$ operation on average). Thus we instantly have a new PQ sorting algorithm: insert all items in the BST, and repeatedly delete the left-most node.

This algorithm is essentially the same as what is often called "tree sort" (originally called "tree insertion sort" by Knuth [8], and attributed to D.J. Wheeler and C.M. Berners-Lee [4]), which inserts all values in a tree and then performs an inorder traversal.

It is good for students to simulate what happens in the insertion phase: the first item is put at the root, and all subsequent items are compared with it. With some guidance, students should recognize this "partitioning" as being equivalent to quicksort, but with comparisons being made in a different order. Knuth made this observation [8], but it is valuable for students to discover this for themselves.

Once the relationship between a BST and quicksort is established, other connections fall out easily; for example, if the input is a sorted list it is a worst case for both the BST and quicksort unless some effort is made to do some balancing. The sorted input causes the BST to degenerate to a linked list and for quicksort it causes the unbalanced partitioning that leads to behavior equivalent to selection sort. We also note that the degenerate linked list is the only non-trivial case where a tree can be both a heap and a BST, and provides a data structure-based link between the worst case of quicksort and the quadratic sorting algorithms. Finally, strictly sorted lists aren't the only worst case for the BST and quicksort; any ordering where the partitioning value is either the maximum or minimum will cause this behavior, so a choice of pivots such as 1, 10, 2, 9, 3, 8 etc. leads to worst-case partitioning. Such inputs also correspond to the worst case for a BST, where the branches are a zigzag rather than a linear list and the depth is $O(n)$. These duals provide yet another opportunity to explore the behavior of algorithms and data structures.

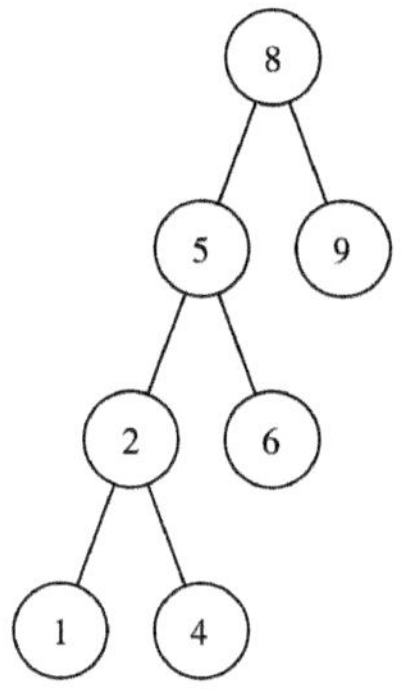

Figure 2: A BST being used to sort the example values

Another relationship that comes from this view is that tree sort can be viewed as an improvement on insertion sort, as follows. The invariant of insertion sort has a "sorted" component that grows with each step in the outer loop, and from a data structure point of view, we are searching for where a value belongs in this component and inserting it. Insertion sort uses a sorted array for this with $O(n)$ time required for insertion, but a BST is a more dynamic structure that can provide $O(\log n)$ searching and insertion times. Finding the insertion point for insertion sort can be improved to $O(\log n)$ time by performing a binary search for the insertion point, but the insertion still dominates with $O(n)$ time because of the linear nature of the array. Substituting a BST for the sorted component transforms insertion sort to tree sort. Thus quicksort, via tree sort, can be viewed as a more efficient way of doing insertion sort by using a better data structure. The usual caveats about keeping things balanced apply to both the BST and quicksort! This pathway from insertion sort to "tree insertion sort" is essentially how Knuth [8] introduced what is now referred to as tree sort.

Returning to heap sort, we note that it will probably have already been taught with a shortcut for the initial n insert operations; the "heapify" operation can be performed in $O(n)$ time if the heap is built bottom-up [6] (Floyd called the improved algorithm "treesort", although it is now usually regarded as the standard version of heap sort, and the name "tree sort" now commonly refers to what was "tree insertion sort"). Despite the improved heapify phase, the heap sort algorithm is still dominated by the $O(n\log n)$ time for the delete-max operations, so asymptotically the shortcut has no effect, and our thought experiment based on the d-heap is still relevant. Similar reasoning applies to performing an inorder traversal for tree sort instead of repeated delete-min operations; the other phase of the sorting will still dominate despite this $O(n)$ optimized version. In fact, the two optimizations provide a nice dual; the first phase of heap sort can be reduced to $O(n)$, as can the second phase of tree sort, but the remaining phase in each case is $O(n\log n)$, so the $O(n)$ component is mere fine tuning and not a fundamental improvement in the sorting algorithm.

4. RELATING OTHER SORTING ALGORITHMS

The d-heap and related priority queues were used in Section 3 above to connect all the commonly-taught sorting algorithms except merge sort (i.e. insertion, selection, heap and quicksort). In this section we will discuss the connection between merge sort and insertion sort so that relationships between all five main algorithms are clear. The connections in Section 3 plus the relationship between merge sort and insertion sort are the main ones that we recommend discussing with students, and there is no need to labor the point by exploring other links. However, in this section we will also note some other connections that occur; these sometimes come up in open-ended discussions with students, and/or can be used as the basis of assessment questions to see if students have understood the algorithms being related.

A direct relationship between merge sort and insertion sort was noted by Merritt [10], who observes that instead of splitting the n items into two lists of size $n/2$, one could perform a "singleton split" into lists of size 1 and $n-1$. Using a constructivist approach, it is worth asking students to imagine such an algorithm; after trying an example they should soon notice that the resulting algorithm is insertion sort since merging a list of size 1 is the same as inserting a value in a list. This can be exercised by considering the worst case (the singleton is larger than everything in the n-1 list) and the best case (it is smaller than everything else). This exposes a correspondence between these cases for merge sort and insertion sort, and exercises the idea that a merge is fastest if one list is exhausted before anything is taken from the other list, and slowest if both lists must be processed to their end.

We can also reverse this reasoning; merge sort can be thought of as an improvement on insertion sort, achieved by batching a group of insertions and pre-sorting them so that the insertion doesn't need to go back to the start of the array to find each insertion point.

A singleton split can be forced in merge sort simply by changing the partitioning point, so to change a standard merge sort program to run as insertion sort only the one calculation needs to be changed. Merritt [10] also noted that a singleton split in quicksort is equivalent to selection sort (which corresponds to the worst case of quicksort), although this occurs by chance and can't be forced by a simple change to the algorithm.

The above is sufficient to relate all our algorithms; however, we now mention some other relationships that might be observed.

We have been considering algorithms as equivalent if they perform the same key comparisons, even if the order of the comparisons is different; for example, this happens for tree sort and quicksort. Another place that this can be observed is between the worst case of insertion sort (a reverse-sorted list) and maximum-selection sort (for which all cases are the same). If we consider the largest item, in both cases it will be compared with every other item in the array; the second largest item is compared with all but the largest, and so on. Therefore both will perform the same number of comparisons ($n(n-1)/2$), and will also be comparing exactly the same pairs of values (that is, all ${}^{n}C_2$ distinct pairs), but in a different order.

In a similar manner, the number of comparisons made in the worst case of merge sort is the same as the best case of quicksort (which also emphasises the merge/quick and insert/select duality). In the worst case of merge sort, a merge will make $n-1$ comparisons to create a list of size n; quicksort always makes $n-1$ comparisons to perform the partition. The best case of quicksort is when the partition makes two even halves, and hence the recursive cases for quicksort are the same size as they would be for merge sort.

Another connection is through the PQ structures: if quicksort is given a reverse sorted list, this corresponds to tree sort where the BST degenerates to a linked list (which is also a 1-heap) with each inserted item being compared with everything that is already in the BST/list/heap. This corresponds to a worst case insertion sort, and we have just established that this performs the same comparisons as a selection sort.

5. CONCLUSION

By linking most sorting algorithms as special cases of a PQ sort (Section 3) and then incorporating some connections already made in the literature (Section 4), we are able to show multiple relationships between sorting algorithms, and in principle, each could have been derived from another by exploring a generalization or extreme case. These relationships provide an opportunity for students to re-visit each algorithm after it has been taught, and explore its performance from a different perspective. This approach shows the strong relationship between algorithms and data structures, and how generalizing an algorithm or data structure can lead to new ones. Because a PQ sort is a simple concept, the derivations are easily taught in a constructivist manner.

The main relationships identified are summarized in Figure 3. The idea of a PQ sort is a simple "black box" approach to the problem; the d-heap PQ then provides us with a range of data structures under a unifying description, leading directly to insertion, heap and selection sort for different values of d. If we use a BST instead of a heap for the PQ, we end up with tree sort, which is essentially equivalent to quicksort (although tree sort can also be thought of as a insertion sort where the sorted component of the array is replaced with a BST). We use Merritt's [10] "singleton split" to link quicksort to selection sort, and merge sort to insertion sort. Batching a number of insertions into a pre-sorted list converts insertion sort to merge sort. Finally, Merritt's [10] view of the two divide-and-conquer algorithms based on whether

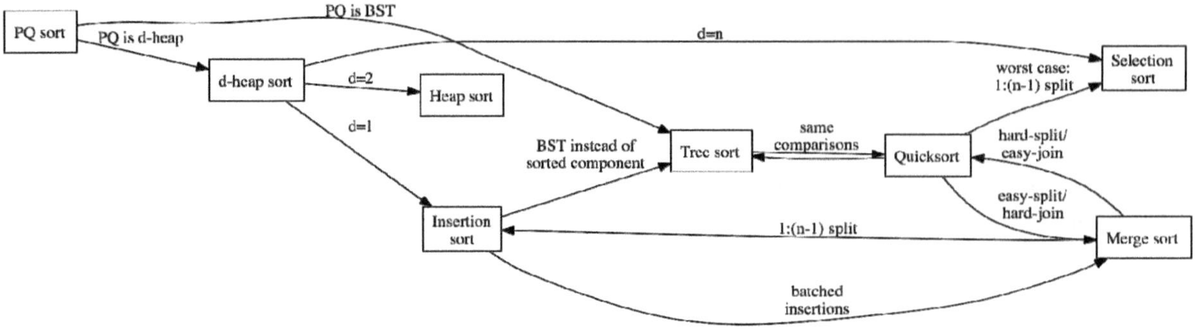

Figure 3. Relationships between common sorting algorithms

the split or join is hardest provides a relationship between quicksort and merge sort.

In the direct relationships we have described above, the various cases for complexity (best, average and worst) are naturally equivalent in terms of the number of comparisons. In addition, we have noted some other equivalences between specific cases:

- the worst case of insertion sort and all cases of selection sort;
- the worst case of merge sort and the best case of quicksort; and
- the worst case of quicksort, which can be seen in tree sort's degenerate BST, which is the same as a 1-heap in this case, which is in turn equivalent to the worst case of insertion sort and therefore also selection sort.

We reiterate that the view of sorting algorithms presented in this paper is not intended for deriving the sorting algorithms from the d-heap when first introducing them, but simply for using this as a thought experiment after the methods have been taught. It can be used to show that they aren't as unrelated as they might appear, to help students perform meaningful exercises relating to the algorithms, and to enable them to remember how they differ and how they are similar.

This approach to showing the relationship between sorting algorithms can inspire students with the elegance behind what can otherwise seen as a random catalogue of algorithms to be learned, and it is good training for computer scientists to always be considering special cases, abstractions, and extreme values.

6. REFERENCES

[1] Aho, A. V., Hopcroft J. E., and Ullman, J. D. 1983. *Data Structures and Algorithms*. Addison-Wesley, Reading, MA.

[2] Astrachan, O. 2003. Bubble sort: an archaeological algorithmic analysis. *SIGCSE Bull.* 35, 1 (Jan. 2003), 1–5. DOI= http://doi.acm.org/10.1145/792548.611918.

[3] Cormen, T. H., Leiserson, C. E., Rivest, R. L., and Stein, C. *Introduction to Algorithms (3rd Ed.)*. The MIT Press, Cambridge, MA.

[4] Douglas, A. S. 1959. Techniques for the recording of, and reference to data in a computer. *The Computer Journal* 2 (1959), 1-9

[5] Dromey, R. G. 1987. Derivation of Sorting Algorithms from a Specification. *The Computer Journal* 30, 6 (1987), 512–518.

[6] Floyd, R. W. 1964. Algorithm 245: Treesort. *Commun. ACM* 7, 12 (Dec. 1964), 701. DOI= http://doi.acm.org/10.1145/355588.365103

[7] Johnson, D. B. 1975. Priority queues with update and finding minimum spanning trees. *Information Processing Letters* 4, 3 (Dec. 1975) 53–57. DOI= http://dx.doi.org/10.1016/0020-0190(75)90001-0.

[8] Knuth, D. E. 1998. *The Art of Computer Programming, Volume 3 (2nd Ed.) Sorting and Searching.* Addison Wesley Longman Publishing Co., Inc., Reading, MA.

[9] Manber, U. 1989. *Introduction to algorithms: a creative approach*. Addison-Wesley Publishing Co., Inc., Reading, MA.

[10] Merritt, S. M. 1985. An inverted taxonomy of sorting algorithms. *Commun. ACM* 28, 1 (Jan. 1985), 96–99. DOI= http://doi.acm.org/10.1145/2465.214925.

[11] Merrit S. M., and Lau, K.-K. 1997. A logical inverted taxonomy of sorting algorithms. In *Proceedings of the Twelfth International Symposium on Computer and Information Sciences*, S. Kuru, M. Caglayan, and H. Akin, Eds. (Bogazici University 1997) 576–583.

[12] Sedgewick, R. 1983, 1988. *Algorithms*. Addison-Wesley Longman Publishing Co., Inc., Reading, MA.

[13] Thorup, M. 2007. *Equivalence between priority queues and sorting*. J. ACM 54, 6 (Dec. 2007), 28. DOI= http://doi.acm.org/10.1145/1314690.1314692.

[14] Weiss, M. A. 1995. *Data Structures and Algorithm Analysis (2nd Ed.)*. Benjamin-Cummings Publishing Co., Inc., Readwood City, CA.

[15] Williams, J. W. J. 1964. Algorithm 232: Heapsort. *Commun. ACM* 7 (1964), 347–348.

[16] Wood, D. 1993. *Data Structures, Algorithms, and Performance*. Addison-Wesley Longman Publishing Co., Inc.

Getting Algorithm Visualizations into the Classroom

Clifford A. Shaffer
Dept. of Computer Science
Virginia Tech
shaffer@cs.vt.edu

Monika Akbar
Dept. of Computer Science
Virginia Tech
amonika@vt.edu

Alexander Joel D. Alon
Dept. of Computer Science
Virginia Tech
alon@vt.edu

Michael Stewart
Dept. of Computer Science
Virginia Tech
cse@vt.edu

Stephen H. Edwards
Dept. of Computer Science
Virginia Tech
edwards@cs.vt.edu

ABSTRACT

Algorithm visualizations (AVs) are widely viewed as having the potential for improving computer science education. However, the rate of AV use and overall impact on education does not match the positive interest in their use that instructors report. Surveys of CS faculty show that impediments to successful use of AVs in the classroom include difficulties in finding quality AVs on desired topics, difficulties in adapting AVs to a given classroom setting, and lack of knowledge on the best way to deploy AVs. This indicates a need for better support for instructors, to get them past these barriers. We seek to provide this support through an online educational community that relies on a new model based less on the "digital library" approach of information gained by going to a site and searching. Instead, the focus is on community-added content through members' discussions, reviews, and ratings of content items. The AlgoViz community effort will better focus the future direction of AV development and use.

Categories and Subject Descriptors

E.1 [**Data Structures**]; K.3.2 [**Computers and Education**]: Computer and Information Science Education

General Terms

Algorithms

Keywords

Algorithm visualization, data structure visualization, online educational community, active learning, animation, interactive tutorial, teaching aid

1. INTRODUCTION

Algorithm (and data structure) visualizations (AVs) are widely viewed as having the potential for improving computer science education. Surveys of instructors over the past decade have shown great support for the concept of AV use in the classroom. Yet the rate of AV use and overall impact on education does not match the interest claimed by instructors. These same surveys show that the impediments to successful use of AVs are related to difficulties in first finding good materials, and then difficulties in deploying them in classes effectively. Fortunately, much progress has been made in recent years. There are many high-quality AVs available—though there are enough poor quality AVs that sorting out the good ones can be time consuming [16]. There is a growing body of research on how to use AVs effectively in the classroom (though getting up to speed on this information is again time consuming). These impediments could be overcome with adequate information about which AVs are of good quality and how they can best be used. From the developers' side, more information about what makes for an effective AV, and which topics are of greatest need, could lead to more effective AVs being produced.

Thus, we find that information and dissemination of best practice plays a key role in the successful deployment of AVs in the classroom. Given that the most needed information is (1) feedback on AV quality (user ratings) and (2) hearing of real experiences with this material in the field, the most effective way to improve instruction is through an active community of AV users and developers interacting to exchange information and experiences.

This paper is organized as follows. Section 2 discusses past surveys of instructor opinions on AVs, and presents the results of a new survey given during SIGCSE'10. Section 3 discusses the role that an online educational community can play in overcoming barriers to adoption of AVs. Section 4 describes the AlgoViz Portal. Section 5 describes our efforts related to moving from a digital library model to an online educational community model. Future plans are discussed in Section 6. Readers interested in background related to the history AVs, their level of availability, and best practices for their use in the classroom are referred to [16, 9, 7].

2. SURVEY RESULTS: A DISCONNECT

Periodic surveys on both instructor interest in AVs and their level of use have been conducted among attendees of education conferences and listservs for more than a decade.

Naps, et al. [9] report on three surveys conducted in 2000. Collectively, they indicate a strong positive view in favor of AV use (over 90%). However, only about 10% of respondents indicated frequent use of AVs in data structures courses at their institutions, while about half to three quarters indicate occasional use of AVs in such classes.

At SIGCSE'10 (held in Milwaukee during March 2010) we conducted a new survey to determine instructor attitudes toward AVs and their use in the classroom. The survey was designed in the spirit of the 2000 surveys reported in [9]. The survey instrument was included in the conference bag distributed to SIGCSE'10 attendees, it was distributed at the AlgoViz Project booth in the exhibition hall, and it was also handed out and collected at a special session [17] on the AlgoViz community effort.

Survey participants (both of our survey and the previous surveys reported) do not reflect a random sample of CS educators. First, they were attendees of various CS education conferences. Second, they probably had some interest in algorithm visualization, since they voluntarily returned the survey. In our case, often this was triggered by a visit to our booth or the special session. Others might have been attracted by the opportunity to win a $25 gift card to Amazon.com that was advertised as a mechanism to increase response rates. Yet, the survey does provide a snapshot of the issues that concern CS instructors regarding AV use, and it serves as a useful comparison to the previous surveys (of similar populations) to see whether anything has changed.

Question 1: Using algorithm visualizations can help learners learn computing science.

- Strongly Agree: 18
- Agree: 23
- Neutral: 2
- Disagree: 0
- Strongly Disagree: 0

This question closely mirrors questions asked in the prior surveys. The results are pretty much the same as 10 years ago. In these and all other interactions that we have had with instructors over the years, they have consistently and overwhelmingly indicated that they think using algorithm visualization in courses is a good idea.

Question 2: Have you used any AVs in a class that you taught in the past two years?

- Yes: 22
- No: 19

At a coarse level, this is not much different from results reported in 2000. The 2000 survey was finer-grained in that it asked for information about level of AV use. The 2000 survey reported about 10% of instructors using AVs in relevant classes on a weekly basis, and over 50% using AVs on at least an infrequent basis (but there is no time period defining "infrequent"). It is not clear that all of the "yes" answers from the present survey refer to what we might consider to be "AVs." But they probably all refer to some sort of dynamic software visualization run on a computer, as was the case in the 2000 survey.

Important technological factors contribute to making AVs easier to use in the classroom than in prior years. More AVs are available than ever before, backed up by improved research studies and improved access both through general Internet search and at the AlgoViz Portal (see Section 4). Increased access to the Internet by students and instructors, both in and out of the classroom, makes AV use more practical. For example, at Virginia Tech, while it has been "possible" to project Internet material from a computer in a class for over a decade, it has only been in the past couple of years that such access has become both ubiquitous and reliable in all of our classrooms. This makes a huge difference in the confidence of mainstream instructors for using such technolgoy, in contrast to early adoptors [4]. From discussions with instructors and from comments on the survey forms, we know that even now not all schools have built up the proper classroom support infrastructure to allow broadcasting of internet presentations in typical classrooms. This is still an evolving technology.

Question 3: What do you see as the greatest impediments to using AVs in your courses?

We have aggregated the text responses into the following broad categories.

- Trouble with finding suitable AVs: 13
- Trouble with integrating AV material into course: 11
- Difficulty of making AVs: 3
- Finding class time to fit AVs in: 2
- Classroom technology limitation: 1
- Question the pedagogical utility of AVs: 1

These results are roughly the same as reported in [7]. We see here that the largest single category is trouble with finding materials. Interestingly, the need for an organized repository for AVs (with some review mechanism) has been recognized since at least 1996 [1]. We can hope that the presence of newer online resources such as the AlgoViz Portal will improve this situation. The second largest category is much harder to deal with. It relates to integrating materials into courses once they have been discovered or created. This is a well-known problem [4]. While it is easy to provide pointers to AVs to students as supplemental material, it is much harder to integrate AVs into lectures, labs, and assignments.

3. AN ONLINE COMMUNITY

As indicated in the surveys, the greatest impediment beyond finding suitable AVs is integrating them into courses. If we hope to increase the penetration of AVs into the classroom, then instructors will need sufficient support to get over this hurdle. While improved access to information about what AVs are available can help, something beyond this seems needed to complete the circle. Instructors need information about how to use AVs in class, and confidence that their use will lead to success. This sort of information will need to come from other instructors as well as education researchers.

The central idea of the AlgoViz Portal is to prototype a new use model for online educational sites, with the goal of establishing an online educational community centered around Algorithm Visualization. The Portal diverges from the old model of an information site as a "digital library" where people come to search a collection. The problem with the traditional model is that users do not get the interaction with other instructors that they need to build confidence in the artifacts. Instructors do not get necessary information about which artifacts are truly of value, and how best to use them. Another problem is that users do not know when new content of interest has been added to the site. One must also recognize that it is difficult for content providers today to improve over the effectiveness of modern search engines for discovering online content. Static digital library "services" typically can be provided by search engines automatically.

The new model embraced by the AlgoViz Portal is to allow the community to add value beyond the base content. This comes as a byproduct of direct communication between community members. While forums are one obvious method for this, for many communities there is a deeper communication involving evaluation of the content (community ratings and recommendations for content entries), and discussions about the content (sharing experiences on how to make the best use of it). This user-based, value-added material is not "content" under the old model, and is generally not captured by the metadata associated with a collection. Yet, in many educational contexts, the user feedback on items in the collection is as important as the collection itself. The reason is that in educational communities, a major concern for instructors is deciding whether a given educational resource is of good quality, and how to use it.

Our analogy is to Amazon.com. While its backbone is a catalog and purchasing infrastructure, Amazon is much more than this from a community standpoint. An important component to Amazon's success is community-generated ratings and reviews, where significant categories such as books, movies, and music have increased sales by as much as 20% due to the value added by these reviews [18]. In the context of educational content, a successful online educational community is much more than a digital library. It must also include community-added content that raises the value of the information. This includes discussion of best practice, and user evaluation for the artifacts represented in the library.

Due to the size of its user base, Amazon has a rich collection of user-supplied product ratings and reviews even though less than one tenth of one percent of their customers provide this information [18]. An online educational community for a topic such as AV use has an additional burden, since it must get a much higher percentage of the potential "market" to actively engage, more like 1 to 10% of the membership, depending on how membership is defined. Fortunately, members of that "market" also have a greater incentive to become active participants.

4. ALGOVIZ.ORG

The *AlgoViz Portal* (`http://algoviz.org`) is intended to be an online hub for educators, developers, and users of algorithm visualizations. It is the successor of the AlgoViz Wiki [20], an older project by the Virginia Tech Algorithm Visualization Research Group.

AlgoViz.org is built on Drupal [2], an open-source content management system written in PHP. The functionality built into the basic Drupal installation, known as Drupal core, can enable a website with features such as forums, blogs, news feeds, comments, and user registration. Perhaps the most important consideration in the selection of Drupal for the CMS powering the AlgoViz Portal is the massive existing body of user-contributed modules, which greatly reduces development time, combined with the ability to create new modules or modify the existing code base if necessary. AlgoViz.org is built on top of a Drupal distribution, Acquia, that packages Drupal core with many popular contributed modules. For its database backend, AlgoViz.org uses a MySQL database driven by the PHP MySQLi (MySQL Improved) Extension.

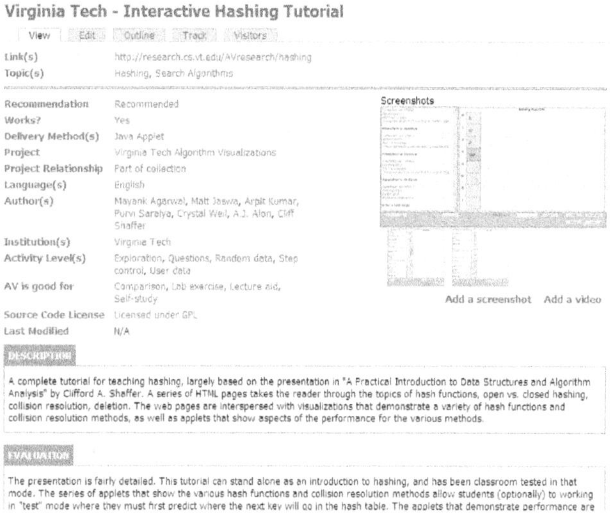

Figure 1: A sample catalog entry.

The main informational resource at the Portal is the *AlgoViz.org Algorithm Visualization Catalog*, a referatory to AVs on the Web. It is not intended to be merely a simple link collection. Each catalog entry contains key details about the AV such as its delivery mechanism, information on the developers and the project (if any) that the AV is part of, an objective description, and a subjective evaluation of the pedagogical value of the AV (see Figure 1). The AV Catalog has expanded in size and scope since its original incarnation as part of the AlgoViz Wiki, and now contains over 500 entries.

Figure 1 shows a sample entry in the Catalog. Additional content includes a description of Activity Level, which specifies how a user may control a particular visualization. The References field is used to list links to academic publications or white papers associated with a particular AV. Users are encouraged to provide Digital Object Identifier (DOI) links as references whenever available. Entries may also include multimedia in several forms: attached Screenshots, embedded Videos, or links to external galleries. Such material would ideally demonstrate how an AV works or even classroom use cases.

The other major informational resource at the Portal is an *annotated bibliography* of the published literature on algorithm visualization and related research. An entry in the bibliography contains information about that publication, including ISSN, ISBN and DOI numbers when available. This information is presented to the user in a tabular format, but may also be displayed in Tagged, XML, or BibTEX form. A link is provided to Google Scholar for most entries. The annotated bibliography currently contains over 500 papers.

The Portal provides several public forums for discussion of AV-related topics. We hope that the forums will be the primary gathering place for members of the AlgoViz.org community, particularly those who are new to the field or who have specific questions.

Instructors report that a major deterrent to their use of AVs is the time and effort they perceive must be expended in integrating existing AVs into existing course content (see [9] and the survey results in Section 2). To help address this issue, the Portal provides a structure called the *field report*, which gives a convenient way for instructors who have used an algorithm visualization in a class to share their experiences. Field reports are designed to supplement the evaluation data in the AV Catalog, since AV ratings in the catalog are not necessarily based on real-world classroom experiences. A field report can thus provide empirical evidence to strengthen or qualify a recommendation. Instructors submitting a field report are asked to describe the lesson in question and how AVs were incorporated into the lesson. They may assess how successful the lesson was as they see fit. They are also asked to provide the following:

- the person or persons who presented the lesson (in case the user submitting the field report is not the same as the presenter(s));
- the institution where the lesson took place; and
- the AV(s) used (as a link in the catalog).

The AlgoViz Project is a primary content contributor to Ensemble [3], the NSDL Computer Science Digital Library. To ensure interoperability between the different repositories in its index, the Ensemble project employs the Open Archives Initiative Protocol for Metadata Harvesting, or OAI-PMH [11]. Under OAI-PMH, actors fall into one of two roles, the data provider and the service provider. A data provider is a repository or collection that structures and exposes contained metadata. A service provider requests metadata via service requests sent to data providers. We have implemented for the AV Catalog an OAI-PMH data provider service that maps catalog entry content to tags in the Dublin Core format. The metadata is thereby made available to Ensemble and other potential OAI service providers.

AV developers can benefit from a source of example AVs to use for reference, including source code. We have established OpenAlgoViz at SourceForge.net [12]. The site has at least two purposes: to provide reference implementations for good quality AVs that others can use to see how things should be done, and to provide a hosting site for AV contributors. OpenAlgoViz has the potential to become a major repository of AV source code in its own right. All entries are open source and are contributed by developers in the AV community. Currently, the repository contains the following contributions: JFLAP from Susan Rodger of Duke University [14]; several algorithm visualizations from Virginia Tech; the JHAVÉ [8] and GAIGS [10] projects from Tom Naps of University of Wisconsin–Oshkosh, the PCIL project [6] from Mississippi State and Tennessee Tech, internationalization libraries [15] from Guido Rößling of Technische Universitat Darmstadt, and XAAL, an XML-based markup language for algorithm animation [5], from Ville Karavirta of Aalto University in Finland.

We routinely monitor AlgoViz Portal site traffic to view user trends using both Google Analytics and native Drupal tools. Since the portal's inception in July 2009, we have received more than 9,800 visits from outside the Virginia Tech domain. Figure 2 shows the monthly visits from July, 2009 to August, 2010. Monthly traffic at the portal has increased by nearly a factor of four during this time. We observed a major spike in activity caused by advertising the site during the SIGCSE 2010 conference. Unfortunately, site traffic data must be interpreted in light of the fact that our site has been split between the AlgoViz Portal and the original AlgoViz Wiki. Until June, 2010, the Wiki contained the

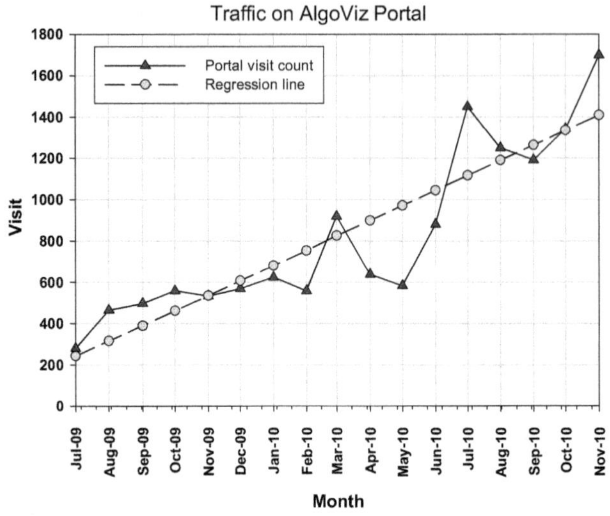

Figure 2: Vistors per month to the AlgoViz Portal, July 2009 (shortly after the Portal was made public) to November 2010. A regression line shows the overall trend.

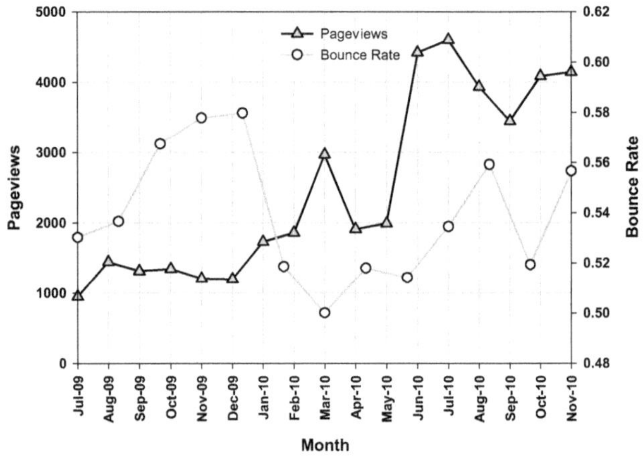

Figure 3: Monthly page views and bounce rates of the AlgoViz Portal, July 2009 to November 2010.

actual catalog (presumably a primary attraction for users). Any visitor moving from the Portal to the Wiki would be considered as a visitor who had left the Portal. A sustained increase in traffic measured for the Portal began in June 2010, when the Wiki catalog was migrated to the Portal.

Figure 3 shows traffic data in terms of page views (the loading of a new page). The average number of page views per visit is about three. The total number of page views is steadily increasing over time. The bounce rate is an estimate of how many visitors left the site after viewing a single page; in most cases that could be the front page. The bounce rate now averages about 54%.

Since July 2009 we have had over 9,000 unique visitors to the Portal. 64% of the visits came from first-time visitors. This could be due to the relative newness of the site. Because of our activities in conferences and public mailing lists, we are likely to get more new visitors at this point. On average, new visitors spend a little more than three minutes in the site while returning visitors spend six minutes.

5. BUILDING THE COMMUNITY

Since a relatively high percentage of the community must actively engage to reach the needed critical mass to sustain community interaction, much of our work focuses on ways to lower the barriers to participation. This includes technology to support easy/automatic login from allied sites (to avoid additional registration or login overhead), a robust notification system to inform users when new information of interest has been provided at the site, and mechanisms to solicit ratings information.

5.1 Community Value Added

An important example of community-added content is a community rating system for AVs in the catalog. Currently, quality assessment information in the catalog comes from:

- An overall ranking given by the catalog editors (Recommended, Has Potential, Not Recommended) on each of four potential uses: lecture aide, self-study supplement, stand-alone use, and debugging aide;
- ratings by users on a five-star basis, similar to product ratings at a site such as Amazon;
- description and review information for the AV;
- field reports; and
- user comments.

While the present incarnation of the catalog gets its primary review information from the catalog editors, in the future the bulk of this material must come from the community to reach its true potential, through users submitting reviews and comments. This in turn will drive recognition of AVs and other content items that can then be sent as "notifications" to community members through their favored notification streams, which will in turn prompt community members to add more value to the community through their own ratings and comments.

5.2 AlgoViz Awards

In 2010 we initiated the AlgoViz Awards, an annual competition intended to provide a number of positive effects. Our initial goal was to help build community interest in the site, and to showcase high-quality AVs. Each year, the winners of the annual awards will be added to our AV Hall of Fame. This should serve as a useful starting point for instructors who want to see what is possible with AVs.

The AlgoViz Awards began with a nomination process starting in June 2009 and closing in October 2009. Any AlgoViz Portal registrant was permitted to nominate an entry. Several AVs were selected by the AlgoViz Project Steering Committee to initially pre-seed the competition. Nominees were assigned to one of three categories: *Standalone AVs in Lower Division Topics* represents AVs that cover topics generally taught in CS1, CS2, and sophomore-level courses; *Standalone AVs in Advanced Topics* represents AVs that cover topics taught in upper division and graduate-level courses; *Online Tutorials and Hypertextbooks* represents AVs that are integrated into a larger learning object, instead of presented alone. These award categories were chosen in part to draw attention to various issues in AV development. In total, fourteen AVs were nominated for an AlgoViz.org Award.

All registrants at the Portal were given the opportunity to vote on the nominated visualizations. The actual voting process involved rating each AV on a five-point scale, where one point represents a poor AV and five represent an excellent AV. Users were permitted to rate as many or as few AVs as desired, and were allowed to change their rating choice on any AV as many times as desired until voting closed (only the final rating on each AV was counted). Voting ended on 31 January 2010. The winners were publicly declared in a video presentation on 13 March 2010 at the SIGCSE conference. The video gave a quick demonstration showcasing the strengths of each winning AV. It is available at `http://www.youtube.com/watch?v=QLT_AKgYJYk`. The second annual AlgoViz Awards includes a category on program visualization tools, and a category on new AVs. Results will be announced during SIGCSE'11.

5.3 Notification

An important way to keep members in touch with the site—and thereby increase participation—is through notification mechanisms. We cannot expect users to routinely come to our site to determine if new content is available, since the overhead for doing so is too high relative to the frequency of change. Instead, we need to notify members of our community whenever "interesting" content appears.

This notification needs to be done in a way that is natural to any given individual, in that it fits in with their normal information flow. For some, that flow takes the form of email or RSS feeds. For others, notification streams come through social networking schemes such as Twitter or Facebook. Each user must have sufficient control in determining what they consider to be "interesting" so that they do not receive too much unwanted information.

Many people opt to use social networking schemes for notification, rather than receive all such information via more traditional email, because those social networking systems are better tuned toward integrating many streams of small, targeted notification (a very short message, typically). As a consequence, notification streams based on changes to the AlgoViz site content need to be fine grained, and targeted to only those recipients that want any given notification. For example, a given user might want to know when certain AV topics are updated in the catalog, or new posts are made to certain subforums at the site, and not others. Thus, we are building an extensive "interest profile" mechanism whereby users can easily select what topics are of interest, and the method by which they wish to be notified about new content. For now, users can control their level of notification by selecting from various twitter or RSS feeds.

6. FUTURE WORK

People are more willing to visit online communities where there is more activity, and are more willing to contribute to communities where they see contribution is the norm [13, 19]. This would seem to argue for minimizing barriers to contribution. Forcing people to register initially, and sign in on return visits, can be a significant barrier to getting started for many people. Many of us are reluctant to invest the overhead of time to register, or give any personal information (especially an email address, which is often the minimum price of admission). So why require this?

Unfortunately, there are many malicious entities on the Internet. The most common is the "link spammer" who attempts to hijack the public's ability to deliver content to a website in order to promote links to unrelated sites, with the goal of boosting the 3rd party site's visibility in search engines. If permitted, these sorts of attacks can dominate the "contributed" content at the site and destroy its usefulness to the targeted community.

For this reason, AlgoViz currently requires potential contributors to register first. But since encouraging content contributions (such as ratings, reviews, and forum posts) is of primary concern, and since registration is a major disincentive to "simple" contributions such as rating an AV, we see an urgent need for lowering this barrier. One way to minimize the need for registration is to accept authentication from other sites. The key information that we actually need is some unique identifier for each visitor, so that we can recognize them as the same person at each return visit. In that way we are able to connect the contributions of the individual over time, and to block malicious individuals. Thus, explicit registration at a community site is not absolutely necessary to its goals. An alternative is shared registration with explicit allied sites (such as the Ensemble portal [3]), OpenID access (not as useful since it still requires initial registration), and automated connection from sites such as Facebook or LinkedIn.

Another approach used by some sites is relaxed registration combined with greater moderation. That is, we could eliminate the requirement for validation by returning an email message. But unvalidated users are the greatest risk for malicious behavior. By sending all contributions by unvalidated users to a moderator before making the contribution public, we can screen these attacks out. Once a user has cleared some number of successful moderation attempts, they can then be flagged as a "trusted" user with no further need for automatic moderation.

We will also study the potential for "social capital" to encourage users to contribute. Many sites are successful by giving some sort of "reward" for contribution in the form of titles in a hierarchy. Those who contribute more get better titles in recognition. While this is seemingly minor, it appears to tap into the innate competitiveness by some people, and the need for validation of authority by others.

7. ACKNOWLEDGMENTS

We gratefully acknowledge support of the AlgoViz Project by the National Science Foundation's CCLI and NSDL programs under grants DUE-0836940 and DUE-0937863.

8. REFERENCES

[1] J. Bergin, K. Brodie, M. Patiño-Martínez, and seven additional authors. An overview of visualization: its use and design: Report of the working group in visualization. In *ITiCSE '96: Proceedings of the 1st Conference on Integrating Technology into Computer Science Education*, pages 192–200, 1996.

[2] Drupal. `http://drupal.org`, 2010.

[3] ENSEMBLE. `http://www.computingportal.org/`.

[4] K. Hew and T. Brush. Integrating technology into k12 teaching and learning: current knowledge gaps and recommendations for future research. *Educational Technology Research and Development*, 55:223–252, 2007.

[5] V. Karavirta. Xaal - extensible algorithm animation language. Master's thesis, Helsinki University of Technology, Helsinki, Finland, Dec 2005.

[6] B. Malone, T. Atkison, M. Kosa, and F. Hadlock. Pedagogically effective effortless algorithm visualization with a PCIL. In *Proceedings of the 39th IEEE international conference on Frontiers in Education conference*, pages 1501–1506, Piscataway, NJ, Oct 2009. IEEE Press.

[7] T.L. Naps, S. Cooper, and twelve more authors. Evaluating the educational impact of visualization. *SIGCSE Bulletin*, 35(4):124–136, 2003.

[8] T.L. Naps, J.R. Eagan, and L.L. Norton. JHAVÉ: An environment to actively engage students in web-based algorithm visualizations. In *SIGCSE '00: Proceedings of the thirty-first SIGCSE technical symposium on Computer science education*, pages 109–113, 2000.

[9] T.L. Naps, G. Rössling, and nine more authors. Exploring the role of visualization and engagement in computer science education. In *ITiCSE-WGR '02: Working Group Reports from ITiCSE on Innovation and Technology in Computer Science Education*, pages 131–152, New York, NY, USA, 2002.

[10] T.L. Naps and B. Swander. An object-oriented approach to algorithm visualization: easy, extensible, and dynamic. In *SIGCSE '94: Proceedings of the twenty-fifth SIGCSE symposium on Computer science education*, pages 46–50, 1994.

[11] Open archives initiative - protocol for metadata harvesting - v2.0. `http://www.openarchives.org/OAI/openarchivesprotocol.html`, June 2002.

[12] OpenAlgoViz SourceForge Site. `https://sourceforge.net/projects/openalgoviz/`, 2009.

[13] J. Preece, B. Nonnecke, and D. Andrews. The top five reasons for lurking: improving community experiences for everyone. *Computers in Human Behavior*, 20(2):201 – 223, 2004.

[14] S. Rodger and T. Finley. *JFLAP - An Interactive Formal Languages and Automata Package*. Jones and Bartlett, 2006.

[15] G. Rößling. Translator: A package for internationalization for Java-based applications and GUIs. In *Proceedings of the 12th ACM SIGCSE/SIGCUE International Conference on Innovation and Technology in Computer Science Education (ITiCSE 2006)*, page 312, Bologna, Italy, 2006. ACM Press.

[16] C.A. Shaffer, M.L. Cooper, A.J.D. Alon, M. Akbar, M. Stewart, S.Ponce, and S.H. Edwards. Algorithm visualization: the state of the field. *ACM Transactions on Computing Education*, 10:1–22, August 2010.

[17] C.A. Shaffer, T.L. Naps, S.H. Rodger, and S.H. Edwards. Building an online educational community for algorithm visualization. In *SIGCSE '10: Proceedings of the 41st ACM technical symposium on Computer science education*, pages 475–476, New York, NY, USA, 2010. ACM.

[18] J.M. Spool. The magic behind amazon's 2.7 billion dollar question. `http://www.uie.com/articles/magicbehindamazon`, March 2009.

[19] S.L. Toral, M.R. Martinez-Torres, F. Barrero, and F. Cortes. An empirical study of the driving forces behind online communities. *Internet Research*, 19(4):378–392, 2009.

[20] Virginia Tech. Data Structures and Algorithm Visualization Wiki. `http://algoviz.cs.vt.edu`, 2006.

Two Experiments Using Learning Rate to Evaluate an Experimenter Developed Tool for Splay Trees

Michael C. Orsega
Department of Computer Science
The University of West Georgia
Carrollton, GA
morsega@westga.edu

Bradley T. Vander Zanden
Department of Electrical Engineering and Computer Science
The University of Tennessee
Knoxville, TN
bvz@eecs.utk.edu

Christopher H. Skinner
Department of Educational Psychology and Counseling
The University of Tennessee
Knoxville, TN
cskinne1@utk.edu

ABSTRACT

We conducted two experiments evaluating Sketchmate, a tool used to teach the splay tree data structure and its algorithms. Learning and learning rates were compared across two groups, one using Sketchmate and the other using paper-and-pencil on practice problems. Results from Experiment I showed that when students used Sketchmate with minimal feedback, there were no significant differences across learning, time spent learning, or learning rate. Experiment II used a version of Sketchmate that provided richer feedback. Results showed similar learning but Sketchmate took significantly less time. Thus when feedback was added, learning rates were significantly greater relative to the paper-and-pencil condition. Discussion focuses on measuring learning rates when evaluating instructional tools.

Categories and Subject Descriptors

K.3.1 [**Computer Uses in Education**]: experimentation; E.1 [**Data Structures**]: Trees

General Terms

algorithms, experimentation, human factors

Keywords

learning rate, feedback, student learning, Sketchmate

1. INTRODUCTION

In addition to enhancing the quality of our work, computer applications are widespread today because they increase efficiency across so many tasks. From communication to organization of data, programs exist to help us accomplish our tasks in less time and perhaps with less effort. Educational software should be viewed in the same light. That is, when designing educational tools, developers should keep track of the amount of time users spend with the tool and calculate an effective learning rate, as this is an important measure of the tool's usefulness [13, 14]. Recent research [1] shows a steady decline in the amount of time full-time students spend studying. A new tool may provide an excellent resource for students to learn the material, yet if it significantly increases the amount of time they spend studying, this tools may not be as useful as its alternatives.

A wide variety of computer programs aimed at instruction exist today. There are games teaching children how to read, lecture presentation software, and interactive practice tools. Programmers have attempted to help students learn a range of different concepts. Researchers spend countless hours developing their tools and then running experiments to evaluate the effectiveness of these applications. Although researchers may measure a variety of variables related to these tools, (e.g., acceptability, ease of use), none of these measures are very important unless the tool enhances student learning. In many instances these measures of learning are assessed with post-activity quizzes or exams. When experimental procedures (e.g., randomization) are used to control threats to internal validity, such studies may provide strong evidence that tool-use caused and/or contributed to learning [4] and support the tool's usefulness.

In this paper we describe two experiments designed to evaluate a newly developed instructional tool called Sketchmate[1]. Sketchmate is a standalone, Java application used to help students learn more about the splay tree data structure and its associated algorithms. We attempted to develop Sketchmate with an intuitive interface so students would not be required to spend a large amount of time learning how to use the application. Additionally, we wanted Sketchmate to provide immediate feedback on incorrect responses, but were concerned about how much extra time would be required reading the details of the more descriptive feedback. Therefore, we developed two versions of Sketchmate: one providing minimal feedback and the other providing a richer set of instruction.

The first experiment compared participants solving exercises using Sketchmate with minimal feedback versus paper and pencil. We measured the amount of time needed to complete the exercise and the score on a subsequent, pop quiz. We then calculated the effective learning rate as the amount

[1]http://www.sketchmate.org

SIGCSE'11, March 9–12, 2011, Dallas, Texas, USA.

of time spent on the exercises divided by the quiz score. The second experiment was identical to the first, except participants used the version of Sketchmate that provided detailed feedback.

2. RELATED WORK ON LEARNING RATES

Although enhancing learning is certainly important, any evaluation of a tool's usefulness must take into account the amount of time spent engaged in instructional activities [15]. School psychology researchers concerned with remedying student deficit have demonstrated the importance of measuring learning rates, or the amount of learning/amount of time spent learning [5, 9, 13, 14, 15]. To highlight the difference in learning versus learning rates, consider an instructor who has the choice of using two different learning tools. Experiments with both tools have shown that they raise student test scores by one letter grade (10%). Thus, based on internally valid experiments one may conclude that both tools cause equivalent learning. Now consider that to occasion the 10% increase on test scores, the first tool requires students to work for 1 hour completing exercises and the second tool only requires 30 minutes. Although both tools enhance learning, learning rates are doubled with the second tool, relative to the first. If an educator were to choose the second tool they may save student time. Also, assuming learning rates are constant, the educator could enhance learning (20% increases) by applying the same amount of time needed for the less efficient tool (i.e., 1 hour in our example) to the more efficient tool [15, 13].

Researchers have conducted several studies comparing interventions using learning and learning rate measures and found that the interventions demonstrating equal or superior levels of learning resulted in inferior learning rates [5, 9, 13, 15]. Consequently, educators who choose a procedure or tool because researchers found it causes greater learning may actually be putting the student at a disadvantage as a different intervention may have caused the same or even more learning in the same amount of time [13]. Based on these learning rate studies [14] we recommended that learning researchers conducting comparative effectiveness studies should include a precise measure of learning time and make relative effectiveness evaluations based on learning rates, as opposed to mere learning.

3. DESCRIPTION OF SKETCHMATE

Our desire to develop a tool providing immediate, corrective feedback led to the development of Sketchmate. This program is designed to be used by a student to complete homework problems on splay trees and their operations. The program begins by loading a pre-made exercise file. Each exercise entry contains the tree structure and the operation to be performed. The user's start time is logged in an external data file. All user actions, such as button clicks and mouse drags, are then logged. This information is used to provide information about how students are thinking about the algorithm's processes and the amount of time students are spending on each problem.

Sketchmate can display two different types of problems: demonstrating one of the six splay steps, or demonstrating a find, insert, or delete operation. The first type is designed to give the students fine-grained practice with the fundamental operations used by splay trees, while the second type of problem is designed to give the students courser-grained practice with how splay operations are used by the various algorithms to re-balance the tree. A description of the two different problem types follows.

3.1 Demonstrating Splay Steps

We sought to mimic the way students would solve these problems with paper and pencil. The advantage Sketchmate provides is that students are no longer required to redraw the entire tree at each step, thus they can spend more time focusing on the algorithms and less time with rote recopying of existing tree nodes.

The six splay steps (zig, zig-zag, etc) are the fundamental actions performed by the main operations (find, insert, delete) to rebalance the splay tree. These splay steps consist of making and breaking existing connections within the tree itself. Users do this in Sketchmate with mouse click actions to break the connections and mouse drags to create connections between nodes (see Figure 1).

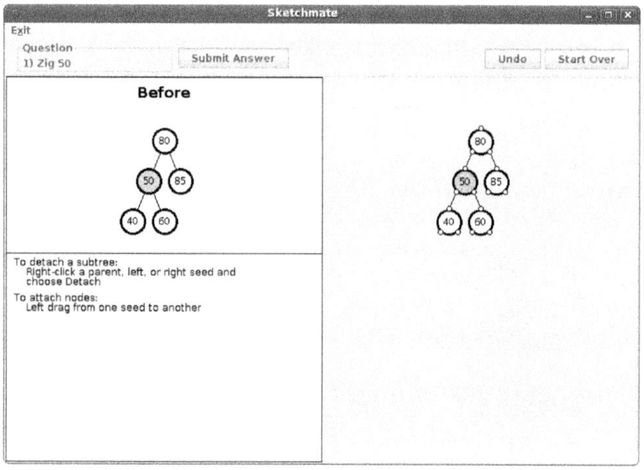

Figure 1: Sketchmate screenshot for an exercise where users demonstrate basic splay operations.

3.2 Demonstrating Find, Insert, and Delete Operations

Building upon their new knowledge from the fundamental splay steps, students can now practice the second type of problem: demonstrating the find, insert, and delete splay tree operations. The instructional idea is that students are initially given an opportunity to practice the fundamental splay steps with the first type of problem (i.e., splay problems) so that they are now in a position to simply apply the appropriate splay step and have the program do it for them. For this reason, six buttons (zig, zag, zig-zig, zag-zag, zig-zag, and zag-zig) are added to the toolbar for the second problem (see Figure 2).

Users can select a node that they are interested in splaying. Once selected, the user is able to click the button associated with the appropriate splay step. When the button is pressed, the animation is performed and the tree is transformed appropriately. If the user attempts any splay step other than the correct one, a dialog box is displayed telling the user that the action is incorrect. This is done because each splay step is only possible on a specific arrangement of

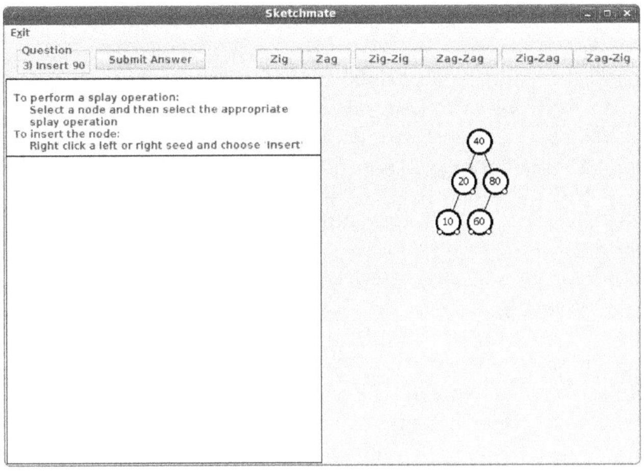

Figure 2: Sketchmate screenshot for an exercise where users demonstrate either a find, insert, or delete operation.

nodes. For example, when the left child of a node is selected, it is not possible to perform a zag splay step because the zag requires the selected node to be a right child.

3.3 Feedback

The initial version of Sketchmate provides only basic feedback in that it prevented users from performing invalid operations but does not explain why the operation is invalid. For example, if a user attempts to perform a zag step on a node that has a left child, Sketchmate displays an error message saying that this is an invalid operation. This version of Sketchmate also alerts the student if they try to submit an answer before performing all of the steps in the operation. Sketchmate displays a dialog box stating "The answer is incomplete. Please try to finish this problem." The dialog box also contains two buttons with the text, "Submit Anyway" and "I will keep trying".

By contrast, the second version of Sketchmate provides more details about user actions. For example, when a user selects a zig step, when the correct answer should be a zag, instead of just displaying a message box stating "Incorrect Action", Sketchmate displays a text description of a zig step and an image to show when it is appropriate. In this manner, detailed feedback is given about their choice and why it is incorrect without actually displaying the answer. The desire behind the richer feedback is so that students will learn from their mistakes and not make them again on subsequent problems. However the drawback with the extra material is that students may spend more time on the exercise, thereby decreasing learning rates [10, 12, 16].

4. SIMILAR TOOLS

There are a variety of tools available with some of the same characteristics as Sketchmate. The majority of these tools appear as either a standalone Java application or a Java applet embedded into a web page. Four examples of these applications are Princeton University's "Growing Tree" [11], University of La Laguna's "Java Models" [6], University of Southern California's "Splay Tree Applet" [7], and New York University's "Binary Search Tree Visualization" [2].

All of these tools provide users with a set of controls for selecting splay tree operations and for navigating through the algorithm steps. All applications allow the user to delete or find a value in a splay tree. Java Models and Growing Tree also give users the ability to insert any value they wish and to control the speed of the animation. However none of these can deliver pre-populated, instructor-generated problems targeted for homework or instruction. Additionally, none of the associated literature for these tools makes mention of the time users spend with the tool or report the resulting learning rates.

Another program, TRAKLA2 [8] is similar to Sketchmate in that it provides automatic grading of the user's work. However the grading is simply an overall score at the end of the problem. That is, there is no feedback on what users did correctly or incorrectly. Instead, it just grades the result and provides a numeric value.

5. EXPERIMENTS

While others have developed tools that contain some similar attributes to Sketchmate, none are specifically aimed at reducing the amount of time spent on the material and thereby increasing learning rates. Additionally, the corresponding literature fails to make specific mention of the amount of time spent with the tool. This seems to be a critical omission because when talking about student learning, the amount learned is important; however, in order to properly evaluate a learning tool or procedure the amount of time needed to achieve that learning must also be taken into account [13, 15].

Each of our experiments involved having students in an introductory data structures class perform a set of lab exercises. Half the students were randomly assigned to use Sketchmate and the other half paper and pencil. To get a baseline measure of learning outcomes and student efficiency, our first experiment used a simplified version of Sketchmate which provided a minimal amount of feedback. The second experiment conducted was identical to the first, with the exception of Sketchmate itself. This version of Sketchmate was designed to provide richer feedback. In both experiments we measured the amount of time to complete the exercise and the number correct on a subsequent pop quiz.

5.1 Subjects and setting

After receiving Institutional Review Board (IRB) approval, we recruited students from an undergraduate course in data structures at a university in the southeastern United States. The first experiment was conducted with 36 students (34 male, 2 female; mean age 22.1). The second experiment was conducted with a new set of 34 students (30 male, 4 female; mean age 21.8). The experiments were run during the semester as part of a class exercise.

The experiments took place using the computers in the students' normal lab classroom in the Computer Science department. All machines had a Pentium 4 processor with 1 GB of RAM and were running the Ubuntu operating system. Participants were provided a copy of the Sketchmate program on a 1 GB USB drive.

5.2 Materials

Experimenters developed one set of 21 splay tree problems. Each problem presented a different splay tree and participants showed the resulting tree after a requested operation. The first 12 problems involved demonstrating basic splay steps such as zig, zag, zig-zag, etc. An example problem where the participant is asked to peform a zig operation on node 50 is shown in Figure 1.

The remaining 9 problems were equally divided between find, insert, and delete operations. Each type of problem was presented multiple times (3 finds, 3 inserts, and 3 deletes) so that students would be able to learn from possible mistakes along the way and correct those mistakes on subsequent problems. Figure 2 shows a question where the participant is asked to insert a node with value 90 into a given splay tree.

Experimenters used screen shots of only the splay trees and the same wording (i.e., "Insert 30") from each Sketchmate problem to develop the paper-and-pencil exercises in an effort to keep the questions as close to the same as possible between groups. No directions were provided on the paper-and-pencil exercises as the students were drawing free-form and therefore did not need any special assistance on using a new tool.

The pop-quiz questions were developed in a similar manner to the paper-and-pencil lab exercises in that a new set of problems was developed for Sketchmate and then screen shots were taken of the splay trees and similar wording was used. However we note that the pop-quiz was conducted during the next lecture period using paper-and-pencil only, even though this methodology put the Sketchmate participants at a disadvantage.

5.3 Design and analysis

A true-experimental, between-subjects, post-test only design [4] was used to test for differences on efficiency and learning for participants using Sketchmate (experimental condition) and paper and pencil (control condition). The dependent variables included the amount of time to complete the lab exercise, the overall pop quiz score, and the learning rate. Independent samples t-tests were used to test for significant differences across dependent variables. All differences were considered significant at the $\rho < 0.05$ level.

5.4 Procedures

The data structures course was structured as a single, combined lecture class with two different lab sections. The experiment took place during the lab sessions in the computer lab. Participants had been given a lecture in class and were given a brief review of splay trees and their operations in the lab. Examples were presented at the whiteboard for the zig, zag, zig-zag, and zig-zig splay steps, as well as one example for each of the find, insert, and delete operations. Participants were encouraged to ask questions as they normally would in a classroom setting. Experimenters gave no demonstration or explanation of Sketchmate or how to use it. Instead participants using Sketchmate were given a USB drive containing the application and a sheet of paper explaining how to start it.

Following the review, researchers distributed the lab exercise. The students were randomly assigned to a group with half of each lab section using Sketchmate and the other half using paper and pencil to complete the exercises. Paper-and-pencil participants were asked to show their work on the paper provided. Also, each was asked to raise their hand at the completion of the exercise so that the experimenter could accurately mark their completion time and collect their work. All paper-and-pencil products were collected and the computer saved Sketchmate responses and the time to complete the exercise on the USB drive, which was then collected. Additionally, experimenters set up a video recorder to record paper-and-pencil participants for a permanent record of completion times.

At the beginning of the next lecture period (less than one week), all students present were given a paper-and-pencil pop quiz on splay tree operations similar to those used in the lab exercise. For example, the lab exercise may have asked the student to show the results of a particular tree after splaying a node with value 5, whereas the pop-quiz asked them to splay a node in a different tree with value 10. We chose to use a pop quiz over an announced quiz in an effort to better control the experiment. That is, we feared that if the students knew a quiz was coming, they might choose to study for it and we would not be able to control 1) the amount of time they spent studying for it, and 2) the method they used for studying for it (Sketchmate or paper and pencil).

Only results from students who completed both the lab exercise and the quiz were used in this study. Although students were told that the exercise and the pop quiz were part of their class grade, any student who submitted work for either the exercise or the quiz received full credit. Also, after the pop quiz, students were given the opportunity to complete the exercise with the other method (Sketchmate or paper and pencil) so as not to put anyone at a disadvantage in their learning. None of the students asked to rework the exercise using the other tool, however after the pop-quiz two students from the Sketchmate group did request a copy of the tool for their own personal use.

The primary experimenter scored all responses for the time to complete the lab and for pop quiz accuracy. Each pop quiz question was given partial credit based on the amount of work shown and the correctness of the result. For example, students who demonstrated the insert operation by inserting the node, but then not splaying the new node to the root only received 25% credit for this answer. A second, independent experimenter also viewed the lab sessions to check for interscorer agreement on completion times for paper-and-pencil participants. Results showed an agreement of completion times within 5 seconds for 97% (36 of 37) of the participants. This experimenter also checked 49% (30 of 59) of all pop quizzes resulting in 97% (29 of 30) agreement. These data suggest that the times and quiz results were scored consistently.

5.5 Results

While the procedures and materials (except for the version of Sketchmate) were the same for both experiments, to keep the data easier to understand we have chosen to report the results into two separate sections: Sketchmate without feedback and Sketchmate with feedback.

5.5.1 *Experiment I: No Feedback*

Table 1 shows the mean and standard deviations across dependent variables for the control and experimental groups. There was no significant difference between those using Sketchmate and those using paper and pencil with regard to completion time ($t(34) = -1.165$, $\rho = .25$), quiz score ($t(34) = -0.27$, $\rho = .979$), or learning rate ($F(1) = 0.463$, $\rho = 0.50$).

Table 1: Student Experiment I Summary Data. SD is the standard deviation.

	Sketchmate		Paper/Pencil	
	n	Mean (SD)	n	Mean (SD)
Time (s)	20	1931 (625)	20	2188 (695)
Quiz (%)	19	70.95 (23.6)	17	71.18 (27.8)
Rate (%/s)	19	0.04 (0.02)	18	0.04 (0.04)

Table 2: Student Experiment II Summary Data. SD is the standard deviation.

	Sketchmate		Paper/Pencil	
	n	Mean (SD)	n	Mean (SD)
Time (s)	17	1453 (362)	17	2332 (488)
Quiz (%)	12	55.00 (26.2)	11	51.18 (19.3)
Rate (%/s)	12	0.04 (0.02)	11	0.02 (0.01)

5.5.2 Experiment II: With Feedback

Table 2 shows the mean and standard deviations across dependent variables for the control and experimental groups. Results showed that participants using this version of Sketchmate with the rich feedback completed their exercises in significantly less time ($t(32) = -5.958$, $\rho < .001$) and had a significantly higher learning rate ($F(1) = 4.412$, $\rho = 0.048$) than those using paper and pencil. However there was no significant difference between the groups based on quiz score ($t(21) = 0.329$, $\rho = .745$).

6. DISCUSSION

We designed the first experiment using Sketchmate giving minimal feedback as a way to get a baseline when comparing the computer to paper and pencil. Although none of the results were statistically significant, we were still encouraged. Prior to the experiment, we were concerned that students using Sketchmate would need extra time and/or instruction in order to simply learn how to use the program. We want to reiterate that students received no instruction whatsoever on how to use Sketchmate. Even though the time differences here were not statistically significant, Sketchmate students were able to complete this set of exercises about 4 minutes faster than those using paper and pencil. We also had concerns that students working with Sketchmate would have difficulties when attempting to complete a paper-and-pencil exercise since the computer would not be present to assist them.

These results suggest that Sketchmate with minimal feedback does not have much of an effect on student learning or learning rates. However, Sketchmate might still be a useful tool as it may provide a different way for students to perform splay tree exercises that does not retard their learning. Results from Experiment II were similar to those from Experiment I and suggest that students performed no better or worse on the pop-quiz when using Sketchmate. However, in Experiment II participants using Sketchmate with richer feedback were able to complete their exercises significantly faster (about 40%) than those using paper and pencil. Therefore, when evaluating using a learning rate measure our comparative effectiveness study shows that Sketchmate with richer feedback significantly enhanced learning rates relative to paper and pencil.

Instructors using Sketchmate could leverage this faster pace by providing students with 30 problems to be solved during a 50 minute lab period, instead of 20. This increased practice can enhance student accuracy, speed of accurate responding, and maintenance of more rapid and accurate responding. Additionally, increasing the number of problems complete should allow educators to present a wider variety of problems which should enhance generalization or students' ability to solve more problem types and novel problems [12]. Alternatively, because students are spending overall less time studying[1], the instructor might choose to assign the same number of problems as they normally would and anticipate getting roughly the same learning outcomes, while demanding less of the students' time.

7. FUTURE RESEARCH

In the current experiments we held tasks constant and allowed time to vary across the Sketchmate and paper-and-pencil conditions. Results suggest that relative to paper and pencil, an instructor may be able to use Sketchmate for a smaller part of a class period and still expect the same amount of student learning. A next step would be to hold time constant across condition and allow the number of problems completed to vary [5]. Such studies may show that Sketchmate results in greater levels of learning in a fixed period of time.

In most, if not all instances, available educational/learning time is constrained. Although educational researchers often provide a careful evaluation of behavior change or learning, they rarely incorporate a precise measure of either time spent learning or learning rate [3]. Consequently, in most instances it is difficult to refer to the professional scientific literature and identify the applications or procedures that will produce the greatest amount of learning in a fixed period of time [5]. As advances in technology often enhance efficiency, technology researchers may be more willing to collect precise measures of learning/instructional time and embrace learning rates as their primary dependent variable. Using precise measures of learning rates to evaluate tool should produce data that are more useful to consumers, who are interested in efficient learning [13]. When comparing tools, measures of overall learning are important; however including measures of learning rates provides a qualitatively different measure. From an applied perspective, these learning rates may be a more relevant metric for objective comparisons [15].

8. SUMMARY

We designed a new tool called Sketchmate to help students learn about splay trees and their algorithms and attempted to leverage the computer's ability to deliver rich, instructive feedback to the student. With the current experiments we evaluated Sketchmate using both learning and learning rate measures as dependent variables as we compared Sketchmate exercises to tradition paper-and-pencil exercises. While education literature shows that immediate feedback increases student learning [16], we were concerned that detailed richer feedback would retard learning because it required users to spend significantly more time to complete the exercise [10].

Our first experiment showed that those using Sketchmate with minimal feedback spent about the same amount of time on the exercises and did not demonstrate better learning of the material than those using paper and pencil. For the second experiment we modified Sketchmate to enhance feedback. Again, participants using the program did not demonstrate a better understanding of the material; however, they did complete their practice exercises quicker, which results in them showing significantly greater increases in learning rates (the same amount of knowledge gained in significantly less time)than those using paper and pencil. Thus, Experiment II showed that instructors could incorporate use of this program in their courses such that students can achieve a similar amount of knowledge with less time spent with the material.

Our research has strong implications for others who are developing educational tools. Specifically, we tend to think that adding corrective feedback or other material to instructional programs will increase the amount of time spent with the tool. However, the current experiments suggest that in some instances including additional time-consuming tasks can enhance, as opposed to hinder learning rates. Additionally, the current study provides a clear example of why learning rate measure may provide a better measure of a tool's effectiveness than learning. We hope that these results will encourage future developers to measure time users spend with their tools and provide learning rate measures when disseminating their results.

9. REFERENCES

[1] P. S. Babcock and M. Marks. The falling time cost of college: Evidence from half a century of time use data. Working Paper 15954, National Bureau of Economic Research, April 2010.

[2] H. Biermann. Binary search tree visualization. Website, 1998. http://www.cs.nyu.edu/algvis/java. (accessed June 1, 2008).

[3] R. Bramlett, G. L. Cates, E. Savina, and B. Lauinger. Assessing effectiveness and efficiency of academic interventions in school psychology journals: 1995-2005. *Psychology in the Schools*, 47(2):114–125, 2010.

[4] D. Campbell and J. Stanley. *Experimental and quasi-experimental designs for research.* Rand McNally College Pub. Co., 1966.

[5] E. Carroll, C. H. Skinner, H. Turner, E. McCallum, and S. Woodland. Evaluating and comparing responsiveness to two interventions designed to enhance math-fact fluency. *School Psychology Forum: Research in Practice*, 1:28–45, 2006.

[6] A. Gogeshvili. Java models. Website, 2002. http://webpages.ull.es/users/jriera/Docencia/AVL/AVL tree applet.htm. (accessed June 1, 2008).

[7] D. Ierardi and T.-W. Li. Splay tree applet. Website, 1996. http://www.ibr.cs.tu-bs.de/courses/ss98/audii/applets/BST/SplayTree-Example.html.(accessed June 1, 2008).

[8] A. Korhonen and L. Malmi. Algorithm simulation with automatic assessment. *SIGCSE Bull.*, 32(3):160–163, 2000.

[9] L. Nist and L. M. Joseph. Effectiveness and efficiency of flashcard drill instructional methods on urban first-graders' word recognition, acquisition, maintenance, and generalization. *School Psychology Review*, 37(3):294–308, 2008.

[10] K. N. Rhymer, C. H. Skinner, S. Jackson, S. McNeill, T. Smith, and B. Jackson. The 1-minute explicit timing intervention: The influence of mathematics problem difficulty. *Journal of Instructional Psychology*, 29(4):305–311, 2002.

[11] C. Sanders, B. Segewick, and K. Wayne. Growing tree. Website, 2002. http://www.cs.princeton.edu/introcs/GrowingTree/GT.jnlp. (accessed June 1, 2008).

[12] C. H. Skinner. *Preventing academic skill deficits.*, pages 61–83. Handbook of child behavior therapy: Ecological considerations in assessment, treatment, and evaluation. Plenum, New York, 1998.

[13] C. H. Skinner. Theoretical and applied implications of precisely measuring learning rates. *School Psychology Review*, 37(3):309–314, 2008.

[14] C. H. Skinner. Applied comparative effectiveness researchers must measure learning rates: A commentary on efficiency articles. *Psychology in the Schools*, 47(2):166–172, 2010.

[15] C. H. Skinner, P. J. Belfiore, and T. S. Watson. Assessing the relative effects of interventions in students with mild disabilities: Assessing instructional time. *Assessment in Rehabilitation and Exceptionality*, 2:207–220, 1995.

[16] C. H. Skinner and E. S. Smith. Issues surrounding the use of self-management interventions for increasing academic performance. *School Psychology Review*, 21(2):202–210, 1992.

Teaching Requirements Engineering to Undergraduate Students

Sriram Mohan
Rose-Hulman Institute of Technology
5500 Wabash Avenue
Terre Haute, Indiana
mohan@rose-hulman.edu

Stephen Chenoweth
Rose-Hulman Institute of Technology
5500 Wabash Avenue
Terre Haute, Indiana
chenowet@rose-hulman.edu

ABSTRACT

Requirements engineering, an integral part of the life of a software engineer, often receives little or no attention in the education of a computer science student. We report on our experiences in constructing an innovative curriculum that utilizes a three tier model of learning that provides students with hands-on experience on the various facets of requirements elicitation and management. This curriculum can be integrated into an existing course on software engineering, software requirements or the senior capstone experience. We believe our experience will be of use to other computer science and software engineering programs that are aiming at introducing requirements in the undergraduate curriculum.

General Terms

Design

Categories and Subject Descriptors

K.3.2 [**Computer and Information Science Education**]: [Curriculum]

Keywords

Software Engineering, Requirements, Education, Curriculum

1. INTRODUCTION

The vital role played by software requirements in the eventual success or failure of a software product has been document by research through the years [6, 7, 14, 19]. A study by the Standish Group[1] paints a very gloomy picture of the state of the software industry. The report reveals that 31% of projects will be canceled before completion and that 52.7% of the projects will cost at least 189% of their estimates. The report also identifies three common factors behind these sobering numbers:

- Lack of user input (13 % of the projects)
- Incomplete requirements and specifications (12 % of the projects)
- Changing requirements and specifications (12 % of the projects)

The report also duly identifies several factors that were common to successful projects. The three most important factors that were commonly cited include:

- User involvement (16% of the projects)
- Clear statement of requirements (14% of the projects)
- Support from upper management (12% of the projects)

A recent study[22] of software organizations in the United States and Australia reveal that requirements continue to be a problem for software development and one of the most common causes of runaway projects.

This problem is further compounded by the cost associated with fixing requirement errors. *"If a unit cost of one is assigned to the effort required to detect and repair an error during the coding stage, the cost to detect and repair an error during the requirements stage is between five to ten times less"* [10].

Software requirements engineering is commonly taught under the aegis of software engineering. The emphasis placed on software engineering in undergraduate education is varied - ranging from optional, to one or two course sequences in software engineering, to coverage through a senior capstone project, to complete degree programs. An analysis of current undergraduate curriculum reveals the following themes:

1. Students typically do not encounter issues of large scale requirements, design, or other principles until their senior year [15].
2. A lack of emphasis on the importance of requirements in computer science education (Most programs tend to cover this area using a couple of class periods) [12].
3. Use of simulated project examples with faculty clients to convey the art/science of requirements in software engineering programs. The simulated experience, while beneficial does not provide the student with a realistic flavor of client-developer interaction and tends to mask some of the challenges in requirements elicitation [12].

As Walker et. al point out [23] "the process of software development is learnt by developing software under conditions similar those used in industry". The importance of using real clients is further confirmed by [2] and [8]. The rest of this paper describes our experiences with a new approach to teaching requirements engineering. This course utilizes a three tiered model of learning and emphasizes hands-on experience with various facets of requirements engineering through interaction with real clients with real needs.

2. EDUCATIONAL CONTEXT

It is important to understand the educational context within which this new course on software requirements has been implemented. We are a four year engineering college with an emphasis on undergraduate education. Currently our department offers undergraduate programs in computer science and software engineering. As a part of these programs, graduating software engineering students are required to complete a year long senior capstone experience. This experience requires students to work on teams of about four students on a project for a client to understand the need for, design, and develop a system that meets the identified needs, and to deliver and refine the system in response to feedback about those needs. Past examples include companies like Microsoft, Omni Software, Turner Broadcasting, Mayo Clinic, Naval Surface Warfare Center, etc.

To help educate students on the skills necessary for a successful senior capstone experience and to provide them with a sound background in software engineering, we require our students to take a series of courses on the following subject areas:

1. Quality Assurance
2. Requirements and human computer interaction
3. Project Management
4. Architecture and Design
5. Construction, Maintenance and Evolution
6. Formal Methods

Over the past couple of years, in order to create an experience similar to those faced by software professionals and to provide our students with more opportunities to work with real clients, we reorganized some of the above courses into a Junior Design Sequence. The courses that comprise the junior design sequence share a common project (similar in idea and execution to that of the senior capstone experience). These courses[1] include the following:

1. Requirements and Human Computer Interaction
2. Project Management
3. Architecture and Design
4. Construction, Maintenance and Evolution

It must be noted that students in the computer science program have the option of pursuing either a senior capstone experience or a senior thesis to complete their graduation requirements. However, irrespective of this choice, the computer science students are required to participate in the junior design sequence through the following courses

1. Requirements and human computer interaction
2. Architecture and Design

[1]It must be noted, that software engineering students would have received a background in quality assurance fundamentals including test-driven development, metrics and quality assurance before they begin the junior sequence.

To align the Junior Projects with the classes the students are taking, we follow a hybrid process. This begins with classical requirements elicitation and documentation, where the students also learn to interact with project stakeholders and hone their verbal and written communication skills. The teams then move into a more iterative development process, regularly delivering successively more refined systems and documentation.

The junior projects tend to have a smaller scope than a traditional senior capstone experience. And because the requirements phase is more structured, Junior Projects can sometimes accommodate projects that might be less clearly defined at the outset. For Junior Projects we favor proposals that can be implemented using object-oriented languages and systems. This constraint supports the educational outcomes of our Software Architecture and Design course, which emphasizes object-oriented design patterns.

3. OUR COURSE ON REQUIREMENTS

We established a curriculum based on our experiences in the industry and by surveying current requirements analysts and software engineers. Given the nature of courses that followed our course in the junior design sequence, we organized the student learning outcomes to target areas of software engineering that highlighted working with the end user and other stakeholders to elicit their needs, define the features and develop a usable interaction experience. Accordingly, the course had the following high level objectives.

Students who successfully complete the course should be able to:

1. Explain the role of requirements engineering and its process.
2. Formulate a problem statement using standard analysis techniques.
3. Determine stakeholder requirements using multiple standard techniques.
4. Produce a specification with functional and non-functional requirements based on the elicited requirements.
5. Decide scope and priorities by negotiating with the client and other stakeholders.
6. Manage requirements.
7. Apply standard quality assurance techniques to ensure that requirements are: verifiable, traceable, measurable, testable, accurate, unambiguous, consistent, and complete.
8. Produce test cases, plans, and procedures that can be used to verify that they have defined, designed and implemented a system that meets the needs of the intended users.
9. Design and prototype user interfaces to validate requirements.
10. Prepare and conduct usability tests to evaluate the usability, utility and efficiency of the developed user interface.

To meet the above learning outcomes, the course covered the following topics:

- Requirement Preliminaries
  - Why requirements?

- Role of requirements in the software life cycle
  - Responsibilities of a software team
- Problem Analysis
  - Identifying need and defining a problem
  - Problem statements and formats
  - Root cause analysis
  - Domain modeling
  - Personas
- Understanding Needs
  - Problems in obtaining requirements
  - Needs versus features versus requirements
  - Interviewing
  - Brainstorming
  - Storyboarding
  - Data gathering and analysis
  - Requirement workshops
- Defining and Refining the Software System
  - Use cases
  - Vision document
  - Non-functional requirements
  - Ambiguous requirements
  - Assessing requirements quality
- Scope Management
  - Scope triangle
  - Managing clients
  - Traceability
  - Managing change
- Interaction Design and Prototyping
  - What is interaction design?
  - Cognition
  - Low fidelity prototyping
  - high fidelity prototyping
- Evaluation
  - Usability testing
  - Analytical evaluation
  - Evaluation frameworks
- The Transition
  - Requirements to design
  - Requirements to testing

We have refined the list of topics mentioned above over the last three years, based on feedback we have received from students, alumni and our industry board of advisors. The transition from requirements definition to system design can be a smooth process if handled in the right manner. We are currently considering the introduction of system sequence diagrams, and operation contracts to assist in the transition of user requirements to provide an ideal launch platform for our course on software architecture and design.

4. TEXTBOOKS

A review of books used in various schools indicates the following books are commonly used:

1. Software Engineering by Ian Sommerville (2010) [21]
2. Software Engineering - A Practitioner's Approach by Roger Pressman (2009) [18]

These two seminal books provide an overview of software engineering, but do not provide an in-depth coverage of the various stages of the software development life cycle. For instance, their coverage on requirements is restricted to a couple of chapters and was not sufficient for our use. Good books on requirements are hard to come by. Our search led us to consider the following books:

1. Requirements Engineering, Processes and Techniques by Gerald Kotonya and Ian Sommerville (1998) [9]
2. Managing Software Requirements: A Use Case Approach by Dean Leffingwell and Don Widrig (2003) [10]

We decided to use the Leffingwell & Widrig text [10] as our primary text due to the in-depth treatment of the list of topics under consideration for the class and the use of a consistent case study throughout the book to explain the various facets of requirements engineering.

The role of prototyping and user interfaces in removing barriers to requirements elicitation is well documented. Our desire to expose students to interaction design as an integral aspect of requirements engineering led us to consider the following books:

1. Interaction Design: Beyond Human Computer Interaction by Helen Sharp, Yvonne Rogers and Jenny Preece (2006) [17]

2. Designing the User Interface - Strategies for Effective Human Computer Interaction by Ben Shneiderman and Catherine Plaisant (2009) [20]

We adopted the text by Sharp, Preece & Rogers [17] as it provides an in-depth coverage of interaction design and evaluating user interfaces. Additionally, the conversational writing style and the use of examples makes it very approachable to undergraduate students in computer science.

5. LEARNING MODEL

Gathering requirements is as much art as it is science. There is no magic formula that can be applied to understand the need behind a system and document the features required in a software system. The technique to use depends on several factors including a) the type of system, b) the technical know how of the clients and the end users, c) the geographical location of the stakeholders. It is not enough to teach students the problems with gathering requirements, the techniques used to elicit, capture, organize and trace requirements. Hands-on experience is particularly important to help students understand the finer details of requirements elicitation. With this in mind, we decided to utilize a three-tier learning model to provide numerous opportunities for our students to practice and develop a mastery of these vital skills. The three tier model includes the following:

1. Tier 1 - In-class Elicitation

2. Tier 2 - Elicitation via Homework Projects

3. Tier 3 - Elicitation through Junior Design

5.1 Tier 1 - In-class Elicitation

We believe that a student's comprehension of the material is greatly enhanced when they are engaged with the material. Each and every technique / concept covered in the class is coupled with suitable active learning exercises that provide a chance for the student to apply the knowledge gained in the classroom.

A common technique utilized in the classroom is the notion of personas; we combine this with mock projects in the first tier of our learning model.

- Mock Projects: We have used mock projects in the classroom to provide context to our discussions. We have organized the discussion on requirements elicitation around project scenarios, where the teaching assistants and the course instructors play the role of client stakeholders and the student teams act as the software developers. The mock projects provide students the ability to apply the software management and development practices they learn in the classroom. It also helps them identify the techniques that are applicable to various project situations. We provide the students with a brief product statement and the student teams then identify the needs, features and requirements as we work our way through the various elicitation techniques and other facets of requirements engineering and interaction design.

  Computer Science is a rapidly changing field and the project scenarios are selected with an eye towards exposing students to new practices and software technologies. For instance, here is a problem statement we used last year:

  A system that integrates micro-blogging services like twitter to run in-class assessments and to gather feedback during class. This could be generalized into a system that integrates with PowerPoint and helps gather student feedback in classes. Faculty can conduct quizzes, gather data via polls, and conduct plus / delta evaluations.

- Personas: A software engineering professional will encounter a wider variety of clients. To give our students a sense of how clients (who think differently and approach problems differently may behave), we developed various persona's [3] (engineers, marketing managers, technophobes and people from different cultures). Students were provided with a description of these persona's and trained faculty played the roles of people with these persona's and students were then required to work in groups to elicit requirements of a very small project. We have enclosed a description of a sample persona:

  Shanice: Went to Indiana University as an undergraduate, majoring in Economics with a minor in Chemistry. Then she started working in the Project Management Department at Eli Lilly in Indianapolis. During her time as manager, Shanice obtained a MS in Information Systems from Kelley School of Business in Indianapolis. She is currently managing a project to change the software for pharmaceutical research and production systems.

5.2 Tier 2 - Elicitation via Homework Projects

We identified homework assignments as a valuable resource to provide students with more opportunities to practice and reflect on requirements gathering. We designed a series of assignments on the simple scenario provided below:

Bank de Fleur *was established in 1875 to assist employees of Fleur Polytechnic to manage their money and investments. It has now grown to be one of the most successful banks in the Wabash Valley.* ***Bank de Fleur*** *has ATM's for convenient access at various locations on campus and in several locations downtown and the adjoining rural areas.. They have recently released plans on redesigning and updating their ATM software to enable a better user experience for their customers and enhance the overall security.*

We enlisted our teaching assistants to represent the bank's management and IT divisions. We also identified some students participating in the senior capstone experience to play the role of the Bank's customers. Each teaching assistant was provided with a list of features and they were instructed to answer only the questions posed by the students.

Feedback was provided by the assistants at the end of an interview session on the student's approach, the questions that were asked and the questions they should have asked. The course instructor provided additional feedback at the very end. The assignments were designed to help the students gain experience in the following areas:

1. Creating a problem statement, identifying stakeholders and constraints
2. Identifying features and tracing features to needs
3. Creating storyboards, data flow diagrams and domain models
4. Identifying actors and creating and refining use cases for the high priority features
5. Creating low fidelity prototypes using post-it notes for the identified use cases.
6. Identifying supplementary specifications such as usability, reliability and performance requirements. Students are also required to identify usability violations on the prototypes from the previous assignment based on the usability requirements and make the necessary changes
7. Developing acceptance test cases based on the identified use cases.
8. Specifying usability and user experience goals
9. Performing usability tests and re-design based on user feedback

5.3 Tier 3 - Elicitation through Junior Design

The Junior design sequence is the final tier of the learning model. The homework assignments and in-class activities were designed to help students apply elicitation and management techniques as they work with real clients on a project. We gather project proposals throughout the year from alumni, from companies that hire our students, from not-for profit organizations and from the campus community. It should be noted that these organizations **do not** pay a fee to participate in the junior design sequence and are appraised of the educational objectives associated with the junior design sequence.

The projects are made available to the students and student opinion on project / team preferences is taken into account in determining the final list of projects. It must be noted that each team (composed of 3 - 4 members) has its own client and project. The team is retained for the entire sequence of classes that comprise the junior design sequence.

Each team is also assigned a teaching assistant who functions as a project manager and provides the team with valuable guidance as they navigate the development lifecycle. Each team has weekly meetings with their client to update them on their progress. Teams also have weekly meetings with their project manager and instructor (if necessary). Agendas and reports are maintained for each meeting, and teams are also required to provide their manager and instructor with weekly stop light reports. The manager has a responsibility similar to a first line manager in a professional situation. Of course, the manager cannot literally fire and hire students, or suggest raises or salary reductions. However, the manager will periodically evaluate each member of the team. This evaluation will be given strong consideration in determining the individual grade for the project.

To help the student teams as they worked on their projects, we divided the work into five distinct milestones as follows

1. Milestone 1: Current System Analysis, Client Stakeholder Analysis, Feature Listing & Problem Statement.
2. Milestone 2: Use Cases, Data Flow Diagrams & Domain Models
3. Milestone 3: Supplementary Specifications: (Non-functional requirements) & Initial user interface design
4. Milestone 4: Change Control Plan, Coding Standards & Acceptance Test Cases and Plan
5. Milestone 5: Usability Test Plan, Test Report and Revised Interface Design

Teams were required to make changes as necessary to various milestones to keep the documents up to date with changing requirements. Students were also encouraged to maintain electronic journals as a reflective exercise. We have also experimented with peer reviews of requirements specifications by other project teams and teams from the senior capstone experience.

Teams were also strongly encouraged to receive feedback on the various milestones from their project managers. We do require teams to turn in a draft to the manager a week prior to the final submission. It must be noted that we had to carefully schedule homework assignments and milestone deadlines to ensure students had sufficient time to receive and incorporate feedback from their homework and in-class exercises on the project.

5.4 Case Study Discussions

The final component of our learning model was the use of discussions revolving around case studies. We introduced case studies and papers (pertinent to requirements) from industry/academia that detail software product success stories and failures. Students are expected to prepare a pre-discussion report that is due before the class session. During the class session, we analyze the case study from the perspective of the concepts learned in the classroom and we try to identify the a) rationale behind the failure, b) key reasons behind the success of a strategy and c) mechanisms to improve the software process. These case studies provide the student with an opportunity to apply their knowledge by reflecting on a real world example. Our list of case studies include the following

1. BAE Automated systems: Denver international airport baggage handling system [13]
2. Why (some) large computer projects fail ? - An analysis of the FAA Advanced Automation System [5]
3. When professional standards are lax: The Confirm failure and its lessons [16]
4. Anatomy of the Boston Big Dig project
5. Requirements engineering challenges in multi-site software development organizations[4]

Most of the above case studies can be either purchased through Harvard Business School or can be purchased as a part of the book - *Software Runaways: Lessons Learned From Massive Software Project Failures* [5].

6. EVALUATION AND DISCUSSION

The classroom processes we have outlined here did lead to junior college students delivering substantial projects at the end of their second or third (of three) terms in the school year. Indeed, the majority of these projects were successful, over three years of experience in using these processes in the requirements course. Failures attributable to incorrect requirements were quite low [3 out of 36]; we believe this was because of the quality work the students did in eliciting and managing the requirements in the course described. They showed their client prototypes early and often, so that misunderstandings about requirements were known early. They did a professional job of trying out their human interface designs on real users in the class, which improved their projects' odds of success. We also believe that they learned to follow good practices for maintaining a relationship with their client, so that they were able to relate realistically with them regarding such things as introduction of changes to requirements after they had begun building the system.

This requirements course was invented largely because the school also has a software engineering major. However, since its inception in 2003, the course always has been a required part of the computer science curriculum, as well. Requirements engineering is not easy to teach to undergraduate majors for a variety of reasons which have been noted by others. As Lethbridge, et al. [11] described teaching soft topics to undergrad CS students, "Anyone who has tried to teach topics such as ethics, quality, process, configuration management, maintenance and requirements will recognize the glassy-eyed appearance in the eyes of some (or most) students. These are critical topics for industrial practice, yet it is a particular challenge to motivate students to feel passionate in these areas, and hence learn what they need to know".

We believe that, if students see clearly the end result of all the work they put into a project, including using their soft skills like requirements engineering, they do appreciate the value of learning these skills. In our junior sequence, they all carry their requirements projects forward into design and development, sufficiently that they can see the importance of the time spent learning to do requirements. That is, we believe the methodology described inherently helps to overcome the problem of students not valuing such material. Further, the use of case studies and in-class discussions on the role of requirements in the software life cycle and the problems caused due to various failures directly attributed to requirements helped emphasize the vital nature of the material and provided the necessary motivation for the students.

We conducted end of the term anonymous evaluations to gauge student feedback about the course. The students were pleased with the outcomes and felt that they gained a lot from the class. They liked the exposure provided to real world practices through the project and conveyed that their level of learning was higher in this class when compared to other courses. Students felt that the the three-tier model of reinforced learning was instrumental in their ability to understand and apply the concepts covered in the classroom. Over the last three years, 104 students completed the surveys and the course averaged the following:

- Quality of learning 4.12/5
- Use of supporting material to reinforce concepts 4.5/5
- Quality of course 4.01/5

Response from the students and alumni on free-from questions is filled with positive feedback about the quality of learning, material and the course in general. More details are not included due to space constraints, but we will be happy to share the results. We include the following comment to convey the expressed sentiments.

"Course homework and activities enforced the concepts we needed to learn. The project really is the best part of this course. It is really cool to work with an actual client, and it feels like we are doing something useful. Unlike other courses, there is some motivation, besides grades, to actually do well on the project. The structure of the course was excellent"

7. CONCLUSION

To be a science, computer science should be based on a firm foundation; in most cases this is taken to include a clear expression of the problem to be solved, such that it leads to a precise resolution. However, most computer science students enter careers in software development, in areas where, usually, clarity of requirements is fuzzy and changing. As we said, this imprecision is known to be a major culprit in the failure of a high percentage of the projects they will embark on. Understanding how to interpret these requirements well is analytical work and lies very close to selecting the proper algorithm and to the art of coding, usually felt to be the core parts of the computer science curriculum. By knowing, as well, the art which goes into requirements elicitation and management, students gain a deeper understanding of the meaning of those requirements. We believe that, even if an undergraduate student's intent is not to become an expert in requirements engineering, their learning of how this expression of the problem comes to be, with real customers, and the vagaries of that work, greatly improve their ability to fit into real software organizations upon graduation.

We also believe that the staged learning of the skills in requirements engineering, which we have outlined here, is a good teaching method for the students to transition into this world they will work in, where problem definition is much less predictable or containable than in the traditional classroom.

8. REFERENCES

[1] Standish group chaos: A recipe for success. *Standish Group International*, 1999.

[2] R. Bruhn and J. Camp. Capstone course creates useful business products and corporate-ready students. *ACM SIGCSE Bulletin*, 2004.

[3] A. Cooper. *The inmates are running the asylum.* SAMS publishing, 2004.

[4] D. Damian and D. Zowghi. Requirements Engineering challenges in multi-site software development organizations. *Requirements engineering*, 8(3):149–160, 2003.

[5] R. Glass. *Software runaways.* Prentice Hall, 1998.

[6] R. L. Glass. How not to prepare for a consulting assignment, and other ugly consultancy truths. *Commun. ACM*, 41(12):11–13, 1998.

[7] R. L. Glass. Frequently forgotten fundamental facts about software engineering. *IEEE Softw.*, 18(3):112–111, 2001.

[8] H. Koppelman and B. van Dijk. Creating a realistic context for team projects in HCI. *ACM SIGCSE Bulletin*, 2006.

[9] G. Kotonya and I. Sommerville. *Requirements engineering.* Wiley Chichester, 1998.

[10] D. Leffingwell and D. Widrig. *Managing Software Requirements: a use case approach.* Pearson Education, 2003.

[11] T. Lethbridge, J. Diaz-Herrera, J. Richard Jr, and J. LeBlanc. Improving software practice through education: Challenges and future trends. 2007.

[12] L. Macaulay and J. Mylopoulos. Requirements Engineering: an educational dilemma. *Automated Software Engineering*, 2(4):343–351, 1995.

[13] R. Montealegre, H. Nelson, C. Knoop, and L. Applegate. BAE automated systems (A): Denver International Airport baggage-handling system. *Harvard Business School Teaching Case*, page 311, 1996.

[14] T. Moynihan. How experienced project managers assess risk. *IEEE Softw.*, 14(3):35–41, 1997.

[15] J. Myers Jr. Software engineering throughout a traditional computer science curriculum. In *Proceedings of the fourteenth annual consortium on Small Colleges Southeastern conference*, 2000.

[16] E. Oz. When professional standards are lax: the CONFIRM failure and its lessons. *Communications of the ACM*, 37(10):29–43, 1994.

[17] J. Preece, Y. Rogers, and H. Sharp. Interaction design: beyond human-computer interaction. 2006.

[18] R. Pressman. *Software Engineering - A Practitioners Approach.* McGraww Hill, 2009.

[19] K. D. Schenk, N. P. Vitalari, and K. S. Davis. Differences between novice and expert systems analysts: what do we know and what do we do? *J. Manage. Inf. Syst.*, 15(1):9–50, 1998.

[20] B. Shneiderman and C. Plaisant. *Designing the user interface - Strategies for Effective Human Computer Interaction.* Addison-Wesley Reading, MA, 2009.

[21] I. Sommerville. *Software Engineering.* Addison Wesley, 2010.

[22] J. Verner, K. Cox, S. Bleistein, and N. Cerpa. Requirements engineering and software project success: An industrial survey in australia and the u.s., 2004.

[23] E. Walker and O. Slotterbeck. Incorporating realistic teamwork into a small college software engineering curriculum. *Journal of Computing Sciences in Colleges*, 2002.

Collaborative Web-Based Learning of Testing Tools in SE Courses

Peter J. Clarke, Jairo Pava, and Yali Wu
School of Computing and Information Sciences
Florida International University
Miami, FL 33199, USA
{clarkep, jpava001, ywu001}@cis.fiu.edu

Tariq M. King
Department of Computer Science
North Dakota State University
Fargo, ND 58108, USA
tariq.king@ndsu.edu

ABSTRACT

One of the main concerns in the software industry continues to be the development of high quality software. This concern will be exacerbated as software systems become more complex. The training of software developers continues to grow in academia since more institutions are offering software engineering (SE) courses. However, the list of topics that are expected to be covered in this course leaves little or no time for topics that focus on developing quality software, such as software testing and the use of testing tools.

In this paper we describe an approach that non-intrusively integrates the use of software testing tools in SE courses. The cornerstone of our approach is the interaction students have with a *Web-Based Repository of Software Testing Tools* (WReSTT) that contains tutorials on testing concepts and testing tools. WReSTT employs both collaborative learning and social networking features that are attractive to students. We present the results of preliminary study performed in two SE courses that show how using the resources in WReSTT can potentially impact the students' understanding of software testing and the use of testing tools.

Categories and Subject Descriptors

K.3.2 [**Computer and Information Science Education**]: Miscellaneous

General Terms

Experimentation

Keywords

Collaborative Learning, Repository, Software Testing, Unit Testing

1. INTRODUCTION

One of the main concerns in the software industry continues to be the development of high quality software. This concern will be exacerbated as the size and complexity of software systems increase. The training of software developers continues to grow in academia since more institutions are offering software engineering (SE) courses. The literature states that most software engineers in industry are not educated in key portions of the SE body of knowledge, including testing [2, 19].

The list of topics that are expected to be covered in SE courses leaves little or no time for topics that focus on developing quality software, such as software testing [2]. Testing continues to be the primary technique used to ensure the development of high quality software, but recent studies [6] indicate that major improvements in software testing are needed. Therefore it is important that innovative ways be developed to encourage students to learn about testing and testing tools without extending the length of the already crowded curriculum. Although we focus on SE courses in this paper, the problem of developing quality software should be addressed in courses earlier in the computing curriculum e.g., CS1-CS3. Clarke et al. [5] describe a three-phase project that supports the integration of testing into programming courses supported by a *Web-Based Repository of Testing Tools* (WReSTT). WReSTT contains tutorials on testing concepts and testing tools.

In this paper we describe an approach that non-intrusively integrates the use of software testing tools in SE courses. The cornerstone of our approach is the interaction students have with WReSTT. Unlike the original version of WReSTT described in [5], the updated version (WReSTT V2) employs the use of both collaborative learning and social networking features that are attractive to students. WReSTT V2 is currently in the beta stage and is still being updated to reflect the improvements recommended by the students in the study. We present the results of a preliminary study performed in two SE courses that use WReSTT V2 as a learning resource. The results show how using the resources in WReSTT can potentially impact the students' understanding of software testing and the use of testing tools. We acknowledge that a more comprehensive study is required before any major claims can be made regarding the impact of using WReSTT in the classroom.

The paper is organized as follows: Section 2 provides a review of the approaches and online resources that support the integration of testing into programming courses. Section 3 describes the structure of WReSTT and its use as a learning resource. Section 4 describes the study and presents the results. Section 5 presents the concluding remarks.

SIGCSE'11, March 9–12, 2011, Dallas, Texas, USA.

2. RELATED WORK

In this section we review some of the approaches used to integrate testing into courses that contain a significant portion of programming, more specifically SE courses. A brief overview for some of the common online resources that can support student learning in software testing is also presented.

2.1 Integrating Testing into Programming

Frezza [11] describes an approach that integrates testing into an introductory software design course. The approach was tried in several instances of the course and the students rated the approach as effective. However, the approach was not able to make up the deficiencies in student programming ability. Barbosa et al. [3] tackle two prominent challenges in software education: (1) making students recognize the relevance of the testing activity, and (2) motivating students to use testing ideas in their projects. The approach, used in an object-oriented development course, was based on the idea of test-driven development. The results of the work indicated that students generally approved of the testing early approach.

Janzen et al. [16] present test-driven learning (TDL) as a pedagogical tool that can be incorporated into multiple levels of the CS and SE curricula. They propose that TDL can be applied early in the CS curriculum and should not compete with other approaches used to teach early programming courses. A survey was conducted using a CS2 course, undergraduate SE course, and a graduate SE course. The results indicated that less experienced students are more open to adopting a test-first approach.

Astigarraga et al. [2] present a study that evaluates software testing as an industry profession and discusses ongoing efforts to advance the status of software testing in academic curricula. The conclusion of the paper recommends changes to the curricula that focus more on test courseware, journals, societies and education opportunities for software test engineering. It is well known in academia that such changes will take a long time to be realized; therefore we propose integrating testing into SE courses by using available web-based resources, collaborative learning, and social networking to attract students to software testing.

2.2 Online Resources

There are several web-based repositories that provide access to learning materials on software testing. We provide a brief description of these repositories below.

CSTER [18]. CSTER, The Center for Software Testing Education and Research, provides materials to support the teaching and self-study of software testing, software reliability, and quality-related software metrics. CSTER has a large repository of content on software testing including video lectures, practice quizzes, drills, and other assessment materials.

OpenSeminar - Module 7 [26]. OpenSeminar is a web-based open courseware platform that enables instructors to collaborate on material for similar courses by sharing links to content. The testing component in OpenSeminar is located in model 7 of the software engineering component, and provides users with examples, lab exercises, lectures (slides) and readings.

Bug Hunt [8]. Bug Hunt is an online tutorial to instill good testing practices through lessons and challenges. Bug Hunt's tutorials provide instructors and students with several features including: immediate feedback, self-paced progression, configurability to accommodate instructor's requirements, and provision of an automatic assessment of student performance.

Ensemble [9]. Ensemble is an NSF NSDL Pathways project to support the distribution of computing education materials. Ensemble provides access to other repositories such as SWENET [20] and CITIDEL [24]. SWENET, The Network Community for Software Engineering Education, is a project to produce and organize high-quality materials supporting software engineering education. One of the Software Engineering Education Knowledge (SEEK) modules in SWENET is Software Verification and Validation (VAV). CITIDEL, the Computing and Information Technology Interactive Digital Educational Library is a resource to discover Computer Science education and research materials.

MERLOT [21]. MERLOT, Multimedia Educational Resource for Learning and Online Teaching, is an online, user-centered, and searchable collection of peer reviewed and selected higher education learning materials. MERLOT is not exclusive to software testing. However, testing material can be found by searching with the browse path "All>Science and Technology>Computer Science" and keywords "Software Testing".

3. USING WRESTT IN THE CLASSROOM

The *Web-Based Repository of Software Testing Tools* - (WReSTT) [27], is one of the components of a project consisting of three phases to integrate software testing into programming and software engineering courses. The three phases include: (1) developing an online portal of learning resources that supports pedagogy in the area of software testing, particularly the use of testing tools; (2) holding a series of annual workshops for instructors that introduce them to software testing techniques and tools available through WReSTT, and (3) performing studies to determine the effectiveness of WReSTT and the instructors' workshop on improving student learning. Clarke et al. [5] describe WReSTT and report on the first instructors' workshop. In this paper we focus on integrating collaborative learning into WReSTT and report the preliminary results of a study performed in two SE courses.

3.1 Overview of WReSTT

WReSTT [27] was developed to support the pedagogical needs of students and instructors in programming and software engineering courses by providing access to a comprehensive and up-to-date set of learning material on software testing tools. Although WReSTT focuses on software testing tools, we also provide links to other repositories containing software testing materials. WReSTT was developed using Drupal [7], a content management system. WReSTT currently contains learning materials for several tools, including: *JUnit* [12] - a unit testing framework and *SWAT* [25] - Simple Web Automation Toolkit, among others. Clarke et al. [5] provide a more complete description of the first version of WReSTT.

3.2 Integrating Collaborative Learning

In Fall 2009 WReSTT was introduced to the students in the undergraduate SE course at Florida International University (FIU) to encourage them to use tools to test the soft-

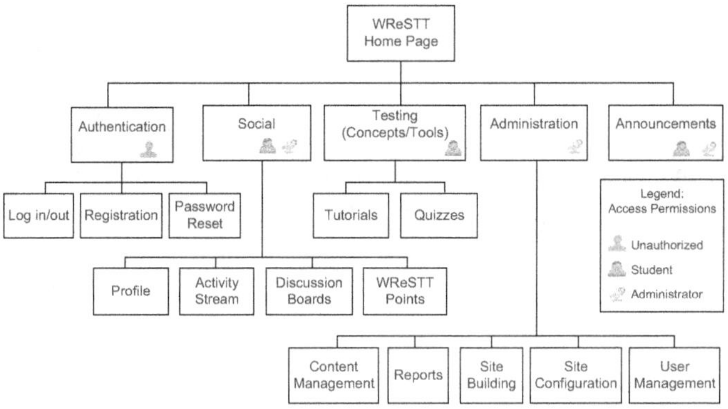

Figure 1: Block diagram of WReSTT version 2.

ware developed for their class projects. Upon completion of the academic semester one of the students in the class, Jairo Pava (second author of this paper), recommended to the WReSTT team that students would be more willing to use WReSTT if: (1) the interface to WReSTT was improved to have more of a social networking tool feel e.g., Facebook [10], and (2) there was a competition for bonus points between project teams to access and complete quizzes based on software testing tutorials. Jairo was invited to be part of the WReSTT team and assisted in the development of a new version of WReSTT that is still being beta tested.

The process of acquiring knowledge, or learning, is largely enhanced by social activity. If there is no interaction, students often feel isolated, overwhelmed, and reluctant to learn [14]. As a result, there has been a great rise in the use of Online Learning Communities (OLC) for instruction through academic and professional training programs on the Internet. An OLC describes a group of people who are dedicated to learning together in an online environment that encourages dialogue, feedback, and reflection. Members of an OLC may be students, professors, tutors, or domain experts who engage in meaningful conversations and work in teams towards a common purpose or objective [15].

A successful OLC uses positive reinforcement, presents new information in motivating ways, and encourages group collaboration. These characteristics correspond specifically to the behavioral, cognitive, and social learning theories which have been empirically proven to be successful for instruction [17]. To increase student motivation, participation, and retention, WReSTT was transformed into a collaborative OLC.

3.3 WReSTT V2 Design

The second version of WReSTT (WReSTT V2) is an OLC and incorporates features of common social networking tools. These improvements are expected to be more attractive to students and will encourage them to use the site more often and promote collaborative learning. Figure 1 shows a hierarchical block diagram of the components in WReSTT V2. The major components are as follows:

- *Authentication* - allows users to log in/off, register for an account, and reset their passwords.
- *Social* - allows users to create a profile, monitor the activity stream, post comments to the discussion boards, and monitor virtual points assigned to users or user teams.

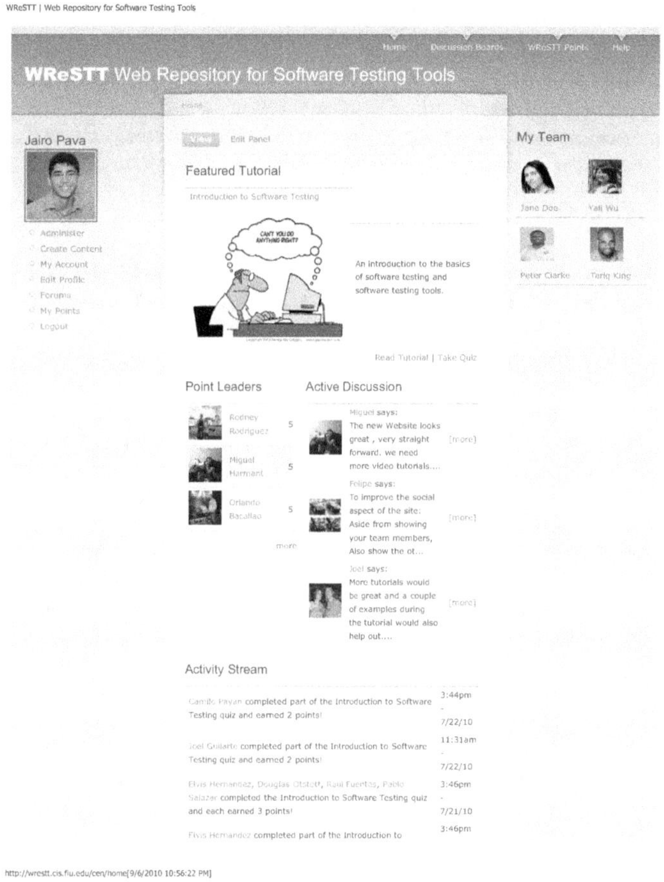

Figure 2: Student's homepage in WReSTT V2.

- *Testing* - contains the tutorials and quizzes for testing concepts and the tools hosted in the repository.
- *Administration* - provides the basic operations to maintain the site including: content management, generation of reports, extending the site, configuration of the site, and management of user accounts.
- *Announcements* - distribute announcements to the registered users of the site.

Building and configuring the Social and the Testing components are the innovative components of the site. Drupal [7], the content management system used to build the site, provides most of the functionality in the other components. Note, however, that these components still need to be configured correctly for WReSTT V2 in order to function properly.

Figure 2 shows the home page for one of the students currently registered on WReSTT V2. On the left side of the page is the picture of the student and the main menu. The right side of the page shows the student's team members and their pictures. The main block in the center of the page is divided into four parts: (1) *Featured Tutorial* - the current tutorial available to the team, there are two links available: one to access the tutorial and the other to take the quiz; (2) *Point Leaders* - the students currently with the most points assigned by the WReSTT V2 system, (3) *Active Discussion* - comments posted by students, and (4) *Activity Stream* - posting showing the recent activities by the users of the system.

3.4 Using WReSTT in an SE Course

The process an instructor would follow to use WReSTT V2 is as follows. At the beginning of the academic semester, the instructor uploads the course roster onto the WReSTT website and places each of the students into virtual WReSTT teams. Each team may contain up to six students. There is no limit to the amount of teams that participate on the WReSTT website. After uploading the roster and forming teams, accounts on the WReSTT website are created, and an e-mail with a WReSTT username and password is delivered to each student. The instructor may then make the tutorials on software testing tools available to the teams either all at once, or as the course progresses through various testing topics.

Each tutorial is followed by a collaborative quiz which all of the students on a virtual team must complete with a grade of 80% or higher to receive virtual points. The quizzes are divided into as many individual parts as there are students in a team. Each student must complete a quiz part using his or her own WReSTT account. A student is rewarded with virtual points for completing an individual quiz part, but must work with his or her team members to ensure that everyone on the team passes their individual quizzes to receive the maximum amount of virtual points. The more tutorials a virtual team reads and the more quizzes the team is allowed to complete, result in more opportunities for its members to accumulate virtual points. WReSTT maintains a count of each of the students' earned virtual points so that the instructor may use these points as extra-credit points towards the students' grades.

Quizzes on WReSTT are divided into two parts. The first part consists of multiple choice questions where the students may use a combination of HTML form elements such as radio buttons, checkboxes, and lists to submit answers that are automatically graded. Students receive immediate feedback on answers and are automatically assigned virtual points from multiple choice questions. The second part consists of short response questions where students are asked to reflect on a concept, and the responses are used to stimulate dialogue on the discussion boards. WReSTT maintains a count of the posts each student makes on the discussion boards and recommends to the instructor the amount of extra virtual points a student should earn.

As a virtual team successfully completes quizzes and is awarded points, other teams are notified of the team's accomplishments through an activity stream on the front page of WReSTT. The names and pictures of the students are posted on the front page along with the name of the tool they have now learned about and the amount of points they have earned as a result of successfully completing the quizzes. A points leader board on the front page is updated to show the name of the student in the class with the highest amount of points on WReSTT to promote a competitive social environment. The students benefit from the competitive environment as they now have more motivation to learn from software testing tutorials, take quizzes, and earn points.

4. PRELIMINARY STUDY

To determine the effectiveness of using WReSTT in the classroom we conducted a preliminary study that involved students in the *CEN 4010 - Software Engineering I* course for the Spring 2010 and Summer 2010 semesters. The students were exposed to both the WReSTT V1 implementation to access the tool tutorials and the WReSTT V2 implementation for collaborative learning. Based on the results of the study we expect to merge both versions of WReSTT. One of the main components in the SE course is the semester long project. To achieve the learning outcomes of the course, students are required to work in project teams, which lends itself to collaborative learning.

Two parts of the study were used to evaluate the improvement of students' understanding of software testing and use of testing tools. The first part focused on the impact WReSTT V1 had on the students' ability to use testing tools in their software projects and be able to demonstrate the use of the tools to the instructor. The second part of the study focused on the impact WReSTT V2 had on promoting collaborative learning and improving the students' conceptual understanding in the area of software testing.

4.1 Data Capture

The data for the study was collected from two sources. The first source was the pre/post test instruments given to the class prior to the testing component of the course being taught, and upon completion of the course, respectively. In addition to the pre/posttest instrument, data was also collected from the grading rubric to evaluate the students' proficiency of testing tools during the demonstration of the software projects. The second source of data was from the WReSTT V2 web site.

The pre/posttest contained four classes of questions: Q(1)-(3) focused on program testing and the use of testing tools, Q(4)-(5) on online resources available to support testing, and Q(6)-(7) assessed the importance of tool support for software testing. The leftmost column of Table 1 shows the closed ended questions from the pre/post test instrument. During the demonstration of the project each student was asked to demonstrate their knowledge of a testing tool if they stated that one or more tools were used during testing.

The data collected from the WReSTT V2 was in the form of WReSTT virtual points. These points were awarded to students as follows: 2 points for completing an individual quiz part; 3 points for being on a team that had all of its members pass their individual quizzes; 1 point for uploading a profile picture; and 1 point for posting on the discussion board. Teams were also awarded bonus points based on the team with the highest point tally in the quizzes and the promptness in completing the quizzes.

4.2 Results

Table 1 shows a summary of the results for the pre/post test for the two semesters (Spring and Summer 2010). Column 1 shows the questions that required discrete answers. Questions 3.b.i, and 6 used a Likert scale ranging from 1 (low) to 5 (high). Row 1 of the tables shows the number of responses of the students that took both the pretest and posttest. In the Spring semester 18 out of 38 (47%) took both tests and in the Summer 24 of 34 (71%).

The data in Table 1 shows that there was a 50% increase in the number of students who used testing tools during their software project from the Spring to the Summer semester. There was also an increase in the number of students using the different types of tools e.g., unit and functional testing tools and code coverage tools. Note however that the highest tool usage (54% of the students) was the unit testing

Question	CEN 4010 - Spring 2010		CEN 4010 - Summer 2010	
	Pretest	*Posttest*	*Pretest*	*Posttest*
Number of Responses:	18 out of 38 (47%)		24 out of 34 (71%)	
2. Have you ever used tools to support testing of programs?	N(15) Y(3)	N(6) Y(12)	N(20) Y(4)	N(6) Y(18)
3.b.i Unit Testing Tool Proficiency	Avg = 4 (1 response)	Avg = 1.7 (8 responses)	Avg = 2.5 (2 response)	Avg = 3.2 (13 responses)
3.b.ii Functional Testing Tool Proficiency	(0 response)	(0 responses)	Avg = 3 (1 response)	Avg = 2.7 (3 responses)
3.b.iii Code Coverage Tool Proficiency	(0 responses)	Avg = 3 (4 responses)	Avg = 3 (1 response)	Avg = 2.0 (6 responses)
4. Do you know of any online resources that provide information on software testing?	N(11) Y(7)	N(5) Y(13)	N(21) Y(3)	N(2) Y(22)
6. How beneficial do you think it is to use tools to support the testing of programs?	Avg = 4.3	Avg = 4.6	Avg = 4.4	Avg = 4.4

Table 1: Results for the closed ended questions in the pretest/posttest instrument. N – No; Y – Yes; Avg – average of scores are out of 5.

Class of Data	Spr. 2010	Sum. 2010
Number of students that participated in the study	22 of 38 (58%)	32 of 34 (94%)
Students that received points	18 (82%)	30 (94%)
Students that received maximum points	2 (9%)	7 (22%)
Students that completed a quiz	22 (100%)	31 (97%)
Students that passed the quiz	17 (77%)	25 (78%)
Students that received maximum points on the quiz	9 (41%)	19 (59%)
Number of teams in class	7	7
All members of team that completed the quiz	1 (14%)	3 (43%)

Table 2: Data collected from WReSTT V2.

tool at the end of the Summer semester. There was a significant improvement in the number of students that became aware of online resources with information on software testing. This was expected since the students were introduced to WReSTT during the class. The last row of table 2 shows that students in both classes generally agreed that it is beneficial to use tools to test programs.

The data in the table with respect to the students' knowledge and skill of using testing tools was validated when the students demonstrated their SE project to the instructor. That is, unlike other SE classes taught in the past, students were able to describe the process of using an automated tool during testing. The students understood concepts such as test setup/tear down, and why it was necessary to explicitly state the expected results of a test. One of the interesting aspects of the study was the variety of testing tools used by the teams. These included unit testing tools - FlexUnit [1], JUnit [12], MbUnit [23], PHPUnit [4], Visual Studio Team System 2008 [22]; functional testing tools - SWAT [25]; code coverage tools - NCover [13]. The most popular tools were JUnit, MbUnit and PHPUnit.

Table 2 contains the data captured from the part of the study that used WReSTT V2. Column 1 shows the class of the data collected, Columns 2 and 3 contain the data for the Spring and Summer semesters, respectively. The percentages presented in Rows 2-6 are based on the students that participated in the study. Of the 38 students in the Spring class only 22 (58%) participated in the WReSTT V2 study, and 32 of the 34 (94%) students participated during Summer. The students who participated in the study and performed tasks to be awarded virtual points were over 80% in both semesters. Similarly, 77% and 78% of the students passed the quiz in the Spring and Summer semesters, respectively. The number of teams that completed the quiz was 14% and 43% for the Spring and Summer semesters, respectively. There was an increase in teams completing the quiz of 29% from Spring to Summer. Out of the seven teams in both semesters, one team completed the quiz in Spring and three teams in the Summer. Based on the results in Table 2, it can be deduced that the main hurdle to overcome is to get all students to participate in the study. If all students do not participate then some teams will not be able to get the maximum number of virtual points.

4.3 Discussion

The results shown in Tables 1, 2 and the anecdotal evidence from the SE project demonstrations, support the claim that using WReSTT in SE classes exposes students to testing tools and improves their practical skills in testing software systems. Prior to the studies related to WReSTT, students in the SE classes at FIU did not use any automated testing tools to test their software projects. One of the main concerns regarding the study is that not enough students participated. One reason for the low participation by students was that the study commenced two-thirds of the way into the semester, which is when testing is introduced into the SE class. Around this time some students were not attending class due to deadlines for projects and exams in other classes. In both the Spring and Summer classes, the percentage of student participation in the study was very similar to the percentage of the student attending class.

The results collected from the WReSTT V2 component of the study are very promising, particularly during the Summer semester. The participation was high, over 80% in both classes, and almost all students took the quiz online. The percentage of the students that passed the quiz was also good, around 77%. Of the students who participated in the study, 41% of the students in the Spring semester and 59% of the students in the Summer semester obtained full points on the quiz. Note that the percentage of teams where all members completed the quiz was low (14% and 43%) due to the fact that some students did not participate in the study or did not complete the quiz in the allocated time. It is evident that using the collaborative learning approach in WReSTT is a factor that can impact students' conceptual understanding of software testing, particularly if bonus points are awarded based on the WReSTT virtual points.

Threats to Validity. The Spring SE class was taught by a new instructor with little expertise in software testing and did not engage the students in using testing tools during the SE class. This may have also contributed to the low participation of the students in the study. This problem was rectified in the Summer SE class with a more experienced

SE instructor who is knowledgeable in the area of software testing. No control groups were used during the preliminary study since there was only one section of CEN 4010 being offered in each semester and it was important to expose all of the students in the course to the testing tools. We plan to repeat the study in the coming semesters when WReSTT is fully implemented and use a control group.

5. CONCLUDING REMARKS

In this paper we describe how the learning resources in a *Web-Based Repository of Software Testing Tools* (WReSTT) may be used to support the teaching of testing in software engineering (SE) courses. The learning resources in WReSTT include tutorials on software testing concepts and testing tools. The tutorials in WReSTT utilize a collaborative learning approach where students are grouped into virtual teams and each team is awarded virtual points based on the completion of specific tasks, such as quizzes. WReSTT contains social networking features that allow students to create profiles, monitor the activities of fellow students and identify who are the points leaders in their class.

A preliminary study was performed with two SE classes, Spring and Summer 2010, to evaluate the effectiveness of using WReSTT in the classroom. The results showed that: (1) most students have never been exposed to an online resource containing software testing learning materials before using WReSTT; and (2) integrating collaborative learning into WReSTT, with the reward of virtual points, can potentially improve students' conceptual understanding of software testing and the use of testing tools during an SE course.

6. ACKNOWLEDGMENTS

This work was supported in part by the National Science Foundation under grants DUE-0736833 (FIU) and DUE-0736771 (FAMU). We would like to thank Dr. Edward L. Jones (FAMU) and the reviewers for their insightful comments on how to improve the paper.

7. REFERENCES

[1] Adobe Open Software. FlexUnit, 2010. http://docs.flexunit.org/index.php.

[2] T. Astigarraga, E. Dow, C. Lara, R. Prewitt, and M. Ward. The emerging role of software testing in curricula. In *Transforming Engineering Education: Creating Interdisciplinary Skills for Complex Global Environments, 2010 IEEE*, pages 1–26, apr. 2010.

[3] E. Barbosa, J. Maldonado, R. LeBlanc, and M. Guzdial. Introducing testing practices into objects and design course. In *Proceedings of CSEET 2003*, pages 279 – 286, mar. 2003.

[4] S. Bergmann. PHPUnit, 2010. http://www.phpunit.de/.

[5] P. J. Clarke, A. A. Allen, T. M. King, E. L. Jones, and P. Natesan. Using a web-based repository to integrate testing tools into programming courses. In *Proceedings of the ACM OOPSLA 2010 Companion*, SPLASH '10, pages 193–200, New York, NY, USA, 2010. ACM.

[6] "CNSS". Software 2015: A national software strategy to ensure u.s. security and competitiveness. Technical report, Center for National Software Studies, 2005.

[7] Drupal Community. Drupal, 2008. http://drupal.org/.

[8] S. Elbaum and K. Stolee. Bug Hunt , 2010. http://esquared.unl.edu/BugHunt.

[9] Ensemble Development Team. Ensemble - Connecting Computing Educators, 2010. http://www.computingportal.org/.

[10] Facebook Team. Facebook, 2010. http://www.facebook.com/.

[11] S. Frezza. Integrating testing and design methods for undergraduates: teaching software testing in the context of software design. In *Frontiers in Education, 2002. FIE 2002. 32nd Annual*, volume 3, pages S1G–1 – S1G–4 vol.3, nov. 2002.

[12] E. Gamma and K. Beck. JUnit, 2008. http://www.junit.org/.

[13] Gnoso. Ncover, 2010. http://www.ncover.com/.

[14] N. Hara and R. Kling. Students' Frustrations with a Web-based Distance Education Course, September 1999. http://www.slis.indiana.edu/CSI/wp99_01.html.

[15] S. Hiltz. Collective learning in asynchronous learning networks. In *Proceedings of WEB 1998*, Orlando, Florida, USA, 1998.

[16] D. S. Janzen and H. Saiedian. Test-driven learning: intrinsic integration of testing into the cs/se curriculum. *SIGCSE Bull.*, 38(1):254–258, 2006.

[17] S. D. Johnson and S. R. Aragon. An instructional strategy framework for online learning environments. In *Education*, pages 31–43, 2002.

[18] C. Kaner. Center for software testing education and research (CSTER), 2010. http://www.testingeducation.org/.

[19] T. C. Lethbridge, J. Diaz-Herrera, R. J. J. LeBlanc, and J. B. Thompson. Improving software practice through education: Challenges and future trends. In *FOSE '07: 2007 Future of Software Engineering*, pages 12–28, Washington, DC, USA, 2007. IEEE Computer Society.

[20] M. J. Lutz, W. M. McCracken, S. Mengel, M. Sebern, G. W. Hislop, and T. B. Hilburn. Swenet - seek category: Software verification and validation (vav), 2010. http://www.swenet.org/browseModules.aspx?categoryID=11.

[21] MERLOT Community. Multimedia educational resource for learning and online teaching (MERLOT), 2010. http://www.merlot.org/merlot/index.htm.

[22] Microsoft Corporation. Visual Studio Team System 2008, May 2010. http://msdn.microsoft.com/en-us/library/ee338734(v=VS.90).aspx.

[23] NUnit.org. MbUnit, May 2010. http://www.mbunit.com/.

[24] C. D. Team. CITIDEL - Computing and Information Technology Interactive Digital Educational Library, 2010. http://www.citidel.org/.

[25] Ultimate Software. SWAT, 2009. http://sourceforge.net/projects/ulti-swat/.

[26] L. Williams. Openseminar: Software engineering: Testing, 2010. http://openseminar.org/se/modules/7/index/screen.do.

[27] WReSTT Team. WReSTT: Web-based Repository for Software Testing Tools, 2010. http://wrestt.cis.fiu.edu/.

Software Studio: Teaching Professional Software Engineering

Tom Nurkkala
tnurkkala@cse.taylor.edu

Stefan Brandle
sbrandle@cse.taylor.edu

Department of Computer Science and Engineering
Taylor University
236 W Reade Av
Upland, IN 46989

ABSTRACT

Software Studio is a studio-based learning (SBL) curriculum designed to train students as professional software engineers. Traditional software engineering courses remain important, but suffer significant gaps in preparing students for professional engagement. We describe our curriculum model, highlight ways in which it fills these gaps, and offer a SWOT analysis. As practical guidance, we reflect on our missteps and successes in implementing Software Studio over the past five semesters. Finally, we suggest future directions for Software Studio.

Categories and Subject Descriptors

K.3.2 [**Computer and Information Science Education**]: Computer science education; D.2.9 [**Software Engineering**]: Management—*life cycle, programming teams*

General Terms

Management, Design

Keywords

Software Engineering, Studio-Based Learning, Software Studio, HFOSS, Capstone Project

1. INTRODUCTION

Computer Science students in traditional programs often receive excellent training in many aspects of software engineering. Important parts of the software life cycle can be exercised in classes and student projects, including requirements gathering, modeling, design, implementation, documentation, and testing. As valuable as such experience is for students, however, there remains a considerable gap between what *students* learn and experience in class, and what *graduates* will experience in their early days as professional software engineers.

SIGCSE'11, March 9–12, 2011, Dallas, Texas, USA.

Studio Based Learning (SBL) promises to help fill this gap. At Taylor University, we have implemented SBL in our Computer Science and Engineering (CS&E) curriculum in a unique form that we call *Software Studio*. In a 2005 proposal to develop the Software Studio curriculum, Bill Toll, CS&E chair, wrote:

> As evidenced by our experience and that of other universities reporting at conferences, it is very difficult to provide an environment where students can consistently produce commercial level production software. ... We believe it is possible to create a structure where students can consistently produce professional quality software.
>
> The dream of this initiative is to create a structure where students can create software that may be used on a production basis by the University for administrative and academic functions, by missions and other non-profit organizations, and by commercial entities.

That dream became reality in the fall of 2008, when we inaugurated Software Studio. This paper describes our experience to date.

2. RELATED WORK

Software Studio took inspiration from prior efforts to teach students to produce professional quality software in the classroom.

Our understanding of software engineering as a *studio* experience originated with the work of Newell Award recipient Richard Gabriel, who compared program design to fine art [4]. Both require talent that can be developed. Although learning information is beneficial, Gabriel proposed that software development is a craft best learned by "doing the thing" and being taught what sets the "extraordinary apart from the ordinary."

Inspiration for a *multi-semester* studio experience came from Ramakrishnan [5], who describes a studio-based, yearlong course at Monash University. Their focus is on teams that "learn by doing," getting help from an advisor if needed. Project teams work for real clients using industry-standard tools and processes. Learning outcomes include teamwork in a professional environment, collaborative learning in an applied context, and the application of high-level critical thinking to solve problems.

A multi-semester experience is also suggested by the work of Allen, et al [1], who describe an early effort to teach students to write production quality software using Extreme Programming. Students rated the experience highly, but because the work was constrained to one semester, only one of three projects was completed, and it contained a significant defect. The unfinished projects each required an additional month of development by two programmers.

Ellis, et al [3] described the need for "real world" experience, asking whether an open source project could deliver it. They suggested that humanitarian service would attract students who are motivated more by a cause than by technology. Our department, with a history of "noble cause projects" that dates to our 1979 founding, embraced this idea of recruiting students to a superior learning opportunity.

Finally, we recommend to the reader an on-line community dedicated to studio-based learning at Auburn University [2].

3. GAPS IN SOFTWARE ENGINEERING EDUCATION

Several serious gaps exist between software engineering student experience and professional software development.

No Product.

A student project is just that—a *project*. It is not a *product* in any meaningful, commercial sense. Such a non-product escapes the scrutiny of sales, marketing, and customer relations. It also is isolated from external forces like press reviews, competing product offerings, market share, and most importantly, user scrutiny.

Independent of such forces, students create throw-away projects. Most such software would not be considered even alpha quality, much less beta quality or production-ready.

Short Duration.

Student projects are artificially time-boxed, typically to a single semester and rarely to longer than an academic year.

In such a short time, there is little need to consider feature sets for future releases or configuration management to maintain multiple supported revisions. Similarly, maintenance and support are effectively ignored, simply because the project will be abandoned in short order.

High Turnover.

Regardless of project duration, students move on, taking their knowledge and experience with them. It is, of course, our goal to graduate high quality software engineers. But the necessary corollary to our success is a talent pool that remains permanently shallow. The wholesale turnover of entire classes of experienced students also means little opportunity for productive mentoring relationships between upperclassmen and students new to the program.

Low Complexity.

The limited duration of projects has a commensurate impact on project complexity. With limited time, students simply cannot create large, complex software, and thus have little experience with code bases of commercial size and scope. A student who finds (justifiable!) satisfaction in a completed program that numbers in the thousands of lines of code is nevertheless ill prepared to engage a code base whose source lines number in the millions.

No Maintenance.

Short duration projects are also immune to the reality of software maintenance. Yet defect repairs and enhancements are likely to be the stock in trade of most newly minted software engineering graduates.

In a software engineering class, we might ask students to trade source code and enhance another student's program. While useful, this is hardly sufficient preparation for the pressure of repairing a software defect uncovered by a major customer whose core business is suffering harm as a result.

No Customer.

The most significant gap is that student projects seldom involve a real customer. Even if a student team is motivated to work for an external customer, it is easy to see why the pool of customers is vanishingly small. No competent IT manager would make a "bet your business" commitment to developers who face all these challenges.

Perhaps adding faculty to a project would calm the fears of potential customers. But without load credit or external funding, few faculty have the time or resources to engage meaningfully with an ongoing project, much less pick up the pieces at the end of a semester or when a particularly productive student engineer has the temerity to graduate.

Lacking a real external customer, the professor can stand in as a mock customer. However, his or her interest in the project's outcome is ultimately pedagogical. Faculty simply have no skin in the game: the project outcome has no impact on his or her market credibility or personal livelihood. Consequently, the interaction between a student team and the "customer" lacks the visceral motivation that drives commercial development.

4. SOFTWARE STUDIO

Our goal for Software Studio is to give students extended experience building non-trivial, production-quality software for real external customers, who will actually *deploy* and *use* the software.

We emphasize HFOSS[1] projects that will make a difference in the broader community—typically in partnership with non-profit, missions, and humanitarian organizations (occasionally including Taylor University itself).

4.1 Curriculum Design

In addition to general education requirements, the Taylor Computer Science and Engineering curriculum consists of required core courses, elective courses, and courses comprising one of several concentrations that we call *tracks*. One such track is *Software Studio*. It consists of a one-semester *Software Engineering* course and *four* consecutive semesters of courses that are also called *Software Studio*.

Software Studio requires instructor permission for admission. The instructor interviews interested students to assess their software development experience, performance in other classes, and their personal maturity. We are looking for students who are self-starters and who demonstrate the ability to perform well without constant oversight.

Students in the Software Studio track normally take *Software Engineering* in their sophomore year and the four semesters of *Software Studio* throughout their junior and senior

[1] *HFOSS* is an acronym for *Humanitarian Free and Open Source Software*

years. The inaugural cohort of Software Studio students entered the program in Fall, 2008 and completed the track in Spring, 2010.

For all four semesters, Software Studio is a four credit course. Assuming a two-to-one ratio between out-of- and in-class activities, we expect students to devote twelve hours per week to Software Studio. Table 1 shows the typical weekly workload of students in the track.

Activity	Hours
Weekly seminar	1
Seminar reading and preparation	1–2
Classroom lab session with instructor	2
Project work with team	8

Table 1: Weekly student workload

4.1.1 Weekly Seminar

In the weekly seminar, students interact with a paper or book chapter selected by the instructor based on historical significance, topical coverage, or immediate need in a current project. Typically, students present the paper or chapter, but the instructor or a guest speaker will sometimes present.

To encourage them to engage with the seminar material, students are required to complete the weekly reading and post to a Moodle discussion forum at least two days prior to the seminar. Posts must include a brief analysis of the material and two relevant questions that the student wishes to have addressed during the seminar. With a two-day lead time, the presenter has time to address student questions during the seminar.

When Software Studio was first conceived, faculty expressed concern that the track would possess insufficient academic content. Reading and analysis in the weekly seminar served to allay these concerns.

4.1.2 In-Class Lab

The classroom lab was not originally part of the Software Studio design. We added it to ensure that all student teams would gather at least once per week at a time convenient for the instructor and other stakeholders to meet with teams.

For example, a team using the Scrum methodology to manage a project might use a lab session for a sprint planning meeting. Another team might invite end users to brainstorm user stories or create wireframes of a proposed interface. At the end of an iteration, a team might meet with their product owner for a sprint review.

4.1.3 Team Software Development

The remaining eight hours of required weekly work find student teams engaged in software development. Teams determine their own schedule and work venue.

Because most heads-down work takes place during off hours in various locations around campus, we require students to maintain a weekly activity log that includes the times they worked and the tasks they accomplished.

4.2 Student Evaluation

The student who presents in the weekly seminar is graded using a rubric that emphasizes understanding the material and recognizing its implications for current projects, discussing questions raised by students in the on-line forum, and interacting with the audience during the presentation.

Other seminar students are graded on their forum posting, which must interact with the material, include relevant questions, and be completed two days prior to the seminar.

The majority of a student grade, however, is based on performance as a software engineer in a team environment. The main criteria employed are these:

1. Sufficient time devoted to the project as documented in the student's activity log. Although there is a possibility of fraud in time accounting, experience has shown that teams hold their members closely accountable in devoting time to the project.

2. Contributions to the project code base. A rough measure of a student's productivity can be derived from the revision control system for each project. Depending on the desired accuracy, we count the number of commits, number of changed lines of code, or similar measures, filtered by the date range for the semester.

3. Quality of the code committed by the student. Using the "blame" feature of a project's revision control system, the instructor can identify blocks of code committed by each student. We employ a coding rubric to assign a grade to each student's code contributions.

4. Subjective measures of student participation on the team, typically gauged informally during in-class lab time. We have sometimes asked students to evaluate their teammates according to criteria students helped define at the beginning of the semester.

Taylor emphasizes student writing and speaking across the curriculum. In addition to presentations and forum postings for the seminar, students in Software Studio I through III compose a 1250–1500 word final experience paper. In Software Studio IV, students write a near-publication-quality paper on their entire Software Studio experience and make a formal, public presentation.

4.3 Projects to Date

To date in Software Studio at Taylor, student teams have completed (or are in the process of building) a variety of software products, including:

- A database-backed web application to support student registration for a multi-campus school

- A syntax checking plug-in for a natural language translation workbench

- A web-based system for intramural sports, including team creation, player sign-up, schedule management, and e-commerce for player fees. Students have elected to make this software available as an open source project.

- An iPhone application to update a global database of missions organizations operating in remote locations around the world

- Tooling to support project management and planning in Software Studio itself (Section 9.4).

4.4 Enrollment

Table 2 shows the number of Taylor students enrolled in Software Studio by semester. Also shown is the number of active teams during each semester.

Semester	Students	Teams
Fall 2008	7	2
Spring 2009	5	2
Fall 2009	8	2
Spring 2010	8	3
Fall 2010	8	3

Table 2: Software Studio students and teams per semester since inception.

5. ADDRESSING THE GAPS

Software Studio addresses the software engineering education gaps identified in Section 3.

Real Product.

All Software Studio *projects* implement a *product* for a real external customer. Students are engaged throughout the project with customer stakeholders, ranging from senior IT management, to product owners, to end users. Customer stakeholders are regularly engaged in planning future project iterations and in evaluating the deliverables from earlier ones. Such scrutiny provides direct and immediate feedback from customers to the development team.

The explicit goal of each project is to create production-quality software that can be deployed in the customer environment. Early in each project, we work with our customer to choose languages, tools, libraries, and platforms that conform to the customer's production environment.

It is possible that a potential customer's requirements necessitate a language or environment that doesn't fit within the overall pedagogical goals of our department. If so, we would decline the opportunity to partner on that project. To date, we have not had to exercise this prerogative.

Long Duration.

Because students enroll in Software Studio for two full academic years, we are able to take on projects with much longer time horizons than a typical student project. Most projects are of shorter duration, but one past project extended four full semesters.

Students see a long-duration project through multiple releases. Students also learn to respond to changes in requirements as customer priorities change over time. Long duration projects also make manifest the need for functional testing, acceptance testing, integration testing, complete documentation, and user training.

Continuity.

Perhaps the greatest impediment to enlisting external customers in an academic project is *lack of continuity* due to normal student turnover. This objection is blunted somewhat by the four-semester duration of the track. However, for production software, losing the brain trust that understands—and can maintain—the software is unacceptable after *any* period of time.

Software Studio address the issue of long-term continuity by ensuring that teams comprise students from both the first and second year of the track (Figure 1). Pairing experienced and new students has several benefits:

- Students are mentored by, and in turn, mentor other students—a key skill in commercial software teams.

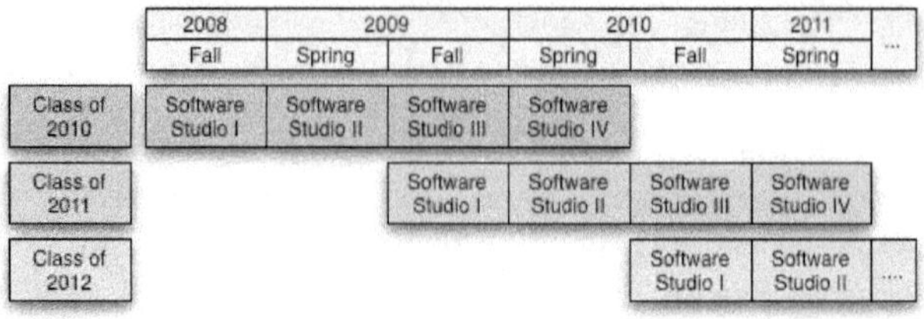

Figure 1: Temporal continuity in Software Studio. First and second year students meet concurrently and work together in project teams.

- Specific product knowledge and lore are passed between "generations" of Software Studio students, providing continuity of conceptually unlimited duration.
- The Software Studio culture is communicated across time from class to class.

A question sometimes raised is whether this model means we're on the hook *forever* for product support and maintenance. There are several answers to this question.

1. Support and maintenance are *intentional* elements of Software Studio, so we want some of this responsibility.
2. We discuss long-term support with our customers when we deploy software in their operational environment. Customers with a mature IT shop may assume or share the maintenance burden.
3. As discussed in Section 9.2, we intend to broaden the Software Studio community so that the entire software life cycle need not be the responsibility of a single institution.

Increased Complexity.

Because Software Studio focuses on a real product over a long duration for a real customer, the code base has time to grow in complexity and sophistication. As a result, students are exposed to software engineering "in the large."

Maintenance Included.

Regular maintenance tasks are the inevitable consequence of long duration projects with large code bases. Software Studio students are regularly exposed to the kind of challenges they are likely to encounter as new graduates in an industry software shop: defect repair, maintenance, and enhancement of large, legacy software packages.

Real Customer.

By closing the aforementioned gaps, Software Studio removes the roadblocks that would otherwise prevent us from engaging in meaningful projects with external customers.

Does this mean that potential customers are willing to "bet their business" on a Software Studio project? No. Although our model address many of the barriers that have kept industry and academia at arm's length, an academic institution cannot commit to hard delivery dates, service level agreements, and the like.

In early discussions with a potential customer, we emphasize our spin on the time-honored trinity of *scope*, *cost*, and *schedule*. While a qualified consultancy or internal corporate software team may be able address all three issues effectively, the same is not true for a student team.

Software Studio satisfies project *scope* with a high level of quality by enrolling strong students managed by qualified faculty. We offer a very low *cost*—free! However, we must flex on *schedule*. Even for the most committed team, the exigencies of full class loads, campus activities, student athletics, and work-study commitments mean that schedules are even more fluid than they often are for the typical commercial software team.

6. MISSTEPS

As we have implemented Software Studio, we have made some missteps. We propose solutions to these problems in Section 9.

6.1 Student $\neq$ Professional

Although we are training students to become software engineering professionals, we sometimes forget that they are still students.

While a mature professional exhibits a consistent, unsupervised willingness to complete assigned tasks, student motivation is often driven by grades. Software Studio grading is fractal—it must be done at the small scale (e.g., forum postings) and the large scale (e.g., semester-long contribution to the code base) in order to keep students on task.

A professional software engineer is motivated over the long term by a looming annual performance review. Student motivation, however, is more fluid—even if grades are given regularly. The professional works to maximize an annual salary adjustment because it will have a long-lasting personal impact. For the student, there will be more grades next week and next semester, and settling for a 'B' today may be worth a few extra hours of sleep.

6.2 Large Tasks

Conventional software estimation practice suggests that work breakdown be continued until tasks are likely to last a few days. Longer tasks are harder to estimate accurately, and shorter ones are troublesome to track. For a professional, a task extending over several days provides clear work direction and a regular sense of accomplishment and closure.

The student context is quite different. As mentioned in Section 4.1, students in Software Studio work about eight hours per week outside structured class time. Rarely do students work eight hours at one sitting, so these hours may be spread over several days during the week. The same task that a full-time professional completes in just a few *days* may thus extend over several *weeks* for a student. As a result, team members lose focus and don't experience the simple joy of checking off tasks regularly.

6.3 Inadequate Tooling

We have struggled to identify effective tooling for software project planning and management in an academic context. We have tried both open-source tools (e.g., Trac) and commercial products (e.g., Mingle) with limited success.

7. KEYS TO SUCCESS

Now in our third academic year of Software Studio, we believe that the following are key to the success of such a program of instruction.

Set Customer Expectations.

As introduced in Section 5, it is critical to set expectations appropriately with potential customers, particularly related to *scope*, *cost*, and *schedule*. To smooth the discussion, we have prepared a short white paper for potential customers that explains the risks and benefits of working with Software Studio.

Choose Appropriate Projects.

The best projects seem to be those that are high enough on a customer's priority list to have significant internal visibility, but have been postponed due to resource limitations. These are not "bet the business" projects. Instead, they are often "nice to have" features that capture the attention of customer management and staff, building goodwill with the Software Studio team.

Communicate Early and Often.

Communication among team members and between the team and the instructor is, of course, critically important. Such communication is largely built in to the course through the weekly lab and seminar. It is also helpful for the instructor to be available by e-mail, on-line forum, or instant messaging, and the importance of "Management By Wandering Around" to keep tabs on students cannot be overstated.

Equally important is communication with customer stakeholders. Most of our projects are managed using Scrum with short-duration sprints—usually two weeks. We engage customer stakeholders with the same frequency in an hour-long meeting that includes the instructor, student team, and customer stakeholders. We demonstrate progress made during the previous sprint and identify product backlog items to be addressed during the next one. A key enabling technology for these meetings is web conferencing, which allows us to demonstrate applications to customer staff.

8. SWOT ANALYSIS

Here, we evaluate Software Studio according to the the standard *SWOT* framework for strategic planning and analysis. As illustrated, SWOT considers helpful and harmful forces of both internal and external origin.

	Helpful	**Harmful**
Internal	Stengths	Weaknesses
External	Opportunities	Threats

Strengths.

We have demonstrated that Software Studio does prepare students to become professional software engineers. We have seen evidence of this fact in high quality products created by student teams, positive feedback from our customers, the ease with which graduates of the program obtain industry employment, and feedback on job performance from managers of graduates.

Weaknesses.

Our long-term ability to train students and deliver value to customers is dependent on our ability to broaden the Software Studio program beyond our walls. If we are unable to do so, we will either fail to meet our educational goal (support and maintenance will overwhelm new development) or we will drive away customers (new development will preclude continuity of support).

Opportunities.
With a demonstrated ability to create production-quality software in the academic context, Software Studio offers the potential to attract grant-funded or for-pay projects.

Should we attract such external funding, we have considered hiring a full-time project manager to oversee Software Studio projects. Funds could also be used to offset teaching load, allowing faculty release time to enhance Software Studio itself, develop relationships with customers, etc.

Threats.
The key threat to date to Software Studio's success has been declining Computer Science enrollment across the country and at Taylor. For the first two years of Software Studio, we enjoyed sufficient student interest to undertake two or three projects per semester (Table 2). This spring, however, only two juniors enrolled in the track, and we subsequently recruited several carefully selected sophomores.

9. FUTURE DIRECTION

This section briefly considers how we intend to improve Software Studio.

9.1 Small Tasks

As discussed in Section 6.2, projects should comprise fine-grained tasks that allow a student to check off one or more completed tasks per work session. A larger number of fine-grained tasks presents a planning challenge, but we hope to address it with appropriate tooling (Section 9.4).

9.2 Distributed Teams

We plan to broaden the teams involved in Software Studio projects in several ways.

Software Studio would benefit greatly from participation by students from other disciplines within our institution. On past projects, we have engaged students from the graphics arts to help with design and layout issues. Possible contributions from students in other disciplines include: business students working with customers to tune up business requirements, writing students creating documentation and product literature, sociology students designing social networking applications, and education students developing training materials for customers.

Large software engineering projects employ multiple, geographically distributed teams, including teams within an organization as well as outsourced and off-shore teams. To introduce students to distributed development, we plan to engage faculty and students at other schools in Software Studio projects.

Most of our interaction with customers has been at the level of requirements planning and stakeholder communication. Software Studio would be enhanced by directly engaging customer software staff in a project. Such an arrangement would improve communication with the customer, help uncover hidden assumptions, and provide mentoring for Software Studio students.

9.3 Student Evaluation

In order to make student evaluation itself be a learning experience, we would like to engage customer staff in the evaluation and grading process.

9.4 Appropriate Tooling

As mentioned in Section 6.3, we have not found project planning and management tools that are well suited to our needs. We have begun a project to develop a tool chain that is friendly to academic teams. Some notable features we are building into this system include: grade assignment at varying levels of detail (Section 6.1), support for task breakdown at a very fine level of granularity (Section 9.1), painless time tracking that is tied explicitly to tasks in the current sprint backlog, scheduling blocks of time during the week when teams can meet as a group (even in the face of crazy student schedules), and support for distributed development by multiple teams (Section 9.2).

10. CONCLUSION

Software Studio at Taylor has proven to be an exciting, novel, and successful approach to educating students in professional software engineering. Students are engaged, enthusiastic, and generally work at a very high level of proficiency and productivity. Because we partner with real-world customers to create production-quality software, students have a clear sense of mission and purpose, which makes the work not only meaningful and rewarding, but *fun*.

The proof is in the pudding: we have seen members of our first cohort of Software Studio students graduate and assume industry positions. Feedback from graduates and their managers regarding the Software Studio experience and its efficacy in preparing students to work as software professionals has been uniformly positive.

11. ACKNOWLEDGMENTS

We are grateful to all of our customer partners to date, but to none more than Tom Young, IT Director at New Tribes Mission. His patience and encouragement have given us great freedom to explore different directions for Software Studio, honing our model while doing our best to serve his organization and others.

Thanks to Software Studio graduates Reece Heinlein, Matt Tamny, and Chet Enright for excellent performance at Taylor and for insightful suggestions on how to improve the track (reflected in Sections 9.1 and 9.2).

12. REFERENCES

[1] E. Allen, R. Cartwright, and C. Reis. Production programming in the classroom. *ACM SIGCSE Bulletin*, 35(1):89–93, January 2003.

[2] `http://iis.cse.eng.auburn.edu/~sbl/index.php`.

[3] H. J. Ellis, R. A. Morelli, T. R. de Lanerolle, et al. Can humanitarian open-source software development draw new students to CS? *SIGCSE 2007*, pages 551–555, March 2007.

[4] R. P. Gabriel. Master of fine arts in software. http://dreamsongs.com/MFASoftware.html, accessed September 10, 2010.

[5] S. Ramakrishnan. Muse studio lab and innovative software engineering capstone project experience. In *Proceedings of the 8th ITiCSE Conference*, pages 21–25, 2003.

Successful K-12 Outreach Strategies

Karen Donathan
Computer Science Department
George Washington High School
Charleston, West Virginia
+1.304.348.7729
kdonathan@kcs.kana.k12.wv.us

Barbara Ericson
Institute for Computing Education
College of Computing
Georgia Institute of Technology
Atlanta, Georgia
+1.404.385.2107
ericson@cc.gatech.edu

Paul Tymann
Computer Science Department
Rochester Institute of Technology
Rochester, New York
+1.585.746.5690
ptt@cs.rit.edu

Henry M. Walker (moderator)
Department of Computer Science
Grinnell College
Grinnell, Iowa
+1.641.269.4208
walker@cs.grinnell.edu

Summary
Much has been written about the decrease in the number of students pursuing computing in colleges. Unfortunately, most students form their (usually negative) opinions of computing long before they reach college [1], so it is beneficial for university faculty who want to increase college enrollment to do outreach aimed at a younger audience. Activities to promote computing among K-12 students can proceed at several levels, occur in various locations, and involve both students and faculty.

College and high school faculty can collaborate in many ways. As teachers of introductory courses, both groups want to generate interest, cover important material, and provide a strong foundation for later work. For example, the AP CS course description includes material that fits well with both high school and introductory college courses. Also, today in both environments, there is much discussion regarding the best approaches for creating excitement and introducing students to computing. Although both faculties need to address common content and utilize active pedagogies, it also is important to acknowledge that college and high school environments are different, and both levels have special opportunities and constraints.

Categories and Subject Descriptors
K.3.2 [**Computers and Education**]: Computer and Information Science Education – *computer science education, curriculum, information systems education, literacy.*

General Terms
Design, Management

Keywords
High school-college collaboration

SIGCSE'11, March 9–12, 2011, Dallas, Texas, USA.
ACM 978-1-4503-0500-6/11/03.

Many college faculty are interested in doing K-12 outreach but often do not know where to start or do not know any successful strategies. The purpose of this panel is to present K-12 outreach strategies that have worked and then to provide the audience with the opportunity to brainstorm with the panelists to explore alternate ideas for outreach and to identify new approaches. Some ideas and strategies come from experiences of high school and college teachers working together as part of the AP CS program, but other approaches extend beyond AP CS.

1. Karen Donathan
College Computer Science faculty and High School Computer Science faculty share many of the same problems: lack of funding, lack of understanding, lack of female enrollment, and lack of training. Because of these shared problems, it should be fairly easy for college faculty to understand why it is sometimes difficult to reach out to high schools for new students.

Budget constraints continue to be the most significant, ever-present problem in secondary education systems. This is the reason that many school systems do not offer quality Computer Science education, even though it should be one of the most important fields of study.

If college faculty members wish to do outreach to recruit more students, they need to start with the teachers, administrators and higher-ups to convince them of the importance of Advanced Placement Computer Science (AP CS) programs. They also need to brainstorm ways for high school teachers to receive funds for training. They could also pair up with nearby high schools in some sort of partnerships. This partnership is truly what is needed for quality CS education.

2. Barbara Ericson
Georgia Tech has been offering summer computing camps for students since 2004. We started with 2 weeks of camps for high school students and added camps for middle school students in 2006 and added camps for elementary school students in 2009. In the summer of 2010 we ran 8 weeks of summer camps for a total of 202 students. There were about 25 students in each camp. The

camps were 40% female and 69% black. The camps have resulted in statistically significant changes in attitudes towards computing. At least two of our current computing students at Georgia Tech attended the camps and trace the decision to major in computing to the camps. In our camps we use PicoCrickets, Pleo robots, LEGO NXT robots, Scratch, Alice, IPRE robots, and Media Computation. We have also provided training and "seed" money to 10 other colleges and universities in Georgia to help them start computing summer camps.

Georgia Tech's Cool Computing day in 2010 was attended by over 300 high school students from 17 schools. Students took a tour of campus, asked questions of a corporate panel, asked questions of a student panel, and listened to a talk by a researcher. All students were asked to fill out a survey about their attitudes towards computing in order to get a raffle ticket before the event started. All attendees received a t-shirt and we raffled off some cool computing gadgets (like I-Pods and GPSs) at the end of the event. One teacher sent us an e-mail after the event saying, "the students talked non-stop on the bus ride home about what they heard and saw today. It was inspiring, fun, and well-organized."

While it is encouraging that students report an increase in interest in computing after our summer camps and Cool Computing Days, we realize that we can't reach every student in Georgia directly. A key part of our strategy is to increase the quantity and quality of secondary computing teachers, especialy AP CS teachers. We offer professional development for teachers in the four computing courses in Georgia that are aligned with the ACM model curriculum. Partially due to these efforts, the number of schools offering AP CS A in Georgia increased from 44 in 2004 to 81 in 2007-2008, but it has been dropping again the last few years due to the economy.

3. Paul Tymann

I have formed a APCS teachers group that meets at RIT once per quarter. At these meetings teachers discuss curriculum issues, teaching techniques, and exchange homework assignment and project ideas. Most high school teachers are isolated at their schools. Many schools have at most one computer teacher. As a result they do not have the opportunity like most college faculty to discuss curricular approaches and share ideas with their colleagues in the office next door. This is a very low cost approach that is appreciated by the teachers that attend.

One outcome of the teachers group meeting is an annual high school programming contest held at RIT. Students from nearby high schools come to RIT for a morning. While the students compete in the programming contest we provide a professional development opportunity for the teachers. Our last programming contest featured an Alice 3 workshop. This has turned out to be an excellent opportunity for high school students to interact with our students and for high school teachers to interact with our faculty.

4. Henry Walker

College students may work with high school students, serving as mentors, role models, facilitators, or tutors. For example, the Grinnell [College] Women in Science student organization, GWIS, runs a Saturday morning series to explore the excitement and possibilities of numerous science disciplines, including computer science. The college students may work with science faculty to brainstorm and plan, but GWIS women are the visible leaders during the sessions themselves.

College and high school faculty can collaborate in many ways. For example, over the years, I have been most fortunate to work with high school and college teachers at AP CS readings, workshops, SIGCSE conferences, and other venues. In each case, I have shared, brainstormed, and learned; and my teaching has benefited from these collaborations.

Yet another area of connection arises when college faculty visit high schools. Most commonly, I have worked with a high school teacher for a day, meeting with the teacher's classes, presenting enrichment talks, and talking informally with students. At other times, I have addressed a school-wide assembly. In both settings, a challenge is to brainstorm with teachers about what themes might be most helpful and then to consider what topics might connect best with high school students.

Finally, in some cases, high school students might enroll in college courses. For example, for many years, with the recommendation of their guidance counselor, high school juniors and seniors in area schools have been able to take up to two courses at Grinnell College at no charge (space permitting). Such an arrangement promotes conversations between college faculty and the area schools, allows high school students to take courses that otherwise would not be available with limited high-school staffing, and provide these students with solid college-level experiences as part of their high-school preparation. In several instances, area students have taken courses in computer science.

Reference

[1.] Commission on Technology, Gender, and Teacher Education, Tech-Savvy: Educating Girls in the New Computer Age, American Association of University Women, 2000. Available online at http://www.aauw.org/research/upload/techsavvy.pdf

Setting the Stage for Computing Curricula 2013: Computer Science – Report from the ACM/IEEE-CS Joint Task Force

Mehran Sahami (moderator)
Stanford University
Computer Science Department
sahami@cs.stanford.edu

Mark Guzdial
Georgia Institute of Technology
College of Computing
guzdial@cc.gatech.edu

Andrew McGettrick
Department of Computer and Information Sciences
University of Strathclyde
andrew.mcgettrick@cis.strath.ac.uk

Steve Roach
University of Texas at El Paso
Computer Science Department
sroach@utep.edu

Categories and Subject Descriptors
K.3.2 [**Computers and Education**]: Computer and Information Science Education

General Terms
Documentation, Design, Standardization.

Keywords
Computing Curricula 2013: Computer Science, CS 2013.

1. SUMMARY
Following a roughly 10 year cycle, the Computing Curricula volumes have helped to set international curricular guidelines for undergraduate programs in computing. In the summer of 2010, planning for the next volume in the series, Computer Science 2013, began. This panel seeks to update and engage the SIGCSE community on the Computer Science 2013 effort.

The development of curricular guidelines in Computer Science is particularly challenging given the rapid evolution and expansion of the field. Moreover, the growing diversity of topics in Computer Science and the integration of computing with other disciplines create additional challenges and opportunities in defining computing curricula. As a result, it is particularly important to engage the broader computer science education community in a dialog to better understand new opportunities, local needs, and novel successful models of computing curriculum.

The last complete Computer Science curricular volume was released in 2001 [3] and followed by a review effort that concluded in 2008 [2]. While the review helped to update some of the knowledge units in the 2001 volume, it was not aimed at producing an entirely new curricular volume and deferred some of the more significant questions that arose at the time. The Computer Science 2013 effort seeks to provide a new volume reflecting the current state of the field and highlighting promising future directions through revisiting and redefining the knowledge units in CS, rethinking the essentials necessary for a CS curriculum, and identifying working exemplars of courses and curricula along these lines.

SIGCSE'11, March 9–12, 2011, Dallas, Texas, USA.
ACM 978-1-4503-0500-6/11/03.

Early discussions in the CS 2013 effort provide several topics that the panel will address:

- *The "Big Tent" view of CS* – As CS expands to include more multi-disciplinary work and new programs of the form "Computational X" are developed, it is important to embrace an outward looking view in computing that sees CS as a discipline actively seeking to work with and integrate into other disciplines. Such a view impacts the definition of CS curriculum as a means for promoting multi-disciplinary work while maintaining a clear identity of the field.
- *Managing the size of the curriculum* – Although the field of Computer Science continues to grow unabated, it is simply not possible to proportionately expand the size of the curriculum. Indeed CS 2001 was successful in reducing the total number of required instruction hours in comparison to Computing Curricula '91 [1]. Similarly, CS 2013 seeks to further reduce the number of required instruction hours in order to promote more flexible models for curricula, without losing the essence of a rigorous CS education.
- *Computational Thinking* – While there has been a great deal of discussion in regard to computational thinking [7], its direct impact on curriculum is still unclear. While we believe there is no "right answer" here, CS 2013 seeks to gain more clarity regarding models by which CS curricula can promote computational thinking for broader audiences.
- *Actual course exemplars as opposed to stylized course guidance* – CS 2001 took on the significant challenge of providing descriptions of stylized courses incorporating the knowledge units defined in that report. While this was a valiant effort, it was felt in retrospect that such course guidance did not have much impact on actual course design. As a result, CS 2013 plans to take a different approach: identifying existing successful courses and curricula as fielded exemplars of how the relevant knowledge units can be addressed in actual programs. This bears some similarity to the recent report by

CRA-E [4], although that report focused specifically on preparing students for research careers.

- *Institutional needs* – Understanding that curricula exists in the context of specific institutional needs, goals, and resource constraints, CS 2013 aims to provide curricular models suitable in a broad range of contexts. This requires not only a curriculum that affords flexibility, but one that is also cognizant of and aligned with upstream (K-12, two year college) and downstream (graduate school, industry) needs and constraints.

Additionally, specific developments in the field in the past decade (such as the pervasiveness of parallel computing and the need for better understanding computer security) as well as issues identified by 2008 Interim Review (such as differing models for knowledge units on Programming Languages) provide additional topics for discussion during this panel.

Importantly, the goal of this panel is not simply to provide an update on the current thinking and state of CS 2013, but to actively engage the community in the discussions and work that will eventually manifest into the published volume. We encourage the community to review and comment on forthcoming drafts of CS 2013 by contacting the committee chairs Mehran Sahami and Steve Roach.

2. MEHRAN SAHAMI

Mehran Sahami is chair of the ACM delegation for the Computing Curricula 2013: Computer Science volume. He is an Associate Professor and Associate Chair for Education in the Computer Science Department at Stanford University, where he recently led a complete revamping of the undergraduate Computer Science curriculum [6].

3. MARK GUZDIAL

Mark Guzdial is a member of the ACM Education Board and the SIGCSE Board of Directors. He is a Professor in the College of Computing at Georgia Institute of Technology and the former Director of Undergraduate Programs in Computer Science and Computational Media. He served on the Computer Science Curriculum 2008 Review Taskforce and also was a principal in the development of Georgia Tech's innovative Threads Computer Science curriculum [5].

4. ANDREW MCGETTRICK

Andrew McGettrick is chair of the ACM Education Board. He is a Professor in the Department of Computer and Information Sciences at the University of Strathclyde. He has been involved in several Computing Curricula efforts, including Computer Science 2001, Software Engineering 2004, Computer Engineering 2004, Overview volume 2006, and was co-chair of the Computer Science Curriculum 2008 Review Taskforce.

5. STEVE ROACH

Steve Roach is chair of the IEEE-CS delegation for the Computing Curricula 2013: Computer Science volume. He is an Associate Professor and Associate Chair of the Department of Computer Science at the University of Texas at El Paso. He was involved in Computing Curriculum Software Engineering 2004 and the Graduate Software Engineering 2009 efforts.

6. REFERENCES

[1] ACM/IEEE-CS Joint Curriculum Task Force. 1991. Computing curricula 1991: Report of the ACM/IEEE-CS Joint Curriculum Task Force, ACM Press, NY.

[2] ACM/IEEE-CS Joint Interim Review Task Force. 2008. Computer Science Curriculum 2008: An Interim Revision of CS 2001, Report from the Interim Review Task Force. http://www.acm.org/education/curricula/ComputerScience2008.pdf

[3] ACM/IEEE-CS Joint Task Force on Computing Curricula. 2001. ACM/IEEE Computing Curricula 2001 Final Report. http://www.acm.org/sigcse/cc2001.

[4] CRA-Education Committee. 2010. Creating Environments for Computational Researcher Education. http://www.cra.org/uploads/documents/resources/rissues/CRA-E-Researcher-Education.pdf

[5] Furst, M., Isbell, C., and Guzdial, M. 2007. Threads™: how to restructure a computer science curriculum for a flat world. In *Proceedings of the 38th SIGCSE Technical Symposium on Computer Science Education* (SIGCSE '07). ACM, New York, NY, 420-424.

[6] Sahami, M., Aiken, A., and Zelenski, J. 2010. Expanding the frontiers of computer science: designing a curriculum to reflect a diverse field. In *Proceedings of the 41st ACM Technical Symposium on Computer Science Education* (SIGCSE '10). ACM, New York, NY, 47-51.

[7] Wing, J. M. 2006. Computational thinking. *Commun. ACM* 49, 3 (Mar. 2006), 33-35.

It Seemed Like a Good Idea at the Time

Jonas Boustedt
Univ. of Gävle, Sweden
jbt@hig.se

Robert McCartney (MC)
Univ. of Connecticut
robert@engr.uconn.edu

Josh Tenenberg
Univ. of Washington
jtenenbg@uw.edu

Stephen Cooper
Stanford University
coopers@acm.org

Daniel D. Garcia
Univ. of California, Berkeley
ddgarcia@eecs.berkeley.edu

Michelle Friend Hutton
Stanford University
mfh@pobox.com

Nick Parlante
Stanford University
nick.parlante@cs.stanford.edu

Brad Richards
Univ. of Puget Sound
brichards@pugetsound.edu

Categories and Subject Descriptors

K.3.2 [**Computer and Information Science Education**]: self-assessment; K.4.2 [**Social Issues**]: employment

General Terms

Design, Experimentation, Human Factors, Measurement, Performance, Verification

Keywords

fiasco, disaster, breakdown, failure, humiliation, doom, gloom, termination

SUMMARY

We often learn of successful pedagogical experiments, but we seldom hear of the the ones that failed. For this special session we solicited submissions from the SIGCSE membership, selected the best from among these, and will have presentations at the session by the selected authors. Our contributions describe pedagogical approaches that seemed to be good ideas but turned out as failures. Contributors will describe their pedagogical experiment, the rationale for the experiment, evidence of failure, and lessons learned.

1. OVERVIEW

This Special Session at SIGCSE 2011, "It Seemed Like a Good Idea at the Time," is a forum for discussion of the failures we have all had, with the hope that others can avoid the paths that led to these unanticipated results. This session is structured like Parlante's "Nifty Assignments" sessions: a set of presenters selected from submissions solicited by a general CFP to the SIGCSE community.

2. OVERALL OBJECTIVE

By presenting these experiences, the authors provide cautionary tales (and some entertainment) to other instructors. By providing a forum for the failed experiment, we hope to encourage risk taking in the classroom, and by focusing on evidence we hope to foster a community with a greater eye for documenting our classroom experiments.

SIGCSE'11, March 9–12, 2011, Dallas, Texas, USA.
ACM 978-1-4503-0500-6/11/03.

3. OUTLINE OF THE SESSION

The session will consist of a brief overview of the session by the moderator stating how submissions were solicited and selected. The body of the session will be short presentations by each presenter, with questions following each presentation.

4. EXPECTATIONS

This will draw a general audience. The audience *might* learn some particular facts, but more likely they will see their own experiences in the experiences of the presenters. They will have fun. Feedback includes questions and discussion after each presentation, plus a lot of buzz for the rest of the conference.

5. SUITABILITY FOR A SPECIAL SESSION

This has been a really special event in the past, and will likely be so this year. Take a look at the archive at http://depts.washington.edu/goodidea/ and see what you think. Summaries of each of the presentations follow.

Self-selected pairs and teams (Stephen Cooper)

During one fall semester, I was teaching both software engineering and an introductory computer science class. Inspired by Laurie Williams at SIGCSE 2003, I decided to try pair programming in my intro class, and add student teams into my software engineering class in the same semester.

In the introductory programming class, I made several mistakes. Students chose their own partners. Partnerships were to persist throughout the semester, for both closed laboratories and programming assignments. And I requested no feedback from the students about the performance of their partners.

Results: Social relationships did not often lead to effective class partnerships. Weak students "rode on the coattails" of their stronger partner. Students didn't successfully complete assignments. And I first learned about student frustrations with their partners in their student evaluations.

Similar to the introductory course pairs, the software engineering students picked their own teams, with the same problems as the freshmen teams. These problems were amplified because the project counted for a large percentage of the students' grades.

Delegating assignments (Dan Garcia)

My TA worked tirelessly to re-work one of our own nifty-like assignments so it was different from last year. After 2 all-nighters he finished, and sent the framework code to the class webmaster, who posted what he received without looking at it. In the TA's exhaustion, he included the answers! We caught the error after it had been out for 12 hours, and scrapped the assignment. The red-faced TA pulled *another* all-nighter to create another re-work, and sent it on to the webmaster to post it. The new project, no surprise, had *tons* of little bugs. My TA spent every waking moment for the next week on the newsgroup, diligently responding to posts. Since he did not summarize these posts on the project site, assuming everyone was reading the newsgroup, all the fixes were tucked away in the nooks and crannies of hundreds of newsgroup responses! Finally, his assignment design was lots of /* Put your code here */ lines interspersed within the framework code, which he created by simply removing key pieces of his solution. Students, therefore, were directly editing his framework, so whenever he updated the framework to fix bugs, students now had a "corrupted copy" and had to cut/paste their changes into the new framework.

It was a perfect storm of unfortunate circumstances and poor decisions.

Drama in lecture (Jonas Boustedt)

The year before this incident, I had conducted a successful exercise in a computer engineering class: a drama exercise in which students act as different objects and the play presents the story of an executing C++ program. The students appreciated this exercise and I felt very successful and happy.

Next year, I had the same class and I wanted to do the same successful drama exercise again. In the middle of a lecture, I told the students about the exercise and I was just dividing the students into groups, when suddenly almost all of them stood up in their rows and walked out of the lecture hall. This was a disaster! I totally lost face.

Groups, it appears, have different dynamics, and have different needs and expectations. The first group was evenly split between men and women, with ages from 20 to 50, and they often asked questions and discussed things. The second group were primarily young cocky 20 year old men who often tried to show off by asking tough questions to test me in class. Certain activities are not suitable for all groups.

On the bleeding edge (Brad Richards)

Developing software for mobile computing devices is all the rage these days, and who am I to drag my feet when the bandwagon is rolling? I imagined a way to use wireless devices in the classroom to help demonstrate and reinforce topics from computer networking: Students would actively participate in exercises introducing routing, for example, by watching "their" routing tables evolve as they exchanged updates with peers in a virtual network. The instructor could modify the topology on the fly for extra educational impact, as well as modify routing tables across student devices. Did I use Android? iPhone? No, this was a decade ago, and I used a brand new gadget called the Cybiko. (Surely you all remember them.)

My tale of woe will describe the realities of introducing bleeding edge technology into the classroom, including dealing with inadequate and broken development tools, the drawbacks of putting technology in the hands of students, the challenges of controlling the classroom environment and, in my case, dealing with the demise of the platform after the materials had been developed!

It's not the technology (Michelle Hutton)

The good idea was a typical introductory, pre-AP program: non-stop computer use, some lecture, and a great deal of time spent with kids using technology to create computer artifacts, such as programs, robots, or animations. The goals of the program were to get middle-school girls enthusiastic about computer science, to provide a broad range of activities that could serve as an entry point to that excitement, and most important, to teach them some important computer science concepts.

While I felt that I was teaching important CS concepts such as algorithm development and efficiency, students consistently commented on the technologies they'd used, rather than anything about the important computer science concepts. "I was proud of learning Flash" was common; "Algorithm development is really interesting" was not.

Students spent a lot of time debugging the technology and were rarely able to focus on deeper ideas, using technology in a superficial way to complete assignments rather than using higher order skills. If the goal is to think about how to solve problems efficiently, the programming was getting in the way.

The technologies garnered a great deal of praise and attention from outside the classroom, but only one time in ten years of teaching did someone comment on a core computer science topic – in order to criticize that I was not spending enough time teaching Q/A style debugging.

Covering it, and lecture-homework spaces (Nick Parlante)

Two good ideas: cover all of the material, and have lecture examples and homeworks fit their natural environments.

Cover it all: You're teaching Java or C++ or whatever, and you take a look at the table of contents of the book. Holy cow, look at all these features; you'll have to move quickly to cover them all! This is a huge mistake.

It's wrongheaded to imagine that you need to cover every feature or idea. Once they are done with your class, months or years later, looking up unknown or forgotten details will be the norm. What's most important is that you come up with an interesting and coherent subset of the material and focus on the most important ideas vigorously. Be very comfortable not covering topics. Focus on doing a great job with the subset you pick.

Lecture space and homework space: The natural space of worked out lecture examples is what fits in the time allowed. You know the main ideas you want to show, and you scale an example down so it fits in the lecture time available. The natural space of homework problems is "hey this is important material and these are CS students, so we're going to come up with something really interesting and kind of difficult."

The very picture of bad CS teaching is a lecture example and a homework problem which seem to be made up by two people who haven't spoken to each other, which of course is exactly what happened.

Analysis of a CS1 Approach for Attracting Diverse and Inexperienced Students to Computing Majors

Jim Cohoon
University of Virginia
Computer Science
Charlottesville, VA
+1 434 982 2210
jpc@virginia.edu

Luther Tychonievich
University of Virginia
Computer Science
Charlottesville, VA
+1 434 924 7605
lat7h@virginia.edu

ABSTRACT

An effective CS1 approach has been developed for encouraging diverse students without prior computer science experiences to select computing majors. Separation of CS1 sections by prior experience level concentrates diverse students in the inexperienced section. Within that section we use several techniques to increase student comprehension and participation, including an integrated lecture/lab, many small examples and assignments, student participation, etc. We discuss the approach and evaluate its performance over a four-year time period.

Categories and Subject Descriptors

K.3.2 [**Computers & Education**]: Computer and Information Science Education – *computer science education, curriculum*; K.4.2 [**Computers and Society**]: Social Issues – *employment.*

General Terms

Management, Measurement, Economics, Human Factors.

Keywords

CS1, diversity, education, introductory computer science, teaching, pedagogy, programming.

1. INTRODUCTION

Computer Science and Computer Engineering confront two problems: decreases in enrollments and in diversity [4, 8]. The decreases result in an important missed opportunity—meeting societal needs for an increasing pool of skilled information technology professionals [20]. The computing homogeneity results in another missed opportunity—using the insights and needs of under-represented groups to discover new technology directions [4, 8].

We reported in 2007 about our first-year computer science (CS) curriculum and pedagogy designed to attract and retain a diverse student body [6]. As an experiment towards both better learning and generating diverse student interest, our department offered a pilot CS1 section aimed at inexperienced programmers. Three years later that course has evolved into a vital part of our curriculum and continuing effort to improve recruiting into the CS major, particularly from under-represented demographic groups. We report here on the evolution, principles, practices, and successes of this course. The successes are four fold:

- Our CS1 curriculum in total has experienced a 30% increase in the number of university students taking introductory course CS1.
- The department now attracts black students at a rate 1.2 times the national average even though our University's percentage of black students is only two-thirds the national average.
- The department now attracts women students at rate 1.6 times the national rate (18.8% versus 11.8%).
- The department has seen an improvement in women, minority, and overall engineering student retention, particularly in the first year.

2. MULTIPLE ENTRY PATHS INCREASE INTEREST AND DIVERSITY

At our institution almost all CS1 students have either not yet declared a major or selected a non-Computer Science major. To satisfy stakeholders from other departments, CS1 is a service course emphasizing programming, currently in the Java language, rather than a general introduction to Computer Science. In return for providing this service, we have the opportunity to interact with and attempt to recruit a much larger population of students than we would were our CS1 course aimed only at students intending a computing major.

CS1 students come with a wide variety of skill levels, ranging from life-long programmers to students without any prior programming experience. Studies indicate that students without prior computing experience are often uncomfortable when classmates demonstrate advanced knowledge of course content [3]. Studies also indicate that women and minorities are more likely to not have a high school computing course [16]. Other research suggests by making the CS1 course more hospitable, a student is more likely to consider a computing major [4].

Our department offers four avenues into the computing major. Some students are advanced enough they can skip CS1 altogether. For the rest, we offer three variants of CS1 with comparable objectives and grading criteria, but which are aimed at students with different levels of prior experience: CS1E for the

SIGCSE'11, March 9–12, 2011, Dallas, Texas, USA.
Copyright 2011 ACM 978-1-4503-0500-6/11/03...$10.00.

experienced, CS1G for the general student body, and CS1X for those without prior exposure to programming concepts.

The general CS1G course is an open-enrollment course servicing the entire university community. The course is structured with large lectures and smaller weekly closed laboratories for all students, as well as homework and examinations. Education research indicates that laboratories provide important experiences that stimulate interest and contribute to successful outcomes for both under-represented and over-represented groups [17]; the closed-laboratory design allows us to better monitor and facilitate student learning in the laboratory setting.

The department first introduced CS1E in Spring 2003. It was offered primarily as a diversity increasing measure [2, 13, and 19] in a manner analogous to the multiple curriculum entry points offered at Carnegie-Mellon [13]. Students in CS1E are expected to be familiar with variables, conditionals, and looping constructs prior to enrolling in the course. Their assignments and grading scales are identical to those in CS1G, but they are free to conduct laboratory assignments in open laboratories at times of their own choosing. Ongoing examination of student outcomes shows that open laboratories do not materially affect these students' abilities to complete course requirements. The freedom of open laboratories provides experienced students with incentive to enroll in CS1E and has a welcomed side effect of reducing departmental staffing costs.

Increasing qualified enrollment in CS1E improved the CS1G course environment—there are fewer advanced students who can intimidate others by demonstrating prior knowledge of course content. To further improve diversity, our department added CS1X to its curriculum starting in Spring 2006. CS101X is designed to encourage the interest and retention of a diverse community [8, 11] and is open only to students with no prior programming experience.

3. CS1X PEDAGOGY

The involvement of CS1X students begins prior to the opening of the semester. As a close-enrollment course, all students personally visit with the instructor to determine their eligibility for the course. In order to be accepted, a student must not have any prior programming experience and must pledge:

- To participate fully in every class meeting.
- To help others learn and improve.
- To raise concerns and questions promptly.
- To honestly consider majoring in computing.

These items are reinforced throughout the course. For example, some assignments require students to converse with their neighbors and come to an agreement on the answer; "I have raised my hand in class"' is a question on an early quiz each semester; students are reminded to add comments to their code noting which other students have helped them; and classroom discussions frequently focus on the options, advantages, and rewards of computing careers [12, 13, 20].

The above pledge is difficult, maybe even impossible, to fully enforce. Our university has a strong emphasis on student honorability that increases our trust in students' pledges; we have had only minor difficulties with students violating the pledge, and these have always been resolved simply by speaking with the students in question. We normally schedule CS1G and CS1X to be offered at the same time in different rooms in order to facilitate placing students who registered for the wrong section; however, we have only moved two students during the last four years and do not anticipate expending effort to keep this schedule in future terms.

CS1X is designed around the motto "baby steps" inspired by the 1991 film *What About Bob*. Although it is possible to perform several actions in a single Java statement, CS1X students are taught to take small steps, generally including only one simple expression, construction, or assignment per statement. Larger combined statements are shown where appropriate, but the emphasis on simple steps helps keep all students engaged by keeping each concept and action distinct.

Another manifestation of the "baby steps" motto is the quantity and size of programming assignments. Initially CS1X had the same small set of weeklong assignments as the other sections of CS1. Because post-semester surveys repeatedly showed students wanted more assignments, recent CS1X courses have assigned 55–65 programming projects, or approximately 1½ assignments per class period. Assignments tend to be smaller and more frequent at the beginning of the semester. For the last third of the semester, there are generally two projects per week (the assignments have become larger and require more effort to do the design and implementation). Recent surveys indicate the students are satisfied with this frequency of assignments.

CS1X lecture and lab sections are integrated into a single set of instructional periods, with computers and the Internet available for all students at all class meetings [1, 16]. The CS1X pilot was held in a computer laboratory, but that environment was not well designed for instruction. All subsequent CS1X course offerings have been held in a tiered, audio-video enabled classroom equipped with tables and sufficient wireless network bandwidth for each student to bring their own notebook computer. The department supplies laptops to students without laptops or to students experiencing difficulties with their own machines.

Approximately two thirds of each instructional period is devoted to discussion and instructor led experiments and the other third to in-class computing experiences—either simple in-class exercises or homework assignments. This integrated format allows the students to reinforce their learning with practice while the instruction is still fresh in their minds.

In order to facilitate in-class exercises, teaching assistants are in attendance at each class meeting. Teaching assistants are primarily computing majors who took CS1X in previous semesters; they are thus familiar with course structure and provide role-models for the students. In addition to providing practical one-on-one assistance to students experiencing difficulties with assignments, teaching assistants are encouraged to comment throughout the instruction. These comments provide additional perspectives on course topics and help preserve a relaxed environment where students are comfortable raising concerns and comments.

Instruction focuses on introducing computing concepts and demonstrating, explaining, and modifying simple code examples. The students examine approximately 150 Java example program and class files over the course of the semester. Students download these examples at the start of class and experiment with them as they are discussed. Discussions are usually dominated by student

Table 1: Participation Demographics

Demographic	Engineering School (n=1738)	Computing Major (n=293)	CS1 (n=1378)	CS1E (n=203)	CS1G (n=965)	CS1X (n=210)
Female	30.7%	18.8%	33.0%	17.2%	29.5%	64.3%
Male	69.3%	81.2%	67.0%	82.8%	70.5%	35.7%
Asian	18.3%	26.3%	17.4%	23.2%	17.2%	12.9%
Black	6.0%	6.1%	5.9%	3.0%	4.6%	14.8%
Hispanic	4.0%	3.4%	3.3%	3.0%	2.8%	5.7%
White	62.6%	57.0%	64.9%	62.1%	67.8%	54.8%
Other	9.1%	7.2%	8.5%	8.9%	7.7%	11.9%

Table 2: CS1 Enrollments

Course	05–06	06–07	07–08	08–09	09–10	10–11
CS1G	479	438	427	543	527	595
CS1E	137	179	131	120	84	130
CS1X	43	100	102	99	130	130
Total	659	717	660	762	741	856

Table 3: CS1 Attraction to Computing Major

Ethnicity	CS1G %	CS1E %	CS1X %	CS1 %
Male	11.9%	31.5%	12.0%	15.5%
Female	7.0%	28.6%	8.1%	9.0%
Asian	18.1%	25.5%	14.8%	19.2%
Black	15.9%	50.0%	9.7%	16.0%
Hispanic	11.1%	50.0%	16.7%	17.8%
White	8.6%	31.7%	8.7%	11.8%
Other	6.8%	27,8%	4,0%	9.4%
Total	10.5%	31%	9.5%	13.4%

questions and participation. Slide decks and lecture-style presentations are generally eschewed in favor of active learning practices [8]. Maintaining student interest is deemed crucial for promoting computing majors.

Just as CS1X begins prior to the opening of the semester, the class culture extends beyond the close of the semester [6]. Students are left with an open invitation to visit the instructor at any time throughout their stay at the university, and reviews prior to beginning CS2 are offered to interested students. While the willingness to provide assistance is shared by most faculty members throughout the school, making the offer explicitly as part of the course's closing moments reinforces the idea that the instructor really does desire to help students succeed, not just in the course but in computing and academia generally.

4. DIVERSE APPEAL OF EXAMPLES

Major class examples and assignments are largely ones for which students express interest in response to on-line surveys. Surveys have been given to students in all sections of CS1, in CS2, and in several workshops for high-school computer science teachers. Table 8 summarizes survey results with respect to student gender and the student-teacher distinction. The survey results show that student interest varies between genders and topics. Each computing application was measured using a Likert scale of 1 to 7 corresponding to extremely uninteresting to extremely interesting, respectively. Of the 195 statistics gathered about 51 applications, only 4 ratings are in the "very uninteresting" range (below 2.5) and only 5 ratings are in the "very interesting" range (above 5.5), indicating that most applications do not have strong negative or positive appeal to students. Teachers were (unsurprisingly) more interested than students, often with significant difference in taste.

As has been observed elsewhere [9, 10, 18], differences in interest exist between genders and between ethnic groups. We found that males were generally more pleased by applications than were females (a 0.38 difference). The applications exhibiting the strongest male biases were rocket payloads (differed by 2.76) and text to speech (1.36); the strongest female biases were for photo mosaics (0.82) and linguistic translation (0.62).

While these findings are only population-level trends and may not apply to particular students, they are useful in selecting examples and assignments that are more likely to appeal to the entire student body. To facilitate selection of applications interesting to both males and females, Table 8 is sorted by the minimum of male and female Likert ratings.

5. SUCCESS OF CS1X

CS1X has now been offered for five years. We have observed the following indicators of success in attracting and retaining all students, particularly those from demographics with traditionally poor representation in computing.

Tables 1 and 2 provide context for our demographics discussion. Table 1 includes the demographics of the school of engineering, the computing majors within that school, and CS1. As expected for a required service course, CS1 enrollment matches the overall school demographics closely. The computing majors are similar, though with a somewhat higher Asian and lower female representation compared to the rest of the school. Table 2 shows the enrollment in each section of CS1 since the inception of CS1X. Though showing fluctuation, there are 30% more CS1 students in the current academic year (2010–11) than five years earlier and the CS1X enrollment has tripled. In addition, because of its capped enrollment hundreds of students were unable to enroll in CS1X.

In addition to the particular successes of CS1X noted in the following sections, we have seen an increase in female and minority enrollment across all CS1 sections.

5.1 Women and Minorities Favor CS1X

In all ten semesters it has been offered, women and minority students continue to be over represented in CS1X, as illustrated in Table 1. CS1X is at least 1.6 times as female as any other section of CS1 with a p-value of 0.01, and is more female than the engineering school overall with a p-value of 10^{-17}. Conversely, CS1G is not statistically different from the engineering school in any demographic and CS1E is more male (p value 10^{-5}). CS1X also has a higher black enrollment compared to the other CS1 sections and to the engineering school with a p value of 0.004.

These trends are consistent with the cultural stereotypes that lead fewer females and blacks to have prior programming experience than males. No preferential bias was given to women and minority students; CS1X enrollment was provided on a first-come first-serve basis to all eligible students with no prior exposure to programming concepts.

5.2 More Students Major in Computing

Diverse students without prior computing experience were attracted to computing majors. A priori, CS1X student intention to major in computing was minimal (we are aware of only one such student out of the 474 to take the course so far), while intended majors accounted for 10–15% of CS1G enrollment and 30–35% of CS1E enrollment. These percentages are approximate and based on an earlier portion of our study because our institution stopped collecting relevant statistics during the time reported.

Table 3 shows the percentage of enrolled students within each section who had not declared a major when they enrolled and later declared a computing major. Numbers here are difficult to compare, as we do not have reliable measures for the number of students in each section predisposed to computing majors. We note that CS1X attracts within statistical error of the same ratio of students as CS1G and CS1 overall. CS1E is considerably higher, which is unsurprising given it attracts only students already familiar with computing. CS1X attraction rate has been on the rise. For over the three prior semesters, 16% of the undeclared students indicated their intention to enroll in a computing major

5.3 Students Continue in Computing

Students who declare a computing major after taking CS1X continue in their major and perform well. Thus far 100% of students who declared a computing major after taking CS1X are either currently continuing in the major or have graduated on time with a computing degree. A CS2 instructor not associated with CS1X observed that on average students from CS1X outperformed both CS1G and CS1E on the first CS2 exam. Former CS1X students have gone on to head the ACM and BSE student chapters and have been accepted into prestigious computing graduate programs and industry leaders in the computing field.

6. STUDENT REACTIONS

As part of assessment for course efficacy, an external independent evaluator has twice conducted CS1X student focus groups. These focus groups included a few general questions, as well as an open discussion period.

In response to general questions, half of CS1X students indicated they intended to take one or more additional computing course. Two-thirds stated the instructor increased their interest in majoring in CS. Over 70% of students stated that the instructor had strongly encouraged them to major in computing. Of the students who intended to major in computing after CS1X, all expressed confidence that they can succeed in the major.

In the open discussion, students expressed the following as what they saw were key elements to course success.

- Regular use of laptops in class, including the integration of lecture and lab;
- Class size (limited to at 70 students);
- Class pace: frequent "baby steps"—mini assignments and small problems—that help students to practice concepts;
- Routine professor-student and student-student interactions;
- Presentation of material: before applying a concept there is an overview of new material along with an indication of its importance towards problem solving.
- Tests that are open-book, comprehensive, and "fair"—the tests were deemed to accurately measure of what they had learned;
- Requiring permission of instructor to enroll—students knew what was expected of them and had a sense of selectivity.

Students also commented, based on experiences with friends, that the other CS1 sections should adopt CS1X learning practices.

One female student commented, "the fact that I got into this class probably changed my life for the rest of my career. [...] now a computer engineer and intended to be a chemical engineer." Another expressed she would feel guilt if she did not major in computing.

In the initial CS1X course offerings students worried whether they would as prepared for CS2 as were students in other sections of CS1. This worry is alleviated by informing students that a CS2 instructor examined student performance on the first CS2 test with respect to CS1 section and reported that on average CS1X students outperformed students who had taken other sections of CS1.

7. EXTENDING CS1X PEDAGOGY

Because Our CS1 structure and CS1X details differ from the "standard" CS1 design in multiple ways, it is difficult to separate the impact of individual elements of CS1X design. In particular, we do not know how much of our success is attributable to the X/G/E split, the increased instructor energy and enthusiasm connected with designing and teaching any new course structure, and the particular pedagogical techniques implemented. To facilitate other institutions hoping to benefit from our experience but lacking the resources to implement all of our practices, we offer the following as more-or-less distinct concepts that we have found useful.

- CS1X is a privilege, not remedial. Two key elements are necessary for this to be true: first, it must cover the same concepts as CS1G so it truly is not "watered-down CS1"; second, it must tailor the instruction style to the students it serves. These two principals in place, it *is* a better fit for the students it serves than is CS1G; treating it as such, with restricted enrollment and explicit expectations, is readily accepted by the students.
- Explicitly and frequently encourage students. We frequently review with students how much they have accomplished in a short time and tell them they can easily master further concepts. Student questions are treated as intelligent recognition of novel material or inadequate explanation, and never as individual inability to master concepts. Students are frequently told they can and should continue and succeed in computing.
- Offer many simple interesting examples of each concept. Offering many examples helps differentiate between the concept taught and the surrounding structure, and helps make that structure familiar and natural. Offering simple examples makes them easier for students to internalize, facilitating the

ability to offer many of them. Offering examples of interest to the students increases their focus and enjoyment of the course.

- Offer short frequent hands-on activities and assignments. Many CS1 courses are taught with a small number of multi-week projects that are designed to exercise the synthesis of course concepts—a valuable learning objective. However, we believe that frequent, small assignments with nontrivial overlap provide the same kind of familiarity and confidence in CS1 as similarly-scoped homework does in mathematics. Assignments due each class also help gauge how rapidly students are mastering each concept, focuses student questions, and indicates where additional instruction is need. No student has yet complained of too many assignments.
- Provide ample help during class. There are always some students who have questions of an individual nature, either about their code or due to individual differences in learning pace and background. Having teaching assistants present in the class to field such questions one-on-one streamlines instruction for the other students and increases the comprehension and confidence of the student having difficulty.
- Facilitate a relaxed, interactive environment. Several elements contribute to this goal: combining lab and lecture, encouraging TA involvement, requesting each student participate in discussion, and making the elicitation and fielding of student questions a higher priority than remaining on schedule. We attempt to make it clear to the students that we are experimenting, mention how their experience differs from other semesters and sections and why. In general, we foster the view that the instructor is an imperfect but interested person working to teach them the best way possible.
- Reorganize teaching to emphasize learning, not traditional concept hierarchies. We believe that the standard structure of CS1 pedagogy is poorly suited for true beginners, and each semester we reorganize topics and emphases to seek a more effective structure. For example, we found that students confused loops with conditionals so we swapped the order in which they were introduced, teaching the "while" construct several weeks prior to the "if" construct. Similarly, we found that ArrayList was a more natural concept for students than arrays, so we teach ArrayList (and other built-in Java objects) early in the term and explain arrays much later as highly restricted ArrayLists. At least once a week the authors of this paper visit together to discuss what seems to be troubling students and what reorganizations, analogies, or exercises might better convey those concepts.

8. ACKNOWLEDGMENTS

We much appreciate the support provided by NSF BPC grant 0739254 to develop CS1X. NCWIT and its extension services are thanked for their analysis of departmental practices and their recommendations for advancing diversity.

9. REFERENCES

[1] Astin, A. W., & Astin, H. S. (1992). Undergraduate Science Education: The Impact of Different College Environments on the Educational Pipeline in the Sciences, ED36240. UCLA.

[2] Bair, B. A., Bhatt, P., Marcus, M., & Valli, M. (2003). *Gendered Perceptions of Programming as a Career.* 4/25/ 2004, www.cse.ohio-state.edu/~bbair/WIC.

[3] Barker, L. J., and Garvin-Doxas, K. (2004). Making visible the behaviors that influence learning environment. *Computer Science Education, 14*(2).

[4] Cohoon, J. M., and Aspray W, J. (eds) (2006). Women and Information Technology, MIT Press.

[5] Cohoon, J. M., Gonsoulin, M., & Layman, J. (2004). Mentoring Computer Science Undergraduates. *Human Perspectives in The Internet Society: Culture, Psychology, and Gender.* WIT Press.

[6] Cohoon, J.P. (2007), An Introductory Course Format for Promoting Diversity and Retention, SIGCSE Technical Symposium, Kentucky, 395-399

[7] Computing Research Association, http://www.cra.org.

[8] Gürer, D. and Camp, T. (2002). An ACM-W literature review on women in computing. *SIGCSE Bull.* 34, 121–127.

[9] Rich, L., H. Perry, M. Guzdial. (2005) A CS1 Course Designed to Address Interests of Women, Technical Symposium on Computer Science Education, 190–194.

[10] Jamieson, L. (1991, May 2001). Women, Engineering, and Community. *Computing Research News,* p. 2 and 16.

[11] Katz, S., Aronis, J., Allbritton, D., Wilson, C., and Soffa, M. L. (2003). A study to identify predictors of achievement in an introductory computer science course. *SIGMIS Conference on Computer Personnel,* Philadelphia, 157–161.

[12] Lips, H. M. (2004). The Gender Gap in Possible Selves: Divergence of Academic Self-Views Among High School and University Students. *Sex Roles, 40*, 357-371.

[13] Margolis, J., & Fisher, A. (2001). *Unlocking the Clubhouse: Women in Computing.* Cambridge, MA: MIT Press.

[14] Nagappan, N., Williams, L., Ferzli, M., Wiebe, E., Yang, K., Miller, C., and Balik, S. 2003. Improving the CS1 experience with pair programming, *SIGCSE Technical Symposium on Computer Science Education*, Reno, Nevada, USA, 19–23.

[15] McDowell, C., Werner, L., Bullock, H. E., and Fernald, J. 2006. Pair programming improves student retention, confidence, and program quality. *CACM* 49, 8, 90–95

[16] Potosky, D. (2002). A field study of computer efficacy beliefs as an outcome of training: the role of computer playfulness, computer knowledge, and performance during training. *Computers in Human Behavior, 18*(3), 241–255.

[17] Prey, J. C., Cohoon, J. P., and Fife, G. (1994). Software Engineering Beginning in the First Computer Science Course. *Software Engineering Education*, 359–374.

[18] Strenta, A. C., Elliott, R., Adair, R., Matier, M., & Scott, J. (1994). Choosing and Leaving Science in Highly Selective Institutions. *Research in Higher Education, 35*(5), 513–547.

[19] Turkle, S., Papert, S. (1990). Epistemological Pluralism - Styles & Voices within the Computer Culture. *Signs,* 128–57.

[20] U.S. Department of Labor, Bureau of Labor Statistics (2006), http://nces.ed.gov/ipeds.

Table 8: Likert-Scale Ratings of CS1 Example Applications

Application	High School CS Teacher	CS Student	Female Student	Male Student	Female – Male	Normalized Student – Teacher
Instant messaging	5.36	5.39	5.38	5.43	–0.05	0.47
Music player	5.30	5.39	5.29	5.71	–0.42	0.53
Photo manipulation	4.90	5.29	5.26	5.36	–0.10	**0.83**
Card games	5.73	5.12	5.15	5.07	0.08	–0.17
Medical diagnosis	3.95	5.14	5.21	5.00	0.21	**1.63**
Music library organizer	4.54	5.04	4.97	5.29	–0.32	0.94
Battleship game	5.00	5.02	4.85	5.43	–0.58	0.46
Connect four	5.33	4.92	4.85	5.14	–0.29	0.03
Mad Lib	–	4.92	4.79	5.21	–0.42	
Sudoku	5.09	4.98	5.06	4.79	0.27	0.33
Password security	5.52	4.78	4.74	4.93	–0.19	–0.30
Travel routing	4.36	4.67	4.65	4.71	–0.06	0.75
Video player	5.05	4.96	4.62	5.79	**–1.17**	0.35
Language translation	4.73	5.06	5.24	4.62	**0.62**	0.77
Engineering applications	4.90	4.81	4.61	5.29	–0.68	0.35
Tic-tac-toe	5.26	4.65	4.59	4.79	–0.20	–0.17
Heart monitor	3.90	4.63	4.65	4.54	0.11	**1.17**
Business applications	4.86	4.59	4.50	4.79	–0.29	0.17
Photo mosaics	4.72	5.08	5.32	4.50	**0.82**	0.80
Exercise training zone	4.19	4.54	4.56	4.46	0.10	0.79
Personality typing	4.68	4.61	4.71	4.36	0.35	0.37
Photo viewer	4.77	4.73	4.88	4.36	**0.52**	0.40
Smart appliances	4.73	4.40	4.29	4.64	–0.35	0.11
Virus protection	4.90	4.52	4.24	5.21	–0.97	0.06
Body mass index	4.73	4.61	4.76	4.21	0.55	0.32
Food dispenser	4.00	4.10	4.12	4.07	0.05	0.54
Science applications	4.71	4.21	4.00	4.71	–0.71	–0.06
Encryption	5.52	4.00	3.94	4.43	–0.49	**–1.08**
Calculator	5.00	4.00	3.91	4.14	–0.23	–0.56
Checkbook register	4.77	3.88	3.88	3.86	0.02	–0.45
Bank account interest	4.34	3.98	4.00	3.86	0.14	0.08
Text to speech	4.38	4.25	3.85	5.21	**–1.36**	0.31
Coin change maker	4.59	3.73	3.74	3.71	0.03	–0.42
Daily jumble	5.09	4.02	4.15	3.71	0.44	–0.63
Bridge capacity	4.30	3.86	3.68	4.57	–0.89	0.00
Spamming	5.10	3.81	3.65	4.23	–0.58	–0.85
Loan calculator	4.40	3.57	3.50	4.00	–0.50	–0.39
Tax computation	4.08	3.58	3.35	4.14	–0.79	–0.06
Text analysis	4.33	3.27	3.15	3.57	–0.42	–0.62
Statistics	3.85	3.33	3.03	4.07	**–1.04**	–0.08
Carbon dating	4.35	3.13	3.03	3.31	–0.28	–0.78
Wind flow	3.89	3.19	2.94	3.85	–0.91	–0.26
Econometrics	3.47	3.02	2.76	3.86	**–1.10**	–0.01
Dungeons & Dragons	–	2.96	2.68	3.64	–0.96	
Readability	4.25	2.98	2.65	3.85	**–1.20**	–0.83
Elevator strategies	4.47	2.63	2.56	3.00	–0.44	**–1.40**
Rocket payload	4.20	3.19	2.38	5.14	**–2.76**	–0.57
Redistricting	3.45	2.63	2.29	3.43	**–1.14**	–0.38
Fractals	4.85	2.39	2.21	3.00	–0.79	**–2.02**
Predator-prey interaction	4.50	–	–	–	–	–
Average:	4.63	4.20	4.09	4.47	–0.37	0.00 (normalized)

Women Build Games, Seriously

Elizabeth Sweedyk
Harvey Mudd College
Claremont, CA
909.607.8360
z@cs.hmc.edu

ABSTRACT

Recruitment of students to Computer Science has been a major focus of effort for educators since the dot-com bust in 2001. Two largely disparate themes in these efforts are women and games. There have been numerous efforts to broaden participation in computer science by attracting women to the field. At the same time, games are increasingly used to attract new students. Our interest lies at the intersection of these methods.

We began using game design/development projects in our software engineering course, CS121, in 2002. The game focus was extremely successful with many of our students. But a nagging minority of students objected to building games, and women tend to be overrepresented in that group.

So while are awed by the power of games to engage and motivate many of our students, we need to ask: Do games in our curriculum reinforce gender stereotypes of Computer Science? Do they foster development of the so-called "Geek mythology?"[7] In short, *must we choose: women or games?*

We argue the answer is no. While traditional game projects may disenfranchise women, our experience shows that serious game projects both attract and engage them. This paper describes our results.

Categories and Subject Descriptors
K.3.2 [**Computer Science Education.**]: Curriculum

General Terms
Design

Keywords
Gender, computer games

1. INTRODUCTION
Recruitment of students to Computer Science (CS) has been a major focus of effort for educators since the dot-com bust in 2001. Two largely disparate themes in these efforts are women and games.

SIGCSE'11, March 9–12, 2011, Dallas, Texas, USA.

There has been a concerted effort in recent years to broaden participation in CS. This work includes studies to understand gendered attitudes toward computer science [7] as well as models for attracting girls and women to computing [8,11] reducing attrition of women in CS programs [4,16,17], and encouraging women to pursue advanced degrees [12].

At the same time, games in CS curriculum have exploded with efforts that include educational games to teach CS concepts [3,9,19], game programming in introductory courses [2,11], game projects in advanced courses like graphics and AI [14], and new degree programs aimed at future game designers [6,18].

We began using game projects in our software development course, CS121, in 2002 [13,14]. The game focus was wildly successful with many of our students. They threw themselves at game projects with an incredible passion and often produced remarkable results. But some of our students objected to building games. It became clear that many non-gamers, those students who lack a passion for gaming, felt disadvantaged by the game focus. And women were over-represented in that group.

So, on one hand, we were awed by the power of game building to engage and motivate many of our students. On the other, we worried that games in our curriculum worked to perpetuate "geek mythology" [7], to reinforce gender stereotypes of computer science, and to disenfranchise our women.

Over the last five years we have initiated several game-related initiatives aimed at attracting and engaging women. This work involved the creation of a new course, IE179 Gender and Computer Games [14,15], summer research and independent study projects involving students in game development, and a reform of our software development course, CS121. Our conclusion is that games in our classroom can disenfranchise women, but they don't have to. In fact, women can be highly motivated to design and develop computer games when the games are "serious," that is they serve some purpose beyond simple entertainment, such as educational games. We find this approach particularly successful when paired with basic training in gender critique.

Harvey Mudd College (HMC) is a small liberal arts college with a focus on science, math and engineering. We offer majors in Biology, Chemistry, Computer Science, Engineering, Math, and Physics as well as joint majors in Bio/Chem, Bio/Math, and Math/CS. We are part of the Consortium of Claremont Colleges and our students can also select an off-campus major at one of the other colleges. This year, for the first time, our in-coming class has more women than men; 101 vs. 96. Computer Science and the joint Math-CS program typically have 30-50 majors each year. We have made a concerted effort to attract women to CS [22] with the result that the number of women majors as well as the percentage of majors who are women has risen substantially in recent years (Figure 1).

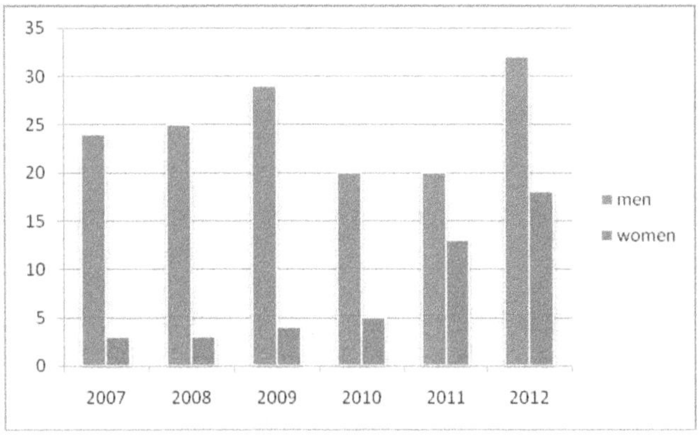

Figure 1 CS and Joint CS-Math majors for graduating classes 2007-2012

2. GENDER AND GAMES

In 1985 Keisler *et al* [10] made the following observations.

> "... we believe computing is more than a set of skills. It is embedded in a social system consisting of shared values and norms, a special vocabulary and humor, status and prestige ordering, and differentiation of members from non-members. In short, it is a culture."

The nature of this culture was more fully elaborated by Margolis & Fisher [7]. They found that many students didn't feel they measured up to the cultural norm of "geek mythology;" in fact 2/3 of the women and 1/3 of the men interviewed felt they had inadequate background and insufficient passion compared to the perceived model student. But these feelings were more likely to make women reconsider their choice of career than men.

Computer games play a central role in geek mythology. Games are the primary mechanism by which boys become interested in technology [1] and the primary reason they decide to major in CS [1,5]. While many women play games, they typically do so less often and with less passion than men.

This was borne out in a survey we conducted of HMC first year students in fall 2010. Students were polled in our introductory CS courses; an intro CS course is required in the first semester for all first-year HMC students but we also draw students from the other Claremont Colleges. Of the 223 students registered in these courses, 208 participated in the study, 116 women and 92 men.

Even among women students at Harvey Mudd—women interested in careers in math, science, and engineering—gameplay habits differ markedly from the men (Figure 2). When asked the average number of hours per week spent playing games in high school, the median choice for women was 0-2 hours, while for men it was 2-5. Further, no women reported playing more than 5-10 hours per week, while 19 men reported play more than 10 hours per week, with 3 playing more than 20 hours per week! Though HMC students don't declare a major until their second year, we asked students whether they had any preferences. When restricted to students who expressed an interest in majoring in CS, gameplay times increased but men still play much more than women (Figure 2).

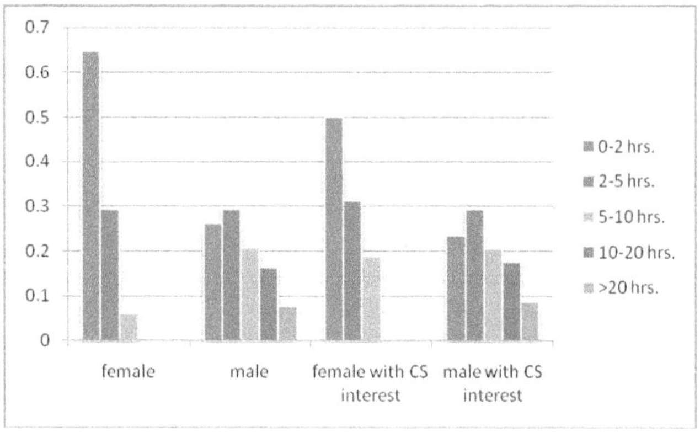

Figure 2 Gameplay hours per week among students in intro CS courses

All but one of our students reported playing games. What these numbers do not capture is the types of games our students play. The Entertainment Software Association (ESA) reports that 40% of all game players are female and that adult women represent a greater portion of the game-playing population (33 percent) than boys aged 17 or younger (18 percent) [20]. These statistics are surprising until one considers games like Bejeweled and Solitaire and online Bridge.

Games are not all created equal. The students in our Gender and Games course argue that casual games like Solitaire are not "real" games. One woman in our gaming survey added a comment *in parentheses* that she played Solitaire, as if she was unsure whether that counted.

What makes a game "real?" Well, for one thing, its price. "Real" games produce most of game industry revenue. But it also matters "who" plays them. Though The Sims is the best-selling game franchise of all times, our students in the Gender and Games course could not agree if it was a "real" game, or for that matter, even a game. [1]

Ultimately, "real" games are played by "gamers," a community with a full-fledged culture and its own shifting and often unarticulated aesthetic. The culture of gaming is overtly male. It is "male," as in the opposite of "female." And while women may play games, they are not very welcome as full-fledged citizens of gaming culture.

While almost half of our male survey participants self-identified themselves as gamers, less than 10% of the women did (Figure

[1] They are not alone. When The Sims was released, a huge debate raged in the gaming community as to whether it was really a game. Even its designer, Will Wright, argued it wasn't a game but rather a "software toy."

3). In fact, although yes and no were the available choices for the question "Do you consider yourself a gamer?" two women wrote in the answer "maybe."

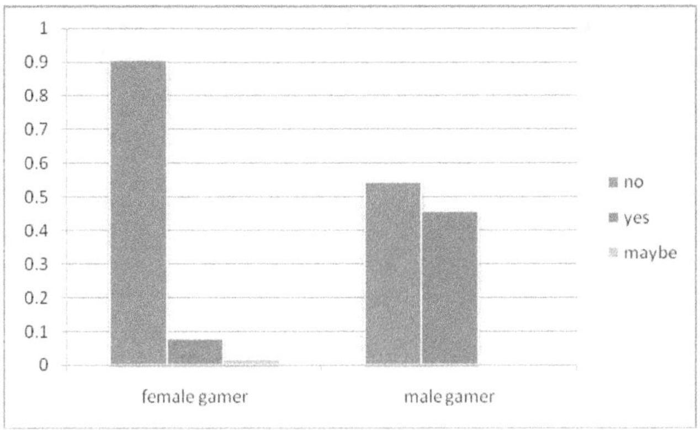

Figure 3 Self-described "gamer"

In addition to a difference in gameplay experience, the men and women in our survey differed in game building experience and interest (Figure 4). Somewhat surprisingly, more than half of our women expressed an interest in taking a game development course.

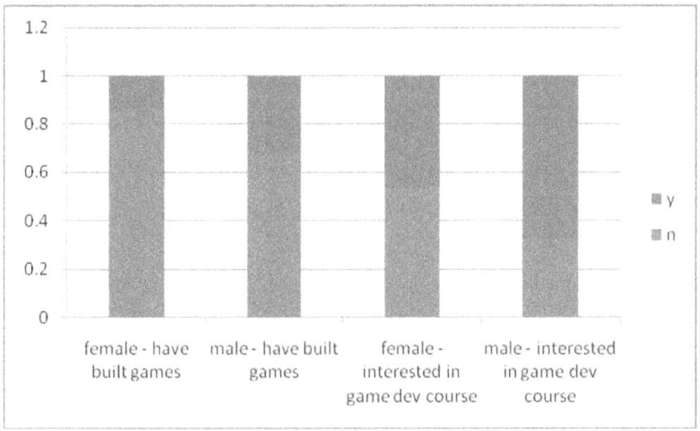

Figure 4 Experience/interest in game development

3. SERIOUS GAMES

All CS students are required to take our software development course CS121. In 2002 we changed the course to focus on game projects [13,14]. Students worked in teams to develop three games across the semester. The first project was a 2D arcade style game built off of an existing game engine; this phase of the course primarily focused on the requirements process. The second project was a 3D one-hole miniature golf game; this part of the course addressed the software design and testing processes. The third project was left to students' discretion; the pedagogical goals during this phase involved project management.

Many of our students were thrilled to be building games. They threw themselves at the projects with great passion and often produced remarkable results; e.g. Elemental Golf was a one-hole miniature golf game that featured four types of balls (earth, wind, fire, and water) with different magical properties, a stunning 3D landscape, and obstacles that included a flying pirate ship (Figure 5).

Figure 5: Elemental Golf created in CS121 Spring 2004

Non-gamers often complained about feeling disadvantaged by the game focus. Their complaints echoed those that Margolis *et al* reported in their landmark study [7]:

> "Our interviews with students, both male and female, are rife with descriptions of a culture and its expectations of who will succeed. The cultural norm of the successful CS student is someone who is at the computer 24/7, living, thinking and breathing computer science."

The students who excelled in our course were almost always avid gamers. (Though being an avid gamer certainly didn't ensure success.) They brought passion, domain knowledge, and often game-building experience to the classroom and non-gamers found it hard to compete. While passion and hard work should garner reward, we inadvertently ascribed these gamers an authority in our classroom by virtue of their participation in gaming culture. And the gamers were always male.

In 2007 we had a surge in the number of women declaring a major in CS. As part of an effort to retain them, we set out to change CS121 with the goal of ensuring equal participation by all students regardless of gender or gaming practices. Rather than eliminating games, we chose to focus on serious game projects.

The new course has evolved over three offerings, fall 2008, fall 2009, and spring 2010. In fall 2008, students self-organized into four teams, one all-women team and three all-male teams. They were asked to develop "serious games" for a real client.

The team of women developed Reign of the Olympians (Figure 6), an educational game to teach Greek mythology to middle school students. The male teams developed PhysGame, a physics-based puzzle game for students at the Mtwango Secondary School in southern Tanzaia, SimServer, a simulation game aimed to teach college students about computer networking, and HMC Orientation, an adventure game for incoming Harvey Mudd students meant to relay college traditions around dorm life.

Figure 6: The Reign of the Olympians created in CS121 Fall 2008

Some of the outcomes of this offering include:

- The team of women consistently spent more time per week working on their project than any of the male teams. For example, over the last two week of the project, each woman worked on average 27 hours on their project while male teams averaged 15-20 hours per person for the same period.
- The team of women students continued to work on the game as an independent study project over spring 2009. Only one male in the class continued work on a game project.
- Three of the women went on to do a year-long game development project for the Imagine Cup Competition.
- In peer evaluations students rated the women's game as the best overall game, the best educational game, and the game with the best premise. The only other category, best executed game, was won by one of the male teams.

In fall 2009, we began a new collaboration with Greg Orr and Joshua Yavor, social science teachers from Hillside Middle School in Kalamazoo, MI. Students in CS121 collaborated over the semester on a single game, Time Mystery Mischief (Figure7). This game was designed by the students to address the middle school learning objective:

> *Explain how historians use a variety of sources to explore the past (e.g. artifacts, primary and secondary sources including narratives, technology, historical maps, visual and mathematical quantitative data, radiocarbon dating, DNA analysis).*

In the game, the player must rescue villagers trapped in the past by a villain with a time machine. The player must find and interpret clues to figure out *when* in time each villager is located.

In spring 2010 we continued our collaboration with the teachers at Hillside Middle School but returned to the 4 team model. In this semester teams worked on the following games:

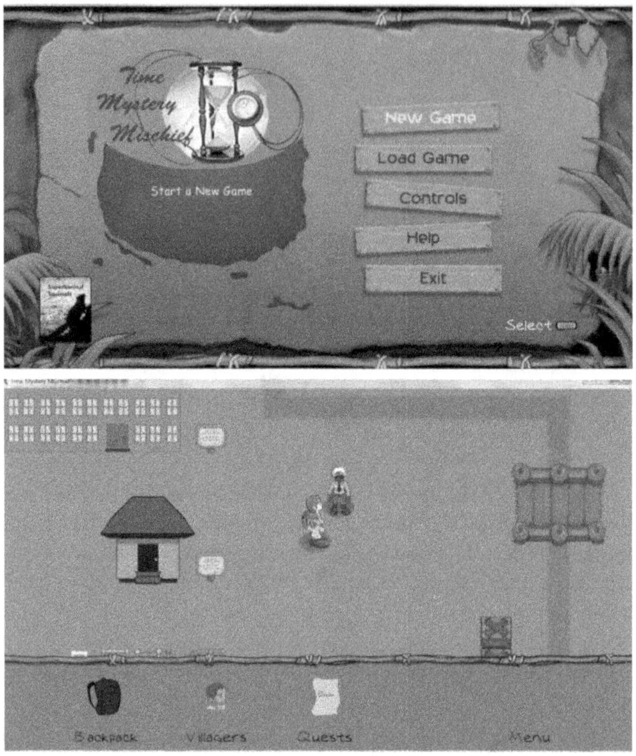

Figure 7: Time Mystery Mischief created in CS121 Fall 2009

- Village Defense: In this turn-based tower defense game, the player must assign Neolithic villagers to tasks such as hunting, building, farming, and protecting the village to ensure the village survives. The game targets the following learning objective: *Explain the impact of the Agricultural Revolution (stable food supply, surplus, population growth, trade, division of labor, development of settlements).*
- Globe Trotter: The player must track a spy who has stolen the school mascot by solving geographical clues. This game addresses the objective: *Explain and use a variety of maps, globes and web based geography technology to study the world, including interregional, regional and local scales.*
- Energy Empire: The player controls a power company and must raise power output without destroying the environment. This game targets the learning objective: *Describe ways the physical environment is modified by human activities, and how those actions are influenced by the values societies place on the Earth's natural resources, physical features, and processes (e.g. changes in the tropical forest environments of Brazil, Peru and Costa Rica).*
- Hectare (Figure 8): The player controls the weather and other environmental factors and must help computer-controlled agricultural communities flourish. This game

addresses the middle school learning objective: *Describe the importance of the natural environment in the development of agricultural settlements in different locations (e.g. available water for irrigation, adequate precipitation and suitable growing season).*

Figure 8: Hectare created in CS121 Spring 2010

In both semesters we surveyed students about the game projects (F2009: 9 women/10 men, S2010: 4 women/8 men). We asked whether serious games made good course projects. The women approved in greater percentages than the men (Figure. 9)

We also asked how involved students felt in the project. Involvement, in general, improved with the changes we made in the spring 2010 offering. But in both semesters women reported being more involved that the men.

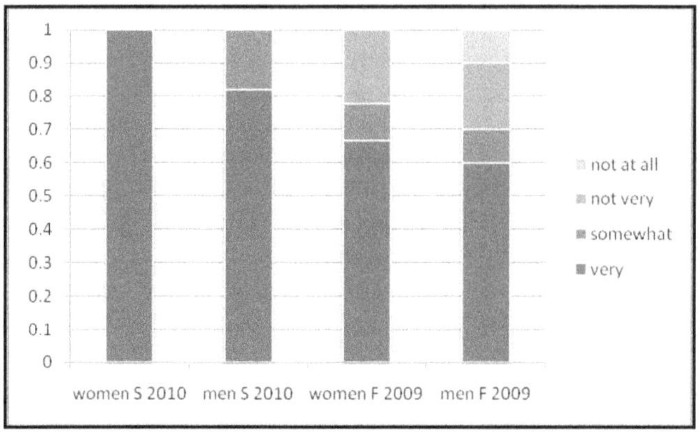

Figure 9 Students surveyed "Do serious games make good projects?"

We have two additional data sets that reflect our women's engagement with serious games. The first is data on the rising interest of women students to work on games as independent study. Independent study projects are typically initiated by students and over the years we have only refused a couple of requests. Figure 10 tracks the growth in game projects involving women over recent years. Though the projects involving male students focused on entertainment and serious games, every project involving a woman has centered on a serious game.

The second data concerns summer research. The CS department typically hires over 50 students each summer to do research on campus. Students apply for all positions through a single form, ranking their preferences. In the summers of 2009 and 2010 we supervised several serious game research projects including a dance game similar to Dance, Dance Revolution but aimed at senior citizens and a game authoring system for children. Figure 11 show how the women and men applicants ranked these projects. Half of the women applicants in 2009 and almost 40% in 2010 gave the serious game projects a 5 (the highest score). The median and average ranking in 2010 was 3 and in 2009 was 3 and 3.25 respectively.

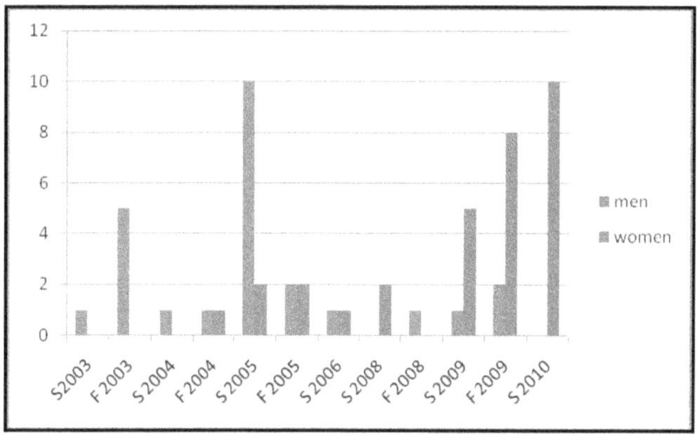

Figure 10: Independent study game projects

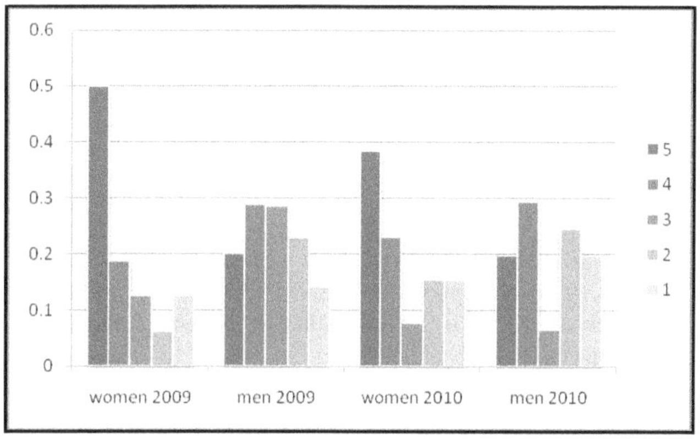

Figure 11 Student ranking of serious game projects for summer research

4. CONCLUSIONS

Games are powerful tools to engage students in Computer Science but they can have adverse effects with non-gamers and particularly with women. Courses that involve the design and development of games as projects can ascribe undue authority to gamers. This may be seen as some implicit endorsement of the values of gaming culture; a culture that dichotomizes gender to the extreme, forcing women into the role of other.

We have found that serious game projects avoid these problems. Women engage with serious games and, by some metrics, they do more enthusiastically than do men,

We plan to continue our study of serious games in the curriculum. We are particularly interested in whether the first year women, who report less interest in game building than the men, have a change of mind when they encounter serious game development in CS121.

5. ACKNOWLEDGEMENTS

Our view of games and gender has been greatly informed by the thoughtful reflections of our students in the Gender and Games course. We thank them greatly. We also thank Greg Orr and Josh Yavor of Hillside Middle School for their tireless efforts as customers to our CS121 students.

6. REFERENCES

[1] AAUW Educational Foundation Commission on Technology, Gender, and Teacher Education, 2000. Tech-Savvy: Educating Firls in the New Computer Age.

[2] Jessica D. Bayliss and Sean Strout, 2000. Games as a 'flavor' of CS1. Proceedings of the 37th SIGCSE Technical Symposium on Computer Science Education, pp500-504.

[3] Tiffany Barnes, Heather Richter, Eve Powell, Amanda Chaffin, and Alex Godwin, 2007. Games2Learn: building CS1 learning games for retention. Proceedings of the 12th annual SIGCSE Conference on Innovation and Technology in Computer Science Education.

[4] Sarah B. Berenson, Kelli M. Slaten, Laurie Williams, Chih-Wei Ho, 2004. Voices of women in a software engineering course: reflections on collaboration. Journal on Educational Resources in Computing (JERIC) Volume 4 , Issue 1 (March 2004) Special Issue on Gender-Balancing Computing Education

[5] Lori Carter, 2006. Why students with an apparent aptitude for computer science don't choose to major in computer science. SIGCSE Bulletin Volume 38 , Issue 1 (March 2006) pp 27 – 31.

[6] CMU Entertainment Technology Center, http://www.etc.cmu.edu/

[7] Allan Fisher and Jane Margolis, 2002. Unlocking the clubhouse: the Carnegie Mellon experience. SIGCSE Bulletin Volume 34, Issue 2 (June 2002), pp 79-83.

[8] Lauren Rich, Heather Perry, and Mark Guzdial 2004. A CS1 course designed to address interests of women. Proceedings of the 35th SIGCSE technical symposium on Computer Science Education (2004), pp 190-194.

[9] John M.D. Hill, Clark K. Ray, Jean R. S. Blair, and Curtis A. Carver, 2003. Puzzles and games: addressing different learning styles in teaching operating systems concepts. Proceedings of the 34th SIGCSE Technical Symposium on Computer Science Education (2003), pp182 –186.

[10] Sara Kiesler, Lee Sproull, and Jacquelynne S. Eccles, 2002. Pool halls, chips, and war games: women in the culture of computing. SIGCSE Bulletin, Volume 34 , Issue 2 (June 2002) pp 159 – 164.

[11] Barbara Moskal, Deborah Lurie, and Stephen Cooper, 2004. Evaluating the effectiveness of a new instructional approach. SIGCSE Bulletin, Vol. 6, Issue 1 (March 2004), pp 75-79.

[12] Shari Lawrence Pfleeger, Pat Teller, Sheila E. Castaneda, Manda Wilson, and Rowan Lindley, 2001. Increasing the enrollment of women in computer science. Proceedings of the 32nd SIGCSE Technical Symposium on Computer Science Education (2001), pp 386 – 387.

[13] Elizabeth Sweedyk and Robert M. Keller (2005). Fun and games: a new software engineering course. Proceedings of ITiCSE 2005.

[14] Elizabeth Sweedyk, Marianne deLaet, James Kuffner, Michael Slattery, 2005. Computer games and CS education: Why and how. Proceedings of SIGCSE (2005).

[15] Elizabeth Sweedyk and Marianne deLaet, 2005. Women, games, and women's games. Phi kappa Phi Journal (Summer 2005).

[16] Linda L. Werner, Brian Hanks, and Charlie McDowell, 2004. Pair-programming helps female computer science students.. Journal on Educational Resources in Computing (JERIC) Volume 4 , Issue 1 (March 2004), Special Issue on Gender-Balancing Computing Education.

[17] Brenda Wilson, 2008. Improving the comfort level of females in the first computer programming course: suggestions for CS faculty. Journal of Computing Sciences in Colleges, Volume 23 , Issue 4 (April 2008) pp 28-34.

[18] WPI Interactive Media and Game Development http://www.wpi.edu/Academics/Majors/IMGD/

[19] Ursula Wolz, Tiffany Barnes, Ian Parberry, and Michael Wick, 2006. Digital gaming as a vehicle for learning. Proceedings of the 37th SIGCSE Technical Symposium on Computer Science Education.

[20] "Essential Facts About the Video and Game Industry," (2007), http://www.theesa.com/facts/pdfs/ESA_EF_2007.pdf

[21] Carol Tarvis, *The Mismeasure of Women*, Touchstone (1993).

[22] Christine Alvarado and Zachary Dodds, "Women in CS: An Evaluation of Three Promising Practices," Proceedings of the 41st ACM technical symposium on Computer science education (2010), pp 57-61.

Contextualized Approaches to Introductory Computer Science: The Key to Making Computer Science Relevant or Simply Bait and Switch?

Jennifer S. Kay
Computer Science Department
Rowan University
201 Mullica Hill Road
Glassboro, NJ 08028
U.S.A.
+1 (856) 256-4593
kay@rowan.edu

ABSTRACT

America's youth perceive Computer Science to be difficult, tedious, boring, irrelevant and asocial. Unfortunately, many traditional introductory Computer Science classes and textbooks do little to improve that image. In contrast, contextualized approaches to teaching introductory Computer Science are very attractive. Instead of writing a leap year program, students can learn about conditional statements by programming a robot to follow a light, or by creating an animation to tell a story, or even by modifying a picture of the college president so that she is wearing a neon orange jacket instead of a navy blue one.

The arguments in favor of contextualized approaches to attract non-Computer-Science-majors to our classes are very persuasive. But what about students who then choose to major or minor in Computer Science? Of course we want to offer them interesting and engaging first courses in Computer Science, and indeed this may help with our efforts to attract more students to our programs. But what happens in subsequent semesters?

The purpose of this paper is to initiate a general discussion on the use of any sort of "cool" new approach into both undergraduate and K-12 Computer Science education. These approaches successfully attract students to study subjects that we ourselves are deeply engaged in. But we need to discuss as a community what happens to students who do choose to major or minor in Computer Science when our individual classes conclude and the rest of their studies commence.

Categories and Subject Descriptors

K.3.2 [**Computers and Education**]: Computer and Information Science Education – *Computer Science Education, Curriculum.*

General Terms

Design, Economics, Experimentation, Human Factors, Management, Theory.

Keywords

Education, contextualized approaches, CS0, CS1, motivation, recruitment, enrollment, retention, interest, robotics, manipulatives, bait and switch.

1. INTRODUCTION

America's youth perceive Computer Science (CS) to be difficult, tedious, boring, irrelevant and asocial [13][31]. Unfortunately, many traditional introductory CS classes and textbooks do little to improve that image. Sure, some of us may be fascinated to learn that the year 2100 will not be a leap year and we may find a recursive solution to the Towers of Hanoi problem truly exciting, but that probably isn't the case for many of our students.

In contrast, contextualized approaches to teaching introductory CS are very attractive. Instead of writing a leap year program, students can learn about conditional statements by programming a robot to follow a light, or by creating an animation to tell a story, or even by modifying a picture of the college president so that she is wearing a neon orange jacket instead of a navy blue one. Some of these approaches have empirical data that demonstrates improved student learning and retention, e.g. [11][21][29].

The arguments in favor of contextualized approaches to attract non-CS-majors to our classes are very persuasive. Forte & Guzdial [11] make a strong case that a basic understanding of programming is an important part of all students' computational literacy and is necessary to understand the underpinnings of what drives much of the culture and environment that our graduates will encounter. With the number of CS-related courses offered in North American high schools on the decline [26], students may not have the opportunity to be exposed to *any* CS concepts before arriving on campus their Freshman year. If CS departments do not offer appealing, introductory-level courses, we are denying a huge population the chance to learn a body of knowledge and approaches to problem solving afforded only through CS.

But what about students who then choose to major or minor in CS? Of course we want to offer them interesting and engaging first courses in CS, and indeed this may help with our efforts to attract more students to our programs. But what happens in subsequent semesters? While there are those who work towards the integration of robots (or media computation, or other contextualized approaches) across the undergraduate Computer Science curriculum, the recent explosion of work in this field has been in elementary courses for majors and non-majors.

The purpose of this paper is to initiate a general discussion on the use of any sort of "cool" new approach into both undergraduate and K-12 CS education. These approaches successfully attract students to study subjects that we ourselves are deeply engaged in. But we need to discuss as a community what happens to students who choose to major or minor in Computer Science when our individual classes conclude and the rest of their studies commence.

2. BACKGROUND

2.1 Contextualized Approaches to Introductory Computer Science

Contextualized approaches to introductory CS can be split into three categories: traditional (non-electronic) manipulatives, robots and other electronic tangibles, and desktop-computer-based tools. This section presents only a few selected examples in each category with an emphasis on those that have empirical studies of their effectiveness. [16] and [23] provide a good starting point for those looking for more detail.

2.1.1 The Use of Traditional Manipulatives in Introductory Computer Science

Traditional non-electronic manipulatives are omnipresent in K-12 education. According to Jean Piaget, children are limited to thinking about things in terms of perceptions and concrete experiences until adolescence. [8] Thus with younger children, one would imagine that the use of physical manipulatives to teach mathematics, for example, would be essential. In fact, regardless of grade level, the use of manipulatives in mathematics classes generally (but not always) results in better performance as well as higher scores on retention and problem solving tests.[3]

Computer Science does have its share of non-electronic physical manipulatives. While objects drawn on paper are ubiquitous, more interesting variations abound: The Computer Science Unplugged project [4] includes activities with oranges, tennis balls, candy, poker chips, tent pegs, and string. The introductory textbook, Concrete Abstractions [6] makes use of paper chains and chocolate candy bars. And of course there is the use of peanut butter, jelly, and bread to introduce the importance of precision in programming (many examples abound, e.g. see [9]).

2.1.2 Robots and other Electronic Tangibles in Introductory Computer Science

Robots have probably been the most popular electronic tangible in CS education ever since Papert and Paterson introduced students to physical Logo Turtles in the early 1970s [12]. There is little doubt that the use of robots in introductory classes can be an effective way to spark an initial interest in Computer Science, recruit students into our classes, and subsequently recruit some of them as Computer Science majors. But are they beneficial? A decade ago, the educational robotics community was shocked when Fagin & Merkle found that the use of robots in an undergraduate core computing course actually reduced students' test scores [10], though they concluded that the fact that students in the robot sections of their course had limited access to work with the robots was a key factor. This conclusion is supported by Huetinck & Munshin [15] who emphasize that in the use of traditional manipulatives, it is important to allow the students to have hands-on time with the manipulatives. If, due to cost or time constraints, students are forced to rely on teacher demonstrations, the benefits of using the manipulatives are reduced.

More recently, an initial study by Summet et. al [30] comparing a CS1 course using robots (in which each student had a personal robot they could use whenever they wished) with a non-robot course showed that the robots did not have a negative impact.

Beyond robots, a variety of input and output devices are incorporated into Introductory CS courses including LEDs, switches, gamepads, pushbuttons, and sensors for everything from tilt and acceleration to temperature, light, and sound, e.g. see [2][18][22][24].

2.1.3 Desktop-Computer-Based Contextual Approaches to Introductory Computer Science

Logo "screen turtles" also date back to the early 1970s. [12] More recently, there has been a flurry of computer-based contextual approaches to introducing Computer Science concepts, many with accompanying textbooks. The Alice Programming environment [1][7][21] introduces students to programming through the creation of 3D animations using a drag-and-drop interface and has been shown to improve students' attitudes towards CS, performance in future courses, and retention in the CS major. Media Computation [11][19] uses the theme of manipulating media, images, music, and animations, to teach concepts from CS1 through Data Structures. This approach has been shown to have positive effects with both non-majors and majors. Scratch [27][28] uses a drag-and-drop approach to introductory programming based on 2D animations. The system is very accessible to an even younger audience; the majority of Scratch users range from ages eight to sixteen. In developing Scratch, the focus was not only on ease of use and enabling individuals to do projects that are meaningful to them, but also on social computing. The upload of programs to the website is easy and encouraged by the design of the system. Once on-line, source code is made available to all, and others are encouraged to experiment with modifying existing code. Scratch's popularity is clear: users upload 1,500 new projects each day.

2.2 The Need to Recruit More Students to Computer Science

While the number of BS degrees in CS continues to decline, there is finally an indication that we are on the road to recovery as CS undergraduate enrollments begin to slowly creep up. [32]

While there are obvious factors like the dot com bust that may explain much of our enrollment crash over the last few years, anecdotal reports also suggest that the advent of No Child Left Behind, and specifically the fact that Computer Science is not an area that students are tested on, may be a factor in the decreased presence of CS at the high school level:

"Here are some of the things kids at Garfield/Franklin elementary in Muscatine, Iowa no longer do: eagle watch on the Mississippi River, go on field trips to the University of Iowa's Museum of Natural History, and have two daily recesses ...

Creative writing, social studies, and computer work have all become occasional indulgences." [20]

More locally, the demographics for the annual high school programming contest held at Rowan University have been changing:

- One regional high school that used to regularly win our contest had all of their programming classes cancelled.
- Another school had all their programming classes cancelled and the freed computers reassigned to No Child Left Behind remedial work.
- One teacher left her high school to teach at a community college because all of her classes were cancelled. [25]

At the same time, the US Bureau of Labor Statistics is projecting that the majority of careers in Computer Science fields are growing much faster than the average for all occupations. [5]

Clearly there is a need to attract more students to Computer Science, and if it is not happening in our schools it may be up to us to introduce the field to our Freshmen. Furthermore, as Computer Scientists, many of us personally feel the urge to evangelize about the subject that we ourselves are so deeply interested in. So how do we capture and maintain student interest?

2.3 The Science of Interest

While the result seems obvious, it is worth noting that educational psychologists have found that the degree of interest a person has in a subject has a powerful influence on his or her ability to learn the material. [14] So assuming that a "cool context" does increase student interest, our gut instinct to incorporate them into our classes is indeed scientifically valid. So what exactly is interest, and how can we create, maintain, and sustain it?

Hidi & Renninger [14] have developed a four-phase model of how a person's interest develops and matures based on empirical studies of interest & learning. The four phases happen sequentially, and the length and character of each phase is influenced by a variety of factors:

- **Phase 1:** Triggered Situational Interest. Some sort of event or information, almost always external, initiates interest.
- **Phase 2:** Maintained Situational Interest. This comes after phase 1 and involves focused attention either over an extended period of time or recurring, and some level of persistence. This phase is almost always externally supported.
- **Phase 3:** Emerging Individual Interest. This phase is "characterized by positive feelings, stored knowledge, and stored value." While this interest is generally self-generated, it requires some continued external support.
- **Phase 4:** Well-Developed Individual Interest. Again this is characterized by positive feelings and an increase in stored knowledge and stored value over phase 3. Phase 4 is typically self generated, but can benefit from external support.

For example, consider two students, Anna and Bob[1] . Both have just graduated from high school, they had similar grades and SAT scores, and no experience with robots or computer programming. Both attend an advising session for undeclared majors the summer before their Freshman year at Our State U, where several faculty members try and recruit them for their classes. Among the classes advertised is an introductory programming class in which students will do much of their programming on small robots. Anna and Bob both watch the professor giving the demonstration. They both find it interesting and both add the handout the professor provides to their ever-growing pile of material they have collected.

After returning to their homes that evening, both Anna and Bob sift through the material they received that day. When Anna gets to the robot programming handout, she thinks about the light-following task the professor demonstrated. She has never really thought about programming before, but the demonstration was kind of cool, and while it seemed quite magical at first, she found the logic behind how the robot followed the light quite satisfying and attractive. She pulls out her laptop and heads over to the URL the professor provided. After some web surfing, she decides to sign up for the course.

In contrast, when Bob sees the robot programming handout, he briefly recalls the various demos in a positive light, but then quickly tosses the paper into the recycle bin and continues on to the others.

Anna and Bob both have a Triggered Situational Interest in robots and computer programming. They are attentive and interested in the professor's demonstrations. But only Anna moves on to Phase 2, a Maintained Situational Interest, which hopefully may progress to Phase 3 as she takes the class in the Fall.

3. THE CONTEXTUAL CONUNDRUM

As illustrated above, an interesting context may provide exactly the trigger that initiates student interest in our field. This would seem to be a strong argument in favor of contextualized approaches to introductory CS courses.

But what then? In my own institution, students like Anna have the option of taking an introductory programming class for non-majors that does use robots. But if Anna decides to become a CS major, she will not have the opportunity to see any robots in her classes again until she takes an advanced elective in her Junior or Senior year.

Of course we're left with an obvious question: is this simply a case of bait-and-switch? Are we introducing students to CS as a fun playground and then subsequently dumping them into the CS quagmire? Or is this insignificant in comparison to the millions of other variables that must exist?

The answer is not at all clear. Given our field's appalling reputation with young people, it seems essential that we work hard to trigger an initial interest in CS. And one would hope that many of those students who are excited enough by an initial course to decide to continue on in the field would discover a love for everything that is Computer Science. But I do have a fear that a student who finds an introductory course accessible and interesting might then declare CS as a major and be subsequently

[1] This case illustration is modeled on one from [14]

overwhelmed by the pace set in our CS1course for majors. Or the student might not be able to succeed in the rigorous mathematics curriculum that we require of our majors. Or the student may simply be disappointed that CS isn't as interesting as they thought it might be.

Of course, any introductory-level course for non majors will provide an incomplete view of the fullness or complexity of the field of study. Some would argue that a student should take the time to review all of the requirements for a given major and consider carefully whether they are making an appropriate choice and that an interesting introductory course should simply serve as the entrance point to further research. But this argument seems a bit unrealistic; I must admit that wasn't how I selected my own major as an undergraduate, and I am confident that the majority of my students don't use that approach either.

4. SEARCHING FOR A SOLUTION

4.1 Context Throughout the Curriculum

One obvious approach would be to extend the context further into the curriculum. For example, the media computation approach offers textbooks through Data Structures [19] and Klassner and Anderson presented an approach to using robots in seven core areas across the CC2001 curriculum [17]

On the one hand, this seems to be the ideal solution to the problem of how to help Anna continue to develop her interest in robotics and computer science. But there are some other factors that should be considered.

First, while I personally find robotics one of the most exciting areas in computer science and perhaps Anna will too, robots are not for everyone. If Bob were to find a different path to the CS major, it is not clear that he would see the addition of robots to several of the required courses in his major beneficial. Indeed, he might even find the recurrence of robots irritating. Perhaps an alternative theme would be of greater benefit to him. Or perhaps he would benefit from a more traditional approach.

Furthermore, it seems likely that the success of any context-based approach across the curriculum depends as much on the quality of instruction as on the context and curriculum. Indeed, according to Huetinck & Munshin [15], "The most significant influence on the successful use of manipulatives is the quality of teacher-conducted instruction in their use." Thus the use of a single context across an entire curriculum would require significant buy-in from the faculty.

Finally, embracing a particular contextual approach throughout the CS curriculum may impose more strict sequencing of courses than might otherwise be necessary. If a student does not successfully complete their algorithms and complexity (using robots) course, should that prevent them from taking operating systems (using robots) the following semester? Will students who transfer to the university from other schools be able to enter the major? What about students who decide after their Freshman year that computer science is actually the major for them, is there any hope that they will be able to complete the program in four years?

4.2 A Personal Perspective

I find it difficult to imagine successfully integrating a single (or even a few) context throughout the curriculum. At the same time, I can't help but feel that we are doing our students a disservice by starting students out with a cool new gadget or tool and subsequently moving back to a keyboard and mouse. As an individual, I can continue to work with a few of the students who are most excited by robots (or animation or music or whatever context we have used in class) after the semester is over and help them maintain and develop their interest. And I suppose it's possible that some of our students continue to "play" in or with the contexts they've been introduced to early on without external support. But I don't see this as a solution.

I have successfully used robots in programming courses for non-majors, and am experimenting with the media computation approach this semester. While I'm impressed by the literature that is beginning to emerge that shows that contextual approaches can improve student success and retention, I'm equally motivated by the simple fact that these approaches are fun and interesting for me.

Have my own students been more engaged, enthusiastic, and successful in my own robot-based courses? It certainly feels to me as though they are, and I believe that as we accumulate more data we will discover that this approach does indeed improve the performance of students in our classes, rather than simply not harming them. But I also question how easy it is to distinguish the effects of a particular pedagogical approach from the effects of having a more engaged and enthusiastic instructor.

4.3 What to Do?

Ambivalent as I may appear, there is no question in my mind that I will continue to use robots and media computation in my own introductory classes for non-majors for the foreseeable future. I do believe it works well for my students. Perhaps it works simply because I am more engaged and enthusiastic about the material than I might otherwise be. But so what? The bottom line is that the early studies do indicate that this approach probably isn't harming my students, and if my engagement results in better teaching, then my students will indeed benefit. Furthermore, there is no requirement that taking on a context means the abandonment of the occasional "traditional" assignment. I do periodically stray from the context I am using and assign my students text-based programming problems. I want them to know that the tools that they are learning are appropriate not only for robots or media but also for figuring out how long it will take to mow a football field or how many friends they can have on facebook before every minute of their day must be dedicated to reading their friends posts.

Should others use contextual approaches? I think that until we find that such approaches genuinely do improve learning, my own answer is for instructors to try out some contexts and see how they feel. If the reaction is "wow, this is cool" then there's no question in my mind they should experiment with them in class. If the reaction is negative, I wouldn't encourage it. But with an instructor who is genuinely neutral about the idea, you'll find me dragging them to watch some of my students' robots dancing around on youtube and to look at pages of images my other students have produced.

4.4 Moving Forward

My goal in writing this paper is to stimulate further discussion among those of us who advocate the use of contextual approaches in introductory Computer Science. I am convinced that they have great value for both non majors and majors, but I do also feel the occasional twinge in my gut that there's something that we as educators are missing. I am hopeful that we can work together as a community to come up with new ideas that will let us support our students throughout their academic careers.

5. REFERENCES

[1] "Alice.org," http://www.alice.org/, accessed July 2010.

[2] "arduino meets processing – PUSHBUTTON," http://webzone.k3.mah.se/projects/arduino-workshop/projects/arduino_meets_processing/instructions/index.html, accessed July 2010.

[3] Clements, D. H. and McMillen, S. 1996, Rethinking "Concrete" Manipulatives. *Teaching Children Mathematics*, 2, 5 (Jan. 1996), 270-279.

[4] "Computer Science Unplugged," http://csunplugged.org/, accessed July 2010.

[5] "Computers Home Page," http://stats.bls.gov/k12/computers.htm, accessed July 2010.

[6] "Concrete Abstractions," http://gustavus.edu/+max/concrete-abstractions-pdfs/index.html, accessed July 2010.

[7] Cooper, S., Dann, W., and Pausch, R. 2003. Teaching objects-first in introductory computer science. In *Proceedings of the 34th SIGCSE Technical Symposium on Computer Science Education* (Reno, Navada, USA, February 19 - 23, 2003). SIGCSE '03. ACM, New York, NY, 191-195. DOI= http://doi.acm.org/10.1145/611892.611966

[8] Driscoll, M. (1982). *Research Within Reach: Secondary School Mathematics, A Research-Guided Response to the Concerns of Educators* (Nov. 1982), National Institute of Education, Washington, D.C.

[9] "EWeek," http://www.eweek.org/site/discovere/activities/pbnj.shtml, accessed July 2010.

[10] Fagin, B. S. and Merkle, L. 2002, Quantitative Analysis of the Effects of Robots on Introductory Computer Science Education, *J. Educ. Resour. Comput.* 2, (4), 2002.

[11] Forte, A., and Guzdial, M. 2005. Motivation and Nonmajors in Computer Science: Identifying Discrete Audiences for Introductory Courses, *IEEE Transactions on Education*, 48(2), 2005, pp. 248-253. http://ieeexplore.ieee.org/search/freesrchabstract.jsp?tp=&arnumber=1427874

[12] Feurzeg, W. 2006. Educational Technology at BBN. *IEEE Ann. Hist. Comput.* 28, 1 (Jan. 2006), 18-31.

[13] Guzdial, M. 2009. Education: Teaching computing to everyone. *Commun. ACM* 52, 5 (May. 2009), 31-33. DOI= http://doi.acm.org/10.1145/1506409.1506420

[14] Hidi, S., & Renninger, K. A. 2006. The Four-Phase Model of Interest Development, *Educational Psychologist,* 41, 2 (2006), 111-127.

[15] Huetinck, L., and Munshin, S. N. 2004. *Teaching Mathematics for the 21st Century: Methods and Activities for Grades 6-12*, (2004), Pearson Prentice Hall.

[16] Kelleher, C. and Pausch, R. 2005. Lowering the barriers to programming: A taxonomy of programming environments and languages for novice programmers. *ACM Comput. Surv.* 37, 2 (Jun. 2005), 83-137. DOI= http://doi.acm.org/10.1145/1089733.1089734

[17] Klassner, F., and Anderson, S., "Lego MindStorms: Not Just for K-12 Anymore," *IEEE Robotics and Automation Magazine*, 10, 2, (June 2003), 12-18.

[18] Lobo, A. F., Baliga, G. R., Bergmann, S., Stone, D., and Shah, A. 2000. Using real-world objects to motivate OOP in a CS1 lab. In *Proceedings of the Fifth Annual CCSC Northeastern Conference on the Journal of Computing in Small Colleges* (Ramapo College of New Jersey, Mahwah, New Jersey, United States). J. G. Meinke, Ed. Consortium for Computing Sciences in Colleges. Consortium for Computing Sciences in Colleges, 144-156.

[19] "Media Computation Teachers Website," http://coweb.cc.gatech.edu/mediaComp-teach#DS, accessed September 2010.

[20] Meier, D. & Wood, G., eds. 2004. *Many Children Left Behind: How the No Child Left Behind Act Is Damaging Our Children and Our Schools*, Beacon Press, 2004.

[21] Moskal, B., Lurie, D., and Cooper, S. 2004. Evaluating the effectiveness of a new instructional approach. In *Proceedings of the 35th SIGCSE Technical Symposium on Computer Science Education* (Norfolk, Virginia, USA, March 03 - 07, 2004). SIGCSE '04. ACM, New York, NY, 75-79. DOI= http://doi.acm.org/10.1145/971300.971328

[22] "Myro Hardware – IPRE Wiki," http://wiki.roboteducation.org/Myro_Hardware#Other_Myro_supported_hardware, accessed July 2010.

[23] Pears, A., Seidman, S., Malmi, L., Mannila, L., Adams, E., Bennedsen, J., Devlin, M., and Paterson, J. 2007. A survey of literature on the teaching of introductory programming. In *Working Group Reports on ITiCSE on innovation and Technology in Computer Science Education* (Dundee, Scotland, December 01 - 01, 2007). J. Carter and J. Amillo, Eds. ITiCSE-WGR '07. ACM, New York, NY, 204-223. DOI= http://doi.acm.org/10.1145/1345443.1345441

[24] "PicoBoard – Sensor Board that works with MIT's Scratch," http://www.picocricket.com/picoboard.html, accessed July 2010.

[25] Provine, D., 2008. Personal Interview, November 13, 2008.

[26] Radev, D., and Levin, L. 2009. Engaging High School Students in Interdisciplinary Studies, *Computing Research News*, 21(4), http://www.cra.org/resources/crn-archive-view/2009/09/

[27] Resnick, M., Maloney, J., Monroy-Hernández, A., Rusk, N., Eastmond, E., Brennan, K., Millner, A., Rosenbaum, E., Silver, J., Silverman, B., and Kafai, Y. 2009. Scratch: programming for all. *Commun. ACM* 52, 11 (Nov. 2009), 60-67. DOI= http://doi.acm.org/10.1145/1592761.1592779

[28] "Scratch: Home: imagine, program, share," http://scratch.mit.edu/, accessed September 2010.

[29] Simon, B., Kinnunen, P., Porter, L., and Zazkis, D. 2010. Experience report: CS1 for majors with media computation.

In *Proceedings of the Fifteenth Annual Conference on innovation and Technology in Computer Science Education* (Bilkent, Ankara, Turkey, June 26 - 30, 2010). ITiCSE '10. ACM, New York, NY, 214-218. DOI= http://doi.acm.org/10.1145/1822090.1822151

[30] Summet, J., Kumar, D., O'Hara, K., Walker, D., Ni, L., Blank, D., and Balch, T. 2009. Personalizing CS1 with robots. In *Proceedings of the 40th ACM Technical Symposium on Computer Science Education* (Chattanooga, TN, USA, March 04 - 07, 2009). SIGCSE '09. ACM, New York, NY, 433-437. DOI= http://doi.acm.org/10.1145/1508865.1509018

[31] Yardi, S. and Bruckman, A. 2007. What is computing?: bridging the gap between teenagers' perceptions and graduate students' experiences. In *Proceedings of the Third international Workshop on Computing Education Research* (Atlanta, Georgia, USA, September 15 - 16, 2007). ICER '07. ACM, New York, NY, 39-50. DOI= http://doi.acm.org/10.1145/1288580.1288586

[32] Zweben, S. 2010. Undergraduate CS Enrollment Continues Rising; Doctoral Production Drops, *Computing Research News,* 22(3), May 2010. http://www.cra.org/uploads/documents/resources/crndocs/issues/0510.pdf

WebMapReduce: An Accessible and Adaptable Tool for teaching Map-Reduce Computing

Patrick Garrity
St. Olaf College
1500 St. Olaf Ave
Northfield, MN 55057
garrity@stolaf.edu

Tim Yates
St. Olaf College
1500 St. Olaf Ave
Northfield, MN 55057
yates@stolaf.edu

Richard Brown
St. Olaf College
1520 St. Olaf Ave
Northfield, MN 55057
rab@stolaf.edu

Elizabeth Shoop
Macalester College
1600 Grand Ave
St. Paul, MN 55105
shoop@macalester.edu

ABSTRACT

WebMapReduce (WMR) is a strategically simplified user interface for the Hadoop implementation of the map-reduce model for distributed computing on clusters, designed so that novice programmers in an introductory CS courses can perform authentic data-intensive scalable computations using the programming language they are learning in their course. WMR currently supports Java, C++, Python, and Scheme computations, and can readily be extended to support additional programming languages, and configured to adapt to the practices at a particular institution for teaching introductory programming. The open-source system is designed to give beginning CS students experience with parallel computing and exposure to concepts of parallelism, at a wide variety of institutions with diverse curricular choices and cluster resources. Potential applications in courses at all undergraduate levels are indicated, and implementation of the WMR software is described.

Categories and Subject Descriptors

D.1.3 [**Programming Techniques**]: Concurrent Programming -- *distributed programming*
K.3.2 [**Computers and Education**]: Computer and Information Science Education -- *Computer science education*
C.5.5 [**Computer Systems Organization**]: Computer System Implementation -- *Servers*
D.2.6 [**Software Engineering**]: Programming Environments -- *Integrated environments*

General Terms

Documentation, Design, Human Factors, Languages.

Keywords

Map-reduce, CS1, introductory course, parallel computing, distributed computing, data-intensive scalable computing, CS curriculum, education

1. INTRODUCTION

In 2004, researchers at Google Corp. published one of the key elements behind the company's meteoric rise to international prominence as a provider of web search and other services, known as the MapReduce system [5]. With this system running on a large computer cluster, Google engineers could perform computations with enormous data, such as the substantial portion of the web that Google includes in web searches, comprising quadrillions of bytes of data. When used with a suitable algorithm, such as the PageRank algorithm for assessing the importance of a web page within a set of pages [2], engineers could perform useful computations in a reasonable amount of time with modest programmer effort. Although MapReduce is a patented, proprietary system, numerous implementations of its underlying algorithmic strategy (which we will call *map-reduce*) have been created, including Apache Foundation's widely-used open-source Hadoop framework [6].

The map-reduce programming model is inspired by a functional programming strategy that LISP programmers have used for decades, in which one function is applied to each element of a list in order to produce a second list, and another function is used to combine the values in the latter list in order to produce a value. Implementations on clusters for processing large data modify this strategy, so that the first function, called the *mapper*, produces key-value pairs, and the second function, called the *reducer*, operates on key-value pairs that have a common key. This supports *data parallelism*: a map-reduce system can launch multiple mappers on different computer nodes in a cluster, each operating on a portion of the large data; and that system can also distribute reducers among different nodes, each handling its own selection of keys. Figure 1 illustrates the behavior of mappers and reducers. Map-reduce implementations such as Hadoop also provide features to support large-scale computations: *fault tolerance* (e.g., by replicating data on a special distributed file system and automatically recovering from crashes of a particular computer during any phase of computation); and *optimization* (e.g., by arranging for local reads and writes by all mappers and reducers, saving network transmission of data for a "shuffling" stage between the completion of mapper computations and the beginning of reducer computations). The resulting system is *scalable*, in that larger data sets can be processed efficiently by adding more nodes and storage to a cluster. In industry, Google, Yahoo, and other companies regularly run MapReduce and Hadoop jobs on clusters with thousands of nodes.

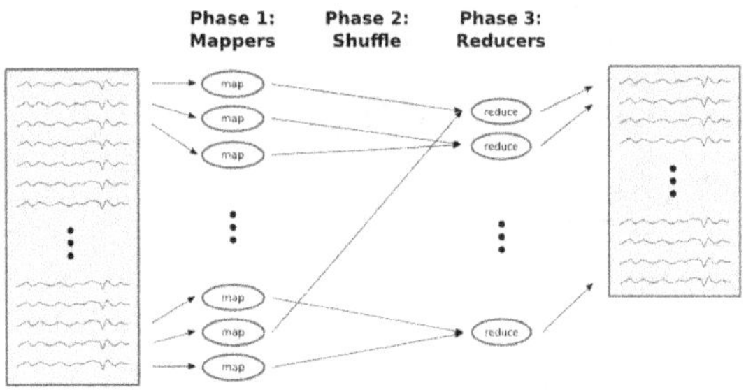

Figure 1. A simplified view of the map-reduce process.

In 2008, Johnson et. al of the University of California at Berkeley described how they teach introductory students about parallelism using a Scheme interface to Hadoop map-reduce computing [9]. The course is taught using a modified version of the STk [13] Scheme interpreter, which they further modified to launch and manage Hadoop jobs on a local cluster. Hadoop mappers and reducers are typically written in Java, so Berkeley used Java-based Scheme interpreter called SISC [12] to carry out Scheme mappers and reducers within a Hadoop job.

Introducing beginning students to concepts of parallelism through map-reduce computing is desirable for several reasons. First, the basic concept of use for the map-reduce framework is simple: in order to run a map-reduce job, a programmer provides only a mapper function, a reducer function, and the data, together with some configuration information. Novice programmers can readily program many useful mapper and reducer routines. Reasoning out the behavior of map-reduce applications naturally brings students to various issues of parallel distributed computing, including the issues described above. Furthermore, map-reduce computing can be a strong motivation for studying parallelism, because of its prominent and growing use in industry, and because of compelling projects that even young students can implement, involving large and interesting data sets.

Scheme, a dialect of LISP, is a natural setting for students to study this functional style of scalable parallel programming. However, other institutions frequently use different languages in their introductory courses. Among these languages is Java, the native language for Hadoop. However, using Hadoop's Java interface for programming mappers and reducers requires programming concepts that are beyond the experience and comfort of many first-course students.

Therefore, we created *WebMapReduce (WMR),* a web-based interface for Hadoop designed to enable introductory and advanced students to program mappers and reducers in several commonly used programming languages. WMR offers the following features:

- The web interface is *strategically simple*, making it accessible for novice programmers but with minimal limitations on the power of Hadoop. Processing terabytes or petabytes of data is still within reach.
- WMR is *extensible and configurable*. At this writing, the system supports writing mappers and reducers in Python, Java, C++, or Scheme, and the system can be extended to support nearly any other programming language. Also, the interface for a given language can be configured for consistency with local preferences.

  For example, one configuration for Scheme mirrors Johnson et al.'s approach to specifying reducers in [9], in which the Scheme addition function + could be a reducer function. In another Scheme configuration, inspired more by Hadoop than LISP, reducer functions receive a stream of values (from key-value pairs with a given key) as an argument, so an iteration that adds those values could be a reducer function. Also, different configurations in C++ might provide different ways to tokenize strings, an operation that might be handled differently at various institutions.
- WMR is *open-source* and can run on *multiple computing platforms*. For example, one may install the system on a local cluster, a standalone computer running Hadoop, or using an Amazon EC2 [1] "cloud cluster," launched from images that are provided on the WMR website [14].

Although we designed WMR for introducing beginning CS students to parallelism, the tool can be used equally well with more advanced students. We hope that the system will help to address the need for teaching parallel computing concepts at all levels of the CS curriculum, through its customizability for particular institutions and through its usability in courses at all levels.

In the remaining sections we will describe the WMR interface, indicate ways WMR has been used in CS courses at two institutions, and explain the system's design and implementation.

2. TOOL DESCRIPTION

WebMapReduce aims to hide implementation details of the underlying map-reduce framework in order to focus on the core programming model. Some of the functions it performs to facilitate this include:

- Providing a web-based GUI rather than a command-line interface
- Using a form for job configuration and translating this to Hadoop's native programmatic configuration
- Compiling and packaging mapper and reducer code (when applicable)
- Storing uploaded input and retrieving and displaying output
- Exposing a simpler programming interface to students

2.1 Language Support and Examples

Support for multiple languages is achieved through a configurable code packaging system, described in more detail in the Design and Implementation section. Each language specifies its interpreter or compiler, as well as an adapter library that is responsible for providing the programming interface for the user. This customizable programming interface gives WMR much of its flexibility and simplicity from the user's perspective: Instructors can tailor it to suit a particular class's experience level, select between a purely-functional or imperative paradigm, or import a library that is familiar to students. The user interface presents a choice of language interface, enabling students to choose among languages they know.

Map-reduce programs in WMR typically consist of two specially-named functions or methods, one each for the map and reduce operations. This, for example, is a word frequency calculator (the "Hello, World!" of map-reduce) written in Python:

```
def mapper(key, val):
  words = key.split()
  for word in words:
    Wmr.emit(word, '1')

def reducer(key, values):
  total = 0
  for count in values:
    total += int(count)
  Wmr.emit(key, total)
```

The `mapper()` function is called for each key-value pair in the input, which in this case consists of a line of text in the key and nothing in the value. First, it splits the line into a list of words. Then, for each one, it outputs a pair where the word itself is the key and a count, 1, is the value. The `reducer()` function is then called for each unique word (key) output from the mapper, receiving an iterator that yields all the values associated with that key. The reducer sums these values to produce the final count, which it outputs in a single "reduced" pair along with the original word.

The programming interface used by the previous example dictates an imperative programming style that mimics (but simplifies) the standard Hadoop approach: the reducer receives of the whole list of values, and results are output through a function call. The next example, in Scheme, is written for an adapter library that follows the style used by Johnson et al. in [9]:

```
(define (make-word-pair word)
  (make-kv-pair word 1))

(define (mapper pair)
  (map make-word-pair
       (string-tokenize (kv-key pair))))

(define (reducer next-value accumulator)
  (+ next-value accumulator))
```

This mapper and reducer (along with the auxiliary `make-word-pair` procedure) perform the same function as the ones in the previous example, but in a purely functional style. The mapper receives a single pair and returns a list of output pairs. The reducer, rather than receiving a list, is called repeatedly on successive values to combine them into the final output. (The `make-kv-pair` and `kv-key` procedures are included for compatibility with Johnson et al.'s interface; they are simply aliases of `list` and `car`.)

As noted by Johnson et al., this style highlights map-reduce's LISP roots, and helps make the concept familiar to Scheme students. The style used is completely determined by the adapter library, and endless variations are possible.

2.2 Interface and Workflow

The WebMapReduce interface guides students through a simple workflow of writing, testing, submitting, and monitoring a map-reduce job. In comparison to the suite of command-line tools used with standard Hadoop, this interface reduces the overhead for students to write their first program.

Figure 2. WebMapReduce job: Screenshot of submission form

The hub of the WMR interface is the job submission form (Figure 2), where users are brought after logging in. The form has three main configuration elements:

- **General information**, including a descriptive name for the job and the language of the mapper and reducer. Other parameters, which are optional and can be safely ignored, are the number of map and reduce "tasks" and a choice between lexicographic and general numeric sort order.
- **Input**. For small files, input can be uploaded or typed directly into the form. For medium to extremely large data sets, there is an option to specify a path to files on the server's distributed file system, where they should be placed beforehand by the instructor.
- **Mapper and reducer source code**. These can be input directly into the form or uploaded as a file.

Once the form is completed, the user has two options: to test the job using a special debugging environment, or submit the job to run in the full map-reduce system. The testing environment (Figure 3) runs the job on a small subset of the input and displays extra information that is difficult or impossible to get from the full map-reduce implementation. Besides helping to locate errors in the code, this can also demonstrate the map-reduce process to students by showing output at both the intermediate and final stages.

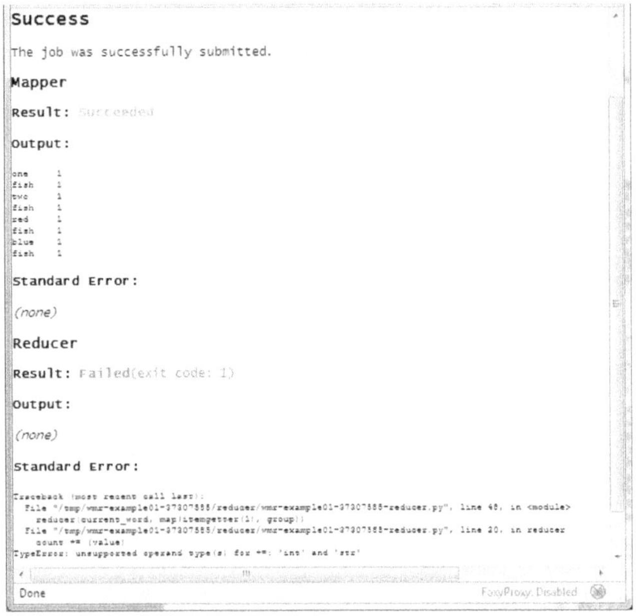

Figure 3. WebMapReduce: Screenshot of test output, showing the result of an error in the reducer.

After the job has been tested and any corrections applied (possibly through several iterations), the user can submit the job to be run with the full input. Since this process can take minutes or potentially even hours depending on the size of the job, WMR presents a status page that the user can refresh to monitor its progress. If the job fails before it completes, the user is notified. Otherwise, the job output is retrieved and displayed upon completion (Figure 4).

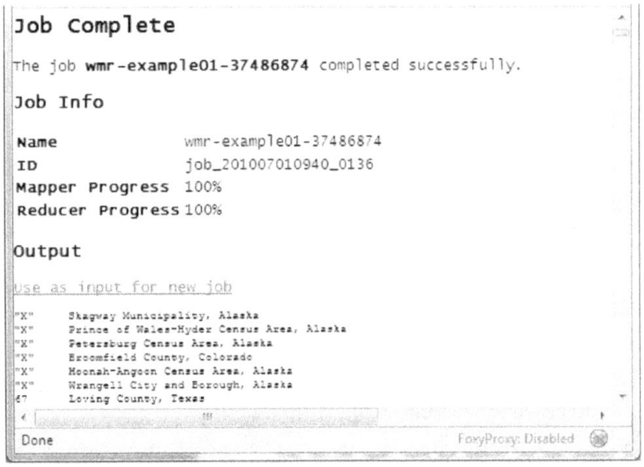

Figure 4. WebMapReduce: Screenshot of final output.

3. USING WMR IN CS COURSES

Although we designed WMR with introductory students in mind, we have found the system very adaptable to a variety of curricular settings. We will outline some of these here, providing some links for more information.

3.1 Introductory Course with Programming

As indicated above, WMR has features for extension to various programming languages and configuration for local pedagogical choices for employing those languages. These features, together with its usability with any cluster platform (including inexpensive cloud computing clusters), make the system a candidate for teaching concepts of parallelism in a wide variety of introductory courses, assuming those courses include beginning programming. We have made available a teaching module for introductory courses that introduces concepts of map-reduce computing, provides elementary hands-on WMR exercises, and discusses more general issues in parallel computing and further strategies for map-reduce computing [10]. Separate versions of that module treat four different programming languages (Java, C++, Python, Scheme). We have informally tested this module at two institutions using various introductory languages, and will conduct formal assessment of this module in Fall 2010 introductory courses at two or more institutions.

Data sets that our introductory students have explored using WMR include collections of classic literary works available from Project Gutenberg [11], the data formerly available for the Netflix prize competition, and snapshots of the complete Wikipedia corpus. Sites such as [4] and [8] provide rich selections of large data sets in many areas of interest.

3.2 Courses in Programming Languages

Because of multi-language support, we have used WMR in a programming language course to introduce a 2.5-day unit on parallel computing. In this context, we exhibited solutions to a single map-reduce problem in multiple languages, inviting a comparison of language practices as well as an initial topic in parallelism. We have made our materials available as part of [3], and are preparing assessment materials.

Note that we strive to produce adapter libraries that represent idiomatic use of each programming language. For instance, reducers traverse their values using language-appropriate iterators in Java and in Python, but streams or LISP combiner functions in Scheme.

3.3 Other Courses

We have used WMR as a quick introduction to parallel computing concepts in other courses as well, such as an intermediate software design course. It has been suggested that WMR could be used in a topics course in parallelism, since substantial map-reduce computing with significant data sets and multiple map-reduce stages could be explored without a steep learning curve, leaving more time for studying other significant forms of parallel computing.

3.4 Project Potential

Because WMR requires only modest CS background, it can readily serve interesting undergraduate projects. We intend to explore such possibilities in final projects for a special section of our introductory course that emphasizes applications to the natural sciences and mathematics. Since some cross-disciplinary projects in our introductory courses have contributed to undergraduate research projects, and since WMR imposes few limitations on the full power of Hadoop map-reduce computing, we hope WMR will prove useful as a prototyping system for advanced parallel computing projects, and perhaps even a production system.

4. PRELIMINARY ASSESSMENT

We have begun formal assessment of teaching materials under development that introduce parallelism to CS1 students using WMR. Here, we report on very preliminary analysis of partial assessment data that we have collected as of early December, 2010. The test population for these data consists of 27 undergraduates taking the introductory course CS 121, *Principles of Computer Science* at St. Olaf College. This course has no prerequisites, and different sections may use different programming languages; nine students were programming in Python, and 18 were programming in Scheme.

The teaching module [10] was assigned as reading and presented in one class hour, including an in-class exercise that involved using WMR, with follow-up discussions in portions of two subsequent class meetings. Two homework sets were assigned and collected during the two weeks after the initial class meetings, which included a Thanksgiving break. Each homework set included three map-reduce programming problems; the first set also included a short answer question about large data sets.

At this writing, 17 students have completed assessment surveys, eight students using Python and nine using Scheme. Students reported completing a mean of 77% of the homework questions in an average estimate of 2.50 hours total effort for two assignments. When asked to rate the difficulty of the WMR homework assignments on a scale of 1 to 5 (3 being "a good level of difficulty", 5 being "far too difficult for me"), seven students rated the difficulty at 3 and the other ten at 4, for an average of 3.59. A few students added verbal comments about the difficulty. None indicated that the map-reduce concepts were beyond them, but some provided feedback for expansions or revisions of the support materials that were uncovered when they worked on their homework. Student use of the WMR system uncovered some unanticipated technical issues; for example, an interaction between Scheme streams (used to deliver values to a reducer function) and Java memory usage occurred when students wrote reducer functions that did not use any of their input values, a case we didn't anticipate. We are responding to these comments, e.g., programming the Scheme interface to WMR to work around that interaction without crashing, and revising our support materials. We also intend to expand the error feedback from WMR's test and production interfaces in response to our classroom observations.

In our test, we found that our Python students apparently found WMR programming easier than our Scheme students (difficulty ratings 3.37 for Python and 3.78 for Scheme). Scheme students reported spending more time on the homework (2.78 hours) than Python students (2.14 hours), although they estimated that they completed a little more of it (82% for Scheme, 71% for Python). However, we now realize that the example Python mapper and reducer functions were quite similar to the programming that our Python students had seen, whereas the Scheme examples included several features that were unfamiliar to our Scheme students (streams, state changes for emitting output rather than delivering return values, string processing such as splitting an input string into words), in addition to the map-reduce concepts themselves.

Since WMR supports customizable programming interfaces, we intend to try Berkeley's more functional approach [9] for programming Scheme mappers and reducers in our next offering, rather than the imperative programming approach we used this semester. Although an imperative approach has algorithmic similarities to map-reduce programming in other languages, the simplicity of Berkeley's approach will reduce the number of new concepts our beginning students must face. We may also precede the map-reduce/WMR presentation with some string processing homework exercises using operations helpful for map-reduce computations, such as splitting lines into words.

Although we discovered these issues in the case of our Scheme students, these concerns indicate the importance of using WMR's customization features to provide an institution's introductory students with a programming style for mappers and reducers that is similar to the programming style used in the rest of the course, whatever the programming language.

5. DESIGN AND IMPLEMENTATION

WebMapReduce is built around the open-source Hadoop map-reduce framework. It is a two part tool that consists of a PHP front end interface and a Java back end server. The server is designed to run on the administration node of a cluster, and the web interface may be hosted by any web server that has access to the back end server. This separation allows greater flexibility in deployment, including indirect access to the Hadoop cluster, which may be behind a firewall. It is, of course, possible to run both on a single machine.

The front end is a simple component that is responsible for authenticating the user, presenting the job submission form, and formatting and displaying results. It forwards requests to the back end using an HTTP-based protocol with XML-formatted responses. This link can be optionally SSL/TLS-encrypted and/or protected with HTTP authentication.

After receiving a job submission request, the back end prepares the provided source code and submits the job to the Hadoop system. It can then, on separate requests from the front end, check the progress of the job, report failures, and display output. The back end can also enforce submission quotas on a total and per-user basis in order to prevent accidental or malicious cluster overload.

Three elements of the system are worth noting: the interaction of the back end with Hadoop, the code processing and language adapter system, and the framework for debugging and testing.

5.1 Interaction with Hadoop

The back end of WMR is implemented in Java in order to permit easy interaction with Hadoop through its API. This is not as straightforward as it may seem, however, since Hadoop is written to function as a command-line tool rather than a library. Many external parameters (environment variables, JVM properties, etc.) must be set for the system to work correctly—parameters that may vary greatly between setups. To address this issue, WMR exploits an ability to run inside Hadoop itself, hosted by Jetty, an embeddable web server used extensively inside Hadoop.

5.2 Language Support

Internally, WMR jobs are run using a modified version of the Hadoop Streaming module. Streaming, a component included in the standard Hadoop distribution, allows jobs to be written in any language by specifying an arbitrary process as the mapper and reducer, sending input through a pipe to the process and reading results from its output stream [7]. Though this interface is flexible, it requires the programmer to write I/O and parsing code for every job, which is too tedious and distracting for novice users.

WMR takes this responsibility away from the student with its system of reusable 'adapter libraries' for each language used on the interface. These libraries implement the common I/O to and from Streaming and, in turn, call the student's code to process the key-value pairs. These libraries can be written to handle various languages and language dialects, giving them the flexibility and control described in earlier sections. WMR's code packaging system adds this adapter library to the user's code in a preprocessing step.

When implementing these adapter libraries, one important concern is maintaining scalability in the I/O code. For instance, the entire list of values for a given key should not be loaded into memory at once, since this list could become very large when processing large inputs. This usually necessitates the use of some sort of iterator instead of a normal list or array.

5.3 Debugging and Testing Jobs

Providing for efficient debugging of map-reduce jobs proved to be a particularly challenging problem. Due to the distributed nature of map-reduce, most errors occur in separate processes or even separate machines. Though Hadoop reports some information about errors back to the main process, much of the more useful data is only available from the remote processes themselves. Hadoop, unfortunately, provides no programmatic way to access these processes.

In order to bypass this limitation, WMR implements a testing environment that mimics the behavior of Hadoop Streaming as closely as possible, while running within a single thread on a single machine. In this envionment, we can collect extra information, such as the error stream and intermediate output, and report it to the user.

This approach has its own disadvantages. Since we cannot mimic all of Hadoop in the testing environment, a job that tests normally may still fail when running in Hadoop—with virtually no useful information when it does. Failures of this kind are often result from mismatches in configuration (e.g., a different version of a library or interpreter on the nodes) rather than bugs in the system itself, so careful administration and thorough testing is often the best remedy. We are considering several possible methods to improve this issue in future releases.

6. CONCLUSIONS AND FUTURE WORK

The map-reduce model for distributed computations involving potentially enormous data provides strong motivation for young CS students to study parallelism, because of its broad applicability and its association with prominent successful corporations. The basic concept of use is simple, and the strategically simplified WebMapReduce interface for Hadoop makes map-reduce computation accessible for beginning programmers, while retaining Hadoop's computational power for large data. The open-source WMR software can operate on various cluster platforms. WMR supports programming of mappers and reducers in multiple languages with customizable configuration, in order to reach a broad array of institutional settings and introductory CS courses. A testing/debugging feature with diagnostic feedback further supports novices learning map-reduce computation. Intermediate and advanced CS undergraduates can also use the system profitably in coursework and realistic projects.

Future work includes modification of Hadoop task management and the Hadoop streaming interface used by WMR, in order to simplify the system's internal operation and maintainability, and to provide better diagnostic information for production (non-testing) map-reduce computations. We also hope to collect feedback on the interface in order to improve usability.

7. ACKNOWLEDGMENTS

Development of WMR was funded by NSF CCLI grant DUE-0942190/0941962, an HHMI grant to St. Olaf College, and additional research support from St. Olaf College. Todd Frederick and Nathaniel Meierpolys implemented an early prototype of the WMR system. We are grateful to the Intel Innovative Software Education Team for providing us with an opportunity to demonstrate WMR throughout SIGCSE 2009.

8. REFERENCES

[1] Amazon Elastic Compute Cloud (Amazon EC2). *http://aws.amazon.com/ec2/*. Accessed: 09-10-2010.

[2] Brin, S. and Page, L. 1998. The anatomy of a large-scale hypertextual Web search engine. *Computer Networks and ISDN Systems*. 30, 1-7 (1998), 107-117.

[3] Concurrency and Map-Reduce Strategies in Various Programming Languages. *http://serc.carleton.edu/csinparallel/modules/concurrency_pl.html*. Accessed: 09-10-2010.

[4] Data.gov. *http://www.data.gov/*. Accessed: 09-10-2010.

[5] Dean, J. and Ghemawat, S. 2004. MapReduce: Simplified Data Processing on Large Clusters. *Operating System Design and Implementation* (San Francisco, CA, December 2004), 137-150.

[6] Hadoop. *http://hadoop.apache.org/*. Accessed: 09-10-2010.

[7] Hadoop Streaming. *http://hadoop.apache.org/common/docs/r0.20.1/streaming.html*. Accessed: 09-10-2010.

[8] Infochimps Data Marketplace. *http://infochimps.org/*. Accessed: 09-10-2010.

[9] Johnson, M. et al. 2008. *Infusing Parallelism into Introductory Computer Science Curriculum using MapReduce*. EECS Department, University of California, Berkeley.

[10] Map-reduce Computing using WebMapReduce. *http://serc.carleton.edu/csinparallel/modules/IntroWMR.html*. Accessed: 09-10-2010.

[11] Project Gutenberg. *http://www.gutenberg.org/wiki/Main_Page*. Accessed: 09-10-2010.

[12] Second Interpreter of Scheme Code. *http://sisc-scheme.org/*. Accessed: 09-10-2010.

[13] STk. *http://kaolin.unice.fr/STk/*. Accessed: 09-10-2010.

[14] WebMapReduce. *http://webmapreduce.sourceforge.net/*. Accessed: 09-10-2010.

Practical Parallel and Concurrent Programming

Caitlin Sadowski
University of California
Santa Cruz, CA, USA
supertri@cs.ucsc.edu

Thomas Ball
Microsoft Research
Redmond, WA, USA
tball@microsoft.com

Judith Bishop
Microsoft Research
Redmond, WA, USA
jbishop@microsoft.com

Sebastian Burckhardt
Microsoft Research
Redmond, WA, USA
sburckha@microsoft.com

Ganesh Gopalakrishnan
University of Utah
Salt Lake City, UT, USA
ganesh@cs.utah.edu

Joseph Mayo
University of Utah
Salt Lake City, UT, USA
u0565813@utah.edu

ABSTRACT

Multicore computers are now the norm. Taking advantage of these multiple cores entails parallel and concurrent programming. There is therefore a pressing need for courses that teach effective programming on multicore architectures. We believe that such courses should emphasize high-level abstractions for performance and correctness and be supported by tools.

This paper presents a set of freely available course materials for parallel and concurrent programming, along with a testing tool for performance and correctness concerns called ALPACA (A Lovely Parallelism And Concurrency Analyzer). These course materials can be used for a comprehensive parallel and concurrent programming course, *à la carte* throughout an existing curriculum, or as starting points for graduate special topics courses. We also discuss tradeoffs we made in terms of what to include in course materials.

Categories and Subject Descriptors

H.3.2 [**Computers and Education**]: Computer and Information Science Education; D.2.8 [**Programming Techniques**]: Concurrent Programming

General Terms

Human Factors, Languages, Performance

1. INTRODUCTION

Once upon a time programmers were taught to write sequential programs, with the expectation that new hardware would make their programs perform faster. In the early 2000s, we hit a power wall [1]. Today, all major chip manufacturers have switched to producing computers that contain more than one CPU [24]. Parallel and concurrent programming has rapidly moved from a special-purpose technique to standard practice in writing scalable programs. The future is upon us, and many undergraduate courses are lagging behind.

Scheduling decisions made by an operating system or a language runtime can dramatically affect the behaviour of parallel and concurrent programs. This makes such programs difficult to reason about, and introduces a whole new set of code bugs students may encounter, such as data races or deadlocks. Students programming for multicore systems also face a new set of potential performance bottlenecks, such as lock contention or false sharing. Concurrency bugs are both insidious and prevalent [8, 14, 16]; we need to ensure that all computer science students know how to identify and avoid them.

We need to start teaching courses that prepare students for multicore architectures now, while concurrently updating the whole curriculum. Since parallel and concurrent programming was previously relevant only to the relatively small collection of students interested in high-performance computing, operating systems, or databases, instructors may need help developing course materials for this new subject. In this paper, we put forward several ideas about how to structure parallel and concurrent programming courses, while also providing a set of concrete course materials and tools.

1.1 Contributions

- We present course materials for a 16 week course in parallel and concurrent programming [2]. We begin by describing the course structure (Section 2), and then discuss the individual units (Section 3).
- We present a testing framework, ALPACA [2], which supports *deterministic* unit tests for parallel and concurrent programs, and allows students to effectively test their concurrent programs. This framework is described in Section 4.
- We discuss tradeoffs we made about what to include (Section 2). We situate these tradeoffs within related work, including comparisons with other courses (Section 5).

2. COURSE STRUCTURE

Practical Parallel and Concurrent Programming (PPCP) is a semester-long course for teaching students how to program parallel/concurrent applications, using the C# and F# languages with other .NET libraries. Taken as a whole,

SIGCSE'11, March 9–12, 2011, Dallas, Texas, USA.

this 16 week (8 unit) course is aimed at upper-division undergraduate students. However, individual units can also be taught *à la carte* and could be integrated into various stages of an existing curriculum. Alternatively, selections from the course materials can form the core structure for an in-depth graduate special topics course.

Parallel and Concurrent.

In the course title, we make a distinction between parallel and concurrent programming. Parallel programming is about improving performance by making good use of the underlying parallel resources of a particular machine (such as multiple cores), or the set of machines in a cluster. Concurrent programming is about improving responsiveness by reacting to simultaneously occurring events (coming from the network, user interface, other computers, or peripherals) in a timely and proper fashion. Programs may exhibit both concurrent and parallel characteristics, thus blurring the distinction; we make such a distinction to emphasize that PPCP includes both parallel and concurrent programming. Other courses may only focus on one of these two facets (Section 5).

Performance and Correctness.

In this course, students learn to write parallel algorithms, and explain (and fix) both performance and correctness bugs. PPCP has a strong emphasis on both correctness and performance, with a slight tilt towards correctness. On the performance side, students will learn how to predict and test parallel speedups, and explain actual performance bottlenecks. On the correctness side, students will develop a vocabulary for reasoning about parallelism and correctness, analyze parallel or concurrent code for correctness, and understand expected invariants in their code.

Breadth-first, Abstraction-first.

PPCP has a breadth-first structure. Since there is not a clear consensus on whether any one parallel or concurrent programming model will emerge as a clear winner [22], we feel that students should be exposed to a variety of paradigms and topics. This course is tilted towards shared memory systems with multiple threads, since we feel it is important to prepare students to succeed in this common case. However, a wide breadth of material is covered, including message passing, data parallelism and even some GPU programming.

This course emphasizes productivity and starts with a high level of abstraction. Abstraction layers, such as the .NET Task Parallel Library (TPL) [15], allow students to quickly write parallel or concurrent programs while avoiding explicit thread management. Figure 1 shows an example generic `ParQuickSort` function which uses `Parallel.Invoke` from the TPL to run quicksort recursively in parallel; programmers do not have to explicitly create or manage threads.

Unfortunately, understanding performance bottlenecks requires moving through abstraction layers. For example, discovering which portions of a program lie along the "critical path" of places where optimizations result in parallel speedup requires analyzing the (high level) task dependency graph for a program, whereas preventing false sharing requires understanding the (low level) cache behaviour. After abstractions are introduced, PPCP shows students how to

```
static void ParQuickSort<T>(T[] arr, int lo, int hi)
            where T: IComparable<T> {
  if (hi-lo <= Threshold) InsertionSort(arr, lo, hi);
  else {
    int pivot = Partition(arr, lo, hi);
    Parallel.Invoke(
      delegate {ParQuickSort(arr, lo, pivot-1);},
      delegate {ParQuickSort(arr, pivot+1, hi);}
    );
  }
}
```

Figure 1: Parallel quicksort with the TPL; Parallel.Invoke() runs a list of delegates in parallel.

break those abstractions when necessary for performance. Students learn the low-level building blocks (such as monitor synchronization and threads) that are combined to build TPL-level abstractions, and the performance effects of these building blocks interacting with a parallel architecture.

Tool-based learning.

PPCP supports a tool-based approach to correctness and performance. We have developed a tool called ALPACA (A Lovely Parallelism and Concurrency Analyzer) which students can use to explore performance and correctness concepts. Students will build an understanding of correctness conditions and performance problems through experimentation. Throughout PPCP, students will regularly analyze their code, including tests of data race detection, deadlock detection and linearizability checking. These tests leverage the CHESS stateless model checker [20] to run unit tests on different thread schedules, increasing the chances that a scheduling-dependent assertion will be tripped. ALPACA tests can also link into a GUI-based performance analysis tool (called TASKOMETER). We believe that this tool-based approach will improve the learning experience by enabling quick and simple analysis to make debugging less frustrating; preliminary observations of students in our Fall 2010 pilot course support this assertion. We have also found ALPACA and TASKOMETER to be extremely useful in debugging our own code. The ALPACA framework is discussed in more depth in Section 4, and is available for download [2].

In addition to ALPACA tool support, the course materials also include slides and lecture notes, which are supported by a selection of programming samples and a recommended textbook. The programming samples include a variety of appealing examples, including small interactive games and visual examples such as ray tracing programs; additional samples are available online [18]. Further reading on course topics can be found in a recommended textbook [6], which is also available online; suggested sections from this textbook are listed at the end of the slides for each lecture and in the lecture notes.

3. UNITS

Figure 2 shows the dependency structure of the eight units. The course material starts at a high level of abstraction by introducing patterns rather than primitives (units 1-4). For example, in the DAG model of parallel computation tasks are represented as nodes and dependencies between parallel tasks are represented as directed edges. This model is presented in Unit 1 and can be used to reason about both performance and correctness in future units. In later units

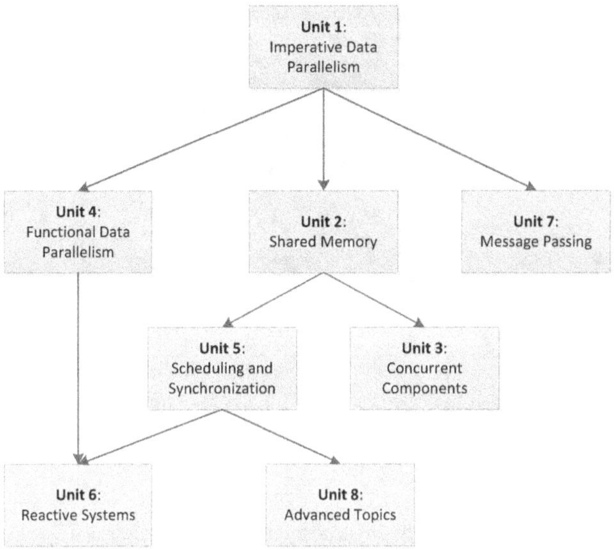

Figure 2: Unit dependencies.

(Unit 5 & 8), these abstractions are peeled back to expose the underlying primitives (e.g. threads and low-level synchronization). PPCP also includes an introduction to message passing (Unit 7) for distributed systems, and a unit specifically focused on concurrency (Unit 6).

3.1 Unit 1: Imperative Data Parallelism

Students are motivated when they initially write programs that demonstrate parallel speedups [13]. Unit 1 introduces data and task parallelism and emphasizes pleasing parallelization of independent loops. This unit teaches students to use abstractions from the TPL, such as Parallel.For loops, which execute iterations in parallel, and lightweight concurrent tasks. It also contains a set of core abstractions that can be used to reason about performance and correctness such as the DAG model of computation and Amdahl's law, which provides an upper bound on the performance gain from parallelizing a sequential program. This unit also introduces the concept of unit testing.

3.2 Unit 2: Shared Memory

Unit 2 is an in-depth look at correctness and performance issues under the shared memory model. This unit introduces the concept of locks and details strategies for preventing data races, including proper synchronization, isolation of data by partitioning across threads, and making shared data immutable. Building on these foundations, Unit 2 then teaches students to identify and fix other concurrency errors such as atomicity violations or deadlocks. This unit also delves into common performance bottlenecks, such as false sharing, data locality, task creation overheads, and synchronization overheads. The last lecture in this unit introduces a selection of high-level design patterns which can be used to avoid concurrency bugs. For example, the producer-consumer pattern reduces data sharing to a thread-safe buffer.

3.3 Unit 3: Concurrent Components

Unit 3 is focused on building thread-safe components, an important skill for many programmers [10]. This unit teaches students how to leverage interface-level specifications and determinism analysis when adding internal parallelism to a component. This unit also discusses important thread-safety concepts (such as linearizability) for reasoning about how concurrent accesses to the same component interact.

3.4 Unit 4: Functional Data Parallelism

Unit 4 emphasizes the nice match between sets and parallelism through mediums such as parallel queries with PLINQ (Parallel Language-Integrated Queries) [17], parallel functional programming with F#, and array parallel algorithms with Accelerator [25]. In the PLINQ section of this unit, students will learn how to write LINQ queries, make them parallel, and get speedup in their programs. LINQ queries provide a distinctive way to structure code and get information from data structures with database-like queries. This data-first view may help clarify the parallelism in an algorithm. Parallel functional programming with F# is an immutability-first programming style which strives to minimize global variables and so prevent errors, such as data races, caused by inadequately protected shared data. Accelerator allows students to harness the power of Graphics Processing Units (GPUs) to quickly run data parallel computations over arrays.

3.5 Unit 5: Scheduling and Synchronization

Unit 5 peels back the abstractions introduced in other units. The first part of this unit is focused on how threads are mapped to cores, and how to synchronize between threads. This unit also covers how high-level synchronization (such as semaphores) can be built from low-level synchronization primitives (such as Interlocked operations). After this, Unit 5 includes a section devoted to correctness issues for the threading model. Students learn to reason about programs as state machines and to build and analyze synchronization protocols. The last section of this unit focuses on how tasks are mapped to threads. This unit concludes with a discussion of the threadpool and scheduling decisions made by the TPL, and strategies for customizing and building a work-stealing scheduler.

3.6 Unit 6: Interactive/Reactive Systems

Unit 6 focuses on reactive programming, where a program must handle many requests from the environment in a responsive fashion. This unit focuses on various patterns for asynchronous programming, building on principles of state machines established in Unit 5. State machines underlie many of the technologies discussed, such as F#'s `async` construct and Reactive Extensions for .NET.

3.7 Unit 7: Message Passing

Unit 7 presents a tutorial on conventional MPI-style message passing programming. We wrote a simplified implementation of MPI [11] inside the C# framework so that students have a more seamless entry to this paradigm and a consistent programming language syntax structure to work with. This unit introduces students to write programs suitable for distributed systems. It also provides a simple formal model of message passing.

3.8 Unit 8: Advanced Topics

Unit 8 is a catchall collection of some advanced topics that can be included as time permits. These topics can also

```
Object[] arr;

public int ProcessArray()
{
  int accum = 0;
  for (int i = 0; i < arr.Length; ++i)
  {
    if (arr[i] != null)
    {
      accum += arr[i].count;
      arr[i] = null;
    }
  }
}
```

Figure 3: Code snippet involving a data race.

```
[UnitTestMethod]
public void ProcessTest()
{
  Console.WriteLine("Processing....");
  Parallel.Invoke(
      () => {ProcessArray();},
      () => {ProcessArray();}
  );
}
```

Figure 4: Sample unit test of the snippet in Figure 3.

be focused on in more depth for a graduate special topics course. Advanced topics currently include a section on memory models, a section that has a detailed focus on caching behaviours, a section on safe strategies for lock-free data structure creation, plus a section on alternative programming models to synchronization such as transactions or revisions [5]. We may add additional topics to this unit, based on feedback from the initial iterations of the course.

4. ATTRIBUTE-BASED TESTING

Concurrency bugs are insidious. They only manifest on particular schedules, and so cannot be found with traditional testing methods. For example, imagine there are multiple simultaneous calls to `ProcessArray()` in the code snippet in Figure 3. These calls may successfully execute hundreds of times before the program crashes. However, it is possible for two threads to simultaneously verify that a particular array entry is non-null, and then one thread tries to access the `count` field after the other thread has nulled out the entry! Testing this method may or may not cause the program to crash with a null pointer exception. Even when an error manifests, it may be extremely difficult to reproduce.

In order to effectively test parallel or concurrent programs, the test suite must somehow control the scheduling of operations, and drive execution down the path of multiple different schedules. This process is called *stateless model checking*.[1] Of course, enumerating all possible schedules would be too slow. CHESS [20] is a stateless model checking framework which uses sophisticated heuristics [19] to decide which schedules to prioritize. In addition, CHESS has built-in analyses which can be used to detect concurrency bugs such as data races or deadlocks.

The ALPACA tool allows programmers to add attributes to unit test methods that enable different types of concurrency error detection and utilizes CHESS to both run the

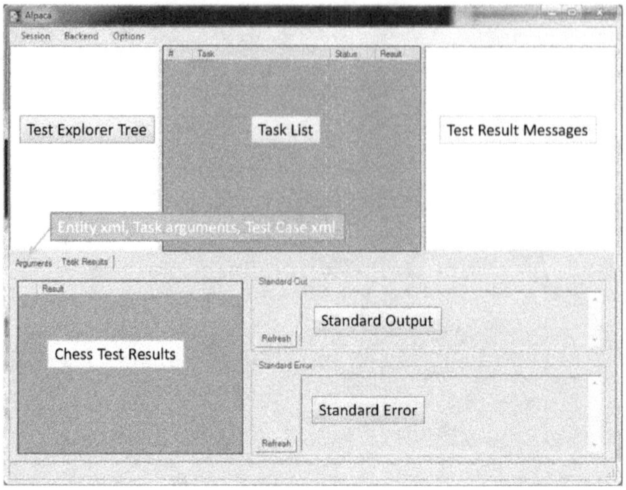

Figure 5: Screenshot of the Alpaca tool

test methods on different schedules and analyze the tests for concurrency errors. Figure 4 shows an example ALPACA test. The `[UnitTestMethod]` annotation tells ALPACA to run the `ProcessTest()` method as a unit test, without any additional concurrency checking.

Once the student annotates test methods with different attributes, the concurrent unit tests can be run in the ALPACA UI (Figure 5). The tree of current test methods is displayed in the top left corner; students can use this tree to select which tests to run and then run them. The task list pane (top center) displays the status of currently executing tests. The test result message pane (top right) displays the result of running each test. More detailed information about the errors found in a particular selected test will display in the chess test results pane (bottom left). The bottom right pane displays standard output or standard error. The performance overhead of logging complete information about thread interactions ("tracing") is too high to be always executing. If a test results in an error state, the student can choose to replay the test with tracing and then interactively explore the thread interactions which led to the bug.

We created ALPACA as a way to make the CHESS research tool suitable for pedagogical use. The research tool originally matched tests to executables in a one-to-one way; this meant that the programmer was responsible for creating a separate executable for each unit test. Now programmers can just annotate methods for testing. Furthermore, the research tool user needed to understand many command-line flags, and set up an XML file for the test suite. Instead of command-line flags, the new framework allows the programmer to specify different test types. We wanted to make the interface completely interoperable for different types of test methods, so we had to change the framework to provide cleaner abstractions, and support multiple test types (such as performance or unit tests).

The ALPACA framework supports several different types of attributes; we briefly overview four of them here:

- `[UnitTestMethod]`
  This attribute tells ALPACA to just run the test, without controlling the scheduling or detecting any extra concurrency errors. This attribute is similar to Visual Studio's `[TestMethod]` attribute.

[1]"Stateless" refers to the fact that there is not a separate explicit model of the program.

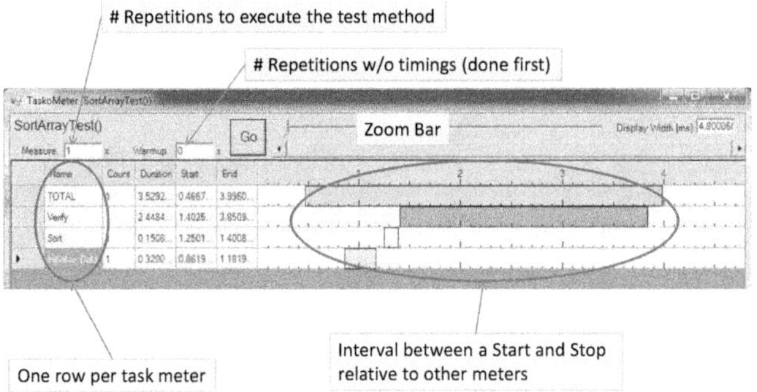

Figure 6: Screenshot of the TaskoMeter tool

- `[PerformanceTestMethod]`
  This attribute will open up the TaskoMeter user interface (Figure 6) upon running the test. The programmer must demarcate code sections where performance measurements are desired. TaskoMeter displays timing information across different threads within these programmer-defined sections.
- `[ScheduleTestMethod]`
  When a test with this attribute is run, it will run under the CHESS direct execution model checker, to test for deadlocks and assertion violations on different schedules.
- `[DataRaceTestMethod]`
  A test with this attribute behaves very similar to one with the `[ScheduleTestMethod]` attribute. However, the system explores less schedules but checks for data races on those observed schedules.

5. RELATED WORK

5.1 Unit Testing in Education

A number of researchers have advocated the inclusion of test-driven development into the computer science (CS) curriculum [12, 21, 23]. However, testing concurrent programs is extremely difficult [14]. Because testing frameworks usually do not control scheduling of multiple threads, the results of testing are nondeterministic. In particular, tests do not necessarily expose concurrency-specific bugs such as data races or deadlocks (Figure 3).

Previous pedagogical tool suites exist [3, 7]. However, Alpaca is unique in being tightly coupled with both a set of course materials and a unit testing framework. Ricken et al. [21] present some examples of concurrent unit tests in ConcJUnit; these examples are suitable for an educational context. ConcJUnit is a framework that ensures that all threads spawned in unit tests terminate, but does not explicitly check for concurrency-specific bugs (such as race conditions). Furthermore, since ConcJUnit tests do not control scheduling, they may be nondeterministic. In contrast, Alpaca tests check for concurrency-specific errors, control scheduler-dependent non-determinism, and run the unit tests on different thread schedules.

5.2 Multicore Curricula

Some researchers have advocated sprinkling parallelism and concurrency throughout the CS curriculum and introducing these topics in introductory courses [9, 4]. Although we believe that concurrency should be better integrated with the entire CS curriculum, doing so requires widespread changes. Additionally, special-purpose parallel and concurrent programming courses can help fill the gaps for current students while introduction of concurrency in introductory courses is phased in. For these reasons, the focus of this paper is on the content and structure for a dedicated parallel and concurrent programming course. However, individual course units could be used *à la carte* at different points throughout a curriculum. Additionally, the Alpaca framework could be used independently from the course materials.

Suzanne Rivore [22] presents a breadth-first course in multicore programming. This course is an upper-division elective which covers three different paradigms: shared memory with OpenMP, pattern-based parallel programming with Intel's Thread Building Blocks (TBB), and a graphics processors (GPU) programming model with nVidia's CUDA library. These three paradigm-focused course subsections were followed by reading technical papers on other advanced topics within parallel and concurrent programming. Performance profiling was also an important part of the code development process for students. Students found that learning the different syntax and style of the three paradigms was challenging. Although PPCP covers a wide breadth of paradigms, these paradigms are presented in an interoperable framework. We discuss shared memory with threads and synchronization in Unit 5, pattern-based parallel programming with the TPL in Unit 1, and GPU programming with Accelerator in Unit 4: all of these programming models use C# syntax and the same development environment.

5.3 Comparison to Other Courses

The University of California at Berkeley and the University of Illinois at Urbana-Champagne both make up the well-funded Universal Parallel Computing Research Center (UPCRC). For this reason, we focus the following section on courses taught at these schools.

GPU-based courses.

Several courses exist which target programming on graphics processing units (GPUs). These include "Applied Parallel Programming" at UIUC, which is focused on CUDA programming tools and scientific computing workloads. We briefly touch on GPU programming with the presentation of Accelerator in Unit 4. However, PPCP is focused on general programming and has more breadth.

Multicore Programming Courses.

Several multicore-themed courses exist, including Berkeley's "Parallel Programming for Multicore" and "Applications of Parallel Computers". These courses are mostly focused on shared memory programming using Posix threads. "Parallel Programming" at UIUC starts with several lectures on MPI, and then moves on to object-based parallel programming (Charm++), followed by OpenMP and a few other language models (such as high performance FORTRAN) and performance bottlenecks.

All the above courses are more focused on parallelism than concurrency and performance over correctness. Also, they do not include the tool support found with Alpaca. Unlike these courses, PPCP leverages the TPL to start at a high level of abstraction, and provides a unified framework for introducing a variety of programming models.

6. FUTURE WORK

A pilot version of PPCP is being taught at the University of Utah in Fall 2010, while this article goes to press. A second pilot will be taught at the University of Washington in Spring 2011. We are collecting survey data from the students enrolled in the initial pilot course; we also have developed feedback surveys for teachers who use PPCP materials and for anyone who reviews the online course materials. We plan to incorporate feedback from these evaluations.

We are working to develop additional materials; we are currently writing more example programs, as well as slides for lab sessions.We are also incorporating new tests into ALPACA, such as MPI analyses.

7. ACKNOWLEDGEMENTS

Special thanks to Sherif Mahmoud and Chris Dern for their support.

8. ADDITIONAL AUTHORS

Additional Authors (Redmond, WA, USA): Madanlal Musuvathi (Microsoft Research, email: madanm@microsoft.com), Shaz Qadeer (Microsoft Research, email: qadeer@microsoft.com), and Stephen Toub (Microsoft, email: stoub@microsoft.com)

9. REFERENCES

[1] K. Asanovic, R. Bodik, J. Demmel, T. Keaveny, K. Keutzer, J. Kubiatowicz, N. Morgan, D. Patterson, K. Sen, J. Wawrzynek, D. Wessel, and K. Yelick. A view of the parallel computing landscape. *Communications of the ACM*, 52(10):56–67, 2009.

[2] T. Ball, S. Burckhardt, G. Gopalakrishnan, J. Mayo, M. Musuvathi, S. Qadeer, and C. Sadowski. Practical parallel and concurrent programming course materials. http://ppcp.codeplex.com/.

[3] M. Ben-Ari. A suite of tools for teaching concurrency. *SIGCSE Bulletin*, 36(3):251–251, 2004.

[4] K. Bruce, A. Danyluk, and T. Murtagh. Introducing concurrency in CS 1. In *Technical Symposium on Computer Science Education (SIGCSE)*, 2010.

[5] S. Burckhardt, A. Baldassion, and D. Leijen. Concurrent programming with revisions and isolation types. In *Symposium on Object-Oriented Programming Systems, Languages, and Applications (OOPSLA)*, 2010.

[6] C. Campbell, R. Johnson, A. Miller, and S. Toub. *Parallel Programming with Microsoft .NET: Design Patterns for Decomposition and Coordination on Multicore Architectures.* Microsoft Press, 2010. http://parallelpatterns.codeplex.com/.

[7] S. Carr, J. Mayo, and C. Shene. ThreadMentor: a pedagogical tool for multithreaded programming. *Journal on Educational Resources in Computing (JERIC)*, 3(1):1, 2003.

[8] S. Choi and E. Lewis. A study of common pitfalls in simple multi-threaded programs. *SIGCSE Bulletin*, 32(1):329, 2000.

[9] D. Ernst and D. Stevenson. Concurrent CS: preparing students for a multicore world. In *Conference on Innovation and Technology in Computer Science Education (ITiCSE)*, 2008.

[10] A. Fekete. Teaching students to develop thread-safe Java classes. In *Conference on Innovation and Technology in Computer Science Education (ITiCSE)*, 2008.

[11] W. Gropp, E. Lusk, and A. Skjellum. *Using MPI: portable parallel programming with the message passing interface.* The MIT Press, 1999.

[12] D. Janzen and H. Saiedian. Test-driven learning: intrinsic integration of testing into the CS/SE curriculum. In *Technical Symposium on Computer Science Education (SIGCSE)*, 2006.

[13] D. Joiner, P. Gray, T. Murphy, and C. Peck. Teaching parallel computing to science faculty: best practices and common pitfalls. In *Symposium on Principles and Practice of Parallel Programming (PPoPP)*, 2006.

[14] E. Lee. The problem with threads. *Computer*, 39(5):33–42, 2006.

[15] D. Leijen, W. Schulte, and S. Burckhardt. The design of a task parallel library. *SIGPLAN Notices*, 44(10):227–242, 2009. http://msdn.microsoft.com/en-us/library/dd460717.aspx.

[16] S. Lu, S. Park, E. Seo, and Y. Zhou. Learning from mistakes: a comprehensive study on real world concurrency bug characteristics. *SIGPLAN Notices*, 43(3):329–339, 2008.

[17] Microsoft. Parallel Language-Integrated Queries (PLINQ). http://msdn.microsoft.com/en-us/library/dd460688.aspx.

[18] Microsoft. Parallel programming samples for .NET 4. http://code.msdn.microsoft.com/ParExtSamples.

[19] M. Musuvathi and S. Qadeer. Iterative context bounding for systematic testing of multithreaded programs. *SIGPLAN Notices*, 42(6):446–455, 2007.

[20] M. Musuvathi, S. Qadeer, T. Ball, G. Basler, P. Nainar, and I. Neamtiu. Finding and reproducing heisenbugs in concurrent programs. In *Symposium on Operating Systems Design and Implementation (OSDI)*, 2008.

[21] M. Ricken and R. Cartwright. Test-first Java concurrency for the classroom. In *Technical Symposium on Computer Science Education (SIGCSE)*, 2010.

[22] S. Rivoire. A breadth-first course in multicore and manycore programming. In *Technical Symposium on Computer Science Education (SIGCSE)*, 2010.

[23] J. Spacco and W. Pugh. Helping students appreciate test-driven development (TDD). In *Symposium on Object-Oriented Programming Systems, Languages, and Applications (OOPSLA)*, 2006.

[24] H. Sutter. The free lunch is over: A fundamental turn toward concurrency in software. *Dr. Dobbs Journal*, 30(3):16–20, 2005.

[25] D. Tarditi, S. Puri, and J. Oglesby. Accelerator: using data parallelism to program GPUs for general-purpose uses. *SIGOPS Operating Systems Review*, 40(5):325–335, 2006. http://research.microsoft.com/en-us/projects/Accelerator/.

Teaching Concurrency-Oriented Programming with Erlang

Ariel Ortiz
Information Technology Department
Tecnológico de Monterrey, Campus Estado de México
Atizapán de Zaragoza, Estado de México, Mexico. 52926
ariel.ortiz@itesm.mx

ABSTRACT

Teaching how to write correct programs is hard; teaching how to write correct concurrent programs is even harder. There is a desperate need for a better concurrency programming model than what most people are currently using. The Erlang programming language might be a step in that direction. This paper provides an overview of Erlang and how it has been successfully used to teach concurrency-oriented programming (COP) in a sophomore level course at the Tecnológico de Monterrey, Campus Estado de México.

Categories and Subject Descriptors

K.3.2 [**Computers & Education**]: Computer & Information Science Education—*Computer Science Education*; D.1.3 [**Programming Techniques**]: Concurrent Programming—*Distributed programming, Parallel programming.*

General Terms

Design, Languages, Performance.

Keywords

Concurrency, Programming, Languages, Erlang, Parallel, Distributed, Functional, Multi-core.

1. INTRODUCTION

Concurrency is a difficult topic. So, as computer science educators, why do we bother with it? The CS2008 Review Taskforce [4] has an answer to this question:

> The development of multi-core processors has been a significant recent architectural development. To exploit this fully, software needs to exhibit concurrent behavior; this places greater emphasis on the principles, techniques and technologies of concurrency. ... Such a view implies that the increased emphasis on concurrency will not be a passing fashion but rather it represents a fundamental shift towards greater attention to concurrency matters. ... The increased ubiquitous nature of computing and computers represents a further factor in heightening the relevance of this topic and again there is every indication that this will only gain further momentum in the future.

Applications will increasingly need to be concurrent if they want to fully exploit continuing exponential CPU throughput gains. Herb Sutter, in his famous article entitled "The Free Lunch Is Over: A Fundamental Turn Toward Concurrency in Software" [16], states that concurrency is the next major revolution in how we write software:

> Different experts still have different opinions on whether it will be bigger than OO, but that kind of conversation is best left to pundits. For technologists, the interesting thing is that concurrency is of the same order as OO both in the (expected) scale of the revolution and in the complexity and learning curve of the technology.

Later in that same article, Sutter asserts the following:

> The mainstream state of the art revolves around lock-based[1] programming, which is subtle and hazardous. We desperately need a higher-level programming model for concurrency than languages offer today.

Joe Armstrong, the main designer of the Erlang programming language, agrees with this assertion, and proposes his solution [2]:

> Using essentially sequential programming languages to write concurrent programs is difficult and leads to the notion that concurrent programming is difficult; indeed writing concurrent programs in languages like Java or C++ which were designed for sequential programming is very difficult. This is not due to the nature of concurrency itself, but rather to the way in which concurrency is implemented in these languages.
>
> There is a generation of languages, which includes Erlang and Oz, in which writing concurrent programs is the natural mode of expression.

2. CONCURRENCY OVERVIEW

2.1 Defining Concurrency

A program is considered to be *concurrent* if it has more than one active execution context (a.k.a. thread of control). According to [15], concurrency has at least three important motivations:

[1]The term *lock-based* refers to synchronization mechanisms such as semaphores, monitors or mutexes.

SIGCSE'11, March 9–12, 2011, Dallas, Texas, USA.

1. **To capture the logical structure of a problem.** Some programs are said to be *embarrassingly parallel*. This means that little or no effort is required to separate the problem into a number of independent tasks. Typical examples include: serving static files on a web server, brute force searches in cryptography, and rendering of computer graphics.

2. **To exploit extra processors, for speed.** In the past, multiprocessor[2] systems used to be expensive and rare. Today they are cheap and fairly common. Many laptops and even some netbook computers currently come with a dual-core CPU. To use these processors effectively, programs must generally be written with concurrency in mind [7].

3. **To cope with separate physical devices.** A program that runs on a group of computers scattered across a network is inherently concurrent. In a similar vein, embedded applications often have separate processors for each of several physical devices. Some examples: medical equipment, home automation, and automobiles.

The term *concurrent* describes a system in which at least two tasks may be underway at the same time. On a single core processor, concurrency can be achieved using time-shared preemptive threads or processes. A concurrent system is *parallel* if more than one task can be physically active at once. To achieve this, a multiprocessor system is required. A parallel system is *distributed* if its processors are associated with devices that are physically separated from one another. Under these definitions, "concurrent" applies to all three motivations. "Parallel" applies to the second and third, while "distributed" applies to only the third [15]. Erlang simplifies the construction of all these types of applications.

2.2 Concurrency-Oriented Programming

Concurrency-oriented programming (COP) is a term coined by Joe Armstrong [2]. He argues that a concurrency-oriented language should offer a good support for concurrency in the same way that an object-oriented language offers good support for objects. In COP, the programmer breaks up the solution of a problem into a number of parallel processes; a concurrency-oriented language should make this easy, while its runtime environment should make it inexpensive.

2.3 To Mutate, Or To Not Mutate

At the end of Part I of [7], there is a "concurrency cheat sheet" that summarizes a set of eleven rules that should be followed in order to write good concurrent code. Although these rules were written specifically for Java, they actually apply to other object-oriented languages that rely on threads and shared memory:

1. *It's the mutable state, stupid.*
2. *Make fields final unless they need to be mutable.*
3. *Immutable objects are automatically thread-safe.*
4. *Encapsulation makes it practical to manage the complexity.*
5. *Guard each mutable variable with a lock.*
6. *Guard all variables in an invariant with the same lock.*
7. *Hold locks for the duration of compound actions.*
8. *A program that accesses a mutable variable from multiple threads without synchronization is a broken program.*
9. *Don't rely on clever reasoning about why you don't need to synchronize.*
10. *Include thread safety in the design process—or explicitly document that your class is not thread-safe.*
11. *Document your synchronization policy.*

Almost all of these rules relate to the difficulties and complexities associated with the synchronization of access to mutable variables and data structures. If mutation is eliminated, most of these problems disappear. Functional programming disallows (or at least discourages) mutation, thus simplifying the development of concurrent programs. Erlang is a functional programming language. When it comes to programming concurrent applications, the consequences of having non-mutable state are enormous. In Erlang, there is no mutable state, there is no shared memory, and there are no locks. This makes it relatively easy to parallelize programs.

3. ERLANG OVERVIEW

Erlang is a general-purpose programming language and runtime environment. Erlang has built-in support for concurrency, distribution and fault tolerance. Named after the Danish mathematician Agner Krarup Erlang, it was developed at the Swedish telecom company Ericsson in the late 1980s. It started as a platform for developing soft real-time software for managing phone switches. It has since been open-sourced and ported to several common platforms. Erlang's minimal set of concurrency primitives, together with its rich and well-used libraries, give guidance to anyone trying to design a concurrent program [10].
In recent years several trade books covering Erlang have been released, including [3, 5, 11]. All of them are geared towards experienced programmers.

3.1 Main Features

Erlang offers some quite interesting features. Here are some of the most relevant ones [6]:

- The language source code is compiled into a platform independent bytecode, which is later executed by a virtual machine (VM).
- A read-eval-print loop (REPL) is provided to allow interactive development and exploration.
- Variables can be bound to a value only once. This is known as "single assignment", and it eliminates several kinds of common concurrency bugs.
- Pattern matching is used to bind variables to values. It can be explicit, as when the `=` (pattern matching operator) is used, or implicit, as when a function call is processed and a function's actual arguments are matched with its formal parameters.
- The type system is strong and dynamic. Variables are not declared. Types are determined at runtime, as is the viability of any operation.

[2]Most common multiprocessor systems today use a symmetric multiprocessing (SMP) architecture. An SMP machine has two or more identical CPUs that are connected to a single shared memory. These CPUs may be on a single multicore chip, spread across several chips, or a combination of both.

- Supported data types include: numbers (integers and floats), atoms, lists, tuples, functions, binaries (untyped arrays), processes, and ports (I/O streams).
- Concurrency is achieved through lightweight processes instead of threads. Unlike threads, processes do not share memory. A typical application can be made from thousands to millions of these extremely lightweight processes. Concurrency belongs to the VM and not the operating system.
- Processes interact only by sending asynchronous messages to each other.
- Location transparency allows sending messages to a process on a local or remote VM using the same semantics.
- Symmetric multiprocessing (SMP) support provides multiple native threads that run Erlang processes. The use of native threads allows machines with multiple CPUs to make effective use of the additional CPUs.
- Garbage collection (GC) is done per process. A system may have thousands of processes, but if GC is only required for a single process, then the collector only touches the heap belonging to that process, thus making collection time practically imperceptible.
- Hot code swapping allows upgrading code without needing to restart an application. This is extremely important for systems that can't tolerate any downtime.
- The standard Erlang distribution comes with the OTP (Open Telecom Platform) framework. OTP is a set of libraries and procedures used for building large-scale, fault-tolerant, distributed applications.
- There are several mechanisms for inter-language working. This means that Erlang code can be combined to work with Java, C++ and quite a few other languages.

Because of its performance characteristics and language and library support, Erlang is particularly good for [10]:

- Irregular concurrency—applications that need to derive parallelism from disparate concurrent tasks.
- Network servers.
- Distributed systems.
- Parallel databases.
- GUIs and other interactive programs.
- Monitoring, control, and testing tools.

On the other hand, Erlang tends not to be well suited for:

- Floating-point-intensive code.
- Code requiring an aggressive optimizing compiler.
- Code requiring non-portable instructions.
- Projects to implement libraries that must run under other execution environments, such as the Java Virtual Machine (JVM) or the Common Language Runtime (CLR).

3.2 Examples

The following examples should give some idea of what Erlang code looks like.

3.2.1 Factorial

Given the mathematical definition for computing the factorial of a positive number n:

$$n! = \begin{cases} 1 & \text{if } n = 0 \\ n \times (n-1)! & \text{if } n > 0 \end{cases}$$

This is how it translates into Erlang code:

```
fact(0) -> 1;
fact(N) when N > 0 -> N * fact(N-1).
```

The `fact` function is implemented by two clauses, separated by a semicolon. The final clause always ends with a period. When `fact` is called, the actual parameters are tested against the patterns in each clause head in turn to find the first match, then the body (after the arrow `->`) is evaluated. Variables, including parameters, are identifiers that must start with a capital letter. The expression after the `when` keyword is a *guard* (a condition that places an additional constraint to the function clause). The value of the final expression in the body is the return value of the call; no explicit `return` statement is needed. As mentioned before, Erlang is dynamically typed, so a call to `fact("boo-boo")` will compile but will raise a runtime exception when an operation with incorrect argument types is attempted.

3.2.2 List Insertion

The following code implements the function `insert`. It takes two arguments: a number N and a list of numbers L in ascending order. It returns a new list with the same elements as L but with N inserted in such a place so as to maintain all the elements of the list in ascending order.

```
insert(N,[]) -> [N];
insert(N,[H|T]) when N < H -> [N,H|T];
insert(N,[H|T]) -> [H|insert(N,T)].
```

The first clause says that if you try to insert a number N into an empty list, the result is a one element list containing N. The second clause says that if you try to insert N into a list, where H is the head (first element) of the list and T is the tail (rest) of the list, and $N < H$, then the result is the list T but with N and H placed at the beginning. If these two clauses do not match (in other words, the list is not empty and $N \geq H$), then the body of the last clause calls itself recursively, inserting N into T; the final result is the list returned by the recursive call but adding H as its head.

3.2.3 Sorting

Using the `insert` function from the previous example, an insertion sort algorithm can be implemented in a fairly straightforward fashion:

```
sort([]) -> [];
sort([H|T]) -> insert(H,sort(T)).
```

The first clause establishes that an empty list is an ordered list. The second clause says that to sort a list, just insert the head of the list into the result of sorting its tail.

3.2.4 Process Handling

The following contrived example demonstrates how to use Erlang's concurrency primitives. Figure 1 is a UML sequence diagram [14] that captures the behavior of what the code does.

```
proc_example() ->
    Proc = spawn(fun () -> do_it() end),
    Proc ! {compute,5,self()},
```

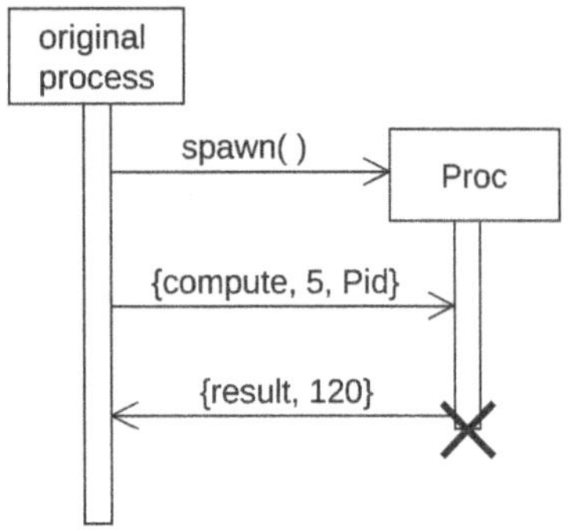

Figure 1: Creating a process, and sending and receiving messages between processes.

```
        receive
            {result,R} -> R
        end.

    do_it() ->
        receive
            {compute,N,Pid} ->
                Pid ! {result,fact(N)}
        end.
```

The spawn built-in function creates a new process, returning its process identifier (pid) to the caller. An Erlang process, like a thread, is an independently scheduled sequential activity with its own call stack, but like an operating-system process, it shares no data with other processes—processes interact only by sending messages to each other. The self built-in function returns the pid of the caller. A pid is required in order to send messages to a process.

The new process starts executing the anonymous function (defined using the fun keyword) specified in spawn and will terminate when that function returns.

Messages are sent with the syntax: *Pid ! Message*. A message can be any Erlang value, and it is sent atomically and immutably. It is conventional to use tuples[3] containing atoms[4] as messages. The message is placed in the receiving process's mailbox, and the sender continues to execute—it does not wait for the receiving process to retrieve the message.

A process uses the receive construct to extract messages from its mailbox. It specifies a set of patterns and associated handler code and scans the mailbox looking for the first message that matches any of the patterns, blocking if no such message is found. This is the only blocking primitive in Erlang. Like the patterns in function clauses, the patterns in receive options match structures and bind new variables. If a pattern uses a variable that has already been bound to a value, then matching the pattern requires a match with that value [10].

In this code, the proc_example function creates a new process (bound to variable Proc), then sends it the request message {compute,5,self()}, and finally waits to receive the response message. The new process starts executing the do_it function, which blocks until it receives the expected message. Once this occurs, it sends the message {result,120} back to the original sender (referred by the Pid variable which got bound to the process identifier returned by the call to self() within the original process). The value 120 is the result of computing fact(N), where N=5.

[3]Erlang tuples are a compound data type with a fixed number of terms. They are delimited with curly braces: {$Term_1$, $Term_2$, ..., $Term_n$}.

[4]An atom is a literal, a constant with a name. They are equivalent to symbols in languages like Lisp or Ruby. They must start with a lowercase letter.

3.2.5 Process Distribution

Creating a process so that it runs on another network node is also pretty straightforward. There is a special version of spawn that takes the name of the node where the new process will be created and run. Additionally, you must provide the module, name, and argument list of the function to be executed. The distributed version of the proc_example function from the last section would be as follows:

```
dist_example() ->
    Proc = spawn(mynode@example.com,
                 mymodule, do_it, []),
    Proc ! {compute, 5, self()},
    receive
        {result, R} -> R
    end.
```

Thanks to location transparency, sending and receiving messages is done just as if all involved processes were running in the local VM.

3.3 Design Principles

In order to achieve a good level of parallelism on a SMP system, Joe Armstrong gives a few recommendations when programming with Erlang [3]:

1. **Use lots of processes in relation to the number of cores.** This will keep the CPU busy. Preferably all the processes should do similar amounts of work.
2. **Avoid side effects.** Side effects are mainly produced by mutating shared memory. A disaster might happen if two threads write to common memory at the same time. Systems with shared memory concurrency prevent this by locking the shared memory while the memory is being written to. The main problem with shared memory is that one thread can corrupt the memory used by another thread, even if the code in the first thread is correct.
3. **Avoid sequential bottlenecks.** This follows Amdahl's law: *The speedup of a program using multiple processors in parallel computing is limited by the time needed for the sequential fraction of the program* [1]. Sometimes certain steps of an algorithm have to be done sequentially and not concurrently. If that is the case, the only solution might be to replace or rewrite the algorithm.
4. **Write "small messages, big computations" code.** The overhead of setting up a process and waiting for a reply should not be greater than the time required by the process to do the computation itself.

3.4 Drawbacks and Alternatives

Erlang is not the silver bullet for concurrent programming. Many issues still arise as noted in [10]:

> All standard errors in concurrent programming have their equivalents in Erlang: races, deadlock, livelock, starvation, and so on. Even with the help Erlang provides, concurrent programming is far from easy, and the nondeterminism of concurrency means that it is always difficult to know when the last bug has been removed.

There are alternative concurrency mechanisms supported by other modern programming languages; some of these might be considered simpler than Erlang's message-passing model, specifically in the context of non-distributed applications. An interesting example worth mentioning is the fairly new Clojure programming language [9]. Clojure is a non-pure functional Lisp dialect that runs over the JVM. It supports threads and shared memory, but it protects the later via software transactional memory (STM). STM is a higher-level approach to thread safety than the locking mechanisms provided by Java and other mainstream languages. Rather than creating fragile, error-prone locking strategies, shared state can be protected with transactions, which are easier to reason about.

4. CLASS EXPERIENCE

In August 2007, the author introduced Erlang and COP in his *Programming Languages* course at the Tecnológico de Monterrey, Campus Estado de México. This course is part of a nine semester Computer Systems Engineering undergraduate program, which basically blends together computer science with software engineering.

The author has been teaching this course since 1994, using several different languages at different moments. The languages that have been used in the past include: Scheme, Prolog, Python and Ruby.

4.1 Syllabus

Students usually take the *Programming Languages* course during their fifth or sixth semester. Its prerequisites include *Data Structures* and *Theory of Computation*. The course syllabus, including the approximate number of classroom hours assigned to each topic, is as follows:

1. General Concepts of Programming Languages (3 hrs.)
2. Functional programming (15 hrs.)
3. Parallel programming (12 hrs.)
4. Distributed programming (9 hrs.)
5. Introduction to Language Translation (9 hrs.)

Erlang is used from topics 2 to 5. At the beginning of the course, students have no previous exposure to Erlang, nor to functional programming for that matter. They start learning the sequential part of Erlang during topic 2. The larger portion of the course, topics 3 and 4, is dedicated to COP.

A semester is comprised of 16 weeks, with three classroom hours per week. About 80% of the classroom time is spent in lectures; the remaining 20% is used for quizzes, exams, and a few collaborative activities. Students are expected to schedule an additional five hours a week for extra class activities on their own.

The course final grade is calculated considering the following items: programming assignments 10%, final project 10%, discussion forums 5%, quizzes 15%, quarter term exams 35%, and a final exam 25%. A student requires a final grade of least 70 out of 100 in order to pass the course.

References [5, 15] are used as textbooks. These books were chosen not only due to the adequacy of their content, but also because students have access to them through the *Safari Books Online* campus subscription [12].

4.2 Extra Class Assignments

During the semester, students are required to use Erlang to develop individually five programming assignments and a final project. A programming assignment consists of three to ten problems. Each problem is solved usually in just a few lines of code. Students are given at least one week to solve each programming assignment.

This is the list of programming assignments:

1. **Recursive Functions.** Students solve problems that require a recursive solution and pattern matching. For example: Write a function that, given a list of elements, returns a new list that results from compressing the original list using the run-length encoding (RLE) algorithm.
2. **Higher-Order Functions.** Students solve problems that require using higher-order functions[5]. For example: Implement functions that allow to do numerical derivation and integration.
3. **Project Euler.** Students select and solve at least ten problems from the *Project Euler* [13] website, which contains a series of challenging mathematical problems of different difficulty levels that can be solved by writing computer programs in any language.
4. **Concurrent Programming.** Students solve problems that involve creating processes, and sending and receiving messages. For example: create a ring of N processes, and send a message M times around all the processes in the ring.
5. **MapReduce Exercises.** Students solve problems that use the MapReduce framework [8] in order to run efficiently on an SMP system. For example: Write a function that determines the IP address of the remote host that has the greatest number of accesses to a certain web server by inspecting the corresponding log files. Students also perform benchmarks to evaluate the performance of their solutions.

The first three programming assignments allow students to develop functional programming skills, while the last two focus on parallel programming abilities.

For the final project, students build a complete text based distributed multi-player game, working in teams of two or three people. This is a fairly challenging activity. A different game is requested each semester. So far, these are the games that have been implemented by students: Tic-Tac-Toe, Connect-4, Dots and Boxes, Crazy Eights, Go Fish!, and Collector. To successfully complete the project, the team members must effectively write functional, parallel and distributed code in Erlang, thus demonstrating a good level of COP proficiency.

4.3 Results Obtained

In the last six semesters, 166 students have taken the *Programming Languages* course with the COP approach using Erlang. 87.35% of those students obtained a passing grade.

[5]A higher-order function takes one or more functions as an input, and/or returns a function as its ouput.

A passing grade guarantees that a student has at least the basic skills needed to write code using the functional, parallel and distributed programming styles.

In order to have a better idea on how students perceive the material covered in the course, the author conducted in the last two semesters a fairly simple anonymous survey. At the end of the course, students were requested to honestly give a score to six statements depending on how closely they resembled their current attitudes and feelings. The possible score values were: 5 ← Strongly Agree, 4 ← Agree, 3 ← Neutral, 2 ← Disagree, and 1 ← Strongly Disagree. These were the statements to be scored:

1. I consider Erlang's concurrency message-passing model to be easier to understand and use than the model supported by C/C++/C#/Java, which uses threads, shared memory and locks.
2. I consider that writing programs that fully take advantage of the parallel facilities offered by multi-core systems is easier to achieve using Erlang than using languages like C, C++, C# or Java.
3. I consider **functional programming** to be easier **in general** than object oriented or procedural programming.
4. I consider that **functional programming** simplifies the development of **concurrent** programs, compared to object oriented or procedural programming.
5. I consider that **functional programming** simplifies the development of **distributed** programs, compared to object oriented or procedural programming.
6. If I had to build a **concurrent** or **distributed** system from scratch, I would most definitely consider using Erlang.

A total of 44 students took the survey. Of those, 84% had already taken an *Operating Systems* course. This is relevant because that course also covers concurrency, but with the traditional model using threads, shared memory and locks. 100% the students also mentioned that they already had some experience using threads in Java, C or C++ from some previous course.

The following table shows the results of the survey. Note that $\overline{x}$ is the arithmetic mean and σ is the standard deviation of the entire population.

Stmt. No.	$\overline{x}$	σ
1	4.34	0.88
2	4.45	0.58
3	3.20	1.14
4	4.34	0.67
5	4.25	0.83
6	4.07	0.75

5. CONCLUSIONS

From section 4.3, it is interesting to note that most students "Strongly Agree" or "Agree" on all statements except for number 3, which also happens to have the largest deviation. It seems that students consider Erlang and functional programming to be good options for COP, but there is disagreement on the general relevancy of functional programming.

When students start using Erlang, it appears to be quite odd to them. But after using it for a while, they start to appreciate its merits. When the semester ends, most students seem to enjoy using it.

Erlang is definitely not a perfect language. But, in the author's experience, Erlang is better suited for teaching concurrency than the alternatives that most instructors are currently using.

The material used for teaching COP and Erlang is available under a Creative Commons Attribution-Noncommercial license at the following URL: *http://www.arielortiz.com/*

6. REFERENCES

[1] G. Amdahl. Validity of the single processor approach to achieving large-scale computing capabilities. *AFIPS Conference Proceedings*, (30):483–485, 1967.

[2] J. Armstrong. *Concurrency Oriented Programming in Erlang.* http://www.guug.de/veranstaltungen/ffg2003/papers/ffg2003-armstrong.pdf Accessed December 6, 2010.

[3] J. Armstrong. *Programming Erlang: Software for a Concurrent World.* Pragmatic Bookshelf, 2007.

[4] Association for Computing Machinery and IEEE Computer Society. *Computer Science Curriculum 2008: An Interim Revision of CS 2001.* http://www.acm.org/education/curricula/ComputerScience2008.pdf Accessed December 6, 2010.

[5] F. Cesarini and S. Thompson. *Erlang Programming.* O'Reilly Media, 2009.

[6] Ericsson Computer Science Laboratory. *Erlang Programming Language, Official Website.* http://www.erlang.org/ Accessed December 6, 2010.

[7] B. Goetz, T. Peierls, J. Bloch, J. Bowbeer, D. Holmes, and D. Lea. *Java Concurrency in Practice.* Addison-Wesley Professional, 2006.

[8] Google Code University. *Introduction to Parallel Programming and MapReduce.* http://code.google.com/edu/parallel/mapreduce-tutorial.html Accessed December 6, 2010.

[9] R. Hickey. *Clojure Website.* http://clojure.org/ Accessed December 6, 2010.

[10] J. Larson. Erlang for concurrent programming. *Queue*, 6(5):18–23, 2008.

[11] M. Logan, E. Merritt, and R. Carlsson. *Erlang and OTP in Action.* Manning Publications, 2010.

[12] O'Reilly. *Safari Books Online.* http://my.safaribooksonline.com/ Accessed December 6, 2010.

[13] Project Euler. *Project Euler Website.* http://projecteuler.net/ Accessed December 6, 2010.

[14] J. Rumbaugh, I. Jacobson, and G. Booch. *The Unified Modeling Language Reference Manual, Second Edition.* Addison-Wesley Professional, 2005.

[15] M. Scott. *Programming Language Pragmatics, Third Edition.* Morgan Kaufmann, 2009.

[16] H. Sutter. *The Free Lunch Is Over: A Fundamental Turn Toward Concurrency in Software.* http://www.gotw.ca/publications/concurrency-ddj.htm Accessed December 6, 2010.

Learning to Love Computer Science: Peer Leaders Gain Teaching Skill, Communicative Ability and Content Knowledge in the CS Classroom

Sarah Hug
ATLAS Institute, Assessment & Research Center
University of Colorado at Boulder
320 UCB
Boulder, CO 80309
1 303 735-0993
Sarah.hug@colorado.edu

Heather Thiry
ATLAS Institute, Assessment & Research Center
University of Colorado at Boulder
Boulder, CO 80309
1 303 735-5172
Heather.thiry@colorado.edu

Phyllis Tedford
Texas A&M University – Corpus Christi
6300 Ocean Drive Unit 5824
Corpus Christi, TX 78412
1 361 825-3711
Phyllis.tedford@tamucc.edu

ABSTRACT
This paper describes the benefits of Peer-Led Team Learning (PLTL), an NSF-sponsored program in the sciences, to peer leaders serving in the Computing Alliance for Hispanic Serving Institutions (CAHSI). Beyond the benefits to students enrolled in the PLTL courses, survey findings show the majority of peer leaders report increased self-efficacy in teaching computer science, improved content knowledge, and better communication and leadership skills following a semester of leading PLTL. Results from this diverse group of leaders indicate no differences in gains between underrepresented minority and majority students, suggesting the program may provide a path for improving retention of underrepresented groups in the field.

Categories and Subject Descriptors
K.3.2 [Computer and Information Science Education]: Computer science education, active learning

General Terms
Human Factors

Keywords
Peer-led team learning, communication skill, cooperative learning, peer mentoring

1. INTRODUCTION
Education evaluation and research have paid much attention to the benefits of peer tutoring and peer leading for the recipients, or so-called "less expert" students, involved in these curricular initiatives. Far less common are studies of the *leaders' development* as they learn to guide students through course content. The role of a peer leader differs from that of a teaching assistant or a professor, and provides unique learning opportunities for those involved. In the words of one peer leader:

SIGCSE'11, March 9–12, 2011, Dallas, Texas, USA.

"I facilitate a cooperative learning environment to where I am not a major authority figure that has control over the student's grades, but rather I am just a peer that is there to help them learn."

In this paper, authors examined the benefits of leading PLTL sessions for the leaders who engage students in computer science-related lessons and activities at CAHSI institutions over the course of five semesters, from the fall of 2007 through the fall of 2009. Our research questions were:

1) Does the act of leading PLTL sessions increase student leaders' teaching self-efficacy in computing? 2) Does the act of leading PLTL sessions increase student leaders' content knowledge in computing? 3) Does the act of leading PLTL sessions increase student leaders' "soft skills" (e.g., leadership, communication, problem solving)?

This paper describes implementation of PLTL in one of the six participating CAHSI computer science departments, details the survey methods employed using an existing instrument vetted based on adequate reliability and validity measurements, and relates quantitative and supporting qualitative evidence of peer leaders' development during the implementation of PLTL. In addition, authors draw possible implications and further directions for this work.

2. PLTL IN THE CAHSI COMMUNITY
The CAHSI academic computing departments have adopted a novel approach to the PLTL workshops first developed by City College of New York in the mid-nineties[1]. PLTL implementation in CAHSI schools focus on cooperative learning as a structured method to support student learning in an active learning-focused, positive classroom environment. Leaders are paid a modest stipend, and are recruited by faculty and by their peers as being knowledgeable in course content. We note that in some cases, classmates recommend students who do not appear to faculty as most knowledgeable—students base their recommendations on peers' ability to communicate concepts. What follows is an example of one CAHSI institution's experience implementing the program, and sets the stage for the data collected from peer leaders across CAHSI campuses.

2.1 ONE CONTEXT: PLTL AT TAMUCC

The Computing Sciences Department at Texas A&M University (TAMUCC) – Corpus Christi established a PLTL program for the introductory computer science courses (CS-1, CS-2, and CS-3) based on the model implemented by Roach and Villa in computer science courses at the University of Texas at El Paso [2]. As a member of CAHSI, TAMUCC institution benefited from the expertise and experience of faculty and instructors who had implemented the program in the past, and as an alliance, had the resources necessary to train the new leaders and instructors.

The PLTL model as implemented throughout CAHSI hinges on the components found in cooperative learning: positive interdependence, individual and group accountability, group processing, social skills, and face-to-face promotive interaction [3]. During the PLTL sessions, students create a learning environment that is far different from the traditional classroom. In this non-traditional setting, cooperation and participation are encouraged over competition and individualism.

At TAMUCC, the peer leaders are CS majors or minors who have completed the introductory course they assist. They attend a day-long training session that is conducted as a cooperative learning environment. During this training, each pair of peer leaders develops the activity to be used during the first PLTL session of the semester based on the lecture schedules provided by the course instructors. Volunteers, usually other non-peer leader students, participate as "students" for this first planned activity. After each peer leader pair has led the "students" through the activity, the "students" and peer leaders candidly review how well the session worked with suggestions for improving the activity discussed as needed.

The peer leaders are required to attend all lectures for the class to which they are assigned. They are also required to attend weekly meetings with the program coordinator for discussion about and peer review of the previous week's activity along with additional training. Each peer leader is required to submit a weekly report to the coordinator on the activity used for that week's session. The reports include "what went well," "what went wrong," and suggestions for improvement. The peer leaders are required to meet regularly with the instructor of the class to which they have been assigned to provide feedback about problem areas they've found during the PLTL sessions.

The activities used during the PLTL sessions emphasize using problem-solving techniques during exercises related to topics covered in lecture. The PLTL sessions occur in a 45-60 minute block of time during the laboratory session of each course. The students in the courses are required to attend the sessions. The students are randomly assigned to work in teams of 3 to 5 people to complete the cooperative learning activity presented to them. There are 2 peer leaders per class who are responsible for creating and facilitating the activities. These activities are designed to be visual, active, and memorable. Since the purpose of these sessions is to reinforce the information covered in lecture rather than introduce new material, the peer leaders are trained to question and assess the teams' approaches and solutions and not simply provide the answers. Since the goal is to make the sessions a truly peer-led environment, the course instructor is not permitted in the room during the PLTL session. The peer leaders encourage the teams to use multiple approaches to solving a problem along with promoting equal participation of all team members.

The description of implementation at TAMUCC is one representative example of how CAHSI computer science and engineering departments are implementing PLTL in an effort to improve instruction.

3. LITERATURE REVIEW

Educational research focused on teachers and students at multiple points in their education shows that teaching concepts to others helps solidify knowledge for the instructor. In describing content to another, one must articulate how a phenomenon occurs in more than one way, and these multiple ways of thinking and talking about a concept prove beneficial to the tutor and tutee [4].

While many researchers have described benefits of PLTL to science students, particularly chemistry students [5 6 7 8 9], the literature regarding leaders' gains has been scarce. Tien, Roth and Kampmeier [10] studied the development of a course to train peer leaders, and report anecdotal evidence of satisfaction from participants in their training program. Amaral and Vala [11] found that students chosen for PLTL leadership roles, even when underprepared at the beginning of their studies, surpassed those deemed ready for chemistry and those underprepared for chemistry who were not mentors in the program.

In an evaluation study across 11 schools, Gafney and Varma Nelson [12] state that leaders saw the experience as promoting their confidence in presentation and teamwork efforts. Leaders gained appreciation for learning styles, small group work settings, and the teaching endeavor. An in-depth qualitative study of peer leaders uncovered the connected ways in which leaders developed cognitively and personally, and how that development corresponded with more practical benefits of PLTL leadership [13].

This paper extends this research base with a focus on a multi-site study of the benefits of peer leading, as described by the leaders themselves. In extending this work, the current study brings the focus on peer leader development to the realm of computer science education. The authors expand upon the study of peer leader benefits through empirical experimentation with a modified version of an existing survey instrument for use with computer science peer leaders that demonstrates reliable measurement of three latent constructs of interest. The work focused on a quantitative study of peer leaders' perceived benefits in three key areas: teaching efficacy, communicative abilities ("soft skills"), and content knowledge, and provides complementary qualitative information to support the claims. The stability of results across genders and ethnicities indicate peer leading may support diversity aims in computer science departments.

4. METHODS

The authors used peer leader surveys to measure the effectiveness of the initiative and to measure potential benefits to leaders. While self-report measures are not the only way to measure benefits of an intervention, they do give an initial indication of how leaders experience the initiative. In fact, research in science undergraduate education shows that self-conception of ability and self-efficacy in technical fields are better predictors of retention in the field than grades [14].

A peer leader survey was adapted from the Science Teaching Efficacy Belief Instrument (STEBI) developed by Riggs and Knochs [15]. The authors chose to use a previously developed survey because of its sound design, psychometric properties, and established usefulness in the educational research literature.

Because the STEBI instrument was designed for pre-service elementary teachers, the items had to be revised to better fit the undergraduate classroom and the role of peer leaders as guides and tutors, not teachers. The authors revised the survey to reflect the discipline of computer science, rather than science in general. Thus eight items that were specific to K-12 teaching were deleted. For instance, one of the deleted items was "I would not invite the principal to evaluate my science teaching." The rest of the twenty-five item STEBI survey was modified to better fit the role of the peer leaders and the computing discipline. For instance, "I am typically able to answer students' science questions" was revised to "I am typically able to answer students' computing questions."

Authors edited a few items more substantially to reflect the role of the peer leader and to fit postsecondary classrooms. For example, "Effectiveness in science teaching has little influence on the achievement of students" was simplified to "I am confident in my ability to motivate students." Six items were added to address specific gains in peer leaders' skills, such as oral communication, leadership, interpersonal, and decision-making skills. Open-ended questions were also added to elicit more detailed, descriptive data about peer leaders' beliefs about their role, and the influence of the peer leader experience on their career aspirations and skill development. Finally, the authors shifted from a five-point to a four-point scale scale, forcing peer leaders' to either agree or disagree with survey items, based on survey research indicating that a neutral point in a scale is not necessary and may detract from collecting real attitudes and perceptions held by respondents [16].

Data were collected at the end of each semester from 89 peer leaders over five college semesters and six institutions using an electronic survey system. Peer leader coordinators and faculty from each school sent the survey to all leaders, ranging from 2 to 10 leaders per institution per semester. Each survey administration measured a semester of work as a Peer Leader—items asked participants to respond based on their leader experience that semester.[1] The majority of items used the following scale: 1= strongly disagree, 2=disagree, 3= agree, 4=strongly agree, 5= I don't know/Not applicable. The rating of "5" was described as missing in the program, so as not to inflate means with irrelevant responses.

Results were calculated using the SPSS statistical package. Mean scores and frequencies are reported with collapsed categories (strongly agree and agree are reported together, as are strongly disagree and disagree). Averaging scores (1-4) created composites for each construct. Reliability for each of the three constructs was calculated using the Cronbach's alpha statistic. Authors used the Analysis of Variance (ANOVA) to measure mean comparisons for each construct based on gender and ethnicity of the leader as well as semester as a leader (new leaders compared with returning leaders). Differences for scale scores are reported where statistically significant at the 0.05 level.

[1] While less than half of leaders had been leaders in past semesters, veteran leaders may have responded to the survey over more than one semester. Students were asked to focus their responses on the most recent semester experience

5. RESULTS

Survey respondents were predominantly Hispanic (44 respondents, 54%), a third were Caucasian (30 respondents, 37%), and a smaller portion were of Indian descent (8 respondents, 10%). The majority of students were in their fourth year of study (44 respondents, 53%), with a quarter of leaders in their third year of coursework (30 respondents, 25%), sixteen percent were sophomores, and the remaining students were freshmen. Leaders who took the peer leader survey were more likely male, as is reflective of gender distribution in computer science and computer engineering departments as a whole (82% male). Three quarters of leaders were in their first or second semester of leading PLTL workshops. Student GPAs averaged 3.16, were reported in only 65 cases, and ranged from 1.9 to 4.0 on a 4 point scale, with 11% in the C range and 57% in the B grade range. The GPAs of leaders were not the deciding factor in recruitment for peer leader positions at CAHSI schools, according to CAHSI faculty—in fact, peer leaders often recruited the next generation of leaders from their classmates who best explained the concepts in small discussion groups, rather than those known to get the best grades on the tests. All leaders were asked to complete the PLTL leader survey at the end of each semester.

5.1 Developing teaching skills in PLTL

Seven items from the STEBI were modified for use with peer leaders to examine growth in teaching skill. While most computing scientists do not intend to pursue teaching careers, the skill of conveying computational ideas to others is certainly useful in many professional roles. Table 1 shows the frequency and proportion of individuals who "agreed" or "disagreed" with the seven statements, and the mean score for each item. The table also shows the composite scores for individuals averaged across the seven items. The Cronbach's alpha (0.85) score shows strong reliability across the items, indicating the scale is robust.

Results show that most students (60-83%) view PLTL as an experience that supports teaching skill development, particularly when "teaching skill" is defined in terms of active learning, where teachers are guiding students rather than simply presenting information. Negatively worded items "I am uncomfortable addressing students' questions" and "When I put more effort into my PLTL lessons, I see little change in students' achievement" show the lowest scores in this construct, and had more "I don't know" and "Not applicable" responses than any other items, a possible indication of confusion based on item wording. ANOVA analyses indicate that returning leaders rated their development of teaching skill slightly higher than beginning peer leaders ($F=4.804$, $\alpha=0.03$). No other statistically significant differences were found across this construct.

In open-ended survey items, leaders described what was difficult about their role in the computer science curriculum. One survey response indicated an understanding of teaching as a difficult skill to master, given students' varied levels of understanding and multiple preferred learning styles.

Table 1: Peer Leaders' Teaching Skill development

Peer Leader's Teaching Skill Development			
Item (N=88)	**Percent Agree**	**Percent Disagree**	**Mean Score (4 point scale)**
Leading PLTL has improved my teaching skills	80%	20%	3.20
I am confident in my ability to help students understand computing concepts	83%	17%	3.17
I generally facilitate PLTL sessions effectively	79%	21%	3.02
I am confident in my ability to motivate students	75%	25%	3.01
I often think of better ways to facilitate PLTL sessions	79%	21%	3.01
*I am uncomfortable addressing students' questions	69%**	31%**	2.93
	(percentage agree is reversed, shows comfort addressing questions)[2]		
*When I put more effort into my PLTL lessons, I see little change in students' achievement	60%**	40%**	2.61
	(percentage agree is reversed, shows greater change in achievement)		
TOTAL = COMPOSITE VARIABLE	**80%**	**20%**	**3.00**

"The main challenge is trying to come up with effective sessions. Every student has a different type of learning style and also learn on different levels. So trying to keep the sessions so everyone is learning is sometimes hard."

Another leader described her effort to be an enthusiastic, group-work oriented, responsive facilitator.

"Strategies I use as a peer leader are to go into each session enthusiastically, talk to the students, put them into small groups, and walk around to make sure the students are working together."

5.2 Leadership and Communication Skill Development

According to the Accreditation Board for Engineering and Technology (ABET), academic programs focused on engineering and technical fields must provide opportunities for students to develop group work skills and the ability to communicate effectively [17]. Peer leaders at CAHSI institutions indicate the program facilitated their development of so-called "soft" skills vital in a team-based, design-oriented industry like computing. Five items were developed based on informal data collected from staff, leaders, and project coordinators during the first semesters of CAHSI's implementation of PLTL. These items were developed deductively, with the theory of how peer leading impacts students driving item development. Cronbach's alpha (0.93) indicates strong relationships among responses to these "soft skill" items. See table below.

[2] Starred items were reversed to better capture overall agreement and disagreement within the construct "teaching skill development".

Table 2.Peer Leaders' Leadership and Communication Skill

Peer Leaders' Leadership and Communication Skill development			
Item (N=89)	**Percent Agree**	**Percent Disagree**	**Mean Score (4 pt scale)**
Leading PLTL has improved my oral communication skills	81%	19%	3.21
Leading PLTL has improved my leadership skills	79%	21%	3.06
I know the steps necessary to effectively communicate computing skills	81%	19%	3.05
Leading PLTL has improved my interpersonal skills (in other words, my ability to cooperate with others)	77%	23%	3.05
**Leading PLTL has improved my decision-making skills[3]	76%	24%	2.91
TOTAL = COMPOSITE VARIABLE	**82%**	**18%**	**3.03**

According to survey data, the majority of students who lead computing PLTL workshops improve in communicative abilities vital to success in engineering professions. Between 76-82% of leaders indicated growth in soft skills related to communicating concepts, leading a team, and making decisions.

One student who gained communication skills as a peer leader described the greatest challenge of leading the workshops:

"I think the greatest challenge for me was actually getting up there in front of everyone and talking to them."

Another peer leader described his role in terms of facilitating knowledge development through cooperative engagement in the content.

"(I serve as a) fellow student that can help other students work in groups, and get a grasp of what CS is all about, (including) how it

[3] For most items, the number of missing data points (in which the respondent answered with Not Applicable or I don't know) is less than 10% of the total data. Items with greater than ten percent missing variables are shown with double asterisks **

is applied, what options they have, and at the same time making things interesting, challenging, using cooperative learning to reach those goals."

5.3 Content Knowledge Development

Perhaps the greatest benefit for leaders is that of increased content knowledge. As leaders consider problems to pose to their students, they must solve them as well as develop strategies for guiding their peers towards deeper understanding. The PLTL leader survey included 5 items related to the peer leader's content knowledge, two of the items explicitly reflecting leaders' *change in content knowledge* attributed to leading peers. Cronbach's alpha (0.79) suggests a moderate to strong relationship among items.

Table 3. Peer Leaders' Content Knowledge Development

Peer Leaders' Content knowledge development			
Item (N=89)	**Percent Agree**	**Percent Disagree**	**Mean Score (4 point scale)**
I understand computing concepts well enough to be an effective peer leader	82%	18%	3.18
I am typically able to answer students' computing questions	83%	17%	3.17
*I question whether I have the necessary skills to facilitate peer-led team learning	82%	28%	3.13
	(percentage agree is reversed, shows respondent does have necessary skills)		
Leading PLTL has increased my computing knowledge	71%	29%	2.94
Leading PLTL has improved my study skills	56%	44%	2.62
TOTAL = COMPOSITE VARIABLE	**82%**	**18%**	**3.04**

Items in this section refer to students' confidence in having content knowledge in general, as well as the impact of leading PLTL on their study skills and computing knowledge. Results show that peer leaders are largely confident regarding their content knowledge following a semester of peer leading (82-83%). A majority of leaders also state the experience increased their content knowledge (71%) and a smaller fraction said it improved their study skills (56%). Anecdotal evidence from conversations with leaders indicates being a peer leader takes time, and that this additional work time may detract from time to study. Comparison across groups indicate returning students develop greater content knowledge based on their peer leading experience ($F=4.774$, $\alpha=0.032$). No other statistically significant differences were found across this construct.

One student described the influence of the program on his interest and knowledge of computing:

"(*Being a peer leader) has sparked my interest in computing even more... my foundations of computer science have been fortified by being a peer leader, I feel more confident about the material, not to mention that I have also learned from the students."*

Another student said:

"(Since becoming a leader) I like teaching, I got more involved, and I feel more comfortable and secure now with my knowledge."

6. DISCUSSION

Results from 89 peer leaders over five college semesters and six institutions signify that leading sessions designed to engage peers in understanding concepts of computer science has clear benefits for the majority of leaders. In particular, peer leaders develop teaching skills, communicative abilities, and content knowledge in their discipline. The modified STEBI seemed to measure constructs of interest to PLTL programs with reliability, and adequate face validity. While current results are based solely on self-report, future studies will incorporate faculty assessment, retention rates in the major, and shifts in leader GPA to see if peer leaders' corroborating data show similar positive impact from the experience. Results show no statistically significant differences by ethnicity or gender, indicating that serving as a leader in peer tutoring may help retention efforts focused on diversifying the technical pipeline. The results of our study indicate that academic departments could benefit students by providing peer-leading opportunities.

This preliminary work provides a modified version of a previously developed tool for measuring student leader gains from their work in PLTL, and suggests further study into retention in computing for those who lead workshops for their peers. The strong confidence in ability and content knowledge of leaders following their experience as leaders, and development of relevant skills and abilities that support computing professionals suggest leading workshops, as well as attending workshops, may improve retention goals. Significant studies of leaders' learning trajectories are needed to better understand the benefits of guiding students in conceptually based learning sessions. Our study provides a first look at how peer leading can positively impact undergraduate students. In the words of one leader:

"As a peer leader, I realized I'm capable of much more, and learned to love Computer Science!"

7. ACKNOWLEDGEMENTS

This work was supported in part by the National Science Foundation through collaborative NSF grants CNS-0540592 and CNS-0837556.

Special thanks to John Fernandez, Ann Gates, Nestor Rodriguez, Richard Alo, Malek Adjouadi, Enrico Pontelli, and Mohsen Beheshti of CAHSI.

8. REFERENCES

[1] Gosser, D.K., Cracolice, M. S. Kampmeier, J. A., Roth, V., Strozak, V.A., and Varma-Nelson P. 2001. *Peer-Led Team Learning: A Guidebook,* Prentice Hall, Upper Saddle River, NJ.

[2] Roach, S., Villa, E., 2007. Reaching out across disciplines: learning from each other to produce more graduates in

computer science, In *Second Annual Technology Workforce Development Workshop: Best Practices 2007*, 6-7, 2007.

[3] Johnson, D. W., Johnson, R. T., & Smith, K. 1991. *Active learning: Cooperation in the college classroom.* Interaction Book Company, Edina, MN.

[4] Ball, D.L, & Bass, H. 2000. Interweaving content and pedagogy in teaching and learning to teach: Knowing and using mathematics. In *Multiple perspectives on teaching and learning mathematics,* J. Boaler Ed. Ablex, Westport, CT.

[5] Loui, M. C., & Robbins, B. A. (2008). Work-in-progress: assessment of peer-led team learning in an engineering course for freshmen. *In Proceedings of the Thirty-Eighth ASEE/IEEE Frontiers inEducation Conference*, Saratoga Springs, N.Y., October 22–25, 2008 (pp. F1F-7–F1F-8).

[6] Biggers, M., Yilmaz, T. & Sweat, M. 2009. Using collaborative modified peer-led team learning to improve student success and retention in intro CS. In *SIGCSE'09*, March 3–7, 2009, Chattanooga, Tennessee, USA.

[7] Horwitz, S., Rodger, S.H., Biggers, M., Binkley, D., Frantz, C.K., Gundermann, D., Hambrusch, S., Huss-Lederman, S., Munson, E., Ryder, B., & Sweat, M. 2009. Using peer-led team learning to increase participation and success of under-represented groups in introductory computer science. In *SIGCSE'09*, March 3–7, 2009, Chattanooga, Tennessee, USA.

[8] Huss-Lederman, S., Chinn, D., & Skrentny, J. 2008. Serious fun:peer-led team learning in CS. In *February 2008* ***SIGCSE Bulletin*** Volume 40 Issue 1.

[9] Sperry, R. A. and Tedford, P. 2008. Implementing peer-led team learning in introductory computer science courses. *J. Comput. Small Coll.* 23, 6 (Jun. 2008), 30-35.

[10] Tien,L., Roth, V., Kampmeier, J. 2004. A course to prepare peer leaders to implement a student-assisted learning method. In *J. Chem. Educ.* 81, 1313–1321.

[11] Amaral, K. E.; Vala, M. 2009. What teaching teaches: mentoring and the performance gains of mentors . In *J. Chem. Educ*, 86, 630–633.

[12] Gafney, L. Varma-Nelson, P. 2007. Evaluating peer-led team learning:a study of long-term effects on former workshop leaders. In *J. Chem. Educ.* 84, 535–539.

[13] Micari, M., Streitwieser, B., & Light, G. 2005. Undergraduates leading undergraduates: peer facilitation in a science workshop program. In *Innovative Higher Education*, 30(4), 269–288.

[14] Seymour, E., and N. Hewitt (1994). *Talking about leaving: Factors contributing to high attrition rates among science, mathematics, and engineering undergraduate majors.* Boulder, CO: Bureau of Sociological Research, University of Colorado.

[15] Riggs, I. M., & Enochs, L. G. 1990. Toward the development of an elementary teacher's Science Teaching Efficacy Belief Instrument. In *Science Education,* 74, 625-637.

[16] Krosnick, J. A. & Fabrigar, L. R. 1997. Designing Rating Scales for Effective Measurement in Surveys. In *Survey measurement and process quality.* New York: Wiley, 1997, pp. 141-64.

[17] ABET (Accreditation Board for Engineering and Technology). 2009. Criteria for accrediting computing programs: Effective for evaluations during the 2010–2011 accreditation cycle. Retrieved August 17, 2010. http://www.abet.org/Linked%20DocumentsUPDATE/Criteria%20and%20PP/C001%201011%20CAC%20Criteria%2011-16-09.pdf .

Lessons Learned from a PLTL-CS Program

Christian Murphy, Rita Powell*
Dept. of Computer and Information Science
University of Pennsylvania
Philadelphia PA 19104
{cdmurphy, powell}@cis.upenn.edu

Kristen Parton, Adam Cannon
Dept. of Computer Science
Columbia University
New York NY 10027
{kristen, cannon}@cs.columbia.edu

ABSTRACT

The Peer-Led Team Learning (PLTL) approach has previously been shown to be effective in recruiting and retaining students, particularly under-represented students, in undergraduate introductory CS courses. In PLTL, small groups of students are led by an undergraduate peer and work together to solve problems related to CS. At Columbia University, the Columbia Emerging Scholars Program has used PLTL in an effort to increase enrollment in CS courses beyond the introductory level, and to increase the number of students who select Computer Science as their major, by demonstrating that CS is necessarily a collaborative activity that focuses more on problem solving and algorithmic thinking than on programming. Over the past six semesters, over 80 students have completed the program, and preliminary results indicate that this program has had a positive effect on increasing participation in the major.

This paper discusses our experiences of building and expanding the Columbia Emerging Scholars program, and addresses such topics as recruiting, training, scheduling, student behavior, and evaluation. We expect that this paper will provide a valuable set of lessons learned to other educators who seek to launch or grow a PLTL program at their institution as well.

Categories and Subject Descriptors

K.3.2 [**Computers and Education**]: Computer and Information Science Education—*computer science education*

General Terms

Human Factors, Measurement

Keywords

Peer-Led Team Learning, Emerging Scholars Program, Outreach, Women in Computer Science, Diversity, CS1

*Dr. Powell is also an Extension Services Consultant for the National Center for Women & Information Technology.

1. INTRODUCTION

Computer specialists are among the occupations projected to grow the fastest and add the most new jobs through 2018, with job prospects in this industry the greatest for those who hold the bachelor degree. The U.S. Department of Labor estimates that there will be 1.4 million technology jobs in 2018, but U.S. universities will be able to provide graduates that qualify for less than 1/3 of these positions.[1] In addition, diversity in computer science is decreasing: only 18 percent of bachelor's degrees in computer science were awarded to women in 2006, and at U.S. research universities, that number was less than 12 percent.[2] This trend underscores the scarcity of diverse insights in undergraduate computer science courses, and calls for an intervention through pedagogy and curriculum to attract a larger sector of students to computing majors.

One effort to recruit and retain students, particularly under-represented students, in undergraduate introductory CS courses is the Emerging Scholars Program (ESP), based on Peer-Led Team Learning (PLTL). Since many students are not exposed to computer science in high school, introductory CS courses (hereafter CS1) are often their first experience. Large, lecture-based classes and complex one-person programming assignments can be daunting to students with no CS background. However, ESP/PLTL encourages active learning, as opposed to the common paradigm of passively listening to lectures in an auditorium filled with hundreds of students. ESP/PLTL supplements traditional science, technology, engineering, and mathematics (STEM) courses in that students meet in small groups (6-8 people) that are facilitated by a student who has recently completed the course. The peer leader presents problems to the group, and then guides students as they collectively brainstorm, discuss and analyze the problems to come to a solution.

Since 2008, Columbia University[3] has offered an ESP/PLTL program for students in its introductory CS course. This enrichment program, called the Columbia Emerging Scholars Program (CESP), is not directly tied to CS1 course content, but is rather aimed at demonstrating to students the breadth of CS topics, using fun and interesting group problem-solving activities. Initial results indicate that CESP has been successful in its goals of increasing retention of students (i.e., the number of students who continue on to CS2) and increasing the number of students who major in CS.

[1]http://www.bls.gov/news.release/ecopro.t06.htm
[2]http://www.cra.org/resources/taulbee
[3]The first author of this paper was previously a graduate student at Columbia.

This paper describes our experiences (both positive and negative) in launching, expanding, and refining CESP over the past three years. Whereas other authors have discussed the theoretical and observed merits of such a program [2, 6, 8], or focused on how to get a program off the ground [4], our intent is to share the general lessons learned so that others who are starting, growing, or modifying a PLTL program can learn from our experiences.

In addition, we present encouraging initial results that demonstrate the effectiveness of CESP: the number of female undergraduates declaring CS as their major has increased since we started the program, and a number of participants have gone on to receive academic awards and honors.

2. BACKGROUND

The ESP concept was initially developed by Uri Treisman at the University of California, Berkeley, in the 1970s to propel the mathematics skills of African-American students by providing them with an honors workshop adjunct to the introductory calculus course to solve challenging problems in group study sessions [7]. Originally called the Math Workshop Program at Berkeley, the program became the Emerging Scholars Program at the University of Texas, Austin, and has been adopted by over a hundred universities and expanded to support courses in the natural and physical sciences and engineering.

ESP/PLTL has long been applied successfully in other STEM disciplines - for instance, the PLTL Workshop Project at City College of New York has been using it in chemistry since the early 1990's. A typical ESP/PLTL program consists of a set of weekly one- or two-hour long workshops adjunct to an academic course, led by an undergraduate workshop leader, or "peer leader", who has been specially trained in PLTL techniques. Workshops may have anywhere from as few as six to as many as 15 participants, and the students work together to solve problems, without the pressure of exams or grades. Over the course of the semester, weekly meetings are held between the peer leader and program coordinators to ensure that the program is on track, that educational goals are being met, and that the peer leader is sufficiently comfortable with the workshop material. At the end of the semester, the coordinators typically perform some evaluation procedure to measure the success of the program, and to make adjustments as necessary.

In Computer Science, ESP/PLTL has been growing in popularity over the last few years due to the success of the Emerging Scholars Program in CS (ESP-CS) endeavor. Funded by an NSF grant, eight universities worked closely together to develop, implement and evaluate a PLTL program for CS1 over three years. They have published detailed findings of their experiences and results [3], as well as modules of course content, to assist other CS departments in starting similar PLTL programs.

In addition to using PLTL, ESP-CS uses targeted recruiting to attract students from under-represented groups. Students who may otherwise be turned off by the stereotype of computer scientists as lone programmers can discover through PLTL that CS is a collaborative discipline that encompasses much more than just coding. Initial studies have shown that students, particularly students from under-represented groups, are much more likely to be drawn to STEM subjects when the material focuses on teamwork rather than on working alone [1, 5].

3. ESP/PLTL AT COLUMBIA

At Columbia, the CS1 course is a large, lecture-style class with a single section of 150-200 students. There are no lab or recitation sections, so students do not have the opportunity to meet in small, structured groups. Many CS1 students have not yet declared a major, since Columbia students typically do not declare until their second year, and the course consists of about 40% women - a much higher proportion than the CS department as a whole, where in 2008 only 16% of majors were women. Clearly many of the female students who complete CS1 are going on to choose other majors. Our objective, then, was to increase female participation in CS beyond the introductory level, by addressing some of the issues that other researchers have claimed may be driving those students away.

On the heels of the successful "PLTL in CS Workshop" at Duke University in 2007, the CS Department at Columbia University funded a pilot program in Spring 2008 to encourage more women to pursue CS as a major. By exposing students to a variety of CS topics early in their education, focusing on collaborative problem solving instead of technical details or coding, and creating a network of undergraduate women interested in computing and technology, the Columbia Emerging Scholars Program aims to increase the number of female students who go on to take CS2 and, ideally, choose CS as their major. CESP is an enrichment program, not directly tied to CS1 course topics, in which students meet for one hour per week in small groups to solve problems, facilitated by undergraduate peer leaders. There are nine workshops over the course of the semester, followed by a reunion event with former CESP participants, which provides a networking opportunity for students, recruiting opportunity for future CESP leaders, and a way to advertise other groups and events in the department.

During the pilot program, two graduate students (the first and third authors of this paper), one faculty member (the fourth author of this paper) and one undergraduate peer leader worked closely to come up with engaging problems from a variety of CS disciplines, including natural language processing, information retrieval, and social networking. The pilot was very successful. In the pilot program's exit survey, all six students said they would recommend ESP to a friend. One student wrote, "These workshops gave me a better perspective of what computer science is. I have learned that it is extremely useful and pertains to problems and issues that are in our daily lives."

Thanks to a seed grant from the National Center for Women & Information Technology (NCWIT) and Microsoft Research, CESP grew to two sections in Fall 2008, and we have continued to hone and expand the workshop content over the past two years. In total, over 80 undergraduates have participated in CESP as students, and 10 have gone on to be peer leaders and/or workshop assistants.

The Columbia Emerging Scholars Program differs from ESP-CS programs at other institutions in a variety of small but significant aspects:

- Rather than being open to the general population of CS1 students, CESP is limited to 12-15 students per semester, meaning that students must go through an application process in order to participate (Section 3.1).
- In its first three semesters, CESP only allowed for female participants; this has since changed, though, and

male students are now invited to participate as well (Section 3.2), and a gender balance is maintained in the coed workshops.

- CESP workshops feature no programming-related material at all, and focus only on CS as an algorithmic problem-solving activity (Section 3.3).

The rest of this section describes these differences further, discusses their influence on the success of the program, and provides suggestions for other educators who are considering developing similar programs.

3.1 Selection

CS1 at Columbia University is a requirement for many engineering students, and acts as a service course for many other departments, so it is taken by students from a variety of backgrounds, including upper-class students who have already declared majors. On the other hand, CESP is explicitly aimed at students who are undecided or potentially interested in CS as a major, so CESP is only appropriate for a subset of CS1 students.

Students apply to CESP via an online form, in which they are asked to indicate the level of their CS background, the majors that they are considering, and how likely they are to take any further CS courses. They are also asked open-ended questions like "why do you want to participate in this program?"

The target CESP candidate is undecided as to her major, and curious about CS. The ideal CESP section has students from diverse backgrounds (some with prior CS experience, some new to CS), with most students from the freshman and sophomore years, if possible.

Typically, we would try to avoid selecting: students who have already decided to major in something else, since this program is not targeted to them; students who seem *too* enthusiastic about CS, since we do not want them to overwhelm or dominate the workshop discussions; and continuing education, upperclassmen, or graduate students, who may be older (sometimes significantly so) than the other students and even the workshop leader.

There have, of course, been incidents when students were not selected for CESP and were very disappointed. It is important that the selection criteria is clearly defined, in case a student escalates her complaint about not being chosen. It is not necessary to publicly declare the selection criteria, but it should be something that is defensible, just in case. Students who are not accepted into the program are encouraged to participate in other organizations such as ACM.

At other institutions, ESP is open-enrollment, i.e., available to all students in the CS1 course who wish to participate; in some, ESP is a mandatory corequisite to CS1. Although these approaches broaden the number of students who are exposed to the benefits of ESP, they may not be appropriate in all cases. At Columbia, the CS1 course typically has up to 200 students per semester; certainly not all of them will benefit from CESP, either because they do not have the right personality to enjoy its collaborative problem-solving nature, or they do not have interest in CS beyond learning how to program. In our case, then, it is preferable that students should have the option of being a part of CESP, which we feel will reduce the number of participants who are merely "along for the ride," and improve the quality of the workshops.

3.2 Coed vs. Women-Only

The initial incarnation of CESP was specifically designed for female students. We feared that male students might tend to dominate the workshops, and wanted to provide the female students with a more comfortable and less confrontational environment. Additionally, we sought to create a community of young women in the CS Department, and use CESP as a stepping stone to other organizations, such as Women in Computer Science and ACM-W.

Restricting CESP to only female students does, of course, raise a number of issues. First, what are the educational, ethical, and legal implications of creating an enrichment program that is limited only to women? We struggled with this issue, fearful that male students would claim that they were not being given equal opportunities. Fortunately (if not somewhat surprisingly), this situation never arose. In fact, university administration supported the program financially under the "diversity" umbrella. However, whether or not a female-only program is acceptable/allowed may differ at other institutions.

Another concern is that the program would be seen - particularly by participants - in a derogatory manner as "remedial Computer Science" or "Computer Science for Girls". It was important for us to address this immediately in the advertising and recruiting efforts, as students may shy away from the program if they feel there is some stigma attached to it. We pointed out that CESP workshops are *not* extra office hours or tutoring sessions, but rather that they are problem-solving sessions with topics that are related to CS, though not directly related to the CS1 course material. We found that by focusing on the enrichment aspect of the program, and the advantages that it provides to students outside the classroom, students quickly realized that they were being presented with a wonderful opportunity.

As we sought to grow CESP, we considered opening the program to male students as well. Before doing so, we polled the students who had participated in the female-only semesters of CESP, and asked "How much did you like having all-female workshops?" We were surprised to find that the number of students who wanted female-only workshops (46%) was about the same as the number who would have been fine with coed workshops (42%). Thus, starting in Fall 2009, we opened up the program to male students, with one all-female section and one coed section, and the program is now fully coed.

3.3 Topics

Since CESP is only open to a subset of students in the CS1 course, we felt it was inappropriate to have the workshops be tied directly to course material, as it would give the participating students an unfair advantage over those who were not in the program. Instead, we try to demonstrate the breadth and variety of fields within CS. The ESP workshop topics we developed include: designing algorithms; encoding and encryption; machine translation; human-computer interaction and usability; social network analysis and graph theory; and hard (NP-complete) problems. These workshops are designed to engage the students in group problem solving, so that they can see that CS is a collaborative activity that is focused on problem solving, not solely on programming.

Many programs similar to CESP include topics related to the programming languages they are learning in their CS1 courses, such as exploring the language's syntax and semantics, how the language works under the covers, or how to implement an algorithm using the language and its APIs. However, we chose to focus workshop content solely on algorithmic thinking and problem solving, since students do a lot of programming in the course already. Although the CS1 course at Columbia is taught using Java, CESP does not include any material related to how to use Java or how Java works. All of the CESP workshops are language-independent.

The students seem to agree with this notion: 50% said they would prefer not to have Java programming covered in the workshops, compared to 33% who said they would. One student preferred not to program in CESP because it taught her that "much is done before programming begins," such as "simply thinking about how to solve the problems." Another agreed that the "thinking aspect [of CS] can get forgotten, lost, trampled over or almost done away with when programming." Last, a student pointed out that she "liked how we focused on theory by just thinking of solutions rather than programming them. The programming language seems more like a chore and doesn't interest me, whereas the theory behind the actual computing does."

Last, we also considered giving the students take-home assignments, either to do in preparation for an upcoming workshop, or to further elaborate upon material covered in previous ones, as is done in ESP programs at some other institutions. Regardless of whether these assignments would be graded or not, or if they were to be done alone or in groups, fully 85% of the students indicated that they would not want take-home assignments included in the program. However, we often provided students with handouts at the end of each workshop, in which we listed books and websites that students could look at if they were interested in learning more about the day's topic.

4. LESSONS LEARNED

As it is the goal of this paper to share our experiences with educators looking to start, grow, or modify an ESP-CS program, this section highlights other lessons we have learned through the administration of CESP.

4.1 Recruiting

Recruiting of students is essential to the program's success, as it is important to attract students who are suited to its open atmosphere and workshop format, but are also not quite sure that they will proceed on to CS2.

One lesson that we have learned is that what appears to be an effective recruiting technique in one semester may not be so effective in another. For example, in the CESP pilot, we announced the program in class and sent out a recruiting email to the female students. We had 19 applicants for six spots, and the students who participated were extremely enthusiastic and since then have been actively involved in programs for women in CS. A year later, though, using the same recruiting techniques, only 15 students applied for 12 spots. As a result, three out of the 12 accepted students had already declared majors other than CS.

At times we have been disappointed with the lack of applicants who are truly interested in CS. In the past, we have sometimes accepted these students into the program to fill out the numbers, but this can backfire. Students who are not particularly interested may refuse to participate, sleep during workshops, or act out, which lowers the morale of the entire workshop. It may be necessary to reduce the number of participating students and then either have smaller workshops (which seems to be preferable) or have one workshop but with a larger number of students.

We have found that in-class announcements can be an effective recruiting technique, and work best when undergraduates (i.e., current workshop leaders and/or last semester's workshop leaders) give part of the talk. One of the best strategies was getting the RA in one of the science/engineering dorms to tell all the CS1 students on her floor. That is, students are more likely to be interested in such a program when they hear about it from a peer, rather than from a graduate student or faculty member.

We suspect also that the program would attract more students if it were institutionalized as a proper course that appeared in the registrar's bulletin of classes. At Columbia, CESP is an extracurricular program for which participating students get one unit of "research credit"; this allows us to select the students we find desirable and to limit enrollment. However, in some cases, freshman advisors who were not familiar with the program have expressed concern about their students participating in CESP, since it did not appear to be a "real" course. Additionally, although the students received one unit of credit, they could not apply it towards the graduation requirements for being a CS major in some cases. If CESP had its own course number and had a description in the course catalog, these problems may be overcome, and more students may choose to apply and participate.

4.2 Setting Expectations

In the early days of CESP, we struggled to properly convey during recruitment what, exactly, CESP was. Whether we advertised it in person or in an email, we knew we only had a few short moments to make a positive impression on the students, who may have thought to themselves "that sounds uninteresting to me" or "the last thing I need is yet another event in my schedule". Even though we specifically focused on the facts that CESP workshops consisted of small groups, that there would be only problem solving and no programming, and that CESP would be a lot of fun, it is possible that some students were turned off by notions that CESP would be tantamount to extra office hours or, worse, extra homework assignments.

Even the students who *did* decide to participate may have had incorrect notions of what CESP entailed. Wrote one in her exit survey, "Based on the descriptions, I had thought it would be more of a lecture style rather than small workshops. I like the way it turned out, but I had no idea when I applied." Wrote another, "I expected there to be more ... programming. It was more that we tackled basic puzzles, [and] just talked about solutions as opposed to what would actually go into a computer [program]."

As mentioned above, we have found that students tend to be more interested in CESP if they hear about it from a former participant, rather than from a graduate student or instructor. This may help in setting the expectations, too: even though the message is the same, it may sink in more when it comes from a peer. Since we started exclusively having undergraduates advertise the program, almost all students have said that CESP matched their expectations, compared to much lower numbers in previous semesters.

It has also been suggested that an "open house workshop" be held for all interested applicants, so that they can see for themselves what a CESP workshop is like before deciding whether to apply. We have not yet tried this but suspect it would at least give the students a solid idea of the PLTL concept, and may help increase the number of applicants. This may require some juggling of schedules, since ideally all participants would apply to, be accepted to, and sign up for CESP before the "add class deadline" (which is at the end of the second week of the semester at Columbia). It may be necessary to do this very early in the semester, perhaps even before first CS1 class meeting.

4.3 Scheduling

In the pilot program in Spring 2008, when we only had six participants, we first selected the students and then tried to find a time for workshops that fit into everyone's schedule. This, of course, does not scale particularly well. In the second semester of CESP, we accepted the top 15 applicants, regardless of their availability, and tried to balance them across two meeting times; however, we ended up with 11 students in one section and just four in another, which clearly was not desirable.

At our university, and supposedly at most others, Friday afternoon workshops seem to work for just about everyone. So now, just like a regular class, we select two times on Friday (maybe early afternoon and late afternoon) and then tell applicants "these are the times". We choose workshop leaders and assistants who can make those times and then, in the application for participants, students choose which time(s) they want to apply for. If they can't make it to either, then they don't get in. This runs the risk of excluding highly-desirable students just because of their availability, but is the only feasible approach for programs of any size greater than just a handful of students.

It is important to work out the weekly meeting times and the semester-long workshop schedule in the beginning of the semester. In CESP, there are nine workshops plus the end-of-semester reunion and party, so there is some wiggle room in the schedule. We have had to be particularly aware of religious holidays (many of which may be observed by the students but not by the university), the Grace Hopper conference, the course midterm, and exam review sessions. By scheduling around these events, we try to minimize students' absences and ensure a consistent attendance rate, which improves the flow of the workshops.

Scheduling is an issue that concerns not just the participating students, but the workshop leaders as well. When selecting peer leaders, we seek students who have enough time at reasonable hours to make both the workshop and any weekly coordinators meeting. As pointed out previously, the best approach has been to set the times in advance, and then find a student whose schedule allows her to be free at those times. In the early days of CESP, we worried that we would not be able to find qualified peer leaders, and in one semester selected a student who had a number of other commitments and did not have a very flexible schedule. Despite the student's enthusiasm and winning personality, she simply was not able to attend all meetings and could not spend adequate time preparing for her workshops. This is definitely a situation to avoid.

4.4 Training

Ideally, the peer leader would be a student who had previously participated in CESP, so that she is already familiar with the PLTL style as well as the material that is covered in each workshop. Of course, familiarity does not necessarily equate to competence or expertise, so it is essential that adequate time is invested at the beginning of the semester to training peer leaders and having them lead sample workshops. This is typically uncomfortable and awkward for the student, but is a good way to be sure that she is ready.

This training should continue over the course of the semester. During weekly coordinator meetings, we try to make sure that peer leaders are comfortable presenting the content themselves. Of course, if one asks a student "are you okay with this material?", she will almost always answer "yes", just to avoid having to present it in front of graduate students or faculty members, even if she really is not prepared. So we have the leaders present the material at the weekly meeting as if they were running the real workshop. This is the only way to know that they really are ready.

4.5 Behavior and Attendance

At the beginning of CESP, students are given a contract that lays out the expectations for how they will behave and participate in the workshops. This contract addresses issues related to using laptops and cellphones, and this policy is emphasized from the very beginning. In CESP, the students have one task and one task only: show up and pay attention for 60 minutes. That's it. No homework, no exams, no preparatory work. So it should be possible for them to be attentive for one hour a week without sending text messages or checking Facebook. There is no reason for students to be using cellphones or laptops during the workshops. A student who is not participating because she is distracted thus becomes a distraction to all other students, as well.

The CESP contract also stipulates that any lateness of more than 10 minutes is considered an absence, and more than two unexcused absences will result in a failing grade (CESP participants earn one point of pass/fail credit). In the very beginning, we emphasize to all students that it is important that they are on time for the workshops, as they cannot really get started until all participants are present.

There have been some occasions when we had to give students a failing grade because they missed (or were significantly late for) more than two workshops. We notify students after the second absence that they are in danger of failing if they miss another workshop or are very late. This adds a bit of administrative overhead during the semester, but will probably help avoid a difficult and uncomfortable situation down the road.

4.6 Discussion vs. Problem-Solving

As discussed above, CESP workshops focus on the algorithmic thinking aspects of computer science, in which students need to work together to devise a solution to a particular puzzle or problem. Often there is a "correct" solution to these problems, though in many cases there may be more than one solution or approach, and part of the workshop is to discuss the tradeoffs between the approaches.

We recently introduced a more open-ended, discussion-based workshop in which the students were asked to consider social issues related to computer science and technology, and then come up with legal or academic policies that made sense to them. We expected that the students would like this workshop very much, as it included topics that are familiar to the students, such as digital copyright laws and online plagiarism. However, in the exit surveys, the workshop was rated second-lowest (out of nine workshops) by the students. Surprisingly, some of the students commented that the workshop did not appear to be about computer science. This was very unexpected, and indicates that we need to broaden the students' concept of what "computer science" is and the issues that they, as computer scientists, will need to address in the future.

4.7 Evaluating the Program

The only way to know whether an Emerging Scholars Program is having a positive impact is to have a formalized way of tracking the students and accumulating both qualitative and quantitative data about their experience in ESP, CS1, and beyond.

At Columbia, all CESP participants fill out online surveys at both the beginning and end of the program that ask questions such as "how likely are you to take another CS course?" or "how likely are you to major in CS?" Ideally, the participating students' likelihood of taking another CS course or majoring in CS would rise after completing CESP, of course. And, supposedly, the increase in likelihood would be greater than the increase (if any) for those students *not* participating in the program.

Note that students' self-reported likelihood of taking another CS course or majoring in CS does not necessarily equate to *actually* taking another CS course or majoring in CS. However, gathering data about students' activities after they leave CS1 often requires assistance from the department or school's administration, and may bring about issues related to privacy. In order to collect that sort of data, we have had to get administrative buy-in beforehand, and make it clear that we wish to be able to answer questions such as "what percentage of CS1 students who did not participate in ESP go on to take CS2?".

For collecting other qualitative data, such as "how much of an impact did ESP have on your decision to take CS2 (or major in CS)?", it is important to stay in touch with ESP alumni so that they will be willing to provide such feedback. In our case, we sent out a survey to all former CESP students (some of whom had participated in the program two years prior), asking questions about the CS courses they had since taken and their impressions of CESP in hindsight, but had only a 33% response rate. Perhaps we would have had a higher response rate if we had set the expectation that we would later on ask such questions, rather than sending out the survey after a long period of no communication at all.

5. RESULTS

Fall 2010 marks the sixth semester of CESP offered as an adjunct to CS1 at Columbia University. Initial evaluation of CESP's impact on enrollment indicates that CESP is increasing women's participation in the computer science major at Columbia. Women's percentage of total computer science majors increased from 9 percent in 2007 to 21 percent in 2010, and to date 45% of CESP students who have declared a major chose Computer Science.

We have also observed that peer leaders benefit greatly from the program, as well, as they grow and gain confidence in themselves as computer scientists. To date, two former CESP peer leaders have participated in CRA-W's Distributed Research Experience for Undergraduates program, and one has earned an honorable mention for the CRA Outstanding Undergraduate Researcher award. Another currently is a software engineer at Microsoft. By all these measures, we consider CESP to be a success.

6. CONCLUSION

Emerging Scholars Programs, based on the Peer-Led Team Learning methodology, have been very effective in improving retention in CS courses and increasing the number of students who choose CS as their major [3]. However, starting, growing, and maintaining a successful program can be a tricky task. In this paper, we have described the Columbia Emerging Scholars Program, from its inception through its expansion, and discussed some of the lessons we have learned along the way. From recruiting and selecting students, to training peer leaders and scheduling meetings, to deciding on workshop topics and evaluation criteria, our experiences have been largely positive and the program has been a success. We hope that this paper will help other educators looking to start programs of their own.

7. ACKNOWLEDGMENTS

The authors would like to thank Remi Moss for her assistance with data collection, as well as Henning Schulzrinne, Shree Nayar, Julia Hirschberg, and Kathleen McKeown for their support and encouragement. We especially extend a special thanks to all the students who have participated in CESP. The Columbia Emerging Scholars Program is funded in part by the National Center for Women & Information Technology and Microsoft Research.

8. REFERENCES

[1] J. M. Cohoon. Toward improving female retention in the computer science major. *Communications of the ACM*, 44(5):108–114, May 2001.

[2] L. Gafney and P. Varma-Nelson. *Peer-Led Team Learning: evaluation, dissemination, and institutionalization.* Springer, 2008.

[3] S. Horwitz and S. H. Rodger. Using peer-led team learning to increase participation and success of under-represented groups in introductory computer science. In *Proc. of the 40th ACM technical symposium on computer science education*, pages 163–167, 2009.

[4] S. Huss-Lederman, D. Chinn, and J. Skrentny. Serious fun: peer-led team learning in CS. In *Proc. of the 39th SIGCSE technical symposium on Computer science education*, pages 330–331, 2008.

[5] R. M. Powell. Improving the persistence of first-year undergraduate women in computer science. In *Proc. of the 39th SIGCSE technical symposium on Computer science education*, pages 518–522, 2008.

[6] C. Stewart-Gardiner. Using peer led team learning to assist in retention in computer science classes. *Journal of Computing Sciences in Colleges*, 25(3):164–171, January 2010.

[7] U. Treisman. Studying students studying calculus: A look at the lives of minority mathematics students in college. *The College Mathematics Journal*, 23(5):362–372, Nov. 1992.

[8] T. T. Utschig and M. Sweat. Implementing peer led team learning in first-year programming courses. In *Proc. of the 38th Annual Frontiers in Education Conference*, pages F3C–13–F3C–18, 2008.

Tutoring for Retention

Joseph A. Cottam, Suzanne Menzel, Janet Greenblatt
Indiana University - School of Informatics and Computing
Bloomington, IN 47405; USA
{jcottam, menzel, jgreenbl}@indiana.edu

ABSTRACT

Peer tutoring is a simple, low-cost intervention that can be implemented in CS1/2 courses. It is hypothesized that peer tutoring helps students build a sense of community, succeed in course work, and build confidence to take further courses in the major. This paper examines the latter two hypotheses by examining the predicted and actual behavior of students in CS1/2. Course performance improvements were observed, which also strongly influence retention in computing-related courses. The measures also point to further research directions, such as social influences and the impact of peer tutoring relative to office hours or online forums.

Categories and Subject Descriptors

K.3.2 [**Computer And Information Science Education**]: Computer Science Education

General Terms

Measurement, Human Factors

Keywords

CS1/2, peer tutoring, recruitment, retention

1. INTRODUCTION

Five years ago, computer science education was in crisis. CS1 enrollments had plunged to a fifth of their previous levels. A variety of programs were quickly implemented at many institutions to try to increase enrollment, improve retention in the program and support student success. At Indiana University, a recruitment initiative, TryIT [15], targeted over one thousand first-year women and included a peer tutoring program to support new recruits. A year and a half later, the peer tutoring program was expanded to cover three courses: CS1, CS2 and a non-major programming course. However, the effectiveness of the peer tutoring program has never been formally examined. Informal observations indicate that concurrently with its expansion, retention rates have risen. Furthermore, student success has increased. This paper approaches these informal observations with more formal methods.

This paper proceeds with an explanation of the basis of our analysis. That is followed by a description of the peer tutoring program. We then examine the questions of "Does peer tutoring improve student performance?" and "Does peer tutoring improve retention?" We conclude with a description of a more detailed study covering more factors that can be used to enrich such recruitment and retention efforts.

2. RELATED WORK

As computer science emerged as a distinct field from mathematics and other engineering disciplines, much attention was paid to predicting success. A number of programming aptitude tests (PATs) were developed and targeted at retraining and certifying professionals in computing-related activities. These PAT batteries strongly correlated with mathematical ability. In the 1980s, the focus shifted from retraining, to predicting success in training, and then to predicting success in computing courses. Factors considered ranged from prior educational experience to psychological factors. The quantity of high school math courses passed (though not necessarily the exact GPA) consistently highly correlated with success in freshman computing courses [2, 7, 8]. This correlation in high school math also held with introductory level college math [1, 8, 10, 16]. Similar correlation to ACT and SAT scores composite score [2,8] emphasize the importance of math education but also the co-importance of language-related skills [13]. College math placement tests at the University of Tennessee at Martin (variants of which exist at most universities) were found to predict the success of students in computing courses [8].

Interesting results from these early studies of prediction include: (1) success in introductory computer science courses is predicted on both logical and linguistic basis [2, 8], and (2) most simple predictors (e.g., SAT, ACT, GPA) can only account for 20-30% of the variability seen in actual course performance [7, 8].

An earlier examination of the peer tutoring program at Indiana University showed a positive trend in retention and overall success rate in CS1 after the introduction of peer tutoring [15]. The degree to which this uptick can be attributed to peer tutoring and external factors was not examined, although the trend has continued. The study presented here looks at the impact of peer tutoring in a more struc-

Figure 1: A peer tutor consults with a CS1 student

tured and detailed way, attempting to provide insight into how much of an impact peer tutoring has and on whom.

3. TUTORING PROGRAM OVERVIEW

For each of the tutored classes, we hire a graduate student supervisor, and three undergraduate students who took the course within the previous two semesters, earned an A or A+, and are currently enrolled in some CS major course. Each week, two of the three tutors for each course lead a session. These sessions run three hours, in the evening, usually one or two days before the week's homework assignment is due. We typically schedule two sessions during exam weeks and towards the end of the semester.

We rely on professor recommendations to identify potential tutors from the students who took the class the previous semester. We choose students with excellent content knowledge, distinct communication skills, and role-model potential. To date, we have hired 53 tutors and 70% have been women. For the supervisor, we hire a graduate student who is familiar with the course but who is not directly involved with the course during the current semester. The supervisor's responsibilities include setting the weekly schedule, training tutors, and approving time cards for the tutors.

A faculty member directs the program; responsibilities include appointing the tutors and supervisors, coordinating the initial training session, scheduling the facilities, setting up the payroll, and assessing the program. The cost of the program is about $1,200 per course per semester.

3.1 Goals

The principle goal of the peer tutoring program is the retention of able students in the class, through future classes, and in the major.

Increase programming self-efficacy: Many students suffer from incorrect estimates of their own absolute and relative ability in computing. This distorted view leads capable students to abandon their studies even when they are performing well. This is especially pronounced in female students [4]. Providing an informal environment for working through homework problems provides a place where students can observe and work with other students, thereby gaining a better understanding of their peers' abilities as related to their own.

Develop community: By providing an environment where students can make friends with others in the major, peer tutoring helps form a community of students. The space is cheerful and inviting, well-lit and appropriately decorated [3], with ten computers and empty tables for those with laptops. A large whiteboard, scrap paper, and comfortable chairs appoint the space. Free snacks (e.g., cookies, chips, muffins, fruit) and drinks are provided at each session. The peer-to-peer nature of the interactions and the important fact that the tutors have no grading responsibilities means the discourse is more balanced than between student and professor. The student and the tutor have a similar status and speak a similar language. The students are more comfortable expressing opinions, more honest about their level of understanding, and more willing to take risks in proposing problem solving strategies [11].

Informal mentoring: The tutoring sessions provide an opportunity for tutors to mentor younger students regarding their next steps. This includes what courses to take, where to find jobs, and information about clubs and activities. Since the tutors are recruited from the pool of students who recently completed the CS course, they act as socially similar peers and role models of successful students.

Model soft skills: The peer tutoring sessions provide an environment where effective problem decomposition strategies are modeled and debugging strategies are emphasized. Tutors are trained in talk-out-loud and pair-programming protocols to model their own thought processes for students. Students are then encouraged to help each other through similar techniques. Critical analysis for debugging and corner case identification are modeled by tutors in these sessions. Students also benefit from working with others to approach programming problems. There are always two tutors in every session, so a tutor has another person to consult with on difficult cases. These "programming in the large" skills, often difficult to convey in lecture and lab formats, are essential to success in computing. Students who develop these skills are more self-sufficient, leading to greater confidence in their abilities and increased retention in the major.

Increase diversity: A desired side-effect of peer tutoring is increasing the participation of women in computing. To this end, we place excellent, qualified women students in the tutoring positions whenever possible. By creating the appearance that women are well represented, we hope to make it a future reality.

4. QUESTION 1: PERFORMANCE

As mentioned in Section 3, peer tutoring is provided to help students develop skills relevant to the course materials. How well the program achieves this goal is the focus of this analysis. Our principle question was, "At what level of tutoring participation, if ever, can performance changes be measured?" We used several measures to both predict and evaluate the performance of individuals in selected courses.

Data Set

Data concerning CS1 and CS2 couses at Indiana University, Bloomington, was collected starting in fall 2009. The data includes three basic components: (1) *a priori* predictors of success (used to identify peers); (2) tutoring logs; and (3) success measurements.

Sessions	0	1	2	3	4	5	6	7	8	9+
Students	186	38	23	20	9	8	7	7	4	11

Table 1: Tutoring counts by session for all semesters (313 total students).

We use three measurements to predict success in computer science courses, identified from earlier literature (see Section 2). The first is an SAT equivalent score calculated by the university at matriculation. SAT equivalent is equal to the SAT score if an SAT score is provided. If an ACT score is provided instead, it is converted to a score in the same range as the SAT using the SAT-ACT Concordance Tables provided by CollegeBoard [5]. SAT-Equivalent will be referred to simply as SAT for the remainder of this document. This measure can be directly translated to other institutions, but loses predictive power as the time since the test was taken increases.

The second indicator is the cumulative GPA of the student at the time of enrollment in the course [17]. This value does not experience the time degradation that SAT scores do since the most recent GPA is always used. However, GPA values cannot be known for first semester freshman. This eliminates 43 people from analysis based on this measure. GPA calculation is fully described on IU Registrar's website [9].

The third indicator is a math skills assessment (MSA) test administered to the majority of incoming students at Indiana University (foreign students do not always take the MSA). MSA is a 26 question, multiple-choice advising tool used, in conjunction with SAT score, to help students select an appropriate college math course. The MSA covers topics in algebra and pre-calculus. (There is a separate test to determine calculus placement that students can elect to take.) MSA scores are indicated by the number of questions answered correctly. Since math and CS skills are correlated [1], MSA has been used by the computer science program to direct new students to appropriate CS courses. The prerequisite for CS1 at Indiana University is "high school precalculus math" (an MSA score of at least 12) and CS2 requires only CS1 or equivalent. The MSA score is the most focused *a priori* indicator used. It suffers from time degradation, like the SAT, and is not as directly portable. However, an informal survey indicates that similar tests exist at many universities and thus a corresponding indicator probably exists. MSA is similar in purpose and construction to the instrument validated as a predictor for computing success at the University of Tennessee at Martin [8].

Tutoring logs indicate which tutoring session students attended. When a student attends a session, they are encouraged (but not required) to sign the log book. Tutoring sessions are typically available once a week during a semester. On average 6 students attend each session, but up to 26 have attended. Though the temporal information has been retained, this study uses only aggregate information. For the purposes of this analysis, a student is considered "tutored" if they attended two or more sessions during the semester. Tutoring data is summarized in Table 1.

Success in a course is determined by looking at three end-of-course values: the homework grade, the final exam grade, and the official course grade. In all three cases, the values were examined as the percentage of total points possible.

Indicators	Predictor Estimate	Tutoring Estimate
MSA Course	1.370***	7.413**
MSA Final	1.964***	.920
MSA Homework	.778	12.957*
SAT Course	.056***	9.306**
SAT Final	0.085***	3.887
SAT Homework	-.001	9.600
GPA Course	5.460***	4.797
GPA Final	7.687***	-3.574
GPA Homework	2.710	16.836**

Table 2: Parameter estimates and significance values for each *a priori* indicator. Individuals were considered "tutored" if they attended two or more sessions. * indicates p less than .05; ** indicates p less than .01; * indicates p less than .001.**

This allows comparison across semesters and course sections where small variations in the total points available occur. This three-part examination of success was conducted to improve the assessment of which skills peer tutoring impacts. The course grade is a composite of all of the skills learned, and often the only grade that students care about. However, the tutoring sessions focused on homework assignments, and thus we expect to see an impact on homework grade more than any other.

The three components of the data set came from separate sources. The *a priori* indicators originate from the registrar and were provided to us by the Associate Vice Provost for Undergraduate Education. Success indicators were collected with the cooperation of the course instructors. Only students who completed the course were considered in this study (though data concerning students who withdrew was also collected). Tutoring attendance was assessed with the help of dated logs. As described in Section 4, each student was encouraged to sign in when attending a tutoring session. These logs were retained and encoded for the purposes of this study. This data set is available upon request to other researchers.

Analysis Performed

The analysis performed was a series of linear regressions with normally distributed errors. All analysis was performed using The R Project for Statistical Computing [12]. In all cases, an interact between tutoring and an *a priori* indicator was considered to predict a success indicator. This leads to a default model with one dependent variable and three independent variables. The default models were considered for simplification using ANOVA analysis with a model that did not include the interaction [6]. In all cases, the simpler model was retained (use of the more complex model will be explicitly noted in discussion), though further simplification to just the dependent variable and tutoring was only warranted for homework grades. A p-value $< .01$ was considered significant for model simplification, but a p-value $< .05$ was accepted for other analysis.

Determing what constituted a "tutored" individual was approached analytically. Exploratory analysis on preliminary data indicated that treating tutored count directly would be problematic. With the full data set, each integral value of tutored counts was considered as a division point for tutored vs. not tutored with respect to MSA. Two

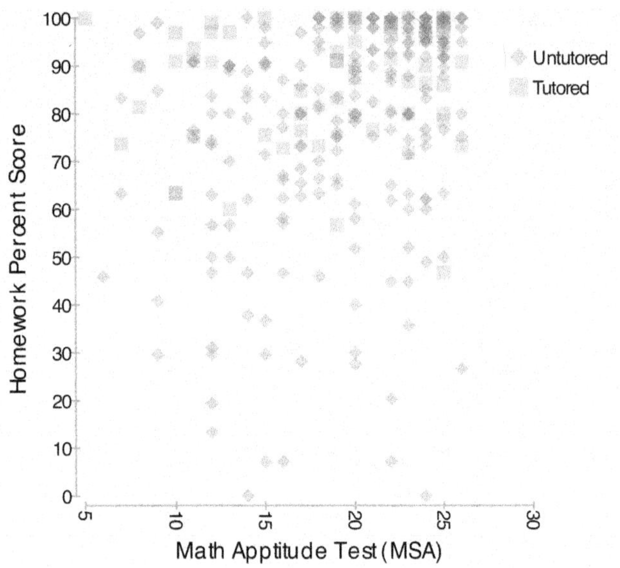

Figure 2: MSA vs expected grade with tutoring highlighted.

or more tutoring sessions attended was selected because this marked the start of a series of significantly impacting values.

Discussion

The analysis performed yielded several interesting results. Parameter estimates and p-value ranges are given in Table 2.

First, earlier work using MSA-like tests, SAT scores and GPA as predictors of success in computing courses is confirmed by our analysis. In all cases, the overall course grade and the final exam scores were significantly predicted by the *a priori* indicator. This analysis further indicates that the CollegeBoard ACT to SAT translations can be used along side of raw SAT scores for this purpose. Interestingly, none of these indicators significantly predicted homework performance. This lack of predictor for homework performance limits any analysis of peer tutoring's impact on homework grades because we have no clear predictor. However, important lessons can still be learned.

Second, tutoring had an significant impact on the course grade in two of the three predictors (SAT and MSA). We consider this an indication that peer tutoring had a positive impact on course performance, however, this effect was secondary to that of the *a priori* predictor. Interpreting the parameter estimate, a 7-9% increase in overall course performance was experienced by tutored students.

Third, peer tutoring did not have a significant impact on final exam grades. The difference between final and course evaluation cannot be used to estimate the impact of tutoring on homework scores because in-class participation, lab assignments and the mid-term also influence the final grade.

Finally, no *a priori* indicator was found to be a significant predictor of homework grades. As an *a posteriori* test, the impact of tutoring count on homework grade was measured and found significant (estimate = 3.169; p-value = .001). This indicates a strong relationship between tutoring and homework grades, approximately 3% per additional session. However, the baseline of this measurement is not known because of the lack of an *a priori* indicator. Furthermore, there is insufficient data at higher session counts to be confident in any analysis (see Table 1).

While pursuing model simplification, the ANOVA comparing the interaction-including model with the simpler models occasionally returned a p-value between .05 and .01. Though below the significance level we established, this warrants further investigation as more data is collected. It indicates that students with certain *a priori* indicator levels also tend to use (or avoid) peer tutoring. This explanation is plausible given that tutoring is one of many study tools and use of employing tools also tends to predict academic success. The lack of significant impact of tutoring when using GPA as a predictor may also be caused by this overlap of study tools and peer tutoring.

Sessions	0	1	2	3	4	5	6	7	8	9	*Totals*
Lost	29	5	5	5	3	0	1	1	0	0	*49*
Retained	66	16	5	4	0	5	2	1	1	1	*101*

Table 3: Tutoring counts vs. retention breakdown for the Fall 2009 semester (150 total students).

5. QUESTION 2: PROGRAM RETENTION

An informal observation of students who participated in peer tutoring indicated that they were more likely to take additional courses in computer science. This analysis investigates this observation more formally.

Data Set

The data sources employed to evaluate program retention are the same as those used in the prior question. A student was considered retained if they were enrolled in CS1 or CS2 and then took any additional majors focused computer science course in the subsequent three semesters. Due to the longitudinal nature of retention, only students enrolling during the fall 2009 semester can be fairly evaluated for retention at this time. This data is summarized in Table 3. A single instructor taught all classes except one section of CS2, which was taught by a professor who followed the same curriculum as the other CS2 section in this study. Information on subsequent course enrollment originated with the university registrar's office, but was provided by the Associate Vice Provost for Undergraduate Education.

Performance in introductory courses is also a strong predictor of retention in a degree program. A minimum level of performance is often a pre-requisite to future courses. Therefore, final course grade was also considered in this analysis. Course performance data was collected from official records kept by course instructors. (Limitations are discussed for all questions in Section 6.)

Analysis

Regression analysis was performed comparing retention in the program to the final grade in the course and participation in tutoring. Final grade was included in the model because it is highly correlated with retention taking further courses in a degree program. Tutoring participation was treated as a continuous variable on the number of times tutoring was attended. Since course retention is a binary variable, a binomial error distribution was used in a generalized linear regression. The original regression used a mixture model with respect to tutoring and final grade, but ANOVA analysis indicated that a simplified two-factor model was sufficient [6]. A p-value of $< .05$ was considered significant.

Discussion

The two-factor model of program retention indicated two informative findings. First, students are retained based on their course score (with p-value of $< .001$). This is a very strong effect, with an estimated impact coefficient of .04. Although not surprising, it does indicate that increases in course score translate into increased retention. Second, the fitted model indicated that tutoring did not significantly impact retention rates. This indicated that, beyond the increase in grade, there was no measurable difference in retention based on attendance at tutoring. Any effect of tutoring on retention independent of course success is expected to be small, and may not be discernible given the small sample size.

Due to small sample sizes over two tutoring sessions, analysis was repeated considering all individuals who had attended two or more tutoring sessions as "tutored." However, this further treatment did not change the lack of significance impact of tutoring on retention.

6. LIMITATIONS

The principle limitation and source of error in this study is the division of tutored and untutored individuals. The tutored individuals are a self-selecting population, so our data represents a convenient sample. Though controls have been established for *a priori* indicators available through the academic setting, many other factors could influence participation in the available tutoring. This includes mundane matters such as scheduling conflicts with the tutoring sessions to more complex matters such as social disposition. This analysis assumes that conflicting factors are shared across the tutored and untutored populations in a comparable fashion.

The second source of error is undercounting of student attendance at tutoring sessions. This comes from two sources. First, students were not required to sign in at a tutoring session. They were originally encouraged with the justification that only attendance counts were desired. As such, approximately 20% of log entries are for "anonymous" or similar placeholders. It is certain that some students did not sign in at all. Second, under-reporting of tutoring is certain because four of the log sheets have been lost. We made no attempt to recover the information on these log sheets, nor to proxy its possible contents analytically. The analysis presented here represents the data as collected. Using an optional sign-in also hides a potentially significant data point: length of stay. Tutoring sessions last three hours, but a person attending for thirty minutes appears the same in the data as one staying the full duration. Total tutoring time likely varies between individuals.

A source of error that impacts the use of composite course grades and homework grades is the lack of controls on when, where and how much of the work is done for the course. As is common, students are expected to do much of the work outside of class, and environment impacts performance. During the second half of CS2 (eight weeks), students work in pairs on a long-term project. Although they must meet certain milestones along the way, they ultimately receive a single project grade for their efforts. The homework grade for CS2 is calculated as a weighted combination of the regular weekly assignments from the first half of the semester and the project grade. An additional confounding factor is that students in CS1 and CS2 are offered an appeal process on their weekly homework assignments. Students may resubmit a homework assignment for a replacement grade within two weeks of its due date. In the extreme case, an F on a homework can be upgraded to a B. Earning a B after appeal is indistinguishable from a B that was originally earned. The impact of the appeal process likely masks some of the effects of tutoring. For this reason, the final exam score is also considered independently, even though homework was the focus of the peer tutoring.

The fourth limitation of this study derives from inaccuracy of *a priori* indicators. The SAT and GPA scores are not specific to computer science, though they do generally predict academic success in a post-secondary setting. The SAT and MSA scores suffer a loss of predictive power as the time between their administration increases. The MSA has not been *formally* validated, but it has been in use at Indiana University for about 30 years. None of the indicators are specifically tailored to computer science. This limitation is unavoidable as no direct predictor of success in computer science is available for the population being studied.

7. FUTURE WORK

Future work divides into three large groups: (1) further analysis with the data set already acquired; (2) acquisition and analysis of more detailed data on CS1 and CS2 students; and (3) studying the impact of tutoring on the larger educational picture.

The existing data includes the dates during the semester students attended tutoring sessions. The presented analysis did not consider this temporal aspect. There are reasons to believe that tutoring is helpful at all stages of the semester. Early on, it may help establish effective study and work habits. Mid-semester is when many foundational concepts are encountered, and the small relative difference between peers might provide the most opportunities for peer teaching. Late in the semester, as homework becomes more challenging, the cooperative aspects of the peer tutoring environment may provide opportunities for students to collectively work through problems they would otherwise abandon. All of these are plausible arguments, but our work has not establish which (if any) effects actually occur. If a reason for difference in early/mid/late semester tutoring can be assessed, an effective difference in impact would help improve resource allocation.

The analysis presented is focused on immediate and objective measures of student performance. However, this does not indicate *how* the effects were achieved. Is it a sense of engagement in the material or the additional skills practice that raises the grade? Do the social aspects of peer tutoring matter to student performance or retention in the program? Understanding how peer tutoring benefits students can guide refinement of existing programs and implementation of new programs. To achieve this, more detailed information about participants in CS1 is required. A pre- and post-survey of educational attitudes, skills self-assessment and interests is being piloted in fall 2010. The survey design builds on the work of Spence [14], who found that mathematics self-efficacy is among the most significant predictors of mathematics achievement. Responses will be analyzed to illuminate (1) a profile of students who opt in to tutoring (independent of the success predictors) and (2) a more detailed examination of the impact of tutoring.

In addition to the short-term continuation rate, we hypothesize peer tutoring improves retention of students in the computer science major. This may be the result of increased success, or of building of a stronger sense of community. Assessing this requires tracking individuals beyond the first few classes. The survey being piloted poses questions about major/minor intentions. Tracking of actual retention can be accomplished through standard educational records, which can also address some questions of performance. Having an *a priori* predicator of success that can be used to estimate success in a course three to four years later would be required for a well-founded assessment of a performance impact of tutoring in CS1 in a later course.

These last two points align with research into the psychological factors of computing and computing education. Tools such as the Myers-Briggs Temperament Indicator and TTS personality measurements have been correlated prior with success in computing courses [1, 16]. Examining these predictors of success and the relative impact of peer tutoring could help indicate how psychological factors influence both participation in and benefits from peer tutoring. Confidence scales developed to assess self-efficacy in math can be adapted to create a confidence scale for programming and we can measure the change in confidence between the tutored and untutored groups.

Independent of the students being tutored, an interesting question is how the peer tutors themselves are impacted by the tutoring program. As mentioned in Section 4, tutors are recruited from those who recently completed the course successfully and have continued in the major. To establish if acting as a peer tutor has an impact on later class performance, CS1 and CS2 grades could be used as a baseline measure for performance and compared to performance while acting as a tutor.

Many of the proposed directions can be targeted to investigate questions surrounding under-represented groups. For example, women are more likely to leave the computer science major, independent of their actual abilities [4]. Assessing the particular impact of peer tutoring on women and other minorities is an important future work.

8. CONCLUSIONS

Informally, peer tutoring has been observed to improve both retention of individuals in the computer science program and student performance in individual classes. Our analysis has validated both of these claims. Given the relatively low cost and known positive impact, further study of the impacts of peer tutoring is warranted. Further study is required to measure and quantify the many perceived intangible benefits the peer tutoring program has on the students, the tutors, and the culture and climate of the computer science program. Beyond studying peer tutoring, we can recommend that peer tutoring programs be expanded, both at Indiana University and other schools.

9. ACKNOWLEDGMENTS

The authors thank Prof. Dennis Groth for providing registrar data and the Open Systems Laboratory for the time and resources that enabled this research. Consultations with the Indiana University Stat/Math consulting center and Prof. Peter Kloosterman in the School of Education were extremely valuable in planning, executing and interpreting this study.

10. REFERENCES

[1] C. A. Alspaugh. Identification of some components of computer programming aptitude. *Journal for Research in Mathematics Education*, 3(2):pp. 89–98, 1972.

[2] P. F. Campbell and G. P. McCabe. Predicting the success of freshmen in a computer science major. *Commun. ACM*, 27(11):1108–1113, 1984.

[3] S. Cheryan, V. C. Plaut, P. Davies, and C. M. Steele. Ambient belonging: How stereotypical cues impact gender participation in computer science. *Journal of Personality and Social Psychology*, 97(6):1045 –1060, December 2009.

[4] J. M. Cohoon and W. Aspray. *Women and Information Technology: Research on Underrepresentation*, chapter 5, pages 137 – 180. The MIT Press, 2006.

[5] CollegeBoard. SAT-ACT concordance tables. `http://professionals.collegeboard.com/data-reports-research/sat/sat-act`, August 2010.

[6] M. J. Crawley. *Statistics: An Introduction using R.* John Wiley & Sons, Inc., 2005.

[7] G. E. Evans and M. G. Simkin. What best predicts computer proficiency? *Commun. ACM*, 32(11):1322–1327, 1989.

[8] E. Gathers. Screening freshmen computer science majors. *SIGCSE Bull.*, 18(3):44–48, 1986.

[9] Indiana Unviersity Office of the Registrar. Gpa calcuation. `http://registrar.indiana.edu/gpacal.shtml`, September 2010.

[10] J. Konvalina, S. A. Wileman, and L. J. Stephens. Math proficiency: a key to success for computer science students. *Commun. ACM*, 26(5):377–382, 1983.

[11] S. Loos, S. Menzel, and M. Poparad. Three perspectives on peer tutoring for CS1. In *Proceedings of the Midwest Celebration of Women in Computing conference*, `http://www.cs.indiana.edu/cgi-pub/midwic/papers/uploads/loos.pdf`, 2005.

[12] R Development Core Team. *R: A language and environment for statistical computing.* R Foundation for Statistical Computing, Vienna, Austria, 2005.

[13] V. L. Sauter. Predicting computer programming skill. *Computers & Education*, 10(2):299 – 302, 1986.

[14] D. Spence. *Engagement with Mathematics Courseware in Traditional and Online Learning Environments: Relationship to Motivation, Achievement, Gender, and Gender Orientation.* PhD thesis, Emory University, 2004. `http://www.des.emory.edu/mfp/SpenceDissertation2004.pdf`.

[15] G. C. Townsend, S. Menzel, and K. A. Siek. Leveling the CS1 Playing Field. In *SIGCSE '07*, pages 331–335. ACM, 2007.

[16] L. H. Werth. Predicting student performance in a beginning computer science class. In *SIGCSE '86*, pages 138–143. ACM, 1986.

[17] R. N. Wolfe and S. Johnson. Personality as a predictor of college performance. *Educational and Psychological Measurement*, (55):177–185, 1995.

Multidisciplinary Computer Science through Conducting Robots

Andrea Salgian
Dept. of Computer Science
The College of New Jersey
Ewing, NJ 08628
+1 609 771 2933
salgian@tcnj.edu

Christopher Ault
Interactive Multimedia Program
The College of New Jersey
Ewing, NJ 08628
+1 609 771 2236
ault@tcnj.edu

Teresa M. Nakra
Dept. of Music
The College of New Jersey
Ewing, NJ 08628
+1 609 771 2759
nakra@tcnj.edu

Yunfeng Wang
Dept. of Mechanical Engineering
The College of New Jersey
Ewing, NJ 08628
+1 609 771 2458
jwang@tcnj.edu

Meredith K. Stone
Independent Evaluator
Lawrenceville, NJ 08648
+1 609 895 1239
MeredithKStone@aol.com

ABSTRACT

In this paper, we describe an ongoing multidisciplinary undergraduate seminar that we have developed, in which student teams build non-human systems that conduct our college orchestra. Students and faculty in the course come from four disciplines: computer science, interactive multimedia, music, and mechanical engineering. This paper describes the course structure, computer science components, final projects, team dynamics, and assessments. We evaluate the results to-date and discuss ongoing revisions and expectations for the future.

Categories and Subject Descriptors

K.3.2. **[Computers and Education]:** Computer and Information Science Education – *Computer science education*; J.2. **[Computer Applications]**: Physical Sciences and Engineering – *Engineering*; J.5. **[Computer Applications]**: Arts and Humanities - *Music*

General Terms

Algorithms, Design, Human Factor.

Keywords

multidisciplinary, robotics, interfaces, music, orchestral conducting

SIGCSE'11, March 9–12, 2011, Dallas, Texas, USA.

1. INTRODUCTION

As we advance into the 21st century, computer science is increasingly playing a central role in other disciplines, from science and engineering to humanities and arts. Nearly all areas of academic and scholarly endeavor now rely on computer software for presenting and conducting academic research. Future generations of scientists, engineers, and artists will benefit from understanding and using principles of computer science and computational thinking [12, 3].

Many of the most pressing problems of the day are best solved using interdisciplinary approaches [8]. However, the standard paradigm in interdisciplinary work is that it requires participants to become fluent in *all* of the participating disciplines, sometimes sacrificing depth for the sake of breadth. A *multidisciplinary* approach modifies this scenario through the participation of specialists from different fields who have the necessary skills to communicate with each other and produce a collaborative solution through a common perspective [2].

Regardless of their subject discipline, 21st-century undergraduates will be better served by a multidisciplinary approach to education, to prepare them for future tasks and environments. Non-computer science majors should become familiar with concepts of computational thinking, while computer science majors should learn to communicate with specialists from other disciplines. Recently, a wide variety of interdisciplinary approaches to computer science education have been developed and described in the literature, ranging from entire programs [6] to interdisciplinary courses that combine computer science with computer games [13], robotics [11], science [4, 2], media [6], and music [5].

In this paper we describe our own implementation of the multidisciplinary approach through an undergraduate seminar entitled "Conducting Robots." Our course brings together students majoring in computer science, mechanical engineering, interactive multimedia and music in a common setting. It is a project-oriented course that fosters critical thinking, creative problem solving, and computational thinking skills through an open-ended team project requiring the synthesis of knowledge in all four core disciplines.

Students work collaboratively to design and develop innovative robotic and graphical conducting systems that can direct an orchestra. Topics taught include robotics, visual music, abstract animation, computer vision, algorithms, data processing, music conducting, and project management. We discuss the course structure in Section 2, and the computer science component in Section 3. We describe some of the students' final projects in section 4, team dynamics in Section 5 and conclude in Section 6.

2. COURSE STRUCTURE

The Conducting Robots course is an ongoing one-semester course that has been offered twice, in the fall and spring semester of the 2009-2010 academic year. Both times the course was cross-listed in the departments of Computer Science, Interactive Multimedia, Mechanical Engineering, and Music, and was taught by a team of four instructors, one from each department (the authors). Throughout both semesters we worked with an independent evaluator to develop and administer student surveys and interviews. In addition, students were asked to keep a reflection journal. From the first weeks of the first semester these tools were used to evaluate the course and modify it based on student feedback.

The main challenge was designing lectures and assignments for students with four different disciplines as a background. All the students were fairly advanced in their own major (junior or senior level), and had varying amounts of knowledge in the other disciplines involved in the course.

Initially, the course was planned as a two-semester course, with a design phase in the fall semester, followed by an implementation phase in the spring semester. The fall semester was going to be filled with lectures in the four subject areas that would provide necessary background in all the four disciplines. The end of the semester was to be spent on the design of an initial prototype that was going to be implemented and refined in the spring semester.

However, early in the fall semester it became apparent that the majority of students would not be able to register for two semesters due to requirements of their majors. Moreover, they were eager to start building prototypes and get hands-on experience. Traditional lectures and assignments in specific subject areas (especially computer science and mechanical engineering) were either difficult for students majoring in other areas, or boring for students already familiar with the field.

Therefore, in the middle of the semester we decided to change the structure of the class and allow students to work in interdisciplinary teams to develop a non-human conductor. Five teams were formed, and with the exception of the mechanical engineering majors (of whom only three were enrolled in the course), each major was represented on each team.

The second time we offered the class (in spring 2010), the number of traditional discipline specific lectures and assignments was significantly reduced. Their content was changed to be less dependent on in-major background, and more relevant to the course-specific project. Students formed (larger) interdisciplinary teams from the first week and started brainstorming design ideas right away. Whether they were working on the final project or on a smaller assignment, they were expected to rely more on their teammates for problem solving, and therefore become more involved in tutoring each other.

Since many of the students were not very familiar with classical music, numerous opportunities were provided to give them exposure. In addition to the regular weekly class meetings, students were required to attend one rehearsal session of the college Orchestra. The instructors arranged for a group trip to see the Philadelphia Orchestra conducted by Charles Dutoit at the Kimmel Center in Philadelphia. Additionally, the conductor of the college Orchestra served as a consultant on this project, and made himself personally available to the students for interviews and discussions about conducting technique.

We also invited guest speakers that provided expertise in different areas required by our project.

3. COMPUTER SCIENCE COMPONENT

In the first semester we introduced the students to computer science and programming through Matlab. The reason for this was that Matlab was required for some of the mechanical engineering content, including forward and inverse kinematics. Students started with simple matrix operations and plotting, and continued with control structures and functions. Due to the limited amount of time, this material was covered in two 3-hour combined lecture/lab sessions. Students worked on two individual assignments that were not related to the conducting robots topic.

Based on student feedback and performance, our approach was different in the second semester. Students continued to use Matlab for mechanical engineering assignments, but this time without control structures and functions. Computer science was introduced through Processing, a Java-based open source programming language and environment for people who want to program images, animation, and interactions [9]. This approach allowed for an easy introduction of algorithms and control structures, as well as computer-based drawing and animation in one 3-hour session. Students worked on a music animation assignment, and while the assignments were individual, they were strongly encouraged to seek help from their computer science major teammates.

Reflection journals and average assignment grades show that the second approach was more successful. Students found it more compelling, as it allowed them to explore computer science in a project-related context. Table 1 shows the average grades obtained by the students on computer science assignments by their major. Not surprisingly, due to their prior background, the best results were obtained by the computer science majors. They were followed by the interactive multimedia majors, due to the closeness of their field to computer science. The weakest results were obtained by the music majors, who were not always able to finish all the requirements, but showed good effort nonetheless.

Table 1. Average Computer Science grades by major

Major	Fall	Spring
Computer Science	92%	96%
Interactive Multimedia	91%	96%
Mechanical Engineering	74%	90%
Music	77%	82%

In addition to being introduced to algorithms and control structures, students gained hands-on computer science experience through their final project. Music majors worked together with computer science majors to develop an abstract description of conducting gestures, and of the music that needed to be conducted. Most teams decided to work with the MIDI file format, which they approached through the Finale music composing and notation software. Some teams wrote their own MIDI parsers, while others used existing sample code. Then computer science majors worked together with interactive multimedia majors to create live animations, and with mechanical engineering majors to program the microcontrollers controlling the robots. Programs were written in a variety of languages, including Java, C, and Processing.

4. THE FINAL PROJECT

The final objective of the course was to have students build non-human conductors based on graphics and robots that could conduct an orchestra. The minimum requirement was that each system should indicate beat patterns, tempo, dynamics and cueing to a human ensemble in real-time.

During the Fall, student teams were formed somewhat late in the semester (around week seven). As a result, the final project deliverables were relaxed a little bit. The 20 students enrolled in the class were divided into five teams. The two teams without engineering majors focused on graphical conducting systems, while the other teams built robotic conductors complemented with graphical visualizations. The robots were built using Lego Mindstorms NXT kits.

Students were encouraged to build general systems that could conduct any musical piece, but for practical purposes (slower tempo, simplicity of cueing, etc.) the conductor of the TCNJ orchestra suggested Beethoven's 7th Symphony, Movement 2. The conducting systems were required to conduct at least one minute of the piece.

Five different prototypes were developed. Testing occurred during two special sessions of our college orchestra at the end of the semester. The quality of these prototypes was judged by the performing musicians who gave scores on a scale of 1 to 10 for the systems' tempo, dynamics, section cuing, conducting style/beat pattern, articulation and level of interaction. Due to the small size of the robotic conductors and the nature of the musical score, only the string section (violins, violas, and celli) of the orchestra attended the rehearsals (25 musicians). The movements of the robotic conductors were also projected on a big screen for visibility. Although it was the first time the course was offered, and it was the musicians' first experience with a robotic conductor, all of the systems worked and obtained satisfactory scores from the orchestra.

Figure 1 shows three of the five conducting systems developed by students in the first semester. *C3* (*Cybernetic Conducting Contraption*, top) was built using the Lego Mindstorms NXT robotic kit, and had two arms. The right arm had two degrees of freedom and was used to conduct beat and dynamics; the left arm had one degree of freedom and was used for cueing. *C3*'s functionality was constrained by the limitations of the NXT kit, which can control only up to three motors.

Ahasimo (bottom left) was a non-humanoid graphic conductor implemented in Processing. It conveyed beats by means of two pulsing circles, while dynamics were controlled by the bar on the right. Its cueing functionality was modeled after the Guitar Hero graphical interface.

GUS (bottom right) was a humanoid graphic conductor implemented in Maya. Just like the robotic conductor *C3*, *GUS* used its right arm to conduct beat and dynamics, while the left arm was used for cueing. Each arm had three degrees of freedom.

The second time we offered the course (Spring 2010), teams formed in the first week of the semester and started brainstorming design ideas right away. This time the teams were larger, with 17 students divided into three teams, each having two mechanical engineering majors. Each team was required to work on systems with both a mechanical and a media component that had to be complementary, rather than redundant. Robots had to be at least half human size, to be visible by the orchestra. Each team picked its own musical piece to conduct at a public concert event with the college orchestra at the end of the semester.

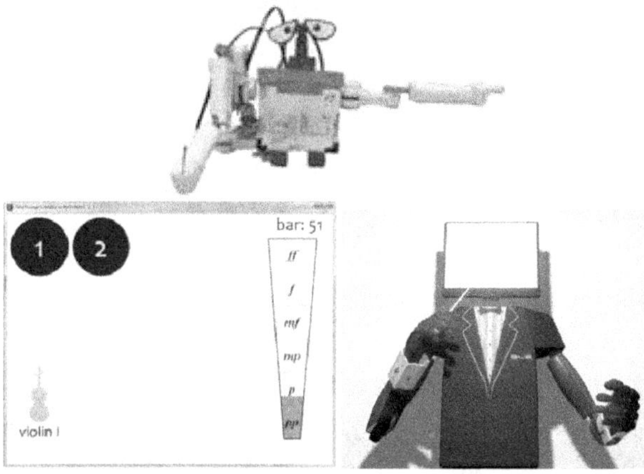

Figure 1. Prototypes built by students in the first semester:C3, Ahasimo, and GUS

As in the previous semester, the robots were evaluated in a demonstration with the string section of the orchestra, and the musicians gave satisfactory scores to all the robots.

Seven of the 17 students enrolled in the spring class also took the fall class. We allowed them to do so because of our initial plan to have a two-semester course. In the future we will not allow students to take the class for a second time.

Figure 2 shows the prototypes built by the students in the second semester. The students in team *C3* from the fall continued in team *C4* in the spring and, although they built a new robot (top right), they benefitted from their experience in the Fall semester. The *C4* robot was still humanoid (like *C3*), but was built using the VEX robotic kit and the Arduino microcontroller. Each arm had three degrees of freedom, and they used a mirrored motion to indicate the beat pattern and tempo. Dynamics were indicated by increasing the size of the gesture of the right arm while the left arm would be raised or lowered. Cues were indicated by the left arm pointing at the appropriate section. Articulation was communicated by the robot with both arms, the smoothness of the gestures corresponding to articulation. The robot also featured two real-time procedural animations implemented in Processing: an animated face for the orchestra, and an additional animation on its back to entertain the audience.

This robot was the only one that could "hear" the orchestra, using the Chuck audio programming language [1] for real time audio processing. The motion of the robot and the facial gesture are adjusted according to the tempo and dynamics played by the orchestra.

ACRE (top right) was the robot with the most advanced mechanical component, due to the fact that the engineering majors on the team were working on this as part of their senior design project as well. *ACRE* is a human size humanoid robot built from scratch without the use of any kits, and uses the Arduino microcontroller. It uses its right arm to indicate the beat pattern, and the left arm to indicate cueing and dynamics.

Instead of using the score of the music, the robot learned to conduct from a video of a human conducting the same piece. The hands were tracked in the video using the system described in [7]. Inverse kinematics was used to define a robot motion that would mimic that of the human conductor.

The robot simulates knee bending through the use of a linear actuator in the lower body, and could turn to face different orchestra sections. In addition, the robot's head displayed a human face that expressed emotional changes according to the score.

The third robot, *Superconductor* (bottom) was not humanoid. It consisted of a "baton" that rotated on a square board with four LED lights. The rotation of the baton, together with the lights, conveyed the beat pattern. The lights could move closer together or further apart suggesting the dynamics. The team composed its own music to highlight the features of the robot.

Figure 2. Prototypes built by students in the second semester: *C4*, *ACRE*, and *SuperConductor*

5. TEAM DYNAMICS

Students worked in multidisciplinary teams of four in the fall, and six in the spring. Every discipline was represented on each team, with the exception of two teams in the fall that did not have any engineering majors.

Students were asked to keep biweekly confidential reflection journals that documented whether they were aware of "aha" experiences and who they learned from throughout the semester. The journals were collected by an independent evaluator who also summarized the results for the instructors.

These journals show that teamwork changed students' perception of their own, as well as the other, disciplines. Music majors started out intimidated by the technical majors whom they referred to as "smart" majors. The realization that these majors didn't have any background in music and conducting was an important boost to their confidence. Students saw quickly that conducting systems could not function without musical expertise.

While engineering and IMM majors came in knowing exactly what their task would be (build a robot or create a visualization of the music), they had to work with the music majors to understand the functionality of the system that was being built.

Indeed music majors were not only clients for the other students on the team, but active participants in the design process. Music students used their skills in musical interpretation (the art of nuance in performance), by making decisions about time-varying aspects in the score. These decisions about elements such as dynamics and tempo are part of the added value that conductors bring to an orchestral performance; the music students were assigned this role. They then documented their decisions and converted them to a quantitative representation that would be machine readable and usable for machine control. For the most part, they relied on the MIDI format for this function; most of the music students used music notation or MIDI sequencing packages such as Finale or Logic. Some created a metaexpression format, redefining MIDI messages for their own purposes.

While all the instructors understood from the very beginning the major role that computer science would play in the project, students were less clear on this point. Both engineering and IMM students came into the class with some knowledge of programming, and believed they were able to put their systems in motion. The presence of the computer science major seemed unnecessary. In addition, at the beginning of the semester computer science majors did not have the technical background necessary to build a robot or to create a visualization, so some of them started out by feeling that their presence was not required for a successful project.

As the semester progressed, students soon realized that computer science was the link that held all the pieces together. A conducting system uses music to guide its movements. Whether it is the actual musical score (possibly with a human conductor's annotations) or information about how a human conductor moves his hands to conduct the piece, the language in which this information is represented differs greatly from the language that controls the artificial system. The role of computer science then is a major one: convert the musical representation into one that can be used by a robot or visualization system.

Since students are required to build systems that can conduct any musical piece, this conversion cannot be done by hand. It requires a general algorithm that can break up any musical piece into small pieces, analyze and convert them into another representation, and put them back together. Students have to use *abstraction* to solve this problem, as well as knowledge from all the areas involved: music, engineering and multimedia. While the computer science major has some expertise in algorithm design and implementation, working with a multidisciplinary team requires him/her to communicate in a language that is understood by everyone. Through this process, CS majors gained a better understanding of their own field, while the other students were introduced to the basics of computational thinking.

From the first semester to the second, we observed a change in the students' approach: during Semester 1, the students generally thought about their non-human conductors as signal generators, whereas during Semester 2, they started to define the conducting function as interacting with the musicians in a mutual feedback loop, and started looking into real-time audio processing concepts.

We believe that improved communication between team members was instrumental in this development.

In addition to reflection journals, we asked students to assess their own and their teammates' teamwork, using a rubric developed based on [10]. This assessment, together with the instructors' perception of students' individual teamwork, was used to determine individual final grades in the course. The attributes in the rubric were:

- Process – includes caring about goals, exhibiting leadership skills, helping the group in setting and meeting goals, and exhibiting consistent on-task behavior
- Communication – includes sharing ideas, encouraging other group members to share ideas, listening skills, incorporating comments
- Interpersonal skills and social interaction – includes involving the whole group in problem solving, actively working together with the group, being aware and respecting the views and opinions of others, empathizing with others' ideas and feelings
- Contributions – includes contributions to decision making, work, and evaluation
- Responsibility sharing – includes active participation, completion of assigned tasks, and ensuring that responsibilities are evenly assigned

Since these evaluations were seen only by the instructors, students did not hesitate to pinpoint those who did not contribute enough to their team.

The change in course structure from the fall to the spring semester was visible in the team dynamics as well. Teams formed and started work earlier, and teamwork was emphasized in assignments throughout the semester. While most students rated their teammates as excellent both times, more students were satisfied with their teammates performance the second time we offered the course (Figure 3).

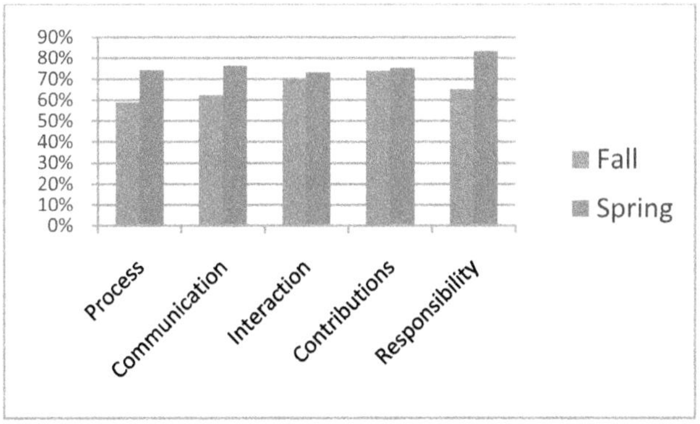

Figure 3. Percentage of teamwork attributes evaluated as "Excellent"

Teamwork issues had to be resolved in the instructor team as well. Given the fundamental differences between science, engineering, and the arts, instructional and grading styles are very different. These differences were sometimes perceived by the students (as indicated in their anonymous reflection journals) as unfair. Arts students felt the lectures were tough and boring when engineering/science topics were delivered by engineering/science instructors. These topics were usually introduced in terms of definition/concept/principle and explained through logic derivation and application examples with proper math background. At the same time, engineering students thought they learned little in arts topics as these were usually introduced through students' discussion in class and often there was no right or wrong answer.

Both students and instructors were surprised to see the different grading styles in arts versus science and engineering. A score of 100% in arts is very rare and is reserved to students to show exceptional creativity. In science and engineering answers are either right or wrong, and a students who answers everything correctly will earn 100%. The judgment and baseline for a good written report is different from engineering and the arts.

For engineering and science majors, a good report is a data-driven, fact-based, and concisely written technical description of what has been done. For arts majors, a good report is a detailed "story-telling" style argument and analysis. At the end of the semester each team was required to submit a 20-page written report detailing the project from the initial design phase to prototyping and testing. We (the four instructors) graded all the reports individually, and realized the challenge in the first semester when we met to discuss the grades. We ended up adjusting our individual grades after deliberations on each report, with the arts instructors leaning towards technical requirements.

6. CONCLUSIONS AND FUTURE WORK

We presented the first two semesters of teaching an on-going undergraduate multidisciplinary seminar entitled "Conducting Robots". Through this seminar, majors from four disciplines, computer science, interactive multimedia, music and mechanical engineering, worked together contributing their own expertise to multidisciplinary teams concentrating on a common goal: building a non-human system that could conduct the college orchestra.

Throughout the two semesters we used student feedback collected by our independent evaluator to reflect on and revise the course. We have found that our original plan to teach the seminar over the course of an entire year was unrealistic given the graduation requirements of our students, and we adapted to the shorter schedule using a hands-on approach that was favored by the students.

Designing lectures that are engaging and challenging to students from such varied backgrounds was another obstacle that we encountered. We tried to keep in-class discussions general, and allowed students to discover and teach each other the details.

Due to the multidisciplinary collaboration our students were able to build working systems at a level that is rare in an undergraduate setting, and is more characteristic of graduate research.

We plan to offer the course two more times, after which we believe that the novelty of building conducting robots will wear off. However, this seminar is meant to be a prototype for multidisciplinary courses that bring together students majoring in different areas. Our preliminary results show that such settings are successful in teaching students computational thinking and creative problem-solving. Future work includes collecting and analyzing additional data to test these findings.

7. ACKNOWLEDGMENTS

The authors would like to thank the orchestra of The College of New Jersey and its conductor Dr. Philip Tate for their collaboration and support. This work was supported by the National Science Foundation under Grant No. 0855973.

8. REFERENCES

[1] cs. princeton.edu 2010. ChucK : Strongly-timed, Concurrent, and On-the-fly Audio Programming Language. Retrieved December 5, 2010 from http://chuck.cs.princeton.edu/

[2] Erkan, A., Hamilton, J., Pfaff, T., and Rogers, M. 2010. Use of Satellite Imagery in Multidisciplinary Projects. *Proceedings of the 41st ACM SIGCSE Technical Symposium on Computer Science Education*, 32-36.

[3] Guzdial, M.. 2008. Paving the way for computational thinking. *Commun. ACM*, 51(8):25–27, 2008.

[4] Hambrusch, S., Hoffmann, C., Korb, J. T., Haugan, M., and Hosking, A. L. 2009. A Multidisciplinary Approach Towards Computational Thinking for Science Majors. *Proceedings of the 40th ACM SIGCSE Technical Symposium on Computer Science Education*, 183-187.

[5] Heines, J. M., Greher, G. R., and Kuhn, S. 2009. Music Performamatics: Interdisciplinary Interaction. *Proceedings of the 40th ACM SIGCSE Technical Symposium on Computer Science Education*, 478-482.

[6] Kessler, R., van Langeveld, M., and Altizer, R. 2009. Entertainment Arts and Engineering (or How to Fast Track A New Interdisciplinary Program). *Proceedings of the 40th ACM SIGCSE Technical Symposium on Computer Science Education*, 534-538.

[7] Nakra, T., Tilden, D., and Salgian, A. 2010. Improving upon Musical Analyses of Conducting Gestures using Computer Vision. *Proceedings of the 2010 International Computer Music Conference*.

[8] National Academy of Sciences, National Academy of Engineering, Institute of Medicine, Facilitating Interdisciplinary Research, ISBN: 0-309-54727-X, 2004

[9] processing.org. 2010. Processing. Retrieved December 5, 2010 from http://processing.org

[10] Smith, H.H., and Smarkusky, D.L. 2005. Competency matrices for peer assessment of individual in team projects. *SIGITE'05: Proceedings of the 6th conference on Information Technology Education.*

[11] White, W. W., and Weinberg, J. B. 2009. Breadth-Last Technical Electives: Integrating the CS Core via Computer Games and Mobile Robotics. *Proceedings of the 38th ACM SIGCSE Technical Symposium on Computer Science Education*, 54–58.

[12] Wing, J. M. 2006. Computational thinking. *Commun. ACM*, 49(3):33–35, 2006.

[13] Wolz, U., Ault, C., and Nakra, T. M. 2007. Teaching Game Design through Cross-Disciplinary Content and Individualized Student Deliverables, Journal of Game Development 2 (2).

Nelson: A Low-Cost Social Robot for Research and Education

Michael Ferguson
ILS Institute, SUNY Albany
1400 Washington Avenue
Albany, New York, USA
ferguson@cs.albany.edu

Nick Webb
ILS Institute, SUNY Albany
1400 Washington Avenue
Albany, New York, USA
nwebb@albany.edu

Tomek Strzalkowski
ILS Institute, SUNY Albany
1400 Washington Avenue
Albany, New York, USA
tomek@albany.edu

ABSTRACT

A social robot is a robotic platform that supports natural interaction with people in a human-scale environment. Such a platform allows interesting opportunities for both traditional Computer Science students and students from other disciplines, such as psychology, philosophy, design and communications. In this paper, we describe a new social robotic platform for educational uses that is equipped with a social face, arms for gesturing, advanced sensory, mobile base, and ROS integration. By using off-the-shelf and rapidly prototyped components, together with open source software, this platform is low-cost, easy to use, and easy to reproduce.

Categories and Subject Descriptors

K3.2 [**Computer and Information Science Education**]: Computer science education; I.2.9 [**Robotics**]: Commercial robots and applications.

General Terms

Algorithms, Design, Experimentation

Keywords

Robotics, ROS, Social Robotics

1. INTRODUCTION

While a number of schools and classrooms are exploring the use of robotic platforms, the focus so far has been on providing students with platforms to explore core programming skills, or the fundamentals of robotics or cognitive science (cf. [3, 7, 5, 11]).

As interest in robots and robotics increases, there is a parallel interest in the *social* component of robotics. The goal for us is to create robots that can work alongside, and collaborate with, humans in real world environments. In order to achieve this successfully, such robots need to be able to interpret and produce a wide range of social functions. This includes principles of human-robot interaction, communication, philosophy, psychology and design.

To explore such human-robot interaction issues, research groups typically create their own 'social robot', robots which have some easily recognizable social characteristics, such as a face which can produce expressions. The drawback with such platforms is that they are often expensive, and the designs are not open source.

With Nelson, our goal is to create a socially capable robotic platform, allowing students to study issues such as human-robot interaction or the communicative requirements for a robot to be deemed socially acceptable. For instance, students might study the social cues that a robot could generate (robot specific communication research) or recognize how the robot's navigation impacts people's impression of it (which we refer to as socially-aware navigation).

In developing Nelson, we set forward a series of design requirements that would be necessary to adequately support the social robotics program we envision. First and foremost, both hardware and software should be open source where possible, and easily modifiable to allow students to expand the platform as they develop new experiments.

Second, the platform should be low cost, so that it is accessible to a wide audience. We used off-the-shelf components whenever possible.

Third, we wanted a platform that would be socially acceptable to a large audience, and so we selected a small number of parameters we believed would fulfill this requirement; for example, we created a robot that was closer to human size, but not so large as to be intimidating, and we required that the robot have some sort of face.

Finally, because we believe that social robots must interact with people in human-scale environments, the robot needed robust sensory to deal with the complex environment of the real world. Additionally, because of the robust sensory, the robot should carry at least its basic processing power onboard.

For those parts which could not be obtained off-the-shelf, we tried to design parts which could easily be manufactured or replicated using known processes, such as 3D printing, laser cutting, or sheet metal fabrication. As different sites would have access to different methods of fabrication, each of Nelson's parts were designed to be made in several ways.

2. RELATED WORK

When talking about robotic platforms in an educational environment, we have to distinguish between hardware platforms and software platforms. The choice of both of these

SIGCSE'11, March 9–12, 2011, Dallas, Texas, USA.

Figure 1: Nelson, a social robot.

elements has a direct correlation with the usability, cost and extensibility of the project in question, and must be considered carefully.

From an educational perspective, there are a number of robot hardware platforms available, each aimed at a particular facet of the educational market. For example, the Scribbler robot[1] is designed as a low cost entry level robot, used by many to teach both fundamental robotics, and as a platform for introducing programming to a wide audience. The LEGO NXT[2] has many of the same principles, but with a larger array of sensing. The iRobot Create[3] is a robust, industrially produced platform with a more limited sensor array but which has a high payload capacity and can easily be extended.

Recently, Aldebaran robotics has produced the Nao robot[4], a humanoid replacement for the now-defunct SONY Aibo in robotic soccer competitions. These platforms are more socially capable than the Scribbler, Create or NXT, but are still fairly small, and very expensive.

The CMU Chiara[5], is a multi-legged open source platform, which is a more capable research platform. However, mobility with the Chiara is still limited due to battery life and weight, and it is primarily designed as a platform to research issues in cognitive science and machine vision.

The RobotCub project[6] is one of the most exciting robotics projects in Europe. Tasked to design and build a robotic platform for future research and education, the consortium has built iCub - at 37" high, the iCub is equivalent in size to a three year old child. It has 53 degrees of freedom, has fully working, grasping hands, as well as visual, auditory and haptic sensory capabilities. The entire design of the iCub, both hardware and software, is freely available under the Free Software Foundation GNU license, however a complete, assembled iCub costs around $200,000.

[1]http://www.parallax.com
[2]http://mindstorms.lego.com
[3]http://www.irobot.com/create
[4]http://www.aldebaran-robotics.com/en/
[5]http://www.chiara-robot.org
[6]http://www.robotcub.org

From a software perspective, there are several packages which attempt to abstract robotic concepts, in a way that makes interfacing with a range of hardware possible. This is attractive on at least two levels. First, students can switch platforms, based on experimental need, e.g. requiring a specific set of sensors or effectors. Second, a user community can create libraries of useful packages and plugins, which can then be exploited or expanded by students, relieving the need to reinvent the wheel at each iteration.

Two of the most successful open-source robot platforms currently available for education are Myro and Tekkotsu. Myro is a Python-based programming environment for introducing programming in a unique and personal way [2]. The software uses the Parallax Scribbler robot with a custom add on board that communicates with as student's laptop over a wireless connection. The Scribbler robot has limited sensory, which includes several floor sensors and a few IR obstacle avoidance sensors. The add-on board has a small camera, however the frame rate is limited. The Tekkotsu system is designed for higher level robotics education, with extensive support for cognitive vision, walking robots, and kinematics [12]. Students use C++ and a custom state machine language to create Tekkotsu programs. Tekkotsu supports only a small set of hardware, currently the iRobot Create, Dynamixel servos, webcams and several custom walking robots.

While each of these platforms offer support for their intended audience, we deemed that neither was the preferred platform for a new robot intended for social robotics as neither addressed the issues of robots operating in real human-scale environments. Instead, we chose to build on the Robot Operating System (ROS), a meta-operating system for robotics [10]. ROS is in use at over 30 institutions, with support for over 25 robotic platforms ranging from the Lego NXT up to advanced mobile manipulators such as Willow Garage's PR2 robot[7]. While its robustness, ease of use, and real-world focus has gained ROS a foothold in research in both University and Industry settings, ROS has not been widely applied to educational settings.

The positive here is that there is a large amount of open-source software available under ROS for interfacing with hardware such as scanning laser range finders and stereo cameras. There is also a large amount of software for advanced tasks such as navigation in human-scale environments. ROS allows the student to choose between several supported programming languages. ROS has an extensive, community-generated wiki, which also has a number of tutorials. In choosing ROS for Nelson's software platform, we accepted that generating some custom code to make ROS more accessible for students was worth the resultant speed up in development time for creating such a platform.

3. INTRODUCING NELSON: HARDWARE

We specifically wanted to design a robot with social capability. For us, this means that it should have a face (and implied through this, a voice, although this is not covered

[7]http://www.willowgarage.com

in this paper), and arms, enough to create expressions and gestures, as well as pick up and put down small objects. Also, it would need sufficient sensory ability to navigate and negotiate small populated environments, such as our labs or office suites. In this section, we detail our approach to these requirements.

3.1 A Low-Cost Face for HRI

One of the most important elements of this robot is the face and head. Some of the more interesting robotic faces, such as that found on the Mertz robot[1] can cost thousands of dollars to build, well beyond the scope of our budget. Instead, we designed a face that can be constructed for around \$150 using either basic hand tools, or a 3D printer.

Nelson's head consists of a 3 degree of freedom neck, and an 7-degree of freedom face. The neck is built out of Dynamixel AX-12 servos, a low cost, strong, and robust actuator that includes easy to assemble brackets. Of the three neck servos, one is devoted to panning the head left or right. The remaining two servos are used to move the head up or down, and forward or backward. This simple neck allows a wide range of motion, and Nelson can appear to be inquisitive by leaning forward towards an item, or afraid by pulling his head back. The range of motion of his head is such that he can easily view people standing a reasonable distance (around 3 feet) in front of him.

The face servos are moving lightweight components and are therefore barely under load allowing us to use tiny micro servos which cost only a few dollars a piece. A number of very small parts had to be produced, however all are designed to be produced on a low-cost 3D printer[8]. Alternate part designs are available that can be created using a laser cutter, or hand cut from sheet material using other tools. The servos are installed such that each eye can pan independently, and a tray holding the eyes can tilt them up and down as a pair. A pair of eyebrows can each be moved up or down independently, and each lip can move up or down independently. This small number of movements can generate a vast array of possible facial expressions, as shown in Figure 2. One actuator that was planned but not yet implemented activates a set of eyelids. Eyelids would likely improve the range of emotions that Nelson can express, however our early approaches were fragile.

As we intended Nelson to be socially acceptable to a wide audience, we paid special attention to his level of realism. In developing Nelson's face, we attempted to keep the features cartoon-like, so as to avoid the uncanny valley effect[4]. Unfortunately, as the robot came together and the software became more sophisticated, we received feedback that we were rapidly approaching that point. Future versions of Nelson may heed some of the other recommendations from[4], such as making a robotic face wider than it is tall so as to make the robot appear less human. Such approaches have worked well on robots such as Willow Garage's PR2, but the results are unclear for robot's with active faces.

3.2 Torso and Arms

We believe that a key requirement for continued interaction is that a robot be closer to human scale. While a tall robot is more susceptible to toppling over, we have designed Nelson with a lightweight upper body and torso, keeping heavy components such as batteries and computers close to the ground. Nelson's torso raises his head to more reasonable height, close to that of a child, and approximately the same size as the iCub robot. This is also an important consideration for sensors, as a camera mounted too close to the ground will wash out when attempting to look up at a person.

[8]http://www.makerbot.com

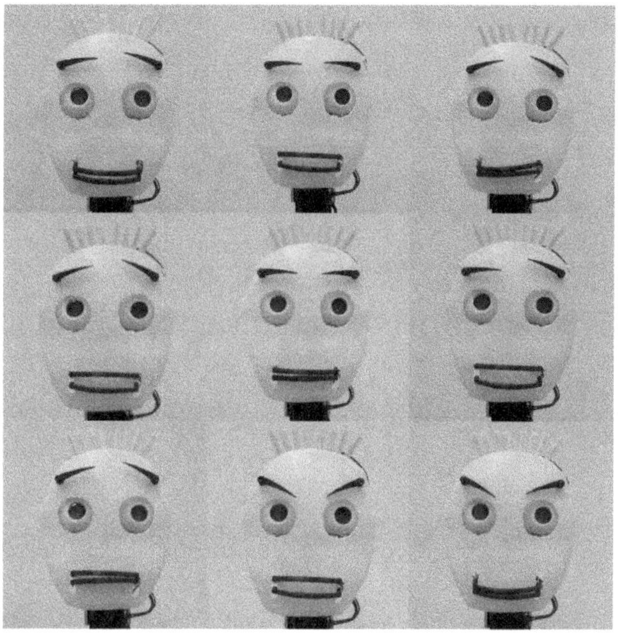

Figure 2: The many faces of Nelson.

A pair of simple arms are attached to the torso. These arms are primarily to aid in gesturing, such as pointing at objects, and conveying expressions although they can be used for simple object manipulation. Each arm includes three servos for moving the arm and an additional servo to create a small gripper. The arms, like the neck, are constructed out of Dynamixel servos, making them inexpensive yet robust.

3.3 Mobility

Because social robots must interact with people in human-scale environments, Nelson has a mobile base, capable of achieving approximately a walking speed. While there are a number of mobile bases with support for ROS, an iRobot Create base was chosen, due to its low-cost, robust operation, and hefty payload capability. The Create is also already widely used in existing educational programs, making it a logical choice.

A custom column mount is built on top of the Create, to which the torso and head are attached. The column mount is built out of low cost electrical conduit, a locally available and inexpensive alternative to the more common but costly aluminum channel found on higher end robots.

3.4 Sensors

Operation in a complex environment requires advanced sensory capabilities. Nelson is currently outfitted with a single webcam above his face, and a unique scanning range

Figure 3: View of the Nelson's arm and chest components.

finder. As ROS is fully integrated with OpenCV[9], creating visual routines is a relatively simple task.

Navigating in human-scale spaces requires that a robot avoid obstacles, especially dynamic ones. Typically, this is done using a laser range finder, however such devices are extremely expensive, typically several thousand dollars. Nelson, uses a lower cost replacement constructed from a $20 infrared range finder and a Dynamixel AX-12, which we call the Planar Meta-Laser (PML). The PML pans the servo, taking readings with the range finder and broadcasting the data in the same format as laser range finders. By broadcasting the data in the same format, we can use existing tools, such as ROS's Navigation Stack [8]. Further details on the usage of the PML are provided later in this paper.

3.5 Controller

All of the servos are connected to a Netbook using a Vanadium Labs ServoStiK. The ServoStiK is a USB interface device that passes serial commands between the PC and the servos, in addition to controlling the PML.

4. INTRODUCING NELSON: SOFTWARE

Having constructed the hardware, we need to implement software for robot control. Building Nelson's software on ROS means that we have easy access to a wide variety of open-source libraries and tools. Reducing the amount of custom code needed to run Nelson makes the platform both more robust and maintainable.

ROS currently supports Python, C++, and Lisp, and there is experimental support for Java and other languages. The ability to allow students a wide choice of languages means that students spend their time developing interesting robotics applications and learning about robotics, rather than debugging the nuances of a language they are not entirely familiar with.

ROS includes a federated model of code distribution, using a single, publicly accessible wiki hosted at www.ros.org, but allowing sites to host their own code repositories. Software is organized into packages, small portions of code that do a specific function, and stacks, which are a collection of related packages. A good example is the *Navigation* stack which provides autonomous navigation capabilities to a mobile base. The stack includes packages such as *costmap 2d* which handles the creation of 2D occupancy grids from sensor data, a separate *base local planner* package then uses this 'costmap' to safely send trajectory commands to the mobile base. ROS uses a distributed computing approach to robots, so each package typically consists of one or more programs that become separate nodes in the runtime graph. This distributed approach, and a large collection of open source software, means that students can often prototype a high level idea in a very small amount of code.

The distributed approach of ROS, and the easy division and communication between different nodes within the runtime graph also promotes collaboration. Robotics is a diverse field, and we expect that each student will choose to focus on one aspect of a social robotic application. ROS makes it easier then for teams of students to collaborate in this manner.

4.1 Servo Control

Vanadium Labs provides an ROS library for interfacing to the Dynamixel servos using a ServoStiK. On top of this library we have built a series of controllers and tools which provide easy access to the face servos and arms.

4.2 Virtual Face

In addition to an embodied version of Nelson's face, we have created a virtual version that interfaces with ROS. The GUI version of Nelson interacts with ROS in exactly the same way as the real face, allowing students to test code in a simulated environment.

5. A COURSE IN SOCIAL ROBOTICS

One principal goal with this platform is to introduce the issues of Human-Robot Interaction to a wide audience, including both students in traditional Computer Science and inviting participation from students from other disciplines. A first iteration of this combined class happened in the spring semester of 2010.

In addition to introducing the technical topics involved with using ROS, and situating our overall human-robot interaction objectives within the field, a major portion of the course is a final social robotics application project. For this final project, CS and non-CS students form teams to create an application, guided by both the technical reality of the robotic hardware and software capabilities and the understanding of social issues in creating such robots. For the first iteration, we had students with psychology and communication majors.

Planning for this application begins with round-table discussions between the two sets of students, with literature reviews on, for example, the importance of social cues, being presented by non-CS students, arriving at a sub-set of behaviors and actions the final robot should perform in order to be socially successful or accepted. Ultimately, the

[9]http://opencv.willowgarage.com

majority of the programming is then left to the CS students, although non-programmers are encouraged to write simple programs for Nelson using the easy to learn Python language.

Our intent is that all students leave a course in Social Robotics with the following:

- A working knowledge of the major issues confronting Human-Robot Interaction and related fields.
- An understanding of the kind of technology currently available for platforms that can operate in human environments. In particular, a solid understanding of the current sensor suites, and their limitations.
- Experience working in a truly interdisciplinary team, especially in the area of creating software requirements when not all members of the team are expert programmers.

5.1 Example Social Robotics Projects

Our social robotic platform provides a number of opportunities for students in both traditional Computer Science and other disciplines to explore interesting topics in Human-Robot Interaction. The next few sections of this paper outline several example projects that have been implemented using this platform, which give a feeling for the wide range of topics that can be explored.

5.1.1 People Detection and Following

People following is an interesting application and active research area which combines mathematical techniques, sensory and perception, and the understanding of human interaction. Robust algorithms for people following typically build on both or either of visual techniques or laser-based detection of legs. Such algorithms also require the use of filters on the candidate points that may be people. Students of Social Sciences can provide valuable input and feedback in this area in how people move and the size and effect of social space (personal versus public space), thus improving such filters.

Nelson's standard applications include a simple person detector which was implemented using the base scanning sensor to find possible candidates, and then a color tracking filter to verify the candidate, such as found in [6]. Even with great sensory, robotic applications can break down in complex environments. In particular, the presence of many people in an environment can cause people tracking to fail. The "Walk With Me" application allows a person to lead Nelson around by the hand, helping him to move in, through, and away from large crowds.

5.1.2 Navigation in Human-Scale Environments

As robots move out of the lab and into the real world, there is an immediate requirement for autonomous robust navigation. Paramount is that the robot be able to deal with obstacles, especially dynamic ones. Since the Planar Meta-Laser (PML) broadcasts its data in the same format as a much more expensive scanning laser, we are able to use ROS's standard costmap modules for local planning and obstacle avoidance.

However, the PML does not provide enough high quality data to construct area maps or to localize the robot. As a semester project several students created a localization routine to supplement the existing ROS navigation software. This localization system uses markers from ARToolkit, placed around the lab. Upon seeing a marker the robot can automatically align itself within a larger map. Students have already applied social robotics constructs in deciding how fast the robot should move, so as not to be a danger to humans in the navigation space, and attempting to make the navigation more fluid and natural, ideally observing social conventions, such as moving to one side in a corridor.

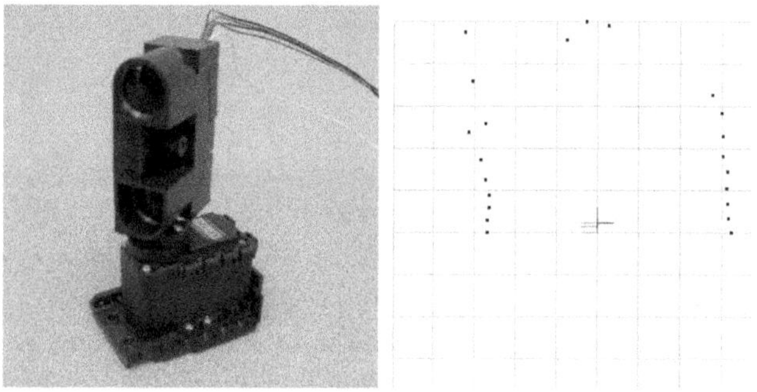

Figure 4: The PML, and a planar scan created with it.

Future work on this low cost navigation system might include refining the global planner, creating a more ROS-like map server, and expanding the local planner to be more people friendly.

5.1.3 Non-Verbal Communications

Several communications majors who participated in Nelson's first deployment immediately wished to address the issue of non-verbal communications. An 'emotional engine' was created for Nelson using emotional dichotomies based on the Circumplex Model of Affect [9]. The emotional engine allows Nelson to automatically react based on his level of stimulation, and his belief of how accurately he was accomplishing his task, base on metrics such as the number of failed attempts at speech recognition or the tone of a person's voice. A graphical-based controller was also implemented to control Nelson's emotional state directly.

Future work in this area could include addressing issues such as response time and eye contact, as well as developing additional metrics for more robust feedback to the emotional engine.

5.2 Discussion

It is hard to formally evaluate the outcome of a single course, held in a single semester. However, it is the impression of the educators involved, and the anecdotal feedback of the student participants, that the course was a great success. The initial round table process produced fascinating interaction between groups of students who would not normally have cause to interact during the course of their academic studies. Students from outside of Computer Science gained access to, and direct experience with, complex computer-based systems, in a way usually out of reach to all but those that major in a computer or engineering field. The course will be offered again in the Spring of 2011, and Nelson will be a major component as the focus for social robotic applications.

6. FUTURE WORK

From a hardware standpoint, while Nelson provides an excellent set of capabilities, there is still more we would like to implement and refine. First and foremost is reducing the number of parts required for the face, and making parts simpler to produce.

We would also like to improve Nelson's sensory. A redesign of the head to better accept a pair of cameras would allow the creation of a low-resolution 3D depth map, which could be very useful for supplementing the PML during navigation, as well as improving people perception. Reduction in the noise of the PML's servo motor is also a top priority, as the noise is currently a distraction when interacting with people. Our current solution has been to throttle back the rate of scanning during interactions, so that the servo becomes quieter.

7. CONCLUSIONS

We have presented a low cost and robust robot that is capable of navigating human-scale environments and interacting with people. This platform presents interesting opportunities to a wide range of interdisciplinary students, and we have started to investigate this through an 'Introduction to Social Robotics' course.

Our wiki (http://robotics.ils.albany.edu) contains videos of Nelson in action, as well as software, build instructions, and part layouts.

8. ACKNOWLEDGMENTS

This work is funded in part by the NSF CPATH program (award number IIS 0722277). We would like to thank our students, who patiently dealt with debugging issues in early versions of Nelson and who implemented the example projects discussed in this paper.

9. REFERENCES

[1] L. Aryananda and J. Weber. Mertz: A quest for a robust and scalable active vision humanoid head robot. In *IEEE-RAS/RSJ International Conference on Humanoid Robots*, November 2004.

[2] T. Balch, D. Blank, M. Guzdial, and D. Kumar. IPRE: Institute for personal robotics in education, 2007. (www.roboteducation.org).

[3] R. D. Beer, H. J. Chiel, and R. F. Drushel. Using autonomous robotics to teach science and engineering. *Communications of the ACM*, 42(6), 1999.

[4] C. F. DiSalvo, F. Gemperle, J. Forlizzi, and S. Kiesler. All robots are not created equal: the design and perception of humanoid robot heads. In *DIS '02: Proceedings of the 4th conference on Designing interactive systems*, pages 321–326, New York, NY, USA, 2002. ACM.

[5] Z. Dodds, L. Greenwald, A. Howard, S. Tejada, and J. Weinberg. Components, Curriculum, and Community: Robots and Robotics in Undergraduate AI Education. *AI Magazine*, 27(1):11–22, 2006.

[6] M. Kleinehagenbrock, S. Lang, J. Fritsch, F. Lomker, G. A. Fink, and G. Sagerer. Person tracking with a mobile robot based on multi-modal anchoring, 2002.

[7] A. N. Kumar. Three years of using robots in an artificial intelligence course: Lessons learned. *Journal on Educational Resources in Computing: Special Issue on Robotics in Undergraduate Education*, 4(3), 2004.

[8] E. Marder-Eppstein, E. Berger, T. Foote, B. Gerkey, and K. Konolige. The office marathon: Robust navigation in an indoor office environment. In *IEEE International Conference on Robotics and Automation (ICRA)*, pages 300–307, 2010.

[9] J. Posner, J. A. Russell, and B. S. Peterson. The circumplex model of affect: An integrative approach to affective neuroscience, cognitive development, and psychopathology. *Development & Psychopathology*, 17:715–734, 2005.

[10] M. Quigley, B. Gerkey, K. Conley, J. Faust, T. Foote, J. Leibs, E. Berger, R. Wheeler, and A. Ng. ROS: an open-source robot operating system. In *Open-Source Software workshop of the International Conference on Robotics and Automation (ICRA)*, 2009.

[11] E. Sklar, S. Parsons, and M. Q. Azhar. Robotics across the curriculum. In *Proceedings of the 2007 AAAI Spring Symposium on Robots and Robot Venues: Resources for AI Education*, 2007.

[12] E. J. Tira-Thompson. Tekkotsu: A rapid development framework for robotics. Master's thesis, Carnegie Mellon University Robotics Institute, 2004. Available online at http://www.tekkotsu.org.

An Introduction to AI Course with Guide Robot Programming Assignments

Nik Swoboda
Universidad Politécnica de Madrid
Boadilla del Monte, Spain
nswoboda@fi.upm.es

Juan Bekios-Calfa
Universidad Católica del Norte
Antofagasta, Chile
juan.bekios@ucn.cl

Luis Baumela
Universidad Politécnica de Madrid
Boadilla del Monte, Spain
lbaumela@fi.upm.es

Javier de Lope
Universidad Politécnica de Madrid
Madrid, Spain
javier.delope@upm.es

ABSTRACT

In this paper we describe a collection of course materials designed to be used in an undergraduate introduction to artificial intelligence (AI) course. These materials include three programming assignments, each touching upon core AI topics, which require that the students build the main functionalities of a guide robot. These assignments were carefully designed to allow the same solution to work both with a robot simulator and an inexpensive web-cam as well as with real robots. An overview of the course and the assignments is given along with references to online versions of the resources developed to teach the course.

Categories and Subject Descriptors

K.3.2 [**Computers and Education**]: Computer and Information Science Education—*Computer science education*; I.2.9 [**Artificial Intelligence**]: Robotics—*Commercial robots and applications*

General Terms

Human Factors, Algorithms

Keywords

Course Design, Artificial Intelligence, Robots

1. INTRODUCTION

Following the same principle presented in [16], the basic premise of this project is to use robotics as an underlying theme for the design of an introduction to artificial intelligence (AI) class.[1] The following is a list of qualities which were considered to be desirable in the design of the course:

- Hardware neutral with the possibility of simulation – Rather than focus on a particular hardware platform, like the use of the popular LEGO®Mindstorms®, we have selected programming tools which are hardware neutral and allow for the use of robot simulators. Furthermore, due to limited lab space and hardware availability we wanted students to be able to effectively work outside the robot lab and using their own computers. (By doing this we also hoped to address the problems reported in [9] as being possibly due to the lack of a simulator, see Section 1.2 for further discussion.)
- Off the shelf robots – Unlike many courses which begin by having the students build a robot, which is the case in many courses using LEGO®Mindstorms®(e.g., [14]) we have chosen to use pre-fabricated robots to focus more of the student's work on the basic subject matter of an AI course.
- Integrated assignments – Rather than have the students complete a number of independent assignments we have opted to include assignments which integrate and later combine to accomplish a single more complex task (much like the "egg hunt" assignments given in [5]). This is to provide continuity between the assignments and motivation for the students to continue with the course work.
- Student failure recovery – The assignments are further designed to allow the student to produce a functioning (though inferior) system even if they are unable to complete some of the assignments.
- Real world environment – A good number of the existing proposals for teaching AI with robots include the need for a specially constructed environment for the

[1] It should be noted that this is also not all that different from Russell and Norvig's use of agents as the basis of their popular AI text book *Artificial Intelligence: A Modern Approach* [23].

robot [15, 3, 5], which require a large dedicated lab space and also make the problems less realistic. The assignments we propose use the hallways and rooms in the vicinity of the robot lab as the workspace of the robot.

As we were unable to find existing proposals for teaching AI which meet these demands, we decided to strike new ground and design a series of course projects from scratch. To do this three programming assignments were created to construct the core components of a guide robot. These assignments are intended to be completed in small groups of 2-3 students and are intentionally open-ended.[2] The main purpose of this paper is to present an overview of the course as well as to share the teaching materials which we have developed.

1.1 Topics covered in the course

AI is concerned with the design of software systems or physical machines that interact with their environment to act rationally in order to accomplish an assigned task [7]. To achieve this goal these systems must have planning, acting and perception capabilities, among others. In this paper we present a course that covers those topics in the *Intelligent Systems* (IS) knowledge area of the ACM Computer Science Curriculum [7] that are essential for controlling our robotic system.

The course is organized around the three modules that compose our system: a navigation module which provides acting and low-level perception, a planning module concerned with knowledge representation and search, and lastly a vision module to detect and recognize markers. The material in the course thus covers the *Fundamental Issues* and *Basic Search Strategies* core IS knowledge units. Elective IS knowledge units also covered are: *Advanced Search* (heuristics, genetic algorithms), *Machine Learning* (neural networks), *Robotics* (sensing, world models, planning, programming, navigation and control, software and architecture) and *Perception* (image formation, object detection and recognition). We do not cover the core IS knowledge unit *Knowledge Based Reasoning*; this is due to the fact that our students have already studied those topics in logic and statistics courses earlier in the curriculum.

1.2 Robots in the classroom

It is generally believed that using robots in the classroom provides an environment where students are more motivated and a context for addressing the complexity of real world problems. Some experimental studies have been conducted to determine the validity of these beliefs but unfortunately the results are mixed.

In [9], rather negative results were presented showing lower test scores and subjective measures (calculated from student surveys) in classes which used robots.[3] Limited, but somewhat more positive results can be found in [24] where it was informally shown that student demand, grades, and understanding improve in robot-based CS1 courses. While in [19] few statistically significant results were achieved with respect to student motivation with the exception of the fact that students in robot-based courses had less extrinsic goal orientation, i.e., that they were less motivated to learn for the purpose of achieving rewards, like for the sake of getting a better grade. Also, the work in [17] shows more homework submissions and higher grades in sections taught with robots. Despite the existence of some published negative reports, our experience coincides with that of many authors who, in general terms, describe the experience of using robots in the classroom as being a positive one.

[2]Thus the course is intended to teach "transversal" or non-computer science skills such as learning how to work in a group and open-ended problem solving skills as well as traditional AI concepts.

[3]In that work the authors hypothesize that these findings could be due to the lack of a robot simulator which forced students to work in a lab.

2. THE UNIFYING THEME OF THE COURSE: A GUIDE ROBOT

The main idea of the course is to group and orient some of the material taught in a typical introduction to AI course to the solving of a realistic, but greatly simplified, problem. It is designed to provide students with the basic skills necessary to program the core functionalities of a *guide robot*, a robot whose main purpose is to assist people in arriving at a given destination in a public space. One example scenario where this kind of a robot could be useful would be:

> Upon arriving at the Madrid International Airport, Mr. Brown is met by a guide robot which leads him to the baggage claim area to collect his luggage and then to the taxi stop for him to take a taxi to his hotel downtown.

In order to accomplish tasks of this sort, we assume that the robot is provided with the following information:

- An accurate and to scale map of the physical space where the robot will be moving including the locations of all fixed obstacles in that environment
- The location and orientation of "markers" in the world which, when visible to the robot, will allow the robot to determine its current location and orientation within the environment
- A model of the visual properties of those markers to allow the robot to recognize them in its environment

Furthermore, we assume that the robot, which can be either a real or a simulated robot[4], has the following basic capabilities:

- Devices to allow the robot to change its location and orientation (e.g., wheels, legs)
- A fixed camera used to search for the presence of markers in the area in front of the robot
- Sensors to detect the presence of obstacles along the heading of the robot (e.g., sonar or laser range sensors)
- Sensors to allow the robot to calculate its location using dead-reckoning (e.g., wheel encoders, gyroscopes and/or accelerometers)

[4]In the case of students working with a simulated robot we suggest that they use a real web-cam to test the vision module of the assignment. This will be further discussed in Section 5.3.

We divide the core functionality of the robot into three modules:

- Navigation – A reactive or low-level planner with the capacity to move from one known location in the environment to another while avoiding obstacles provided that there are no convex obstructions in that path.
- Planning – A global planner with the capacity to use a map of the environment to determine the shortest path from a given location to a goal.
- Vision – A marker recognition system with the capacity to recognize to determine the relative location and orientation of markers in the environment of the robot.

Lastly, to increase the feasibility of the project we make some general simplifying assumptions:

- The robot always begins the task with a marker in its field of view (thereby allowing the robot to localize at startup).
- The floor space where the robot roams is all in the same plane.
- The human and the guide robot do not need to interact directly.
- The robot can execute the task without needing to recharge.

3. COURSE OVERVIEW

We assume that approximately four weeks of in class time is spent in presenting the material related to each of the three modules taught in the course. Further class time is alloted to an introduction to AI, the programming environment, and the robots as well as to sessions where students discuss problems they have encountered with the assignments and share experiences. We now present further details of the three modules.

3.1 The Navigation Module

The navigation system is responsible for guiding the robot to a desired position by following a collision-free path. The students are given the assignment of developing the navigation system through the evolution of an Artificial Neuron Network (ANN) [20]. The ANN's inputs are the robot's perceptions (sonar readings and robot heading) and the ANN's output is the robot's angular speed. Optionally, the robot's linear speed can also be obtained by applying a similar procedure. Figure 1 shows the expected robot behavior in a simulated environment.

A simple perceptron is suggested as the ANN model and students are encouraged to try more complex models if the results are not successful. Several conventional activation functions are also provided.

An evolutionary strategy for training the ANN must be designed as a part of this assignment. Students receive an initial scheme of this evolutionary strategy that must be adapted and optimized for this particular problem. Also, we recommend that they experiment with changes in several of the scheme's parameters and features such as: the size of the population, whether elitism improves the solution, the

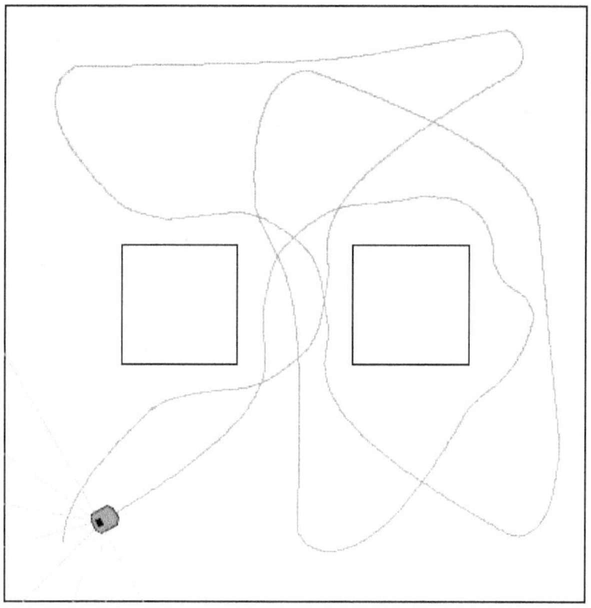

Figure 1: A robot guided by an evolved ANN in a simulation: the robot must visit a list of way-points by following a free-collision trajectory

initial values for the weights and bias, the fitness function, etc.

It should be noted that this assignment bears some similarity to that presented in [11] which uses different kinds of neural net topologies and Bayesian networks to learn the detection of obstacles using infrared and light sensors.

3.2 The Planning Module

The planning module is responsible for finding the shortest path from the robot's current location to a goal location. To do this the module applies a search algorithm to the information contained in the map of the environment of the robot. In this section of the course there is a strong emphasis on the trade-offs involved in selecting a knowledge representation and a search algorithm based upon the desired properties of the resulting system. Students are presented with a number of methods for representing 2-D space along with search algorithms and begin working with a somewhat naive implementation of an occupancy grid spatial representation and a dynamic-programming search algorithm. Then students are given the "open-ended" assignment of improving upon this implementation. To give the students some basic direction, the following suggestions are made:

- Use a watershed-like algorithm to segment the occupancy grid to construct a labeled topological graph (also sometimes called the Voronoi graph).
- Implement the A^* search algorithm to plan routes through the topological graph.

Even if the students follow these suggestions there are still a number of important decisions which need to be made including: deciding upon the number of way-points used to represent the path and the principles used to select those way-points.

Figure 2: Detecting the "Ground Transportation" [1] marker

3.3 The Vision Module

The goal of the vision module is to provide the robot with sensing capabilities to detect and estimate its position relative to a set of known landmarks. In order to use realistic markers and to continue in the airport metaphor, we decided to use the "symbol signs" designed by AIGA and the U.S. Department of Transportation for use in airports and other transportation centers (see [1]). This problem may be solved using publicly available software, e.g., Artoolkit [13, 2]. Nevertheless, we decided to use a more general, albeit computationally more demanding, approach to familiarize the student with a set of key concepts related to object recognition and robust estimation.

Representing objects using local descriptors of the object's appearance is one of the most successful recent results of work in Computer Vision, with SIFT (Scale-invariant feature transform) [18] being the most prominent representative of this approach. Applications include object and place recognition, robotic mapping and navigation, image stitching, 3D modeling, gesture recognition, video tracking, and match moving, among others. To detect and recognize landmarks we introduce the student to the problem of scale-invariant blob detection, using the scale-normalized determinant of the Hessian, and description, using SURF (Speeded Up Robust Features) [4]. This solution is based on the SURF implementation available in OpenCV [21]. A screen shot of the system detecting the "Ground Transportation" marker can be found in Figure 2.

Once detected and recognized, we can compute the relative position of the the robot to the landmark by fitting a homography to the known planar structure of the landmark. If the camera intrinsics are known, then the relative positions of the landmark and robot can be immediately obtained from the estimated homography [12]. Here again we use OpenCV [21] to calibrate the robot camera and robustly fit the homography using the RANSAC algorithm (Random Sample And Consensus) [12].

4. COURSE DETAILS

4.1 Student prerequisites

We assume that students taking the course have a solid background in basic Computer Science concepts and have had at least two or three courses including intensive programming experience. A typical CS undergraduate would take a course of this nature in his or her third or fourth year.

4.2 Programming environment

We use Pyro (Python Robotics) [6] as the programming platform for the assignments. Though we do not assume that our students have Python programming experience, we have found that after a brief introduction to Python programming they quickly become able programmers. Pyro and its robot simulator work well in Linux, Windows and in MacOsX. Furthermore Pyro includes an interface to Player thereby allowing the same code to control a simulated robot as well as all robots supported by Player (see [22] for a list of supported hardware). Player itself is designed to only run on Unix systems, but as we assume that students will be working with the physical robots in a laboratory and with the simulation at home, this was not problematic. For image capture and processing we use OpenCV [21], which is also cross-platform and somewhat hardware neutral with respect to video capture.

4.3 The programming assignments

Students begin the semester with a working prototype of the guide robot system. This prototype includes "toy" implementations of all of the core modules which provide the basic functionality needed to solve the task using a simulated robot. Throughout the semester students replace each of these modules with code of their own to improve its functionality and robustness.

Though it might seem counter-intuitive to provide the students with a working prototype from the start, this was done for a number of reasons. In addition to building the core modules, a lot of work is required to program a working system, and much of this work is not directly related to the material covered by the course. By providing a working system the students have access to the complete system if needed, but in most cases they can treat large portions of code as "black boxes". Also by providing trivial implementations of the modules that the students will need to develop, students are able to see how those modules interact with the other parts of the system and again this simplifies the work expected from the student. A screen-shot of the initial system is shown in Figure 3. We will now describe the initial system at more length.

For its navigation module a simple algorithm is given to move the robot from one location to another. In a nutshell, this algorithm works by rotating the robot until approximately the correct "as the crow flies" heading is achieved and then advances while making small heading corrections. This algorithm does not deal with obstacles in the path, nor does it produce very fluid movements (the robot stops completely to make hard turns).

The given planning module consists of our own modifications to the occupancy grid implementation included in Pyro, see Section 4.2, along with Pyro's naive implementation of a dynamic-programming path searching algorithm

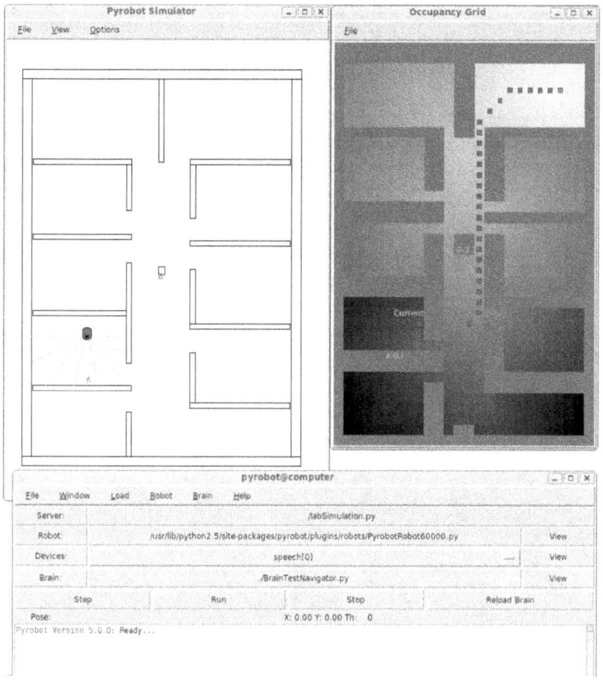

Figure 3: A screen-shot of the initial system

(the algorithm is based upon Thrun et al. [25]). Given a goal in the occupancy grid based representation of the robot's environment it uses value iteration to calculate the distance from each cell to the goal. Then path planning is simply a "downhill" search from any cell to the goal.

In place of the vision module, we rely upon the simulation to provide the locations of the "visible" markers relative to the robot.[5] Thus, no real image processing is done by the module and therefore students must begin the semester by working with a robot simulator.[6]

4.4 Online resources

Online copies of the resources which we have developed to teach the course can be found at: `http://airobotics.ucn.cl/`. These resources include the initial implementation of the system given to the students, slides used in lectures to present the core concepts behind each of the modules, along with images and videos.

5. COURSE EXPERIENCES

5.1 On using real robots

We have taught the course using the Erratic Robot [8]. The Erratic includes an on-board PC running Linux, wheel odometry, sonar range sensors, and an optional fire-wire camera. Students work at desktop computers in the lab or on their own laptops connected to the robot using SSH through WIFI. In this manner they can run Pyro and all task processing on-board the robot. An image of the Erratic robot realizing the task can be found in Figure 4.

Figure 4: The Erratic robot realizing the task

The decision to use robots in a course of this nature does entail a good deal of additional work for the faculty involved. Assuming that students will share the robots, maintaining these machines with their on-board PC's is similar in many ways to maintaining a laboratory of desktops. Problems including account creation, system updates, and hardware failures need to be addressed. Furthermore, measures might need to be taken to supervise the laboratory to prevent the theft of robots or their parts.

5.2 Real vs. simulated robots

Students are provided with a simulated world which was built to scale from architectural drawings of the area around the robot lab. Thus, working with both simulated and real robots was not very problematic though we have observed some significant differences between the behavior of the simulated sonar sensors in the Pyrobot simulator and the real sensors. These differences did cause a few problems when moving from the simulator to the real robot. For example, navigating around door frames was more difficult using the real robots than in the simulation. Despite these small problems students were able to work both at home using the simulator and in the lab with the real robots without much trouble.

5.3 Using only simulated robots

The course can also be taught without the use of real robots. In this case students work exclusively with the robot simulator included with Pyro and use inexpensive web-cams to test the vision module. But doing this means that students are not able to integrate the vision module into the final solution. It is also possible to use images from simulated cameras in a 3-D simulator, like Gazebo [10], but that results in much less realistic images. Furthermore, many image processing challenges, like those due to illumination and noise, are almost eliminated in that setting.

6. CONCLUSIONS AND FUTURE WORK

We acknowledge that employing the assignments presented here in an introduction to AI course results in a programming intense course. By far the most common comment that we have received regarding the course was that it was a "lot of work", but at the same time course survey results showed

[5]Reasonable assumptions regarding the field of view and resolution of a typical camera as well as the maximum distance and angle for successfully recognizing markers of approximately 20x20cm are used to make the detection of markers in the simulation more realistic.

[6]Artoolkit [13, 2] was used to implement a second basic image processing module but it was not used with the students due to its level of complication and a general desire to keep the initial system as simple as possible.

that the course satisfied the students' expectations. Despite the work load, we believe that using a "realistic" problem and real robots really does motivate students to learn, work hard, and to produce high quality work.

The course materials which we provide should be considered to be "work in progress" and we plan to post additions and improvements to the course web page as they are implemented and tested. In the immediate future we plan to make modifications to the Pyrobot simulator to make its sonar readings more realistic and improvements to the vision module to increase the distance at which it can accurately recognize markers.

7. ACKNOWLEDGMENTS

Nik Swoboda was funded by Spanish Ministerio de Educación through the grant 2008-05624/TIN. Juan Bekios and Luis Baumela received support from the Consolider Ingenio Program, project CSD2007-00018. Luis Baumela was also funded by the Spanish Ministerio de Educación under contract TIN2008-06815-C02-02.

8. REFERENCES

[1] Aiga - symbol signs. Retrieved July 16, 2010 from http://www.aiga.org/content.cfm/symbol-signs

[2] Artoolkit homepage. Retrieved July 16, 2010 from http://www.hitl.washington.edu/artoolkit/

[3] J. Baltes and J. Anderson. Leveraging mixed reality infrastructure for robotics and applied ai instruction. In *Proceedings of the Twenty-Fourth AAAI Conference on Artificial Intelligence*, 2010.

[4] H. Bay, A. Ess, T. Tuytelaars, and L. V. Gool. Speeded-up robust features (surf). *Computer Vision and Image Understanding*, 110(3):346 – 359, 2008.

[5] R. D. Beer, H. J. Chiel, and R. F. Drushel. Using autonomous robotics to teach science and engineering. *Communications of the ACM*, 42(6):85–92, 1999.

[6] D. S. Blank, D. Kumar, L. Meeden, and H. A. Yanco. The pyro toolkit for ai and robotics. *AI Magazine*, 27(1):39–50, 2006.

[7] Computer science curriculum 2008: An interim revision of cs 2001. Retrieved September 7, 2010 from http://www.acm.org/education/curricula/ComputerScience2008.pdf

[8] The erratic robot. Retrieved July 16, 2010 from http://www.videredesign.com/

[9] B. S. Fagin and L. Merkle. Quantitative analysis of the effects of robots on introductory computer science education. *ACM Journal on Educational Resources in Computing*, 2(4):1–18, 2002.

[10] Gazebo - 3d multiple robot similator with dynamics. Retrieved July 16, 2010 from http://playerstage.sourceforge.net/gazebo/gazebo.html

[11] L. Greenwald, D. Artz, Y. Mehta, and B. Shirmohammadi. Using educational robotics to motivate complete ai solutions. *AI Magazine*, 27(1):83–95, 2006.

[12] R. Hartley and A. Zisserman. *Multiple View Geometry in Computer Vision*. Cambridge University Press, second edition, 2004.

[13] H. Kato and M. Billinghurst. Marker tracking and hmd calibration for a video-based augmented reality conferencing system. In *IWAR '99: Proceedings of the 2nd IEEE and ACM International Workshop on Augmented Reality*, page 85, Washington, DC, USA, 1999. IEEE Computer Society.

[14] F. Klassner. A case study of lego mindstorms'™suitability for artificial intelligence and robotics courses at the college level. *SIGCSE Bulletin*, 34(1):8–12, 2002.

[15] A. N. Kumar. Using robots in an undergraduate artificial intelligence course: an experience report. In *FIE '01: Proceedings of the Frontiers in Education Conference, 2001. 31st Annual*, volume 2, pages T4D–10–14, Washington, DC, USA, 2001. IEEE Computer Society.

[16] D. Kumar and L. Meeden. A robot laboratory for teaching artificial intelligence. *SIGCSE Bulletin*, 30(1):341–344, 1998.

[17] T. Lauwers, I. Nourbakhsh, and E. Hamner. Csbots: design and deployment of a robot designed for the cs1 classroom. *SIGCSE Bulletin*, 41(1):428–432, 2009.

[18] D. G. Lowe. Distinctive image features from scale-invariant keypoints. *International Journal of Computer Vision*, 2(60):91–110, 2004.

[19] W. I. McWhorter and B. C. O'Connor. Do lego®mindstorms®motivate students in cs1? *SIGCSE Bulletin*, 41(1):438–442, 2009.

[20] S. Nolfi and D. Floreano. *Evolutionary Robotics: The Biology, Intelligence, and Technology of Self-Organizing Machines*. MIT Press/Bradford Books, Cambridge, MA, 2000.

[21] The opencv wiki. Retrieved July 16, 2010 from http://opencv.willowgarage.com/wiki/

[22] Player - supported devices. Retrieved July 16, 2010 from http://playerstage.sourceforge.net/doc/Player-2.0.0/player/supported_hardware.html

[23] S. Russell and P. Norvig. *Artificial Intelligence: A Modern Approach*. Prentice Hall, Upper Saddle River, NJ, USA, third edition, 2009.

[24] J. Summet, D. Kumar, K. O'Hara, D. Walker, L. Ni, D. Blank, and T. Balch. Personalizing cs1 with robots. *SIGCSE Bulletin*, 41(1):433–437, 2009.

[25] S. Thrun, A. Bücken, W. Burgard, D. Fox, T. Fröhlinghaus, D. Hennig, T. Hofmann, M. Krell, and T. Schmidt. Map learning and high-speed navigation in rhino. In D. Kortenkamp, R. P. Bonasso, and R. Murphy, editors, *AI-based Mobile Robots: Case Studies of Successful Robot Systems*, pages 21–52. MIT Press, Cambridge, MA, 1998.

Keynote Talk

A Computer Scientist Goes to Washington: How to be Effective in a World Where Facts are 10% of the Equation

Susan Landau
Radcliffe Institute for Advanced Study, Harvard University
susan.landau@privacyink.org

Abstract

Government's role in computer science is much larger than funding agencies. Digital rights management, net neutrality, and cybersecurity are hot topics in Washington, hot topics where regulation or legislation may have major impact on the computer systems we develop and enjoy. Yet the rules governing DC are very different than the rules that govern science and engineering, and learning how to operate in a world where facts are only ten percent of the equation can be a challenging experience for someone more accustomed to proving theorems and building systems. I'll describe what it takes for a nerd to be effective in the world of government, and give some specific examples in the hot area of cyberwar.

Categories & Subject Descriptors: K.3.2 [Computers and Education]: Computer and Information Science Education – computer science education

General Terms: Legal Aspects, Security

Bio

Susan Landau's book "Surveillance or Security? The Risks Posed by New Wiretapping Technologies" (MIT Press) was published in February 2011, and she is spending 2010-2011 as a fellow at the Radcliffe Institute for Advanced Study at Harvard University. From 1999-2010 Landau was a Distinguished Engineer at Sun Microsystems Laboratories, where she worked on security, cryptography, and policy, including surveillance and digital-rights management issues. Landau is coauthor, with Whitfield Diffie, of "Privacy on the Line: the Politics of Wiretapping and Encryption"" (MIT Press, original edition: 1998; rev. 2007), and author of numerous computer science and public policy papers, as well as op-eds on cybersecurity and encryption policy. She is a member of the National Research Council's Computer Science and Telecommunications Board, serves on the advisory committee for the National Science Foundation's Directorate for Computer and Information Science and Engineering, and on the CSIS Commission on Cyber Security for the 44th Presidency. She received her PhD from MIT, her MS from Cornell, and her BA from Princeton.

SIGCSE'11, March 9–12, 2011, Dallas, Texas, USA.
ACM 978-1-4503-0500-6/11/03.

Top Issues in Providing Successful Undergraduate Research Experiences

Hans-Peter Bischof
Rochester Institute of Technology
Rochester, NY 14623
hpb@cs.rit.edu

Jacob D. Furst (moderator)
DePaul University
Chicago, IL 60604
jfurst@cdm.depaul.edu

Daniela S. Raicu
DePaul University
Chicago, IL 60604
draicu@cdm.depaul.edu

Susan D. Urban
Texas Tech University
Lubbock, TX 79409
susan.urban@ttu.edu

ABSTRACT

Undergraduate research is becoming increasingly common in colleges and universities, and, to support this, there is a need to have best practices and forums for promoting exchange of ideas. In particular, a working group at a recent National Science Foundation (NSF) Computer and Information Science and Engineering (CISE) Research Experiences for Undergraduates (REU) sites PI's meeting identified four important issues in undergraduate research: 1) how to design a good research project, 2) how to prepare students for research, 3) how to measure outcomes of undergraduate research and 4) incentives for undergraduates to publish as result of their participation in research.

The panelists have all served as PIs or Co-PIs on NSF REU projects in computing and have mentored many undergraduates in a large variety of research projects both in REU settings as well as during the regular academic year. They will each address one of the issues identified above, and share their expertise in addressing the issue, providing solid guidance to anyone interested in promoting undergraduate research. A significant amount of time will be set aside for audience participation and discussion.

Categories and Subject Descriptors

K.3.2 [Computer and Information Science Education]: Computer science education

General Terms: Design

Keywords

Undergraduate research, computing problems

1. BACKGROUND

In the past ten years many universities have significantly changed their general education to address some of today's most intellectual challenges, such as changing demographics of the undergraduate population, shifts in knowledge, technological advances, and increasing emphasis on "transferable" skills. Most of the changes addressing these challenges relate to increased writing (65% of the research universities), preparing students for global environment (60%), fostering interdisciplinary programs (53.4%), and enhancing and facilitating research experiences (39%) [4].

Research experiences for undergraduates can be provided under different settings including advanced courses and seminars, senior projects, honor thesis, and summer/academic-year undergraduate research programs [5, 6, 9, 10]. The research experiences benefit the students engaged in research as well as the faculty and host institutions. Students expand upon their personal/professional skills, intellectual preparations, professional socialization, and also enhance their preparation for graduate school along with career clarification and confirmation [7]. On the institutional side, involving undergraduates in research also helps with the faculty development and potentially even student retention [1-3, 8].

To provide these benefits to the students and to the academic institutions, the faculty mentors have to design good strategies for overcoming various challenges such as insufficient student preparation/background to work on specific projects in a certain amount of time, misunderstanding of the research process, and lack of interaction with peers, all of them coupled with demanding faculty research agendas that impose high expectations on the undergraduate students' work. Therefore, this panel will focus on how the lessons learned by the panelists in mentoring undergraduate research assistants can be grouped into four important issues, and how these issues and their solutions are applicable to undergraduate research in any academic environment.

2. THE PANELISTS

Dr. Hans-Peter Bischof serves as PI of the REU site in Computer Science at Rochester Institute of Technology, where students work on different aspects of an interdisciplinary project to analyze and visualize the simulation of galactic events such as the formation of galactic nuclei and super massive black hole mergers. He will address the issue of how to design a good research project for undergraduate research students. He will discuss the importance of accounting for the wide diversity of possible participants, and of generating research projects that are scalable and relevant. He will discuss the importance of projects

SIGCSE'11, March 9–12, 2011, Dallas, Texas, USA.
ACM 978-1-4503-0500-6/11/03.

that fit both the students' skill sets and their expectations. Finally, he will discuss the flexibility required to ensure that students, research projects and mentors all fit together.

Dr. Daniela S. Raicu serves as the PI of the Medical Informatics Experiences (MedIX) REU Site at DePaul University, where students address research in medical informatics, with emphasis on imaging informatics. Dr. Raicu will address the issue of preparing students for research. She will discuss the importance of creating a positive work environment, such as making sure students have access to labs, equipment, libraries, and previous work in terms of code, technical reports, and research papers. She will also discuss more research-related preparation, including designing tutorials to cover not just the technical information students will encounter, but also tutorials to introduce students to searching for articles, tutorials educating students on giving presentations, and tutorials providing guidance on writing papers from formulating a research hypothesis and creating a comprehensive literature review to writing the results and future work sections.

Dr. Jacob D. Furst serves as co-PI of the MedIX REU Site at DePaul University. Dr. Furst will address the issue of measuring outcomes of undergraduate research. He will discuss the importance of measuring success in different ways, to include student self-reports of attitude and satisfaction, mentors' assessment of the value of the work to a larger research agenda, and the number and kind of publications that result from the undergraduate work. Specifically, he will discuss the kinds of questions that can be asked of students (and the importance of asking the questions both before and after the research experience) and what forms of useful feedback mentors can supply. Finally, he will discuss follow-up surveys that can be used to track long-term success of undergraduate research participants. He will also serve as the moderator of the panel.

Dr. Susan D. Urban serves as co-PI of the REU Site Program on Software Engineering and Service Composition at Texas Tech University, where students address research in three main areas: software specification, self-managed embedded software systems, and service-composition and recovery in service-oriented environments. Dr. Urban will address the issue of incentives for getting undergraduate researchers to publish. She will discuss the importance of having participants go through the process of publishing their research by working with faculty and graduate students. She will also discuss the need for mentoring undergraduate researchers with respect to the graduate school application process and the role that the research experience, coupled with publications on research results, play in helping to distinguish graduate applications of undergraduate researcher applicants from those of other applicants.

3. SESSION OUTLINE

The moderator will introduce the panelists and provide motivation for the panel. Each panelist will speak for 10-12 minutes on the issue identified above. The emphasis of each speaker will be on 1) motivating why the specific issue is important to successful undergraduate research, 2) providing specific guidance on how to achieve success with the issue, and 3) explaining how the lessons learned in NSF REU sites can be applied more generally to undergraduate research in other environments. The remainder the time will be used for questions and discussion.

4. ACKNOWLEDGMENTS

The student research described by the panelists was supported by the National Science Foundation under grant Nos. 1005212, 0851743, and 0755407.

5. REFERENCES

[1] Beck J., Buckner B., and Nikolova O. Using Interdisciplinary Bioinformatics Undergraduate Research to Recruit and Retain Computer Science Students. SIGCSE'07, Covington, Kentucky, USA, 2007.

[2] Dahlberg T., Barnes T., Rorrer A., Powell E., and Cairco L. Improving Retention and Graduate Recruitment through Immersive Research Experiences for Undergraduates. SIGCSE'08, Portland, Oregon, USA, 2008.

[3] Hislop G.W., Ellis H.J., Tucker A.B., and Dexter S.. Using open source software to engage students in computer science education. In SIGCSE '09: Proceedings of the 40th ACM technical symposium on Computer science education, 2009.

[4] Katkin, W.F. and Potash D. Redefining Undergraduate Education: Issues and Challenges in General Education. AAC&U Workshop on Curricular Responses to Academic and Societal Challenges of the Next Three to Five Years, 2007.

[5] Knox D.L., DePasquale P.J., and Pulimood S.M. A Model for Summer Undergraduate Research Experiences in Emerging Technologies. SIGCSE'06, Houston, Texas, USA, 2006.

[6] Krilowicz B., Johnston W., Sharp S.B., Warter-Perez N., and Momand J. A Summer Program Designed to Educate College Students for Careers in Bioinformatics. CBE—Life Sciences Education, Vol. 6, 74–83, 2007.

[7] Laursen S., Hunter A-B., Seymour E., Thiry H., Melton G. Undergraduate Research in the Sciences: Engaging Students in Real Science. Willey Publisher, July 2010.

[8] Peckham J., Stephenson P., Hervé J.Y., Hutt R., and Encarnação M. Increasing Student Retention in Computer Science through Research Programs for Undergraduates. SIGCSE'07, Covington, Kentucky, USA, 2007.

[9] Raicu D.S., Furst J.D. Enhancing Undergraduate Education: A REU Model for Interdisciplinary Research. SIGCSE 2009: The 40th ACM Technical Symposium on Computer Science Education, Chattanooga, TN, March 4-7, 2009.

[10] Walker E.L. and Slotterbeck O.A. Integrated research components: a practical and effective alternative to senior projects. J. Comput. Small Coll., 22(1), 2006.

Report on Qualitative Research Methods Workshop

Sue Fitzgerald
Metropolitan State University
St. Paul, MN 55106
+1 651-793-1473
sue.fitzgerald@metrostate.edu

Renée McCauley
College of Charleston
Charleston, SC 29424
+1 843-953-3187
mccauleyr@cofc.edu

Vicki L. Plano Clark
University of Nebraska-Lincoln
Lincoln, NE 68588
+1 402-472-9108
vpc@unlserve.unl.edu

Categories and Subject Descriptors
K.3.2 [**Computing Milieux**]: Computers and Education - Computer and Information Science Education

General Terms
Human Factors

Keywords
Computer science education research, qualitative research methods, mixed methods.

1. SUMMARY
This special session will recap qualitative research design and analysis as discussed during an NSF-sponsored two-part workshop for computer science education researchers held in 2009-2010. Several workshop participants will illustrate the use of qualitative methods by describing their research projects. They will briefly present their methodologies, analyses and findings. Attendees will be encouraged to ask questions about how qualitative methods can be used in their own research projects.

2. OBJECTIVES OF THE SESSION
The primary objective of this session is to provide the SIGCSE attendees with information on qualitative research methods and to demonstrate their applicability to computer science education research. Attendees will see examples of projects which use common qualitative research methodologies and will have an opportunity to ask questions.

Research in education is different from research in the physical sciences, which traditionally involves only quantitative methods. Qualitative methods focus on uncovering the motivations and understandings of the participants. Today, education research has evolved to include qualitative as well as quantitative explorations.

Common types of qualitative research include grounded theory, ethnography, phenomenology, narrative research, and case studies [2]. Qualitative research data is often collected via interviews, observations, diaries or transcripts. In qualitative approaches, the researcher relies on the opinions, views and actions of participants; asks broad, general questions; collects data consisting of spoken words, writing or pictures; and analyzes the data looking for themes. Many computer science educators are unfamiliar with or uncomfortable with qualitative methods. This session seeks to change that.

SIGCSE'11, March 9–12, 2011, Dallas, Texas, USA.
ACM 978-1-4503-0500-6/11/03.

3. OUTLINE
The session leaders will present a brief overview of qualitative research methods. Attendees will be provided with a list of resources that can be of immediate use. Next, four groups of researchers, who attended the workshop, will summarize their research, from research plan to results. Each group will discuss their work and respond briefly to questions (see sections 4-7 for descriptions of the projects that will be presented). Additional time for questions will be given at the end of the session.

4. STUDY #1: NOVICE PAIR DEBUGGING
Laurie Murphy, Renee McCauley, Brian Hanks, Sue Fitzgerald

Our project focuses on an important aspect of pair programming —*pair debugging*. Debugging is difficult for novices and the dialog pairs naturally engage in presents an ideal context for studying debugging. To gain a better understanding of the nature of that dialog, particularly the differences between successful and unsuccessful pairs, we used the qualitative research method *discourse analysis*.

We based our initial analysis on an earlier study [4] that found a link between *transactive discussion* and successful learning in children. Transactive discussion "extends, paraphrases, refines, completes, or critiques the partner's reasoning or the speaker's own reasoning" [4, p. 362]. Transactive discourse analysis involves coding statements into the following categories: feedback request, paraphrase, justification request, juxtaposition, completion, clarification, extension, critique and integration.

We collected audio, video and screen capture data from five pairs of university-level introductory programming students as they debugged Java programs. Results are discussed in [3] and revealed that extensions, feedback requests, critiques and completions were the most frequently observed types of transactions, while other types were rarely detected. Pairs who talked more and used completion transactions more often attempted to debug more programs, but those who critiqued more frequently successfully debugged more programs.

5. STUDY #2: STUDENT SELF-EVALUATION

Ruth Anderson, Colleen Lewis, Ken Yasuhara

Our work focuses on understanding factors affecting undergraduate entry into the field. We study intro CS students' experiences with and beliefs about computer science and how these influence major choice. By interviewing students for their first-hand perspectives, we identify ways educational institutions can help students make informed decisions about majoring in CS.

Our work employs the qualitative method of Grounded Theory, which is well-suited for exploratory research that aims to generate understandings or hypotheses about a process. This method privileges the interviewed students' accounts and allows for the development of a complex theory that might not be suggested by prior work. We conducted 30 semi-structured interviews with students taking introductory CS classes at the University of Washington, Seattle and the University of California, Berkeley. The interviews explored students' experience in their current course and their interest in pursuing computer science.

The interviews were transcribed and iteratively analyzed to identify and refine themes within the data. Students' discussion of their self-evaluation emerged as a theme, and factors affecting self-evaluation became the focus of further data analysis. The product of our research project will be a theory that describes the process of students' self-evaluation and how it is influenced by a variety of factors.

6. STUDY #3: STUDY HABITS OF CS 1 STUDENTS

Donald Chinn, Judith Sheard, Angela Carbone, Mikko-Jussi Laakso

Our project investigates how students in CS 1 study: where they study, how often they study, what kinds of activities they engage in when they study, whether they work in groups, and the ways in which they use class resources to help them study. Our goals are not only to understand the range of study strategies students employ and those that seem to work for them, but also to provide information to CS 1 instructors who design learning environments that students will use and benefit from.

We used a mixture of quantitative and qualitative methods. We developed a survey to ask students about their background and study habits. We used the results of the survey to develop questions for semi-structured interviews with 12 students. For the qualitative part of the analysis, we used Grounded Theory to analyze the transcripts of the interviews. The end product of the analysis will be a model or theory that explains the choices students make when deciding where, how, and how much to study, and which includes factors that influence these choices.

From survey data, we discovered study activities that were correlated with success in the course and uncovered some gender differences [1]. Subsequent interviews allowed us to categorize the methods by which students study. Our analysis will guide us in designing a new set of questions for another round of interviews.

7. STUDY #4: PLANNING AND THE NOVICE PROGRAMMER

Julie Johnson and Jon Wellons

In our long range research agenda we design activities and scaffolds to teach and support the meta-cognitive skills needed by novice programmers to achieve early success in programming. This qualitative study used a systematic approach to observe and explain the complex process of planning among novice programmers. We also wanted to demonstrate how student interviews could be used for more than just the course on which they were commenting to yield insights into more general aspects of the programming experience.

Ten volunteers from an Introduction to Engineering course described their experiences during several programming assignments, what type of plan they created, how detailed it was, and how it was adapted. Interview data was then coded and student comments were categorized for further analysis. We employed a grounded theory approach to analysis of the data.

From our analysis we developed three emerging theories that warrant further research.

- **Theory I:** Novice programmers attempt to adapt problem-solving strategies from other domains, such as mathematics or essay composition.
- **Theory II:** Planning by means of pseudocode is achievable for novice programmers.
- **Theory III:** Students who planned their programs are more likely to report a positive experience in the class.

8. ACKNOWLEDGMENTS

We thank the National Science Foundation for making the Qualitative Research Methods Workshop possible via DUE CCLI grant #0923592. Any opinions, findings, and conclusions or recommendations expressed in this material are those of the authors and do not necessarily reflect the view of the National Science Foundation.

9. REFERENCES

[1] Chinn, D., Sheard, J., Carbone, A., and Laakso, M.-J. 2010. Study Habits of CS 1 Students: What Do They Do Outside the Classroom? *Proceedings of the Twelfth Australasian Computing Education Conference* (Brisbane, Australia, January 2010). ACE2010. Australian Computer Society Inc., 53-62.

[2] Creswell, J. W. 2007. Qualitative Inquiry and Research Design: Choosing among Five Approaches, Thousand Oaks, CA: Sage Publications.

[3] Murphy, L., Fitzgerald, S., Hanks, B., and McCauley, R. 2010. Pair Debugging: A Transactive Discourse Analysis. In *Proceedings of the Sixth international Workshop on Computing Education Research* (Aarhus, Denmark, August 9-10, 2010). ICER '10.

[4] Teasley, S. D. 1997. Talking About Reasoning: How Important is the Peer in Peer Collaboration? In Resnick, L. B., Saljo, R., Pontecorvo, C., and Burge, B. (Eds.) *Discourse, Tools, and Reasoning*. Springer-Verlag, Heidelberg, Germany, 361-384.

NCATE Standards for Preparation of Secondary Computer Science Teachers

J. Philip East
University of Northern Iowa
Computer Science Department
Cedar Falls, IA 50614-0507
1 319-273-2939
east@cs.uni.edu

Charmaine Bentley
F.D. Roosevelt High School
525 Bonnie View Rd.
Dallas, TX 75203
1 972-925-6800
charmainebently@gmail.com

Joe Kmoch
Milwaukee Public Schools
1035 E. Colfax Pl
Whitefish Bay, WI 53217
1 414-964-6892
joe@jkmoch.com

Stephen Rainwater
The University of Texas at Tyler
3900 University Boulevard
Tyler, TX 75799
1 903-566-7235
srainwater@uttyler.edu

Chris Stephenson
CSTA
2 Penn Plaza, Suite 701
New York, NY 10121
1-800-401-18799
cstephenson@csta.acm.org

SUMMARY

This special session serves two purposes. It provides a progress report on the revision of the NCATE Standards for the Preparation of Secondary Computer Science Teachers and seeks input from computing education professionals on the proposed revisions. The Standards and their role in evaluating teacher preparation programs will be explained, the proposed revision discussed, and process for providing input explained.

Categories and Subject Descriptors

K.3.2 [**Computing Milieux**]: Computer and Information Science Education – *accreditation*.

General Terms

Human Factors, Standardization, Legal Aspects.

Keywords

Teacher preparation. NCATE Standards. Secondary Computer Science.

1. SESSION OBJECTIVES

NCATE (National Council for Accreditation of Teacher Education) is the primary accrediting body for programs that prepare pre-college teachers. Since about 1990, there has been a set of standards for programs that prepare secondary computer science teachers. Those Standards are currently being revised (for the third time) by ISTE and CSTA and input is being sought concerning the proposed revision. The objectives of this session are to explain the Standards and their use and to provide SIGCSE community members the opportunity to examine and respond to the proposed revisions.

Some who encounter the Standards have been known to consider them to be curriculum guidelines for either high schools or teacher preparation programs. They are neither. Rather, they are similar to ABET (Accreditation Board for Engineering and Technology) and CSAB (Computing Sciences Accreditation Board) standards and are used to assess college programs; in this case, programs that prepare teachers. The Standards address both computer science content and educational practitioner skills. Programs for the preparation of teachers always have a substantial education component that is often offered in or administered through colleges/schools/departments of education rather than in computer science. Accurately conveying this background information is a major goal of the session and necessary for informed input.

The other objective of this session is to provide discussion of the proposed revision to the Standards—both its form and content—that will enhance the input that session participants might provide. NCATE mandates some structural elements in standards documents that constrain the content of particular sets of standards. Once the constraints are outlined, discussion of the contents can occur.

Ultimately, the goal is to receive as much input as possible on the proposed revision to the Standards. The input will occur via an on-line survey rather than in this session. However, the committee conducting the revision will use the discussion in this session as context for interpreting the input received on the survey.

2. SESSION OUTLINE

We plan a discussion-oriented session in which the information described above will be presented with questions and comments during the presentation. Thus, time estimates are approximate.

- Session & participant introduction (5 minutes)
- Standards explanation (10 minutes)
  - NCATE and the standards process
  - Standards use in evaluating teacher education programs
  - Possible/typical structure of teacher education programs
- Structure of the Standards (5 minutes)
- Presentation and discussion of the proposed Standards revision (25 minutes)

SIGCSE'11, March 9–12, 2011, Dallas, Texas, USA.
ACM 978-1-4503-0500-6/11/03.

- Free/non-directed discussion and questions (20 minutes)
- Providing feedback/input on the Standards and expected committee activity (5 minutes)

3. EXPECTATIONS

Attendees will become better/well informed about the NCATE standards and better prepared to submit their input on the proposed revisions.

4. SUITABILITY

It is appropriate that this session be included in the Symposium because SIGCSE has vital interest in pre-college computing education. Understanding that context is important for SIGCSE members wishing to have a relationship with educational professionals at the secondary level or to influence those educators. The accreditation of programs that prepare computing teachers is an important part of that context.

5. STANDARDS OUTLINE

NCATE specifies the structure of all standards documents. Each must address four educational **principles** and have at most seven **standards** which include at most 28 **elements** (in total). Included below is an outline of the draft revision.

PRINCIPLE I. KNOWLEDGE OF CONTENT.

Standard I.A. Abstraction and data representation.

- **I.A.1.** use of primitive data types.
- **I.A.2.** static and dynamic data structures.
- **I.A.3.** information & data representation; storage & retrieval; files, spreadsheets, databases, Web, cloud, ...
- **I.A.4.** modeling and simulation to solve real-world problems.

Standard I.B. Algorithm design, development, and testing.

- **I.B.1.** proficiency in a high-level programming language.
- **I.B.2.** complex logical expressions using Boolean operators and functions.
- **I.B.3.** design and test algorithms and programming solutions.
- **I.B.4.** analyze algorithms using complexity, efficiency, aesthetics, and correctness.
- **I.B.5.** select appropriate data structures to solve problems.
- **I.B.6.** two or more programming paradigms.
- **I.B.7.** two or more integrated development environments.
- **I.B.8.** one or more software development models.

Standard I.C. Digital devices, systems and networks.

- **I.C.1.** logic gates and basic machine architecture.
- **I.C.2.** data representation and organization at the machine level.
- **I.C.3.** operating systems and networking.
- **I.C.4.** computer networks and mobile devices supporting communication and collaboration.

Standard I.D. Role and impact of computing in modern world.

- **I.D.1.** social, ethical, and legal issues and impacts, and attendant responsibilities of computer scientists and users.
- **I.D.2.** contributions of computer science to current and future innovations in sciences, humanities, the arts, and commerce.

PRINCIPLE II. EFFECTIVE TEACHING AND LEARNING STRATEGIES.

Standard II.A. Plan and teach computer science lessons/units.

- **II. A.1.** problems and methodologies supporting active and authentic learning.
- **II.A.2.** collaboration in lesson plans/units and assessments.
- **II.A.3.** effective use of multiple forms of media.
- **II.A.4.** culturally relevant activities, lessons, and assessments.
- **II.A.5.** problematic concepts and constructs in computing.

PRINCIPLE III. EFFECTIVE LEARNING ENVIRONMENTS.

Standard III.A. Environments for effective teaching and learning in classrooms and on-line learning.

- **III.A.1.** safe and effective use of hardware, software, peripherals, and networks.
- **III.A.2.** supporting learning.
- **III.A.3.** supporting equity and accessibility.

PRINCIPLE IV. PROFESSIONAL KNOWLEDGE AND SKILLS.

Standard IV.A. Ongoing professional development and life-long learning.

- **IV.A.1.** societies, organizations, and groups for professional growth and resources.
- **IV.A.2.** evolving social and research issues relating to computer science.

6. ACKNOWLEDGEMENTS

Two organizations are working together to revise the Standards—SIGCT (the Special Interest Group for Computing Teachers of ISTE, the Specialty Professional Association collaborator with NCATE) and CSTA (the Computer Science Teachers Association). One committee member Joanna Goode of the University of Oregon was unable to attend the conference.

Recognizing Computational Thinking Patterns

Ashok Basawapatna
University of Colorado Boulder
Department Of Computer Science
Boulder, CO. 80303
(720) 838-5838, 001
basawapa@colorado.edu

Kyu Han Koh
University of Colorado Boulder
Department of Computer Science
Boulder, CO. 80303
(303) 495-0357, 001
kohkh@colorado.edu

Alexander Repenning
University of Colorado Boulder
Department of Computer Science
Boulder, CO. 80303
(303) 492-1349, 001
ralex@cs.colorado.edu

David C. Webb
University of Colorado Boulder
School of Education
Boulder, CO. 80303
(303) 492-0306, 001
dcwebb@colorado.edu

Krista Sekeres Marshall
University of Colorado Boulder
School of Education
Boulder, CO. 80303
(303) 999-5736, 001
krista.marshall@colorado.edu

ABSTRACT

End-user game design tools are effective in motivating and exposing students with no prior programming experience to computer science. However, while there is good evidence that these environments are effective motivators, the question remains what do students actually learn? For our purposes, using AgentSheets, we would like to know if students can apply the knowledge obtained from programming games to creating science simulations. Specifically, we want to better understand if students are able to recognize *Computational Thinking Patterns* (CTP) from their game programming experience. Computational Thinking Patterns are abstract programming patterns that enable agent interactions not only in games but also in science simulations. Students and teachers who participated in a game design summer institute were administered a Computational Thinking Pattern Quiz (CTP Quiz). This quiz tested the participants' ability to recognize and understand patterns in a context removed from game programming. We found that participants, for the most part, were able to understand and recognize the patterns in a variety of contexts.

Categories and Subject Descriptors

K.3.2 Computer and Information Science Education

General Terms

Algorithms, Design, Experimentation, Human Factors.

Keywords

University Programming Education, Middle School Computer Education, Scalable Game Design, Computational Thinking, Computational Thinking Patterns, Transfer, Student Observation.

1. INTRODUCTION

Currently end-user video game design is a popular way to teach programming to students who have little or no prior programming experience [1,2,3]. The allure of using video games to introduce students to programming partly lies in students' natural interest in video games, but also, in that certain game design tools allow students to create games relatively quickly as compared to conventional programming languages [4]. To put this in perspective, a student using AgentSheets, the end user rapid game prototyping environment we employ, can make their first 'Frogger' game within 5 hours [5].

Much research has shown the teacher effectiveness of using end user game creation as a motivational tool to get students interested in Computer Science [4,6]. There has been less research, in general, on the actual knowledge/skills students acquire. For example, implicit in these studies is the idea that students learn "Computational Thinking" [7]. However, the definition of Computational Thinking at the present time is abstract at best [8]. For this method of instruction it is essential we concretely define what exactly we expect students to learn. In other words, for Computational Thinking to become a notion that is actionable, teachers require more than just abstract definitions of what Computational Thinking is or is not.

A different way to think about Computational Thinking is to move beyond its definitions towards a more pragmatic conceptualization. In one of the many schools participating in the Scalable Game Design project, one teacher came up with an interesting idea. After glancing at some of the current definitions of Computational Thinking, he indicated that he still did not quite understand what Computational Thinking really was, but he had an expectation. He would want to be able to walk up to a student participating in game design and ask:

"Now that you can make Space Invaders, can you also make a science simulation." [9]

To put it another way, the teacher's expectation is that the student should be able to use their programming knowledge to solve real world problems. The ability to create scientific simulations should be an important benefit of thinking computationally and an indication of STEM proficiency.

For our purposes, any useful educational benefit obtained through end-user game design would have the following properties:

Educational Characteristics of Game Design:

1) Enables students to ***transfer*** their skills to science simulations and/or mathematical models
2) Is based on concepts that are easily ***recognizable*** a and ***usable*** by both instructors and students
3) Is automatically ***measurable*** for evaluation and progress tracking purposes.

The above specifications initially motivated us to look at the elements of game programming that enable transfer to science simulations. This led us to define Computational Thinking Patterns, which are abstracted programming patterns that are learned by students when they create games and can readily be used by students to model scientific phenomena [5]. For example, in Frogger, students must program a truck-frog collision; this situation, wherein two agents physically collide, can be used to model molecules colliding or even a car crash. The following table shows some example games and their corresponding Computational Thinking Patterns. It should be noted that these patterns are a work in progress and this table is by no means comprehensive.

Table 1 Games and their corresponding Computational Thinking Patterns [5]

Games	Computational Thinking Patterns
Frogger	Generation, Absorption, Collision, Transportation
Sokoban	Push, Pull
Centipede	Generation, Absorption, Collision, Push, Pull
Space Invaders	Generation, Absorption, Collision
Sims	Diffusion, Hill Climbing

The following is a brief description of selected Computational Thinking Patterns and how they relate to game programming and STEM simulation design. For a more in-depth description of these and other patterns please see [5].

Generation: To satisfy this pattern, an agent is required to create another agent; in real life, for example, raindrops emanate from clouds. Analogously, in predator/prey science simulations, animals breed to create new animals. Conversely, the ***Absorb*** pattern is when one agent deletes another agent.

Collision: The collision pattern occurs when two agents physically collide. In real life, a car crashing into another car is an example of a collision. In science simulations atoms can collide with other atoms to make new elements.

Transportation: In the transportation pattern, one agent carries another agent. In real life a car transports a person. In science simulations red blood cells transport oxygen molecules to parts of the body.

Diffusion: Diffusion allows for the "scent" of an agent to be dispersed around a level. In real life, the scent of freshly baked bread originating from the kitchen is present in other rooms. In a science simulation diffusion can be used to depict how heat is transferred from one side of a heated metal bar to the other side.

Hill Climbing: An agent employing a hill-climbing algorithm looks at neighboring values of interest and moves towards the one with the largest value. These values could be, for example, the "scent" of another agent. In real life, mosquitoes hill climb the smell given off by humans.

One possible method of evaluating Computational Thinking in the classroom, in the context of end user game programming, is evaluating the ability of teachers and students to understand and make use of these Computational Thinking Patterns. Previous research has indicated that students do indeed use these Computational Thinking Patterns to implement science simulations of their own [5,11]. Further research into automatically recognizing which patterns a student has used to implement a game/simulation yielded an analysis called the Computational Thinking Pattern Graph [10]. The Computational Thinking Pattern Graph employs an approach similar to Latent Semantic Analysis to create a graph that depicts the Computational Thinking Patterns used to program a given game [12]. Basically, the underlying code of a game or simulation is compared to canonical Computational Thinking Patterns coded in the same programming language. For instance, the dimension of collision indicates if there is some code exhibiting a similar pattern to a canonical implementation of two object colliding. The following figure is a Computational Thinking Pattern graph of a student's Frogger implementation as compared to the tutorial Frogger.

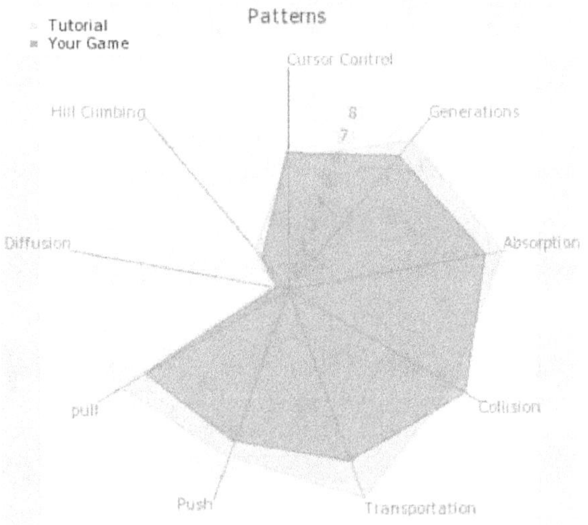

Figure 1: Computational Thinking Pattern graph. Depicts the Computational Thinking Patterns for a student's implementation of Frogger as compared to the tutorial's implementation.

This graph is one way to visually evaluate the Computational Thinking Patterns students use in a game. For example, using Figure 1, a teacher could readily see that, to a large extent, the student was able to successfully implement all the Computational Thinking Patterns necessary for Frogger. Therefore, the graph seems to indicate the student has met a high level of proficiency in the end user game design task; this relates to point 3 of the above Educational Characteristics of Game Design. Furthermore, previous research has indicated this transfer between games and simulations seems to occur [5,11]. This relates to point 1 of the Educational Characteristics of Game Design. However, the question still remains whether the user can now recognize and re-implement these patterns in the context of a STEM simulation.

To put this another way, though the Computational Thinking Pattern graph shows that teachers can teach and students can implement these patterns, a real educational question arises as to whether the students and teachers truly understand what is being learned. In order for students to implement and teachers to teach these Computational Thinking Patterns in another context, they must first be able recognize and understand these patterns. This relates to point 2 in the above Educational Characteristics of Game Design. For example, given that a class has finished the Frogger unit, are the students able to recognize that to model a car crash simulation they would employ the same collision pattern that they used in Frogger? Specifically, the research question we are asking is "To what extent are these Computational Thinking Patterns accessible and useful to teachers teaching game design and students learning game design." To help gain better insight into this question, we developed the *Computational Thinking Pattern Quiz*.

The Computational Thinking Pattern Quiz starts with several videos that depict one or a combination of Computational Thinking Patterns. The last question of the Computational Thinking Pattern Quiz is a paragraph specification of a given science simulation, and game designers are asked to list the Computational Thinking Patterns that should be used to implement this simulation. The videos and paragraph description questions allow us to see if game designers can, and to what extent, recognize various Computational Thinking Patterns outside the context of game programming. Therefore, the Computational Thinking Pattern Quiz could be an important aspect of evaluating what students actually learn from end-user game programming as well as method of evaluating the usability of Computational Thinking Patterns themselves.

2. METHOD

In the summer of 2010 a National Science Foundation-funded 2-week Summer Institute was held at the University of Colorado, Boulder. The goal of this Institute was to present to middle school teachers and community college students methods of using game design to teach computer science and Computational Thinking in middle school classrooms across the state of Colorado, and sites in Texas, Alaska and South Dakota. Specifically, this Institute was held as part of NSF funded iDREAMS Scalable Game Design project which has, thus far, educated over 2,000 students in Colorado.

There were 2 groups that participated in the Summer Institute. Group 1 consisted of participants who had not participated in the 2009 Summer Institute. This group attended the Summer Institute for the entire 2-week session. Group 2 was made up of participants who had experienced the prior Summer Institute in 2009, therefore, they were only present for the second week session of the Summer Institute. Group 2 had completed everything Group 1 did in a previous Summer Institute and thus, by week 2, both groups were at comparable levels of expertise. Teachers in both Groups 1 and 2 came from diverse backgrounds; for example, participant teachers taught everything from computer science to Spanish to accounting. Moreover, community college students were also from diverse backgrounds such as computer science, creative writing, art, and philosophy.

The curriculum for the Summer Institute exposed all the participants to multiple Computational Thinking Patterns. In week 1, participants programmed Frogger, Sims, and Space Invaders (refer to Table 1 to see the Computational Thinking Patterns implemented in these games). In week 2, the participants implemented two science simulations and the game Pacman (which uses the patterns diffusion and hill climbing).

At the end of the Institute, all participants were given an 8 question Computational Thinking Pattern Quiz. The first 7 questions involved video of real-life phenomena relating to patterns participants programmed in previous games. The final question of the quiz was a paragraph description of a predator/prey model and asked the participants to list and describe all the Computational Thinking Patterns necessary for implementation. The following section covers these 8 questions more in-depth.

2.1 Computational Thinking Pattern Quiz

As mentioned above, the Computational Thinking Pattern quiz has 8 questions, 7 of which are video of real life phenomena that resemble in-game Computational Thinking Patterns and one of which is a specification for a predator/prey simulation. The questions were administered online and the 43 participants were given an hour to complete the quiz. The descriptions of the questions are as follows.

Question 1 is a video of 2 people sledding down a hill. At the end of the video one of the sledders collides with a person standing at the bottom of the hill. The patterns depicted in this video are 'transportation' and 'collision' and the participants were specifically asked how this related to something in the "Frogger" game. Figure 2 depicts sequential screenshots of this video as an example as to what these videos looked like. Participants were given credit if they correctly identified either one of the patterns.

Figure 2 Sequential screenshots from question 1 of the Computational Thinking Pattern Quiz wherein 2 sleds 'transport' 2 people down a hill and one of the sledders 'collides' with a person at the bottom of the hill.

Question 2 depicted a marching band coming out of a tunnel and again asked participants to say how this was similar to the "Frogger" game they programmed (i.e.: the tunnel in the "Frogger" game 'generates' trucks).

Question 3 depicts a 'collision' between two soccer players. Again participants are asked how this is similar to something they programmed in "Frogger" (i.e.: when the truck hits the frog).

Question 4 depicts a hot-dog eating contest and asks the participants how this is similar to something they programmed in "Pacman" (i.e.: the "Pacman" eats or 'absorbs' the pellets)

Question 5 depicts several football players chasing after a player with a football and the participants are asked how this relates to something they programmed in "Pacman" (ie: the ghosts 'hill climbing' of Pacman's 'diffused' scent resembles the players running after the person with the football). As for Question 1, which also depicted 2 patterns, describing either pattern yielded a correct answer.

Question 6 is a video depicting one type of liquid being 'diffused' in another type of liquid and participants were asked to state how this was similar to "Pacman" (ie: Pacman's scent is diffused around the level so the ghosts can track Pacman).

Question 7 is a video that depicts marathon runners running towards the finish line and participants were asked to describe how this resembles something in the Ant Foraging simulation they used earlier in the week (ie: runners running towards the goal is visually similar to ants following a pheromone scent to food and/or taking food back to the nest).

Question 8) As mentioned above, Question 8 was a written paragraph that described a predator/prey simulation, and participants were asked to talk about all the Computational Thinking Patterns they would use to create this simulation. The specification of the simulation was as follows:

"This simulation involves the Predator Prey relationship between the Fox and the Rabbit. The Foxes find and eat Rabbits when they are hungry. Otherwise, Foxes will breed with other Foxes to create new Foxes. The Rabbits also breed with other Rabbits to create new Rabbits. Finally Rabbits, when hungry, seek out and eat grass."

Based on what participants experienced at the Summer Institute, we would expect the following patterns to be identified as necessary to complete the simulation:

- Generation because the animals breed creating new animals.
- Absorption because the foxes eat (or absorb) rabbits and the rabbits eat grass.
- Diffusion because the rabbits diffuse a scent around the level.
- Hill Climbing because the foxes follow the rabbit's diffused scent and the rabbits seek out grass when hungry.

Unlike Question 1 and Question 5, in Question 8 participants were specifically asked to list all the patterns they thought would be necessary to implement the predator/prey paragraph description. Therefore, Question 8 was out of 4 points.

Participant answers to all questions were given in paragraph long-answer format, and the answers were categorized and coded. As mentioned above, participants were awarded a correct answer if they named or described an intended Computational Thinking Pattern for a particular question, with the exception of Question 8 which was out of 4 correct answers.

3. RESULTS

Table 2 depicts the average scores for each question. In general, the results show that participants were able to understand and recognize Computational Thinking Patterns in a different context; the average score for all questions was over 78%, and for the first 7 questions, the average score was over 84%. This is remarkable since the participants came from diverse backgrounds and had minimal instruction on Computational Thinking Patterns before they took the quiz.

The nature of responses took two main forms. Some participants named the specific Computational Thinking Pattern that was shared between both the game and the Computational Thinking Quiz video. Other participants actually described the interaction in the video that was similar to the patterns. Both were deemed correct answers. The specific results are as follows.

The first three question refer to how the videos (described above) resemble something the participants had seen in Frogger.

Question 1 depicted two people sledding down a hill and with a sledder collision at the bottom. Surprisingly, every participant got one of the two Computational Thinking Patterns leading to every participant getting the question right. Some participants even wrote both Computational Thinking Patterns though it was specifically not required by the question. This is not too surprising since collision and transport are both taught in Frogger, the first game everyone learns (and the one that is most taught by participants in their respective schools). The following answer is indicative of a correct answer to both patterns:

"The people are being transported by the tubes and the announcer is hit (collision) like the frog and the truck."

Question 2 was a video of a marching band coming out of a tunnel. As with Question 1, the participants correctly identified this pattern as the average score was 93%. The following correct answer is representative of how many participants described the game/video similarity:

"Generation of trucks, logs, turtles is similar (sic) to the tunnel generating people so to speak."

Question 3 depicted a scene from the 2004 World Cup where one player infamously head-butts another player. 88% of the participants correctly identified the Computational Thinking Pattern. Though many people described this pattern, fewer people were able to correctly name or describe this Computational Thinking Pattern than in prior questions. The reason for this might lie in the fact that in the video one player head-butts another player in the context of a soccer game which could lead to participants adding information from their own experiences or knowledge of, in this case, soccer to answer the question. For example, a typical incorrect answer looked as follows.

Table 2 Average score of participants for each question in the Computational Thinking Quiz. The numbers in parenthesis denote the total possible points for a given question

	Q1 (1)	Q2 (1)	Q3 (1)	Q4 (1)	Q5 (1)	Q6 (1)	Q7 (1)	Q8 (4)
Participants	1	0.929	.881	.952	.976	.951	0.846	3.14

"It could be either the guy getting a red flag . . . or a third agent keeping track of a loss."

The participant refers to aspects of a soccer game (red card cheating vs. cheating in Frogger and referee scoring) that are not explicitly shown in the video. Everything this participant alluded to is correct, but is not the simple 'collision' pattern we were looking for in this case. Ambiguity brought about by the implied video context is a shortcoming of the Computational Thinking Pattern Quiz. The typical correct answer resembled the following.

"There is a collision with two different team members just as the car collides with the frog. . ."

Questions 4 through 6 deal with how the videos are similar to the game Pacman. The answers to this portion of the quiz were for the most part all correct; this might be due to the fact that Pacman was one of the most recent games the participants had programmed so it was fresh in their minds.

Question 4 depicted a hot dog eating contest. This question was answered correctly by 95% of the participants; most people seemed to understand that hotdogs being eaten by a person was similar to how Pacman absorbs the pellets. This is one of the main patterns in Pacman. Furthermore, absorb is a simple pattern that is also shared in other games such as Frogger when a truck is absorbed by a tunnel at the end of the road; thus, participants were very familiar with this particular pattern. A typical answer for Question 4 looked as follows:

"PacMan eats pellets and they erase, just like the hot dogs erase when they are eaten."

Question 5 was a video of a football player being chased by other football players. This question had 2 answers, if the participants answered or described hill climbing or diffusion they were awarded a correct answer. Similar to Question 4, everybody basically answered Question 5 correctly (98%). An indicative correct answer given by participants is as follows.

"Both are seeking - the football players are seeking the player with the ball and the ghosts are seeking Pacman."

Question 6 examines the similarity between one liquid diffusion into another liquid and how Pacman's scent is diffused across a level. Unlike the liquid, Pacman's diffused scent is invisible making the contextual leap more challenging. However, participants still uniformly understood the connection between this Computational Thinking Pattern of diffusion in Pacman and the diffusion of one liquid into another as 95% of participants got this question right. The following is a common participant answer we came across

"This shows the diffusion of the dye which represents the scent we assigned to pacman."

Question 7 referred to an Ant foraging simulation that the participants modified.

Question 7 depicted marathon runners running on a path towards the finish line much like the ants in the ant simulation followed pheromones to food and followed an implicit path back to the nest once finding food. Of the first 7 questions this is the one that participants had most trouble with as only 85% of participants got it right. As with Question 3, this question might have suffered from ambiguity relating to the video as participants may not have understood the significance of a person travelling on a path (something they see in everyday life and possibly deem as not notable). For example, the following incorrect answer was given by one participant:

"This is similar to the ant simulation because they both have a large number of similar "agents" moving around quickly."

This answer completely disregards any notion of agents moving on a path in favor of how the video matches the overall aesthetic of the ant simulation. In contrast, the correct answers all noticed the trail aspect of the video. A common correct answer participants provided is as follows:

"The runners are behaving like the ants after they have located some food. They are all heading in the same general direction as fast as they can."

Note that the second answer is somewhat similar to the first answer but focuses on the idea of seeking which involves the diffusion and hill climbing Computational Thinking Patterns.

Question 8 deals with the specification of a predator/prey science simulation. As mentioned above, the patterns needed to correctly implement this simulation are generate, absorb, hill climbing, and diffusion. Of all the Computational Thinking Quiz questions, we thought Question 8 would be the most challenging and the most indicative of whether participants could actively recognize and transfer the Computational Thinking Patterns they learned in prior game development to a science simulation. Surprisingly, the results were positive. 20 of the 43 participants were able to name or describe all 4 computational thinking patterns. An excerpt representative answer from this group is as follows

"You would use collaborative diffusion, the fox will hill climb to find a rabbit, the fox will then absorb the rabbit. . . When one (of the) foxes are stacked on another fox it will generate a new fox."

An additional 13 participants were able to correctly identify 2-3 correct patterns. Many of these participants missed the less complex patterns such as absorb and generate while correctly pointing out the more sophisticated patterns of hill climbing and diffusion. A typical answer from this group is as follows:

"Foxes and Rabbits use DIFFUSION/HILL CLIMBING in order to find their food sources, or you can have it be based on random movement. Foxes and rabbits will GENERATE new versions of themselves when they're with another one of their species, also found by either diffusion or random movement. I would make the rabbits/foxes give off a low level of scent for "heat" . . ."

It is hard to say why this would be the case. A possible reason might be that since absorb and generate are simpler patterns, they are easier to overlook. 9 participants were able to name one Computational Thinking Patterns and only 1 participant was not able to name any. Given the performance on prior quiz questions, it could be that these participants were able to correctly recognize the patterns in different contexts visually but were not yet at the level where they could recognize the patterns from a more abstract English description.

Though participants did well in the Computational Thinking Pattern Quiz, there are a few issues with using this as a method of evaluation for Computational Thinking Patterns. The first, as referred to in Question 3 and Question 7, is the possible video ambiguity as to the specific Computational Thinking Pattern they would use to program a specific phenomenon. Sometimes participants added their own knowledge to the context of the video. Other times participants referred to shared actions that happened both in the video and the previous game they programmed; however, these were not at the generalized level of Computational Thinking Patterns, but rather, at a more specific implementation level or more of an aesthetic similarity between the video and the previously programmed game. In Question 8, wherein participants were given a specification and asked to list the Computational Thinking Patterns they would use for implementation, participants sometimes overlooked some of the more obvious patterns to describe the more complex patterns involved. It could be that if these participants actually programmed the predator/prey simulation they would, in fact, readily recognize and implement all the patterns correctly as the missing patterns would be made more explicit (i.e.: grass would not disappear when eaten by rabbits leading them to implement the absorb pattern). Even with these problems, the Computational Thinking Pattern Quiz is a good first step towards evaluating if students recognize what they learn from game programming as well as validating the usefulness of Computational Thinking Patterns themselves.

The Computational Thinking Quiz results imply that in 1 to 2 weeks time the diverse participants in the Summer Institute were able to recognize Computational Thinking Patterns in a variety of different contexts. The fact that middle school teachers and community college students could relatively easily pick up on these patterns helps to support point 2 in the Educational Characteristics of Game Design above wherein we ask if the educational elements are readily recognizable and understandable by teachers to students. This coupled with prior research showing that Computational Thinking Patterns can be used for automatic evaluation and that students tend to transfer these patterns when creating simulations, indicates that Computational Thinking Patterns are one way to measure the educational benefit of end-user game design.

4. CONCLUSION

Claiming an educational benefit through end-user game design necessitates the ability for students to gain tangible and measurable Computational Thinking skills in order to be useful in the classroom. For our purposes, our expectation of whether Computational Thinking has occurred is based on whether students are able to transfer the knowledge they gained from game programming to science simulations. We define Computational Thinking Patterns as the specific units of transfer between games and science simulations. In this paper, we show that Computational Thinking Patterns are readily recognizable and understandable by teachers and community college students across different contexts, which is an important step in showing the usefulness of Computational Thinking Patterns in the classroom.

Future research will look at other ways to make Computational Thinking Patterns more explicit in the programming process, identify more useful Computational Thinking Patterns, and develop further evaluations of student learning and methods of evaluating the usefulness of patterns themselves. We will administer the Computational Thinking Quiz to over 2000 middle school students during the 2010-2011 school year. Results from the quiz will further inform this research.

5. ACKNOWLEDGMENTS

This material is based in part upon work supported by the National Science Foundation under Grant Numbers No. 0833612 and DMI-0712571. Any opinions, findings, and conclusions or recommendations expressed in this material are those of the authors and do not necessarily reflect the views of the National Science Foundation. A special thanks to Andri Ioannidou for all her help and invaluable advice.

6. REFERENCES

[1] Cooper, S., Dann, W., Pausch, R., Cooper, S., Dann, W., and Pausch, R., Teaching Objects-first In Introductory Computer Science, In Proc. SIGCSE 2003, Reno, Nevada, USA, 2003

[2] Peppler, K. and Kafai, Y. B., Collaboration, Computation, and Creativity: Media Arts Practices in Urban Youth Culture. In C. Hmelo- Silver & A. O'Donnell (Eds.), In Proc. Computer Supported Collaborative Learning, New Brunswick, NJ, USA, 2007

[3] Repenning, A., Excuse me, I need better AI! Employing Collaborative Diffusion to make Game AI Child's Play. In Proc. ACM SIGGRAPH Video Game Symposium, Boston, MA, USA, ACM Press, 2006.

[4] Sturtevant, N. R., Hoover, H. J., Schaeffer, J., Gouglas, S., Bowling, M. H., Southey, F., Bouchard, M., and Zabaneh, G. 2008. Multidisciplinary students and instructors: a second-year games course. In proc 39th SIGCSE Technical Symposium on Computer Science Education, Portland, OR, USA, 2008.

[5] Basawapatna, A. R., Koh, K., and Repenning, A. 2010. Using scalable game design to teach computer science from middle school to graduate school. In Proceedings of ITiCSE '10. ACM, Bilkent, Turkey 2010.

[6] Squire, K., Video games in education. International Journal of Intelligent Simulations and Gaming, (2) 1. 2003

[7] Ruthmann, A., Heines, J. M., Greher, G. R., Laidler, P., and Saulters, C. 2010. Teaching computational thinking through musical live coding in scratch. In Proceedings of the 41st ACM Technical Symposium on Computer Science Education Milwaukee, Wisconsin, USA, March 10 - 13, 2010. SIGCSE '10.

[8] National Academy of Sciences on Computational Thinking. Report of a Workshop on The Scope and Nature Computational Thinking, National Academies Press, 2010

[9] Repenning, A., Webb, D., and Ioannidou, A., "Scalable Game Design and the Development of a Checklist for Getting Computational Thinking into Public Schools", Proc. SIGCSE' 10, ACM Press, WI, USA, 2010

[10] Koh, K., Basawapatna, A., Bennet, V., and Repenning, A., "Towards the Automatic Recognition of Computational Thinking For Adaptive Visual Language Learning," to appear in Proceedings of the 2010 Conference on Visual Languages and Human Centric Computing (VL/HCC 2010), IEEE Computer, Madrid, Spain.

[11] Basawapatna, A., and Repenning, A., "Visualizing Student Game Design Project Similarities", In Proc. Diagrams 2010, Portland, Oregon, USA 2010.

[12] Landauer, T. K., Foltz, P. W., and Laham, D., Introduction to Latent Semantic Analysis. Discourse Processes, 25, 1998, 259-284.

Initial Experience with a Computational Thinking Course for Computer Science Students

Dennis Kafura, Deborah Tatar

Department of Computer Science
Virginia Tech
{kafura, tatar}@cs.vt.edu

ABSTRACT

Experience with the first offering of a computational thinking course for computer science (CT4CS) students is reported. The course is grounded in student interaction with fundamental, recurring concepts suggested by comparison with two sets of computer science principles. By using specialized, freely available tools and physical simulations it is possible to provide concrete, tangible learning experiences that neither require knowledge of nor the overhead of programming. Student end-of-term reflections indicate that the course deepened and broadened their understanding of computer science even when they had previously encountered a topic, and improved their computer science vocabulary.

Categories and Subject Descriptors

K.3.2 [**Computers and Education**]: Computer and Information Science Education

General Terms

Design, Experimentation

Keywords

Computational thinking, curriculum,CS0, pedagogy

1. INTRODUCTION

Like many departments across the country, the Department of Computer Science at Virginia Tech has worked to revamp the entry points to its undergraduate curriculum. A particular focus of concern has been the widespread perception that computer science is "just details of programming." This effort has included restructuring the sequence of programming courses, introducing an optional media computation first course, and adding an early required non-programming course in problem-solving.

Another, as yet experimental, approach is a "computational thinking" first course referred to as CT4CS. The name CT4CS is used because the conception of this course draws on the general computational thinking concern for promoting an early and deeper understanding of critical notions of computation [7, 10, 20, 21]. But this project differs from other efforts because it focuses on students interested in computer science as a likely area of study. Thus, rather than developing computational thinking for and embedded in other disciplines, we are interested in computational thinking as a core component and attractive aspect of computer science itself. Courses in computational thinking that target other fields of study (science, engineering, liberal arts, etc.) are clearly needed and well motivated. While the goal of computational thinking to help students develop "ways to think like a computer scientist" [20] is universally valuable, this goal is especially critical to students learning to become practicing computer scientists.

The overarching goal of this course is to create learning experiences that allow prospective computer science majors to encounter recurring, fundamental concepts in computer science early in their study. Through these experiences students explicitly learn a number of critical principles but, perhaps more importantly, develop a cognitive model for and underlying intuitions and mental models about computational phenomenon. In this way, students develop an initial, albeit incomplete, framework for their future study of computer science, a framework that aids them in recognizing connections across courses which may otherwise go unnoticed. From a pedagogical standpoint, this approach builds on Bransford's notion of contrasting cases [1] which emphasizes that learning is aided by seeing the introduction of new ideas as a solution to a pre-existing problem. Students, therefore, are better positioned to recognize key ideas later on, integrate them into the particulars of more advanced courses, and enrich their epistemologies throughout the course of their studies. Instructors across the computer science curriculum can also assist students integrate and deepen their understanding by explicitly referencing the concepts. The course objectives were to:

- better inform prospective majors about the nature of computer science,
- engender a set of intuitions, perspectives, thought processes, or mental models that are indicative of how computer scientists view the world and conduct the practice of their work,
- introduce recurring, fundamental concepts and structures – ideas that appear, perhaps implicitly, in several different contexts in computer science, and
- develop a more sophisticated computer science epistemology, including key vocabulary.

These goals are, of course, to be understood in the context of a single semester introductory course.

SIGCSE'11, March 9–12, 2011, Dallas, Texas, USA.

A feature of CT4CS is that it does not require prior knowledge of and does not use programming. The decision to avoid programming was motivated by four considerations. First, to convincingly illustrate that computer science is "more than just programming," the course allows students to encounter basic principles of computation without reference to programming. Second, in the absence of programming, the students' full time and energy is focused more clearly on the concepts because these concepts are not confounded with the extraneous details of how these concepts are expressed in a given programming language. Third, avoiding programming helps to diminish the effect of the students' prior, usually programming experience on their opportunity to learn the concepts presented in the course. The course can deepen the knowledge of students with prior experience and simultaneously reach students without such background. Fourth, the strict avoidance of programming was adopted to ensure that the course design would explore the curriculum space as distinct from possible from programming approaches, including media computation style approaches.

Nonetheless, CT4CS allows *concrete and tangible* work to be done involving material drawn from every level of the curriculum. The work is described as concrete and tangible for three reasons. First, in some cases the students are able to *construct* artifacts or systems of interacting elements and explore their behavior. Students encounter not only the abstract idea but are able to undertake practical work that embodies and explores the idea. Second, in some cases the students are introduced to a specific encoding (notation) so that their thinking about an idea can be externalized, shared, and comment on. Third, in some cases the students were involved in conducting physical simulations that engaged them in manipulating physical objects representing aspects of a concept in material form. Examples of the concrete and tangible work included in the course are: using a finite-state machine simulator to develop a gene acceptor based on the genetic code presented in a junior level computational biology course, using a taxonomy modeling tool to represent the relationships of real-world examples that students would encounter in senior level courses in databases or information retrieval, using a Petri net simulator to study classical synchronization and protocol problems that students encounter in junior or senior level operating systems and networking courses, and using a lambda calculus evaluator to deal with issues of binding that are explicit in junior or senior level courses in programming languages or compilers and which are implicit in programming courses.

Section 2 provides a description of the course topics and tools. Section 3 compares CT4CS to other related approaches. Section 4 evaluates the course using student feedback from an end-of-term questionnaire. Section 5 draws some conclusions based on the evaluation and the comparison to other approaches.

2. COURSE DESCRIPTION

The course was offered as an alternative to an existing required introductory class. Students self-selected to register for the course which met over a 15-week semester in two 75-minute sessions each week. The room was outfitted with small round tables to accommodate in-class work by teams of two or three students. An overview of the course topics is given in Table 1. The time devoted to each topic is measured in weeks. One week consists of two 75-minute classes and the associated time students spend working on assignments and readings outside of the class meetings. Additional information can be found at: http://www.cs.vt.edu/~kafura/ComputationalThinking .

Broadly, the topics are divided into two categories were based on a definition of computer science that emphasizes the representation (modeling) and manipulation (via engineered systems) of information that is inherent to scientific, natural, social, and others kinds of systems. The modeling topics focus on how information is used to represent the attributes and relationships of real-world artifacts and systems. The engineering topics focus on issues related to the construction of computational systems.

2.1 Modeling Topics

The modeling topics focused on state and behavior, abstraction, and relationships. Finite state machine diagrams were used to explore the importance of stateful behavior, recognizing that in a given state the system is only capable of certain actions, that the observed behavior of a system arises from its transitions among its possible states, and that reactive behavior occurs when the system interacts with an external world that drives the system from one state to the next. A particular kind of state-oriented system is an acceptor. Using a tool (JFLAP [11]), the students were able to build and test acceptors for various kinds of structured data including one that performed a simple form of gene recognition (allowing a discussion of the relationship of computer science to biology). The graphical form of an acceptor was also related to a text-based form using BNF grammars. The abstraction topic studied how artifacts have a rich set of attributes, that representing an artifact depends on the point of view of the modeler, and that there are a variety of graphical and textual forms for representing the abstraction. A physical simulation engaged the students in the modeling of a book: identifying different modeler points of view and creating attributes that are relevant from each point of view. The relationships topic looked at very basic ideas of knowledge representation. Using Protégé [14], the students were able to define the attributes of a collection of entities (pizzas) and observe what inferences could be made automatically about the categorization of the entities.

2.2 Engineering Topics

The engineering part of the course consisted of five topics. The notion of concurrency and the problems of concurrency control were introduced by a physical simulation where the students acted out a scenario of updating a shared memory and observing the loss of consistency. The modeling of the correct synchronization for several problems (traffic lights, reader-writer) was done using a graphical tool (Snoopy [15]) for editing and executing Petri nets. Snoopy was also used to illustrate "layers of abstraction." A simple layered system was built for the AB protocol. Using the Petri net tool, the students modeled a noisy channel, the AB protocol layer, and a bi-directional channel layer. The last four engineering topics focused on concepts related to programming languages and software systems. First, the lambda calculus was used both to explore the ideas of binding and scope as well as give some insight into the theory of programming languages and computation. A graphical tool for composing and evaluating lambda expressions (LambdaTeacher [12]) was used. Second, testing of software systems was undertaken using two exercises.

Weeks	Topic		Tools/Methods
.5	Modeling	Definition of computer science	Guided discussion
2		State and Behavior	Applet; tool for creating and exercising an acceptor (JFLAP); BNF grammar; BNF visualizer
2		Abstraction: modeling/design perspective	Physical simulation; UML diagrams, Venn diagrams, XML, tree diagrams
1.5		Relationships	Tool (Protégé) for representing, inferring, and visualizing relationships; ontologies
1	Midterm exam and return/review		
1.5	Engineering	Concurrency	Physical simulation; tool (Snoopy) to create and simulate Petri nets
1		Abstraction: engineering perspective	Layered systems; tool (Snoopy) to build layered protocol
2		Binding, scope, theory: lambda calculus	Tool (Lambda Teacher) for editing and evaluating lambda expressions
1		Testing	Testing applet for simple (triangle classification) problem; Exercise (Web-CAT) for more complex (sentence parsing) problem
1		Debugging	Puzzle (Sudoku) tool with history and backtracking
1		Memory, pointers, data structures	Physical simulation; C syntax
.5	Review, Course evaluation		

Table 1: CT4CS Course Overview

The first exercise allowed the students to enter test cases for a program to classify triangles (as equilateral, isosceles, or scalene). The tool used provided code coverage statistics and error detection percentages against a hidden collection of correctly and incorrectly programmed solutions. The second exercise involved the development of test cases for a grammar-based sentence parser. An automated system (WebCAT [19]) developed at Virginia Tech was used to run the test cases against a model solution and provide code coverage feedback. The third topic, debugging, explored unwinding a sequence of decisions to find a flawed decision that led to an erroneous state. A system for solving Sudoku puzzles [18] was used to present the students with an incorrectly solved puzzle. The tool provided a history and navigation controls so that students could "debug" the puzzle's incorrect solution. The last of the four topics was data structures. A physical simulation of a linear computer-like memory was conducted. The students were engaged in finding ways to map a tree structure (built of index cards and strings) into a linear memory. Notions of representing relationships via adjacency in memory and pointers arose from this simulation. The syntax of C was used to show how these ideas could be represented in a programming language.

3. COMPARISON

The CT4CS course can be compared with other computational thinking courses, definitions of the principles of computation, and repositories that provide resources for teaching topics in computer science.

CT4CS differs from other computational thinking approaches in one or both of two ways. First, some computational thinking courses are focused on students majoring in fields other than computer science (e.g, [8] focusing on science majors). These courses are valuable and seek to portray computation through topics and terms meaningful to other fields. CT4CS focuses exclusively on computer science majors and the terms of reference and topics that have the most impact on their future learning. Second, many courses use some form of programming either in lexical (e.g., [6]) or graphical (e.g., [17]) form. CT4CS explicitly avoids the use of programming languages so that the students can be engaged in topics that might be difficult to approach via programming. Admittedly the absence of a programming capability also limits some topics that can be approached in CT4CS. However, this is a tradeoff that seems reasonable given the topics that are addressed and the fact that the students will have multiple subsequent chances to encounter other important computing ideas. The specific computational thinking courses cited above are only representatives of many other similar courses from which CT4CS is differentiated in the ways just noted.

In comparison to principles of computing, CT4CS embodies five of the seven Big Ideas defined in the College Board's CS Principles and employed five of their seven computational thinking practices [2]. Specifically, CS4CS shows that computing is a creative human activity (Principle 1) by the creation of tangible artifacts, involved the use of abstraction to reduce information and detail (Principle 2), demonstrated knowledge creation (Principle 3) via ontologies, examined systems and networks (Principle 6) via concurrency and protocols, and illustrated how computing enables innovation in other fields via the use of examples from, for example, biology in the gene recognizer. The course used abstraction and models (Practice 3), analyzed problems and artifacts (Practice 4), connected computation with other fields (Practice 6), and engaged students in teamwork (Practice 7). Additionally, the course involved the creation of computation artifacts (Practice

2). While *programming* artifacts were not created, numerous other *computation* artifacts were created among which were test cases, UML diagrams, XML encodings, data structure declarations, BNF grammars, Petri nets, acceptors, lambda expressions, and an ontology. We believe that these kinds of artifacts deserve to be considered on an equal par with programming artifacts for several reasons. First, doing otherwise devalues the real work that computer scientists invest in the creation and use of these artifacts. Second, we are trying to counter the stereotype that limits computer science to programming. This stereotype is reinforced when we value only programming artifacts. Furthermore, we often deny students' early exposure to the very elements that make computer science of enduring interest during the bulk of most computer scientists' careers. Last, our experience in the course indicates that these non-programming artifacts enable student learning.

Another set of principles is Denning's framework [4], one axis of which is a set of computing practices and the other axis of which is a set of principles for design and mechanics. The topics in the CT4CS course have strong overlap with the elements of this framework. Specifically, the coordination and communication elements of mechanics resonate with the concurrency and engineering abstractions in the CT4CS class; the automation element is reflected in the relationships topic where automatic deduction of relationships is seen; to a lesser extent the computation element is touched on by the lambda calculus and the recollection element by the topic on data structures. The relationship of the CT4CS topics to the design aspects was centered on the simplicity element, showing how abstraction is used to simplify the description of artifacts. The practices axis contained two elements that related to topics in CT4CS. Many of the topics in the "engineering" half of the course relate well to the "engineering systems" practice. Similarly, many of the topics in the "modeling" half of the course relate well to the "modeling and validation" practice.

Finally, there are repositories of materials for teaching computing, perhaps the best exemplar of which is the Computer Science Unplugged collection [3]. CT4CS shares with the "unplugged" materials the goal of providing tangible and concrete experience about computing concepts without programming. A important difference between the two is the academic level of the audience which dramatically influences the level of sophistication of the topics and the presentation of these topics. Nonetheless, there might be contributions that CT4CS can make to the unplugged repository and there may be materials or ideas that can be adapted from the repository for use in future offerings of CT4CS.

4. EVALUATION

The observations reported in this section are based on the students' answers to a questionnaire. All of the 15 students, three of whom were female, were in their second semester at Virginia Tech. The questionnaire was administered on the last regularly scheduled class meeting. The students were told in advance of the general nature of the questionnaire (though not the specific questions). The questionnaire was distributed in electronic form and completed anonymously by students using their personal laptops. The students were not provided lists of course objectives or the course topics. The students had the full class period (75 minutes) to complete the questionnaire along with two other short standard course evaluations. All of the students completed the questionnaire before the end of the class. The questionnaire was divided into two parts: a student profile and student reflections. The student profile consisted of five questions about the student's background and interests in computer science. The student reflections contained eleven free response questions about various aspects of the course. The number of students in the class is not sufficient for statistical analysis but qualitative analysis of the results and the student reflections offers insights into student experiences. Furthermore, the argument for this approach lies only partially in precisely what was learned during the semester, and more fully in the way it is thought to smooth the path towards the future. However, the reflections offer important insight into the students' experience, and if their experiences are insufficiently good, then the long-term benefits of the approach are moot.

The students as a whole had substantial prior experience in computer science. Two-thirds of the class had programming experience of at least one semester and almost half of the class (7 of 15) had at least a full year of experience. This experience was typically described as an AP CS course using Java. There were only two students who had neither high school CS experience or completed a CS class at VT. There was only one student who had no prior CS coursework (in high school or at VT) and was not taking another CS class concurrently.

Observation 1: *The students reported that the course topics deepened their knowledge and perspective on computer science.* A third of the students (5 of 15) indicated that the course had a deep impact on their appreciation for or approach to computer science. This was expressed variously as gaining insight into the "why" behind programming, better understanding of what it means to be a computer scientist, or enabling future problem-solving with a deeper understanding of computing. Another group (3 of 15) reported more generically that they learned new concepts related to computing. A third group (3 of 15) reported that the course reaffirmed or clarified concepts that they already understood.

Observation 2: *The students reported that the course offered a number of new (to them) concepts and/or improved their understanding of concepts they had already seen.* Eight specific ideas were mentioned as being new. Four of these ideas (grammars/acceptors, finite state machines, Petri nets and concurrency, lambda calculus) were identified in this way by over half of the class (at least 8 out of 15). A minority (5 out of 15) identified two other topics (abstraction, ontologies) in this way. Two other topics were identified as new to the students by smaller groups (testing – 3 out of 15, debugging 2 out of 15). A strong majority (10 of 15) of the class reported that the class had improved their understanding of a concept that they had previously encountered. Students (6 out of 15) also reported that they had previously encountered the concepts of abstraction, generalization, or modeling but found that the course improved their understanding of these concepts.

These responses are meaningful in two ways. First, the identified concepts are fundamental to computing and, thus, progress in deepening students' understanding of these concepts is meaningful. Second, despite the high overall level of experience, the students found the course presented a number of new ideas or deepened their appreciation of ideas they had already encountered. Thus, the course content seemed to "stretch" and/or deepen the students' understanding of computer science. For example, one student reported that the course provided a "deeper look into not only *how* to model things, but *why* we model them that way" (italics in student's comment). A smaller group (3 of 15) reported similar gains in understanding of concurrency issues and another group (3 of 15) cited improvement in their understanding of testing/debugging. There was a small amount of overlap among these three groups (due to students citing more than one topic area); in total the three groups above accounted for two-thirds of the class (10 of 15).

Observation 3: *The students reported that a number of course topics strongly engaged their interest*. Overall, there were 22 reasons given for why a particular idea was cited by a student as being of interest. The number or reasons is more than the number of students because some students citied more than one idea as being interesting.

A majority of the students (8 of 15) reported that concurrency was the most interesting idea they encountered in the class. The reasons for their choice of this idea varied and included: utility (dealing with real life or practical situations), challenging, involved logic or problem solving, novelty (something not thought about before). Another group (4 of 15) identified the ideas of grammars and finite state machines as among the most interesting. The given reasons behind their choice included logic and problem-solving, and utility (dealing with real life or practical situations). A smaller group (3 of 15) identified data structures as the most interesting topic citing utility (2 of 3) and novelty as their reasons. These same reasons were cited by a similarly sized group (3 of 15) for the ideas related to testing/debugging.

These reasons can be categorized as utility (can be applied to real-life problems, will be useful in future work), logic/problem-solving (can be approached in a logical fashion, requires structured thinking, engages problem-solving skills), challenge (offered a mental challenge to think about), and novel (the idea or some aspect of the idea was new, a new way of thinking about the idea). The distribution of the reasons suggests that the students found interesting ideas that they could see as having high utility (cited 9 of 22 times), novelty (6 of 22), logic-problem solving (5 of 22), or challenging (2 of 22). While these results had a high degree of overlap, their diversity is very important. There is no single reason that a person should be interested in computer science. To the contrary, the goals of this class and of other changes to our computer science curriculum, is to bring people with a wide scope and perspective as well as deep engineering capabilities into computer science.

Furthermore, it is interesting to note that a single topic (e.g., concurrency) may appeal to different students for different reasons, making the task of designing an appropriate set of topics more promising -- and more challenging. The student feedback also gave good guidelines for determining how to improve the presentation of current topics or what aspects to look for in new topics.

Observation 4: *The students reported that the course helped them develop a better vocabulary for explain computer science issues.* A strong majority of students (12 of 15) reported that the course had improved their technical vocabulary. The degree of improvement was variously described, ranging from "definitely" to "somewhat". Two students did not believe that their vocabulary was improved and one student was not sure. This spread in reactions may be due to the fact that the word "vocabulary" means different things to different people. Vocabulary is an interesting metric because it represents utility both for itself and also as an indicator of the students' epistemology, that is, their notions about the interconnected web of ideas inherent in computer science, some of which are well captured in particular specialized words or phrases.

Observation 5: *The students reported that the physical simulations were useful to their learning.* As described in Section 2, the course pedagogy included three physical simulations illustrating ideas related to abstraction, concurrency, and data structures. The students unanimously believed that the physical simulations were useful. Eighty percent (12 of 15) of the students gave unqualified support for the value of the physical simulations. Twenty percent (3 of 15) noted that the simulations took too much time to conduct or were seen as being useful only to those who had not yet taken a CS class. This feedback is meaningful because it might be the case that (relatively) new university students would find the activity of a physical simulation not sufficiently sophisticated for a college-level course.

Observation 6: *The students expressed divided opinions on the ordering of this course with respect to an introductory programming course in computer science.* The single strongest opinion (7 of 15) was that this course should come before a programming course. Three of these students believed that this course would help form ways of thinking that would make a programming course easier. Two students believed that the ideas in this course were presented in a more abstract or less detailed way than these concepts would appear in a programming course so it was useful (or necessary) to take this course first. Two students gave no reason. However, others (4 of 15) indicated that there was equal value in taking this course before or after an introductory programming class. The one student who explained this choice pointed to the mutual reinforcing of concepts between this course and a programming course, believing that there was value in such reinforcement working in either direction. Two students believed that this course should be taken after a programming class. Both these students believed that the practical grounding achieved in a programming course was necessary before approaching these concepts in a more abstract way in this course. One student found it useful to be taking this class concurrently with a media computation programming class. One student offered no opinion.

While there was a near majority who favor taking this course before a programming course, the variety of opinion and reasons suggested that there is some latitude in where the course could be positioned in the overall curriculum. The students' reasons could be interpreted to mean that the choice depends on a student's learning style more than any prior study, or that the students, most of whom had taken programming before or concurrently, had difficulty imagining the counter-factual case. Pragmatically, other scheduling constraints (on the individual student or the institution) may also play a role in determining when the course is taken.

5. CONCLUSIONS

The experience with the initial course offering convinced us that a computational thinking course for computer science students was a viable concept. We found it possible to provide practical, concrete, learning experiences about a variety of important computing concepts using tools and physical simulation rather than programming. Student feedback suggests that the course fulfilled its specific course objectives to:

- better inform students about the nature of computer science (observation 1)
- to help develop intuitions and mental models (observation 2)
- present fundamental concepts as gauged by the comparison with two sets of principles of computing (see section 3)
- develop better epistemologies, as indicated by vocabulary (observation 4)

The student feedback also indicated that the physical simulations were very useful to student learning (observation 5), and that a course like this one could be flexibly positioned with respect to a programming course (observation 6).

Our own experience in teaching went beyond these specifics to suggest that students used the experience to encounter ideas in a way that would more firmly fix elements of computational thinking in their minds and render the treatment of these ideas in subsequent courses more tractable, more marked, and more profound.

We do not believe that the particular set of topics used in this first offering is the "right" set; but the experience seems to confirm the notion that a non-programming computational thinking course for computer science students is viable.

We are exploring the development of CT4CS in two ways. First the collection of topics presented in the course can be expanded. Other topics that we are investigating are in machine learning [16], natural language processing [13], ideas related to networks and behavior [5], and social networks [9]. Second, the examples used in class and in assignments can be enriched to better illustrate the connections of computation with other interesting problem domains similar to the use of gene recognition in conjunction with acceptors. We are interested in receiving suggestions and ideas on either of these improvements from the community.

6. ACKNOWLEDGMENTS

We would like to thank and acknowledge the contributions to the course of Denis Gracanin (finite state machine applet), Steve Edwards (testing applet and WEbCAT assignment), and Joon S. Lee (Sudoko system).

7. REFERENCES

[1] Bransford, J. D., Franks, J. J., Vye, N. J. and Sherwood, R. D. New approaches to instruction: Because wisdom can't be told. Cambridge University Press, City, 1989

[2] College Board, CS Principles, http://csprinciples.org/

[3] Computer Science Unplugged. See: http://csunplugged.org/

[4] Denning, P. J. 2003. Great principles of computing. *Commun. ACM* 46, 11 (Nov. 2003), 15-20. DOI= http://doi.acm.org/10.1145/948383.948400

[5] [NB] Easley, David and Kleinberg, Jon Networks, Crowds, and Markets, Cambridge University Press, 2010, a pre-publication draft is available at http://www.cs.cornell.edu/home/kleinber/networks-book/networks-book.pdf

[6] Freudenthal, E. A., Roy, M. K., Ogrey, A. N., Magoc, T., and Siegel, A. 2010. MPCT: media propelled computational thinking. In *Proceedings of SIGCSE'10* (Milwaukee, Wisconsin, USA, March 10 - 13, 2010). ACM, New York, NY, 37-41. DOI= http://doi.acm.org/10.1145/1734263.1734276

[7] Guzdial, M. 2008. Education: Paving the way for computational thinking. *Commun. ACM* 51, 8 (Aug. 2008), 25-27. DOI= http://doi.acm.org/10.1145/1378704.1378713

[8] Hambrusch, S., Hoffmann, C., Korb, J. T., Haugan, M., and Hosking, A. L. 2009. A multidisciplinary approach towards computational thinking for science majors. In *Proceedings of SIGCSE'09* (Chattanooga, TN, USA, March 04 - 07, 2009) ACM, New York, NY, 183-187. DOI= http://doi.acm.org/10.1145/1508865.1508931

[9] HarambeeNet: The SocialNets in Education Project, see: http://harambeenet.org/modules.html

[10] Henderson, P. B., Cortina, T. J., and Wing, J. M. 2007. Computational thinking. *SIGCSE Bull.* 39, 1 (Mar. 2007), 195-196. DOI= http://doi.acm.org/10.1145/1227504.1227378

[11] JFLAP, http://www.jflap.org/

[12] Mason, K. An Interactive Interpreter for Expressions in the Lambda Calucus, Honors Paper, Department of Computer Science, University of Adelaide, November, 1997.

[13] Natural Language Toolkit, see: http://www.nltk.org/

[14] Protégé, http://protege.stanford.edu/

[15] C Rohr, W Marwan, M Heiner: Snoopy - a unifying Petri net framework to investigate biomolecular networks; Bioinformatics 2010 26(7): 974-975. http://www-dssz.informatik.tu-cottbus.de/index.html?/software/snoopy.html

[16] Russel, Ingrid and Markov, Zdravko, Machine Learning Experiences in Artificial Intelligence: A Multi-Institutional Project, see: http://uhaweb.hartford.edu/compsci/ccli/index.htm

[17] Ruthmann, A., Heines, J. M., Greher, G. R., Laidler, P., and Saulters, C. 2010. Teaching computational thinking through musical live coding in scratch. In *Proceedings of SIGCSE'10* (Milwaukee, Wisconsin, USA, March 10 - 13, 2010). ACM, New York, NY, 351-355. DOI= http://doi.acm.org/10.1145/1734263.1734384

[18] Sudoku player: http://poet.cs.vt.edu/tuple_games/

[19] WebCAT http://web-cat.org/WCWiki/WebCatWiki

[20] J. Wing, Viewpoint-Computational Thinking, *Commun. ACM* 49,3 (March 2006) 33-3.

[21] J. Wing, Computational thinking and thinking about computing, *Philosophical Transactions of the Royal Society*, A, 2008, 366, pp. 3717-3725. DOI=10.1098/rsta.2008.0118

A Model for Piloting Pathways for Computational Thinking in a General Education Curriculum

Charles Dierbach[1], Harry Hochheiser[2], Samuel Collins[3], Gerald Jerome[4], Christopher Ariza[5], Tina Kelleher[6], William Kleinsasser[7], Josh Dehlinger[1], Siddharth Kaza[1]

[1]Department of Computer and Information Sciences, Towson University

[2]Department of Biomedical Informatics, University of Pittsburgh

[3]Department of Sociology, Anthropology, and Criminal Justice, Towson University

[4]Department of Kinesiology, Towson University

[5]Music and Theater Arts, Massachusetts Institute of Technology

[6]Department of English, Towson University

[7]Department of Music, Towson University

{cdierbach, scollins, gjerome, tkelleher, wkleinsasser, skaza, jdehlinger}@towson.edu; harryh@pitt.edu; ariza@mit.edu

ABSTRACT

Computational thinking has been identified as a necessary fundamental skill for all students. University curricula, however, are currently not designed to provide such knowledge to a broad student population. In this paper, we report on our experiences in the development of a model for incorporating computational thinking into the undergraduate, general education curriculum at Towson University. We discuss the model in terms of eliciting faculty interest, institutional support, and positive student response. In the first two years of this NSF-funded three-year project, we have developed, piloted and assessed five computational thinking general education courses – an Everyday Computational Thinking course, and four discipline-specific computational thinking general education courses. Initial assessments show promising and significant student, instructor and administration interest in computational thinking as a basis in courses covering multiple disciplines within the general education curriculum.

Categories and Subject Descriptors

K.3.2 [**Computers and Education**]: Computer and Information Science Education – *curriculum.*

General Terms

Experimentation

Keywords

Computational Thinking, Curriculum Design.

SIGCSE'11, March 9–12, 2011, Dallas, Texas, USA.

1. INTRODUCTION

In her seminal paper [1], Jeannette Wing states that, "computational thinking is a fundamental skill for everyone" and that along with "reading, writing, and arithmetic, we should add computational thinking to every child's analytical ability." Her paper has spawned many discussions on the definition and importance of computational thinking. Among these is an ongoing series of workshops by the National Academies of Sciences on the scope and nature of computational thinking, as well its cognitive and educational dimensions [2]. As a result, computational thinking has emerged as a focal point in computer education initiatives with the goal of exposing *all* students, at *all* educational levels, to the fundamental concepts of computation. The National Science Foundation has funded projects over the past few years for the incorporation of computational thinking at the university level, and has recently solicited projects for funding at the K-14 levels.

The approach that we have taken for exposing a wide range of university students to the concepts of computational thinking is to incorporate such concepts into a diverse set of general education courses at Towson University. We piloted this approach with the vision of computational thinking someday becoming a standard general education category in the undergraduate curriculum at all academic institutions nationwide. In light of this vision, we set the following goals for this project:

- To provide a viable and replicable means of incorporating computational thinking into the undergraduate general education curriculum for all undergraduate students.
- To demonstrate the intrinsic importance of computational thinking as a part of the general education of all undergraduate students to the academic administration of Towson University, and ultimately other academic institutions nationwide.

In this paper, we discuss a model developed for meeting these goals, and describe our experiences in implementing this model. Specifically, we found the following to be fundamental questions to the success of the project:

1. How to find pathways to incorporate computational thinking in an existing general education curriculum?
2. How to garner faculty interest in including aspects of computational thinking into existing courses and/or develop new courses utilizing computational concepts?
3. How can computational thinking concepts be effectively woven into various disciplines?

Finally, we report the success of achieving expected outcomes of the project.

2. THE PROPOSED MODEL

2.1 Finding Pathways and Seeking Advocates

We discovered that the current general education requirements for all undergraduate students at our institution were under major revision. This provided a clear opportunity for including computational thinking in the general education curriculum and therefore provided a "pathway" for exposing all students to computational thinking concepts.

In order to make this happen, it was important to get key advocates to buy into our vision. We received enthusiastic support from the chair of the task force for the development of new general education requirements, as well as the deans of the six undergraduate degree-granting colleges of the university. We found that there was a planned new category requirement called Towson Seminar that all freshman students would have to select a course from. The Everyday Computational Thinking course that we envisioned was a perfect fit for this new requirement.

In reflecting back on this stage of the project, it is clear that both the proper timing of events (i.e., the institution's development of a new general education curriculum), as well as early support from those that could facilitate the process, were key factors in any success achieved.

2.2 Generating Faculty Interest

Next, we needed to know that there was sufficient interest from faculty of other non-STEM disciplines in the connections of computational thinking to their areas. Without this, the development of the discipline-specific computational thinking courses would not be possible. Personal contacts with colleagues across campus were made in diverse areas including Geology, Health Sciences, Economics, English, Sociology and Music

In order to generate faculty interest in computational thinking and identify potential collaborators, special informational sessions were held for each of the six undergraduate degree granting colleges, supported by the respective deans. The sessions were held in the fall of the first year of the project. At these sessions, we informed the faculty about computational thinking and relayed the current, national efforts at making computational thinking part of the knowledge of all students. Attending faculty members were then invited to propose a discipline-specific computational thinking course and were told that selected proposals would be given summer support for full course development.

We were fortunate to have a colleague and advocate from the music department on campus who had already been teaching a course titled "Creative Programming and Programming Creativity — Introductory Computer Science for Artists," which explored procedural and conceptual approaches to creative expression. This course served as an exemplar discipline-specific computational thinking course and was described and demonstrated at each of the informational sessions by the faculty member teaching the course.

Looking back at this step, we did not anticipate the level of interest in computational thinking that the informational sessions revealed across disciplines. We also found that having an existing advocate outside of computer science to illustrate how computational thinking can be incorporated into another discipline was very helpful.

2.3 Establishing Faculty Collaboration

Following our initial fall semester of informational meetings, we held a January workshop to help those interested faculty to develop their computational thinking related course proposals. These workshops provided an opportunity for interested faculty to collectively explore and share ways in which computational thinking concepts could be infused into specific topics from various disciplines. From these collaborations, faculty were encouraged to pursue and submit course proposals. This led to the submission of eight proposals (all except one from departments outside of the STEM disciplines) of which four were selected. Faculty whose proposals were accepted were made a "faculty fellow" on the project and provided summer stipends to develop and pilot their course during the following academic year. The four discipline-specific computational thinking courses developed were: Computational Thinking and the Humanities; Computational Thinking: Creative Work with Audio and Video; Revolutionary Networks; and Computational Thinking: Developing Life Skills for Weight Management. These courses, as well as the Everyday Computational Thinking course, are depicted in Figure 1.

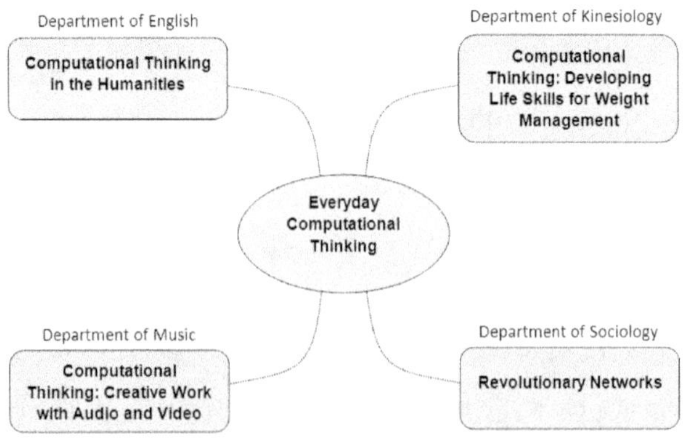

Figure 1. Computational Thinking Courses

From this step, we now recognize that the workshop held to help guide faculty in the development of a discipline-specific computational thinking course was a crucial part in assuring that appropriate proposals would ultimately be developed. We found that, even at this stage, some interested faculty did not have a clear understanding of computational thinking and how its concepts could be woven into their disciplines.

2.4 Development of a Common Set of Course Objectives

After the selection of the course proposals, two additional workshops were held over the following summer. These workshops were for helping each faculty fellow with the development of their course materials, as well as the development of a set of computational thinking-related course objectives. It was found that simultaneous discussions of courses by all faculty fellows helped shed insight into the development of each individual faculty fellow's course and course objectives. The common set of computational thinking course objectives developed is given in Figure 2.

After completing the computational thinking course, the student will be able:

1. To develop and/or evaluate computational models, and apply such models to a particular problem, or problem domain.
2. To create and/or apply algorithms, and determine the appropriateness of various algorithmic techniques for a given problem
3. To distinguish between problems that can and cannot be solved computationally, either theoretically or practically.
4. To evaluate a given algorithm or model, and specify appropriate criteria used.
5. To apply and reflect on the application of established computational thinking methods and models to tasks, problems and investigations in specific domains or disciplines.

Figure 2. Common Computational Thinking Course Objectives

It was the intention that each discipline-specific course would have an associated set of objectives that were drawn from at least some of the common computational thinking course objectives, specialized to the particular topics of each such course. We present these sets of objectives in the following.

2.5 Piloting of Courses

Each of the five computational thinking courses were offered through the Honors College on campus except for one, the Revolutionary Networks course. Since the planned new general education curriculum, and specifically the new Towson Seminar course was not yet in place, the Honors College provided a receptive environment of their relatively quick approval and offering.

Each of the courses were offered the following academic year. In the fall, the Everyday Computational Thinking; the Computational Thinking and the Humanities; and the Computational Thinking: Creative Work with Audio and Video courses were offered, with enrollments of 16, 12 and 10 respectively. (The Creative Work with Audio and Video course was limited to 10 students because of limited resources for the course.) In the following spring semester, the Revolutionary Networks; and the Computational Thinking: Developing Life Skills for Weight Management courses were offered, with enrollments of 29 and 19, respectively. (Honors courses are allowed a maximum enrollment of 20 students.) Ninety-four percent of the students completed the courses, and all those remaining in the course passed the course.

3. THE COURSES

In this section, we provide the course objectives for each of the computational thinking courses developed, modeled on the common set of objectives provided in Figure 2. The major challenge faced by the faculty fellows was to coherently weave in computational thinking concepts into their course topics. Complete syllabi and general information about the project can be found at http://triton.towson.edu/~compthnk.

First, we give the course objectives for the Everyday Computational Thinking course in Figure 3.

After taking this course, students will be able to:

1. Identify and/or generate alternate representations of problems and data for various everyday problems.
2. Develop and/or evaluate the effectiveness of various computational models in everyday problem solving.
3. Analyze the time complexity of a simple algorithms applied to everyday problem solving.
4. Cite and explain various examples of unsolvable and intractable problems.
5. Identify the use of and/or apply problem decomposition, recursion, approximation and heuristics in everyday problem solving.
6. Apply appropriate algorithmic techniques in everyday problem solving
7. Apply concepts of graph theory to networks in different domains, including social networks and maps.
8. Identify opportunities for the use of concurrency and/or parallel processing in everyday problem solving.

Figure 3. Everyday Computational Thinking Course Objectives

This course contained Honors students from various disciplines and with almost exclusively no prior computing-related courses. Each student worked on a semester project of their choosing in which computational problem solving can be employed. Each topic had to be an everyday problem that can benefit from a computational approach and not one that is inherently computational. Examples of such project topics included the job of a restaurant hostess in seating customers with consideration of how many and what size tables are available, the number of table that each server currently has, the reservations schedule, etc.; a heuristic method for finding one's way home when lost in a city such as Washington, D.C; and the optimal placement of a new bridge across the Chesapeake considering multiple factors, including ground softness, environmental concerns, accessible roadways, etc. The general theme of the course was viewed as "executable abstractions," leading to discussion of algorithmic strategies, limits of computation, computational models and the structuring of data. These concepts were elucidated in specific areas of application such as coordination systems, evolutionary computation, cryptography, social networks, computer simulation, and artificial intelligence.

In Figure 4, we give the course objectives for the Computational Thinking in the Humanities Course.

After taking this course, students will be able to:

1. To apprehend how a range of text-analyses methods and tools can be used for humanistic inquiry.
2. To apply basic graph, networks and systems principles, to place representational dynamics into perspective.
3. To design, use and work with various mapping and modeling tools.
4. To learn how algorithms can be used to delimit and test generic conventions and to generate language experiments.
5. To develop an understanding of challenges associated with applying technology in the arts and humanities.

Figure 4. Computational Thinking in the Humanities Course Objectives

In this course, students investigate, through classic and contemporary readings, how computational concepts can be used to deepen our perspective on and understanding of cultural artifacts and literary texts. The topics covered in the course include Borges' engagement with issues of abstraction and modeling, Carroll's interest in making and breaking rules for language games, Hardy and Faulkner's use of maps to orient their imaginative worlds, Poe's fascination with code, encryption and hoaxes, and Pynchon's experimentation with the ways chance and randomness affect a subject's search for meaning.

Virtual environments and popular tools like Facebook are utilized in the course to enable students to model a well-known text, such as Shakespeare's *Romeo & Juliet*, to place the social network of the characters and the events that transpire into a range of perspectives that generate fresh possibilities for adaptation, analysis and interpretation (using graph, network and systems theories). Conversely, students reflect on the ways artists and writers (such as Asimov and Gibson) have explored the limitations of computational thinking for understanding human emotions and experiences. Assignments allow class participants to choose an assigned story, film, play or poem to blog, encode, map, model, sample, simulate, storyboard, visualize, and text-analyze.

The objectives of the Computational Thinking: Creative Work with Audio and Video course are given in Figure 5.

After taking this course, students will be able to:

1. Demonstrate understanding of computational thinking principles as applied to the creative use of interconnected multimedia.
2. Demonstrate understanding of basic principles and methods for input, control, interconnection, and output of audio and video information based on recorded data and rendered output models.
3. Demonstrate understanding of how sonic and visual information can be modeled through analysis, decomposition, abstraction, and alternate forms of representation in computational systems.
4. Demonstrate the ability to design basic audio, video, and graphic processing systems in Max/MSP/Jitter.
5. Use reflective writing to enhance learning.

Figure 5. Creative Work with Audio and Video Course Objectives

This course explores hands-on introduction to computational thinking applied to creative problems using software that integrates audio and video data and processing. The course introduces students to thinking in terms of how sounds and visual information can be represented, interconnected, and developed for creative and expressive uses within the context of computational methods and abstractions. The course does not require any previous background in musical notation or music theory.

The objectives of the Revolutionary Networks course are given in Figure 6.

After taking this course, students will be able to:

1. Discuss the social and cultural characteristics of networks.
2. Demonstrate the ways in which networks allow people to form connections with each other in a variety of contexts.
3. Be able to analyze networks using concepts drawn from the social sciences and from the computer sciences (e.g., ties, range, density) in order to characterize the quality of agent/alter interactions and the efficacy of the network in promoting its avowed goals.
4. Utilize models for understanding computer-mediated social networks (e.g., small world, random network, etc.).
5. Understand the challenges involved in scaling social network analysis for web-based social networking.
6. Construct visualizations of computer mediated social networks using different techniques (e.g., sociograms).
7. Speculate on the future of "network thinking" in information society.
8. Critically reflect on the effects of "information society" changes on the lives of the student herself and the people around her.
9. Understand the usefulness of computation in: 1) solving problems posed by social networks and 2) suggesting alternatives to existing computer-mediated social networks.

Figure 6. Revolutionary Networks Course Objectives

In this course, networks are discussed through at least two modalities, the first as a kind of social fact emerging through the actions of networked individuals; the second as a concept "good to think with," a way of theorizing about the self and social life. "Network thinking" is argued as the basis for all kinds of social structures—from social networking software to 1-minute dating happy hours. Implicit in this is the argument that an anthropological approach to computer-mediated social networking founders if it confines itself to anthropological theory and methods. The course introduces a variety of tools drawn from the computer and information sciences. The goal is to give students an introduction to both computational and non-computational methods for studying networks in order to provide a robust characterization of the network as a pervasive, cultural form, and to do so in such a way that students are able to generate their own, variously hybridized approaches. Over the course of the semester, students characterize ICT-mediated networks they themselves have enjoined using all of the concepts, theories and tool introduced through class.

Finally, we give the course objectives of the Computational Thinking weight management course in Figure 7.

After taking this course, students will be able to:

1. Use model building, algorithmic development and programming, define realistic steps towards weight management in your own life, taking into consideration your social and built environments.
2. Demonstrate the use of algorithmic techniques to overcome specific barriers to lifestyle based weight management.
3. Explore gaps between model building and life events as it relates to lifestyle based weight management.
4. Discuss the utility of individualized models for optimal weight management behavior from a public health perspective.

Figure 7. Developing Life Skills for Weight Management Course Objectives

This course explores obesity and healthy weight management from a public health perspective. It reviews scientific evidence of the impact of obesity and evidence based approaches to healthy weight management. Students develop a basic understanding of computational thinking and how it can be applied to develop a better understanding of the relationship between individuals, behaviors and the environment as it relates to healthy weight management.

4. PROJECT ASSESSMENT

In order to assess our progress in incorporating computational thinking concepts into the general education curriculum, as well as to evaluate the effectiveness of our model to garner and maintain institutional interest in computational thinking, we describe progress evaluation results related to the project objectives.

4.1 Assessment Design

The evaluation of the project was overseen by an independent evaluator who prepared all assessment materials, including student, instructor, and administrator surveys. We focused on three primary evaluation questions during the pilot stage of the discipline-specific computational thinking courses:

1. Did 75% or more of the students in the class demonstrate knowledge of CT concepts at the end of the semester?
2. Did 75% or more of the students in the class perceive the course as valuable?
3. Did school administrators think that CT courses were an important part of the curriculum?

Knowledge of computational thinking concepts (to address Question 1) was measured using a "computational thinking grading rubric" that incorporated questions on the concepts of modeling, abstraction, algorithms, tractability and other core ideas. Instructors were asked to map assignment solutions, student responses, and student discussion in class to the rubric to gauge the level of knowledge demonstrated by students. At the end of the semester, the project evaluator interviewed each instructor to gather data on how the students performed.

Question 2 was measured using self reported end of semester student surveys. The value perceived by students was operationalized with questions such as "Did you enjoy the class?" and"Would you recommend the class to others?" The answers were measured on a Likert scale.

Question 3 was measured using a survey sent to deans and department chairs. The survey included seven questions gauge the level of interest in, understanding about, and commitment to computational thinking using a Likert scale.

4.2 Assessment Results

In this section, we describe the results of the assessment as they pertain to the three evaluation questions.

4.2.1 Question 1 – Knowledge of Computational Thinking Concepts – Instructors' Perspective

Though instructors did not use the grading rubric for all assignments, they agreed that at least 75% of the students in their class demonstrated knowledge of computational thinking concepts. Deeper analysis of instructor feedback is in progress, however, interviews with the evaluator revealed the following observations:

- Explanation of computational thinking and its relevance to the subject matter early in the course is critical for student success
- Active learning assignments were very effective for the subject matter
- Student assignments were important for the discovery and understanding of computational thinking concepts

4.2.2 Question 2 – Perceived Value of Computational Thinking Course – Students' Perspective

Assessment of student evaluations indicated that the vast majority of students enjoyed and/or saw the value of the discipline-specific computational thinking course taken. At the same time, 45% of students reported having some degree of confusion in the class. Such a level of confusion is not unexpected, given the nature of the material and the fact that each course was a first-attempt for each instructor. The fact, however, that the majority of students had a positive view of the subject matter is an encouraging result. We believe comprehensive analysis of student surveys after the courses are offered a second time would lead to better results.

4.2.3 Question 3 – Value of Computational Thinking Courses in the Curriculum – Administrator Perspective

A number of administrators had some degree of interaction with the project. This included two deans, an assistant dean, two department chairs and a director of research services. It also included an interim provost at a local institution, who had invited us to present our experiences with the project. The result of this survey is shown in Figure 8. As can be seen, a majority of administrators answered that they would recommend computational thinking courses to colleagues and that computational thinking has a role in general education.

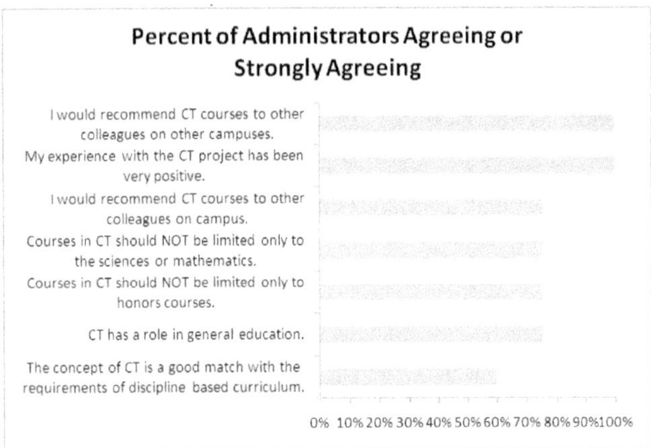

Figure 8. Administrators Assessment of Project

4.3 Achievement of Stated Goals

The specific goals for this project were: to provide a viable and replicable means of incorporating computational thinking into the undergraduate general education curriculum for all undergraduate students to learn; and, to demonstrate the intrinsic importance of computational thinking as a part of the general education of all undergraduate students to the academic administration of Towson University, and ultimately other academic institutions nationwide. We believe that each goal was met. Towards the first goal, this paper described:

- A high-level of interest in the course proposals were received from non-STEM disciplines, demonstrating the viability of infusing computational thinking concepts throughout the undergraduate general education curriculum.
- The discipline-specific computational thinking course objectives for the five piloted course, allowing for replicability and use as future examples.
- Encouraging results in student evaluations of the developed computational thinking courses, supporting the viability of inclusion in a general education curriculum.
- Perceived learning of computational thinking concepts by at least 75% of students in all the piloted classes, illustrating the viability of inclusion in a general education curriculum.

Towards the second goal, the results in Figure 8, indicates that those administrators connected to this project recognize the intrinsic importance of computational thinking as a part of the general education of all undergraduate students.

5. ONGOING WORK

The positive reception of the piloted courses by the instructors, students and administrators has led to the reoffering of the Everyday Computational Thinking course and two of the discipline-specific courses to be offered again during the 2010-2011 academic year. Additionally, a fourth course is planned to be offered during the following academic year.

6. SUMMARY

A model for piloting pathways of computational thinking into the undergraduate general education curriculum has been utilized for the development of five new computational thinking courses at Towson University. The results of this project show promise for being able to infuse computational thinking concepts among a wide range of diverse areas of study at other institutions, ensuring that all students have exposure to concepts of computational thinking. In particular, faculty members from a diverse range of disciplines showed interest in the project, and were able to develop courses in their areas with infused computational thinking. The majority of students found the material interesting/relevant, and there was positive feedback from the administrators connected to or aware of the project.

7. ACKNOWLEDGEMENTS

This research was supported by the National Science Foundation under CNS CPATH-CDP grant # 0829661. We would also like to acknowledge the support and encouragement for this project from the Honors College at Towson University.

8. REFERENCES

[1] Wing, J. M. 2006. Computational Thinking. In *Communications of the ACM*, 49(3):33-35.

[2] Report of a Workshop on the Scope and Nature of Computational Thinking, The National Academies, 2010.

A Course on Probability Theory for Computer Scientists

Mehran Sahami
Computer Science Department
Stanford University
Stanford, CA 94305
sahami@cs.stanford.edu

ABSTRACT

During the past 20 years, probability theory has become a critical element in the development of many areas in computer science. Commensurately, in this paper, we argue for expanding the coverage of probability in the computing curriculum. Specifically, we present details of a new course we have developed on *Probability Theory for Computer Scientists*. An analysis of course evaluation data shows that students find the contextualized content of this class more relevant and valuable than general presentations of probability theory. We also discuss different models for expanding the role of probability in different curricular programs that may not have the capacity to teach a full course on the subject.

Categories and Subject Descriptors

K.3.2 [**Computers and Education**]: Computer and Information Science Education – *Computer science education.*

General Terms

Algorithms, Theory, Human Factors, Design.

Keywords

Probability Theory, Computing Curricula, Discrete Mathematics

1. INTRODUCTION

During the past two decades, probability theory has come to play an increasingly important role in many areas of computer science. Understanding probability theory is not only useful for simulations, but it is becoming an essential tool for analyzing large-scale systems and is used as an integral part of many computing applications. Probability is also the cornerstone for most machine learning (a.k.a. data mining) techniques used to build predictive models from huge volumes of data. In this paper we describe a course on *Probability Theory for Computer Scientists*, explaining why such a course is needed and showing the efficacy of teaching this material in a computing context.

In Section 2, we present a case for why knowledge of probability theory and machine learning is critical for students studying computing today. Addressing this point, we describe a course on *Probability Theory for Computer Scientists*, which has been successfully offered three times in the past two years at Stanford University. The course is detailed in Section 3. We discuss the computing-specific applications presented in this course, distinguishing it from traditional courses in probability theory often taught in Mathematics or Statistics departments. Section 4 gives a comparative analysis of course evaluation data from several different probability theory courses at Stanford, providing evidence for the efficacy of a computing-centric course as opposed to general courses in probability theory. We conclude in Section 5 with thoughts on how themes from this course may be adopted in other contexts at other institutions.

SIGCSE'11, March 9–12, 2011, Dallas, Texas, USA.

2. THE NEED FOR PROBABILITY THEORY IN COMPUTING CURRICULA

Work in computing increasingly relies on probability theory as a tool for analysis and data modeling. Furthermore, probability theory now plays a foundational role in making advances in many areas of computing. For example, while probability was once simply used as a tool to analyze the average running time of algorithms, it has now become a central tenant in developing a new class of *randomized* algorithms [14]. In the area of Systems, probabilistic analyses of network routing and machine failures have become essential elements for building robust large-scale distributed systems, and will continue to become more important with the growth of "cloud computing". Much work in Artificial Intelligence is now based on probabilistic formalisms, encompassing work in reasoning, robotics, natural language understanding, and machine learning [18]. Specifically, the widespread use of data mining techniques for analyzing large data sets involves algorithms grounded in probability theory. Even application areas such as Graphics make use of random sampling in image rendering and work in Human-Computer Interaction involves probabilistic models of uncertainty in user behavior.

Despite the growing importance of probability theory in computing, the role of probability in the computing curriculum has remained relatively minor. Although both Computing Curricula (CC) 1991 and 2001 [1, 2] include probability as one of several topics to be included as part of a discrete math course, CC 1991 provides little guidance on the depth of coverage and CC 2001 suggests only six total hours of instruction. While some institutions suggest (or sometimes even require) that students take a full course in probability theory, the designated courses are often surveys taught in Mathematics or Statistics departments and do not offer any computing-specific applications. As a result, even students who receive a full course in probability theory are often at a loss with regard to how it relates to problems in computing, and this lack of context means students may less effectively learn and apply the material [6]. This point is further corroborated (later in this paper) by an analysis of data comparing the *Probability for Computer Scientists* course described here with several more traditional courses in probability theory.

Nevertheless, the importance of probability theory has not been lost in the Computer Science Education community, as some have previously suggested the incorporation of more concepts from probability into early computing courses [7]. However, that discussion focused more on the use of randomness to generate problem simulations in CS0 and CS1 courses as opposed to a formal treatment of probability theory in computing.

More recently, Anderson [4] has argued for combining probability with computing, suggesting a course in *Simulation, Probability and Statistics* as a means for students to satisfy a college "quantitative reasoning" requirement. The suggested course focuses primarily on building simulations, which is certainly useful, but quite different in content, applications, and goals from the course we present here.

Several textbooks on probability and statistics in computing have also been introduced in the past few years. Some of these texts [12, 16] are not introductory in nature, requiring previous coursework in probability. Other texts with a more introductory flavor [5, 10] tend to focus on simulation and queuing theory, without giving much, if any, coverage of machine learning.

While building randomized simulations is itself an important goal, the use of probability theory as a foundation for machine learning (i.e., building statistically valid models of data for prediction and insight) is a more central problem in the foreseeable future. A recent report by the NSF Task Force on Cyberlearning [15] points to the need to "prepare students for the data deluge" by giving them the mathematical tools to analyze data as part of their training in computing. The report goes on to state that "some of the world's largest companies (Google, Yahoo, Microsoft, Amazon, eBay) are struggling" with how to productively identify and exploit patterns in large amounts of data. The need for computer scientists with experience in statistical data analysis is also reported in a recent Wall Street Journal article [21], stating that "technology companies... are in hot pursuit of a particular kind of employee: those with experience in statistics and other data-manipulation techniques." Indeed, the article goes on to quote an executive at a high-tech recruiting firm who states that engineers "with strong statistics backgrounds will earn up to 20% more than generalist engineers", reflecting the strong industrial demand for software engineers with statistical modeling skills.

The ever-present discussions of Computational Learning also point to the importance of probability theory and machine learning. This point is forcefully made in Wing's seminal paper [22], which states that "machine learning has transformed statistics. Statistical learning is being used for problems on a scale, in terms of both data size and dimension, unimaginable only a few years ago. Statistics departments in all kinds of organizations are hiring computer scientists." As a result, we believe that giving students in computing a deep understanding of probability theory, grounded in real computing applications, is becoming increasingly important. From both the standpoint of preparing students for research in the field as well as meeting industrial demands, there is a need to give students greater preparation in probability theory and machine learning methods. We describe a course aimed at addressing this need presently.

3. A COURSE ON *PROBABILITY THEORY FOR COMPUTER SCIENTISTS*

3.1 Historical background

During the past two years we have taught three offerings of a course entitled *Probability Theory for Computer Scientists* at Stanford University. The course was created as part of recent curriculum revision of our undergraduate Computer Science program [19] and is a core class required for all CS majors. Prior to the curriculum revision, we required all CS majors to take a full quarter-long course in probability theory. Students could select any one of three classes to satisfy this requirement (all of which are rigorous calculus-based courses):

1. *Theory of Probability* – Offered by the Statistics department, this course provides a general introduction to probability theory without a computational component.
2. *Intro. to Probability and Statistics* – Offered by the program in Computational Mathematics, the course provides an engineering perspective on probability. The course uses MATLAB for computational work.
3. *Probabilistic Analysis* – Offered by the Management Science and Engineering department, the course emphasizes probabilistic model building and uses Microsoft Excel for computational work.

While all of these courses provide students with significant exposure to probability theory, even from various engineering perspectives, we often heard that students had difficulty recalling and applying the material from these courses in subsequent computing classes (e.g., algorithms, artificial intelligence, etc.). Since the probability courses were developed for more general audiences, they, understandably, provide no motivating examples that are computing-specific. Moreover, the computational work provided in some of the courses is more focused on simulation and does not address the issue of analyzing data to build predictive models (i.e., machine learning).

To remedy this issue, we developed a new course, specifically for computer science students, which we describe shortly. As mentioned previously, the new course is now required for all our undergraduate computer science students (and is also strongly suggested for Masters students who may not already have a solid background in probability). CS students no longer have the option of taking the other three probability courses, although students who took such a course prior to the availability of our new class were "grandfathered" into satisfying the requirement.

3.2 Course Prerequisites

As with the other probability course options previously available, the new course requires a background in calculus, which was already a mathematics requirement for our program. However, the new course, being aimed at computer scientists, also has CS2 as a prerequisite. CS2 provides a critical level of background in computing that allows for excellent contextually-relevant motivating examples in the probability course. For example, the probabilistic nature of hash functions, insertions or look-ups into ordered data structures (e.g., lists, binary search trees), and the randomized selection of pivots in QuickSort all provide rich examples that we analyze in our new course. Furthermore, by having CS2 as a prerequisite, we guarantee that all students have a

Table 1. Weekly outline of *Probability Theory for Computer Scientists* course

Week	Topics	Sample of Motivating Examples
1	Counting, Combinatorics (Combinations/Permutations), Intro. to probability, Sample spaces, Axioms of probability	Counting degenerate Binary Search Trees, Sharing a birthday, Likelihood of poker hands, Sampling computer chips for defects
2	Conditional probability, Bayes Theorem, Independence, Discrete random variables, Expectation, Variance	Analyzing hash table load, Email spam detection, Arrangements of bit strings, HIV testing, "Monty Hall problem", Value of lotteries
3	Discrete probability distributions (Binomial, Multinomial, Poisson, Geometric, Negative Binomial, Hypergeometric)	Flipping coins, St. Petersburg paradox, Error-correcting codes, Packet corruption in networks, Web server overload
4	Continuous random variables and probability distributions (Uniform, Normal, Exponential), Joint distributions	Disk crashes and expected lifetime, Likelihood of error in digital/analog conversion, Probabilistic text analysis
5	Independent random variables, Conditional distributions and independence, Expected algorithm running times	Distributing requests in a cluster, Recommendation engines, Hash tables as "coupon collecting", QuickSort expected running time
6	Covariance, Correlation, Conditional expectation, Moment generating functions	Computer cluster utilization, Analyzing recursive functions, Simple predictive models, Optimizing hiring (software engineers)
7	Inequalities (Markov, Chebyshev, Chernoff, Jensen), Law of Large Numbers, Central Limit Theorem	Analyzing midterm scores, Modeling a risky investment, Estimating algorithm clock running time via repeated trials
8	Prior probabilities, Parameter estimation (Method of moments, Maximum likelihood, Maximum a posteriori)	Number of idle machines in a computer cluster, Estimating probabilities from rolling dice, "Two envelopes" problem
9	Intro. to Machine Learning, Naive Bayesian classifier, Logistic regression, Simple Bayesian networks, Utility	Predicting tomorrow's weather, Email spam filtering, Simpson's paradox in data analysis, Utility of lotteries
10	Computational generation of probability distributions, Monte Carlo simulation	Generating other distributions using only the `rand()` function, Algorithms for random shuffles, Monte Carlo integration

reasonable foundation in programming. This allows for class examples and homework problems that involve the direct probabilistic analysis of code. Moreover, it allows us to have significant programming projects, where students implement algorithms that build predictive models of real-world data and then analyze the results of their programs.

3.3 Course Details

3.3.1 Structure

The *Probability Theory for Computer Scientists* course is taught during a 10 week quarter, and has three 75 minute lectures (including interactive demonstrations) each week. A weekly outline for the course is shown in Table 1, showing both the topics covered as well as a sampling of the examples that are used to motivate the material in class. A complete set of course slides providing detailed course contents is available on the web [3].

3.3.2 General introduction to probability

As seen in Table 1, the topical coverage of the course during the first seven weeks aligns with many traditional probability theory courses. In fact, the textbook [17] we have used for our course is a general probability text that is also used in two of the other three probability courses taught at Stanford (previously mentioned).

What distinguishes our course during the first seven weeks is that the vast majority of examples used to motivate and explain the various topics covered are drawn from computer science. For example, in the first week, while we examine the traditional problems of computing the probability of various poker hands (via counting) or determining the probability that two people in a room share the same birthday, we also examine the number of degenerate (i.e., linear) Binary Search Trees that can be generated to show how slowly that number grows in comparison to the total number of possible Binary Search Trees. The following week, we analyze the well-known "Monty Hall" problem [13], but also look at questions related to how evenly elements are likely to be spread across buckets in a hash table. In the weeks following, there is a steady stream of real-world computing problems presented, including how error-correcting codes are used to increase the probability of robust communication in networks, determining the probability that web servers will become overloaded under particular distributions of requests, how probability is used in recommendation engines and email spam filters [20], as well as showing how to analyze the expected running time of algorithms.

These examples significantly engage students as they see the role probability plays in many of the computing technologies presented in their other courses as well as applications they use on a regular basis (e.g., email, on-line shopping). More importantly, by seeing probabilistic concepts in a domain that students are already familiar with, they have a framework to better assimilate the salient aspects of the new information they receive. They are no longer learning probability in a vacuum (using the common notion of "balls and urns"), but can directly relate it to real problems in computing they will likely have to face. By learning to identify which probabilistic aspects of a problem (e.g., independence, conditioning, etc.) give rise to which issues in real computing applications, they come away better prepared to tackle problems in the future. Moreover, they gain a greater appreciation for the significant role that randomness plays in a domain that they tend to think of as strongly deterministic.

During the course, we do also discuss classic problem set-ups in probability, such as "coupon collecting" and reasoning about distinguishable vs. indistinguishable "balls" in urns. However, each of these cases is also directly related to applications in computing. In this way, students not only see the general concepts, but also look at analogous computing-specific examples to gain a firm grounding of how such problems arise in the real world. As a result, they gain experience mapping general concepts to solutions of actual problems, a key ingredient missing in the general probability courses students were previously taking.

3.3.3 *Introducing Machine Learning*

The last three weeks of the course leverage what students learned during the prior seven weeks to introduce them to Machine Learning, specifically building classification models from data. *Classification* is the task of predicting a particular discrete value (i.e., the "class" or "prediction output") as a function of a set of observed input variables. For example, we might consider building a model to predict if the weather tomorrow will be "sunny", "overcast", or "rainy" based on variables that can be measured today (e.g., average temperature, humidity, if the sky is currently cloudy, etc.). Such prediction models are "learned" (i.e., parameters are estimated) using historical data to help determine how the prediction output is probabilistically related to the input variables. Another common example of classification in a computing context is the detection and filtering of email spam. Indeed, most modern email servers treat spam detection as a classification problem, where the server must classify each email message as "spam" or "legitimate" based on characteristics of the message (e.g., the sender, the words contained in the messages, which SMTP server it was received from, etc.)

Prior to discussing classification tasks, however, in week 8 of the course we get students to understand that in real-world applications of probability, the parameters for distributions (e.g., mean, variance, covariance, etc.) are not given, but rather must be estimated from data. This begins a week of in-depth investigation of various parameter estimation techniques and their mathematical properties. It also provides a natural context for discussing Bayesian techniques and the role of subjective prior probabilities. Indeed, some students have difficulty grappling with the general notion of subjective probabilities at first. But through grounded examples we show how people naturally make use of such probabilities and how they are mathematically incorporated into probabilistic inference, giving students a concrete, yet formal treatment that they are more comfortable with. Moreover, we explain various probabilistic smoothing techniques as forms of parameter estimation with the incorporation of subjective prior probabilities (e.g., Laplace smoothing [11]).

Armed with knowledge about how data can be used to (computationally) estimate parameters of probability distributions, students are then introduced to the classification task and specific probabilistic models for addressing this problem. Specifically, we focus on the Naive Bayesian classifier [8] and Logistic Regression models [9]. We start with the Naive Bayesian classifier, as this model is simple to understand. Given a set of n input variables $X_1, X_2, ..., X_n$, the Naive Bayesian classifier predicts the class (output) c_i that maximizes the probability $P(X_1, X_2, ..., X_n, \text{Class} = c_i)$ over all choices of i (i.e., all possible values of the discrete output variable) under the assumption that all the input variables are independent of each other, conditioned on the variable *Class*. More formally, the Naive Bayesian classifier predicts the output c_i given by:

$$\underset{c_i}{\operatorname{argmax}}\ P(X_1, X_2, ..., X_n \mid \text{Class} = c_i) \cdot P(\text{Class} = c_i)$$

under the "Naive Bayes assumption" that:

$$P(X_1, X_2, ..., X_n \mid \text{Class} = c_i) = \prod_{j=1}^{n} P(X_j \mid \text{Class} = c_i)$$

Importantly, this model shows the power of conditional independence (which students learned about earlier in the course) as a means of reducing the number of parameters needed to be estimated in the model from exponential to linear in n (the number of input variables). Computer science students, already having an appreciation for the extreme difference between exponential and polynomial running times, quickly appreciate how the simplifying assumption made in the Naive Bayes model can lead to a dramatic change in the efficiency of probabilistic inference.

After presenting the Naive Bayesian classifier, students then see the Logistic Regression model, which has many mathematical similarities to Naive Bayes, but a few critical differences that prevent its parameters from being estimated analytically (as can be done with Naive Bayes). As a result, Logistic Regression immediately forces a computational solution in which parameters are optimized using gradient descent over a convex objective function. To better understand the differences between the two models and gain hands-on experience with the issues that arise in doing actual data analysis, students implement both Naive Bayes and Logistic Regression and estimate their parameters using provided real-world data sets (described in more detail below).

The course concludes with a discussion of how various probability distributions (e.g., Poisson, Normal, Exponential) may be computationally generated using only the uniform random distributions that are provided by a function such as the C standard library's **`rand()`**. This also provides an opportunity to discuss in detail the generation of pseudo-random numbers and the strengths and weaknesses of various random number generation techniques. Along the same lines, we also discuss how algorithms for common tasks involving randomization, such as shuffling a deck of cards, are often *incorrectly* implemented by programmers, as we can rigorously analyze the properties of such algorithms that on the surface are easily mistaken for producing a truly random shuffle (where all permutations of the cards are equally likely). Finally, we show how Monte Carlo simulation (making use of various random number generators) can be used to approximate the solution to many mathematical problems (e.g., evaluating an integral). Thus, while we do discuss simulation (which is also a topic touched on at other points in the course as well), it is not meant to be the central theme of the course.

3.3.4 *Demonstrations*

While the course is organized using primarily a traditional lecture-based format, the lectures also include a number of computer and interactive demonstrations to give students a better grounding in the material. These demonstrations include the "classics", such as selecting a student from the class to actually try the "Monty Hall problem" using three envelopes (where one contains money and the other two are empty), as well as determining if two students in the class have the same birthday.

We also consider more modern examples, such as providing a computer simulation of how sampling distributions are generated to show the Normality of such distributions as predicted by the Central Limit Theorem. While the Central Limit Theorem is one of the most powerful results in probability, it is often misapplied by those confused by the difference between a *sampling* distribution and the *underlying* distribution that the samples are drawn from. To clarify this issue, we play a simple game where students (in front of the class) roll 10 fair 6-sided dice to see if they can roll a total less than 25 or greater than 45 (and thereby win a prize). This demonstration allows students to map theoretical concepts to a physical process (i.e., the 6-sided die represents the underlying distribution, the 10 rolls represents a sample from the distribution, and the average of the 10 rolls is a value from the sampling distribution of the mean), allowing them to better remember the material. The physical demonstration is then reinforced by the computer application which they can use to try various other underlying distributions and see that the sampling distribution of the mean tends to always be Normal. Students report that class demonstrations help them better remember the material, especially when they have the opportunity to follow-up on them afterwards.

3.3.5 Assignments

There are six assignments in the course, spanning a range of problem modalities. Most assignment problems are word problems that involve analytically deriving a mathematical result based on appropriately modeling the probabilistic dynamics of the problem. What distinguishes such problems from a more traditional probability course is that a large majority of them involve realistic problems in computing, such as analyzing the distribution of elements in hash tables and determining request distributions to web sites. Also, in such problems, students are encouraged (but not required) to write simulation programs to verify their answers. Several assignment problems also involve the direct analysis of code. For example, students may be asked to determine the expected running time of a stylized recursive algorithm or determine if an algorithm is correct with respect to modeling some probabilistic process.

In the final portion of the course, where the focus shifts to Machine Learning, students are required to implement various learning algorithms (specifically, the Naive Bayesian classifier and Logistic Regression, as mentioned above) and test their implementations using real-world data sets. In the past, students have built models using data to predict Congressmembers' political affiliation based on their voting records as well as tackling medical diagnosis tasks, such as determining if a patient has a heart abnormality based on tomography (X-ray) data. Other tasks considered for future courses include building an email spam filter or predicting the locations of splice junctions in DNA.

Students have their choice of implementing their algorithms in Java, C/C++, or R (a functional statistical modeling language). All of the students in the course are expected to have worked with Java or C/C++ previously (as a result of CS2 being a prerequisite). We also allow R as an option for programming assignments as we have recently started to offer an optional one unit adjunct lab course entitled *Statistical Programming with R*.

The R course provides two main benefits for students. First, it provides them with an opportunity to see a more direct relationship between programming and the statistical theory they are learning, as the topics covered in the R course mirror those covered in the probability course. This parallel structure also allows many examples in the R course to be relevant to building computational simulations to verify analytical results of problems in the probability course. Second, the course provides a convenient way to expose students to functional programming in a context which is not just about learning programming, but motivated by solving real statistical problems.

4. COURSE EVALUATION ANALYSIS

To evaluate the efficacy of our course, we compare end-of-quarter student evaluation data from our *Probability Theory for Computer Scientists* course against all three other probability theory courses taught at Stanford. Since we want the data from the three other probability theory courses to reflect evaluations from CS students (to create a more direct comparison to the population of our new course), we consider every offering of the other three courses in the year and a half *prior* to the introduction of our new course (Fall 2007-08 through Winter 2008-09), when a substantial portion of the population of those other courses would still be CS students. We then compare the data we have on every offering of our new course over the immediately following year and a half period (Spring 2008-09 through Spring 2009-10). We denote the courses compared as follows:

- *Theory of Probability* – Denoted **TP**. The course was offered three times from Fall 2007-08 through Winter 2008-09. A total of 184 student evaluations were collected.
- *Intro. to Probability and Statistics* – Denoted **IPS**. The course was offered twice from Fall 2007-08 through Winter 2008-09. A total of 191 student evaluations were collected.
- *Probabilistic Analysis* – Denoted **PA**. The course was offered twice from Fall 2007-08 through Winter 2008-09. A total of 163 student evaluations were collected.
- *Probability Theory for Computer Scientists* – Denoted **PCS**. The course was offered three times from Spring 2008-09 through Spring 2009-10. A total of 277 student evaluations were collected.

In the evaluation data, we examine questions specifically related to the value of the course and the relevance of course content, which we believe are the most meaningful indicators for comparing across courses in this context. Using a 5-point scale (5 = Excellent, 4 = Very Good, 3 = Good, 2 = Fair, and 1 = Poor), students rated several course criteria. Table 2 presents these criteria (column 1), and the average score received in each of the 10 class offerings (columns 2 through 11 in the table each represents a distinct offering of a course). It is worth noting that *every* offering of the *Probability Theory for Computer Scientists* course (**PCS 1/2/3**) ranks higher on all of the five criteria than *any* of the more general probability theory courses.

To determine the significance of these results, we compute t-tests between the data for each of the four courses under consideration. Since it is infeasible to report the results of comparing every class offering versus every other class offering, we first pool the student evaluation data on a *per course* basis. This also provides the benefit that data is focused more on the content of the course in general as opposed to the particulars of any one offering. The pooled per-course data is given in columns 12 through 15 of Table 2. We compute t-tests (unpaired, heteroscedastic, two-tailed) on the pooled data for PCS vs. TP, IPS, and PA, respectively. The t-test results (p-values) are given in columns 16 through 18 of Table 2. On every criteria, PCS scores statistically significantly higher than any of the other probability courses with $p < 0.001$, providing strong evidence that students find the contents of the new course more relevant, valuable, and related to their studies in computing.

Table 2. Student evaluation and t-test results for probability courses.

Criteria \ Course Offering	TP (1)	TP (2)	TP (3)	IPS (1)	IPS (2)	PA (1)	PA (2)	PCS (1)	PCS (2)	PCS (3)	TP (all)	IPS (all)	PA (all)	PCS (all)	PCS vs. TP (all)	PCS vs. IPS (all)	PCS vs. PA (all)
The quality of the course content	3.60	3.58	4.17	4.29	4.06	3.41	3.84	4.53	4.32	4.51	3.80	4.18	3.60	4.45	< 0.001	< 0.001	< 0.001
Set out and met clear objectives announced for the course	3.00	3.57	4.22	4.44	4.23	3.60	3.76	4.62	4.57	4.61	3.58	4.34	3.67	4.60	< 0.001	< 0.001	< 0.001
Emphasized conceptual understanding and critical thinking	3.36	3.50	4.01	4.20	4.14	3.45	3.81	4.52	4.41	4.56	3.63	4.17	3.61	4.49	< 0.001	< 0.001	< 0.001
Related course topics to one another	3.17	3.52	4.14	4.31	4.24	3.40	3.72	4.59	4.45	4.79	3.61	4.27	3.54	4.57	< 0.001	< 0.001	< 0.001
Selected course content that was valuable and worth learning	3.37	3.50	4.21	4.25	4.07	3.28	3.64	4.55	4.51	4.69	3.70	4.13	3.43	4.56	< 0.001	< 0.001	< 0.001
# Evaluations (N)	75	43	66	102	89	90	73	131	101	45	184	191	163	277			

It is also worth noting that while the class was originally designed for CS students, it does attract a number of non-CS majors who report that they are interested in the Machine Learning aspect of the course, which is not available in the other probability courses.

5. CONCLUSIONS

Probability theory and machine learning will continue to grow in importance for students studying computing. We believe the course presented here helps effectively prepare students for applying probability in computing contexts and using it as a tool for data analysis and modeling. The comparative analysis of course evaluation data shows that students are finding the new course content to be more relevant and valuable than more general courses in probability. Materials from our course are available on-line and have been freely distributed in various educational forums. Indeed, we have already learned of at least one other university planning to offer a course this coming year modeled on the one described here, and several other programs that are considering similar courses in the future.

Understanding that some CS programs cannot justify a full course in probability, we would encourage an expanded coverage of the topic with more computing-relevant examples in existing discrete math courses. In such contexts, we believe that probability can be taught using only *discrete* variables, which also provides sufficient foundation for discussing topics from Machine Learning (parameter estimation and Naive Bayes). In fact, such a treatment can be provided without requiring a background in calculus.

Alternatively, some schools have reported that they are planning a move toward the model described here by restructuring existing course offerings. For example, rather than requiring a full course in *Automata Theory and Computability*, these topics are now covered in a condensed treatment in an existing discrete math course (in place of probability) and the probability material is expanded into a separate course (perhaps with the inclusion of some additional topics). We believe there will be many models that will work for providing expanded coverage of probability theory in the computing curriculum.

6. REFERENCES

[1] ACM/IEEE-CS Joint Curriculum Task Force. 1991. Computing curricula 1991: Report of the ACM/IEEE-CS Joint Curriculum Task Force, ACM Press, NY.

[2] ACM/IEEE-CS Joint Task Force on Computing Curricula. 2001. ACM/IEEE Computing Curricula 2001 Final Report. http://www.acm.org/sigcse/cc2001.

[3] http://ai.stanford.edu/users/sahami/cs109/

[4] Anderson, S. D. 2007. A course on simulation, probability and statistics. *SIGCSE Bull.* 39, 1 (Mar. 2007), 110-114.

[5] Baron, M. 2006. *Probability and Statistics for Computer Scientists*, Chapman and Hall/CRC Press.

[6] Carraher, T. N., Carraher, D. W., and Schliemann, A.D. 1985. Mathematics in the streets and in the schools. *British Journal of Developmental Psychology* 3.

[7] Ginat, D., Anderson, R., Garcia, D., and Rasala, R. 2005. Randomness and probability in the early CS courses. In *Proc. of SIGCSE '05*, 556-557.

[8] Good, I. J. 1965. *The Estimation of Probabilities: An Essay on Modern Bayesian Methods*. MIT Press, Cambridge, MA.

[9] Hosmer, D. W. and Lemeshow, S. 2000. Applied Logistic Regression (2nd Ed.), John Wiley & Sons, Hoboken, NJ.

[10] Johnson, J. 2008. *Probability and Statistics for Computer Science*, John Wiley & Sons, Hoboken, NJ.

[11] Lidstone, G.J. 1920. Note on the general case of the Bayes-Laplace formula for inductive or a posteriori probabilities. *Trans. of the Faculty of Actuaries* 8.

[12] Mitzenmacher, M. and Upfal, E. 2005. *Probability and Computing: Randomized Algorithms and Probabilistic Analysis*, Cambridge University Press, New York, NY.

[13] http://montyhallproblem.com/

[14] Motwani, R. and Raghavan, P. 1995. *Randomized Algorithms*, Cambridge University Press, New York, NY.

[15] NSF Task Force on Cyberlearning. 2008. Fostering Learning in the Networked World: The Cyberlearning Opportunity and Challenge. http://www.nsf.gov/pubs/2008/nsf08204/nsf08204_1.pdf

[16] Ross, S., 2001. *Probability Models for Computer Science*, Academic Press, San Diego, CA.

[17] Ross, S., 2009. *A First Course in Probability (8th Ed.)*. Prentice Hall, Englewood Cliffs, NJ.

[18] Russell, S. and Norvig, P. 2009. *Artificial Intelligence: A Modern Approach (3rd Ed.)*, Prentice Hall, Englewood Cliffs, NJ.

[19] Sahami, M., Aiken, A., and Zelenski, J. 2010. Expanding the frontiers of computer science: designing a curriculum to reflect a diverse field. In *Proc. of SIGCSE '10*, 47-51.

[20] Sahami, M., Dumais, S., Heckerman, D., and Horvitz, E. 1998. A Bayesian Approach to Filtering Junk E-Mail. In *Learning for Text Categorization: Papers from the 1998 Workshop*. AAAI Press Technical Report WS-98-05.

[21] Vascellaro, J. E., April 8, 2010. *New Hiring Formula Values Math Pros: Region's Employers Seek Statistical Experts Over Computer-Science Generalists*. Wall Street Journal (San Francisco Bay Area).

[22] Wing, J. M. 2006. Computational thinking. *Commun. ACM* 49, 3 (Mar. 2006).

Mathematical Induction is a Recursive Technique

Robert L. Scot Drysdale
Department of Computer Science
Dartmouth College
Hanover, NH 03755
scot@cs.dartmouth.edu

ABSTRACT

Many students find that proof by induction is one of the most difficult topics in discrete mathematics. Even students who are able to write inductive proofs in a Discrete Mathematics course often find it difficult to write inductive proofs in Data Structures, Algorithms, Theory of Computation, and other computer science courses. Part of the reason for this is that discrete mathematics courses tend to emphasize weak induction over the natural numbers, but strong induction over recursively defined structures is much more useful in computer science.

This paper argues that learning and using proof by induction is easier if the recursive nature of proof by induction is made explicit, especially for students familiar with recursion. It can be useful to view an inductive proof as a template for a recursive program that takes a specific instance as a parameter and generates a complete direct proof for that instance. The abstract idea of assuming and invoking an inductive hypothesis is replaced by the concrete idea of making a recursive call to prove a lemma. Viewing induction as a recursive process allows us to give a rule for determining what base cases need to be proved in strong induction and simplifies creating correct inductive proofs.

Categories and Subject Descriptors

G.2 [**Mathematics of Computing**]: Discrete Mathematics

General Terms

Theory

Keywords

Proof by induction, Discrete mathematics, Pedagogy

1. INTRODUCTION

Many students have great difficulty understanding proof by induction. This conclusion is supported by research in mathematical pedagogy [7, 5, 6]. Even students who appear to understand proof by induction in a Discrete Mathematics course may find it difficult to use it to solve problems in Data Structures, Algorithms, Theory of Computation, and other CS courses.

Part of the problem is that proof by induction is usually presented as weak induction, and is introduced as a method of proving properties about natural numbers. One version of Peano's fifth axiom for defining the natural numbers says that to prove a property P for all natural numbers one can prove P(0) (the base case) and prove that $\forall n(P(n) \implies P(n+1))$ ([12], p. 277). Thus it is no surprise that a mathematician would view proof by induction as being weak induction on the natural numbers. Strong induction is covered as a generalization of weak induction, and usually receives much less attention.

This presentation does not adequately prepare a student for the uses of proof by induction in computer science. The technique is often used to prove properties about recursively defined data structures (e.g. binary trees), recursively defined sets (e.g. the set of strings generated by a formal grammar), or recursive programs. These applications usually require strong induction over recursively defined structures. The structures can be mapped to natural numbers (e.g. a binary tree can be mapped to its depth or number of nodes), but this adds an extra layer of complexity to the proof and actually obscures what is going on. It is clearer to think about induction as a technique that works on a recursively defined structure. The natural numbers are just a particular recursively defined structure.

Proof by induction need not be presented as an axiom. The Well Ordering Principle is equivalent, and if it is chosen as an axiom we can use it to prove the correctness of proof by induction. In fact, about half of the texts in the bibliography of this paper note the equivalence of proof by induction and the well ordering principle, and most of them use the well ordering principle to justify either weak or strong induction via a proof involving the smallest counterexample [1, 9, 11, 12, 13, 16, 20, 23, 24, 25, 29].

Another fact that can be used to prove the correctness of proof by induction is "Recursion Works." That is, if a program solves an instance of a problem by making recursive calls to smaller instances of the problem and using the results of these calls to solve the bigger instance, it will compute the correct answer as long as the method of building a solution from solutions to smaller problems is correct, the base cases are solved directly, and all recursive decompositions lead to base cases in a finite number of steps.

SIGCSE'11, March 9–12, 2011, Dallas, Texas, USA.

Using "Recursion Works" as an axiom may seem strange, although it it precisely what we depend on in computer science courses when we teach about recursion. Stating it with mathematical rigor is not as easy as stating Peano's Fifth Axiom or the Well Ordering Principle, but that is not the point. The point is that many computer science students have more experience with recursion than induction, and their experience teaches them that recursion works. Thus this is an easy axiom for them to accept and understand.

This paper is directed at those teaching induction to students familiar with recursion, and the approach is not recommended for Computer Science students who study proof by induction before recursion. However, the points made in Section 3.3 about the advantages of decomposing big problems into smaller ones rather than growing small problems into bigger ones still hold.

We can view a proof by induction that a property P is true for all x as a recursive schema for generating a complete, horribly detailed direct proof of $P(x)$ for any specific instance x. A base case x is handled by printing out a direct proof of $P(x)$. Invoking the inductive hypothesis on a smaller instance y becomes a recursive call to prove the lemma $P(y)$. The proof of the inductive implication explains how to use this lemma (or several lemmas) as the basis for a proof of $P(x)$. The program prints out this proof, specialized to the given instance x. The proof of the inductive hypothesis becomes a proof of the correctness of the program, assuming that "recursion works." This program will generate a proof for any given instance x. The existence of a program that will print out a complete direct proof of the property $P(x)$ for any x means that $P(x)$ must be true for all x.

To be concrete, suppose that we want to prove some property P for all binary trees. We could write a procedure that would take as its parameter a particular tree T and generate an exhaustive direct proof of $P(T)$. In the process it might use the fact that P is true for T_l and T_r, the left and right subtrees of T. But rather than assuming $P(T_l)$ and $P(T_r)$ as the inductive hypothesis, it would call itself recursively on T_l and T_r to generate complete proofs of $P(T_l)$ and $P(T_r)$. It would use these facts as lemmas in proving $P(T)$.

This recursive view of induction (break the big case into one or more smaller cases and use them as lemmas in proving the big case) can help students generate inductive proofs. This approach avoids some of the pitfalls that arise from the "grow up from the base cases" approach for generating inductive proofs. It also gives a concrete rule for resolving the common question, "What base cases do I need to prove in strong induction?"

Most of the ideas in this paper appear to a greater or lesser extent in various discrete mathematics texts ([12, 21, 28, 29], among others). The title of the paper comes from [15], p. 187. However, these ideas are not widely known in the CS education community, and judging from comments in talks with colleagues and discussions on various mailing lists, they are rather controversial. (Some of the concerns about using this approach will be addressed later.) This paper tries to explain why these ideas are useful, and is intended to spark discussion on whether it would be wise to incorporate them into Discrete Mathematics courses designed for computer scientists. It is not an attempt to recommend particular Discrete Mathematics textbooks. The ideas can be used in any Discrete Mathematics course if the students are comfortable with recursion, independent of the text chosen.

2. HOW PROOF BY INDUCTION IS TAUGHT IN DISCRETE MATH TEXTBOOKS

How is proof by induction covered in Discrete Mathematics texts? There are so many texts on this topic that finding and reading copies of all of them is infeasible. This paper considers the texts that my colleagues and I had on our shelves plus those in the Dartmouth library. This misses many texts, but should be a reasonable sample.

All but one of these texts begin the section on proof by induction by introducing weak induction on the natural numbers [1, 2, 3, 4, 8, 9, 10, 11, 13, 14, 15, 16, 17, 18, 20, 19, 22, 21, 23, 24, 25, 26, 27, 28, 29]. That is, they say that there are two parts to an inductive proof that some property $P(n)$ is true for all positive integers n. The first is to prove the base case $P(1)$ (or $P(0)$ [28] or $P(n_0)$ for some fixed n_0 [2, 4, 11, 17, 21, 26, 29]). The second is to prove the implication:

$$\forall n(P(n) \implies P(n+1)).$$

The exception is [12], which starts with strong induction.

Weak induction is useful for proving mathematical formulas, but it is not sufficient for most computer science applications. Computer scientists must often prove things about recursively defined structures. A binary tree is either empty or it consists of a root with a left child and a right child, both of which are binary trees. A list is empty or it consists of a first element and a "tail," which is a list. BNF grammars recursively define sets of strings. Computer scientists also use induction to prove the correctness of recursive programs and of solutions of recurrences.

In most of these cases the natural way to decompose a problem is to use the recursive definition to get one or more smaller problems, and these smaller problems are often much smaller than the original problem. In these cases what is needed is strong induction. In strong induction, when trying to prove $P(n)$ one is allowed to assume that P is true for all smaller cases. That is, the implication is:

$$\forall n(\forall k(k < n \implies P(k)) \implies P(n))$$

Unfortunately, most discrete math books that I examined devote much less space to strong induction than to weak induction. Some don't mention it [14, 19, 20, 27]. Others merely define strong induction, and then give no examples [3, 18] or a single example [1, 4, 8, 9, 17, 22], devoting a page or two to the subject. (Some of these books use the technique in proofs later in the book, but here I am reporting what appears in the section or sections devoted to proof by induction.) A student who understands weak induction well but who does not understand strong induction is not well prepared for inductive proofs in computer science.

A smaller subset of the books discuss structural induction. They note that induction is a property of recursively defined structures, rather than just of the natural numbers [12, 15, 21, 28, 29]. They consider examples including binary trees, triangulated polygons, a grammar that generates strings of balanced parentheses, and two-coloring line maps. The inductive hypothesis need not involve natural numbers. It can be of the form, "In proving that property P is true for a structure x we assume that P is true for all substructures involved in the recursive definition of x."

The idea is that when one decomposes a recursively defined structure, the substructures are automatically smaller than the whole. Thus it is possible to define strong induction by saying, "Assume that the inductive hypothesis holds for all recursively defined proper substructures" without referring to natural numbers. Gries and Schneider discuss this idea rigorously and in great detail, proving that proof by induction works on partially ordered sets that are noetherian (have no infinite decreasing chains) ([12], p. 230).

3. A RECURSIVE VIEW OF PROOF BY INDUCTION

There are strong similarities between proof by induction and recursion. Both deal with base cases. Both solve a general case by utilizing results from smaller cases. For many students both seem to be circular.

Many computer science students have much more experience with recursion than they have with proof by induction. They have learned from experience that "recursion works." We can take advantage of this understanding of recursion by presenting proof by induction in terms of recursion.

As was mentioned in the introduction, an inductive proof of a property P can be viewed as a description of a recursive program that generates a complete direct proof for any instance x that it is given. Base cases are proved directly. When the proof invokes the inductive hypothesis to claim that a property P is true for a smaller instance y, the program makes a recursive call to generate a complete, direct proof of $P(y)$. In effect the program treats $P(y)$ as a lemma and then proves it in detail. Once the lemmas are proven it prints out the proof of the inductive implication, specialized to the specific instance. Because we can create a program that can print out a complete direct proof of $P(x)$ for any instance x, the proposition must be true for every instance.

This process of converting an inductive proof to a recursive program is illustrated in the next section.

3.1 Proving Integers are Products of Primes

A common example of proof by strong induction is to prove that every integer greater than 1 can be written as a product of prime numbers. (About half of the texts in the bibliography used this example.) We use this example to demonstrate how an inductive proof can be translated into a recursive program that generates a complete direct proof for any integer greater than 1.

3.1.1 The Inductive Proof

The following inductive proof is taken from [28].

PROOF. The induction hypothesis asserts that for arbitrary n, for every k such that $2 \leq k < n$, k can be written as a product of prime numbers.

On the basis of this assumption we must show that n can be written as a product of primes. The proof is by cases.

Case 1: If n is a prime, then n is such a product of one prime.

Case 2: If n is not a prime, then $n = ab$, where $2 \leq a, b < n$. By the induction hypothesis, both a and b can be written as products of primes and therefore their product can be written in this form. □

3.1.2 The Recursive Program

The following Java method generates a proof of the theorem for any integer greater than 1. It assumes the existence of a method `isPrime` that returns true if its argument is a prime and a method `findDivisor` that returns some divisor of its argument n that is strictly between 1 and n, assuming that n is composite.

```
public static void generateProof(int n) {
  if(isPrime(n)) {
    System.out.println(n + " is prime, " +
    " so is a product of a single prime.");
  }
  else {
    int divisor = findDivisor(n);
    int quotient = n / divisor;
    System.out.println ("In order to prove that "
      + n + " is a product of primes\n  we prove"
      + " that " + divisor + " and " + quotient +
      " are products of primes.");
    generateProof(divisor);
    generateProof(quotient);
    System.out.println("Having proved that " +
      divisor + " and " + quotient +
      " are products of primes,\n" +
      "  we conclude that " + n + " = " +
      divisor + " * " + quotient +
      "\n  is a product of primes.");
    }
}
```

This program mirrors the inductive proof above. Where the proof asserts that a divisor must exist, the program finds one. Where the proof invoked the inductive hypothesis, the program makes a recursive call to prove in detail what the inductive hypothesis asserts.

Calling `generateProof(60)` generates the following output:

```
In order to prove that 60 is a product of primes
  we prove that 6 and 10 are products of primes.
In order to prove that 6 is a product of primes
  we prove that 2 and 3 are products of primes.
2 is prime, so is a product of a single prime.
3 is prime, so is a product of a single prime.
Having proved that 2 and 3 are products of primes,
  we conclude that 6 = 2 * 3
  is a product of primes.
In order to prove that 10 is a product of primes
  we prove that 2 and 5 are products of primes.
2 is prime, so is a product of a single prime.
5 is prime, so is a product of a single prime.
Having proved that 2 and 5 are products of primes,
  we conclude that 10 = 2 * 5
  is a product of primes.
Having proved that 6 and 10 are products of primes,
  we conclude that 60 = 6 * 10
  is a product of primes.
```

This proof is painfully detailed. It repeats proving things that have already been proved (e.g. that 2 is prime). A human being would never want to read such a proof for a number with many factors. The advantage to this proof is that there is never a need to assume an inductive hypothesis. When a proposition is needed (e.g. that 10 is the product of primes) it is proved directly. The existence and correctness of this program show that for any $n > 1$ there exists a direct proof that n can be expressed as a product of primes. Therefore any $n > 1$ can be expressed as a product of primes.

3.2 Why Viewing Induction as Recursion Can Aid Student Understanding

Papers studying how students learn proof by induction find that the difficulties arise mostly in understanding and using the implication $\forall n(P(n) \implies P(n+1))$ [5, 6, 7]. (These papers studied weak induction.) They claim that understanding proof by induction requires the ability to view this implication both as an object that can be reasoned about and as a process of passing from $P(n)$ to $P(n+1)$. Students must be able to move easily from one view to the other, or to be able to hold both views simultaneously. Many students find this very difficult. They don't understand why assuming $P(n)$ when proving $P(n+1)$ (viewing the implication as a process) isn't assuming what they are trying to prove (viewing the implication as an object to be reasoned about). The authors use Piaget's theory of learning to claim that understanding the dual views of the implication requires a high level of sophistication.

Viewing a proof by induction as a recursive program eliminates the need to assume the inductive hypothesis when proving the implication. Instead of saying, "We now invoke the inductive hypothesis" we instead say, "We prove this lemma via a recursive call." Students comfortable with recursion find it natural to assume that a recursive call will do what it is supposed to do. Instead of having to understand the abstract subtleties of assuming the inductive implication, the student needs to understand that a recursive call will correctly generate a proof. A recursive call is much more concrete than invoking the inductive hypothesis. Students can actually run the program and see that it generates a detailed proof for every instance that they try.

A number of people have raised the objection that testing the program for a finite number of cases does not prove anything. I agree. They argue that the correctness of the program must be proved via proof by induction. I disagree. The correctness of the program must be proved via something very similar to an inductive proof. But where the inductive proof says, "Assume the inductive hypothesis" the alternate proof says, "Assume that recursion works, so this recursive call will generate a proof of the lemma." In both cases they are using the truth of the inductive hypothesis. In one case they assume it because that is what you do in a proof by induction, and Peano said it works. In the other case it is true because they have a program that will generate a proof for them. Some students who balk at assuming an inductive hypothesis are comfortable saying, "This is true because I have a program that proves it for me."

The program is not the proof. The argument that the program can be written and is correct is the proof. Students write what are really inductive proofs, but they now have a concrete model for what it means to "invoke the inductive hypothesis." It means calling a recursive theorem prover to prove what is needed.

3.3 Other Advantages to the Recursive View of Proof by Induction

Proof by induction is often viewed as a "building up" process, where one starts with the base case and builds up to reach the other cases. The metaphors used for describing induction include climbing a ladder [9, 27], knocking over a row of dominos [13, 19, 21, 24], having a line of people pass a secret [9, 24], and marking an infinite set of numbered blocks [16]. This often works well for weak induction, but "building up from base cases" is usually not the most effective way to come up with a correct strong inductive proof. Thinking recursively ("breaking down" an instance into smaller instances of the same type) usually works better.

There are at least two advantages to thinking about proof by induction recursively. First, it gives the student a rule to answer the common question, "What base cases do I need to prove?" Second, viewing an inductive proof recursively gives guidance on how to write the inductive proof, and it avoids a common error.

3.3.1 Recursive Decomposition Determines the Base Cases

Most discrete mathematics books do not give much guidance on how to determine the base cases in a proof by induction. Most give a definition of strong induction that has a single base case $P(1)$ (or $P(0)$). They later present an example such as, "Prove that every amount of postage of 12 cents or more can be formed by using just 4-cent and 5-cent stamps" [24]. (Seven of the books in the bibliography use a "make postage out of stamps" example or a similar one with coins or envelopes [10, 11, 12, 13, 16, 21, 24].) The inductive implication in this case is $P(n) \implies P(n+4)$.

Suddenly $P(12)$, $P(13)$, $P(14)$, and $P(15)$ are presented as the base cases. The explanation given is, "We need to prove these cases separately since the inductive step, which shows that $[P(12) \wedge P(13) \wedge \cdots \wedge P(n)] \implies P(n+1)$, only holds when $n \geq 15$" [24]. Why does it not hold for smaller n? Thinking of growing from base cases, the reasoning goes, "Which $n \geq 12$ cannot be obtained by adding 4 to some $n' \geq 12$?" It is easier to view this recursively. There the reasoning is, "To prove $P(n)$ I need to recursively prove $P(n-4)$. This recursive call is invalid when $n - 4 < 12$. For which n is $n - 4 < 12$?" The answers are the same, but the second seems easier to understand.

Viewing proof by induction recursively gives a concrete rule for determining whether an instance is a base case or a general case. Base cases are cases where the recursive decomposition fails (the case is too small to be decomposed or the decomposition results in a recursive call to an instance not included in the inductive hypothesis). The base cases must be proved separately, because the general proof using the inductive hypothesis does not work for them [12, 29].

This leads to conclusions that may seem strange at first. Consider the proof given above that every integer greater than 1 can be written as a product of primes. Using this definition of a base case we conclude that every prime number is a base case [29]! It may seem strange to have an infinite number of base cases. However, this view is more reasonable than proving $P(2)$ as the base case, then having an inductive case that says, "There are two cases to consider, when $n+1$ is prime and when $n+1$ is composite. If $n+1$ is prime, we see immediately that $P(n+1)$ is true" ([24], but thirteen other texts in the bibliography have similar proofs). Instead of separating the proof into primes and composites, this approach considers primes as part of the inductive case, but does not use the inductive hypothesis in proving that primes are products of primes. The base case $n = 2$ is superfluous, because 2 is a prime and is already covered. We would not write a recursive program with cases $n = 2$ and $n > 2$, and then have sub-cases when $n > 2$. Why should we prove the $n = 2$ case separately in an inductive proof?

The program above did not have three cases, because

Stanat and McAllister's proof did not have three cases. Their definition of strong induction includes only the implication, and has no base cases [28]. They note that when $n = 0$ there are no $P(k)$ with $k < n$, so $P(0)$ must be proved without any help from the inductive hypothesis. They say that this approach "only requires that we establish a single hypothesis, but this often requires a proof by cases." Unfortunately, this changes the question "What are the base cases?" to "What are the cases that require separate proofs?" We now have an answer: cases where the recursive decomposition fails.

3.3.2 *Recursive Decomposition as a Guide to Inductive Proofs*

If the induction is on a recursively defined structure (e.g. a binary tree), it is almost always correct to base the decomposition of the problem in the proof on the recursive decomposition of the structure. We teach students to do this when writing recursive programs. By regarding inductive proofs as recursive processes they can apply this experience to guide them in writing inductive proofs.

Viewing induction in terms of breaking a larger problem into similar subproblems also avoids a subtle error. I will illustrate this error by using an example from a data structures course that I taught.

We studied binary trees, and one of the things that I proved in class was the relationship between the number of internal and external nodes in a binary tree. In a complete binary tree each node has either zero or two children. The nodes with zero children are called leaf nodes or external nodes. They correspond to null pointers (or to empty tree objects) in a binary tree data structure. The nodes with two children are the internal nodes.

I proved the following theorem in class: If n is the number of internal nodes in a binary tree and e is the number of external nodes, then $e = n+1$ for any complete binary tree. I used strong induction as follows.

PROOF. The base case is a single external node, where $n = 0$ and $e = 1$, so the theorem holds in this case.

Given a binary tree T which has at least one internal node, remove the root. This leaves two smaller subtrees, a left subtree T_l and a right subtree T_r. Because these trees are smaller than T, we can use the inductive hypotheses to assert that $e_l = n_l + 1$ and $e_r = n_r + 1$, where the l and r subscripts limit the nodes counted to the left and right subtrees, respectively. But $e = e_l + e_r$ and $n = n_l + n_r + 1$, because the root that was removed was an internal node. We can conclude that

$$\begin{aligned} e &= e_l + e_r \\ &= (n_l + 1) + (n_r + 1) \\ &= (n_l + n_r + 1) + 1 \\ &= n + 1 \end{aligned}$$

Thus the theorem is true by mathematical induction.[1] □

[1]An alternate inductive proof of this theorem removes an internal node, all of whose children are external nodes. However, to do this proof rigorously one must first prove that such a node exists. The recursive definition of a binary tree tells us that a binary tree which is not a single external node consists of a root with a left and right child, so we can use this decomposition without having to prove that the decomposition is possible.

A similar formula holds for complete d-ary trees, where each node has either zero or d children: $e = (d-1)n + 1$. I asked students to prove this formula on a midterm exam. I expected their proofs to parallel the one above, and most of them did. However, perhaps a quarter of the class came up with the following ingenious "proof."

The induction is on d, the degree of the tree. When $d = 2$ the formula reduces to the theorem proved in class, so the base case is true. For the inductive case, assume that the formula holds for a d-ary tree. Adding an external node as a child to each internal node creates a $(d+1)$-ary tree. This operation increases the number of external nodes by n while leaving the number of internal nodes unchanged. Thus the number of external nodes for a $(d+1)$-ary tree is $((d-1)n + 1) + n = dn + 1$, so the theorem is proved by induction for all $d \geq 2$.

This is a valid proof. However, what it proves is that the formula holds for any d-ary tree where no internal node has more than two internal nodes as children. It does not prove that the formula holds for a 3-ary tree consisting of a root with three internal nodes as its children, because there is no way to construct such a tree by adding external children to a binary tree.

This shows the danger of thinking of proof by induction as a process of growing small instances into bigger instances, rather than thinking of taking a big instance and recursively decomposing it into smaller instances. When proving formulas such as $\sum_{i=1}^{n} i = n(n+1)/2$ using weak induction it seldom matters whether you think of growing from n to $n+1$ or recursively decomposing the sum by removing the last term. But when doing strong induction on structures the difference is significant. When growing from smaller instances to larger ones it is necessary to prove that every possible larger instance can be constructed using the specified method. In the "proof" above only a subset of the d-ary trees could be constructed by adding external children.

This extra proof is not needed if one starts with a large instance and decomposes it recursively. Because the instance one begins with is a general one, the decomposition automatically deals with all instances. The equivalent mistake to the one my students made would be to start with a general d-ary tree and to remove an external node child from each internal node. But when it is worded this way it is obvious that this approach fails when there is a node that has no external node children. Furthermore, this is not a natural way to recursively decompose a d-ary tree.

In short, trying to "grow" a smaller problem into a larger one requires a separate proof that the approach will construct all possible larger instances. This proof is seldom given. Thinking about recursively decomposing the problem leads more naturally to a correct inductive proof, and avoids the need for an additional proof that the construction method can build all instances.

4. EXPERIENCE

I have been using this approach to teach proof by induction to computer science students familiar with recursion for about 6 years. I present it as an alternate way to view proof by induction, as a supplement to the standard approach of invoking the inductive hypothesis. I also teach my students to recursively decompose problems rather than to build up. My observation is that this approach works better, but I have not done controlled studies. I realize that such subjective anecdotal evidence is of limited value in assessing whether this method works better than the usual one, but my intention is to spark thought and discussion about how we teach proof by induction. I invite interested readers to do formal studies and report the results.

5. CONCLUSIONS

Discrete mathematics courses that put substantial emphasis on teaching strong induction are most useful to computer science students. Ideally they will teach induction on recursively defined structures and sets as well as on the natural numbers. Computer scientists will be doing inductive proofs on recursively defined structures more often than they will be doing proofs on natural numbers, and requiring them to express such proofs in terms of natural numbers only complicates the process.

Students should approach inductive proofs by thinking recursively, especially when using strong induction. The first question is how to recursively decompose large instances into smaller instances. This approach is usually more effective than thinking about how to grow smaller instances into a bigger one. Students should not think about base cases until after they have proved that if a proposition P is true for all smaller instances it is true for a large instance. Once they have developed this proof they should ask under what circumstances the recursive decomposition breaks down. These are the base cases that need to be proved separately. Recursively decomposing is more likely to lead to a correct proof than "building up" from smaller cases.

Students who understand recursion can use recursion to understand induction. An inductive proof can be converted into a recursive program that generates a complete direct proof for any given instance. The original inductive proof now becomes a proof of correctness for the program, but instead of assuming an inductive hypothesis we assume that recursion works. This makes the process concrete and avoids what researchers have reported as the most difficult part of understanding proof by induction.

6. ACKNOWLEDGMENTS

I would like to thank students in sections of CS 8, CS 18 and CS 21, on whom I tried out this approach to teaching proof by induction. Discussions with Ed Dubinksy, Ken Bogart, and Cliff Stein helped me develop the approach that I describe in this paper. Kim Bruce and anonymous reviewers made useful suggestions that improved the presentation.

7. REFERENCES

[1] J. Anderson. *Discrete Mathematics with Combinatorics.* Pearson/Prentice Hall, Upper Saddle River, New Jersey, 2004.

[2] K. Bogart. *Discrete Mathematics.* D. C. Heath, Lexington, Massachusetts, 1988.

[3] J. Bradley. *Introduction to Discrete Mathematics.* Addison Wesley, Reading, Massachusetts, 1988.

[4] J. A. Dossey, A. D. Otto, L. E. Spence, and C. V. Eynden. *Discrete Mathematics.* Addison Wesley, Boston, 2002.

[5] E. Dubinsky. Teaching mathematical induction i. *Journal of Mathematical Behavior*, 5(1):305–317, 1986.

[6] E. Dubinsky. Teaching mathematical induction ii. *Journal of Mathematical Behavior*, 8:285–304, 1989.

[7] E. Dubinsky and P. Lewin. Reflective abstraction and mathematics education: The genetic decomposition of induction and compactness. *Journal of Mathematical Behavior*, 5(1):55–92, 1986.

[8] S. Galovich. *Introduction to Mathematical Structures.* Harcourt Brace Jovanovich, San Diego, 1989.

[9] L. J. Gerstein. *Discrete Mathematics and Algebraic Structures.* W. H. Freeman and Company, New York, 1987.

[10] J. L. Gersting. *Mathematical Structures for Computer Science.* W. H. Freeman and Company, New York, 1999.

[11] E. G. Goodaire and M. M. Parmenter. *Discrete Mathematics with Graph Theory.* Pearson/Prentice Hall, Upper Saddle River, NJ, 2006.

[12] D. Gries and F. Schneider. *A Logical Approach to Discrete Math.* Springer-Verlag, New York, 1993.

[13] R. P. Grimaldi. *Discrete and Combinatorial Mathematics: An Applied Introduction.* Pearson/Addison-Wesley, Boston, 2003.

[14] R. Haggarty. *Discrete Mathematics for Computing.* Addison-Wesley, Harlow, England, 2002.

[15] D. Hunter. *Essentials of Discrete Mathematics.* Jones and Bartlettl, Sudbury, MA, 2009.

[16] R. Johnsonbaugh. *Discrete Mathematics.* Pearson/Prentice Hall, Upper Saddle River, New Jersey, 2005.

[17] B. Kolman, R. C. Busby, and S. C. Ross. *Discrete Mathematical Structures.* Pearson/Prentice-Hall, Upper Saddle River, NJ, 2009.

[18] L. Lovasz, J. Pelikan, and K. Vesztergombi. *Discrete Mathematics: Elementary and Beyond.* Springer, New York, 2003.

[19] M. Marcus. *A Survey of Finite Mathematics.* Houghton Mifflin, Boston, 1969.

[20] J. Matousek and J. Nesetril. *Invitation to Discrete Mathematics.* Clarendon Press, Oxford, 1998.

[21] S. Maurer and A. Ralston. *Discrete Algorithmic Mathematics.* A. K. Peters, Ltd., Wellesley, MA, 2004.

[22] J. L. Mott, A. Kandel, and T. P. Baker. *Discrete Mathematics for Computer Scientists.* Reston Publishing Company, Reston, Virginia, 1983.

[23] R. C. Penner. *Discrete Mathematics: Proof Techniques and Mathematical Structures.* World Scientific, New Jersey, 1999.

[24] K. H. Rosen. *Discrete Mathematics and its Applications.* McGraw-Hill, Boston, 1999.

[25] K. A. Ross and C. R. B. Wright. *Discrete Mathematics.* Prentice Hall, Englewood Cliffs, New Jersey, 1985.

[26] S. Sahni. *Concepts in Discrete Mathematics.* Camelot, Fridley, Minnesota, 1981.

[27] A. B. Shiflet. *Discrete Mathematics for Computer Science.* West Publishing Companyl, St. Paul, 1987.

[28] D. F. Stanat and D. F. McAllister. *Discrete Mathematics in Computer Science.* Prentice-Hall, Englewood Cliffs, New Jersey, 1977.

[29] C. Stein, R. L. Drysdale, and K. Bogart. *Discrete Mathematics for Computer Scientists.* Addison Wesley, Boston, 2010.

Teaching Discrete Structures: A systematic review of the literature

Thomas Whelan
Dept of Computer Science
National University of Ireland
Maynooth, Co. Kildare, Ireland
thomas.j.whelan@nuim.ie

Susan Bergin
Dept of Computer Science
National University of Ireland
Maynooth, Co. Kildare, Ireland
susan.bergin@nuim.ie

James F. Power
Dept of Computer Science
National University of Ireland
Maynooth, Co. Kildare, Ireland
jpower@cs.nuim.ie

ABSTRACT

This survey paper reviews a large sample of publications on the teaching of discrete structures and discrete mathematics in computer science curricula. The approach is systematic, in that a structured search of electronic resources has been conducted, and the results are presented and quantitatively analysed. A number of broad themes in discrete structures education are identified relating to course content, teaching strategies and the means of evaluating the success of a course.

Categories and Subject Descriptors

K.3.2 [**Computers and Education**]: Computer and Information Science Education—*Computer science education, Curriculum*; G.2.0 [**Mathematics of Computing**]: Discrete Mathematics—*General*

General Terms

Human Factors

Keywords

Computing curriculum, discrete structures, discrete mathematics

1. INTRODUCTION AND MOTIVATION

The 2008 ACM Computer Science curriculum provided the standard definition of discrete structures as *foundational material* for computer science, that is required by many other areas in the syllabus [1]. The curriculum defines 43 core hours of topics, covering sets, logic, counting, graphs and probability.

However, in attempting to implement such a curriculum, many decisions remain for the educator. For example, frequently a choice must be made of which sub-topics to cover, bearing in mind the particular needs of a given programme, and the possibility that some topics may be covered elsewhere in the curriculum. Beyond this, the correct strategies for teaching and assessment must also be worked out. Finally, the ACM curriculum documents, while firmly based on years of experience, do not themselves provide a guide to the literature available in the field.

In this paper we address the last of these points, providing a literature survey, in order to provide a basis for addressing the others. In particular, we present the results of a *systematic* literature review of the teaching of discrete structures, based on the guidelines outlined by Kitchenham and Charters for performing literature reviews in software engineering [20]. Our evaluation contains cues from other sources of analysis, in particular the meta-analysis presented by Valentine [44].

The starting point of our review is to identify the main *research questions:*

Question 1: What approaches have been taken to designing the curriculum for discrete structures courses?

Question 2: What teaching methods have been employed in these courses?

Question 3: How has the success in teaching discrete structures courses been evaluated?

Rather than presenting the entire systematic literature review process, this paper provides an overview of the process and a summary of the results; fuller details can be found in the associated technical report [48].

We believe this review will be of interest on at least three levels: first, as as a review of the literature spanning many decades of teaching discrete structures, second at the meta-level, providing a meta-analysis of publications in the area, and third at the meta-meta level, as an example of applying the systematic review process applied to CS education.

Phases of paper selection and analysis

The paper selection strategy proceeded in three phases:

Phase 1: Use an automated search engine to identify papers that deal with topics relevant to our research. For simplicity we have restricted our search to *electronically-available* resources, but, given the topic, we do not believe this to be a major limitation of our review. This phase is described in Section 2.

Phase 2: Manually filter the results based on reading the abstracts, in order to identify the subset of these papers that are relevant to our research questions. This phase is described in Section 3.

Phase 3: Extract and synthesise the research by reading the remaining papers. Section 4 presents the results of this phase, discussing some common themes in the literature concerning course structuring, delivery and evaluation.

SIGCSE'11, March 9–12, 2011, Dallas, Texas, USA.

2. AUTOMATED SEARCH RESULTS

The **search space** for sources consisted of, in order, the *ACM Digital Library* (ACM DL), *ACM Guide to Computing Literature* (ACM Guide) and the *Google* search engine. All searches were carried out between July and September 2010.

It quickly became apparent that both "Discrete structures" and "Discrete mathematics" were good search terms for the kind of papers we wanted. Beginning with these search terms (referred to as "base terms" from now on) we also tried searches including the phrases "teaching", "education" or "learning" to enhance the search precision.

2.1 Search Results

When displaying results in the ACM DL there are two options. The first, "Sort by" was left at its default setting ("relevance"), while the second, "Form" was set to "condensed form", which contains 50 paper titles per page.

Since the search for each of the base terms returned about 20,000 papers, we needed to establish a cut-off point for manual filtering. In the remainder of this paper, we use a cut-off density of 4%: that is, we did not consider more pages of results after two or less papers in a page of fifty were judged relevant. In total, 65 papers were manually identified by title alone from the ACM DL.

The ACM Guide contains over 1.2 million citations from over 3,000 publishers, enabling a larger search space than the ACM DL alone. However, many of the results were not relevant to the topic or the research questions, or did not have a readily available on-line copy. Only two new papers were found in the ACM Guide (references [24, 50]).

The final search strategy used the search engine *Google*, keeping in mind that many results returned from such a search engine will not be relevant and/or academically published. In order to counteract this, the base terms were only ever queried along with either "teaching", "education" or "learning". All queries were done as individual words and also as complete phrases, and the results were examined manually up to the 5th page. Interestingly, having removed unrefereed or non-relevant sources such as lectures and coursework, no new papers were identified by this search.

Following these searches a total of 67 unique papers were identified by title alone as meriting further analysis.

2.2 Analysis of search terms

Table 1 shows the results of searching the ACM DL using the base terms and their extensions. As can be seen, the vast majority of relevant papers were retrieved using the two base terms, with the extra terms yielding just six new papers in total, only two of which were unique.

Figure 1 contains a bar chart showing the distribution of relevant papers retrieved, broken down by search term over five year periods. In this bar chart, when a paper was found using more than one search term its score was divided between these terms. From this figure it can be seen that whereas "discrete structures" was the dominant term until 1985, since then "discrete mathematics" has become more common, with an increasing number of these being additionally qualified by one of the secondary search terms.

Table 1: Numbers of ACM DL papers judged relevant based on examining the results using various search terms.

Search Term	Number of Papers		
	Inspected	Accepted	Added
Discrete Structures	100	18	
+ Education	150	11	+1
+ Learning	50	2	+0
+ Teaching	150	14	+2
Discrete Mathematics	200	55	
+ Education	250	24	+1
+ Learning	200	21	+1
+ Teaching	150	30	+1

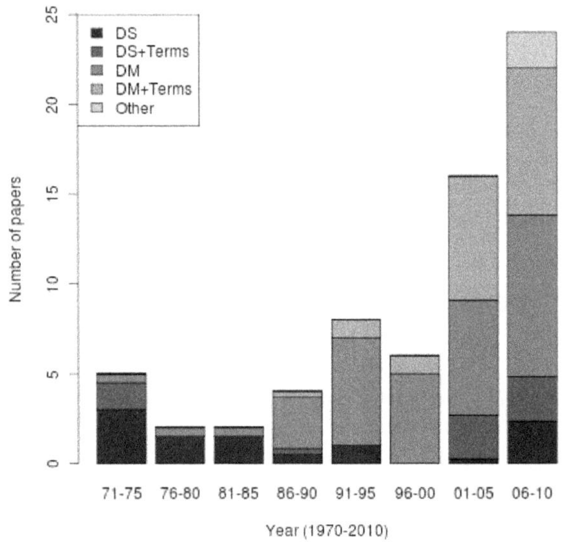

Figure 1: Distribution of relevant papers from the ACM DL by search term. Each bar represents the number of relevant papers in a given five-year period; subdivided by the search term used.

3. FURTHER MANUAL FILTERING

Following their selection by title, the 67 papers were then manually filtered by reading their abstracts and determining whether they contained information relevant to the research questions. The main reason for rejection of a paper in this phase was the *nature* of the paper (e.g. book review, poster and discussion sessions, documentation) rather than the content. This phase resulted in the exclusion of a further 20 papers, leaving 47 papers for full consideration.

Precision and Recall

In order to measure the exactness and completeness of our search for sources we can calculate the *precision* and *recall* associated with each search term. *Precision* is defined as the number of relevant documents retrieved by a search divided by the total number of documents retrieved by that search, while *recall* is defined as the number of relevant documents retrieved by a search divided by the total number of existing relevant documents (which should have been retrieved).

Calculating *precision* requires determining the total number of documents retrieved by a search, but there are a number of possible choices here. For example, the search of the ACM DL for the term "discrete mathematics" yielded 19,013 papers, but only 200 were actually examined by title, using the 4% density cut-off mentioned above. Thus, dividing by

Table 2: Precision and recall values for each search term, (total relevant = 47 abstract-filtered papers)

Search Term	Papers Retrieved	Papers Relevant	Percentage Precision	Recall
DS	23,855	13	0.05	27.66
DS+E	2,401	10	0.42	21.28
DS+L	6,128	1	0.02	2.13
DS+T	1,407	12	0.85	25.53
DM	19,013	38	0.20	80.85
DM+E	1,695	18	1.06	38.30
DM+L	3,374	17	0.50	36.17
DM+T	1,094	25	2.29	53.19

19,013 gives a slightly lower result than is fully accurate, but dividing by 200 inhibits comparison with other terms whose density may have reduced at a different rate. Bearing this caveat in mind, Table 2 uses the full total figure to facilitate comparison between search terms.

Table 2 gives the precision and recall values as percentages, assuming that the relevant papers are the 47 remaining after filtering based on abstract. As can be seen from this tables, the terms "discrete mathematics teaching" and "discrete mathematics education" provide the most precise search terms. Consistent with the results shown above in Figure 1, the term "discrete mathematics" provides the greatest recall value, yielding 81% of the final 47 relevant papers.

Source of publications

Finally, Table 3 shows a breakdown of the 67 title filtered papers according to the search term used and the source of the publication. Just under three-quarters of the relevant papers came from four sources, with the top eight sources accounting for nearly 90% of the papers. These results must be qualified by noting that most came from the ACM DL, thus causing a natural clustering, but are nonetheless broadly in line with expectations.

4. ANALYSIS AND SYNTHESIS

Having acquired the 47 source papers, the final step is to read, analyse and synthesise the results. While we cannot provide universal recommendations for any syllabus in the subject, we hope to at least provide a framework within which they can be worked out.

In this section we discuss the research in teaching discrete structures under five broad *themes*:

- **Whether** discrete structures should be taught as a single course, or have its content distributed over multiple courses.
- **When** students should study discrete structures
- What should the material be linked with: we have identified two main overlapping areas: **with programming** and **with data structures**.
- **How** should the course be taught; in particular, what teaching methods have been identified.

Table 4 presents a summary of the papers by each of these themes, and Figure 2 shows the distribution of the themes over time.

A further theme, the *evaluation of course success*, is discussed at the end of this section.

Whether to teach DS

This somewhat existential question is not so much related to whether the topics in discrete structures should be taught, as to whether they should be taught in a single course, or moved into the courses where they are applied. Examples include moving logic into software verification or formal methods or moving all study of trees and graphs into data structures. Similar questions arise when considering the mathematical techniques relevant to computer science, such as calculus or statistics, and appear across a large time span, from Berztiss, Tremblay and Manohar in the 1970's to Fleury and Neff in the 1990's and 2000's [6, 43, 12, 32].

It is highlighted quite frequently that one of the main ideas of teaching students discrete structures is to prepare them for more theoretical content they meet in courses later on [25, 27], which brings up the question that if computer science majors are finding the content too difficult or aimless so early in their studies, why not push it back to "where it belongs"? With Tremblay and Manohar for example, counting techniques, permutations and probability are omitted from their discrete structures course (although part of the curriculum) as they are covered in other courses [43].

A more novel approach is taken specifically by Neff [32], where parts of the discrete structures course are outsourced and the subject is then taught with an approach of rather than "Here's the tools, you'll need them sometime", it says "Here's a computer science problem we need to solve, what tools do we need to solve it?".

Table 3: Place of publication for the 67 title-filtered papers, broken down by search term used.

Place	DS	DM	Other	Total	Cum
SIGCSE	7.5	14.5	2	24	36%
JCSC	1	11	0	12	54%
SIGCSE Bulletin	3	5	0	8	66%
ITiCSE	0	4	0	4	72%
JERIC	0	4	0	4	78%
SIGACT News	0	3	0	3	82%
CCSC	0	2	0	2	85%
CSC	0.5	1.5	0	2	88%
Others	1	5	2	8	100%
Total	*13*	*50*	*4*	*67*	

Table 4: Themes covered in the 47 abstract-filtered papers (some papers cover multiple themes).

Category	Sources	Total
Whether to teach DS	[3, 4, 6, 8, 12, 32, 43]	7
When students should learn DS	[2, 3, 4, 6, 8, 13, 18, 22, 25, 26, 27, 29, 35, 36, 37, 46, 47]	17
With programming?	[5, 7, 10, 14, 15, 16, 23, 28, 30, 31, 33, 39, 41, 45, 49, 50]	16
With data structures?	[4, 5, 6, 11, 22, 28, 31, 34, 39, 40, 45, 49]	12
How to teach DS	[2, 5, 7, 9, 10, 14, 16, 21, 24, 32, 33, 37, 41, 42, 45, 49, 50, 51]	18

When students should learn DS

It is acknowledged that discrete structures is just a basis for the more specialised computer science topics which students may not encounter for quite some time [6]. Thus a conflict arises between teaching discrete structures early in the syllabus or late, potentially allowing for greater depth, but causing difficulties for subjects that depend on it [25].

Marion draws us back to our previous point about dismantling the subject, but instead segments the course rather than completely dissolving it [27]. This can allow an easier introductory course for discrete structures and a subsequently more in-depth course later on when students are more experienced. But the appreciation of the subject is always a problem early on, with a difficulty noted in teaching students material that they believe they may never use [13]. If discrete structures is to serve as a basis for a wide variety of more in-depth modules later on, it needs to justify its existence by demonstrating its necessity and application.

DS with Programming

A number of papers describe curricula that involve coding up a discrete structures related problem. One approach uses real world examples in order to aid students in the applicability of what they are being taught and motivate them to excel at the course work [39]. Martin proposes allowing students to implement an algorithm of their choice which they learnt in their discrete structures course, enforcing their understanding of the material [28]. Cigas and Hsin, introduce the use of *specification* for problems; one of the primary applications of the logic learnt in discrete structures [10].

There is also the opportunity to exploit the link between discrete structures and declarative programming languages. For example, Berry describes a more advanced application of coding involving the use of Scheme [5]. As a language which contains elements of functional programming there is already a clear link between this approach and the *functions* aspect of discrete structures. Similarly, Hein outlines the use of FP, ML and Prolog to teach students discrete structures concepts [15]. Clearly, an issue here is how this interacts with the teaching of programming and language paradigms in the syllabus as a whole.

McMaster *et al.* draw the conclusion that teaching discrete structures with programming makes the subject easier for students - or at least for those students who already know how to program [31]. Implementing a theory learnt in discrete structures as a program requires a full understanding of it, rather than the regurgitation of a rote learnt mathematical proof. However, it is important not to turn discrete structures into another programming course, since omitting the theoretical material could lose much of the intended flavour of the subject.

DS with Data Structures

Another noticeable feature of many of the papers reviewed is an apparent crossover between topics covered in discrete structures and data structures (CS2). The ACM curriculum for discrete structures contains a number of intersections with data structures such as graphs and trees and such a crossover (as well as some others) is further explored by Decker and Ventura [11].

Even though the context in which these topics are to be studied is different between the two subjects, this again raises questions regarding the coherence of a discrete structures course in a syllabus. A number of the papers note that the concept of coding up actual algorithms in discrete structures is very similar to the way in which data structures are studied [39, 28, 5, 31]. Teaching an inductive structure such as a list or tree, and then asking students to implement them, particularly in a functional language [34], is similar to implementing these as data structures, albeit often with different motivation and analysis mechanisms.

A different angle on this issue arises from studies of factors influencing student success at discrete structures. There is significant coupling between data structures and discrete structures when evaluating student performance [6, 40, 34, 11], giving strong support to closely examining this link in a syllabus.

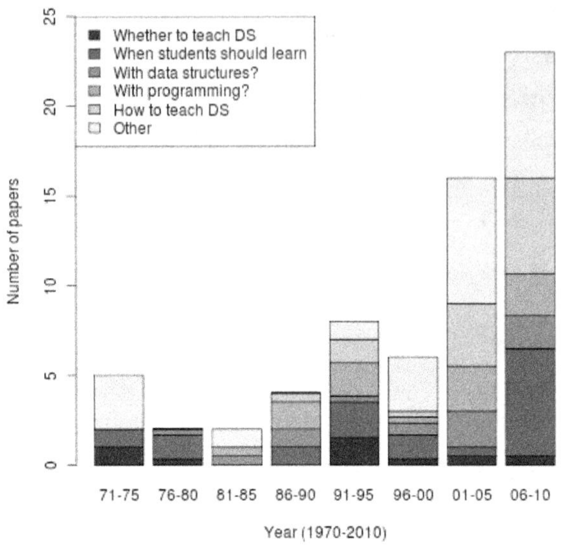

Figure 2: Distribution of topics over time. Each bar represents the number of relevant papers over a five-year period, subdivided by the topic covered.

How to teach DS

Finally, in response to the uncertainties of educating students in discrete structures a number of teaching methods are described in the literature.

There is much focus on reducing the unfamiliarity of the subject. For example Zeng and Jiang builds on the foundation of staying in a student's comfort zone when introducing a new idea [51]. This appears to ease students into the formality of certain areas of discrete structures. Berry, Cigas and Hsin use visual tools to try to reduce the complexity for students [10, 5]. Exploitation of a student's familiarity with programming is also an interesting way to tackle teaching problems since students may be a lot more comfortable in a software engineering setting than in a pure mathematical one in which discrete structures is sometimes presented. To deal with unfamiliar notation, a simple reinforcement of exactly what a symbol means can uncloud a problem for a student, allowing them to focus on understanding the theory rather than the theory's representation [21].

The collaborative approach discussed by Buchele takes a more traditional pen and paper approach but the increased student engagement can certainly be seen as beneficial [9]. Collaborative homework also enables mingling of those who understand certain concepts and those who don't, hopefully making the educational experience "viral". Similarly, Neff suggests that a problem-directed approach can go some way to tackling the appreciation and motivation problems with discrete structures [32].

It is interesting that while the previous themes explored the relationship of discrete structures with other subjects, many of the papers on approaches to teaching seek to exploit this relationship positively.

Table 5: Ways of evaluating course success.

Category	Sources	Total
Grade Based Statistics	[11, 19, 30, 34, 35, 40, 50]	7
Survey Based Statistics	[9, 26, 28, 37, 38, 42, 45]	7
Anecdotal Feedback	[6, 7, 8, 14, 16, 17, 21, 24, 31, 41, 43]	11

4.1 Evaluation of Course Success

Given that a very large number of papers discuss some kind of discrete structures course it is important to analyse the ways in which these courses are evaluated. We found that a total of 25 papers discussed some form of evaluation, though this varied between papers. Overall we can identify three broad categories of information regarding the evaluation of a teaching approach: based on student grades, based on a quantitative analysis of student feedback, and based on anecdotal information from students. The papers falling into each of these three categories are shown in Table 5.

Notably, it appears that statistics in some cases can be quite sparse when it comes to discrete structures. With Martin for example, a set of 20 students may not tell us as much as a set of 100 students would when it comes to certain questions [28]. Going by statistics alone, in taking radical approaches such as scattering discrete structures course content to later on modules we effectively move into unknown territory. For this reason, it is necessary to collect a significant amount of statistics for a wide variety of approaches taken to teaching the subject. Having said that, there are some more sizable data sets which analyse the final grades for students [11, 34, 40].

As well as these grade-based statistics there are also some survey-based course evaluations which provide more anecdotal type feedback on courses [28, 9]. This anecdotal type evaluation is a lot stronger in some papers than in others, sometimes with just a sentence or two given for student thoughts on a course [6, 21, 31, 43]. There appears to be quite some variety in course evaluation techniques and as a result it can be difficult to fully evaluate, much less compare, course outcome analyses.

5. CONCLUDING REMARKS

This paper has presented a review of research on discrete structures teaching. Since the initial submission of this paper our search parameters were extended to include the ERIC collection, however this did not result in any significant changes to this review; details can be found in the associated technical report [48].

We hope this work will be of use as a reference point for those preparing to teach discrete structures, and as an example of a systematic literature review in CS education.

6. ACKNOWLEDGEMENTS

This work was partially funded by the National Academy for Integration of Research, Teaching and Learning (NAIRTL).

7. REFERENCES

[1] ACM/IEEE. Computer science curriculum 2008: An interim revision of CS 2001. Report from the interim review task force, ACM and the IEEE CS, Dec. 2008.

[2] V. L. Almstrum, P. B. Henderson, V. Harvey, C. Heeren, W. Marion, C. Riedesel, L.-K. Soh, and A. E. Tew. Concept inventories in computer science for the topic discrete mathematics. In *Working group reports on ITiCSE on innovation and technology in CS education*, pages 132–145, Bologna, Italy, 2006.

[3] D. Baldwin, B. Marion, and H. Walker. Status report on the SIGCSE committee on the implementation of a discrete mathematics course. In *35th SIGCSE Tech. Symp. on CS Education*, pages 98–99, Norfolk, VA, 2004.

[4] D. Baldwin, C. H. Smith, P. B. Hendersen, and V. Vadisigi. CS1 and CS2 (panel session): foundations of computer science and discrete mathematics. In *31st SIGCSE Tech. Symp. on CS Education*, pages 397–398, Austin, TX, 2000.

[5] J. Berry. Improving discrete mathematics and algorithms curricula with LINK. In *2nd Conference on Integrating Technology into CS Education*, pages 14–20, Uppsala, Sweden, June 1997.

[6] A. T. Berztiss. The why and how of discrete structures. In *6th SIGCSE Tech. Symp. on CS Education*, pages 22–25, July 1976.

[7] S. Bridges. Graphics assignments in discrete mathematics. In *24th SIGCSE Tech. Symp. on CS Education*, pages 83–86, Indianapolis, IN, 1993.

[8] D. T. Brown. Discrete mathematics II. *SIGCSE Bulletin*, 25(4):13–17, 1993.

[9] S. F. Buchele. Increased student participation in a discrete mathematics course. *J. of Comp. Sci. in Colleges*, 20(4):68–76, Apr. 2005.

[10] J. Cigas and W. J. Hsin. Teaching proofs and algorithms in discrete mathematics with online visual logic puzzles. *J. Educ. Resour. Comput.*, 5(2), June 2005.

[11] A. Decker and P. Ventura. We claim this class for computer science: a non-mathematician's discrete structures course. In *35th SIGCSE Tech. Symp. on CS Education*, pages 442–446, Mar. 2004.

[12] A. E. Fleury. Evaluating discrete mathematics exercises. In *24th SIGCSE Tech. Symp. on CS Education*, pages 73–77, Apr. 1993.

[13] D. Gries, M. Eckmann, A. Erkan, and J. Heliotis. Discrete mathematics/structures: How do we deal with the late appreciation problem? *J. of Comp. Sci. in Colleges*, 24(6):110–112, June 2009.

[14] V. J. Harvey and S. H. Rodger. Editorial for the special issue on software support for teaching discrete mathematics. *J. Educ. Resour. Comput.*, 5(2):1, 2005.

[15] J. L. Hein. A declarative laboratory approach for discrete structures, logic, and computability. *SIGCSE Bulletin*, 25(3):19–25, Sept. 1993.

[16] P. B. Henderson. Discrete mathematics as a precursor to programming. In *21st SIGCSE Tech. Symp. on CS Education*, pages 17–21, Washington D.C., 1990.

[17] P. B. Henderson. Reflections on teaching discrete math for the first time. *SIGCSE Bulletin*, 39(2):24–24, 2007.

[18] P. B. Henderson, R. DeCoste, and K. L. Huggins. Preparing to teach discrete math for the first time. In *Working group reports on ITiCSE on Innovation and technology in CS education*, pages 20–21, Bologna, Italy, 2006.

[19] L. Jamba-Joyner and W. F. Klostermeyer. Predictors

for success in a discrete math course. *SIGCSE Bulletin*, 35(2):66–69, 2003.

[20] B. Kitchenham and S. Charters. Guidelines for performing Systematic Literature Reviews in Software Engineering. Technical Report EBSE 2007-001, Keele University and Durham University Joint Report, 2007.

[21] J. Krone. Meeting the challenges of discrete mathematics for computer science: the power of symbols. *J. of Comp. Sci. in Colleges*, 23(1):31–37, Oct. 2007.

[22] M. D. LeBlanc and R. Leibowitz. Discrete partnership: a case for a full year of discrete math. In *37th SIGCSE Tech. Symp. on CS Education*, pages 313–317, Houston, TX, 2006.

[23] G. M. Levin. ISETL: a language for teaching discrete mathematics (abstract). In *ACM Annual Conference on Cooperation*, page 455, Washington, D.C., 1990.

[24] Y. Li. A new approach to teaching logic in discrete mathematics. In *9th Intl. Conf. for Young Computer Scientists*, pages 2432–2437, Nov. 2008.

[25] B. Marion. Discrete mathematics: support of and preparation for the study of computer science. In *Seventh annual CCSC Midwestern Conference on Small Colleges*, pages 190–199, Dec. 2000.

[26] B. Marion. Final oral report of the SIGCSE committee on the implementation of a discrete mathematics course. In *37th SIGCSE Tech. Symp. on CS Education*, pages 268–269, Houston, TX, 2006.

[27] W. Marion. Discrete mathematics for computer science majors - where are we? How do we proceed? In *20th SIGCSE Tech. Symp. on CS Education*, pages 273–277, Feb. 1989.

[28] K. E. Martin. The role of discrete structures and operations research in a computer science curriculum. *SIGCSE Bulletin*, 16(4):4–6, Dec. 1984.

[29] W. D. Maurer. An alternative to group theory in the discrete structures course. *J. of Comp. Sci. in Colleges*, 21(5):110–115, 2006.

[30] J. W. McGuffee. The discrete mathematics enhancement project. *J. of Comp. Sci. in Colleges*, 17(5):162–166, 2002.

[31] K. McMaster, N. Anderson, and B. Rague. Discrete math with programming: better together. In *38th SIGCSE Tech. Symp. on CS Education*, pages 100–104, Mar. 2007.

[32] N. Neff. Problem-directed discrete structures course. In *41st SIGCSE Tech. Symp. on CS Education*, pages 148–151, Mar. 2010.

[33] D. Nohl. Using an automated reasoning program as a CS application in discrete mathematics. *J. of Comp. Sci. in Colleges*, 22(4):7–13, 2007.

[34] R. L. Page. Software is discrete mathematics. In *8th Intl. Conf. on Functional Programming*, pages 79–86, Aug. 2003.

[35] B. T. Pioro. Introductory computer programming: gender, major, discrete mathematics, and calculus. *J. of Comp. Sci. in Colleges*, 21(5):123–129, 2006.

[36] R. E. Prather. Another look at the discrete structures course. In *6th SIGCSE Tech. Symp. on CS Education*, pages 247–252, Feb. 1976.

[37] D. A. Schoenefeld and R. L. Wainwright. Integration of discrete mathematics topics into the secondary mathematics curriculum using Mathematica: a summer institute for high school teachers. In *24th SIGCSE Tech. Symp. on CS Education*, pages 78–82, Indianapolis, IN, 1993.

[38] A. Settle and C. Settle. Graduate student satisfaction with an online discrete mathematics course. *J. of Comp. Sci. in Colleges*, 21(1):79–87, 2005.

[39] B. Setzer. A lab course for discrete mathematics. In *47th Annual Southeast Regional Conf.*, Mar. 2009.

[40] J. R. Sidbury. A statistical analysis of the effect of discrete mathematics on the performance of computer science majors in beginning computing classes. In *17th SIGCSE Tech. Symp. on CS Education*, pages 134–137, Feb. 1986.

[41] D. E. Stevenson, M. R. Wick, and S. J. Ratering. Steganography and cartography: interesting assignments that reinforce machine representation, bit manipulation, and discrete structures concepts. In *36th SIGCSE Tech. Symp. on CS Education*, pages 277–281, St. Louis, MO, 2005.

[42] K. Sutner. CDM: Teaching discrete mathematics to computer science majors. *J. Educ. Resour. Comput.*, 5(2):4, 2005.

[43] J. P. Tremblay and R. Manohar. A first course in discrete structures with applications to computer science. In *4th SIGCSE Tech. Symp. on CS Education*, pages 155–160, Feb. 1974.

[44] D. W. Valentine. CS educational research: a meta-analysis of SIGCSE technical symposium proceedings. In *35th SIGCSE Tech. Symp. on CS Education*, pages 255–259, Norfolk, VA, 2004.

[45] R. L. Wainwright. Introducing functional programming in discrete mathematics. In *23rd SIGCSE Tech. Symp. on CS Education*, pages 147–152, Kansas City, MO, 1992.

[46] J. S. Warford. An experience teaching formal methods in discrete mathematics. *SIGCSE Bulletin*, 27(3):60–64, 1995.

[47] J. Waxman. Reflections on B3, discrete structures. *SIGCSE Bulletin*, 7(2):51–54, 1975.

[48] T. Whelan, S. Bergin, and J. F. Power. Discrete structures teaching: A systematic literature review. Technical report, Department of Computer Science, National University of Ireland Maynooth, NUIM-CS-TR-2010-01, Sept. 2010.

[49] M. R. Wick and P. J. Wagner. Using market basket analysis to integrate and motivate topics in discrete structures. In *37th SIGCSE Tech. Symp. on CS Education*, pages 323–327, Houston, TX, 2006.

[50] W. Xiuguo. Discrete mathematics teaching reformation: Adding experiments. In *Intl. Workshop on Education Technology and Computer Science*, volume 2, pages 566–569, 2009.

[51] H. Zeng and K. Jiang. Teaching mathematical proofs to CS major students in the class of discrete mathematics. *J. of Comp. Sci. in Colleges*, 25(5):326–332, May 2010.

Teaching Operating Systems as How Computers Work

Peter Desnoyers
Northeastern University
360 Huntington Ave.
Boston, MA 02115
pjd@ccs.neu.edu

ABSTRACT

The "Computer Systems" course at Northeastern University is an MS-level core course which attempts to teach students *how computers work*, through a behavioral approach to the concepts involved in operating systems and their interface to the hardware. As an operating system is typically the first reactive system which students encounter in their studies, the goal of the class is to develop an understanding of the tools and reasoning which are involved in understanding and working with the internals of such a system, whether it be a conventional operating system or (as is more commonly found in industry) a consumer product, networking device, or other embedded system. This course is currently in its third year with enthusiastic responses from students, especially those who have been able to apply its lessons in co-operative work assignments, and an undergraduate class teaching substantially the same material is currently underway.

Categories and Subject Descriptors

K.3.2 [**Computers and Education**]: Computer and Information Science Education; D.4.7 [**Operating Systems**]: Organization and Design

General Terms

Design, Experimentation, Human Factors

Keywords

operating systems, computer science education

1. INTRODUCTION

CS5600, Computer Systems, begins with a simple demonstration — a ridiculously simple one, in fact. The projector displays the console of a computer which has been booted into Linux in text mode; the instructor types the keystrokes 'l', 's', and return. At the beginning of the semester virtually every student can describe what this is doing—listing the files in a directory. By the end of the class, the goal of this class is that these students learn *how* this happened—e.g. the operation of the keyboard driver and scheduler to deliver input to the shell, the virtual memory operations needed to demand page the `ls` executable, and the file system layout, implementation, and actions necessary to locate and enumerate a particular directory.

In effect the goal of this class is to teach students how computers work. For a simple enough computer, this understanding might be obtained through an understanding of the hardware. For any general-purpose computer today, however, most of its working parts are virtual and reside as software components within the operating system.

The approach this class takes to teaching its material matches this goal, as well. The class does not teach how a computer operating system is structured, or what its most important concepts are - it tries to teach *how it works*. In particular, by this we refer specifically to the causal chains of events which occur in response to stimuli such as user requests, and which as a whole comprise its behavior.[1]

This goal is reflected at all levels within the course. Lectures emphasize event-by-event walkthroughs to illustrate concepts. Material is presented in order from low-level components up, so that higher-level behaviors may be seen as combinations of previously-learned lower-level ones. Assignments are used to illustrate these behaviors, with test scripts or other oracles provided so that students may identify correct behavior. Finally, evaluation on exams is done in a way which emphasizes exposition of system behavior in response to state and stimuli, rather than descriptive or computational problems.

With the introduction of this revised course, enrollment has increased by 60%, while the pool of eligible students has remained roughly constant. A university-wide change from paper to online course evaluations coincident with the first offering of this course prevents direct comparison with previous versions; however, evaluations have been well above average, with many students describing the new syllabus and format in highly enthusiastic terms.

2. BACKGROUND

CS 5600, Computer Systems (previously CS G112) in the College of Computer and Information Science at Northeastern is a core course in the professional MS program - students

[1]We note that an operating system is often the first reactive system which students see in their studies, requiring them to be introduced to the idea of reasoning about the evolution of system state given a sequence of inputs over time.

SIGCSE'11, March 9–12, 2011, Dallas, Texas, USA.

must take either this or Managing Software Development as one of 8 courses. In addition, most students undertake a cooperative assignment in industry as part of their degree; a significant fraction of the students in this course have already been on co-op. The students are primarily international, with a broad range of undergraduate preparation that may or may not have included an operating systems course or exposure to the C programming language.

Prior to 2008 the class was a traditional operating systems concepts class. Anecdotal evidence indicated that the class was not meeting the needs of students—enrollment was low, and co-op employers had commented on students' lack of operating systems background. With a change of instructor, the course was re-focused to emphasize topics which would be of long-term use for students pursuing careers in embedded systems, such as networking and storage devices, which represent a significant number of co-op and career opportunities for students in the College.

3. BEHAVIOR AS A PRIMARY CONCEPT

The class is structured around operating system behavior for several reasons. First, because it fits the intuitive idea of "how it works". Part of the goal of the class is to make students comfortable working "under the hood", as would be the case in embedded fields such as consumer or network devices; the author believes that the form of operational understanding emphasized in this class is a key factor in achieving this familiarity. In addition we wish to teach principles that are general, rather than specific to an individual operating system, and while structure and abstractions may vary from one OS to another, behavior such as response to a page fault remains relatively constant.

The level of abstraction at which this behavior is described varies according to the complexity of the interaction. Thus the discussion of keyboard input in the first lecture would serve as a detailed design for the keyboard driver of the simple machine being described, while when discussing virtual memory and demand paging we refer to reading a block from a file (itself a complicated process) as one operation.

Assessment of student comprehension of these behavioral concepts poses a set of challenges. Programming assignments when successfully completed result in code which when executed will reproduce the behavior in question, but do not necessarily prove understanding of the behavior by the student. For in-class exams the problem is worse, as typical problems involving calculation or description fail to capture the behavioral aspects of a system at all.

Instead we place a heavy reliance on questions which ask for pseudo-event traces in response. Like pseudo-code, these questions ask for a description at a prescribed level of detail, in this case describing the sequence of actions which unfold given a specified starting state and stimulus. An example of such an assessment is shown in Figure 1, where students are asked to trace the virtual memory operations which occur as several lines of machine code are faulted in and executed.

In contrast, programming assignments are designed to illustrate the behavior patterns being studied, as well as assessing the students' knowledge of these patterns. For the most part the assignments are accompanied by test scripts; successfully completion of all tests should correspond to full marks on the assignment. The assignment thus acts as a simulator, reproducing the behavior the student heard described in lecture, or failing tests until corrected if that understanding proves to be incorrect.

The diagram below shows the page tables in physical memory for two address spaces [...]
The operating system view of address space 2 is shown on the right - note that the shared page is mapped read-only so that it can be copied on write, while 05000000 is demand-paged from disk and BFFF0000 is allocated on demand.
[diagrams omitted]
We begin execution in the following state:

```
PC = 05000000
SP = BFFF0FFC
```

The code to be paged in starts with the following 3 instructions:

```
MOV *(06000100) -> EAX
PUSH EAX
MOV EAX -> *(06000300)
```

Give the sequence of events which occur during the execution of these three instructions. Specifically describe each of the following events when they occur:

- instruction attempts - indicate which insn.
- instruction completions
- page faults - indicate which insn. faulted (1st MOV, PUSH, or 2nd MOV), whether an I or D fault, and for D faults, the fault address.

[...]

Figure 1: Behavior-based exam questions

4. LOADING AND CONTEXT SWITCHING

The beginning of the class is designed to help students develop a mental model of an operating system and programs in memory on a simple machine, and be able to walk through the steps involved in loading a program, invoking OS functions, and context switching. For this purpose we define a simple machine, executing only on the blackboard. Thus we do not need to fully define the CPU; instead we give only its assembly language instructions – the basic MOV, CALL, etc. found on most CPUs, with numbered registers and fixed-length instructions for simplicity.

For our purposes the key characteristic of this machine is its set of simple I/O devices mapped into the top of its 16-bit address space. At present these consist of a text-mode 80x24 video display buffer, a keyboard controller, a primitive disk controller, and 4 serial ports for multiprocessing.

Rather than taking a top-down approach, we begin with a very simple "bare-metal" program, copying the string "Hello World" to the display buffer, as shown in Figure 2. Starting with this program, which may easily be understood in its entirety with little effort, we proceed in stages to develop a simple single-user system, transitioning from assembler to pseudo-code when appropriate. Hardware-specific functionality is split into separate procedures, and then segregated to a separate region of the memory space to allow loading of programs; loading is done by a simple command line which allows the user to specify disk blocks and then begin execution. Next we introduce a system call vector at a well-known location, as well as its software interrupt equivalent,

```
frame_buf   eq     F000
str         .db    'Hello World'
len         eq     11

begin:      MOV    #frame_buf → R0
            MOV    #str → R1
            MOV    #len → R2

loop:       MOV    *(R1++) → R3
            MOV    R3 → *(R0++)
            SUB    1 → R2
            JMP    NZ, loop

done:       JMP    done
```

Figure 2: Our first program

```
switch( uint16 *oldsp, uint16 newsp)
_switch:  PUSH  R7 (caller-saved)
          PUSH  R6
          MOV   *(SP-8) → R0
          MOV   SP → *R0
          MOV   *(SP-10) → SP
          POP   R6
          POP   R7
          RET
```

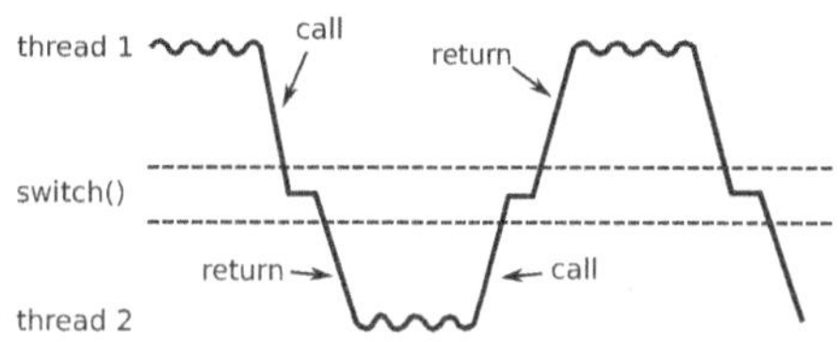

Figure 3: Alternate context switching depictions

providing a stable interface for binary compatibility across instances of the OS.

We then describe the concept of a command-line shell which uses OS functions to load and execute other programs, hardware interrupts and their application in buffering keyboard input, and a file system using a directory of {name, start, length} tuples in block 0. At this point we have explained a system of roughly the sophistication of MS-DOS 1.0, a contemporary description of which is part of the assigned reading. [8]

Using the motivating example of the 4 serial ports with attached terminals, we review subroutine linkage and stack frames and introduce context switching and multiprogramming. On a simple system such as this, process state can be pushed onto the stack and represented by nothing more than a saved stack pointer value, allowing context switches to be easily walked through on the blackboard. Drawing on the prior description of hardware interrupts, a timer device is then introduced, and with that, preemptive context switching.

In each iteration of the system there is an emphasis on the memory map, using the classic organization of code at the bottom, heap growing up, and stack growing down. This organization is used to present the memory map for the multitasking system, leading to a discussion of methods for loading programs at this differing locations in memory—separate compilation, load-time fix-up, position-independent code, and segment registers.

In practice most students have a great deal of difficulty with context switching; although they understand the concept, they have trouble following the exact sequence of events which occur. This difficulty is seen regardless of prior preparation or experience; we believe that it is because a context switch function, which is called in one thread but returns in another, breaks a fundamental programming abstraction which is more deeply ingrained in the more experienced students. We have found it helpful to present multiple ways of visualizing the context switch process, including both the low-level instructions themselves as well as higher-level views of behavior, as shown in Figure 3.

The assignment for this section of the class involves writing a user-space loader, context switching between threads, and scheduling multiple threads to respond to user input. Students are provided with a code framework which creates an executable data segment and two network connections, as well as functions for switching the stack pointer and initializing a stack. In addition, a build script is provided which extracts the contents of simple ELF executables in binary form which may be easily loaded into memory and invoked, as well as an assembler file which defines a vector table these "micro-programs" can use to invoke functions within the main executable.

Students must write several micro-programs and a simple shell to load and execute them, as well as the "system calls" such as `println()` which are invoked through the vector table. Next they implement context switching between two threads, and finally implement a thread context switch, and modify their input routine to switch between two threads as user input is received on the network connections.

For many students this assignment is a high point of the class — although tiny, they have written an operating system of their own. Where in prior classes they were looking down at the interface to the OS, by creating a sort of micro-OS with basic functions, they become able to look at the remainder of the class as elaborations on top of this base.

5. SYNCHRONIZATION

Having introduced threads and preemptive switching, the concept of race conditions is described via the classic bank balance update example. We walk through the operation of a spinlock at the memory transaction level, and show how to construct a mutex using spinlocks or interrupt disabling in conjunction with a thread scheduler.

For the remainder of the section on synchronization we focus on abstract synchronization primitives rather than lower levels. Using classic problems such as bounded buffer for motivation, we introduce semaphores, monitors, and deadlock.

This is in a sense the most practical unit of the class, as it is likely that most students will have to write and debug threaded code at some point in their career. As such, there is a strong focus on best practices and rules of thumb, e.g.:

- Logical association of mutexes with data, rather than code sections; we therefore downplay the term "critical section".
- Safe handling of shared variables, through means such as creating local copies before releasing a lock.
- Use of lock ranking to avoid deadlocks.

Although semaphores are introduced early on, the primary synchronization mechanism used in this class is the

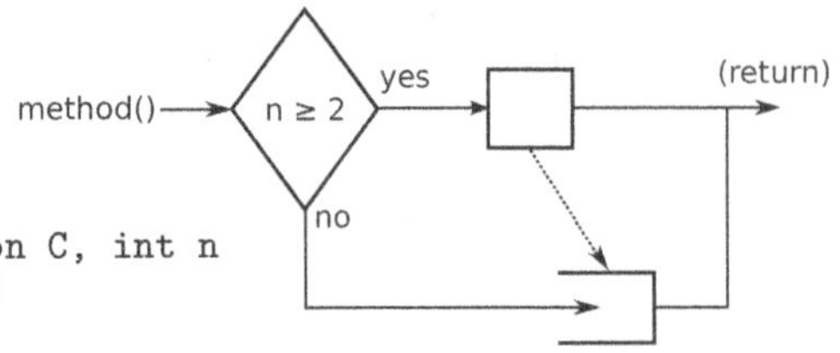


```
monitor
  condition C, int n
  method()
    n++
    if n >= 2
      signal C
    else
      wait C
```

Figure 4: Graphical illustration of synchronization

monitor. We do this for both practical and philosophical reasons. First, monitors are the more likely form in which students will later encounter concurrency control, in either Java (as synchronized objects or re-entrant locks from *java.utils.concurrent*) or Posix threads *pthread_cond* operations. More importantly, we believe monitors are more pedagogically sound, as the intuitive understanding of how a semaphore works must be violated (by calling `wait` in one thread and `signal` in another) in order to use it for any but the simplest of problems.

We focus on reasoning about the operation of multiple threads, an area which presents difficulties for even experienced programmers. Rather than understanding *the* order of events which will occur, students must learn to understand *all possible* orders of events. To cope with this, we introduce a flowchart-based graphical notation for visualizing the flow of control in multiple simultaneous threads, as shown in Figure 4. Although not as precise as the n-dimensional state graphs used in e.g. Bryant and O'Hallaron [2], the ability to visualize multiple threads moving through a 2-dimensional network provides students with an effective metaphor to understand the state space of a multi-threaded system. [2]

We augment this section with a review of continuous-time Markov models, providing students with another tool to reason about state-based behavior. This allows us to give the following assignment:

- Write a pseudo-code description of a monitor-based solution to a concurrency problem (e.g. the sleeping barber)
- Translate this solution into C using Posix thread condition variables, and execute this solution.
- Run the same solution as an event-driven simulation using a virtual-time thread scheduler, with additional instrumentation to gather state occupancy and throughput statistics.
- Finally, formulate the problem as a Markov model and solve the balance equations, deriving expected state occupancies and transition rates.

A significant problem in assigning multi-threaded programming assignments is that unlike the single-threaded case, student observation of program behavior appears to do little to dispel misconceptions about the operation of a particular piece of code; instead, they often need to be shown by some other means that it is operating incorrectly. Using the approach described here, we are able to provide an oracle to test the Markov model solution (e.g. selected digits from the decimal solution), and once students have successfully solved that portion of the problem, they may in turn use it to verify operation of their code.

[2]Graph representations of concurrency (e.g. Petri nets) have a long history, however a review of current textbooks shows no examples of their use in teaching introductory concurrency concepts.

6. VIRTUAL MEMORY

Virtual memory plays a central role in modern operating systems, and without understanding it much of the operation of these systems must remain an unknown black box. We therefore focus heavily on this topic, covering the range from hardware mechanisms through software policies and algorithms.

Early on we introduced the use of segment registers for run-time relocation of executables; we now examine per-process memory protection, leading to simple base-and-bounds translation hardware. A walk though several examples leads to the necessity of separate user and supervisor modes, along with mechanisms (e.g. software interrupts) to allow controlled transitions into supervisor mode. At this point we have covered all the infrastructure needed to understand the non-file system portions of the original Unix paper [14] which is assigned for reading.

There is a brief (and very conventional) discussion of heap allocation strategies (first/best/next fit, buddy) and external and internal fragmentation. These problems motivate the introduction of paged translation. Students become familiar with the steps involved in address translation via page tables, as well as use of a TLB to achieve acceptable performance. To reinforce this knowledge we ask students to (a) given a specified table, describe the steps needed to translate a particular address, and (b) for a specified memory map, construct a page table to implement it.

The central idea of this unit is virtual memory, though, rather than address translation. We thus describe the concept of operating system virtual memory areas, and the page fault handling necessary for demand allocation, copy-on-write, and demand paging. As before, the emphasis is on understanding of the sequence of steps involved, as illustrated in the test question shown in Figure 1.

We describe hardware virtualization next, which is perhaps the most conceptually difficult subject in the class. At this point At this point we have erected enough infrastructure that we can describe the difficulty of the problem—i.e. why one operating system cannot be run directly on top of another. The first solution presented is full software emulation, as in e.g. Bochs [5], which despite its practical complexity is conceptually an almost trivial fetch-switch-execute loop. From this we proceed to the trap-and-emulate strategy used on CPUs meeting the Popek & Goldberg virtualization requirements [10], and finally discuss software and hardware techniques for virtualizing non-virtualizable CPUs such as the x86 series. [11]

The homework for this unit is split between paper exercises, in particular pseudo-event traces, and a programming assignment. Creating meaningful programming assignments for this unit is a challenge, as pure user-mode projects are very restrictive, while a kernel-mode assignment would require an amount of development and debugging infrastructure which really needs to be amortized over multiple assignments. To date our assigment requires students to use the `mprotect` system call and a `sigsegv` handler to emulate actual page faulting. They then implement several different page replacement policies - FIFO with differing working set sizes, and the VMS LRU approximation [6] using FIFO replacement from the working set and a victim cache with LRU replacement.

7. I/O AND BLOCK DEVICES

In traditional operating systems classes the block storage layer is woefully under-represented in comparison to the attention it receives in both industry and academia. In this portion of the class we focus on the block interface both internally and externally, again paying close attention to the sequences of operations involved, which are typically the crucial determinants of performance.

On the host side of the interface we focus on driver architecture and the performance characteristics of buses such as PCI and PCI-e. We calculate what I/O performance would be for simple memory-mapped devices given typical bus latencies, and use this to motivate the discussion of a typical I/O device using DMA, a descriptor queue, and interrupts. We discuss driver architectures, and put these together to provide students with a picture of the operation of blocking I/O from the application, through the OS and down through to the PCI bus, and back.

Disk drives are then discussed, from the point of view of performance. The goal here is to give students a basic understanding of the mechanical and geometric properties which determine performance—rotation speed, seek time, and zone density. The primary focus of this portion of the class, however, is on features which may be provided on the device side of the block interface. After a brief discussion of transports (SCSI, Fibre Channel, USB, etc.) we cover standard RAID levels (RAID0, RAID1, RAID4 and RAID5) as well as logical volume management (snapshot, migration, storage virtualization) and storage de-duplication.

To date the assignment for this unit has been combined with that for virtual memory. Students are given specifications for a small but otherwise representative disk drive—rotational speed, zones and sectors per track in each zone, and seek time as a simple function of tracks moved. They must then write a timing simulator, which may be validated against a provided sample sequence. Finally they use a page fault trace collected during the virtual memory portion of the assignment, and use their simulator to determine performance of that trace on the specified drive.

On-paper assessment for this unit is a work in progress; to date it has focused on RAID systems and students' understanding of their operation and performance. Thus they may be asked to indicate the sequence of underlying disk operations in response to reads and writes at the volume level, or to calculate the time taken for certain operations, given specified disk seek and transfer parameters.

8. FILE SYSTEMS AND SECURITY

These are the final sections in the class; to date file systems has been covered first, building on top of the discussion of block devices, with security last. However this order may be revised, as permission checking has been an area of significant confusion in the file system assignment.

Unlike other portions of the class, we begin at an abstract level, presenting the ideas of file system namespace and operations. We do this in order to solidify students' intuitive notions of file and directory, providing a firm basis for discussing concepts such as hard and soft links, inclusion of devices in the file system namespace, and Win32 (device-rooted) vs. Unix (single root) path names.

Kernel implementation of file systems is covered briefly, covering dispatch at the file operations level (e.g. to device driver methods) and at the VFS level. The primary focus, however, is on the externally-visible file system structure. We characterize file systems by their solutions to the following problems:

- Free space management: Do they use linked lists (i.e. the original UNIX file system), a bitmap, some array-based equivalent such as a file allocation table, or extent lists?
- File organization: We discuss contiguous files (e.g. ISO 9660), allocation table-based linking, direct/indirect block structures such as used by most UNIX file systems, and extent lists.
- Directory entries and file meta-data: What information is stored about a file? Is there a separation between file meta-data (i.e. i-node) and directory entry?
- Robustness: Here we discuss file system checking, as well as the operation of log-structured file systems and file system journalling.

The assignment for this unit is typically the most intensive one of the semester. Students are given the definition of a simple file system using a file allocation table and UNIX-like file names and attributes, along with several sample disk images, a `mkfs` utility, and test scripts. In addition to this they are given skeleton code to read and write blocks from a disk image file and to interface with the Linux FUSE (File system in USEr space [13]) library.

Given these materials, students create an implementation of the specified file system, which they are able to mount and use on a Linux system. As with prior assignments, students are provided with test suites which may be used to verify their solutions, so that with sufficient effort most teams should be able to obtain full marks.

On-paper assessment of students' understanding focuses on operations across the block interface boundary, as well as the role of buffering in optimizing these interactions, for both FAT and i-node/indirect block organizations. Thus students might be asked for the sequence of reads necessary for certain operations, and of the effect of e.g. a small buffer cache vs. an i-node cache on the number of operations, or to contrast the worst-case overhead for FAT vs. indirect block organizations for retrieving a block at a large offset within a file.

The final unit, security, is quite brief. It focuses on security mechanisms found in common operating systems (i.e. UNIX, Windows) and covers user/group permissions, access control lists, and capabilities as used in Posix and Windows. The goal of this unit is for students to be able to construct user/group permissions and access control lists to implement a given access policy, a skill which many (although by no means all) students enter the class with.

9. COMPLICATIONS

One of the particular issues with this course, as with many other operating system classes, is the use of C for programming assignments. For many students this is their first exposure to an unsafe language, yet we wish to use class time for teaching course content rather than the assignment language. To some extent this problem has been ameliorated by student use of Valgrind [7] to detect memory bugs. Unfortunately this is not always feasible; in particular, valgrind is unable to differentiate a user-constructed context switch from a severe memory error. To complement valgrind, we are currently working on a set of grading-enforced style rules — e.g. all pointer variables must be initialized to a valid value or NULL— which we hope will further reduce problems.

The other major issue is that of grading. Due to the open-ended nature of the exam questions and cascading effects of errors, considerable judgment is required to assign marks in a way that reasonably reflects a student's performance. The assignments are similarly subject to a wide range of often subtle errors; in both cases it has been difficult for graduate teaching assistants to achieve the desired quality of grading on their own. (This may change as the course matures.) Our solution to date has been the use of "grading parties", where TAs and the professor mark papers, agree on an ordering of answers, and then assign grades accordingly.

As with any novel course, textbook support is problematic. To date we have used Silbershatz et al. [12], and are using Bryant and O'Hallaron [2] in an undergraduate version of the class, but neither is a good fit. Silbershatz is too abstract, avoiding hardware details, although its treatment of synchronization and file systems fits well. Bryant and O'Hallaron cover more hardware details, but not file systems and concurrency are poorly covered. The gap between the textbook and class material has been filled with readings from the literature, as well as student-produced scribe notes and lecture videos posted on the course website.

The use of lecture videos has been highly successful. These are low quality videos, made using consumer-grade equipment operated by the TA, who also typically edits them for posting. Although no doubt responsible for a small drop in course attendance, many students report that the videos have been a valuable study aid.

10. DISCUSSION

In order to provide students with an in-depth exposure to the concepts in this class, certain compromises have been made. Chief among these is the use of user-mode programming assignments, rather than kernel code running on simulated, virtual, or real hardware. This is a deliberate decision, as the goal of these exercises is to illustrate particular issues and mechanisms, not to teach students how to work with a large body of systems code. The largest amount of "scaffolding" required for the CS 5600 assignments is 600 lines of actual code (including headers) for the file system assignment, compared to 4500 lines for project0 in GeekOS [3, 4], or over 7000 for just the scheduler in a recent Linux kernel.

The only area in which this has presented significant difficulty is the virtual memory assignment, where the mprotect/sigsegv mechanism has a number of deficiencies when compared to the equivalent functions in the kernel. With work we believe this may be remedied, either with better support code, or by moving the entire assignment into kernel mode under e.g. QEMU.

The notion of starting from the bottom up in a computer systems class is not new; in particular, Patt and Patel [9] begin at the lowest level with digital logic. After the hardware level, however, their focus turns directly to application programming, while CS 5600 leaves discussion of hardware implementation to digital design classes, but focuses almost exclusively on the layers underneath the application.

Unlike Bryant and O'Hallaron's Introduction to Computer Systems [2, 1], CS 5600 does not attempt to describe those aspects of a computer system which every application programmer will interact with. This is in part due to purpose of the class; as an elective core, it is taken by students with an interest in low-level programming. In addition, however, we consider some aspects of this material to be a fundamental part of any engineering-oriented computer science education.

The class is still evolving, and this paper does not exactly reflect any single semester of CS5600, but rather those portions which have been successful in the past and are being retained, as well as several new approaches which have been tested in a more advanced version of the same class (CS7600) and will be introduced to CS5600 this year.

The author is in the process of revising class and scribe notes into a form which may be used as a text for this class, either alone or in combination with another text. These materials will be made available under an open documentation license on the author's web page, where existing materials such as prior lecture videos and the pedagogical machine description may be found.

11. REFERENCES

[1] Bryant, R. E., and O'Hallaron, D. R. Introducing computer systems from a programmer's perspective. In *SIGCSE* (Charlotte, NC, 2001), ACM, pp. 90–94.

[2] Bryant, R. E., and O'Hallaron, D. R. *Computer Systems: A Programmer's Perspective.* Prentice Hall, Aug. 2002.

[3] Hovemeyer, D. GeekOS. http://geekos.sourceforge.net/, 2010.

[4] Hovemeyer, D., Hollingsworth, J. K., and Bhattacharjee, B. Running on the bare metal with GeekOS. In *SIGCSE* (Norfolk, VA, 2004), ACM.

[5] Lawton, K. P. Bochs: A portable PC emulator for Unix/X. *Linux J. 1996*, 29es (1996), 7.

[6] Levy, H. M., and Lipman, P. H. Virtual memory management in the VAX/VMS operating system. *Computer 15*, 3 (1982), 35–41.

[7] Nethercote, N., and Seward, J. Valgrind: a framework for heavyweight dynamic binary instrumentation. In *SIGPLAN* (San Diego, CA, 2007).

[8] Paterson, T. An inside look at MS-DOS. *Byte Magazine 8*, 6 (1983), 230–252.

[9] Patt, Y. N., and Patel, S. *Introduction to Computing Systems: From Bits and Gates to C and Beyond.* Osborne/McGraw-Hill, 2000.

[10] Popek, G. J., and Goldberg, R. P. Formal requirements for virtualizable third generation architectures. *Commun. ACM 17*, 7 (1974), 412–421.

[11] Robin, J. S., and Irvine, C. E. Analysis of the intel pentium's ability to support a secure virtual machine monitor. In *USENIX Security Symposium* (Denver, Colorado, 2000), pp. 10–10.

[12] Silberschatz, A., Galvin, P. B., and Gagne, G. *Operating System Concepts.* Wiley, July 2008.

[13] Szeredi, M. FUSE: filesystem in userspace. http://fuse.sourceforge.net/, 2010.

[14] Thompson, K., and Ritchie, D. M. The UNIX timesharing system. *Communications of the ACM 17*, 7 (1974), 365–375.

Structured Linux Kernel Projects for Teaching Operating Systems Concepts

Oren Laadan
Dept of Computer Science
Columbia University
New York, NY 10027
orenl@cs.columbia.edu

Jason Nieh
Dept of Computer Science
Columbia University
New York, NY 10027
nieh@cs.columbia.edu

Nicolas Viennot
Dept of Computer Science
Columbia University
New York, NY 10027
nviennot@cs.columbia.edu

ABSTRACT

Linux has emerged as a widely-used platform for enabling hands-on kernel programming experience to learn about operating system concepts. However, developing pedagogically-effective programming projects in the context of a complex, production operating system can be a challenge. We present a structured series of five Linux kernel programming projects suitable for a one semester introductory operating systems course to address this issue. Each assignment introduces students to a core topic and major component of an operating system while implicitly teaching them about various aspects of a real-world operating system. Projects are of modest coding complexity, but require students to understand and leverage core components of the Linux operating system. The learning benefits for students from this approach include learning from real-world operating system code examples by expert kernel designers and gaining software engineering experience managing production code complexity. We have successfully used these structured Linux kernel projects to teach over a thousand students in the introductory operating systems course at Columbia University.

Categories and Subject Descriptors

D.4.0 [**Operating Systems**]: General; K.3.2 [**Computers and Education**]: Computer and Information Science Education—*computer science education*

General Terms

Design, Experimentation, Human Factors

Keywords

Operating systems, computer science education, open-source

1. INTRODUCTION

Kernel programming projects provide crucial hands-on experience for helping students to understand operating system concepts. Linux has emerged as a widely-used platform for teaching operating systems because of its many advantages. Its open-source software base and widely available development tools make it easy for students to access its internals. It provides students the ability to explore a real production operating system, not just a toy system, thereby also enhancing skills that can be immediately applied in the workforce after graduation. It is already maintained by real developers for real users, so there is no need to invest any effort maintaining a separate pedagogical operating system. It provides real code examples by real developers for students to learn from by example.

However, developing effective programming projects that teach students systematically about real-world operating system design and implementation in the context of a production operating system can be a challenge. Production operating systems are large, complex pieces of software. To gain a broad understanding of operating systems, it is useful to have hands-on experience with several different major components of an operating system. However, the sheer size of these systems makes them difficult to understand. It may be tempting to create projects that only touch on fringe aspects of a production operating system to avoid its complexity. However, fringe projects do not provide the opportunity to learn about the core functionality of the kernel. Production operating systems are also not primarily designed as teaching tools, but instead to be used in commercial deployment. Such operating systems are already fully functional and do not have major missing subsystems that students can design and implement. Redesigning several major subsystems of a production kernel may also not be feasible in the time constraints of a course.

We present our efforts at Columbia University over the past decade to leverage the benefits of Linux and address the challenges of designing kernel programming projects that provide educational value for an operating systems course. We have developed a structured series of five Linux kernel programming projects that exposes students to core components of a production operating system with modest coding complexity. These projects start with the basics of writing system calls and understanding the structure of processes, progress into synchronization which is necessary for understanding other aspects of operating system design and implementation, then explore three core operating system components in processor scheduling, virtual memory, and file systems.

Our projects are designed to require students to read and understand core components of the operating system to make the modifications necessary to complete the projects. At

SIGCSE'11, March 9–12, 2011, Dallas, Texas, USA.

the same time, the coding complexity is modest enough for groups of students with no previous operating systems background to successfully complete the projects in less than a few hundred lines of code. In addition to learning about the operating system components themselves, the projects are designed to implicitly teach students about various aspects of operating system structure and understanding how to modify a large code base and manage its complexity.

We have successfully used these structured Linux kernel projects to teach over a thousand students in the introductory operating systems course at Columbia University. We describe our experiences using these projects and analyze various aspects of students' submitted solutions. We demonstrate that the designed coding complexity of the projects is achieved as example project solutions are each under 400 lines of code and students' submitted solutions on average fall within the same range. We also demonstrate that common programming errors in students' submitted solutions become notably less frequent in subsequent projects as later projects reinforce the concepts taught in earlier projects, demonstrating that the projects provide an effective framework for progressive learning.

2. KERNEL PROGRAMMING PROJECTS

The kernel programming projects focus on five core topics in operating systems: system calls and processes, synchronization mechanisms, processor scheduling, virtual memory, and file systems. The topics and order of topics are intentionally chosen as they introduce key operating system concepts and build on one another. In particular, system calls and processes start with less complex components of the operating system and introduce students to basic kernel structures. Synchronization is next as understanding proper use of synchronization mechanisms is a prerequisite for being able to design and implement all other operating system components. Processor scheduling builds on the knowledge students have gained on the structure of processes from the first assignment and the use of synchronization on the second assignment. Virtual memory is deferred until the fourth assignment to only then focus on one of the most complex aspects of a production operating system. File systems is last among the assignments to follow the ordering of topics reflected in most common textbooks.

The assignments are carefully designed so that a group of students with no previous operating systems background can implement a correct solution in a few hundred lines of code. We accomplish this by choosing specific, scope-limited assignments that require intimate understanding of how the existing operating system kernel operates. It is not uncommon for students to spend at least as much time studying and understanding existing kernel code as they do implementing their solutions. Once students understand the relevant mechanisms in the stock kernel well, the implementation itself is fairly straightforward in terms of kernel code.

For the assignments, we direct students to pay careful attention to the handling of errors and unexpected conditions, including resource unavailability, security restrictions, and invalid inputs. While this is important for programming in general, this is particularly important for kernel code. Unlike user-space programs, the operating system kernel may not simply give up and terminate when it encounters an error. For example, when user-space programs terminate, their memory is implicitly freed, but the kernel must explicitly clean up all used resources such as locks held and memory allocated when an operation fails. Furthermore, given the increasing dominance of multicore systems, we require that students generate code in a manner that is SMP-safe. To do proper testing, students must generate test programs in user-space that demonstrate the correctness of their kernel code, including identifying corner cases.

2.1 System Calls and Processes

System calls lay the foundation for the interface between processes and the operating system. Processes are the main abstraction for application programs and the most important entity managed by the operating system. The first kernel project teaches students about basic concepts related to system calls and processes by adding a new system call. We design the project to acclimate students to Linux kernel programming including the development environment such as how to compile and install a new kernel and how to apply debugging techniques.

Both system calls and processes are good topics for a first kernel assignment because of their simplicity. Adding a new system call does not require in-depth knowledge of any kernel subsystem, and accessing process data is fairly straightforward. Moreover, both are fundamental notions that will be used in all of the remaining assignments.

To teach students about the basics of processes, the system call should perform a task that requires access to the kernel process data so that students can learn about the internal representation of processes in the kernel. We focus on process relationships, creation and termination of processes, and how process properties are inherited. Because in this assignment the students are not yet familiar with synchronization methods, we provide template code to handle synchronization and instruct the students to configure a uniprocessor kernel.

While there are many choices about what a system call might perform, we suggest designing the assignment to teach students about two key concepts in addition to the technical details of adding a new system call. First, the system call should involve data transfer to or from the calling program to illustrate the kernel-space versus the user-space view of memory. Second, to exercise handling of unexpected conditions in the kernel, we ask students to identify possible error conditions and select meaningful values to return in response. This also teaches how errors are propagated to the calling program. These two concepts exemplify important differences between implementing system calls and standard library calls in user-space.

Example assignment: system calls (1). One example assignment is to have students write a new system call that outputs records about descendant processes of a given process in DFS order. Each process record consists of some information about the process, such as its process identifier (PID), state and runtime statistics, and the PIDs of its parent, first child, and next sibling. The system call takes three arguments: the PID of the top process, a buffer to store the data, and an integer that indicates the size of the buffer.

Pedagogically, this assignment helps students develop a useful mix of skills. Students learn to traverse the process hierarchy and collect data about individual processes. They learn how to copy data back to user-space. They learn how to use basic kernel data structures, especially kernel linked list structures, which are used throughout the core components of the kernel. They learn how to handle bad input (e.g., invalid PID) or failed memory allocations in a graceful manner. Finally, in testing the code, students need to produce process trees of specific forms, e.g. flat, deep, or very large trees, which improves their knowledge about process creation mechanisms and process relationships.

Example assignment: system calls (2). Another example assignment is to have students write two different types of system calls, one that modifies the behavior of existing system calls and the other to understand how processes run. The first system call accepts two integer arguments used to set a maximum limit on the number of bytes that can be read or written in a single invocation of the *read* and *write* system calls. This can be useful for testing the correctness of a user-space program in handling unexpected behavior of *read* and *write* system calls. The second system call accepts two arguments–a buffer and its size–and fills the buffer with a sequence of records describing when the caller was scheduled to run. Each record indicates the start-time and end-time of a scheduling period. Records are reported only once, and data older than one minute is discarded to avoid memory pressure.

While the first example assignment provides more experience with manipulating process list structures, this assignment provides experience with modifying the kernel process structure. In this example assignment, both system calls require adding a new field to the process structure in the kernel. Students need to adjust process creation code to correctly inherit (or not) the new fields by a child process. The second system call also requires adjusting process termination for proper cleanup and provides students some insight into the notion of context-switches.

2.2 Synchronization

Synchronization mechanisms are at the heart of an operating system's ability to function safely and correctly in the presence of concurrent or interleaving access to shared state. The second kernel project teaches students about synchronization and race conditions by implementing new kernel synchronization primitives. Students are assumed to be able to write system calls and use kernel list structures from their experience with the first project.

The new primitive is a high level primitive to be implemented using Linux's basic synchronization building blocks. We aim to achieve two learning objectives. First, students will learn about and gain first-hand experience with the native basic kernel synchronization primitives such as spinlocks, atomic counters, and wait queues. This is useful not only for this assignment, but also for all of the following assignments. Second, students will become familiar with higher level synchronization concepts such as fairness and the thundering herd, instead of re-implementing an already existing mechanism in the kernel.

To further deepen students' understanding of the topic, we introduce in the assignments three additional twists that we feel are often overlooked in operating systems classes. First, we introduce the notion of reference counting for shared resources by designing the new synchronization primitive to have global scope so that it is visible to all processes. To protect the validity of the new primitive in the presence of concurrent create, access, and destroy operations, a solution must maintain a reference count for the primitive and allow an object to be released only by the last user. Second, we direct students to select appropriate kernel primitives to produce a solution that is *correct* and *efficient*, in this order. For instance, students should prefer a spinlock over a semaphore if and only if they do not expect the process that holds it to block (sleep) on it. Finally, on occasion it is useful to forbid the use of certain synchronization primitives, either to avoid trivializing the assignment, or to guide students toward a path to a solution.

Example assignment: synchronization (1). One example assignment is to have students implement a synchronization barrier primitive that allows multiple processes to block on an event until some other process triggers the event. When a process triggers the event, all processes that are blocked on the event are unblocked; the operation has no effect if no processes are blocked. This is accomplished with four new system calls: `eventopen` to create a new event and return an event identifier; `evenclose` to destroy an event and notify all blocked processes; `eventwait` to block on an event; and `eventsig` to unblock all processes waiting on an event. The scope of an event is system wide so that any process may access an event by its identifier.

In this assignment we encourage students to leverage the kernel *wait queue* primitive and to learn from the many existing examples in the kernel that show how to use it properly. We also remind students that a reference count must be used to protect against concurrent access, using either explicit synchronization or atomic types. Finally, students are required to write a test program for their code. The test program should show that the kernel functions work for the usual cases, for example, with one process waiting, and also for corner cases such as a call to `eventsig` with no processes or multiple processes waiting, multiple concurrent calls to create a new event, a call to `eventclose` when processes are waiting, and a call to `eventclose` that coincides with an `eventsig` or `eventwait` call to the same event instance.

Example assignment: synchronization (2). Another example assignment is to have students implement a user-space policy mutex mechanism. The mutex primitive is provided by the kernel, but the policy for deciding which task to run in case of contention is determined by a user-space daemon that picks the task that gets the mutex when available. This is accomplished with six new system calls: `mutex_open` to create a new mutex and return its identifier; `mutex_close` to close a mutex; `mutex_down` and `mutex_up` to grab and release the mutex, possibly blocking if already taken; `mutex_list` to fill a buffer with the list of all mutexes in the system and their waiters; and `mutex_grant` to grant a given task that waits for a mutex access. The latter two system calls are intended to be used by the user-space daemon. The scope of a mutex is system wide so that any process may open it by its name, but each task has its own set of mutex identifiers.

This example assignment introduces three additional elements compared to the previous example. First, because mutex identifiers are per process, the students learn about the idea of a descriptor table, conceptually similar to the file descriptor table. Furthermore, they combine skills from the assignment on system calls to implement this table as an extension to the in-kernel process structure, which reinforces their knowledge. Second, we restrict students to use only spinlocks and atomic counters, as using the native mutex primitive would trivialize the assignment. Finally, moving some functionality to user-space (specifically, the policy that determines the order in which waiting tasks gain access to a mutex) is useful for two reasons. First, working in user-space makes it easier to debug and experiment with different policies, e.g., to avoid the thundering herd effect. Second, through this split of functionality, students learn about the tradeoffs and possibilities in designing operating system interfaces and deciding on the boundary between the kernel and user-space.

2.3 Scheduling

Scheduling is a key concept crucial for an operating system to provide time-sharing and multitasking, while considering metrics such as throughput, response time, and fairness. The third kernel project teaches students about scheduling by having them modify the existing Linux kernel scheduler to add a new scheduling policy. Recent Linux kernels are particularly amenable to this approach because they provide a framework designed for adding new scheduling policies, as well as several existing scheduling policies which can be used as examples for implementing new scheduling policies.

The new scheduling policy can be any new policy, but we have several learning objectives to achieve. Students will learn about and gain first-hand experience with the structure of a kernel scheduler and how scheduling algorithms fit within the context of that structure. Students will learn how processes switch among different states of execution, such as sleeping, runnable, and running, and how those state transitions are handled as part of scheduler functions. Students will learn how multiple scheduling policies are typically supported by a common scheduling mechanism. Students will learn about what scheduling parameters can affect scheduling and how they are set or modified over time.

This is the first assignment that requires students to deal with a more substantial kernel subsystem, but the scheduler code is localized to just a few files and the assignment still only involves modification of only a relatively modest number of lines of kernel code. For simplicity, one can focus on uniprocessor scheduling policies to avoid the additional multiprocessor scheduling complexity of managing distributed processor queues and load balancing among them. The assignment builds on the previous two kernel programming projects as students need to write new system calls to control the scheduler and they need to be careful to protect kernel data structures with proper locking mechanisms.

Example assignment: scheduling (1). One example assignment is to have students implement a User-Weighted-Round-Robin (UWRR) scheduling policy. It operates by switching, round-robin, among users with runnable processes, giving each user a share of the CPU when it is that user's turn. The scheduler uses a hierarchical scheme to choose which process to run: first, a user is chosen, then, a process associated with that user is chosen. Each user has an associated weight that determines the proportional share allocation of that user. This scheduler was chosen both because it is easy to understand and implement, and because students can easily see why such a scheduling policy might be useful. It also does not cause starvation of processes if implemented correctly, making it easier for students to debug.

Example assignment: scheduling (2). Another example assignment is to have students implement a Container-Weighted-Round-Robin (CWRR) scheduling policy. It operates in a manner similiar to the UWRR scheduling policy, but with Linux containers being used as the grouping mechanism for processes instead of user identifiers. Process containers are a powerful isolation mechanism that is increasingly being included in production operating systems, so this assignment provides an opportunity for students to learn about this mechanism in the context of scheduling.

2.4 Virtual Memory

Virtual memory is another fundamental concept in operating systems. The fourth kernel project teaches students in detail about virtual memory and the paging system by having them implement mechanisms to measure and visualize how memory pages are managed and used, and then create programs that produce different memory access patterns.

We focus on measuring and visualizing how memory pages are managed and used, as opposed to implementing new virtual memory mechanisms. Because the virtual memory subsystem is typically the most complex part of the operating system, it can be difficult to cover any portion of it in any reasonable depth. We chose not to focus on relatively isolated parts of the virtual memory subsystem, such as memory allocators or the page replacement policy. Instead, we focus on mechanisms related to memory pages to cover a wider range of topics central to virtual memory including page table management, page faults, copy-on-write, and address translation as just a few examples. Implementing new virtual memory management mechanisms that cover these topics would be difficult for students to do in a reasonable amount of time for a production operating system. Our measurement mechanism approach focuses on students gaining working knowledge of the kernel's memory subsystem. Once students understand the stock kernel well, the implementation itself is fairly straightforward and requires under a few hundreds lines of new kernel code.

Example assignment: virtual memory (1). One example assignment is to have students implement a mechanism to visualize how memory pages are used by modifying the kernel so that the `/proc/[PID]/maps` file show additional information about pages in each memory region. For each memory region displayed we add a string that represents all the pages of that region, such that each page is denoted by a '.' if not present, a '1-9' for the page reference count if less than 10 if the page is present, or 'x' otherwise.

This assignment is useful because it helps students become thoroughly familiar with virtual memory concepts like the page table and paging, and process memory layout. To test their solutions, students must write user-space programs that generate memory regions with specific patterns, such as only not present pages ('......'), all pages with a given reference count ('222222'), and even arbitrary valid strings. By writing test programs that produce different memory usage behaviors, students gain further insight into virtual memory internals. Finally, we reinforce the knowledge by also requiring students to examine the output of `/proc/[PID]/maps` for common programs and explain the role of each region displayed (e.g., code, stack, heap), its page table mappings, and how that data differs between different programs.

Example assignment: virtual memory (2). Another example assignment is to have students implement a framework to track the *working set* of processes, and then add a new system call to report to user-space the data collected. The system call fills a user supplied buffer with records. Each record describes a single memory region and carries a bitmap of the pages accessed recently in that region. Regions without recently accessed pages are not reported. The system call then resets the monitored state to start collecting only new data.

One way to approach this assignment is to use the hardware access bit of the page table as an indication to whether a page was accessed. Because this flag is also used and reset by other functions in the kernel, students must study the related code and understand the implications of changes they introduce. For simplicity, students are allowed to ignore changes to address space layout such as due to mapping new memory regions, as long as their code does not crash. However, we do require students to identify the respective system calls and discuss the changes required to accommodate their effects, to raise students' awareness to this caveat.

Example assignment: virtual memory (3). Another example assignment is to have students implement a framework to track the *modified set* of processes. This is a variation of the previous example. The modified set is similar to the working set, but includes only pages that were modified, not just accessed. As before, students also add a system call to report the data collected to user-space and reset the monitored state.

Unlike before, using the hardware access bit of the page table is insufficient to track the modified set as it does not indicate whether a page is modified when accessed. Rather, students need to alter the page table of the process and convert all writable pages to be write-protected so that write accesses are intercepted. When a write-fault occurs, the kernel records the page address and restores the original protection of said page. By implementing this mechanism and writing test programs that produce write-faults, read-faults followed by writes, writes without faults, and copy-on-write faults, students experiment with and demonstrate knowledge about the page fault handler mechanism.

2.5 File Systems

Files are the other main abstraction other than processes that are managed by operating systems. As a fifth kernel project, we have students implement extensions to an existing file system code. This assignment requires students to gain practical understanding of how the virtual file system (VFS) infrastructure is designed, which is the key file system abstraction layer that every file system designer needs to understand. The project also gives students an opportunity to learn about the underlying file system realization of some VFS methods.

Disk-based file systems can be very complex, so we focus on implementing pseudo file systems. Pseudo file systems do not represent real, physical storage, but instead reside entirely in main memory and store files and directories that represent runtime information, such as `procfs`, `sysfs`, `ramfs`, and `devpts`, to name a few. Pseudo file systems make good candidates for pedagogic purposes: not only are they an effective platform to practice file system development, but they are also often used to report other kernel state and thus expose students to additional kernel mechanisms. To ease students into a successful solution we provide a skeleton implementation of a pseudo file system, saving the gory details of developing one from scratch.

Example assignment: file systems (1). One example assignment is to have students implement a pseudo file system to show the users currently running on a system, and the processes that they own. When mounted, the top level directory contains subdirectories that correspond to active users and are named after the respective user identifier. Each subdirectory holds two files: *"proc"* lists the processes of that user, and *"signal"* provides a way to signal all the processes of a given user in an atomic manner. In this way, students learn not only about file system principles, but also about users and groups. Moreover, a correct solution requires students to apply skills acquired from the second project on synchronization to manage race free access to shared objects.

Example assignment: file systems (2). Another example assignment is to have students implement a pseudo file system that gives information about the process hierarchy, by mirroring the tree structure. In this file system, directories correspond to processes and are named after the respective process's PID. Each directory holds one file *"status"* which contains select information about the process, and as many subdirectories as it has children. An advantage of this variation on the previous example is that it builds directly on skills and code developed in the first project on system calls and processes. By presenting an alternative mechanism to achieve the same goal, we illustrate the design options available to operating system builders, and foster comparisons between the two approaches in terms of usability and implementation difficulty.

3. EXPERIENCES

We have taught the introductory operating systems course at Columbia University using these Linux kernel projects for about a decade. Over a thousand students have taken this course. We assign five projects for a semester course, one project for each of the core topics: system calls and processes, synchronization, scheduling, virtual memory, and file systems. Students work in teams of two or three and are given two weeks to complete each project. We currently provide a VMware virtual appliance for doing the kernel project assignments, which can be easily deployed and run on students' personal computers without interfering with any existing software already on the students' computers. A distributed version control system is used to provide reliable storage for students' homework assignments, support students working together on group homework assignments, and manage the submission and grading of homework assignments. The experience of both students and instructors has been quite positive [4, 7].

An important consideration in designing the projects was to keep the coding complexity modest enough for groups of students with no prior experience with operating systems to successfully complete the projects with reasonable effort. To assess our approach in this aspect, we compared the size of our example solutions for a representative set of projects, to the average size of the students' solutions. The results are given in Table 1 in lines of code after stripping comments and blank lines. The results show that in all the projects,

Project	Example solution	Students' solutions
System calls and processes	146	164
Synchronization	353	465
Scheduling	399	389
Virtual Memory	66	63
File System	132	120

Table 1: Projects solutions sizes in lines-of-code

our proposed solution requires under 400 lines of code, and in nearly all cases students produce solutions of comparable size. The exception is the assignment on synchronization, where students produced more complicated solutions for the problem, with approximately 30% more lines of code on average. Producing an example solution in advance was an important step in the process of designing the specifics of assignments to estimate the expected complexity, and instrumental to ensure that it would be possible for students to complete with a reasonable limited amount of time coding.

It is also noteworthy to examine common errors encountered in the students' solutions as an indication to how students' knowledge and skills evolve as they proceed from one project to the next. For instance, two common mistakes in the first assignment on system calls were lack of input argument validation and incomplete error handling. However, they became notably less frequent in subsequent projects in which students had to repeatedly code additional system calls. Similarly, two common mistakes in the second assignment on synchronization were omitted locking around access to shared data and allowing a process to sleep while holding a spinlock. These errors became increasingly scarce later on, even though virtually all subsequent projects required repeated use of similar synchronization techniques. In this context, arranging the order of projects according to their dependencies is crucial to produce an effective framework for progressive learning.

Finally, although many students find kernel-level programming very difficult at first, they often say the work investment is warranted because they are learning a useful and applicable skill. We have received many comments from alumni who say the course turned out to be most useful course to them after graduation.

4. RELATED WORK

Courses that involve kernel-level projects with production operating systems have gained popularity in recent years; in 2005, 14% of the top 100 computer science schools reported using the Linux kernel in some form in their undergraduate operating systems course [1]. Nieh *et al* [6, 7] presents some early work on teaching operating systems by programming directly with the Linux kernel. Our work builds on this prior work and experience by describing a new, more structured series of Linux kernel projects with extensive examples for teaching core operating system concepts. Our work also leverages this prior work by using virtual machines to provide the necessary infrastructure to enable students to do kernel-level development.

Other Linux kernel projects have also been used for teaching. The SOFTICE [2] project advocates Linux Kernel Modules (LKM) to enhance students' hands-on experience. However, LKMs provide a narrow view of the kernel with a limited set of interfaces, and thus severely restrict the potential scope of projects. Lawson *et al* [5] describe one project in which students modify a custom Linux kernel designed to run on the iPod. Hess *et al* [3] describe some projects taught during six terms, with a course assessment. However, these projects lack structure and are suboptimal in that they may oversimplify a topic or focus on a simpler but tangential kernel component, degrading the utility of the assignment. We address these issues by providing guidelines and rationale for designing new projects to achieve specific learning objectives, as well as multiple examples from five core topics of operating system concepts. The examples are carefully chosen to meet the objectives and ease students incrementally into the world of kernel programming.

5. CONCLUSIONS

We have developed a structured series of Linux kernel projects for teaching operating system concepts. The projects progressively introduce students to core topics and major components of operating systems, namely system calls and processes, synchronization, scheduling, virtual memory, and file systems. At the same time, they implicitly teach students about various aspects of a real-world operating system and managing the code complexity of a large software system. The projects require students to understand and leverage core components of the operating system while keeping the coding complexity modest. We presented guidelines and rationale for designing new projects to achieve specific learning objectives, and provide examples of eleven different projects that can be used.

Our experiences teaching over a thousand students in the introductory operating systems course at Columbia University demonstrate the pedagogical value of these kernel projects in practice. We have shown that the designed coding complexity of the projects is achieved as example project solutions are each under 400 lines of code and students' submitted solutions on average fall within the same range. We have also shown that common programming errors in students' submitted solutions become notably less frequent in subsequent projects as later projects reinforce the concepts taught in earlier projects, demonstrating that the projects provide an effective framework for progressive learning.

6. ACKNOWLEDGMENTS

This work was supported in part by NSF grants CNS-0905246, CNS-0914845, and CNS-1018355.

7. REFERENCES

[1] C. L. Anderson and M. Nguyen. A Survey of Contemporary Instructional Operating Systems for Use in Undergraduate Courses. *Journal of Computing Sciences in Colleges*, 21(1):183–190, 2005.

[2] A. Gaspar and C. Godwin. Root-kits & Loadable Kernel Modules: Exploiting the Linux Kernel for Fun and (Educational) Profit. *Journal of Computer Sciences in Colleges*, 22(2):244–250, 2006.

[3] R. Hess and P. Paulson. Linux Kernel Projects for an Undergraduate Operating Systems Course. In *Proceedings of SIGCSE 2010*, Milwaukee, WI, Mar. 2010.

[4] O. Laadan, J. Nieh, and N. Viennot. Teaching Operating Systems Using Virtual Appliances and Distributed Version Control. In *Proceedings of SIGCSE 2010*, Milwaukee, WI, Mar. 2010.

[5] B. Lawson and L. Barnett. Using iPodLinux in an Introductory OS Course. In *Proceedings of SIGCSE 2008*, Portland, OR, Mar. 2008.

[6] J. Nieh and Özgür Can Leonard. Examining VMware. *Dr. Dobb's Journal*, pages 70–76, Aug. 2000.

[7] J. Nieh and C. Vaill. Experiences Teaching Operating Systems Using Virtual Platforms and Linux. In *Proceedings of SIGCSE 2005*, St. Louis, MO, Feb. 2005.

LINQ ROX! Integrating LINQ into the Database Curriculum

Suzanne W. Dietrich [1]
dietrich@asu.edu
[1]Division of Mathematical and Natural Sciences
Arizona State University
Phoenix, AZ 85069-7100

Mahesh Chaudhari [1,2]
mahesh.chaudhari@asu.edu
[2]School of Computing, Information, and Decision Systems Engineering
Arizona State University
Tempe, AZ 85287-8809

ABSTRACT
The Language INtegrated Query (LINQ) language is a declarative query language integrated within an object-oriented programming language that provides a unified paradigm for querying relations, objects, and XML (ROX). This paper describes a suite of exercises, from cooperative in-class activities to larger-scale graded assignments, for incorporating LINQ into the database curriculum. These exercises support various student learning outcomes and illustrate the applicability of LINQ by querying the same database enterprise across the ROX data models.

Categories and Subject Descriptors
H.2.3 [**Database Management**]: Languages – Query languages.

K.3.2 [**Computers and Education**]: Computer and Information Science Education – Computer science education.

General Terms
Languages

Keywords
Databases, Object Relational Mapping, LINQ, SQL, XML

1. INTRODUCTION
Today's applications typically require the integration of relational and XML data within an object-oriented programming language (OOPL). The interaction between the underlying OOPL and the data has typically been managed by providing a call-level interface, which has a specific application programming interface (API) that the programmer uses to orchestrate the interactions between the OOPL and the data using method calls and string representations of queries. Besides call-level interfaces, there are several object-relational mapping (ORM) approaches that introduce a layer of abstraction to integrate the OOPL and the relational database, such as the Java Persistence API (JPA) [20].

SIGCSE'11, March 9–12, 2011, Dallas, Texas, USA.

In an ORM, annotations within the class definition provide a mapping between the objects and relations. LINQ [6], which stands for Language INtegrated Query, is a declarative query language that is seamlessly integrated into object-oriented programming languages supported by the .NET Framework. LINQ is more than an ORM approach, since LINQ can query data stored as relations, objects, and XML (ROX).

Several questions may arise at this point. Does LINQ replace SQL? No. LINQ works with the industry-standard SQL. LINQ queries over relational data sources are automatically converted to SQL by the underlying framework. Is LINQ a fad? No. LINQ bridges the gap between databases and OOPLs. LINQ promises to be successful based on its underlying formalism of functional programming and its extensibility to define query providers. What about LINQ being proprietary to Microsoft technologies? Besides the (default) query providers that allow LINQ to query objects, relations, and XML, third parties are already building query providers for LINQ to query: Amazon [16], Google, mySQL, PostgreSQL, and Oracle [6]. Also, LINQ has been successfully used in applications developed in a UNIX-based operating system using the Mono [19] library, which is an open-source implementation of the .NET framework for building cross-platform applications.

There has been some literature describing the use of LINQ as an object query language in a database course [10] and as a gentle introduction to XML and databases [11]. The goal of this paper is to describe the experience with various exercises across the ROX paradigms to illustrate how LINQ may be incorporated into an already crowded database curriculum [2]. The LINQ framework is briefly introduced in Section 2 along with the database enterprise. Sections 3 through 5 describe the various exercises and learning outcomes for LINQ to Objects, LINQ to SQL, and LINQ to XML, respectively. These exercises range from cooperative in-class activities to larger-scale graded assignments and can be tailored by the database educator to fit their needs. These exercises have been incorporated across various courses in a database curriculum, and a discussion of this LINQ experience concludes the paper in Section 6.

2. LINQ OVERVIEW
LINQ's integration into imperative languages (e.g., C# and Visual Basic) of the .NET Framework 3.5 is based on a framework of language extensions, which include implicitly typed local

variables, extension methods, object initializers, anonymous types, and lambda expressions.

The paper uses the EMPLOYEE TRAINING enterprise from [9] as a scenario to illustrate the use of LINQ over ROX. The enterprise maintains a record of the training courses taken by employees. Each training course is associated with one technology area, and a technology area has a designated employee as a leader. Figure 1 provides a corresponding UML class diagram. The Takes class represents an association class, storing the date that an Employee took the TrainingCourse. The representation of Takes as a reified association facilitates the discussion of the enterprise across all three data models.

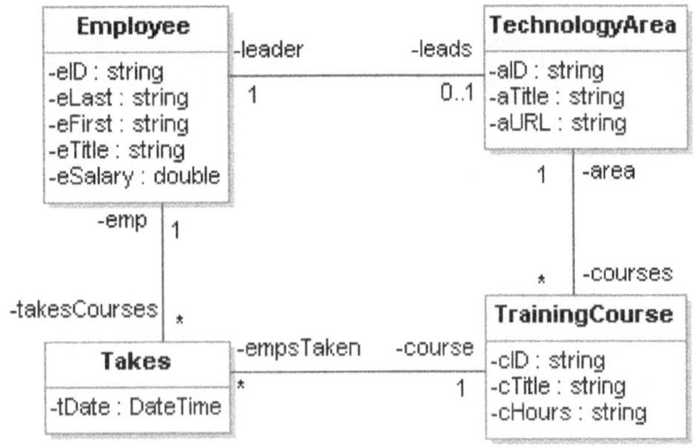

Figure 1. Employee Training UML Class Diagram

As an example, consider the following LINQ query expression that returns employees who earn more than $75,000, displaying the result in descending order by salary:

```
var empsMoreThan75K =
   from e in employees
   where e.eSalary > 75000
   orderby e.eSalary descending
   select new { salary = e.eSalary,
                name  = e.eLast + ", " + e.eFirst,
                title  = e.eTitle };
```

This query illustrates the query comprehension syntax of LINQ that resembles SQL clauses, although the order of the clauses corresponds to the underlying evaluation. The var keyword allows the declaration of implicitly typed variables whose type is derived from the LINQ query expression. The select clause in the above example illustrates the use of anonymous types and object initialization, since the type returned is created on the fly and this anonymous type is initialized using the *by name* object initialization feature.

The query comprehension syntax is converted to the underlying functional extension method syntax, where the familiar SQL keywords are implemented as extension methods. An extension method is a static method of another class that can be called as an instance method of the class itself. The extension method syntax for the above LINQ query is:

```
employees
  .Where(e => (e.eSalary>75000))
  .OrderByDescending(e => e.eSalary)
  .Select(e => new { salary = e.eSalary,
                     name  = ((e.eLast + ", ") + e.eFirst),
                     title   = e.eTitle } )
```

C# uses the => syntax for lambda expressions that allow for the passing of parameters to anonymous functions, such as passing the employee to the anonymous filtering predicate in the Where extension method. The full details of LINQ are beyond the scope of this paper. Readers are referred to papers for database educators [10] and books [6, 16] for more information. However, there are sample LINQ queries used throughout the presented exercises that will provide additional insight into the LINQ language.

For all of the exercises presented in the following sections, the free LINQPad tool [4] provides a formative environment for students to learn and use LINQ. LINQPad provides a lightweight interactive development environment for students to experiment with LINQ in C# (as an alternative to using Visual Studio). LINQPad also supports all three ROX paradigms for querying in LINQ. (Sample files are made available on the author's Web site.)

3. LINQ TO OBJECTS

Learning outcomes for coverage of object-oriented databases (OODB) usually include the implementation of an inherently object-oriented enterprise using an OODB. A typical approach is to have students use in-memory objects first and then to extend the assignment to a persistent OODB, such as the open-source db4o database [8].

Once the classes have been implemented and verified with the conceptual model, the database must be populated. Using the object initialization feature, properties can be initialized *by name* rather than *by position* as with a typical constructor:

```
var emp111 = new Employee { eID = "emp111", ... };
var emp321 = new Employee { eID = "emp321", ... };
var dbArea = new TechnologyArea { aTitle = "Database", ... };
```

In OODBs, there is usually a mechanism to refer to the collection of objects of a particular type, known as an *extent*, to facilitate querying the database. For an in-memory implementation, an employees extent can be defined using an array:

```
Employee[] employees = { emp111, emp321, ... };
```

For a persistent OODB implementation, there is no need to create an extent as the database automatically provides this capability. Assuming that the variable db references a db4o database, the Set method stores the object in the database (e.g., db.Store(emp111)), and the Query method retrieves objects from the database (e.g., db.Query<Employee>() retrieves all Employee objects). To provide a name for the extent, a simple LINQ query can be posed:

```
var employees =  from e in db.Query<Employee>() select e;
```

Once the database is populated, the database instance should be validated. In SQL, the primary key, unique, not null, and referential integrity constraints are specified as part of the DDL. In an OODB, the data definition language is the programming language, and OOPLs do not inherently support all of these database constraints. Before the DDL was added to the SQL standard in 1992, these constraints were verified using queries over the relational database. Similarly, the students can write LINQ queries to verify these constraints on an OODB. Figure 2 provides a sample collection of validation rules for the employees extent that extends an example found on the Web [5]. The original example validated one employee for non-null and non-empty strings as well as constraints on numeric fields. Figure 2 also illustrates primary key/uniqueness, participation, and cardinality constraints. The variable invalidEmployees returns a collection of Employee instances that do not satisfy all of the validation rules.

```
Func<Employee, bool>[] validEmployeeRules =
{
// String not null validation: repeat for each String
  e => !String.IsNullOrEmpty(e.eID), ...
// not null: repeat for each required reference property
// participation is not required in leads or takesCourses
// validate numeric values
  e => e.eSalary > 0,
// uniqueness constraint
  e => (from Employee emp in employees
          where emp.eID == e.eID
          select emp).Count()==1,
// Verify instance of 1:1 relationship
   e => e.leads == null || e.leads.leader == e,  // lazy evaluation
// Verify instance of M:1 relationship
   e => (from Takes t in e.takesCourses
          select t.emp).All(te => te == e)
};

var invalidEmployees =
  from Employee e in employees
  where !validEmployeeRules.All(rule => rule(e))
  select e;
```

Figure 2. Validation Rules for Employees

The primary key or uniqueness constraint verifies that there is only one Employee object with the eID of the employee e by checking that the count of objects with that eID is 1. Referential integrity constraints are inherent in the specification of the underlying object model. For example, the leader property for the TechnologyArea is a reference to an Employee. For required or total participation in an association, a validation rule checks that a property is not null, such as the leader property for TechnologyArea.

The validation of the enterprise includes the verification that the associations are populated correctly. The Employee validation rules include checking 1:1 and M:1 associations. The leads 1:1 association check uses lazy evaluation to verify that if an employee leads a TechnologyArea then the leader of the TechnologyArea must be that employee. The takesCourses property verification checks that all Takes objects indicating the courses that an employee has taken are linked back to that employee. For a 1:M association, consider that a TrainingCourse is in one TechnologyArea and that a TechnologyArea has many TrainingCourses. To verify that population, check that the TrainingCourse c is in the set of courses associated with its TechnologyArea:

```
c => (from TrainingCourse tc in c.area.courses
        select tc).Contains(c)
```

To verify a direct M:N association, which does not exist in this EMPLOYEE TRAINING enterprise (the M:N between Employee and TrainingCourse uses Takes as an association class to store the date attribute of the association), consider an association between customers and bank accounts in a fictitious bank enterprise. The following checks that an account a is contained in the collection of accounts for each owner of the account:

```
a => (from Customer c  in a.owners  select c).All(cust =>
        (from Account acct in cust.accounts select acct).Contains(a))
```

Once the database instance has been validated, the students can be given query specifications to answer over the OODB. An important aspect of the queries is to require a nested (non-1NF) result so that students can be exposed to non-relational results.

Before using LINQ, the object database curriculum necessarily had more of an emphasis on OOPLs, since the OOPL is the language used to define, populate, validate, and query the database. With the introduction of LINQ and the availability of the LINQPad tool for formative feedback, students now have the opportunity to more easily experience a declarative query language for objects, since the OQL standard [7] was only available in research prototypes. Now the OODB coverage emphasizes the declarative features of LINQ for validation and querying, and student projects use LINQ as a declarative query language with the db4o OODB.

If there is not enough time to have the students implement the scenario and the learning outcome is to query an OODB using LINQ, a verified implementation and population of main memory objects can be given to the students as the basis for querying. The implementation of the classes can be supplied as a dll file, and a LINQ file provided for population and verification. Students can then be given a short assignment to answer queries over objects in main memory to explore the LINQ language.

LINQ can also be explored in the context of LINQ to SQL, where the from clause iterates over the tuples of a table.

4. LINQ TO SQL

Since OOPLs are used to implement today's applications, it is important for students to experience an ORM approach to querying relational databases as a learning outcome for an advanced database course. LINQ to SQL is an ORM approach that can be viewed as automatically creating wrapper objects for the relations and allowing for the attributes to be referenced using dot notation.

Students in a typical database course will have an assignment to query a relational database in SQL to answer various types of queries, involving select-project-join (SPJ), negation, aggregation (count, min, max, sum, avg), grouping, and division. These same queries can be used in a companion LINQ assignment. Figure 3 gives the relational schema for the EMPLOYEE TRAINING enterprise, and Figure 4 shows LINQ queries for such an assignment [9]. These queries illustrate various features of LINQ including existential (Any) and universal (All) quantifiers, join, grouping, returning a single element (Single), and Contains.

employee(eID, eLast, eFirst, eTitle, eSalary)
technologyArea(aID, aTitle, aURL, aLeadID)
trainingCourse(cID, cTitle, cHours, areaID)
takes(eID, cID, tYear, tMonth, tDay)

Figure 3. Relational Schema for Employee Training

LINQ to SQL provides a mechanism to retrieve the SQL equivalent to the LINQ query. For example, the SQL equivalent generated for the employeesWithMinSalary query shown in Figure 4 is given here with minor renaming of aliases and formatting changes to improve readability:

```
SELECT    e.eID, e.eLast, e.eFirst, e.eTitle, e.eSalary
FROM      employee AS e
WHERE     e.eSalary = (( SELECT min(m.eSalary)
                         FROM employee AS m ))
```

```
var dbTrainingCourses =
  from c in trainingCourse
  where c.areaID == (from a in technologyArea
                     where a.aTitle == "Database"
                     select a.aID).Single()
  select new {c.cID, c.cTitle, c.cHours};

var empsWhoTookDatabaseCourses =
  from e in employee
  where takes.Any(t => t.eID == e.eID &&
             dbTrainingCourses.Any(db => db.cID == t.cID))
  select new {e.eID, e.eLast, e.eFirst, e.eTitle};

var empsWhoDidNotTakeAnyCourses =
  from e in employee
  where !takes.Any(t => t.eID == e.eID)
  select new {e.eID, e.eLast, e.eFirst, e.eTitle};

var empsWhoTookCoursesInMultipleTechnologyAreas=
  from e in employee
  join t in takes on e.eID equals t.eID
  join c in trainingCourse on t.cID equals c.cID
  group c.areaID by e into g
  where g.Distinct().Count() > 1
  select g.Key;

var employeesWithMinSalary =
  from e in employee
  where e.eSalary == employee.Min(m => m.eSalary)
  select e;

var empsWhoTookAllDBCourses =
  from e in employee
  where dbTrainingCourses.All(db =>
         (from t in takes
          where t.eID == e.eID
          select t.cID).Contains(db.cID))
  select e;
```

Figure 4. LINQ to SQL Queries

Students can be asked to compare and contrast their SQL solution to their LINQ solution and then to the equivalent SQL. This provides students with an opportunity to practice necessary skills of reading queries and reflecting on the various solutions. A cooperative group exercise can extend the learning outcomes to include query optimization by discussing the relative performance of various approaches to evaluating the query.

5. LINQ TO XML

Learning outcomes for an XML and database course typically include the examination of the features of XML-enabled relational databases and the definition, transformation, and querying of XML data.

Most relational database products support an XML type and the ability to return a query result in XML format. A hands-on exercise for the students would be to compare and contrast this capability for well-known database products, such as Oracle and SQL Server, with the capability provided by LINQ.

Figure 5 shows a desired XML result for a query over relational data that finds employees earning the minimum salary using queries expressed in LINQ, Oracle, and SQL Server. Due to space limitations, the details of the established Oracle and SQL Server approaches cannot be discussed in detail. However, LINQ uses a functional construction approach to construct the elements and attributes, typically as part of the select clause, using XElement and XAttribute constructors. Each constructor takes a name as the first argument and the value as the second argument. Students have found LINQ easier to use to return results in XML format than Oracle or SQL Server due to their familiarity with SQL and the new operator in OOPLs.

Additional assignments can be given to write queries involving nesting of the resulting XML for various types of queries as a basis for a comparison of the XML construction capabilities of queries using LINQ, SQL/XML, and FOR XML. The resulting XML can be used in subsequent assignments to explore LINQ queries over XML data where the from clause iterates over a collection of elements.

XML Result

```
<minSalaryEmployees minSalary="36369.00">
  <employee>
    <name>First369 Last369</name>
    <title>Software Engineer</title>
  </employee>
</minSalaryEmployees>
```

LINQ to SQL

```
var minEmpSalary = employee.Min(e => e.eSalary);

var minSalaryEmployees =
  new XElement("minSalaryEmployees",
    new XAttribute("minSalary", minEmpSalary),
    from e in employee
    where e.eSalary == minEmpSalary
    select new XElement("employee",
               new XElement("name", e.eFirst + " " + e.eLast),
               new XElement("title", e.eTitle)));
```

Oracle using SQL/XML

```
select xmlelement("minSalaryEmployees",
         xmlattributes(min(e.eSalary) as "minSalary"),
         xmlagg(xmlelement("employee",
           xmlforest(e.eFirst || ' ' || e.eLast as "name",
                     e.eTitle as "title"))))
  from employee e
  where e.eSalary = (select min(eSalary) from employee);
```

SQL Server FOR XML clause

```
select (select min(eSalary) from employee) as "@minSalary",
   (select e.eFirst + ' ' + e.eLast as "name",
           e.eTitle as "title"
    from employee e
    where e.eSalary = (select min(eSalary) from employee)
    for xml path('employee'), type)
for xml path('minSalaryEmployees');
```

Figure 5. XML Results in LINQ, Oracle & SQL Server

The LINQ query in Figure 5 illustrates the use of the XElement type in the creation of an XML element. The XElement type also provides methods to load and navigate XML data, which are used in LINQ to XML queries.

Initially, the XML data is loaded into main memory using the Load method:

```
XElement empDB = XElement.Load(@"empTraining.xml");
```

In this example, the empTraining.xml data is assumed to be in an element-based representation of the employee table where each relational attribute is an element in the XML, which is nested within an enclosing element for each tuple:

```
<employeeTable>
    <employee>
      <eID>111</eID>
      <eLast>Last111</eLast>
      <eFirst>First111</eFirst>
      <eTitle>Database Administrator</eTitle>
      <eSalary>75111</eSalary>
    </employee>
    ...
  </employeeTable>
```

Once the XML data is loaded, the collection of elements for the from clause in the LINQ query can be obtained using the Elements or Descendants methods of the XElement type. These methods provide access to the immediate children or descendants, respectively. For example, a LINQ query can define a named extent employees to retrieve the descendant nodes with the name employee:

```
var employees = empDB.Descendants("employee");
```

The Element method provides access to a named element of a node, and is necessary when using untyped XML. (If you have typed XML with an associated XSD, LINQ uses dot notation to access the element.) Figure 6 provides a corresponding LINQ query over XML data that finds the employees with the minimum salary as in Figure 5 for LINQ to SQL. In untyped XML, the element values are considered to be text. The syntax, (int) e.Element("eSalary"), casts the value of the eSalary attribute to an integer. Figure 6 also shows the corresponding XQuery. Students can explore the query capabilities of LINQ and XQuery through an assignment with various queries that provide a basis for comparison of the XML query languages. LINQ can also be used as an introduction to querying (and transforming) XML [11].

LINQ to XML

```
var minEmpSalary =
  (from e in employees
   select (int) e.Element("eSalary")).Min();

var minSalaryEmployees =
  new XElement("minSalaryEmployees",
      new XAttribute("minSalary", minEmpSalary),
    from e in employees
    where (int) e.Element("eSalary") == minEmpSalary
    select new XElement("employee",
             new XElement("name", e.Element("eFirst").Value + " "
                                  + e.Element("eLast").Value),
               new XElement("title", e.Element("eTitle").Value)));
```

XQuery

```
let $minEmpSalary := min(//employee/eSalary)
return
  <minSalaryEmployees minSalary = "{$minEmpSalary}">
  {
   for $e in //employee
   where $e/eSalary = $minEmpSalary
   return
    <employee>
     <name> {data($e/eFirst)} &#32; {data($e/eLast) } </name>
     <title> {data($e/eTitle)} </title>
    </employee>
  }
  </minSalaryEmployees>
```

Figure 6. LINQ to XML and XQuery

6. DISCUSSION

LINQ provides a solution to the ROX impedance mismatch, where fundamentally different data models of relations, objects, and XML are typically used in the different tiers (data, business, presentation) of a three-tier distributed architecture. LINQ is based on a theoretical foundation of functional programming [17] and through this formalism is able to unify programming against the disparate ROX data models.

This paper has provided a suite of exercises for integrating LINQ within the database curriculum, as part of the broader impact of a grant in which the LINQ framework is used to explore several research issues within a heterogeneous distributed system. These LINQ exercises have been used in various database courses by the author, although only a brief introduction to LINQ is possible in the first database course due to time constraints. There are more opportunities to explore LINQ in an advanced database class. The specific topics covered in such a course appear to vary widely but may include databases and the Web, object databases, and XML [12] as well as data warehousing and mining [18]. Due to small class sizes, a formal assessment of this LINQ integration is difficult. However, the introduction of LINQ appears promising. Students in the advanced database class appear to learn LINQ quickly, typically in one class session. The comparison exercises of LINQ with the generated SQL equivalent query provide valuable insight into SQL for the students, especially for queries that result in the use of grouping or temporary tables in the underlying SQL. When covering LINQ to XML, the students apply LINQ handily to XML based on their familiarity with SQL and the new operator from OOPLs. Since LINQ's from-let-where-orderby-select syntax resembles XQuery's FLWOR expression, students appear to understand XQuery more quickly if they already know LINQ. When covering object databases, the ability to provide hands-on querying with LINQ is essential, since OQL was never implemented in a commercial product. Since LINQ is relevant across all three data models, this wide applicability should provide various opportunities for database educators to introduce LINQ in their classes.

Another challenge that educators can take on is the integration of LINQ outside of the database curriculum. A programming language course for computer science majors usually exposes students to rule-based and functional programming. This course may use Haskell, LISP, ML or Scheme as the representative functional programming language. One idea is to use LINQ to expose students to functional programming concepts, industry practice, and database technology all at the same time. This goal is compatible with CS Curriculum 2008 [1] that adds a requirement of exposure to different programming paradigms.

The impact of LINQ is still in its infancy. There are several visions for LINQ in both industry and research. LINQ is being evaluated by the Object Database Technology Group at OMG for its potential in the new Object Database standard [22]. Also, the latest research directions for databases [3] include declarative programming languages and the report specifically mentions LINQ as one of the languages. There has been much earlier work on the integration of declarative query languages with object-oriented languages, known as deductive object-oriented databases (DOOD) [21]. One such effort led to a product known as Validity [14], which was not widely adopted. However, LINQ is integrated into multiple, popular OOPLs, and is more likely to be successful.

Another vision is that LINQ will provide a bridge between database developers and programmers by improving developer productivity through its declarative paradigm and ease of use for rapid prototyping. However, there are always trade-offs. Although LINQ is declarative, a developer must still be aware of its underlying implementation for performance and security considerations [16]. Typically, LINQ to SQL is used for rapid prototyping and testing the application with a SQL Server database, and LINQ to Entities is used to deploy the application in a production environment that may integrate a variety of databases [13].

Why is LINQ important? LINQ brings the advantages of declarative querying from established database technology to object-oriented programming. The declarative language describes the properties of the information to be retrieved rather than procedurally specifying how to retrieve it. The database system infers the type of the query result from the specification. One may be able to envision an analogy between the importance of LINQ and the importance of databases. Why are databases important? Databases provide a useful tool for efficient, shared access to persistent data for many enterprises, providing a higher-level of abstraction than writing a storage system from scratch using files. Similarly, LINQ provides a higher level of abstraction for querying across the ROX data models. This enables the developer to use LINQ as a tool, unifying the three paradigms that are integrated within the same application or across the enterprise. Instead of integrating the technologies by calling numerous methods over disparate APIs, the LINQ framework provides a declarative language and determines how to execute the query. Just as databases are not always a viable solution due to the associated overhead, the applicability of LINQ as a solution should similarly be considered.

The experience with using LINQ within a database curriculum has been a positive one, supporting the learning outcomes presented for each exercise. The use of LINQ may also support program outcomes by exposing students to functional programming. The use of the free, lightweight LINQPad IDE provides a straightforward formative environment for students to experiment with LINQ. Graduating students are receiving employment in industry positions that utilize LINQ. LINQ is also being explored in database research [15]. LINQ's acceptance by both industry and research strongly motivates its inclusion in the database curriculum.

7. ACKNOWLEDGMENTS

This material is based upon work supported by the NSF under Grant No. CSR-0915325.

8. REFERENCES

1. ACM/IEEE-CS Interim Review Task Force. 2008. Computing Science Curriculum 2008: An Interim Revision of CS 2001. ACM and the IEEE Press.
2. Adams, E. S., Granger, M., Goelman, D., and Ricardo, C. 2004. Managing the Introductory Database Course: What goes in and What comes out? *Proc. SIGCSE Technical Symposium on Computer Science Education.* pp. 497-498.
3. Agrawal, R. et al. 2009. The Claremont Report on Database Research. *Commun. ACM.* 52, 6, June 2009. pp. 56-65.
4. Albahari, J. 2010. LINQPad. http://www.linqpad.net. Retrieved 9 Sep 2010.
5. Anonymous. 2008. The Standard LINQ Operators. http://www.odetocode.com/Articles/739.aspx. Retrieved 9 Sep 2010.
6. Calvert, C. and Kulkarni, D. 2009. *Essential LINQ*. Addison-Wesley Professional.
7. Cattell, R. et al (ed.). 2000. *The Object Data Standard ODMG 3.0*. Morgan Kaufmann.
8. Db4objects by Versant. 2010. http://www.db4o.com/. Retrieved 9 Sep 2010.
9. Dietrich, S. W. 2001. *Understanding Relational Database Query Languages*. Prentice Hall.
10. Dietrich, S. W. and Chaudhari, M. 2009. The Missing LINQ between Databases and Object-Oriented Programming: LINQ as an Object Query Language for a Database Course. *Journal of Computing in Small Colleges*. Volume 24, Number 4. pp. 282-288.
11. Dietrich, S. W. and Chaudhari, M. 2010. The LINQ between XML and Databases: A Gentle Introduction. *Journal of Computing in Small Colleges*. Volume 25, Number 4. pp. 158-164.
12. Dietrich, S. W., Urban, S. D. and Haag, S. 2008. Developing Advanced Courses for Undergraduates: A Case Study in Databases. *IEEE Transactions on Education*. Volume 51, Issue 1. pp. 138-144.
13. Dot Com Infoway. 2010. LINQ to SQL vs. ADO.NET Entity Framework. http://www.dotcominfoway.com/blog/linq-to-sql-vs-ado-net-entity-framework. Retrieved 9 Sep 2010.
14. Friesen, O., Lefebvre, A., and Vieille, L. 1996. VALIDITY: Applications of a DOOD System. *In Proceedings of Extending Database Technology*. pp. 131-134.
15. Grust, T., Mayr, M., Rittinger, J., and Schreiber, T. 2009. FERRY: Database-supported Program Execution. *In Proc of the 35th SIGMOD international Conference on Management of Data*. pp. 1063-1066.
16. Marguerie, F., Eichert, S. and Wooley, J. 2008. *LINQ in Action*. Manning. 2008.
17. Meijer, E. 2007. Confessions of a Used Programming Language Salesman: Getting the Masses Hooked on Haskell. *OOPSLA*. pp. 677-694.
18. Murray, M. and Guimaraes, M. 2008. Expanding the Database Curriculum. *Journal of Computing in Small Colleges*. Volume 23, Number 3. pp. 69-75.
19. Novell. 2010. Mono. http://www.mono-project.com/, Retrieved 9 Sep 2010.
20. Oracle Sun Developer Network. 2007. Java Persistence API. http://java.sun.com/developer/technicalArticles/J2SE/Desktop/persistenceapi/. Retrieved 9 Sep 2010.
21. Sampaio, P. R. F. and Paton, N. M. 1997. Deductive Object-oriented Database Systems: A Survey. *Proc. of Rules in Database Systems*. pp. 1-19.
22. Zicari, R. ed. 2008. Object Database Systems: Quo vadis? http://www.odbms.org/blog/2008/05/object-database-systems-quo-vadis/. Retrieved 9 Sep 2010.

Using a Student Response System in CS1 and CS2

A.T. Chamillard
Computer Science Department
University of Colorado at Colorado Springs
Colorado Springs, CO 80933-7150
719-255-3150
chamillard@cs.uccs.edu

ABSTRACT

Professors are continually exploring ways to increase the engagement of their students, but are sometimes concerned that doing "fun" things in class could adversely affect student learning. Over the course of several semesters, we had the same professor teach several CS1 and CS2 courses for computer science and game development majors. As part of his classroom approach, the professor used a student response system to engage the students in the flow of the lecture. In this paper, we examine the relationships between student participation using the student response system and student performance in the course assessments. We also explore the relationship between each student's perceived mastery of course topics and their demonstrated mastery of those topics on the Final Exam. Finally, we explore several differences between the multiple courses included in the study.

Categories and Subject Descriptors

K.3.2 [**Computers and Education**]: Computer and Information Science Education – *computer science education, self-assessment.*

General Terms

Engagement, Measurement, Performance, Experimentation.

Keywords

Student response system, student performance, student engagement, computer science curriculum.

1. INTRODUCTION

Trying to find ways to engage students in course lectures and other course activities can be a challenging endeavor. As educators, we want to ensure that including "fun" class activities designed to increase student engagement do not have a negative effect on actual student learning. In this paper, we discuss the integration of one engaging technology – a student response system – into several CS1 and CS2 courses. We examine the relationships between student participation with that system and student performance on course assessments, and we also use the collected data to study how well the students' perceived understanding of particular course topics corresponds to their assessed understanding of those topics.

The University of Colorado at Colorado Springs (UCCS) has offered a computer science degree since the early 1980s. CS 115, Principles of Computer Science, is the CS1 course required of all computer science, computer engineering, and mathematics majors. In Fall 2007, UCCS began offering a Bachelor of Innovation™ in Game Design and Development (GDD). GDD 120, Introductory Programming for Game Developers, is the CS1 course required of all GDD majors. GDD 220, Data Structures and Algorithms for Game Developers, is the CS2 course required of all GDD majors.

We offer distinct CS1 and CS2 courses for the CS and GDD majors because of language differences (Java vs. C#), the desire to use XNA Game Studio in the GDD courses (which requires C#), and the desire to use game development examples as an integral component of the GDD courses.

Over the course of the study reported here, which includes the Fall 2007, Spring 2008, and Fall 2008 semesters, the same professor taught three sections of CS 115, one section of GDD 120, and one section of GDD 220. In all these classes, we used the i>clicker student response system [6].

The i>clicker student response system, like many such systems, let's the students in the class participate in class activities using a device much like a simple television remote. A receiver station attached to the professor computer through a USB connection receives the student responses, with the i>clicker software archiving the student responses and summarizing those responses for immediate examination. A response device and the receiver station are shown in Figure 1. This is a portable and easy-to-use configuration that lets us avoid some of the technological problems that can arise using response systems [11].

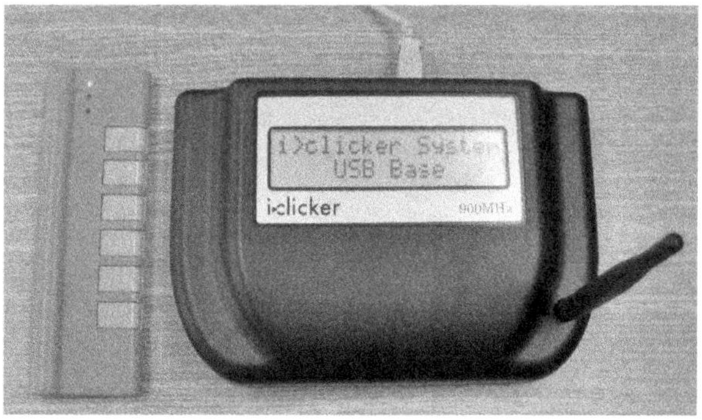

Figure 1. i>clicker System

SIGCSE'11, March 9–12, 2011, Dallas, Texas, USA.

Student response systems can be used in a variety of ways: to take attendance, to quiz students on their understanding of particular key lecture points, to simply keep students engaged during the class period, and even to assign programming pairs for lab assignments. As we integrated this technology into these courses, we were curious about the relationships between each student's participation using the student response system and that student's performance on key course assessments.

We believe this paper provides two significant contributions to computer science educators. First, our analysis results indicate a strong, consistent relationship between student participation using a student response system and student performance on course assessments, leading us to recommend that others consider this approach. Second, our analysis indicates a significant lack of student ability to self-assess their mastery of course topics, yielding a suggestion that professors help students work on their self-assessment skills.

The following sections examine related work in this area, describe the composition of our analysis dataset, discuss our analysis results for a variety of questions, and present our conclusions.

2. RELATED WORK

There is a growing body of literature discussing the use of student response systems in the classroom, including reviews of that literature [7] discussing the benefits and challenges associated with this technology. Only 6 of the 67 papers included in the cited literature review addressed using student response systems in "mathematics or computer science," so continued study in the computer science domain seems warranted; we do note, however, that the reviewed literature excluded conference publications, a significant outlet for computer science education research. Although the reviewed literature generally showed a positive impact on student learning, we note that some studies have shown no statistically significant effect from using clickers [12]. Numerous of the reviewed studies indicated the positive effects of having students actively engage in the learning process through use of this technology; active student engagement was our primary goal for integrating this approach into our courses.

Numerous educators have reported on their experiences using student responses systems, laptops, tablets, and other mobile devices in the classroom [1, 3, 4, 5, 9, 13, 15] or have hypothesized effective scenarios for using such systems [14, 18]. The student response system approach has even been used in distance education to implement a response system for 23 geographically-separated classrooms [17].

While we recognize that there are deeper possibilities for integrating these systems into the learning process, we chose an approach in which the system is used as an engagement tool rather than (directly) as a learning one. This is in direct contrast to the proposed uses presented by some authors [9]. We also note that student response to the use of clickers in a wide range of classes is generally positive [8, 16].

Cutts and Kennedy [3] found that a higher number of responses from a student indicated higher course assessment performance for that student independent of the correctness of the responses; the results reported below are consistent with that observation, though Cutts and Kennedy focus most of their discussion on the effects of using the technology to support a formal learning cycle rather than quantitative analysis of their results. Although some universities have pursued system-wide deployment of student response systems [10], UCCS has a variety of different systems in use at this time, with a small minority of instructors using them.

3. DATASET

In this section we discuss the characteristics of our analysis dataset. For all the courses in the study, we only included the students who completed the course; students who dropped a course during the semester are not included in the dataset.

The Spring 2008 offering of CS 115 included 30 students in a wide range of majors. Although only two of the students were officially computer science majors, preengineering students comprised 13 (43.3%) of the students in the class; students who are pursuing an engineering degree but do not meet all the engineering entrance requirements (typically in math and science) are designated as preengineering majors until they clear those requirements at UCCS. Although it is not possible to know exactly which major these students are pursuing, 41% of the survey respondents for the anonymous end-of-semester survey indicated computer science as their major. It is therefore reasonable to assume that approximately 12 of the students in that class were computer science majors. Other majors included computer engineering (5 students), electrical engineering (2 students), and a variety of other majors. The Fall 2007 offering of CS 115 included 30 students with 9 computer science majors, 8 computer engineering majors, and various other majors. The Fall 2008 offering of CS 115 included 12 students with a distribution of majors similar to that in Spring 2008. There are 72 students in the combined set of all CS 115 students included in the study.

The Spring 2008 offering of GDD 120 included 34 students. 20 of those students were officially game development majors, with an additional 8 students designated as preengineering students. The majority of the preengineering students reported that they were also planning to pursue the game development degree.

The Fall 2008 offering of GDD 220 included 17 students. Because GDD 120 is a prerequisite for GDD 220, the majors for those students are similar to those for the GDD 120 course.

4. PARTICIPATION AND PERFORMANCE

In this section we discuss our analysis of the relationships between student participation and student performance on course assessments. Student participation is measured as a percentage calculated as the number of class sessions in which the student provided i>clicker responses throughout the semester divided by the total number of class sessions in which i>clicker questions were asked throughout the semester. Details of the course assessments are discussed in the analysis sections for each course.

In the classes included in this study, 10% of a student's grade was based on class participation. Participation extends beyond mere attendance for the lectures, because the students are required to respond to i>clicker questions throughout each lecture. While it is possible to use the i>clicker software to identify the correct answer to each question and only give "credit" to students who answer the question correctly, we took a different approach. Because our primary goal is to merely encourage participation, any response counts. That actually opens up interesting possibilities for amusement during the lecture as students (often)

Table 1. Statistically-Significant Correlations

Course Assessment	CS 115, Fall 2007	CS 115, Spring 2008	CS 115, Fall 2008	GDD 120, Spring 2008
Homework Assignments	0.71**	0.68**	0.66*	0.68**
Lab Assignments	0.80**	0.88**	0.88**	0.66**
Programming Assignments	0.81**	N/A	N/A	0.54**
Lab Practica	N/A	N/A	0.76**	N/A
Mid-Term Exam		0.52**		
Final Exam	0.69**	0.57**		0.38*
Course Percentage	0.82**	0.72**	0.63*	0.63**

answer E for a question that only has choices A through D or when the professor (rarely) doesn't include letters for the choices and the students act as though they don't know what to do. In general, the questions included the correct answer, an answer that would seem correct to a student without a firm grasp of the topic, an answer that was a bit further off, and a ridiculous answer that was clearly wrong.

Because both the student participation and the student performance on course assessments are measured on the interval scale, we can use the Pearson correlation coefficient (r) to examine the linear relationship between these variables. The coefficient ranges from –1.0 to 1.0, with a coefficient magnitude close to 1.0 indicating a strong linear relationship and a magnitude close to 0.0 indicating a weak linear relationship.

It is important to note that correlation does not imply causality. Our analysis is not intended to prove that increased participation causes improved performance where we find statistically-significant correlations between the two. We therefore point out that the analysis below is an exploration of the relationships between class participation and student performance rather than a claim of causality.

4.1 CS1 Courses

The CS 115 and GDD 120 courses both cover the standard CS1 topics. The course assessments for the CS1 sections included in the study include homework assignments, lab assignments, short programming assignments, lab practica, a mid-term exam, a final exam, and overall percentage in the course.

The homework assignments were programming assignments designed to be completed in one to two hours by a typical student. The lab assignments were completed by two students working as pair programmers, and each lab assignment was completed in a 75-minute class period. The short programming assignments were programming problems designed to be approximately twice as hard as the homework assignments, though in GDD 120 this was a single larger assignment developing a small number guessing game. The lab practica are in-lab exams designed to evaluate each student's programming skill; see [2] for further discussion of this approach. We used overall percentage for each of the course assessments as the measure of student performance for that assessment. For example, a student with grades of 75%, 80%, and 85% for the three lab practica would have an 80% performance measure for the lab practica course assessment. The 10% for class participation is included in the overall course percentage, though its effect on the 100% possible in the overall course percentage is small.

The statistically-significant correlations for each CS1 section are shown in Table 1. Correlations that are significant at the 0.05 level are marked with a single asterisk (*) and correlations that are significant at the 0.01 level are marked with two asterisks (**). Table cells for correlations that were not statistically significant are left blank, and table cells for which the given course assessment was not included in that section are marked as Not Applicable (N/A).

Before discussing specific results, we note that we discovered statistically-significant correlations between student participation and student performance on course assessments for 19 of the 23 possible correlations. The fact that almost 83% of the correlations were statistically significant indicates an important and consistent relationship between student participation and performance.

The correlation between participation and lab assignments is the highest correlation for two of the sections, the second highest for one section, and third highest for the final section. For the lab assignments, we used the i>clickers to assign students to pairs for the assignment. That means that a student needed to be present and respond with their i>clicker to get above a 0 on a lab. The high correlation between participation and lab assignment grade is probably affected by that process. We do note that some pairs were formed manually (if students forgot their i>clickers) and there was of course variation in student performance on the labs themselves.

The correlations for overall percentage in the course range from 0.63 to 0.82 and were statistically significant for all the CS1 sections included in the study. We actually believe this to be the most significant result in terms of pedagogy, because this correlation indicates a very strong relationship between student participation during the lectures and student performance across all the course assessments. This result also indicates that using the i>clickers in an entertaining way rather than "grading" each student response seems to be an effective approach, though we of course do not know if the correlation would be even higher if we did take the graded questions approach.

The correlations for homework assignments ranged from 0.66 to 0.71. Because these assignments are evenly spread across the semester, students turn in a homework assignment approximately every third class lecture. We believe the consistently high correlation reflects the benefits of student attendance and participation continuously throughout the semester. The same explanation applies to the high correlation for programming assignments in the Fall 2007 offering of CS 115.

The correlations for the final exam are the lowest correlation in two of the classes, the second lowest in a third, and not statistically significant in the fourth. The correlations for the mid-term exam were only significant for one course (in which case it was the lowest correlation). The weakness of these correlations may be at least partially caused by the fact that the other course assessments represent an averaging of student performance across a variety of turn-ins during the semester, while the exams are completed at a single point in time. On the other hand, it can certainly be argued that student performance on exams is a critical measure of student learning, so the lack of strong correlations for the exams calls into some question the possible beneficial effects of using the i>clickers in these courses. Given the different types of assessment methods used in the courses included in the dataset, we believe this area merits further study to examine why the use of i>clickers correlates more strongly with some forms of assessment than with others.

The results for the Fall 2008 offering of CS 115 are weaker than those for the previous offerings of CS 115. This is somewhat confusing, though it is possible that the smaller size of this section (12 students rather than 30 students in the other two sections) could have some effect on the results.

The correlations for GDD 120 tend to be smaller than those for the CS 115 offerings. We believe that this is a result of the characteristics of the participation percentage distributions. For example, for the Spring 2008 offering of CS 115 the participation percentage distribution has a mean of 68% with a 27% standard deviation, while the GDD 120 distribution has a mean of 80% with a 21% standard deviation. The course assessment distributions in the GDD 120 course generally have variances similar to those for the comparable assessments in the Spring 2008 offering of the CS115 course, so correlating the higher participation distribution with a smaller variance to the course assessments in GDD 120 yields lower correlation coefficients.

4.2 CS2 Course

The course assessments for the GDD 220 course in Fall 2008 consisted of homework assignments, lab practica, a mid-term exam, a final exam, and overall percentage in the course. The homework assignments and lab practica were similar to those for CS 115, though of course covering CS2-level topics.

The results for this course were disappointing compared to the other courses. The only statistically-significant (at the 0.05 level) correlation was with the mid-term exam (-0.58), and the correlation was negative. In fact, all the correlations between student participation and course assessments were negative.

These results are obviously very different from those discussed for the other course sections in the study. One possible explanation is that 15 of the 17 students included in the GDD 220 data were also included in the GDD 120 data. It may be the case that student participation is related to student performance when such technology is "new," but has a reduced impact in later courses using the same technology. That explanation seems inconsistent with anecdotal evidence that students continued to be engaged by the technology, but it is possible.

Another interesting pattern in the data is that several of the strongest students very rarely attended class (and therefore had low participation), while some of the students struggling with the course material made sure they attended (and participated in) each lesson. This behavior would also lead to the observed negative correlations.

A third possible explanation is that using student response systems may be an effective student engagement technique in early courses, but not for later ones. CS2 is obviously still an early course, so this particular explanation would merit further data collection and analysis before any general conclusions could be drawn.

5. PERCEIVED AND ACTUAL TOPIC UNDERSTANDING

In this section we discuss our analysis of how well the students' perceived understanding of particular course topics corresponds to their assessed understanding of those topics. On the final class meeting prior to the final exam, we asked students to self-assess their understanding of specific course topics on a 5-value Likert scale. To determine each student's actual understanding of those topics, we mapped the topics to one or more questions on the final exam and calculated a percentage for the student for that topic. Although we realize that there are certainly other ways to assess student understanding of these topics, the temporal closeness of the self-assessment and the actual exam and the fact that both of these activities were after most, if not all, student learning in the course had taken place make this a reasonable approach.

5.1 CS1 Courses

The 10 topics of interest for the CS1 courses (CS 115, GDD 120) come directly from the expected course outcomes developed by the department to support ABET accreditation activities. We did not have a mapping between each of the 10 topics and questions on the final exam, however, because we assess those outcomes across all the course assessments in a course rather than only on the final exam. In all, for the four CS1 course offerings included in this study, we calculated correlation coefficients for 29 mappings between self-assessed and final exam-assessed course topics. This analysis yielded the four statistically significant results (all for Spring 2008 courses) shown below.

Table 2. Self-Assessed and Actual Correlation Results

Topic	CS 115	GDD 120
How selection (if, switch) and looping (while, for) work	0.55	0.50
The difference between a class and an object	Not on final exam	0.50
How method resolution works	Not on final exam	0.51

The latter two topics were not included on the CS 115 final exam because we pursue an objects early approach in that course. Although questions on those topics were included on the mid-term exam in CS 115, we did not include them in our analysis for consistency.

Despite the fact that we did discover four statistically significant results, we believe that the more important observation is that for 25 of the 29 mappings there was not a statistically significant correlation between student perceptions of their mastery of a topic and their assessed mastery of that topic on the final exam.

There are a variety of explanations for this phenomenon. The most obvious explanation is that the students have not yet developed sufficient computer science or game development maturity to be able to really tell how well they understand particular topics in those domains. Given that for 15 of the 29 mappings the mean perceived understanding was above 4 (out of 5) and the means for the actual student understanding for those same mappings ranged from 34% to 79%, we believe that this is the most likely explanation, and that students are more likely to overestimate rather than underestimate their understanding.

It is also possible, however, that some students that self-assessed poor knowledge on particular topics in class then went to thoroughly review (or learn) those topics as they prepared for the final exam. Given the evidence that students are more likely to overestimate their knowledge, this seems to be a less compelling explanation than the one discussed above.

5.2 CS2 Course

We had 6 separate topics that we analyzed for the CS2 course (GDD 220). For the single CS2 section included in this study, we calculated correlation coefficients for those 6 mappings between self-assessed and final exam-assessed course topics. This analysis did not yield any statistically-significant correlations. This result – that students did not accurately self-assess their understanding of specific course topics – is consistent with the results discussed above.

6. CROSS-COURSE COMPARISONS

There are a number of interesting questions we can ask about student participation and student performance that lead to comparisons between the courses included in the study.

We caution, however, that there are several factors in addition to the course participation and the domain for the class examples that could significantly affect these cross-course examples. For example, CS 115 was taught using an objects early approach in which students begin extending existing classes in their first assignment. GDD 120 was taught using an objects late approach because of the relative scarcity of CS1 books that use C# (this has been remedied through the use of an instructor-written textbook for the course). The differences between these approaches could certainly contribute to some of the analysis results below. Despite the many similarities between Java and C#, the choice of programming language and the available IDEs for the chosen languages could also have an effect. GDD 220 covered CS2-level data structure and algorithm analysis topics, so that course has even more extensive differences with the CS1 courses included in the study.

Although we use sound statistical techniques to analyze the course data from these courses, this section should be viewed more as a preliminary exploration of these questions rather than an opportunity to provide general conclusions about the subject courses.

6.1 Participation Percentages

Our first question is "Are students more likely to participate in one course over another?" We can answer this question by comparing the means of the participation percentage distributions for two distinct courses to try to reject the null hypothesis that the samples could have been drawn from the same distribution. There are a variety of tests that can be used to conduct these statistical comparisons; we chose to use the Kolmogov-Smirnov Z test because it is very robust over differences in the shapes and locations of the sample distributions.

We compared the distributions for the three different possible course pairings: CS 115/GDD 120, CS 115/GDD 220, and GDD 120/GDD 220. None of the pairwise comparisons of these distributions yielded statistically-significant results. These results indicate that students were statistically just as likely to participate in CS 115, GDD 120, and GDD 220.

6.2 Course Performance

Our second question is "Do students perform better on course assessments in one course over the other?" We explore this question using the Kolmogov-Smirnov Z test for the three course pairings as described in the previous section. We did not find any statistically-significant results for the GDD 120/GDD 220 pairing.

For the CS 115/GDD 120 pairing, we found two statistically-significant results: programming assignments and the mid-term exam. The mean for the programming assignments in CS 115 was 61% while the mean for the programming assignments in GDD 120 was 81%, so GDD 120 students performed significantly better on those assignments than CS 115 students. We do not believe this result carries much weight, however, because the GDD 120 programming assignment contained specific step-by-step instructions for completing their programming assignment while the CS 115 programming assignments were less detailed.

The difference in performance on the mid-term exam is of more interest, because the mid-term exams in CS 115 and GDD 120 have many similar questions. The mean for the mid-term exam in CS 115 was 65% while the mean for the mid-term exam in GDD 120 was 57%. CS 115 students performed significantly better on the mid-term exam than GDD 120 students.

For the CS 115/GDD 220 pairing, the only statistically significant result was for the homework assignments. The mean for the homework assignments in CS 115 was 50% while the mean for the homework assignments in GDD 220 was 68%. This result is interesting, because the homework assignments in GDD 220 are more advanced than those in CS 115, leading us to expect worse performance from the GDD 220 students. On the other hand, CS 115 is typically the first programming course for those students, while GDD 220 students have successfully completed CS1 (GDD 120) before attempting GDD 220. Perhaps the correct explanation for this result is that GDD 220 students have more programming experience than CS 115 students and are therefore more able to complete the homework assignments. We also note that the transition between the CS1 and CS2 courses is where we anecdotally observe significant attrition. Our result may also reflect this "weeding out" effect.

7. CONCLUSIONS

The statistical analysis results presented above exploring the relationships between student participation using a student response system and their performance on course assessments yielded statistically significant results for 20 out of 28 comparisons. Given our approach using the i>clickers as an engagement tool rather than an explicit teaching tool, we believe these results show that simply engaging the students as participants in our lectures is sufficient to yield a strong and positive relationship with student learning in 19 out of 20 of those cases. We again caution that correlation is not causality, so our claim is not that student participation results in better student learning, but we do find the positive relationships to be of significant interest in their own right.

We also found that a student's perceived understanding of a particular course topic rarely corresponded with their assessed understanding of that topic on the final exam. These results were consistent across all three courses included in the study, with only 4 of 35 correlations yielding statistically-significant results. Computer science educators could use this insight to help students learn how to more effectively assess their understanding of specific course concepts. One possible approach would be to have students self-assess their understanding of each programming assignment topic before attempting the assignment, then comparing their self-assessment to their assignment grade and/or the time it takes them to complete the assignment.

We observed significant enthusiasm on the part of the students in response to the i>clicker use in these courses. Cutts and Kennedy [3] report that typically about 80% of students with clickers responded to any given question in their study; analysis of a random sample of detailed session data indicates our response rates averaged in the 94-100% range for each question. We also have students who decorate their i>clickers with magic markers, affix stickers to their i>clickers to customize their appearance, and even discuss (though thankfully haven't yet implemented) crafting Velcro armbands so their i>clickers are always convenient for use. While we recognize the deeper possibilities available from using student response systems, we believe the results reported here indicate that even using them in a largely entertaining way can lead to a strong and positive relationship with student learning. We suggest that other computer science educators consider using this engaging technology as part of their teaching approach as well.

8. REFERENCES

[1] Ayu, M.A., Taylor, K., and Mantoro, T. Active learning: Engaging students in the classroom using mobile phones. In *Proceedings of the 2009 IEEE Symposium on Industrial Electronics & Applications (ISIEA 2009)*, 2, Kuala Lumpur, Malaysia, October 2009, 711-715.

[2] Chamillard, A.T. and Joiner, Jay K. Using lab practica to evaluate programming ability. In *Proceedings of the 32nd SIGCSE Technical Symposium on Computer Science Education*, Charlotte, NC, February 2001, 159-163.

[3] Cutts, Q.I. and Kennedy, G.E. Connecting learning environments using electronic voting systems. In *Proceedings of the 7th Australasian Conference on Computing Education*, Newcastle, New South Wales, Australia, 2005, 181-186.

[4] Denning, T., Griswold, W.G., Simon, B., and Wilkerson, M. Multimodal communication in the classroom: What does it mean for us? In *Proceedings of the 37th SIGCSE Technical Symposium on Computer Science Education*, Houston, TX, March 2006, 219-223.

[5] Esponda, M. Electronic voting on-the-fly with mobile devices. In *Proceedings of the Thirteenth Annual Conference on Innovation and Technology in Computer Science Education*, Madrid, Spain, 2008, 93-97.

[6] Iclicker.com. 2010. i>clicker: The Decision is Simple, Retrieved November 29, 2010 from http://www.iclicker.com/dnn/

[7] Kay, R.H. and LeSage, A. Examining the benefits and challenges of using audience response systems: A review of the literature. *Computers & Education*, 53(3):819-827, November 2009.

[8] Lantz, M.E. The use of 'Clickers' in the classroom: Teaching innovation or merely an amusing novelty? *Computers in Human Behavior*, 26(4):556-561, July 2010.

[9] Lazar, A. Engaged learning in a computer science course. *The Journal of Computing Sciences in Colleges*, 23(1):38-44, October 2007.

[10] Lichti, S.M. Purdue's system wide deployment of a classroom response system. In *Proceedings of the 34th Annual ACM SIGUCCS Conference on User Services*, Edmonton, Alberta, Canada, 2006, 196-200.

[11] Murphy, T. Success and failure of audience response systems in the classroom. In *Proceedings of SIGUCCS 2008*, Portland, Oregon, October 2008, 33-37.

[12] Morgan, Robin K. Exploring the pedagogical effectiveness of clickers. *InSight: A Journal of Scholarly Teaching*, 3:31-36, 2008.

[13] Pargas, R.P., and Shah, D.M. Things are clicking in computer science courses. In *Proceedings of the 37th SIGCSE Technical Symposium on Computer Science Education,* Houston, TX, March 1-5, 2006, 474-477.

[14] Sanseverino, M. Pedagogy that clicks: "Clickers" in the CSC classroom. In *Proceedings of the 15th Western Canadian Conference on Computer Education (WCCCE 2010)*, Kelowna, British Columbia, Canada, 2010.

[15] Simon, B., Anderson, R. Hoyer, C., and Su, J. Preliminary experiences with a tablet PC based system to support active learning in computer science courses. In *Proceedings of the Ninth Annual Conference on Innovation and Technology in Computer Science Education (ITiCSE 2004)*, Leeds, UK, 2004, 213-217.

[16] Taneja, A. The influence of personal response systems on students' perceived learning outcomes and course satisfaction. *The Journal of Computing Sciences in Colleges*, 25(2):5-11, December 2009.

[17] Tiwari, D., Sehgal, R., Bansal, J., and Murthy, S. Clicking away the distance from education. In *Proceedings of the 2010 International Conference on Technology for Education (T4E)*, July 1-3, 2010, 17-23.

[18] Wilkerson, M., Griswold, W., and Simon, B. Ubiquitous presenter: Increasing student access and control in a digital lecturing environment. In *Proceedings of the 36th SIGCSE Technical Symposium on Computer Science Education*, St. Louis, MO, February 2005, 116-120.

Effectiveness of Cognitive Apprenticeship Learning (CAL) and Cognitive Tutors (CT) for Problem Solving Using Fundamental Programming Concepts

Wei Jin
Dept. of Computer Information Sciences
Shaw University
Raleigh, NC 27601
(919) 546-8376
wjin@shawu.edu

Albert Corbett
Human-Computer Interaction Institute
Carnegie Mellon University
Pittsburgh, PA 15213
(412) 268-8808
corbett@cmu.edu

ABSTRACT
In this paper, we describe our approach in addressing learning challenges students experience in introductory programming courses. We combine two effective instructional methodologies to help students learn to plan programs prior to writing code: Cognitive Apprenticeship Learning (CAL) and Cognitive Tutors (CT). In the CAL component, the instructor models program planning in class and paper handouts are used to scaffold program planning in homework assignments. In CAL-CT, the program-planning process is also supported by a computer tutor which provides step-by-step feedback and advice. The results show that the combined CAL-CT approach yielded substantial gains over traditional instruction. Its advantage over the CAL-Only approach is also significant.

Categories and Subject Descriptors
K.3.2 [**Computers & Education**]: Computer & Information Science Education – *Computer Science Education, Curriculum.*

General Terms
Design, Experimentation, Human Factors

Keywords
CS1, Cognitive Apprenticeship Learning, Cognitive Tutors, Introduction to Programming, Pedagogy, Scaffolding

1. INTRODUCTION
Shaw University is the oldest Historically Black University in the south and its mission is to provide higher education to those who otherwise would not have such an opportunity. Since there are substantial performance gaps among students and many students are not well-prepared for college, it faces special challenges in helping all students to learn and progress.

Our project started with the observation that many of our students specifically "freeze" and do not know where to start with programming assignments. Many educators have observed the difficulties that students have with mastering programming [14] and many innovative approaches have been proposed. We had previously tried several methods, such as peer collaboration, which may be effective for different student population, but we did not observe much effectiveness.

Our approach is to use computer tutors to support students and help them develop problem solving strategies that they can use independently in the future. These tutors simulate a human instructor who demonstrates how to approach a programming problem and guides students through problem solving processes. Through numerous guided practices, we hope that eventually the problem analysis and solving process will become students' habits and they can use them automatically in their independent problem solving.

This approach fits our students' needs. Guidance tutors, which start students off with a problem analysis, then guide students through an expert problem-solving process in a step-by-step fashion, seem to be the most appropriate. As it turns out, guidance tutors are relatively easy to implement, because they follow specific problem solving strategies.

In fact, our approach is a combination of the Cognitive Apprenticeship Learning (CAL) model and Cognitive Tutors (CT). Both have been shown effective at helping students improve problem solving skills in domains that require abstract thinking (see Section 2 for detail).

The study presented in this paper is an extension of previous work [11], which focused on the very basic programming concepts – variables and basic statements. First, in addition to variables and basic statements, currently we have developed computer tutors for if statements and for loops. Second, the tutors in the previous report [11] only provide students with planning guidelines on how to solve a problem (writing a program). In contrast, our current tutors will help students step-by-step in planning and writing complete programs.

In this paper we report an evaluation of three learning approaches, CAL-CT (CAL with Cognitive Tutor support), CAL-Only (CAL with paper worksheets) and no-CAL (conventional problem solving), based on student test scores collected over several semesters. The data show that both the CAL-CT and the CAL approach have improved student test scores. On average, test scores for students in the CAL-CT group are 53% higher than

SIGCSE'11, March 9–12, 2011, Dallas, Texas, USA.

students that benefitted from CAL-Only instruction and 64% higher than students in the no-CAL group.

The remainder of the paper is organized as follows: In Section 2, we discuss the rationales for our approach in the context of CAL and CT and other related work. We describe the CAL component in Section 3 and the CT component in Section 4. We evaluate the effectiveness of CAL and CAL-CT in Section 5. We will summarize conclusions and future work in Section 6.

2. RATIONALES AND RELATED WORK

2.1 Cognitive Apprenticeship Learning (CAL)

Cognitive apprenticeship learning (CAL) models traditional apprenticeship learning, which has successfully trained individuals in various trades and professions [5]. Students learn complex skills by practicing in real life problem-solving settings. In addition to explaining how to perform a task, the teacher demonstrates how to perform the task (modeling), gives individualized guidance and feedback to the apprentice during practice (coaching), and gradually reduces the amount of help given as the apprentice develops proficiency in the task (fading). During this process, the teacher also provides scaffolding tools to guide the apprentice in the performance of the task, which are discarded as the apprentice becomes more adept.

The cognitive apprenticeship learning model helps students acquire abstract skills. Since abstract skills engage thinking processes that are "invisible," the teacher articulates expert thought processes to students. The description of these problem-solving processes and strategies provides organizational scaffolds for students and helps them acquire higher-level skills. In addition, instructors may use other materials, such as specially designed problems or worksheets to guide the student during practice [9]. In contrast, traditional forms of instruction are much less explicit with the problem-solving process. They often present students with models of complete answers that give no indication of the decision-making process and have little or no coaching component.

2.2 Cognitive Tutors (CT)

Cognitive tutors are an educational technology with characteristics similar to human tutors. They are most effective at developing skills that can only be gained through applying knowledge in a problem solving context. These skills are often the higher-level skills in Bloom's Taxonomy [3], such as knowledge application and synthesis, which are the skill levels that students need to reach to master programming.

Cognitive tutors pose complex problem-solving tasks to students and provide the individualized advice students need to succeed [1, 2, 6, 12]. Cognitive tutors are based on an understanding of both domain knowledge and problem-solving strategies. This knowledge is represented as a "cognitive model" in the cognitive tutor [1], an expert system which can solve the problems in the many ways that students solve them. As a student works, the cognitive model is used to follow the student's step-by-step solution and provide accuracy feedback. The tutor does not automatically provide detailed advice; instead students have the opportunity to reflect on and correct their own mistakes. However, if the student asks, the cognitive model is also employed to provide advice on how to accomplish each problem-solving step.

Cognitive tutors have been shown to speed learning by as much as a factor of three and yield an achievement effect size of about one-standard deviation compared to conventional instruction [2]. This is about twice the effect of typical human tutors [7] and about half the effect of the best human tutors [4].

2.3 Our Approach: CAL-CT

The cognitive apprenticeship learning model is an instruction methodology; cognitive tutors are computer programs. Combining these two approaches has advantages over using either approach alone. The advantages of CAL-CT over CAL-Only are as follows:

- Cognitive tutors make it possible for students to receive more individualized "coaching" outside of classrooms/office hours.
- Use of automatic tutors encourages students to actively participate in learning by limiting the fear of mistakes.
- Availability of help is immediate, which is made possible by the hints made available to students by automatic tutors.

2.4 Other Related Work

There have been various related approaches to automatic tutoring in programming that have had some success, for example, natural language dialog to help students develop pseudo code [13], reverse engineering to determine whether a program satisfies goals and then provide relevant hints [18], use of filling-blanks to focus on crucial part of the program [15], debugging tutors to help master programming concepts [8], and machine learning to determine grasp of knowledge and present learning materials adaptively [17]. Some enhanced IDEs also have tutoring features, such as identifying syntax/logic/style errors and providing feedback that is more meaningful [10, 16].

3. THE CAL COMPONENT

The CAL component is a step-by-step problem solving process to guide students in the right direction and help them develop habits to think as experienced programmers. We have developed instruments (e.g. worksheets) that help students follow this process. We emphasize that these forms are effective only if instructors model how to use them in problem solving through multiple examples and demonstrate how to convert information in a worksheet into a program.

3.1 Variables and Basic Statements

Problem solving involves three steps: (1) mental visualization of how the program interacts with a user, (2) variable analysis, and (3) flow analysis. Step 2 extracts essential information from step 1: the inputs the user will provide for the program and the outputs the program will calculate and give to the user. Step 3 determines the order of data processing. We previously developed a worksheet that explicitly supports variable analysis and flow analysis activities in program design, as described in [11]. For variables and basic statements, a paper-and-pencil worksheet was developed with three sections: Program I/O, Variables, and Flow. In the first section, students determine the relevant data items and whether each data item is an input or output of the program. In the next section, students choose a variable name and type for each data item. In the third section, students determine the program actions, which include getting input values from user and computing and displaying output values. The worksheet provides the framework for students to think. It is most effective to introduce the worksheets in the classroom where an instructor models their use and summarizes after students spend some time working on a sheet.

3.2 If Statements

Figure 1 shows a correctly completed CAL worksheet for an IF statement. The problem description and the shaded areas are provided to students and the rest are blanks that students need to fill out. This worksheet again divides the program planning process into several sections: (1) Case analysis: A case is the set of situations under which the program should perform the same actions. Eventually a case will be specified by a logic expression, but during step 1, students describe each case in plain English. (2) Exclusiveness/order analysis: Students indicate if the cases in the program are exclusive of each other (that is, if only one can be true at any given situation). Exclusive cases can be implemented as one multi-branch if statement. If cases are non-exclusive, they should be implemented as independent if statements. (3) Logic expressions and actions: Students convert their English case descriptions into formal symbolic expressions for the tests and actions and at the bottom of the page assemble these components into one or more if statements.

Since variables are a topic for Basic Statements, when students reach the topic of if statements, they already achieved certain fluency. Here students have freedom to choose a proper variable name for a data item as long as consistency is maintained throughout the worksheet. Students also need to bring their work product (in the last blank space) into a program to compile, debug, and test. The worksheet itself only provides a framework for students to think and it is still up to students to figure out the details themselves.

3.3 Loops

Iteration is a challenging topic. Our observation is that students have trouble condensing actions into a compact loop format. The problem is not with loop syntax, but with how to abstract the sequence actions into a set of statements that will be executed repeatedly.

Our problem solving process helps with this abstraction. Figure 2 shows a correctly completed worksheet for loops. Similar to Figure 1, the problem description and the shaded areas are provided to students and the rest are blanks that students need to fill out. It involves the following steps: (1) Students describe the solution as a sequence of actions in plain English. (2) Then students specify a sequence of C++ statements that implement the actions identified in step 1. (3) In the next, key phase, students find the patterns among the sequence of C++ statements and abstract them into a set of C++ statements, which can be executed repeatedly to produce the same behavior as the sequence in step 2. Finally, students (4) determine how to stop the loop, and (5) determine how to set up the variables before the loop and the actions to perform after the loop. Students have freedom to choose a proper variable name for a data item as long as consistency is maintained throughout the worksheet.

Challenges: The problem solving processes and the accompanying worksheets presented above provide off-line scaffolding for modeling and coaching on how to construct programs to solve problems. They guide students and scaffold them in following a good analytical process. However, our classroom experience is that while some students can make good progress, some required additional help and some still didn't know what to do. For the last group, it is difficult to conduct one-on-one coaching during a class period. In addition, in our instructional experience, worksheets would not be effective at all outside the classroom for this group of students. Frequently these students failed to submit homework assignments due to their inability to use these worksheets independently.

Problem: If a student is a first-year and GPA is 3.0 and up, he gets *good starter* award. If GPA is 3.5 and up, he gets *dean's list* award.

Case Analysis

ID	Categorization of the Cases	Actions of the Cases
1	Student is a first-year and GPA is 3.0 or up	Student gets good starter award.
2	Student's GPA is 3.5 or up	Student gets dean's list award.

Exclusiveness/Order Analysis

Are the above cases exclusive to each other?	No
If no, please list the order of cases:	Order does not matter.

Logic Expressions and Actions

ID	Logic Expressions	Actions
1	classification==1 && gpa >= 3.0	cout << "Good Starter Award." << endl;
2	gpa >= 3.5	cout << "Dean's List Award." << endl;

Put the If Statement(s) Together

If the cases are exclusive, please use one multi-branch if-else statement. Otherwise, use independent if statement for each case.

```
if (classification == 1 && gpa >= 3.0) {
    cout << "Good Starter Award." << endl;
}
if (gpa >= 3.5) {
    cout << "Dean's List Award." << endl;
}
```

Figure 1: Pre-programming Analysis for Ifs

Problem: Calculate 2 + 4 + 6 + … + 10000 and display the result.

Describe the solution in sequence of actions (plain English):

Add 2 to sum
Add 4 to sum
…
Add 10000 to sum

Translate the above actions into C++ statements:

```
sum = sum + 2;
sum = sum + 4;
...
sum = sum + 10000;
```

Abstract into a set of same statements that can be repeatedly executed:

```
sum = sum + num;
num += 2;
sum = sum + num;
num += 2;
...
```

Condition that the loop should stop:

```
num > 10000
```

The condition that the loop should continue (reverse condition):

```
num <= 10000
```

Variables to set up before the loop:

```
sum = 0;  num =2;
```

Actions after the loop:

```
cout << "2+4+6+...+10000 = " << sum << endl;
```

Figure 2: Pre-programming Analysis for Loops

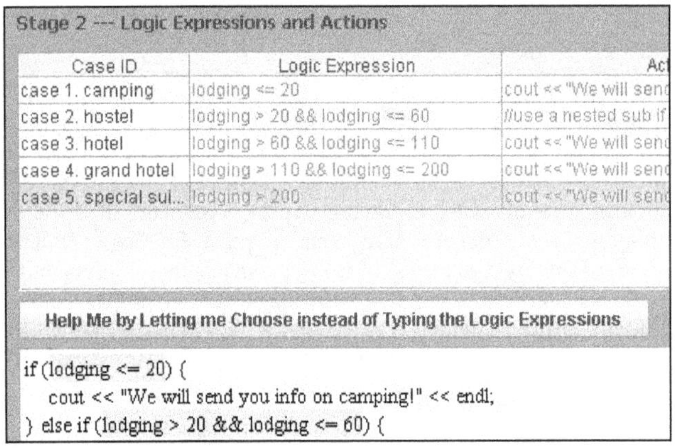

Figure 3: Snapshot of a Tutor Interface

4. THE CT COMPONENT

Our approach to address the challenge described at the end of Section 3 is to use Cognitive Tutors that interact with students within the framework of the cognitive apprenticeship learning model. The tutors provide the step-by-step support each student needs to complete each planning and programming task successfully. The tutor indicates whether each student action is correct or incorrect. If incorrect, students can request a hint as to why it is wrong. Some decisions, such as variable names and logical expressions, require students to type in the answers, but most decisions are multiple-choice. Figure 3 displays a snapshot of a part of the tutor interface during a step in solving a programming problem using if statements. The students can either type in the logic expressions or, after repeated failure, may request the tutor to present a multiple-choice menu from which to select a logic expression.

Program construction is divided into several stages. The if-statement tutor, for example, consists of the four stages. In stage (1), the student identifies the cases in a programming problem (selects English descriptions from menus). In stage (2), shown in Figure 3, the student enters logic expressions and actions for the cases. In stage (3) the student determines whether each logic expression can be simplified. The part of a logic expression that would be always true when it is evaluated can be safely removed. Logic expressions in a multi-branch if statement can often be simplified. Finally, in stage (4) students repeat stage 1-3 for if statements that will be nested in the top-level if statement. After students make correct answers for a stage, the tutor displays a partially completed program that incorporates the decisions the students have made for that stage. For the example in Figure 3, the logic expressions and actions the student enters at the top of the screen are incorporated into an actual if statement at the bottom of the screen. This way, a program is gradually constructed/refined based on students' decisions. Students will observe how their decisions in each step contribute to the construction of the program. After students finish the program, they can copy and paste the program into a standard IDE (e.g. Microsoft Visual Studio) to compile and test.

5. EFFECTIVENESS EVALUATION

These CAL and CAL-CT learning activities were incorporated into introductory programming courses at Shaw University and in this report we use student test scores to evaluate these interventions for each of the three programming topics across semesters (Fall 2007 – Spring 2010). For each of the three constructs, Variables & Basic Statements, Ifs, and Loops, all the students in the same semester used one of the learning approaches: No-CAL (the baseline), CAL-Only, or CAL-CT. Table 1 shows student assignment by semester.

Table 1: Student Assignment by Semester

	Basic Statements	If	Loops
Fall'07	CAL-Only	No-CAL	
Spring'08	CAL-Only	CAL-Only	No-CAL
Fall'08	CAL-Only	CAL-Only	CAL-Only
Spring'09	No-CAL	No-CAL	No-CAL
Fall'09	CAL-CT	CAL-CT	CAL-Only
Spring'10	CAL-CT	CAL-CT	CAL-CT

For each topic, the instructor introduced the programming construct in class and then students completed some program-tracing and syntax-debugging activities. At this point, a pretest was given to students. That is, at this point, students had learned the syntax of a programming construct but had not any programming experience for that construct. After the pretest, students worked on some programming problems in class. In the CAL-Only and CAL-CT conditions, the teacher demonstrated the use of the CAL worksheets in completing these example programs. Students then completed a homework assignment consisting of a set of problems in which they wrote programs.

- In the No-CAL condition, students completed the set of programming homework problems without any additional scaffolding.
- In the CAL condition, CAL worksheets were made available for the homework assignment and students were encouraged, but not required, to use the worksheets to help design the programs.
- In the CAL-CT condition, students completed a small set of homework problems and CAL worksheets were made available for that purpose. Students then completed a set of programming exercises in the CAL-CT environment. Note that there is no CT-Only approach for two reasons: (1) the classroom use of worksheets is in common to CAL CAL-CT by design, and (2) we wanted to conduct a within-student analysis of the "added value" in going from CAL worksheets to the CT environment, as discussed under section 5 "Learning Progress in the CAL-CT condition."

Following each homework assignment, the instructor reviewed the answers in class in all conditions. Finally, students completed a posttest in class. The test questions were all problem-based, asking students to write complete programs. We collected student test data over multiple semesters and tried to keep the test problems for each construct as similar as possible across semesters. We used self-developed and expert-inspected grading rubrics to evaluate student tests and generate test scores. Since our focus is problem solving, our rubrics give more weight (points) to students' approach to solving problems than to program syntax. Table 2 shows the number of students in each condition who participated in the study.

Table 2: Number of Students in Each Group

Condition	Basic Statements	If Statements	Loops
No-CAL	7	35	36
CAL-Only	55	35	19
CAL-CT	39	31	9

Figure 4 displays average posttest scores for the three learning conditions for each of the three programming topics and overall. As expected, students in the CAL-CT group scored higher than students in the other two conditions for each of the three topics and this overall result is significant by a non-parametric test of independent probabilities, $p < 0.04$.

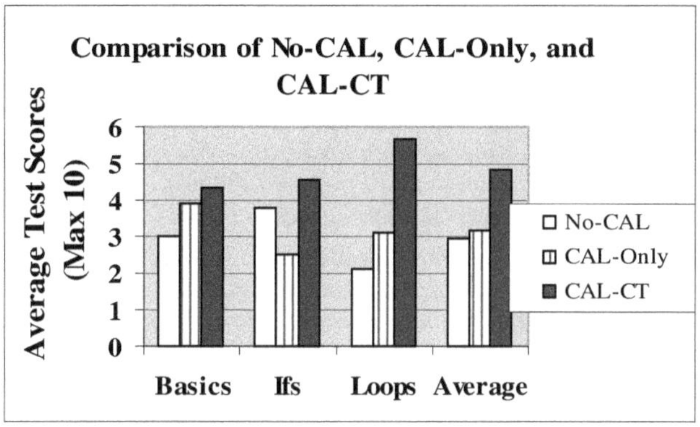

Figure 4: Posttest Comparisons among Three Groups

For the Loop construct, the differences among the groups were quite large. Posttest scores in the CAL-CT group were 82% higher than in the CAL-Only group, which in turn were 48% higher than the No-CAL baseline group. In a between-subject ANOVA, the main effect of learning condition is reliable, $F(2, 61) = 5.02$, $p < .01$. In pair-wise comparisons, the difference between CAL-CT and CAL-Only is reliable, $p < .04$, as is the difference between CAL-CT and No-CAL $p < .01$, while the difference between CAL-Only and No-CAL is not significant.

For the If construct, posttest scores for the CAL-CT group were 22% higher than in the No-CAL condition and 82% higher than in the CAL-Only condition. In a between-subject ANOVA, the main effect of group type is marginally significant, $F(2, 98) = 2.22$, $p < .12$, and the only significant pair-wise difference is between the CAL-CT and CAL-Only groups, $p < .05$. We believe that the close similarity of an example with the posttest solution led to the high posttest scores for Fall'07 (part of No-CAL), which caused the "skew" that No-CAL outperforms CAL.

Finally, for Variable & Basic Statements, the differences among the three groups were much smaller and in a between-subjects ANOVA, the main effect of group is not significant. In fact, the CAL-Only group for basic statements is not strictly CAL only because this group has used preprogramming analysis tutors as reported in [11]. These tutors are much simpler. They helped students fill out the preprogramming analysis worksheet without leading students to the final solutions (complete programs).

Learning Progress in the CAL-CT condition. In the CAL-CT condition, pretests and intermediate tests were used to examine how students made progress in learning. Students completed programming problems on these tests analogous to the posttest problems. For the Variables & Basic Statements construct, each student took a pretest before the homework assignment and completed an intermediate test after working on the initial set of problems with CAL worksheets and before beginning the CAL-CT problems. For the If construct, each student completed either a pretest or an intermediate test. For the Loop construct, each student completed an intermediate test.

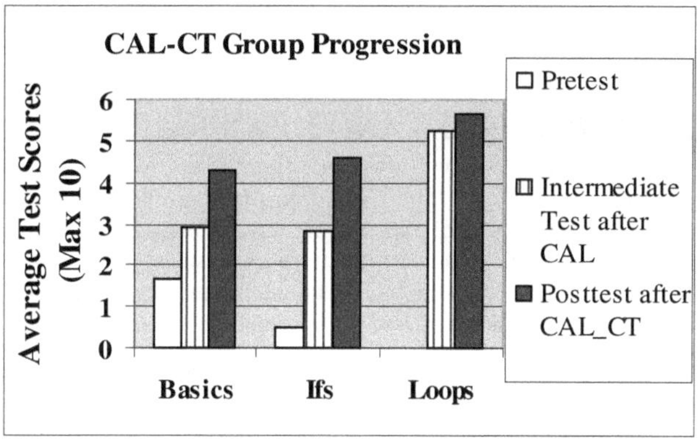

Figure 5: Student Performance Progression (CAL-CT)

Figure 5 displays the results of the pre-, intermediate and post tests. For both the Variables & Basic Statement constructs and the If construct, the learning activities with off-line CAL worksheets alone yielded substantial learning gains between the pretest and the intermediate test. This gain for Variables & Basic Statements is reliable in a paired-sample t-test, $t(20) = 2.75$, $p < .02$ and the gain for Ifs is marginally reliable in an independent-sample t-test, $t(26) = 2.61$, $p < .08$. For these two constructs, the Cognitive Tutor CAL-CT activities yielded substantial additional learning between the intermediate test and posttest. These respective gains were reliable in paired-sample t-tests, $t(35) = 3.34$, $p < .01$ and $t(19) = 2.62$, $p < .02$. In contrast, for the Loop construct, CAL-CT problem solving yielded little additional learning between the intermediate test, which followed the use of off-line CAL worksheets, and the posttest, and the difference between the two tests is not significant. This latter result is surprising since, as we've seen, the CAL-CT group posttest scores are reliably higher than the CAL-Only posttest scores (Figure 4).

Table 3: Student Surveys – Full or High Agreement

Survey Questions	No-CAL (28)	CAL-CT (24)
Felt motivated to come to every session.	57%	75%
Felt motivated to complete all hw assignments.	64%	79%
The instruction was very different from other courses.	67%	71%
The instruction was high quality.	68%	92%
The materials were excellent.	57%	88%
The course increased the excitement I have on learning C++ programming.	54%	71%
This course convinced me to stay a computer science major or to become on.	46%	50%
This course kept me or made me become interested in a CS career.	64%	71%
This was the best course I took this sem.	29%	33%

Table 3 shows student survey data collected during Spring 2009 (No-CAL) and Spring 2010 (CAL-CT). Students rated their agreement with each statement on a 5-point scale. Table 3 displays the percentage of students who "fully" or "highly" agreed with each statement. Clearly CAL-CT students tend to have more positive attitudes toward the course activities. A higher percentage of CAL-CT students than No-CAL students fully or highly agreed with every statement. The biggest differences between the two groups were for the 4th and 5th questions, "The instruction in this course was high quality," and "The course materials were excellent," and both of these differences are significant at the .05 level in a z-test of the difference between two independent samples.

6. CONCLUSION AND DISCUSSION

CAL-CT combines two effective approaches for developing problem solving skills. The CAL-style preprogramming analysis allows students to model experts' analytical thinking and problem solving processes and helps them to mature as programmers. Online tutors give students individual attentions which are usually not available outside classrooms and keep them moving forward.

The CAL-CT Tutors are based on Java Swing technology and can be delivered to students easily online through either Java Applets or Java Web Start. Tutors are designed to be flexible enough to make it easy to incorporate new problems. Teachers can specify programming problems/solutions and tutor behaviors using text files without any programming.

We will add tutors for more programming concepts and develop adaptive problem delivery mechanisms to better fit individual student's needs. Our ultimate goal is to develop an engaging CAL-CT curriculum to help students master programming skills.

7. ACKNOWLEDGMENTS

This material is based upon work supported by the National Science Foundation under Grant No. 0837505.

Our thanks to Yingqi Wang for assistance in developing the tutors, Susan Rodger and Sung-Sik Kwon for their tutor-interface suggestions and Barry Nagle for designing student surveys.

8. REFERENCES

[1] Anderson, J. R., Conrad, F. G., and Corbett, A. T. 1989. *Skill Acquisition and the LISP Tutor*. Cognitive Science 13(4), 467-505.

[2] Anderson, J. R., Corbett, A. T., Koedinger, K. R., and Pelletier, R. 1995. *Cognitive Tutors: Lessons Learned*. J. of the Learning Sciences, 4(2), 167-207.

[3] Bloom, B. S. and Krathwohl, D. R. 1956. *Taxonomy of Educational Objectives: The Classification of Educational Goals, by a committee of college and university examiners*. Handbook I: Cognitive Domain. New York, Longmans, Green.

[4] Bloom, B. S. 1984. *The 2 sigma problem: The search for methods of group instruction as effective as one-to-one tutoring*. Educational Researcher, 13(6), 4-16.

[5] Collins, A., Brown, J. S., Newman, S. E. 1989. *Cognitive Apprenticeship: Teaching the Crafts of Reading, Writing and Mathematics*. In L. Resnick (Eds.), Knowing, Learning and Instruction, Essays in Honor of Robert Glaser. Erlbaum, Hillsdale, NJ.

[6] Corbett, A. T. and Anderson, J. R. 1995. *Knowledge tracing: Modeling the acquisition of procedural knowledge*. User Modeling and User-Adapted Interaction, 4, 253-278.

[7] Corbett, A. T., McLaughlin, M. S. and Scarpinatto, K. C. 2000. *Modeling student knowledge: Cognitive tutors in high school and college*. User modeling and user-adapted interaction, volume 10, 81-108.

[8] Fernandes, E. and Kumar, A. N. 2004. *A Tutor on Scope for the Programming Languages Course*. ACM SIGCSE Bulletin, volume 36, issue 1 (March 2004), 90 -93.

[9] Heller, P., Keith, R., and Anderson, S. 1992. *Teaching Problem Solving Through Cooperative Grouping. Part 1: Group versus Individual Problem*. American Journal of Physics, Volume 60, Issue 7 (July 1992), 627-636.

[10] Hristova, M., Misra, A., Rutter, M., and Mercuri, R. 2003. *Identifying and Correcting Java Programming Errors for Introductory Computer Science Students*. SIGCSE'03: Proceedings of the 34th SIGCSE technical symposium on Computer science education, 486-490.

[11] Jin, W. 2008. *Pre-programming Analysis Tutor Helps Students Learn Basic Programming Concept*. SIGCSE'08: Proceedings of the 39th SIGCSE technical symposium on Computer Science Education, 276-280.

[12] Koedinger, K. R. and Corbett, A. T. 2006. *Cognitive Tutors: Technology brings learning science to classroom*. In K. Sawyer (Ed.), the Cambridge Handbook of the Learning Sciences, Cambridge University Press, 61-78.

[13] Lane, H. and VanLehn, K. 2003. *Coached Program Planning: Dialogue-Based Support for Novice Program Design*. SIGCSE'03: Proceedings of the 34th SIGCSE technical symposium on Computer science education, 148-152.

[14] McCracken, M. et al. 2002. *A multi-national multi-institutional study of assessment of programming skills of first-year CS students*. SIGCSE Bulletin, Vol. 34, No. 1 (March 2002).

[15] Odekirt-Hash, E. and Zachary, J. L. 2001. *Automated Feedback on Programs Means Students Need Less Help from Teachers*. SIGCSE'01: Proceedings of the 32nd SIGCSE technical symposium on Computer Science Education, 55-59.

[16] Shaffer, S. C. Ludwig 2005. *An online programming tutoring and assessment system*. Inroads --- The SIGCSE Bulletin, Volume 37, Issue 2 (June 2005), 56-60.

[17] Soh, L. K. 2006. *Incorporating an Intelligent Tutoring System into CS1*. SIGCSE'06: Proceedings of the 37th SIGCSE technical symposium on Computer science education, 486-490.

[18] Song J. S., Hahn, S. H., Tak, K. Y. & Kim, J. H. 1997. *An intelligent tutoring system for introductory C language course*. Computers & Education, Volume 28, Issue 2 (February 1997), 93-102.

Can AlgoTutor Change Attitudes toward Algorithms?

Jungsoon Yoo Sung Yoo Suk Seo Chrisila Pettey
Computer Science Department
Middle Tennessee State University
United States
01-615-898-2397
csyoojp@mtsu.edu

ABSTRACT

The ability to design an algorithm is one of the most important learning outcomes of a computer science program. Unfortunately, not only is learning how to design algorithms a challenging task, but many students believe that algorithm design is not an important part of problem solving. To address this challenge and hopefully change student attitudes, we developed AlgoTutor, a web-based algorithm development tutoring system. AlgoTutor's primary components are the algorithm composer and the algorithm tracer. A third component, ProgramPad, was added to show the connection between algorithms and code. This paper presents the results of experiments that assessed AlgoTutor's effectiveness in changing student attitudes about algorithm development. The results show that students who used AlgoTutor in CS-I were more likely to realize the importance of algorithm design in problem solving and to have confidence in their own algorithm development abilities.

Categories and Subject Descriptors

K.3.1 [**Computer Uses in Education**]: Computer-assisted instruction, Computer-managed instruction, Online learning.

General Terms

Design, Management, Human Factors.

Keywords

algorithm development, learning environment.

1. INTRODUCTION

In beginning computer science classes we introduce "algorithm development prior to coding" as an essential task for problem solving. We teach what is involved in the algorithm development stage in classroom lectures as well as in computer laboratories. We emphasize the importance of algorithm development, and students are frequently required to include an algorithm for programming assignments. However, we have observed that many students ignore this step and fail to acquire algorithm development skills. We think that this is due to two reasons: lack of appreciation of the worth of algorithm development and lack of ability to construct algorithms [9]. Students in introductory computer science classes often feel that there is no need to develop an algorithm for problem solving. This attitude prevents them from building a habit of developing algorithms prior to coding and from acquiring algorithm development skills. There has been a lot of interest in engaging students in programming activities by using visual systems such as Alice or Scratch [2,3,7]. However, there is no tool for practicing algorithm development as a prerequisite of coding as well as helping them learn algorithm development skills.

We have developed an algorithm development tutor (AlgoTutor) for Computer Science (CS) I and II classes [6] [9]. AlgoTutor is a Web-based tutoring system that enables introductory computer-programming students to build algorithms using the top-down design strategy with abstraction refinement. The system can also help students use the bottom-up approach by reusing the algorithms created previously. However, problem solving using a computer programming language such as C++ involves several steps. AlgoTutor also addresses issues that arise in these steps (e.g., verifying the correctness of an algorithm or converting an algorithm to code). In this paper we will show that using AlgoTutor helps students build confidence in algorithm development and recognize the value of algorithm development in problem solving.

In the following section, we discuss steps involved in problem solving using a computer programming language as well as issues related to these steps. In Section 3, we describe the components of AlgoTutor including the algorithm composer, the algorithm tracer, and ProgramPad which automatically generates C++ code from an algorithm developed in the composer. Section 3 also describes the experiments conducted along with the results and lessons learned. Section 4 reports the results of student surveys conducted to assess the effectiveness of AlgoTutor and the students' attitude toward algorithm development. We conclude with future directions of the research.

SIGCSE'11, March 9–12, 2011, Dallas, Texas, USA.

2. PROBLEM SOLVING PHASES

Problem solving using a computer programming language such as C++ is a complex task which involves several steps:

step 1. Understand the problem specification.
step 2. Develop an algorithm for the problem.
step 3. Verify the correctness of the algorithm by tracing each step of the algorithm.

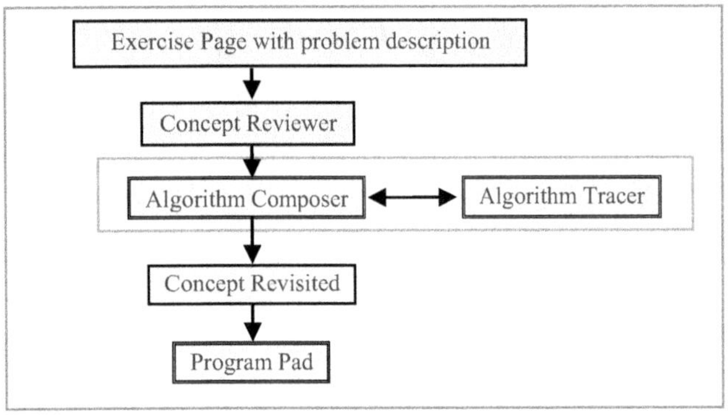

Figure 1. Components of the AlgoTutor system.

step 4. Convert the algorithm into a C++ program.
step 5. Verify whether the converted program is syntactically correct.
step 6. Test and debug the program's correctness.

Steps 5 and 6 are done with the help of compilers and debuggers; however, steps 1 through 4 are typically done manually. In this paper, we describe the system that we have developed to help students with these manual steps (see Figure 1).

In step 1, students need to understand the problem specification by reading the problem description. Additionally, any skills and/or concepts required to solve this problem have to be reviewed/acquired. AlgoTutor uses the concept reviewer component to help students review concepts required and clarify the problem specifications.

The algorithm composer which is the main component of AlgoTutor can help students develop an algorithm for step 2 [6]. Algorithms are constructed by assembling instructor defined pseudo code (pre-defined operations) and control structures via a graphical drag-and-drop interface. The automatic assessment tool in AlgoTutor uses the instructor's solution(s) to give the student online feedback.

For step 3, we have developed an algorithm tracer that can be used for a certain category of problems (usually simple, small problems). The algorithm tracer allows students to verify the correctness of their algorithm by providing visual tracing of the student algorithm.

Once an algorithm has been developed for the problem, students need to figure out what kinds of programming skills are necessary to convert the algorithm to a program. AlgoTutor uses the concept revisited component to help students review the required programming concepts.

For step 4, we have developed another component of AlgoTutor called ProgramPad. ProgramPad converts most of the operations/steps in the student developed algorithm into C++ code, and provides an interface for completing the program. Using ProgramPad, the student can then see the connections between the algorithm that is developed using the composer and the program that is implemented from the algorithm. In Section 3, the algorithm development process using each of the components of AlgoTutor is described.

3. ALGORITHM DEVELOPMENT

The AlgoTutor system has been developed to address the undesirable attitude that developing algorithms prior to writing code is not necessary [9]. In Section 4.2, we will show evidence that students who used AlgoTutor in CS-I appreciate the usefulness of algorithm development and are more confident in developing algorithms. But in this section we will describe each of the components of AlgoTutor along with some experiences we have had with our students.

3.1 Concept Reviewer and Concept Revisited

AlgoTutor starts the tutoring session by providing a problem description as an exercise in a lab. Before students start constructing an algorithm, AlgoTutor uses the concept reviewer component to help students review concepts required to solve the problem and clarify the problem specifications. For example in solving the binary search problem, we asked students to figure out the correct search sequence given the key and the array values. Additionally, we asked students to identify the condition that indicates the situation when the key is not in the array. After the algorithm development phase is completed, AlgoTutor uses the concept revisited component to help students review the required programming skills.

Questions used in these components are presented online in multiple choice or short answer format, and the student responses are graded with appropriate feedback. We have used these two components to evaluate understanding of the problem specification and programming skills as well as for assessment of student learning.

3.2 Algorithm Composer

The Algorithm Composer is the core component of AlgoTutor. This component allows algorithms to be constructed by assembling pre-defined operations and control structures via a graphical drag-and-drop interface. AlgoTuor divides the algorithm design process into two phases. The first phase called the operation selection phase involves knowing which operations to use and in what order to use them. In the second phase called the parameter mapping phase, the student must map the variables in the generic operations to problem specific values.

Figure 2 shows a snapshot of the algorithm composer that solves the problem of drawing a triangle using a nested loop. The available operations and variables are both displayed in the right pane using tabs. A working algorithm under development is displayed in the left pane, which is composed by dragging operation tiles and variable tiles from the right pane [6].

The AlgoTutor system provides online grading and feedback so that students can check immediately whether or not their algorithm is correct and what mistakes, if any, they made. When the "Compare my ordering w/ teacher's" button is clicked, the system will highlight the last correct operation tile in blue and the first incorrect operation in red so that a student can fix the error and complete the algorithm. If they run into a problem that cannot be resolved on their own, students can use a lifeline which will provide the next correct step.

3.3 Algorithm Tracer

In a typical CS-I course much of the teaching effort is expended in teaching correct syntax and use of the programming

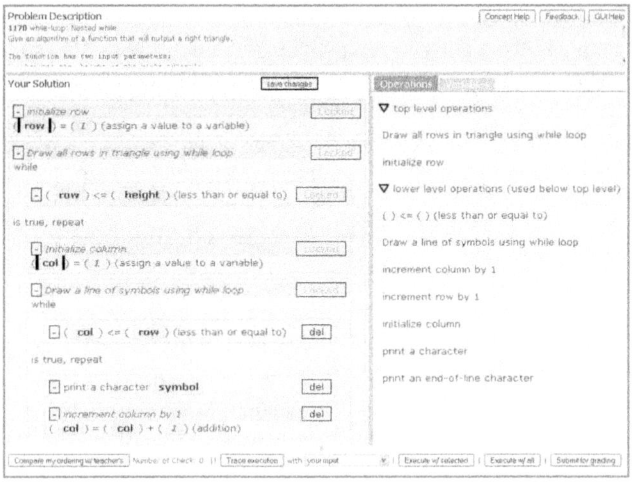

Figure 2. A snapshot of the algorithm composer that solves the problem of drawing a triangle using a nested loop.

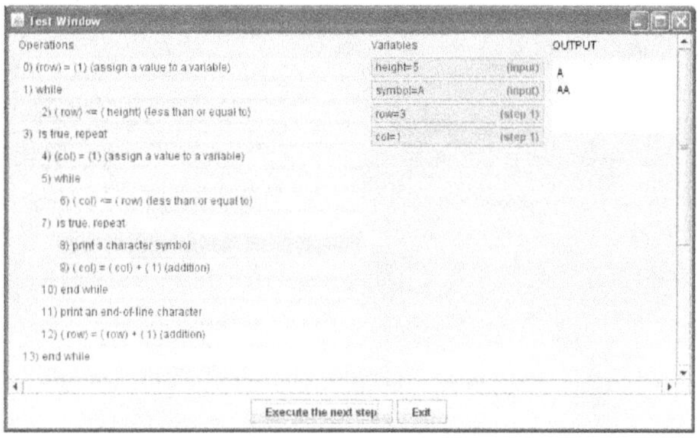

Figure 3. A snapshot of the algorithm tracer for the algorithm in Figure 2.

environment. The high overhead of learning syntax and a programming environment can distract students from focusing on the primary goal, i.e., learning the process of designing an algorithm for problem solving. Shackelford [8] observed that the details of a particular programming language tended to "annoy and distract attention from the core issue of algorithmic problem solving." Furthermore, even when they learn to construct algorithms on paper, novice students are typically unable to follow the execution of the algorithm to check for its correctness. Algorithm Tracer addresses these issues.

To run the algorithm tracer, the student first selects a test input from the combo box located adjacent to the "Trace execution" button in the algorithm composer, as shown in Figure 2. A trace may require values for input problem parameters and/or the input stream, the student can provide their own values or use one of the test data sets provided by teachers. The algorithm tracer visualizes the execution of the algorithm by stepping one operation or control structure part at a time. The student can follow the control flow and monitor changes in variable values.

Figure 3 shows a snapshot of the algorithm tracer for the algorithm shown in Figure 2. The tracer interface is divided into four panes: the algorithm pane, the variable pane, the output pane and the control panel. The algorithm pane shows a listing of the current algorithm in a format similar to that of the composer. Operations are numbered for reference during execution of the algorithm. The next operation to be executed is highlighted as shown in Figure 3 (step 8). The variable pane shows a listing of all currently defined local variables with their current values. The last operation step that modified the value of that variable is shown in parenthesis to the right of the value. For input problem parameters, "input" is shown instead. The output pane shows output from the execution as it progresses. The control panel lies along the bottom of the window.

The algorithm tracer allows students to verify the correctness of their algorithm by providing visual tracing of the student algorithm. When a student submits an algorithm for grading, it will be run against a known correct solution for all predefined test cases. The outputs for each test case are compared and the student receives a score that is the percentage of all test cases that matched. These grading runs are performed without visualization, i.e. no diagnostic information will be provided. Students can also execute the algorithm with selected data to see the output of the execution without tracing by clicking the "Execute w/ selected" button in Composer.

Experiences with Algorithm Tracer

We used AlgoTutor with the algorithm tracer for while-loop labs. Participants in these studies were students enrolled in the CS-I classes in the fall of 2009 and the spring of 2010 at our school. Each of these labs contained four problems. We used pre-tests and post-tests to measure the effectiveness of these labs (and the outcome of the experiments was positive), but we could not isolate the effect of the algorithm tracer from the algorithm composer [10]. To assess the students' perception of the usefulness of the algorithm tracer, an exit survey response was collected online after the second lab. The survey question was "The tracing feature helped me verify my algorithm." A total of 111 students participated in the exit survey, and 77% of the students (85 out of 111) agreed or strongly agreed with the question and only one student disagreed.

The exit survey also asked students to provide any comments related to their experience with the system. The following are typical positive comments provided by students:

- If there happens to be an error, it helps to be able to see where the algorithm goes wrong.
- I really really like tracing.
- The trace function is very helpful. For me, it's the best feature by far. I wish there were more traceable examples, even outside of lab, that I could access for studying and comprehending programs.
- It was very helpful to find out the errors if the algorithm was incorrect

Negative comments were mostly related to very specific situations such as a system glitch which has since been addressed, misunderstanding a problem specification, or inability to solve that specific problem.

Currently the algorithm tracer can only be used for a certain category of problems whose algorithms consist of traceable operations. These operations are implemented so that the execution can be visualized. We are planning to expand the set of traceable operations in the future. In the following subsection, we will describe another component of AlgoTutor called ProgramPad which addresses step 4 of the problem solving process, "convert the algorithm into a C++ program."

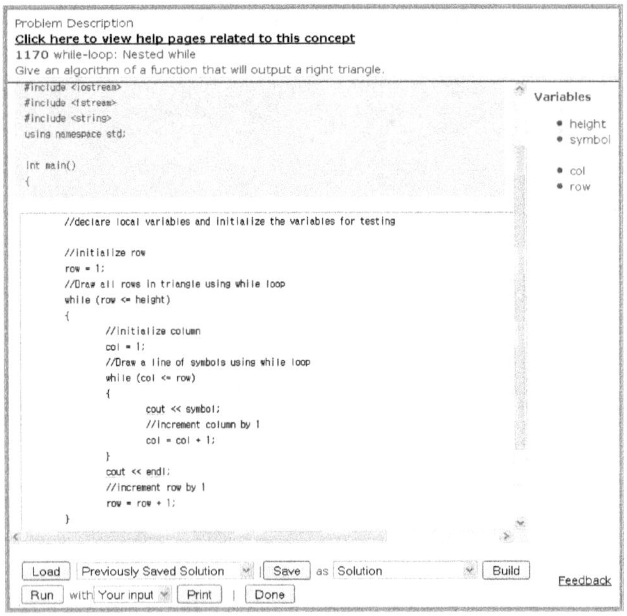

Figure 4. A snapshot of ProgramPad.

3.4 ProgramPad

The main target student group of ProgramPad is students in CS-I classes. The algorithm developed using the composer eventually needs to be converted to code for implementation. Students in CS-I often do not see the relationship between the algorithm and the code. For this reason, we have developed another component of AlgoTutor called ProgramPad. ProgramPad converts most of the operations/steps in an algorithm into C++ code, and provides an interface for completing the program.

Figure 4 shows a snapshot of the program pad for the algorithm that solves the problem of drawing a triangle using a nested loop. ProgramPad displays the problem description in the top pane for students to review the problem specification. The problem parameters and local variables used are displayed in the variable pane on the right. The program pane on the left is used to either convert the student algorithm developed in the composer into C++ code or to load the previously saved code. Along with the capability of converting the algorithm to C++ code, ProgramPad also provides most of a simple integrated development environment's capabilities: edit, save, load, build, run, and print. The control panel displays the buttons related to these features.

ProgramPad can be used in two ways: 1) as the main function that solves the problem or 2) as a function that is called by a driver. Each operation used in AlgoTutor has corresponding C++ code which is either a primitive statement or a function prototype. For example, "print variable" is converted to "cout << variable;" and "print a right triangle of height h with symbol s" is converted to "void PrintTriangle (int h, char s);" An operation with a function prototype is an abstract operation that is not atomic and is viewed as a function in C++. This allows us to convert an algorithm with abstract operations into a program with multiple functions.

Programming concepts related to functions are not easy for novice programmers. They typically have difficulties differentiating between the function parameters and local variables and/or between arguments in a function call and parameters in the corresponding function definition. In addition, students are often confused with the concepts of returning a value from a value-returning function and outputting a value with an output statement. Similarly, they have trouble distinguishing between input-parameters and input statements.

ProgramPad can also be used for more complex problems which contain subproblem(s). For example, the problem of drawing a trapezoid can be solved by using an abstract operation "draw a line of symbols." This operation is a problem which students have already solved. When ProgramPad is invoked for drawing a trapezoid, it automatically provides function prototypes and most of the function definitions which are then automatically converted using the algorithms developed in the algorithm composer as well as the driver that uses these functions.

Repeatedly practicing on problems similar to the above problems using ProgramPad can help students learn the programming concepts while understanding the connection between the algorithm and the corresponding program. Unlike the algorithm composer, ProgramPad does not provide automatic grading. Students can complete and test the program, which has been converted from their algorithm, using their own input values. The program can be printed for grading and/or for help.

Table 1. : Students' responses to the survey questions after using ProgramPad (A for agree, N for nuetral, D for disagree in %).

Questions	A	N	D
While concept related			
This exercise helped me learn how to check input errors using a while loop.	79	18	3
Function concept related			
This exercise helped me understand pass-by-value parameter. For example, the value parameter n can be used as a loop control variable.	66	29	5
This exercise helped me understand pass-by-reference parameters. For example, reference parameters can be used to return multiple values.	62	28	11
Top-down/bottom-up strategy related			
This exercise helped me learn to develop a top-level algorithm without worrying about details.	61	33	6
ProgramPad related			
Did ProgramPad help you understand the process of developing a program using the algorithm for this problem?	81	18	2

Experiments with ProgramPad

We used AlgoTutor with ProgramPad for several labs including while-loop, function, and array concepts. Participants in these studies were students enrolled in the CS-I course in the fall of 2009 and the spring of 2010. There were several classes taught by three teachers. To assess the students' perception of the usefulness of the ProgramPad system, exit survey responses were collected online after each problem. Table 1 shows the survey results categorized by concepts that the exercise addressed. Some of the questions are programming concept specific and others are problem solving related or ProgramPad related. Not all exercises were done by all classes, so each question has 22 to 130 responses. The actual survey questions have 5 options: strongly agree, agree, neutral, disagree, and strongly disagree. However, we merged strongly agree and agree as well as strongly disagree and disagree for simplicity.

The data shows that survey results for the while-loop are better than the function. We think it is because the function programming concept is more difficult than the while-loop concept. However, more than 62% of the students agreed for all the questions related to the function concept. For the question related to problem solving strategy, 61% of the students found it useful/helpful. More than 80% of the students agreed that ProgramPad helped them understand the process of developing a program using an algorithm.

4. STUDENT SURVEYS

4.1 How effective is AlgoTutor?

At the end of the 2009 fall and 2010 spring semesters, we also conducted a written exit survey to obtain student feedback for the AlgoTutor system. Table 2 shows a part of the questionnaire used in the exit survey for the algorithm composer and ProgramPad. Questions 1 through 5 refer to the algorithm composer and Questions 6 through 8 are for ProgramPad. Participation in the exit survey was voluntary, and a total of 111 students participated. The student responses are summarized in Table 2. From that data we see that roughly 80% of the students agreed or strongly agreed with "Selecting operations from the provided list helped you figure out the solution," and "The process of choosing parameters helped you figure out the solution." This shows that two phases in the algorithm composer, the operation selection phase and the parameter mapping phase, helped students figure out the solution. We also received favorable responses on ProgramPad.

The exit survey also gave students an opportunity to comment. The following are typical comments provided by students.

Table 2. : A part of the exit survey questionnaire and the survey results. (A for agree, N for nuetral, D for disagree in %).

Survey questions	A	N	D
1. Not worrying about C++ syntax helped you concentrate on problem solving.	71	21	7
2. Selecting operations from the provided list helped you figure out the solution.	79	12	9
3. The process of choosing parameters helped you figure out the solution.	83	12	5
4. The algorithm tutor helped you organize your thoughts and develop an algorithm.	80	10	9
5. The algorithm tutor helped you understand the process of developing an algorithm.	78	13	9
6. Being able to see the C++ code that corresponds to my algorithm helped me understand the algorithm/program.	75	19	6
7. Being able to execute the program for my algorithm and to see the output helped me understand the algorithm	73	21	6
8. The ProgramPad helped you bridge the gap between the algorithm development and the implementation of the algorithm.	59	27	13

Comments on Algorithm Composer

- It really helped me organize my thoughts, and at times it provided an algorithm solution to the one I had in mind.
- We don't have to worry about typos and we can focus on solving the problem rather than stressing out over semi-colons and other syntax errors, and trace execution was very helpful.
- I enjoyed the visual representation of nesting. Nesting was a harder concept to grasp, especially trying to trace execution before using AlgoTutor.
- It developed a foundation to understand how to start analyzing the problem first, than being able to code the program was more clear.

Comments on ProgramPad

- I liked that it helped see how a program is made from an algorithm.
- It was a good way to get real coding experience without having to write the entire program yourself.
- You actually got to see the code and then you got to finish it.
- It did help show the connection between the AlgoTutor and actual coding
- I got to see the algorithm I just made into C++ form

There were some constructive criticisms that will be used to improve the system. Most of the personal conversations with students were very positive and we are quite encouraged to know that students were able to learn a new programming concept and reinforce their learning using the AlgoTutor system.

4.2 Can we change the student's attitude toward algorithm development?

As we mentioned in an earlier section, we observed that students often think developing an algorithm prior to coding is not necessary. They are also lacking algorithm development skills. To find out whether AlgoTutor addresses these two issues, we conducted a survey during the first class of CS-II in the fall of 2010. A total of 52 students participated in this survey. Roughly half of these students used AlgoTutor in CS-I (Group 1), while the other half (Group 2) had not used the system previously.

The survey was designed to assess the students' attitudes toward "lack of appreciation of the worth of the algorithm development phase" and "lack of ability to construct algorithms." Table 3 summarizes the results that were statistically significant.

Specifically, Table 3 shows that more students in group 1 (students who used AlgoTutor in CS-I) responded that they are confident in developing an algorithm than students in group 2 (students who did not use AlgoTutor previously). It also shows that more students in group 1 found that developing an algorithm helped in solving programming tasks than students in group 2. One way ANOVA tests were conducted to determine if there were any significant differences between the two groups and both results are statistically significant with the 95% confidence level.

From the results we reported in this paper, we claim that using AlgoTutor in CS-I helps students:

- Learn proper problem solving processes
- Learn how to develop an algorithm for a problem
- Learn the value of algorithm development
- Develop confidence in algorithm development

Table 3. : Students' responses to the attitude survey questions (percent of students who either agree or strongly agreed).

Questions	Group1	Group2
I know how to develop an algorithm for a programming assignment.	54%	21%
I found it easier to solve a programming task with an algorithm than without it.	63%	29%

5. RELATED WORK

The drag-and-drop features of Alice were a major inspiration in the design of the AlgoTutor interface. While Alice [2] and Scratch [3] [7] allow for the creation of engaging animated content, we used a simpler visualization method for illustrating the algorithms typically encountered in an introductory programming course. The visualization technique provided by ALVIS Live! [4] is at the correct level of abstraction, but it does not provide relief from the burden of language syntax. Even though, there has been some work on automatic code generation from design patterns [1] or an object model like a UML class drawing diagram tool [5] which represents the logical structure of the class templates, none of the systems uses the abstract algorithm to generate code.

While other teaching tools have been developed with similar features, most have been developed as stand-alone applications running on the end user's computer. With AlgoTutor, we chose to create a web-based application that is hosted on a central server and runs within a web browser. This approach allows easy deployment and access from locations outside the lab. Because all data is stored centrally, it is easy to develop tools for instructors and to analyze student performance and behavior.

6. CONCLUSION AND FUTURE WORK

Acquiring the ability to design an algorithm for a problem is one of the most important learning outcomes of computer science courses. Unfortunately, not only is learning how to design algorithms a challenging task, but many students believe that algorithm design is not an important part of problem solving. We developed AlgoTutor to address this challenge and hopefully change student attitudes toward algorithm design.

AlgoTutor trains CS-I students to start the problem solving process with algorithm design. Using the algorithm tracer in AlgoTutor, the system then helps students learn how to trace an algorithm by visualizing the execution of a student algorithm. Using ProgramPad in AlgoTutor, students can see the connection between the algorithm that is developed using the algorithm composer and the converted C++ program. Even difficult programming concepts such as function parameters and array concepts can be addressed using ProgramPad.

Our survey results show that students feel that AlgoTutor helped them organize their thoughts and develop algorithms. But more importantly, students who used AlgoTutor were significantly more likely to appreciate the importance of algorithm design and to have confidence in their ability to develop an algorithm. In the upcoming semesters we plan to run more experiments with new features such as reviewing related concepts and problem specifications. We are also investigating ways to promote student thinking and engaging student interest by adapting to each individual student's learning.

7. ACKNOWLEDGMENTS

This research was supported by the NSF CCLI grant DUE-0737257.

8. REFERENCES

[1] Budinsky, F.J. Finnie, M.A., Vlissides, J.M., and Yu, P.S. (1996). "Automatic Code Generation from Design Patterns" *Object technology*, vol. 35, No. 2.

[2] Cooper, S., Dann, W., & Pausch, R. (2000) Alice: A 3-D tool for introductory programming concepts. In Proceedings of the 5th Annual CCSC Northeastern Conference 2000, Ramapo, NJ.

[3] Fesakis, G. and Serafeim, K. (2009). Influence of the familiarization with "scratch" on future teachers' opinions and attitudes about programming and ICT in education Volume 41 , Issue 3 (September 2009), ITiCSE '09, Pages 258-262.

[4] Hundhausen, C.D. and Brown, J.L. (2007). What You See Is What You Code: A 'Live' Algorithm Development and Visualization Environment for Novice Learners. *Journal of Visual Languages and Computing* 18(1), 22-47.

[5] Niaz, I.A. and Tanaka, J. (2004) "Mapping UML Statecharts to Java Code", in *Proc. IASTED International Conf. on Software Engineering (SE 2004)*, Innsbruck, Austria, pp. 111-116.

[6] Pettey, C., Yoo, J., Yoo, S., Seo, S., Dong, Z., (2009). A Tool for Promoting Algorithm Development in Introductory CS Classes, Proceedings of ED-MEDIA 2009, pp 87-95, Honolulu, Hawaii.

[7] Resnick, M., Maloney, J., Monroy-Hernández, A., Rusk, N., Eastmond, E., Brennan, K., Millner, A., Rosenbaum, E., Silver, J., Silverman, B, and Kafai, Y. (2009). "Scratch: programming for all". Communications of the ACM , Volume 52 Issue 11.

[8] Shackelford, R. L. (1997). "Introducing computer science fundamentals before programming". In FIE '97: Proceedings of the Frontiers in Education Conference, 1997. on 27th Annual Conference. Teaching and Learning in an Era of Change., Washington, DC, USA, pp. 285-289 vol.1. IEEE Computer Society.

[9] Yoo, J., Dong, Z., Yoo, S., Seo, S., and Pettey, C. (2009). "Improving Student Performance by Enforcing Algorithm Development" Proceedings of ED-MEDIA 2009, pp 119-127, Honolulu, Hawaii.

[10] Yoo, J., Pettey, C., Seo, S., and Yoo, S. (2010), Teaching Programming Concepts Using Algorithm Tutor. Proceedings of ED-MEDIA 2010, Toronto, Canada.

Teaching Tips We Wish They'd Told Us Before We Started, Small College Class Edition

Daniel D. Garcia (moderator)
University of California, Berkeley
777 Soda Hall, Berkeley, CA 94720-1776
+1 510-642-9595
ddgarcia@cs.berkeley.edu

Zachary Dodds
Harvey Mudd College
301 Platt Boulevard, Claremont, CA 91711
+1 909-607-1613
dodds@cs.hmc.edu

Timothy Huang
Middlebury College
642 McCardell Bicentennial Hall
Middlebury, VT 05753
+1 802-443-2431
huang@middlebury.edu

Samuel A. Rebelsky
Grinnell College
1116 8th Avenue
Grinnell, IA 50112
+1 641-269-4410
rebelsky@grinnell.edu

SUMMARY

"Be an opener of doors for such as come after thee..."
– Ralph Waldo Emerson, 1844

At the SIGCSE Symposium in 2007, we presented a panel in which seasoned teaching faculty from four large, PhD-granting universities shared the teaching tips we wished we'd known before starting our careers [1]. The difference from earlier "Teaching Tips" panels [6] was that our suggestions were meant to be hidden gems less often highlighted by our colleagues or by some of the best-known teaching resources [2, 3, 4, 8, 10, 11]. We clustered our tips into several categories: **Lecturing**, **Office** (hours), **Staff** (mentoring), **Exams** (authoring & administering), **Labs** (authoring & running), **Section** (TA-led discussion), **Projects** (and homework; authoring & supporting), and **Meta** (advice spanning categories). The session was received quite well, and the audience contributed many of their own teaching tips throughout the presentation.

Since all of the presenters in 2007 regularly taught large, hundred-student classes, many of their suggestions (e.g., lecturing in a large venue or managing an army of teaching assistants) were not relevant to the experience of teaching small classes. Quite a few attendees suggested there be a follow-up session with presenters who could address the challenges specific to small college or university classes. To that end, we present the "Small College Class" edition, with seasoned educators who have expertise teaching smaller classes at their university or college. The position statements that follow offer a random sampling of two of these "hidden" pearls; presenters will share many more during the session, and time will be provided for audience participation. We'll endeavor to capture all the tips for an online collection. Complementing the categories above, we have added two more that capture the intimate setting of small classes:

- **Classroom** (organization, interactions, and incentives)
- **Personal** (fostering relationships).

SIGCSE'11, March 9–12, 2011, Dallas, Texas, USA.
ACM 978-1-4503-0500-6/11/03.

Categories and Subject Descriptors

K.3.2 [**Computer and Information Science Education**]: Computer Science Education

General Terms

Documentation, Experimentation, Human Factors, Management

Keywords: Computer science education, teaching tips

1. DANIEL D. GARCIA

Activate students' slow-motion effect (Lecturing) I don't remember much of 4th grade. However, one day I had the fortune of performing with my chorus at Lincoln Center in New York City, and I remember the entire experience as if it were yesterday. Neuroscientist David Eagleman calls this the "slow-motion" effect, where significant experiences turn your memory from a sieve into a high-fidelity recorder [9]. The lesson is: when there's something critical they need to learn, do something to trigger their unconscious, high-resolution brain recording. Stand on the table! Take them on a relevant field trip to a museum or local company.

Know them all … now (Personal) In small classes, you're sure to know them all by the end of the term. Do so as soon as possible, through repeated use of fun icebreakers like *the big wind blows* [7], *data processing* [5], *stupid human tricks* (e.g, sharing a unique skill), and other games. Provide an incentive to the student who knows the names of everyone in the room first; see if you can beat them to the punch (enrollment lists are often available before the term starts). Create a mini-bio, have all your instructional staff fill it out and put their answers online, then ask your students to affix a photo and fill one out too. Class bios should be visible only to your staff unless the student "opts in" to a slightly public (class-only) or fully public option (web). Host a potluck the first week of the term and play games together!

2. ZACHARY DODDS

Celebrate idiosyncrasies (Personal) In a small classroom, we strive to make time and space that will include more of both students' and instructor's personalities – beyond the stage personas that tend to dominate in large-crowd interactions. Assignments and in-class exercises with an open-ended, personal component are helpful here: media-based and dialog/text-based problems can both work. Even our first week's CS1 assignment, a text-based rock-paper-scissors, leads to surprising and amusing variations – when encouraged. Sharing the results with the class further fosters camaraderie. Regardless of the details, celebrating the idiosyncrasies of all of a class's members helps to reinforce that learning and teaching is primarily about people, not content.

The most important 20 minutes (Lecturing, Personal): I believe the most important 20 minutes of class time is the 10 minutes before the scheduled class begins and the 10 minutes after it ends. By being completely set up well ahead of time, an instructor can chat with students as they arrive – that span is a great way to know what big projects *other* classes are imposing that week, how the school's water-polo team is doing, or how the weekend's "dis-orientation" party fared. In fact, starting 5 minutes early – preferably with student-suggested content such as the latest (family-friendly) YouTube meme, facebook group, or, for the higher-brow, New York Times article – can help the segue into the day's material and provide students added incentive to make it by the starting time. Similarly, the 10 minutes after class offer a chance to re-connect personally with individuals who might have looked either too disconcerted (or not disconcerted enough) with the day's material. Positioning yourself between the class and the primary exit, at the very least, offers the opportunity to send everyone off with an invitation to come back for the next meeting!

3. TIMOTHY HUANG

Tiered goals (Exams): For take-home exams with programming problems, give tiered goals with increasing point values. For example, writing code to find an object in a maze might be worth 20 points, adding code to paint a path from the starting point to the objects might be worth 25 points, and writing code to find two objects and the path between them might be worth 30 points. Tiered goals make it easier for students of all levels to make progress and feel a sense of accomplishment on problems, and they facilitate faster and more consistent grading.

Organize debates (Lecturing): In my OS course, I break the class into three teams and hold three debates between each pair of teams on topics of current interest (e.g., net neutrality or open vs. closed mobile platforms) over the course of the term. The team not debating forms the jury and votes on a winner at the end. The debate format encourages students to dig deep into the topic and to work together on how best to argue for a particular position.

4. SAMUEL A. REBELSKY

Make mistakes (Classroom) Too often, we (teachers in lecture, textbooks, whatever) describe a problem, show the approach to take, and then present the corresponding code. Students wonder why it's not as straightforward for them as it is in the book. So… *make mistakes, and make them enthusiastically*! Choose the wrong algorithm. Write code with bugs in it. The mistakes you show in processes can make students more comfortable making their own and more comfortable making suggestions that may be wrong.

Involve students in collaborative problem-solving processes (Classroom) Particularly in introductory courses, students are often uncomfortable with the process of going from a vague problem statement to a working and verified solution. One of the advantages of a small class is that we can actively model the process, by calling on students with a series of questions. You can call on students by name, taking advantage of what you know about their strengths and weaknesses, or simply let students volunteer to answer each question. Have a set of stock questions ready (e.g., "What would that mean for the current example?"). You should, of course, be willing to accept the occasional "I don't know". However, one important aspect of such an exercise is that students need to learn to take risks and be willing to make mistakes. That means that you also need to be willing to take the time to follow a few incorrect paths.

5. REFERENCES

[1] Astrachan, O., Parlante, N., Garcia, D. D., and Reges, S. 2007. Teaching tips we wish they'd told us before we started. In *Proceedings of the 38th SIGCSE Technical Symposium on Computer Science Education* (Covington, Kentucky, USA, March 07 - 11, 2007). SIGCSE '07. ACM, New York, NY, 2-3. http://doi.acm.org/10.1145/1227310.1227314

[2] Bain, K. *What the Best College Teachers Do.* Harvard University Press, Cambridge, MA, 2004.

[3] Boice, R. *Advice for New Faculty Members.* Allyn & Bacon, Needham Heights, MA, 2000.

[4] Davis, B.*Tools for Teaching, 2/e.* Jossey-Bass, SF, CA, 2009.

[5] Fluegelman, A. *More New Games!* Dolphin, NY, 1981.

[6] Grissom, S., Naps, T., Parlante, N., and Lawhead, P. 2001. Practical teaching tips from around the world. In *Proceedings of the Thirty-Second SIGCSE Technical Symposium on Computer Science Education* (Charlotte, North Carolina, United States). SIGCSE '01. ACM, New York, NY, 419. http://doi.acm.org/10.1145/364447.364807

[7] group-games.com. *Big Wind Blows Game.* www.group-games.com/ice-breakers/big-wind-blows-game.html

[8] McKeachie, W. J. Mckeachie's *Teaching Tips: Strategies, Research And Theory for College And University Teachers.* Houghton Mifflin, Boston, MA, 2005.

[9] NPR. *Why a Brush With Death Triggers the Slow-Mo Effect.* www.npr.org/templates/story/story.php?storyId=129112147

[10] Reis, R. M. *Tomorrow's Professor: Preparing for Careers in Science and Engineering.* IEEE Press, New York, NY, 1997.

[11] Royce, D. *Teaching Tips for College and University Instructors: A Practical Guide.* Allyn & Bacon, Needham Heights, MA, 2000.

Understanding NSF Funding Opportunities

Scott Grissom
National Science Foundation
sgrissom@nsf.gov

Sue Fitzgerald
National Science Foundation
scfitzge@nsf.gov

Victor Piotrowski
National Science Foundation
vpiotrow@nsf.gov

Jan Cuny
National Science Foundation
jcuny@nsf.gov

Joan Peckham
National Science Foundation
jpeckham@nsf.gov

Harriet Taylor
National Science Foundation
htaylor@nsf.gov

Daniel Menelly
National Science Foundation
dmenelly@nsf.gov

Mimi McClure
National Science Foundation
mmcclure@nsf.gov

SUMMARY
This session highlights programs in the National Science Foundation's (NSF) Education and Human Resources (EHR) and Computer and Information Science and Engineering (CISE) directorates. The focus is on providing descriptions of several programs of interest to college faculty, and discussing the requirements and guidelines for programs in these areas. It includes a description of the proposal and review processes as well as strategies for writing competitive proposals. Participants are encouraged to discuss procedural issues with the presenters.

Categories and Subject Descriptors
K.3.2 Computer and Information Science Education

General Terms
Documentation.

Keywords
Grants, awards, proposals, National Science Foundation, education.

1. INTRODUCTION
NSF supports projects to improve education in science, technology, engineering, and mathematics through several programs in its Education and Human Resources (EHR) directorate, as well as in its research directorates, including Computer and Information Science and Engineering (CISE). This forum presents a description of some education-related programs in the EHR and CISE directorates, and enables participants to interact with the presenters concerning specific project ideas that could be appropriate for the various programs.

2. SPECIFIC PROGRAMS DISCUSSED
Complete details about each of the following programs can be found on the NSF websites for the Division of Undergraduate Education (DUE) [1], the Directorate for Computer & Information Science & Engineering (CISE) [2], and the Office of Cyberinfrastructure (OCI) [3].

SIGCSE'11, March 9–12, 2011, Dallas, Texas, USA.
ACM 978-1-4503-0500-6/11/03.

2.1 Advanced Technological Education (ATE)
ATE is a program specifically geared for community colleges, or for four-year schools working closely with community colleges. This program focuses on improvement in the "education of science and engineering technicians at the undergraduate and the secondary school levels. [2]" Specific technological fields include computer and information technology, cybersecurity, forensics, and telecommunications.

2.2 Transforming Undergraduate Education In Stem (TUES)
TUES supports innovation in student learning in the classroom, and improvements in educational practice. Particular emphasis in TUES is on creating new learning materials and strategies, developing faculty expertise, implementing education innovations, assessing student achievement, and conducting research on undergraduate STEM education. The NSF showcase presents innovative TUES projects.

2.3 Cyberinfrastructure Training, Education, Advancement And Mentoring (CI-TEAM)
The programs of OCI offer significant educational elements. One program in particular, CI-TEAM, is focused on the education and workforce development needed to prepare our citizens for success. OCI serves directly under the Office of the Director of the NSF, and thus is not a part of any other directorate. OCI supports research and development of the cyberinfrastructure (CI) needed to support a cyber-enabled and scientific society, and the education and training required to sustain and support the CI. The current foci are on big data, HPC (high performance computing), and virtual organizations including attention to the development of networks, software, security, and algorithms to support the above. In all of our efforts we collaborate across NSF and with other government agencies as our work is highly interdisciplinary in nature.

2.4 Federal Cyber Service: Scholarships for Service (SFS)

This program seeks to increase the number of qualified students entering information assurance and computer security and to increase the capacity of the US higher education enterprise to continue to produce professionals in these fields. The SFS program is has two tracks: (1) the Scholarship Track that provides funding for scholarships to students in information assurance and computer security, and (2) the Capacity Building Track that provides funding for professional development of information assurance and computer security faculty and for the development of academic programs in these fields.

2.5 Information Technology Experiences for Students and Teachers (ITEST)

While there are four main components to ITEST, the two most likely to be of interest are youth-based projects for students in K-12, and comprehensive projects for K-12 teachers and students. "It is anticipated that projects funded under the ITEST program will not only increase interest in IT through the creation of effective student education programs in both school and non-school contexts, but also maintain interest through supportive activities that include parental involvement, career exploration, externships, research, and multi-year programs."

Two other programs in the Division of Research on Learning in Formal and Informal Settings (DRL) for supporting K-12 students and teachers are Informal Science Education (ISE) and Discovery Research K-12 (DRK-12). These will both be briefly covered.

2.6 Research Experiences for Undergraduates Sites (REU Sites)

Research experience is one of the most effective ways of attracting talented undergraduates to, and retaining them in careers in science and engineering, including careers in teaching and research. The REU Sites program aims to provide appropriate and valuable educational experiences for cohorts of 8-10 undergraduate students in the summer through participation in research and professional development activities. REU projects involve students, most who are from other than the host institution, in meaningful ways in ongoing research programs or in research projects specifically designed for the REU program. REU projects feature high-quality interaction of students with faculty and/or other research mentors and access to appropriate facilities and professional development opportunities.

2.7 Scholarships in Science, Technology, Engineering and Mathematics (S-STEM)

This program makes grants to institutions of higher education to support individual scholarships of up to $10,000/year for academically talented, financially needy students, majoring in science and engineering disciplines. It is expected that scholarship recipients will achieve at least one of the following by the end of the scholarship award period: (1) receive an associate, baccalaureate, or graduate degree in one of the S-STEM disciplines; (2) transfer from an associate degree program to a baccalaureate degree program or from an undergraduate program to a graduate program in one of the S-STEM disciplines; or (3) successfully complete a stage within an associate, baccalaureate, or graduate degree program in one of the S-STEM disciplines.

2.8 STEM Talent Expansion Program (STEP)

STEP grants fall into two categories of activities. Type 1 activities are aimed at implementing recruitment or retention strategies that will lead to a measurable increase in the number of students obtaining STEM degrees in baccalaureate or associate degree programs or completing credits toward transfer to a baccalaureate degree program in STEM fields at community colleges. Type 2 activities focus on educational research on factors affecting associate or baccalaureate degree attainment in STEM.

3. WRITING COMPETITIVE PROPOSALS

NSF programs are quite competitive but there are simple strategies you should be aware of when writing proposals to improve your chances of success. First and foremost, read the Program Solicitation carefully. Your goal is to help reviewers quickly understand *what* you intend to do and that you have given sufficient thought of *how* you intend to do it. Organize the proposal to address the essential components described in the solicitation. Use headings, boldface and bulleted lists to help the reader quickly understand the organization of the proposals. Address each point thoroughly but succinctly. And finally, start well before the submission deadline. Include sufficient lead time to allow colleagues to provide feedback and for your research office to approve the proposal. Specific directions for completing your proposal can be found online [4].

4. REFERENCES

[1] http://nsf.gov/div/index.jsp?div=DUE

[2] http://nsf.gov/dir/index.jsp?org=CISE

[3] http://nsf.gov/dir/index.jsp?org=OCI

[4] http://nsf.gov/funding/preparing/

Role and Value of Quantitative Instruments in Gauging Student Perspectives in A Computing Curriculum

Henry M. Walker
Grinnell College
Grinnell, Iowa 50112-1690
walker@cs.grinnell.edu

Ali Erkan
Ithaca College
Ithaca, NY 14850, U.S.A.
aerkan@ithaca.edu

Mark Guzdial
Georgia Institute of Technology
Atlanta, GA, 30332-0280
guzdial@cc.gatech.edu

Steve Cooper
Purdue University
West Lafayette, IN 47907-2015
coopersc@purdue.edu

Categories and Subject Descriptors

K.3.2 [**Computer and Information Science Education**]: Curriculum, Computer Science Education

General Terms

Theory

Keywords

Survey instrument, perspectives, attitudes, beliefs, expectations

1. SUMMARY

From our perspective, introductory courses generally represent a blend of elements, such as:

- practice with problem solving (perhaps with programming as a mechanism to help students make their solutions precise),
- coverage of technical elements and details (perhaps with an emphasis on proficiency in some programming language),
- preparation for later courses (e.g., experience with control structures and simple data structures for intermediate level computing courses or experience in C for engineering or physics),
- overview of the scope of the discipline (sometimes called a "breadth-first perspective"),
- connections with one or more application areas (sometimes discussed as making computing relevant),
- identification of social and ethical issues of computing (e.g., placing computing in a broad framework),
- clarification of what it means to be a computing professional (e.g., what do computing folks actually do),
- shaping of attitudes and perspectives on the computing discipline (e.g., correcting misconceptions or developing a sense of professionalism).

Further, students often enter college with pre-conceived notions of what the field of computing entails, and unfortunately many of these images are misguided. For example, many incoming students seem to believe that computing primarily involves some combination of surfing the Web, hacking, and playing video games. Their expectations of the study habits and learning techniques that would make them successful at their intended major are also spread across the spectrum.

In this special session, we will discuss the role and value of quantitative instruments in gauging student perspectives in the context of these issues. After creating the appropriate context (section 2), we will discuss the road educators have travelled in creating such instruments (section 3) as well as review one based on a variation of a survey developed by the University of Maryland Physics Education Research Group (section 4). Finally, we will present the importance of gathering this information (for curriculum design) from the perspective of grant agencies (section 5). After the presentation of the four speakers and before the start of our general discussion, we will invite our audience members to fill out the survey form for a particular instrument. If we are collectively on the same page, then our responses may be used to establish a baseline to which students progress can be compared.

2. Henry M. Walker

My role on this panel is to consider the role of attitudinal studies of students as they progress through a computing curriculum. Unfortunately, in my experience, many discussions of introductory computing courses become side-tracked by low-level details and anecdotal vignettes. For example, it seems to me that many arguments regarding the use of one programming language or another in CS1 depend upon underlying assumptions regarding the merits of a specific problem-solving paradigm, the significance of specific technical constructs (e.g., the relative merits of iteration versus recursion), and the need for proficiency in a favorite language as preparation for later courses.

With the interest in recruiting a broad range of students to the field and to encourage students who try an introductory course, I think computing faculty need to review various underlying assumptions. For example,

- What really are the important underlying elements that should be emphasized at the introductory level?

SIGCSE'11, March 9–12, 2011, Dallas, Texas, USA.
ACM 978-1-4503-0500-6/11/03.

- How can introductory courses connect with diverse groups of incoming students, and how do alternative introductory courses provide a strong foundation in key areas for future work?

Computing faculty likely need to sort out priorities for the entire curriculum, including introductory courses. However, student attitudes and perceptions are important in appealing to diverse populations and shaping course details. Likely different schools enroll different groups, so what works in recruiting and retention for one school may be quite different from what works at another institution. Further, interests and perspectives of faculty differ, and instructors will likely be most effective when they can work for their individual strengths. The challenge for computing educators is to find a balance that works well in each local environment.

3. Mark Guzdial

Computing education research has focused for 30 years on measuring the knowledge and attitudes of students entering our field, in part, to explain the overall dismal performance. From Elliot Soloway's pioneering work in the 1980's, through the working group efforts led by Mike McCracken and Raymond Lister, to the individual dissertation efforts by Michael Caspersen and Allison Elliot Tew, we have ample evidence that students do not understand what computer science is, and when they leave their first semester, a surprisingly large percentage of them still won't know. These efforts were not wasted. Far from it – they form the rungs of the ladder for us to climb to a new level of computing education.

Physics education was able to make dramatic improvements once they had a validated measure (Hestenes' Force Concept Inventory) that the community of educators accepted. Once a yardstick is established, we can start doing the hard work of making progress on that yardstick. We need reliable, validated measures that we can all agree on, so that we can start working at getting better results on those measures.

Not a single one of the large-scale, multi-institutional studies of CS1 knowledge has ever resulted in an average passing grade. But with solid tests, we can start to develop new teaching methods that lead to better student learning and performance. The importance of having a bar is that now we can see what we need to rise above.

4. Ali Erkan

As stated in section 2, students enter CS education with different attitudes, beliefs, and expectations. Yet, in my experience, they are mostly unified in these three dimensions as they graduate. One of my interests has been to identify the points (between admission and graduation) at which notable levels of convergence occur. Consequently, in the context of a recently initiated multi-disciplinary project, my team and I focused on a number of questions that address the following questions:

- Can we adapt a tested survey instrument from physics education to locate the points at which students converge?
- Do CS educators have a unified set of attitudes, beliefs, and expectations associated with a conventional curriculum?
- If there is no single unified set within CS educators, then can we identify field-specific "clusters" among ourselves?

Our work involved the adaptation of the Maryland Physics Expectations Survey (MPEX) instrument [1, 2] and its use in a number of introductory and intermediate courses. My role on this panel is to present this tool and to show results drawn from four different courses.

5. Steve Cooper

Since curriculum development could be based on external funding, it is important for those who initiate such projects to express the justification as well as the consequences of their efforts using quantitative, reliable, and objective instruments. My role in this panel is to provide a perspective from the funding angle, particularly regarding the way in which NSF operates.

6. SESSION INFORMATION

Our goal is to have a contextualized discussion on how quantitative instruments can help us better understand our students as they go through a computing curriculum. The session will start with short perspectives from the session presenters, followed by the administration of a particular instrument, followed by a general discussion (we will do our best to maximize the time allotted for the discussion). We think this is an important topic because we believe in the role of accurate and meaningful data in curriculum design.

We expect the intended audience to be anyone who has interest in curriculum design and/or student perspectives. The instrument to be demonstrated will be made available online as well as in print.

The brief perspectives from the session presenters as well as the intended subsequent discussion makes our plans unsuitable to be considered as a paper. The presence of the activity moved us in the direction of a special session rather than a panel.

7. REFERENCES

[1] E. F. Redish, R. N. Steinberg, and J. M. Saul. The distribution and change of student expectations in introductory physics. In *The Changing Role of Physics Departments in Modern Universities*, number 399 in AIP Conference Proceedings, pages 689–698, 1997.

[2] E. F. Redish, R. N. Steinberg, and J. M. Saul. Student expectations in introductory physics. *American Journal of Physics*, (66):212–224, 1998.

Kinetic Art and Embedded Systems: A Natural Collaboration

Erik Brunvand
School of Computing
University of Utah
elb@cs.utah.edu

Paul Stout
Department of Art and Art History
University of Utah
paul.stout@gmail.com

ABSTRACT

We describe a cross-disciplinary collaborative course that pairs computer science and engineering (CSE) students with art students to engage in joint engineering design and creative studio projects. These projects combine embedded system design with sculpture to create kinetic art. We believe that this is a natural pairing of two disparate disciplines, and one that provides distinct educational benefits to both groups of students. In this paper we describe the course content, the collaborative process, the materials used in the class, and experience with a pilot version of the course taught in Fall 2009 at the University of Utah.

Categories and Subject Descriptors

K.3.2 [**Computer and Information Science Education**]: Computer Science Education

General Terms

Design, Experimentation

Keywords

Kinetic art, embedded systems, collaborative curricula, studio-based learning

1. INTRODUCTION

Jim Campbell is an artist living and working in San Francisco. According to a recent monograph on his work he is "... acknowledged as a masterful new media artist, adept at manipulating the base materials of electronics and computers into visual haiku of the information age." [9] He has been producing thought provoking and cutting-edge kinetic art for the past 20+ years. On his web site [7] he has a wry take on a "Formula for Computer Art", a snapshot of which is shown in Figure 1. The web-based version of Campbell's Formula is animated with many potential inputs and outputs scrolling by. The essential notion of Campbell's Formula is that as a broad category, kinetic art generally takes

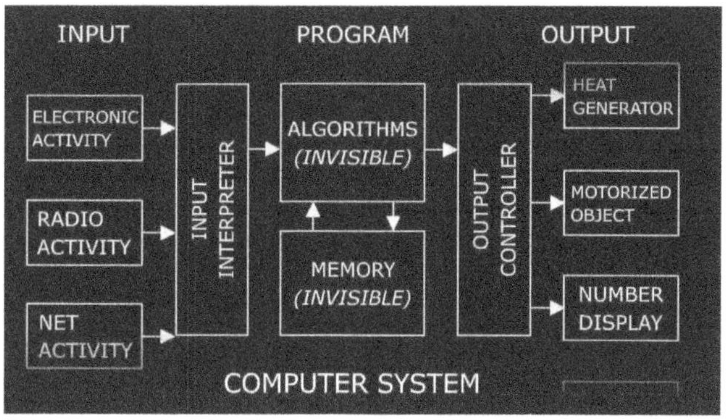

Figure 1: Jim Campbell's Formula for Computer Art [7]

some input from the real world (e.g., a sensor of some sort capturing environmental data in proximity to the artwork), processes it in an invisible way, and based on that input and processing, produces some output that is visible as the artwork itself.

Kinetic art contains moving parts or depends on motion, sound, or light for its effect. The kinetic aspect is often regulated using microcontrollers connected to motors, actuators, transducers, and sensors that enable the sculpture to move and react to its environment. But, distinct from other types of computer art, the computer itself is usually not visible in the artwork. It is a behind the scenes controller. An *embedded system* is a special-purpose computer system (microcontroller) designed to perform one or a few dedicated functions, often reacting to environmental sensors. It is embedded into a complete device including hardware and mechanical parts rather than being a separate computer system.

Kinetic art using embedded control is a marriage of art and technology. Artistic sensibility and creativity are required for concept and planning, and computer science and engineering skills are required to realize the artistic vision. In the project-based semester-length class we describe in this paper computer science and engineering (CSE) students work together with art students to build collaborative kinetic art pieces. Students explore interfacing of embedded systems with sensors and actuators of all sorts, along with real-time/interactive programming techniques and interrupt driven system design. They also explore physical and conceptual aspects of machine-making as a fine-art sculpture process.

The overall goal of the course is to enhance the educational experience for both groups of students. From the CSE side we encourage students to apply their technical skills in a context that is explicitly non-technical. This can allow students the freedom to try a wide range of approaches to a particular problem. In the process, engineers are exposed to a variety of aesthetic and creative concepts that would not normally be part of an engineering curriculum. Artists explore programming and engineering in a context that is more conducive to their learning style because it is directed at art-making. Both groups of students gain practical experience in design-thinking which is quite distinct from the computational thinking that is usually more associated with CSE. By requiring that the project groups include both engineers and artists, the students contribute to their own learning and creative growth through peer teaching. The multi-disciplinary teams allow both groups of students to experience a very different approach to problem solving because of their different fields. Learning to communicate across disciplines, and perhaps just as importantly respect each other's skills and contributions, is vitally important for successful collaboration. The overall result is that both student groups gain significant and unusual benefits that they can apply to a wide variety of aspects in their respective disciplines.

2. CURRICULUM

Our collaborative course is listed both as a CS course and as an Art course. The course is an upper division undergraduate course in both departments so we can assume that the CSE students are capable programmers and that the Art students are capable 3d artists. Students sign up for the course in their own discipline, but the classes meet together and the instructors team-teach all sessions. As we were planning the course this presented some challenges, mostly as we considered the amount of background material that each group of students might need in the other group's field of study. We considered breaking the class into two groups for the first part of the semester with the artists studying CS topics and the CSE students studying art. In the end we decided to keep all students together throughout the semester with the hope that students would rise to the occasion to contribute peer teaching to the curriculum when appropriate. We also considered the other extreme of pairing students at the beginning of the course, but were concerned that students from each discipline would rely too much on their counterpart and not attempt some of the material themselves.

The overall curriculum consists of review topics and individual assignments for the first four to five weeks of the semester, followed by a group project phase using a studio-based instruction model. This worked quite well in the pilot course. The topics covered include the following:

Computer Science and Engineering Topics
- Programming fundamentals
- Electronics fundamentals
- Input sensors (switches, potentiometers, resistive sensors including light, temperature, flex, etc., rangefinders, optical switches, etc.)
- Output actuators (servos, DC motors, stepper motors, LEDs, relays, switching transistors, etc.)
- Programming reactive systems
- External chip interfacing with protocols such as SPI
- Interrupt programming

Art and Design Topics
- Art history review of kinetic art
- Discussion of contemporary kinetic artists (Jim Campbell, Jack Dollhausen, Arthur Ganson, Rebecca Horn, Dan Rozin, Sabrina Raaf, Alan Rath, Peter Vogel, etc.)
- Formal elements of 3d art such as aesthetics, proportion, and balance
- Material studies (plastic, metal, paper, wood, etc.)
- Mechanical linkages and physical construction
- Concepts and meaning in art
- Artistic design process

Note that for each group of students, some of these topics will be review, and some will be brand new. For example, the first programming lab session is basic review for the CSE students, but may be the first time an art student has attempted to write a program of their own. From the other side, the fundamentals of 3d art is a review for the art students, but is perhaps the first time a CSE student has considered the ideas. While this has the potential to be "boring" to some of the students, we were pleasantly surprised in the pilot class that students seemed willing to take the reviews seriously, and help out during the hands-on activities.

Class proceeds with a set of individual assignments of gradually increasing complexity in both engineering and artistic aspects. These assignments introduce new programming concepts, give students experience with the range of sensors and actuators they can use, and practice building sculptural art pieces. After this phase, the students are partitioned into teams of three to four students where each team includes both engineers and artists. The teams proceed to work on two or three collaborative projects during the course of the semester. In our pilot offering of the course in 2009 we used teams of three and shuffled the teams after each project so that all students worked with a variety of different students throughout the semester.

An obvious question about the curriculum is how the subjects covered compare to a traditional CSE embedded systems course. Clearly because of the added art content, our kinetic art course cannot cover the same range of purely CSE material. In terms of strictly CSE content we cover interfacing to sensors and actuators in much more detail than our regular embedded systems course, but do not cover as much material related to assembly programming, advanced C programming, program optimization, or analysis of embedded programs.

The class culminates in a gallery show of the projects. This is a powerful motivator for the student groups to create interesting, thoughtful, and most importantly finished works by the end of the semester. A gallery show not only adds to the art students' portfolios, it can be an interesting resume line for the CSE students as well. We worked with the gallery in the Department of Art and Art History after the course in Fall 2009, and based on the success of that show are negotiating with other galleries in Salt Lake City for a show after this Fall's offering of the course.

2.1 Studio Art Educational Models

Pedagogical modes in engineering and fine art are typically quite different in both direct and subtle ways. One major difference is the use of studio-based instruction in the fine arts. Studio-based learning emphasizes collaboration, design-thinking, interaction, and learn-by-doing approaches. It forms the core of most fine art and design curricula [16, 21]. At the core of a studio-based curriculum are the ideas of exploring a multitude of design alternatives (design thinking) and the evaluation of those designs through peer group critiques (collaboration). These peer critiques serve a very different role for the student from graded assignments or even from engineering design reviews. Because students are discussing, evaluating, and critiquing each other's work, this can create a much more collaborative, supportive, and less hierarchical learning environment than traditional engineering courses with lectures and individually completed lab assignments.

Our course includes peer design critiques at both formative and completed project phases. This is natural for the art students, but can be intimidating to the CSE students at first. We found that it takes a few critique sessions for the CSE students to feel comfortable with the process. Because the designs are not "regular" CSE projects, we feel that this environment allows the CSE students to more comfortably adjust to the critique process. That is, because the subject of the critiques is (for the most part) art, their CSE skills are not necessarily on the line.

Although studio-based curricula are the norm in fine arts and design fields (such as industrial design, architecture, graphic design, etc.), they are not common in engineering. Recently there have been some intriguing studies on how a more collaborative [4, 35, 27, 10] or studio-type curriculum [21, 6, 19, 20, 17] might be adapted for CSE. We find these approaches very interesting from a broader CSE point of view, but view them as essential for our proposed kinetic art curriculum. One of our ongoing curriculum development challenges is to fit the programming, computing, and engineering construction course content into this type of exploratory, collaborative studio environment. A longer term goal is to contribute to the growing body of knowledge about how a studio model meshes with a broader CSE curriculum.

2.2 Enhancing Creativity

Computer scientists and computer engineers who exhibit high levels of creativity and interdisciplinary design vision are highly valued in their communities, and are often identified with leadership roles in research, development, and education. Creativity is clearly a tremendous asset when faced with a challenging problem, and students who can work across disciplines are a natural fit for many areas of CSE studies. However, students with this powerful combination of traits are seen as somewhat rare in CSE. One of the exciting ancillary benefits of this kinetic art and embedded systems course is the potential to enhance the creativity of our CSE students.

In this course, technical students are encouraged to apply their technical skills in a context that is explicitly nontechnical. This not only forces students to think about problems and solutions in a very different way, but also gives them an environment where they can feel able to propose and explore solutions where aesthetics are a primary goal, not engineering costs and practicalities. This freedom to explore "impractical" solutions is, we believe, a powerful creativity enhancer. One interesting model of creativity defines enhanced creative problem solving in the following way: "Creativity is demonstrated by the generation of many potential solutions instead of gravitating quickly toward a single and (usually) familiar solution that is not necessarily the optimal one." [11]

Thinking outside the normal scope of engineering projects can have a profound impact on how engineers and computer scientists approach all their designs. Students who have more creative, artistic design in their engineering vocabulary should be able to design better human interfaces, make systems more usable, extendable, and testable, and be more willing to take novel and unconventional approaches. We think of this as extending the palette available when considering the design of a new system, whether that system is software, hardware, mechanical, or a combination of all. There are a number of researchers who report that interdisciplinary collaborations are a powerful catalyst for creativity [27, 8, 4, 35].

Another aspect of creative problem solving is embodied in the actual construction of a physical artifact. The root of the word "creativity" itself implies the creation of something. There is evidence that creativity is enhanced by engaging in studio courses where the projects involve physical artifacts [12, 10, 32, 18].

3. COURSE FACILITIES

The primary facilities required for a course of this type are studio space that supports the exploration and construction of moderately complex 3d assemblages, a variety of sensors and actuators that the students can use, and a microcontroller platform for control.

In terms of studio space our class is able to use the 3d design studios in the Department of Art and Art History. This includes separate wood and metal shops, as well as open studio space for project construction. In terms of sensors and actuators, we received a small grant from the University of Utah Teaching Committee to support our pilot class in Fall 2009 and used that, in part, to stock our lab with initial supplies. A modest class fee for subsequent classes will be used to restock and acquire a variety of components for the lab. These components (servos, motors, LEDs, light sensors, resistors, etc.) are for the most part quite inexpensive ranging from a few pennies to a few dollars each.

For the microcontroller platform there are a variety of choices available. The choice of a controller can have a large impact on the class because the control of the kinetic art is critical, and different controllers have quite different features and programming environments. We have chosen to use the Arduino embedded controller and associated programming environment [2]. The Arduino is an open-source electronics prototyping platform based on an Atmel AVR 8-bit microcontroller. The hardware is open-source in the sense that all details of the controller board are made freely available so that users can build their own if they choose. The software integrated development environment (IDE) for programming the Arduino hardware is also called Arduino, and is a set of C-language functions designed to be relatively easy for any user to quickly write programs that use the Arduino hardware to sense and control the physical world.

Although the Arduino contains many interesting I/O properties and features, it is quite affordable. The basic board we are using is the Arduino Duemilanove which has 14 digital I/Os, 6 Analog inputs, 1 UART, and a variety of other features on a 2.7 X 2.1 inch board and costs around $30 (See Figure 2). The development and programming environment

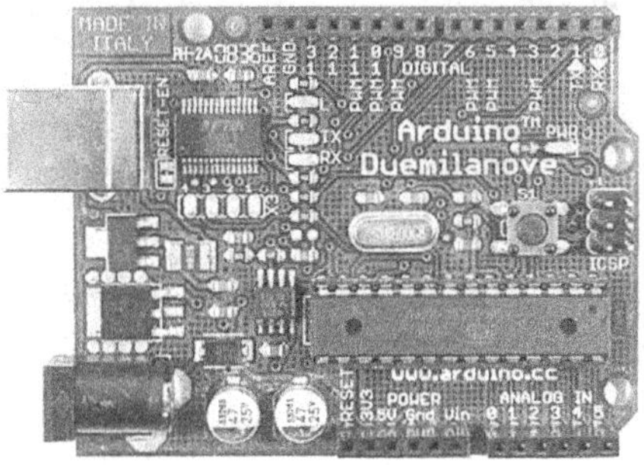

Figure 2: An Arduino Duemilanove board which is based on the AVR ATmega 328p microcontroller.

is open source and available free of charge in PC, Mac, and Linux versions. The Arduino programming IDE is really C/C++, but with a set of useful functions predefined for the user. The back-end of the IDE is the gcc compiler [15] which means that advanced users can use the full C/C++ programming language, and access all the internal features of the Atmel chips. Because Arduino hardware is programmed through the USB port of the host computer (acting as a serial interface), no additional programming hardware needs to be purchased.

Although the Arduino is a relative newcomer to the microcontroller world (compared to PIC and Basic Stamp, for example), it already has a wide following which results in many informative web sites that students can access [13, 14, 25]. There are also a number of books that describe using Arduino for controlling and sensing the physical world [29, 22, 5].

4. PILOT COURSE

A pilot version of the course was taught by the authors in Fall semester 2009. The enrollment was fairly small with six CSE and three art students participating. All aspects of the curriculum in Section 2 were covered, and a total of three group projects were completed by each of the three interdisciplinary teams. Because of the small class size, we were able to shuffle the teams such that every student worked on a team with every other student at some time during the semester, and all teams consisted of both artists and engineers. The course culminated with a gallery show in the Gittins Gallery in the Department of Art and Art History in January 2010. The show consisted of all nine group project pieces and was widely viewed as a successful show by other faculty in both departments (see Figure 3 and http://www.eng.utah.edu/~cs5968/pictures).

Some details of a few of the final kinetic art projects from Fall 2009 are:

***Relic*:** This large floor-standing piece (seen in Figure 3) was constructed of wood and metal with stepper motors, light bulbs, and electronic (Arduino) control. Standing in front of the piece the viewer sees a triangular themed structure with a dim light in the center casting a shadow of some gears on the wall behind. There are two metal plates on either side of the piece with hand prints on them inviting the viewer to place their hands there. The piece sends a very low voltage signal through those plates to sense the capacitance of the person and increases the light output when someone is touching the plates. As more people join hands and make a human chain between the plates, the light grows brighter and the gears turn casting a dynamic shadow on the wall. Drone-like sound effects are also played during this process. The piece is meant to evoke the idea of a mystical relic that responds to cooperation by the viewers. The more viewers join the human chain, the brighter and more dynamic the relic becomes.

***Cars*:** In this piece a large eight foot square white board was set up as a table. On the table are two small remote control cars, stripped to their chassis, and each dragging a white board marker. The cars are controlled by Arduinos hidden under the table. The turning and direction of the cars is changed in response to characters received on internet RSS feeds so that the patterns drawn on the white boards are in some way a physical representation of the data coming across that internet feed. By placing paper under the cars a permanent record of the drawing can be made.

***Flowers*:** In this piece eight kinetic flowers (each around 18" in diameter) were constructed from plastic, foam, paint, and servos controlled by an Arduino (see Figure 3). At the center of each flower is a light sensor. When left on their own the petals of the flowers move slowly up and down in a random fashion that looks calm. When a viewer moves close enough to change the amount of light on the sensor however, the flowers become agitated and exhibit a variety of different frightened or angry behaviors until the viewer backs away.

***Windchime*:** This piece consists of a wind chime constructed from copper tubing for the chimes, and a decorative metal housing as the support. At the center of the chimes is a metal striker. As the striker hits each of the chimes, a switch connection is made and a different set of LEDs in the main housing illuminates. A gentle breeze provides a constantly changing set of sounds and colors.

The student evaluations of the course were very positive with numeric scores above the department and college averages. The most striking thing about the comments was the degree to which students in each demographic group were positive about the experience of working on such wildly multi-disciplinary teams. Some representative student comments include: "It was really great to learn how to work with other students (art, cs, ece) like on the job." "I really enjoyed the open interaction that all the students had with each other and with the instructors." "I learned a great deal about electronics and embedded programming that I had not learned previously in my engineering courses. For me, it put into practice and solidified what we covered in the earlier engineering courses."

We are encouraged that the enrollment in our Fall 2010 course is more than double our Fall 2009 course. The course web page is available at http://www.eng.utah.edu/~cs5968. One of the main lessons we learned in the pilot course was that without individual practice in all aspects of the kinetic

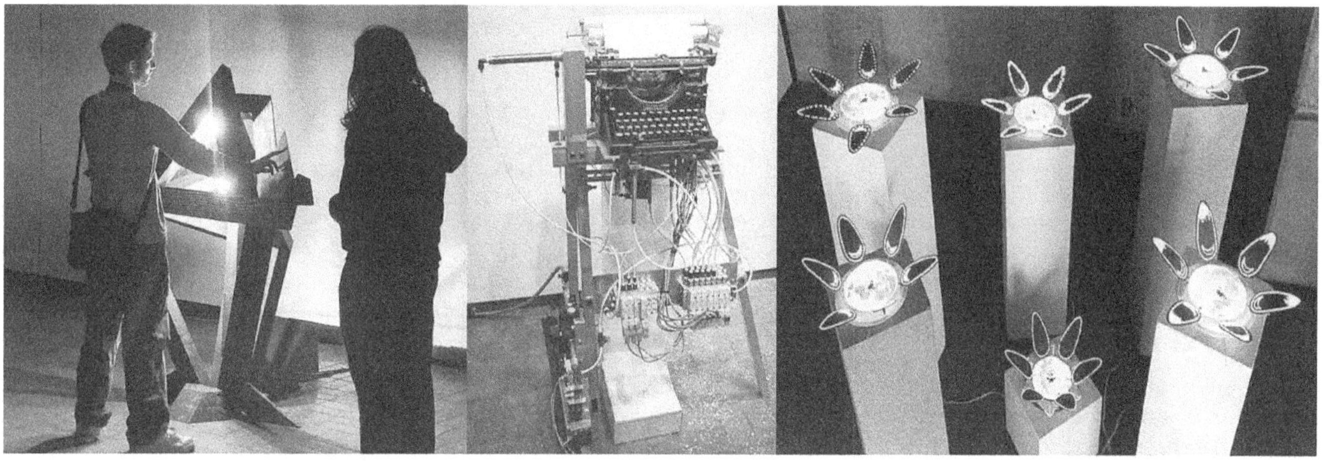

Figure 3: Three of the nine finished projects from *Invisible Logic*, the gallery show from Fall 2009. From the left they are *Relic* (wood, metal, light bulbs, motors, electronic control), *Underwood 1910* (metal, typewriter, pneumatic actuators, electronic control), and *Flowers* (plastic, paint, servos, electronic control)

art design process, multi-disciplinary teams tended to naturally slip into predefined engineering/art roles. In our second offering we are adding more extensive individual projects before forming teams, and will monitor the teams carefully to judge team participation in all aspects of the projects.

Another lesson is that the more hands-on practice with the materials, the better. We have a variety of sensors and actuators available for the students, but in the end most art pieces used a small subset of them, mainly servos, LEDs and light sensors. This is partly because those components already provide a great deal of flexibility in how they can be integrated into the kinetic art, but it likely also because they were the components most prominently featured in our initial hands-on labs. For our current offering of the course we plan to increase the number and type of components used in the preliminary labs to see if that will result in a wider range of components being used in the final projects.

One lesson that may translate to many other types of CSE courses is how valuable the process can be of building small throw-away non-serious prototypes. Students in the Fall 2009 semester commented on how liberating it was to sketch rough ideas and try things out on breadboards in class just to see how the components behaved without worrying about making every test a completed assignment. As described earlier, one intriguing definition of creativity is how many designs are explored before a final solution is settled upon. A kinetic art project, along with the ongoing design critiques in the studio class model, is a perfect opportunity to explore creativity in this way.

5. RELATED WORK

The general area of collaboration between arts and technology is quite rich, but many educational collaborations are targeted specifically at finding ways to introduce technology to artists, designers, and other non-technical or younger audiences (e.g.,affordable Alice [1, 23], Scratch [33, 26], Processing [30, 31], etc.). We have found only a few examples of using arts to enhance engineering. Some of those have already been referenced in this paper and include exploration of how interdisciplinary collaboration in general enhances engineering problem solving [4, 35], how studio-based courses make sense as a model for computing courses [12, 21, 6], and how the process of making tangible artifacts enhances engineering problem solving [10, 32, 18, 3].

The program most directly related to our Kinetic Art and Embedded Systems course is the successful Artbotics program at UMass Lowell [24, 28, 34], initiated in 2006. This is quite a similar program in some respects. Its main activity involves a curriculum using art and robotics (similar to kinetic art, although it is not described in that way) to help attract new students to computing disciplines. They are also connected with a local museum that organizes shows of the student's work. There are many small, but important, differences between Artbotics and our proposed course, but one major difference is that Artbotics is primarily an after school program and summer camp for high school students. Artbotics is also somewhat more focused on the robotics aspects of the projects than the fine-art aspects of the projects although this is admittedly somewhat subjective.

6. CONCLUSIONS AND FUTURE DIRECTIONS

Our collaborative course builds on the powerful connection between embedded control and kinetic art. This pairing seems like a natural fit, and one with high potential for intriguing results. Engineers are rarely taught to think about artistic, conceptual, and aesthetic outcomes, and artists are not usually taught to think about engineering issues in creating an artistic artifact. The studio model is an intriguing model for more general CSE education, but it is perhaps best experienced in a true studio course. A focus on design thinking also seems to us to be a natural complement to computational thinking.

There are many opportunities for this sort of collaboration. Many media in the fine arts require the equivalent of engineering problem solving to master. Kinetic art is the most obvious (and thus is the choice for this course), but sculpture, printmaking, photo, new media, video, installation art, interactive art, and digital media all have aspects that would be amenable to collaboration of this sort.

Enhanced collaboration between these colleges that are

usually thought of as quite distant could have a profound impact on how both engineers and artists are educated. Our broader goals are to use this as a building block for further connections between the College of Engineering and the College of Fine Arts at the University of Utah, and to serve as a model that could be adopted at any number of other educational institutions. Further connections could engage a much wider range of engineering and fine arts students, and explore further fascinating synergies in creative problem solving in both engineering and fine arts.

7. ACKNOWLEDGMENTS

We thank the University of Utah Teaching Committee for their support of our pilot course in Fall 2009.

8. REFERENCES

[1] The Alice web page. http://www.alice.org.

[2] Arduino home page. http://www.arduino.cc.

[3] D. Avrahami and S. E. Hudson. Forming interactivity: a tool for rapid prototyping of physical interactive products. In *DIS '02: Designing Interactive Systems*, pages 141–146, London, England, 2002.

[4] E. E. Ayiter, S. S. Balcisoy, M. Germen, and S. Artut. Propagating collaboration: an instructional methodology for artists and engineers. In *SIGCHI C&C '07*, Washington, DC, USA, 2007.

[5] M. Banzi. *Getting Started with Arduino (Make: Projects)*. Make Books, 2008.

[6] L. J. Barker, K. Garvin-Doxas, and E. Roberts. What can computer science learn from a fine arts approach to teaching? In *SIGCSE '05*, St. Louis, Missouri, USA, 2005.

[7] J. Campbell. Artist's web site. http://www.himcampbell.tv.

[8] L. Candy and E. Edmonds. *Explorations in art and technology*. Springer-Verlag, London, UK, 2002.

[9] S. Dietz, editor. *Jim Campbell: Material Light*. Hatje Cantz, 2010.

[10] E. Y.-L. Do and M. D. Gross. Environments for creativity: a lab for making things. In *SIGCHI C&C '07*, pages 27–36, Washington, DC, USA, 2007.

[11] E. Edmonds and L. Candy. Creativity, art practice, and knowledge. *Commun. ACM*, 45(10):91–95, 2002.

[12] E. A. Edmonds, A. Weakley, L. Candy, M. Fell, R. Knott, and S. Pauletto. The studio as laboratory: combining creative practice and digital technology research. *Int. J. Hum.-Comput. Stud.*, 63(4-5):452–481, 2005.

[13] The world famous index of arduino and freeduino knowledge. http://www.freeduino.org.

[14] L. Fried. Arduino tutorial. http://www.ladyada.net/learn/arduino.

[15] Gcc, the GNU compiler collection. http://gcc.gnu.org.

[16] L. N. Green and E. Bonollo. Studio-based teaching: history and advantages in the teaching of design. *World Transactions on Eng. and Tech. Edu.*, 2(2):269–272, 2003.

[17] D. Hendrix, L. Myneni, H. Narayanan, and M. Ross. Implementing studio-based learning in CS2. In *SIGCSE '10*, Milwaukee, Wisconsin, USA, 2010.

[18] S. E. Hudson and J. Mankoff. Rapid construction of functioning physical interfaces from cardboard, thumbtacks, tin foil and masking tape. In *UIST '06*, Montreux, Switzerland, 2006.

[19] C. Hundhausen, A. Agrawal, D. Fairbrother, and M. Trevisan. Integrating pedagogical code reviews into a CS1 course: an empirical study. In *SIGCSE '09*, Chattanooga, TN, USA, 2009.

[20] C. Hundhausen, A. Agrawal, D. Fairbrother, and M. Trevisan. Does studio-based instruction work in CS1?: an empirical comparison with a traditional approach. In *SIGCSE '10*, Milwaukee, Wisconsin, USA, 2010.

[21] C. D. Hundhausen, N. H. Narayanan, and M. E. Crosby. Exploring studio-based instructional models for computing education. *SIGCSE Bull.*, 40(1), 2008.

[22] T. Igoe. *Physical Computing: Sensing and Controlling the Physical World with Computers*. Course Technology PTR, 2004.

[23] C. Kelleher, R. Pausch, and S. Kiesler. Storytelling Alice motivates middle school girls to learn computer programming. In *CHI '07*, pages 1455–1464, San Jose, California, USA, 2007.

[24] H. J. Kim, D. Coluntino, F. G. Martin, L. Silka, and H. A. Yanco. Artbotics: community-based collaborative art and technology education. In *SIGGRAPH '07: Educators Program*, San Diego, California, 2007.

[25] T. Kurt. Todbot blog. http://todbot.com/blog/.

[26] D. J. Malan and H. H. Leitner. Scratch for budding computer scientists. In *SIGCSE '07*, Covington, Kentucky, USA, 2007.

[27] L. Mamykina, L. Candy, and E. Edmonds. Collaborative creativity. *Commun. ACM*, 45(10):96–99, 2002.

[28] F. Martin, H. J. Kim, L. Silka, H. Yanco, and D. Coluntino. Artbotics: Challenges and opportunities for multi-disciplinary, community-based learning in computer science, robotics, and art. In *Workshop on Research in Robots for Education*, Robotics Science and Systems conference, June 2007.

[29] J. Noble. *Programming Interactivity: A Designer's Guide to Processing, Arduino, and openFrameworks*. O'Reilly Media, Inc., 2009.

[30] Processing web site. http://processing.org/.

[31] C. Reas, B. Fry, and J. Madea. *Processing: A Programming Handbook for Visual Designers and Artists*. The MIT Press, 2007.

[32] O. Shaer, M. s. Horn, and R. j. k. Jacob. Tangible user interface laboratory: Teaching tangible interaction design in practice. *Artif. Intell. Eng. Des. Anal. Manuf.*, 23(3):251–261, 2009.

[33] The Lifelong Kindergarden Group at MIT. The Scratch web page. http://scratch.mit.edu/.

[34] H. Yanco, H. J. Kim, F. G. Martin, and L. Silka. Artbotics: Combining art and robotics to broaden participation in computing. In *AAAI: Resources for AI Education*, Stanford, CA, March 2006.

[35] Y. Zhang and L. Candy. An in-depth case study of art-technology collaboration. In *SIGCHI C&C '07*, Washington, DC, USA, 2007.

Cooperative Expertise for Multidisciplinary Computing

Ursula Wolz
The College of New Jersey
Dept. of Computer Science
Ewing, NJ 08528
+1 609 771 2766
wolz@tcnj.edu

Lillian (Boots) Cassel
Villanova University
Dept. of Computing Sciences
Villanova, PA 19085
+1 610 519 7341
cassel@acm.org

Thomas Way
Villanova University
Dept of Computing Sciences
Villanova, PA 19085
+1 610 519 5033
thomas.way@villanova.edu

Kim Pearson
The College of New Jersey
Dept of English
Ewing, NJ 08528
+1 609 771 2692
kpearson@tcnj.edu

ABSTRACT

As the need for multidisciplinary computing education continues to increase, consideration for distributed expertise will become critical to implementing a successful curriculum. A model of *cooperative expertise* is presented in which faculty maintain responsibility for their own course, creating and evaluating assignments for their students that support learning in their colleagues' courses as well. We present outcomes of an experiment to implement this model at two geographically separated institutions through three courses (two at one institution, one at the other), by faculty in computer science, media and English. Results reported include faculty analysis of student achievement in each course and student surveys of attitudes toward multidisciplinary collaboration. Overall, it appears that student learning and attitudes are enhanced by the experience.

Categories and Subject Descriptors

K.3.2 [**Computing Milieux**] Computer and Information Science Education

K. 4.0 Computers and Society

General Terms

Human Factors

Keywords

CS Education, Multidisciplinary Computing, Writing and Computing, Distributed Expertise, Cooperative Expertise.

1. INTRODUCTION

This paper describes an experience undertaken as part of an NSF CPATH funded project on Distributed Expertise. That concept evolved from an earlier project, funded through NSF CCLI, to investigate the potential for collaboration in bringing enhanced expertise to teaching computer science [1,2]. Our previous research demonstrated that many computer science departments do not have sufficient human resources to adequately teach every area of computer science, unrealistically stretching faculty expertise and resources. We found that instructors cope by emphasizing the part of the subject with which they are most comfortable for them and skipping those for which they lacked confidence. We received enthusiastic support by CS faculty for potential collaboration with subject area experts who could augment local resources. However, there were challenges involved that made direct collaboration impractical at the time. We were able to explore resource sharing in CITIDEL [3,4] and Ensemble [5,6] but were unable to fully address collaborative teaching models.

In the ensuing decade, the computing education landscape has changed, yet these needs remain the same. While the number of students who pursue a computing major has declined, the breadth of computing has increased, as had the need to expose a larger constituency to computing concepts and skills. Perhaps most importantly, we in the computing disciplines have begun to recognize the contributions other disciplines offer to us.

The project reported here suggests the potential for collaborative, cooperative teaching across disciplines. A model is presented in which faculty participants come from different educational institutions and from different disciplines. Three integrated upper level courses are described: a software engineering course for computer science majors (SE-VU), a multidisciplinary video game course primarily for media and computer science majors (VG-TCNJ), and an interactive storytelling course for media majors (IS-TCNJ). How these disparate groups interacted and built on each other's abilities gives us insights into creating collaborative efforts among faculty and among students. The results presented suggest that disciplinary boundaries do not have to limit learning and workforce potential.

The course syllabus construction process, the execution of that syllabus in a coordinated fashion, the non-didactic pedagogy as well as novel approaches to student assignments require a high degree of flexibility as well as some abdication of control on the part of the instructors. The payoff is evidence of authentic student learning of both technical skill and communication (soft) skills. Key issues are (1) an emphasis on large scale deliverables, to which students from all three classes contribute, (2) clear boundaries on expectations for individuals, both faculty and students so that assessment gives credit where credit is due, (3) a commitment to the notion that students learn from each other without everyone having to do the same assignment.

2. COOPERATIVE EXPERTISE

Cooperative Expertise is one of three Distributed Expertise [7] models we have identified. It is a model in which faculty and students in distinct courses identify and share expertise with faculty and students in other courses to support learning goals in both courses. Ideally, cooperative expertise is bi-directional. In a cooperative model all involved benefit both from learning from the expertise of others and from the experience of sharing expertise with others.

2.1 Models of Distributed Expertise

Our three models of Distributed Expertise define the center and endpoints of a spectrum of collaborative approaches to sharing expertise in education [7]. The models are

- Remote Expert with Local Facilitator, where faculty expertise resides at one institution and benefits faculty and students at another institution;
- Cooperative Experts, where faculty at two collaborating institutions exchange mutually beneficial expertise with the other; and
- Special Resource, where expertise is shared in more of a one-time or guest instructor format, or through recorded materials shared through a repository.

The experience described in this paper is an example of cooperative experts, the CE model, extended to include more than two faculty members and more than two course offerings at two institutions.

2.2 Coordinating Syllabi Via Deliverables

A key concern to facilitating mutually supportive collaboration is balancing individual responsibility with dependence on resources. Ultimately, within the constraints of mainstream higher education, accountability for instruction and assessment must rest with the instructor of record. This is particularly critical for classroom instruction where outside forces (e.g. institutional expectations) may not completely embrace a collaborative cooperative model. An instructor takes responsibility for the course syllabus. A student takes responsibility for completing assignments. Cooperative class expectations for both the instructor and student must provide "fault tolerance," that is, fall-back mechanisms for resource failure – when an instructor or student on whom your work relies, fails to deliver in the expected manner.

To address this in the cooperative model, we designed curriculum for three co-dependent courses, where each faculty member was fully responsible for just one course. Furthermore, assignments were designed to provide enrichment for the other courses, but no assignment was created that depended upon deliverables from students outside the immediate course.

Two face-to-face meetings of the collaborating faculty members, prior to the start of the semester, provided an opportunity to negotiate where, when and how student assignments could support learning between courses. Tentative course schedules and syllabi were then shared in order to coordinate timing of collaborative activities. Rather than coordinating presentation of content and skills (e.g. who was presenting in whose course and when), the syllabi were structured around three shared deliverables that would contribute to illustrating learning goals for all three courses. All three courses contributed to design documents and prototype implementations of the following:

- A sprite editor for producing 2-D animation strips.
- A story engine for interactive storytelling.
- A two player game engine played between a mobile device and console device.

2.3 Multidisciplinary Computing

The TCNJ faculty members have been active participants in multi-disciplinary computing experiences for almost a decade [8,9]. A two-semester upper level experience in game design and implementation continues to provide the anchor. The VG-TCNJ course described here is that second semester course. A firm principle of this experience is that each student brings personal expertise to the enterprise as well as highly personalized learning goals within the framework of broad course objectives. One of those objectives is for students to demonstrate, through deliverables and reflective essays, how diverse expertise contributes to the software enterprise. In past years we have drawn on assignments from other courses at TCNJ including animation, artificial intelligence and interaction design. The deliverables, however, were defined entirely within the games course, with individual students in the other courses choosing to do major projects based on specifications defined by the games students to augment the game implementation. The work done outside the course in recent years was never mission-critical, but provided augmentation to the target prototype implementation in the form of game level designs, character development, and sample agent action enhancements.

In Academic Year 2008-2009, the authors created a cooperative experience between our two institutions. The VG-TCNJ course, taught by Wolz and Pearson was paired with a pilot introductory game design class at Villanova taught by Way. Both courses were open to all majors. Our perspective in that experience was to "outsource" technical development from the VG-TCNJ to the more experienced computer science students in the introductory games course at Villanova. This was a very different model from prior experiences at TCNJ because the outsourced programming work was expected to be mission-critical. Results reported in detail in [7] confirm that students learned to appreciate multidisciplinary cooperation. However, the VG-TCNJ deliverables were completed without any significant contribution from the Villanova students. As a means of self-protection (in order to deliver prototypes) the VG-TCNJ students gradually moved the outsourced components to the status of background and augmentation, just as their peers had in prior semesters.

2.4 Responsibility and Accountability

The mixed success of the prior year led the instructors to analyze how to support better cooperation and collaboration between students. This is a problem in any partnered approach to technology skills development. Because the US undergraduate experience is entrenched in an individualistic accountability tradition (e.g. grades), there is an inherent tension between the goals of collaboration and accountability. While industry is searching for computing expertise that includes the ability to "play well with others", the pedagogy of the traditional classroom, especially across institutions, is antithetical to this goal.

Our solution was to explicitly design in a balance between sharing and student self-protection. The structure of our cooperative experiment held to the following:

1) Each assignment would be assessed by the faculty of record for the course in which the student was enrolled, using rubrics and criteria that were solely the responsibility of that instructor.

2) Assignments in a particular class, whether to the group or an individual, had to have a clearly defined objective related to the learning goals of that course (e.g. no busy work, no exploitative 'grunt' work to support another course.)

3) Deliverables assigned in one course should not be mission critical to deliverables in another course; that is, a student's ability to complete an assignment should not be dependent upon the work of a student in another course.

In retrospect these principles seem obvious, and can be applied in a single cooperative classroom as well. However, despite our own extensive experience with multidisciplinary computing classrooms, we did not fully appreciate their importance until we were immersed in the cross-institutional experience.

3. Cooperative Curriculum

Three courses, each led by a different instructor and taken by different students, offered an interesting prospect for interaction and cooperative learning:

VG-TCNJ, the **Game Implementation** course at TCNJ is a spring semester experience in video game development that focuses on project management and software implementation. It follows a fall course in which game engine architecture and game design are emphasized through the development of a robust design document that includes a game story, interface design, and media prototyping (e.g. graphics, sound and music.) This upper level course requires permission of instructor and is cross-listed in Computer Science and Interactive Multimedia, attracting students from majors across campus.

SE-VU, the **Software Engineering** course offered at Villanova University is taken in the second semester of the junior year, and is a software specification and design course that provides students with a theoretical and practical background in the topic while preparing students to apply their educational experiences to their career.

IS-TCNJ, Interactive Storytelling is an advanced class in the Professional Writing focus area of the Interactive Multimedia major at TCNJ. Students are required to consider the ways in which the use of interactive technologies and media create new possibilities and challenges for storytellers. Students create and critique stories that aspire to blend the principles of narrative theory with elegant software design.

3.1 Course Objectives

Course objectives and learning goals were tailored to the cooperative agenda. The principal Cooperative Expertise objective for students in SE-VU is to simulate real-world software engineering practices of software design, specification, consultation, evaluation and testing through practical and collaborative exercises that benefit students in the other two courses. A secondary objective is to expose students to faculty and student expertise in game design and interactive storytelling, to place software engineering concepts within the context of concrete applications.

As a self-contained unit, VG-TCNJ focuses on multidisciplinary cooperation and highly individualized learning to accomplish a technical task. Students learn project management via an immersive experience. A major goal of this class is developing an appreciation for the complex skill set required to produce a highly interactive piece of computing software. The principle objective with regard to cooperative expertise was to provide students with insight into distance communication in the project cycle.

The learning goals for IS-TCNJ expect students to identify and classify interactive stories, both in terms of their interactive features and their narrative structures. Students are expected to analyze and critique the technical and design features of interactive narratives on the basis of their contributions to storytelling, and examine and apply existing interactive multimedia tools to the creation of interactive narratives. Students also are expected to discuss and hypothesize ways in which this genre of storytelling might evolve. They should be able to understand and make reasoned arguments about the social, cultural and ethical value of interactive storytelling techniques and artifacts. As such, this course was expected to provide realistic clients for the software engineering course, and game designer expertise for the games course.

3.2 Enrichment Assignments

Specific enrichment activities were assigned to students in the collaborating courses. These were designed to provide all students involved with opportunities to support the learning of students in other courses while applying the skills and experience learned in their own courses. These enrichment assignments were broken down as follows.

SE-VU supports VG-TCNJ through:

- Design evaluation of a sprite editor software specification by the entire SE-VU class.
- Specific SE-VU student team project to design and implement a prototype sprite editor tool, which included a software design and implementation phase, in-class demonstration of prototypes, based on needs analysis by members of VG-TCNJ.
- Consulting on iPhone programming, primarily identifying student expertise, discussing what might be needed.
- In-class discussion of story and game engines to support design documents developed by VG-TCNJ.

IS-TCNJ supports VG-TCNJ

- Provide literary analysis of the game story, highlighting concepts of genre, narrative structure and story consistency.
- Via sample stories developed in a prototype story engine developed by Wolz, articulate relationship between story engines and game engine logic system. Provide insight into data structures to support complex story.
- Contribute to discussions of level elaboration and overall story consistency.

SE-VU supports IS-TCNJ

- Interactive story evaluation of four stories from usability and software design perspectives, include code review of IS-TCNJ student work in Flash, Scratch and Processing.
- Evaluation of existing free and open source interactive storytelling engines by one student.
- Collaboration on a software requirements and design specification of an interactive storytelling engine.
- In-class discussion of distributed collaboration on interactive storytelling projects.

VG-TCNJ supports IS-TCNJ:

- Provide the interactive story for a two-person game as a test-bed for literary analysis.

- Provide consulting services via code review with regard to logic implementation of assigned interactive stories (e.g. provide technical expertise in implementing stories within the Wolz story engine prototype.) Analyze shortcomings of Wolz story engine based on experience with game story.
- Provide real-world opportunities for interactive storytelling students to elaborate on level concepts (e.g. flesh out interactivity and narrative in the game levels.)

VG-TCNJ supports SE-VU:

- As client for the sprite editor, research existing technology.
- Contribute design perspective to story engine development based on implementation of game story.
- Create design specifications for data communication needs for two player cross-platform game (web-based Java applet and iPhone), soliciting technical expertise from SE class.

IS-TCNJ supports SE-VU:

- Provide client perspective for storytelling engine.
- Provide opportunity for code critique on engine.
- Provide feedback on sprite editor usability for storytelling.

4. RESEARCH METHODOLOGY

This is what we set out to do:

***Objective**: To demonstrate how three courses, each with its own learning outcomes can be coordinated to enhance learning and support faculty expertise in a multidisciplinary manner through the development of three deliverables: an iPhone game (based on a design developed in a Fall Game Design course at TCNJ), a Sprite editor, and a Storytelling Engine.*

***Methodology:** Course activities will require individual students to coordinate with peers in other classes to complete development of the three deliverables. Expertise sharing will be documented, with the expectation that it will be reciprocal; that is, no class will act solely as client, consultant or developer.*

4.1 Report on Deliverables

Outcomes were as expected, but with some surprises. The cross-collaboration took the responsibility for directing deliverables development away from the instructors as expected; however, the deliverables envisioned by the instructors at the onset were not delivered: instead the influence of client feedback on all three projects pushed technology design and implementation in unanticipated directions. Furthermore, learning goals were satisfied in ways not anticipated by the instructors.

A sprite editor design was produced; however, the focus of the ultimate design, influenced heavily by the animators in the games course, was significantly different from that initially conceived by the software engineering students. Whereas the SE-VU students wanted to focus on cutting up a sprite sheet (a document that holds all of the possible positions of a sprite) into individual animation cells, the VG-TCNJ animators needed the inverse system: a way to take individual drawings created in Photoshop and merge them into a sprite sheet. Low-level specification of layout on the sheet, agreement on number of drawings per animation, granularity of animation and a host of other details with which animators are intimately acquainted, were communicated to the design team at Villanova in SE-VU course.

The IS-TCNJ students made good use of Wolz' prototype story engine. Some of them developed programming expertise as they by coding extensions. The VG-TCNJ class did analysis of how to take a story narrative and translate it into a data structure and logic. A student in the VG-TCNJ class led an effort by the SE-VU students to extend the story engine to include necessary elements to support game design. Thus, students in all three classes were engaged in the conversations about the boundaries between interactive story and game design. While this project was not a major focus in any of the three classes with regard to explicit deliverables, it became a point of departure for curricular issues in all three classes: in SE-VU regarding assumptions about design specifications; in IS-TCNJ regarding linear versus interactive storytelling; and in VG-TCNJ regarding the implementation of a story concept as a logic and data structure.

Contrary to expectations for "outsourcing" and "expert consulting," the VG-TCNJ students were unable to derive much technical expertise on iPhone programming from the SE-VU class. Instead they were very dependent upon the IS-TCNJ students to developing a plausible game. In retrospect this reaffirms some of the social dynamics of the previous year when the remote class was considered an outsourcing site. Both years the remote students did not have ownership of the implementation development – they were not responsible for a particular component or block of code. The lag time in contacting them, as well as the lack of establishing trust over distance, meant that the VG-TCNJ students relied on each other in face-to-face meetings, rather than try to invoke distance communication technology. We posit that the heavy influence of undergraduate culture came into play here. Despite herculean efforts on the part of the instructors to forestall it, the students in all three classes still did major work at the last moment, typically through the night prior to the next class meeting. The reality of the undergraduate experience trumped our best efforts The TCNJ classes met at the same time, while the Villanova class met on a different day. This may have influenced these outcomes, and we will address in the future.

The major lesson learned by the instructors was to promote a pedagogy akin to agile design: exploit resources as need emerges. Do not over-commit to teacher-driven concept learning, but focus on the holistic themes of the course goals. Survey results reported in Section 5 confirm the success of this approach.

4.2 Impact on Student Content Learning

Based on student project work, final exam results and observations in the classes, all three instructors are confident in saying that students met the learning goals for each course. As summarized above, the collaboration provided a vehicle for "real world" experience in how client expertise influences specification changes. We were able to recover from faulty vision, misunderstanding and simple bad luck and still produce three solid products: (1) a design specification for a useful sprite editor, (2) a proof of concept for an interactive storytelling engine, (3) a prototype of a mobile/console two player game.

We posit that this sort of collaboration is perhaps more realistic than connecting with an industrial or non-profit client. Under those circumstances there is very little wiggle room if the design and implementation process goes wrong. The artificial timeframe of a semester course does not provide the flexibility of delayed roll out that can occur in an industrial setting. Furthermore, both in our model and an industrial partnership, the students are learning skills while implementing them. In both cases this significantly complicates milestone predictions, but adjusting is easier when both partners are in an academic setting.

We further assert that the collaborative approach improves upon the industrial client model because students in all three classes have an opportunity to experience both the client and developer side of the process. This was particularly important in the interactive storytelling course. These students programmed in a version of Java called Processing. They delivered product that was critiqued by the technical classes. Such experiences will become increasingly important in a 21st century liberal education.

4.3 Impact on Student Soft Skills Learning

Surveys were administered at the end of the semester. Twenty two Villanova students responded, twenty five at TCNJ (19 in Games, 6 in Storytelling.) Table 1 confirms our objectives that students will gain from the cross-collaborative experience. At Villanova they overwhelmingly believe that there was value added by cross-institutional collaboration, with half agreeing at TCNJ. Tables 2 through 4 show more details of the perceptions of the students at each institution. Because two classes at TCNJ participated in the experience, there is a distinction between their view of local and remote collaboration. Students saw how computing applied across fields and how the skill set learned be applies in the real world of work. Overall students were positive about the experience.

5. ANALYSIS AND SUMMARY

Table 1 indicates that the Villanova students definitely gained from this experience. We attribute the lower impact of the interdisciplinary experience on the TCNJ students to the fact that over half of them had already taken at least one cross-listed course in media in which students bring a range of expertise. At both institutions, students overwhelmingly responded that they gained a perspective on the ubiquity of computing, as well as an appreciation for the range of skills learned and how they can be applied beyond the classroom setting.

Tables 2 – 4 provide detail on the subtle attitudes toward the developer/client model. The Villanova students, who were in a traditional software engineering class, reported that their interactions with the TCNJ students added significantly to the value of the learning outcomes. With regard to soft skills, the students' perspective on learning is primarily positive. The complexity of collaboration provided invaluable experience to all of the students and the faculty. Analyzing this in greater depth will require more time for review and more space for reporting. The TCNJ student outcomes were a bit more subtle. While they did not overwhelmingly believe Villanova contributed to deliverable completion, they did overwhelmingly believe that (1) their classroom experience was enhanced; (2) it enhanced skills development, and (3) contributed to how they seek out expertise.

Traditional undergraduate education is lecture-based, and especially in STEM fields students often work on projects with well-known solutions. Major universities can provide more collaborative exposure to the "real world" of collaborative product development and research. As we focus on multidisciplinary studies we have an opportunity to create models of pedagogy that exploit local and remote resources in a manner that provides a less hierarchical, teacher-centered learning experience. Especially in a field as dynamic as computer science, this is critical. Our collaboration this past year has been a pleasure for the instructors and a true learning experience for our students.

6. ACKNOWLEDGMENTS

This work is supported by NSF CISE IS-0829616 and CPATH 0935942. Any opinions, findings, and conclusions or recommendations expressed in this material are those of the authors and do not necessarily reflect the views of the National Science Foundation. Credit for our tables goes to Kathleen Nazar.

7. REFERENCES

[1] Cassel, L.N. and D. Kumar 2002. A state of the course report: computer organization & architecture. In *Proceesings of 7th annual conference on innovation and technology in computer science education.* (Aarhus, Denmark June 24-26 2002), ITiCSE '02: ACM, New York, NY, 175-177, DOI=http://dx.doi.org/10.1145/637610.544466

[2] Cassel, L.N., G. Davies, and D. Kumar, 2002. *The Shape of an Evolving Discipline, in Informatics Curricula and Teaching Methods*, L.N. Cassel and R. Reis, Editors. Kluwer Academic Publishers: Florianópolis Brazil,. 131-138.

[3] Cassel, L.N., et al. 2004. CITIDEL: The Computer and Information Technology Interactive Digital Education Library. 2002 [cited 2004 February 8]; Available from: http://www.citidel.org

[4] Cassel, L.N., et al. 2003. Report on the NSF major educational funding initiative for a National Science, Technology, Engineering, and Mathematics Education Digital Library (NSDL) with special emphasis on the Computing Education component. *Proceedings of the 34th SIGCSE technical symposium on computer science education.* (Reno, Nevada, February 12 – 23, 2003) SIGCSE '03 ACM, New York, NY. 301-302, DOI=http://dx.doi.org/10.1145/611892.611910

[5] Carpenter, B.S., et al. 2010 Multiple sources with multiple portals: a demonstration of the ensemble computing portal in second life. *Proceeding of the 10th Annual Joint Conference on Digital Libraries* (Gold Coast, Queensland, Australia June 21-25 2010) JCDL 2010, ACM, New Yourk, NY. 397 DOI=http://dx.doi.org/10.1145/1816123.1816199

[6] Fox, E.A., et al. 2010 Ensemble PDP-8: eight principles for distributed portals. *Proceeding of the 10th Annual Joint Conference on Digital Libraries* (Gold Coast, Queensland, Australia June 21-25 2010) JCDL 2010, 341-344. DOI= http://dx.doi.org/10.1145/1816123.1816174

[7] Way, T., et al., 2010, A Distributed Expertise Model for Teaching Computing Across Disciplines and Institutions., in The 2010 International Conference on Frontiers in Education: Computer Science and Computer Engineering 2010: Las Vegas, Nevada.

[8] Wolz U, C. Ault and T. M. Nakra, 2007 Teaching Game Design through Cross-Disciplinary Content and Individualized Student Deliverables, *The Journal of Game Development,* 2(1), Feb. 2007.

[9] Wolz U, and S. M. Pulimood, 2007 An integrated approach to project management through classic CS III and video game development, in *Proceedings of the 38th SIGCSE technical symposium on computer science education.* (Covington Kentucky, March 8-10, 2007) SIGCSE '07 ACM New Your, NY 322-326, DOI= http://dx.doi.org/10.1145/1227310.1227422

Table 1: Survey Results on Cross-Institutional Multidisciplinary Collaboration

Respondents who Strongly Agree or Agree	Villanova #	Villanova %	TCNJ #	TCNJ %
I believe that collaborating with another university as part of a class adds value to my educational experience.	18	86%	7	50%
This course has helped me see how computing can be applied across other fields.	16	73%	12	86%
This course has provided me an opportunity to see how skills can be applied beyond the classroom setting in the world of work.	19	86%	12	80%

Table 2. Villanova University Student's Assessments of their Experiences Working with TCNJ Students.

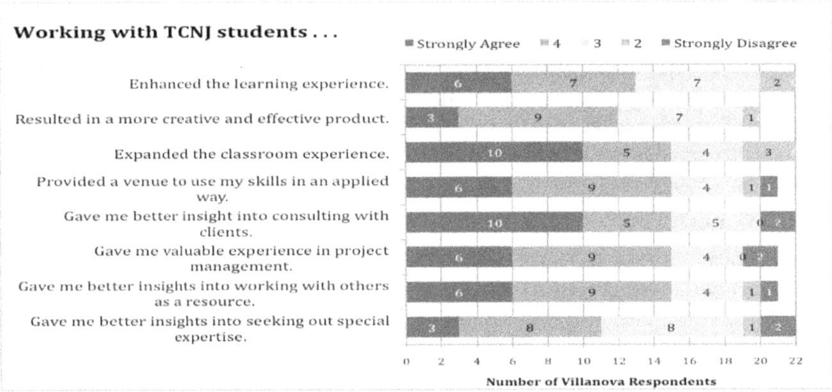

Table 3. TCNJ Students' Assessments of their Experiences Working with Villanova Students.

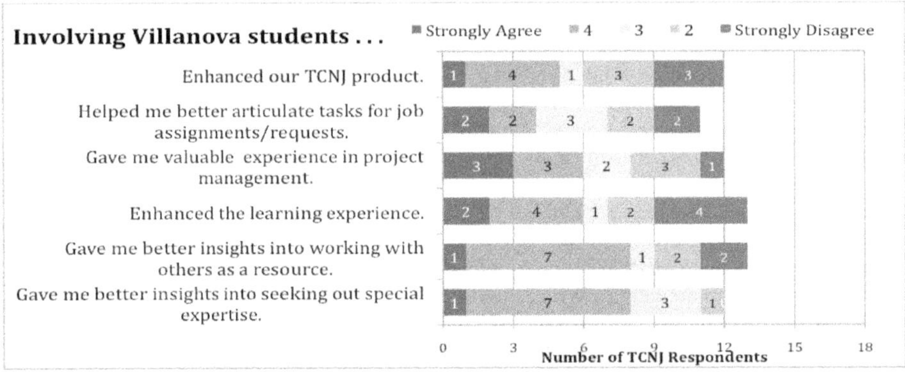

Table 4. TCNJ Students' Assessments of their Experiences Working with other TCNJ Students.

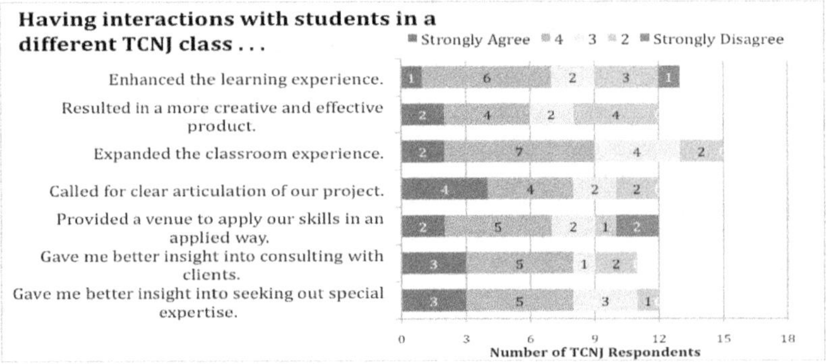

Teaching Biologists to Compute using Data Visualization

Kay A. Robbins
Department of Computer Science
University of Texas at San Antonio
One UTSA Circle, SA, TX 78249
1-210-458-5543
krobbins@cs.utsa.edu

David M. Senseman
Department of Biology
University of Texas at San Antonio
One UTSA Circle, SA, TX 78249
1-210-458-5543
david.senseman@utsa.edu

P. Elizabeth Pate
Interdisc. Learning and Teaching
University of Texas at San Antonio
One UTSA Circle, SA, TX 78249
1-210-458-7442
elizabeth.pate@utsa.edu

ABSTRACT
The accelerating use of computation in all aspects of science continues to widen the gap between student skills and expectations. Currently, computation is taught using one of two approaches: teach students a standard programming language (e.g., FORTRAN, JAVA or C) perhaps augmented by support tools such as Alice or teach them to use a program such as MATLAB by formulating and solving math problems. Both approaches have high failure rates for students hindered by poor mathematics training and weak logic skills. This paper describes an alternative approach that introduces students to computing in the context of data analysis and visualization using MATLAB. Our goal is produce computationally qualified young scientists by teaching a highly relevant computational curriculum early in their college career. The course, which integrates writing, problem-solving, statistics, visual analysis, simulation, and modeling, is designed to produce students with usable data analysis skills. The course is in its third year of implementation and is required of all biology majors at the University of Texas at San Antonio.

Categories and Subject Descriptors
K.3.2 [Computer and Information Science Education]: Curriculum, Computer science education

General Terms: Algorithms, Experimentation.

Keywords
Data Analysis, MATLAB, Visualization, Biology.

1. INTRODUCTION
In a recent editorial, Cooper and Cunningham [1] discussed the notion of teaching computer science in context and urged computer science educators to recognize the importance of "computational thinking" in a successful education [10]. They promote a broad view of computer science and encourage the development of computing capabilities in students outside of computer science as well as building a broad viewpoint for computer science students. ITiCSE'09 Working Group 6 [5] defines the notion of "computationalist thinking" and articulates six concepts (modeling, abstraction, interpretation, scales and limits, simulation, and automation) that characterize and unite computational endeavors.

Providing a context for learning in the CS0-CS2 sequence underpins approaches such as Alice [2], media computation [4] and graphics-based curricula [7]. Studies have shown these approaches have been effective motivators and can provide good foundational programming skills.

Our own thinking on this issue evolved from the computational and statistical trends driving the field of biology as well as our experience managing a project that matched undergraduate biologists with quantitative partners (math or stat majors) to work on research teams conducting biological research. These students spent considerable time on data analysis activities for which they were singularly unprepared. In thinking about how to change the biology curriculum to make it more quantitative, we realized that computing was an important aspect of the transformation, but a single traditional computing course did little to remedy the deficiencies in the requisite student skills.

We envisioned an approach in which we taught computation by having students work on real data analysis problems. We selected MATLAB as a platform because of its high-level data analysis and user-interface support. However, most traditional MATLAB courses and textbooks emphasize formulas and target students with some mathematical training.

An exception is the Wright State EGR 101 which uses a combination of mathematics, computation and experiments to engage students in solving engineering problems at the freshman level [5]. Their course is noteworthy in several respects. They introduce MATLAB as an exploratory and computational tool to solve specific engineering problems that students will encounter in later courses. The beginning half of the course only uses high school mathematics, but the problems introduced are significant engineering problems. However, in contrast to the course proposed here, EGR 101 emphasizes analytical problem-solving rather than data analysis and does not have the teaching of programming skills as an objective.

The remainder of this paper has the following organization. Section 2 provides an overview of the curriculum, Section 3 describes course evolution, Section 4 discusses teaching issues, and Section 5 presents concluding remarks.

SIGCSE'11, March 9–12, 2011, Dallas, Texas, USA.

2. COURSE ORGANIZATION

CS 1173 Data Analysis and Visualization Using MATLAB is moving into its third year of implementation and is required of all biology majors at our university. The course has College Algebra as its prerequisite and students typically take the course in their sophomore or junior year, although advising encourages them to take the course as early as possible.

2.1 Topics

The course focuses around building skills in three areas: data analysis, computation, and scientific process. Specifically, we target the following skills.

Quantitative and data visualization skills:

- Display data using appropriate visualizations (e.g., histograms, pies, scatter graphs) and their combinations.
- Understand and use basic statistical indicators for data (e.g., mean, standard deviation, median, tests of significance).
- Make correct and relevant assertions about data.

Computational skills:

- Develop programs that use variables, relational expressions, loops, functions, and logical indexing.
- Apply basic functions (e.g., sum, difference, exponential, log) appropriately and in context.
- Manipulate data structures such as lists, tables, and strings.

Scientific skills:

- Formulate and test hypotheses about data.
- Use modeling to study scientific questions.
- Understand how to acquire and analyze data.

Figure 1 gives a week-by-week listing of the major topics with focus questions shown in italics. In the first five weeks, students learn to write scripts, call functions, and use the basic statistical indicators. We integrate rudimentary writing in the form of making correct assertions about the data throughout the course. After the midterm exam, we move to more complex programming skills needed in actual data analysis and to statistical analyses beyond mean, median, and correlation.

2.2 Course delivery

The course is offered in a 55-seat computer classroom, and each student has his/her own computer (currently multicore with 24" monitors running Windows XP). The room is equipped with iTALC classroom control software, which we find useful for locking screens and projecting demonstrations when the details on the main projectors are not visible to students sitting in the back of the room. We also use the ClassQue [8] software extensively for administering short exercises and reviewing student answers. In addition to the instructor, generally one or two assistants are in the classroom. We try to hire undergraduates with good interaction skills who have previously done well in the course.

1 Basic data visualization in MATLAB
Introduction to the MATLAB workspace, basic plotting and editing of line graphs, loading files, saving plots, legends, figure captions, annotations, color, `plottools`
How do I get started using MATLAB?

2 Effective use of line graphs, bar charts, and pies
Line graphs, pie charts, bar charts, stacked bar charts, sum function, percentage calculations
How can I display trends and relationships?

3 Combining plots to compare data sets
Insets, multiple axes, units, bar charts maximum, minimum, mean, median, mode
How can I combine graphs for effective comparisons?

4 Rates of change
Plots of ratios, difference, per capita, slope and rate of change, rate of change per capita, fractions of the whole
How can I characterize rates of change?

5 Scatter plots and logarithmic axes
Scatter plots, curve-fitting, correlation, logarithmic axes
How can I determine whether two variables are related?

6-7 Project and midterm

8 Vector indexing and program control
Relational expressions, logical vectors, loops, if-else
How can I extract information based on data values?

9 Depictions of spread
Histograms, cumulative probability distributions, box plots, interquartile range, percentiles, standard deviation
How can I depict the distribution of data values?

10 Depictions of error
Error bars, standard error of the mean
How can I depict uncertainty and variability in data?

11 Hypothesis testing and confidence intervals
One sample and two sample t-tests, confidence intervals
How can I determine whether an experimental group is significantly different from the control group?

12 Modeling
Using difference equations and other models
How can I simulate biological and other systems?

13 Real data (optional)
Dates, low-level I/O, missing values
How can I analyze real data?

14-15 Review

Figure 1: Week-by-week topic list

2.3 Course curriculum details

We have organized the course around lessons, labs, projects, and in-class activities. Our goal is to develop a hands-on course that includes significant problem solving as well as programming and writing. The course is designed to produce students with usable data analysis skills.

2.3.1 *Lessons*

We cover each major topic of Figure 1 in two lessons that introduce the material and give a core set of examples. We try to cover two lessons per week, which includes the students working through the lessons and participating in various in-class activities. The instructor gives some explanation at the beginning and during each lesson. Students can work through the lesson examples to see the process before fully grasping the details. Lessons provide models for how students should do their own computations.

2.2.2 *Laboratories*

The laboratories use the material from the lessons, but require students to apply the results of the lessons. Students can get help and are encouraged to collaborate on the laboratories. A lesson might have an example of using the mean function with an explanation of what it did and allow the student to try it out and observe the results. The follow-on laboratory asks students to compute the average for another data set and output it. A nearly identical statement would appear somewhere in the lessons (applied to different data).

2.2.3 *Projects*

Projects require extension and more application of material in an independent way. In a project, the student must decide what to do in addition to figuring out "how" to do it. The current version of the course has two projects: a graphical analysis of an existing data set and a statistical analysis of a more complex data set.

We typically use an epidemiological data set (such as diabetes or tuberculosis where the data is broken down by age group and by race) from the CDC or other government source for the data analysis project. Students may select any combination of graphs they choose to display the data, as long as they display all of the data and they choose combinations that enable them to make appropriate written observations about the data.

3. EVOLUTION OF COURSE MATERIALS

3.1 Lessons

We wrote the initial lessons while offering the course for the first time in the fall 2008 semester. In the initial version of the course, the laboratories and projects used real biological data, but most of the lessons used the non-biological traffic data set, `count.dat`, that comes with the MATLAB distribution.

Since its initial offering, we have revised the lessons several times as illustrated by two versions of an example from an early lesson shown in Figure 2. The top EXAMPLE 2, which came from the initial version of the course offered in the fall 2008, asks students to extract a variable to hold the first column of the `count` array. The example refers to the traffic data set, and the instructions describe the action in terms of arrays. The column corresponds to the traffic from intersection 1, as reflected by the variable name, but the example does not make the relationship explicit.

The bottom EXAMPLE 2, which comes from the current version of the course, uses a well-known biological data set [11], childhood diseases in New York City for the years 1931-1971. The example describes the variable in terms of its meaning (measles cases from 1931) rather than as a row or column of an array.

EXAMPLE 2: Separate array columns into variables
Type the following in the Command Window:

```
    % Create variable for first column of count
 inter1 = count(:, 1);
```

EXAMPLE 2: Define appropriate variables for analysis

```
    % Measles cases in 1931 (row 1 of measles)
 measles1931 = measles(1, :);
```

You should see a `measles1931`variable in the Workspace Browser. The `measles1931` variable holds a 12-element row vector containing the monthly measles cases for 1931.

In the space below:
Define a variable called `mumps1942` that contains the monthly case counts of mumps for the year 1942.

Figure 2: Evolution of lesson examples. Top version is from first offering and bottom version is from the current offering.

After describing the expected results in terms of the data, the example asks the students to produce a similar MATLAB statement pertaining to a different row of a different array. As they work through this example, students learn to define variables (the assignment statement), to extract array rows and columns, and to associate meaning with rows and columns.

3.2 Use of FAQ-style questions

In a lecture-style course, instructors often present very detailed explanations of how things work and why. While this may work for an orderly and measured presentation of material, we have found that such a "waterfall" strategy does not work well for an immersion-style laboratory course. The second lesson already asks students to define variables, extract rows and columns from arrays, sum rows and columns of arrays, plot data using line graphs, and to make meaningful interpretation of data. We can present the details about how things work, but students are not ready to listen.

Instead, we have adopted the use of FAQ-style (Frequently Asked Questions) for delivering explanations as shown in Figure 3. During the class period students work through the lesson and we give a brief overview of the lesson objectives, ask and answer questions to test student understanding, and walk around and help students who are stuck.

After the lesson, students read over an associated questions page or FAQ that dissects and explains each statement in the lesson. Most of the important statements have many associated questions covering issues ranging from MATLAB syntax to the meaning of the commands. Our original format included the FAQ with the lesson in a single-column format with the answer following the question in italics. We now have a separate FAQ for each lesson that mirrors the examples and uses a two-column format with the question in bold on the left and the answer on the right. Students indicate that they go back to the FAQ many times.

3.2.4 *Sleep diary case study*

The second project has evolved into a major case study that we use throughout the course. We ask students to track their sleep

EXAMPLE 7: Adding columns to summarize data

```
%Sum columns to calculate monthly totals
measlesByMonth = sum(measles);
```

Question	Answer
What does `sum(measles)` do?	This command adds up each column of `measles`.
How big is `sum(measles)`?	Since `measles` is an array with 41 rows and 12 columns, the result will be a single row of 12 entries.
Does `sum(measles)` differ from `sum(measles, 1)`?	They are the same in this case. The second parameter refers to the first non-singleton dimension.

Figure 3: FAQ-style questions to present explanations.

patterns by keeping a 3-week sleep diary starting in the third week of the semester. Students record their bed times, their wake up times, whether they used caffeine that day and whether they woke up to an alarm and enter this information into a spreadsheet. This exercise exposes students to the vagaries of data collection. The entered data must meet rigid formatting guidelines, or the computer programs that use this data will crash. We grade this assignment as a gateway (full credit or nothing) and do not accept student data until it passes the verification tests.

We then consolidate, anonymize, and combine the data for all students (typically around 150 students in 3 or 4 sections). We email subject numbers to the students for use in comparing their particular sleep patterns to those of the class as a whole. We used this data for a number of examples in the lessons, a laboratory, and for the second project. We formulate questions such as "Are men's sleep patterns different than women's?" and discuss whether our cohort is representative of all people or of particular subsets.

In the final project, students compare their sleep diaries to those of the rest of the cohort. Students are free to select the statistics and graphs to compute within certain guidelines. They are also required to prepare a technical report evaluating the results of this analysis, reflecting on their sleep patterns, and discussing how these patterns and choices might influence their performance.

4. OTHER CONSIDERATIONS

4.1 Cell mode and scripting

MATLAB has a weakly dynamically typed scripting language that supports a variety of data structures. Most operations support arrays and other complex types, eliminating the need for loops in many of the usual data analysis situations. The power of the scripting language makes MATLAB scripts very compact but it requires some sophistication to use effectively. We spend a fair amount of class time having students work through simple examples by hand to make sure that they understand what is happening in the code.

MATLAB supports a mode of execution called Cell Mode. A MATLAB script is broken into cells by separating blocks of code by lines that start with %%. MATLAB can execute the code in any cell independently of the rest of the script using the current contents of the workspace. Users can break a script down into cells in any way they choose. Cell Mode encourages incremental development and testing. The lessons, which consist of 8 to 10 core examples, have each example in a separate cell so that we can execute each one independently of the rest of the script. Students can also examine the workspace variables and their values while executing the cells.

In the initial conception of the course, we envisioned using the MATLAB `plottools` and code generation to gently introduce students to scripting. We found however, that after a few hours of doing figures with `plottools`, students began to find the process very tedious. In later versions of the course, we have nearly eliminated the use of `plottools`. Instead we introduce MATLAB functions such as `title`, `legend`, and `xlabel` almost immediately. We then emphasize the importance of correct labeling of graphs rather than the visual details such as font selection. We did not anticipate that biology students with no programming experience would so easily adapt to scripting nor that they would so readily recognize the savings in time and effort such scripting affords.

4.2 Mathematics and statistics background

While the students in the biology program at our university are required to take a biocalculus course and a biostatistics course, this required MATLAB data analysis course only has college algebra as a prerequisite. While some of the students have completed their mathematics requirement, most have not. This presents challenges as well as opportunities.

We deal with 2D arrays from day one, but we stick to a spreadsheet metaphor during the course, referring to tables and lists rather than matrices. The analysis techniques covered in the course only require element-wise operations and are not difficult for students, once they master the notation.

We heavily rely on students knowing the equation of a line given two points. Students first meet this equation in the first week when we talk about what a line graph really is (lines connecting successive pairs of points). We meet the equation of a line again in the lessons on rates of change, where we use slopes and geometry rather than talking about derivatives. We emphasize the units of x and y when discussing rates of change. Lines are also an important element in the discussion of linear fits.

Many students are weak in their understanding of logarithms and exponentials. We do not approach this topic in a traditional manner. Rather, our discussion of logarithms emphasizes the use of log scales to view a collection of items that range in scale from small to large. We also talk about exponential growth in the context of graphs, discussing the fact that curves undergoing exponential growth appear linear on a semi log scale.

We do not assume much in the way of statistical background beyond knowing what the average is. We hand calculate means and medians as well as standard deviations. The course introduces the notion of a population and a sample in geometric terms.

The most difficult topic for students by far is the notion of hypothesis testing and the t-test. MATLAB has nice built-in functions for one-sample and two-sample t-tests. These functions have three return values: h (an indicator of whether to reject the null hypothesis), a p-value, and a confidence interval for the mean or difference of the means. We apply the t-test in many different situations and interpret the results without explaining the basis of the t-test in any detail.

As part of the statistical part of the course, we explain that the t-test assumes samples drawn at random from a normally distributed population. We discuss how well these assumptions are satisfied and apply visual and analytical tests for normality.

4.3 Role of hand calculations

We feel that pencil and paper calculations provide an essential check for students to make sure that they really understand what they are doing. Every day we ask students different types of review questions such as the following:

a. Given the array `A = [1,5,2;6,2,3]`, what is `sum(A)`?

b. The variable `horseTemp` represents a `24 × 5` array containing the core body temperature in degrees Centigrade for five different horses over a 24-hour period. Write a MATLAB statement to define a variable `horse1` containing the temperature measurements of the first horse.

Question a. is a routine syntactical question that determines whether the student understands the MATLAB `sum` function. Students also have to understand the comma and semicolon notation for expressing arrays in order to answer the question.

Question b. determines whether a student understands how to extract a column from an array and how to use an assignment statement. The question has extraneous information and requires more than just syntactical understanding.

We also give a few hand-calculation homework problems that we check off as completion grades and go over in class. For example, we ask students questions about the table at the left such as:

Day	Beach 1 CFU/100ml	Beach 2 CFU/100ml
1	10	20
5	80	20
6	30	50
8	20	40
10	50	30

a) Find the maximum daily count for Beach 1.

b) Find the fraction of Beach 2's count that occurred on Day 6.

c) Find the percentage of Day 5's count that occurred on Beach 1.

After going over the answers, we write MATLAB code to calculate the quantities.

4.4 Modeling

We incorporate modeling in several ways. We introduce linear models in the lesson on linear fits, scatter plots, and correlation. We do several examples using linear fits to make predictions about the data. For example, one of the labs looks at cricket chirps versus temperature to assess the accuracy of a "cricket thermometer", a well-known backyard science project. We also read the famous Nature paper by Dawson and Reid [3] that uses linear fits to derive an equivalence between alcohol consumption and sleep deprivation.

During the statistics unit, we perform simulation experiments to measure how closely the mean or standard deviation of a sample reflects the mean or standard deviation of the underlying population. We sometimes do simulations using nonlinear difference equations and reproduce the bifurcation diagrams.

4.5 Writing

Requiring students to articulate their understanding through writing is an important tool for developing higher-level data analysis skills and for assessing student understanding of these concepts. As the course has evolved, we have incorporated a writing component that is manageable for both students and instructors. We define the following levels of writing:

- **Level 1 (mechanics)** includes grammar, spelling and sentence construction that can be addressed to a significant extent by spelling checking and grammar checking tools.
- **Level 2 (facts)** includes correct and informative interpretation of the data.
- **Level 3 (insight)** involves making connections among multiple pieces of information and describing relationships in a broader context.

Our goal is for students to write consistently at Level 2 with a smidgeon of Level 3. We require students to use Microsoft Word with grammar checking turned on and forbid them to use the word "it". We can check these requirements mechanically and find they are sufficient for students to meet the Level 1 requirements. We require students to submit major writing assignments through Safe Assign on Blackboard to eliminate plagiarism.

In the initial versions of the course, we required students to write half page reports in conjunction with various labs and assignments. We found that poor writing confounded our ability to pick out logic errors. Our graduate student graders, many of whom were non-native English speakers could not deal with the grading. We now do most of the writing (except for the final project reports) in the form of bullet points. TAs cut and paste incorrect bullet points into the grading program comment box and assemble all of the incorrect answers in a single file to give to the instructors. They do not offer corrections. The instructors can use the file as the basis for in-class writing exercises.

An important insight that we have gained while working through our writing strategy is that it is relatively easy to demonstrate bad writing— students provide a rich example set. However, we have found it essential to model good writing before we ask them to do their own writing. In particular, instructors must give many examples of good observations about data in a variety of contexts in order for students to be successful.

4.6 Classroom management

Keeping students on task in a computer classroom is always a challenge. Installation of the ITALC classroom control software helped a lot. Pacing is everything, and we have found that it is important to have activities available for the early finishers (or get them to help the other students). Attempted use of distracters went way down after we put a strong statement in the syllabus about classroom courtesy and stated cell phones and other devices used during class were subject to confiscation.

5. DISCUSSION

This paper describes the design, implementation, and evolution of a data-driven computing curriculum for undergraduate biologists. The project is well into the implementation phase, and we have offered 11 sections of the course taught by six different instructors. We are entering into the summative evaluation phase of the project. We have developed a complete set of teaching materials including lessons, lecture plans, laboratories, projects, and teaching notes, all of which are available on the web at http://www.cs.utsa.edu/~cs1173. The course materials have undergone a number of rewrites as we have learned what works and what does not. The course includes a writing component and discussion of actual scientific literature. The remainder of this paper is a summarization in the form of a FAQ.

Can this course be done without MATLAB? Ans: One of the problems with traditional programming courses and languages is that you have to work very hard to do anything useful. It takes most of the semester in a beginning course for students to reach the point of being able to read values from a file into an array in a typical beginning Java, C, or C++ course. Graphing takes an extraordinary amount of work. Students can do little computation that is useful to a working biology lab after taking a traditional programming course. Our students have useful data analysis skills after completing this course. Our students learn a lot about computers, programming, and debugging along the way. Other environments such as SciLab, Octave, or SciPy or even Excel [9] could be adapted to integrate programming and data analysis. We do rely on the strong debugging and visual data browsing support provided by the MATLAB IDE that MATLAB substitutes don't always have.

Can this course be done without a computer classroom? Ans: We don't think so. There are some attractive possibilities with having two students share a computer instead of having each student at his or her own computer. However, the course material requires students to have extensive hands-on experience with someone readily available to help when they become stuck or confused.

Does this course have to be about biology? Ans: No. We could easily substitute data sets from the other sciences, engineering, psychology, and economics for those used in the current examples to change the orientation of the course. We choose the particular data analysis techniques to reflect common usage in biological papers. However, we do not have any examples related to genetics or bioinformatics in the current version of the course. A course designed specifically for physicists or engineers should probably have more modeling and less statistics.

Could this course be offered as a hybrid course? Ans: Maybe. While we do not think that a course offered entirely online is feasible, some combination of computer lab and online course may be possible. After the first few weeks, students are able to work through the lessons independently. Their difficulty comes from trying to adapt the code to slightly new situations. A hybrid course would require a collection of video demonstrations and probably additional online material.

Can we make connections to other courses? Ans: We are trying. The statisticians are planning to make this course a co-requisite for the required biostatistics course so that students will have a common computing background. When we first start introducing some of the statistical concepts such as the concept of normality and the t-test, students without statistics feel they should have statistics first. However, we have found that having the statistical background really does not appear to have a strong influence on how well students do. They appear to benefit from acquiring a more geometric grasp of the concepts before listening to the mathematical explanations from their statistics course.

This course is a prerequisite for a required junior level course in physiology. Work has begun on redesigning the curriculum for that course and we hope to modify some of the examples to be physiological in nature. In particular, we plan to develop some examples using a model of the heart that students see in biocalculus and use for some analysis units in physiology.

6. ACKNOWLEDGMENTS

This work was supported by NSF grant 0837248.

7. REFERENCES

[1] Cooper, S. and Cunningham, S., 2010. Teaching computer science in context. *ACM Inroads*, 1, 1, 5-8, http://doi.acm.org/10.1145/1721933.1721934.

[2] Dann, W., Cooper, S., and Pausch, R. 2008. *Learning to Program with Alice*, 2nd Ed. Prentice-Hall, 2008.

[3] Dawson, D. and Reid, K. (1997). Fatigue, alcohol and performance impairment. *Nature*, 388, 235.

[4] Guzdial, M. and Ericson, B. 2007. *An Introduction to Computing and Programming with Java: A Multimedia Approach*. Prentice-Hall.

[5] Isbell, C. L., Stein, L. A., Cutler, R. Forbes, J. Fraser, L. Impagliazzo, J., Proulx, V., Russ, S. Thomas, R. and Xu Y. 2009. (Re)defining computing curricula by (re)defining computing. *ACM SIGCSE Bulletin*, 41, 4, 195-207, http://doi.acm.org/10.1145/1709424.1709462.

[6] Klingbeil, N. W., Mercer, R.E., Rattan, K.S., Raymer, M. L. and Reynolds, D. B. 2006. The WSU model for engineering mathematics education: Student performance, perception and retention in year one. *Proc. 2006 ASEE Illinois-Indiana and North Central Conference*, Fort Wayne, IN, April 2006.

[7] Matzko, S. and Davis, T. A., 2008. A graphics-based approach to data structures. *ITiCSE'08, ACM SIGCSE Bulletin*, 40, 3, 109-113, http://doi.acm.org/10.1145/1597849.1384302.

[8] Robbins, S., 2011. Beyond clickers: Using ClassQue for multidimensional electronic classroom interaction. *ACM SIGCSE*, to appear.

[9] Vacher, L. and Larner, E. 2010, Spreadsheets across the curriculum 1: The idea and the resource. *Numeracy,* 3, 2, 6.

[10] Wing, J. M. 2006. Computational thinking. *Communications of the ACM,* 49, 3, 33-35.

[11] Yorke, J. A. and London, W. P. 1973. Recurrent outbreaks of measles, chickenpox and mumps. *American Journal of Epidemiology*, 98, 6, 453-468.

τέχνη Trees: A New Course in Data Structures

Andrew T. Duchowski
School of Computing
Clemson University
Clemson, SC 29634-0974
duchowski@clemson.edu

Robert Geist
School of Computing
Clemson University
Clemson, SC 29634-0974
geist@clemson.edu

Robert Schalkoff
Department of Electrical &
Computer Engineering
Clemson University
Clemson, SC 29634-0915
rjschal@clemson.edu

James Westall
School of Computing
Clemson University
Clemson, SC 29634-0974
westall@clemson.edu

ABSTRACT

The τέχνη method is an approach to undergraduate computer science education that is based on cognitive constructivisim, in the sense of Piaget, and which invokes several course design directives that include re-combining art and science, problem-based learning, problem selection from the visual problem domain, and cognitive apprenticeship. The paper describes a new τέχνη course in *data structures*. It includes a full comparative assessment of the realized improvement in student problem solving capability and, for the first time, cognitive authenticity in problem selection, in that the course problem is a variation on a very recent research result.

Categories and Subject Descriptors

K.3.2 [**Computers and Education**]: Computer and Information Science Education—*Curriculum*

General Terms

Design, Experimentation, Human Factors

Keywords

computer graphics, curriculum design, problem-based instruction, ray-tracing, τέχνη

1. INTRODUCTION

The τέχνη project provides an unusual, perhaps radical, alternative to the standard design of the computing curriculum for the bachelor's degree in computer science. As described by Davis et al. [4, 5], it is built on a foundation of *cognitive constructivism* and draws directly from Piaget [13], Dewey [6], and Rousseau [15] in its basic tenets:

- Learning is an active process of constructing individual knowledge.
- Learning occurs when observations differ from expectations, and new models must be constructed as accommodations.
- Teaching is the process of invoking and supporting these constructions.

Nevertheless, this foundation alone is an insufficient specification of method. The τέχνη designers specify pillars, upon which courses should be designed and taught:

- *re-combining art and science* An original motivation for the τέχνη design was (and is) effecting a reconnection of divergent branches in the U.S. educational system, art and science. The word, τέχνη, is the Greek word for *art*. It shares its root with τεχνολογία, the Greek word for *technology*. The lateralization of brain functions need not be enforced by curriculum. Addressing single problems that require linear reasoning, spatial manipulation, and visual processing can offer bi-lateral engagement, with its attendant creativity and originality.

- *problem-based learning* Problem-based learning is well-known [7], and its use is widespread. Carefully designed problems demand that learners acquire self-directed learning strategies, critical knowledge, and the problem-solving proficiency needed for effective progress in deriving solutions. The τέχνη method differs from other problem-based learning methods in the size and scope of the problems addressed. It calls for one, large-scale problem per semester.

- *visual domain* Problems are chosen from the fields of computer graphics and visualization. Human society is increasingly visually-oriented, and visual problems quickly capture the attention and interest of young students. Further, in his discussions on visual communication, Cunningham [3] observed that the tools of thought for effective problem solving, as well the attendant communication skills for group efforts, were extremely well-supported by computer graphics. Cunningham's work was a principal motivating factor in the original τέχνη design.

- *cognitive apprenticeship* Resnick [14] observed that the time-honored master-apprentice relationship could be transferred from the arena of physical skills to that of cognitive skills,

SIGCSE'11, March 9–12, 2011, Dallas, Texas USA

given an appropriately designed learning environment. Process is the key, rather than any artificial balance in the roles of master and apprentice. There is great value in observation of a master at work. Original solutions to challenging problems, including missteps and erasures, carry a vitality that is missing in solutions that have been cleaned and polished for presentation in more formal settings. Of course, such vitality will only appear if the cognitive demands on the master are authentic. Thus the ideal problems for τέχνη courses are those that challenge both student and instructor.

The entire philosophical basis of the τέχνη method, as well as the results of instructional experiments with introductory courses, have been presented in several papers, e.g. [4, 5, 10], and in the dissertation by Matzko [9].

We present here the results of teaching a new, τέχνη-based course in *data structures* at Clemson University during the Fall semester of 2009. In addition to the new course design, we offer two important extensions of previous efforts. First, we include the results of a full, comparative assessment of the realized improvement in student problem-solving capability. The assessment instruments were designed prior to the beginning of the course(s), and included pre-test and post-test evaluations with linear regression models. Second, for the first time we have invoked full cognitive authenticity in problem selection. The semester-long problem is a variation on graphics research results that were published only one year earlier.

2. DATA STRUCTURES

A Data Structures course is a standard component of most undergraduate curricula in computing. The topic remains a specific requirement for CAC/ABET accreditation in the 2009-2010 cycle [2]. The conventional approach to Data Structures, as typified by the popular book of Weiss [17], is breadth-first, wherein a wide range of structures are considered, hypothetical cases in which each might be useful are proposed, and some elementary algorithm analysis is offered. The breadth of topic, combined with the time constraints of the standard semester course, allows consideration of only elementary examples. The students are well aware that they are solving toy problems in series.

The τέχνη course, in contrast, is depth-first. Investigations into data structures are driven by real needs for adequate execution time, as experienced by student teams in solving a real problem. Elementary algorithm analysis is augmented by profiling code prototypes to obtain a priori runtime estimates of proposed solutions. This approach sacrifices some breadth of coverage, but students gather a first-hand understanding of the real use and real value of a variety of data structures. Seeking new structures as new problems arise should become a natural process for them.

To use an analogy from the construction industry, in a classical course students practice hammering nails, practice sawing 2×4s, learn that a nail gun is faster than a hammer, and learn that a SKIL saw is faster than a hand saw, but at the conclusion of the course they have not a clue as to how to build a house. In the τέχνη course, the instructor leads student teams in building houses. The students learn of the tools available and develop the skills to use them within a context of purpose.

3. STUDENT BACKGROUND

Data Structures (CPSC 212) is the third course for undergraduate majors in the School of Computing at Clemson University. It is a 4-hour course, with 3 lecture/discussion sessions and a single 2-hour lab session each week. It is typically taken by first semester sophomores. At the beginning of the semester, students were randomly assigned to one of two sections. The *conventional* section was taught by author Duchowski using a conventional approach which followed the topics and order of the Weiss [17] textbook. The τέχνη section was taught by author Geist.

Figure 1: Example 102 scene.

Because the τέχνη curriculum design was in place during the 2008-2009 academic year, students who had completed the first two courses had already experienced (the joy and) the difficulty of solving large, semester-long problems, had significant experience with C, and had some experience with C++.

The semester-long, τέχνη problem of the second course, CPSC 102, is writing a ray tracer to generate synthetic images. The scene of Figure 1 is typical of the output, although orientations that are not axis-aligned, such as the view and the cube placement, may not have been covered by all sections. Stronger students might have added additional light sources, textures (photos mapped to scene geometry), and more interesting, though still elementary, objects.

4. THE NEW PROBLEM

The new problem for τέχνη Data Structures builds on the ray tracer from the second course. Of course, some students had not completed this course, and others who had completed it no longer had copies of their final code. A generic ray tracer, written in C and capable of generating the scene of Figure 1, was distributed to all students on the first day. The course goal, also presented on first day, was then to build a C++ ray tracer to generate scenes such as those shown in Figure 2. These scenes, taken from [8], are also synthetic, but, obviously, they are much more complex. Rather than a handful of polygons or surfaces, each of these scenes contains more than 250,000,000 triangles.

The apparent impossibility of the task at hand is then easily described. Simple arithmetic shows the folly of the effort. Anti-aliasing will demand a minimum of about 5 rays per pixel, but most of these rays will generate another, to determine whether the object hit by the ray is in a shadow. The images of Figure 2, at 896×672 pixels, will thus each require approximately 6,021,120 rays. To find the first visible triangle, each ray must be tested against each triangle, i.e., approximately 3×10^{12} tests. The fastest, most efficient ray/triangle intersection test is given by the Möller/Trumbore algorithm [11]. By placing CPU cycle counters into the calling code, one can determine an accurate measure of execution time for this

(a) Target scene rendering

(b) Rendering with pine trees rather than beech trees

Figure 2: Sample renderings

test. On a fast, modern CPU, it takes approximately 85 ns. So, if the time for texture lookup and overhead is ignored, this will take at least $3 \times 10^{12} \times 85 \times 10^{-9} = 255{,}000$ seconds, i.e., 3 days. Even if the students are willing to accept substandard images obtained by using only one primary ray per pixel, this will still take 14 hours.

It was then revealed to the students that each of the images of Figure 2 was actually ray-traced in less than 1 second. "How is this possible?" was the universal response. The short answer is "Data Structures," and the long answer is the course content.

4.1 Phase 1

The course begins with a code review of the distributed ray tracer, which is available online at http://www.cs.clemson.edu/~geist/212/rt.v0zup.c. This includes discussion of C structures, arrays, linked lists, and function pointers. It also includes an orientation to 3D geometry, including a discussion of dot and cross products and their geometric interpretation, and translation and rotation operators (expressed as triples of dot products) that are necessary to move objects (such as trees) into desired positions within an overall scene.

A forest is built from many trees, and each tree is built from many leaves. The first assignment is an elementary increment: modify the distributed C ray tracer to produce a C++ ray tracer that will generate an image similar to that of Figure 3. The distributed ray tracer, though strictly C code, will compile under g++, but assignment requirements included replacement of all function pointers, structs, and unions. As noted earlier, students work in self-selected teams, with a limit of 4 students per team. The only significant problem in this phase is handling the leaf geometry. It is implemented as a pair of texture-mapped triangles, arranged as a single rectangle. The texture (photo) contains more than just the color channels (r,g,b) for the leaf. It contains an alpha channel that determines per-pixel visibility within the photo. Thus, if a ray/triangle intersection test determines that a texture-mapped triangle was hit, the appropriate pixel in the photo must be examined to determine whether the intersection was within the leaf boundary. If so, the leaf color from the photo is used. If not, a miss is reported. Finding the appropriate pixel within the photo requires a discussion of interpolation, and handling the 4-channel photo requires a discussion of parsing large, externally-supplied files of relatively simple format. The portable pixmap format (.ppm) was used for all textures/images. A simple extension to the P6 format allowed 4 bytes per pixel.

Figure 3: Assignment 1.

The transition to C++, begun with this phase, was generally seen as a relief, rather than a burden. The ray tracing problem is a natural one for object-oriented solution. Operator overloading for vector operations on points and colors offers significant savings, and the different geometries (triangles, boxes, spheres, and texture-mapped versions of each) are conveniently handled as derived classes with with virtual methods and polymorphic operators.

4.2 Phase 2

In the second phase, the students were asked to ray trace a single tree, such as that shown in Figure 4. Models for several tree species ([12]) were supplied in the form of .obj files. This phase occupied most of the semester. Parsing .obj files is far more complicated than parsing simple, 4-component .ppm images. Once parsing, with attendant focus on fast I/O, is mastered, the real fun begins. The image of Figure 4 contains only two textures, but it contains almost 500,000 triangles. From Phase 1, the students know how to render linked lists of texture mapped triangles, and so the natural inclination is to build a linked list of triangles and ray trace as before.

The students were given a full class period to come to the realization that each ray cannot be tested against each triangle, and so the scene geometry must be partitioned to avoid intersection tests. Thus the kd-tree [1], a balanced, binary tree of axis-aligned splitting planes, is introduced. Construction of such trees alone invokes interesting sub-problems such as the often repeated task of finding the median of a very long list of items (triangle vertices). The natural approach proposed by students is to sort the list and select the middle item. This leads to a discussion of sorting techniques and their comparative performance on very large tasks. During the development of quicksort, it is observed that the same basic compare-and-swap operation used in quicksort could be used to build a an

Figure 4: Assignment 2.

Figure 6: Example (with permission) from student C. J. Corsi

$O(N)$ algorithm to find the median! This linear algorithm is then integrated into the kd-tree construction. Although sorting per se is ultimately abandoned for the ray tracing task, the students become quite knowledgeable on the topic.

Building the kd-tree also requires recursive traversals. Since the correctly constructed kd-tree is complete, a discussion of the advantages of heap representation is conducted.

Traversing the kd-tree to find a reduced collection of triangles to be ray-tested is a delicate operation that requires ray-plane intersection tests and an auxiliary stack to hold pointers to potential candidates, but the search and the need for the stack are easily motivated with a 2D analogy drawn on the classroom white/black board. Pseudo-code for the traversal is show in Figure 5. Execution time

```
(t_min,t_max)=intersect(ray,bounding_box)
stack.push(root,t_min,t_max)
while(not stack.empty):
    (node,t_min,t_max) = stack.pop
    while(not node.is_leaf):
        a = node.splitaxis
        t_split = (node.splitvalue - ray.origin[a])/(ray.dir[a])
        (one,two)=order(ray.dir[a],node.left,node.right)
        if(t_split≥t_max)
            node=one
        else if(t_split≤t_min or t_split<0)
            node=two
        else
            stack.push(two,t_split,t_max)
            node=one
            t_max=t_split
    for triangle in node.triangles:
        t_hit = min(t_hit,intersect(ray,triangle))
    if t_hit < t_max
        break
return t_hit
```

Figure 5: Stack-based kd-tree traversal for ray tracing

that is $O(logN)$ versus that which is $O(N)$ becomes truly meaningful when N reaches the levels found in this task.

4.3 Phase 3

Phrase 3 requires ray tracing a miniature "forest" consisting of multiple species of trees with multiple instances of at least one species. Only one copy of each species' geometry was allowed. The other instances contain only rotation and translation information. The entire scene is represented as a kd-tree of bounding boxes, each leaf of which contains a list of one or more bounding boxes, each of which contains either a simple geometry list or another kd-tree representing a physical tree. Correct handling of normals to surfaces was a delicate matter. Each surface, e.g. a physical tree leaf, had a normal with respect to its defined geometry at the point of ray-surface intersection. This normal had to be combined with the normal to the enclosing bounding box, set during placement of the tree, in order to yield the correct world-coordinate normal.

The students were encouraged to be creative in their designs and reminded that there was no "correct" or "incorrect" final image. A sample student image is shown in Figure 6.

This somewhat singular focus on the structures needed for ray tracing forests did not completely preclude other, more traditional topics from the discussions. Brief forays into AVL trees, red-black trees, hashing, and dynamic programming were also made, after front-loading the structures and methods necessary for the ray tracing task. The lab sessions were used primarily to reinforce understanding of these auxiliary topics and components of the C++ language.

Finally some discussion of mapping highly parallel tasks such as ray tracing to the relatively new SIMD architectures (GPUs) was offered.

5. ASSESSMENT

Assessment of the principal, desired accommodation, an ability to solve real problems, is extremely difficult within the classroom setting. Results of assignments that extend over multiple class periods have questionable validity. Instead, we developed ABET-like embedded instruments which were incorporated into the τέχνη course (treatment) and the *conventional* course in both pre-test and final exam. Two analyses were carried out. First, a t-test was used on the per-student change in score from the pre-test to the final exam. The null hypothesis for this test was:

H_0: There is no benefit to the τέχνη method.

Second, a linear regression analysis was conducted using 3 regressors, the pre-test score, the standard constant for such tests (1), and

Table 1: Change from pre-test to final exam

section	mean change	standard dev.	population
τέχνη	0.02	0.26	24
conventional	-0.13	0.28	17

T = 1.7269, α=0.05, reject H_0

a *class* value, which was set to 1 for the τέχνη class and 0 for the *conventional* class. The estimated coefficient of *class*, if significant, is then an indicator of the value of the τέχνη method. Thus, if F denotes the score on embedded final exam questions, P the score on pre-test questions, C the class, and E the error, the linear model was

$$F = \beta_P P + \beta_C C + \beta_K 1 + E$$

All pre-test questions and all final exam embedded questions were multiple choice, to avoid any bias in grading and issues of partial credit. Pre-test questions were largely focused on C code-reading. An example is shown in Figure 7. Embedded final exam

```
If the following code:
#include <stdio.h>

void myfunc(int a)
{
if(a >= 0){
        printf("%d ",a);
        a–;
        myfunc(a);
        }
return;
}

main()
{
int b = 5;
myfunc(b);
printf("\n");
}
were compiled and executed, which of these would appear on stdout?
```

1. no output - infinite recursion
2. compile error
3. 5 4 3 2 1 0
4. 5 4 3 2 1
5. 1 2 3 4 5
6. 0 1 2 3 4 5
7. none of these

Figure 7: Sample Pre-test question

questions avoided those areas specific to the τέχνη section. In particular, there was no mention of kd-trees, ray-object intersection tests, or parsing .ppm or .obj files. Rather, questions focused on C++ code-reading, algorithm execution time order, and solving small problems. An example question is shown in Figure 8.

In Table 1 we show the results of the t-test on the change from pre-test to final exam. The embedded questions on the final exam(s) were, of course, decidedly more difficult than those on the pre-test, and so the magnitude of the mean change per section is, by itself, not significant. Nevertheless, the difference between sections is significant. It should also be noted that the sections suffered different attrition rates, and so the final populations were no longer the same size.

In Table 2 we show the results of the regression analysis. The coefficient of determination (R^2) was 0.196928. The most important

What is the length of the shortest path from S to T in this network?

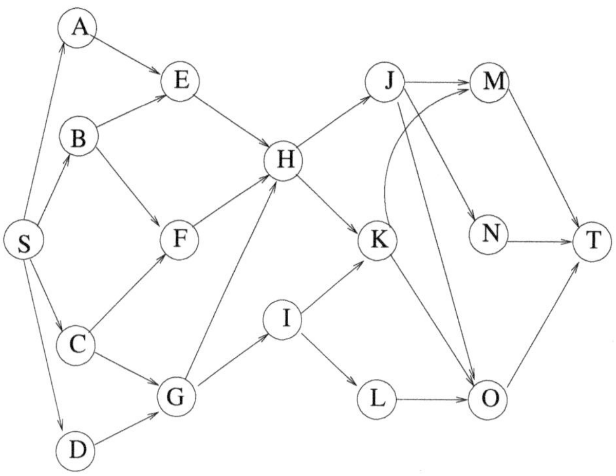

1. 10
2. 11
3. 12
4. 13
5. 14
6. 15
7. 16
8. 17
9. 18
10. 19

Figure 8: Sample Post-test question

Table 2: Regression analysis on embedded final exam scores

regressor	estimate	standard dev.	t-ratio	p-value
constant	0.499446	0.106333	4.697	0.000034
pre-test	0.062996	0.143390	0.439	0.6629
class	0.176040	0.059004	2.984	0.0050

coefficient estimate is that for the class regressor, in that it shows the benefit accrued from the τέχνη treatment, which was significant at the 1% level (p=0.0050).

An indirect assessment was also carried out. Walker and Fraser [16] observed that numerous studies report a strong correlation between traditional student outcomes (e.g. grades, test scores) and perceptions of classroom environments. The latter can be measured with unobtrusive and time-saving survey instruments. Walker and Fraser used factor analysis on field tests to develop a survey instrument of 34 ratings on six scales, instructor support, student interaction and collaboration, personal relevance, authentic learning, active learning, and student autonomy. Their instrument was targeted at distance education.

We constructed a survey instrument with 19 questions that were a composite of those suggested at http://oerl.sri.com/. The topics included satisfaction, effectiveness, opportunity to learn, assignments, and engagement. Sample questions and mean scores thereon are shown in Figure 9.

A positive correlation between attitude and post-test (embedded final exam question) results, favoring the τέχνη treatment, was found on all questions except one. Those in the τέχνη class more strongly favored the future use of a different set of software examples. Apparently, the singular focus held inadequate variation.

· I feel my classroom experience in this course generated enthusiasm for the subject.
1) Very little 2) A little 3) Somewhat 4) A lot 5) A great deal
τέχνη: 3.90 *conventional*: 3.00

· I feel my software development experience in this course generated enthusiasm for the subject.
1) Very little 2) A little 3) Somewhat 4) A lot 5) A great deal
τέχνη: 3.14 *conventional*: 2.69

· I feel the software development experience in this class used real-world examples.
1) Very little 2) A little 3) Somewhat 4) A lot 5) A great deal
τέχνη: 3.52 *conventional*: 2.38

Figure 9: Sample survey questions and results

6. CONCLUSIONS

We have presented the design of a new course in *data structures*, a design that is consistent with the goals and foundations of the τέχνη method [4, 5, 9]. The single, semester-long, driving project is construction of a C++ ray tracer that is capable of rendering, in less than a minute, scenes that are built from more than a million triangles. The driving project forces deep, performance-related investigations into many of the areas that are covered by traditional data structures courses, but often covered at a much more superficial level.

In addition to the course design, there are two important contributions of this effort. First, a formal, comparative evaluation between the τέχνη method and the traditional method of teaching data structures was conducted. At the beginning of the Fall semester of 2009, data structures students were each randomly assigned to one of two classes, which were then taught that semester, one with each method. Both pre-tests and post-tests were administered. The post-tests took the form of selected multiple choice questions that were embedded in the final exams of both classes. Analysis included a t-test on the score change from pre-test to post-test and linear regression where the regressors included the pre-test score and a class value (0 = *conventional*, 1 = τέχνη), whose coefficient then estimated the benefit of the τέχνη treatment. Both the t-test and the regression analysis yielded statistically significant results showing that the τέχνη method provided better learning outcomes. An attitudinal survey was also carried out, and it showed, in general, more positive attitudes associated with the τέχνη treatment, although a notable exception was the interest of the τέχνη students in seeing a more varied collection of examples.

The second important contribution was the first achievement of cognitive authenticity in τέχνη problem selection. The chosen task was only one year removed from research results of the instructor, and thus it represented an area of both high interest and significant challenge.

The overall evidence in support of the τέχνη method is compelling. Nevertheless, caveats are in order. We believe that we have provided a fair comparison, but it is difficult, perhaps impossible, to control for instructor bias, motivation, interest, and enthusiasm, even if the same instructor were to teach both classes, and, of course, we used different instructors. Moreover, we must acknowledge that teaching with this method requires substantially more effort than a traditional, textbook-directed approach. If that same additional effort were devoted to any other alternative method, would the result not also be quite positive? Finally, we have observed push-back from members of our own faculty whose research specialties are outside visual computing. They are both uncomfortable with venturing into visual computing and unconvinced that appropriate rewards will be attached to the substantial additional effort that must be expended.

Still, we remain hopeful that the additional benefits to student learning outcomes, such as observed here, will ultimately carry the day.

7. ACKNOWLEDGMENTS

This work was supported in part by the U.S. National Science Foundation under Award 0722313.

8. REFERENCES

[1] J. L. Bentley. Multidimensional binary search trees used for associative searching. *Commun. ACM*, 18(9):509–517, 1975.

[2] Computing Accreditation Commission. 2009-2010 criteria for accrediting computing programs. http://www.abet.org/Linked Documents-UPDATE/Criteria and PP/C001 09-10 CAC Criteria 12-01-08.pdf, 2008.

[3] S. Cunningham. Graphical problem solving and visual communication in the beginning computer graphics course. *ACM SIGCSE Bulletin*, 34(1):181 – 185, 2002.

[4] T. Davis, R. Geist, S. Matzko, and J. Westall. τέχνη: A first step. *ACM SIGCSE Bulletin*, 36(1):125 – 129, 2004.

[5] T. Davis, R. Geist, S. Matzko, and J. Westall. τέχνη: Trial phase for the new curriculum. *ACM SIGCSE Bulletin*, 39(1):415 – 419, 2007.

[6] J. Dewey. *Experience and education*. The Macmillan Company, New York, 1938.

[7] B. Duch, S. Gron, and D. Allen. *The Power of Problem-Based Learning*. Stylus Publishing, LLC, Sterling, VA, 2001.

[8] R. Geist and J. Steele. A lighting model for fast rendering of forest ecosystems. In *Proc. of the IEEE Symposium on Interactive Ray Tracing (RT08)*, pages 99–106, and back cover, Los Angeles, California, August 2008.

[9] S. Matzko. *τέχνη and Quest-Oriented Learning*. PhD thesis, Clemson University, 2008.

[10] S. Matzko and T. Davis. Using graphics research to teach freshman computer science. In *SIGGRAPH '06: ACM SIGGRAPH 2006 Educators program*, page 9, New York, NY, USA, 2006. ACM.

[11] T. Möller and B. Trumbore. Fast, minimum storage ray-triangle intersection. *Journal of Graphics Tools*, 2(1):21–28, 1997.

[12] G. Organic-Software. Xfrogplants v 2.0. http://www.xfrogdownloads.com/greenwebNew/products/productStart.htm, 2008.

[13] J. Piaget. *The development of thought: equilibration of cognitive structures (translated by A. Rosin)*. Viking Press, New York, 1977.

[14] L. B. Resnick. Learning in school and out. *Educational Researcher*, 16(9):13–20, 1987.

[15] J.-J. Rousseau. *Émile (translated by B. Foxley)*. Dutton, New York, 1955.

[16] S. Walker and B. Fraser. Development and validation of an instrument for assessing distance education learning environments in higher education. *Learning Environments Research*, 8:289–308, 2005.

[17] M. A. Weiss. *Data Structures and Algorithm Analysis in C++*. Pearson/Addison-Wesley, Boston, MA, USA, 3rd edition, 2006.

Student Attitudes and Motivation for Peer Review in CS2

Scott Turner
Department of Math and Computer Science
UNC Pembroke
Pembroke, NC
scott.turner@uncp.edu

Manuel A. Pérez-Quiñones, Stephen Edwards
Department of Computer Science
Virginia Tech
Blacksburg, VA
{perez, edwards}@cs.vt.edu

Joseph Chase
Information Technology
Radford University
Radford, VA
jchase@radford.edu

ABSTRACT

Computer science students need experience with essential concepts and professional activities. Peer review is one way to meet these goals. In this work, we examine the students' attitudes towards and engagement in the peer review process, in early, object-oriented, computer science courses. To do this, we used peer review exercises in two CS2 classes at neighboring universities over the course of a semester. Using three groups (one reviewing their peers, one reviewing the instructor, and one completing small design or coding exercises), we measured the students' attitudes, their perceptions of their abilities, and how many of the reviews they completed. We found moderately positive attitudes that generally increased over time but were not significantly different between groups. We also saw a lower completion rate for students reviewing peers than for the other groups. The students' internal motivation, as measured by their need for cognition, was not shown to be strongly related to their attitudes nor to the number of assignments completed. Overall, our results show a strong need for external motivation to help engage students in peer reviews.

Categories and Subject Descriptors

K.3.2 [**Computers and Education**]: Computer and Information Science Education – *Computer science education.*

General Terms

Measurement, Design, Experimentation, Human Factors

Keywords

Peer Review, Peer Assessment, Computer Science Education, Learning, Attitude, Engagement

1. INTRODUCTION

Like all other disciplines, computer science students need experience with the fundamental concepts within the field, need practice with professional activities, and need opportunities to develop their learning skills. Designing and writing programs is one typical way of dealing with this issue, but it generally does not meet all of the students' needs. While programming is an essential skill, it is not the only necessary skill for the students to learn and it does not always reinforce crucial ideas. That is, students may produce working programs while misunderstanding key concepts [18].

Peer review has been suggested, by a number of people, for a number of reasons, as an additional learning activity in computer science. It can be used to address programming concepts [17] and is a common professional activity [1, 8, 16], for example reviewing papers for conferences. Reviewing involves the active use of the higher levels of Bloom's taxonomy [2] and can provide students with a rich opportunity for learning. They can see authentic uses of core concepts and have a chance to incorporate the new ideas (good or bad) into their own body of knowledge [10, 16]. These qualities suggest that peer review could be a very valuable part of the curriculum.

There are, however, a number of issues (administration, reliability, etc.) that need to be dealt with in a successful review process. One of these issues centers on the attitudes of the students towards the review process. Since students may feel that computer science is about programming and that activities that are not programming are not useful to their advancement in the discipline [12], they may be reluctant to engage in the activity. Less engagement means fewer opportunities to learn.

With this in mind, we studied peer review in two CS2 classes over the course of a semester. We explored student attitudes towards peer review and internal motivation to engage in the activity. Specifically, we were evaluating student reactions to the review process, their belief in its effectiveness, and their perception of their own skills. These measures were compared over time and between two different implementations of the review process to provide a more detailed picture of how students responded to the assignments.

2. RELATED RESEARCH

Peer review is a topic that has often been explored for use in the computer science curriculum. Research has covered the benefits of peer review and the students' reactions to the process. There have also been a number of studies involving the creation of peer review systems and the viability of computer mediated reviewing. From the literature, some of the studies have investigated how closely student reviews matched other students or instructor reviews [5, 19], basic student motivation and attitudes towards peer review [9, 19, 21], systems for performing reviews [13, 21], and improvements in student projects [8].

It is important to note that how the reviewer benefits and grows from the process is commonly overlooked in literature. A sizable portion of the research focuses on how to provide software solutions to ease the implementation of the process. Other work looks at how

SIGCSE'11, March 9–12, 2011, Dallas, Texas, USA.

the extra feedback affects those being reviewed. How the reviewer learns and otherwise benefits while reviewing is not typically central to the literature. More specific to this work, the reviewers' attitudes, how they change over time, and how well the reviewers engage in the reviews need to be more thoroughly investigated. Because some of the research suggests that the implementation of a review and the materials used can influence the review's outcomes [14, 21], it would also be beneficial to compare reactions between different reviews implementations.

The available work on student motivation and attitudes does partially meet our goals but the focus of that work typically is on the system being tested and the perceived fairness of the reviews. Generally, the studies are also not compared over time or between implementations and do not look at whether the students completed the assignments or not. By addressing these issues we can get a more complete understanding of how students react to the peer review process.

2.1 Peer Review Theories and Frameworks

Peer review is active, authentic, provides opportunities for higher-level thinking [2], and can be used to explore programming concepts in a non-programming way [17]. It can be used as a way to add variety to a lecture-based class, as a thought-provoking homework, as a basis of group discussion, or in a number of other ways.

There are several educational theories that can be used to explore the idea of peer review. One way to look at the process is from a cognitive viewpoint. Bloom's taxonomy [2] can be used for this. Peer review supports higher-level learning skills such as synthesis, analysis, and evaluation. Piaget [11] and Vygotsky [4] provide a (social) constructivist approach to peer review. Peer review is an active process that engages the students in learning and gives them some ownership in their instruction. Having access to other peoples' work can provide new perspectives that challenge the students' and help them identify fallacies they currently possess and provide an opportunity for negotiation of meaning. By working together in this way, students will be able to accomplish and learn more than they could alone. There are also many ways to implement it. Topping [15] provides a 17 dimension topology that can be used to describe and explore peer review activities.

In our study, we focused on Topping's *Product/Output*, *Objectives* and *Directionality* dimensions (see Table 1). While we are not actively changing the *Product/Output* dimension, it has important implications on our work. Reviewing designs and programs is not the same process as reviewing a term paper or a musical score. The concepts being reviewed and the methods being used (such as reading or running code) can be very different. This limits the value of the results from other fields. To understand how reviewing programs helps students, we have to have them review programs.

We are, however, actively manipulating the *Objectives* and *Directionality* (which looks at whether a student is a reviewer or both a reviewer and reviewee) in the study by changing who the students review: their peers or their instructor. This affects the motivation for doing the reviews, the amount of social interaction, and, to some extent, the type of learning occurring. In a *peer* review, students may be more motivated to review their classmates because they feel they are providing useful feedback. It also provides an opportunity for community building and social learning. In a *training* review, where the student reviews instructor-provided material, there is reduced social interaction but there is also an opportunity to learn how to review programs before assessing classmates. It also reduces worries about poorly done or incorrect feedback. This may provide a different level and type of motivation to the students. In both cases, the students can still learn programming concepts and professional skills, but with a somewhat different emphasis.

Table 1. Subset of Topping's Peer Review Topology [15]

Dimension	*Description*
Product/Output	The work being reviewed. This includes papers, programs, diagrams, presentations, performances, etc.
Objectives	The reason for performing the review. This could be to provide more feedback, to reduce the teacher's grading load, to allow the students to see other possible solutions, etc. Students and teachers may or may not have similar objectives.
Directionality	The logic of who is reviewed by whom. This could be one-way, where a student gives a review but is not reviewed, reciprocal, where pairs could review each other, or mutual, where everyone gives and receives a review from someone in the group.

2.2 Student Attitudes towards Peer Review

Numerous studies have addressed the students' attitudes. Some focused on the how well they liked peer review software [9, 13]. Other research provided basic attitudinal information [1, 6] through questionnaires that covered if peer review was helpful and if it was motivating. In these cases, students were reasonably accepting of the process and the peer interaction.

A few studies provided more detailed explanations. Xiao and Lucking used a wiki in a teacher preparation course to compare two approaches to peer review based on the students' impressions of the system and their attitudes about the review process [21]. The results showed a difference in satisfaction depending on the review method. This indicates that implementation can affect attitudes. In this case, requiring more work improved their satisfaction.

Sivan [14] explored, in non-technical classes, student acceptance of peer review. Unlike other approaches, this paper compared the student attitudes based on their experience with peer review and whether they were allowed to help write the review criteria. From the results, those with experience in peer review and those who could influence the review criteria had better opinions of the process. This shows that both training and amount of control can influence attitudes.

In a teacher in-service course, Wen and Tsai [20] compared attitudes before and after a series of reviews. While the students' measured opinions were relatively good (i.e. on average, higher than neutral), they decreased significantly over time. This contrasts with Sivan's [14] results on students who have reviewing experience. There may be many interacting influences on the students' attitudes.

In general, the researchers found that students were accepting of the review process but these findings have some limitations. Many of the studies did not compare the results to anything. Others were done in settings that are significantly different from computer science. The literature indicates a relationship between attitudes and the implementation of the reviews, so it is important to gauge the students' acceptance as the reviews are applied in different settings and with different goals.

2.3 Need for Cognition

The need for cognition [3] measures a person's desire to engage in complex thinking. Someone with a high need for cognition would likely have more internal motivation to perform tasks that involve problem-solving or are otherwise intellectually challenging. Since peer review is a complex task that involves analysis and evaluation of materials, it is reasonable to assume that those with a high need for cognition would engage more in the process. They may also have a better attitude towards the activity than those with a low need for cognition.

3. METHOD

All participants (n=134) were students in selected CS2 courses at two neighboring universities. There were 64 students at one university and 70 from the other. Although this was a CS2 course, their class level varied from freshman to senior, but most of the students were in the lower levels. Most were Computer Science majors (75%). There were a total of 13 females in the study.

For each class, the reviews were designed to fit into and support the educational goals of the class. To that end, the reviews were a mixture of code and design reviews. We had each reviewer evaluate two designs or programs for each activity using a rubric to guide them. The same rubric was used for each review.

Before doing any of the reviews, students were asked to complete an initial online attitudinal survey. They then completed four review or controlled assignments that were worked into the routine of the class. These assignments were given as homework and the students were graded on their completion. After the completion of an assignment, students were given brief feedback about the quality of their work. At the end of the semester, they were asked to take a second questionnaire about their attitudes towards the review process. This used a methodology similar to that found in Hay, Wells et al. [7]. The intervention occurred in four assignments spread over roughly ten weeks of classes.

3.1 Questionnaires

The questionnaires covered topics that included the students' need for cognition (short form) [3], their perceptions of working with peers, their feelings about the value of their peers' input, their self-efficacy (perceived skill level compared to the class), their fears about peer review, and demographic information.

The questionnaires were intended gauge the students' attitudes towards review, and their self-efficacy. The need for cognition [3] questions were intended to highlight some of the internal motivation for working on their reviews and was only in the first questionnaire. The other questions were concerned with the students' comfortable level when working with their peers and when reviewing programs, with how useful they though the process and their peers' feedback was, and with how they perceived their own skill level. These questions were not taken from standard measures, but parts of the survey are similar to one by Wen and Tsai [20]. Other surveys in the literature contained similarly worded questions [6, 21]. Student ids were also collected so that their responses could be linked to the other data in the study. This was suitably anonymized for the data analysis.

3.2 Groups

The same three groups were used at both universities: a Peer review group, a Training review group, and a Control group. The Peer group reviewed their classmates. Reviewer assignments were made randomly and anonymously but they were specifically told that they were reviewing classmates. The Training group evaluated materials provided by the instructor and were also made aware of their origin. All of the resources for the Training group were modified to have some strong and some weak points without obviously being a "good" or "bad" project. The control group completed homework assignments that were typical for the course. These included extra design or coding work that were designed to take about as long as the review tasks so that each group had roughly the same time on task. Groups (separated by university) ranged in size from 15 to 26. We used random and non-random assignment to groups as best fit the class. We tested the non-randomly assigned students' understanding of OOP concepts using concept maps (see [17]) and all of the participants' need for cognition scores across groups and schools. We found no significant differences.

3.3 Data Analysis

From the survey, we calculated the students' need for cognition [3] and five values that measured their attitudes and level of self-efficacy (see Table **2**).

We took the differences between the pre- and post-questionnaires values so that we could look at the change in attitudes after having completed multiple reviews. The number of study assignments (reviews, extra design/coding work) that the students completed was recorded as well. This was used as a basic measurement of engagement to determine if students were more likely to turn in the review assignments. We also correlated the students' need for cognition with their attitudes to explore if this internal motivation to engage in thinking was influencing their engagement in peer review, a process that involves considerable thinking.

Table 2. Values for Student Attitudes and Self-efficacy

Value Name	*Description*
Comfort Level Working with Peers	Comfort level in reviewing and being reviewed
Perceived Skill Level	Opinion of their programming skills (self-efficacy)
Perceived Use of Peer Review	Peer review's value for improving code and designs
Value of Peers' Feedback	Value of the students' feedback versus the instructor's
Comfort Level Reviewing Programs	Comfort level in reviewing programs and designs

4. RESULTS

Values were compared between the schools and the groups in the study using a t-test or an ANOVA as appropriate. To look at the effects at each university, we performed the between group tests again after dividing the data by school. A post hoc analysis was completed on all significant results, as needed.

4.1 Attitudes between Groups

To better understand how the different types of review (peer or training) is related to the students' perception of the review process, we compared the attitudinal data from the surveys across the groups. We grouped the responses into five values (see Table 2). Differences between the groups in the post-survey or in the difference between the surveys would be an indication that the type (peer or training) of review has an impact on how students perceive the process.

We first compared the students' responses by school to see if there was an attitudinal discrepancy. We then compared the pre-survey (as a baseline), the post-survey, and the changes between the two surveys by group.

When comparing attitudes between schools, we found two differences, one in the pre-survey and one in the post-survey. We did not find any significant differences in how the attitudes changed. In the pre-survey, we found that the perceived skill level at Univ-2 was significantly higher than at Univ-1 ($p<0.05$). The average at Univ-1 was slightly on the negative side while Univ-2 was somewhat positive. It should be noted that the students at Univ-2 had noticeably better background knowledge and consistently outperformed Univ-1 in a number of ways [17]. There is not a significant difference in the post-survey results. Students at Univ-1 seemed to have gained a relatively large amount of confidence over the semester (see Fig. 1).

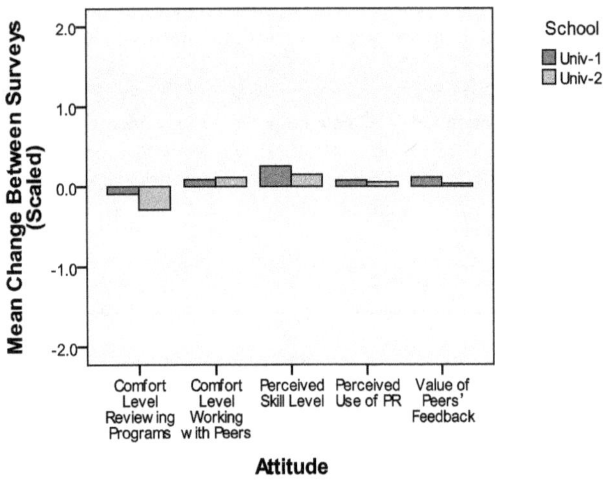

Fig. 1. Changes in Attitude by School (Scaled)

In the post-survey, we found a difference in how comfortable students were in reviewing programs. In this case, students at Univ-1 were more comfortable reviewing programs than students at Univ-2 ($p<0.05$). This is a change from the pre-survey and is due to a decrease in the value for students from Univ-2. Both schools' values decreased but Univ-2's was noticeably (if not significantly) larger (see Fig. 1). This may indicate that the students realized that reviewing programs is difficult and reevaluated their confidence in doing so.

Having examined the differences by school, we explored the differences by groups. We found no significant differences in the combined data set or just with the values from Univ-1. This was true for the pre-survey, post-survey, and the changes between them. For Univ-2, we found a difference in the comfort level for reviewing programs after the review process. The ANOVA was significant ($p<0.05$) but the post hoc tests were not at $\alpha = 0.05$ (Control > Training: $p = 0.077$, Peer > Training: $p = 0.095$).

Over all, the attitudes towards peer review, before and after, were slightly positive. This is similar to the results obtained by Wen and Tsai [20]. Generally, the attitudes improved over time except for the comfort level for review programs which decreased. However, we did not see any real differences between groups. The Peer and Training groups do not seem have a better or worse opinion of the process and were not significantly different from the Control group.

4.2 Study Assignments Completed

As a measure of the students' engagement, we looked at the number of study-related homework assignments (reviews or design/coding exercise) that the students completed. It can be reasonably argued that students more interested and engaged by the assignments will more likely turn them in. We first compared this value between schools. Since each class had its own set of policies and its own learning environment, we wanted to determine if these were affecting the number of items completed. This did not seem to be the case. While students at Univ-2 tended to complete more assignments, it was not significant ($\alpha > 0.05$).

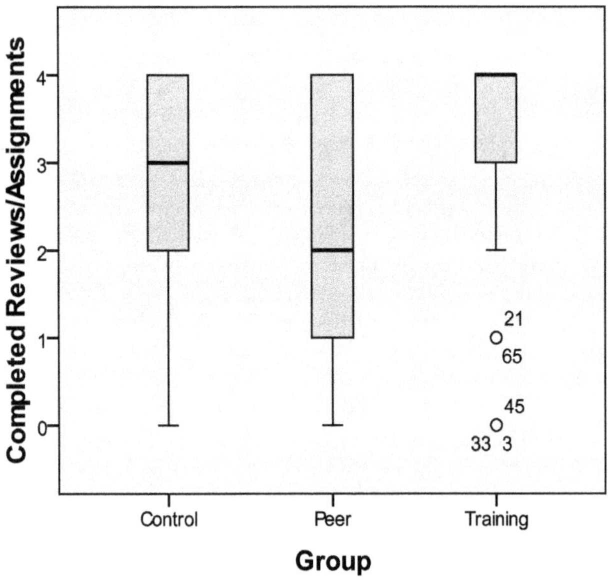

Fig. 2. Completed Study Assignments by Group (All)

Using Oneway ANOVAs, we compared the number of completed assignments by group. As a whole data set and with just Univ-2, the Training group turned in a higher number of review assignments than the Peer group ($p<0.005$) (see Fig. 2). Univ-1 did not have a significant difference ($p = 0.058$), but followed a similar pattern. Looking at the data, the Peer group consistently had the lowest completion rate. We also looked at the differences between the groups on the first study assignment (a review or a design/coding exercise). We did find a difference here, as well. We found that students in the Peer group were less likely to turn it in than either of the other two groups ($p<0.05$) even though the groups seemed to be comparable in terms of initial knowledge and need for cognition scores.

Based on these results, there appears to be a difference in engagement between the groups. It appears that students reviewing other students have less of a tendency to complete their work. It may be that students in the Peer group do not feel the same kind of pressure to turn in an assignment because it is not directed to the instructor. It could be that they feel that this is not their responsibility and that the instructor will provide feedback anyway. This highlights the need for external motivation if peer reviews are used. Training reviews seem to be sufficiently motivating on their own.

4.3 Attitudes and the Need for Cognition

Since peer review can involve complex thinking, we wanted to test if the students' need for cognition (a measure of the desire to engage in complex thinking) was related to their attitudes towards peer review. We correlated this value with the attitudinal values calculated from the survey to gain more information about how students perceive the process and if the internal motivation associated with the need for cognition is an influence.

We found a few significant weak to moderate correlations between the need for cognition and the comfort level for reviewing programs and their perceived skill level. These relationships differed somewhat between schools. These results are not wholly unexpected as students that enjoy thinking will likely be more comfortable in a thinking task and more confident in their thinking abilities. What we did not find was evidence that the need for cognition was related to the students' feelings about working with peers, about the value of their feedback, or if peer review was of any real use. We also did not find a link between the need for cognition and the number of reviews completed. It seems that this measure of internal motivation is not associated with their attitudes towards the social aspects of the review or with doing the reviews. It may be that external motivators would be more effective to get students to engage in the process.

5. CONCLUSIONS

When examining the group's effect on the students' attitudes towards peer review, we found that there were very few differences between groups in the students' stated attitudes. Aside from one difference found in Univ-2, the pre- and post-surveys showed no real differences between groups. The students' opinions were also fairly neutral. Opinions of the value of the reviews, of working with their peers, and of their received feedback did not seem to have much influence on whether they completed the reviews or how much effort they put into them. While there was some positive change over time, it was not much. There were also no real differences between those that reviewed and those that did not. They did not seem particularly motivated to engage in the assignments.

However, when looking at the number of study assignments completed by the students in each group, we see a definite trend for the peer group to do less than the other two. While the differences were not always significant, the discrepancies are apparent. There seems to be, at this level, a *lack of motivation to review peers*. They may think that the instructor will provide the students with reviews, so their reviews are not really needed. This might be an aspect of *social loafing*.

From our results, it seems that external motivation is needed for the review process. Students at this class level do not seem to be internally motivated to engage in the process. This conclusion was supported when we looked at the relationships of the attitudes towards peer review and the students' need for cognition. We found a relationship with their self-efficacy in the forms of their perceived skill level and in their comfort level for reviewing programs but with nothing else. The need for cognition, as a measure of internal motivation to think, did not appear to be strongly related to the students' desire to complete the reviews or otherwise engage in them.

There are signs, however, that the students' attitudes changed to better match their ability level. This was seen when looking at their comfort level for reviewing programs compared to the measures of their understanding of the material [17] and in the changes of how willing students were to participate in reviews. One positive aspect of the reviews is that it may have shown students that they did not understand everything they thought they did.

Overall, it seems that, for the situations we looked at, that the review process was not very engaging on its own as a thinking task or as a way to interact and help out other students. We found no evidence that the type of group improved student attitudes even compared with those who did not review. Indeed, it seems that reviewing peers could decrease their incentive to engage. This should be considered when implementing a review assignment.

These results provide a better understanding of how the CS2 student may react to the review process. It highlights the need for external motivation and for monitoring of the process. If students are not or only half-heartedly completing the reviews, then they are missing out on a valuable learning experience. Social incentives, class credit, or other types of rewards may be needed. More research is required to explore how to best motivate the students to engage in the activities so that they can benefit from it.

6. REFERENCES

[1] Anewalt, K. Using peer review as a vehicle for communication skill development and active learning. *J. Comput. Small Coll.*, 21, 2 (2005), 148-155.

[2] Bloom, B. S. *Taxonomy of educational objectives*. Allyn and Bacon, Boston, MA, 1984.

[3] Cacioppo, J. T. and Petty, R. E. The need for cognition: Relationship to attitudinal processes. *Journal of Personality and Social Psychology*, 42 (1982), 116-131.

[4] Doolittle, P. E. Vygotsky's Zone of Proximal Development as a Theoretical Foundation for Cooperative Learning. *Journal on Excellence in College Teaching*, 8, 1 (1997), 83-103.

[5] Falchikov, N. and Goldfinch, J. Student Peer Assessment in Higher Education: A Meta-Analysis Comparing Peer and Teacher Marks. *Review of Educational Research*, 70, 3 (2000), 287-322.

[6] Gatfield, T. Examining Student Satisfaction with Group Projects and Peer Assessment. *Assessment & Evaluation in Higher Education*, 24, 4 (1999), 365 - 377.

[7] Hay, D., Wells, H. and Kinchin, I. Quantitative and qualitative measures of student learning at university level. *Higher Education*, 56, 2 (2008), 221-239.

[8] Hundhausen, C., Agrawal, A., Fairbrother, D. and Trevisan, M. Integrating pedagogical code reviews into a CS 1 course: an empirical study. In *Proceedings of the Proceedings of the 40th*

ACM technical symposium on Computer science education (Chattanooga, TN, USA, 2009). ACM Press.

[9] Liu, E. Z.-F. and Yuan, S.-M. A study of students' attitudes toward and desired system requirements of networked peer assessment system. *International Journal of Instructional Media*, 30, 4 (2003).

[10] Papalaskari, M.-A. Peer evaluation in an algorithms course. In *Proceedings of the Proceedings of the 8th annual conference on Innovation and technology in computer science education* (Thessaloniki, Greece, 2003). ACM Press.

[11] Piaget, J. *The Psychology of Intelligence.* Harcourt and Brace, New York, 1950.

[12] Schulte, C. and Magenheim, J. Novices' expectations and prior knowledge of software development: results of a study with high school students. In *Proceedings of the Proceedings of the first international workshop on Computing education research* (Seattle, WA, USA, 2005). ACM.

[13] Silva, E. and Moriera, D. WebCoM: a tool to use peer review to improve student interaction. *J. Educ. Resour. Comput.*, 3, 1 (2003), 1-14.

[14] Sivan, A. The Implementation of Peer Assessment: an action research approach. *Assessment in Education: Principles, Policy & Practice*, 7, 2 (2000), 193-213.

[15] Topping, K. Peer Assessment Between Students in Colleges and Universities. *Review of Educational Research*, 68, 3 (1998), 249-276.

[16] Trytten, D. A. A design for team peer code review. In *Proceedings of the Proceedings of the 36th SIGCSE technical symposium on Computer science education* (St. Louis, Missouri, USA, 2005). ACM Press.

[17] Turner, S. A., Pérez-Quiñones, M. A., Edwards, S. and Chase, J. Peer Review in CS2: Conceptual Learning. In *Proceedings of the 41st SIGCSE Technical Symposium on Computer Science Education* (Milwaukee, Wisconsin, March 10-13, 2010). ACM Press.

[18] Turner, S. A., Quintana-Castillo, R., Pérez-Quiñones, M. A. and Edwards, S. Misunderstandings about Object-Oriented Design: Experiences Using Code Reviews. In *Proceedings of the 39th SIGCSE Technical Symposium on Computer Science Education* (Portland, Oregon, USA, 2008). ACM Press.

[19] van Hattum-Janssen, N. and Lourenco, J. M. Peer and Self-Assessment for First-Year Students as a Tool to Improve Learning. *Journal of Professional Issues in Engineering Education & Practice*, 134, 4 (2008), 346-352.

[20] Wen, M. L. and Tsai, C.-C. University Students' Perceptions of and Attitudes Toward (Online) Peer Assessment. *Higher Education*, 51, 1 (2006), 27-44.

[21] Xiao, Y. and Lucking, R. The impact of two types of peer assessment on students' performance and satisfaction within a Wiki environment. *Internet & Higher Education*, 11, 3/4 (2008), 186-193.

Applying Data Structures in Exams

Briana B. Morrison
So. Polytechnic State University
Marietta, GA USA
1-678-915-4295
bmorriso@spsu.edu

Mike Clancy
Univ. of California, Berkeley
Berkeley, CA USA
clancy@cs.berkeley.edu

Robert McCartney
University of Connecticut
Storrs, CT USA
robert@engr.uconn.edu

Brad Richards
University of Puget Sound
Tacoma, WA USA
brichards@pugetsound.edu

Kate Sanders
Rhode Island College
Providence, RI USA
ksanders@ric.edu

ABSTRACT
It is important for students to be able to select and apply the appropriate data structure for the problem to be solved. Testing this knowledge on exams can be difficult, however. We examined 59 data structures final exams and found only 36 that contained questions involving the application of data structures. To promote assessment of this knowledge in the data structures course, we present a framework for classifying *apply* exam questions, with illustrations from the exams collected. We then show how a number of questions can be developed by varying a single rich *apply* question along the dimensions of this framework.

Categories and Subject Descriptors
K.3.2 [**Computers and Education**]: Computers and Information Science Education –*Computer Science Education*

General Terms
Algorithms, Measurement

Keywords
CS2, data structures, exams, apply, assessment

1. INTRODUCTION
Courses in data structures have been offered in computer science programs for a long time; it was one of the core courses proposed in the first ACM curriculum guidelines, Curriculum 68 [1], and has existed in one form or another in every curriculum recommendation since. The topics suggested in 1968 include many that are still familiar in data structures courses, including lists, stacks, strings, trees, and graphs.

The exact expectations for students in data structures courses vary, but generally include understanding what operations the standard data structures provide, alternative ways to implement these structures, their performance characteristics, and how they might be applied in solving problems. In this paper, we focus on questions that require students to apply their data structures knowledge to solve problems, "*apply questions*" for short. These questions were relatively rare in our dataset. In the hopes of facilitating development of *apply* questions, we present a framework for classifying them with examples from our data, and suggestions for generating new questions by varying a single question along the dimensions of our framework.

This paper is structured as follows. In Section 2 we provide background, discussing a similar analysis of data structures questions, work that proposes greater emphasis on application in data structures courses, and work relating assessment to course content. In Section 3 we discuss an approach for categorizing exam questions along a number of dimensions of variation. In Section 4 we use these dimensions to categorize a fairly substantial (and challenging) problem taken from a data structures exam, and illustrate how different exam questions can be produced by varying a problem along these dimensions. These variations can be used to change the difficulty of a problem and to shift the problem's emphasis. We conclude in Section 5 by discussing how our findings can be used by classroom instructors.

2. BACKGROUND
Simon et al. [9] analyzed the stack and hashtable questions in a large dataset of data structures exams drawn from 14 schools over a 36-year period. These exams included true-false, multiple-choice, short-answer, and essay questions, as well as questions where students are asked to draw diagrams or write code. Focusing on the stack and hashing questions (about 19% of the questions by points), the researchers developed a classification scheme that sorted the questions based on their position relative to the interface, that is, whether they required knowledge of the implementation, only of the operations provided, or of the operations and how to apply them to solve a problem. They found relatively few application questions and no clear increase in the number of such questions over time.

The scarcity of *apply* questions even in the recent exams was surprising, given the literature. Before the advent of frameworks such as the Standard Template Library in C++ and the Java Collections Framework, CS2 courses necessarily emphasized the implementation of data structures over their application. But by 2003, Tenenberg [10] argued that students would be better served by learning how to use frameworks or libraries. The following year, Lister et al. [8] acknowledged the growing "implement" versus "apply" debate, urging instructors to first consider why

SIGCSE'11, March 9–12, 2011, Dallas, Texas, USA.

they teach the data structures course. The 2007 LACS model curriculum [4] recommends that liberal arts students should learn to both *apply* and *implement* data structures. By the time Yarosh and Guzdial described their media-computing approach to CS2 [11], the idea of emphasizing data structures' application over implementation was treated as mainstream – they had moved on to asserting that one needs a compelling context in which to *apply* data structures. Similarly in 2009, when arguing that it was time for a third "generation" of CS2 (one in which the emphasis is on applying and extending frameworks), Ernst et al. [6] took it for granted that the "second generation of this course focused on using these basic data structures to solve meaningful problems …"

Biggs' theory of constructive alignment [2] advocates an educational approach in which student assessment activities connect with the intended outcomes of the course. If educators are practicing constructive alignment, final exam questions should therefore reveal something about an educator's objectives for the course. Even if faculty are not employing constructive alignment, the questions shed light upon what students are implicitly being told is important. Boud [3] observed that "Assessment methods and requirements probably have a greater influence on how and what students learn than any other single factor", and Gibbs et al. [7] found similar results when surveying studies of student learning: "Whether or not what it is that assessment is trying to assess is clearly specified in documentation, students work out for themselves what counts – or at least what they think counts, and orient their effort accordingly. They are strategic in their use of time and 'selectively negligent' in avoiding content that they believe is not likely to be assessed."

3. PROPOSED FRAMEWORK

From the original collection of 88 exams, for this work we examined a subset of 59 final exams from 10 different institutions. We selected exams that had been identified as potentially having questions that fell into one of the two "*apply*" categories used in [9], either *Apply-given* or *Apply-select*. An *Apply-given* question requires the student to know or explain how a given data structure could be used to perform some task, where the task is beyond simply calling a given sequence of data-structure routines. An *Apply-select* question requires the student to choose an appropriate data structure for a specific task as well as knowing or explaining how to apply it. *Apply* questions may ask students to select the most appropriate data structure based on algorithm efficiency, so long as students are not required to have specific implementation details and encapsulation is not broken.

Each researcher reviewed a subset of the 59 exams and identified all "*apply*" questions. The "*apply*" questions were collated and features of their design space began to emerge. Each question was classified within each of the dimensions (given or select, single or multiple data structure, recognizing or generating code, and length and type of question). Here we propose a framework for defining these possible dimensions of *apply* questions using examples from our dataset to illustrate.

3.1 Given / Select Dimension

Although *Apply-given* and *Apply-select* are presented above as a binary choice, they are two ends of a spectrum. Below, we give some examples to illustrate the range, ordered from the *Apply-given* end of the spectrum to *Apply-select.* Variations that can affect a problem's difficulty are described as well.

One kind of ***Apply-given*** problem asks the student to use a known ADT to write another method for the same ADT. For example:

> The diameter of a tree is the maximal number of vertices on a path from one vertex in the tree to another. (The diameter of an empty tree is 0.) [some examples given][1] Note in particular that the relevant path does not necessarily include the root of the tree.
>
> Write a BinaryTree method named diameter that returns the diameter of the tree. Assume that each tree node contains its height in a field named myHeight.

A student might be required to use a single known data structure to solve a problem *unrelated* to that ADT:

> Show how to implement the stack ADTs [sic] using only a priority queue and an additional integer variable.

Another example requires students to work on *two* known structures:

> Consider a composite data structure to represent an inventory of items, declared as follows. It contains as private data members [a list of name-cost pairs, sorted by cost, and a hash table of these pairs, indexed by name]
>
> Items are identified uniquely by name; *i.e.* there shouldn't be two items with the same name. Elements of the sortedByCost list appear in decreasing order by cost, except that if there are more than one item with the same cost, those items appear in the list alphabetically by name. The corresponding items should also all be represented in the hash table, which is accessed by hashing a name, then searching the corresponding chain for a pointer to the item with that name.
>
> [Gives rationale for consistency checking, then the student is asked to implement two consistency checks for these data, defined as:]
>
> Duplicate check: no two items represented in sortedByCost should have the same name; no two items represented in hashTable should have the same name.
>
> Correspondence between components: Every item represented in sortedByCost should also be represented in hashTable, and vice-versa.

Near the middle of the spectrum are *Apply-given* problems where students are provided a set of possible data structures from which to choose, as in:

> Which of the following would be best suited as part of the implementation of the back button on a Web browser?
>
> a. a Stack b. a Queue c. a Priority Queue d. a List e. a Tree f. a Dictionary

This is still considered an *Apply-given* question as the alternatives are chosen from an explicit set.

[1] Due to length restrictions, we use square brackets here to replace parts of the exam questions with comments.

Apply-select questions require students to choose at least one ADT or data structure, as in the following set of questions:

> Give the **abstract data type** and **data structure (implementation)**, if it makes a difference, that would be used to implement each of the following:
>
> 1. Finding a BFS spanning tree
> 2. Finding a DFS spanning tree
> 3. Heap
> 4. Simulation of airplanes waiting to land
> 5. Algebraic expressions without parenthesis

Context can make problems requiring the selection of a single data type more challenging. For example:

> Your company, Nocturnal Avionics, is designing a new web browser. Your task is to reimplement its "Back" and "Forward" capabilities. These should work as follows: [problem includes description of Back and Forward behavior, plus available methods from old browser that is to be extended]
>
> Specifically, do the following parts:
>
> (a) Explain your design in general: What data do you store, what sort of structure(s) will you use, and when will you store and retrieve data? When do you enable and/or disable the buttons? How do you detect when this should be done?
>
> (b) Complete the class definition. Remember to add 1) any necessary instance variables, 2) any initialization code in the constructor, and 3) methods for back(), forward(), and getAndDisplayPage().

Moving along the spectrum, some problems require multiple data structures, with some unknown and perhaps some given, for example:

> Given below and on the following pages is the framework for a program to escape from a maze. (A sample maze is shown on the right.) In pseudocode sufficiently detailed that a fellow student could convert it immediately to Java, complete the search method.
>
> Make clear what data structures you're using for auxiliary storage. (A hash table will be useful.) Don't use recursion. Assume that the maze is large enough to make a solution that involves linear searches impractical.

In other problems, little or no guidance is provided as to what data structures are needed: see, for example, the problem in Section 4.

Summarizing, the *Apply-given – Apply-select* continuum ranges from tasks performed on known structures to choosing a data type from a given set to problems requiring multiple unspecified data structures.

A similar continuum might be used to describe some of the more algorithmic problems, from more to less guidance. At one end, problems might ask for modification of some code (for example, one problem asked students to modify given topological sort code to find the longest path in a directed acyclic graph) or an algorithm (another problem asked students to modify the Prim-Jarnik algorithm for minimum spanning tree to be efficient when all edge weights are 1 or 2). At the other end, the student might be given little guidance beyond a definition, as in the following:

> A triangle in a simple undirected graph $G=(V,E)$ is a set of 3 distinct vertices u,v,w such that (u,v), (v,w), and (u,w) are all edges in E. Describe an efficient algorithm for testing whether a given graph G with n vertices and m edges has a triangle. To receive full credit, the algorithm must run in $O(n+m)$ time.[2]

3.2 Single / Multiple Dimension

Most of the *apply* questions concentrated on a single data structure, assessing student understanding of that specific structure. Examples of this type include using a stack to balance parentheses, using a queue to simulate a bank teller line, or using a binary search tree to represent a spell-checker. Questions may ask the student to write the solution algorithm, select the correct algorithm, or select the correct (single) data structure for the solution.

The other end of this spectrum is represented by questions that involve multiple data structures for the application solution. These questions generally follow a pattern of describing the application domain (bookstore, medical database, stock transactions) followed by a description of possible implementation solutions involving one or more data structures (e.g., a linked list for storing book information, an array for storing room information and a binary search tree for patient information). Students are asked to select the best solution for specific operations (adding books, printing by ISBN number, etc.) or for the overall solution. Most of these questions test the student's knowledge of the efficiency of operations of specific or combinations of data structures.

Examples of problems involving multiple data structures where efficiency was not the primary question were similar to those examples given in Section 3.2. In these questions, it is the use of the data structure that is being assessed. There was also a single question that asked students to increase the efficiency of a graph algorithm by writing the pseudocode solution, including identifying any and all data structures used in the solution, a combination of both use and efficiency.

3.3 Recognizing / Generating Dimension

This dimension applies specifically to questions that involve reading or writing code (including pseudocode). It is common for the coursework component of CS2 to contain programming assignments through which students demonstrate their ability to apply data structures. It should therefore not be surprising that questions involving code also appeared on the exams in our sample. Code questions ranged in format from problems requiring students to write substantial amounts of code, to multiple-choice questions in which students were to select a code sequence with the desired effect. We refer to the former as *generate* problems, and the latter as *recognize* problems, since students must at least recognize which code sequence correctly applies a data structure.

The most involved of the *generate* questions required that students complete non-trivial programming tasks such as extending a web browser class and adding functionality to the

[2] The authors believe this should be $O(n*m)$ time.

forward and back buttons, for example, or implementing the backtracking search mechanism in a program that packed collections of virtual rectangular blocks as compactly as possible. Students were not given any guidance as to which data structures might be useful.

A variety of approaches for reducing the complexity of code-writing questions were observed. Some problems allowed students to write answers in pseudocode, for example. Other questions explicitly specified which data structures should be used. (*E.g.* "Write code to sort an array of integers using a priority queue." or "Determine if parentheses are balanced using a stack.") We also saw problems where students were asked to *modify* existing code instead of creating it from scratch. For example, the problem asking students to modify a topological sort routine so that it instead returned the longest path in a DAG.

While most problems involved standard data structures, some tested students' abilities to apply structures that they had presumably never seen. (One such problem introduced a data structure for representing 2D bitmaps and asked students to solve problems involving pixel placements.) Some problems asked students to apply data structures to *themselves* — extending a Set class to include methods for union and intersection, but implementing them in terms of existing Set operations, for example.

At the other end of the spectrum, *code recognition* problems assess whether students understand the behavior of code provided by the instructor. Two different variations on this theme were observed in the sample exams: Multiple-choice problems in which students selected the code sequence with the correct behavior, and problems where the instructor asked questions about code presented to the students. An example of the former presented four different Scheme expressions and asked students to circle the answers that performed a specified database query correctly. An example of the latter problem style showed a list-processing procedure and asked about its behavior when adding new items to a list.

In the set of sample exams we inspected, *code generation* problems appeared much more frequently than *code recognition* problems. One might speculate that *recognize* problems, while being simple to grade, are more challenging to construct, or perhaps instructors are simply less familiar or less comfortable with this problem style. Parsons problems, which present students with all of the lines of code required to solve a problem but require students to *sequence* those lines properly, might be a useful addition to the repertoire as well. [5]

3.4 Length Dimension

Many *apply* questions are quite long. Their length may be part of the reason we found relatively few of them. Longer questions require greater creative effort from instructors and in addition, can place a higher cognitive load on students.

There is a strikingly wide variation in the length of the *apply* questions we found, however, from several lines to several pages. We discuss one of the longer questions in detail in Section 4. In this section, we include several illustrations of shorter questions.

Here's a short multiple-choice question:

> Which of the following would be best suited for use as part of a program modeling the arrival of patients to an emergency room in a hospital?
>
> a. a Stack b. a Queue c. a Priority Queue d. a List
>
> e. a Tree f. a Dictionary

A group of brief short-answer questions was given above in Section 3.1. All the student would need to read to answer one of these, for example, is the following:

> Give the **abstract data type** and **data structure (implementation)** if it makes a difference, that would be used to implement each of the following: ...
>
> 4. Simulation of airplanes waiting to land

One very short code question involved using the tree ADT to write an additional operation:

> Write a recursive definition to determine if a tree is a two-tree.

The following short essay question involved the game of Go:

> Go is a two-player game, played on a square board consisting of a number of crossing lines (usually 9x9, 13x13, or, for official tournaments, 19x19). Each move in the game involves placing a small stone on the intersections of two of the lines. If a group of stones becomes surrounded by stones of the opposite colour, they are removed. Stones are not otherwise moved. The player with the most stones on the board at the end is the winner.
>
> For example, the board below shows the state of play after each player has moved twice. [image omitted]
>
> Outline how you might represent the state of a Go board in Java.

3.5 Type-of-Question Dimension

The *apply* questions we found were not just open ended code questions. We found multiple-choice, short-answer, and essay questions that also involved applying data structures. Additional questions can be obtained by varying a question's format. For example, compare the web-browser multiple choice question and the Nocturnal Avionics example from Section 3.1.

Another way to classify *apply* questions is according to their application domain. One of the reasons for the length of some *apply* questions is that they involve a long description of their domain. We saw two ways in which the difficulty of writing (and reading) long questions might be avoided. One solution for the instructor is to "parameterize" the domain. For example, there were questions involving collections of student, medical, bookstore, airline, and restaurant information. An instructor who writes a good question about organizing or searching through one of these collections could generate many additional questions by simply varying the domain.

A second solution is to use the methods of one data structure or ADT to build another method for the same ADT or a new ADT. A compact example of this type of question is the implementation of a stack using a priority queue example found in Section 3.1.

These questions have the advantage that the domain (data structures) is covered in the class itself, so a lengthy explanation is generally not required. They are both simpler for the instructor to write and shorter for students to read. On the other hand, if used exclusively, they might give the impression that data structures are not useful outside the course itself.

4. EXAMPLE AND VARIATIONS

We close with a relatively rich exam problem (shown in Table 4.1), which yields several interesting variations.

The framework just described classifies this problem as follows:

- *Apply-select*: Potential data structures for a solution include a hash table, a binary search tree, and a sorted array.
- Multiple data structures: The USPS list and the mailing.
- Generating: Student is asked to write code.
- Length: The problem is 263 words long.
- Type of question: A solution involves pseudocoding the algorithm (code) and analyzing it (essay).

Problem

The U.S. Postal Service gives price discounts to businesses that pre-sort their outgoing mail according to the route taken by a mail carrier. To assist a business in the sorting process, they provide a list of addresses visited by the mail carrier arranged in the order that he or she would visit them. Each address is a character string, for instance, "[82 Main St.]" or "[395 Maple]".

Suppose you are a programmer in a business that wishes to save money on its mailings. You are in charge of a data base, each record of which contains an address that matches one of the addresses in the Postal Service's list. Each mailing is sent to a subset of the addresses in the data base. You are to design a pseudocode algorithm that, given a list of the addresses for a mailing, sorts them according to their ordering in the Postal Service list.

The algorithm you are to design has two steps:

1. Preprocess the Postal Service list in such a way as to make step 2 as efficient as possible.
2. Rearrange the elements of the mailing as just described.

Your design should include an estimate of the algorithm's running time in terms of `m`, the number of addresses in the mailing, and `p`, the number of addresses in the Postal Service list. Step 2 should run as quickly as possible in the big-Oh sense. Step 1 need not be efficient at all. There are no memory constraints on the algorithm. Assume that the Postal Service list is much larger than the mailing.

Table 4.1: A sample of a rich, medium-length question.

One obvious modification to move the problem somewhat from "*select*" closer to "*given*" is to add the statement "With a suitable preprocessing step, the processing step can be done in `O(m log m)`, where `m` is the size of the mailing."

In the abstract, this problem involves two sequences, one sorted and the other not. Variations arise from strengthening or weakening the order of the sequences. For example, if both are unsorted:

> You are given two sequences `S1` and `S2` of keys (not in any particular order) with the length of `S1` approximately twice the length of `S2`. Provide a pseudocode algorithm that determines if every element of `S2` is also in `S1`. Your algorithm should run as quickly as possible in the big-Oh sense.

A correct solution to this problem involves the same preprocessing as the Postal Service problem, but a simpler processing step. This moves the problem from requiring multiple data structures to requiring just one. It is also shorter (53 words).

To move the problem from "*generate*" to "*recognize*," the instructor could include all or part of a solution, plus incorrect variations on the solution, and ask the student to choose the correct version.

Another variation involves a change in domain. For example, we might consider a sequence of pairs, each pair representing information on a freeway exit sign:

> Exits from United States interstate highways each have a name and an exit number. The name is typically a town or city name. The number is often the distance in miles from a base point, either the start of the freeway or a state boundary. (Examples may be found by Googling "interstate highway sign".)
>
> Design a data structure for storing a sequence of exits, each exit consisting of a String name and an int distance. The constructor for the data structure need not run efficiently; however, your design should make the following operation as fast as possible ...

Candidates for the operation to optimize include the following, ordered roughly from easiest to hardest:

- Given the name of an exit, return the corresponding distance from the base point.
- Given an exit number, return the name of the exit.
- Given a distance from the base point, find the nearest exit.

This problem could be categorized as an *Apply-select*, single data structure, *generation* of code. It could also be stated as a multiple-choice problem, where students are given the operations and asked to match them with the data structure used (hash table or binary search tree) or the corresponding running time.

5. DISCUSSION

When asked the purpose of a Data Structures course, most instructors would include in their answer "Teaching students about different data structures with the goal of having students select the most appropriate data structure for the application problem." Many instructors include implementation of specific data structures, as is evidenced by the number of implementation questions found in the original analysis [9]. Fewer assess the students' ability to *apply* these same data structures within application problems. If our goal is to ascertain whether our students can select and apply appropriate data structures, then our test questions should reflect that goal.

This paper offers guidance and encouragement to instructors wishing to assess the data structure-application component of their courses. It demonstrates, by summarizing the different dimensions represented by a collection of CS2 exams, that there are numerous approaches for testing students' ability to *apply* data structures: We can ask them to apply data structures by giving them a specific data structure for the solution, or by asking them to select the most appropriate data structure for a problem domain. We can ask students to *apply* a single data structure, or use multiple data structures in the solution to test deeper understanding. We can ask them to *recognize* correct solutions to the application problem, or to *generate* the solution from their knowledge.

Problems involving applying data structures to another domain are typically lengthy, requiring more time for the student to both read and understand the question. However, once the application domain information has been presented, instructors have the option of asking several questions covering that single application problem. Different data structures can be proposed for the solution, different operations can be emphasized, students can be asked to not only select the answer, but to defend their response. *Apply* questions can be structured into any type of question, from multiple choice, to short answer, to generating code solutions.

We would encourage CS2 instructors to develop one or more "deep" application questions which can then be altered in various ways to assess different knowledge and allow re-use of the question in future terms. Re-use can also occur by shifting domains, as illustrated in Section 4.

"Good" *apply* questions in the data structures course presuppose a "good" set of programming projects. A good programming project, from the standpoint of *apply* questions, would be those that have multiple solutions, are modular, and represent an instance of a standard pattern (e.g. backtracking search, tree processing, database implementation). Questions then arise naturally from tweaking the problem specifications or addressing a related problem. Basing the exam question on work the students have already seen uses the context to reduce the length of the exam problem statement.

6. ACKNOWLEDGMENTS

The authors would like to thank all the instructors who shared their final exams and the NSF for supporting the DCER project. This material is based upon work supported in part by the National Science Foundation under grant number CNS 0734761. Any opinions, findings, and conclusions or recommendations expressed in this material are those of the authors and do not necessarily represent the views of the National Science Foundation.

7. REFERENCES

[1] Atchison, W. F., Schweppe, E. J., Viavant, W., Young, D. M., Conte, S. D., Hamblen, J. W., Hull, T. E., et al. (1968). Curriculum 68: Recommendations for academic programs in computer science: a report of the ACM curriculum committee on computer science. *Communications of the ACM, 11*(3), 151-197.

[2] Biggs, J. (1999). What the Student Does: teaching for enhanced learning. *Higher Education Research & Development*, 18(1), 57.

[3] Boud, D. J. (1989). The role of self-assessment in student grading. *Assessment & Evaluation in Higher Education*, 14(1), 20-30.

[4] Consortium, L. A. C. S. (2007). A 2007 model curriculum for a liberal arts degree in computer science. *J. Educ. Resour. Comput.*, 7(2), 2.

[5] Denny, P., Luxton-Reilly, A., & Simon, B. (2008). Evaluating a new exam question: Parsons problems. In *Proceeding of the 4th international Workshop on Computing Education Research* (pp. 113-124). Sydney, Australia: ACM.

[6] Ernst, D. J., Stevenson, D. E., & Wagner, P. J. (2009). Hybrid and custom data structures: evolution of the data structures course. In *Proceedings of the 14th annual ACM SIGCSE conference on Innovation and technology in computer science education* (pp. 213-217). Paris, France: ACM.

[7] Gibbs, G., & Simpson, C. (2004). Conditions under which assessment supports students' learning. *Learning and Teaching in Higher Education*, 1(1), 3-29.

[8] Lister, R., Box, I., Morrison, B., Tenenberg, J., & Westbrook, D. S. (2004). The dimensions of variation in the teaching of data structures. In *Proceedings of the 9th annual SIGCSE conference on Innovation and technology in computer science education* (pp. 92-96). Leeds, United Kingdom: ACM.

[9] Simon, B., Clancy, M., McCartney, R., Morrison, B., Richards, B., & Sanders, K. (2010). Making sense of data structures exams. In *Proceedings of the 6th international workshop on Computing education research* (pp. 97-106). Aarhus, Denmark: ACM.

[10] Tenenberg, J. (2003). A framework approach to teaching data structures. In *Proceedings of the 34th SIGCSE technical symposium on Computer science education* (pp. 210-214). Reno, Nevada, USA: ACM.

[11] Yarosh, S., & Guzdial, M. (2008). Narrating data structures: The role of context in CS2. *J. Educ. Resour. Comput.*, 7(4), 1-20.

IASSim: A Programmable Emulator for the Princeton IAS/Von Neumann Machine

Barry Fagin
Dept. of Computer Science, US Air Force Academy
2354 Fairchild Drive
USAFA, CO 80840
1-719-333-7377
barry.fagin@usafa.edu

Dale Skrien
Dept. of Computer Science, Colby College
5851 Mayflower Hill
Waterville, ME 04901-8858
1-207-859-5851
djskrien@colby.edu

ABSTRACT

In this paper, we describe a programmable emulator for the Princeton IAS/Von Neumann machine. The emulator is historically accurate, preserving the quirks and eccentricities of the machine. It is also user-friendly and robust, suitable for undergraduate architecture and programming classes as a teaching tool. Users can write non-trivial programs in IAS assembly code or machine code. We present some examples here, and discuss assignments from its first use in two undergraduate classes. IASSim is a Java application publicly available at no cost.

Categories and Subject Descriptors

C.0 [**Computer Systems Organization**]: General – *instruction set design, modeling of computer architecture.*

General Terms

Measurement, Design, Standardization, Languages, Verification.

Keywords

Emulation, IAS Machine, Von Neumann Architecture, Courseware, Computer Architecture.

1. INTRODUCTION

In 2009, the first author began development of a "Great Ideas in Computer Science" course, designed for a special academic program at the US Air Force Academy. Courses in this program were intended to engage students directly with the fundamental ideas and fundamental figures in the discipline under study. The "Great Ideas" chosen by the author, presented in historical order, were 1) Computation as calculation, 2) Computation and its limits as articulated by Turing, 3) Computation as a physically realizable idea, 4) Programming languages and software, 5) Computational complexity, 6) Cryptography, and 7) The future of computing. Reading materials chosen included Babbage's work on the Difference Engine [3], Turing's original paper on computation [12], Rivest, Shamir and Adelman's paper on public key cryptosystems [8] and so forth. All students read and discuss the original papers, and do "hands-on" assignments intended to acquaint them with the associated ideas as directly as possible.

SIGCSE'11, March 9–12, 2011, Dallas, Texas, USA.

For block (3), the obvious choice for reading material was Burks, Goldstine and Von Neumann's technical report [4]. So for the corresponding assignment a close encounter with the Princeton Institute for Advanced Study (IAS) computer seemed appropriate. Preliminary inquiries, however, indicated no emulators or comparable tools existed. Fortunately, the second author had developed an extendible microprogrammed simulator "CPU Sim" [10] that could implement a wide variety of architectures and instruction sets. This led to collaborative development of IASSim, a "frozen" offshoot of CPU Sim that faithfully models assembly language programming on the original IAS machine. This tool is described here.

2. PREVIOUS WORK

A large variety of computer simulators have been developed for educational purposes [6,7,11,14]. Such simulators have value in environments where resources are limited and the actual computers are not available for study. They are also valuable in introductory courses, in which the study and programming of real architectures would be too complex and time consuming.

Most simulators imitate a specific architecture. Some simulate very simple ones [9] that give beginning students a feel for how CPUs work. Others simulate real modern architectures, such as the MIPS machine [13]. Many such simulators are discussed in two issues of JERIC [1,2]. Simulators allow you to study the architecture of and write programs for computers that no longer physically exist, except possibly in museums. For example, there are simulators for the PDP-8 [2] and the EDSAC [5]. Unfortunately, no simple simulator could be found by the authors for the IAS architecture. This led to the creation of IASSim.

3. THE IAS MACHINE

The IAS machine is named after the Princeton Institute for Advanced Study, where it was developed by a team headed by the mathematician John Von Neumann. Von Neumann had met Alan Turing during the latter's short stay at Princeton, and was very interested in bringing Turing's ideas to life by building an actual computer. While there will always be controversy regarding who built the "first" computer, the technical report [4] describing the IAS machine is generally regarded as the first and most authoritative publication of the general ideas used in computers today. We therefore chose it and the machine it describes as the "Great Idea" that would best illustrate humanity's attempts to

Table 1: The IAS Instruction Set

inst name	opcode	description
S(x)->Ac+	1	copy the number in Selectron location x into AC
S(x)->Ac-	2	same as #1 but copy the negative of the number
S(x)->AcM	3	same as #1 but copy the absolute value
S(x)->Ac-M	4	same as #1 but subtract the absolute value
S(x)->Ah+	5	add the number in Selectron location x into AC
S(x)->Ah-	6	subtract the number in Selectron location x from AC
S(x)->AhM	7	same as #5, but add the absolute value
S(x)->Ah-M	8	same as #7, but subtract the absolute value
S(x)->R	9	copy the number in Selectron location x into AR
R->A	10	copy the number in AR to AC
S(x)*R->A	11	Multiply the number in Selectron location x by the number in AR. Place the left half of the result in AC and the right half in AR.
A/S(x)->R	12	Divide the number in AC by the number in Selectron location x. Place the quotient in AR and the remainder in AC.
Cu->S(x)	13	Continue execution at the left-hand instruction of the pair at Selectron location x
Cu`->S(x)	14	Continue execution at the right-hand instruction of the pair at Selectron location x
Cc->S(x)	15	If the number in AC is >= 0, continue as in #13. Otherwise, continue normally.
Cc`->S(x)	16	If the number in AC is >= 0, continue as in #14. Otherwise, continue normally.
At->S(x)	17	Copy the number in AC to Selectron location x
Ap->S(x)	18	Replace the right-hand 12 bits of the left-hand instruction at Selectron location x by the right-hand 12 bits of AC
Ap`->S(x)	19	Same as above, but modifies right-hand instruction
L	20	Shift the number in AC to the left 1 bit (new bit on the right is 0)
R	21	Shift the number in AC to the right 1 bit (leftmost bit is copied)
halt	0	Halt the program (see paragraph 6.8.5 of IAS report)

AC: Accumulator
AR: Arithmetic Register

first realize computation with actual machines. We used it as the guideline in designing IASSim.

Table 1 shows the instruction set of the IAS machine, as originally described in [4]. This is also the instruction set of IASSim. To recreate the "look and feel" of the original, and to emphasize the origins of programming in mathematics, IASSim preserves the opcode notation as described by the original authors. Original terminology is also preserved, for example, in the description of a memory cell as a "Selectron location". Opcodes are identical to those originally described in [4]. Contrary to present practice, the source of an instruction is on the left, destination on the right.

The IAS machine organizes memory into 4K words of 40 bits each. In a quote worth pointing out to students, the authors of the IAS architecture noted "this memory capacity exceeds the capacities required for most problems that one deals with at present by a factor of about 10" [4]. They chose a 40-bit word size since it gave about 12 decimal places of accuracy, "higher than what is required for the great majority of present day problems" [4]. In this machine, 40-bit integers are stored in 2's complement notation.

Floating point numbers were not supported in the IAS machine. It is worth pointing out and discussing Von Neumann's views on this topic [4] in the classroom. In a nutshell, Von Neumann believed that the costs were not worth the benefits. If you could not keep track of where the binary point belonged during your calculations, you had no business using a computer.

Instructions use 20 bits and so two instructions fit in one word. Halfwords that are used as instructions store the opcode in the left 8 bits, and use the remaining 12 as an address or instruction operand. Instructions and data are co-resident in memory, one of the fundamental contributions of this machine to computer science. Instructions are fetched one pair at a time, and executed from left to right within the word and from lower addresses to higher, unless branching interrupts the normal flow.

The IAS machine has two programmer-visible registers: The Accumulator (AC or A in the table) and the Arithmetic Register (AR or R in the table). Both are 40 bits wide. The AR is set only by a special load instruction or one of two arithmetic instructions; the AC is the more common target. Instructions 13 and 14 are unconditional branches, while 15 and 16 provide conditional branching. Instructions 18 and 19 are used for indexing, which the IAS machine achieves through self-modifying code.

The IAS machine does not include any instructions for handling I/O and so all data must be loaded into memory directly (either manually or via assembly pseudoinstructions) before the program is executed. IASSim includes an option for the programmer to specify the target load address.

The original IAS report does not specify a halt instruction. However, paragraph 6.8.5 states "There is one further order that the control needs to execute … which will tell the computer to stop and to flash a light or ring a bell." In that spirit, we have provided a HALT instruction with a zero opcode that will stop computation and ring a bell. Mercifully, the auditory component of this instruction can be disabled by the user.

```
; adds up the values n+...+3+2+1(+0) in a loop and stores
; the sum in memory at the location labeled "sum"

loop:
          S(x)->Ac+     n       ;load n into AC
          Cc->S(x)      pos     ;if AC >= 0, jump to pos
          halt                  ;otherwise done
          .empty                ;a 20-bit 0
pos:      S(x)->Ah+     sum     ;add n to the sum
          At->S(x)      sum     ;put total back at sum
          S(x)->Ac+     n       ;load n into AC
          S(x)->Ah-     one     ;decrement n
          At->S(x)      n       ;store decremented n
          Cu->S(x)      loop    ;go back and do it again

n:        .data 5               ;will loop 6 times total
one:      .data 1               ;constant for decrementing n
sum:      .data 0               ;where the running/final total is kept
```

Figure 1: Summing numbers from 1 to n on the IAS Machine

4. A SAMPLE IAS PROGRAM

The IAS machine had no assembly language or assembler, and so coding needed to be done in machine language. However, to simplify programming and to make it more useful as a teaching tool, we have provided a basic assembly language and assembler as part of IASSim.

Figure 1 shows how the IAS machine could be programmed to sum the numbers from 1 to *n*, where *n* is stored in a memory location. IASSim supports labeling of memory locations. Labels are terminated with a colon. Each instruction and operand corresponds to a 20-bit halfword. Comments are indicated with a semicolon.

The `.data` pseudoinstruction converts its operand to a 40-bit binary number and stores it at the current memory location. The `.empty` pseudoinstruction stores a 20-bit zero at the indicated halfword. Because all instruction fetches are 40 bits at a time, and because alignment errors are difficult for beginning students to catch and debug, the IASSim assembler enforces labels and branch targets to align with word boundaries. The `.empty` pseudoinstruction enables programs to comply with this requirement.

5. RUNNING PROGRAMS WITH IASSim

The opening screen of IASSim is shown in Figure 2. Memory contents appear in the large window on the left. Only a small number of 40-bit words are shown below, but the size of memory is user-configurable.

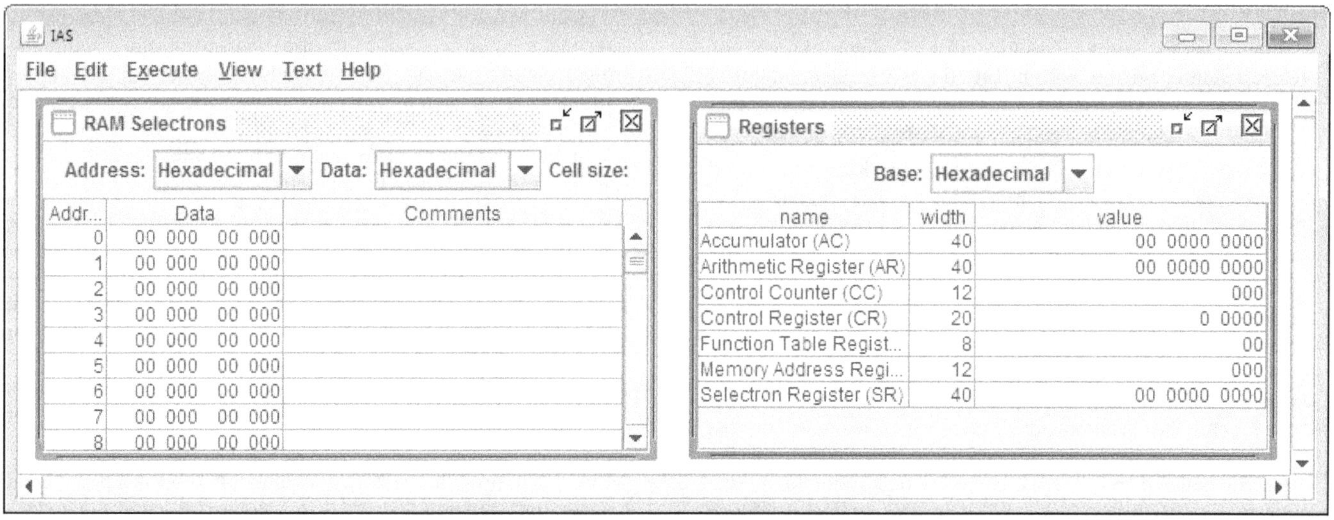

Figure 2: Opening Screen of IASSim

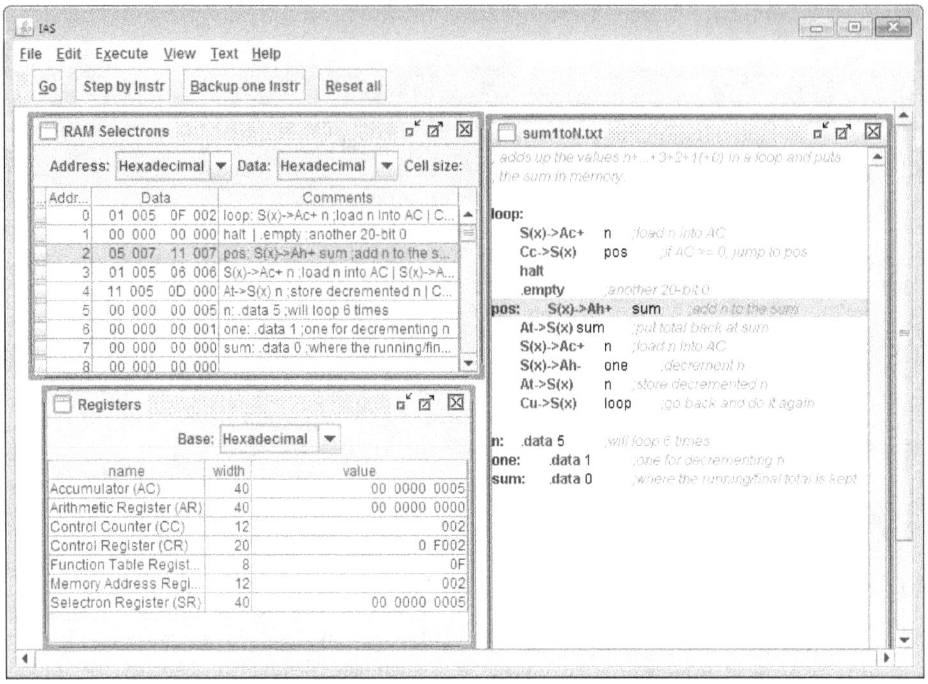

Figure 3: After Executing the First Two Instructions

In addition to the previously mentioned AC and AR registers, the Registers window also permits students to view some internals of the machine, as an aid to understanding and debugging. Consistent with our emphasis on historical accuracy, we employ the authors' original terminology. The Control Counter is what we now call the Program Counter. The Control Register holds the currently executing instruction. The Function Table Register holds the current opcode, the Memory Address Register the current memory address, and the Selectron Register the current data value being read from or written to memory.

Assembly language programs like that of Figure 1 can be created using either the built-in text editor or an external editor and stored as text files. The built-in editor has syntax highlighting specifically designed for IAS assembly language.

Program windows can be opened from the "File" menu, and then assembled and loaded from the "Execute" menu. The RAM Selectrons window shows each instruction halfword loaded into memory, with the upper eight bits of opcode visually separated as an aid to learning.

Placing the simulator into "Debug" mode enables setting break points and allows single step execution of the program forward or backward. After two instructions are executed, the resulting screen is shown in Figure 3. Note that the value of *n* (5) is now loaded into the accumulator. Since the contents of the accumulator are positive, execution will continue at the instruction labeled "pos:" This can be verified by examining the value of the Control Counter. The instruction at the branch target has not yet been fetched, so the Control Register still holds the previous instruction executed. When in debug mode, the next instruction to be executed is always highlighted in the program window and the Rams Selectron Window

Programs may be executed to completion at any time by pressing "Go". At the end of execution, 15 (the sum of the numbers from 1 to 5) is stored in the memory location corresponding to the label "sum:", the Control Counter holds the address of the halt instruction, and the simulator highlights the empty halfword after it.

6. IASSim TECHNICAL DETAILS

IASSim is based on CPU Sim [10], a Java application that the second author created for use in introductory computer organization classes. It was modeled on the STARTLE simulator developed by J. Kerridge and N. Willis [7]. CPU Sim was designed to simulate many different CPU architectures, including simple accumulator-based architectures, RISC architectures, and stack-based architectures such as the JVM.

When using CPU Sim, the user can specify a previously saved architecture or can create a new one. In the latter case, the user specifies the CPU features such as the number and width of registers, the size of main memory, the instruction set, and the layout and implementation of the instruction set using microinstructions. Once a CPU architecture has been specified, the user can write and run assembly language and machine language programs for that architecture within the CPU Sim environment.

CPU Sim provides standard debugging tools such as break points and stepping forward and backward through the code to inspect and optionally change the values in registers or memory at any point.

IASSim was created by modifying CPU Sim to simulate only the IAS architecture. Quite a few modifications were necessary because of the IAS's non-standard features, such as 40-bit words containing either a 40-bit data value or two 20-bit instructions. To keep IASSim as simple as possible, many menus and menu items used in CPU Sim to allow the user to modify the architecture were removed from IASSim.

7. TEACHING INSIGHTS

7.1 Using IASSim in a "Great Ideas" Course

As mentioned previously, the first author used IASSim in a "Great Ideas" computer science course, taught to freshman cadets at the US Air Force Academy. Although most of these students had some computer programming in high school, the course had no formal prerequisites other than admission into the USAFA Scholars Program, a program designed to identify the top forty or so cadets in each class based on their academic potential. The course is not required for the computer science major, and although any student enrolled may declare the CS major in their sophomore year (the typical time for cadets to declare), it is expected that most will not.

Students in this course read the original IAS tech report [4], and then used IASSim as a vehicle to explore humanity's first attempts to build actual prototypes of Turing's Universal Computing Machine [12]. Students had written their own Turing machines using a tool developed at USAFA, designed to follow Turing's notation and style as much as possible. Although many students had taken some computer programming in high school, for some their construction of Turing Machines was their only programming background prior to tackling this assignment.

Nonetheless, all students successfully completed ten IAS assembly language programming assignments. These included summing two or three numbers, finding the maximum of two or three numbers, polynomial evaluation, adding a scalar to a vector, multiplying a vector by a scalar, primality testing, and using Von Neumann's algorithm in [4] to calculate reciprocals.

Students reported a range of 3 to 15 hours of effort to complete all 10 problems, with an average of around 7 hours. The class average was 95%, with three perfect submissions. A histogram of their performance on the IAS programming task is shown below.

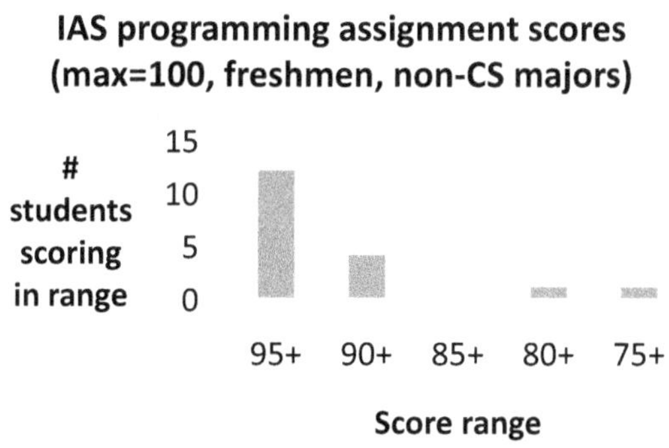

These results should be interpreted with caution. Students in the Academy Scholars program are an extremely bright and motivated group. Nonetheless, the fact that a group of college freshmen with a wide variety of academic interests were able to perform so well in writing assembly language programs for a 60-year-old computer suggests that IASSim is a useful and effective teaching tool.

7.2 Using IASSim in a CS Course

The second author used IASSim in his computer organization class in the spring of 2010. The 23 students had already been using CPU Sim for a month before the IASSim assignment was given, and so they felt very comfortable with the IASSim package. A brief (6 paragraph) introduction to the IAS architecture was given and a sample program was provided that found the larger of two integers. Then the students were given assignments to find the largest of 3 integers, evaluate a cubic polynomial, and copy a value into a series of consecutive locations in memory.

Scores on this assignment are shown below:

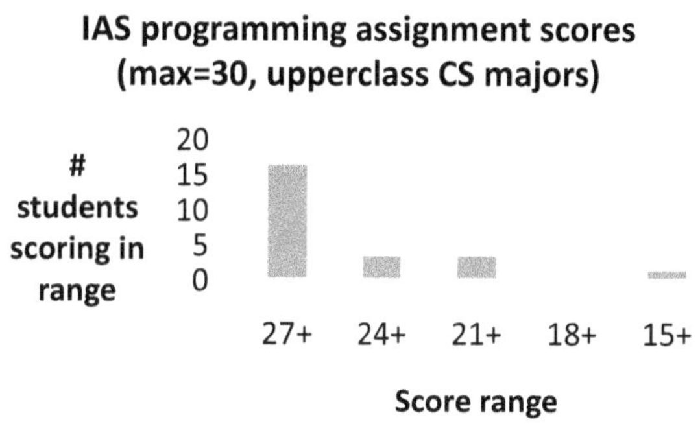

The students were asked to keep track of the amount of time it took them to complete these assignments. The average was about 4 hours for all three assignments, with the times ranging from 1.5 hours to 7 hours. These numbers were not significantly out of line with previous and later CPU Sim assignments. It appears that, because of previous exposure to the CPU Sim package, simple accumulator based architectures, and self-modifying code, the students took the IASSim assignments in stride with no complaints and no significant difficulties.

7.3 Educational Impact

Although the tool is still fairly new and has only been used in two courses at two institutions, we have some evidence of its educational utility.

We have, for example, performance data from IASSim's use on graded tasks. The results clearly show that students (albeit in some cases very bright and highly motivated ones) can use a 60-year-old instruction set architecture to accomplish programming tasks, and can do so with a reasonable amount of effort.

Qualitatively, we have also seen some evidence of pedagogical value in using IASSim. Students who work with a "real" architecture that is nonetheless limited to 12-bit addresses gain an immediate and practical insight into the relationship between address space and computational power. The awkwardness of the "left" and "right" instructions in the IAS also helps students appreciate modern architectures and provides an appreciation for simplicity and regularity in engineering design.

One particularly unconventional feature warrants special mention. Memory addresses in the IAS architecture can only come from instruction fields (it has no index register). Since addresses for array accesses are not normally known at compile time, array indexing requires the address fields of instructions to change while the program runs. Hence if you are working with vectors on the IAS machine (as the original designers did), you must employ self-modifying code.

We believe challenging students with a programming problem for which the only answer is self-modifying code provides a very useful historical and technical perspective. The historical perspective illustrates that even towering intellectual figures don't always get the right answer the first time around. Sometimes, only the experience of working with a system will show a better way to solve a problem.

The technical perspective is relevant today. Self-modifying code is so frowned-upon as a programming practice that it is seldom, if ever taught, and never to beginning programmers. However, virtually all of the most sophisticated viruses work by modifying their own instructions. Students who have written at least some simple self-modifying assembly language routines will have a much better understanding of how viruses work once they encounter them. Particularly given the profession's increased interest in teaching computer security issues more vigorously and earlier in the computing curriculum, we believe this insight to be particularly useful.

Finally, the IAS ISA can start a good discussion about hardware/software tradeoffs in computer architecture. What did the designers do at the gate level, and what did they leave for software? What technology was available to them, and how did that influence their decision? The answers are different today, but the questions, as always, remain the same.

We hope other faculty will use IASSim and report their experiences to us.

8. CONCLUSIONS AND FUTURE WORK

For faculty and students with experience in assembly language programming, programming with IASSim is a trip back in time. You find yourself bemoaning the existence of a single register, grimacing at the extra memory traffic, and wistfully longing for an index register. Writing self-modifying code to accomplish vector processing definitely takes some getting used to.

But for students with no background in assembly, the small instruction set and simplicity of the architecture make it an attractive first platform, independent of its historic interest. The behavior of each instruction is clearly defined, and there is seldom more than one way to accomplish a task, so even if the program seems inefficient by modern standards the correct solution is discoverable by a sufficiently bright and motivated student.

In the future, IASSim could also serve as a useful tool to illustrate numerous issues in high-level language programming. Shortly after submission of this paper, the first author developed JVNTRAN, a very simple high-level language, and an accompanying compiler that generates IAS assembly code. This compiler is being integrated into IASSim, with the eventual goal of supporting JVNTRAN/IASSim classroom assignments.

Beginning programmers who must solve programming problems in both assembly language and a higher level language could learn first-hand about the forces that led to the emergence of high level languages in the first place, an important goal in a "Great Ideas" course. More advanced students could be assigned the task of writing their own compiler for JVNTRAN. Speaking from experience, the authors can attest that they will learn in dramatic fashion the impact of architectural decisions on compiler design!

IASSim is available for download at http://www.cs.colby.edu/djskrien/IASSim/. Source code will be freely provided to anyone interested in inspecting or improving it. We hope a user community will develop that will find bugs, report experiences, develop assignments, and suggest features for future releases.

9. ACKNOWLEDGMENTS

The authors wish to thank our students in "Computer Organization" (Colby) and "Introduction to Computing, Scholars Section" (USAFA) for their service as beta testers.

10. REFERENCES

[1] *ACM Journal of Educational Resources in Computing (JERIC),* Vol 1, No. 4, December 2001.

[2] *ACM Journal of Educational Resources in Computing (JERIC),* Vol. 2, No. 1, March 2002.

[3] Lardner, D., "Babbage's Calculating Engine", *The Edinburgh Review,* Vol. 59, 1834, pp 263-327.

[4] Burks, A. et. al., "Preliminary Discussion of the Logical Design of an Electronic Computing Instrument", Report to US Army Ordnance Department, 1946.

[5] Campbell-Kelly, M. "The EDSAC Simulator", http://www.dcs.warwick.ac.uk/~edsac/ [accessed July, '10]

[6] Grunbacher, H., "Teaching Computer Architecture/ Organization Using Simulators," *IEEE Frontiers in Education Conference (FIE),* 1998, pp 1107-1112.

[7] Kerridge, J.M. and Willis, N., "A Simulator for Teaching Computer Architecture," *ACM SIGCSE Bulletin,* Vol. 12, No. 2, July 1980, pp 65-71.

[8] Rivest, R. et. al., "A Method for Obtaining Digital Signatures and Public-Key Cryptosystems", *Communications of the ACM* **21** (2): pp 120-126.

[9] Schweitzer, D. and Boleng, J., "A Simple Machine Simulator for Teaching Stack Frames", *Proceedings of the 41st SIGCSE Technical Symposium on Computer Science Education,* September 2010, pp 361-365.

[10] Skrien, D., "CPU Sim 3.1: A Tool for Simulating Computer Architectures for Computer Organization Classes", *ACM Journal of Educational Resources in Computing,* Vol. 1, No. 4, December 2001, pp 46-59.

[11] Tangorra F., "The Role of the Computer Architecture Simulator in the Laboratory," *ACM SIGCSE Bulletin,* Vol. 22, No. 2, June 1990, pp. 5-10.

[12] Turing, A, "On Computable Numbers, With an Application to the Entscheidungsproblem", *Proceedings of the London Mathematical Society* **42**: pp 230–65. 1937.

[13] Vollmar, K. and Sanderson, P., "MARS: An Education-Oriented MIPS Assembly Language Simulator," *ACM SIGCSE Bulletin*, Vol. 38, No. 1, March 2006, pp 239-243.

[14] Wolffe, G. S. et. al., "Teaching Computer Organization/Architecture with Limited Resources Using Simulators", *Proceedings of the 33rd SIGCSE Technical Symposium on Computer Science Education*, September 2002, pp 176-180.

A Full System x86 Simulator for Teaching Computer Organization

Michael Black
American University
4400 Massachusetts Ave NW
Washington, DC 20016
(202) 885-2011
mblack@american.edu

Priyadarshini Komala
American University
4400 Massachusetts Ave NW
Washington, DC 20016
pk7551a@student.american.edu

ABSTRACT

This paper describes a new graphical computer simulator developed for computer organization students. Unlike other teaching simulators, our simulator faithfully models a complete personal computer, including an i386 processor, physical memory, I/O ports, floppy and hard disks, interrupts, timers, and a serial port. It is capable of running PC software such as FreeDOS, Windows, and Minix, and can run as a Java applet. Graphical user interfaces allow students to view and modify the processor, memory, disks, and hardware devices at runtime. The simulator includes a processor development utility that allows students to design their own datapath and control units, and run their custom processor alongside the x86 processor. The paper describes labs where students use the simulator to write x86 assembly programs, device drivers, hardware controllers; and design both simple and pipelined processors.

Categories and Subject Descriptors

C.0. [**Computer Systems Organization**]: General

General Terms

Design, Experimentation.

Keywords

Simulator, x86.

1. INTRODUCTION

Computer simulators are important tools for teaching computer organization. Simulation software allows students to observe the internal workings of the processor, memory, and devices while executing their programs; make changes during run-time; and, in some cases, test their own hardware designs. Simulators can teach assembly and machine language programming, datapath and control design, pipelining and advanced architectures, and digital design. They provide a safe environment for experimenting with operating systems. And they give students a better appreciation for the complexity of their own computers.

Many simulators have been developed over this last decade. They range from highly detailed cycle-accurate processor models intended for graduate students and researchers (such as Superscalar [8], to simplified models intended for undergraduate students (such as SPIM or WinDLX [15,13]), to full-system PC emulators for safely running software (such as Bochs or Dosbox [6,10]). A 2002 survey paper [20] listed several simulators for undergraduate courses, and more have been created since.

We have developed yet another computer simulator for teaching undergraduates. Why did we do this? After surveying existing teaching simulators, we found that few faithfully model a full personal computer. Most are specifically written to teach a particular concept, either datapath design, or assembly programming, or pipelining. Peripherals and I/O are generally neglected. Simple RISC instruction sets, such as MIPS, are preferred to x86. These specialized simulators are excellent for teaching their particular material. But they do not allow students to run existing software, develop assembly programs that can run natively on their own computer, observe the interplay between devices, and generally see how their actual personal computer works. PC emulators, in contrast, do run familiar software and operating systems, but are not easily modified and hide the underlying hardware, making them unsuitable for a computer organization course. The next section lists some of the better simulators we found and their focuses and limitations.

Our simulator models the function of a personal computer. It models the full instruction set of an i386 processor, both 16-bit and 32-bit mode. It simulates physical memory, hard and floppy drives, interrupts, keyboard, VGA video, and a serial port. The simulator has been tested with MS-DOS, FreeDOS, Windows 3, and Minix 1. Table 1 gives a complete list of components fully modeled.

Table 1. Hardware Components Modeled

16-bit Real-Mode	Floppy controller
32-bit Protected-Mode	Hard disk controller
Physical Memory	Interrupt controller
CGA Video	Interval Timer
CMOS	Keyboard
DMA	Serial Port
BIOS ROM	VGA Video

The simulator includes a set of user interfaces, one for each hardware component. Each user interface shows a graphical representation of the component and the contents of its internal buffers or registers. Reads and writes to the component are both graphically highlighted and explained in a status bar at the bottom. Several of the interfaces also allow the user to modify the component during runtime. Section 3 describes these user interfaces in detail.

Additionally, the simulator allows users to experiment with their own processor designs. We wrote a datapath development tool to allow students to assemble and connect microarchitecture blocks (such as registers, ALUs, and muxes). Using our control development tool, the user can then create a control state machine and specify datapath behavior. During simulation, students can swap the x86 processor with their own processor, and observe it work and interact with the physical memory and I/O devices. This processor development tool is also described in Section 3.

The simulator is written entirely in Java and can be downloaded and executed as a single JAR file. It can also be run from a webpage as an applet. The simulator is being freely distributed under the GNU license. We are currently teaching (in the Fall of 2010) an introductory computer organization course using the simulator. Upon the course's completion, both the simulator and the course labs will be made publicly available.

2. PREVIOUS SIMULATORS

Before starting development, we surveyed existing freely available or published teaching simulators. An undergraduate computer science student, who had not yet taken a computer organization course, was hired to download and experiment with each simulator, and document her experiences and opinions. This allowed to us to gauge which user interfaces appeal to students starting a computer organization course, and determine which features to include and which to omit.

Table 2. Notable Existing Simulators

Name	Year	Inst Set	I/O	Advanced	
WebMIPS	2004	MIPS		5-stage pipeline	[7]
ProcSim	2005	MIPS		datapath editor	[12]
SimuProc	2004	x86-like	console		[19]
K Scalar	2001	Alpha		superscalar pipeline	[17]
WinMips64	2010	MIPS		configurable pipeline	[18]
WinDLX	1992	DLX		5-stage pipeline	[13]
emu8086	1997	8086	drives		[16]
PCSpim	1990	MIPS	console		[15]
Microprocessor Simulator	2003	Custom x86-like	timer, key		[1]
MiniMIPS	2004	MIPS		5-stage pipeline	[3]
HDLDLX	2004	DLX		5-stage pipeline	[2]
IECS	2000	Custom	dma	virtual memory, cache	[9]
p88110	2009	Custom		superscalar, cache	[11]

Table 2 lists the simulators that were found to have the most appealing interfaces, or had features that inspired our work, and lists which hardware components are modeled. SPIM is a venerable earlier simulator that has the very useful feature of showing and tracking code, stack, and data at once in separate frames, and includes a built-in assembler. We considered these essential features. Procsim is a datapath design utility that inspired our own. It also outputs its datapath to XML code, a design choice we decided to imitate. Emu8086 is the best example we could find of an x86 teaching simulator. However, it is limited to 16-bit code and does not model many I/O devices. Several simulators depict a pipeline (usually the DLX pipeline); however the student found these simulators either bewilderingly complex or excessively simple. We decided not to hardcode a pipeline GUI, but to make it possible instead for students to construct pipelines using the datapath developer.

We also surveyed several personal computer emulators before deciding to write our own from scratch. Bochs, Dosbox, and Java PC (JPC) [14] influenced us the most, and are all released under the GNU license. Bochs, possibly the "gold standard" of PC emulators because it faithfully runs newer operating systems, is very lengthy and complex. Dosbox is easy to use, but is heavily optimized for speed, and is hardwired for DOS (for example, it does not run a BIOS ROM image, but simply mimics common BIOS calls.) JPC appeared to be the most suitable for our project. It is cleanly written in Java, handles several operating systems, and can run as an applet. We nevertheless decided to write our emulator ourselves so that it would be simple to modify and work with our user interfaces. However, we closely paralleled JPC's emulation methodology, associating one Java class with each physical device, and decoding x86 instructions into microinstructions before executing them. For three hardware devices, the Floppy Controller, Interrupt Controller, and DMA controller, we chose to adapt JPC's code rather than write them from scratch.

After surveying these simulators, we decided that several elements would be essential:

* It must run a preexisting PC operating system
* It must include the basic I/O devices: video, keyboard, disk
* Students must be able to easily load, assemble, and simulate their x86 assembly code
* It must have a split screen view that allows the user to simultaneously see register contents, instructions, the console, and data
* It must be possible to view the datapath and observe the movement of data values
* Students must be able to design their own processor and simulate it

3. THE SIMULATOR

A screenshot of the simulator is shown in Figure 1. It can be run as a large single window with many frames (in applet or standalone form), or as multiple windows. When run as a single window, it consists of a large frame showing the console, a scrollable side panel containing several small frames, an optional keyboard frame at the bottom, and basic control buttons (Play, Pause, Step). A menu bar allows the user to open additional GUIs in the side panel.

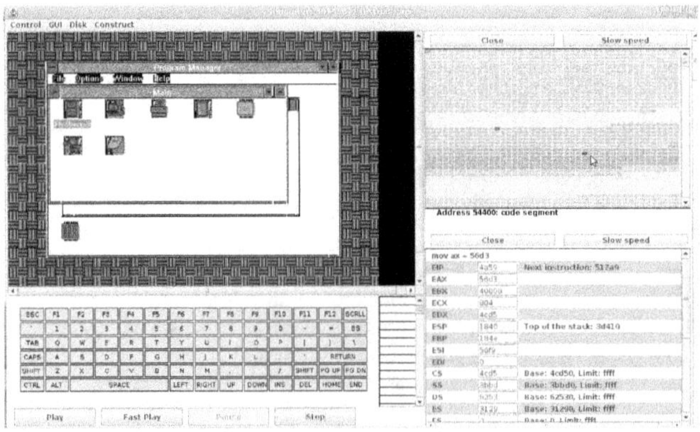

Figure 1: Main Simulator Window, Running Windows 3.

3.1 User Interfaces

3.1.1 Boot

When the simulator is started, the user is given a boot window. The user can select hardware devices to include, GUIs to open, and the disk images to use.

3.1.2 Processor

Two GUIs are dedicated to the x86 processor, and are shown in Figures 2 and 3. The first allows the user to view and edit the contents of all the registers and flags. The assembly code of the current instruction is shown at the top of the frame. The second GUI, which opens in a larger frame over the console, depicts a simple non-pipelined datapath of the processor. When open, the GUI is updated on each CPU cycle. The instruction register at the top shows how a i386 instruction is decoded from prefix, opcode, MOD/RM, SIB, displacement, and immediate bytes. Buses carrying data are highlighted with their data values drawn adjacent, registers read are colored green, and registers written to are colored red. A description of the action taken is given in the status bar.

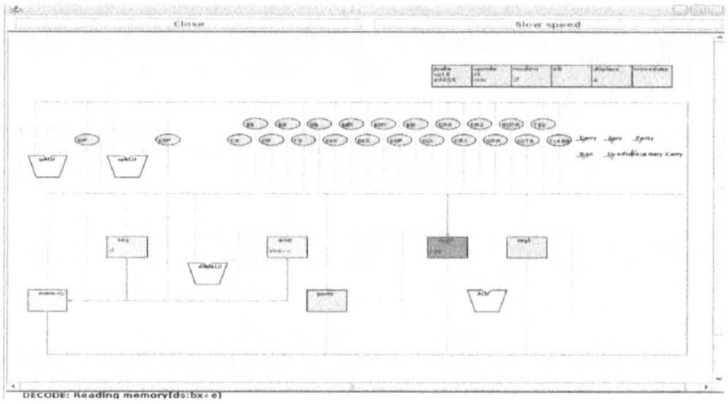

Figure 2: Processor GUI

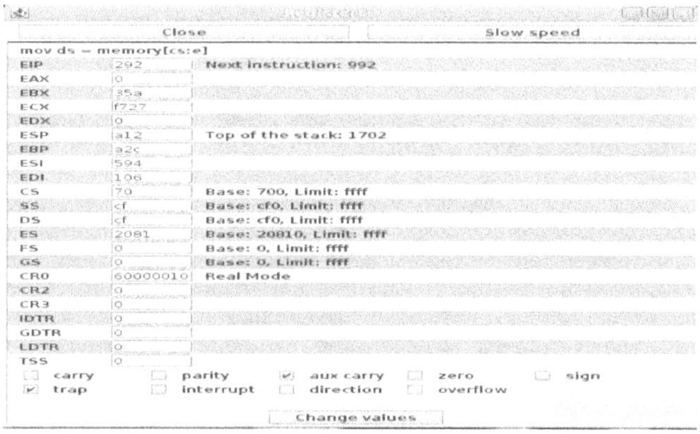

Figure 3: Register GUI

3.1.3 Physical Memory

There are two memory GUIs, shown in Figures 4 and 5. The first GUI depicts all of physical memory, broken into 1kB blocks, and color coded based on purpose: base RAM, extended RAM, BIOS ROM, Video BIOS, nonexistent. A further color coding, updated dynamically during runtime, specifies which blocks belong to the code segment, stack segment, and data segment; a brighter color is used for the current instructions, top of the stack, and last data access. When the mouse is moved over a block, its purpose is described in the status window.

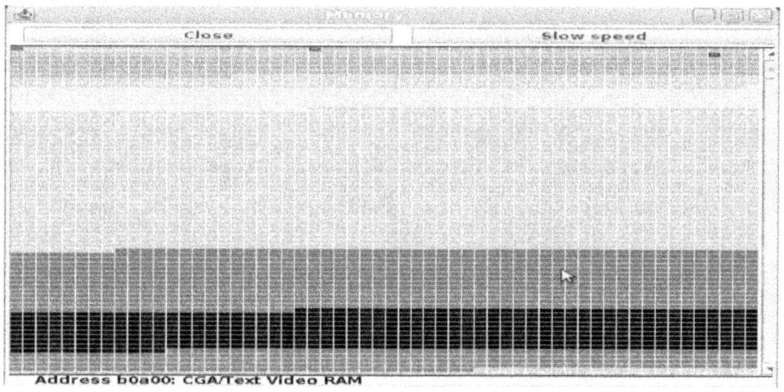

Figure 4: Physical Memory GUI

When the user clicks on a block, or types an address into the status window, a second GUI opens for that block. The GUI shows the address, memory contents, and an interpretation of the block's contents. If the block belongs to the code segment the corresponding x86 instruction is given; the data segment, an ASCII decoding; the stack segment, the name of the register from where the value was pushed. The user can modify any byte by clicking on it and entering an alternative value. By right-clicking on a byte in the instruction memory, a user can set a breakpoint at that instruction.

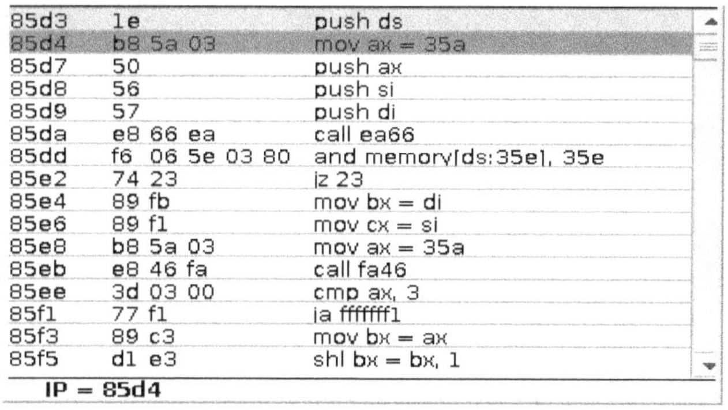

Figure 5: Instruction and Data Memory Views

3.1.4 Disks

Figures 6 and 7 show the two disk GUIs, which are the same for both hard and floppy disks. The first GUI depicts the disk platter, showing track and sector bounds. When a sector is read or written, the corresponding block is lit up in green or red respectively, and the current track is highlighted in white. Disk parameters are given in a legend in the top corner.

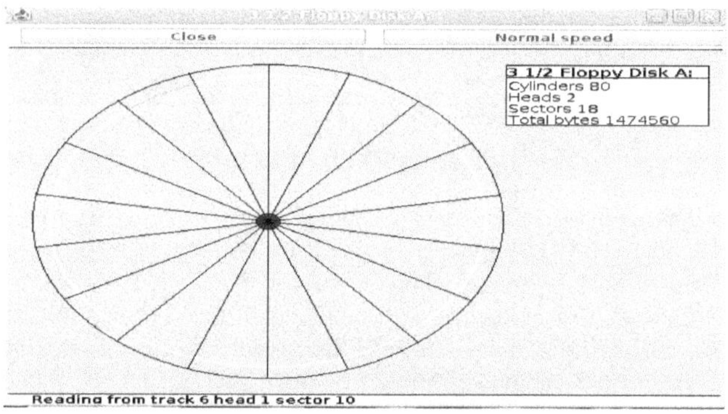

Figure 6: Disk GUI

The second GUI shows the purpose of the disk blocks. If a simulated disk image contains a FAT-12 or FAT-16 file system, the blocks are color coded, showing Boot, FAT, Directory, file, and free sectors. When the user moves the mouse over a block, or a block is accessed by the simulator, the corresponding file is identified and shown in the status window, and all blocks belonging to the file are highlighted. When the user clicks on a block, a block editor opens, allowing the user to modify the individual bytes.

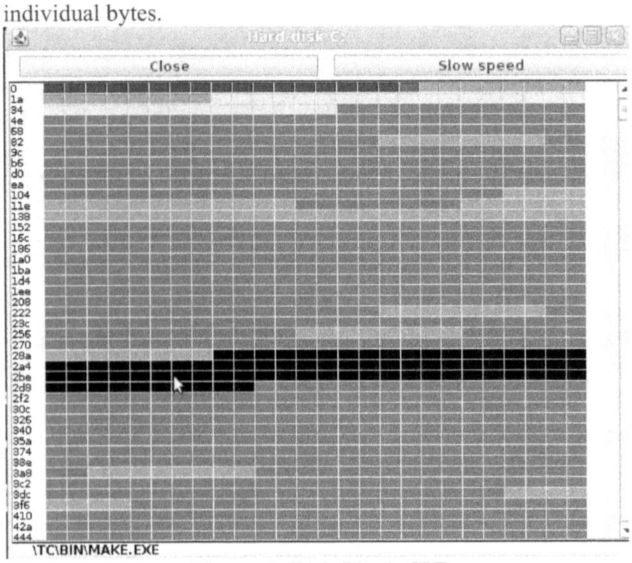

Figure 7: Disk Block GUI

3.1.5 *I/O Ports*

Figure 8 shows the I/O port interface. All allocated ports have a row showing the port address, the device claiming it, the port's purpose for that device, and a breakdown of the individual data bits. Ports accessed by the simulator are highlighted dynamically, and the user can read or write to a port and edit individual bits.

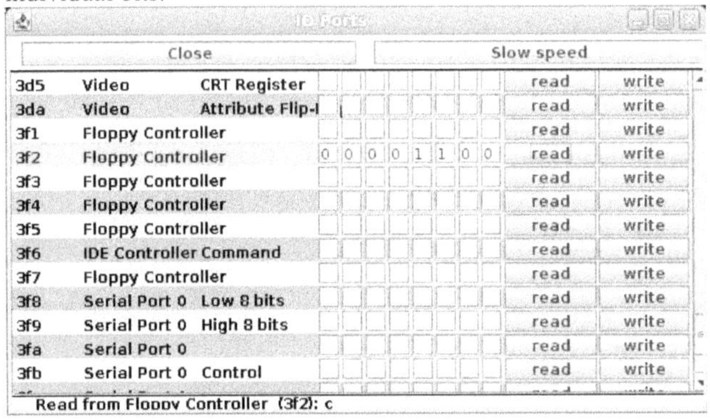

Figure 8: I/O Port GUI

3.1.6 *Keyboard*

The keyboard GUI occupies a fixed place at the bottom of the main simulator window, shown earlier in Figure 1. It shows the keys of an 80-key keyboard, the contents of the keyboard buffer, and the keyboard status. When the user types into the console, the keyboard reflects the key strokes by highlighting the keys. When the user moves the mouse over a key, the keyboard status bar tells its keycode. At other times, the status field tells the contents of the keyboard's internal status registers.

3.1.7 *Interval Timer*

The simulator includes a programmable interval timer modeled on Intel's 8253, shown in Figure 9. The timer is depicted as a clock, with a second-hand showing its countdown, and "12:00" representing an interrupt. The timer's data value (0 or 1) is depicted by shading the clock face white or gray. The timer's mode (one-stop, retriggerable) is described in the timer's status field.

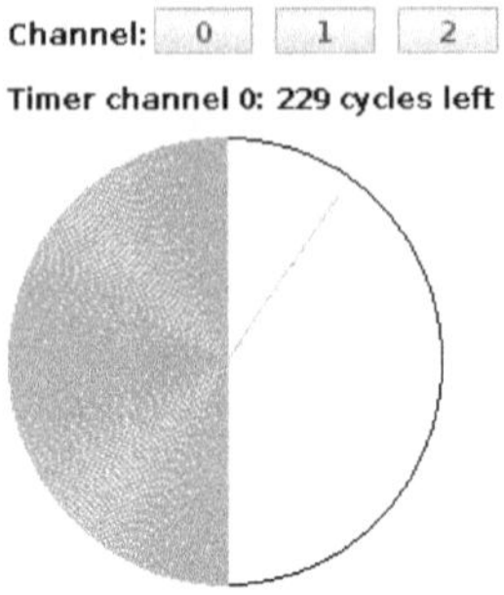

Figure 9: Timer GUI

3.1.8 *Serial Port*

Figure 10 shows the serial port interface. The GUI shows bytes recently transmitted and received, and breaks the byte currently being transferred into individual bits (including parity, start, and stop). A sketch of a DB9 connector shows the pins, and the RS-232 function of each pin is described in a mouse-over. By clicking in the appropriate field, the user can transmit or receive a byte, and change the serial port parameters. Currently under development is a "Connect" button that interfaces the simulated serial port to the actual /dev/ttyS0 port (at present this only works on Linux systems).

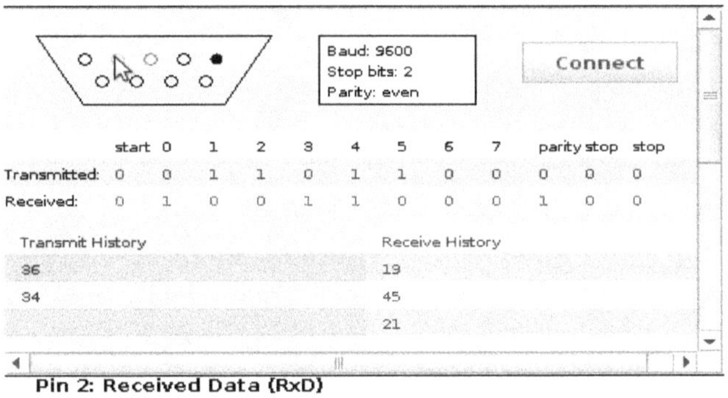

Figure 10: Serial Port GUI

3.1.9 *Breakpoints*

The simulator allows the user to set breakpoints. Using a GUI, shown in Figure 11, a student can pause the simulator on a variety of events, including watching for particular register value, a memory or port access, an interrupt, or a cycle count. The simulator also parses breakpoint equations given in text form.

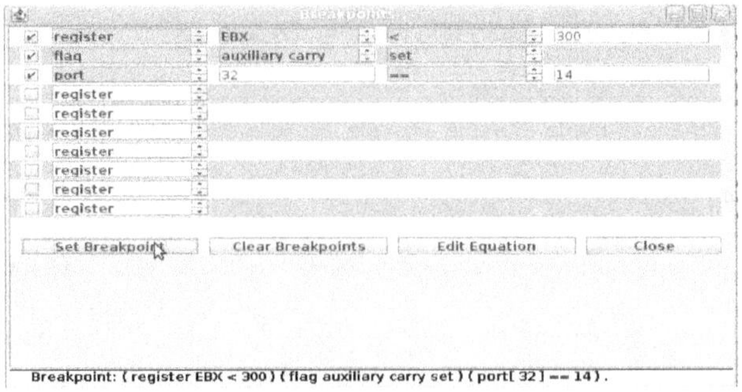

Figure 11: Breakpoint Editor

3.1.10 File Transfer

Students can transfer files to and from their PC to the simulated disk images with a File Transfer GUI. If the Borland Turbo C or Turbo Assembler are installed under Freedos on the simulated hard disk image, the GUI also allows students to compile or assemble their programs. (Both of these applications are currently being distributed for free.) A similar GUI allows students to make fresh disk images. The user can specify whether the image is a floppy or 10MB hard disk, and install FreeDOS on the image.

3.2 Processor Development Tool

The Datapath and Control Developers allow students to design their own custom processor. While intended to be simple for beginning students to use, they offer sufficient capability for students to simulate pipelined or out-of-order processors. The Datapath Developer gives an interface, loosely modeled after Microsim PSpice and similar circuit design tools, to allow students to draw their own datapath. It consists of two frames: a canvas that opens over the console, and a toolbox that opens in the side panel. Figure 12 shows a screenshot of the Developer along with a simple datapath of a two-instruction computer.

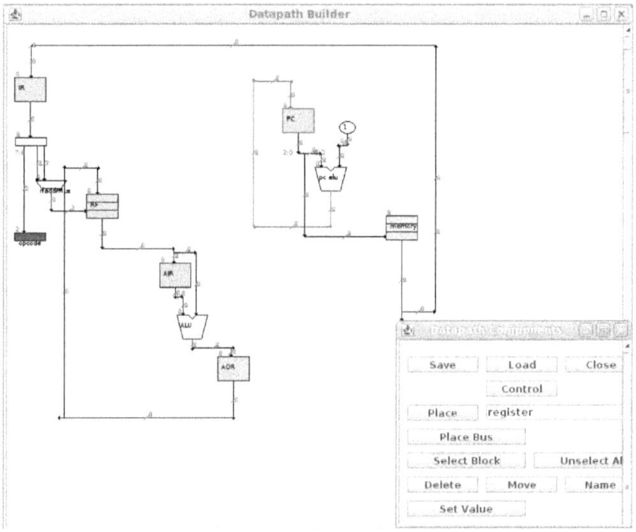

Figure 12: Datapath Developer

Using the toolbox, students can select and place a variety of microarchitecture components: registers, register files, multiplexors, decoders, bus splitters, extenders, and joiners, lookup tables, ALUs, control unit inputs, adders, and constant values. Two additional components allow students to interface their datapath with the physical memory and the I/O ports. Each component is given a name and a bit-width. Students can then draw buses connecting the components. Each bus is automatically set to carry the bit-width of the component sourcing it. Datapaths are converted to XML form and can be saved to and loaded from a text file.

The Control Developer, shown in Figure 13, also consists of a canvas and a toolbox, and allows students to design a finite state machine for sending control signals to the datapath. Displayed as rows of different colors, the user can specify one or more control paths (which run simultaneously to allow pipelining), consisting of one or more states. Each state consists of one or more microinstruction rows, and one or more next state rows. When a microinstruction or next state row is placed, a list of control inputs are automatically gathered from the Datapath Developer, and the user can specify which control input value should activate that row. Furthermore, when the microinstruction row is placed, the user is a given a list of control outputs. The user can choose a direction for each mux, a behavior for each ALU, and whether to clock each register. Like the datapath, the Control Developer translates the control states to XML form, allowing the users to load and save them to a text file.

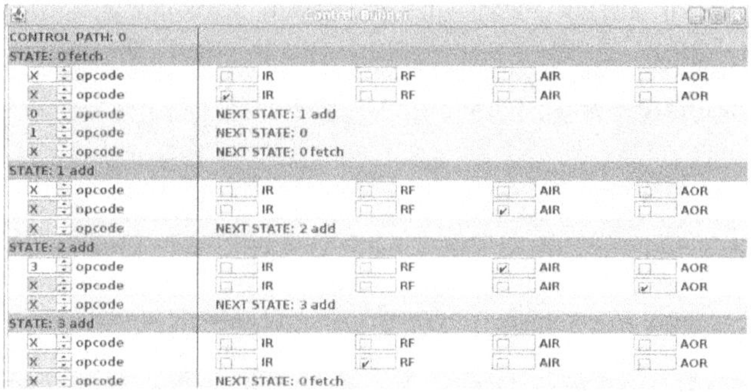

Figure 13: Control Developer

Once the user has created a datapath and control, a Custom Processor unit can be created. All components are given a data value, initially 0, but changeable by the user. The custom processor runs alongside the x86 processor, parsing and stepping through the control states, and communicating to the same memory and devices as the x86 processor.

We modeled dynamic processor swapping after the system used in some of the early dual-processor personal computers (specifically the Zenith Z-100). By writing to an unused port (currently port FF), the simulator can enable or disable the x86 processor and the custom processor. This allows a student to write a machine code program for their custom processor, load it into the simulated file system, and using an x86 wrapper program that loads the custom machine code and writes to the port, automatically run their program on their own processor.

4. LABS

We are developing a series of labs for Computer Organization that use the unique capabilities of our simulator, which we are testing with 18 students this semester. These labs are briefly synopsized as follows:

Assembly Programming: Students write simple x86 assembly programs that use MS-DOS I/O system calls. They load the program to the simulator's disk image containing Freedos and Turbo Assembler 1, assemble it, and run it. Students can debug their work by setting breakpoints at the beginning of their program, opening the register GUI and the code, stack, and data memory GUIs, and single stepping through it.

Device Programming: Students write a simple graphical animation program (a moving car) in x86 assembly. This involves configuring the interval timer, modifying the interrupt vector table and making their own timer interrupt routine, switching the video to graphics mode, and writing to video memory. Because the simulator accurately models a PC, the students then run the same program on their own laptops.

Hardware Control: Students use the simulator, running on a Linux computer with a serial port, to control hardware. Students connect a line driver and shift register to the serial port, and write software that turns on and off LEDs connected to the bits of the shift register.

Processor Design: Building on existing computer organization labs [4], students design their own instruction set and datapath. They then build it on the simulator and run simple programs on it.

Pipeline Design: Students are given a tiny MIPS-like instruction set. They construct a 5-stage DLX-like pipeline and control, simulate it, and analyze the instructions-per-cycle performance of their processor.

We additionally plan to develop a series of labs that use the simulator in an operating systems course. The following two are possible examples:

Reverse Engineering: Students take an existing application (such as Turbo C, Scandisk, and Windows 3.0), and determine which files and disk sectors it accesses, which memory it uses, and what interrupt calls it makes. Students modify the application's machine code so that it calls their own routine during runtime.

Operating System Design: Students build a small operating system similar to this [5] and test it on our simulator instead of Bochs. With our simulator the students can track register values and memory use, and potentially complete a more advanced system.

5. FUTURE WORK

We designed our simulator to be simple and modular so that advanced students can easily build additional features, including new user interfaces. Below are some of the additional components we hope to construct:

Additional Hardware: In the near term, we plan to add a mouse, ethernet port, USB port, memory protection, and a two-level cache to the simulator.

Advanced Processor Architectures: We plan to create a set of templates for our Datapath Developer, including a DLX pipeline and a superscalar MIPS processor. We also plan to update our current 386 processor to a more modern Core 2 Duo, with 64-bit instructions and multicore.

Improved Processor Developer: We plan to add power and latency modeling to the processor developer, making it a useful tool not only for undergraduates but also beginning computer architecture researchers.

6. ACKNOWLEDGMENTS

This work was made possible by NSF CCLI grant 0941057.

7. REFERENCES

[1] Bauers, C. N. 2003. Microprocessor Simulator v5.0. http://www.softwareforeducation.com/

[2] Bečvář, M. 2004. Teaching Basics of Instruction Pipelining with HDLDLX. Workshop on Computer Architecture Ed.

[3] Bem, E. Z. and Petelczyc, L. 2003. MiniMIPS: a simulation project for the computer architecture laboratory. 34th SIGCSE Technical Symposium on Computer Science Education, February, 2003.

[4] Black, M. 2008. A Processor Design Project for a First Course in Computer Organization. American Society for Engineering Education Annual Conference, June 2008.

[5] Black, M. 2009. Build an operating system from scratch: a project for an introductory operating systems course. SIGCSE Technical Symposium on Computer Science Education, 2009.

[6] "Bochs - The Open Source IA-32 Emulation Project" 2009. http://bochs.sourceforge.net/

[7] Branovic, I., Giorgi, R., and Martinelli, E. 2004. WebMIPS: a new web-based MIPS simulation environment for computer architecture education. 2004 Workshop on Computer Architecture Education.

[8] Burger, D., Austin T_M. 1997. The SimpleScalar Tool Set, Version 2.0., University of Wisconsin-Madison Computer Sciences Department, Technical Report #1342.

[9] Djordjevic, J., Milenkovic, A., Grbanovic, N. 2000. An Integrated Educational Environment for Teaching Computer Architecture and Organization. IEEE Micro.

[10] DOSBox - an x86 emulator with DOS. http://dosbox.com

[11] Garcia, Rodriguez, Perez, Garcia. 2009. p88110: A Graphical Simulator for Computer Architecture and Organization Courses. IEEE Trans. on Education.

[12] Garton, J. 2005. ProcessorSim – a visual MIPS R2000 Processor Simulator. http://jamesgart.com/procsim/

[13] Grunbacher and Khosravipour. 1996. WinDLX and MIPSim pipeline simulators for teaching computer architecture, IEEE Symposium on Engineering of Computer-Based Systems.

[14] JPC - The Pure Java x86 PC Emulator. http://jpc.sourceforge.net/

[15] Larus, J., SPIM: A MIPS32 simulator, http://www.cs.wisc.edu/~larus/spim.html

[16] Margolin, Yuri. 2010. Emu8086. http://www.emu8086.com/

[17] Moure, J. C., Rexachs, D. I., and Luque, E. 2002. The KScalar simulator. J. Educ. Resour. Comput, Mar. 2002.

[18] Scott, M. 2010. WinMips64. http://www.computing.dcu.ie/~mike/winmips64.html

[19] Vlaye Software. 2004. SimuProc. http://sites.google.com/site/simuproc/

[20] Wolffe, G., Yurcik, W., Osborne, H., and Holliday, M. 2002. Teaching Computer Organization/Architecture with Limited Resources using Simulators. ACM SIGCSE Bulletin Volume 34 , Issue 1 Pages: 176 - 180.

[21] Z-100 Technical Manual. Heath / Zenith Data Systems, Benton Harbor, MI, 1982.

IBCM: The Itty Bitty Computing Machine

A one-week module to teach machine language in computing courses

Aaron Bloomfield
University of Virginia
aaron@virginia.edu

William Wulf
University of Virginia
wulf@virginia.edu

ABSTRACT

We present the development and implementation of the Itty Bitty Computing Machine (IBCM), a machine language designed specifically to be taught to lower-level undergraduate students. The presentation of the material takes about one-week of lecture, and allows understanding of all the concepts of machine language without having to deal with the complexity of modern machine language implementations, such as x86 and MIPS. A number of pedagogical aspects are addressed concisely via IBCM, such as treating all data as untyped and performing arithmetic on instructions.

While we are not the first to introduce a short machine language module, we do provide a number of benefits over older versions: a modern browser-based implementation, a full set of pedagogical tools, and a decade of experience teaching this module. All of the necessary materials, including compilers, simulators, and documentation, are available online and licensed through Creative Commons licenses.

Categories and Subject Descriptors

D.3.m [**Software**]: Programming LanguagesMiscellaneous; D.2.6 [**Software Engineering**]: Programming Environments

General Terms

Languages

Keywords

machine language, pedagogy

1. INTRODUCTION

Understanding machine language is vital for any computer science undergraduate. While all undergraduate programs will have their students understand this topic by graduation, the question persists as to how and when best to introduce these concepts to the students. Some institutions have a separate assembly language course that touches on machine language, whereas others include it in a computer architecture course. We are not aware of any institutions that have an entire required computer science course dedicated to machine language. We recognize that hardware-based computer engineering curricula, including ours at the University of Virginia, will have such material as upper-level courses. These courses tend to be specialized computer hardware or computer engineering courses, and are typically not required for a computer science degree.

We present a pedagogical module designed to teach machine language in a single week in a low-level undergraduate course. While the depth of knowledge obtained by the students is limited due to the short time spent on the topic, the students are still able to understand the fundamental concepts. This allows machine language to be introduced to the students early in the curriculum, with a more detailed approach potentially taught in later classes.

We have developed a machine language that we have called the Itty Bitty Computing Machine, or IBCM. This language is intended to be very simple – there are only 16 commands. Yet it is still fully functional, and is a Turing complete programming language.

SIGCSE'11, March 9–12, 2011, Dallas, Texas, USA.

2. RELATED WORK

We are certainly not the first to propose a simplified machine language as a pedagogical tool. Andrew Tanenbaum's original 1984 text, *Structured Computer Organization* – now in its 5th edition – presents the Mic-1 micro architecture and the Mac-1 machine language [10]. Indeed, the Mac-1 machine language has many similarities with IBCM – this is not surprising, as there are many common elements that must be present in all small instruction set machine languages. Further research in that decade presented implementations of those languages [5, 6]. The Mic-1 simulator, which is focused on assembly language, is available online [9]. Simulators for the Mac-1 machine language do exist, but seem to be independently developed, and without a modern set of implementation software.

A number of high quality simulators exist at the assembly level. Pep/8 [11, 12] is a 16-bit CISC architecture designed to teach assembly language concepts. While it can be used for machine language – and can trace program execution at the machine language level – the primary pedagogical design is at the assembly language level. Another example is SPIM, which is a full featured MIPS 32-bit simulator [4].

Additional research on machine language simulators has

often focused on the register transfer level [7], or is restricted to a single client operating system [1].

More recent research by Stone has focused on a similar machine language implementation [8]. Although developed independently, our research can be seen as an extension of Stone's, as we add a number of additional aspects: significant pedagogical tools, a fully downloadable package so this system can be used in any course, a proof of Turing completeness, and a discussion of pedagogical concerns.

We are not aware of any machine language simulators that are available with the set of modern tools that we present with IBCM.

3. THE IBCM LANGUAGE

The Itty Bitty Computing Machine is an accumulator-based machine language with 16-bit two's complement integer arithmetic. There are no registers other than the accumulator. IBCM has 4096 words of memory, and each word is also 16 bits.

All instructions are likewise 16 bits: the first four bits are the opcode, and the rest are interpreted differently, depending on the opcode. The instruction format can be seen in Figure 2.

0 1 2 3	4 5	...	15	
0 0 0 0	(unused)			halt
0 0 0 1	I/O op	(unused)		I/O
0 0 1 0	shift op	(unused)	count	shifts
opcode	address			others

Figure 2: IBCM instruction format

An opcode of 0x0 halts the IBCM. The remaining 12 bits are not used by this instruction, and can hold any value.

An opcode of 0x1 will perform either an input or output operation. All input is written to the accumulator, and all output is read from the accumulator. The two bits following the opcode specify which operation: the 5th bit specifies either a read (if 0) or a write (if 1), and the 6th bit specifies if the value being read or written is a four digit hexadecimal word (if 0) or an ASCII character (if 1).

An opcode of 0x2 will perform a shift operation on the bits in the accumulator. The bit following the opcode specifies whether the operation is a shift (if 0) or a rotate (if 1). A rotate takes the bits that "fall" off one "end" of the 16-bit word, and move them to the empty spots on the other "end" of the word. The 6th bit of the instruction specifies if the shift or rotate operation is to the left (if 0) or right (if 1). The last 4 bits of the 16-bit word (called 'count' in Figure 2) specify how many bit positions the shift or rotation should move.

The remaining 13 opcodes (0x3 to 0xf) are classified as 'address' instructions, as the remaining 12 bits generally specify the memory address that the opcode will use. A few of the instructions do not need the 12 bit address: in particular, the `not` and `nop` operations. All of 13 these 'address' instruction opcodes are shown in Figure 1. In that figure, note that `a` represents the accumulator register, and `mem[]` represents memory. Of these 13 operations, the first 8 manipulate data, and last 4 perform program flow control; the `nop` instruction does nothing. Note that `PC`, the program counter, is the address of the current instruction being executed.

An IBCM file is simply a text file, and the simulator only reads in the first 4 bytes of each line; the remaining characters on the line are ignored. In the sample program that is shown below (in Figure 4), additional opcodes are used for clarity. These are so that one can read an assembly-like opcode for each line.

- `dw` (for "declare word"), for declaring variables
- `readH` and `printH` are for reading or writing a hexadecimal value
- `readC` and `printC` are for reading or writing an ASCII character
- `shiftL` and `shiftR` are for the shifts
- `rotL` and `rotR` are for the rotations

All the functionality of a modern procedural programming language can be implemented using IBCM. Conditionals (if-then-else) are implemented through comparing a number!– or a number minus a constant!– to zero, and using the various jump commands (`jmp`, `jmpe`, `jmpl`) to access the different parts of the conditional. As in any assembly or machine language, iteration is achieved through looping, such as the `jmp` command. Subroutines can be implemented through the `brl` instruction, which stores the return address in the accumulator upon jumping to the subroutine start address. The `brl` command is discussed in more detail below, as well as an IBCM example that uses subroutines.

A specific design decision with IBCM was to include only basic operations – for example, multiplication and division are not included, but can be replicated by using repeated addition or subtraction. We wanted students to see that any program, no matter how complicated, can be broken down into very simple instructions. Indeed, this is the point of the concept of Turing machines, but they are often not taught when students are first seeing machine language.

4. EXAMPLE PROGRAMS

We present one example IBCM program in its entirety here in Figures 3 and 4. We discuss two other programs in this article, and their full program listings can be found online [2].

The first program will compute the sum of the integers 1 through n, where n is read from the keyboard; the resulting sum is printed to the screen. The program then halts after printing the sum. The C++ code for the program is shown in Figure 3 – this is presented to help show the conversion to IBCM.

```
int main(void) {
  int n, s = 0;
  cin >> n;
  for ( int i = 0; i <= n; i++ )
    s += i;
  cout << s << endl;
}
```

Figure 3: C++ summation program

The IBCM program is shown in Figure 4. Note that the only part of the program that the simulator reads in is the

Hex	Opcode	HLL-like meaning	English explanation
3	load	a:= mem[addr]	load accumulator from memory
4	store	mem[addr] := a	store accumulator into memory
5	add	a := a + mem[addr]	add memory to accumulator
6	sub	a := a - mem[addr]	subtract memory from accumulator
7	and	a := a & mem[addr]	bitwise 'and' of memory and accumulator
8	or	a := a | mem[addr]	bitwise 'or' of memory and accumulator
9	xor	a := a ⊕ mem[addr]	bitwise 'xor' of memory and accumulator
A	not	a := ~a	bitwise complement of accumulator
B	nop		do nothing (no operation)
C	jmp	goto addr	jump to 'addr'
D	jmpe	if a = 0 goto addr	jump to 'addr' if accumulator equals zero
E	jmpl	if a < 0 goto addr	jump to 'addr' if accumulator less than zero
F	brl	a := PC; goto addr	set accumulator to PC; jump (branch) to 'addr';

Figure 1: IBCM instructions

first four characters on the line. The rest of the line in the text file is solely for comments. The column headers shown in the figure are heavily abbreviated to fit in the width of a column, but are, in order: the actual 4 hexadecimal digit memory value, the hexadecimal location (used for determining jump targets and variable addresses), the label (used to refer to jump and variable targets), the opcode (from Figure 1), the target address (which refers to a given label), and any English comments.

Mem	Loc'n	Label	Opcode	Adr	Comments
C006	00		jmp	init	jmp past vars
0000	01	i	dw		int i
0000	02	s	dw		int s
0000	03	n	dw		int n
0001	04	one	dw		
0000	05	zero	dw		
1000	06	init	readH		read n
4003	07		store	n	
3004	08		load	one	i = 1
4001	09		store	i	
3005	0A		load	zero	s = 0
4002	0B		store	s	
3003	0C	loop	load	n	if i>n, jmp xit
6001	0D		sub	i	
E016	0E		jmpl	xit	
3002	0F		load	s	s += i
5001	10		add	i	
4002	11		store	s	
3001	12		load	i	i += 1
5004	13		add	one	
4001	14		store	i	
C00C	15		jmp	loop	goto loop
3002	16	xit	load	s	print s
1800	17		printH		
0000	18		halt		halt

Figure 4: IBCM summation program

Another program that was developed computes the product of two numbers, x and y, through a recursive multiplication subroutine that uses only addition. Both x and y are read from the keyboard, and the resulting product is printed to the screen. The program is just over 100 lines of IBCM opcodes, and is available online [2].

The C++ code for the multiplication program can be seen in Figure 5. We did not create a tail recursive `multiply()` routine, as the IBCM compiler and language is (intentionally) far too simple to optimize for tail recursion.

```
int mult(int x,int y) {
  if ( y == 0 )
    return 0;
  else
    return x+mult(x,y-1);
}
```

```
int main(void) {
  int x, y;
  cin >> x;
  cin >> y;
  cout << mult(y,x)
       << endl;
}
```

Figure 5: C++ multiplication program

This IBCM program creates a stack similar to x86: the stack starts at the end of addressable memory, and grows downward. An activation record is created for each recursive call, which consists of the two parameters and the return address – other fields typically in an activation record (e.g., backup of registers) are not necessary in IBCM. The `brl` instruction was used to allow for subroutine calls – the return address is saved in the accumulator, and is stored on the stack immediately upon subroutine activation. We were able to run the program with the second parameter (which is decremented in each recursive call) set as high as 1,243 (0x4db), beyond which point IBCM runs out of available memory for the stack.

This recursive multiplication program is beyond what we would expect of a student to be able to program after a one-week introduction to IBCM. However, it is very illustrative of two important points about IBCM. One is that complex functionalities (such as multiplication) can be achieved by using only the simple capabilities available in IBCM (such as addition). The other is that subroutines are fully realizable in IBCM.

5. TURING COMPLETENESS

We were conflicted as to how much to discuss about Turing completeness in this article. IBCM is similar to a Random Access Stored Program (RASP) machine [14], which is itself Turing complete, so it is perhaps not surprising that IBCM is also Turing complete. However, we felt that breaking down a complex task (a Turing machine simulator) and programming it into IBCM was a worthwhile task to discuss,

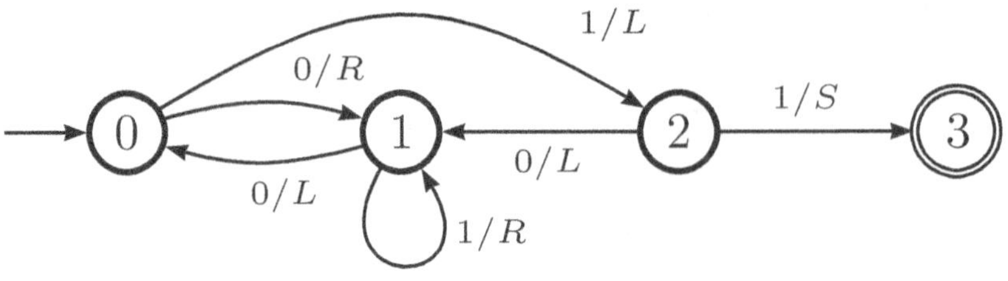

Figure 6: Four state Busy Beaver automaton

as it emphasizes a primary design goal of IBCM – that you can take any program and write it in IBCM.

Obviously, no physical computer with a finite amount of memory can be truly Turing complete. Thus, we will instead show that the IBCM computational model is Turing complete.

We define the *IBCM computational model* as the same IBCM computer defined above, but allowing any sized integer to be held in a single memory location, as well as having an infinite amount of memory. Thus, other fields that make up part of a given instruction, such as the 'address' or 'count' fields (see Figure 2), can also hold any size integer.

Given this model of computation, we will show how to simulate a Turing machine in IBCM. Hopcroft and Ullman [3] define a Turing machine as a 7-tuple $M = \langle Q, \Gamma, b, \Sigma, \delta, q_0, F \rangle$ where:

- Q is a finite set of states
- Γ is the finite set of allowable tape symbols
- $b \in \Gamma$ is the blank symbol
- $\Sigma \subseteq \Gamma \setminus b$ is the set of input symbols
- $\delta : Q \times \Gamma \rightarrow Q \times \Gamma \times \{L, R\}$ is the transition function
- $q_0 \in Q$ is the initial state
- $F \subseteq Q$ is the set of final states

We will make two modifications to the above definition, to allow for ease of implementation in IBCM. We will allow a no-shift transition of S (in addition to L and R), which will not move the tape. The Turing machine programs allowed by the no-shift are equivalent to the ones described above [15]. Furthermore, we will define f, a single final state, which all states in F move to on a no-shift transition.

To represent the transition functions in IBCM, we will represent state $q \in Q$ and symbol $\Sigma \in \Gamma$ each as a (16-bit) word in IBCM. Thus, states and symbols will be a single integer each. While this limits the number of states (and symbols) to $2^{16} = 65,536$ in our IBCM implementation, it is not limited in the formal IBCM computational model. Thus, one can encode any amount of states, symbols, and transition functions into IBCM's memory.

To simulate a Turing machine, we will define an arbitrary memory location to represent the current state of the Turing machine, and another arbitrary memory location to contain the current address of the head of the tape. The transition function quintuples, δ, will start at a specific (but arbitrary) memory address, take up five words each, and will contain the five parts listed above $(Q, \Gamma, Q, \Gamma, \{L, R, S\})$. The tape itself will start at different arbitrary memory location. Furthermore, we define a initial state q_0 and a (single) final state f. The blank symbol b will be an arbitrary value, such as -1 (0xffff in 16-bit 2's complement integer).

Any Turing machine that requires a significant amount of tape will need to be a one-way tape Turing machine, as the program code and state transitions will lie at a lower address than the initial head position. Thus, only a finite amount of tape space is available in the lower memory address direction. The particular automaton example that we provide, below, uses a two-way tape, but that is because we know the finite amount of tape space necessary. Note that one-way tape Turing machines are equivalent in computational power to two-way tape Turing machines [3].

What is needed, then, is an IBCM program that will iterate through the following steps:

- Read the current state s, initially set to the start state. If the current state is the (single) final state, then exit.
- Read the current head position.
- Read the current input symbol t at the head position
- Search the list of transition functions until the appropriate one is found, based on the current state s and the input symbol t.
- Perform the action specified in the transition function by updating the state s, writing the specified symbol to the tape position, and then moving the tape left or right (or, on an S, not at all).

We have developed such a program, which we describe here. The full listing of the program is available online [2]. The program consists of 67 IBCM commands, and 15 variables – note that numeric constants are considered variables in an IBCM program. This program only used half of the instructions: `halt`, `load`, `store`, `add`, `sub`, `nop`, `jmp`, and `jmpe`.

To test the Turing machine, we choose a four state Busy Beaver automaton, which is described in more detail in the Wikipedia page on Turing machine examples [16]. The Mealy machine finite automaton is shown in Figure 6. For each transition, the input symbol (0 or 1) is shown, along with the tape direction to move (L, R, or S). Note that in this automaton, upon each transition a 1 is written to the output tape; this is not shown in the figure to improve clarity. Also recall that the S transition means to not move the tape, and is used only on the transition to the final state.

Our implementation can utilize a two-way tape, although the tape in one direction is finite. We define memory address 1 as the current state variable, and address 2 to store the location of the current head position. The transitions start at address 0x060, as our program takes up 82 (or 0x052) instructions. The states are numbered as per the diagram in Figure 6, with 0 being the initial state and 3 being the final state. The program has constants that specify both the initial and final states of the automaton.

The encoding of the automaton shown in Figure 6 is very straightforward. The transition from 2 to 1, executed on an input symbol of 0, will print 1 to the tape and then move the tape to the left. The quintuple to be encoded is $Q \times \Gamma \rightarrow Q \times \Gamma \times \{L, R, S\}$. The respective values for this transition are $2, 0, 1, 1, 0$; we map the integer values $\{0, 1, 2\}$ to, respectively, the transition directions $\{L, R, S\}$.

6. PEDAGOGY

IBCM was originally developed to complement our CS 3 course entitled *Program and Data Representation*, which is still taught today. This course shows how one represents both data and program code from high levels – such as abstract data types – all the way down to the lowest (software) level, which is the IBCM machine language.

IBCM allows students to easily make the mental connection between assembly opcodes and the machine language that they get translated into. At the University of Virginia, we follow the presentation of IBCM with a two-week introduction to assembly language. This allows students to understand both machine language, as well as a modern processor's assembly language (we use Intel x86), without having to delve into the details of x86 machine language.

Students are exposed to a number of concepts during the IBCM module that they often have not seen previously. They become aware that in both assembly language and machine language, data is untyped, and the operations on the data determine the type – this is quite different than the typed high-level programming languages to which they are accustomed. By this point in our course, students have been exposed to how a 32-bit value can be interpreted either as a two's-complement signed integer or an IEEE 754 floating point number.

Another concept taught through IBCM is self-modifying programs. A non-trivial IBCM program requires arithmetic on instructions – in fact, only the first example program shown in Figure 4 did not use this feature. Array indexing, for example, requires starting with a `load` instruction, and adding to that value both the base address of the array and the current index. This value is then stored in memory which is shortly thereafter executed. The second example program provided to the students uses this feature. While many systems explicitly try to prevent self-modifying code, as that is an exploit used by a significant amount of malware, it is still a concept that the students should be familiar with.

The development of self-modifying IBCM programs leads to another pedagogical goal of the course: the interplay between data and program code. Indeed, there is little difference between data and program code, other than the values (obviously), and how it is interpreted (and, in modern systems, what segment of an executable in which the data is found). This concept seems trivial to instructors, but is one that students who have only programmed using high-level languages are often unfamiliar with.

What IBCM does not teach, of course, is how binary machine language instructions are executed on the processor. Understanding of this material is typically beyond all but senior-level undergraduate courses; at many institutions, this is also outside the standard computing curriculum.

7. RESULTS

At the University of Virginia, this module is taught about half-way through our CS3 course, which is where we teach data structures. Our CS1 and CS2 course are both in Java. At this point in the CS3 course, the students have learned to implement a number of data structures in C++. We introduce machine language using IBCM for one week, follow that with two weeks of assembly programming (x86), and then return to C++ for the remainder of the semester. The lectures used to teach IBCM typically take three 50-minute class periods. This is followed by an IBCM lab the following week. All of the lecture slides and labs are available online [2].

We have taught machine language using IBCM in our CS3 class for over a decade. Student reactions to IBCM have varied greatly. With the usage of the modern tool set presented in this article, those reactions have generally been positive, as shown below While they often do not like being constrained to such a limited set of instructions, they see the purpose of learning machine language, and generally enjoy the IBCM assignments. We have found that the quality of the software tools is directly related to student perception of IBCM – in the past, when our IBCM simulator was less refined, student reaction was significantly more negative.

Objective comparison with other programming languages, including assembly language, are difficult due to the vast differences between both the capabilities and the required learning curve. We have instead focused on subjective assessment. In the most recent semester in which IBCM was used (fall of 2010), six questions were asked of the students. All questions were asked on a Likert scale, where 1 means strongly agree, 2 is agree, 3 is neutral, 4 is disagree, and 5 is strongly disagree. For all the questions, $n = 89$.

The first two questions focused on how much the students felt they learned from the IBCM module. The middle two questions focused on the ease of use and enjoyability. And the last two questions focused on how worthwhile this module was, both for this course and future courses.

Question	Avg	Stdev
IBCM increased my understanding of the basics of machine language	1.67	0.58
IBCM increased my understanding of how computers work at a low level	1.89	0.65
IBCM was easy to use, once I got the hang of programming in it	1.92	0.88
I enjoyed learning IBCM	2.01	0.98
Considering what was taught, IBCM was a worthwhile module to have in this course	1.75	0.68
IBCM should be used in future iterations of this course	1.76	0.72

The results clearly show that the module was generally well received. The lowest score, enjoyment of learning IBCM, still was in the 'agree' category.

8. MATERIALS AVAILABLE

We have developed and made available a wide range of materials for the purpose of teaching the IBCM module. The materials are all released under various Creative Commons licenses. They are available online [2], and consist of:

- A PowerPoint slide set to introduce the concepts during a lecture-based course. This 42 slide set takes about three 50-minute lectures to present.
- A *Principles of Operation* document, which describes the IBCM computer and language, and how to write a program. It covers similar content to the lecture slides.
- Sample programs, one of which was shown in Figure 4, above. We also provide sample programs on array indexing, for example. All the programs mentioned in this article are available online.

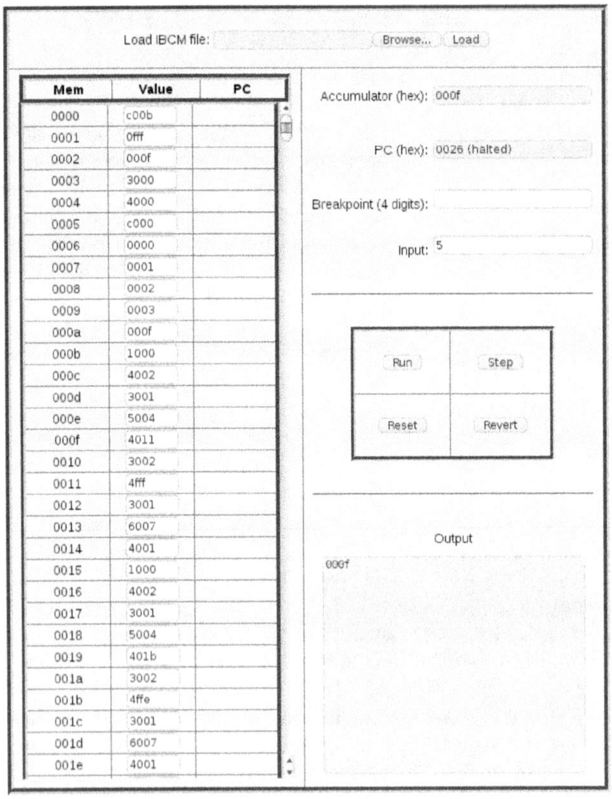

Figure 7: Web-based IBCM interface

- Sample student assignments, which require students to write additional IBCM programs beyond the sample programs provided. One of the assignments is to write a quine, or an IBCM program that will print itself out – the smallest quine produced is nine IBCM commands.
- An online PHP/Javascript simulator, which is the primary way that the students program in IBCM. This is shown above in Figure 7. The PHP is used to allow loading of an IBCM program from a text file; the Javascript implements the IBCM simulator in the browser itself. The simulator works across all major browsers on all major operating systems.
- A C++-based command-line program, which can both compile and execute IBCM programs. Not surprisingly, this is much faster than the online simulator. This is particularly useful for automated compilation and execution of IBCM programs for grading, or for very long programs, such as the recursive multiply routine described above.

Furthermore, a GUI-based tool for executing IBCM programs is available separately [13]. This tool allows for drag-and-drop loading of IBCM files into the GUI, and compiles natively for each operating system.

We very specifically have not developed an IBCM assembler, which would take in the opcodes in an assembly language format and output hexadecimal machine code. The purpose of IBCM is to teach the students machine language; given an IBCM assembler, this module ends up being just a different assembly language for the students to learn.

9. CONCLUSION

We have used IBCM for over a decade at the University of Virginia in our CS3 class. During that time, we have refined it into the pedagogical tool presented here. With the set of current pedagogical tools provided, we have found it to be an effective means of teaching the basic concepts of machine language without having to go into the complexity of modern machine languages that is beyond the scope of a lower-level undergraduate course. All of the necessary materials are available online for adoption at other institutions.

10. REFERENCES

[1] B. Lewis Barnett, III. A visual simulator for a simple machine and assembly language. In *SIGCSE '95: Proceedings of the twenty-sixth SIGCSE technical symposium on Computer science education*, pages 233–237, New York, NY, USA, 1995. ACM.

[2] Aaron Bloomfield. Itty bitty computing machine online. `http://www.cs.virginia.edu/~asb/ibcm/`.

[3] John E. Hopcroft, Rajeev Motwani, and Jeffrey D. Ullman. *Introduction to Automata Theory, Languages, and Computation.* Addison-Wesley Publishing Company, 3rd edition, 2006.

[4] James Larus. SPIM: A MIPS32 Simulator. `http://pages.cs.wisc.edu/~larus/spim.html`.

[5] Jerry E. Sayers and David E. Martin. A hypothetical computer to simulate microprogramming and conventional machine language. *SIGCSE Bull.*, 20(4):43–49, 1988.

[6] Delmar E. Searls. An integrated hardware simulator. *SIGCSE Bull.*, 25(2):24–28, 1993.

[7] Dale Skrien and John Hosack. A multilevel simulator at the register transfer level for use in an introductory machine organization class. *SIGCSE Bull.*, 23(1):347–351, 1991.

[8] Jeffrey A. Stone. Using a machine language simulator to teach cs1 concepts. *SIGCSE Bull.*, 38(4):43–45, 2006.

[9] Andrew Tanenbaum. Mic-1 download website. `http://www.ontko.com/mic1/`.

[10] Andrew S. Tanenbaum. *Structured Computer Organization.* Prentice Hall PTR, Upper Saddle River, NJ, USA, 1984.

[11] J. Stanley Warford and Chris Dimpfl. The pep/8 memory tracer: visualizing activation records on the run-time stack. In *Proceedings of the 41st ACM technical symposium on Computer science education*, SIGCSE '10, pages 371–375, New York, NY, USA, 2010. ACM.

[12] J.S. Warford. *Computer Systems.* Jones & Bartlett Learning, 2009.

[13] Jacob Welsh. JWelsh's useful programs. `http://www.eemta.org/~jwelsh/progs/`.

[14] Wikipedia. Random access stored program machine. `http://en.wikipedia.org/wiki/Random_access_stored_program_machine`.

[15] Wikipedia. Turing machine. `http://en.wikipedia.org/wiki/Turing_machine`.

[16] Wikipedia. Turing machine examples. `http://en.wikipedia.org/wiki/Turing_machine_examples`.

Exploring Careers While Learning Alice 3D: A Summer Camp for Middle School Girls

Heidi C. Webb
Penn State University
University Park, PA
16802 U.S.A.
+ 1 814-863-2478
hcw120@ist.psu.edu

Mary Beth Rosson
Penn State University
University Park, PA
16802 U.S.A.
+ 1 814-863-2478
mrosson@ist.psu.edu

ABSTRACT
We discuss a study conducted during a summer program for middle school girls that emphasized possible future careers that rely on computer technology. During the weeklong camp middle school girls created an original computer project, visited campus computer labs and listened to invited speakers – all with computer technology as the central theme. This paper discusses the program, girls' reactions to their experiences, and the projects they created during the summer camp.

Categories and Subject Descriptors
K.3.0 [**Computers and Education**]: General Education

General Terms
Design, Human Factors

Keywords
middle school girls, careers, Alice 3D, summer camps

1. INTRODUCTION
Throughout middle school, high school and college students listen to peers, role models and other external influences when considering their studies and future careers. For young women, many external sources reflect or reinforce gender-specific stereotypes, suggesting that computer science or related professions are best reserved for men. One result is that the proportion of women in these professions has been steadily declining.

Where should we intervene? The issue is complex because it involves many factors including family, friends, teachers, curricula and technology. Interventions have included after-school programs [4, 8, 9, 20], summer institutes [22, 24], novel software systems [19, 33] and teacher training [3, 25, 26]. For instance, across the United States there are many opportunities for young people during the summer months to attend camps and workshops in topics that range from computer technology to sports. The technology programs being held at instructional institutions such as private academies and universities are a means to help young people gain confidence in working with technology, teaching them to have fun with computers and exposing them to potential careers with computer technology [5, 9-14, 17].

Studies have been conducted in Greece, Australia, England and other countries to try to determine students' motivations for pursuing careers in computer science; effects of role models or mentors; and whether future job security in the field influences youth in thinking about future careers [28]. Studies have shown that high school students rank computer science 7th in preferred majors, with psychology, medicine, engineering and law amongst the top four [27]. It is interesting that computer science is ranked so poorly, given that majors in the top four have computer technology embedded in them and information technology is needed in many aspects of medicine and engineering. However, the issue involves more than exposing students to Computer Information Science (CIS); there are skills, feelings, a sense of belonging and other factors that play a role in the learning of young people.

SIGCSE'11, March 9-12, 2011, Dallas, Texas, USA.
Copyright 2011 ACM 978-1-4503-0500-6/11/03...$10.00.

Children learn best when they are involved and active in their learning environments [16, 23, 29]. Learning occurs naturally when children interact with people in their environment, for example cooperating on activities with peers. For this reason summer technology programs where children can interact with others in a relaxed atmosphere, working together and alone to learn new skills are popular with both young people and their parents.

In the United States, middle school normally comprises grades 6-8; students are in the age range of 10-14. At this age, most children have reached the level of cognitive development that would enable them to comprehend and work with abstractions, a key prerequisite for many introductory computer science activities [29]. Middle school students are also beginning to experience more freedom in their academic selections, and are being encouraged to think about college and other career preparation activities [1, 7, 15]. These characteristics make it an ideal time for introducing some simple programming concepts, in an effort to help girls see how such activities might play a role in their future.

We designed a summer workshop with an exploratory research orientation; our primary goal was to see how middle school girls might react to a visual programming environment and to understand their problems and successes. We also had a more specific interest in whether and how we might inject career thinking into the introductory programming activities; we anticipated that if girls were able to see how their personal inclinations about future jobs could be melded with computer activitiess, they might be more likely to see a role for computers and information technology as part of their future education and careers. In the balance of the paper, we describe the summer program that we designed to introduce novel technology skills to middle school girls, and then briefly summarize the projects and reflections we obtained from the girls. We close with a short discussion of the implications we see in our findings.

2. SUMMER CAMP DESIGN
During the summer of 2009 a summer camp using Alice 3D (www.alice.org) was offered for middle school girls at a large Northeastern University. We focused on middle school girls because of the cognitive and social development associated with

this age group [21]; the freedom to modify their class schedule with electives (U.S students); and the creation of social groups based on academics and after school activities (for instance students in chess club tend to socialize with other club members, cheerleaders with cheerleaders, etc.) [7, 15].

The primary focus during the workshop was to provide enough knowledge and skills about programming in Alice that the girls would be able to design and complete a personal project (Table 1); the projects were shared with parents and others on the final day. Except for this final day, each 1 ½ - 2 hour morning lesson comprised introductory remarks to motivate the new concept(s), followed by code or tool walkthroughs. After lunch the girls had approximately 2 hours to work on their own projects, with continuous access to the instructor and assistants for help when needed. Guest speakers were scheduled for the mornings and the lab tours in the afternoon. From comments received from the first day, we decided to reduce the time for lunch to a half hour so the girls would have more time to work on their projects and still enjoy the lab tours.

Table 1. Overall workshop structure

Weekday	Lesson	Tour	Speakers
Monday	Getting Started Basics (objects, methods, Alice 3D, storyboards)		
Tuesday	Events, more on methods, working with the camera	Create IT Lab	Privacy; Fashion Design
Wednesday	Functions, Conditionals	Visualization Lab	Security
Thursday	Timers and Scores		Medicine
Friday	No lessons, final touches before Parent Showcase		

To introduce more information about professional activities related to the use computer technology we organized two lab tours and four guest speakers to be held after the first Getting Started day of the camp for three days of the workshop. All guest speakers were females who described their use of computers in their work activities (final column in Table 1). Studies have shown that young girls may not have the information needed to adequately plan for future technology or science careers [18, 31].

2.1 Alice Project Activities

The choice of projects for students who are first learning about technology and software is an important challenge. On the one hand, students may become disillusioned if they are unable to complete an assignment, if they are unable to use with the technology provided, or do not understand why a piece of technology or software is needed to complete a task. On the other hand, if the activities are too artificial or simplistic, the students may reject them as trivial or meaningless. For this reason we encouraged the girls to create their own original stories or games during the week. In support of this overall project, we provided introductory demonstrations, coaching, and exercises that included examples for the girls to use. These activities were done using practice projects so their experimentation would not "mess up" their current working copies of their own story or game projects.

An effective project for learning Alice has two components: a question which motivates the learners' activities, and carefully designed supporting activities that will produce a final product that addresses these questions [2]. In this summer camp, except for the first day while the girls were learning the basics of the Alice environment, they developed a game or story concept they generated at the beginning of the week: On the first day they were assigned to write a short story (no more than one paragraph). This story was intended to help them envision what they would like to work on for the rest of the camp and to serve as the driving force for the rest of the week's activities. Importantly, we asked them to think about jobs or careers that seem interesting to them, or other aspects of their future lives, and to try to work these ideas into their stories. In this way we encouraged the girls to think of Alice as a play to explore "career-related" stories.

Working from these stories the girls built their games or stories in Alice. Not surprisingly, as they began these more extensive projects they generated many "How do I...?" style questions. Thus starting on the second day, the previously scheduled lessons were revised to address common questions. Throughout the week exercises were tailored to help the girls successfully complete their projects for the family showcase at the end of the week (Table 1).

2.2 Surveys

In addition to attending sessions and working on projects, camp participants completed brief surveys prior to beginning the camp (as part of the research consenting process) and on the final day. The pre-camp survey included a small amount of background information (e.g., age, grade) as well as several scales aimed at probing girls' knowledge of and interest in computer-related activities and careers. The post-camp survey included a repeat of some of these scales but also asked girls to react to their project activities at the camp. Furthermore, at the end of each day (except Friday) the girls submitted reflections by writing open-ended responses to the prompts "What did you like best?" and "What did you like least?"

Three scales in the pre-camp survey were drawn from the literature [6, 30]. The first was *CS Careers*; it asks for ratings concerning knowledge of computer-related careers, likelihood of choosing such a career, satisfaction doing work with computers and similar questions. A second was *Positive Stereotypes*, a set of items probing the extent to which people who work in computer-related jobs are believed to be "creative", "smart", and "hardworking". The third was the *Computer Playfulness* scale, where the participant rates how well seven adjectives (creative, inventive, playful, etc) describe how she feels when doing things with a computer.

The post-camp survey included three rating scales created to assess the participants' feelings of success with Alice programming (confidence they understood the tools they were using; confidence they developed a good game; and extent to which they had fun). It also repeated four of the *CS Careers* items from the pre-camp survey. All rating scales used values from 1-7 (e.g., 1=Very Strongly Disagree, 7=Very Strongly Agree).

3. RESULTS

Forty-six girls attended the workshop; we obtained research consents for 42. Though the camp was advertised for middle school girls, one girl was 9 and another was 14; the remainder were 10–13 years old, with an overall average of 11.6 (SD=.96).

3.1 Initial Attitudes and Career Orientation

We used the pre-camp survey to collect background information about the girls (e.g., age) and to probe their initial views about computer activities and computer-related careers. The means and standard deviations for CS Careers-1, Positive Stereotype, and Computer Playfulness appear in Table 2. Each of these is an index created by averaging the contributing items, after first confirming acceptable internal reliability (Cronbach α is reported for each along with the sample size).

Table 2. Computer-related attitudes from pre-camp survey

CS Careers-1 (α=.76, n=41)	Pos Stereotype (α=.81, n=41)	Playfulness (α=.80, n=41)	CS Positivity (α=.82, n=41)
4.9 (sd=.97)	5.2 (sd=.94)	5.1 (sd=.86)	5.1 (sd=.78)

Not surprisingly, these three pre-camp indices are intercorrelated. Because we found that the girls had some difficulty with the vocabulary in the Playfulness scale, and because it was correlated with Positive Stereotypes (r=.39), we simplified the analysis by creating a combined index called *CS Positivity*, comprised of the three stereotype items and the seven playfulness items. The resulting scale had high internal reliability (α=.82); the mean and standard deviation are shown in the fourth column of Table 2.

Note that these initial ratings tend to be positive (4 is the neutral value). This might be due to a general positivity bias in use of such scales or may reflect a self (or parental) selection bias in the population of girls who attend summer camps like this.

3.2 Post-Camp Reactions

In contrast to the pre-camp survey, the post-camp questions were intended to explore participants' reactions to the camp activities and to determine what if any effect these activities might have had on their attitudes about computer-related careers. Recall that our hope was to demonstrate to these girls that they can integrate enjoyable computer-based activities with their interests in careers or other future activities.

As described in Section 2.2, three rating scales were used to gather general reactions to the camp – whether they understood the use of Alice; whether they felt they had created a good game project; and whether they had enjoyed themselves. The associated mean values and standard deviations appear in the first three columns of Table 3.

Table 3. Post-camp reactions and career attitudes

Understood (n=38)	Good Project (n=38)	Had Fun (n=37)	CS Careers-2 (α=.82, n=37)
5.8 (sd=1.2)	5.4 (sd=1.5)	6.1 (sd=1.2)	5.2 (sd=1.2)

We were pleased to observe that each of the three mean values is greater than neutral point of 4 on the scale (t-values of 9.7, 5.5, 10.1, respectively, p<.001 in all three cases). We also found that the ratings were strongly correlated, suggesting that they could be combined into a single index that we named *Felt Success*. The internal reliability of this three-item scale was high (α=.81) and the mean value was 5.7 (sd=1.1). As we had noted informally while observing the girls at work, most of them had a good time and felt that they had learned a lot.

The fourth column in Table 3 presents the internal reliability and mean values for CS Careers-2; recall that these ratings are for the same four items assessed in the pre-camp survey. A quick comparison of the two tables suggests that the participants' orientation to computer-related careers increased, but the mean difference does not reach significance (t(37)=1.9, p-.07). Thus it seems that while many of the girls enjoyed the camp activities, the overall impact on career attitudes was modest at best.

To investigate the possible relationships among initial attitudes and the girls' post-camp reactions, we conducted two exploratory regression analyses. In the first we regressed Felt Success on the two pre-camp survey variables of CS Career-1 and CS Positivity. We found that only the latter predicted feelings of success (F(1,36)= 8.2, p<.01), in a model accounting for 18.5% of the variance). This was surprising, as we expected that girls who started out with a stronger orientation toward CS careers would be more engaged and learn more from the camp; however at least in this small sample, it appears that beliefs like "people who choose careers in information technology are smart" or "I often feel creative when I work on computer projects" were better predictors of post-camp feelings of success.

The second regression considered Felt Success, CS Career-1 and CS Positivity as predictors for CS Career-2. The resulting model was quite strong, accounting for 57.7% of the variance (F(2,35)= 23.9, p<.001). In this model, both CS Career-1 and Felt Success were significant predictors. The predictive value of CS Career-1 is not surprising – this simply demonstrates self-consistency in girls' career orientation when assessed at two different times. However, the independent contribution of Felt Success suggests that the camp activities may have also affected subsequent interest in CS careers.

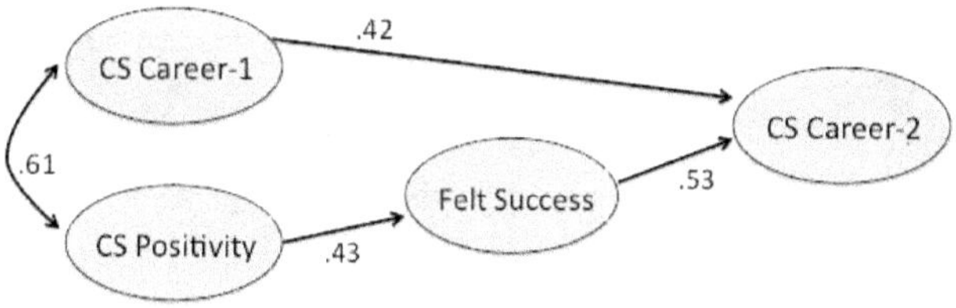

Figure 1. Exploratory path model for CS Career beliefs

By integrating the two exploratory regression models, we can construct a preliminary path model (Figure 1). The model conveys the two sets of relationships: each node is a variable in the model, and the arrows show the presence of significant predictive relationships (the numerical annotations are the standardized beta values, an indicator of relationship strength). Note that the model in Figure 1 is not one that we hypothesized and tested; rather it is a representation that summarizes patterns we discovered in the survey data. Future studies might test the model in a more systematic way or work to build a more elaborate model.

3.3 Story Narratives

At the beginning of the week the girls were encouraged to create a story or game that depicted a career they might eventually pursue someday. To aid in the development of their first screens, the girls were instructed to start by writing a short paragraph. Looking over these early stories, we found that 24% of the girls incorporated some ideas about future careers into their projects.

For example, one girl incorporated her interest in becoming a veterinarian by telling the story of curing a small kitten in a Vet's office (Figure 2). Another girl was interested in meteorology and centered her story around a tornado with people needing to be rescued. We found these to be interesting responses to our request for career-oriented projects. While not all the girls focused on what people did on a day-to-day basis in careers, they did feature characters in occupational roles (e.g., the marine biologist character in Figure 3). This may have occurred because the girls are interested in these types of careers but are unable to express what people actually do on a day to day basis when they are on the job. However, the integration of occupational roles does illustrate that a focus on careers was of interest to some of the girls and we plan to expand on this concept in future workshops or seminars.

Figure 2. Vet's Office

Figure 3. Marine biologist.

In general a popular project narrative or theme was the rescue of a person or item by a knight or magical creature. Some girls had few ideas for career-related projects, so they simply adapted an example from one of the beginning lessons and built their story around those characters. On occasion the girls who had developed career-themed stories could not find suitable characters in the library, so they also reused characters introduced in lessons throughout the week. These findings suggest that additional career-orienting activities might be helpful for future workshops; for instance we might introduce a few popular ones via stories.

3.4 Alice Projects

Of the 42 girls who agreed to be research participants, only 33 submitted projects at the end of the week to the instructor. This was partly due to the girls wanting to add "one more thing" and also the general excitement of having their families join us for the showcase of projects. Of these 33 projects, 9 reflected some connection to an occupational role as described in the original story narratives. The extent to which a career-oriented story was "programmed" varied significantly among these projects. As seen in Figure 2, one girl literally programmed her story about a vet operating on a kitten. Once she began the project she found many story-relevant objects and behaviors already available in the Alice library.

In contrast, other career-related projects made relatively light use of the girls' story concepts. The marine biologist project (Figure 3) features a professional character, but her behaviors are just those available for swimmers in the library. The teacher character in Figure 4 is played by the generic "Alice" object and conducts her activities largely through speech bubbles. It may be that the introduction of more "career-related" characters and behaviors would enhance girls' development of such narratives.

The use of sound and color showed up on many of the projects and in Figure 4 each scene the teacher has speaks in different colored speech bubbles. The daily reflections reflected these creative goals from the very beginning as many options were presented, "*I like how I can personalize the game so much.*" and "*I enjoyed searching through all the objects and looking at all our choices for characters in our story/game the most.*"

Figure 4. Teacher with multi-color speech bubbles

Figure 5. Zombie extras

On occasion a girl who wrote a story with a career theme had trouble finding a particular character for her story and resorted to using characters introduced in lessons throughout the week. As one girl stated when asked what she liked least about the day, "*Seeing how many objects you don't have.*" This may be why an occasional zombie, mummy or ghost showed up in a project that began with a career theme (Figure 5).

All of the projects had some form of interactivity for the viewer (i.e., the end user), but only two can be considered a "game". To be classified as a game, the project needed user activity, rule(s) and an end goal. The game involving the marine biologist required the user to select all the fish within 10 seconds; the game with the meteorologist had the character rescue all animals and people before the hurricane hit. Most of the projects were an interactive story that is, a story that plays out but stops at points for input from the viewer or user. For instance, the vet story included a second scene where the viewer can click on various objects to make the cat meow or end the story. More than half of the girls programmed user input using both the keyboard and mouse. For example, in one story the characters would begin speaking if the user pressed Tab; users could also use the mouse to move around the world by moving the camera. A problem with this manipulation was that the character speaking might no longer be in view even though it was still talking. This tended to be a frustration we had trouble avoiding throughout the week.

4. DISCUSSION

In this paper, we have briefly summarized a study conducted during a summer camp for middle school girls. As observed in another study of middle school girls using Alice [32], our students eagerly built in interactivity and narrative goals in their projects; they presented their work with pride in the final day showcase for family and friends. The girls left at the end of the week with smiles on their faces, quickly capturing phone numbers and email addresses from each other, and with parents asking for more information on the Alice programming tool so their daughters could continue working on their projects.

Our survey results offer a picture that is consistent with the general observations of girls engaged with and enjoying their project work. Although self-reported orientation to careers in computing showed only a modest increase by the end of the camp ($p=.07$ for the pre-post difference), we did discover an interesting pattern of relationships among initial attitudes and reactions to the camp activities. Feelings of success (confidence, fun) were predicted by generally positive attitudes about computing and computer professionals, but not CS career orientation. However initial career orientation combined with feelings of success to predict final ratings of CS career orientation. This pattern of results suggests that while the Alice projects may not have been equally engaging for all girls, those who did find them engaging were more likely to feel increased positivity about CS careers.

Though we observed plenty of smiles, we also acknowledge that there is considerable room for improvement for workshops of this sort. Some of the girls were receptive to the request to think about future careers, as indicated in the ways they integrated these ideas into their projects; however not all the girls were able (or wanted) to do this. It may be that some needed additional scaffolding at the start of such an activity rather than a simple request to write a short story that includes something about careers. Having a short discussion at the end of the first day in which different girls talked about "what they want to do" might have helped all the girls get engaged more readily.

Another lesson concerns the types of career topics or themes presented to girls from this age population; we saw this in reactions to the guest speakers. Recall that the camp featured a series of guest speakers who discussed their work in medicine, security and fashion design, commenting on the role of technology in such jobs. Although we did not probe the girls' reactions to these talks in detail, their daily reflections suggested the most positive reaction was to the fashion design speaker, as in "*I liked listening to the guest speaker. She had some pretty interesting things to say!*" We also noticed that this guest speaker was the only one who combined her interest in a 'non-technology' related career to computers; this seemed to inspire some girls to include models, fashion store owners and seamstresses into their stories. In contrast, one girl commented about the medical professional, "*I'm not at all interested in that form of career.*" Others mentioned in their personal reflections that their least favorite part of the day was a guest speaker who talked about computer security.

Approximately one quarter of the girls tried to create stories or games that had career-related characters or themes; in the future we will consider how to encourage such thinking more broadly. Furthermore, we do not have enough data to determine whether or how much having career elements in an Alice project influenced how the girls felt about the overall experience. We used several mechanisms to encourage the girls to consider career interests in the context of Alice project work and it will remain for future work to disentangle their influences.

The girls also wanted more time to work on their own projects. While a few found it interesting to visit the campus labs, many were not pleased to interrupt their project work. We are uncertain how to avoid this in the future; perhaps having the lab tours prior to any exercises and individual work may help the girls with their frustrations of being pulled away from their projects. Or, it may simply be that working on the projects is more beneficial than other activities like lab tours. Again, future work will be needed to examine these workshop design tradeoffs.

5. FUTURE WORK

More work is required to understand how to better involve students, especially middle school students, in solving technology-related problems that are personally relevant. Guest speakers, lab tours and project examples need to relate to the age level of the participants attending the program. Solving relevant, meaningful problems is beneficial for all age groups. Although thoughts about potential careers may be emerging the middle school age, it is important to maintain an atmosphere of fun.

We are currently working on the development of mini-workshops which are 1-2 hours in length to introduce middle school girls to key programming concepts. Our approach is to begin each workshop with a pedagogical example that introduces a new concept and that can then be customized, revised or expanded by the girls. We have observed in our experiences thus far that long days can be overwhelming and can lead to frustration. Incorporating these mini-workshops into an after school or Saturday program for young girls who meet regularly would provide the girls the time needed to learn the task, the opportunity to meet others like themselves who like to create interactive stories and perhaps give other girls a chance to give computers a try.

6. ACKNOWLEDGMENTS

We thank Jessica Purdum, Valerie Werth, Emily Enslin and Terri Cummings for their assistance throughout the week and Jan Mahar and the University staff for logistics support. This work was supported by the University's Equal Opportunity Planning Committee (EOPC) and by the NSF under the Broadening Participation in Computing initiative (CNS-0634337).

7. REFERENCES

[1] Blackhurst, A. and Auger, R. Precursors to the Gender Gap in College Enrollment: Children's Aspirations and Expectations for Their Futures. *Professional School Counseling*, 11, 3 2008), 149 - 158.

[2] Blumenfeld, P. C., Soloway, E., Marx, R. W., Krajcik, J. S., Guzdial, M. and Palincsar, A. Motivating Project-Based Learning: Sustaining the Doing, Supporting the Learning. *Educational Psychologist*, 26, 3/4 (Summer/Fall91 1991), 369.

[3] Bruckman, A., Biggers, M., Ericson, B., McKlin, T., Dimond, J., DiSalvo, B., Hewner, M., Ni, L. and Yardi, S. "Georgia

computes!": improving the computing education pipeline. In *Proceedings of the Proceedings of the 40th ACM technical symposium on Computer science education* (Chattanooga, TN, USA, 2009).

[4] Clegg, T., Gardner, C., Williams, O. and Kolodner, J. Promoting learning in informal learning environments. In *Proceedings of the Proceedings of the 7th international conference on Learning sciences* (Bloomington, Indiana, 2006). International Society of the Learning Sciences.

[5] Craig, M. and Horton, D. Gr8 designs for Gr8 girls: a middle-school program and its evaluation. In *Proceedings of the Proceedings of the 40th ACM technical symposium on Computer science education* (Chattanooga, TN, USA, 2009).

[6] Creamer, E., Burger, C. and Meszaros, P. Characteristics of high school and college women interested in information technology. *Journal of Women and Minorities in Science and Engineering*, 102004), 67-78.

[7] de Bruyn, E. H. and Cillessen, A. H. N. Leisure Activity Preferences and Perceived Popularity in Early Adolescence. *Journal of Leisure Research*, 40, 3 2008), 442-457.

[8] Denner, J., Werner, L., Bean, S. and Campe, S. The Girls Creating Games Program. *Frontiers: A Journal of Women Studies*, 26, 1 (03 2005), 90-98.

[9] Goldman, R., Eguchi, A. and Sklar, E. Using educational robotics to engage inner-city students with technology. In *Proceedings of the Proceedings of the 6th international conference on Learning sciences* (Santa Monica, California, 2004). International Society of the Learning Sciences.

[10] Groover, T. R. Using games to introduce middle school girls to computer science. *J. Comput. Small Coll.*, 24, 6 2009), 132-138.

[11] Hardnett, C. R. Gaming for middle school students: building virtual worlds. In *Proceedings of the Proceedings of the 3rd international conference on Game development in computer science education* (Miami, Florida, 2008).

[12] Hu, H. H. A summer programming workshop for middle school girls. *J. Comput. Small Coll.*, 23, 6 2008), 194-202.

[13] Javidi, G. and Sheybani, E. Digispired: digital inspiration for interactive game design and programming. *J.Comput.Small Coll.*, 24, 3 2009), 144-150.

[14] Kelleher, C., Pausch, R. and Kiesler, S. Storytelling alice motivates middle school girls to learn computer programming. In *Proceedings of the Proceedings of the SIGCHI conference on Human factors in computing systems* (San Jose, California, USA, 2007).

[15] Kiuru, N., Aunola, K., Vuori, J. and Nurmi, J.-E. The Role of Peer Groups in Adolescents' Educational Expectations and Adjustment. *Journal of Youth and Adolescence*, 36, 8 2007), 995-1009.

[16] Kolodner, J. L. Educational implications of analogy - A view from case-based reasoning. *Am. Psychol.*, 52, 1 (Jan 1997), 57-66.

[17] Lau, W. W. Y., Ngai, G., Chan, S. C. F. and Cheung, J. C. Y. Learning programming through fashion and design: a pilot summer course in wearable computing for middle school students. In *Proceedings of the Proceedings of the 40th ACM technical symposium on Computer science education* (Chattanooga, TN, USA, 2009).

[18] Linda S Kekelis, Ancheta, R. W. and Heber, E. Hurdles in the Pipeline: Girls and Technology Careers. *Frontiers: A Journal of Women Studies*, 26, 1 2005), 99 - 112.

[19] Maloney, J. H., Peppler, K., Kafai, Y., Resnick, M. and Rusk, N. *Programming by choice: urban youth learning programming with scratch.* ACM, City, 2008.

[20] Nicholson, H. J., Collins, C. and Holmer, H. Youth as People: The Protective Aspects of Youth Development in After-School Settings. *Annals of the American Academy of Political and Social Science*, 5912004), pp. 55-71.

[21] Piaget *Intellectual Evolution from Adolescence to Adulthood.* Karger AG, City, 2008.

[22] Pivkina, I., Pontelli, E., Jensen, R. and Haebe, J. Young women in computing: lessons learned from an educational & outreach program. In *Proceedings of the Proceedings of the 40th ACM technical symposium on Computer science education* (Chattanooga, TN, USA, 2009).

[23] Resnick, M. Distributed constructionism. In *Proceedings of the Proceedings of the 1996 international conference on Learning sciences* (Evanston, Illinois, 1996). International Society of the Learning Sciences.

[24] Rodger, S. H., Hayes, J., Lezin, G., Qin, H., Nelson, D., Tucker, R., Lopez, M., Cooper, S., Dann, W. and Slater, D. Engaging middle school teachers and students with alice in a diverse set of subjects. In *Proceedings of the Proceedings of the 40th ACM technical symposium on Computer science education* (Chattanooga, TN, USA, 2009).

[25] Saad, A., He, L., Reed, J., Strauser, E. and Hannigan, P. *Ossabest: a comprehensive itest project for middle and high school teachers and students*. ACM, City, 2008.

[26] Starks, J. Organizing a tech camp for teachers. In *Proceedings of the Proceedings of the 4th conference on Information technology curriculum* (Lafayette, Indiana, USA, 2003).

[27] Stockard, R., Klassen, M. and Akbari, A. Computer science higher education pipeline. *J. Comput. Small Coll.*, 20, 3 2005), 102-113.

[28] Tsagala, E. and Kordaki, M. Critical factors influencing secondary school pupil's decisions to study computing in tertiary education: Gender differences. *Education and Information Technologies*, 12, 4 2006), 281-295.

[29] Vygotsky, L. S. *Mind in Society: The Development of Higher Psychological Processes*. Harvard University Press, City, 1978.

[30] Webster, J. and Martocchio, J. J. Microcomputer playfulness: Development of a measure with workplace implications. *MIS Quarterly*, 16, 2 1992), 201-226.

[31] Weisgram, E. S. and Bigler, R. S. Girls and science careers: The role of altruistic values and attitudes about scientific tasks. *Journal of Applied Developmental Psychology* 272006), 326-348.

[32] Werner, L., Denner, J., Bliesner, M. and Rex, P. Can middle-schoolers use Storytelling Alice to make games?: results of a pilot study. In *Proceedings of the Proceedings of the 4th International Conference on Foundations of Digital Games* (Orlando, Florida, 2009).

[33] Werner, L. L., Campe, S. and Denner, J. Middle school girls + games programming = information technology fluency. In *Proceedings of the Proceedings of the 6th conference on Information technology education* (Newark, NJ, USA, 2005).

Camps on a Shoestring: How We Survived a Summer

Deborah L. Dunn
Stephen F. Austin State University
Department of Computer Science
Nacogdoches, TX
(936) 468-2508
ddunn@sfasu.edu

Robert G. Strader
Stephen F. Austin State University
Department of Computer Science
Nacogdoches, TX
(936) 468-2508
rstrader@sfasu.edu

Michael M. Pickard
Stephen F. Austin State University
Department of Computer Science
Nacogdoches, TX
(936) 468-2508
mpickard@sfasu.edu

ABSTRACT
As we are well aware, there has been a significant nationwide decline in enrollment for computer science programs, as well as other STEM fields. One of the primary reasons the lack of participation and diversity in the STEM fields is becoming increasingly important is the potentially adverse effect it may have on the U.S. work force. Many successful programs have been put in place to combat this decline. But how do the small regional universities with limited resources and a limited "audience" (with limited resources) contribute to the field? In this paper we will discuss the mechanisms that may be implemented for smaller schools to address the decline in CS enrollment. This includes the ability to put in place programs which could allow more educators to become a part of the solution.

Categories and Subject Descriptors: K.3.2
[**Computers and Education**]: Computer science education – *tools and curriculum, computer science education*

General Terms
Management, Design, Experimentation, Languages.

Keywords: Computer Science Education, Teacher Training, STEM, Camps, Robotics, Storytelling, Outreach.

1. INTRODUCTION
All students (K-16) need to be exposed to new ideas for their long term education and to deal with current (and future) trends in technologies. There is a need for basic STEM understanding even if the student is not interested in pursuing a career in a STEM field. Thus the goal is two-fold -- we want to introduce those students interested in STEM to the concepts and tools for future growth and we want to provide an appropriate view of technology for those who will not continue directly in a STEM field, but whose lives will be directly or indirectly influenced by STEM developments. One way to handle this need is through camp offerings. The approaches we have taken involve enrolling individual students (campers) and K-12 teachers (workshop participants) in programs designed to increase exposure to various technology trends. The future approach will be to continue with the current offerings, but begin addressing a wider variety of groups and mentors (teacher-student pairs).

SIGCSE'11, March 9–12, 2011, Dallas, Texas, USA.

2. BACKGROUND
There are numerous studies and associated statistics regarding enrollment trends, underrepresented groups, and diversity in the field of computer science [2, 4, 7, 8, 14, 19]. Studies have been performed which examine the characteristics that seem to hinder students' interest in technology [11, 12, 19]. The primary inhibiting factors cited are the lack of knowledge about what the field has to offer and the lack of role models.

In recent years, summer camps targeting middle and high school students have been popping up across the country. Studies have shown that participation in these programs has increased awareness of the computer science discipline (e.g., [1, 9, 18]). In some instances, they may have resulted in modest enrollment increases in the field of computer science [17] and many believe that increased interest in computer science may be attributable to these types of activities [3, 9, 17].

Although we hope to increase interest in computer science through summer camps, we also believe that all students should also be exposed to technology and the computer science discipline during their middle and high school years on a regular basis. This can be achieved by developing role models competent in the technology field. Several studies indicate that middle and secondary school students select their future career based on those of their role models, both at home and in school [2, 13, 15]. Participants in the surveys specifically cite the lack of role models in technology fields as the primary reason for not choosing computer science as an area of study. A second factor affecting interest in technology is the lack of exposure to professionals in the fields of computer science. Given this lack of exposure, students don't have a clear picture as to what the fields truly are and what they have to offer [5, 10]. Our research activities, therefore, focus on measuring the effect of introducing technology and working with K-12 educators to integrate technology into their classrooms, as well as exposing middle and high school students to the computer science discipline.

Successful programs have been developed and implemented to create professional development workshops for teachers [3, 16], and to fund summer camps for elementary, middle and secondary school students [3, 6, 15, 18]. These programs are used to increase interest and participation in STEM areas. However, how can this be accomplished if your resources and those of your prospective audience are limited?

3. CAMPS ON A BUDGET
3.1 Constraints
Important concerns for the development and presentation of camp experiences is the set of constraints that are involved in such

offerings. The following is a selected list of limitations that may be encountered.

Financial constraints can be a dual problem -- limits on the participants and limits on the host institution. Elite residential camps can cost thousands of dollars for the participants (i.e., CMU Robotics Academy, http://www.education.rec.ri.cmu.edu/, and IDtech camps, http://www.internaldrive.com/). Although these provide an excellent experience, the high cost and the focus on those planning a career in one of the STEM fields can significantly limit participation. For the local host institution, camp offerings may be an outreach or extension activity with limited support from the home institution or may be initiated by a small number of individuals with no direct support.

Time constraints can have a significant impact. One concern is the amount of time that is devoted to a topic before it becomes a class rather than a "fun" camp activity. Also, there is usually a limit to the amount of time that sponsors (those conducting the camps) have to devote to camp. In addition, scheduling is a major issue with sports camps, band camps, and similar academic camps, as well as teacher preparation activities all competing for the same few weeks during the summer. If the activity is spread over a regular term or academic year, numerous conflicts can also arise.

Personnel demands may require a large staff including a director for overall control, budget, and scheduling issues; a technical coordinator for tools, kits, and coordination of concepts and ideas related to STEM fields; instructors/presenters for the actual activities; and assistants to help with problems, both technical and behavioral. Locating or developing qualified individuals can take time and delays are particularly critical in the case of assistants. Early in the spring semester, we began discussions with several students whom we thought might be appropriate to assist with the camps. Often it is difficult to find students willing to devote a portion of their summer to work with the program, especially if they do not live in the immediate area. However, we were able to provide a stipend that made it an attractive summer option.

Facility constraints can limit work areas, presentation areas, break and food areas, and venues for entertainment or physical activities. Equipment and software issues are a major concern with the need to monitor security and replace failing equipment quickly. Our temporary successful solution in the area of equipment was to seek donations, but that will be difficult to continue or to scale upward.

Participant constraints can include dates (conflicts with other camps and activities as indicated above), times (such as mornings vs. afternoons vs. "all day"), family activities (vacations or trips), day care, logistical support (transportation issues), and the camp duration.

Geographic considerations include limited access to local businesses and industries, which provide work opportunities and other support for students interested in STEM or learning about STEM fields.

3.2 The Development Process

The process that we chose to undertake is indicated by the timeline in the Table 1.

Table 1. Camp/Workshop Timeline

Task	Comments
Investigate funding opportunities	In addition to national funding sources, we investigated state and local sources, including our home institution.
Brainstorm camp offerings	We produced a survey for the surrounding schools to determine what might be appealing to students and teachers. This was completed approximately one year in advance so that we could determine the number and types of camps/workshops to be offered.
Outline camp ideas	Shortly after tabulating the survey results, we presented a selected list of offerings to the local school district. This was done in order to receive feedback on offerings, timings, and other information.
Begin the implementation plan for camps	After determining the camp/workshop offerings, we began developing brochures, soliciting funding/donations, and general publicity.
Investigate teacher opportunities	Approximately 6-8 months prior to the summer, we began the process of determining what was necessary to award continuing education credit for teachers. In addition, the local school district provided grant funding for students and teachers to attend the program.
Pilot study	In March, we implemented a 2-day pilot study using a local Girl Scout troop. This enabled us to get feedback on timings, activities, and age appropriateness of the camp.
Prepare camp/workshop	Shortly after the pilot study, we finalized the camp/workshop descriptions, fine tuning of timing, and a determination of additional resources required.
Develop plans for evaluation and dissemination	This was vital for an ongoing program. We used pre and post surveys along with informal feedback.
Implementation of camps and workshops	This should be done well in advance (6-8 months). Our checklist included: • arrange for venue (will include facilities and housing if camps are residential) • schedule camps and workshops • purchase hardware, software, and other resources • arrange for instructors • hire and train assistants • advertise camps/workshops • conduct camps/workshops
Project Wrap Up	Evaluation, dissemination, future plans

Although not universal, for camps on a shoestring many if not most of these steps will need to be completed. The complete timeline should also include an indication as to the person responsible for the task and the status of each task as the project progresses.

3.3 Our Implementation

A short survey was designed to determine the needs and interest of the local K-12 teachers and their perception of the interest of students in the local school district. Each of the potential camps/workshops was described for the teachers and the description of each is included in Table 2.

Table 2. Camp/Workshop Descriptions

Name	Description
Introduction to Storytelling Using Virtual Worlds	This utilizes an animated programming environment first developed at Carnegie-Mellon University. Attendees will learn to quickly and easily create applications using a 3D virtual world tool.
A Taste of Computer Science in the Modern World	This emphasizes the use of computers in the classroom including development of multimedia presentations, effective internet research, database design and development, and how to establish a web presence.
Introduction to Robotics	Fundamental concepts of robotics, including robot construction and programming.
GIS and Computing	Held in cooperation with the Columbia Regional Geospatial Center, this session would involve mapping, remote sensing, geographical information systems, and associated computing.
Introduction to Games and Simulation Using Greenfoot	Introductory programming, design, modeling, graphics, storytelling, and game development are among the topics.

The first survey question targeted the teachers and was designed to measure their desire for offerings that support their work (see Figure 1). The second question allowed the teachers to indicate where they felt middle school student interest might be focused (see Figure 2). The average rating was calculated based on the category "Non Interest at all" being a 0 and "Sign me up today!" being a 5. Additional questions covered the type of camp (resident vs. day), the times offered (day and month), and the grade levels our camps should target (middle school vs. high school).

From the point of view of the teachers, it is clear that there is a significant divergence of interests. For the proposed camp offering with a teacher (mentor) and a student this was a disappointing result. An even more disappointing result however is the very high percentage of responses in the "no interest at all" column, especially for teachers. Also of interest to us was the discrepancy between what the teachers would like (basically use of fundamental tools to use in their classroom), what teachers thought the students would like (those same tools), and what the students are actually interested in (robotics and storytelling).

Based on the results of the district survey indicated above, offerings were divided into two groups: workshops for teachers, and camps for the students. The first group included workshops on the Microsoft® Office tools Excel® and PowerPoint® and developing instructional Web pages with about a dozen participants each. The small size was primarily due to a structural problem in the dissemination of information at the district level.

The second group included robotics camp offerings using the Lego® Mindstorms® NXT platform and a storytelling camp offering using Alice (CMU, www.alice.org). The goal of each of these camps was to present STEM concepts, tools, and ideas in an enjoyable way that allowed for open inquiry and experimentation with immediately available help and feedback in a two-person team based environment. The appropriate competition or demonstration, along with the post evaluation survey indicated that the campers

1. Please indicate your interest level in each of these opportunities:

	No interest at all	Somewhat interested	Interested	Very Interested	Sign me up today!	Rating Average	Response Count
"Introduction to Storytelling Using Virtual Worlds"	40.2% (35)	20.7% (18)	14.9% (13)	13.8% (12)	10.3% (9)	2.33	87
"A Taste of Computer Science in the Modern World"	26.4% (23)	21.8% (19)	25.3% (22)	17.2% (15)	9.2% (8)	2.61	87
"Introduction to Robotics"	58.6% (51)	20.7% (18)	12.6% (11)	3.4% (3)	4.6% (4)	1.75	87
"GIS and Computing"	50.0% (44)	25.0% (22)	12.5% (11)	4.5% (4)	8.0% (7)	1.95	88
"Introduction to Games and Simulation Using Greenfoot"	30.3% (27)	21.3% (19)	28.1% (25)	11.2% (10)	9.0% (8)	2.47	89
						answered question	91
						skipped question	0

Figure 1. Teacher Interest

2. Please indicate the level of appeal each of these opportunites might have to middle school students:							
	No appeal at all	Might appeal to some students	Many students would be interested	Most students would be very interested	Students will sign up as soon as possible!	Rating Average	Response Count
"Introduction to Storytelling Using Virtual Worlds"	10.9% (7)	37.5% (24)	32.8% (21)	15.6% (10)	3.1% (2)	2.63	64
"A Taste of Computer Science in the Modern World"	3.2% (2)	30.2% (19)	46.0% (29)	19.0% (12)	1.6% (1)	2.86	63
"Introduction to Robotics"	4.7% (3)	23.4% (15)	35.9% (23)	29.7% (19)	6.3% (4)	3.09	64
"GIS and Computing"	8.1% (5)	37.1% (23)	32.3% (20)	21.0% (13)	1.6% (1)	2.71	62
"Introduction to Games and Simulation Using Greenfoot"	4.8% (3)	15.9% (10)	36.5% (23)	31.7% (20)	11.1% (7)	3.29	63
						answered question	64
						skipped question	27

Figure 2. Teacher Perception of Student Interest

enjoyed their experience and mastered the appropriate concepts. A typical day's schedule consisted of an introduction (usually the only "lecture-like" activity with a very short duration); design and construction activities; a break; construction and programming activities; lunch; a movie/video or similar activity; a break; experimentation, contest or demonstration activities; and a summary/preview presentation. Presentations were generally done with pictures, photos, and diagrams. Lists and prose were kept to a minimum. Each day (except the last) a newsletter with pictures of each participant was sent home with the student.

3.4 Project Funding

We were fortunate that grant money was available from the local school district for support of teachers to attend the workshops. The cost of the workshops varied, depending on the number of days, but our charge was $75 per day. Other surrounding school districts also funded the cost of teachers to attend the workshops and several teachers from surrounding school districts provided their own funding. Thus, although no money was available for us to provide incentives such as teacher stipends, the costs associated with attending the workshops for many were covered externally. An additional workshop for robotics and "data logging" experimentation was held for teachers. This offering had a very low enrollment and, while successful, will need to be repeated with more participation. Workshops costs were for snacks, a box lunch, insurance (a requirement of our institution), and workshop materials.

We were also fortunate to be in a situation such that grant funds were available from the local school district to support many of the students who attended the camps. The school district offered a series of "Learning Camps" through the district and our camps were listed as part of that program. This enabled us to reach students who otherwise would have been unable to attend the camps for financial reasons. We charged $225 per camp, with each camp lasting four days. We provided snacks, lunches at the cafeteria, insurance, camp materials, T-shirts, and prizes. We also paid a student assistant to help during the camps.

Two companies provided additional funding for the summer camps and teacher workshops. One company (located approximately 140 miles from the university) provided T-shirts (for the teacher workshops), bags, pens, pencils, highlighters, and notepads. Another local company provided ten new Dell laptops (approximately $700 each). Both of these companies are strong supporters of the university and recruit our computer science graduates on a regular basis.

Finally, it is important to explore internal funding opportunities. We received money to purchase hardware and software from the Office of Research and Sponsored Programs. Most colleges have some variation of this program and they are an excellent source of support, both financially as well as providing feedback regarding potential funding sources. We were also able to obtain funding to purchase additional hardware and software from the Provost and Vice President for Academic Affairs. These grants were used to assist us with the pilot study and with the subsequent camps and workshops. The Department of Computer Science provided the materials necessary for brochures, posters, mailings to school districts, and course materials.

Of course, one of the most important levels of support is that of the faculty members who coordinated and participated in the program. We were quite fortunate to have the support of the Provost and Vice President for Academic Affairs. Outreach programs are particularly important to our institution (as is true of many regional universities), so we were able to obtain support in terms of funding summer salaries for two faculty members to develop and implement the summer program. Without this support, the program would not have been implemented. It is our hope that within three years the program becomes self-sustainable.

3.5 Project Coordination

Despite the fact that resources are limited, it is imperative that effective project coordination is in place. The project coordinator is responsible for all aspects of the program. The obvious factors are program development, staffing, registration and billing, and scheduling. However, it also includes funding issues, facility coordination, food services, parking, insurance, and any other issues that will (and we underscore WILL) arise. And of course, with all of these elements there is a certain level of paperwork involved. Fortunately, discipline issues were minimal and did not add to the administrative overhead.

4. RESULTS

Four teacher workshops were developed and conducted over the course of two weeks in early June. The teachers represented five schools from the local school district (one high school, two middle schools, and two elementary schools) and two schools outside of the local area. The workshops addressed an interest in the tools and techniques that are helpful to teachers on a daily basis. These workshops were well received by the participants who commented on learning many new things even through several of them had been using these tools for years. However, this did bring out a critical problem concerning the quality and quantity of equipment and software available to the participants at their home institutions for ongoing support.

Three summer camps were developed and conducted in June and July. The students represented 11 schools, some of which are part of the local district, while several were located in other school districts (including one student from a distant metropolitan area). Students were representative of public schools, private schools, and home schooling. Almost 40% of the participants were females, and less than 25% were minorities.

There were two robotics camps offerings targeted at slightly different middle school age groups. The camp was centered around a two person team with each having one robotics kit, a support tool kit (pens, pencils, flashlight, notepads, ruler, etc.) and a laptop computer. Because of the nature of the robotics kits, this organization worked well and allowed considerable flexibility in the problem solving approaches a team could take. All teams worked together on the initial building and programming exercises. For the challenges and the contest, some teams chose to work on the body construction and the programming together while other teams specialized with one member doing the design and construction of the platform while the other member focused on programming a solution to the task. All teams remained relatively stable (including one "switch" and "switch back") and generally worked well together. When one team member was tired the other member generally took over. The final activity was a contest (robot race) to which the parents were invited, pictures were taken, and prizes awarded. Pre- and post-surveys were administered, with questions pertaining to mobile robots, hardware concepts, and software concepts. For both camps, there was a 67% improvement in terms of concepts of mobile robots. During the first camp, there was an increased understanding of hardware (24%), but a decrease in terms of software (-20%). During the second camp, the timing of the post-survey was adjusted, which resulted in better results. Hardware understanding increased 57%, while software understanding increased 33%.

The storytelling camp using Alice was focused on an individual approach with each camp participant learning the tool and creating their own content. Although each participant completed a common series of exercises, each story was unique. Limited concepts and ideas concerning character development, plot features, and setting issues were introduced. Much of the time was spent on learning tools and there was quite a bit of interaction among the participants as they moved from station to station to see what others had done. Most of the content development was guided by the exercise examples or the participant's own interests. The final activity was to invite the parents of the campers to a showing of each of the stories. A final "quiz" was administered to test their understanding of Alice and programming concepts. The average score was over 80%, with only two questions receiving an average score less than 75%.

5. CONCLUSIONS

In general, we found that it was possible to conduct successful teacher workshops and summer camps on a shoestring. We found that looking first and foremost to the institution was a viable option. Most institutions have the means available to provide funding for promising projects and/or programs. We sought funding from the academic "side" of the institution, as well as the research "side". In addition, public schools across the nation are looking for avenues to improve technology in the school systems. Often they have many opportunities to secure funding for teacher development and student programs and are merely looking for a source to partner with in order to exploit the available opportunities.

The teacher workshop program provides just as much (if not possibly more) promise for research opportunities as the camps for middle and high school students. Studies specifically cite the lack of role models in technology fields as the primary reason for not choosing computer science as an area of study. A second factor affecting interest in technology is the lack of exposure to professionals in the fields of computer science. This became crystal clear during the teacher workshop program. How do we facilitate the integration of technology into the classroom when there is no room in the curriculum? How do we deal with introducing technology into the K-12 classroom when their resources are limited? Many expressed concern that we were teaching with software that they would not be able to use when they returned to their own campus.

Of more concern is the fact that many of the academic curricula are "full" with required courses leaving no room for computer science. The career technology curriculum may have some room (and funding), but background and preparation needs must be matched carefully. Those of us in higher education are quite insulated from the requirements placed on teachers at the K-12 level. Academic requirements, measurements and testing requirements, professional development requirements, and much more place heavy demands on the teachers. To the extent possible, these workshop and camp offerings can provide additional expertise and facilities that may be unavailable to a small school district.

The student camp program provided much needed feedback in terms of target age, activities that are successful as well as those that are not so successful, and timing for future camps. Although we included rising 6th graders in the camps, it was determined that for a 5-day, 8 hour camp, this was a bit young. Future camps will target rising 7th graders and older.

In general, the workshops and camps were successful based on the formal and informal feedback received. We are now in the process of evaluating the changes necessary or desired to improve future camp offerings based on this feedback.

5.1 Future Work

Based on the high interest indicated in Figure 2, a multimedia camp offering with a gaming theme is currently under development. This camp is planned around learning tools and building music and art assets in a game environment. The issues of privilege level for software, quality of support tools, and Internet access are concerns that need to be addressed. From a creative standpoint, the largest concern is working in a controlled environment with sophisticated tools for an extended period of time and then moving into an unstructured environment to create a new experience through experimentation.

In addition, a more advanced robotics camp is under development which will provide an opportunity to introduce more advanced STEM concepts. We are also exploring the possibility of joining with other campus entities to form a STEM center which would extend the expertise and role models available to teacher and student participants. Finally, we are exploring additional funding opportunities for teacher and student stipends.

6. ACKNOWLEDGMENTS

This project was conducted under grants from the Stephen F. Austin State University Research Enhancement Program and, the Provost and Vice President for Academic Affairs' Innovation in Teaching - Activities Involving Undergraduate Research Program. We would also like to extend our thanks to the Nacogdoches Independent School District, Reynolds and Reynolds, and Elliott Electric Supply for their support of the program.

7. REFERENCES

[1] Adams, J. Alice, Middle Schoolers & The Imaginary Worlds Camp, *Proceedings of the 38th SIGCSE Technical Symposium on Computer Science Education (ACM SIGCSE Bulletin)*, Volume 39, Number 1 (March 2007), 307-311.

[2] Balcita, A., Carver, D., and Soffa, M. Shortchanging the Future of Information Technology: The Untapped Resource, *Inroads (ACM SIGCSE Bulletin)*, Volume 34, Number 2 (June 2002), 32-35.

[3] Bruckman, A., Biggers, M., Ericson, B., McKlin, T., Dimond, J., DiSalvo, B., Hewner, M., Ni, L., and Yardi, S. "Georgia Computes!": Improving the Computing Education Pipeline, *Proceedings of the 40th SIGCSE Technical Symposium on Computer Science Education (ACM SIGCSE Bulletin)*, Volume 41, Number 1 (March 2009), 86-90.

[4] Camp, T. The Incredible Shrinking Pipeline, *Communications of the ACM*, Volume 40, Number 10 (October 1997), 103-110.

[5] Carter, L. Why Students with an Apparent Aptitude for Computer Science Don't Choose to Major in Computer Science, *Proceedings of the 37th SIGCSE Technical Symposium on Computer Science Education (ACM SIGCSE Bulletin)*, Volume 38, Number 1 (March 2006), 27-31.

[6] Cliburn, D., Weisheit, T., Griffith, J., Jones, M. Rackley, H., Richey, E., and Stormer, K. Increasing the Interest of Elementary Age Students in Computer Science through Day Camps, *Proceedings of the 2004 ASCUE Conference*, June 6-10, 2004, Myrtle Beach, SC.

[7] Cohoon, J. Must There Be So Few? Including Women in Computer Science, *Proceedings of the 25th International Conference on Software Engineering*, (May 2003), 668-674.

[8] Cohoon, J. Toward Improving Female Retention in the Computer Science Major, *Communications of the ACM*, Volume 44, Number 5 (May 2001), 108-114.

[9] Craig, M., and Horton, D. Gr8 Designs for Gr8 Girls: A Middle-School Program and its Evaluation, *Proceedings of the 40th SIGCSE Technical Symposium on Computer Science Education (ACM SIGCSE Bulletin)*, Volume 41, Number 1 (March 2009), 221-225.

[10] Cukier, W., Shortt, D., and Devine, I. Gender and Information Technology: Implications of Definitions, *Inroads (ACM SIGCSE Bulletin)*, Volume 34, Number 4 (December 2002), 142-148.

[11] Fisher, A., and Margolis, J. Unlocking the Clubhouse: The Carnegie Mellon Experience, *Inroads (ACM SIGCSE Bulletin)*, Volume 34, Number 2 (June 2002), 79-83.

[12] Fisher, A., Margolis, J., and Miller, F. Undergraduate Women in Computer Science: Experience, Motivation and Culture, *Proceedings of the 28th SIGCSE Technical Symposium on Computer Science Education (ACM SIGCSE Bulletin)*, Volume 29, Number 1 (March 1997).

[13] Jepson, A. and Perl, T. Priming the Pipeline, *Inroads (ACM SIGCSE Bulletin)*, Volume 34, Number 2 (June 2002), 36-39.

[14] Mahmoud, Q. "Revitalizing Computer Science Education", *IEEE Computer* (May 2005), 98-100.

[15] Moorman, P. and Johnson, E. Still A Stranger Here: Attitudes Among Secondary School Students Towards Computer Science, *Proceedings of the 8th Annual Conference on Innovation and Technology in Computer Science Education (ACM SIGCSE Bulletin)*, Volume 35, Number 3 (June 2003), 193-197.

[16] Peterson, L. and Benham, D. Overview of the CyberTech-ITEST Project: An Initiative to Attract and Prepare Underrepresented Students for Tomorrow's Careers in the Computing Sciences, *Proceedings of the 37th SIGCSE Technical Symposium on Computer Science Education (ACM SIGCSE Bulletin*), Volume 38, Number 1 (March 2006), 453-455.

[17] Pivkina, I., Pontelli, E., Jensen, R. and Haebe, J. Young Women in Computing: Lessons Learned from an Educational & Outreach Program, *Proceedings of the 40th SIGCSE Technical Symposium on Computer Science Education (ACM SIGCSE Bulletin)*, Volume 41, Number 1 (March 2009), 509-513.

[18] Pollock, L., McCoy, K., Carberry, S., Hundigopal, N., and You, X. Increasing High School Girls' Self Confidence and Awareness of CS through a Positive Summer Experience, *Proceedings of the 35th SIGCSE Technical Symposium on Computer Science Education (ACM SIGCSE Bulletin)*, Volume 36, Number 1 (March 2004), 185-188.

[19] Wardle, C. and Burton, L. Programmatic Efforts Encouraging Women to Enter the Information Technology Workforce, *Inroads (ACM SIGCSE Bulletin)*, Volume 34, Number 2 (June 2002), 27-31.

Introducing Computer Science to K-12 through A Summer Computing Workshop for Teachers

Jiangjiang Liu
Department of Computer Science
Lamar University, Beaumont TX 77706
001 (409) 880-7741
Jane.liu @lamar.edu

Cheng-Hsien Lin
Department of Sociology, Social Work, and Criminal Justice
Lamar University
Beaumont, TX 77706
001 (409) 880-8339
cheng-hsien.lin@lamar.edu

Ethan Philip Hasson and Zebulun David Barnett
Department of Computer Science
Lamar University
Beaumont, TX 77706
001 (409) 880-7741
{ephasson, zdbarnett} @lamar.edu

ABSTRACT

In this paper, we describe a one-week summer computing workshop for teachers to improve computer science education in K-12. Our workshop focuses on using Scratch and Alice, two programs used to make simple games and animations, to introduce computing concepts to teachers in computer, technology, math, and science at all K-12 levels to expose students to computing at an early age and to reach more students. During the workshop the teachers developed curriculum materials for the subjects they will teach in the following semesters with the help of our workshop tutors. We present our workshop strategies, lessons learned, and assessment results in this paper.

Categories and Subject Descriptors

K.3.2 [**Computers and Education**]: Computer and Information Science Education – *computer science education, information systems education, curriculum.*

General Terms

Design, Experimentation, Human factors.

Keywords

Computer science education, computing education K-12 outreach, K-12 teacher training, computing workshop.

1. INTRODUCTION

The Bureau of Labor Statistics predicts that the demand for computer and mathematical occupations will grow more than twice as fast as the average for all occupations in the U. S. over the next decade [1]. However, in recent years the number of degrees earned in computer science (CS) has been decreasing. According to the Higher Education Research Institute (HERI) at the University of California, Los Angeles (UCLA), between 2000 and 2005 there was a 50% decline in the number of newly declared CS majors and a 70% decline in the number of incoming freshmen who expressed an interest in CS majors [5]. A similar steep decline has been reported in the Computing Research Association (CRA) Taulbee Survey during the 2000's. As a result, we might face a shortfall in the computing workforce in the next decade. Even though the 2008-2009 CRA Taulbee Survey reported a two-year increase of 14% in the total number of undergraduate majors with a broader number of degree programs included in the statistics, the College Board discontinued the Advanced Placement (AP) Computer Science "AB" course following the May 2009 exam administration due to the low participation in that course [5]. Therefore, the education crisis in computer science still draws critical attention and compels us to produce more computer scientists.

SIGCSE'11, March 9–12, 2011, Dallas, Texas, USA.

2. RELATED WORK AND OUR CONTRIBUTIONS

K-12 teachers play an important role in preparing students for college and helping them thrive in the 21st-century global workforce. In this section, we first present successful work that has been done on K-12 teacher training to improve computer science education. Then, we discuss our contributions.

2.1 Related work

In 2004, UCLA started a yearly program called the Summer Institute for Advanced Placement Computer Science (APCS) teachers [10]. The course consisted of a series of lectures and curriculum development opportunities. Additional learning materials were made available online to supplement the knowledge gained during the course. As a result of this program, the number of students in APCS courses in Los Angeles Unified School District (LAUSD) tripled.

In 2010, Marquette University led the Computational Thinking for the Sciences workshop, a three-day summer workshop for high school science and mathematics teachers. The goal of the workshop was to emphasize the deep connections between the natural sciences, mathematics, and computer science through activities and simulation development. The program used VPython, a visual extension to the popular Python programming language. The hope was to broaden computational thinking to the natural sciences and attract new students to employ the computational tools they will utilize in the future. The teachers left the workshop better able to understand and teach computer science concepts. It was proof that simple simulations, conditional logic, functions, and graphics could be taught in a very short period of time [1].

Saint Joseph's University became the site at which the Teacher Enrichment in Computer Science course was based **Error! Reference source not found.**. The course spanned two weeks; the first focused on teaching Alice itself while the second allowed teachers in attendance to develop Alice-based curricula that would engage their students. In the year this program started, only nine students were enrolled in AP CS courses, but due to the ongoing effort, that number rose to thirty-three for the 2008-2009 school year.

The Georgia Institute of Technology put in an effort to improve the aging computer science education pipeline currently employed in the state of Georgia by offering a series of teacher workshops to influence CS teaching styles in a positive manner [3]. Participants were presented with example texts, lecture slides, and assignments to greatly reduce the time needed to develop individual curriculum. Half of the participants reported they had been able to effectively use the knowledge and materials gained from the workshop.

Carnegie Mellon University offered the CS4HS and CSbots programs which targeted high school computer science teachers [2, 12]. Many workshop materials are shared on the CS4HS website and the CS4HS model has now spread to many other universities.

Through the medium of bioinformatics, Winona State University conducted a computer science based workshop geared for K-12 science teachers between 2006 and 2008 [12]. Because the creation of teaching materials was the main focus of this workshop, teachers were encouraged to participate in the development of bioinformatics curricula that would meet Minnesota state standards for K-12 science education. In the span of three years, thirteen of the fifteen participants were able to use the materials created during the workshop to enrich their teaching styles and content.

2.2 Our contributions

Our work builds upon some of the successful strategies for teacher workshops mentioned in the related work. During the 2009 NSF-BPC (National Science Foundation Broaden Participation in Computing) annual meeting, we were given many suggestions with regard to workshop organization, recruitment, and lecture development by the Georgia and UCLA projects. The Georgia project offered many useful lecture materials for reference. Next, we briefly discuss our main contributions.

1. Much of the related work that was referenced targeted high school computer science teachers. However, most students that enter high school have already lost interest in computer science. Therefore, our workshop targeted teachers in computer, technology, math, and science at all K-12 levels to expose students to computing at an early age and to reach more students.
2. A ready-to-use flash drive with all workshop materials was provided to each workshop participant. The workshop materials included Scratch and Alice software, software installation instructions, workshop presentations, and a pre-/post-test for each lecture session. In addition, curriculum materials developed by the teachers were added at the end of the workshop, and the participants kept the flash drives and will use the materials in their own classes in following semesters.
3. The afternoon sessions were dedicated to curriculum development; the teachers used knowledge that they gained during the workshop to develop their own curriculum materials they could directly take back and use in their classrooms. The materials are also available on our program website for other K-12 teachers. During this curriculum development time, our department undergraduates and graduate students served as tutors to aid the participants if they were ever confused or unsure.
4. All workshop materials were prepared by two undergraduates under the guidance of the computer science faculty. The guidance was exceptional, and they learned a tremendous amount while running the workshop. They developed and presented all the materials for the workshop. In addition, we have partnered with two on-campus NSF-sponsored programs. Both programs provided the support of workshop tutors, which offered great help to the teachers without any computing background.
5. Workshop assessment was conducted by an outside program evaluator, and all assessment forms are available if any other programs would like to adopt them for their own use.
6. All workshop materials were organized based on different topics and workshop lectures were videotaped. Teaching and lecture assessment materials are available online, which makes it easy for other programs to adopt these materials for one-day, two-day, and week-long workshops.

3. WORKSHOP ORGANIZATION

3.1 Recruitment, objectives, and schedule

We built partnerships with school districts in the surrounding areas of our university, especially districts with a majority of minority and economically challenged students. The workshop targeted K-12 teachers who teach computer, science, technology, and math in our partner school districts. The snapshot of surrounding school district profiles is given in Table 1. Most of the school districts have a large population of minority and economically disadvantaged students.

Table 1: Snapshot of District Profiles

Students	Beaumont	Port Arthur	Orange	Bridge City
Total Students	19,463	9,263	2,655	2,516
African American	63.9%	50.9%	65.3%	0.4%
Hispanic	14.1%	37.2%	5.6%	8.3%
White	18.8%	4.9%	28.2%	87.7%
Economically Disadvantaged	66.4%	84.5%	77.9%	31.5%
Teachers by Highest Degree Held	**Beaumont**	**Port Arthur**	**Orange**	**Bridge City**
Bachelors	72.0%	80.0%	85.5%	90.1%
Masters	26.5%	19.5%	14.5%	9.9%

In order to help the teachers understand fundamental computing concepts, we made the following workshop objectives.

1. Program Structure and Flow of Execution: be able to identify the start of the program and trace its path.

2. Objects: know what makes up an object and how it can be used to simplify program design.
3. Methods/Functions: know how and when to create a separate method to accomplish a small, recurring task.
4. Conditional Branches: how they affect the normal flow of execution based on the value of a Boolean expression.
5. Variables: know how to create, change, and use three basic types of variables: numbers, strings, and Booleans.
6. Loops: how they can be used to repeat a sequence of steps until a certain condition is met.
7. User Input: how to accept and use data and keystrokes supplied by the user to trigger events, call methods, and store information about the user for later use in the program.
8. Boolean Logic: understand core Boolean operands such as NOT, OR, and AND and how they can be used in while loops or conditional branches.
9. Parallel Processing: know how to use parallel processing and how to handle some issues associated with it.

Computing concepts for each session and workshop schedule are given in Table 2 & 3. All afternoon sessions were curriculum development sessions for the first three days. Participants worked on the curriculum materials that they can use in the subjects they will teach in the following semesters. On the fourth day, each participant presented and shared their work with the other participants in order to get feedback and finish the project on the fifth day.

Table 2. Computing Concepts by Session

Session	Computing Concepts
Scratch 1 (SS-1)	Objects, blocks, flow of execution
Scratch 2 (SS-2)	User input
Scratch 3 (SS-3)	Conditional Branching
Scratch 4 (SS-4)	Loops/Repeats
Scratch 5 (SS-5)	Variables
Scratch 6 (SS-6)	Boolean Expressions, Message Passing, Arrays
Alice 1 (AS-1)	Blocks, objects, methods, loops
Alice 2 (AS-2)	Conditional Branching
Alice 3 (AS-3)	Boolean Variables
Alice 4 (AS-4)	Parallel processing, inequality, functions
Alice 5 (AS-5)	Boolean logic, while loop, custom functions
Alice 6 (AS-6)	Conditional branching, parallel processing, methods, loops

3.2 Teaching materials - Scratch

The first session went as planned. All of the participants were attentive and able to follow the outline we devised with little trouble. Due to the highly organized layout of Scratch's user interface, becoming familiar with the program takes very little time. The concepts of blocks and scripts were simple enough to understand and visualize, but the idea of objects (referred to as sprites in Scratch) took them a while longer to wrap their heads around. However, it would have taken much more time if we had used a non-visual programming language such as Java or C++. Visual programs like Scratch are very helpful for beginners when it comes to learning the object-oriented programming paradigm. Results of the post-test indicate that participants' knowledge of general programming concepts grew substantially after this session. Since the first session was only thirty minutes in length, we were unable to include a programming project at the end.

Table 3. Workshop Schedule

Schedule	**Day**				
	Mon.	Tue.	Wed.	Thur.	Fri.
9:00am-9:30am	Opening Session	SS-4	AS-1	AS-4	CD
9:30am-10:00am	SS-1				
10:00am-11:00am	SS-2	SS-5	AS-2	AS-5	CD
11:00am-12:00pm	SS-3	SS-6	AS-3	AS-6	Closing Session
1:00pm-3:00pm	Curriculum Development (CD)	CD	CD	Curriculum Presentation	

In session 2, participants were shown how to gather input from the user and how that input can be used to affect a running program. They were also introduced to the problems that arise when invalid input is accepted by a program. These concepts, while basic to experienced programmers, were eye-opening to the participants in the workshop, which garnered new-found respect for the programs they use on a daily basis and the programmers that created them. At the same time, the almost magical aura felt by non-programmers when dealing with the inner-workings of computers began to vanish, and they realized that they too would be able to tell the computer what to do in a way they had not dreamed of before. The project for session 2 encouraged the participants to create a short story driven by user input. After the session two project had been completed, the participants were eager to begin work on their own projects, which would later become the material they would use in their classrooms. Session two lasted twice as long as we had anticipated, which pushed session three into the evening curriculum development time-slot. This was an ongoing problem throughout the workshop that forced us to drop half of the Alice sessions.

Session 3 focused on conditional branching as a way of altering the normal flow of execution in a program based on a Boolean expression. With this knowledge, the participants were able to start work on their question and answer games, using if/else blocks to handle right and wrong answers. Even though complex programs could now be made, the programs grew quickly and became unmanageable.

In session 4, we introduced the concept of loops in Scratch. This had been the missing piece in many of the participant's projects and was quickly adopted to minimize the number of blocks needed and provided functionality not possible without loops. The participants spent quite a bit of time working on the session project, which had required the generation of a grid using three nested loops. At this point, the participants began to express interest in seeing how other participants, as well as the instructors, had implemented their designs and started to appreciate elegant, well-formed programs.

Variables were the primary topic of Session 5. Participants were shown how to create, change, use, and delete variables through the use of multiple examples. By storing input in variables, the participants realized that data could be used more than once in whatever order desired. The session project showcased behavior not possible without the use of variables, taking the average of a set of values entered by the user. This idea was later used as the basis for the curriculum project of one of the participants.

Session 6 contained the most complex concepts covered in the workshop. Participants were introduced to advanced Boolean expressions, message passing, and arrays. Boolean expressions did not receive very much attention during or after the session. This was probably a result of the lack of need of advanced Boolean expressions in their own programs. Message passing, however, turned out to be quite useful. It allowed two or more sprites to "talk," which had not been possible since the explanation of objects in session one. After completing the project designed to showcase the power of message passing, participants wasted no time incorporating the functionality in their curriculum development projects. In hindsight, the inclusion of arrays was probably unwise during a workshop that only lasted a single week. Participants wishing to use arrays in their project had a difficult time with the actual implementation and had to rely heavily on the assistance of the tutors. Even so, the performance of the participants was remarkable considering the vast amount of information they had received in such a short period of time.

3.3 Teaching materials - Alice

After the Scratch sessions, all of the core computing concepts had been introduced and discussed; this made it easier for the participants to learn Alice for the remainder of the workshop. Alice, a more advanced programming environment, appeared relatively user un-friendly in comparison to Scratch, which caused most participants to redirect their attention and time back to their Scratch-based curriculum projects. Due to the amount of content in the Scratch sessions, we were unable to cover half of the planned materials for Alice sessions in the five-day schedule of the workshop. Therefore, Alice is not discussed much in this paper.

4. WHAT WORKS AND WHAT DOES NOT

4.1 What works

The workshop's success is to be credited to the strengths identified by the participants in their assessment answers, interviews, and comments. The characteristic most highly praised was the tutors assigned to each participant. The tutors were right beside the participants for the duration of the workshop, always ready to help and encourage. The participants appreciated the fact that instead of giving them the answer or showing them what to do, the tutors would ask questions to encourage the participants to think for themselves and learn from experimentation. This is a crucial skill to not only computer scientists, but all educated people regardless of field.

The organization of the Scratch sessions was also appreciated by the participants. Based on a concept-by-concept progression, the sessions were easy for everyone to understand and keep up with. The content in each session built on the content taught in the previous sessions, forming a strong framework on which to link related concepts together in order to memorize and utilize them to create the desired program behavior. The projects at the end of the sessions proved to be extremely useful for the participants. Even though the time allowed for the project was often overrun, the hands-on experience was necessary to solidify the concepts in their minds while at the same time, causing them to feel good about themselves when a project was completed successfully. Curriculum development time was frequently used as an extension of the session project development time to complete difficult projects or modify existing projects in creative ways that often could then be incorporated into curriculum ideas.

The inclusion of the presentation slides and notes on the flash-drive of each of the participants turned out to be a great idea. Participants who were having trouble keeping up with the current presentation were able to refer to previous slides in the session and even previous sessions to figure out what they had missed or misunderstood.

Even if the end goal of the workshop is to provide K-12 students with a better education in the field of computer science, or science in general, the immediate goal is to further educate the teachers themselves so they can pass that knowledge on to their students. Teachers know that children in school greatly enjoy "playing" on computers. By using Scratch to teach curriculum, students are more apt to participate and equate fun with learning. For most teachers present, this was the first time they had been exposed to programming in any form that, in some respect, is like being shown a new way of thinking: computational thinking. Programming forces you to break large, complex problems down into much smaller ones that can be easily solved; this allows you to put the small solutions together in such a way so that the original problem is solved. This is an impossible skill to master in a single week, but one week is certainly long enough to experience a taste of what is possible. To quote one of the attendees in the post–workshop interview, "What a difference 5 days makes because you come in knowing nothing, a blank slate, tomorrow is our last day, we feel like geniuses now." This is the kind of thinking that will inspire future generations of students to continue to love knowledge and keep searching for answers.

Participants were strongly encouraged to apply concepts they had learned during the morning sessions to projects they felt would be useful in their respective classrooms. Since the goal of this workshop is to better prepare K-12 students for college, the time devoted to curriculum development is crucial, as it ensures the teachers will be able to use their knowledge of Scratch to enrich their students' learning experience. This opportunity turned out to be the high-point of the day for most participants and gave them a chance to really put their new knowledge to work. Project ideas were very creative and often incorporated characters, stories, animations, and sounds. Some of the final projects are summarized in Table 4.

4.2 What does not work

While the workshop as a whole was a success, there are always things that could be done to improve the experience and learning potential of the five day period allowed. A common complaint among the participants was the inability for them to work on their curriculum development projects at their place of residence during the week. Some of the participants had to travel many miles in order to attend the workshop and had decided to stay at local hotels for the duration. Once these participants had returned to the

Table 4. Curriculum Developed during Workshop

Curriculum Material	Subject	Grade
Scratchy Takes a Test, earth science quiz	Science	5th
Learning to Skip Count by a Variety of Numbers, players count by twos, threes, etc.	Mathematics	$2^{nd} – 8^{th}$
Teaching Math Concepts Using Interactive Games, players average sets of numbers	Mathematics	$6^{th} – 8^{th}$
Cartesian plane review, animation explaining Cartesian plane terminology	Mathematics	7th & 8th
"Danger Zone" interactive book quiz	Reading (Students with learning disabilities)	9th - 12th

hotel at the end of each day, they had nothing to occupy their time until the next day. They expressed great interest in taking their projects with them on the provided flash-drives to fix bugs and go over the presentations again to further cement the concepts in their minds. Since the flash-drives were collected by us at the end of the day to back-up their project files and journal entries, we were unable to grant them permission to keep them at the end of the day.

Another issue made known to us during the workshop was the vastly different style of the Alice sessions. While the Scratch sessions had been concept oriented, the Alice sessions were presented in a step-by-step fashion that chronicled the creation of a small game. The concept-first approach turned out to be a very natural, progressive way to learn which none of the participants had a problem with; however, many participants were quick to voice their displeasure after going through the first Alice session. In addition to the style change, the end-of-session projects were also dropped. This meant that the participants were no longer able to immediately apply what they had learned during the session, leaving many formerly eager participants feeling overwhelmed and unprepared for later sessions.

At the end of the workshop, it was the general consensus among the participants that while Scratch and Alice are interesting and useful programs, they should not have both been presented in the same week. After three days at the workshop, the participants were beginning to feel comfortable with Scratch and were eager to learn more about it and continue working on their Scratch-based projects. When Alice was introduced on the fourth day, they found themselves trying to divide their time between the two, and as a result, most disregarded Alice completely in order to continue working with Scratch. It should be noted that this decision was not based on their perception of Alice's potential usefulness in a K-12 classroom, but simply the manner in which it was thrust upon them at the last minute. Most participants expressed an interest in returning to a later workshop in which Alice would be its sole focus to properly learn and appreciate this unique program.

5. ASSESSMENT RESULTS

An outside program evaluator worked with us and developed a pre-/post-workshop survey with 58 questions, post-workshop interview, and pre-/post-test with 5 questions for each lecture session. We received thirty-two applications and accepted twenty applicants. In total, seven teachers participated in the workshop. Of the participants that submitted a pre-workshop assessment, five hold a bachelor's degree and one has a master's degree. The grade level distribution turned out quite even: two participants teach high school, two teach junior high school, and one teaches elementary school. Their teaching areas range from math, computer lab, reading, science, biology, and even special education. Of the questions in the assessment, one questioned the participant's competency in the programs being used throughout the workshop. The majority answered they were unfamiliar and unsure of the potential of both Scratch and Alice. In another portion of the survey, the participants were required to rank themselves on their understanding of the objectives of the workshop.

The pre-/post-surveys we gave at the beginning and end of the workshop allowed the participants to rank themselves in their conceptual knowledge of the items taught. With a total score of 50, the average score was 19 and the highest score was 38 for the pre-workshop scores. The second highest score was 22 and the participant with the lowest score totaled 10. The post-workshop assessment yielded impressive results. Two participants ranked themselves 50 out of 50, and the others more than doubled their score. The low after the workshop scored a 31 but this score was three times their pre-workshop assessment score.

After the workshop, participants also took part in a face-to-face interview to determine how effective the workshop had been. Six out of seven participants strongly agreed that the workshop increased their computer-related knowledge and skills, while all seven indicated that they plan to incorporate Scratch into their classroom curriculum. In the interview, multiple participants suggested that Scratch and Alice should be separated into two separate weeks to allow enough time to properly cover both programs. All participants greatly appreciated the assistance the one-on-one tutors were able to provide and the hands on activities that were so vital in their learning; without them, the workshop would not have been as successful as it was. We also developed a number of questions to measure the amount of material the participants would take away from the workshop. We did this by creating pre-/post-questions to test their knowledge of the subject discussed during the session. Table 5 shows average percentage increases ranging from 8.06% to 123.96%. This survey was created alongside a five-scale rubric that was used for grading. The rubric is given in Table 5.

6. CONCLUSIONS

We describe a one-week summer computing workshop for teachers to improve computer science education in K-12. Our workshop focuses on using Scratch and Alice to introduce computing concepts to teachers in computer, technology, math, and science at all K-12 levels to expose students to computing at an early age and to reach more students. During the workshop, the teachers develop curriculum materials for the subjects they will teach in the following semesters. Based on the pre-/post-workshop assessment results, the participants were able to indicate their confidence in the concepts presented in the workshop. In the pre-workshop assessment, the results indicate a confidence level average of 19 out of 50. However, the average post-workshop assessment score was 42 out of 50, indicating a 121% increase in confidence level. A similar change was observed upon analysis of the pre-/post-tests (graded by workshop instructors) for each session. Participants scored an average 2.77 out of 5 on the pre-session tests, but that score rose to 4.24 on the post-session test, which resulted in a 62.76% knowledge level increase.

Table 5. Pre-Test and Post-Test Assessment Results

Session	Pre-Test Average score/ per participant in each session	Post-Test Average Score/per participant in each section	Score changed (percentage increased)
SS-1	1.86	4.16	+2.3(123.96%)
SS-2	2.14	4.39	+2.24(104.76%)
SS-3	2.72	4.5	+1.78(65.75%)
SS-4	3.72	4.43	+0.71(19.10%)
SS-5	3.86	5	+1.14(29.53%)
SS-6	2.27	4.16	+1.89(83.01%)
AS-1	2.07	3.48	+1.41(67.87%)
AS-2	3.53	3.82	+0.29(8.06%)

Rubrics:

1. Posses no understanding of the concept
2. Posses very little understanding of the concept
3. Posses little understanding of the concept
4. Posses moderate understanding of the concept
5. Posses complete understanding of the concept

7. ACKNOWLEDGMENTS

This project was supported by a US National Science Foundation grant #0846053. All opinions reflected in this paper are those of the authors and not necessarily those of NSF.

8. REFERENCES

[1] Ahamed, S. I., Brylow, D., Ge, R., Madiraju, P., Merrill, S. J., Struble, C. A., and Early, J. P. 2010. Computational Thinking for the Sciences: A Three Day Workshop for High School Science Teachers. In Proceedings of the 41st ACM Technical Symposium on Computer Science Education (Milwaukee, Wisconsin, USA, March 10 - 13, 2010). SIGCSE '10. ACM, New York, NY, 42-46. DOI= http://doi.acm.org/10.1145/1734263.1734277.

[2] Blum, L. and Cortina, T. J. 2007. CS4HS: An Outreach Program for High School CS Teachers. In Proceedings of the 38th SIGCSE Technical Symposium on Computer Science Education (Covington, Kentucky, USA, March 07 - 11, 2007). SIGCSE '07. ACM, New York, NY, 19-23. DOI= http://doi.acm.org/10.1145/1227310.1227320.

[3] Bruckman, A., Biggers, M., Ericson, B., McKlin, T., Dimond, J., DiSalvo, B., Hewner, M., Ni, L., and Yardi, S. 2009. "Georgia computes!": Improving the Computing Education Pipeline. In Proceedings of the 40th ACM Technical Symposium on Computer Science Education (Chattanooga, TN, USA, March 04 - 07, 2009). SIGCSE '09. ACM, New York, NY, 86-90. DOI= http://doi.acm.org/10.1145/1508865.1508899.

[4] Bureau of Labor Statistics, 2009. Occupational Outlook Handbook, 2010-2011 Edition. DOI=http://www.bls.gov/oco/oco2003.htm.

[5] College Board, 2008. Important Announcement about AP Computer Science AB, April 2008. DOI= http://apcentral.collegeboard.com/apc/public/courses/teachers_corner/195948.html.

[6] Computing Research Association Taulbee Survey, 2010. Computing Degree and Enrollment Trends. DOI= http://www.cra.org/govaffairs/blog/wp-content/uploads/2010/03/CRATaulbee-2010-ComputingDegreeandEnrollmentTrends.pdf.

[7] Cooper, S., Dann, W., and Harrison, J. 2010. A K-12 College Partnership. In Proceedings of the 41st ACM Technical Symposium on Computer Science Education (Milwaukee, Wisconsin, USA, March 10 - 13, 2010). SIGCSE '10. ACM, New York, NY, 320-324. DOI= http://doi.acm.org/10.1145/1734263.1734371.

[8] Ericson, B., Guzdial, M., and Biggers, M. 2007. Improving Secondary CS Education: Progress and Problems. In Proceedings of the 38th SIGCSE Technical Symposium on Computer Science Education (Covington, Kentucky, USA, March 07 - 11, 2007). SIGCSE '07. ACM, New York, NY, 298-301. DOI= http://doi.acm.org/10.1145/1227310.1227416.

[9] Goode, J. 2008. Increasing Diversity in K-12 Computer Science: Strategies from the Field. In Proceedings of the 39th SIGCSE Technical Symposium on Computer Science Education (Portland, OR, USA, March 12 - 15, 2008). SIGCSE '08. ACM, New York, NY, 362-366. DOI= http://doi.acm.org/10.1145/1352135.1352259.

[10] Goode, J. 2010. Connecting K-16 Curriculum & Policy: Making Computer Science Engaging, Accessible, and Hospitable for Underrepresented Students. In Proceedings of the 41st ACM Technical Symposium on Computer Science Education (Milwaukee, Wisconsin, USA, March 10 - 13, 2010). SIGCSE '10. ACM, New York, NY, 22-26. DOI= http://doi.acm.org/10.1145/1734263.1734272.

[11] High Education Research Institute (HERI), 2006. CIRP Freshman Survey. University of California at Los Angeles. DOI= http://www.gseis.ucla.edu/heri/freshman.html.

[12] Lauwers, T., Hamner, E., and Nourbakhsh, I.. 2010. A Strategy for Collaborative Outreach: Lessons from the CSbots Project. In Proceedings of the 41st ACM technical symposium on Computer Science Education (Milwaukee, WI, USA, March 10-13, 2010).SIGCSE '10. ACM, New York, NY, USA, 315-319. DOI= http://doi.acm.org/10.1145/1734263.1734370.

[13] Lin, C., Zhang, M., Beck, B., and Olsen, G. 2009. Embedding Computer Science Concepts in K-12 Science Curricula. In Proceedings of the 40th ACM Technical Symposium on Computer Science Education (Chattanooga, TN, USA, March 04 - 07, 2009). SIGCSE '09. ACM, New York, NY, 539-543. DOI= http://doi.acm.org/10.1145/1508865.1509050.

Panel

CS Fulbright Experiences Abroad

Joel Adams
Calvin College
Dept of Computer Science
Grand Rapids, MI 49546
+001-616-526-8666
adams@calvin.edu

Brent Baas
Dept of Computer Science
LeTourneau University
Longview, TX 75607
+001 903 233 3341
brentbaas@letu.edu

Suzanne Buchele (Moderator)
Dept of Math and Computer Science
Southwestern University
Georgetown, TX 78626
+001 512 863 1361
bucheles@southwestern.edu

PANEL SUMMARY

The Fulbright Scholar Program is the flagship academic exchange program of the U.S. Department of State that provides the opportunity for U.S. Scholars to teach and/or conduct research at institutions abroad. Every year, approximately 1100 American scholars travel to approximately 125 countries to lecture, conduct research, and participate in a wide variety of academic and professional activities for one or more academic terms, up to one year. The Fulbright Scholar program is open to US Citizens with a Ph.D. or equivalent professional or terminal degree and university teaching experience [1]. In this panel, three computer science professors who have completed a total of five Fulbright grants in the last 12 years offer their experiences, anecdotes, and insights of the Fulbright Scholar program. The goal of the panel is to promote and inform the CS Education community about benefits of the Fulbright Scholar program, address questions or misconceptions regarding the program, and present realistic expectations for both the application process and the program itself. Each of the three panelists will present a 15 minute overview of their Fulbright experiences, leaving ample time for an interactive question and answer period.

Categories and Subject Descriptors

K.3.0 [**Computers and Education**]: General

General Terms

Experimentation

Keywords

Fulbright, exchange programs, academic exchange, teaching abroad, intercultural learning, Africa, developing countries.

Joel Adams, *Calvin College*

Joel is Professor and Chair of the Department of Computer Science at Calvin College. He has been fortunate enough to receive two Fulbright grants: a 1998/99 10-month Fulbright lecturing/research grant to the *University of Mauritius* (which was subsequently extended to 13 months), and a 2005 5-month lecturing/research grant to the *Technology University of Iceland* (TUI), now the School of Engineering of *Reykjavik University*.

Both Mauritius and Iceland are island countries (with *very* different climates). Joel enthusiastically recommends visits to island countries, as they have most of the same problems to solve as mainland countries, but different (fewer) resources with which to do so. Between their resource differences and their isolation from mainland influences, the people of island countries may solve a given problem very differently from their mainland counterparts, making them fascinating places to visit.

In Mauritius, Joel taught courses on *GUI Design* (Java), *Computer Organization*, *Compiler Construction*, and a faculty seminar on Java. He also worked on a computer networking research project, and mentored faculty members who were working on their PhDs. The first day of classes, Joel was surprised to find that about half of the students in his CS classes were women. This delightful surprise led to a collaborative research project with two Mauritian colleagues and two publications [2][3].

In Iceland, Joel taught courses on *GUI Design* (Java) and *Distributed Computing*. He also consulted with the school's administration about CS curriculum, and mentored upper-level students in building a Beowulf cluster.

Joel found that after being a "stranger in a strange land" on a Fulbright, he has greater empathy for his international students here in the US. He also found that by allowing a person to spend an extended period of time in a country, a Fulbright grant allows a person to make more friends and come to a deeper understanding of a country's people and culture than is possible as a tourist.

Joel's wife Barbara and his two sons Roy and Ian accompanied Joel on both grants. On arrival in Mauritius, Roy was 2 years old; Ian was 2 months old, so schooling was not an issue. Mauritius has a British-style health care system, so getting immunizations and other medical care was not a problem. In Iceland, Roy was in 3rd grade and Ian was in 1st grade. Both attended a neighborhood school where instruction was in Icelandic, with *Icelandic as a Second Language* courses. In Mauritius, the family lived in an ocean-side bungalow and bought a pickup truck for transportation; in Iceland, they lived in a Reykjavik apartment and used public transit. Neither grant was stress-free for their family, but both of these periods are remembered as among the best of their lives.

SIGCSE'11, March 9–12, 2011, Dallas, Texas, USA.
ACM 978-1-4503-0500-6/11/03.

Brent Baas, *LeTourneau University*

Brent is a Professor and Chair of the Department of Computer Science at LeTourneau University. He was awarded a 10-month Fulbright Scholar lecturing/research grant to *Mekelle University* in Mekelle, Ethiopia for the 2002-2003 academic year. With little knowledge of Ethiopia, and even less of the reclusive northern region of Tigray, Brent was able to secure a letter of invitation from *Mekelle University* in support of his application for a multi-discipline award. Initial contact with *Mekelle University* was difficult, complicated by poor written English skills, long email delays, and frustrating phone connections.

Brent was assigned to the Electrical Engineering Faculty in the school of Engineering on the Arid Campus on a plateau overlooking the city. In addition to teaching several courses for the department, he was given partial responsibility for the operation of the Computer Center, which in turn was responsible for the campus-wide computer literacy program.

Throughout the course of the year, Brent was assigned a variety of additional responsibilities as Ethiopian faculty members received funds to study abroad, and administrators were away from the campus. Encouraged by the strong interest among students in computing, he wrote a number of technology-related articles for the school newspaper and helped to develop a Computer Science stream in the Electrical Engineering curriculum. One of the highlights of the year was the formation of and participation in the weekly activities of SOTA, the student special interest group in computing.

Brent went to Ethiopia with his wife and three children ages 11, 8, and 5, eight laptop computers, and four forty-pound boxes of books. Due to the lack of English-speaking schools in the city of Mekelle, his wife homeschooled the children. In spite of numerous challenges, including electricity and water outages, for both himself and more frequently for his family, they all cherish their memories of being cultural ambassadors. A deep respect and empathy for the people and cultures of northern Ethiopia continue to make an impact on their lives.

Suzanne Buchele, *Southwestern University*

Suzanne is an Associate Professor of Computer Science in the Mathematics and Computer Science at Southwestern University. She was awarded a 10-month lecturing/research grant to *Ashesi University College* in Accra, Ghana for the 2006-2007 year. She first heard of Ashesi, a relatively new Ghanaian University attempting a liberal arts model of education, through a SIGCSE mailing list posting, and began email correspondence with Ashesi University officials about 6 months prior to beginning the Fulbright application process. At Ashesi, Suzanne taught four computer science classes and advised undergraduate thesis students. In addition, she helped institute a computer science department review of courses and students, helped found an administrative academic programs committee, and helped the University move toward an Honor Code policy (which the University adopted in 2008). Partway through the first year, she applied to the Fulbright program to renew the grant for a second year, which was granted for 2007-2008.

During the second year, in addition to teaching computer science classes and advising thesis students, Suzanne was asked to fill in as Acting Dean of Academic Affairs due to the unexpected temporary leave of the existing Dean. As Acting Dean, she was responsible for all adjunct and regular faculty and the overall academic program, and participated in weekly Executive Committee meetings, which deliberated on all major decisions of the University. In addition to being able to serve the University in a time of need, the professional growth Suzanne experienced by being propelled into a Dean position at a foreign University was monumental.

In research and professional work, during the first year Suzanne organized a group of undergraduate students to investigate the One Laptop Per Child Project and its possible application to Ghana. Work continued with one student through the first summer, which culminated in a paper co-authored with the student [4]. The second year, OLPC began work with the various ministries to bring a pilot program to Ghana. Suzanne was included in initial meetings with OLPC and Ghana ministry representatives, and helped organize a workshop in October 2007 for ministry and educational professionals to learn more about the OLPC project. As the OLPC project moved forward, Suzanne served on the Implementation Team for the OLPC pilot projects in Ghana. As part of the team, she helped implement the Accra pilot consisting of one 4th grade class, and worked closely with those students and their teacher.

Suzanne was accompanied to Ghana by her husband, a pastor who took family leave and participated in missionary and ministerial activities during their stay in Ghana, and their three children (aged 15, 14, and 11 at the start of their two years), who attended an American International School in Accra. The entire family enjoyed the vibrancy of the culture, the kindness of the people, and the spiciness of the food. After a time, power outages, which were frequent, became inconsequential. Water is still treated as a scarce resource in the family, even after the return to plentiful running water flowing right from the tap. Although professionally Suzanne's Fulbright experience was extremely fruitful and informative, she believes that the personal benefits to herself and her family were of equal or greater value.

ACKNOWLEDGMENTS

Our thanks to the United States Department of State and the Fulbright Scholar program for giving us the opportunity to teach and research abroad.

REFERENCES

[1] Council for International Exchange of Scholars (CIES) Fulbright, http://www.cies.org/about_fulb.htm, accessed Aug 12, 2010.

[2] Adams, J., Baichoo, S., and Bauer, V. An Expanding Pipeline: Gender in Mauritius. Proc. of the 34th SIGCSE Technical Symposium on Computer Science Education (February 2003). 59-63.

[3] Adams, J., Baichoo, S., and Bauer, V. Women Embrace Computing in Mauritius. Encyclopedia of Gender and Information Technology. Idea Group Reference, Hershey, PA, 2006. 1258-1266.

[4] Buchele, S. and Owusu-Aning, R. The One Laptop Per Child (OLPC) Project and Its Applicability to Ghana. In Proceedings of the 2007 International Conference on Adaptive Science and Technology (Accra, Ghana, December 10-12, 2007). ICAST '07, IEEE Press, 113-118.

CS Principles: Piloting a New Course at National Scale

Owen Astrachan (Moderator)
Computer Science
Duke University
Durham NC 27708
1 919 660 6522
ola@cs.duke.edu

Tiffany Barnes
Computer Science
University of North Carolina, Charlotte
Charlotte NC 28223
1 704 687 8577
tiffany.barnes@uncc.edu

Daniel D. Garcia
Electrical Eng. & Computer Science
University of California, Berkeley
Berkeley CA 94720
1 510 517 4041
ddgarcia@cs.berkeley.edu

Jody Paul
Mathematical & Computer Science
Metropolitan State College of Denver
Denver CO 80202
1 303 556 8435
jody@acm.org

Beth Simon
Computer Science & Engineering
University of California, San Diego
La Jolla CA 92093
1 858 534 5419
bsimon@cs.ucsd.edu

Larry Snyder
Computer Science & Engineering
University of Washington
Seattle WA 98195
1 206 543 9265
snyder@cs.washington.edu

SUMMARY

Since 2008, the National Science Foundation, in collaboration with the College Board, has been developing a "Computer Science: Principles" curriculum to "introduce students to the central ideas of computing and computer science, to instill ideas and practices of computational thinking, and to have students engage in activities that show how computing and computer science change the world" [1]. We report on the initial pilot of the CS Principles curriculum at five universities in 2010-2011. Beginning in fall 2011, additional colleges will pilot the course while five high schools will teach CS Principles as a rigorous Advanced Placement (AP) high school course with an associated exam. It is important to note that this is in addition to, not as a replacement for, AP Computer Science A, a Java programming course.

In this special session, suitable for both college and high school faculty, the five instructors from the 2010-2011 pilot institutions will describe their classes, the piloting experience (teaching under a microscope), and the successes and failures of their offerings. Emphasis will be placed on the following: mapping the CS Principles curriculum to the specific needs of a college or university, and how others can use or modify the existing materials for pilots at their schools.

Categories and Subject Descriptors

K.3.2 [**Computers and Education**]: Computer and Information Science Education – *computer science education*

General Terms

Measurement, Experimentation, Standardization

Keywords

principles, advanced placement, AP, pilot class, general education, concepts, fluency, high school, big ideas, computational thinking, introductory course

SIGCSE'11, March 9–12, 2011, Dallas, Texas, USA.
ACM 978-1-4503-0500-6/11/03.

1. INTRODUCTION

High school computing courses are generally limited to two choices: AP Computer Science A (an introductory programming course) or a vocational class emphasizing application skills such as using a spreadsheet or word processor. Although useful, neither of these types of courses illustrate the richness and intellectual depth of Computer Science. If we can excite future generations about computing, we have a chance to empower them to become leaders and innovators in our rich and rewarding field. However, since public education in the US is decentralized, where each state controls its curriculum, there is little chance of a consistent, high quality curriculum emerging quickly.

The most feasible path to introducing a high quality, rigorous CS curriculum in high schools is by leveraging the existing Advanced Placement (AP) infrastructure [3]. AP curricula are set by a central process described by the National Research Council [2], and implemented by the CollegeBoard.

This special session reports on progress towards answering the "what" and "how" of teaching essential computing principles to all (major and non-major) students by hearing from instructors at the five campuses involved in the first round of pilots for the new AP Computer Science Principles curriculum. The classes are all different, designed to map the curriculum onto local needs.

2. THE PROCESS

The CS Principles Curriculum has been developed over several years using a process that College Board developed in response to the NRC report to define the core topics [2]. The development of AP CS Principles was headed by a commission of ten members, including college and high school faculty, who produced documents and rationale for topic selection [1]. That process was overseen by a larger Advisory Committee [4].

The driving document for the CS Principles curriculum development, "CS Principles: Big Ideas," articulates seven big ideas (shown in Table 1) as well as their underlying key ideas and supporting concepts.

Table 1. AP CS Principles is founded on 7 Big Ideas and 6 Computational Thinking Practices

Big Ideas
1. Computing is a creative human activity that engenders innovation and promotes exploration
2. Abstraction reduces information and detail to focus on concepts relevant to understanding and solving problems
3. Data and information facilitate the creation of knowledge
4. Algorithms are tools for developing and expressing solutions to computational problems.
5. Programming is a creative process that produces computational artifacts
6. Digital devices, systems, and the networks that interconnect them enable and foster computational approaches to solving problems
7. Computing enables innovation in other fields including science, social science, humanities, arts, medicine, engineering, business
Computational Thinking Practices
1. Analyzing effects of computation
2. Creating computational artifacts
3. Using abstractions and models
4. Analyzing problems and artifacts
5. Communicating processes and results
6. Working effectively in teams

Having developed the guiding documents for the curriculum, the next step was to convert them into a course syllabus, assignments, readings, exercises, exams, etc. Five campuses were selected as pilots in the 2010/2011 academic year (Table 2). The experiences, materials, and results from these first pilots will inform a second round of pilots scheduled for 2011/2012 academic year. These pilots will include a larger set of colleges and at least five high schools. The following year, it is anticipated that many more colleges and high schools will offer the course. An Advanced Placement CS Principles exam is targeted for a first offering in 2015.

3. FIVE PILOTS

The five piloting instructors and schools are:

- Tiffany Barnes, University of North Carolina, Charlotte (UNCC)
- Dan Garcia, University of California, Berkeley (UCB)
- Jody Paul, Metropolitan State College of Denver (MSCD)
- Beth Simon, University of California, San Diego (UCSD)
- Larry Snyder, University of Washington (UW)

Table 2. Comparison of the 2010/2011 Pilot courses

School	Name	Programming Language(s)	Size	Contact Hours
UNCC	The Beauty and Joy of Computing [5]	Scratch, GameMaker	~30	45
UCB	The Beauty and Joy of Computing [6]	BYOB based on Scratch	76	98
MSCD	Living in a Computing World [7]	Scratch	20	60
UCSD	Fluency w/Information Technology [8]	Alice + Excel	575	50
UW	CS Principles [9]	Processing + Python	~40	50

4. SPECIAL SESSION

Moderated by Owen Astrachan, co-chair of the AP CS Principles Commission, the special session will be a round table discussion among the piloting faculty about the experiences of the pilots. Topics to be discussed include:

- Mapping the defined curriculum into a class of local interest
- Programming language choices – vision and second thoughts
- Recruitment and engagement of under-represented students
- Catalog of what worked well, what could work better and what to avoid at all costs
- Experiences teaching a class with everyone watching
- Open source resources developed for the class

Time will be reserved for audience questions and discussion.

The "special session" designation is ideal because the instructors and not giving a position or critiquing their classes. The idea is a rapid interchange among instructors, navigated by the moderator and driven by audience concerns and input. Think of a post-semester conversation by faculty who just taught the same class.

NOTE: Another special session on the 10K Teacher's Effort will be proposed. If that session is chosen, it would be best if this session could follow that one (or at the very least, not overlap).

5. REFERENCES

[1] CS Principles Web Site: http://www.csprinciples.org

[2] NRC, *Learning and Understanding: Improving Advanced Study of Mathematics and Science in U.S. High Schools,* 2002 http://www.nap.edu/openbook.php?record_id=10129

[3] Supporting CS Principles Web Site: http://csprinciples.cs.washington.edu

[4] AP CS Principles Development Process http://csprinciples.cs.washington.edu/theprocess.html

[5] UNCC Course Web Site http://www.cs.uncc.edu/~tbarnes2/ComputingJoy.html

[6] UCB Course Web Site: http://inst.eecs.berkeley.edu/~cs10/

[7] MSCD Course Web Site: http://livinginacomputingworld.org/

[8] UCSD Course Web Site: http://cseweb.ucsd.edu/~bsimon/

[9] UW Course Web Site: http://www.cs.washington.edu/homes/snyder/pilot/CSPdev/

Hands-On Networking Labs With Embedded Routers

Dennis Brylow and Kyle Thurow
Marquette University
MSCS Department – Cudahy Hall
1313 W. Wisconsin Ave., Milwaukee, WI 53233
{brylow,kthurow}@mscs.mu.edu

ABSTRACT

We present extensions to the Embedded Xinu educational operating system that, when coupled with a target device like the Cisco-Linksys WRT54GL, provide for an extremely attractive hands-on laboratory platform in network courses. We present classroom and research lab evidence for the usefulness of this platform as a network education tool, and discuss its significance in the context of a wide spectrum of competitor systems. This project is part of a larger effort to bring cost-effective, hands-on embedded system laboratory experiences into systems courses throughout the undergraduate computer science core.

Categories and Subject Descriptors

C.3 [**Special-Purpose and Application-Based Systems**]: Real-time and embedded systems; K.3.2 [**Computer and Info Science Education**]: Curriculum

General Terms

Experimentation

Keywords

Computer Networks, Systems education, Embedded Xinu

1. INTRODUCTION

In an increasingly wired world, it is essential that faculty have access to powerful, flexible tools for supporting hands-on networking education. Many such tools exist, running the gamut from network simulators and emulators to virtualized and distributed environments. The old-fashioned direct solution – simply plugging a device into the network which students can use to explore the many levels of networking software – has fallen out of favor in many cases because of vexing issues involving security, privacy, flexibility, and the overall difficulty of capturing the full complexity of modern networks.

SIGCSE'11, March 9–12, 2011, Dallas, Texas, USA.

Our work offers an inexpensive and portable combination of hardware and software that provides a powerful direct solution for networking education, while fitting into a much larger effort to weave hands-on embedded laboratory experiences throughout the whole of the undergraduate systems curriculum.

This paper presents 4 main contributions:

- Extensions to the Embedded Xinu educational operating system that, when coupled with a target device like the Cisco-Linksys WRT54GL, provide for an extremely attractive hands-on laboratory platform in networking courses,
- Evaluation of classroom use of our platform for "Build Your Own Stack" laboratory assignments,
- Support for the transport layer socket API used to build network applications on Xinu, and
- Evidence of our platform's suitability for internetworking laboratory activities, including Internet packet routing and inexpensive emulation of network conditions.

The next section offers a brief comparison of our work with some of the many alternative network education tools currently available. Section 3 describes the technical contributions that were required to make full use of the wired networking capabilities of our platform. Section 4 presents the categories in which we have evaluated the use of our platform in the classroom and in the reseach lab. Finally, the paper summarizes and concludes.

2. RELATED WORK

The vast body of prior and related work software tools in support of networking education falls into four primary categories: simulators, emulators, virtual solutions, and direct solutions. Our work falls into the last category – a real embedded operating system that supports direct student access in support of pedagogical goals.

Simulators model specific network properties, usually with a significant abstraction of detail, for lecture demonstrations or fixed laboratory exercises. The NS [13] and NS-2 simulators are designed to allow the user control over how traffic is routed. Simulators can be excellent pedagogical tools for teaching the properties they are designed to model, but cannot be readily applied to other classes of networking properties as direct solutions can.

Emulators model properties of the end-to-end network itself, rather than the host systems connected to them. NIST Net [6] models elaborate statistical properties of Internet traffic and congestion, providing a high-quality test environment both for researchers developing new protocols, and students learning how to evaluate protocols. Direct solutions such as our work can include emulator components, but the reverse is not true; an emulator alone cannot support the breadth of pedagogical activities featured in many modern networking courses.

Prior work by Pan [15] uses the `tc` utility on embedded Linux with WRT54GL router hardware to construct an inexpensive, embedded networking laboratory. Our work differs in that we use the Embedded Xinu instructional operating system on our routers, a much lighter-weight solution for students to learn. Our solution does not require a special kernel patch of the host Linux systems, and is capable of far more than simple network emulation. In addition, our solution provides for an amortized cost of lab construction, in that the Embedded Xinu / WRT54GL platform has been shown to support improvements in student learning in many non-networking courses, including hardware systems / computer organization [2], operating systems [3], embedded systems [4], and compiler construction [14].

DummyNet [5] is another emulator solution that has been recently ported to the OpenWRT distribution of embedded Linux for wireless routers. By contrast, our emulator component is deliberately designed with limited embedded resources and networking pedagogy in mind.

The rise of cheap, effective virtualization has been a great boon for pedagogical networking tools, as it offers easy solutions to age-old laboratory problems like security, privacy, and flexibility. The Virtual Distributed Ethernet (VDE) system [11] provides a general framework for students to test their own network protocols, network tools and security systems. VDE operates in user mode, emulates the many components of an Internet, and can interoperate with real networks. Such virtual solutions excel at offering enhanced security and flexibility over direct solutions such as our work. However, our work has the advantages of being highly portable, cost-effective relative to powerful server hardware, and ultimately more realistic. Our equipment is designed to operate at or near 10/100 line speeds, and does not suffer from the significant virtualization penalty. Most importantly, experience working with real hardware should not be undersold. Examples abound of protocol implementations and device drivers that work well on a virtualized platform, but fail to work at all on real hardware.

The Virtual Network System (VNS) [7] has been successfully used in undergraduate networking courses at Stanford and Johns Hopkins to teach router implementation in software. Further, it has supported a graduate-level networking hardware/software course [8] for designing Internet routers. The VNS paper cited above also provides a thorough bibliography of network course environments circa 2005, and breaks down existing systems into four broad categories: support for transport level experiments; support for link or network level experiments; support for easier access to network traffic for analysis; and support for Internet router experiments. One of our primary contributions in this work is the modernization and revival of the venerable Xinu network stack, which has been used to support activities in all four of these broad categories for more than a decade, rather than just the one.

TinkerNet [17], is one of the few other widely-known direct solutions for supporting networking laboratories. Closely related to the Xinu laboratory lineage in some ways, TinkerNet "provides direct, real-world access to Ethernet packets, and gives students the features necessary to implement an OSI network stack from the data link layer all the way up through the application level." Our work differs from TinkerNet in cost and space requirements, and in flexibility, particularly with regard to multiple network interfaces being available immediately.

Embedded Xinu is a reimplementation of the venerable Xinu operating system [9] on modern RISC hardware. Xinu has been ported to more than half a dozen platforms, but Embedded Xinu is the first ANSI-standard C port for modern RISC hardware. Our work differs from the original Xinu project primarily in our emphasis on cheap consumer hardware and portable, freely-available software tools that support a wide spectrum of hands-on, undergraduate systems courses at institutions that otherwise could not afford a comparable investment in laboratory infrastructure.

In summary, a wide spectrum of tools are available to support hands-on network education. Our direct solution offers greater flexibility than simulation and emulation tools, as well as some desirable advantages over the recent proliferation of virtual networking environments. Nevertheless, these tools need not be mutually exclusive; the best-equipped networking laboratory may feature a careful selection of tools from all of these categories.

3. EMBEDDED TEACHING PLATFORM

Cisco's popular WRT54GL wireless router has for years been a favored platform for home networking enthusiasts and Linux hackers, because of its low cost, wide availability, and great flexibility. The addition of a serial port for debugging (under $10 of extra hardware, plus a little soldering) grants users control over the boot process of the router hardware, to a degree that they can easily redirect the device to updated firmware images, or upload a completely fresh operating system image into RAM in only a few seconds.

Nevertheless, while extremely cost- and space-effective, building a hands-on laboratory environment with these devices still requires investments of equipment and time. In this section, we present the unique advantages that make the Embedded Xinu / WRT54GL platform combination such a compelling choice for teaching networking courses.

3.1 Modern Ethernet Device

The Broadcom BCM5253 System on a Chip ("SoC") within the WRT54GL router includes a BCM47xx family network interface ("NIC") for the wired 10/100 MB Ethernet connections. Members of this ubiquitous NIC family appear in many commodity networking devices, including both embedded systems and Ethernet adapters for PCs. Device drivers are thus widely available for both proprietary and open source operating systems, making this a good choice for study in a course that touches on software issues in the lowest layer of the networking stack.

The hardware has a memory-mapped set of control and status registers, providing for an easy and direct programming interface for beginners. The Ethernet controller features asynchronous operation with independent, interrupt-driven packet transmitting and receiving DMA (direct memory access) rings, as well as a programmable MAC, extensive performance counter registers, and configurable watermark levels. In short, it is an embedded NIC with all of the principle features that students might study on a mainstream PC or laptop NIC.

Instructors of a networking course with emphasis on hardware issues have the option of taking advantage of the advanced features present on this NIC, while more software-focused instructors can assign a basic device driver to their students (under 750 lines of C code,) or skip this level altogether and use the production Embedded Xinu driver we have provided to begin accessing Ethernet frames directly.

3.2 Programmable Switch Hardware

When shipped from the factory, WRT54GL routers are configured to act as a gateway between a local, private, home network, and a public address on the network of an Internet Service Provider (ISP). The jacks on the back of the router are labeled accordingly, with four LAN (Local Area Network) ports and a distinctly marked WAN (Wide Area Network) port for connection to the ISP. The four LAN ports are configured as a *hub*, which is to say that any traffic arriving at one of the four LAN ports can be echoed to the other ports, thus providing connectivity not only between home PCs and the router, but also between the multiple home PCs. Conceptually, this corresponds to Figure 1.

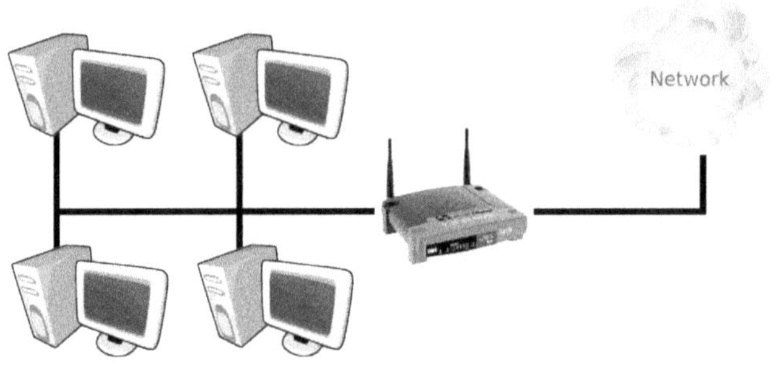

Figure 1: Default hub configuration of network ports

While some routers have networking hardware that fixes the device into this standard configuration, others, like the WRT54GL, feature sophisticated programmable switch components that can be configured for more advanced configurations. For example, the Broadcom "Robo Switch" [1] in our chosen router can be programmed to treat each of the five external Ethernet jacks as a separate interface with its own MAC and IP address, as shown in Figure 2. Our extensions to the Embedded Xinu educational operating system allow students and faculty to reconfigure the programmable switch into new and more useful configurations.

An inexpensive platform with up to five independent Ethernet interfaces opens up a wide range of new possibilities for networking laboratory exercise design. While the simplest examples of hands-on assignments for an undergraduate course can be accomplished on a single host with a single NIC, multiple interfaces enable activities with inline traffic measurement, packet forwarding, route propagation, traffic shaping, network address translation, and easier emulation of Internet phenomena like packet loss, delay, duplication and congestion control.

A number of important technical challenges were overcome to enable full use of the programmable switch component. First, Embedded Xinu commands were written to communicate with the switch hardware, and an interface for monitoring the switch configuration from the text-based Xinu shell was devised. Figure 3 shows the Xinu shell's view of the programmable switch's VLAN (Virtual Local Area

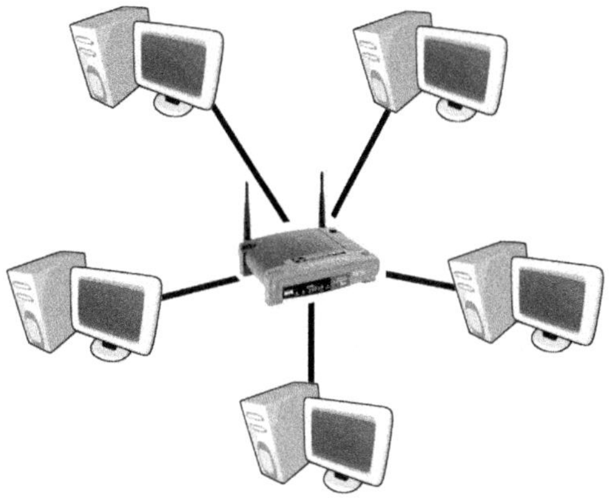

Figure 2: Advanced configuration with five independent network ports

Network) table. The listing shows the default switch configuration, which consists of two table entries, labeled "VID 0" and "VID 1."

```
xsh$ vlanstat
VLAN Switch Status:
    Control 0:E0, 1:0E, 2:00, 3:00, 4:40, 5:08
VLAN Table
    VID  0: 0 1 2 3 5*
    VID  1: 4 5*
    Default Port 0 tag: 0x0000
    Default Port 1 tag: 0x0000
    Default Port 2 tag: 0x0000
    Default Port 3 tag: 0x0000
    Default Port 4 tag: 0x0001
    Default Port 5 tag: 0x0000
```

Figure 3: VLAN status displayed by Xinu shell

Each VLAN is assigned physical interface ports from the switch, numbered zero through five. Conceptually, interfaces zero through three correspond to the four external LAN ports, unfortunately labeled LAN one through four on the external plastic casing of the router. Switch port four corresponds to the external WAN interface on the router. Switch port five is the inward-facing interface that provides connectivity with the embedded MIPS processor. From the processor's perspective, there is only one wired Ethernet interface. However, the switch uses 802.1Q VLAN Tagging [12] to add port identification data into the Ethernet frames, so they are easily demultiplexed according to physical interface by the operating system software.

The asterisks next to port five in the VLAN Table of Figure 3 indicate that the inward-facing switch port is configured to leave the VLAN tags in place; the other ports will strip off the tags before the Ethernet frames actually leave the router.

The programmable switch supports up to 16 VLAN table entries, and thus can be easily configured for each physical interface to exist on its own VLAN, with its own default tag. On the outgoing side, our multiplexing Xinu device driver adds in 802.1Q tags to automatically forward Ethernet frames to the correct external interface. The size of the VLAN table in the switch leaves the possibility of even more elaborate configurations, including tagged VLANs bridging across switches on different routers. We leave experiments with these bridged configurations as future work.

Once reconfigured for five independent interfaces, it is now trivial to build interlocking networks where packets will be forwarded through several real hops to reach their destination router. Some care must be taken before wiring up these kinds of configurations, however. If a router is powered up in its default "hub" state when wired in a configuration that assumes independent interfaces, multiple links between the same switch will cause immediate routing loops that will echo traffic back and forth between the hubs at a rate that can overpower other devices or trigger shutoff conditions in managed switches. For this reason, the default switch configuration stored in non-volatile RAM should be altered to prevent hub behavior. This is easily accomplished through standard firmware access via the serial port.

4. EVALUATION

In this section, we present the three groups of networking-related teaching activities that we have "test-driven" for evaluation in the past three years.

4.1 Build Your Own Stack

A large category of network curriculum tools fall into the category of "Build Your Own Stack" support, where students develop, test, and measure protocol implementations ranging from the link layer (ARP) up to the transport layer (UDP and/or TCP).

We evaluated our platform's suitability for stack-building activities across three different sessions, including two offerings of an operating systems course (spring 2009 and spring 2010), and a special topics course on embedded systems development (spring 2008).

Our operating systems course follows the Embedded Xinu construction sequence of projects followed by several other schools, and first described in [3]. Student teams build significant sections of their own O/S components over the length of the term, reinforcing topics discussed in lecture. At our institution, this course now also includes several weeks of introductory networking material, and we conclude the term with a final project that adds networked functionality to the students' operating system implementations.

Students are given our Embedded Xinu network device driver for the WRT54GL platform, and are expected to build up basic ARP and ICMP echo client and server functions into their system. Students work in teams of two for two weeks; a complete solution can be accomplished in under 200 lines of code for the ping and ARP clients, and another 100 lines for the ping server. (This is a small amount of code for typical assignments in this course, but the cognitive load is high given the switch to networking topics.)

Qualitatively, student enthusiasm is high for this project, and an improvement over the non-network-centric final assignment used in previous terms.

Quantitatively, student performance on this project is low normal. The spring 2009 session (40 students) earned an aggregate score of 26.4 out of 40 for the assignment, and spring 2010 (36 students) earned 25.3 out of 40. These are both below the multi-year aggregate project average of 27.6 out of 40, but not by a large margin. One important mitigating factor to consider is that this assignment is one of the last tasks completed by the roughly half of the students in the final week of their senior year; long term tracking suggests that projects in this final slot on the syllabus suffer significantly from "senioritis" effects, regardless of the topic.

As an indirect measure, students participating in the course voluntarily completed an anonymous, IRB-approved assessment instrument asking them roughly 40 questions about their learning experience in the course. In 2009, 33 out of 40 students participated; in 2010, 30 out of 36 participated.

Five of the survey questions were relevant to evaluating the students' learning experience with regards to the networking extensions we added to Embedded Xinu:

Q6: The lab assignments helped you learn the course material.

Q10: The topics covered will be useful to you in the future, beyond this course.

Q18: You understand basic O/S components involved in network communication.

Q34: You are able to work with the Embedded Xinu environment.

Q35: You are able to work with WRT54GL wireless routers.

Responses were on a five-point scale, ranging from *(1) Strongly Agree* to *(5) Strongly Disagree.*

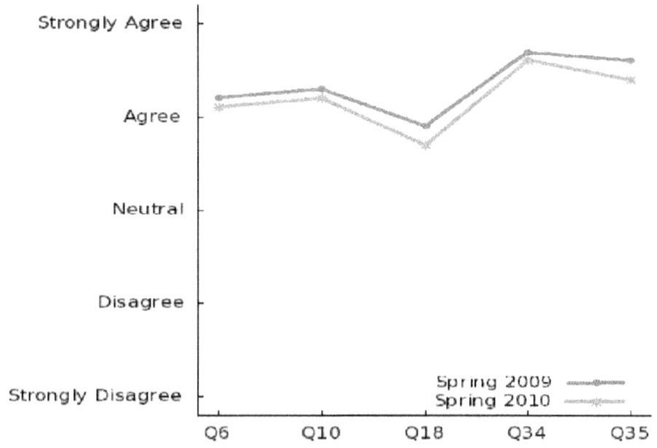

Figure 4: Student Evaluation Scores

As shown in Figure 4, agreement was quite high, despite the fact that the third item corresponded to a single two-week assignment.

A third course offering also sheds light on the Build Your Own Stack approach using our extensions to Embedded Xinu. An offering of a special topics course on Embedded Systems in spring of 2008 included a sequence of several assignments focused on the networking capabilities of the WRT54GL. Our Embedded Xinu networking contributions were used for the course, as reported in [4]. Student teams worked on a packet sniffer, ARP and ICMP, UDP and DHCP. One group implemented a significant portion of TCP, an ambitious task for any undergraduate course. The evaluation in that paper demonstrated that the Embedded Xinu platform on WRT54GL routers enabled an engaging and rewarding learning experience, using both direct and indirect measures.

4.2 Network Programming

A second major category of networking courseware consists of tools that support network programming. Students are typically assigned tasks that depend on an existing protocol stack to build network applications.

To support these types of activities, we have built a socket

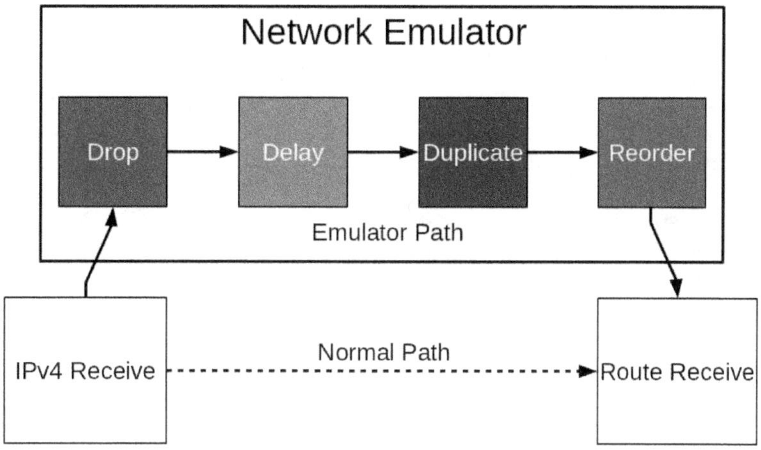

Figure 5: Embedded Xinu network emulator

API compatible with the infrastructures presented in popular networking textbooks, such as [10].

Our socket API for Embedded Xinu provides the following stream-oriented functions.

- socket(family, type, protocol)
  Returns a fresh datagram or stream device.
- send(socket, data, len, flags)
  Sends stream data.
- recv(socket, buffer, len, flags)
  Receives stream data.
- close(socket)
  Closes a socket, cleans up resources.
- connect(socket, servaddr, len)
  Establishes a connection from a client to a server.
- bind(socket, locaddr, len)
  Binds a socket to a protocol port.
- listen(socket)
  Places socket in passive listening mode.
- accept(socket, clientaddr, len)
  Returns new socket and connection info for client.

Additional library functions provide message-oriented calls.

A full assessment of student learning with these tools is currently being carried out in an offering of Networking and Internets, but our protocol stack has already been taken for several "test drives" in the past three years.

Two undergraduate students implemented a telnet client and server for the Embedded Xinu / WRT54GL platform in summer of 2009 as part of a research experiences for undergraduates program. Their contribution has subsequently been combined into the latest release of the Embedded Xinu open source project as a demonstration. Another student has completed a masters thesis project relying on our datagram facility to transport telephone voice data over the network (voice over IP), and a fourth student has implemented both a simple webserver for a class project and a TFTP client as an example application for the open source release.

4.3 Internet Routing and Emulation

A third category of networking courseware is concerned with Internetworking issues, particularly packet forwarding (Layer 2 and 3 routing). Many solutions have been proposed to provide either simulated, emulated, or virtualized interfaces for students to work on the software components that are responsible for managing traffic as it crosses the Internet. Using the contributions we describe in the previous section, the Embedded Xinu / WRT54GL platform provides a perfectly natural alternative to more expensive and complex solutions. Each router device can have up to five independent interfaces; it is trivial to connect them together in a configuration that allows genuine packet forwarding in arbitrary chains.

Our update of the Embedded Xinu networking stack includes routing tables, and can be configured to act as an internet router/gateway with all five interfaces residing on distinct subnets.

The traditional pitfalls of using real networking hardware for this kind of activity must still be addressed. Student-controlled gateways running route propagation protocols and sniffing traffic must be carefully isolated from the production network. While this is a daunting task for a classroom full of PCs, full isolation becomes much more tractable when the target machines are cheap, low-power, and can be stacked by the dozen in a few cubic feet near a dedicated switch.

Other solutions have struggled with the control channel problem. How does one maintain effective administration over a set of student-controlled host devices when the test network itself (or "warzone") is an unreliable medium? In our laboratory design, an "out of band" administrative serial connection handily solves this problem, providing reliable control independent of network state.

A methodical assessment of this technology as a teaching tool is currently underway in a fall 2010 offering of our Networking and Internets course. Early evaluation by undergraduate volunteers in the past three years have already shown that layer-3 routing is perfectly feasible within the limited resources of the embedded platform, and we have every reason to expect that the deployment of these tools in our classroom will be well-received.

One of the ways we have evaluated the effectiveness of this platform as an Internetworking development environment is through the development of a network emulation layer, as shown in Figure 5.

Many tools exist for simulated or virtualized Internet emulators, all of which aim to reproduce hostile packet traffic conditions of the real Internet in a controlled setting. By leveraging our five interfaces and packet forwarding capacity, the platform becomes a simple, portable emulator device that can be physically interposed between other network hosts with minimal effort. The current system provides basic implementations of four common emulator features:

- **Packet Drop** takes a user specified percentage and discards that percentage of forwarded packets via pseudo-random number generation.
- **Packet Delay** takes a user specified percentage and a timing range. The Packet Delay module postpones a percentage of packets randomly and holds them for a random interval within the specified range.
- **Packet Duplication** takes a user specified percentage and range. The specified percentage of forwarded packets are selected for duplication, and a random number of duplicates are released within the specified time range.
- **Packet Reordering** takes a user specified percentage and swaps that percentage of randomly chosen packets with the next packet forwarded through the emulator.

The simple shell-based interface for the network emulator component features sliding configurable percentages, giving the user a visual percentage bar for each module and on the fly configuration.

This network emulator was constructed and evaluated last year as an entry in the undergraduate division of the ACM Student Research Competition, and the student responsible advanced to the semi-finals round [16].

5. SUMMARY AND CONCLUSIONS

We present extensions to the Embedded Xinu educational operating system on the Cisco-Linksys WRT54GL wireless router that provide students with direct access to a modern Ethernet controller with asynchronous DMA rings, and up to five independent wired interfaces. This platform has served as a basis for classroom and laboratory activities ranging from protocol building at each layer of the stack, to network application construction, to Internet routing and emulation.

Our modernization and revival of the venerable Xinu educational operating system provides an inexpensive, flexible tool for supporting hands-on embedded system activities in systems courses throughout the undergraduate computer science curriculum. However, the obvious network-centric nature of this ubiquitous consumer router makes network education a particularly rich vein of possibilities. Our tools and curriculum materials are freely available at [18].

5.1 Future Work

As mentioned earlier, full assessment of a semester length course on networking is currently taking place in fall of 2010; we expect this will offer further insight into the advantages and weaknesses of this platform as a teaching tool.

Meanwhile, continued work on the emulator component of our system will include more elaborate modeling of expected real world network conditions, a module for throughput rate control, and finer grain control over emulation settings based on vlan/incoming/outgoing packet status.

5.2 Acknowledgments

The authors are grateful to George Corliss, who team teaches the operating systems and networking course, and to the many students who have participated in our courses or contributed back to the Embedded Xinu system.

6. REFERENCES

[1] Broadcom Corporation. BCM5325e product brief, May 2004. URL `http://www.broadcom.com/collateral/pb/5325E-PB00-R.pdf`.

[2] D. Brylow. An experimental laboratory environment for teaching embedded hardware systems. In *WCAE 2007: Workshop on Computer Architecture Education*, pages 44–51. ACM Press, June 2007. ISBN: 978-1-59593-797-1.

[3] D. Brylow. An experimental laboratory environment for teaching embedded operating systems. In *SIGCSE 2008*, volume 40, pages 192–196, 2008. ACM.

[4] D. Brylow and B. Ramamurthy. Nexos: A next generation embedded systems laboratory. *SIGBED Review*, 6(1), January 2009.

[5] M. Carbone and L. Rizzo. Dummynet revisited. *SIGCOMM Computer Communication Review*, 40(2):12–20, 2010.

[6] M. Carson and D. Santay. NIST Net: a Linux-based network emulation tool. *SIGCOMM Computer Communication Review*, 33(3):111–126, 2003.

[7] M. Casado and N. McKeown. The virtual network system. In *SIGCSE '05*, pages 76–80. ACM, 2005.

[8] M. Casado, G. Watson, and N. McKeown. Teaching networking hardware. In *ITiCSE '05*, pages 208–212. ACM, 2005.

[9] D. E. Comer. *Operating System Design: The XINU Approach.* Prentice Hall, 1984.

[10] D. E. Comer. *Computer Networks and Internets.* Prentice Hall, 5th edition, 2008.

[11] M. Goldweber and R. Davoli. VDE: an emulation environment for supporting computer networking courses. In *ITiCSE '08*, pages 138–142. ACM, 2008.

[12] IEEE. Standard 802.1q-2005, virtual bridged local area networks, 2005. URL `http://standards.ieee.org/getieee802/download/802.1Q-2005.pdf`.

[13] S. B. Lee, E. Bajaj, L. Breslau, D. Estrin, K. Fall, S. Floyd, P. Haldar, M. H, A. Helmy, J. Heidemann, P. Huang, S. Kumar, S. Mccanne, and H. Yu. Improving simulation for network research. Technical report, University of Southern California, 1999.

[14] A. Mallen and D. Brylow. Compiler construction with a dash of concurrency and an embedded twist. In *to appear in SPLASH (formerly OOPSLA) '10: Companion to the 25th ACM SIGPLAN symposium on Systems, Programming, Languages, and Applications: Software for Humanity*, October 2010.

[15] J. Pan. Teaching computer networks in a real network: the technical perspectives. In *SIGCSE '10*, pages 133–137, New York, NY, USA, 2010. ACM.

[16] K. Thurow and D. Brylow. A network emulator on Embedded Xinu. ACM Student Research Competition, poster and presentation, March 2010.

[17] T. Winters, R. Ausanka-Crues, M. Kegel, E. Shimshock, D. Turner, and M. Erlinger. Tinkernet: A low-cost and ready-to-deploy networking laboratory platform. In *Eighth Australasian Computing Education Conference (ACE2006)*, Conferences in Research and Practice in Information Technology. Australian Computer Society, 2006.

[18] Project Nexos / embedded Xinu wiki, 2007. `http://xinu.mscs.mu.edu/`.

Introducing Networking and Distributed Systems Concepts in an Undergraduate-Accessible Wireless Sensor Networks Course

Sami Rollins
Department of Computer Science
University of San Francisco
San Francisco, CA, USA
srollins@cs.usfca.edu

ABSTRACT

The field of wireless sensor networks is growing rapidly and there is increasing interest in providing students with a foundation in the area. Curriculum in the field, however, is fairly limited and most courses reach only advanced graduate students. Undergraduate students typically lack the background, for example in distributed systems and networking, to digest the topics and assignments of a standard wireless sensor networks course. In this work, we present our approach to teaching wireless sensor networks to undergraduates and introductory graduate students. We discuss a unique, integrated approach to introducing relevant distributed systems and networking concepts in the context of wireless sensor networking applications. The course provides students who have never previously implemented a networked application with the necessary background to implement sensing applications on the Java SunSPOT sensor. It also provides a structured introduction to prerequisite concepts, such as distributed coordination algorithms, so that students can read and understand research papers. Our experience suggests that there is ample opportunity to expand curricula in sensor networking and reach a broader population of students.

Categories and Subject Descriptors

K.3.2 [**Computers and Education**]: Computer and Information Science Education; C.2.1 [**Computer-Communication Networks**]: Network Architecture and Design

General Terms

Human Factors

Keywords

wireless sensor networks, distributed systems, networking

1. INTRODUCTION

The field of wireless sensor networks is growing rapidly. Only a few years ago, work in the field was devoted to hardware and network protocols and only expert researchers attempted to build actual sensor systems. In recent years, the field has become much more broad. Pervasive devices such as mobile phones are touted as the next sensing platform [7]. Moreover, devices such as Sun's SunSPOT platform [10] have made programming sensor systems much more accessible. Whereas a few years ago one might have had to build the sensor device itself before programming it, today platforms such as the SPOT provide a complete networking stack and set of sensors, including light, temperature, and accelerometer, that can be easily programmed using a straightforward Java API. This has made sensor networking much more accessible to a broader population.

Curriculum in the field, however, is still fairly limited. Most courses on sensor networks reach only advanced graduate students. Textbooks and other resources for teaching sensor networks typically focus on low-level details such as radio communication, and are perhaps more appropriate for an electrical engineering curriculum [13, 4]. Further, though many sensor networks courses focus on having students read research papers, undergraduate and introductory graduate students often do not have the relevant background to digest such materials without a bit more preparation. Finally, more junior students have often not been introduced to relevant networking and distributed systems concepts, such as socket programming or concurrency, required to understand and implement sensing applications.

In this work, we present a unique approach to introducing general networking and distributed systems concepts using sensing applications as an overarching theme. We first discuss the challenges of designing such a curriculum for undergraduate and introductory-level graduate students, particularly in a liberal arts environment. We then provide an overview of our course and describe three crosscutting modules: our first module introduces network communication and socket programming by having students implement a simple sensing application; our second module introduces concurrency and multi-threaded programming by having students implement a duty-cycling algorithm for a sensor; our final module uses a layered approach to introduce distributed coordination and link-layer algorithms in order to prepare students to understand research papers on MAC protocols in sensor networks. We conclude with a discussion of our observations of the most and least successful elements of our course.

2. STUDENT PREPARATION AND THE LIBERAL ARTS ENVIRONMENT

The computer science department at the University of San Francisco (USF) is similar to that of many liberal arts colleges. We have a very small undergraduate program, with under 40 majors, and a mid-sized Master's degree (MS) program, with roughly 60 majors. This type of environment poses a number of challenges with respect to curriculum design:

- **Large General Education Requirement** - Our undergraduate students have a significant general education requirement, leaving limited room for computer science elective courses. Our major requires only 10 computer science courses total, and students take only one upper-level core course in each of three areas: systems, applications, and theory and languages.
- **Underprepared Students** - Our undergraduate curriculum is fairly horizontal; we have designed the curriculum to avoid long prerequisite chains and encourage more students into the major. Additionally, elective courses are often offered every other year and students end up taking courses when they are available, which is not necessarily the ideal time in their education. The result is that undergraduate students are often somewhat underprepared for upper-level courses. Similarly, our MS students come from extremely diverse academic backgrounds and many are unprepared for typical graduate-level courses in their first year.
- **Limited Course Offerings** - The combination of limited staffing and low enrollment results in the department offering a limited number of courses each semester. We generally have graduate students enrolled in upper-division undergraduate courses and undergraduates will often take our graduate courses as electives. This results in a need to provide an integrated curriculum that can meet the needs of several levels of student.

More specifically, the wireless sensor networks (WSN) course offered at USF enrolls a variety of students at the undergraduate and graduate level. Most students taking the course have not had a networking or distributed systems course. In contrast to advanced graduate students who might take a more typical WSN course, our students are underprepared in the following areas:

- **Basic Knowledge of Networking** - Most of the foundational work in the area of WSN centers around networking algorithms and a central topic in our WSN course is communication protocols. Students who have never taken a networking course are unfamiliar with the Internet protocol stack and the protocols that exist at each layer. Without this background, they may struggle to understand lectures and readings on topics such as MAC-layer protocols in sensor networks.
- **Basic Knowledge of Distributed Algorithms** - Similar to networking, much of the seminal work in WSN applies distributed algorithms that have existed for years. Two notable areas include topology control and time synchronization. Students can gain significant benefit from having some foundational knowledge of these areas before delving into a WSN paper.
- **Sockets** - A significant portion of students enrolling in WSN have never implemented an application that communicates over a network, wired or wireless. For those who have, many have only utilized frameworks such as Rails or Servlets, which hide the low-level communication details from the developer.
- **Threads** - Nearly all students who have taken WSN struggle with concurrency and multithreaded programming. Surprisingly, even for students who have previously implemented a thread scheduler as part of an operating systems course, multithreaded programming in WSN poses a challenge.
- **Programming Proficiency** - A meta-challenge we face is overall programming proficiency. Incoming MS students, in particular, often lack basic programming skills, and many students may lack knowledge of the particular language chosen for a given course.

Table 1: Overview of topics covered.

Topic	Number of Class Periods
Concurrency and Multithreaded Programming	2
General Networking Concepts	2
Coordination Algorithms and Media Access Control	2
Error Control and the Link Layer	2
Topology Control	2
Routing	2
Time Synchronization	1
Reliability and the Transport Layer	1
Participatory Sensing	2
Applications	2

Our WSN course has been designed with these characteristics in mind. The remainder of this paper describes our course and the unique approach we take to introduce broader concepts in the context of WSN.

3. COURSE OVERVIEW

The Wireless Sensor Networks (WSN) course at USF is a 15-week, undergraduate-accessible course that introduces several general computing concepts using wireless sensor networks as an overarching example application. The course has been offered twice to date.

The course takes a networking-centric approach to WSN. Table 1 outlines the main topics covered in the course and the number of class periods typically devoted to each topic. Below we overview several choices made in the design of the course:

Lecture/Discussion Format.

Class periods typically alternate between interactive lecture and class discussion of research papers. Because there are no good comprehensive resources (e.g., books) that cover all of the necessary topics, lecture periods provide students with a broad overview of each area. Elements discussed in the lectures include the broad research challenges and the algorithms or approaches from other areas (e.g., networking and distributed systems) that may apply. We follow a lecture with a class discussion of a research paper on the given topic. Even undergraduate students with little experience digesting research papers respond favorably to this approach. The lecture periods prepare the students for reading the paper and the discussions allow us to achieve some depth with regard to the topic.

SunSPOTs.

The course uses Sun's Small Programmable Object Technology (SPOT) sensor platform [10]. The SPOT is a Java-programmable sensing device that comes equipped with several sensors including a light sensor, accelerometer, and temperature sensor. The SPOTs provide basic networking and use the AODV protocol for communication [9]. Each SPOT also has two switches that can be toggled, and 8 LEDs. This platform is ideal for a teaching environment. Students who have knowledge of Java can easily begin programming without the learning curve associated with similar technology such as the Mote [8].

Programming-Centric Assignments.

Students are given a substantial amount of programming to reinforce concepts taught in the class. The most recent offering of the course required 3 laboratory assignments and 4 significant programming projects. Our students typically respond positively to this approach. Not only does it reinforce learning of the material, it prepares our students for development jobs, which is the career path chosen by most of them.

4. CROSSCUTTING MODULES

The primary contribution of our approach to teaching WSN is a set of crosscutting modules that use sensor networks as an overarching context in which to introduce general networking and distributed systems concepts. In this section, we describe three modules that are most representative of our approach. We first describe two programming assignments that introduce the concepts of sockets and threads, respectively. We then describe a lecture and discussion module that illustrates our approach to introducing relevant networking and distributed systems concepts to lay the foundation for a more detailed discussion of a research paper.

4.1 Network Communication

Network communication is a fundamental tool used in virtually any sensing application. Traditionally, socket programming is introduced in a networking course or, as is the case in our curriculum, a software engineering course. A UDP Pinger, as described by Kurose and Ross [5], is a typical laboratory assignment used to familiarize students with sockets. The assignment asks students to implement a simple client and server; the client sends a simple ICMP message to a server and determines the round trip time based on the response received. This type of assignment gives students a solid understanding of how communication works. They see first hand that, as Kurose and Ross describe, the server program must first be running and have opened the "door" for communication before it can be contacted by the client. They also gain an understanding of the life cycle of a client-server connection.

Unlike a typical graduate course on WSN, which might assume that students are already comfortable with network programming, our WSN course elevates communication primitives to a first-order topic. We spend roughly half of a lecture period (which are 105 minutes) discussing the basics of radio communication and looking at examples using the SunSPOT API. Students are then asked to practice what they have learned by implementing a simple WSN application that requires client-server communication. In the most recent incarnation of the course, students implemented a client application that samples and reports the temperature on a sensor at a regular interval. Students also implemented a server application that collects data from all sensors and records the reading along with the date/time and the address of the sender[1].

Network communication is perhaps the simplest and most straightforward example of a general topic that can be easily integrated into a WSN course. We spend only half a lecture period to introduce the topic and students are able to implement a simple sensing application that illustrates the same concepts as would a traditional client-server application. Students then build upon this application over the course of the semester and, eventually, produce a more complex sensor system.

4.2 Multi-threaded Programming

The topic of concurrency and threads can appear in many different computer science courses. Though the topic is often covered in detail in a distributed systems course, students might also encounter this topic in an operating systems course and, more recently, parallelism has started to appear in lower-level courses. At USF, for example, students are required to take an introduction to parallel computing course in the sophomore year and threads are also a topic covered in our sophomore-level software engineering course. Assignments in these courses might include the implementation of a multi-threaded web server, or sorting using MPI.

We have found that, even after seeing threads in one or two lower-level courses, students often struggle to understand the intricacies of their operation. In part, the problem stems from a lack of compelling assignments that are guaranteed to expose potential issues that arise with threads. An assignment such as a multi-threaded web server, for example, may require little coordination between threads, particularly if any shared data is stored in a database such as mysql. Additionally, testing strategies for multi-threaded programs can be tricky. If the assignment works, e.g., serves web pages correctly, students may not take the extra step to verify that threads are created and shut down appropriately, or that they interleave correctly.

In WSN, students must use threads extensively for their work. Students report that the *duty cycling* assignment is the most useful assignment in our WSN course. The key

[1]SunSPOT devices are addressed using a 64-bit IEEE address.

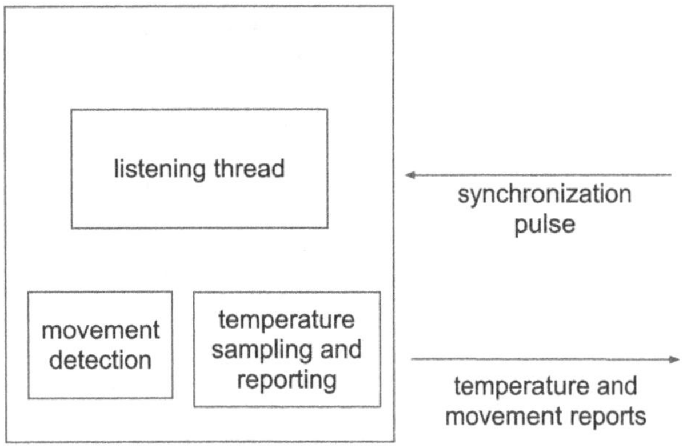

Figure 1: Duty cycle assignment architecture.

element of the assignment is an algorithm to cycle the sensors such that they are on for n seconds and in a suspended or low-power state for n seconds. Moreover, each sensor must be synchronized, at a very coarse level, with the other sensors in the system.

We prepare students for the assignment by devoting two lecture periods to discussing concurrency and multi-threaded programming. This is necessary as some students, particularly our incoming graduate students, have never previously seen the concepts. For most students, this is enough preparation, though a few students typically require a significant amount of help from the instructor or TA when implementing the assignment.

Figure 1 illustrates the components of the assignment. During the on periods, all sensors sense two elements: (1) sensors periodically sample and report their temperature to a base station and (2) sensors use their accelerometers to detect movement and report any movement to a base station. To ensure that all of the sensors' on periods are roughly synchronized, i.e., to mitigate clock drift, the base station periodically sends a synchronization pulse that indicates when the next sleep period should begin. Though students are free to design their own implementations, students often choose to use at least three threads, one to control each of the components in Figure 1. In order for the sensor to enter a suspended state, all threads, including all system-level threads, must be blocked. This is one of the most challenging aspects of the assignment.

Students find that this assignment gives them a significantly better understanding of multi-threaded programming. Students need not develop complicated test suites as they can immediately see whether the sensors enter and leave the suspended state when required. Below we highlight several key lessons of the assignment:

- **Thread Lifecycle** - Students must have a keen understanding of when threads are blocked and when they are runnable. If a single thread is in a running or runnable state, the sensor will not suspend. Similarly, if a thread unexpectedly becomes runnable during the suspend period then the sensor will exit the suspend period prematurely. Through this assignment, students learn how to tightly control a thread's operation.

- **Inter-thread Communication** - To ensure that all threads enter a blocked state at the same time there must be some communication between them. Students often make the mistake of having each thread use an independent timer to determine when to sleep and wake. They quickly discover that this approach does not work as the threads will not be synchronized and the sleep cycles end up being shorter than required. This problem is typically solved by having a single thread act as a *main controller*. This thread determines when the sensor should sleep and wake, and communicates this information to all other threads appropriately.

- **System-Level Threads** - One of the most challenging aspects of this assignment centers around control of system-level threads that are not started by the user-level program. In particular, the SunSPOT sensors have a routing manager that maintains a routing table and forwards messages within a mesh network. The routing manager must be effectively disabled in order for the sensor to enter a suspended state. Students learn a significant amount from figuring out that system-level threads can prevent suspend of the sensor and from figuring out how to control the system-level threads in order to achieve the desired behavior.

4.3 Coordination and the MAC Layer

Because the field of sensor networks is still somewhat immature, most of the literature in the field is restricted to research papers published in computer science conferences. While advanced graduate students may be able to read and digest a paper published at SenSys or Infocom, undergraduates and new graduate students typically lack much of the necessary background to thoroughly understand the ideas proposed. To fully understand and appreciate the benefits of a MAC-layer algorithm such as S-MAC [12], for example, students must have a broad understanding of both distributed coordination algorithms and general MAC-layer protocols.

Our solution to this problem is to take a layered approach to introducing research papers in WSN. Whereas in a typical WSN course students might be expected to read and discuss a new paper every lecture period, we generally devote two lecture periods to each paper. In the first lecture period we introduce the relevant distributed and networking concepts that underlie the solutions proposed by the paper. Once students have this foundation, they are asked to read the paper and discuss it during the subsequent lecture period.

Figure 2 provides an overview of our approach to introducing MAC-layer protocols in sensor networks. In our last incarnation of the course, students read Ye, Heidemann, and Estrin's paper on the S-MAC protocol [12]. We introduced the paper with a lecture covering coordination algorithms in distributed systems, MAC-layer protocols in more traditional networks, and an overview of the challenges of designing MAC-layer protocols in wireless networks. More specifically, our lecture covered mutual exclusion algorithms including time division multiple access (TDMA), frequency division multiple access (FDMA), server-controlled polling algorithms, and ring-based algorithms. Once students understood these broad algorithms, we introduced a conceptual overview of media access control and discussed traditional MAC-layer algorithms such as Ethernet. With this foundation, we then introduced several challenges, including energy efficiency, that arise in the design of MAC protocols for wireless networks.

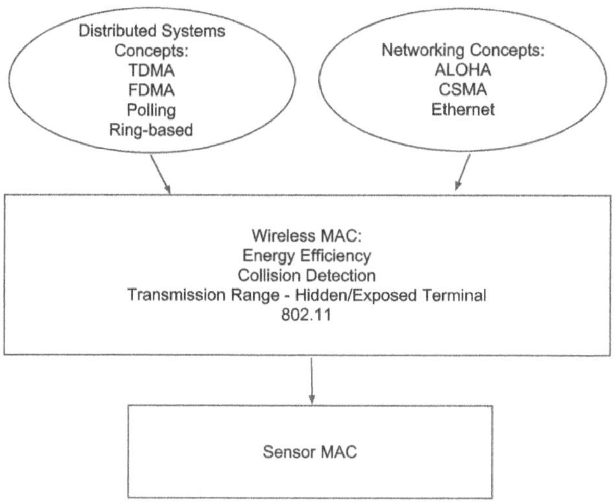

Figure 2: Approach to preparing students to read about MAC-layer protocols for sensor networks.

Though we are unable to cover each of these topics in as much detail as we would in a distributed systems or networking course, one lecture period has provided sufficient time to overview the important elements of each area. With this foundation, students are able to read and understand the assigned research papers. For some papers, students are even asked to implement versions of the proposed algorithms. While we have not done any formal evaluation, we also believe that this approach will have a positive impact for students who subsequently enroll in a distributed systems or networking course.

5. OBSERVATIONS

Our general observation is that the unique approach of integrating distributed systems, networking, and WSN concepts into the same course has been successful. In this section, we highlight several notable elements of the course.

5.1 Tangible Systems

One of the most educative aspects of the course is the experience of building actual sensing applications using physical devices. A sensing application is both inherently distributed and requires networked communication in order to function. By giving students lots of hands-on programming exercises with the SunSPOT sensors, they simply cannot avoid gaining experience with both distributed and networking concepts.

More specifically, to provide a tangible illustration of routing algorithms the routing lecture includes a physical demonstration of the path a packet takes through the sensor network. The demonstration works as follows: each student takes a sensor and positions him or herself somewhere in the classroom. The instructor initiates the send of a packet from a base station node located at the front of the classroom. Based on the color of the LEDs on the sensors, students can see which nodes participate in path discovery and which nodes route the packet. This is an extremely useful exercise and gives students a tangible view of how routing works.

5.2 Iterative Assignments

An approach that has had mixed success is the use of assignments that are iterative—each assignment builds on the previous. We originally thought this approach would be very successful. It allows students to first practice basic skills, such as socket or thread programming, and then asks them to build on top of what they have done to produce a more sophisticated application. We expected students would appreciate not having to start from scratch for each assignment, and that they could build a final application with a significant amount of functionality and complexity.

The reality, perhaps not surprisingly, is that students are frequently unable to complete assignments satisfactorily, which means they are at a disadvantage starting the next assignment. This has been incredibly frustrating for students, and needs to be resolved in future iterations of the course. One solution under consideration is to provide students with solutions to each assignment after it is due. Student can then either build upon their own solution, or the one provided by the instructor.

5.3 Student-Chosen Projects

Each semester we have given students the freedom to propose their own final project for the course. Students can either extend the application they have been building over the course of the semester, or they can choose a completely new project. One of the most exciting successes of the course has been to witness the creative and interesting set of projects proposed by the students. While some students choose the safe bet and implement a small extension to an existing project, some students really try to integrate all they have learned and try something new.

Students have proposed several notable projects in the two semesters the course has been taught. A popular proposal is the use of the sensor as a controller, either for a computer-based game or another device such as a Lego robot. While this assignment does not integrate many of the distributed and network concepts students learn in the course, students often use it as an opportunity to integrate concepts from other courses, for example using Artificial Intelligence techniques to do gesture recognition. Several students have also proposed projects that involve significant experimentation and evaluation. They draw upon what they learn reading and evaluating papers and design and execute experiments to compare different types of sensor network algorithms. Finally, one of the more fun projects was an *automated race monitoring system*. A group of students designed a sensing application and web service to track a runner's movements (speed, etc) and report the results via a web application. The students worked tirelessly on the application, testing running up and down the hallways and getting other students excited about taking the class in the future!

5.4 Room for Improvement

There are several notable areas where we feel the course could be improved. First, in both iterations of the course we have taken a bottom-up approach. We first talk about relevant technologies, i.e., the SunSPOT hardware, and then take a networking-centric approach moving from the MAC layer to the application layer. Though applications of sensor networks, such as RACNet [6], tend to be the topics students enjoy most, they often seem "burnt out" by the time we cover the related papers. We would like to explore whether students have enough foundation surrounding the specific challenges and proposed solutions in sensor networks to understand the relevant papers if we were to structure the course in a top-down fashion.

While we do offer students the experience of using actual devices to develop real sensing applications, in the end their applications are only prototypes and they miss the experience of interacting with an actual deployment. We would like to find a feasible way of having students either build and deploy an application over the course of the semester, or otherwise engage with a deployment provided to them. There are several critical skills they would gain from the experience. They would, for example, have to deal with real failures in a long-running system.

6. RELATED WORK AND CONCLUSION

There has been increased interest in making material traditionally taught in graduate courses accessible to undergraduates. As Albrecht points out [1], knowledge of distributed systems concepts is becoming critical and undergraduate students are often underprepared for careers in research and development without a foundation in this area. Hnatyshin and Lobo [3] highlight the importance of engaging students in computer networking by providing hands-on exercises to illustrate key concepts. More specifically in the area of sensor networks, Tyman, Bulusu, and Mache underscore the increasing importance of wireless sensor networks and point out that there is a need to make sensor networks accessible to undergraduates [11]. They also point out that with the advent of sensor technology like the Java-programmable SunSPOT, this is imminently possible. Finally, Forster and Jazayeri [2] describe their hands-on approach to introducing undergraduate students to sensor networks to prepare them for jobs in industry.

Our work presents an integrated approach to introducing networking and distributed systems concepts using sensing applications as an overarching motivation. We describe our experience with introducing concepts such as network communication and concurrency by having students implement applications on the SunSPOT sensor platform. We further discuss our success using a layered approach to engage undergraduate students in the process of digesting research papers. Particularly in a small, liberal arts department such as ours, our approach is ideal for introducing students to a broad range of advanced topics.

7. REFERENCES

[1] Jeannie R. Albrecht. Bringing big systems to small schools: distributed systems for undergr aduates. In *SIGCSE '09: Proceedings of the 40th ACM technical symposium on Com puter science education*, pages 101–105, New York, NY, USA, 2009. ACM.

[2] Anna Förster and Mehdi Jazayeri. Hands-on approach to teaching wireless sensor networks at the undergraduate level. In *ITiCSE '10: Proceedings of the fifteenth annual conference on Innovation and technology in computer science education*, pages 284–288, New York, NY, USA, 2010. ACM.

[3] Vasil Y. Hnatyshin and Andrea F. Lobo. Undergraduate data communications and networking projects using opnet and wireshark software. In *SIGCSE '08: Proceedings of the 39th SIGCSE technical symposium on Computer science education*, pages 241–245, New York, NY, USA, 2008. ACM.

[4] Holger Karl and Andreas Willig. *Protocols and Architectures for Wireless Sensor Networks*. John Wiley & Sons, 2005.

[5] James F. Kurose and Keith W. Ross. *Computer Networking: A Top-Down Approach*. Addison-Wesley Publishing Company, USA, 3rd edition, 2005.

[6] Chieh-Jan Mike Liang, Jie Liu, Liqian Luo, Andreas Terzis, and Feng Zhao. Racnet: a high-fidelity data center sensing network. In *SenSys '09: Proceedings of the 7th ACM Conference on Embedded Networked Sensor Systems*, pages 15–28, New York, NY, USA, 2009. ACM.

[7] Emiliano Miluzzo, Nicholas D. Lane, Kristóf Fodor, Ronald Peterson, Hong Lu, Mirco Musolesi, Xiao Eisenman, Shane B. an d Zheng, and Andrew T. Campbell. Sensing meets mobile social networks: the design, implementation and e valuation of the cenceme application. In *SenSys '08: Proceedings of the 6th ACM conference on Embedded netw ork sensor systems*, pages 337–350, New York, NY, USA, 2008. ACM.

[8] Crossbow Motes. `http://www.xbow.com`.

[9] Charles E. Perkins and Elizabeth M. Royer. The ad hoc on-demand distance-vector protocol. pages 173–219, 2001.

[10] SunSPOTs. `http://www.sunspotworld.com`.

[11] Damon Tyman, Nirupama Bulusu, and Jens Mache. An activity-based sensor networks course for undergraduates with sun spot devices. *SIGCSE Bull.*, 41(1):34–38, 2009.

[12] Wei Ye, John Heidemann, and Deborah Estrin. An energy-efficient mac protocol for wireless sensor networks. In *Proceedings of the IEEE Infocom*, pages 1567–1576, New York, NY, USA, June 2002. USC/Information Sciences Institute, IEEE.

[13] Feng Zhao and Leonidas Guibas. *Wireless Sensor Networks: An Information Processing Approach*. Elsevier/Morgan-Kaufmann, 2004.

Follow the River and You Will Find the C

Jae Woo Lee
Dept. of Computer Science
Columbia University
New York, NY, USA
jae@cs.columbia.edu

Michael S. Kester
Dept. of Computer Science
Columbia University
New York, NY, USA
msk2117@columbia.edu

Henning Schulzrinne
Dept. of Computer Science
Columbia University
New York, NY, USA
hgs@cs.columbia.edu

ABSTRACT

We present a one-semester transition course intended to bridge the gap between a Java-based introductory sequence and advanced systems courses. We chose to structure our course as a series of lab assignments that, while independent, are also milestones in a single main project, writing a web server from scratch. By anchoring the course on a single real-world application, we were able to provide depth, instill good programming practices, give insight into systems, and generate excitement.

Categories and Subject Descriptors

K.3.2 [**COMPUTERS AND EDUCATION**]: Computer and Information Science Education—*Curriculum, Computer science education, Information systems education*

General Terms

Design, Human Factors, Languages

1. INTRODUCTION

Current trends in the introductory computer science sequence follow the objects-first paradigm. Java is the language of choice in most cases [10], while some have argued Python as a good alternative [9]. Others have resisted the trends and remain committed to a traditional imperative-first or even functional-first approach. The subject remains an ongoing debate [11, 7, 8, 17] and the authors take no position in this paper. Rather, we address a concrete problem that arises as a consequence of choosing objects-first.

Our school has adopted the objects-first approach. Specifically, it follows the three course sequence recommended by CC2001 [6]. This conversion, however, created a gap in knowledge as the students progress to upper level courses like operating systems and computer graphics, where they need a command of C and the UNIX environment.

This "gap problem" seems common among our peer schools. The nationwide decline in enrollment has forced educators to seek ways to attract and retain students. This has led to many changes in the introductory sequence the most prominent of which is the shift to the objects-first paradigm [13]. On the other hand, the upper level courses have largely remained the same, in part because retention of students is less of a concern, and in part because the focus is on the current body of knowledge rather than pedagogy. Most schools that opt for objects-first offer a transition course aimed at bridging the gap. A review of the curricula of our peer schools showed that transition courses typically attempt to cover too many topics. This either limits the course to a cursory treatment of the material, which may leave the students underprepared for advanced coursework, or results in a course where success requires substantial prior programing experience. Such a course would alienate many promising future CS majors.

This paper presents a C-based introductory systems programming course [1] designed to avoid common problems associated with transition courses. We explore the principles of our course design in Section 2. We present a detailed layout of our course in Section 3. We discuss survey results and student experiences in Section 4. Lastly, we summarize our contribution in Section 5.

2. DESIGN PRINCIPLES

In our search for a suitable model for our transition course, we found surprisingly little research about structuring such a course. We feel this is largely based on two factors. First, a typical introduction to UNIX and C is probably considered fairly bland from an educational research standpoint. On a more practical level, the shift to objects-first is a relatively new phenomenon, so educators have yet to come to a consensus on the effect it has on the CS curriculum.

Our course is designed as a single project with milestones, each of which we call a *lab*. Each lab constitutes a step toward completion of the project without explicitly referring to it as such. Students are given one to two weeks to complete each lab assignment, and are expected to work independently. Shortly after each due date a fully commented solution is provided. This course overlaps with the last semester of the introductory sequence, which is, introduction to programming (CS1), object-oriented design (CS1.5), and data structures and algorithms (CS2), each taught in Java. Our school recommends our course be taken concurrently with CS2.

For the single-project approach to be most effective, it is critical to achieve four sub-goals. (*a*) *Don't forgo depth.* Upon completion of this course, the students should be ready

SIGCSE'11, March 9–12, 2011, Dallas, Texas, USA.

for Linux kernel programming in our school's operating system course [20], which requires a strong C and UNIX background. (*b*)*Focus on doing it right.* We emphasize writing bug-free code, rather than simply producing the required results. (*c*)*Lay out the big picture.* At the end of the course the students should have a clear concept of how a complex software system works. (*d*)*Don't be boring.* The students should experience the joy of programming.

We chose writing a web server from scratch as our big project. Each lab, though self-contained, contributes an individual part of the system, either with subsystem code or a fundamental concept. This structure also affords us a surprising degree of breadth as we incorporate concepts from data structures, databases, operating systems, networking, and multi-tier server architectures. This is similar in spirit to "teaching breadth-first depth-first" as put forth by Murtagh [19, 18]. He advocates, rather than teaching the normal wide ranging topics found in a CS1 course as a disjoint set, exploring them as a whole through the lens of a single subfield, computer networking.

Building a web server from scratch is far more effective in motivating students than completing programming exercises. Literature supports that students respond far more enthusiastically to working with production software than pedagogic software [14]. Our students reported exultation when they saw a web page appear in Firefox, served by code they wrote (achieving sub-goal *d*). The *surprise* they experience from building something large and real at this early stage has a lasting impact on their education [21].

We address the remaining sub-goals in a similar fashion. The web server was required to communicate with a back-end server and generate pages dynamically. As such, students thoroughly learn how web-based multi-tier software architectures work (*c*). Coding a web server requires a strong command of C (*a*). We put an emphasis on proper memory management (*b*). Memory errors are a primary source of bugs for novice C programmers [16].

3. THE COURSE

In this section, we describe the course implementation. There are ten lab assignments. The completed web server is lab 7. In a way, the course forms a narrative following a typical structure of a drama: an exposition (labs 1-3) to lay the groundwork of what is to come, a rising action (labs 4-6) to bring the participants ready for the climax (lab 7), a falling action (lab 8) to wind down the climax, and a resolution (labs 9-10) to close the course.

3.1 Exposition

Labs 1-3 introduce the basic tools and skills needed in later labs. At the completion of this section of the course, students will be familiar with the most common UNIX commands, be able to use pointers, and understand the linked list data structure.

Lab 1: UNIX Basics, SVN, and Make

"The beginning is the most important part of the work." - Plato

Lab 1 provides an introduction to three components critical to the remainder of the course: UNIX, SVN, and Make. We help the students set up their shell environments, and introduce them to the UNIX man pages, encouraging them to learn new commands as they encounter them. We provide a short tutorial on SVN, which the students are required to use throughout the semester. In the first semester we taught the class, the students were expected to learn Make on their own from the online documentation, which proved to be insufficient as a tutorial. In subsequent semesters, we provided a tutorial during lecture. In both cases, we provided a heavily commented solution for future use as a template.

The deliverable for lab 1 was a trivial program. The goal was simply to introduce the tools that would become the buttresses of their C programming repertoire.

```
int main(int argc, char **argv)
{
    if (argc <= 1) return 1;
    char **copy = duplicateArgs(argc, argv);
    char **p = copy;

    argv++;
    p++;
    while (*argv) {
        printf("%s %s\n", *argv++, *p++);
    }
    freeDuplicatedArgs(copy);
    return 0;
}
```

Figure 1: The main function provided in lab 2.

Lab 2: Pointers and Arrays

"It can be hard to teach them in half an hour, but we can give them a few pointers..." - Scott Morrison

Lab 2 builds a solid understanding of pointers and arrays in C. For example, the most challenging problem in lab 2 asks the students to properly create and destroy a copy of the `argv` structure. The students are given the main function of a program called `twecho`, shown in Figure 1, which echoes each command line argument twice, once verbatim and once capitalized. The students are asked to implement the two functions it calls: `duplicateArgs` and `freeDuplicatedArgs`. The former duplicates the `argv` structure into a newly allocated structure and the latter frees the structure. Writing the two required functions, without making any memory errors, requires a solid understanding of how to allocate and destroy a non-trivial memory structure. It also requires an understanding of how to manipulate pointers to access and modify data in memory locations.

In this lab we introduce Valgrind [5]. Valgrind is a error checking utility that detects memory leaks, overrunning array bounds, and a number of other common errors. Valgrind enables the identification of memory errors in a program even when the program appears to work. This is consistent with our *focus on doing it right.* Lab submissions that produced the correct results at the expense of memory errors were heavily penalized.

The initial foray into memory management tends to be challenging for beginning C students. As such, we allowed ample time for this assignment, the teaching staff provided significant support to help the students during office hours, and a class mailing list provided a forum in which the students could discuss common problems. Our goal was not only to help them get their code working, but also to make them understand it.

```
struct Node {
    struct Node *next;
    void *data;
};
struct List {
    struct Node *head;
};
struct Node *addFront(struct List *lst, void *data);
struct Node *findNode(struct List *lst, const void *dataSought,
    int (*compar)(const void *, const void *));
```

Figure 2: An excerpt from lab 3's header file.

Lab 3: Implementing a Linked List

"In all planing you make a list and you set priorities."
- Alan Lakein

Lab 3 introduces the students to data structures in C by having them implement a singly linked list. While this is a typical assignment in a C programming course, we present it in a manner consistent with our prevailing principles. We specify the prototypes, some of which are shown in Figure 2, and we provide a comprehensive test driver program. The students are required to run the test driver using Valgrind in order to make sure that their implementation is free of memory errors.

We also introduce two new concepts: callback functions and libraries. Several linked list functions rely on a pointer to function, such as the **findNode** function shown in Figure 2. The students follow a tutorial to build a library from their linked list implementation, which they are required to use in subsequent labs.

The linked list follows pointer semantics. Each node holds a **void*** to a generic data item, but does not manage the lifetime of that item. The interface of the linked list is revisited later in lab 10, which asks the students to wrap the pointer-based linked list in a new value-based interface using C++.

3.2 Rising Action

Labs 4-6 focus on details that are essential to the ultimate goal of writing a web server. The topics include I/O, process management in UNIX, TCP/IP, Sockets, and HTTP.

Lab 4: Standard Input and Output

"A library is thought in cold storage."
- Herbert Samuel

The lectures at this point cover I/O in C. Topics include standard input and output streams, redirection and pipes in UNIX, formatted I/O functions, and file I/O. These concepts are exercised in lab 4. The students must implement *MdbLookup*, a program that searches through a message database. The message database is a binary file in which each record has a simple structure of two fields, name and message which are limited to 15 and 23 characters respectively:

```
struct MdbRec {
    char name[16];
    char  msg[24];
};
```

When the program starts, every message of the database is read into memory using the linked list from lab 3. The program then enters a loop prompting the user for a search string and matching it with the records. An empty string, which can be input by simply pressing *Enter* at the prompt, matches all records.

Lab 5: Turning MdbLookup into a server

"The old pipe gives the sweetest smoke."
- Irish Proverb

At this point we have concluded our discussion of C, and shift focus to UNIX and TCP/IP networking. During lecture, we give a brief overview of operating systems and TCP/IP networking, without going into detail. The main focus is to convey to the students the concept of "layers." We first explain the layers in software systems: OS kernel, system calls, library functions, and applications. We then introduce the five layers of the Internet protocol stack, again with limited detail. The sockets API is an interface between layers 4 and 5, which allows us to treat layers 1 through 4 as a black box. The students had no problem with these concepts because of their daily experiences with operating systems and the Internet. We also introduce the concept of processes, and how a new process in UNIX is created using **fork** and **exec**.

Here we introduce Netcat [2], a command line program that creates a TCP socket and connects it to the standard I/O. The incoming end of the TCP connection is connected to **stdout** and the outgoing end of the TCP connection is connected to **stdin**. It can run as either a client where it will initiate a connection, or server where it will listen on a port. The client mode operation is similar to that of Telnet.

Lab 5 demonstrates how to combine the MdbLookup program and Netcat in a pipeline forming a network server without sockets programming. We provide the pipeline and the command to make a named pipe:

```
mkfifo mypipe
cat mypipe | nc -l -p 40000 | mdb-lookup > mypipe
```

The standard input and output of MdbLookup is connected to those of a Netcat session using pipes. Netcat in turn connects its standard input and output streams to a socket connection. The students are asked to wrap the pipeline in a shell script and control the script from a parent program which calls **fork** and **exec**.

One of the goals here is to convey to the students the central tenet of UNIX: small is beautiful [12]. A complex task is broken up into small building blocks, and the standard I/O paradigm makes it possible to connect them together.

Lab 6: Sockets Programming and HTTP

"From now on, I'll connect the dots my own way."
- Bill Watterson

Lab 6 covers two topics that are needed to implement a web server: sockets programming and HTTP. During lecture, we walk through simple TCP client and server examples. The server echoes back strings sent from the client.

The first part of lab 6 asks the students to write a version of MdbLookup server using sockets. There is actually very little code to write. They combine the lab 4 program and the TCP echo server example to make the MdbLookup server. The solution we supplied merged the two programs and required fewer than 20 lines of modifications.

The second part of lab 6 asks the students to write a limited version of Wget [3], a command line program that downloads a given URL. The students were only required to implement basic single file download functionality. In preparation for this part, we demonstrated how HTTP works by capturing the dialog between a web browser and server.

First, we use Netcat in client mode to pose as a web browser. We connect to a real website and take note of the headers generated by the server. Next we use Netcat in server mode to see what headers the browser had sent.

3.3 Climax

Lab 7: Writing a Web Server

"If we fix a goal and work towards it, then we are never just passing time." - Anna Neagle

Lab 7 is the culmination of all efforts up to this point. It is a serious undertaking, but the students have all the necessary tools and background. The assignment is to code a web server that implements a subset of HTTP 1.0. The server handles GET requests for static content. The server does not send a `content-type` header, but modern browsers can usually detect the types of the incoming files, enabling the retrieval of HTML pages with images.

In addition to static pages, the server is required to return dynamic content, specifically MdbLookup records. The web server provides an HTML front-end to the MdbLookup server from lab 6. The web server maintains a persistent TCP connection to the MdbLookup server. GET requests in the form of `/mdb-lookup?key=`*`string`* trigger the web server to query the MdbLookup server. The web server formats the returned messages into an HTML table.

3.4 Falling Action

Lab 8: Writing an Apache Module

"It's easier to find a new audience than to write a new speech." - Dan Kennedy

Now with one of the most intense aspects of the course out of the way, the students are given a task that may have seemed daunting at the beginning of the course. They must reimplement the HTML front-end of MdbLookup server using an Apache module. They compile and install an Apache web server, and write a module to connect to the MdbLookup server. Many students were surprised to find that this is in fact one of the easier labs. It was treated as extra credit.

Software Architecture: The Big Picture

"Details create the big picture." - Sanford I. Weill

This is an appropriate time to reexamine the labs from a software architecture point of view. We show the students how the evolution of MdbLookup reflects the various forms of software architecture:

- Lab 4: command line, confined to the local database
- Lab 5: server, put together using Netcat and pipes
- Lab 6: server, coded using the sockets API
- Lab 7: web-based server, written from scratch
- Lab 8: web-based server, written as an Apache module

The students now have a clear understanding of what a multi-tier client-server architecture entails. They can immediately understand other popular web-based architectures such as Linux-Apache-MySQL-PHP, commonly referred to as LAMP, or Java EE [4]. Our evolutionary approach was constructed conscientiously in order to teach the students how to look at systems from an architectural point of view. This enables the students to dissect a complex software system by identifying the components and understanding the connections between them.

3.5 Resolution

After lab 8, we have about three weeks left in the semester. The students are introduced to C++ at this point. Given the limited time, we focus on one aspect of the language: object construction and destruction. The interplay between memory allocation and object lifetime is often poorly understood, even by those students who use C++ regularly. The lack of a precise understanding of that issue is often the source of bugs. A solid understanding of object lifetime is the foundation for using more advanced C++ features such as inheritance and templates.

Lab 9: Object Construction and Destruction in C++

"High aims form high characters, and great objects bring out great minds." - Tryon Edwards

In lecture, we study a basic C++ string implementation, *MyString*, which has two data members:

```
class MyString {
public:
    ...
    // member functions
    ...
private:
    char *data;
    int len;
};
```

This canonical example of a C++ class shows how constructor, destructor, copy constructor, and assignment operator should perform memory management. We call these member functions the *Basic4*.

Lab 9 helps the students gain a precise understanding of when each of the Basic4 is invoked. We inserted trace output statements in the Basic4 functions of the MyString class. We ask the students to analyze the trace output when the following function is called, identifying precisely at what point each of the Basic4 is invoked and on which object, including unnamed temporaries:

```
MyString add(MyString s1, MyString s2)
{
    MyString temp(" and ");
    return s1 + temp + s2;
}
```

The `-fno-elide-constructors` flag for the `g++` compiler is used in a Makefile that we provide to the students. The flag makes sure that the compiler generates all copy constructor calls; otherwise the compiler will optimize away some copy constructor calls for temporary objects. Lab 9 also asks the students to provide definitions to some of the member functions and operators that the course-provided version left unimplemented.

Lab 10: Linked List Redux

"Experience isn't interesting until it begins to repeat itself." - Elizabeth Bowen

In lecture, we cover the template container classes in the standard C++ library including `vector` and `list`. We emphasize the important semantic difference between these containers and the linked list we implemented in lab 3. The standard containers provide "value semantics," that is, an item is copied and held by value in the container. In contrast, the linked list from lab 3 only held a pointer to a given object.

The first part of lab 10 tests the students' understanding of this difference. It asks them to write a linked list class in C++, called *StrList*, that holds MyString objects. The challenging requirement is that they need to use the linked list class they implemented in lab 3 as the underlying engine. In other words, the students were required to wrap the lab 3 linked list with a new C++ interface that provides value semantics. For example, one of the member functions that they were asked to implement:

```
void StrList::addFront(const MyString& str)
```

must call:

```
struct Node *addFront(struct List *list, void *data)
```

Being able to switch from value semantics to pointer semantics, and vice versa, represents a significant challenge to the students. As with lab 3, a comprehensive test driver was provided and Valgrind-clean execution was mandatory.

Lab 10 also gives the students a glimpse of working with legacy code. While the first part asked them to wrap a piece of legacy code with a new interface, the second part asks them to do the opposite, namely, keep the new interface and upgrade the implementation. It asks them to turn StrList into *TList*, a template class that can hold data types other than MyString. The underlying engine is no longer based on the lab 3 code, but replaced by the standard C++ `list` template container class. By using the following two typedefs,

```
typedef string MyString;
typedef TList<string> StrList;
```

the students were able to use the same test driver provided in the first part without modification.

SmartPtr: Java-style Object Reference in C++

"We live in an instant-coffee world. Sometimes real-world solutions take a little longer." - Mike Conaway

By this time, the students appreciate the difficulty of object lifetime management in C/C++; they appreciate the benefit of being able to pass around object references in Java without worrying about deallocating the object. We end the course by examining a reference-counted smart pointer class in C++, *SmartPtr*, that can mimic the semantics of Java object references.

A SmartPtr instance is initialized with a pointer to a heap-allocated object–a pointer returned by the `new` operator–and takes over the lifetime management of the given object. The SmartPtr instance is passed around by value. When it is copied, the copy constructor increments the reference count. The SmartPtr's destructor decrements the reference count, and calls `delete` on the underlying object only when the reference count goes to zero. We draw comparisons between a SmartPtr and a Java reference. Although the mechanisms are different (reference counting for a SmartPtr and garbage collection for a Java reference), the effect is the same: you can copy and return an object reference freely without worrying about deallocating the underlying object.

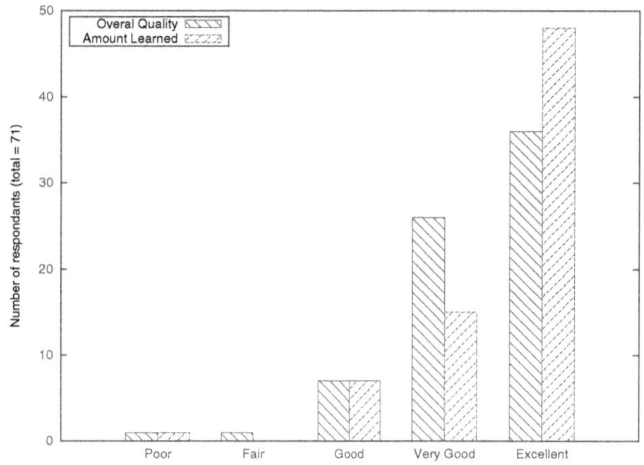

Figure 3: Survey: Overall Quality & Amount Learned

4. STUDENT EXPERIENCE

We taught this course for three consecutive semesters: Spring 2008, Fall 2008, and Spring 2009. The student enrollments were 30, 46, and 49, respectively. The majority of the students were prospective or declared CS majors. Figure 3 shows the results from two relevant questions from the end-of-semester course evaluations. It indicates that student reaction to the course has been overwhelmingly positive.

We implemented several methods to mitigate the demanding workload. We ran a class mailing list, where the students were encouraged to help each other but were forbidden from posting code. This was obviously helpful to those struggling but was equally helpful to those providing guidance as they learned through teaching.

We structured the course rigidly. The lab descriptions clearly laid out the steps needed to complete the assignments correctly. This reflects our viewpoint that, in a C-based introductory systems course, precise direction is more valuable than encouraging creativity. One drawback to this approach was that plagiarism was more difficult to detect.

In order to evaluate our students' performance in the operating systems course (OS), for which our class was designed as preparation, we conducted an additional survey. Among the 40 respondents, 15 went on to take OS. We compared the GPA of those 15 students to that of all OS students from Fall 2008 to Spring 2010, during which all 15 took OS. Our students bettered the four semester average for OS: 3.14 to 2.99. This result is by no means scientific, but we are bolstered by the fact that our students did not perform poorly, especially considering that OS classes are generally comprised of more than 75% graduate students, many of whom have significant industry experience.

Our core mission in education is to engage students and get them excited about CS. This mission, by nature, is difficult if not impossible to evaluate. Perhaps more telling is the personal observations of our students. One student reported that our course "was critical to [his] success in [operating systems]." He went on to describe that many of his peers lacked enough background knowledge in C, and ended up dropping OS. The most gratifying comment we received came from a student who was majoring in Applied Physics, took our course in his third year, and fell in love with CS.

He took as many CS courses as he could in his forth year and was admitted to a top Ph.D. program [15].

> "Due to this course *alone*, I found myself fully-prepared for subsequent coursework in databases, operating systems, and software engineering. [...] We were tacitly taught a lesson in iterative development - we built the server part-by-part, with the requirement of having a working (tested) system at each stage in development. Along the way, I developed skill in efficiently managing a large codebase (in C) on the UNIX commandline - something invaluable in my systems work in graduate school."

5. SUMMARY

We present a one-semester course intended to bridge the gap between a Java-based introductory sequence and advanced systems courses. By anchoring the course on a single real-world application, we were able to provide depth, instill good programming practices, give insight into systems, and generate excitement.

Our contribution is twofold. First, we propose a course organization technique and demonstrate its efficacy. Traditionally classes are structured as either a term project with milestones, or a series of homework assignments testing individual topics. We combine the two approaches. From the outside, our course seems to consist of ten independent assignments, but in fact, they are milestones to a single main project. This technique can be applied to other CS courses. Second, we use this single-project approach to implement a transition course addressing the "gap problem" caused by the shift to objects-first. The course effectively transitioned our students from the introductory Java sequence to upper level systems courses. We present a detailed description of the course material, which others can adapt for their own classes.

Acknowledgments

The authors would like to thank Prof. Angelos Keromytis for providing his previous course materials which gave the foundation for this course, and Prof. Jason Nieh and Prof. Junfeng Yang for their help with the evaluation. We also thank our students and TAs for their effort and feedback.

6. REFERENCES

[1] COMS W3157 Advanced programming, Columbia University. `http://www1.cs.columbia.edu/~jae/cs3157/2009-1/syllabus.html`.

[2] GNU Netcat. `http://netcat.sourceforge.net/`.

[3] GNU Wget. `http://www.gnu.org/software/wget/`.

[4] Java EE at a glance. `http://java.sun.com/javaee/`.

[5] Valgrind. `http://valgrind.org/`.

[6] The Joint Task Force on Computing Curricula. "Computing Curricula 2001". *Journal of Educational Resources in Computing*, 1(3), 2001.

[7] O. Astrachan, K. Bruce, E. Koffman, M. Kölling, and S. Reges. Resolved: objects early has failed. *SIGCSE Bull.*, 37(1):451–452, 2005.

[8] K. B. Bruce. Controversy on how to teach CS 1: a discussion on the SIGCSE-members mailing list. *SIGCSE Bull.*, 37(2):111–117, 2005.

[9] R. J. Enbody, W. F. Punch, and M. McCullen. Python CS1 as preparation for C++ CS2. In *SIGCSE '09: Proceedings of the 40th ACM technical symposium on Computer science education*, pages 116–120, New York, NY, USA, 2009. ACM.

[10] J. Forbes and D. D. Garcia. "...But what do the top-rated schools do?": a survey of introductory computer science curricula. In *SIGCSE '07: Proceedings of the 38th SIGCSE technical symposium on Computer science education*, pages 245–246, New York, NY, USA, 2007. ACM.

[11] J. Gal-Ezer, T. Vilner, and E. Zur. Has the paradigm shift in CS1 a harmful effect on data structures courses: a case study. *SIGCSE Bull.*, 41(1):126–130, 2009.

[12] M. Gancarz. *The UNIX philosophy*. Digital Press, Newton, MA, USA, 1995.

[13] A. Gaspar, N. Boyer, and A. Ejnioui. Role of the C language in current computing curricula part 1: survey analysis. *J. Comput. Small Coll.*, 23(2):120–127, 2007.

[14] R. Hess and P. Paulson. Linux kernel projects for an undergraduate operating systems course. In *SIGCSE '10: Proceedings of the 41st ACM technical symposium on Computer science education*, pages 485–489, New York, NY, USA, 2010. ACM.

[15] N. Knight. personal correspondence, 2009. UC Berkeley.

[16] E. Lahtinen, K. Ala-Mutka, and H.-M. Järvinen. A study of the difficulties of novice programmers. In *ITiCSE '05: Proceedings of the 10th annual SIGCSE conference on Innovation and technology in computer science education*, pages 14–18, New York, NY, USA, 2005. ACM.

[17] R. Lister, A. Berglund, T. Clear, J. Bergin, K. Garvin-Doxas, B. Hanks, L. Hitchner, A. Luxton-Reilly, K. Sanders, C. Schulte, and J. L. Whalley. Research perspectives on the objects-early debate. *SIGCSE Bull.*, 38(4):146–165, 2006.

[18] T. P. Murtagh. Teacing breadth-first depth-first. In *ITiCSE '01: Proceedings of the 6th annual conference on Innovation and technology in computer science education*, pages 37–40, New York, NY, USA, 2001. ACM.

[19] T. P. Murtagh. Weaving CS into CS1: a doubly depth-first approach. In *SIGCSE '07: Proceedings of the 38th SIGCSE technical symposium on Computer science education*, pages 336–340, New York, NY, USA, 2007. ACM.

[20] J. Nieh and C. Vaill. Experiences teaching operating systems using virtual platforms and linux. In *SIGCSE '05: Proceedings of the 36th SIGCSE technical symposium on Computer science education*, pages 520–524, New York, NY, USA, 2005. ACM.

[21] L. Thomas, C. Zander, and A. Eckerdal. Harnessing surprise: tales from students' transformational biographies. In *SIGCSE '10: Proceedings of the 41st ACM technical symposium on Computer science education*, pages 300–304, New York, NY, USA, 2010. ACM.

Computer Literacy as Life Skills for a Web 2.0 World

Jane Turk
La Salle University
1900 West Olney Avenue
Philadelphia, PA 19141
215-951-1094
turk@lasalle.edu

ABSTRACT

This paper presents an innovative computer literacy course that focuses solely on developing skills needed for life in a networked world in which one must protect oneself from identity theft, be careful posting on social networks, and use credit and debit cards wisely. The course emphasizes ethical responsibility and information literacy. Its target audience, first-year, non-computer science majors, learn what they need to know to use technology safely, effectively, efficiently, and ethically. The course is grounded in active learning, such as posting in a class wiki, and critical thinking. It is a radical alternative to a traditional software packages approach.

The paper documents the need for this course, *The Digital Person*, and its blend of content and pedagogy. Data from three years of offering the course provide an assessment of its effectiveness and value to those who have taken it. A review of SIGCSE literature in the last ten years finds no representation of this creative approach.

Categories and Subject Descriptors

K.3.2 [**Computing Milieux**] Computer and Information Science Education, Literacy

General Terms

Design, Experimentation.

Keywords

Computer literacy, general education, non-majors, ethics, critical thinking, information literacy, class wiki, SENCER.

1. INTRODUCTION

1.1 Overview of *The Digital Person*

This paper describes a new approach to computer literacy that focuses on developing ethical responsibility and information literacy in the context of issues such as privacy, social networks, intellectual property, e-waste and protecting one's computer and identity. Pedagogy, an essential element in course design and development, emphasizes active learning and explicit development of critical thinking. Students "go public" with their knowledge in a class wiki, which becomes a resource on several topics.

CSC 153 – *The Digital Person* was created for first-year, non-computer science majors, to provide them with the knowledge and skills needed to make good choices in a data-driven, networked world. The course gets its name, with permission, from the book by Daniel Solove, of George Washington Law School [18].

The course fulfills the core computer literacy requirement. It was first offered in Fall 2007 to majors in communication; speech, language, and hearing; digital art and multimedia design; and English. Given a choice between *The Digital Person* and the traditional software packages course, described in 1.2 below, the chairs of these departments determined that the new course would well serve the needs of their students. Such students now can choose between the two courses.

This paper describes the experience of teaching thirteen sections of *The Digital Person* over three academic years.

The remainder of this section explains why the course was developed, with emphasis on the pedagogy, and how it works, including student assessment. It also explains how and why topics were selected. Section two situates the course within relevant literature, noting that a course like this is not represented in SIGCSE publications in the last ten years. Section three presents examples of topics and associated instructional strategies. Section four provides post-course feedback from student evaluations, survey results, and letters to future students. Sections five through seven chronicle evolution over three years, lessons learned in course creation, and on-going objectives.

1.2 Why Create *The Digital Person*?

There are huge holes in what is taught to many first-year non-computer science majors. My university and many other institutions did not include key issues of privacy, as well as assessing accuracy of information and protection from identity theft. Computer literacy was generally defined for non-computer science majors in terms of facility in *using* a computer, specifically facility in using packages like Microsoft Office and a web browser. The CS0 plan of presenting general principles of computer science in a breadth-first manner has not been discussed, nor would it likely be approved, at the level of general education.

Table 1 below lists the content of the current traditional computer literacy course, designed more than a decade ago.

Table 1. Content of a Traditional Computer Literacy Course

fundamental computer concepts
file management
information literacy • criteria for evaluating web pages • electronic searching
mechanics of word processing, spreadsheet, and presentation software

Table 2 lists the topics in *The Digital Person* course. The new course emphasizes computer skills essential for safe and wise use of social network, credit, and other forms of information—skills needed for a life time. No side-by-side contrast of these two courses is possible because of the radical content difference.

Table 2. Content of CSC 153 – *The Digital Person*

collection, use, and misuse of personal data • identity theft and phishing • credit agencies and FICO scores • social networks
thinking critically
information literacy • criteria for evaluating web pages • evaluating the accuracy and reliability of information and using it ethically
copyright
protecting your privacy • legal framework • protecting your computer • protecting the privacy and reputation of others
Internet/Web • storage of Web pages and queries
current issues • proper disposal of a computer and cell phone • multitasking • texting while driving

1.2.1 What Topics to Include and Why?

The initial set of topics was derived from topics generally included in an undergraduate course in legal, social, and ethical issues for computer science majors.

Core topics such as privacy, ethical use of technology, copyright, and identity theft are part of the body of knowledge defined in the ACM CS Curriculum for 2001 [3] and 2008 [4].

Information literacy is an essential component of any computer literacy course. Rockman defines information literacy broadly as "a set of abilities that allow a person to recognize when information is needed and to effectively and efficiently act on that need"[17]. The information literacy component was defined in consultation with the Library Instruction Coordinator who teaches three classes on that topic.

Section 1.3 below explains the role of explicit development of critical thinking in this course. Section 3.1 explains use of a class wiki as a means of recording and sharing student work.

The initial course description also listed "current issues." This category gave the course flexibility to deal with emerging topics. Electronic voting was an important topic in the run-up to the 2008 presidential election. Electronic health records were examined in the spring of 2009. As the sub-prime loan crisis exploded, study of credit cards was expanded to consider repayment of credit card debt under outrageous interest rates, and the effects of failure to pay on one's credit score. When a Rutgers freshman killed himself after web publication of his private life, we addressed ethical behavior on the Internet in the light of this tragedy. These are issues students need to know in our high-powered technological world and use for a life-time—"computer life skills."

Proper disposal of a computer and cell phone is a "computer life skill," and, in fact, a neglected one. Initially, two classes dealt with e-waste. Current study has expanded to three.

Many students do not question their ability to multi-task efficiently and effectively. I determined from the start that the course should present the research data on multitasking and challenge students to question whether they can read and understand Orwell's *1984* while texting, IMing, or listening to music, and whether driving while texting should be banned.

Ethical behavior is a key component throughout the course. Sara Baase describes ethics as the study of what it means "to do the right thing" [5]. This course uses students' intuitive grasp of the common good rather than theoretically based ethics. The intent is to inform students on a particular topic and motivate them "to do the right thing" for others. The contexts generally lead to action or no action without need for the rigor and nuances of ethical theory. For example, when dealing with e-waste, students watch videos that show unprotected people in Guiyu, China or in Nigeria burning motherboards to retrieve small amounts of minerals or gold. The U.S. is the likely source of the old computers since most other nations ban dumping computers on third world countries, and the U.S. does not. Doing the right thing translates to making an effort to find an honest computer recycler, as well as asking if you really need that new cell phone or computer.

1.2.2 The Importance of Computer Life Skills

Ninety-six percent of seventy-nine students entering *The Digital Person* course during the 2009-2010 academic year did not know the meaning or use of a FICO score. This score determines the interest rate on loans and mortgages: the higher the score, the lower the rate. Often, auto insurance companies include it in determination of a customer's rate. A FICO score (currently 620) is the cut-off for sub-prime designation.

Phishing is often directly associated with identity theft. Successful phishers employ user name, password, and other information to access accounts in banks, social networking sites, and the like. Seventy-seven percent of incoming students to the course lacked familiarity with the term "phishing."

Social network use among freshmen is significant. The seventy students in *The Digital Person* course who completed both pre- and post-course surveys during the 2009-2010 academic year reported an average daily use of 1.83 hours at the beginning of the semester, and 2.22 hours at the end. Incoming freshmen often have no idea of the permanency of data they post on the Web, as well as the accessibility and proliferation of data through friends.

1.3 *How* to Teach It—the Pedagogy

The "*how*" of this new course is based on the SENCER (**S**cience **E**ducation for **N**ew **C**ivic **E**ngagements and **R**esponsibilities) model [2]. SENCER is a largely NSF-funded program for science teachers. The SENCER model emphasizes teacher development to get students hooked and draw them into the basic themes of their science courses. SENCER helps teachers to define learning objectives more clearly, to develop effective assessment, to employ active learning, and to teach critical thinking, so that student action flows from their knowledge. The SENCER model provided the pedagogical framework for *The Digital Person.*

This pedagogy is not new and not unique to SENCER. My initial attendance at a SENCER conference coincided with development of the content of the new course and persuaded me to determine that pedagogy was an equal partner with content in the design and implementation of *The Digital Person.*

The essential guideline for *The Digital Person* is that students take responsibility for their learning and be actively involved. The course itself is driven by learning objectives; each lab, worksheet, and assignment begins with a statement of the learning objectives. Activities are structured to develop the focus of the objectives and to demonstrate mastery. Section 3 provides examples The wiki http://thedpforsigcse.wetpaint.com makes available reading assignments, paper assignments, labs, worksheets, and the course description/syllabus.

The course is taught in a lab, so each student works at a computer. The banks of stations provide natural small groups. The instructor's station connects to projection equipment and a large smart board. Students meet for 75 minutes twice a week. The number of computers (24) provides a natural cap on section size.

Each section has its own wiki, designated as public so parents, friends, and other students can read the postings. Authors are associated with entries using first name and last initial format, to protect privacy. Students "go public" with their knowledge through their wiki postings. Mostly, the postings are small group work, preceded by individual information gathering and small group reflection and discussion. Each group can immediately see what others have posted. This is particularly effective since small groups often work on different topics; e.g., how and where to re-cycle cell phones; how and where to recycle or re-use computers. The instructor can also enlarge and project one group's work so the entire class views it as individuals in the group explain it.

Additional teaching/learning strategies include small group discussions, individual reading and writing assignments, videos followed by discussion, instructor presentation, and guest speakers.

Writing is a significant component. Students write to:

- report on individual labs
- post work of small groups to the wiki
- fulfill about ten reading and writing assignments
- author two or three papers.

This emphasis on student writing in *The Digital Person* helps to differentiate it from a traditional, packages-oriented computer literacy course.

1.4 Student Assessment

The Digital Person has no tests and no final examination. The course grade has the following components:

- reading and writing assignments (35%)
- worksheets and lab reports (35%)
- papers (25%)
- participation in each class and the wiki (5%)

Assignment 1, for example, focuses on chapter 1 of the *Blown to Bits* text [1]. The learning objective is to paraphrase the authors' seven koans or paradoxes to explain aspects of the digital explosion. Tasks include reading chapter 1 slowly, for comprehension, paraphrasing each koan, then writing a personal reflection on the chapter, noting which koan was of particular interest to them.

The assignment is worth 10 points. Criteria on which the assignment is graded are:

10 Descriptions are complete, correct, in your own words. They display understanding of the underlying koans and include thoughtful expression. The personal reflection is thoughtful and complete. There are no spelling errors. You followed all directions.

9-6 Descriptions/reflection show good but not complete understanding or incomplete expression.

5-1 Descriptions are lacking in completeness, accuracy, or understanding. Fewer than the specified minimum number are given, or personal reflection is missing or incomplete.

0 Material is copied and pasted, with possibly minor word changes.

Papers are assessed similarly. Lab reports are assessed by parts. For example, one of the learning objectives of the Credit Card and Credit Scoring Lab is: compare and contrast interest accrued on credit card debt using different monthly payment methods. Students complete a credit card repayment chart, calculating how much interest is paid and how long it takes to pay off $8000 in debt, using interest rates of 8, 12, 19, and 28%, paying only the minimum or paying a fixed amount. Students then state their conclusions. This section has a specific point value.

Worksheets are "check-off labs:" A student who attends class and actively participates gets full credit without having to submit an electronic or hard copy. The instructor can note student involvement during the class. A student who misses class must submit evidence of doing the work to get credit.

Almost all classes have a component that is graded.

2. COURSE DEVELOPMENT

2.1 Literature Review

The literature in ACM's Digital Library describes at least three broad categories of computer literacy courses. One approach is described by Hoffman and Vance as "a functional definition of knowledge according to which students are proficient with a personal computer and Internet applications" [12]. A second approach to non-major courses is identified as CS0. Such courses survey the discipline of computer science in a breadth-first manner [6]. A third approach includes applied computing courses for a general education population such as a case study approach [14] or a web programming and graphics course [9].

Recent publications describe courses that are breaking out of the more traditional computer literacy mold. Elliot Koffman and his panel described five new approaches, including courses entitled: *Computers, Information and Society*; *Privacy and Trust in Cyberspace*; and *Mathematical and Technological Literacy* [13]. These courses seem to have a common thread of incorporating underlying computer science topics, such as building a database. Hoffman and Blake describe a course titled *Introduction to Internet Studies* [11]. The social component of the course deals with social, cultural, and ethical issues. Other components focus on computer literacy, information literacy, and study of Internet technology, history, and applications. Purewal, Bennett, and Maier propose a course with a significant focus on ethics and service-learning in the context of current computing issues [16]. They situate their new course in the introductory computer science curriculum—for majors.

No SIGCSE publication—Proceedings, Bulletin, or *Inroads*—in the last ten years has described a computer literacy course like *The Digital Person*: solely focused on developing computer life skills (as illustrated in Table 2), with emphasis on ethical responsibility and information literacy, targeted at first-year, non-computer science majors, and providing evidence of its effectiveness. Epperson's recently published investigation of computer literacy mentioned no such course [7].

3. BLENDING TOPICS AND PEDAGOGY: SELECTED EXAMPLES

3.1 Introduction to Our Class Wiki

A class wiki enables public sharing of students' knowledge. It acquaints students with the process used by Wikipedia while letting them determine their own rules for use. One class meeting early in the term focuses on adapting Wikipedia's rules to the class wiki.

The learning objectives of this first meeting are:

1. identify the key policies/pillars of Wikipedia and use these as the basis for determining the policies that apply to our class wiki
2. summarize the history of Wikipedia: who, what, why; overall mission; how staffed; how financed
3. enter into and use our class wiki

In small groups, students focus on the 5 Pillars of Wikipedia [21]. Each small group chooses from each pillar a guideline to which they are willing to commit, and phrases it in their own words. Next, they study Wikipedia's Policies [22], adding to their previous statements, if necessary. Each group produces five guidelines for their use of the wiki, which they post to the wiki.

Small groups discuss the postings, with each group suggesting one set of guidelines for adoption. Last, the class reaches agreement on a single set of guidelines.

3.2 Critical Thinking

The critical thinking presentation and lab are scheduled for two classes early in the second month of the semester. Student learning objectives are identifying and using each of the six higher level thinking skills, as defined by to the American Philosophical Association in 1990: interpretation, analysis, evaluation, inference, explanation, and self-regulation [8].

The first class meeting includes a presentation on critical thinking that defines each of the higher level thinking skills and provides examples. Students are challenged to provide simpler definitions of each skill as well as other examples.

In the second class meeting, students read Tracy Mitrano's "Thoughts on Facebook" [15] with the additional learning objective of identifying the pros and cons of using Facebook. They use specific critical thinking skills to answer questions about the reading. Questions include:

- In your own words in one sentence, **interpret** the meaning of caching.
- "Think not only about what identity you create for yourself online, but also how you represent others." **Analyze** this statement, including specific examples of behavior on Facebook that could offend or damage others.
- **Infer** from the reading 2 or 3 guidelines to use in posting or providing information on the Internet.

Each student downloads a copy of the worksheet using Blackboard and answers using Word. Finally the class as a whole discusses the answers and reflects on what they have learned about personal information posted on Facebook.

Exercises, worksheets, and assignments in succeeding classes—as well as my in-class questions—use the same APA critical thinking skills. Students gradually apply the skills, often without prompting. In particular, they gain facility in "inferring," a word none of them had used earlier.

3.3 Intellectual Property

The overall learning objective for this topic is using critical thinking skills to determine whether or not, for its Books project, Google is violating copyright when it scans the full text of books still under copyright. Jeffrey Toobin's article in the New Yorker, "Google's Moon Shot," is required reading [20].

To learn the context and meaning of copyright and fair use, students use only .gov sites—generally the U.S. Copyright Office—to answer worksheet questions. We discuss answers in detail to clarify copyright, copyright infringement, and fair use. We view the 2003 segment "*The Right to Know vs. the Need to Pay*," from PBS's *Now* [19]. This video deals with the conflict between the public domain and fair use, on one hand, and copyright, particularly copyright held by large entertainment companies, on the other.

In their paper assignment, students must answer the question: **Is the library component of Google Book Search fair use or copyright infringement?** There is no clear right answer. Students need to understand copyright, fair use, and copyright infringement, as well as the library component, a subset of Google Book Search. This is a difficult assignment, both for the students to answer and for the teacher to grade.

The Google Books example was relevant and timely. As a court settlement nears in fall of 2010, the controversy has waned. Emphasis on the basics of copyright and fair use shifts now to the context of remixing.

4. POST-COURSE FEEDBACK

4.1 Evaluations

In the 2009-2010 academic year, seventy students evaluated the course using the university's course evaluation Likert scale, where 5 = Strongly Agree and 1 = Strongly Disagree. Selected items are presented in Table 3.

Table 3. Average student ratings of selected items

Item	Rating
Hard work was required to get good grades	3.9
I was intellectually stimulated	4.2
I increased my knowledge of the subject	4.6
Rate the overall value of the course to your learning	4.2

In open-ended feedback on evaluations, words that occurred frequently were: informative, interesting, and relevant. "Protecting ourselves," "staying safe on the computer," and "learning dangers" occurred several times. One student stated that "the course was relevant to society today and to the age group specifically." Another wrote: "The contemporary topics made the course pertinent and kept us focused."

4.2 Pre- and Post-Course Surveys

On the first and on the last day of class, students took an instructor-developed survey to assess current knowledge or behavior. Each composed an identifying number to match pre- and post-surveys without any other personally identifying information. The pre-course survey provides data about the incoming class; e.g., of seventy-nine students who started the course during the 2009-2010 academic year, 92.4% use the same password on different sites, and 27.8% have a credit card.

Use of both surveys identifies large scale changes only. Table 4 lists the percentage of students who indicated lack of understanding of a concept by answering False on the pre-survey and later indicated understanding by answering True on the post-survey. Statistics reflect students who completed both pre-and post-course summaries in course offerings during the 2009-2010 academic year.

Note that Section 1.2.2 refers to pre-course knowledge; e.g., 77.2% of incoming students did not understand phishing at the beginning of the course. Table 4 counts those who did not know something at the beginning of the course but did learn it by the end; e.g., 77.9% understood phishing at the end.

Table 4. Pre- and Post-Course Knowledge

Statement	Percentage of Students Who Needed to and Did Learn the Concept
I am familiar with the term "e-waste" and I understand its meaning	88.2%
I know the meaning or use of a FICO score	87.9%
I am familiar with the term "phishing" and I understand its meaning.	77.9%
I am familiar with cookies used in web browsing.	39.7%

4.3 Letters

On the last day of class each out-going student wrote a letter to those who would take the course in the following semester with advice on how to get the most out of the course. The idea is attributed to Laurie Fathe at one of the SENCER workshops. Letters can be signed or anonymous. In-coming students read these letters on the first day of class in the following semester.

By far, the largest category of suggestions (71%) dealt with the perceived importance and helpfulness of the course; e.g., "Don't take this course lightly because what you learn in it can end up being information that you really can use during your lifetime to protect yourself." The next largest group (47%) stressed the importance of keeping up with assignments and submitting them on time; e.g., "One suggestion is to get your assignments done when you get them so you won't be up late the night before they are due." Attending class was suggested in 30% of the letters.

Other tips included: "It is very interactive, and you need to pay attention and work hard to get a good grade," and "Take the class and assignments seriously, because everything you will learn in this class is important and relevant to your life."

5. EVOLUTION

Reflection on the experience of three years and the response of students has led to changes in text, depth, instructor involvement, and topics.

The course was first offered in the 2007 – 2008 academic year with no required text. The university library's online databases and Web sources provided readings. However, such separate sources lacked the depth and continuity of focus one finds in a book such as Solove's *The Digital Person* [18] or Grossman's *High Tech Trash* [10]. Both of these books were required for the course offerings during the 2008 – 2009 academic year. About three or four chapters of each were used in assignments and class work.

Solove's book was published in 2004, and many endnotes refer to sources even older. In 2008, Hal Abelson, Ken Ledeen, and Harry Lewis published *Blown to Bits*. They say that the book "emerged from a general education course we have taught at Harvard, but it is not a textbook" [1]. *Blown to Bits* and *High Tech Trash* are required for the 2009 – 2010 academic year.

The perceived relevance of several topics as well as the wellspring of material—particularly online videos—led to a decision to place more emphasis on and go deeper into several topics. During the 2009 – 2010 year, three class meetings were devoted to each of the following: credit cards and credit scores, e-waste, multitasking, and copyright.

As students demonstrate their ability to take responsibility for their learning, the instructor can more fully vest them with that responsibility by motivating learning and providing activities that lead to it. Only two instructor presentations, one on critical thinking skills and another on privacy laws, were done in the 2009 – 2010 year. Similarly, current labs rely more on students to find reliable sources than did the original labs. Guidelines still may be given; e.g., use only .gov sites in learning about copyright.

Topics emerge over time. In the semesters leading up to the November, 2008 election, two classes were devoted to problems of computerized voting. Classes on multitasking were expanded in the past year to include recently published research on the danger of texting while driving.

6. LESSONS IN COURSE CREATION

A key lesson is consulting with faculty, particularly those involved in course delivery, to ensure that the course meets student needs. In addition to the faculty of my department, I sought input from the Director of the Library, the Library Instruction Coordinator, and the Director of Freshman Writing. As a result, the Library Instruction Coordinator agreed to teach three classes on information literacy topics each semester. The Director of Freshman Writing provided background in appropriate writing assignments for first semester freshmen. A post-doctoral writing expert has provided on-going assistance in creating and evaluating writing assignments.

Careful documentation is essential. Keeping a detailed and up-to-date log or course portfolio including background readings, learning objectives, videos, labs, and assignments will be especially helpful for an instructor new to teaching the course.

7. ON-GOING OBJECTIVES

Major on-going objectives include:

- encouraging growth in sensitivity to the ethical dimensions, particularly in use of technology, so that students are motivated to act in response to learning; e.g., cyberbullying and what should be responsible use of the technology.
- learning strategies to develop discussions at a deeper level—seeking substance and meaning, rather than just comprehension.
- keeping the course challenging: exploring questions that stimulate and engage, and that motivate on-going interest.

8. REFERENCES

[1] Abelson, Hal, and Ledeen, Ken and Lewis, Harry. 2008. Blown to Bits. Addison Wesley.

[2] *About SENCER*: Overview. http://www.sencer.net/About/projectoverview.cfm.

[3] Association for Computing Machinery. 2001. Computing Curricula 2001: Computer Science. *ACM Educational Activities.* Retrieved Dec 4, 2010 from http://www.acm.org/education/education/curric_vols/cc2001.pdf .

[4] Association for Computing Machinery. 2008. Computer Science Curriculum 2008. *ACM Educational Activities.* Retrieved Dec 4, 2010 from http://www.acm.org/education/curricula/ComputerScience2008.pdf.

[5] Baase, S. 2008. A Gift of Fire, 3rd ed. Pearson Education.

[6] Cliburn, D. 2006. *A CS0 Course for the Liberal Arts.* SIGCSE Bull. 38, 1 (March 2006), 77-81. DOI= http://doi.acm.org/10.1145/1121341.1121368

[7] Epperson, A. 2010. *Computer Literacy Revisited: A Comprehensive Investigation of Computer Literacy.* Inroads. 1, 2 (June 2010), 30-33. DOI= 10.1145/1805724.1805736

[8] Facione, P. 2007. *Critical Thinking: What It Is and Why It Counts.* http://assessment.gmu.edu/ctac/documents/facione%20what&why2007.pdf.

[9] Gousie, M. 2006. *A Robust Web Programming and Graphics Course for Non-Majors.* SIGCSE Bull. 38, 1 (March 2006), 72-76. DOI= http://doi.acm.org/10.1145/1121341.1121367

[10] Grossman, E. 2006. High Tech Trash. Island Press.

[11] Hoffman, M. and Blake, J. 2003. *Computer Literacy: Today and Tomorrow.* JCSC 18, 5, 221-233.

[12] Hoffman, M. and Vance, D. 2005 *Computer Literacy: What Students Know and From Whom They Learned It.* SIGCSE Bull. 37, 1 (Feb. 2005), 356-360. DOI= http://doi.acm.org/10.1145/1047344.1047467

[13] Koffman, E. et al. 2007. *New Paradigms for Introductory Computing Courses.* SIGCSE Bull. 39, 1 (March 2007), 67-68. DOI=http://doi.acm.org/10.1145/1227310.1227336

[14] Marks, J., Freeman, W. and Leitner, H. 2001. *Teaching Applied Computing without Programming: A Case-Based Introductory Course for General Education.* SIGCSE Bull. 33, 1 (Feb. 2001), 80-84. DOI= http://doi.acm.org/10.1145/364447.364547

[15] Mitrano, Tracy. *Thoughts on Facebook* http://www.cit.cornell.edu/policy/memos/facebook.html

[16] Purewal, T., Bennett, C, and Maier, F. 2007. *Embracing the Social Relevance: Computing, Ethics, and the Community.* SIGCSE Bull. 39, 1 (March 2007), 556-560. DOI= http://doi.acm.org/10.1145/1227310.1227496

[17] Rockman, I. and Associates. 2004. Integrating Information Literacy into the Higher Education Curriculum. Jossey-Bass.

[18] Solove, D. 2004. The Digital Person. New York University Press.

[19] *The Right to Know vs. the Need to Pay.* Jan 17, 2003. PBS *Now*

[20] Toobin, J. Feb 5, 2007. *Google's Moon Shot.* The New Yorker.

[21] Wikipedia: Five Pillars. http://en.wikipedia.org/wiki/Wikipedia:Five_pillars.

[22] Wikipedia: List of Policies. http://en.wikipedia.org/wiki/Wikipedia:List_of_policies.

Exploring the Appeal of Socially Relevant Computing: Are Students Interested in Socially Relevant Problems?

Cyndi Rader, Doug Hakkarinen, Barbara M. Moskal and Keith Hellman
Colorado School of Mines
Department of Mathematical & Computer Sciences
1500 Illinois St.
Golden, CO 80401
crader, dhakkari,bmoskal,khellman@mines.edu

ABSTRACT

Prior research indicates that today's students, especially women, are attracted to careers in which they recognize the direct benefit of the field for serving societal needs. Traditional college level computer science courses rarely illustrate the potential benefits of computer science to the broader community. This paper describes a curricula development effort designed to embed humanitarian projects into undergraduate computer science courses. The impact of this program was measured through student self-report instruments. Through this investigation, it was found that students generally preferred projects that they perceived as "fun" over the projects that were social in nature. This may, in part, be due to the fact that it was difficult to reduce socially relevant problems to a level that beginning students could easily comprehend. This made it difficult to capitalize on the appeal of socially relevant problems in the early computer science courses.

Categories and Subject Descriptors

K.3.2 **[Computers and Education]:** Computer and Information Science Education - *computer science education, curriculum*

General Terms

Design, Experimentation

Keywords

Computer science education, gender, broadening participation, socially relevant computing, student projects

1. INTRODUCTION

It is well known that a large gender gap exists in Computer Science [5][8]. Given the increasing role of computers in our society and the estimates of opportunities for software engineers[17], capable women who overlook Computer Science as an option may be limiting their access to lucrative and rewarding careers. Furthermore, researchers have argued that women contribute ideas which are different from their male counterparts, which leads to innovation within a given field of study[19]. The lack of female participation may therefore be detrimental to Computer Science as a field [3]. Several studies have sought to understand why women opt out of CS (e.g., [10][23]). Additionally, over the last decade there have been numerous efforts to combat this problem, including interventions at the middle school, high school and college levels (e.g., [1][9][7][22]).

Margolis and Fisher completed an extensive study of female career preferences and found that women are attracted to fields in which they recognize the broad social impacts [8]. The Margolis and Fisher study is frequently cited and has contributed to the current understanding of what aspects of various fields attract female participation. Furthermore, Buckley et al. report that the number of undergraduate degrees awarded in the social sciences is four times that of CS [4], even when gender is not considered. This may indicate that today's students, males and females, prefer fields in which they recognize the immediate contribution of their work to society.

In 2003, the Colorado School of Mines (CSM) implemented a Humanitarian Engineering program funded by the Hewlett Foundation [16]. This academic program seeks to prepare undergraduate engineering students for careers that benefit the underserved, global community. Through an interdisciplinary collaboration, a sequence of courses was designed and implemented to support engineering students in developing an understanding of the ethical, cultural, historical and technical dimensions of engineering work as it applies to community development in the United States and abroad. Students in the Humanitarian Engineering program use their engineering skills to solve the basic living challenges faced by many of the world's people, such as scarce water resources. This program was found to be very appealing to women [20]. Recognizing the attraction of this program to female students, the decision was made to attempt to transfer this appeal to the CS program. A goal of the current effort was to demonstrate through humanitarian examples that a CS degree can result in a career that has a broad, positive impact on society.

2. RESEARCH QUESTIONS

This paper explores two research questions:

1. Do students express increased interest in performing programming tasks embedded in a humanitarian/ socially relevant context? How does this level of interest compare to their interest in other types of projects?
2. Assuming students *are* interested in humanitarian topics, can we develop programming assignments that effectively capitalize on that interest?

SIGCSE'11, March 9–12, 2011, Dallas, Texas, USA.

3. APPROACH

Student ratings for programming assignments depend on a number of factors, including not only their interest in the topic but also the complexity and length of the lab, amount of background knowledge required, and quality of explanation by the instructor. To isolate the effect of topic choice from the other factors, we developed two surveys. We originally hypothesized that students, especially females, would prefer assignments that illustrate the potential for computer applications to benefit society. Other researchers have conjectured that the use of real-world topics would make assignments more compelling [2][24][21]. A number of researchers have also suggested that students are attracted to game assignments [6][13]. The purpose of the first survey was to solicit direct feedback from students regarding potential programming assignment topics that we categorized as humanitarian, practical, and non-practical. Based on the survey results, we refined our hypothesis and developed a second survey. These surveys are described in sections 3.1 and 3.2.

The primary task for the current project was to embed humanitarian projects into the CS curricula. Based on the experiences of the Humanitarian Engineering Program [20] and prior research [8], we anticipated that these projects would appeal to female students because they illustrate the broader impacts of CS on society. Our goal was to develop a sequence of CS courses, one at each academic level, which contained a humanitarian component. This design would allow interested CS students to experience a different humanitarian project within each academic year of their degree program. The first two courses selected to contain humanitarian components were Introduction to Programming Concepts (CS1) and Software Engineering. The CS1 course is required for a number of majors on campus, not just Computer Science (e.g., mathematics and engineering students must take CS1). Students in the Software Engineering course are generally pursuing either a major or minor in CS. Self-report instruments were used to assess the appeal of the humanitarian assignments immediately after the students completed them. A description of the projects is included in section 3.3.

3.1 Topic Survey 1

The initial survey was created by generating a list of approximately 30 programming projects found in introductory Computer Science textbooks [15][18] as well as through a brainstorming session among the researchers. Each project was given a title which was summarized through two-line descriptions. To relate student preferences to our hypothesis about social relevance, the projects were placed into one of three categories: humanitarian (H), practical but not humanitarian (P), or not practical (N). The project descriptions were independently coded into the three categories by two individuals not associated with this project. To minimize the impact of a bias interpretation, the coders were provided the names of the categories and a list of project descriptions in random order. No category definitions were provided. After the projects were classified, 15 descriptions were selected for the survey, 5 from each category. Within each category, preference was given to those that had the strongest agreement among coders.

This survey was administered at the end of the semester to 78 students, including 13 females, in four different courses: CS1, Data Structures, Software Engineering and Programming Languages. For each topic, the students selected from the following response options: “I definitely would like to do this project,” “I might like to do this project,” “I would rather not do this project,” and “I definitely would not like to do this project.”

3.2 Topic Survey 2

The survey results for topic survey 1 (presented in section 4.1) did not provide substantial support for the appeal of humanitarian projects. Since it is possible that students may enjoy humanitarian projects in general, but not the particular selection of projects in topic survey 1, a second survey was developed to further explore students' preferences. This survey was motivated in part by the hypothesis that students would be more interested in topics to which they could personally relate, which other researchers have called socially relevant with a "little s" [4].

The survey began with eight project descriptions to which the students responded with the same Likert scale answers as the first survey. Our goal was to devise descriptions that would represent humanitarian projects, projects that were likely to have personal relevance to the students, and projects with a technology focus. The survey concluded with students ranking seven categories of project topics: real-world applications, humanitarian applications, games, social networking software, software with technology (wiimotes, cell phones, etc.), educational software and recruiting software. This instrument was administered to 26 students, only one of whom was female, in a senior level Programming Languages course.

Project descriptions for both surveys are included in the Results section of this document.

3.3 Humanitarian Programming Assignments

This section describes the humanitarian programming assignments that were created for inclusion in CS1 and Software Engineering (SE). Table 1 provides a brief description of each project, including the purpose of the project and a list of the CS concepts introduced or reviewed through the project. Our goal was to develop applications which portrayed real-life situations (albeit in a simplified manner) and which illustrated how computer programs can be used to benefit society.

Table 1. Humanitarian assignments

Title/Description	CS Topics
CS1 Search and Rescue (SAR) Program used classes to represent a lost hiker and different types of searchers on a 2D grid. Students were challenged to develop a strategy more effective than random search.	Classes, arrays, 2D arrays
SE Search and Rescue (SAR) Program displayed a map with icons representing different types of search teams. Team movements were simulated and displayed on the map.	UML, JUnit, Subversion, Design patterns
SE Disaster Management (DM) Program accepted input from the user to simulate messages from a text message system. Messages were located on a grid using clickable icons. Messages were displayed sorted by location or priority.	Same as SAR

The Search and Rescue (SAR) project was implemented in CS1 with 71 students, including 17 females (24%). As mentioned above, the CS1 course is required by a number of majors. Of the 71 students, only 8 (11%) were CS majors. The majority of the students (50%) were engineering majors. A version of SAR was implemented in Software Engineering (SE) with 26 students, including 2 females. Twenty-three of the students (88%) were CS majors. The Disaster Management project (DM) was also implemented in Software Engineering, with 14 students, including 1 female. Twelve of the students (85%) were CS majors.

In the CS1 course these assignments were, unintentionally, longer and more open-ended than many of the other CS1 assignments. For the Software Engineering course the assignments were used as final projects and were roughly equivalent in complexity to projects used during other semesters.

The student surveys used to assess these projects consisted of open and closed response and basic demographic questions. Our goal with these surveys was first to determine whether the assignment was appealing to students, and then to use the individual criteria to further analyze what factors may have affected their level of interest.

4. RESULTS

This section begins with an analysis of the results from the two topic surveys and concludes with a discussion of the results of embedding humanitarian projects into our CS courses.

4.1 Topic Survey 1

For survey 1, each of the Likert scale levels was converted to a numerical score for analysis purposes. A coding of "1" reflected a rating of "I definitely would not like to do this project" and a coding of "4" reflected a rating of "I definitely would like to do this project." In other words, a higher rating reflected greater interest in the given project. An average for each question was calculated across female and male students for each description. The topics were then placed in order from highest average rating to lowest.

Table 2 provides a description of each topic along with its rank for each gender. A score of "3" and above, based on the previously defined Likert scale, indicates a willingness on the part of the students to complete the described project. Given this, we considered an average score of 3.0 or greater to reflect a positive evaluation for the project. Seven of 15 topics for females received a ranking of 3.0 or greater, while only three of the 15 topics received an average score of 3.0 or greater for the males. Rankings associated with a score of 3.0 or higher are underlined in Table 2.

Based on these survey results, many students of both genders were attracted to the simple, non-practical topics, such as N1, "Tic-Tac-Toe" and N5, "Death by Sweetener." The appeal of games to today's students has been previously documented [6][25][11][14] and further evidence to confirm that appeal is provided here.

Although women did indicate greater interest in humanitarian projects than did males, with two of the five topics receiving an average score of 3.0 or greater, these were not the projects with the greatest overall appeal. This result appears to challenge prior research which suggests that today's students, especially females, are attracted to socially relevant topics. However, Buckley et al. [4] further divided the category of socially relevant between personally relevant and relevant to society at large. Two topics ranked favorably by females were a grade calculator and an exercise calorie counter. Both of these might be considered personally relevant.

Table 2. Classified topics survey results

Description	Female Rank	Male Rank
Humanitarian		
H1. Zimbabwe inflation estimator	11	14
H2. Search and rescue	<u>3</u>	4
H3. Low income house affordability	10	12
H4. HIV infection rate	<u>7</u>	15
H5. Aquatic ecosystem destruction	12	7
Practical		
P1. Prime number finder	9	5
P2. Zip code decoder	13	<u>3</u>
P3. Grade calculator	<u>5</u>	6
P4. Exercise calorie counter	<u>6</u>	9
P5. Selection sort	15	10
Non-Practical		
N1. Tic-Tac-Toe	<u>1</u>	<u>1</u>
N2. Metric ton of cereal	<u>4</u>	11
N3. Random response generator	8	8
N4. Replace "he" with "he or she"	14	13
N5. Death by Sweetener	<u>2</u>	<u>2</u>

The humanitarian laboratory which received the highest ranking for both males and females was H2, "Search and Rescue." This project may have had personal relevance to the students given that within the local area search and rescues are a common element of the evening news. Possibly, students find humanitarian projects appealing when the project topics also have personal relevance.

4.2 Topic Survey 2

Based on the results of the first survey, the second survey sought to discover whether students found projects that were designed to be of personal relevance more appealing than the other projects. This survey included several topics that students in a User Interface Design course had chosen for their final projects. The theory behind including these problems was that students may have more insight into the creation of problems that appeal to other college students than do members of the faculty. Table 3 lists the project descriptions and displays the percentage of student responses that fell in the two top Likert scale categories ("I would definitely like to do this project" and "I might like to do this project"). The reader will note that this table was not subdivided by gender, because at this level of CS we only had one female student. The table is ordered based on the student rankings, rather than based on the ordering of the topics as listed on the survey.

Table 3. Humanitarian and personally relevant survey results

Description	Yes %	Maybe %	Positive %
Software to control a robot	78	22	100
System to simulate disaster management coordination efforts	9	91	100
Educational software for students in a developing country	22	74	96
Software to help K-12 teachers learn about a new topic	17	65	82
Budget program to help college students manage their finances	9	65	74
Tracking system to monitor bears removed from residential areas	17	56	74
Dietary intake monitoring for chronic kidney disease patients	4	70	74
Scheduling software for Habitat for Humanity site	22	48	70

The final component of this survey was to have students rank order seven categories of potential project topics. The results of this component of the survey are displayed in Table 4. A "1" indicates the greatest interest and a "7" the least interest. This table indicates the percentage of students that ranked a given project within each category level. In some cases, the totals for the table rows do not add to 100% due to rounding error. As with table 3, these topics are listed in order of preference and do not match the order they were listed in the survey. For this survey no project descriptions were included, so students could apply their own interpretation of the categories.

Table 4. Project Categories Ranked by Students

Category	1	2	3	4	5	6	7
Games	48	17	0	9	9	9	9
Use technology (e.g., cell phones, wii mote)	13	26	17	9	9	17	9
Real-world	9	17	35	13	17	4	4
Social networking	9	13	9	17	22	4	26
Humanitarian	9	9	13	22	9	13	26
Educational software	0	17	17	26	17	17	4
Recruiting software	0	9	22	9	22	17	22

4.3 Humanitarian Projects

Three humanitarian projects were tested in the CS curricula. Since Search and Rescue (SAR) was the highest-rated humanitarian project in topic survey 1, a version of SAR was implemented in both CS1 and Software Engineering. The Disaster Management (DM) project was also implemented in the Software Engineering class.

Student feedback was collected via a survey consisting of four multiple choice questions to assess the appeal and design of the specific project, four questions to garner students' preferences for real-world and humanitarian projects, and one question to determine students' general desire to program.

Table 5 shows the percentage of students who answered each question affirmatively. Questions have been paraphrased to fit in table format. Overall, student reaction was more positive in Software Engineering than CS1. Students' dissatisfaction with the assignments in CS1 may be due in part to the complexity, as only 53% of students indicated the level of difficulty was appropriate or too easy. A number of students also found the instructions to be inadequate. On a positive note, 21% of the students in the CS1 course spent additional time on the project because they were interested in the topic. For the Software Engineering course, over half of the students indicated they spent additional time.

Table 5. Humanitarian Project Results

Description	CS1	SE SAR	SE DM
Project was interesting	54	88	93
Level of difficulty OK	53	100	93
Instructions were OK	46	n/a	n/a
Student spent additional time because project was interesting	21	54	57
Project shows real-world problem	85	96	93
Student likes realistic projects	93	100	93
Project shows CS application that can benefit society	76	92	93
Student likes socially-beneficial projects	79	88	93
Student generally likes to program	65	100	93

The survey also solicited input from students regarding whether the assignment conveyed a real-life application of CS and whether it conveyed an application that could be used to benefit society. The majority of students did think the assignment was realistic (85 to 96%) as well as socially relevant (76 to 93%). Most students also claimed that they were interested in real-world problems (93 to 100%) and applications that benefit society (79 to 93%).

These surveys also included open-ended questions which partially explained the students' ratings. One question asked what aspects of the assignment made it difficult. The second question asked which components of the project made it interesting. In response to the first question, the students in the CS1 class indicated that the Search and Rescue project had too many parts and relied too heavily on prior knowledge. Some found the directions confusing and the time requirement to be extreme. One student explained, "I had a tough time connecting the dots with this assignment. The concepts individually are not at all difficult to understand on their own, but using all of the required concepts in a cohesive manner and one which would not produce a compiler freak out was an area where I felt further instruction was necessary."

In response to the second question, the CS1 students indicated that they found the SAR project interesting because it illustrated a real-life application. One student explained, "It was cool to find a real life application for all the stuff we had been learning in class. It really put a lot of the concepts together into one program." Other students indicated that they enjoyed open-ended nature of the problem, "The idea of having a grid and being told to search whatever way we wanted. It is a cool concept to see how different search patterns yield different results."

The same open-ended questions were asked with respect to the SAR and the DM projects in the Software Engineering course. Responses to both projects fell into the following general categories: students who enjoyed learning specific programming functionality, those who enjoyed the larger scope of the project, and those who were interested in the topic and/or real-world applications. One student explained the Search and Rescue project as follows, "Bringing a lot of concepts together and trying to meld them in one big project presented an interesting challenge." Another student indicated, "I'm a hiker, so I know how useful such a tool as this program could be. It was like something we would make when we get out in to the real world."

5. CONCLUSIONS

The results of this investigation are interesting in that they potentially challenge current recommendations.

Our first research question was whether students expressed interest in socially-relevant problems, and how that level of interest compared to their interest in other areas. When asked directly, the majority of students did indicate that they like programming assignments that show how CS can be used to benefit society. It is interesting that the CS1 respondents had the lowest approval rating (79%), compared to 92% and 93% for students in the Software Engineering courses.

In the comparison to other types of assignments, humanitarian projects did not fare as well. In the first topic survey, the top two projects for both genders were a game (Tic-Tac-Toe) and a simple, non-practical project (Death by Sweetener). Two humanitarian projects (Search and Rescue and HIV infection rate) were given a positive rating by females, but none of the humanitarian projects received a positive rating from the males.

In the second topic survey, seven of the eight topics listed could be considered socially or personally relevant. The top ranked project was the one non-humanitarian project with a technology focus (controlling a robot). This result may lend support to the use of robots as a recruiting tool, as proposed by a number of researchers (e.g., [22][12]). On a positive note, all project descriptions in the second survey received a positive rating of at least 70%. However, in the ranking of project categories, humanitarian projects were ranked 5 out of 7, with games receiving the top rank.

Our second research question was whether we would be able to develop programming assignments to effectively capitalize on students' interest in humanitarian projects. Our efforts were successful in Software Engineering, with 88% and 93% responding positively to the SAR and DM projects, respectively. However, only 54% of the students in the CS1 course, including 47% of the females, indicated that they found the SAR project appealing. In general, the humanitarian problems were open-ended when compared to the other problems in the courses. Although a number of students in the Software Engineering commented that the open-ended nature of these projects was a positive aspect, almost 50% of the CS1 students stated that the project was too complex or difficult to understand. The low approval rating for SAR in CS1 may also be partially attributed to the fact that CS1 is a required course and many students who complete this course do not enjoy programming. As shown in table 5, only 65% of the students in CS1 like to program, compared to 93% and 100% in the two sections of Software Engineering. This particular project was programming intense.

Finally, we must note that there are a number of issues that limit the scope of our results. The primary issue is the lack of female participation. The first topic survey included 13 females (17%), and 17 females (24%) programmed the SAR project in CS1. But the second topic survey and both programming projects in Software Engineering had very limited participation by females. Furthermore, the second project survey was administered to Computer Science students in a senior course. The preferences of these students may not match those of the students we are hoping to recruit.

An obvious issue with the CS1 programming assignment is the level of difficulty. As other researchers have noted (e.g., [6]), students tend to prefer assignments that they perceive as easy and fun, and avoid problems that are too open ended. To make the humanitarian projects more appealing, we would need to create assignments that are at the same level of difficulty and require the same level of programming skills as the other problems in the course. Given the low level of programming sophistication for most students in the introductory course, this presents a difficult challenge. Humanitarian problems are complex by nature. Unlike game assignments, students may not have any prior experience with humanitarian issues. Simplifying the constraints on such problems tends to result in assignments that are unrealistic, with no recognizable social relevance. Additionally, the research presented here indicates that the students may not deem this effort of addressing humanitarian issues as intrinsically interesting.

6. ACKNOWLEDGMENTS

The current project is funded through the National Science Foundation (CNS-0739233); the opinions and ideas expressed in this paper are that of the authors and do not necessarily reflect that of the NSF. We want to thank our teaching assistants who have helped to develop and deploy the humanitarian projects.

7. REFERENCES

[1] Adams, J.C. 2010. Scratching middle schoolers' creative itch. *Proceedings of the 41st ACM technical symposium on Computer science education* (Milwaukee, Wisconsin, USA, 2010), 356-360.

[2] Astrachan, O. 2007. Head in the clouds. *SIGCSE Bull.* 39, 4 (2007), 23-23.

[3] Balcita, A.M. et al. 2002. Shortchanging the future of information technology: the untapped resource. *SIGCSE Bull.* 34, 2 (2002), 32-35.

[4] Buckley, M. et al. 2008. Socially relevant computing. *Proceedings of the 39th SIGCSE technical symposium on Computer science education* (Portland, OR, USA, 2008), 347-351.

[5] Camp, T. 1997. The incredible shrinking pipeline.

Commun. ACM. 40, 10 (1997), 103-110.

[6] Cliburn, D.C. and Miller, S. 2008. Games, stories, or something more traditional: the types of assignments college students prefer. *Proceedings of the 39th SIGCSE technical symposium on Computer science education* (Portland, OR, USA, 2008), 138-142.

[7] Cohoon, J.M. 2002. Recruiting and retaining women in undergraduate computing majors. *SIGCSE Bull.* 34, 2 (2002), 48-52.

[8] Fisher, A. and Margolis, J. 2002. Unlocking the clubhouse: the Carnegie Mellon experience. *SIGCSE Bull.* 34, 2 (2002), 79-83.

[9] Graham, S. and Latulipe, C. 2003. CS girls rock: sparking interest in computer science and debunking the stereotypes. *Proceedings of the 34th SIGCSE technical symposium on Computer science education* (Reno, Navada, USA, 2003), 322-326.

[10] Jepson, A. and Perl, T. 2002. Priming the pipeline. *SIGCSE Bull.* 34, 2 (2002), 36-39.

[11] Kurkovsky, S. 2009. Engaging students through mobile game development. *Proceedings of the 40th ACM technical symposium on Computer science education* (Chattanooga, TN, USA, 2009), 44-48.

[12] Lauwers, T. et al. CSbots: design and deployment of a robot designed for the CS1 classroom. *Proceedings of the 40th ACM technical symposium on Computer science education* (Chattanooga, TN, USA), 428-432.

[13] Lewis, M. et al. 2009. Introductory programming courses and computer games. *Proceedings of the 40th ACM technical symposium on Computer science education* (Chattanooga, TN, USA, 2009), 204-205.

[14] Lewis, M. et al. 2009. Introductory programming courses and computer games. *Proceedings of the 40th ACM technical symposium on Computer science education* (Chattanooga, TN, USA, 2009), 204-205.

[15] Main, M. and Savitch, W. 2004. *Data Structures and Other Objects Using C++.* Addison Wesley.

[16] Moskal, B. et al. 2008. Humanitarian engineering: Global impacts and sustainability of a curricular effort. *International Journal of Engineering Education.* 24, 1 (2008), 162-174.

[17] Occupational Outlook Handbook, 2010-11 Edition: Computer Software Engineers and Computer Programmers. *http://www.bls.gov/oco/ocos303.htm.*

[18] Savitch, W. 2007. *Problem Solving with C++.* Addison-Wesley.

[19] Shepherd, L. 1993. *Lifting the Veil: The Feminine Face of Science.* Shambhala Publications.

[20] Skokan, C. and Gosink, J. 2005. Gender Participation in Humanitarian versus Traditional Multidisciplinary Senior Design Projects. *American Society for Engineering Education Conference* (Portland, OR, June 2005), 12-15.

[21] Stevenson, D.E. and Wagner, P.J. 2006. Developing real-world programming assignments for CS1. *Proceedings of the 11th annual SIGCSE conference on Innovation and technology in computer science education* (Bologna, Italy, 2006), 158-162.

[22] Summet, J. et al. 2009. Personalizing CS1 with robots. *Proceedings of the 40th ACM technical symposium on Computer science education* (Chattanooga, TN, USA, 2009), 433-437.

[23] Teague, J. 2002. Women in computing: what brings them to it, what keeps them in it? *SIGCSE Bull.* 34, 2 (2002), 147-158.

[24] Wicentowski, R. and Newhall, T. 2005. Using image processing projects to teach CS1 topics. *Proceedings of the 36th SIGCSE technical symposium on Computer science education* (St. Louis, Missouri, USA, 2005), 287-291.

[25] Wolz, U. et al. 2009. Girls do like playing and creating games. *Proceedings of the 40th ACM technical symposium on Computer science education* (Chattanooga, TN, USA, 2009), 199-200.

Increasing Engagement and Enrollment in Breadth-First Introductory Courses Using Authentic Computing Tasks

Ryan L. McFall
Hope College
Dept. of Computer Science
Holland, MI 49423
1-616-395-7952
mcfall@hope.edu

Matthew DeJongh
Hope College
Department of Computer Science
Holland, MI 49423
1-616-395-7429
dejongh@hope.edu

ABSTRACT

The breadth-first approach to teaching introductory computer science is one way of dispelling the common misperception that programming is the sole task of the computer scientist. The breadth-first approach is particularly useful in courses for non-majors. Hands-on activities that make up laboratory assignments for these courses tend to focus on learning to program or simulations of program execution. These activities unfortunately fail to build on the foundations laid by a breadth-first approach, and serve to perpetuate the computer science = programming misperception. We have developed a set of laboratory activities which are based on what we call *authentic computing tasks*: everyday tasks that students want to know how to accomplish. Example tasks include image editing, operating system installation and configuration, and building home computer networks. Explicit connections are made between these authentic computing tasks and the computer science concepts being covered in the lecture portion of the course. The course has experienced dramatic increases in enrollment, and we have evidence that students see the connections, rather than coming to believe that performing computing tasks well is the essence of computer science.

Categories and Subject Descriptors

K.3.2 [**Computer and Information Science Education**]: Curriculum, Computer Science Education

General Terms

Human Factors

Keywords

Computer Fluency, General Education, Introductory Courses, Enrollment

1. INTRODUCTION

The need for increasing the level of participation in Computer Science programs is well known. Not only does the quantity of students matter, but the caliber of students needs to be improved as well [1]. One of the more obvious ways to accomplish this is to expand the pool of people taking introductory computer science courses. Since computer science is not taught in a large percentage of high schools, many students enter college never having considered computer science as a possible degree option. Compare this with the physical sciences, which have broad representation in the K-12 curriculum.

Students (and their parents) often have misconceptions about the types of careers available to those who have degrees in computer science and information technology [2]. Frequently these misconceptions include the notion that all computer scientists do is write programs, study the computer for its own sake or troubleshoot and maintain computer hardware and software [3]. These narrow definitions of computer science as a profession likely contribute to the lack of interest in computer science as a major, particularly among women.

The world's increasing dependence on technology means we must seek to do more than attract additional computer science *majors*. Technological fluency should be included along with reading and mathematics as skills that *all* citizens should have. In the past, technological fluency has frequently meant familiarity and proficiency with tools such as word processors, spread sheets, and information repositories such as the World Wide Web and digital libraries. As technology permeates everyday life the definition of fluency will need to be expanded.

For example, Jeannette Wing [4] defines *computational thinking* as "having the confidence we can safely use, modify, and influence a large complex system without understanding its every detail." She further states that "Computational biology is changing the way biologists think. Similarly, computational game theory is changing the way economists think; nanocomputing, the way chemists think; and quantum computing, the way physicists think." It is likely that students majoring in sociology, psychology, nursing and many other disciplines will also begin to see computational thinking as important. Introducing more students to Computer Science will help further the advancement of other disciplines by introducing them to computational approaches.

Introductory courses are often the lens through which students perceive a discipline; therefore it is important for these courses to provide an engaging and accurate representation of the field. We believe it is imperative that laboratory activities be based on students' interests and be applicable to everyday life. We call such activities **authentic computing tasks**. Our goal is to use authentic computing tasks as part of an introductory course to:

SIGCSE'11, March 9–12, 2011, Dallas, Texas, USA.

- use students' personal interests to draw them into the course.
- show students the variety and intellectual challenge of computer science as a discipline.
- prepare students to be able to use computational thinking in their chosen careers.

The most recent IEEE/ACM recommendation for introductory computer science courses includes a particular approach known as "breadth-first" [5]. The goal of this approach is to expose students to a wide variety of topical areas, widening their narrow perceptions of what it means to study computer science. This approach is popular, with many articles describing its implementation (for example, [6] and [7]). Textbooks also exist to support the breadth-first model, including Brookshear [8], Dale/Lewis [9] and Snyder [10]. While finding a way to tie the topics together in a consistent and natural way can be difficult at times, a breadth-first approach still seems to be a valid and popular option.

Unfortunately, the laboratory activities that accompany such breadth-first topical courses do not incorporate the same level of breadth. A survey of the literature [7, 11-13] shows that the "hands on" activities associated with breadth-first courses almost always fall into 1 of 2 categories: (1) laboratories in which learning to program is the primary focus and (2) laboratories in which the activities are primarily simulation oriented, focusing on learning about the computer itself

Most of these courses attempt to make these approaches appealing to students. For example, many [14-16] have reported on the use of the popular programming environment Alice [17] in introductory courses and its impact on student perceptions of programming. Similarly, Georgia Tech originated an approach with media computation [18], increasing interest in and motivation for programming. Other approaches have students learning to build interactive web sites using technologies like JavaScript [19] and ASP.NET [15], attempting to build on student interest in and familiarity with the World Wide Web.

Because students enjoy these approaches to learning programming, we applaud these efforts, and have in fact incorporated both Alice and media computation into our own introductory course. However, courses that focus primarily on programming tend to perpetuate the misconception that all computer scientists do is program. To successfully introduce the breadth of computer science, these approaches need to be supplemented with authentic, non-programming oriented activities. A recent study [20] found that "teaching concepts in appealing contexts and relating material to students' prior knowledge and interests is positively associated with retention."

In this paper we describe several laboratory activities based upon authentic computing tasks, including setting up home networks, setting up and configuring an operating system, installing device drivers, and image processing through the use of Photoshop Elements or the GIMP. We also describe programming activities, such as extending the functionality of iTunes in useful ways, which can serve to teach programming in a context that students consider valuable. We have used these activities in conjunction with a breadth-first course for a year now, and we have seen significant increases in enrollment. Evidence shows that students understand how the tasks relate to, and not define, computer science.

2. LAB ACTIVITIES

2.1 General Format of Each Activity

In order to implement our approach, between summer 2009 and summer 2010 we have developed a total of 11 laboratory activities that meet the criteria described in the previous section. A lab manual was developed, with each activity containing the following sections:

Pre-lab reading: This section contains an overview of the lab activities, important background information about the tasks to be completed during the lab, and a glossary of relevant terms. In addition, it contains a "Connections" section which discusses how the lab's tasks connect to the more conceptual content covered in the lecture portion of the course.

Instructions: This section contains the step-by-step instructions needed to complete the lab activities. By design, this section does not attempt to explain why each step is necessary; this is left to the pre-reading so that the instructions during lab can be as easy to follow as possible.

Focus Questions: These questions are designed to help students think about what they've done during the lab, and how the lab activities tie in to the more conceptual content presented during the lecture portion of the course.

Lab Notebook: Students are required to create an on-line "lab notebook" consisting of one web page for each lab session. This section of the lab manual tells students what they are to include on each web page, for example, adding snapshots of artifacts they have created, explaining concepts related to the lab activities, and connecting the lab activities to what they've learned in the lecture portion of the course. This has turned out to be one of the best features of the class – students leave with a concrete summary of the work they have done in a medium they are excited about.

The presence of the "Connections" and "Focus Questions" sections is particularly important. We have argued against laboratory activities that focus *exclusively* on programming since we believe they perpetuate misconceptions about the nature of computer science. There is a danger in our approach that a different, but equally problematic, misconception will be perpetuated, namely that students will see the *use of computers and computer applications* as equivalent to studying computer science. The "Connections" and "Focus Questions" are designed to ensure that students see a direct connection between the lab activities and the more abstract material covered in the lecture. As described in section 3.1.3, data from student survey responses indicate that the inclusion of the "Connections" and "Focus Questions" sections has successfully avoided reinforcing this misconception.

2.2 Overview of the lab activities

The following sections give brief summaries of a selection of activities we have developed and discuss how the lab tab tasks relate to the conceptual material from the course.

2.2.1 Web

Lab #1 walks the students through the creation of their own web page using Microsoft Expression Web. The web page includes personal information, outlines the student's hobbies, and explores places they have been or would like to go. The page contains text, images, video, and links to other pages. The students also learn to alter their page's background, text formats and other properties using Cascading Style Sheets. Finally, they synchronize their site so it can be viewed on the internet.

2.2.2 Photoshop

Labs #2 and 3 take students through the creation of a collage composed of student chosen pictures, either personal pictures, or ones from Wikimedia Commons. This collage is constructed both with and without using Photoshop's collage wizard. They learn to customize the collage's background and apply effects to their pictures. They also learn various image manipulation tools and use Photoshop's searching capabilities to find pictures.

Many introductory text books begin by explaining how information can be stored using the binary system. Manipulating the pictures in the collage using Photoshop helps students connect the abstract concepts in the textbooks to a more familiar application, illustrating the benefits of representing information digitally. Since a collage is frequently made up of both photographs (raster graphics) and text (vector graphics), we point out how the choice of representation makes a difference in what can be done with the different types of graphics.

These activities show students applications of a variety of computer science concepts. Attaching keyword tags to photos shows how Photoshop operates as a database. Applying photo effects such as converting images to black and white and creating background gradients illustrates how color can be easily manipulated when in digital format.

2.2.3 Programming using BlueJ

Labs #4 and #5 explore programming using the media computation approach espoused by Guzdial et. al. [18] . By focusing on digital image manipulation, students are prompted to think about the algorithms they encountered through the use of Photoshop in the previous two labs. Since they are manipulating the RGB values of the pixels, these labs also reinforce their understanding of data representation issues. Focus questions after the lab explore image processing concepts, such as what it means to compute the distance between two pixels, and how a "blue screen" can be used to super-impose one image on top of another.

2.2.4 Operating Systems

Lab #6 walks the students through the process of installing both the Vista and Linux operating systems (OS). In this way they learn about the role of operating system as *resource manager*. For example, they use disk partitioning to separate the operating system from their data. Partitioning the hard drive is a useful technique and provides a concrete example of the resource manager role.

Students also search for and install device drivers for hardware not initially supported by the OS. A second role is to provide an interface between applications and hardware through the use of device drivers; students may frequently need to install drivers for new devices they wish to use with their personal computers.

Example focus questions from this lab ask the students to think about how a computer can be dual booted into multiple operating systems. In particular, they are asked to provide a description of what the boot loader instructions would look like when dual booting.

Lab #7 Another role of the operating system is to provide *services* to application programs. This is an abstract concept that students find difficult to connect to their experience. This lab introduces students to the digital ink/handwriting recognition abilities of the Tablet PC through the OneNote application, an electronic journal, and Google Calendar applications. Students see the benefits of centralizing the handwriting recognition functionality in the OS, rather than implementing it in each application individually.

Additionally, this activity introduces an experimental aspect of computer science. Each student handwrites a portion of the Declaration of Independence, converts it into text, and evaluates the accuracy of the handwriting mechanism. They do this in two ways: first by writing the entire document and converting it as a whole to text, and then by converting each individual word. These two methods allow them to measure the importance of *context* to the recognition algorithm. Students then collaboratively build a Google Docs spreadsheet indicating which words were recognized incorrectly for each student.

Lab #8 returns to examining the operating system's role as resource manager to help students understand how the operating system can provide the crucial abstraction of *files* and *directories*. Students work with a tool designed to explore the way that data are structured on a disk using the FAT12 file system. This lab could be expanded to look at other file systems to help students understand what is involved in transferring files between computers running different operating systems.

2.2.5 Networks

Labs #9 and 10 guide the students through the set-up of both wired and wireless home networks. Teams of two students receive a router, printer, Roku Soundbridge music player, and two laptops. They learn how to configure the router, connect the Soundbridge and computers to their network, how to share files/printers, and some of the technical intricacies of computer networks. The network protocol stack is an excellent example of the use of abstraction, a fundamental concept in Computer Science. Each configuration task targets a different layer of the network protocol stack to illustrate the role each layer plays.

In the wireless portion of the lab, students secure the network through the use of encryption, applying a MAC address filter and turning off SSID broadcast. Port forwarding and dynamic DNS are used to allow access to network devices from outside the private network. SSID broadcast and MAC address filtering complement the concepts learned in Lab #9, and port forwarding and dynamic DNS further illustrate the details of the network protocol stack. Focus questions for this laboratory use *Wireshark* to help students unravel the protocol stack.

Lab #11 revisits programming by guiding through the implementation of a seemingly simple game, *Simon Says*, in the Alice programming environment. While the media computation exercises primarily focus on reinforcing image representation issues, this lab gets more into the details of programming. After completing the game, students examine a simple Perl script written by one of the authors that provides an RSS feed for a web site that does not provide its own feed. This RSS feed is used with the Soundbridge music player from labs 9 and 10.

3. ANALYSIS

Our goals in developing this course included (1) increasing enrollment in undergraduate computer science courses; (2) increasing the number of students who take subsequent courses in computer science; (3) increasing the technological fluency and attitudes towards technology of the general student population; and (4) helping students gain a better understanding of the nature of Computer Science. In this section, we examine the degree to which the course has successfully met each goal.

3.1.1 Impact on Enrollment

In the current environment, increasing enrollment in Computer Science courses is a high priority. The course has now been offered twice (Fall 2009 and Spring 2010), and Fall 2010 is currently in process. Table 1 shows enrollments for 3 semesters using the previous version of the course, which focused almost exclusively on programming tasks, compared to 3 semesters using the authentic computing tasks approach described here.

Old Version		New Version	
Term	**# enrolled**	**Term**	**# enrolled**
Spring 2008	11	Fall 2009	23
Fall 2008	13	Spring 2010	26
Spring 2009	6	Fall 2010	47

Table 1: Enrollments for past 6 semesters

As can be seen from the table, enrollments in the course have improved dramatically, exposing significantly more students to computer science. Table 3 outlines the most common reasons Spring 2010 students decided to take the course. While many enrolled to fulfill a science requirement, it is significant that so many students expressed an interest in the subject matter and its usefulness in other courses as reasons for enrolling. The fact that the course was recommended by friends is also encouraging.

It is particularly noteworthy that for Fall 2010, 21 of the 47 students enrolled are returning students. The fact that so many returning students have signed up seems to indicate that the "word on the street" about the course is positive. Having 26 incoming first year students is also encouraging as it increases the pool of potential majors and minors. In the past, students tended to sign up for Computer Science more towards the end of their academic careers. This meant that even if they decided they liked Computer Science, they were unable to continue on at that point in their career.

Reason	**Fall '09**	**Spring '10**	**Fall '10**
Fulfills science core requirement	18	20	32
Content seems interesting	15	17	22
Will be useful to me in other college courses	6	9	21
Heard it was interesting	1	6	0
Fit into my schedule	5	9	8
Recommended by professor, advisor or counselor	2	5	6
Recommended by a friend	1	3	1

Table 3: Reasons for enrollingin the course

Our second enrollment-based goal was to increase the number of students taking one or more subsequent computer science courses after completing the introductory course. Out of the 49 students who took the course during 2009-10, 6 of them have enrolled in one or more subsequent courses. To the best of our knowledge, at most 1 of these 6 was even considering studying computer science before taking this course. If this percentage can be maintained, we can expect to see 9-10 students take our traditional CS1 course each year, which is a major improvement.

3.1.2 Technological Fluency and Attitudes Towards Technology

In order to measure the impact on student attitudes towards technology, we gave a modified version of the Motivation and Strategies for Learning Questionnaire [21] at the beginning and end of the semester during Spring '10 (due to time constraints, the instrument was not ready to be administered as a pre-test during Fall '09 but it was administered as a posttest). Out of the 26 students enrolled in Spring 2010, 16 of them completed both the pretest and posttest.

The MSLQ contains questions that are grouped in three scales: *intrinsic motivation*, *task value* and *self-efficacy*. All responses to the questions are on a scale of 1 (not at all true of me) to 7 (very true of me), with higher scores representing more desirable results. Table 2 summarizes the average scores for each of the three scales, as well as the average change.

Scale	Pre-test	Post-test	Change
Intrinsic motivation	4.81	4.83	0.02
Task value	5.74	5.38	-0.36
Self-efficacy	5.26	5.42	0.16

Table 2: Results of MSLQ for Spring 2010

As can be seen in the table, modest gains were made in self-efficacy, while there was little change in intrinsic motivation. The fact that a relatively large change in task value is seen is cause for concern. Table 4 shows the data for the individual questions making up the task value scale.

When examining the data, we noted that two students had particularly large decreases on almost all of the questions. These two students' responses were quite different from most of the other students. Therefore, in Table 4 we have included an analysis of the average responses to the task value questions both with and without those two students. As can be seen in the table, the impact of these two students' responses on the overall average is significant; the average overall change is only -0.08 when the two outliers are not included.

The last column in Table 4 indicates **how many** students had responses that decreased, stayed the same, or increased for each of the task value questions (the two outliers are included in this column). This computation ignores the magnitude of the response, which the average does not. In this case, we see that for most of the questions, either no change or an increase was seen in the majority of students. On the task value questions as a whole, half of the students showed a decrease while the other half showed no change or an increase.

Question	Pre/Post/Change		-/0/+
	All students	Outliers eliminated	
I think I will be able to use what I learn in this course in other courses.	5.75/ 5.63/ -0.13	5.71/ 6/ 0.29	7/5/4
It is important for me to learn the course material in this class.	6.25/ 5.25/ -1	6.21/ 5.71/ -0.5	6/7/3
I am very interested in the content area of this course.	5.56/ 5.13/ -0.44	5.79/ 5.5/ -0.29	5/9/2
I think the course material in this class is useful for me to learn.	5.81/ 5.63/ -0.19	5.93/ 5.93/ 0	6/5/5
I like the subject matter of this course	5.5/ 5.5/ 0	5.71/ 5.93/ 0.22	3/8/5
Understanding the subject matter of this course is very important to me.	5.56/ 5.13/ -0.44	5.71/ 5.57/ -0.07	7/6/3
Overall	5.74/ 5.38/ -0.36	5.85/ 5.77/ -0.08	8/2/6

Table 4: Responses to task value questions

While we would like to see more students with an increase in their perceptions of the value of learning the course material and their interest in it, it should be noted that the scores for these items start out quite high, with an average response of 5.74 on a scale of 1 to 7. With such high initial responses, it is not surprising to see the scores decrease. A final value of 5.38 (5.77 without outliers) still indicates a high level of interest by the students. We will be continuing to administer the MSLQ for at least the next year, and will monitor the task value questions with particular interest.

3.1.3 Helping Students Understand the Nature of Computer Science

In order to measure how well students were able to see the connections between the laboratory tasks and lecture, we asked students on the post-survey to describe how each of the lab activities they completed was related to the concepts discussed in lecture. These connections had been made explicit in the lab activities, and including these questions on the post-survey allowed measurement of how well students internalized these connections. If students understand these connections, it is less likely that they hold the misconception that computer use = computer science.

Many of the responses we received were encouraging, demonstrating that students had indeed been able to make the connections between the "practical" lab activities and the "theoretical" lecture content. Here is a sampling of the responses we received:

- The pictures, texts, background, and other content that I used in Photoshop are stored using bitmaps and geometric structures. Each pixel in each picture is stored using individual values for red, green, and blue in a location on the files of the computer. The binary system is used for this storage, making the process much easier and more efficient.
- This lab showed us a lot about what we had been talking about with the operating systems in the lecture portion. I thought it was good to see two different sides of how operating systems function, because it seemed to complete the lesson better.
- In the lecture the concept of networks was just that, a concept. In the lab, it was made real. I discovered that a network is a lot simpler than it seemed when we learned about it in the lecture.
- Programming with Alice was a fun way to learn about how to program. In lecture we learned that computers cannot think on their own, so you need to tell them exactly how to perform tasks.
- This lab made programming languages more accessible. I was able to fully understand what the computer has to see when it executes a program although, I do understand that the computer doesn't see the programming language, it sees the machine language or binary equivalent.

A locally developed course evaluation instrument gives evidence that we have been successful in helping students understand that being proficient at using computers does not mean that one is a computer scientist. For example, in response to the question "What advice would you give a friend who is planning to take this course" one student notes that "he [the instructor] really wants to make sure you actually understand the material and are making connections to the lecture section of the class" while another stated "Use class time effectively and always keep in mind connections to lecture." When asked "What did you find beneficial about this course", the following responses were given:

- I think it really helped me understand what exactly is going on in a computer by hearing about it in lecture, but then also going to lab and getting to see how computers function.
- Making connections with the lecture section of the course.
- I found the lab helped me tie in what I was learning in lecture effectively.

While not all students made comments such as these, it does seem students perceive that our goal in teaching them computer science was not that they become better computer users.

4. POTENTIAL PROBLEMS WITH OUR APPROACH

There are two potential difficulties inherent in the approach to teaching a general education computer science course in the way we have described. The first, perpetuating the misconception that being proficient at using computers is equivalent to being a computer scientist, has already been mentioned but is worth reiterating. We believe that the proficient computer user misperception can be avoided by having faculty explicitly address the question several times, in the course syllabus as well as during class time. We have some data to indicate that we are successfully dealing with this problem, but we will continue to monitor students' perceptions of computer science.

The second potential barrier to widespread adoption of this approach is the issue of cost. Some of our labs require students to have access to machines in ways that are not typically granted to students. For example, lab #3 involves students installing and configuring an operating system. This obviously destroys whatever operating system and applications are currently installed. Imaging tools such as Norton Ghost can potentially alleviate this problem; however, not all schools may have infrastructure to support this type of environment. The equipment needed for the networking laboratory includes a printer for every pair of students, as well as a networkable music player, which may also be problematic.

The cost of software is also potentially prohibitive. We have decided to use commercially available software such as Photoshop Elements, rather than free-of-charge software such as the GIMP because we believe students will be more engaged if they are taught using familiar software.

There are a couple of approaches that could be used to address the cost issue. First, the network lab could be modified to build a network composed strictly of computers, rather than the other devices we have chosen to include. While such a lab might lose some of its authenticity and appeal to students if this was done, many of the networking concepts could still be examined using a subset of the equipment. Software costs can be reduced by using free-of-charge software when possible. Students may actually appreciate learning about these free alternatives.

5. SUMMARY

In this paper we have presented an argument for basing laboratory activities in breadth-first introductory computer science courses on authentic computing tasks related to students' intrinsic interests. We have outlined examples of such activities, and described the results of using those activities at our institution. These results indicate that students are attracted to our approach and are able to make connections between the lab activities and the lecture content.

While there are some potential drawbacks to our approach, they are not insurmountable and we believe the course's appeal and success will make efforts to avoid the drawbacks well worth the time and resources. The lab activities are freely available; contact the first author for more information..

6. ACKNOWLEDGMENTS

Work on this project was supported by a grant by the Howard Hughes Medical Institute as part of Hope's Science Education Scholars program. Joshua Andrews was supported by this grant and helped develop and test the activities during the summer of 2009. Students Brenda Cuellar and Amy Alvine also helped evaluate some of the materials. Our approach to the course was inspired by the success of a similarly themed course in the Engineering Department at Hope. This course, *Science and Technology of Everyday Life*, was developed and implemented by Professor John Krupzcak. We are grateful for his inspiration and willingness to share his ideas and approaches with us.

7. REFERENCES

[1] Gates, W. H., III *Testimony by Mr. William H. Gates III.* City, 2008.

[2] Cassell, L., McGettrick, A., Guzdial, M. and Roberts, E. The current crisis in computing: what are the real issues? *ACM SIGCSE Bulletin*, 39, 1 2007), 329.

[3] Yardi, S. and Bruckman, A. *What is computing?: bridging the gap between teenagers' perceptions and graduate students' experiences*. ACM, City.

[4] Wing, J. M. *Computational Thinking*. City, 2006.

[5] Engel, G. and Roberts, E. *Computing Curricula 2001 Computer Science Volume*. ACM/IEEE, City, 2001.

[6] Cliburn, D. C. A CS0 course for the liberal arts. *ACM SIGCSE Bulletin*, 38, 1 2006), 77.

[7] Phillips, A. T., Stevenson, D. E. and Wick, M. R. Implementing CC2001: a breadth-first introductory course for a just-in-time curriculum design. *SIGCSE Bulletin*, 35, 1 2003), 238.

[8] Brookshear, J. G. *Computer Science, An Overview*. Greg Tobin, 2005.

[9] Dale, N. and Lewis, J. *Computer Science Illuminated*. Jones and Bartlett, 2004.

[10] Snyder, L. *Fluency with Information Technology, Skills, Concepts, and Capabilities*. Addison Wesley, 2008.

[11] Burch, C. and Ziegler, L. Science of computing suite (SOCS): resources for a breadth-first introduction. *ACM SIGCSE Bulletin*, 36, 1 2004), 437.

[12] Hill, J. S. and O'Neal, M. Introductory-level computer science courseware. *Journal of Computing Sciences in Colleges*, 20, 6 2005), 31.

[13] Whaley, T. Including a web/database unit in CS0. *Journal of Computing Sciences in Colleges*, 20, 5 2005), 295.

[14] Anewalt, K. Making CS0 fun: an active learning approach using toys, games and Alice. *Journal of Computing Sciences in Colleges*, 23, 3 2008), 98.

[15] Mosskal, B., Lurie, D. and Cooper, S. Evaluating the effectiveness of a new instructional approach. *SIGCSE Bulletin*, 36, 1 2004), 75.

[16] Powers, K., Ecott, S. and Hirshfield, L. M. Through the looking glass: teaching CS0 with Alice. *ACM SIGCSE Bulletin*, 39, 1 2007), 213.

[17] Cooper, S., Dann, W. and Pausch, R. Alice: a 3-D tool for introductory programming concepts. *Journal of Computing Sciences in Colleges*, 15, 5 2000), 107.

[18] Guzdial, M. A media-computation course for non-majors. *ACM SIGCSE Bulletin*, 35, 3 2003), 104.

[19] Reed, D. Rethinking CS0 with JavaScript. *ACM SIGCSE Bulletin*, 33, 1 2001), 100.

[20] Barker, L. J., McDowell, C. and Kalahar, K. Exploring factors that influence computer science introductory course students to persist in the major. *SIGCSE BulletinGCSE*, 41, 1 2009), 153.

[21] Pintrich, P. R. and DeGroot, E. V. Motivational and self-regulated learning components of classroom academic performance. *Journal of Educational Psychology*, 821990), 33-40.

Breadth in Depth

A 1st Year Introduction to Parallel Programming

Thomas R. Gross
Department of Computer Science
ETH Zurich
8092 Zurich, Switzerland
thomas.gross@inf.ethz.ch

ABSTRACT

There is a debate on when and how to teach parallel programming in the undergraduate curriculum. We try to structure the debate along a number of dimensions and then present the solution that we adopted for an engineering-oriented curriculum. We added an introduction to parallel programming to the list of mandatory classes in the 2nd semester. The class exposes students to three styles of parallel programming: threads with shared memory, CSP-style message passing, and OpenMP-based parallel programming. Within these models, the class aims to focus the student's attention on communication as the key issue in parallel programs. Explicit communication (or their absence) causes correctness problems, implicit communication (e.g., when accessing shared data in different threads) forces the student to understand when updates are globally visible. An introductory class early in the undergraduate curriculum has a number of benefits and disadvantages, which are discussed in this paper. A preliminary evaluation after two editions of this course indicates that the design goals are met but also points to several issues that other institutions may want to consider.

Categories and Subject Descriptors: K.3.2 [**Computer and Information Science Education**] Computer Science Education; D.1.3 [**Concurrent Programming**] Parallel programming

General Terms: Design

Keywords: CS education, parallel programming, software engineering

1. INTRODUCTION

Many papers, panels, and keynote presentations have repeated that current and future computing systems are parallel computers. Computer science students must learn not only how to construct a sequential program but must also learn how to master parallel programming. As a result many institutions have included mandatory or elective courses on parallel (or concurrent) programming[16, 3, 19] in the undergraduate curriculum or have made special efforts to introduce parallelism concepts into the existing courses[7, 4].

But whereas many educators and practitioners agree that parallel programming is important and should be included, there is a lot less agreement on the topics that should be thought, if the material should be part of a separate course (or courses), and when to position the course(s) on this topic in the curriculum. The questions that were posed at the (first) panel on Parallel Computing Education at Supercomputing'91 still have not found a universally accepted answer[17]. This paper does not provide a definite answer either (nor is it likely that there will be a definite answer anytime soon, if ever) but attempts to add to the discussion by presenting another approach that has been implemented in an engineering-oriented computer science curriculum. We start with the rationale and discuss the concerns.

1.1 Options

When debating what parallel programming topics to teach and when to teach them within the context of an undergraduate curriculum there are a number of questions to address. What do we expect the student to gain from attending a class? Of course none of these questions have only two answers that one must choose from - often the realities of an institution's curriculum require a compromise.

1. What is the *target audience*? Who are the customers of the course? All Computer Science majors? Bachelor or Masters students? Future application experts, e.g., in a program on Computational Engineering and Science? How close to graduation are the students?

2. What is the *target platform*? Is there a specific parallel system (either because your institution provides access to this system or you anticipate that this kind of platform will be most important for your students)? Are there specific tools or programming languages that are important for other classes?

3. What should be the *course content and scope*? How many hours of lecture and lab can be tolerated (or are expected) by your audience? How can you balance coverage of principles and an exposition to current tools or current practice?

I try to address some of these questions below. The answer to the last question (what is the scope in credits or hours) is specific to any institution. To provide some frame

SIGCSE'11, March 9–12, 2011, Dallas, Texas, USA.

of reference I assume that – regardless of level and target audience – such a course on parallel programming should take up approximately 1/5 of the students time. Approximately means that in some institutions it may be a 1/4; i.e. the course could be one of four or five courses taken by a student in a semester. Within the context of the European Credit Transfer System (ECTS), such a course yields about 6 - 8 credits. (The ECTS system defines a full load for a semester to be 30 credits.) In practice, such a course would include about 180 min of lectures per week in a semester of about 14 weeks, with ample opportunities (and requirements) to participate in labs, work out homework assignments, and time for practical programming. No doubt, is is possible to design a good class on parallel programming with more or fewer credits (and, therefore, higher or lower expectations on the time a student can spend on this topic).

1.2 Target audience

If the participants are Computer Science students, the emphasis should be on principles, with more emphasis on principles the earlier the class is placed in the curriculum. There exist today many Computer Science programs that differ significantly in the kind (and depth) of topics that are included in the curriculum. It would be surprising if these different programs all agreed on the contents of a class on parallel programming. Programs with an emphasis on computer systems or software engineering may include a class that is different from a class that serves programs with emphasis on visual computing and graphics or human-computer interaction. If the class audience consists of students that will use parallel systems as a platform for application development then the principles and abstractions that are covered in a class on parallel programming must be reinforced by appropriate application-oriented techniques and tools[14].

1.3 Target platform

The proliferation of multicore (and soon manycore) processor components provides ample motivation to pursue parallel programming as such components are used in many systems. On one hand this situation presents a unique opportunity: if students own a laptop (many or all of them do at many institutions) then they own and operate a parallel computer. These computers are small-scale symmetric shared-memory multiprocessor (there are 2 to 4 cores to execute independent instruction streams, each core has access to all memory cells, and the access time is roughly the same for all cores and all memory cells). The abundance of parallel computers at the students' disposal is great as it allows students to experience first-hand the problems of parallel computing. Even a simple parallel program that is incorrect has a good chance to expose the bug on the student's system and therefore motivates students to learn about parallel programming. So a course with this situation in mind might emphasize a simple view of parallel systems (different execution units with a shared, easily accessible memory system).

But there are two problems with this story: once the number of cores increases, the computer system architecture may provide the programming abstraction of a shared memory but the actual computer system implementation presents non-uniform access times. I.e. the computer system is a NUMA (Non-Uniform Memory Architecture) system, and programmers ignore the distance between execution units and the storage system at their peril. Even today's 8-core systems are no longer symmetric with regard to memory access time or memory bandwidth, and larger systems will likely be even more asymmetric. The other issue is related to the other end of the spectrum: if you consider large-scale parallel systems, with tens of thousands of cores (or more), then the programming model used on these platforms is message passing: MPI [10] is the de-facto standard of programming high-end parallel systems.

Graphics processors (and their friends like Cell-based systems) provide another option, and a number of groups have used CUDA [6] as a platform for parallel computing[16]. These systems also provide easy access to a large(r) number of cores with impressive peak performance. Unfortunately the programming support for these system is low-level with limited portability, even from one generation of graphics processors to the next.

1.4 Course content

When designing a class, it is never easy to find a balance between theory and practice, regardless of subject area. To complicate the discussion in the context of parallel programming, there are multiple dimensions of theory (parallel algorithms, formal models of parallel computing, ...) and a wide range of practical issues (computer architecture, programming languages, libraries, performance monitors, tuning tools, ...) that an instructor can choose to include or ignore.

The wide range of programming languages, libraries, and tools complicates the situation tremendously, and in many cases, there is a steep learning curve. To complicate matters further, some popular tools (e.g., CUDA, OpenMP [5], MPI) are only loosely connected to a theoretical foundation, and new tools and languages are introduced frequently. Students must gain experience in parallel programming, but it is not wise to devote a significant part of a semester to learn a tool or programming language that is never used again. On the other hand, any practical (lab-oriented) component of a class on parallel programming is bound to use some tool, with its associated overhead.

2. BREADTH-FIRST AT A BASIC LEVEL

ETH decided to include a mandatory class on parallel programming early in the curriculum. Students starting in the fall of 2008 or later must take the "Introduction to Parallel Programming" in their 2nd semester. There exist several other classes for more advanced students (seniors, or seniors/masters). Some of these courses concentrate on specific platforms (e.g., MPI for computational scientists, MapReduce for information systems students), others cover parallel algorithms or multiprocessor programming based on the later chapters on the book by Herlihy and Shavit[11]. By offering a mandatory course early in the curriculum, the department wanted to ensure that all students are exposed to the problems of parallel processing[1].

The overall goal of the class is to teach the students how to write correct parallel programs To structure the class and

[1]The depressing story of the Therac-25 incidents[15], and the slow progress in eliminating similar problems in software development, should serve as a warning: a computer science graduate should at least identify potential data races and call in an expert if he or she is not skilled in programming a parallel system.

to expose the student to the wide range of options in parallel programming we use three widely-used programming models as guiding principle. We look at multithreading with shared memory as an example of programming with explicit and implicit communication steps. A program may use synchronization to force an ordering (or to avoid a data race) or may cause implicit communication as a consequence of accessing an object shared between multiple threads. We explore message passing as an extreme approach to allow only explicit communication and allow the students to experience the benefits and pain of this programming model. Finally, we use OpenMP as an approach that combines user hints with runtime scheduling. Students experience how some computations can be parallelized with a few hints, how difficult it is in other cases to determine if such hints are legal, and how much time can be spent on uncovering the consequences of a faulty hint. The focus on programming models also appears to be a reasonable preparation for a later discussion of parallel patterns[13].

Students should understand the important role of communication (implicit communication through assignments to shared data, explicit communication by sending or receiving messages). To appreciate the difficulties associated with the use of shared data, the students must delve into variable assignments so that a discussion of update visibility is possible. To understand the dangers of circular waiting in message passing, the students must understand that data transfers incur time. The desire to teach these issues led to the "in depth" exposure of the various programming styles.

But there was also another goal for an early class on parallel programming: the curriculum provides the students with many options and as a consequence, there are not many unifying themes that students can use to organize the vast amount of material that a student is expected to master. Parallelism will be a critical issue for many future software development efforts. And, as has been noted by others, various aspects of parallelism are often introduced in other courses. A class on operating systems may cover semaphores and threads, a class on databases may cover similar concepts, and classes on networks or computer architecture may also devote a significant part of their lectures to discuss threading and its variants. So by moving the basic concepts to a single class, we allow on one hand other courses to focus on more advanced topics and at the same time allow the student to realize that the concepts (or at least some of them) are useful in many contexts.

We therefore designed a class that provides breadth (a decision made by others in a similar situation as well[16]) but we chose a different level. Rather than exploring different programming languages, we want students to understand the core issues of parallel programming. So the class aims to provide breadth at a rather deep level. It is important that students understand that communication is a key problem and there exist several options to express communication (or to trigger communication).

2.1 Platform issues

To keep the faculty and the students sane, we try to minimize the overhead that is associated with introducing new languages - ideally, students can explore these topics within the context of a single programming language. As a target system, we use the student's laptop, although we provide also laboratories for those students that do not own or carry a laptop. These laboratories contain dual-core systems (dual-boot Windows and Linux) as well as a smaller number of 4-core and 8-core systems (Linux).

2.2 Non-topics

The flip side of using the student's computers is that it is difficult (often impossible) to see any performance improvement due to multiprocessing. With only two cores available, it is often the case that a parallel program is slower than the sequential one. While this is a worthwhile learning experience, this situation does not make it easy to motivate students to embrace parallel systems. We address this situation in three different ways: we make available – later in the course – larger systems with multiple cores. We look for application programs that show some speedup (the poor performance is often not due to parallelism overhead but due to memory system effects; if multiple tasks or threads create cache conflicts, the benefits of parallelism are overshadowed by slowdowns due to memory traffic). Finally, we sidestep performance optimization and delay the in-depth discussion of optimizations and tuning to later semesters.

Performance optimization is clearly important for parallel programming, and it has been argued that this topic should be in an integral part of any class on parallel programming[8]. Clearly the motivation for parallel computing is to obtain a faster solution than can be provided by a sequential system (or to obtain a better solution than could be obtained on a sequential system). But covering performance optimization requires that students know a fair bit about computer architecture and possibly about compilers, as the details of the memory organization and the optimizations chosen by the compiler have a great influence on application performance.

In light of the early nature of this class, we do not cover all aspects of the memory model for multithreaded systems[1]. Our goal is to teach the students to write correct programs, not programs that can be optimized well or that use performance-oriented functions or methods. E.g., in the context of Java, we rely only on the simple methods for classes in a package like java.util.concurrent.atomic and hide the "weak" methods from the students. Since we do not cover performance optimization this simplification appears to cause no problem.

3. COURSE STRUCTURE AND CONTENTS

We use Java for all programs in this class, to meet our goal to use a single programming language for the course. While the use of Java for threads may not require further discussion, the use of Java for message passing and OpenMP deserves a few comments. JCSP is a Java implementation of CSP (and more) that has also been used by other courses (e.g.,[12]). Our experience is mixed: although the implementation is fine, JCSP provides more than we need in this course. JOMP is a preprocessor-based OpenMP variant for Java. The current release does not support OpenMP 3.0 and includes no support for nested parallelism. As the development of JOMP seems to have stopped we are implementing a performance-competitive version. Neither JCSP nor JOMP are performance-sensitive implementations,but this is not a problem for our course (that pushes performance optimization into later courses).

We considered C++ or C# as alternative languages. But only Java allowed us to consider all three programming models in the context of a single programming language (we did not want to ask students to deal with the details of more than one new language in this course). Almost 3 years have passed since the original design of this course was done, and there has been considerable development regarding C++ and C#. Now that we have gained experience with Java, a future edition of this course may be based on C# or C++.

3.1 Topics

The class format is two lectures of 90 min each for 14 weeks. Table 1 lists the topics for each week. To increase cohesion, we use a few simple application kernels as running examples – these are revisited for each programming model – and include a simple simulation example (Game-of-Life) to show how parallelism is used in a larger context.

The two application kernels are mergesort and (dense) matrix multiplication. Both kernels are simple and easy to understand yet at the same time allow a discussion of various tradeoffs. In the assignments we do not ask the students to optimize their programs, so useful constructs like thread pools are not given much time. Some students pursue these directions anyhow, and we then discuss these approaches in the recitation groups led by the teaching assistants. However, as this material is not part of the syllabus, only a subset of the students may hear about these topics.

The hardest part in discussing threads and programming with a shared-memory data space is dealing with the visibility of updates. Since we do not want to discuss the complete memory model we focus on the use of "synchronized" methods. These methods establish global visibility of previous updates and allow the students to concentrate on the correctness of their programs.

The Game-of-Life example illustrates that in many programs the "parallel part" may only be a small part of the complete program. (Depending on the metric and the implementation, about 10% of the program is devoted to dealing with parallelism.) Some students complained about this fact and felt that material "unrelated" to parallel programming should not be covered or included in a class on parallel programming[2]. However, the majority of the students liked the (trivial) example. The implementations of mergesort and dense matrix multiplication produce unimpressive output, so a problem that shows even simple output is appreciated (other institutions have successfully based their courses on parallel programming on graphics and animations[3]). The Game-of-Life assignment provides a bridge to the event driven programming practiced in many user interfaces and graphics projects and is included also for this reason.

4. DISCUSSION

4.1 Evaluation

We solicited feedback from the students of two years (2009, 2010). The survey was done anonymously. The students of the first edition (2009) were contacted two semesters after taking the course (to find out if any of the topics had indeed been revisited by other classes, as was hoped for by the curriculum design committee), students of the second edition (2010) were contacted about 3 months after the course had ended. About 45% of the 2009 students responded; for the 2010 students, the nominal return rate was higher (70%).

A response rate of 45% might appear low but ETH employs a model for student selection that is different from the model used by North American institutions. Enrollment in the 1st year is open to all students with an appropriate high school diploma; an exam at the end of the first year serves as a "delayed entrance exam" to decide who is allowed to continue. In Computer Science (at ETH), approximate half of the first year students do not pass this exam. So a response of 45% after one year means that we obtained a response from about 70% of those students that are still at ETH one year after the class (either because they passed the first-year exam or because they still have a chance to pass this exam). As the 2010 survey was taken prior to the first-year exam it is impossible to know the success of the respondents on the first-year exam.

Overall, the success rate for this course is about the same as the success rates for the other exams that make up the first-year exam.

4.2 Recurring themes

56% of the students of the first edition of this course reported that at least one of the topics from the introduction to parallel programming had reappeared in a later class. (31% were not sure, only 10% stated that no topic had reappeared). The topics that were listed as recurring are

- Locking (event queues, read-write locks, fairness)
- Semaphores
- Threads, shared memory programming, synchronization
- OpenMP

These topics resurfaced in several subsequent classes: operating systems, networks, system programming, computer systems lab, databases, advanced classes on parallel programming, software architecture, networks. Given that there were only two semesters that followed the 2009 edition of the class, we are happy with this result; as the students complete their B.S. program, we expect to add additional courses and topics to these lists.

4.3 Evolution

When asked what topics should be emphasized or de-emphasized in future editions, the responses (absolute numbers) were as follows. Of the 2010 population, 9 students make suggestions for additions, 20 students make suggestions to drop/de-emphasize material. The corresponding numbers for 2009 are 7 and 10. A number of topics find supporters and detractors.

The topic with the greatest number of requests to drop or de-emphasize are Java-specific issues. More than half of the 2010 students who responded to this question suggested that Java-related issues be dropped (to put this in perspective, less than 20% of the 2009 students made this suggestion). Of course, it is important to recall that in both populations, less than 25% of the students responded to this question.

[2]Anecdotal evidence suggests that the main reason for this complaint is that these students felt that they had to spend significant time on issues that (most likely) would *not* be part of the all-important first-year exam, which decides on their future as Computer Science students.

Week	Lecture	Lab/assignment
1	Intro, parallel Algorithms	Warm-up
2	Java issues	Java practice
3	Locks	Bounded buffers for multiple threads
4	Condition queues	Mergesort
5	Visibility	Dense matrix multiplication
6	Safety and liveness	
7	Semaphores	Read-Write locks
8	Message passing	Dining philosophers
9	CSP	Mergesort
10	Programming with channels	Game-of-Life
11	Problem decomposition for parallel computing	
12	OpenMP	Proving program properties
13	OpenMP	Dense matrix multiplication
14	Models	Proving program properties

Table 1: Summary of course schedule.

Topic	Decrease Coverage	Increase Coverage
Message passing	2	0
OpenMP	4	3
Locks	5	2
Java/graphics	12	1
Java.util.concurrent		4
Reasoning about programs	5	1
Other		3

Table 2: Requests to change course content.

The use of Java deserves a bit of further discussion. In 2010, 36% of the student self-assessed their knowledge of Java to be "good enough to write a Java program of the scope/complexity of Game-of-Life" or better at the start of the semester. In 2009, the corresponding percentage is 31%. This assessment is a little surprising as the 1st semester uses a different programming language (Eiffel, an object-oriented programming language with static typing). In both years, about a quarter (2009: 27%, 2010: 23%) have no prior knowledge of Java, and for this reason, we include at the start of the semester extra lectures and labs to ease the path of these students. Not surprisingly, the reduction of the treatment of "Java issues" is requested by the segment of the student population that has already prior Java experience. Our response is that in future editions of this class we will form recitation groups based on the students' prior knowledge of the implementation language and add more lectures outside of the course to assist those without prior Java knowledge.

Table 2 summarizes the results. Several students requested other languages, with C++ and Erlang receiving the most support.

4.4 Other issues

The course provides breadth but does not produce students that can immediately solve large-scale real-world parallel programming problems. The omission of performance optimization is one serious shortcoming.

The focus on low-level aspects has also the positive side-effect of improving the student's programming skills. After a first semester that emphasized an object-oriented introduction to programming, later classes (e.g., on operating systems, compilers, computational science) desired that students have a better understanding of program construction. So the introduction to parallel programming in the same semester as the class on "Data Structures and Algorithms" (the local instantiation of CS-2) serves as another vehicle to teach students the constructive aspects of programming. By exploring parallel implementations of mergesort after sorting has been covered earlier in the semester in CS-2, this topic is reinforced and the students investigate another aspect of sorting.

It is too early to evaluate the impact of this class on other classes in later stages of the curriculum. Several classes (on networking and on object-oriented programming concepts) removed material covered in this class. One instructor noted that his course is built on the assumption that students are familiar with parallelism (resp. concurrency) and anecdotal evidence suggest that this assumption is met. The use of Java has been received warmly; one instructor noted that in the networking class, there is a significant difference between "before" (the addition of this course to the curriculum) and now. For others (e.g., software engineering project) no difference was noted or there is no issue (as those classes use C or C++).

The absence of a single textbook that addresses this level of parallel programming is an issue. We recommend (and draw material from) the books by Herlihy and Shavit[11], Goetz et. al.[9], and Ben-Ari[2]. The later chapters of the first two books provide material for later classes as well. Nevertheless, the students seem reluctant to use books as studying tools. Only about 20% of the students admit in the evaluation that they use a book (the above three books receive the largest numbers of mentions). Anecdotal evidence from discussions with other instructors, at ETH and elsewhere, suggests that other classes have the same experience. Even if a course is based on a well-designed textbook (by authors who were recognized for their contribution to Computer Science teaching), the percentage of students that actually reads the book is also about 20%.

15 years ago, teaching a class on parallel programming required a substantial investment in computing infrastructure (see, e.g., Schaller at al. for a discussion[18]). The situation has changed a lot – students now own parallel computers. But whereas Schaller et al. anticipated that separate courses

on parallel programming would disappear (because the subject will be included in many places in the curriculum), there has been such a growth in concepts and techniques that we think it may be a while before these authors' prediction is realized.

5. CONCLUSIONS

Teaching parallel computing to undergraduates in their first year is a challenge. But the benefits outweigh the disadvantages. By exposing all students to the problems early on we capture the student's attention while they are still entering the field. A benefit is that students know about parallelism as an option and when future classes come along, they are aware of parallelism.

By discussing different parallel programming models we prepare the student for later. The student has a higher-level view than can be obtained if a class covers immediately specific programming tools. When the student encounters MPI later on, MPI is seen as a specific implementation of a general programming style. (And as students have understood the advantages and disadvantages of message passing, they can appreciate the many special functions included in MPI to allow a programmer to optimize performance.)

One effect of placing the course early is that we excite students. There is a small gap between the course content and leading edge developments, and students recognize that the topics that are covered in this course are hot. No other discipline can provide 1st-year students a similar opportunity. Students in physics or civil engineering must master a much larger body of prerequisites before they can be exposed to the leading edge. The Computer Science students that participate in such a class have a front-row view of an exciting evolving part of the field.

Acknowledgments

I thank the reviewers for detailed feedback and suggestions. I appreciate the comments by Susanne Cech Previtali and Christoph von Praun on earlier drafts of this paper. I benefited from discussions at the Computing Frontiers 2010 workshop on "Teaching Parallel Programming" organized by Stephanie Brumat. I am grateful to my colleagues Gustavo Alonso, Peter Mueller, Timothy Roscoe, and Peter Widmayer who provided feedback on the course and its relationship to other classes in our program. Finally, I thank the teaching assistants and students of "0024 - Introduction to Parallel Programming" (Spring 2009 and 2010) for their comments and patience. The development of the course was supported, in part, by a gift from Intel Corp.

6. REFERENCES

[1] S. V. Adve and H.-J. Boehm. Memory Models: A Case for Rethinking parallel languages and Hardware. *Commun. ACM*, 53(8):90–101, 2010.

[2] M. Ben-Ari. *Principles of Concurrent and Distributed Programming (2nd ed)*. Addison Wesley, Harlow, UK, 2006.

[3] K. B. Bruce, A. Danyluk, and T. Murtagh. Introducing Concurrency in CS 1. In *SIGCSE '10: Proc. 41st ACM Technical Symp. Computer Science Education*, pages 224–228, New York, NY, USA, 2010. ACM.

[4] D. P. Bunde. A Short Unit to Introduce Multi-Threaded Programming. *J. Comput. Small Coll.*, 25(1):9–20, 2009.

[5] B. Chapman, G. Jost, and R. van der Pas. *Using OpenMP: Portable Shared Memory Parallel Programming*. MIT Press, Cambridge, MA, 2008.

[6] Nvidia Corp. *Nvidia CUDA (C Programming Guide Version 3.1.1)*. Santa Clara, 2006–2010.

[7] D. J. Ernst and D. E. Stevenson. Concurrent CS: Preparing Students for a Multicore World. In *ITiCSE '08: Proc. 13th Annual Conf. Innovation and Technology in Computer Science Education*, pages 230–234, New York, NY, USA, 2008. ACM.

[8] A. L. Fisher and T. Gross. Teaching Empirical Performance Evaluation of Parallel Programs. In *SIGCSE '92: Proc. 23rd SIGCSE Technical Symp. Computer Science Education*, pages 309–313, Kansas City, MO, March 1992.

[9] B. Goetz with T. Peierls, J. Bloch, J. Bowbeer, D. Holmes, and D. Lea. *Java Concurrency in Practice*. Addison Wesley, 2006.

[10] W. Gropp, E. Lusk, and A. Skjellum. *Using MPI: Portable Parallel Programming with the Message-Passing Interface (2nd ed)*. MIT Press, Cambridge, MA, 1999.

[11] M. Herlihy and N. Shavit. *The Art of Multiprocessor Programming*. Morgan Kaufmann, Burlington, MA, 2008.

[12] D. Jackson. A Mini-Course on Concurrency. In *SIGCSE '91: Proc 22nd SIGCSE Technical Symp. Computer Science Education*, pages 92–96, New York, NY, USA, 1991. ACM.

[13] M. C. Jadud, J. Simpson, and C. L. Jacobsen. Patterns for Programming in Parallel, Pedagogically. In *SIGCSE '08: Proc. 39th SIGCSE Technical Symp. Computer Science Education*, pages 231–235, New York, NY, USA, 2008. ACM.

[14] D. A. Joiner, P. Gray, T. Murphy, and C. Peck. Teaching Parallel Computing to Science Faculty: Best Practices and Common Pitfalls. In *PPoPP '06: Proc. 11th ACM SIGPLAN Symp. Principles and Practice of Parallel Programming*, pages 239–246, New York, NY, USA, 2006. ACM.

[15] N. G. Leveson and C. S. Turner. Investigation of the Therac-25 Accidents. *IEEE Computer*, 26(7):18–41, 1993.

[16] S. Rivoire. A Breadth-First Course in Multicore and Manycore Programming. In *SIGCSE '10: Proc, 41st SIGCSE Technical Symp. Computer Science Education*, pages 214–218, New York, NY, USA, 2010. ACM.

[17] N. C. Schaller. Panel: Parallel Computing in the Undergraduate Computer Science Curriculum. In *Supercomputing '91: Proc. 1991 ACM/IEEE Conf. on Supercomputing*, page 148, New York, NY, USA, 1991. ACM.

[18] N. C. Schaller and A. T. Kitchen. Experiences in Teaching Parallel Computing—Five Years Later. *SIGCSE Bull.*, 27(3):15–20, 1995.

[19] G. Wolffe and C. Trefftz. Teaching Parallel Computing: New Possibilities. *J. Comput. Small Coll.*, 25(1):21–28, 2009.

Encouraging Parallel Thinking through Explicit Coordination Modeling

Sirong Lin and Deborah Tatar
Center for Human-Computer Interaction
Department of Computer Science
Virginia Tech
Blacksburg, Virginia 24061
silin@vt.edu, tatar@cs.vt.edu

ABSTRACT

Parallel thinking is a mindset that allows people to create support for activities that happen concurrently in a program. It crosscuts extant computer science boundaries, including parallel processing, network programming and multi-user systems, indeed, any system that involves the distribution and reintegration of work. Recent efforts to integrate parallelism across the CS curriculum begin to address the support of parallel thinking. We approach the pedagogy of parallel thinking by teaching students to *model coordination explicitly* using a specialized coordination language. We report a study of an experimental class taking this approach, finding that advanced CS students lack a good understanding of coordination but that the explicit modeling of coordination can address this lack.

Categories and Subject Descriptors

K.3.2 [**Computers and Education**]: Computer and Information Science Education

General Terms

Design, Experimentation, Human Factors

Keywords

Parallel thinking, pedagogy, TupleSpace, coordination modeling, parallelism, parallel computing, distributed computing

1. INTRODUCTION

As the computing world moves towards multi-core technologies, parallelism, though not a new concept, is, appropriately, attracting pedagogical attention. Multi-core technologies challenge almost every aspect of our assumptions about how computers operate and how they can operate more efficiently. Furthermore, connectivity is now a bread-and-butter business in computer science and complex connectivity implies parallel machines and parallel user actions. And ubiquitous and pervasive computing brings parallelism into the everyday experiences of non-computer scientists. Designing for virtually everyone on the planet is an essential and heavy responsibility.

Some argue that parallelism should be more than an advanced elective topic in CS. Indeed, Blelloch [3] has gone so far as to argue that for teaching parallelism from the start and embedding it throughout the curriculum with the idea of getting students to think about parallelism as the most natural form of computation and sequential computation as a special case. We agree that we need to encourage a *parallel thinking* mindset much earlier in the curriculum and broadly through multiple CS courses.

We define parallel thinking as a mindset that includes all the elements required to allow computer scientists to think about and implement support for activities that are allowed to happen concurrently in a program.

1.1 Support for a Pedagogy of Parallelism

In the past, most pedagogical attempts to improve teaching of parallel programming created new curriculum to make parallel programming techniques and algorithms easier to understand and learn, or developed new tools [2, 23, 26] to reduce difficulties in programming. For example, Robbins [26] reported using remote logging for teaching concurrency to help students visualize, understand, and debug concurrent programs.

Most recently, the pedagogical trend has been to integrate parallelism into the entire CS curriculum [13, 14, 16], from the entry-level courses. Ernst and Stevenson [14] attempted to increase students' exposure to concurrency early and often in their curriculum through multi-threading programming. Wittman [13] also reported integration of concurrency into the freshmen courses through threaded programming. Their challenge was how to bootstrap concurrent programming with students having early, weak programming knowledge and skills. These were good steps of training students in a parallel thinking mindset. However, to program with concurrency concepts such as threads by the end of the first semester required acceleration in teaching Java in the first month [13]. Forcing parallel constructs could actually complicate the transition to parallel thinking in the sense that students may not learn either sequentiality or parallel thinking well. Furthermore, Wrinn [13] pointed out that curriculum design in parallelism education cannot keep up with the rapid development of hardware. Educators are trying to anticipate the state of parallel systems. These problems raise the questions "what essentials in parallelism should be taught?" and "how to integrate these essentials into the CS curriculum, early and broadly?". Last year, a SIGCSE'10's panel discussion called for ideas and solutions to "re-frame parallelism using simpler concepts, preferably ones that students can think about and understand in a natural way" [1].

We suggest solutions to these issues by sharing our experience teaching and studying an experimental class encouraging parallel thinking. In particular, we pick out a fundamental aspect of parallelism that we believe underlies much of the pedagogical challenge, *modeling coordination*, and we concentrate on that. We

SIGCSE'11, March 9–12, 2011, Dallas, Texas, USA.

propose that if coordination is understood well, other aspects of parallelism (syntax, optimization, efficiency, control, etc.) will be seen as solutions to the problems posed by the basic situation. Thus, we are proposing a pedagogical sequence, in the spirit of Bransford's notion of contrasting cases [4], that starts by raising questions that it does not fully answer, leaving a conceptual gap for later instruction to fill in.

In alignment with the previous research, we also find that relatively advanced CS students do not understand coordination well. However, we find that by (1) teaching a coordination language that explicitly separates the coordination model from the computational model and (2) grounding students' imagination in familiar real world concepts and experiences, we can allow students to encounter their conceptual barriers in both design and implementation.

2. STUDY OF PROGRAMMERS' COGNITION

2.1 Coordination, Parallelism and Computer Science

Our focus on coordination is not new. Denning [11] identified coordination as one of the five "windows" of computing mechanics into the realm of computing. He defines it as "multiple entities cooperating toward a single result". In this context, *communication,* a relevant concept to coordination, was defined as "sending messages from one point to anther". At their simplest, communication and coordination involve only two actors; however, we are interested in situations that involve more complex networks.

Parallelism is the natural way to solve complex problems in human problem-solving history: when one problem becomes too complex to solve by one person (e.g. specialist), we divide the problem into small subtasks, and each subtask can be conquered separately. In computing, parallelism becomes a natural topic when computer scientists pursue a way to run programs faster, no matter the goal is to keep multiple cores in a processor productive in calculating, or perform a complicated search over a distributed database. Despite many differences between parallel computing and distributed computing, one common aspect is the need of managing the physically independent processes, either processors or computers (over networks), to collaboratively achieve a common goal or accomplish a large task. From this perspective, both parallel programs and distributed programs are coordinated programs [10]. Coordinating these individual entities through allocating subtasks (the individual entity will finish the task asynchronously) and facilitating the communication to synchronize individual subtask is the central problem in the coordinated activities.

In early 1990s, Carriero and Gelernter, the authors of TupleSpace, anticipated "parallelism will become, in the not too distant future, an essential part of every programmer's repertoire." [10] Twenty years later, their claim has become true and been accepted by more and more people in the field. However, their claim of "coordination — a general phenomenon of which parallelism is one example — will become a basic and widespread phenomenon in computer science" has not been yet given enough attention.

To identify the process of learning that prevents programmers from more spontaneously and successfully approaching the design and development of parallel-distributed coordinated systems to support complex human interaction and coordination, we use a TupleSpace-based class to identify the cognitive challenges that programmers encounter in designing and programming parallel-distributed coordinated activities. The pedagogical goal was to examine the ways to help student programmers better learn collaborative system design and development. In this paper, we focus on discussing the results related to pragmatic meaning of training CS students with "parallel thinking".

2.2 TupleSpace — a Coordination Language

Gelernter and Carriero brought attention to coordination in the computing field by promoting a specialized language, TupleSpace. Originally known as Linda [9], TupleSpace can handle complex coordination issues with simple atomic operations: *out*, *in*, and *read.* It allows coordination of different processes or machines by writing/reading structured data, in the form of a Tuple, to/from a common, globally-shared, associatively addressed memory space [20]. Template (a Tuple with one or more field unspecified) matching, i.e., contents matching, is used to search and return Tuples in/from the shared memory space. This interaction mechanism enables very loosely coupled communication in destination, space, and time [17].

The most significant benefit of using TupleSpace is to separate the coordinative activities from computational activities and create separate models — a coordination model and a computational model [15]. The role of a coordination model is to glue separate computational activities into an ensemble. The advantage of separation is its orthogonality, which further enables the generality and portability of the language. Therefore, TupleSpace can be added to any programming language, such as Java and C/C++. By using a specialized language, programmers can easily focus on thinking about coordination through the explicit exchange of resources.

TupleSpace has been used to successfully solve a number of coordination problems in the past thirty years in parallel computing (e.g. [8, 29]), distributed computing (e.g. [7, 20, 25]), and Human Computer Interaction (HCI) (e.g. [19]). The concept was implemented as network middleware, e.g. TSpaces by IBM, JavaSpaces by Sun, in the past as well. Most of these efforts treated TupleSpace as an underlying infrastructure to support the distributed structure. We explore TupleSpace as an infrastructure to support coordination.

2.3 The Class Design and Implementation

The experimental class, *Designing Distributed, Networked Activities for Learning,* was taught in the Department of Computer Science at Virginia Tech in Fall 2005 and subsequently in Fall 2006. The researchers engaged in teaching and studying the 4000-level semester-long experimental class. We tracked fourteen intermediate to advanced level CS students' learning and using TSpaces, an implementation of TupleSpace, to design and develop multi-user, distributed, fine-grained collaborative systems. All students were in the fourth year of an undergraduate major or the first year of the graduate program in Computer Science at a technically oriented research-one university. Our students successfully designed and implemented a number of game-like coordinated systems, though not effortlessly.

The class in the first year consisted of 31 sessions (75 minutes per session), held twice/week. Four of the class sessions were dedicated to the students working on the team projects. Students spent the first half of the semester learning background support and systems, TupleSpace concepts and programming, practicing design, and programming collaborative activities through various exercises and assignments. The teaching materials included Java, Eclipse and Swing/SWT tutorials, TSpaces programming materials from IBM website, published papers in HCI, CSCW, or CSCL areas (e.g. scenario based design (SBD), coordination, learning theory, education design, design rational, etc.), class lecture slides, sample programs and videos of users. The project vision was delineated as being one of Mock or Playground-like games, rather than more familiar computer games [6]. In the second half of the semester, class activities were devoted to support of design and implementation of the team projects, which involved all phases of design and implementation of a classroom pedagogical activity or a simple, multi-player, coordinated game. All teams (the students worked in pairs) produced working, playable games that varied in the kind of connectivity employed: Apples-to-Apples, Hangman, Pictionary®, the Algorithm Enactor, Collaborative Crossword, Krypto, and MathBingo [27].

Six senior undergraduates and eight first-year graduates in the CS program registered in our class and participated in the study. They received and signed informed consent letters. A separation was maintained between their grade in the class and their participation in the research, such that they could drop out of the research at any time without losing class credit, while none did.

Based on their programming expertise and education background, the students could be considered intermediate if not experienced programmers. However, as is often the case in Computer Science, they varied in knowledge and skills. Furthermore, they were all novices as coordination designers and programmers. Although many had created web pages, they did not have any experience thinking about coordination among users. One had previously designed or implemented a distributed multi-user application.

2.4 Research Approach

Following design-based research [5, 18] approach, data were collected primarily during the first class offering in 2005 with some supplementation from the second year. To maximize methodological triangulation and ensure the noting of potentially important phenomenon [18], multiple data collection methods were used. Research data include: (a) observation notes and videos of every class session, (b) semi-structured face-to-face interviews with open-ended questions conducted at the beginning and the end of the class, (c) documentation of in-class exercise and assignment programming source code, documentation, and reports, (d) documentation of email messages and class website board discussions, and (e) questionnaires and surveys.

Data analysis was guided by Grounded Theory, which uses a systematic set of procedures to develop an inductively derived theory about a phenomenon [12]. By combining these research data, summary tables of classroom activities and between-class progress were made; important classroom events were identified in the videotapes; the interviews were transcribed for analysis; the progress of project development was outlined from in-class discussion, assignments, and code registration. The data were coded and a series of codes were generated based on our research questions supported by the use of qualitative data analysis software, NVivo. Different categories of observed behavior emerged through multiple rounds of coding.

3. FINDINGS

The major findings from the study are that: (1) the overwhelming majority of students started with an undeveloped imagination for coordination that affected their initial project design; (2) some students initially lacked the technical competence to model and implement coordinated activities; (3) TupleSpace appeared to help all students focus on and develop their understanding of coordination issues; and (4) familiar social coordinated activities catalyzed students' imagination about coordination.

3.1 Undeveloped Imagination for Coordination

With limited knowledge of distributed multi-user applications, the students encountered a variety of sociological and technological challenges in the class [21]. Among these challenges, almost all students showed an undeveloped imagination of what was entailed in coordination. This lack emerged primarily in design phase but also required instructional attention in implementation phase.

The students showed great interest in examples of coordinated activities, and started to acquaint themselves with the concept of coordination. However, their preliminary project designs revealed that they used a fundamentally linear approach to address distributed activities. Almost all initial designs, for example:

(1) failed to provide a coordination mechanism.

A successful game implementation requires not only the support for game moves, e.g. laying down a card, but also the support for the interactions among multiple players. Game players need necessary information from each other to take different actions or have a satisfactory playing strategy at different stages during a game, e.g. either in a storyboard form or via the design of the appropriate Tuples protocol. However, the initial design ignored the necessities of supporting such a decision making process, or the exploration of alternatives. For example, the Krypto™ game involved a group of players collaboratively arranging five numeric cards and four arithmetic operator cards to calculate a target number. The designers initially proposed the support of strict turn taking, in which one person would lay down a card, then the next player, and so forth. This implementation did not pay enough attention to the essential coordination among players and neglected the fact: laying down each card severely constrained the possible solutions. The first players were under-constrained, while the last players were typically left with an unsolvable problem.

(2) failed to take advantage of parallelism.

Like Krypto™, the collaborative Pictionary™ and Collaborative Crossword games initially followed a pattern in which multiple players acted in strict sequence, although the primary benefit of making these games distributed was that multiple players could act at the same time.

Another way that initial designs failed to take advantage of parallelism was that students did not envision the idea that other players (like other processors!) might be waiting for something to do. For example, the first proposal for Collaborative Crossword puzzle game involved each player waiting while all the other players took turns choosing a clue and then entering a word. The only way that one player would know what another player had accomplished was when the entire word appeared on his/her screen. Failure to envision the "wait state" of the players was one example of a system element that needed more consideration.

(3) manifested difficulty envisioning all the resources on which the system could draw.

Another important system element that needed to be addressed was the choice of coordination paths. The collaborative games were intended to be played face-to-face, by human beings. This meant that the most ordinary of human capacities, such as talking, not only could be used, but constituted part of the fun. Yet all students initially proposed to implement separate IM-like channels as coordination paths among players. As a result, in games like Crossword Puzzle, rather than telling the other person that they had made a mistake, one person would write a message to the person next to her/him. While there was nothing *a priori* wrong with implementing such systems, neither was it a rational decision. It was an unexamined assumption that added a large implementation component without improving the coordinated nature of the game by anyone's criteria.

These design impulses suggested that students brought strong presumptions and values into the design process, and that these presumptions and values did not initially include the envisionment of passing resources back and forth among multiple parties. They did not have deep understanding of coordination models.

In the implementation phase, some students also had difficulty envisioning the distributed structure. Even when students understood the mechanics of EventRegisters and Callbacks (a request for the client program to be notified on the occurrence of certain events), they had difficulty envisioning the sequences and flow created by the combinations of normal TupleSpace operations, posting Callbacks, and receiving them: "the user logs in, Callback would happen, I know that part. But after Callback happens, what happens next, you know, what happens to the information from Callbacks, like locally, what happens in TupleSpace" (P01, post-class interview, December 04, 2005). Their superficial knowledge of Callbacks needed to be stretched.

3.2 Undeveloped Modeling of Coordinated Activities

The advantage of using a coordination language, like TupleSpace, to model coordinated activities is to let the coordination model handle coordinative issues, and the computational model to handle computational issues that do not require coordination and communication. As we found from the experimental class, a number of students had difficulty differentiating these two models. For example, some students:

(1) used a shared resource, implemented as a Tuple, in both the coordination model and computational model, at different times.

Creating Tuples and using them to create the underlying communication protocol is the process of building the coordination model. Tuples form the coordination model and indicate coordination needs. In Krypto™, two types of Tuples, AnswerNumTuple and AnswerOpTuple were created to represent the number cards and operator cards. These Tuples were supposed to appear only in the coordination model when the end-user made his/her solution public. However, they were also used in computational model when an end-user moved a card around on his/her screen without showing the change to others. This design led to other users losing their own private work (attempts to move cards in their own screen) without a notification when one user broadcasted his/her change.

(2) used a Tuple to represent aspects of the program that were not coordination resources or that contained mixed information about different resources. For example, in Pictionary™ activity, GameCreatingTuple had mixed information about the game and users.

Furthermore, the difficulty in imagining the underlying structure also revealed that a few students lacked the imagination of what actions should be counted as "local" events, things done by a single user's machine, thus in the computational model; and what should be counted as "remote" events, things done by other users and reported to the central TupleSpace server, thus in the coordination model.

3.3 TupleSpace Helped Students Understand and Concentrate on Coordination Issues

Students were encouraged to use TupleSpaces constructs in the TSpaces language to conceptualize coordination and its operations to form the internal communication protocols for each design and programming assignment. Students' feedback about their learning experience with TupleSpace and the analysis of their Tuple design showed that TupleSpace helped all students focus on coordination issues.

First, students reported that the TupleSpace's concept and basic operations were easy to understand and use. Almost every team reported that TupleSpace ultimately simplified their coordination design. Evidence of growth in understanding coordination was that many teams reduced the number of Tuples in the final design as they realized that coordination was simpler than they originally thought. Second, TupleSpace facilitated students' conceptualization of coordination activities at both end-user level and system level. For instance, Apples-to-Apples® is a game that involves red and green "apple" cards that are resources that may be passed from one player to the group or vice-versa. The Apples-to-Apples team designed seven Tuples that delineated the coordination they wanted to implement through the computer; PlayerAnswerTuple conveyed information passed between end-users (e.g. player's selection of a red apple card); RedAppleTuple and GreenAppleTuple were used to represent available resources in the game (i.e. red/green apple cards). Two students particularly pointed out in their interviews that they were "abstracting data that is for interaction" with the help of TupleSpace. Pedagogical benefits of TupleSpace included that it:

(1) represented physical space analogues naturally.

As a shared virtual space, TupleSpace can expressively represent: (a) the different resources, i.e. objects in the physical space, which can be defined by different types of Tuples; (b) the amounts of each resource, which can be reflected by the number of instance for each type of Tuple (represented by a Tuple class).

(2) optimized the grain size in coordination to a right level.

TupleSpace helped students to find appropriate level of data abstraction — defined a proper grain size for coordination. For instance, in the Collaborative Crossword Puzzle activity, different players solved a puzzle by working on different clues. One person could take a clue and fill in the answer in the board while others worked on other clues. Thus, conflict could exist between two clues if they shared a cell in the grid. The team changed the grain size of a Tuple from "clue" to "cell" in the design stage, thereby simplifying the implementation of both the underlying data structure and the corresponding UI.

(3) hid parallel and networking details from students.

TupleSpace (and some extensions in TSpaces) hid many implemental details, such as sockets and threads. Similarly, many general parallelism terms such as race condition and locking did not appear in the class discussion. These simplifications helped students concentrate on facilitating coordination, which is also useful for other courses.

3.4 Familiar Social Coordinated Activities Can Catalyze Students' Imagination of Coordination

Familiar social coordination activities were brought into the class as a reference frame to catalyze students' imagination. The activities:

(1) inspired students' ideas of designing interesting and effective features to support coordination. Some students played familiar collaborative board games while others observed.

(2) helped students focus more clearly on a setting of coordination between multiple parties. We brought in videos of children playing playground games and also read anthropological accounts of game playing which focus on negotiation, rule and role creation as a crucial component. The students were encouraged to think of coordination through playground game play [22].

(3) helped students identify problems in the designs, e.g. why strict turn-taking does not work under certain circumstance. We asked them to act out (engage in the game and play) their own designs team by team. As in the familiar HCI technique of designing with paper user interfaces [28], students could use paper, cards, and whatever else they needed, as if the end-users were interacting with the computer user interface and each other. By passing pieces of paper back and forth to represent the exchange of resources of different types, students could understand the processes more easily. They witnessed the details and the whole of their activities, the necessity of certain technical features, whether the end-user coordination was interesting or fun, and the interplay of information shown on the screen and that spoken out loud. They also could see (and hear!) people who were "abandoned" or had nothing to do for long periods of time. These experiences highlighted the effects of the coordination and computational models and implementation issues such as the grain-size and nature of sharing. It also helped them see whether their implementation schedule was realistic.

4. DISCUSSION

Our findings confirm that the students had difficulty imagining both coordinative activities and separating a model of coordinative activities from other aspects of computing. However, by calling coordination out explicitly, via the creation of a TupleSpace model and in conjunction with familiar reminders of ordinary coordinative experiences, they were able to improve. By cultivating imagination for coordination, we also promoted parallel thinking. We created opportunities in which design decisions about coordination in a parallel context can be made the subject of critical reflection.

TupleSpace gave students the tools to create models. The initial models were incomplete and unsatisfactory, but within a semester every team was able to implement a working game with both coordinative and computational models.

4.1 Using a Coordination Language in Coordinated System Design

As expected, TupleSpace played an important role in our class. First, it helped students differentiate coordination issues from computational ones, so that a coordination model could be created. Second, through the design of expressive resource types, amounts and limits, it effectively helped students envision the virtual space (system) that they built. Third, it facilitated the consideration of coordination grain size. Last, students were not overwhelmed by a complex language or by the need to handle cumbersome programming tasks, e.g. creating sockets connection, overhead of managing threads.

TupleSpace laid the groundwork. However, the students still had difficulty knowing what to do with coordinative capacities. Few students were initially able to identify potential coordination features in a collaborative activity. Familiar social activities such as games helped them envision the systems more clearly. Other more technical approaches are possible. For example, we could teach related knowledge and techniques such as identifying dependencies; however, we believe that drawing on more fundamental human experiences might draw a wider range of students into a deep understanding of concurrency.

4.2 Coordination is Fundamental in Parallelism Education

Students faced different challenges in conceptualizing coordination: presumptions about coordination, difficulty that they had envisioning that players might have gaps in their activities, and difficulty they experienced envisioning the sequences and flow created by the combinations of normal TupleSpace operations and distributed events. The capacity to envision the coordinative situation, what supports it, what detracts from it, and how it could work better constitutes the mindset of parallel thinking that is essential for further development. We suggest that coordination should be an early focus in teaching parallelism. Focus on coordination should concentrate on basic concepts and mechanisms related to concurrency, rather than relatively mutable technical details.

4.3 Collaborative Games — a Familiar Way of Teaching Parallelism

Games have been used to teach different topics in computer science. We used collaborative playground and board games first because they naturally involve rich coordinated features, e.g. communication need, negotiation process, resource allocation and limitation. Second, they are familiar from childhood. Many parallelism concepts and techniques, such as synchronization/asynchronization communication, one-many/ many-many interaction, and resource/task dependence are easily understood in such a context. Similarly Neeman, Lee, etc. [24] successfully taught non-computer scientists with analogies and storytelling (e.g. Jigsaw Puzzle) to illustrate key concepts in parallel computing to avoid technical details. Compared with these, coordinated games have richer coordination features and can give students an experience akin to "direct manipulation".

5. CONCLUSION

Our study of student programmers' conceptualization of the design and development of multi-user, parallel-distributed, coordinated systems promoted a parallel thinking mindset through the focus on coordination. Students encountered a raft of technical and imaginative problems in such a way that they were able to make progress on them and come to understand the area more deeply. The implications for CS education are that (1) coordination should be taught as a fundamental topic in parallelism education; (2) explicit modeling coordination is crucial to coordinated system design and development; and (3) familiar social coordination activities can be used to catalyze students' imagination of coordination in a natural way.

6. ACKNOWLEDGMENT

This work was supported by NSF ITR/IERI Grant #REC 0427783. Thanks to all the members of the Tuples project, and CS4984 from Fall semester, 2005.

7. REFERENCES

[1] J.C. Adams, et al. Multicore Education: Pieces of the Parallel Puzzle. In *Proceedings of the 41st ACM technical symposium on Computer science education (SIGCSE'10)*. ACM, New York, NY (2010). 194-195.

[2] M. Ben-Ari. A Suite of Tools for Teaching Concurrency. In *Proceedings of the 9th annual SIGCSE conference on Innovation and technology in computer science education (SIGCSE'04)*. ACM, New York, NY (2004). 251-251.

[3] G.E. Blelloch. Parallel Thinking. In *Proceedings of the 14th ACM SIGPLAN symposium on Principles and practice of parallel programming (PPOPP'09)*. ACM, New York, NY (2009). 1-2.

[4] J.D. Bransford, et al., *New Approaches to Instruction: Because Wisdom Can't Be Told*, in *Similarity and Analogical Reasoning*. 1989, Cambridge University Press: New York, NY, USA. 470-497.

[5] A.L. Brown, *Design Experiments: Theoretical and Methodological Challenges in Creating Complex Interventions in Classroom Settings*. Journal of the Learning Sciences, 1992. **2**(2): 141-178.

[6] M. Brynskov & M. Ludvigsen. Mock Games: A New Genre of Pervasive Play. In *Proc. DIS 2006*. ACM Press (2006). 169-178.

[7] G. Cabri, L. Leonardi, & F. Zambonelli, *Mars: A Programmable Coordination Architecture for Mobile Agents*. Internet Computing, IEEE, 2000. **4**(4): 26-35.

[8] N. Carriero & D. Gelernter. Applications Experience with Linda. In *Parallel programming: experience with applications, languages and systems*. ACM, New York, NY (1988). 173-187.

[9] N. Carriero & D. Gelernter, *Linda in Context*. Communication of the ACM, 1989. **32**(4): 444-458.

[10] N. Carriero & D. Gelernter, *How to Write Parallel Programs: A First Course*. 1990: MIT Press. 232.

[11] P.J. Denning. Great Principles in Computing Curricula. In *Proceedings of the 35th SIGCSE technical symposium on Computer science education (SIGCSE'04)*. ACM, New York, NY (2004). 336-341.

[12] E. Dunican, *A Framework for Evaluating Qualitative Research Methods in Computer Programming Education*, in *The seventh Annual Workshop of Psychology of Programming*. 2005: Brighton, England.

[13] D. Ernst, et al. Preparing Students for Ubiquitous Parallelism. In *Proceedings of the 40th ACM technical symposium on Computer science education (SIGCSE'09)*. ACM, New York, NY (2009). 136-137.

[14] D.J. Ernst & D.E. Stevenson. Concurrent Cs: Preparing Students for a Multicore World. In *Proceedings of the 13th annual conference on Innovation and technology in computer science education (ITiCSE'08)*. ACM, New York, NY (2008). 230-234.

[15] D. Gelernter & N. Carriero, *Coordination Languages and Their Significance*. Communications of the ACM, 1992. **35**(2): 97-107.

[16] J.R. Graham, *Integrating Parallel Programming Techniques into Traditional Computer Science Curricula*. SIGCSE Bulletin, 2007. **39**(4): 75-78.

[17] R.A. Gregory, *Distributed Programming Languages*, in *Proceedings of the ACM '82 conference*. 1982, ACM.

[18] C.M. Hoadley, *Design-Based Research Methods and Theory Building: A Case Study of Research with Speakeasy*. Educational Technology, 2005. **45**(1): 42-47.

[19] B. Johanson & A. Fox, *Extending Tuplespaces for Coordination in Interactive Workspaces*. Journal of Systems and Software- Special issue: Ubiquitous computing, 2004. **69**(3): 243-266.

[20] T.J. Lehman, et al., *Hitting the Distributed Computing Sweet Spot with Tspaces*. Computer Networks: The International Journal of Computer and Telecommunications Networking, 2001. **35**(4): 457-472.

[21] S. Lin & D. Tatar. Beyond Current Social Computing: Challenges to Complex Coordinated Systems Design? In *Proceedings of the ACM Conference on Computer-Supported Cooperative Work (CSCW '10), CSCW Horizon*. ACM New York, NY (2010). 557-566.

[22] S. Lin, et al. Learning When Less Is More: "Bootstrapping" Undergraduate Programmers as Coordination Designers. In *Proc. PDC2006*. (2006).

[23] C. McDonald. Teaching Concurrency with Joyce and Linda. In *Proceedings of the twenty-third SIGCSE technical symposium on Computer science education (SIGCSE'09)*. ACM, New York, NY (1992). 46-52.

[24] H. Neeman, et al., *Analogies for Teaching Parallel Computing to Inexperienced Programmers*. The SIGCSE Bulletin, 2006. **38**(4): 64-67.

[25] A. Omicini & F. Zambonelli, *Co-Ordination of Mobile Information Agents in Tucson*. Internet Research: Electronic Networking Applications and Policy, 1998. **8**(5): 400-413.

[26] S. Robbins. Using Remote Logging for Teaching Concurrency. In *Proceedings of the 34th SIGCSE technical symposium on Computer science education (SIGCSE'03)*. ACM, New York, NY (2003). 177-181.

[27] J. Roschelle, et al., *Ink, Improvisation, and Interactive Engagement: Learning with Tablets*. Computer, 2007. **40**(9): 42-48.

[28] R. Sefelin, M. Tscheligi, & V. Giller. Paper Prototyping - What Is It Good For?: A Comparison of Paper- and Computer-Based Low-Fidelity Prototyping. In *Ext. Abstracts CHI 2003*. ACM Press (2003).

[29] R.A. Whiteside & J.S. Leichter. Using Linda for Supercomputing on a Local Area Network. In *Proceedings of the 1988 ACM/IEEE conference on Supercomputing*. IEEE Computer Society Press (1988). 192-199.

Modules in Community: Injecting More Parallelism Into Computer Science Curricula

Richard Brown
St. Olaf College
rab@stolaf.edu

Elizabeth Shoop
Macalester College
shoop@macalester.edu

ABSTRACT

Given the recent emergence of multi-core and distributed computing that is transforming mainstream application areas in industry, demand is rising for teaching more parallelism and concurrency in CS curricula. We argue for teaching these topics incrementally in CS courses at all undergraduate levels, and propose a comprehensive approach involving flexible teaching modules with experiential programming exercises, technical and instructor supplementary materials, and an online community of educators to support adopters and module contributors. Progress on developing these materials and online resources is reported.

Categories and Subject Descriptors

K.0 Computing Milieux/General; K.3.2 Computer Science Education

General Terms

Performance, Human Factors.

Keywords

Parallelism, Multi-core Computing

1. INTRODUCTION

For the foreseeable future, the dominant factor in CPU hardware performance will be the number of cores per CPU package, not speedup within an individual core. To some extent, this shift leaves programming as we know it behind: since about 2006, software performance improvements can no longer ride on the coattails of Moore's Law unless programs exploit the parallelism of multi-core processing [12]. Currently, most computer science (CS) curricula focus on sequential computation, with the study of parallelism typically consigned to a handful of systems and architecture courses. To prepare their students for the manycore world that will be standard during their careers, CS educators must urgently increase the prominence of parallel computational concepts and programming in their courses.

Even without the advent of commodity multi-core computing, there would still be rising demand for CS graduates who know about parallelism because of the rise of mainstream distributed computing applications in many sectors of industry, especially in web-based services. Beginning about 10 years ago, Google engineers applied the classical map-reduce functional programming strategy to peta-scale computations in a high-performance, fault-tolerant software system that runs on large computer clusters, in order to power the massive computations needed for their search engine and ultimately most of their diverse product offerings today. When Yahoo! engineers subsequently developed Hadoop, an open-source implementation of the map-reduce strategy, they made *data intensive scalable computing (DISC)* accessible by any company or university that had access to sufficient cluster resources. With the availability of cloud computing resources such as Amazon EC2 that could be rented for pennies per hour per core, DISC computations are now within reach of small businesses and colleges, even individuals. Industry and research have only begun to tap the possibilities of widely available and affordable cluster resources equipped with map-reduce or other distributed parallel computation strategies.

Long before the current era of multicore, cluster, and DISC computing, several educators reported their successful efforts to integrate parallel topics into their undergraduate curricula [9][10][15][16][18][11]. These efforts were based on use of certain parallel equipment at each institution, and the earliest point in the curriculum where parallelism was introduced was the second course in the major. Many others have been successful at introducing advanced-level elective courses dedicated to parallel computing, perhaps as part of a specialized concentration for the undergraduate CS major [1][17]. Because computer scientists and software developers can no longer take advantage of Moore's dividend, educators must now take on the work of these pioneers, learn from their efforts, and work together to infuse our curriculum with parallelism. Some CS educators have recently begun this charge by suggesting ways to introduce parallel concepts and problems into early courses in the curriculum [7][5].

As another step towards enabling CS programs to begin incrementally working more parallelism into their courses, we are producing *flexible teaching modules* that can be used in multiple course and institutional contexts, together with *parallel platform packages (PPPs)* of documentation and software to support hands-on assignments on module concepts. Each module includes learning objectives, comments on contexts for its use, expository text, student exercises, and assessment tools. We seek to develop a community of CS educators around these modules through web-based resources with support frameworks. We have begun this process with a site called *csinparallel.org*. Our goals for the community of educators include feedback and supplementation of the initial modules, contribution of new modules and platform packages from the community, and mentoring and support for new users of these materials. The combination of modular materials and a supportive community of peers is designed to make it practical for CS programs to introduce parallel computing gradually, in multiple courses at all levels of the undergraduate curriculum, including courses such as CS1 that have not

SIGCSE '11, March 9–12, 2010, Dallas, Texas, USA.

traditionally treated parallelism, taught by professors who may not have expertise in parallel computing.

In this paper, we will first discuss our rationale and describe modules that are completed and under development so far, then present our approach to developing a supportive community of educators, before turning to assessment strategies for this effort.

2. MODULES AND PLATFORM PACKAGES

Assuming a well-established and urgent need universally to teach more parallelism in CS curricula, how shall we satisfy that need?

2.1 Taking a modular approach to parallelism

Much of the newly needed parallel computation content would be a diversion from the syllabus of a course in Operating Systems or Computer Architecture, which suggests either requiring CS majors to take a separate course in parallel computing or incorporating parallelism into other courses in the curriculum. We argue for the latter for several reasons: in order to reach non-majors as well as CS majors; to reflect the far-reaching importance of these shifts towards parallelism; and in order to teach the material in a spiral fashion, which education research identifies as an especially effective way to teach CS. The report of an ITiCSE 2010 working group elaborates on these points [3]. We support the introduction of parallelism in CS courses at all undergraduate levels, and we seek to provide materials that can be used flexibly in multiple course contexts.

Every institution has its own approach to teaching CS, expressed in its own courses and degree requirements, and implemented in the context of local interests by that institution's faculty with their individual areas of expertise, using available teaching and computational resources. The challenge of creating teaching materials usable for rapidly injecting parallelism at all undergraduate curricular levels in CS at a wide range of institutions leads us to create materials for learning parallelism with the attributes such as the following:

- compatible with many institutional approaches to teaching CS;
- flexible for use in many potential courses;
- require only incremental change in a course's syllabus;
- minimize the time investment required of instructors who seek to deploy those materials, including those instructors who are not specialists in parallel computing; and
- as simple and quick as possible to deploy in a course.

These attributes lead us to create online modular teaching materials supported by supplements for instructors and by platform-specific assistance for "hands-on" experiential learning exercises. If such teaching modules incorporate a range of programming languages and make minimal prerequisite assumptions, they will have wide compatibility with CS programs and flexibility for use in multiple course contexts within such programs. Modules that minimally require only a day or two of class time can be added to a course at incremental cost in terms of class meeting time. Supplementary materials, and especially an effective online community of support (as described in Section 3 below), will help instructors to insert content on parallel computing into courses that often have not traditionally included such topics. Likewise, platform-specific supports, such as the "parallel platform packages" and "platform resources" described in Section 2.3 below, combined with online community support, will expedite and simplify the installation and use of parallel computation resources that students will need in order to learn about parallelism by experiencing it first-hand.

Textbooks represent an alternative to standalone teaching modules. Courses and curricula typically change together with textbooks used in those courses, and we anticipate that increased parallelism will soon begin to appear in texts for various courses at all levels of the CS curriculum, as has already begun in texts for Operating Systems and Architecture-related courses. But the CS education community needs to respond immediately in order to prepare current students for the knowledge about parallelism they will need upon graduation. Writing, distributing, and improving online modules can be much faster than producing new textbooks, and in this case we need that speed. Also, a collection of suitably designed modules can reach a wide range of course and curricular settings, filling the gap in time while the various textbooks used in those settings are updated with parallelism.

2.2 An initial collection of Modules

At this writing, we have fully or partially completed six teaching modules for introducing topics in parallelism in various courses that may not traditionally have included such material.

Below, we provide description and discussion of our experience with these modules, stating learning goals and focusing on the content of expository documents for students. In Section 2.3 we describe additional parallel platform resources and support to accompany the modules.

2.2.1 Map-reduce computing using WebMapReduce

Learning goals:

- Students should be able to identify basic forms of data parallelism in computational problems.
- Students should be able to distinguish between sequential and parallel computation, and identify the practical significance of each.

Brief description: Intended for introductory CS courses that involve programming, with support for several common introductory languages (Java, Python, C++, Scheme).

Discussion: This module introduces *data-parallel* computation (single program applied in parallel to multiple data sets) and related concepts, with programming exercises to carry out map-reduce computations using the WebMapReduce (WMR) platform package (see section 2.3). Expository teaching materials for students motivate map-reduce computing, citing both prominent applications in industry and potential for use in interdisciplinary student project that may involve large data, then present map-reduce computing with examples in a particular introductory language. Programming exercises reinforce the concepts presented in the reading, then proceed to explore practical features of WMR that could be useful for student projects. Non-programming exercises explore additional concepts related to parallelism, such as multi-tasking.

This is the first module we developed. We have taught prototype versions of this module in several versions of our introductory courses at both of our institutions, using Python and Scheme languages, typically as a two-day unit. Note that WMR is extensible to other choices of programming language, and the language interface can be tailored to local conventions and practices.

2.2.2 *Intermediate Introduction to Parallel Computing*

Learning goals:

- Given a description of a problem to solve, students should be able to discriminate whether it requires a data parallel or task parallel solution
- Given a description of a parallelizable algorithm, students should be able to apply the principle of Amdahl's law to determine the maximum speedup of that algorithm using N processors.
- Given a language-specific library and an associated back-end platform, students will be able to implement at least one simple algorithm with data parallelism and at least one simple algorithm using task parallelism
- Students will be able to discriminate DISC from other forms of parallel computation, describe the operation of the map-reduce strategy for DISC in general terms, and list significant applications of DISC in industry.
- Given an example of parallel code, students will be able to identify race conditions and describe how to remove those race conditions using a synchronization primitive

Brief description: Provides general background in parallel computation that is common to one or more subsequent modules. Programming language-independent; intended for students in a second or later CS course.

Discussion: We consider this to be a *concept module*, whereas most of the other modules listed are *application modules*. This Intermediate Introduction module gathers concepts of parallel computing that other modules require, including terminology, a discussion of speedup (including Amdahl's Law), communication options, and conceptual issues such as fault tolerance and mutual exclusion. At this writing, exercises are under development.

2.2.3 *Concurrent Access to Data Structures*

Learning goals:

- Students should be able to define what a thread-safe data structure object is.
- Given a definition of an object, students should be able to distinguish whether it is properly thread-safe or not and why.
- Students should be able to describe how locking is used to ensure proper concurrent access to data structures and how deadlock is avoided.
- Given a problem that can be improved using parallel access to shared data, students should be able to use built-in thread-safe classes to implement parallel solutions and determine the speedup of their solution.

Brief description: Applies task parallelism to a web-crawling problem, using Java threads and standard Java thread-safe data structures.

Discussion: This module may be presented as a laboratory, in which a sequential web spider program written in Java is parallelized using Java threads together with thread-safe queue and hash table data structures provided in the standard package java.util.concurrent.

Our test offerings of this module include a Data Structures course at one of our institutions and a Client-Server Applications course at the other.

2.2.4 *Multicore Programming with Intel's Manycore Testing Lab*

Learning goals:

- Students should be able to identify issues with attempting to use parallel computing techniques when using multiple threads
- Students should be able to identify differences in the performance of their solutions in manycore computing

Brief description: Explores race conditions and other aspects of shared memory multi-core computation, using C++ programming. Two parts are offered, using OpenMP then Threading Building Blocks (TBB).

Discussion: This module may be presented as a one- or two-part laboratory. The first part uses a single OpenMP line to carry out a simple programming loop in parallel, indicating an approach to parallelizing sequential code. A naïve first attempt leads to an obvious computational error due to a *race condition* (from multiple cores updating a shared memory location), and a remedy is provided and explained. Students observe performance speedup when they increase the number of cores used in the computation. The second part introduces parallelization of the same simple loop using Intel's Threading Building Blocks (TBB) instead of OpenMP.

Programming for this module is intended for the Manycore Testing Lab that (currently) provides access to a 32-core computer, available to members of Intel's Academic Community (free). The minimal programming prerequisites for the OpenMP portion of this module make it accessible for courses in CS that include C++ programming as early as a second course.

2.2.5 *Concurrency and map-reduce strategies in various programming languages*

Learning goals:

- Students should be able to discriminate strategies of how programming languages implement parallelism and concurrency
- Students should be able to implement map-reduce computing using several programming languages

Brief description: Introduces map-reduce computing to intermediate or advanced CS students using WebMapReduce, then explores how different programming languages provide the capability to compute in parallel.

Discussion: This module was developed for a programming languages course, but it could also support a course or project that includes map-reduce computing or considers structures for providing parallel computation in high-level languages. Exercises are under development at this writing.

2.2.6 *Parallel Sorting Algorithms*

Learning Goal:

- Given a theoretical Parallel Random Access shared memory model (PRAM), a particular memory access model, and an interconnection network, students should be able to develop an algorithm for sorting a large collection of N data items.

Brief description: Suitable for use in an algorithms course; uses background material from the Intermediate Introduction (2.2.2.).

Discussion: This is in part a concept module that describes how to reason about and design various parallel versions of merge sort. It begins with an introduction to the theoretical PRAM machine as the basis for formulating parallel algorithms (a technique that has long been used in the study of parallel algorithms). It is designed to be expanded to include other sorting techniques, such as quicksort, and includes exercises.

2.3 Parallel Platform Packages and Platform Resources

We offer *Parallel Platform Packages (PPPs)* and *Platform Resources (PRs)* to support the computational infrastructure needed for hands-on module exercises. Their purpose it to provide simplified programming interfaces or introductory documentation for standard parallel computing resources.

We currently have created one simplified-interface PPP, called *WebMapReduce (WMR)* [http://webmapreduce.sourceforge.net/]. This provides strategically simplified access to the open-source Hadoop [http://hadoop.apache.org/] implementation of map-reduce computation. Direct programming of Hadoop requires sophisticated Java or C++ programming that puts the system beyond the capability of a beginner. WMR's design makes it feasible for introductory programming students to carry out true Hadoop computations, in the programming language they are learning and with an interface they can comprehend.

WMR also makes map-reduce computing convenient for students at any level beyond the introductory CS course, for brief inclusion in more advanced courses (as indicated in the *Concurrency and map-reduce strategies in various programming languages* module) or for independent or course-related projects. The WMR system is an open source project that can be operated over a local, shared, or cloud-based cluster, assuming installation access to that cluster.

Our other PPPs created to date provide resource materials for standard parallel programming resources, such as OpenMP, TBB, and MPI. Besides links to standard online references, each PPP includes a brief introductory documentation describing key concepts for a resource in the context of the *Intermediate Introduction* module (see 2.1.2), and discussing one or more coding examples illustrating features of that resource. These introductory documents provide a uniform starting point for new users of those platforms, written for an audience of intermediate CS students who often have less experience than much of the existing standard documentation expects.

Whereas PPPs have student end-users as their audience, Platform Resources (PRs) support installation and management of parallel computing resources, intended for technicians and systems support personnel. Documentation for installing WMR on a cluster falls in this category. Other PRs developed to date describe a cloud-computing system images with WMR pre-installed, intended for launching temporary teaching clusters on Amazon's EC-2 service, and a document describing installation of a *virtual cluster* on teaching laboratory machines, on which cluster computations can take place simultaneously with ordinary classroom and laboratory use of the equipment, comparable to [4].

3. BUILDING A COMMUNITY

To support the broad and diverse community of CS educators seeking to teach parallelism in courses that have not traditionally included it, we perceive a need for websites that offer far more than repository services. On our site, *http://csinparallel.org*, we make our modules and related materials available and provide a way for educators to discuss them, share their own materials, and get technical help. We will provide rationale for the need we perceive for such a site, and indicate site features that seek to address it.

3.1 A Case for Community-Building Platforms

The industry shifts indicated in Section 1 create an urgent need for new materials to teach more parallel computing in the CS curriculum. The usual publication cycle, from conference papers and workshop presentations to textbook incorporation, has begun to respond to that need. But we argue that the publication cycle is not sufficient to meet that need in the short run, for several reasons. First, if every present-day undergraduate CS student at every academic level must rapidly gain exposure to parallelism, then CS educators must develop and deploy all of those curricular resources in a short amount of time—more quickly than the cycle can respond. Second, as shown in [2], the software environments for parallel computing (both multicore and distributed/cloud) will evolve rapidly as academic researchers and industry developers find new strategies for wielding parallel computing resources. The scale and pace of this dynamic evolution of software environments seems likely to outpace the publication cycle. Lastly, it is important for educators to share information about the effectiveness of various approaches as we work to include parallelism in our curricula.

To handle this rapid pace of change, we CS educators will benefit from web-based *community-building platforms* that offer additional services and features to support our communal efforts. For example, a community of educators teaching CS1, perhaps using a particular language or approach, will be the best group to provide what that community needs to bring parallelism into CS1, with assistance from those having prior expertise in parallelism. We envision support resources that provide open and inviting environments, in which prior parallel computing knowledge or experience is *not* a prerequisite.

3.2 Some Initial Community-Building Features and Practices

There are significant issues to be considered when building an online community of educators. For example, submitters must retain intellectual property rights to materials, and should receive some sort of recognition for their efforts. Also, sites should enable easy searching and sharing, along with support for dialog between people. We will describe some initial features of our site that work toward these goals.

The site encourages use and dissemination of submitted materials for non-commercial purposes, as long as the author is attributed, adopting the Creative Commons license 'Attribution–NonCommercial–ShareAlike 3.0' [6] for intellectual property rights. While participating in such a community seems unlikely carry the wide recognition of traditional conference publication, perhaps lesser forms of recognition will make a start in the short term. For example, we will provide a letter of support to any contributor to our site who requests one.

The site adopts a strategy of sharing between educators that was pioneered by Manduca and colleagues for improving undergraduate education in the geosciences, called the Science Education Resource Center (SERC) [14][13][8]. Based on a study of how higher education teachers prepare for courses and how SERC portals have been used over time, they assert that sites for sharing teaching resources must have two key features:

- materials should be tagged and able to be searched by topic, so they can be found easily
- faculty should be able to communicate with each other and share ideas and materials easily

We have adopted this philosophy by building our site on SERC's technology and adding features we see as important to the effort of transforming CS education to include more parallelism. Our site contains information grouped into three primary categories, which were described in detail in section 2:

- teaching modules
- information about necessary parallel software packages needed with certain modules
- information about parallel platforms (types of physical hardware) that can be used with particular parallel software packages

When contributing modules to the site, submitters choose from a set of predefined characteristics, which act as meta-data for narrowing future searches (see Figure 1). This provides the capability for tagging modules, but with a controlled vocabulary of tags. Users looking for new materials can narrow their searches according to these tags. After administrators screen for spurious submissions, contributed material is immediately available.

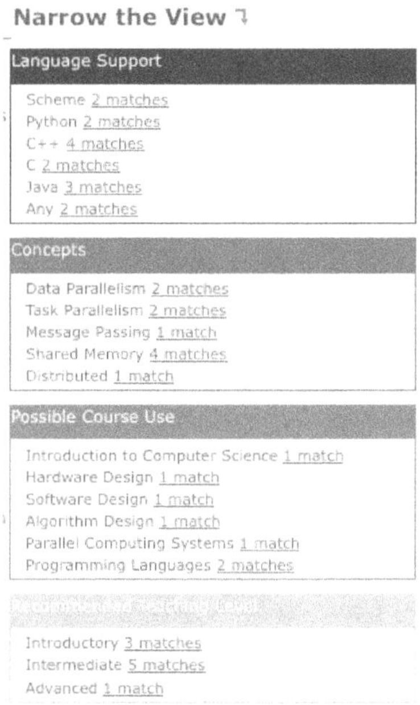

Figure 1. Sidebar on module summary page

The site encourages communication in many ways. For example, submitters of materials may conveniently suggest additions to the tag vocabulary, so that it may evolve over time. Visitors may post questions about modules, packages, and platforms. Also, visitors who have registered can choose to be notified when new posts about a module appear (daily, weekly, monthly digests). We anticipate that further developing effective communication strategies will become a central focus in our future work.

Finally, the csinparallel.org site is convenient to use. Materials within each category have a common format, for easy viewing by visitors. New submissions can be created by any visitor using a content management system (CMS) designed to make submission simple using a WYSIWYG editor.

The remainder of this section describes features of our three categories of materials.

3.2.1 Teaching Modules

Submitters place information about each module into the following categories:

- Title and Summary Description (used on the page listing all modules)
- Learning Goals associated with the module
- Context for use (educational level, type of course, class size, e.g.)
- Full Description with teaching materials used (submitters upload files)
- Teaching notes
- Suggested assessment instruments
- Additional resources (links to other related resources)

These categories enable visitors to determine how a module might fit their particular courses and curricula. All material submitted by an instructor ends up on one page with the same structure as every other module page. At the bottom of each module is a discussion area where visitors can post comments about the use of these modules or any issues or questions they may have.

3.2.2 Parallel Platform Package Information

Along with the teaching modules, the site contains pages about the parallel packages that may be needed for a module, or that may be of interest when creating new materials. These were described in Section 2. Like the module pages, there are meta-data tags associated with these pages, as shown in Figure 2, and visitors can submit new package information.

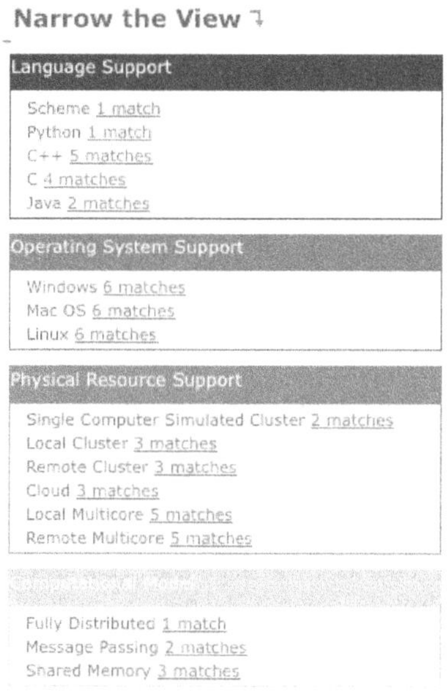

Figure 2. Tags applied to pages about parallel packages

3.2.3 Platform Resources Information

There is an area of the site devoted to providing information about both available external resources and how to set up hardware platforms, such as a local cluster of workstations, for teaching parallel computing using particular teaching modules. To enable communication about technical issues, we maintain a separate professionally managed forum, linked from this area and the sidebar on all pages, where users can direct their questions about hardware or platform packages to us or anyone else who chooses to join the forum. We see this ability for educators to discuss technical issues or problems they encounter with others as key to supporting adoption of parallel teaching materials.

4. ASSESSMENT

As part of the process for creating modules, we have developed learning objectives for them, indicating the types of gains in understanding that we expect students to make. Therefore, an important aspect of this endeavor to create teaching modules is to determine whether they meet the learning objectives that we envision for them. In this section we describe our methodology for assessment.

We have begun to use these modules in several courses in the curricula at each of our institutions. We used our learning objectives while preparing the material for each of the modules. We are writing assessment questions designed to ascertain whether students have grasped basic knowledge we expect to come from some modules, and also whether they can conceptually use that knowledge and apply it to new situations described to them. We plan to administer a pre-test before a module is used in a course and a post-test at the end of a course. We will use the results to determine learning gains and to provide a formative assessment for improving the module content and use in subsequent courses. We will be conducting the first of these assessments in the Fall of 2010 in eight courses between our two colleges. We will provide these assessment instruments on *csinparallel.org* for each of the modules.

We plan to introduce these modules in several courses that our students take for the major. We will also gather some demographic data from each student regarding what courses they have taken previously and when. After gathering this information for several semesters, we plan to report on student learning gains over time, as they are exposed to the concepts in different contexts.

5. CONCLUSION

We are adopting an incremental, modular approach to introducing parallel computing concepts and experiential exercises at all levels of the CS curriculum, as a strategy for addressing the urgent need for all CS students (including non-majors) to learn parallelism. Modules and support materials are designed for flexible use in diverse course and institutional settings, and for ease of adoption. Support materials include learning objectives for each module, notes for instructors, and documentation and software for the computational platforms needed for hands-on learning of parallel computing. We seek the creation of a supportive online community of educators who share and encourage efforts to teach more parallelism in more CS courses through this modular approach, including instructors without particular expertise in parallelism. We describe six teaching modules that are now in production or under development, and illustrate how others in the community could contribute modules and support material using our site. We plan to continue developing modules and assess them for how well students have met the learning objectives for them.

6. ACKNOWLEDGMENTS

This work was supported by a joint NSF CCLI grant DUE-0942190/0941962. We would like to thank Sharon Lane-Getaz of St. Olaf College for her assistance generating the assessment instruments.

7. REFERENCES

[1] Adams, J., Nevison, C. et al. 2000. Parallel computing to start the millennium. *Proceedings of the thirty-first SIGCSE technical symposium on Computer science education* (Austin, Texas, United States, 2000), 65-69.

[2] Asanovic, K., Bodik, R. et al. 2009. A view of the parallel computing landscape. *Commun. ACM.* 52, 10 (2009), 56-67.

[3] Brown, R., Shoop, E. et al. 2010. Strategies for Preparing Computer Science Students for the Multicore Worl. *ITiCSE 2010 Proceedings*. (2010).

[4] Brown, R.A. 2009. Hadoop at home: large-scale computing at a small college. *Proceedings of the 40th ACM technical symposium on Computer science education* (Chattanooga, TN, USA, 2009), 106-110.

[5] Bruce, K.B., Danyluk, A. et al. 2010. Introducing concurrency in CS 1. *Proceedings of the 41st ACM technical symposium on Computer science education* (Milwaukee, Wisconsin, USA, 2010), 224-228.

[6] Creative Commons — Attribution-NonCommercial-ShareAlike 3.0. *http://creativecommons.org/licenses/by-nc-sa/3.0/*. Accessed: 09-05-2010.

[7] Ernst, D.J. and Stevenson, D.E. 2008. Concurrent CS: preparing students for a multicore world. *Proceedings of the 13th annual conference on Innovation and technology in computer science education* (Madrid, Spain, 2008), 230-234.

[8] Fox, S., Manduca, C. et al. 2005. Building Educational Portals atop Digital Libraries. *D-Lib Magazine*. 11, 01 (2005).

[9] John, D.J. 1992. Integration of parallel computation into introductory computer science. *SIGCSE Bull.* 24, 1 (1992), 281-285.

[10] John, D.J. 1994. NSF supported projects: parallel computation as an integrated component in the undergraduate curriculum in computer science. *SIGCSE Bull.* 26, 1 (1994), 357-361.

[11] Kurtz, B.L., Kim, C. et al. 1998. Parallel computing in the undergraduate curriculum. *Proceedings of the twenty-ninth SIGCSE technical symposium on Computer science education* (Atlanta, Georgia, United States, 1998), 212-216.

[12] Larus, J. 2009. Spending Moore's dividend. *Commun. ACM.* 52, 5 (2009), 62-69.

[13] Manduca, C.A., Fox, S. et al. 2006. Digital Library as Network and Community Center. *D-Lib Magazine*. 12, 12 (2006).

[14] Manduca, C.A., Iverson, E.R. et al. 2005. Influencing User Behavior through Digital Library Design. *D-Lib Magazine*. 11, 05 (2005).

[15] Meredith, M.J. 1992. Introducing parallel computing into the undergraduate computer science curriculum: a progress report. *SIGCSE Bull.* 24, 1 (1992), 187-191.

[16] Nevison, C. 1995. Parallel computing in the undergraduate curriculum. *Computer*. 28, 12 (Dec. 1995), 51-56.

[17] Schaller, N.C. and Kitchen, A.T. 1995. Experiences in teaching parallel computing—five years later. *SIGCSE Bull.* 27, 3 (1995), 15-20.

[18] Toll, W.E. 1995. Decision points in the introduction of parallel processing into the undergraduate curriculum. *Proceedings of the twenty-sixth SIGCSE technical symposium on Computer science education* (Nashville, Tennessee, United States, 1995), 136-140.

Animal Tlatoque: Attracting Middle School Students to Computing through Culturally-Relevant Themes *

Diana Franklin
Phillip Conrad
Computer Science Dept.
UC Santa Barbara
franklin,pconrad@cs.ucsb.edu

Gerardo Aldana
Chicana/o Studies Dept.
UC Santa Barbara
gvaldana@chicst.ucsb.edu

Sarah Hough
Gevirtz Graduate School of Education
UC Santa Barbara
sarahh@education.ucsb.edu

ABSTRACT

A popular approach to introducing students to computer science is to involve middle-school students in engaging programming activities. One challenge in such a program is attracting students who are not already positively predisposed to computing.

In order to attract a diverse audience, we developed a summer program based on culturally-relevant themes that appealed to our two target audiences, females and Latina/os. This paper describes our success in developing and implementing a computing curriculum and recruiting materials for a 2-week summer camp integrating two themes, animal conservation and Mayan culture. Scratch programming was used to engage students in creating animations about animals and Mayan culture, allowing them an interdisciplinary experience that combined programming, culture, biology, art, and storytelling.

Our recruiting efforts resulted in an application pool that was 73% female and 67% Latina/o, with only 6.5% in neither group. We had 34 students complete the program. Pre- and post- surveys showed that the number of students citing computer science as their top choice for a career doubled and interest in computer science as a career more than tripled.

Categories and Subject Descriptors

K.3.2 [**Computers and Education**]: Computer and Information Science Education; K.4.m [**Computers and Society**]: Miscellaneous—*Diversity and Outreach*

General Terms

Design, Human Factors

Keywords

diversity, K-12 education, outreach

*Tlatoque (Tlah-TOH-keh)—'speakers'—used as titles by Aztec rulers

SIGCSE'11, March 9–12, 2011, Dallas, Texas, USA.

1. INTRODUCTION

The demand for computer scientists far outweighs the number of students pursuing computer science, and this gap is projected to grow[16]. To satisfy this demand, we must broaden participation in computer science to students who are not already predisposed to pursuing computing careers—and whose parents may not encourage them to choose computer science. This poses a two-fold challenge. First, how do we recruit students to an outreach activity they might not be interested in or aware of? Second, how do we keep their attention long enough to not only see that computer science is fun, but change negative impressions they may have about the field?

There has been a wealth of development of outreach activities designed to give students a taste of computer science without months of training. These range from simple programming with new programming languages like Scratch[14] and Alice[6], to learning about machine instructions by building LEGOs with instructions[10], to learning about different CS concepts through non-computer-based activities in CS Unplugged[5]. While these are all important pieces to solving the puzzle, a single outreach event is not sufficient to provide the transformative experience we want from students not already predisposed to computer science.

We chose two large pools of students who are not currently choosing computer science—females and Latina/os. We then designed a program that appeals to the target groups and their parents, both in recruitment and throughout participation, similar to UC Irvine's program[11], which is targeted at Native Americans. Culture and math have been paired in math tutoring via Wayan Outpost[4] and many projects in ethnomathematics.

The Animal Tlatoque Summer Camp is a 2-week summer camp for middle school students that combines two themes with computing: animal conservation and Mayan culture. We designed an interdisciplinary curriculum, including animals, culture, computing, art, and storytelling. Computing projects were carefully chosen to gradually build skills and confidence, culminating in capstone experiences of animating a story, implementing a virtual pet, and/or contributing to the simulation of a Mayan ball game. In addition, long-term academic assistance and tracking is being provided by Bridges to Pathways, an existing on-campus program that runs after-school study sessions, parent information sessions, and college preparedness assistance.

As part of the National Science Foundations's Broadening Participation in Computing program (bpcportal.org), the overarching goal of the Animal Tlatoque Summer Camp is to increase the number of US students pursuing computer science, particularly among two underrepresented groups: females, and Latina/os. The project employs the following strategies:

- Providing positive exposure to computer science
- Increasing participants' skills and self-confidence in computing
- Increasing participants' openness to a career in Computer Science.

The rest of the paper is organized as follows. We begin with the motivation behind our themes in Section 2. We describe the curriculum in Section 3. Section 4 gives some logistics in how we ran the camp. Next, we present the results of our recruitment and camp implementation efforts in Section 5. Finally, Section 6 provides our conclusions and future directions.

2. MOTIVATION

Our summer camp has two specific goals: (1) to attract the target audience with themes that appeal to both parents and children[2, 12, 15], and (2) to engage participants in activities that allow them to experience many facets of computer science. We have integrated two themes that are intended to appeal to Latina/o and female children and their parents: Mesoamerican cultural history[1] and conservation of endangered species.

Attracting Parents: Studies have found that foreign-born parents are concerned that their children will lose their ethnic identity and culture[15, 20, 19]. In the outreach programs we have been associated with, we have found this sentiment to be corroborated anecdotally. At UCSB outreach events, the authors have often heard parents voice their gratitude for programs that teach their children about their home countries in ways that are not taught in public schools.

Santa Barbara is also an ideal test-bed for attracting parental interest based on conservation. Some in Santa Barbara consider their community as the "birthplace of the environmental movement," which gathered steam after a devastating oil disaster caused by an offshore drilling accident in January 1969[8].

Attracting Students: A 1996 national study on Latino Youth found that YLA (Young Latino Americans) are "extremely interested in maintaining a connection with their culture; 67% agree that this is something that is important to them and nearly half of YLA have the desire to form a stronger connection to their Latino culture."[1] Again, such opinions are borne out by current outreach programs in local junior high schools. A program directed by Aldana was introduced into Santa Barbara Junior High School in 2008. That program combined Mayan hieroglyphic writing with ceramic art and the chemistry of the ceramic firing process. By the end of the calendar year, the voluntary, not-for-credit class grew from 18 students to 35.

The theme of endangered species was chosen to tap into two interests of young females—having a positive impact on the world and working with animals. Females tend to choose majors that have a positive impact[21, 7, 18], and we want to attract those females in order to show them how computing can be used to help solve problems with high social impact. In addition, young females have a strong attraction to animals. In Canada and the United States, women constitute approximately 80% of the veterinary college student population[13]. In fact, our theme was inspired by a current stuffed animal-based web phenomenon called Webkinz™, an interactive web environment tied to small stuffed animals that experienced 1.9 million unique visitors in December 2006[9].

[1] Mesoamerica extends from Central Mexico to parts of Honduras, including Olmec, Teotihuacan, Maya, and Aztec cultures.

3. CURRICULUM

Our curriculum has five components: Mayan culture, art, Scratch programming, CS unplugged activities, tours, and guest speakers. The first three areas are integrated, allowing animations to be created that directly related to the art and Mayan culture lessons. The CS unplugged activities are used to introduce concepts of computer science that the Scratch projects do not cover, and tours and guest speakers are provided to inspire students and introduce academic preparation programs. The remainder of this section provides more detail about each of these components.

On the first day of class, each pair of students is assigned an endangered animal from the Mesoamerican geographical region. They then research basic information about that animal. All of the projects for the rest of the camp are in the context of their animal.

3.1 Mayan culture

Two principles guided the determination of the Mayan cultural activities integrated into the program. First, the activities provided material that would be used in the Scratch programming activities, including drawings and narratives. Second, activities highlighted STEM fields within ancient Mayan culture to demonstrate a relevance of science and technology across cultures and across time.

Mayan counting: Mayan numeration is vigesimal, or base 20, evidenced in records of Mayan hieroglyphic writing. We introduce beans, toothpicks, and shells to provide a manipulable version of calculation using the hieroglyphic bar-and-dot notation. This activity is linked to a binary numbers CS Unplugged activity to provide students exposure to non-decimal computation.

Mayan glyphs: The ancient Mayan writing system is hieroglyphic in which individual glyphs represent vowels or syllables and are combined within glyph blocks and grids of blocks to compose words and sentences. In Mayan books, or codices, glyphic texts often accompanied illustrations to which they were related. Students learn to write the name of their animal in Mayan hieroglyphs and then imitate codex images in their Scratch animations.

Mayan ballgame: One version of the ancient Mayan ball game included elevated rings through which the ball infrequently passed. Students learned about the ball game and then focused on the physics of projectile motion. The next part of this activity involved the launching of water balloons of the same weight and with the same velocity at different angles. Students graphed the measurements of several launches.

Mayan stories: Students participate in a "scavenger hunt" in the library to find Mesoamerican or Native North American myths that made reference to their animals. These stories are summarized and transformed into storyboards as the basis of their second required Scratch animation.

3.2 Scratch Programming

Scratch programming projects are chosen to provide concrete milestones while gradually introducing more programming concepts. The first three projects involve their assigned animal (name poem, story, virtual pet), and are completed by all students. For the fourth project, students are offered a choice between implementing a virtual pet in Scratch, or helping to design a game based on the Mayan Ball game. In all cases, students are encouraged to integrate Mayan art and culture into their projects. culture lessons.

Name Poem: Students write a name poem for their animal and implemented this as a Scratch animation (an idea adapted from[22])–providing an opportunity to learn sequential instructions and event-driven programming. For example, "fish" might become Friendly, Intelligent, Shy, Hairless. When each letter is clicked, the adjective appears. In addition, the fish might swim across the screen in response to pressing the space bar.

Animal Information: Students completed an animation to teach others about their animal. This involves placing many pictures of their animal in two different scenes, one the natural habitat and another of their choice. They record the animal's sounds, narrated information, and add buttons to switch between scenes. All action is in response to user input. This project reinforces the lessons from the name poem and adds control flow (to control the scenes) and audio.

Animating a Story: Students then animate a story about their animal. First, students are taught about Mayan codices, the folded books in which Mayan stories were recorded. The students are also given an opportunity to research Mayan mythology and stories connected with their assigned animal. Finally, the students are invited to animate a story about their animal using the Scratch skills learned so far. These animations are posted on a website to share with friends and family.

Virtual Pet: For the virtual pet project, we teach the students how to make a finite state diagram illustrating the emotional states of their animal as well as how actions transition the pet from state to state, building on a clever virtual pest assignment[17]. Students are then given a simple virtual pet implemented in Scratch in order to demonstrate the additional skills needed for this project. Students then replace the pictures with their own animal pictures and add states and transitions to the code. This is a very challenging project in if-else if statements because the next state depends on both the current state and the action.

Mayan Ballgame: Students work with an undergraduate programmer to design the next steps in a Mayan ballgame. A skeleton program was provided, and students brainstorm with the programmer to decide what they should add to the game. This helps to show how design decisions and creativity are an important part of software development.

3.3 Art

The purpose of the art lessons was to directly support the Scratch animation projects as well as to show that programming projects are creative not only in their design, but also in their implementation.

Drawing animal heads: Students begin by looking at the outlines of different animal heads and identifying what specific shapes identify those animals. They then look at examples of Mayan depictions of animals. Finally, they draw examples of their own animal's head for use in the name poem.

Drawing animal bodies: In order to expand the artwork for the animal information project, students look at the shapes that are used to draw different types of animal bodies.

Drawing landscapes: Next, students work on the backgrounds of their projects, choosing appropriate habitats in which to place their animals. They look at perspectives and vegetation. They can then substitute their own drawings for the "stock" backgrounds chosen in their Scratch projects.

Drawing emotions: Finally, students are given 20 facial expressions of a cartoon fish and asked to identify which emotion goes with each one. They analyzed how simple differences in the eyebrows, eyes, and mouth make major differences in the emotions. They are then given the opportunity to draw their own animal with the same facial characteristics–this is incorporated into the various scratch animations. This is especially relevant to the virtual pet project. where the animal's expression changes to indicate its mood.

3.4 Extras

In addition to the main lessons, we schedule a CS unplugged activity, tour, and/or guest speaker at least once a day. The purpose is to show a broader view of computer science, to educate about careers, and to introduce students to academic preparation programs.

CS Unplugged: Our curriculum incorporates many CS unplugged activities, including counting to 31 on one hand (binary), KidFax (pictures as numbers), Secret messages (writing with numbers), sorting weights, parallel sorting, Muddy Roads (shortest path), and the Routing and Deadlock game (networking).

Guest Speakers / Tours: During the 2010 camp, we had two guest speakers. One was a female graduate student in electrical engineering who develops underwater sensors and communication. The second was from the UCSB program Bridges to Pathways a program that gives students academic advice and invites students to participate in their academic counseling and college preparation program. The students also went on tours of , the Allosphere[3], an immersive interactive environment utilizing 3-d glasses that allows the user to interact with touch, sound, and a video game controller, the Santa Barbara Zoo, and the Marine Science Institute.

4. CAMP DESIGN

During Summer 2010, Animal Tlatoque was offered as a full-day, 2-week camp with free bussing. The full fee was $200. Most students qualified for free or reduced school lunches and had their tuition waived. All other students requesting a scholarship paid $100. This included 10 days with full lunches, breakfast bar, mid-morning snack, and a field trip to the zoo.

Thirty-six students started the camp, and 34 finished the camp. The remainder of the statistics in this paper cover the 32 students whose parents gave informed consent for their children's information to be used for research purposes. The students sometimes worked as a single group, and other times were split into two groups of about 16-18 students each. Each group was led by a graduate student with expertise in Mayan culture and experience with outreach in the

Ethnicity	Applied Elementary	Applied Middle	Participated Elementary	Participated Middle
Males				
African Am	0	0	0	0
Asian	0	0	0	0
Caucasian	2	1	2	0
Latino	5	4	4	3
Native Am	0	1	0	1
Females				
African Am	1	0	1	0
Asian	1	2	1	2
Caucasian	7	4	4	4
Latina	19	3	12	3
Native Am	2	0	2	0

Table 1: Demographics of Applicants and Participants. Some participants have multiple ethnicities.

Latina/o community. The graduate students were assisted by six undergraduates—one Chicana/o studies major and five computer science majors. All of the CS majors were not yet in upper-division courses; thus the camp provided an internship opportunity at a point in their academic program where it is difficult for them to compete for CS-related summer internships and research projects.

Students used pair programming for all computer-based projects and had individual supplies for paper-based tasks. We attempted, whenever possible, to pair students with similar academic backgrounds and ages. The least successful pairings were when we were unable to do so.

Conversations between the students and the undergraduate staff indicate that the students were very satisfied with the camp. Many students asked if they could attend next year. The next section presents our survey results.

5. RESULTS

In this section, we evaluate how well we achieved our two specific goals: (1) attracting underrepresented minorities to our camp (specifically, females and Latina/os), (2) increasing the chances that participants will pursue computer science as a career.

5.1 Recruiting

We recruited in two ways. For 7th graders and older, UCSB has direct access to school records. So, to recruit 7th graders (future 8th graders), we sent fliers to all females and Latina/os with GPAs of at least 3.0. For the elementary schools, we distributed fliers to all 5th and 6th graders at many elementary schools, specifically targeting those with high Latina/o populations and high percentages of students who were at or above grade level in math and science.

Table 1 shows the demographics of the participants. Some students are counted twice if they are of mixed heritage. Out of 46 applicants, only 3 are outside of our target population, even though a large majority of the applications were distributed to elementary schools with students of both genders and several ethnicities.

On the application, we had an open-ended question asking why the student wanted to attend our camp. Some students cited one or more of our themes as the reason. Figures 1 and 2 show the breakdown between three themes—computer science, animals, and Mayan culture.

As we had expected, interest in computer science was

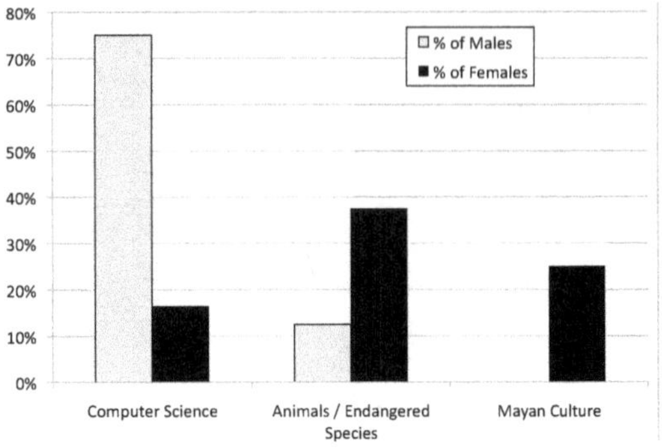

Figure 1: Reasons for choosing Animal Tlatoque camp, broken down by gender

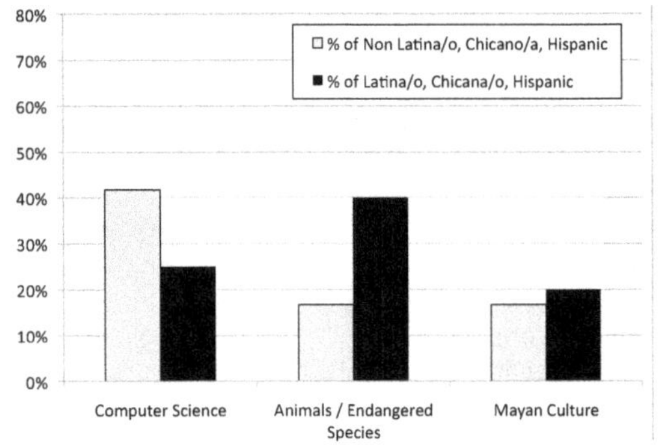

Figure 2: Reasons for choosing Animal Tlatoque camp, broken down by ethnicity

dominated by males, and interest in animals and endangered species was dominated by females. Females were also much more interested in Mayan culture than in computer science. Therefore, our non-computing themes were very successful in attracting females into our program. The data showed nearly the same level of interest in Mayan culture among the Latina/o and non-Latina/o students in our program—though our sample size is too small to draw any strong conclusions,

5.2 Interest in Activities

During the camp, we polled the students as to what activities they had enjoyed so far. We also used pre- and post-surveys to measure students self-perceived learning and interest in overall camp activities.

Prior to the camp, students were asked what specific camp activities interested them. Post camp they were asked to choose what would interest them now they know what each camp component entailed. Figure 3 shows the results of this survey. We can see that before the camp, many of the activities were fairly evenly identified, with creating computer games and learning about animals being the top activities. After the camp, the absolute level of interest increased significantly, and the top choices became much more even with the rest. Learning about animals remained the top choice. We were happy to find that the students were even more satisfied with the activities after having experienced them, and that the non-game computing tasks (as well as others) became more important to the students.

On days three, five and seven of camp participants were asked to select their two favorite and one least favorite activities from a given list. Scratch programming was a favorite

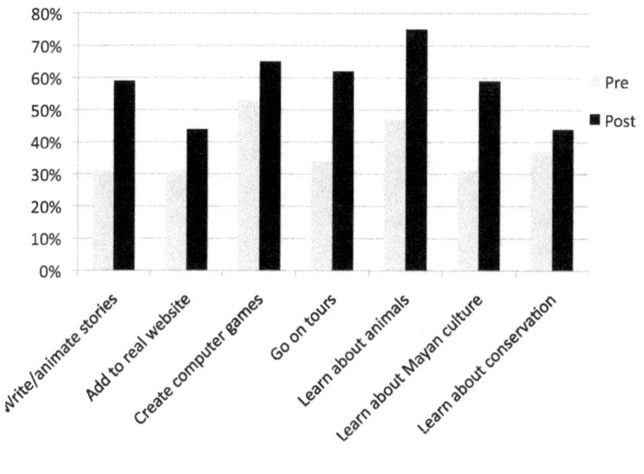

Figure 3: Interest in camp activities, before and after camp

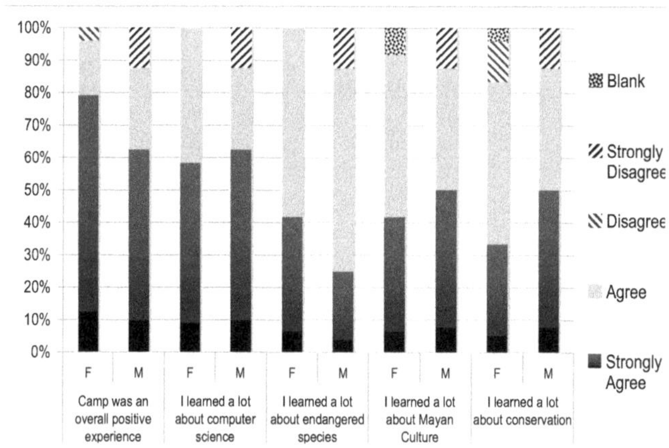

Figure 4: Student self-reported learning, broken down by gender

activity for the most participants (13), even beating out a water balloon slingshot activity (10). Their least favorite activities were learning the binary and Maya number systems (10) and a linear graphing activity (3) (because they were "too hard" and "too much like school"). Further examination found no correlation between their success in learning the Mayan and binary systems. Many students had no least favorite activity.

5.3 Student Learning

At the end of the camp, students were asked whether the camp was an overall positive experience, as well as how much they felt they learned about various subjects. Figure 4 shows the results. All but two students agreed or strongly agreed that the overall experience of the camp was a positive one. Thirty-one of the participants agreed or strongly agreed that they learned a lot about computer science. Overall, students felt they learned about all of the subjects. Students felt they learned they learned the least about conservation and endangered species, which were not as developed this first year.

5.4 Career Aspirations

We asked several questions on our surveys to find out students' views of whether specific groups could or should be-

Question	Pre-Camp	Post-Camp
CS possible career	7	21
CS first choice	3	6
Not capable of being CS	3	0
CS inappropriate for girls	2	0
Boys better at CS	7	5
Girls better at CS	7	0

Table 2: CS attitudes surveys summary

come computer scientists, as well as whether they themselves would be interested in becoming a computer scientist.

In the pre-survey, females were less likely to think females could or should become computer scientists, as well as less likely to want to become one. Post-camp, most of these attitudes had disappeared. Table 2 summarizes the results of these questions, and we give more details on the responses below.

One item on the Pre and Post Animal Tlatoque Survey asked participants to select all of the careers that they had considered for themselves from a list of options. Pre camp, 7 (22%) of the 32 participants chose computer science as a possible career option from a list. Asked which was their first choice from the options they selected, 3 (9%) of the participants selected computer science. Post camp, 21 (65%) participants selected computer science as a career choice with 6 (18%) of these participants choosing it as a first choice. Of the 21 interested participants, 11 had originally given their reason for coming to camp as other than related to computers.

All six of the participants who chose computer science as their first choice of career option expressed an interest in signing up for the Pathways program. Ten of the 21 participants who chose CS as a possible career choice will be first-generation college graduates. All but one of these participants had not thought of CS as an option for them before attending this camp.

Another indicator of participant interest in computer science was a Likert item that asked them to rate the extent to which they agree with the statement: I am excited about taking computer science classes in high school. Not much pre-post change occurred on this variable. Pre camp 27 participants agreed or strongly agreed with the statement: I am looking forward to taking computer science classes in high school. Post camp, 3 participants changed their disagree to agree, and one of the participants who originally chose strongly agree changed their response to disagree.

Finally, three of the Likert items on the Pre and Post Animal Tlatoque Survey were designed to assess participant attitudes about self in relationship to computer science by indicating the extent to which they agreed with the following statements:

1. I think that I could become a good computer scientist if I chose that goal for myself.

2. Who do you think is better at computer science—boys, girls, or neither?

3. Computer science/learning about computers is an appropriate subject for both boys and girls to pursue.

Pre camp, 3 female participants didn't think that they would be able to be a computer scientist. By the end of camp 2 of these girls had decided that they could and 1 decided that she would become a computer scientist.

Pre camp, 3 boys and 4 girls believed that boys were better than girls at computer science. Post camp, one of these boys and one of these girls changed their beliefs to neither. Pre camp, 7 girls believed that girls were better than boys at computer science. Pre camp, 2 of these girls indicated that they didn't think computer science was an appropriate career choice for girls. Post camp, these beliefs changed.

These survey questions show that the Animal Tlatoque Summer Camp had a large impact on students' views of computer science. Many students who had never never considered a career in computing were now interested in computing, and several students who had gender-based stereotypes about their skills or the suitability of computer science found that they could, and wanted, to pursue such a career. In addition, we were successful at interesting students in the Pathways campus advising program. The major factor we did not change was interest in taking computer science courses in high school. This shows a tremendous success in both the recruitment strategies and the implementation of our program.

6. CONCLUSIONS AND FUTURE WORK

Our approach, to mix culturally-relevant themes and computing, was very successful in both attracting students in target populations and improving their opinions of computer science as a career. Our recruiting efforts resulted in an application pool that was 73% female and 67% Latina/o, with only 6.5% in neither group. We had 34 students complete the program. Pre- and post-surveys showed that the number of students citing computer science as their top choice for a career doubled and interest in computer science as a career more than tripled. This impact is significant considering how few of our students were initially interested in pursuing computer science. Our surveys show that students ended the camp more confident in their computing skills, more positive about computer science as a field, and much more likely to pursue a computer science career.

We have funding to continue the camp for at least two more summers ('11, '12). Our plans for next year include expanding the conservation and endangered species component.

A logical extension to this work would be a program for high school students focused on engaging applications such as social networking or cell phone applications. Such a program could bridge the gap between our success with middle school students, and the college years, inspiring a new generation of computer scientists.

7. ACKNOWLEDGMENTS

We would like to thank our anonymous reviewers for their thoughtful comments.

This work is supported by the National Science Foundation BPC Award CNS-0940491 to Franklin, Aldana, and Conrad, CAREER Award CCF-0855889 to Franklin, and the Chicana/o Studies Institute.

8. ADDITIONAL AUTHORS

Additional authors: Natalie Avalos Cisneros (Department of Religious Studies), Felicia Lopez, Angelina Gonzalez(Chicano Studies Institute), Alejandro Hernandez, Sarah Jones, Joni Rae Lopez, Cindy Lu, Nataly Moreno, Pablo Ortiz, Martin Rochin, Stephanie Smith (Department of Computer Science.)

9. REFERENCES

[1] First national study on latino youth. *HispanicVista*, 2006.

[2] G. Aikenhead. Students' ease in crossing cultural borders into school science. *Science Education*, 85(2):180–188, March 2001.

[3] X. Amatriain et al. The allosphere: Immersive multimedia for scientific discovery and artistic exploration. *IEEE MultiMedia*, 16(2):64–75, 2009.

[4] I. Arroyo et al. Effects of web-based tutoring software on students' math achievement. In *AERA*, 2004.

[5] T. Bell, I. H. Witten, and M. Fellows. *Computer Science Unplugged*. 2006.

[6] W. Dann, S. Cooper, and R. Pausch. Making the connection: programming with animated small world. *ITiCSE*, 2000.

[7] H. Etzkowitz, C. Kemelgor, and B. Uzzi. *Athena Unbound: The Advancement of Women in Science and Technology*. Cambridge University Press, 2000.

[8] D. Haier. '69 oil spill leaves mark on sb environmentalism. *Daily Nexus*, 2005.

[9] C. Hawn. Time to play, money to spend. *Business 2.0 Magazine*, 2007.

[10] C. S. Hood and D. J. Hood. Teaching programming and language concepts using legos. In *ITiCSE*, pages 19–23, June 2005.

[11] U. Irvine. Summer institute in computer science.

[12] C. Lee. Why we need to re-think race and ethnicity in educational research. *Educational Researcher*, 32(5):3–5, June 2003.

[13] J. Lofstedt. Gender and veterinary medicine. *The Canadian Veterinary Journal*, 44(7), July 2003.

[14] J. Maloney, L. Burd, Y. Kafai, N. Rusk, B. Silverman, and M. Resnick. Scratch: A sneak preview. *Second International Conference on Creating, Connecting and Collaborating through Computing*, January 2004.

[15] J. Moschkovich. A situated and sociocultural perspective on bilingual mathematics learners. *Mathematical Thinking and Learning*, 4(2/3), 2002.

[16] B. of Labor Statistics. Occupational outlook handbook.

[17] J. L. Popyack, A. Shokoufandeh, and P. Zoski. Software design and implementation in the introductory cs course: Javascript and virtual pests. In *CCSC '00*, 2000.

[18] S. V. Rosser. *The Science Glass Ceiling*. Taylor and Francis, 2003.

[19] F. A. W. S P Wakil, C M Siddique. Between two cultures: A study in socialization of children of immigrants. *Journal of Marriage and the Family*, (43):929–940, 1981.

[20] U. A. Segal. Cultural variables in asian indian families. *Journal of Contemporary Human Services*, (72):233–242, 1991.

[21] V. Valian. *Why So Slow? The Advancement of Women*. MIT Press, 2005.

[22] U. Wolz, M. Stone, S. M. Pulimood, and K. Pearson. Computational thinking via interactive journalism in middle school. In *SIGCSE*, 2010.

K-12 Game Programming Course Concept Using Textual Programming

Ville Isomöttönen
Department of Mathematical Information Technology, University of Jyväskylä, Finland
ville.isomottonen@jyu.fi

Antti-Jussi Lakanen
Department of Mathematical Information Technology, University of Jyväskylä, Finland
antti-jussi.lakanen@jyu.fi

Vesa Lappalainen
Department of Mathematical Information Technology, University of Jyväskylä, Finland
vesal@jyu.fi

ABSTRACT

Several programming environments have been constructed to facilitate novice programming at K-12 and CS0/CS1 levels. The environments can be roughly divided into those using visual or textual programming. This paper presents a K-12 game programming course concept based on textual programming. The concept is based on an easy-to-use C# library, called Jypeli, built on top of Microsoft XNA Framework. The library tries to maintain advantages of visual programming and avoid challenges of textual programming. In particular, the library helps beginners to program their first games in a short period of time and without a heavy syntactic load. The course concept and an initial evaluation consisting of student feedback and a literature rationale are presented.

Categories and Subject Descriptors

K.3.2. [**Computers and education**]: Computers and Information Science Education—*Computer Science Education*

General Terms

Languages, Experimentation

Keywords

K-12 teaching, game programming

1. INTRODUCTION

The starting point of our work is similar to that described by Garlick and Cankaya [7]: student decline in computer science has yielded a variety of strategies to improve enrollment rates. They mention objects-first (cf. [12]), improving materials, CS0 courses, and using games as the strategies. The strategy we followed is the arranging of pre-programming courses with a game theme. More precisely, we deliver computer science to K-12 (principally middle school aged) students with a week-long game programming course to promote positive experiences in science and computing, held at the University of Jyväskylä.

Sung [21] identifies several ways how the game theme has been incorporated into a curriculum: students learn with games but do not program them, students are given individual game themed programming assignments to teach isolated topics, or faculty engages in extensive game development based on a custom library, game engine, new programming language etc. Our approach resembles the last one but is an extra-curricular summer activity targeted towards K-12 students.

Within the game theme, our work belongs to the research track which studies how novice programming can be facilitated with a particular environment. Widely acknowledged novice programming environments exist. These include syntax free visual programming environments, e.g. Alice and Scratch, that let users create micro-worlds and animated movies. While experiences with these environments have been very positive (e.g. [18], [24], [17]), transition from these environments to object-oriented textual programming may be difficult [19].

Our course concept is based on an easy-to-use C# library, called Jypeli, that necessitates textual programming but avoids an excessive syntactic load. The library is built on top of Microsoft XNA framework. Jypeli is available as a DLL at `https://svn.cc.jyu.fi/srv/svn/npo/tags/2.4.5/lib/` and the source code is found at `https://trac.cc.jyu.fi/projects/npo/browser/trunk/Jypeli`[1]. Jypeli library is distributed via MIT license.

During the summers 2009 and 2010 almost 150 middle school students spent a week on our programming course making simple graphical games using textual programming with Jypeli library. This necessitated altogether six course instances plus one camp instance outside the university campus. Student feedback was carefully collected at each instance. This paper describes the course concept including Jypeli library and the teaching approach, and then presents an initial evaluation based on the student feedback and a literature rationale. Our principal aim has not yet been studying student learning but developing an engaging course concept.

SIGCSE'11, March 9–12, 2011, Dallas, Texas, USA.

[1] For readers interested in translating Jypeli class documentation into a language other than Finnish, we want to offer our best support. Please contact the authors.

2. RELATED WORK

Choosing a programming environment is not an easy task for a pre-university instructor. Both visual and textual environments have their strengths. Visual programming environments refer here to syntax-free programming aimed to foster novice engagement [6] and textual programming to traditional code writing. In this section we'll cover some experiences of these two groups of programming environments.

There are plenty of visual programming environments available, the two widely acknowledged being Alice[2] and Scratch[3]. Researchers have found several benefits in using visual programming at pre-CS1, CS1 and CS2 levels. Moskal et al. [17] report on improved student performance, retention rates, and attitude and beliefs in computer science. Wang et al. [24] found a better comprehension of fundamental programming concepts. Kelleher and Pausch report on improved motivation of middle school girls [10]. Overall, the superiority of visual programming has been explained by its way to begin with concrete and gradually move to an understanding of the abstract [5] — this idea appears to be in line with Bloom's Taxonomy [1].

Drawbacks have as well been reported. Wang's et al. [24] results indicate that visual programming might not improve students' perception of programming, but may rather have a negative effect on it. Powers et al. [19] suggest that the object model in Alice may lead to misconceptions and that there is a transition problem when moving to a traditional programming language.

Learning with textual programming seems to compare to learning with visual programming. Garlick and Cancaya [7] report results from a CS1 experiment in which a pseudocode approach was compared to Alice. They examined student enjoyment and understanding of basic programming constructs (e.g. control statements and loops), and found that the pseudocode approach worked better. The authors conclude that the students perhaps did not associate Alice to real programming and that the graphical environment might work better with younger students. Lewis [14] reports that 6th grade students who were exposed to either Logo or Scratch demonstrated a similar interest in computer science. Regarding the students' learning, there was no statistically significant difference with loops, but the students using Scratch performed better with conditionals.

Moreover, there are indications that young students can do textual programming. Sánchez-Ruiz and Jamba [20] report on an elementary school experiment where 4th and 5th graders were able to write code and enjoyed seeing their code in action, while the students disliked programs not working, fixing errors, and syntax. G. Kacmarcik and S. G. Kacmarcik [8] have made similar observations on grades 5–8 on learning real-world computer programming by introducing C language to voluntary participants. Wright and Cockburn [25] found that children read programs written in conventional-style notation more efficiently than programs written in English.

To summarize, success and drawbacks have been reported both with textual and visual programming. Textual programming allows novices to directly deal with programming fundamentals while visual programming illustrates difficult abstract concepts with concrete examples. The former suffers from introducing too much syntax load for novices and the latter from being too far from traditional programming and current mainstream industry tools.

This dilemma motivates our work that belongs to the textual programming category but still aims to make the starting of programming sufficiently easy with a particular programming library. We acknowledge the different purposes and advantages of the reviewed approaches. For example, some concepts of our library are motivated by Alice. The variance in the reported experiences (see above) also indicates that the focus must be given not only on tools but teaching approach and materials used with the tools. We will describe our teaching approach together with the Jypeli library.

3. COURSE CONCEPT

This section describes Jypeli library and how students were taught in the course.

3.1 Motivation to start developing Jypeli

Our objectives with developing Jypeli were programming with mainstream tools, promoting proper programming conventions, and transferability to mobile devices and game consoles. Before starting to develop Jypeli we briefly examined whether any existing environments suited our needs. We principally considered Greenfoot[4] and ACM Java Task Force[5]. We found them impressive but chose to develop our own library nonetheless. This is discussed in the following.

Greenfoot is a framework and an IDE for creating two-dimensional grid assignments in Java. ACM Java Task Force is a class library that simplifies programming of GUIs, graphics, and IO. After starting our project we found out about XGC1 class library [22] built on top of XNA. XGC1 brings the game themed assignments to CS1 level. We noticed that these environments lack one or more of our objectives. For example, physics modeling is missing or event handling requires writing many conditionals. XGC1 could have provided us with a proper starting point for further development but was not known to us at the start of our project.

We have now noticed that developing of our own library has allowed us to give detailed technical support for students and to add features to the library on students' request during the courses. This is in line with our goal of promoting positive experiences in the field.

3.2 Jypeli library

Jypeli library is built on top of Microsoft XNA Game Studio 3.1 runtime environment and class library (hereafter briefly XNA), which is Microsoft's attempt to free game developers from writing "repetitive boilerplate code" [16]. As an IDE we used Visual C# 2008 Express and Professional editions. To ease the phase of getting started, we also created some Visual Studio project templates. A project template contains the necessary links to XNA and Jypeli libraries.

In terms of Kelleher's and Pausch's [9] taxonomy on novice programming environments, the basic idea of Jypeli library is to *simplify the language* and *provide a motivating context*. With respect to the former, Jypeli library is an API that encapsulates low-level details of XNA and C#. For example,

[2] `http://www.alice.org`
[3] `http://scratch.mit.edu`
[4] `http://www.greenfoot.org`
[5] `http://jtf.acm.org`

while XNA necessitates the programmer to take care of target devices and routines for initializing, loading, unloading, updating, and drawing the game content, Jypeli hides the device handling and encapsulates the basic routines into a single method. The code example below demonstrates how adding a white ball to the screen with Jypeli takes *two* lines of code in one method after creating a new project template. `PhysicsObject` constructor takes width, height, and the desired shape as parameters.

```
1  using System; using Jypeli;
2
3  public class BallGame : PhysicsGame {
4    protected override void Begin() {
5      PhysicsObject ball =
         new PhysicsObject(40, 40, Shapes.Circle);
6      Add(ball);
13   }
18 }
```

Regarding the motivating context, we complemented the game theme with a taste of realism. As the physics modeling was not included in XNA, we included Physics2D.Net library in Jypeli. With our ball example, we can now make the ball move by adding few more lines after line #6.

```
7      Vector impulse = new Vector(200, 0);
8      ball.Hit(impulse);
9      Level.CreateBorders();
```

After giving the impulse the ball keeps bouncing inside the borders, conforming to the laws of physics. Collisions are also implemented using events, so it would be easy to change the ball's color each time it hits the wall, for example. With adding the physics modeling to Jypeli we were able to incorporate middle and high school physics concepts, like vector, gravity and friction, into teaching and tutorials.

Another issue that facilitates programming with Jypeli is that XNA's event polling loop was replaced with an event-driven model. In practice this means that a use of complex if and loop structures is decreased dramatically. Below we continue our example by adding a gamepad control to move a paddle downwards.

```
10     PhysicsObject paddle =
         new PhysicsObject(40, 40, Shapes.Rectangle);
11     Add(paddle);
12     ControllerOne.Listen(
         Button.DPadDown, ButtonState.Down,
         MovePaddle, "Move paddle downwards",
         new Vector(0, -100), paddle);
...
14   void MovePaddle(Vector v, PhysicsObject paddle)
15   {
16       paddle.Push(v);
17   }
```

Adding more listeners for other directions (and other buttons) is simply done by adding a new line in the same way as the line #12, just by changing the parameter values. The quoted parameter value in the line #12 is automatically set as an on-screen help text.

Moreover, we note that with modern IDEs such as Visual C# the programmer does not need to remember that much of the syntax details as there is lots of intelligence embedded in the IDEs (e.g. IntelliSense in Microsoft products).

3.3 Teaching approach

The course consisted of lectures, a tutorial and exercises, design and implementation of a game, and demonstrations, in the given order.

The lectures were 30–45 minutes each. The purpose of the lectures was to orient to programming thinking and get acquainted with basic programming concepts and language syntax. There was a maximum of two lectures per day, about 7 hours in total.

During the first afternoon of the course, all students programmed a *Pong game*[6] by following our tutorial consisting of seven phases, each addressing a particular programming concept (e.g. variables, procedures, etc.). There were also a bunch of exercises available for those who assimilated the content of the tutorial rapidly. The purpose of these was to practice the syntax of C# language and to get familiar with the common programming structure. The code written in the tutorial and the exercises could be utilized later on when students started writing the code for the game. The time reserved for these activities was about 6 hours.

Designing and coding the game was naturally the most anticipated part of the course. Each student was guided to make a story or a plot (verbal design) and to draw a sketch (visual design, see Figure 1) for the game. In addition, students had a chance to design and draw their own character for the game. The stories and sketches were shared in the course wiki. About 12 hours were budgeted for the design and implementation.

All the above activities were supported with a motivated teaching team and comprehensive learning materials available in the course wiki. The materials included basics of wiki, programming terminology, general programming tips, instructions for setting up Jypeli environment, the Pong game tutorial, instructions on working with Jypeli class library, and tips for further reading.

The teaching team consisted of a good mixture of technical knowledge and pedagogical expertise. There were 5–6 teachers available for the students on each course. The technical expertise of the teaching team guaranteed that students' design ideas could be carried on. From the pedagogic viewpoint students were not only supported but given sufficient space to experiment with the exercises. For example, when they had produced some game content they were prompted to manipulate it (e.g. size) to discover the role of variables.

On the final day of the course each attendee demonstrated the game to the rest of the class and lively discussions followed. Students voted for the best game which was rewarded with a small prize.

4. INITIAL EVALUATION

A survey was conducted at the beginning and end of each course instance. Data was collected with questionnaires. The final version of the questionnaire included a total of 27 quantitative and 11 open-ended questions. The quantitative questions were designed using a five point Likert scale with the following options: "strongly disagree" (1), "disagree", "not agree nor disagree", "agree", "strongly agree" (5). A few questions were added in 2010, and some questions were rephrased during the summer 2010.

[6]One of the earliest arcade video games. The tutorial is found at `https://trac.cc.jyu.fi/projects/npo/wiki/Pong/Part1`.

The paper reports selected parts of the questionnaire data. In Section 4.1 we describe student background information and their prior conceptions on programming. Section 4.2 describes students' overall perceptions of the course (with three Likert scale questions), challenges and a potential change in their conception of programming (with two Likert scale questions and two open-ended questions), and interest to further study computing/science (with one Likert scale question). We categorized students' answers to open-ended questions and calculated the frequencies of answers in each category.

4.1 Pre-questioning, student background

Demographic data is given in Table 1. A total of 150 students started the course. Gender distribution was uneven, but well-known in the gaming context: in 2009 we had seven (16 %) girls of 45 and in 2010 six (6 %) of 105 students. Across both years, the age median was 14 years, the mean 14.1, the youngest participant being 11 years and the oldest 17 years. In 2009 three students and in 2010 two students dropped out making the total drop-out rate 3.3 %.

Table 1: Student background

Year		2009	2010	Both
N		45	105	150
Girls		7 (16 %)	6 (6 %)	13 (9 %)
Age	**(mean)**	13.8	14.2	14.1
	(median)	13	14	14
	(youngest/oldest)	12/16	11/17	11/17
Dropouts		3 (6.7 %)	2 (1.9 %)	5 (3.3 %)

More than three out of four students (77.8 %) had none or little earlier programming experience, but nearly three out of five (57.9 %) thought they were skilled computer users. Nearly half of the students (45) reported that they had tried some language, mainly Java (20), Basic (17) and C++ (17) (asked only in 2010).

On the question "Programming is no easy matter" (asked only in 2010) the mean was 3.09 with 1.0 standard deviation. However, 46 out of 93 respondents (49 %) did not agree nor disagree. This suggests that students really did not know what to expect out of programming. The open-ended questions "What individual issues do you consider to be difficult ("easy", respectively) in programming" confirm this, since the most common response was simply "I don't know".

4.2 Post-questioning, student feedback

Overall satisfaction on all the seven course instances was very high: the mean in 2009 was 4.71 and in 2010 4.56. The course fulfilled the students' expectations well: the mean in 2009 was 4.1, in 2010 it was 3.9. Of all students 85 % would recommend the course to their friends (asked only in 2010).

On the open-ended question "For me the hardest thing on this course was ..." 42 % of the answers related to "learning a new language", "writing code" or "language syntax". Students seemed to have difficulties in writing faultless code, particularly in finding defects. However, on the question "Programming is harder than I had thought" 48 % disagreed, 32 % agreed and 20 % gave neutral answer (asked only in 2010).

On the question "My conception of programming changed during this course" 49 % of the students agreed, 22 % disagreed and 29 % did not agree nor disagree (asked only in 2010). The students could comment on their answers (open-ended question) — here are few of the typical answers.

> `[Student:]` *I thought it would be harder*
> `[Student:]` *Game programming can be really fun*
> `[Student:]` *I didn't expect it to be writing the actual code*
> `[Student:]` *I expected it to be more complicated*
> `[Student:]` *More difficult than I expected*
> `[Student:]` *Didn't change, I've programmed for some time*

What's interesting is that of those 47 answers that were informative, 23 (49 %) indicate that the students who had had a negative slant against programming demonstrated a positive attitude by the end of the course. For example,

- students thought that programming would be more complicated,
- game programming was easier than expected, and
- programming was more fun than expected.

This suggests that though learning a new language and writing faultless code was a tough thing to do — maybe even laborious and unpleasant — students did find it a little less troublesome and more fun than they had expected.

The question "I'm interested in applying for studying science/computing" was put in the pre- and post-questionnaires. When compared, we notice a small rise in the mean figure, and in the number of students who agreed with the question (see Table 2). Another interesting finding is that the course seemed to have had an even stronger effect on those students who were initially *not interested* in studying computer science (see Table 2).

Table 2: "I'm interested in applying for studying science/computing". Pre- and post-results compared.

	Pre	Post	+/-
Agree or strongly agree	37.9 %	43.6 %	5.7 %
Disagree or strongly disagree	27.9 %	17.9 %	-10.0 %
Mean	3.16	3.41	.25
Std dev	1.19	1.16	-.03

Students' achievements varied a bit since some students had programmed before. An example of the game programmed by two 9th graders is given in Figure 1. More screenshots are found in the course wiki[7].

4.3 Literature rationale

In this section, a couple of theoretical viewpoints are foregrounded from literature, which, we assume, may explain the positive feedback.

The teaching approach outlined in Section 3.3 is in line with constructivist assumptions. Constructivism assumes a gradual knowledge acquisition process implying that the teacher must ensure that students have sufficient prior knowledge for their learning tasks [2]. Here the lectures and exercises aim to ensure that each student knows of the structures and syntax of the language, thus have the sufficient initial

[7] `https://trac.cc.jyu.fi/projects/npo_pelit/wiki/valmiitpelit/2010/31`

knowledge. Moreover, here students are first guided with a tutorial to ease the transition to the actual game design and implementation. The support that is gradually decreased is known as scaffolding in constructivist literature [4], derivable from Vygotsky's zone of proximal development (ZPD) [23]. ZPD means the distance between what a learner can achieve alone and with assistance, being then a conceptual tool to understand those areas of learning that are currently maturing [23, p. 78]. The experimental nature of doing the tutorial and exercises, i.e., the sufficient space given for the students' learning, can be argued with the constructivist concept of discovery learning [3].

More rationale is sourced from Maehr's work on meaning and motivation [15]. Maehr examines motivation with the concept of *personal investment*, which is determined, among other things, by the sense of self in a given situation. The sense of self again can consist of subjective judgments about one's own competence. Here the students start with a tutorial and observe what it takes to make a simple game. They notice that they are actually able to write code that yields something observable. Maehr also presents that personal investment is dependent on the perceived action possibilities in the given situation. Here the sufficient technical knowledge of the teaching team enabled addressing of students' design ideas and the space was left for students' experimenting. These viewpoints may enhance student motivation and therefore their performance.

Furthermore, the process of designing and implementing games can be fairly associated to creativity, which has been acknowledged as a pathway to computer science [11]. It is thus possible that here incorporating creativity has helped engage a part of the students and made them more interested in science and computing.

5. CONCLUSIONS AND FUTURE WORK

This paper described a K-12 game programming course in which a particular library (Jypeli) made it possible to use mainstream textual programming language. Our experiences from seven course offerings suggest that textual programming and professional tools are not insuperable obstacles for middle school students learning basic programming concepts. Nearly half (49 %) of the students responded that it was easier than they had expected, and students' overall satisfaction was very high. The 5-day program did also have a little influence on students' will on being geared towards studying computer science in the future.

As cited in Section 2, young students have been observed to be capable of writing code [20]. Also, learning results when using textual programming seem to compare with results when using visual programming [14]. Our experiences are in line with these observations, adding that with an appropriate teaching approach (e.g. scaffolding) students are able to make progress in a short period of time even though using textual programming. It must be noted that our students attended voluntarily and got lots of support from instructors, both of which likely had an effect on the positive outcome. Based on the students' achievements, feedback, and the literature rationale on the teaching approach, we assume that both making programming sufficiently easy with Jypeli and the sufficient and supportive teaching played an important role here.

The collected qualitative data discloses that the usual novice challenges are still in place: writing of structured

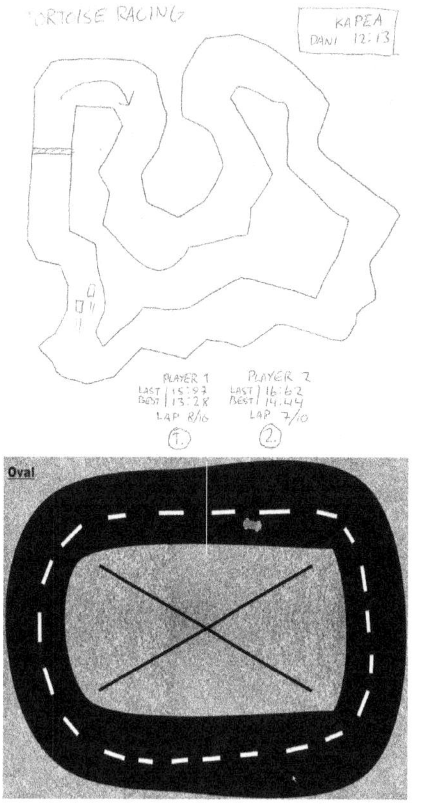

Figure 1: A sketch and a screenshot of a game

solutions, understanding how programs are executed, syntax, and debugging [9]. However, based on the students' achievements and the observed overall satisfaction, we conclude that we have sufficiently overcome the basic challenges and do not even expect or aim to get totally rid of them with this kind of teaching approach.

Another possible drawback with professional tools is the rather burdensome start-up phase including downloading, installing, and setting program preferences. At this point we don't have a package for installing the environment, XNA, libraries, and project templates, but the students need to download and install these separately in a certain order. This can lower the students' interest to continue game programming at home.

We acknowledge that this is not a comparative study and our aim here is to report one possible way to successfully deliver computer science to K-12 students. To better understand K-12 students' ability with textual programming in a motivating context, an interesting future goal would be to test this approach as a compulsory course in an authentic middle school setting. A short-term research interest for us is to observe the transition from the use of Jypeli to the traditional Java programming environment. Jypeli has already been piloted in one CS1 offering with positive experiences, and in near future we are able to observe students' progress from CS1 with Jypeli to CS2 with Java, Eclipse, and JUnit/ComTest [13].

6. ACKNOWLEDGEMENTS

This study and the programming course presented in this paper were partly funded by Technology Industries of Finland Centennial Foundation. We wish to thank the developers of Jypeli library Tero Jäntti, Tomi Karppinen, Janne Nikkanen, Simo Haatainen, and Tuukka Puranen. Moreover, we thank Professor Kelvin Sung for his encouragement and insightful comments on this paper.

7. REFERENCES

[1] L. W. Anderson, D. R. Krathwohl, P. W. Airasian, K. A. Cruikshank, R. E. Mayer, P. R. Pintrich, J. Raths, and M. C. Wittrock. *A Taxonomy for Learning, Teaching, and Assessing: A Revision of Bloom's Taxonomy of Educational Objectives, Abridged Edition.* Allyn & Bacon, second edition, 2000.

[2] M. Ben-Ari. Constructivism in computer science education. *Journal of Computers in Mathematics and Science Teaching*, 20(1):45–73, 2001.

[3] J. Bruner. The act of discovery. *Harvard Educational Review*, 31(1):21–32, 1961.

[4] J. S. Bruner. Early social interaction and language development. In H. R. Schaffer, editor, *Studies in Mother-Child Interaction*, pages 271–289. Academic Press, London, 1977.

[5] W. Dann and S. Cooper. Education: Alice 3: Concrete to abstract. *Commun. ACM*, 52(8):27–29, 2009.

[6] S. Fincher, S. Cooper, M. Kölling, and J. Maloney. Comparing Alice, Greenfoot & Scratch. In *SIGCSE '10: Proceedings of the 41st ACM technical symposium on Computer science education*, pages 192–193, New York, NY, USA, 2010. ACM.

[7] R. Garlick and E. C. Cankaya. Using Alice in CS1: A quantitative experiment. In *ITiCSE '10: Proceedings of the fifteenth annual conference on Innovation and technology in computer science education*, pages 165–168, New York, NY, USA, 2010. ACM.

[8] G. Kacmarcik and S. G. Kacmarcik. Introducing computer programming via gameboy advance homebrew. In *SIGCSE '09: Proceedings of the 40th ACM technical symposium on Computer science education*, pages 281–285, New York, NY, USA, 2009. ACM.

[9] C. Kelleher and R. Pausch. Lowering the barriers to programming: A taxonomy of programming environments and languages for novice programmers. *ACM Comput. Surv.*, 37(2):83–137, 2005.

[10] C. Kelleher and R. Pausch. Using storytelling to motivate programming. *Commun. ACM*, 50(7):58–64, 2007.

[11] M. Knobelsdorf and R. Romeike. Creativity as a pathway to computer science. *SIGCSE Bull.*, 40(3):286–290, 2008.

[12] M. Kölling and J. Rosenberg. Objects first with Java and BlueJ (seminar session). *SIGCSE Bull.*, 32(1):429, 2000.

[13] V. Lappalainen, J. Itkonen, V. Isomöttönen, and S. Kollanus. Comtest: A tool to impart TDD and unit testing to introductory level programming. In *ITiCSE '10: Proceedings of the fifteenth annual conference on Innovation and technology in computer science education*, pages 63–67, New York, NY, USA, 2010. ACM.

[14] C. M. Lewis. How programming environment shapes perception, learning and goals: Logo vs. Scratch. In *SIGCSE '10: Proceedings of the 41st ACM technical symposium on Computer science education*, pages 346–350, New York, NY, USA, 2010. ACM.

[15] M. L. Maehr. Meaning and motivation: Toward a theory of personal investment. In R. E. Ames and C. Ames, editors, *Research on Motivation in Learning*, volume 1, pages 115–144. Academic Press, Orlando, Florida, 1984.

[16] Microsoft. Next generation of games starts with XNA, `https://www.microsoft.com/presspass/press/2004/mar04/03-24xnalaunchpr.mspx`, retrieved September 2nd 2010, 2004.

[17] B. Moskal, D. Lurie, and S. Cooper. Evaluating the effectiveness of a new instructional approach. In *SIGCSE '04: Proceedings of the 35th SIGCSE technical symposium on Computer science education*, pages 75–79, New York, NY, USA, 2004. ACM.

[18] P. Mullins, D. Whitfield, and M. Conlon. Using Alice 2.0 as a first language. *J. Comput. Small Coll.*, 24(3):136–143, 2009.

[19] K. Powers, S. Ecott, and L. M. Hirshfield. Through the looking glass: Teaching CS0 with Alice. *SIGCSE Bull.*, 39(1):213–217, 2007.

[20] A. J. Sánchez-Ruíz and L. A. Jamba. FunFonts: Introducing 4th and 5th graders to programming using Squeak. In *ACM-SE 46: Proceedings of the 46th Annual Southeast Regional Conference on XX*, pages 24–29, New York, NY, USA, 2008. ACM.

[21] K. Sung. Computer games and traditional CS courses. *Commun. ACM*, 52(12):74–78, 2009.

[22] K. Sung, M. Panitz, C. Hillyard, R. Angotti, D. Goldstein, and J. Nordlinger. Game-themed programming assignment modules: A pathway for gradual integration of gaming context into existing introductory programming courses. *IEEE Transactions on Education*, 2010. To appear.

[23] L. S. Vygotsky. *Mind and society: The Development of Higher Mental Processes.* Harvard University Press, Cambridge, MA, 1978.

[24] T.-C. Wang, W.-H. Mei, S.-L. Lin, S.-K. Chiu, and J.-C. Lin. Teaching programming concepts to high school students with Alice. In *Frontiers in Education Conference, 2009. FIE '09. 39th IEEE*, pages 1–6, 2009.

[25] T. Wright and A. Cockburn. Evaluation of two textual programming notations for children. In *AUIC '05: Proceedings of the Sixth Australasian conference on User interface*, pages 55–62, Darlinghurst, Australia, 2005. Australian Computer Society, Inc.

Introducing Computational Thinking in Education Courses

Aman Yadav
Dept of Educational Studies
Purdue University
West Lafayette, Indiana, USA
amanyadav@purdue.edu

Ninger Zhou
Dept of Educational Studies
Purdue University
West Lafayette, Indiana, USA
zhoun@purdue.edu

Chris Mayfield
Dept of Computer Science
Purdue University
West Lafayette, Indiana, USA
cmayfiel@cs.purdue.edu

Susanne Hambrusch
Dept of Computer Science
Purdue University
West Lafayette, Indiana, USA
seh@purdue.edu

John T. Korb
Dept of Computer Science
Purdue University
West Lafayette, Indiana, USA
jtk@purdue.edu

ABSTRACT

As computational thinking becomes a fundamental skill for the 21st century, K-12 teachers should be exposed to computing principles. This paper describes the implementation and evaluation of a computational thinking module in a required course for elementary and secondary education majors. We summarize the results from open-ended and multiple-choice questionnaires given both before and after the module to assess the students' attitudes toward and understanding of computational thinking. The results suggest that given relevant information about computational thinking, education students' attitudes toward computer science becomes more favorable and they will be more likely to integrate computing principles in their future teaching.

Categories and Subject Descriptors

K.3.2 [**Computer and Information Science Education**]: Curriculum

General Terms

Experimentation, Measurement

Keywords

Computational Thinking, K-12 Education, Non-Majors

1. COMPUTATIONAL THINKING IN K-12

Wing suggested that "computational thinking" (CT) is a fundamental skill of analytical thinking for everyone, not just for computer scientists [10]. She described computational thinking as "solving problems, designing systems, and understanding human behavior, by drawing on the concepts fundamental to computer science." Wing also pointed out the untapped potential of computational thinking for K-12 education by stating, "To reading, writing, and arithmetic, we should add computational thinking to every child's analytical ability."

A report on computational thinking by the National Research Council (NRC) advanced a similar idea, that CT is a cognitive skill which the "average person is expected to possess" [5]. Similarly, Bundy suggested that computational thinking concepts have been used in other disciplines via problem solving processes, and that the ability to think computationally is essential to every discipline [4]. The pervasiveness of computational thinking concepts dictates the importance of exposing students to such notions early in their school years and helping them to become conscious about when and how to apply this essential skill.

The NRC report also highlighted "(1) that students can learn thinking strategies such as computational thinking as they study a discipline, (2) that teachers and curricula can model these strategies for students, and (3) that appropriate guidance can enable students to learn to use these strategies independently." Teacher education is one discipline where computational thinking will have significant impact. As we prepare future educators to present their subject areas using ideas from computational thinking, K-12 students will have greater exposure to computing in general.

In this paper, we describe the implementation of a CT module in two sections of a core education course required for all elementary and secondary education majors. We present a pre- and post-assessment of the education students' understanding and attitude of computational thinking, which measured the influence the CT module had on them. In particular, only 20% of the students on the pre-survey described computing as, "the process of solving problems" as compared to 70% on the post-survey. On the pre-survey, 30% of the students agreed that computing relates to any or all fields, and the percentage increased to 62% on the post-survey. Overall, the CT module helped the students understand that (1) they can teach computing concepts in K-12 classrooms without the use of computers, and (2) CT concepts can be incorporated across all disciplines.

Computational thinking in education has the potential to significantly advance the problem-solving skills of K-12 students. However, literature on implementing computational thinking in a K-12 setting is still relatively sparse. There

SIGCSE'11, March 9–12, 2011, Dallas, Texas, USA.

have been a number of workshops on integrating computational thinking at the high school level [1, 6, 7]. But there is little research that has systematically and comprehensively examined the influence of computational thinking on pre-service teachers (i.e., education students).

Exploratory investigations have demonstrated how exposure to computational thinking enhances the way students approach problems. For example, Lewandowski et al. illustrated the idea of "commonsense programming" for students without programming experience [8]. Students were asked to propose solutions to avoid selling theater tickets for the same seat twice at multiple box offices. The results showed that 69% of the solutions correctly identified a race condition, which indicated that the students were indeed equipped with a natural but undeveloped understanding for solving problems computationally.

Several researchers have made the effort to introduce CT to in-service computer science high school teachers during workshop sessions that promote the awareness of integrating CS across all subject areas [3]. The high school teacher participants were reported to have extended their understanding of the scope of CS and considered CS as more than just programming. More importantly, a comparison of the pre- and post-survey indicated that the realization of the importance of "developing computational thinking skills for all aspects of life" emerged as a result of the workshop.

An important step for successfully integrating computational thinking into the K-12 curriculum is to prepare future teachers to teach it. Section 2 briefly describes our efforts to showcase a variety of CT concepts to pre-service teachers. In Section 3, we present a summary of our pre- and post-survey, which demonstrates a positive change of attitude among the students. We conclude the paper with an overall discussion in Section 4.

2. OVERVIEW OF THE CT MODULE

We developed a one-week computational thinking module for the course "Learning and Motivation," which is required for all elementary and secondary majors. The course introduces future K-12 teachers to basic concepts of classroom management, learning styles, student motivation, and assessment. The main content of the course includes theories of learning and motivation, the role of formal and informal assessment in fostering learning and motivation, and ways to adapt instruction both to individual students and differences in social, cultural, and contextual factors.

Since computational thinking naturally includes problem solving and understanding human behavior, it fits well with the topics already covered in class, such as probabilistic reasoning, algorithms and heuristics, and hypothesis testing. We replaced the originally presented unit on problem solving and critical thinking with new lectures on computational thinking. The purpose of the CT module was not only to expose students to ideas in computing, but to show how these ideas can be used in their future teaching careers as well.

Faculty and students from educational studies and computer science jointly developed the lecture material. Special emphasis was placed on highlighting the core concepts of computational thinking, while presenting material the students could relate to and easily apply in a K-12 classroom. The module was presented around the middle of the semester, and students had not been exposed to CT material in earlier lectures. Before the CT module was introduced, students had primarily studied educational theories on how people learn.

The CT lectures provided students with an overview of computational thinking and engaged them in activities that showcased CT principles. Students worked in pairs and each pair was given a "clicker" to provide responses. See the appendix for an outline of the lectures and clicker questions. The original slides are available on our website[1].

The first lecture introduced students to the definition of computational thinking and five basic CT concepts: problem identification and decomposition, abstraction, logical thinking, algorithms, and debugging. The concepts were introduced through examples, activities, and clicker questions. For example, debugging was discussed by asking students to troubleshoot the scenario of a lamp not working when they get home from school, but was working in the morning. Students used clickers to respond to a sequence of questions to locate the problem in order to make the lamp work again.

The second lecture focused on the role of computational thinking in day-to-day life, and emphasized the importance and application of CT in K-12 education. We discussed how problem-solving, abstraction, and critical thinking can be introduced in a classroom setting. The lecture highlighted how computational thinking is a useful tool for dealing with ill-defined problems, where there might not be a clear-cut solution and information needed to solve the problem may be missing. The lecture also presented information on how to teach algorithms through kinesthetic activities and gave an example of recursion. Several members of our project acted out the Towers of Hanoi (for $n = 5$). Finally, we provided examples of computational thinking in core content areas, such as science and humanities.

3. ATTITUDE SURVEY RESULTS

We assessed the students' attitudes toward computing and their understanding of computational thinking through a pre- and post-survey surrounding the CT module. All 155 students from the two sections of the course were emailed a link to the survey. 100 students — 78 female and 22 male — completed both the pre-survey the week before the CT module and the post-survey during the week after the CT module. As a motivation to participate, extra credit was given to students who completed both surveys (the pre- and post-surveys were anonymous, but linked together via answers to security questions).

The surveys consisted of sixteen multiple-choice questions (on a Likert scale from strongly agree to strongly disagree) and four open-ended questions — see the appendix for the complete post-survey. An external evaluator was responsible for collecting and validating the data. We analyzed the responses for patterns and significant differences between pre- and post-surveys. The most interesting results came from the participants' open-ended responses, which we present in this section.

Just over half of the students who responded (55) were preparing to teach at the elementary level; the remainder (45) at the secondary level. Approximately 80% of the elementary education participants were female (44 vs. 11), while at the secondary level, over 75% were female (34 vs. 11). About 65% of the students enrolled responded to the survey.

[1] `http://cs4edu.cs.purdue.edu/comp_think`

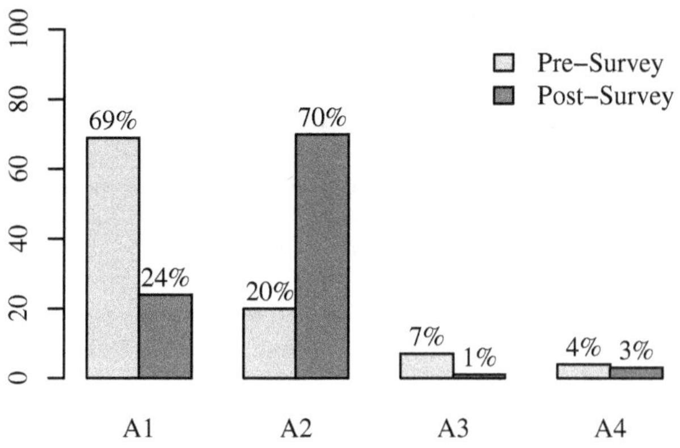

A1: To use computers and/or technology to solve a problem and make tasks easier
A2: The process of solving problems (use of computer or technology not mentioned)
A3: The study of computers
A4: Other

Figure 1: Participants' view of computing

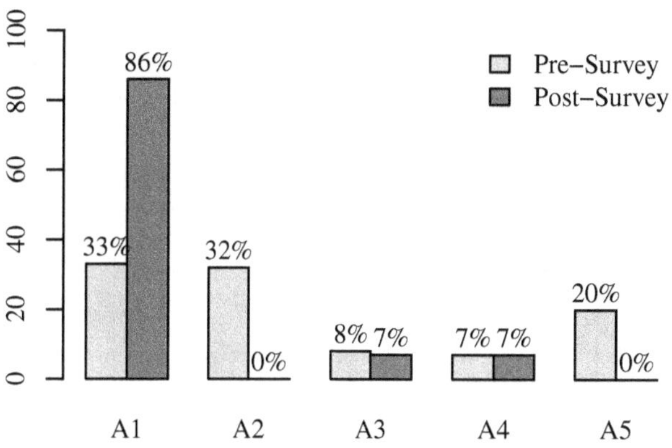

A1: The process of solving problems
A2: To use computers and/or technology to solve a problem or make tasks easier
A3: The study of computers; solving problems like a computer
A4: Other
A5: Not sure

Figure 2: Participants' view of CT

3.1 Participants' View of Computing

Survey participants were asked to describe their view of computing and its purpose. The basic trends of the participants' responses differed greatly from the pre- to post-survey, as shown in Figure 1. (Not all percentages add up to 100% due to blank responses.)

On the pre-survey, a majority (69%) of the participants' responses contained themes that viewed computing as *solving problems or making tasks easier through the use of computers and/or technology.* For example, one student stated, "Computing is the use of computers or some other form of technology to solve a problem. Its purpose is to help solve problems that might be more difficult to solve without some form of technology." Only 20% of participants' responded viewing computing and its purpose as *the process of solving problems (use of computer or technology not mentioned).* The following comment highlights computing as a process of solving problems without the use of computers or technology: "Computing is the science of solving a problem using some pre-set method that has been established. Its purpose is to assist us in solving everyday problems we might be faced with." Finally, 7% of the students reported computing as the study of computers. For example, "Being able to use and apply computer skills to daily life. These skills can run from typing to using different applications and software in many different areas."

In the post-survey, a majority of the participants' responses (70%) reflected the basic trend that viewed computing as *the ability/knowledge/process used to solve problems and make tasks easier (use of computer or technology not mentioned).* For example, a student highlighted this view of computing stating, "Computing is where you logically think something through. Its purpose is so that students can explore to find an answer to a problem." Another student reported, "I believe that computing does not necessarily involve working with computers but working to solve any type of problem. Its purpose is to calculate equations and problems to formulate a correct result." On the other hand, 24% viewed computing as *solving problems or making tasks easier through the use of computers and/or technology.* This view is highlighted by the following comments: "Computing is using technology or computer software to aid in solving problems. Its purpose is to make difficult tasks easier and simpler." Only one participant reported computing as the study of computers.

By de-emphasizing technology and encouraging algorithmic thinking, the lectures helped the education students understand that computational thinking doesn't always require the use of computers to solve problems.

3.2 Participants' View of CT

In both the pre- and post-survey, participants were asked to define computational thinking from their point of view. Figure 2 summarizes the basic trends in the participants' responses between the pre- and post-surveys. Although answers varied, we found basic trends among them. One third (33%) of participants' responses in the pre-survey reflected trends that viewed computational thinking as "the process of problem-solving," which increased to 86% on the post-survey. In addition, responses used more specific terminology and examples (e.g., pre-survey response: *process of solving problems,* post-survey response: *process of solving problems using algorithms, etc.*).

On the pre-survey, 20% of participants responded that they "didn't know" what their view on computational thinking was, and on the post-survey, none of the participants responded that they "didn't know." Additionally, on the pre-survey, where almost one third (33%) of participants' responses reflected trends regarding computational thinking as "the use of computers or technology to solve a problem or make tasks easier," none of the participants' responses on the post survey reflected the idea that computers and technology absolutely must be involved in the definition of computational thinking.

In short, many more students identified the relationship between problem solving and computational thinking after receiving the CT module.

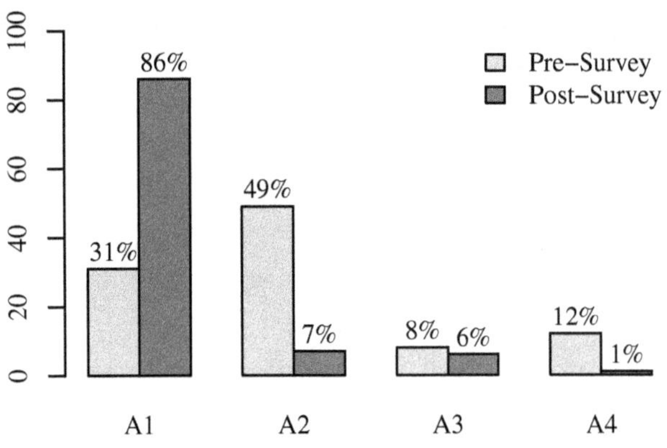

Figure 3: Integrating CT into the classroom

3.3 Integrating CT into the Classroom

Survey participants were also asked how computational thinking can be integrated into the K-12 classroom. Figure 3 summarizes their responses. On the pre-survey, almost half of the participants' responses reflected the view that in order to integrate computational thinking into the classroom, computers and technology were needed. In contrast, only 7% of participants' responses reflected that trend on the post-survey.

During the one week module, many students realized the benefits of understanding CT principles and being able to apply them more systematically as a problem solving technique. This change in attitude is also reflected in the question on whether CT promotes problem solving and critical thinking skills. The responses switched from 31% agreeing to 86% of the participants agreeing. Also, it seems every student had some concept about computational thinking after the module, as reflected by the "don't know" category.

In summary, we saw almost a three-fold increase in the number of education majors who now hold the opinion that computational thinking could be used to enhance problem solving activities in a K-12 classroom.

3.4 Relationship to Other Fields

We also asked the students about the relationship of computational thinking to other disciplines. While 30% indicated that "Computational thinking relates to any or all fields" in the pre-survey, that number rose to 62% in the post-survey. In addition, over 95% of the survey participants either agreed or strongly agreed with the following statements: "Computational thinking *can* be integrated into classroom education in other fields," "Computational thinking *should* be integrated into classroom education for other disciplines," and "Having background knowledge and understanding of computer science is valuable in and of itself."

As future work, we plan to embed computational thinking modules in content area courses and teaching methods courses, including hands-on training in how to implement kinesthetic activities like *Computer Science Unplugged* [2].

4. DISCUSSION

Results from the two surveys suggest that the CT module was effective overall in increasing the students' awareness of computational thinking. Specifically, the post-survey responses were more sophisticated and showcased students' understanding that computational thinking was more than using computers and technology. Students also had a better grasp of how computational thinking can be integrated into their future teaching by promoting problem solving and critical thinking skills (i.e., not by merely using computers).

These findings have important implications for incorporating computational thinking in education as well as other subject areas. Given that computational thinking is becoming a fundamental skill for the 21st century, it is important to introduce it in disciplines outside of computer science and at the K-12 level. Specifically, computational thinking concepts must appear as early as the primary grades, and then continue through the secondary grades and beyond [9]. One way to do this is to incorporate computational thinking modules into core education courses to expose future teachers to this idea. Results from the current work suggest that such an approach has the potential to change future teachers' understanding of computational thinking and how it can be integrated in their classrooms.

In summary, we have shown that given relevant information in computing, education students' attitude toward computing becomes more favorable. They also see applications of computing principles in their careers more readily. We plan to repeat the CT module in "Learning and Motivation" and are also developing an online version of the module for "Introduction to Educational Technology," another course required of all education majors. We hope that our approach to CT modules will attract education students into computing courses that emphasize computer science principles, as well as traditional programming courses.

5. ACKNOWLEDGEMENTS

This work was supported by the NSF CPATH program under grant CNS-0938999 and through a gift from State Farm. We especially thank Courtney Brown for her help with the administration of the two surveys. We also appreciate the CS4EDU team and the anonymous reviewers for their thoughtful feedback on the paper.

6. REFERENCES

[1] V. Allan, V. Barr, D. Brylow, and S. Hambrusch. Computational thinking in high school courses. In *SIGCSE*, 2010.

[2] T. Bell, I. H. Witten, and M. Fellows. Computer science unplugged. http://csunplugged.org/, December 2006.

[3] L. Blum and T. J. Cortina. CS4HS: An outreach program for high school CS teachers. In *SIGCSE*, 2007.

[4] A. Bundy. Computational thinking is pervasive. *Journal of Scientific and Practical Computing*, 1:67–69, 2007.

[5] Committee for the Workshops on Computational Thinking. *Report of a Workshop on The Scope and Nature of Computational Thinking*. The National Academies Press, 2010.

[6] D. D. Garcia, C. M. Lewis, J. P. Dougherty, and M. C. Jadud. If ________, you might be a computational thinker! In *SIGCSE*, 2010.

[7] P. B. Henderson, T. J. Cortina, and J. M. Wing. Computational thinking. In *SIGCSE*, 2007.

[8] G. Lewandowski, D. Bouvier, R. McCartney, K. Sanders, and B. Simon. Commonsense computing (episode 3): Concurrency and concert tickets. In *ICER '07: Proceedings of the Third International Workshop on Computing Education Research*, 2007.

[9] J. A. Qualls and L. B. Sherrell. Why computational thinking should be integrated into the curriculum. *Journal of Comp. Sci. in Colleges*, 25:66–71, 2010.

[10] J. Wing. Computational thinking. *Communications of the ACM*, 49:33–35, 2006.

APPENDIX

A. OUTLINE OF THE CT MODULE

Lecture 1: Computational Thinking and 21st Century Problem Solving

1. Object lesson: driving directions
    - "How do you get from school to the mall?" Clicker questions 1–2
    - "How did you think about the problem?" CT concepts: *Algorithm, Efficiency*
    - "What if the main road was closed?" CT concepts: *Debugging*
    - "How do computers solve this problem?" CT concepts: *Abstraction, Automation*
2. What is computational thinking?
    - An approach to *problem solving* which uses abstraction to create *algorithmic solutions* which can be automated with computation.
    - A *fundamental skill* used by everyone by the middle of the 21st century (i.e., just like reading, writing, and arithmetic).
3. Daily examples of CT
    - Looking up names in a phone book
    - Buying movie tickets (multiple lines)
    - Clicker question 3
    - CT is ..., CT is *not* ...
4. Concept #1: Abstraction
    - "CT is reformulating a seemingly difficult problem into one we know how to solve."
    - People standing in line → *Queue*
    - Cafeteria plates → *Stack*
5. Concept #2: Logical Thinking
    - Inductive reasoning: observation → pattern → hypothesis → theory
    - Deductive reasoning: theory → hypothesis → observation → confirm
6. Concept #3: Algorithms
    - Activity: "peanut butter and jelly sandwich"
    - Explain "write it/ do it" (Science Olympiad)
    - Homework: "swap puzzle" on cs4fn.org
7. Concept #4: Debugging
    - Clicker questions 4–5
    - Discuss reasoning behind each answer

Lecture 2: Computational Thinking in K-12

1. Review of previous lecture
    - Clicker questions 1–3
    - CT Concepts: decomposition, abstraction, logical thinking, algorithms, debugging, automation
    - More definitions for CT
2. Why is CT important for K-12?
    - Enhances problem solving techniques
    - Moves students beyond technology literacy
    - CT is a higher-level cognitive process
3. CT and problem solving strategies
    - *Heuristic*: an experience-based strategy that facilitates problem solving
    - *Algorithm*: a specific sequence of steps that guarantees a solution
4. How do you teach algorithms?
    - Demonstrate specific procedures; apply examples
    - Help students explain their thinking and debug
    - Role play: Towers of Hanoi
5. Using technology to motivate CT
    - Facebook friend network visualization
    - Google's public data explorer
    - Amazon/Netflix/etc recommendations
    - "What other tools have you seen?"
6. Applying CT to any content area
    - Science, Social Studies, Economics, ...
    - Social Sciences, Medicine, Humanities, ...
7. The big picture
    - CT is a fundamental skill for *everybody*
    - State of computing in secondary education
    - Highlight "CS Principles" proposed AP course

B. CLICKER QUESTIONS

Lecture 1 (Intro to CT)

1. How extensive were your directions?

[A] One step (e.g., type "mall" into GPS or Google Maps)
[B] Two steps (e.g., from downtown take bus #4)
[C] Several steps (e.g., head east on SR-15 to 3rd Street)
[D] A detailed, turn-by-turn route (e.g., from the union)
[E] None of the above (e.g., "Man, I was way off!")

2. How did you figure out the driving directions?

[A] Knew them already; simply "recalled" the route
[B] Sketched out a high-level map on paper
[C] Thought about several ways, picked one
[D] Texted a friend when no one was looking
[E] Modeled the entire city as an undirected graph, solved the "single-pair shortest path problem," and applied it to the source and destination

3. What is the quickest way to serve 20 pizzas to 60 hungry students?

[A] One table with pizzas (the usual case)

[B] Five tables with four pizzas each

[C] People stay put and pizzas are passed around

[D] Four servers bringing the pizza around

Scenario: You come home and the desk lamp in your apartment stopped working (it worked in the morning).

4. What is your first step to solve the problem?

[A] Check if the lamp is turned on

[B] Check if the light bulb is working

[C] Check if the lamp is plugged in

[D] Check if the outlet is working

[E] Check if there is power in the room

Scenario: You checked A-E and it is still not working.

5: What do you do next?

[A] Buy a new lamp

[B] Call your mother/friend/landlord/etc

[C] Use your roommate's lamp

[D] Repeat steps A-E from before

[E] Forget about the problem for the day

Lecture 2 (Review of CT)

1. What are the two main ideas of computational thinking?

[A] Abstraction and Automation

[B] Algorithm and Analysis

[C] Debugging and Logical Thinking

[D] All of the above

2. Computational thinking relies on the use of computer programs.

[A] True

[B] False

3. Computational thinking mainly involves computer science and has little impact on other subject areas.

[A] True

[B] False

C. POST-SURVEY

Indicate whether you (1) strongly agree, (2) agree, (3) disagree, or (4) strongly disagree.

1. Knowledge of computing will allow me to secure a better job.
2. My career goals do not require that I learn computing skills.
3. I doubt that I can solve problems by using computer applications.
4. I expect to use software in my future educational and career work.
5. I can achieve good grades (C or better) in computing courses.
6. The challenge of solving problems using computer science appeals to me.
7. I expect to use computer applications for future projects involving teamwork.
8. I can learn to understand computing concepts.
9. I am not comfortable with learning computing concepts.
10. I expect to use computing skills in my daily life.
11. I hope that my future career will require the use of computing concepts.
12. I think that computer science is interesting.
13. I will voluntarily take computing courses if I were given the opportunity.
14. Computational thinking can be integrated into classroom education in other fields.
15. Computational thinking should be integrated into classroom education for other disciplines.
16. Having background knowledge and understanding of computer science is valuable in and of itself.

Open-ended questions

1. In your view, what is computing? What is its purpose?
2. In your view, what is computational thinking?
3. How can we integrate computational thinking in the classroom?
4. How does computational thinking relate to other disciplines and fields? Please provide specific examples.

CodeWrite: Supporting Student-Driven Practice of Java

Paul Denny, Andrew Luxton-Reilly, Ewan Tempero, Jacob Hendrickx
Department of Computer Science
The University of Auckland
Auckland, New Zealand
{paul,andrew,ewan}@cs.auckland.ac.nz,jhen095@aucklanduni.ac.nz

ABSTRACT

Drill and practice exercises enable students to master skills needed for more sophisticated programming. A barrier to providing such activities is the effort required to set up the programming environment. Testing is an important component to writing good software, but it is difficult to motivate students to write tests. In this paper we describe and evaluate CodeWrite, a web-based tool that provides drill and practice support for Java programming, and for which testing plays a central role in its use. We describe how we have used CodeWrite in a CS1 course, and demonstrate its effectiveness in providing good coverage of the language features presented in the course.

Categories and Subject Descriptors

K.3.2 [**Computers and Education**]: Computer and Information Science Education—*computer science education*

General Terms

Design, Human Factors

Keywords

CodeWrite, contributing student pedagogy, assessment, online, student-generated content, constructive evaluation

1. INTRODUCTION

One innovative approach for encouraging students to practice programming and to focus on testing is to challenge them to develop a shared repository of short programming exercises. Students develop associated test cases for the exercises they author, and receive immediate feedback on their own code when solving exercises created by their peers. This learning activity is supported by CodeWrite, a web-based tool. We report here on our experience using CodeWrite in a Java-based CS1 course.

Learning to program, as with any skill, requires practice. Syntax must be mastered, principles need to be understood, and techniques for problem solving need to be developed through regular effort. Programming is a practical subject and consequently much of the learning takes place at a computer while students tackle assignments or lab exercises, both of which are common forms of assessment in introductory programming courses [7]. However, due to their scope, assignments often require background reading or related contexts to be understood before a student can make progress. Similarly, lab exercises may require students to download resource files or configure their programming environment before code can be written. While writing complete programs is critical for developing basic design skills, it can be complemented by the repetitive practice of fundamentals. Drill and practice activities have a low cognitive load, but enable students to master the skills prerequisite for solving more sophisticated programming assignments [13]. CodeWrite presents students with a large repository of short programming exercises with which they can practice. They can begin writing code immediately, and can use the tool from any computer with a browser and network connection.

An important component of writing good software is the ability to design and execute effective tests. The teaching of testing in academia has begun to mature [3], however there is still debate as to how it should be taught and when it should be introduced in a curriculum [16, 17]. A barrier to integrating testing into the first year programming course is that beginners may struggle to appreciate the purpose of testing — it needs to be incentivized. A study by Barrio-canal et al. into whether students enjoy writing test cases reported that, when given the choice, only 10% of the class developed tests for their assignments [2]. Testing is central to the way CodeWrite works as exercise authors begin by defining the set of tests that characterize their exercise. Only once these test cases have been developed, and the exercise author has contributed an implementation that satisfies the tests, is the exercise available to other students. The incentive for developing test cases is clear as they are necessary to automatically verify and provide feedback on code submitted by the class.

In CodeWrite, students are responsible for developing the exercises which are shared with their classmates, a pedagogical approach called constructive evaluation [11]. CodeWrite shares some of the benefits offered by peer review, a learning activity that has been used successfully in a range of contexts over many years [1, 10]. One specific advantage of peer review in programming courses is that a student is exposed to a variety of solutions to a problem they have also solved. Chinn suggests this may enable students to recognize there are multiple correct solutions to a given problem [8], thus advancing them in Perry's scheme of intellectual development [15]. A comparison of solutions can reveal alternative techniques for writing code that may be more succint and easier to understand than their own. Once students successfully answer an exercise in CodeWrite, they are given access to the solutions for that exercise contributed by their peers. Students can then take part in a light-weight peer review process where they rate the quality of the exercise, provide feedback to the exercise author in the form of comments, and endorse solutions contributed by their peers.

In this paper, we describe the CodeWrite tool and report on its use in a CS1 course at the University of Auckland. Our primary focus is the language feature coverage of the exercises in the CodeWrite repository, and the variety and feature coverage of the submitted solutions.

2. RELATED WORK

Palma [13] emphasises the importance of building confidence using drill and practice, particularly for female students, before progressing on to writing larger sections of code. Plentiful opportunities for drill and practice are provided by Parlante's CodingBat tool (previously named JavaBat) [14]. CodingBat is a web-based system that includes a database of exercises expressed as short descriptions of the specification for a single method. Students using CodingBat need only write the method body, and they get immediate feedback in the form of passed or failed test cases that are highlighted green or red. In addition to the large bank of available exercises, course instructors may author their own exercises. The purpose of CodingBat is to build student skill and confidence by presenting them with many practice problems, and unlike larger assignments that may include a realistic context and backstory [19], it is not intended to motivate the bigger picture of Computer Science. Confidence building is also the motivation behind Edmonson's use of proglets [5]. Well designed proglets allow students to focus on a single aspect of a programming problem, highlighting fundamentals and helping students build confidence before being asked to produce "assignment quality" code.

Incorporating software testing into the curriculum continues to be a challenge in academia [3]. Test driven development (TDD) has been suggested as a process that offers promise in the classroom, and a growing body of evidence to support its use sits alongside a number of innovative tools [6, 18] to realize its benefits. Test driven learning (TDL) is a somewhat more general approach that proposes introducing testing early and has been successfully employed in first-year programming classes [9, 4]. The goal of TDL is to encourage students to think about the kinds of errors that may occur in their code, and to develop tests to ensure such errors are not present.

The CodeWrite tool presented in this paper emphasises testing by requiring exercise authors to define test cases prior to implementation, presents opportunities for peer feedback and comparison, and provides students with many simple confidence-building exercises for drill and practice.

3. CODEWRITE

When developing a new exercise in CodeWrite, a student provides both a brief and a detailed description of the purpose of a method. The brief description is displayed as a preview to students selecting an exercise to answer from the repository (figure 1). The detailed description is shown once an exercise is selected to be answered, and should include all the information necessary to complete the method definition. Ideally, this description should include several examples of inputs and output for the method. The exercise author then defines the method signature. The return type of the method is selected from a drop-down list. The method name should ideally be descriptive of the task and up to 5 parameters can be defined, again with their types being selected from a drop-down list. The types are restricted to a subset of the most commonly used primitive types, arrays of these types, Strings and String arrays.

Figure 1: List of available exercises, indicating which have been successfully completed (green), attempted (red), or not attempted (gray).

Next, the test cases must be defined. CodeWrite displays several rows of empty input and output text boxes, derived from the method signature. Each row corresponds to one test case, and the student types the input values and the output value directly into the empty boxes on a row to define one test case. Initially three rows are shown, but the form is expandable and the student can add up to 10 test cases if they wish.

Once the form is submitted, the exercise is in a pending state. Before the exercise is visible to other students in the class, the author must provide an implementation of the method that passes all of the test cases they have defined. If any issues are detected at this stage, the student can edit the exercise. Once an implementation that passes all provided test cases has been provided, the exercise becomes available to other students in the class.

A student practicing writing code with CodeWrite can sort the exercises chronologically or by the quality ratings assigned to the exercises by their peers (figure 1). Once an individual exercise is selected, the detailed description of the exercise is displayed, and a text area is shown beneath

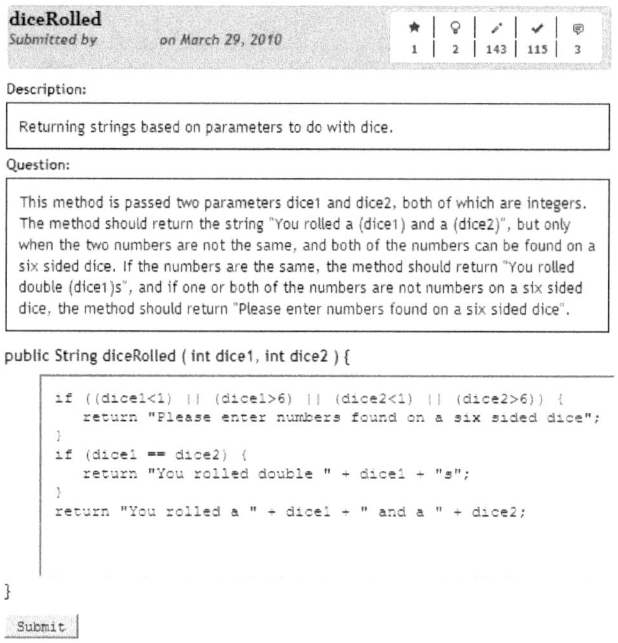

Figure 2: A student enters their solution to an exercise into the text-box provided.

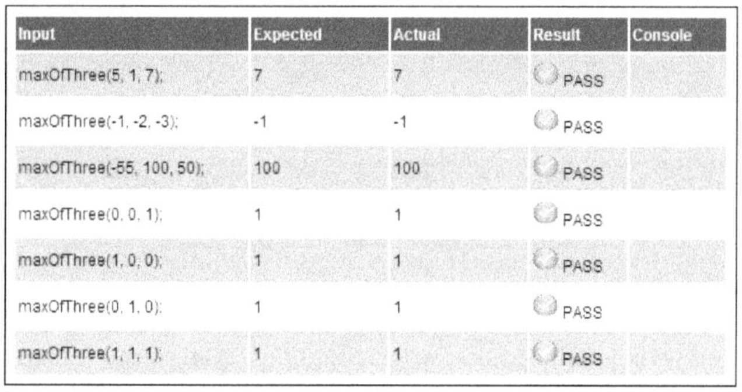

Input	Expected	Actual	Result	Console
maxOfThree(5, 1, 7);	7	7	PASS	
maxOfThree(-1, -2, -3);	-1	-1	PASS	
maxOfThree(-55, 100, 50);	100	100	PASS	
maxOfThree(0, 0, 1);	1	1	PASS	
maxOfThree(1, 0, 0);	1	1	PASS	
maxOfThree(0, 1, 0);	1	1	PASS	
maxOfThree(1, 1, 1);	1	1	PASS	

Figure 3: Feedback to student indicating test case results for submission.

the method signature into which the student can type their implementation, as shown in figure 2.

Upon submitting their answer, all of the test cases are shown and the student receives immediate feedback about which of the test cases passed or failed (figure 3). If the code contains a syntax error, the compiler message is shown to the student. There is no limit on the number of attempts that a student may make, and once all of the tests pass the exercise is highlighted green to indicate successful completion. Following this, the student is able browse all successful answers submitted by other students for that question (figure 4).

4. METHODOLOGY

4.1 Context of use

The COMPSCI 101 course at the University of Auckland is a 12 week CS1 course in Java taken primarily by students intending to major in Computer Science. Students attend three one-hour lectures and one two-hour lab session per

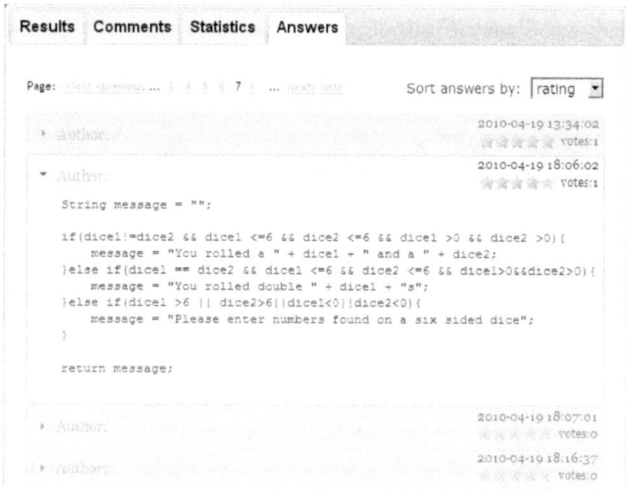

Figure 4: Browsing other successful solutions.

week. CodeWrite was introduced to the class at the end of Week 4 by way of a 10 minute demonstration in the lecture. Attendance in lectures is not compulsory (typically attendance rates are around 50% of enrolled students) so a short document was also prepared that included several screenshots and explained the basic process of authoring an exercise with test cases and submitting a solution to an existing exercise. The topic of "methods and parameter passing" was introduced during the lectures of Week 3, and students were given relevant exercises during the lab sessions of Week 4. Therefore when the CodeWrite activity was introduced to the class, students already had some practical experience writing methods.

Students were required to contribute one exercise, and to successfully answer 10 exercises (all test cases passing) to meet the participation requirements of the activity. They were not restricted regarding the content of the exercise, other than being asked to target only language features that had been covered in class. A categorization of these language features is given in Table 1.

Table 1: Java language features learned by students

Feature	Example syntax
Assignment	`=`
Arithmetic	`+,-,*,/,++,+=,...`
API use	String.substring(), Math.max(), Integer.parseInt(), ...
Relationals	`==, <, <=, ...`
Logicals	`&&, ||, !`
Conditionals	`if, else if, else`
Arrays	`[], .length`
Loops	`for, while, do`

Completing the participation requirements contributed 1% towards the final grade of a student. Although they were given 4 weeks to complete this activity, only 2 of these weeks were during the semester as there was a 2-week mid-semester break during this time. The final deadline for the activity, the end of Week 6, was the day of the mid-term test for the course that contributed 15% of the final grade.

4.2 Research questions

Our primary focus in this paper is to investigate how well the CodeWrite activity supports students in practicing the language features taught in the course. Specifically, our investigation considers the 8 language features in Table 1 and the extent to which these have been used by students when solving CodeWrite exercises.

> RQ1: Do the exercises in the CodeWrite repository encourage the use of all of the features of Java the students have been taught?

This question addresses the concern that students may have built a repository of exercises that does not require students to practice the complete range of language features. We say a question encourages the use of a feature if there is at least one successful submission for the question that makes use of the feature. For each feature, we calculate the total number of questions in the repository in which it is used.

> RQ2: When solving exercises from CodeWrite, do students use the full range of features they have been taught?

This question addresses the concern that even if the repository does offer good coverage of the language features, many students may not practice with the full range. We say a student uses a feature if there is at least one successful submission by the student that makes use of the feature. For each feature, we calculate the total number of students in the class who have practiced using it. We also, for each student, determine the number of features used by that student.

> RQ3: Are students exposed to a variety of solutions for a given exercise?

Once a successful submission for an exercise has been made, the student is able to see how their peers have answered the same exercise. The greater the variety of these solutions, the greater the opportunity for comparison and for making judgements about their quality. For this analysis, we considered solutions to the ten exercises with the greatest number of successful solutions. We measured variety by looking at the length and complexity of successful solutions to each of these exercises.

5. RESULTS

In this section we summarize the overall use of the system and report on our analysis of the code students have submitted while using CodeWrite.

In the results given below, we removed from our analysis any student that did not sit the final exam. Also, during data collection, there was a short period of time where one of the CodeWrite modules stopped functioning correctly. Submissions made by students during this time were recorded, however students did not receive feedback on their submissions. We have removed from our analysis all student submissions where feedback was not correctly received (amounting to 3.9% of total submissions). Table 2 summarizes the number of solutions that were submitted by students across 280 available exercises.

The majority of the students in the course logged in to CodeWrite and submitted at least one successful solution, however, relatively few students met the requirements of the assessment task (i.e. authored 1 exercise and submitted successful solutions to 10 exercises). We speculate perhaps that 1% of the final grade was insufficient motivation for a majority of the students. A summary of the number of students using CodeWrite is given in table 3.

Table 2: Summary of CodeWrite repository contents

Description	N
Total number of passing submissions:	3939
Total number of failing submissions:	4708
Total number of non-compiling submissions:	11604
Total number of submissions:	20251

Table 3: Summary of the students using CodeWrite

Description	N
Students with exam marks	437
... and submitted something to CodeWrite	330
... and a successful CodeWrite solution	299
... and met the requirements	138
... and answered more than required	102

5.1 Do the exercises in the repository encourage use of all the syntax taught?

If a student has used a language feature in a successful solution to an exercise, then we consider that the exercise has encouraged the student to practice with that feature. Since there are many possible solutions for a given exercise, we categorized the exercise as pertaining to a given topic if there was any occurrence of the corresponding Java language feature in any of the successful submissions to that exercise. The columns labelled *Questions* in table 4 summarize the number and percentage of questions that have had at least one successful solution containing a language feature corresponding to each topic.

From the table we can see that 88% of the exercises have at least one solution that uses the assignment operator. Although this is unsurprising given that assignment is a simple and common language feature, we see that 52% of exercises evoke the use of a conditional in at least one solution, one quarter of the exercises have a solution that uses a loop, and 17% of the exercises have a least one successful solution that uses an array. We believe that this shows good evidence that the exercises provide ample opportunities for students to use

Table 4: Number and percentage of students that practiced each topic

Topic	Questions		Students	
N	280	%	299	%
Assignment	247	88	286	95
Arithmetic	215	76	283	94
API use	181	64	282	94
Relationals	161	57	265	88
Logicals	69	24	206	68
Conditionals	147	52	257	85
Loops	72	25	159	53
Arrays	49	17	72	24

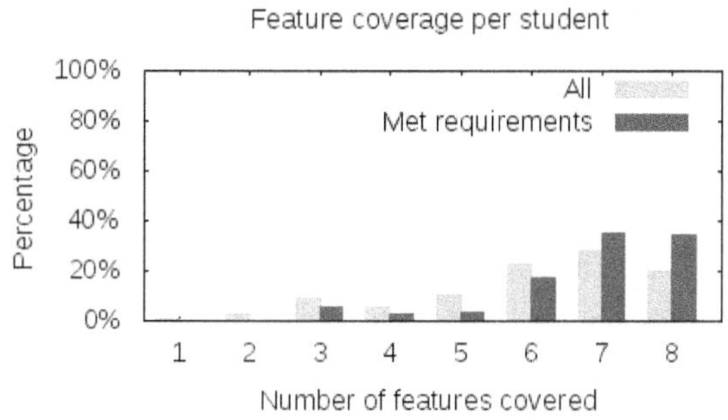

Figure 5: Percentage of students using a given number of features in successful solutions.

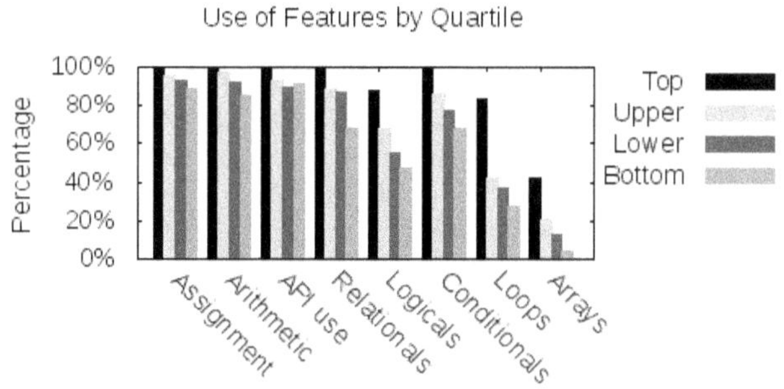

Figure 6: Percentage of students using a specific feature in successful solutions per quartile.

the full range of language constructs they have been taught. We also note that arrays and loops were covered in Week 5 of the course, one week prior to the activity deadline, and hence students had less exposure to these topics than those taught earlier.

5.2 Do students practice the full range of topics taught when solving exercises?

The columns labelled *Students* in Table 4 show the number and percentage of students that have practiced a given topic.

We can see that the majority of students used language features corresponding to most topics in the course, although "harder" topics have been used by fewer students. Slightly more than half (53%) of the students submitted at least one solution that used a loop, and almost one quarter (24%) wrote code that used an array.

Figure 5 shows how many topics an individual student covered over all successful submissions made by that student. Each cluster shows the proportion of students whose submissions covered a particular number of topics. The left bar in each cluster (light grey) considers all 299 students who made at least one successful submission, whereas the right bar (dark grey) considers only the 138 students who met the course requirements for use of CodeWrite (i.e. contributed at least 1 and successfully answered at least 10 exercises). So, 28.4% of all students covered 7 of the 8 topics, whereas 35.5% of those who met the requirements covered 7 of the 8 topics. 87.7% of students who met the requirements of the CodeWrite activity practiced with at least 6 of the 8 language features.

Figure 6 shows the breakdown of the *Students* column in Table 4 by quartile. Each cluster corresponds to one of the topics, with the first bar being for the top quartile and the 4th bar for the bottom quartile. So for the "Arithmetic" topic, 99% of the students in the top quartile submitted a solution that passed all tests and used some form of arithmetic, whereas the results for the other quartiles were 97%, 92%, and 85% respectively. This pattern of decreasing use of features across quartiles reflects the decreasing participation rates by each quartile.

5.3 Are students exposed to a variety of solutions?

To answer this question, we considered the ten exercises with the greatest number of successful solutions. For each, we examined the variability of the non-comment, non-blank number of lines of code (loc) and the Cyclomatic Complexity Number (CCN) [12] of their successful solutions. These solutions are visible to a student once an exercise is successfully answered.

Table 5 summarizes these two metrics for each of the ten most popular exercises. From this table, we can see that there is substantial variation in the number of lines of code for most questions, and that the CCN (i.e. the control flow) shows substantial variation for most exercises. However, some exercises, such as *getPower* and *gstRate* show little variation in CCN.

We can conclude that students using the CodeWrite system are likely to encounter a variety of different successful solutions to the same problems.

Table 5: Variety of answers submitted to the ten most popular exercises

Question	N	loc min	loc max	loc avg	ccn min	ccn max	ccn avg
maxOfThree	244	1	16	3.20	1	7	1.44
willEatFood	192	1	14	5.35	1	9	3.06
isOddSum	190	1	11	5.23	1	6	1.86
minOfSix	182	1	17	4.22	1	17	1.35
getInitials	116	1	14	3.93	1	5	1.05
getBackwStr	105	1	11	5.87	1	4	2.00
diceRolled	102	3	18	8.74	3	15	7.07
gstRate	76	1	6	2.05	1	1	1.00
interlveStr	85	5	31	13.04	3	15	4.45
getPower	66	1	5	1.61	1	2	1.02

5.4 Gender differences

Although it wasn't one of our research questions, we investigated the degree to which male and female students engaged with CodeWrite. Of the students who sat the exam (i.e completed the course), 22.2% were female. We noted that 22.7% of the students who submitted at least one solution were female, consistent with the percentage of female students in the course.

6. DISCUSSION

As noted above, the solutions varied in length and complexity, indicating different solution approaches from quite naive to very sophisticated. For example, one exercise, named `getLettersNotUsed`, required students to calculate all of the letters not used in a particular String, and return these unused letters. One of the less sophisticated solutions to this

```
String unusedLetters = "";
if ((text.indexOf("a")==-1) && (text.indexOf("A")==-1)) {
  unusedLetters = unusedLetters + "a";
}
if ((text.indexOf("b")==-1) && (text.indexOf("B")==-1)) {
  unusedLetters = unusedLetters + "b";
}
if ((text.indexOf("c")==-1) && (text.indexOf("C")==-1)) {
  unusedLetters = unusedLetters + "c";
}
....
if ((text.indexOf("z")==-1) && (text.indexOf("Z")==-1)) {
  unusedLetters = unusedLetters + "z";
}
return unusedLetters;
```

Figure 7: Excerpt of successful solution to `getLettersNotUsed` (reformatted for space).

problem involved a sequence of 26 conditional statements, each of which included a test for both upper and lower case characters. An extract of this is shown in figure 7. The student who developed this solution, would immediately have access to other solutions, including a more elegant example that first converts the input to lower case and utilizes character codes within a loop.

Upon submitting a solution to an exercise, students are shown all test cases for the exercise. The intent is to provide guidance, and to encourage students to complete the exercise so that they may move on to another. We observed a very small number of cases where students created a passing solution to an exercise simply by looking at the test cases and writing a conditional statement that returned the expected value given the appropriate input. Tools such as CodingBat, where the exercises are prepared by an instructor, prevent such reverse engineering by including private test cases that are not seen by the student. One difficulty with this approach in CodeWrite is that students could (either accidentally or maliciously) contribute a private test that makes the exercise unsolvable without knowing what the test is. One possible solution, to prevent reverse engineering of solutions, would be to hide a single test case chosen at random for each student.

7. CONCLUSIONS AND FUTURE WORK

In this paper, we have described the CodeWrite tool and demonstrated its effectiveness in providing good coverage of the language features presented in a CS1 course. Examination of a repository of 280 exercises indicated that all course topics were covered (with 17% of the exercises encouraging use of arrays, and up to 88% encouraging use of variable assignment). We found that students practicing with CodeWrite would develop code covering many of the topics taught in the course (nearly 90% of those students answering at least 10 exercises practiced with at least 6 of the 8 topics). Exercises in CodeWrite also attracted a variety of solutions, all of which are viewable by students upon submission of their own successful solution.

Future work will investigate whether use of CodeWrite as a drill and practice tool has an effect on the confidence and performance of students tackling larger programming assignments and formal examinations.

8. REFERENCES

[1] R. Ballantyne, K. Hughes, and A. Mylonas. Developing procedures for implementing peer assessment in large classes using an action research process. *Assessment and Evaluation in Higher Education*, 27(5):427–441, 2002.

[2] E. G. Barriocanal, M.-A. S. Urbán, I. A. Cuevas, and P. D. Pérez. An experience in integrating automated unit testing practices in an introductory programming course. *SIGCSE Bull.*, 34(4):125–128, 2002.

[3] C. Desai, D. Janzen, and K. Savage. A survey of evidence for test-driven development in academia. *SIGCSE Bull.*, 40(2):97–101, 2008.

[4] C. Desai, D. S. Janzen, and J. Clements. Implications of integrating test-driven development into cs1/cs2 curricula. In *SIGCSE '09*, pages 148–152, 2009.

[5] C. Edmondson. Proglets for first-year programming in java. *SIGCSE Bull.*, 41(2):108–112, 2009.

[6] S. H. Edwards. Improving student performance by evaluating how well students test their own programs. *J. Educ. Resour. Comput.*, 3(3):1, 2003.

[7] S. H. Edwards, J. Börstler, L. N. Cassel, M. S. Hall, and J. Hollingsworth. Developing a common format for sharing programming assignments. *SIGCSE Bull.*, 40(4):167–182, 2008.

[8] E. F. Gehringer, D. D. Chinn, M. A. Pérez-Qui nones, and M. A. Ardis. Using peer review in teaching computing. In *SIGCSE '05*, pages 321–322, 2005.

[9] D. Janzen and H. Saiedian. Test-driven learning in early programming courses. In *SIGCSE '08*, pages 532–536, 2008.

[10] A. Luxton-Reilly. A systematic review of tools that support peer assessment. *Computer Science Education*, 19(4):209–232, Dec 2009.

[11] A. Luxton-Reilly and P. Denny. Constructive evaluation: a pedagogy of student-contributed assessment. *Computer Science Education*, 20:145–167, 2010. Accepted for publication.

[12] T. J. Mccabe. A complexity measure. *Software Engineering, IEEE Transactions on*, SE-2(4):308–320, 1976.

[13] P. D. Palma. Viewpoint: Why women avoid computer science. *Commun. ACM*, 44(6):27–30, 2001.

[14] N. Parlante. Nifty reflections. *SIGCSE Bull.*, 39(2):25–26, 2007.

[15] W. Perry. *Forms of Intellectual and Ethical Development in the College Years.* Holt, Rinehart, Winston, New York, 1970.

[16] T. Shepard, M. Lamb, and D. Kelly. More testing should be taught. *Commun. ACM*, 44(6):103–108, 2001.

[17] J. Spacco and W. Pugh. Helping students appreciate test-driven development (tdd). In *OOPSLA '06 Companion*, pages 907–913, 2006.

[18] J. Spacco, W. Pugh, N. Ayewah, and D. Hovemeyer. The marmoset project: an automated snapshot, submission, and testing system. In *OOPSLA '06 Companion*, pages 669–670, 2006.

[19] D. E. Stevenson and P. J. Wagner. Developing real-world programming assignments for cs1. In *ITICSE '06*, pages 158–162, 2006.

e-Learning Experience using Recommender Systems

Jesus Bobadilla, Antonio Hernando, Angel Arroyo
Universidad Politécnica de Madrid, Crta. De Valencia, Km. 7
28031 Madrid, Spain
+34 913365133
jesus.bobadilla@upm.es, ahernando@eui.upm.es, aarroyo@eui.upm.es

ABSTRACT

This paper presents the results obtained using a real e-learning recommender system where the collaborative filtering core has been adapted with the aim of weighting the importance of the recommendations in accordance with the users' knowledge. In this way, ratings from users with better knowledge of the given subject will have greater importance over ratings from users with less knowledge.

In the same way, we validate the results obtained and we adjust, with just one parameter, the weight that should be awarded, in each specific e-learning recommender system, to the ratings of the users with the best reputation.

The results obtained show a notable improvement regarding traditional collaborative filtering methods and suggest balanced weightings between the importance assigned to users with more or less knowledge.

Categories and Subject Descriptors

K.3.2 [**Computer and Information Science Education**]

General Terms

Experimentation.

Keywords

Recommender Systems; e-learning; collaborative filtering.

1. INTRODUCTION

The social web is leading to positive changes in the way we approach many different aspects of our everyday lives. Nowadays, we often take into consideration the opinions, experiences, tastes and information provided by other people that we do not even know, but whom we turn to more and more when doing our shopping, planning our holidays, choosing the films we watch, selecting the news we read, etc. Of course, in general, we do not base our opinions on the information provided by just one user or even a few users, but rather, we immerse ourselves in a series of searches via one or more web 2.0 websites in order to obtain information that we did not know and that it would be hard to find on non-social websites (e.g. the story of the entertaining late-night chats with the owner of a house who rents out rooms in a national park in New Zealand). We just need to find various congruent comments in order to make a decision on whether to stay at that place or not and, in general, we will make the right decision and will add our experience and comments to reinforce the choice of that destination by future travelers.

Therefore, the social web helps us in our everyday lives as it enables us to access all kinds of information that is not necessarily institutional or structured, provided by any other person. It represents progress made in the existing possibilities regarding traditional websites; however, throughout their rapid expansion, social webs have come across the same problem as their non-social predecessors: sifting out suitable information from a huge and growing number of opinions, posts, photos, videos, texts, etc.

The tools most commonly used to search for the information that best adapts to our expectations are still the traditional search engines (Google, Yahoo,…); we can also see a social tendency to gather in social mega-webs (the most famous of which is Facebook) where we are much more likely to find what we are looking for. With addition of powerful technology compatible with the above-mentioned tools we have recommender systems (RS); At present, recommender systems (RS) comprise an important collaboration tool among Web 2.0 users [21,25,19], providing services that enable accurate recommendations to be made to internet users who have been previously defined according to their preferences in a certain field.

Nowadays, the most broadly-studied RS focus on recommending films [23,2,24] based on votes previously made by users, who have therefore defined their preferences on a limited number of these films. Nevertheless, RS have been introduced to a greater extent in the collaborative systems environment and they cover a large number of applications [4,12] in which it is useful to receive recommendations based on the preferences of a group of users with similar tastes or needs to those of each individual that makes use of these systems; in the commercial environment, the most widely demanded RS applications are those that refer to e-commerce [20,8,31].

Traditionally, papers published in the area of RS research have been based on studies of general validity, which can be equally applied to any type of RS and are normally based on results obtained using existing public databases (which usually contain film ratings). However, it is now possible to find studies focusing on different specific types of RS, such as e-learning RS [26,11,10,17,14,3].

The basic principle of RS is the expectation that the group of users similar to one given user, (i.e. those that have rated an important number of elements in a similar way to the user) can be used to adequately predict that individual's ratings on products the user has no knowledge of. This way, a trip to Senegal could be recommended to an individual who has rated different destinations in the Caribbean very highly, based on the positive ratings about the holiday destination of "Senegal" of an important number of individuals who also rated destinations in the Caribbean very highly. This suggestion (recommendation) will often provide the user of the service with inspiring information from the collective knowledge of all other users of the service.

In short, the internal operating core of RS is based on carrying out collaborative filtering (CF) [1,16] starting from the ratings expressed by a group of users about a group of items, the aim is to select users who have the most similar ratings or tastes to those of the individual who is using the system at any one time. In general, the objective is to suggest a series of elements to the individual, on which this individual have not shown a preference but which have been very highly rated by an important proportion of the group of users with similar preferences to the individual.

The quality of the results offered by a RS greatly depends on the quality of the results provided by its CF [1] phase; i.e. it is essential to be capable of adequately selecting the group of users most similar to a given individual. Two main different approaches are available to tackle this important task: memory-based methods and model based methods.

Memory-based methods [7,22,30], use metrics [14,30] that are directly applied to the data matrix that contains the ratings made by the set of users of the system on the set of items available. The current RS for commercial use employ memory-based methods due to their robustness, predictability and efficiency.

Model based methods use data to create a model: bayesian classifier [9], neural network [18], fuzzy system [32], etc. and from this model they predict the clusters of similar users. Model based methods are generally found in the research stage, in the implementation of recommender systems for non-commercial use.

Although a great variety of metrics capable of implementing the CF have been published, most of the systems only use two ways of measuring the distance between users: cosine and Pearson correlation. This is due to the fact that these metrics have obtained the best results in various research projects and that their behavior in RS is satisfactory.

Regardless of the method used in the CF stage, the technical objective generally pursued is to minimize the prediction errors, by making the accuracy [15,28,13,27] of the RS as high as possible; nevertheless, there are other objectives that need to be taken into account: avoid overspecialization phenomena, find good items, credibility of recommendations, precision and recall measures, etc.

Memory-based methods work on a table of U users who have rated I items. The prediction of a non-rated item i for a user u is computed as an aggregate of the ratings of the K most similar users (k-neighborhoods) for the same item i, where $\widetilde{K}$ denotes the set of k-neighborhoods.

2. COLLABORATIVE FILTERING PROPOSED FOR E-LEARNING

We propose a reflection on part of the existing differences, from the learning perspective, between a well-known non-collaborative knowledge source: the Encyclopedia Britannica and another collaborative source that is equally well-known: Wikipedia. One of the most notable differences lies in the confidence inspired by the information provided in the Encyclopedia Britannica compared to that provided in Wikipedia, as a result of the reputation of those who develop it and of the reliability of the sources. That is a very positive part of the information in traditional education, strongly based on reputation. Due to its actual philosophy, Wikipedia lacks a reputation mechanism comparable to traditional means of knowledge, however, it is capable of providing almost immediate updates, varied points of view, very useful additional information, links to alternative knowledge sources and in general all the benefits provided by immediate and collaborative information.

A conciliatory and balanced approach between the two extremes could be a version of Wikipedia where all the information has its place but is linked to a reputation 'index' of each of the articles based on the level of knowledge of those who write and/or endorse them. At present, Wikipedia can be considered as a sub-set of the proposed Wikipedia where everyone has the same reputation index; based on these ideas, the CF that we will develop will be based on the possibility of awarding greater reputation 'indexes' to users with greater knowledge in subjects on which each e-learning RS is based. In this sense, the existing RS can be considered as a sub-set of the ones we propose.

One of the ideas underlined in the philosophy of the actuation of the RS is based on the equality between its users, not only on their possibilities of access to the service, but also above all with regards to the contribution by each one of them to the recommendations that the rest could receive. The usual RS generate the recommendations for each user based on the ratios supplied by the users with contributions most similar to them.

The equal treatment between users is adequate and convenient in the majority of the RS, for example, there is no reason, in advance, to believe that one user is more qualified than another to offer recommendations about movies, journeys, blogs, etc. However, there exists a group of RS in which this situation does not make so much sense. The RS of e-learning are the most paradigmatic in this asymmetric situation; in these RS one can easily make a distinction between advanced and novice users, for example between the ratios generated by teachers and those generated by students, or those supplied by advanced students (for example final years) and those who are starting their studies.

The CF filtering method used can be obtained from the paper [5] in which it is developed the fundamental underlying principal in the CF method proposed together with the equations that uphold it. In the following sections of this paper we explain the design of experiments carried out, we list the results obtained and we explain the conclusions we have reached on applying this CF method to an e-learning RS currently in operation.

3. RECOMMENDER SYSTEM EXPERIMENT DESIGN

In order to test the CF method proposed we have used an e-learning RS that has been in operation for 2 years. In this period of time, ratings have been received from 243 students on 224 aspects (44 written documentations of teaching units + 44 proposed exercises + 44 knowledge validation tests + 88 external information sources + 4 lecturers), all of which were in 9 training courses with the subjects: "communications with Java language" and "development of web applications with Java".

The external information sources (books, on-line documents, websites, etc.) offer 2 references of complementary information to the actual course documentation in each of the teaching units.

The students' ratings have been collected throughout each course to gauge their opinion, in a range from 0 to 5, on the suitability of each of the 224 aspects rated as a means of assimilating the knowledge proposed in each of the teaching units or throughout the whole course in the case of rating the lecturers.

The students' profile was qualified engineers or students in the final year of engineering with a good knowledge of programming in languages other than Java. The technical level of the students in one of the courses (communications) on average was higher than that of the students of the second course. No students have taken part in both courses. The maximum time period permitted to make a rating on a teaching unit was one week after it had finished. The rating of the lecturers was carried out at the end of the course.

Although participation in the RS was not obligatory, due to the interest shown by the lecturers and the students themselves, the end result has led to a much higher ratings percentage than can be found in any public RS database, which has made it necessary to gauge the impact of working with a ratings matrix R that is not very sparse [29,6].

From the students' point of view, our e-learning RS allowed them to receive personalized recommendations on the suitability of the documentation sources for the classes, which meant they had an idea about which of the 3 documentations for each class would best adjust to their preferences. In the first course, the students had recommendations based on the ratings of their classmates and of the lecturers. In the other courses, the recommendation was also processed considering the ratings of students from previous courses.

The matrix R of ratios consists of the 224 elements rated. The matrix C of scores consist of a number of elements $T=88$ and is formed by the marks obtained by each student in the 44 exercises proposed plus the 44 knowledge validation tests, all of which corresponds to the 44 teaching units. As new courses were held, the number of rows in matrices R and C gradually increased to finally reach the total of 243 students participating in this RS.

Once the courses had ended and matrices R and C were complete, we went on to assess the classic factor of accuracy of the RS by calculating the Mean Absolute Error (MAE) and the measure of dispersion of that mean figure: the percentage of perfect predictions and the percentage of bad predictions [30], by using Pearson Correlation adapted to the CF. After this, we tested the results using the equations designed to be used in the e-learning RS.

4. RESULTS

Figure 1 shows the results of the Mean Absolute Error (MAE) obtained by applying the traditional CF techniques to the data of our e-learning RS (black graph with squares) and the equivalent results using values of α 0.3, 0.5 and 0.7.

The parameter α (with the range of 0 to 1) serves to adjust the weight that we give to the values rated by each user with regards to the weight that we give the evaluations by the users with better scores. Expressed in another way, the parameter (1-α) allows variation of the importance given to the evaluations by people with greater knowledge (scores).

The value of α 0.3 considers to a greater extent the recommendations of users who have a better reputation (or knowledge, in the context of this paper), whilst by using the value of α 0.7 the recommendations of the users that have a better reputation lose a great deal of importance; the value of α 0.5 represents a balance between both tendencies.

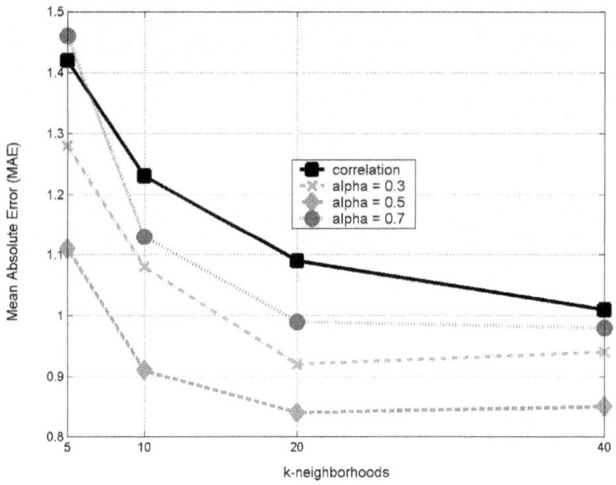

Figure 1. Evolution of the Mean absolute Error (MAE) using the correlation metric compared with the proposed metric in different values of the α and k-neighborhoods parameters.

The study is carried out using k-neighborhood values: 5, 10, 20 and 40, which allows us to emphasize the most representative values for such a small database and also to show the tendency in the results when the number of k-neighborhoods increases.

As we can see in figure 1, with the exception of k = 5 & α = 0.7, in all the values processed the error (MAE) is reduced by testing the accuracy of the recommendations using different values of α. The best results are obtained by balancing (α = 0.5) the importance of the users' reputation in the recommendation process. This result indicates that, by making this specific RS, we achieve the best estimate by weighting by approximately 50% the ratings of the users with the best knowledge.

This result can be explained by reflecting on the necessary balance that should exist between the choice of users (k-neighborhoods) with sufficiently similar ratings to those of the user who will receive the recommendation as regards the choice of users for whom, despite being less similar, the ratings should be more suitable.

In order to illustrate the previous concept, we can take a look at the following example: In line with my ratings on tourist destinations, a traditional RS could recommend Cancun (Mexico) for my beach holiday in September, which fits in with the ratings that I will have made in the RS: beach, hot, nightlife, etc. however, several experts from travel agencies have given this destination a negative rating at the end of the summer due to the high probability of hurricanes in the area. For the RS to make a recommendation almost exclusively in line with the ratings of these experts would make no sense, as I would probably not have the same taste (ratings) as them (they will not be similar to me), but it is a very good idea to take into account (with certain weighting α) their ratings to avoid unwise recommendations from users that are very similar to me, who may be less well informed (in this case about the hurricane season).

Figure 2 shows the percentages obtained of perfect predictions. We consider a perfect prediction to be each situation in which the prediction of the value recommended for one user in one e-learning item matches the value rated by that user for that e-learning item. As an example: we would achieve a perfect prediction when the RS is capable of recommending, with a value of 4, written documentation of a teaching unit that the user has rated with a 4. This process is only carried out to obtain the graphs shown, as the regular recommendation process only recommends items not rated by the users.

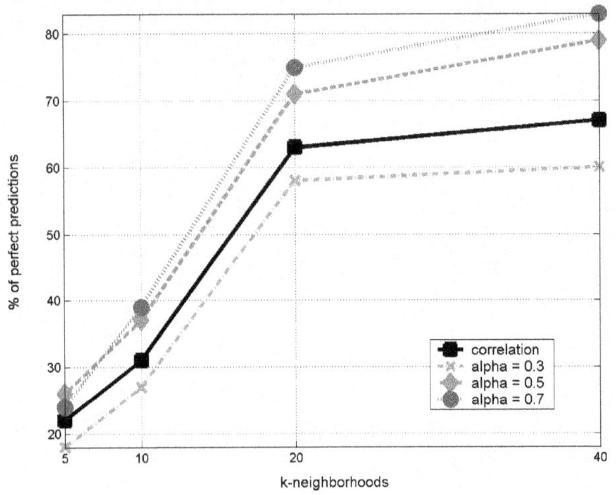

Figure 2. Evolution of the percentage of perfect predictions using the correlation metric compared with the proposed metric in different values of the α and k-neighborhoods parameters.

The results shown in Figure 2 lead us to establish that, in this RS, it is not advisable to excessively weight the ratings of users with a better reputation ($\alpha = 0.3$), because we lose the capacity to make correct predictions; however, it is very useful to consider the ratings of these users with a better reputation using more balanced values (around $\alpha = 0.6$), with which we manage to improve the results compared to the use of traditional CF techniques (show in black with squares).

Figure 3 shows the percentages obtained of bad predictions. We consider a bad prediction to be each situation in which the prediction of the value recommended to one user in one e-learning item is different by more than 2 points from the value rated by that user for that e-learning item.

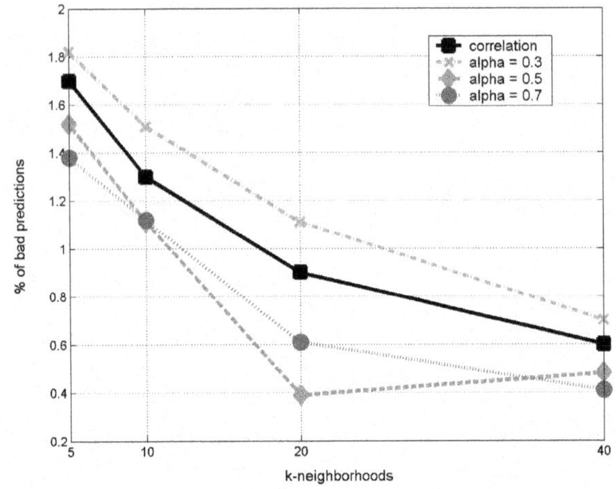

Figure 3. Evolution of the percentage of bad predictions using the correlation metric compared with the proposed metric in different values of the α and k-neighborhoods parameters.

The situation shown in Figure 3 is repeated, in the sense that here it is also counterproductive to overrate the opinions of the experts, but is highly advisable to take them into account in a moderate way (around $\alpha = 0.6$). In this way, we manage to reduce the percentage of bad predictions as regards the traditional results of the RS (shown in Figure 3 as "correlation").

As we can see, the proposed method of CF adapted to e-learning improves the results of traditional CFs. Moreover, we can provide an approximate average value of how much it is improved by percentage. In Figure 1, by observing the numerical values of the MAE we can determine average improvements of around 17%; this percentage is approximately maintained when we take a closer look at Figures 2 and 3, which leads us to establish a generalized improvement of around 17% when we use the proposed CF system on our e-learning RS.

5. CONCLUSIONS

The recommender systems of e-learning allow the possibility of weighting the importance of the ratings that each user generates, depending on their level of knowledge. In order to implement this concept we provide a new measurement for similarity between users x and y, which we call *importance* and we accompany it with the necessary equations in order to validate the results and adjust each e-learning RS by assigning a greater or lesser importance to users with better knowledge.

The results obtained with our e-learning RS have been very positive; we have achieved improvements of around 17% in the levels of accuracy (MAE) and in the percentages of perfect predictions and bad predictions. The empirical results have also shown the advisability of using balanced values in the importance assigned to users with higher levels of knowledge, in such a way that this new source of knowledge is taken into account, but without excessively compromising the similarity of the k-neighborhoods chosen to make each user's recommendations.

A well defined field of investigation exists in CF when the nature of the recommender systems allows the incorporation of weighting in the importance of each one of the users, and the collaborative systems of e-learning are named to lead the developments in this new field of investigation.

6. REFERENCES

[1] Adomavicius E. & Tuzhilin, A. 2005. Toward the Next Generation of Recommender Systems: a survey of the state-of-the-art and possible extensions, *IEEE Transactions on Knowledge and Data Enginnering*, 17(6), 734-749.

[2] Antonopoulus, N. & Salter 2006. J. CinemaScreen Recommender Agent: Combining Collaborative and Content-Based Filtering, *IEEE Intelligent Systems*, 35-41.

[3] Balasundaram, S. R. & Ramadoss, B. 2006. Object Oriented Analysis Learning Tool using Collaborative Learning, *in the 7th International Conference on Information Technology Based Higher Education and Training*, 811-816.

[4] Baraglia, R. & Silvestri, F. 2004. An Online Recommender System for Large Web Sites, *in Proceedings of the*

IEEE/WIC/ACM International Conference on Web Intelligence, 199-205, 10.1109/WI.2004.10158.

[5] Bobadilla, J., Serradilla, F. & Hernando A. 2009. Collaborative Filtering adapted to Recommender Systems of e-learning, *Knowledge Based Systems*, 261-265, doi: 10.1016/j.knosys.2009.01.008.

[6] Bobadilla, J. & Serradilla, F. 2009. The incidence of Sparsity on Collaborative Filtering Metrics, *Australian Database Conference ADC*, 92, 9-18.

[7] Bobadilla, J., Serradilla, F. & Bernal, j. 2010. A New Collaborative Filtering Metric that Improves the Behavior of Recommender Systems, *Knowledge Based Systems*, 520-528, doi: 10.1016/j.knosys.2010.03.009.

[8] Chen, L.S., Hsu, F.H., Chen, M.C. & Hsu, Y.C. 2008. Developping recommender Systems with the Considersation of Product Profitability for Sellers, *in Proceedings of Informaton Sciences*, vol. 178, 1032-1048.

[9] Cho, S.B., Hong, J.H. & Park, M.H. 2007. Location-Based Recommendation System Using Bayesian User's Preference Model in Mobile Devices, *Lecture Notes on Computer Science*, 4611, 1130-1139.

[10] Denis H. 2007. Managing Collaborative Learning Processes in e-Learning Applications, *in Proceedings of the 29th International Conference on Information Technology Interfaces*, 345-350.

[11] Drachsler H., Hummel G. K & Koper R. 2007. IRecommendations for learners are different: applying memory-based recommender system techniques to lifelong learning, *the SIRTEL workshop at the EC-TEL*, 17-20.

[12] Fesenmaier, D.R., Gretzel, U., Knoblock, C., Paris, C., Ricci, F., Stabb, et al. 2002. Intelligent Systems for Tourism, *Intelligent Systems*, 17(6), 53-66.

[13] Fuyuki, I., Quan, T.K. & Shinichi, H. 2006. Improving Accuracy of Recommender Systems by Clustering Items Based on Stability of User Similarity, *in Proceedings of the IEEE International Conference on Intelligent Agents, Web Technologies and Internet Commerce*, 61-61, Digital Object Identifier 10.1109/CIMCA.2006.123.

[14] Gang, C. , Ruimin, S., Jiajun, W. & Zeyu, C. 2007. Collaborative Education Model and Its Application in E-learning, *in Proceedings of the the 6th IEEE/ACIS International Conference on Computer and Information Science*, 856-860.

[15] Giaglis, G.M. & Lekakos 2006. Improving the Prediction Accuracy of Recommendation Algorithms: Approaches Anchored on Human Factors, *Interacting with Computers*, 18(3), 410-431.

[16] Herlocker, J. L., Konstan, J.A., Riedl, J.T. & Terveen, L.G. 2004. Evaluating Collaborative Filtering Recommender Systems, *ACM Transactions on Information Systems*, 22(1), 5-53.

[17] Hu J. & Zhang W. 2008. Community Collaborative Filtering for E-Learning, *International Conference on Computer and Electrical Engineering ICCEE 2008*, 593 – 597, Digital Object Identifier 10.1109/ICCEE.2008.144.

[18] Ingoo, H., Kyong, J.O. & Tae, H.R. 2003. The Collaborative Filtering Recommendation Based on SOM Cluster-Indexing CBR, *Expert Systems with Applications*, 25, 413-423.

[19] Janner, T. & Schroth, C. 2007. Web 2.0 and SOA: Converging Concepts Enabling the Internet of Services, *IT Pro*, 36-41.

[20] Jinghua, H., Kangning & W., Shaohong, F. 2007. A Survey of E-Commerce Recommender Systems, *in Proceedings of the International Conference on Service Systems and Service Management*, 1-5, 10.1109/ICSSSM.2007.4280214.

[21] Knights, M. 2007.Web 2.0, *IET Communications Engineer*, 30-35.

[22] Kong, F., Sun, X. & Ye, S. 2005. A, Comparison of Several Algorithms for Collaborative Filtering in Startup Stage, *In Proceedings of the IEEE networking, sensing and control*, 25-28.

[23] Konstan, J.A. ,Miller, B.N. & Riedl, J. 2004. PocketLens: Toward a Personal Recommender System, *ACM Transactions on Information Systems*, 22,(3), 437-476.

[24] Li, P. & Yamada, S. 2004. A movie recommender system based on inductive learning, *in Proceedings of the IEEE Conference on Cybernetics and Intelligent Systems*, 1, 318-323, Digital Object Identifier 10.1109/ICCIS.2004.1460433.

[25] Lin, K.J. 2007. Building Web 2.0, *Computer*, 101-102.

[26] Loll, F. & Pinkwart, N. 2009. Using Collaborative Filtering Algorithms as eLearning Tools, *42nd Hawaii International Conference on System Sciences HICSS '09*, 1-10.

[27] Manolopoulus, Y., Nanopoulus A., Papadopoulus A.N. & Symeonidis P. 2007. Collaborative Recommender Systems: Combining Effectiveness and Efficiency, *Expert Systems with Applications*, (34) 4, 2995-3013, doi:10.1016/j.eswa.2007.05.013.

[28] Nayak, R., Weng, L.T. & Xu, Y. 2005. An Improvement to Collaborative Filtering for Recommender Systems, *in Proceedings of the IEEE International Conference on Computational Intelligence for Modelling, Control and Automatitation*, 1, 792 – 795, Digital Object Identifier 10.1109/CIMCA.2005.1631361.

[29] Papagelis, M., Plexousakis D. & Kutsuras, T. 2005. Alleviating the Sparsity Problem of Collaborative Filtering Using Trust Inferences, *Lectures Notes on Computer Science*, 3477, 224-239.

[30] Sanchez, J.L., Serradilla F., Martinez E. & Bobadilla, J. 2008. Choice of Metrics used in Collaborative Filtering and their Impact on Recommender Systems, *in Proceedings of the IEEE International Conference on Digital Ecosystems and Technologies DEST*, 432 – 436, Digital Object Identifier 10.1109/DEST.2008.4635147.

[31] Xu, B., Zhang, M., Pan, Z. & Yang, H. 2005. Content-Based Recommendations in E-Commerce, *in Proceedings of Computational Science and its Applications*, 3481, 946-955.

[32] Yager, R.R. 2003. Fuzzy Logic Methods in Recommender Systems, *Fuzzy Sets and Systems*, 136(2), 133-149.

A Web-based Generation and Delivery System for Active Code Reading

Daniel Hoffman and Ming Lu
Department of Computer Science
University of Victoria
PO Box 3055 STN CSC
Victoria, BC V8W 3P6
Telephone: 250-472-5768
FAX: 250-472-5708
{dhoffman,luming}@cs.uvic.ca

Tim Pelton
Department of Curriculum and Instruction
University of Victoria
PO Box 3010 STN CSC
Victoria, BC V8W 3N4
Telephone: 250-721-7803
FAX: 250-721-7598
tpelton@uvic.ca

ABSTRACT

In Computer Science courses, we ask students to write a lot of code. All too often, the resulting code quality is poor. While it is widely believed that students would write better code if they spent more time reading code, it is difficult to get students to read code effectively. We present a web-based application supporting generation and delivery of quizzes designed to evaluate and improve code reading skills.

Categories and Subject Descriptors

K.3.2 [**Computers and Education**]: Computer Science Education

General Terms

Algorithms, Human Factors

Keywords

CS1, code reading, active learning, web-based tool

1. INTRODUCTION

Writing computer software is hard. You must maintain control over many details and numerous complex relationships, in both the programming language and the application domain. While Computer Science students write a lot of code, the quality of the code is often poor: the students have misunderstandings about their programs and about the programming language features they are using.

Active code reading is a special case of active learning. Many instructors believe that students would write better code if they spent more time reading code, and already do ask students to read code. Unfortunately, the reading tends to be unfocused and little is learned. We lack precise goals and practical evaluation mechanisms for code understanding. Many students simply do not know how to learn much about a program by reading it.

We present *C-doku*, a web-based application intended to support evaluation and improvement of code reading skills. The application takes a sequence of computer programs, each displayed as an HTML "web form" with a few actual inputs or outputs in the code replaced by text fields. The student completes the fields; the solution is then checked automatically and feedback is provided immediately.

Although *C-doku* has many potential uses, in this paper we focus on one scenario. In a second-year Software Engineering course, we regularly provide code focusing on some language feature or programming technique, e.g., C strings or linked lists. We want to know if the students have studied and understood the code. To do so efficiently, we want a tool which can measure that understanding automatically. Both presentation and marking must be automated. Finally, the tool must be suitable for a lab environment, where a student taking the marked exam can see the displays of his/her neighbors.

In Section 2, we present related work. Section 3 describes the tool features as seen by a student taking a *C-doku* quiz and Section 4 explains the features available to authors for quiz generation. Section 5 describes our experience with the tool in a second-year Software Engineering course. Section 6 summarizes the principles on which *C-doku* is based.

2. RELATED WORK

The psychology literature contains reports that active retrieval is a more effective learning strategy than simple repetition [8]. Industrial software reviews have been shown to benefit from a question-based, active-learning approach [14].

Active learning has long been advocated in the Computer Science education community [11, 16]. A variety of approaches have been used to engage students. Liu has shown how to improve learning outcomes by replacing traditional lectures with a 50/50 split between lectures and question-based work sheets [10]. Wu's castle [6] is a graphical role-playing game for teaching students about the execution behaviour of loops. Students can set various loop parameters, e.g., index start and end values. To retain student interest, execution is carried out by animated characters. With PeerWise [5], a web-based tool for active learning, students collaboratively create multiple choice questions. Use of the tool

SIGCSE'11, March 9–12, 2011, Dallas, Texas, USA.

correlates positively with later exam performance. Peer instruction [15], long used in Physics instruction, was adapted to programming courses in Java. Clickers are used in lecture to answer questions focusing on previously assigned readings and exercises.

Some approaches to active learning incorporate automated checking of student work. GraphPad [13] is a web-based tool aimed at graph data structures. Students draw graphs which are compared to the instructor's solution automatically using a graph isomorphism algorithm. The tool also captures student interactions at the pen-stroke level for later study by the instructor. Kumar [9] presents a web-based tutor aimed at teaching C++ pointers. The tutor presents C++ code with a pointer error; the student must identify the variable and line number of the error. Both practice and marked mode are supported. The tutor is part of the problets framework [2]. A *C-doku* prototype was described previously [7]. The version described in this paper extends that work with support for two languages (C++, Java and Python), the addition of two question types (*Liar-liar* and *Find-the-failure*), and the data and analysis presented in Sections 5.2 and 5.3.

3. TOOL FEATURES: DELIVERY

C-doku evaluates code-reading skill with quizzes containing four simple question types. We present the game features by example, with two trivial examples focusing on the tool features and one additional example to illustrate typical use.

Figure 1(a) shows the screen layout for *Input-output*, the first of the question types supported by *C-doku*. On the left side is a C program containing definitions of the functions `min` and `main`. In `main`, the value returned by `min(1,2)` is written to the standard output. Under the heading **`Standard output`** is a text field. The student is asked to supply the correct value (`1`) and then click the *Check answer* button. To check the answer for correctness, the code is executed once, reading from the standard input values shown on the display and capturing the actual output. The answer is correct if the output captured from the execution and the output on the display are the same.

Figure 1(b) shows *Bullseye*, the second question type supported by *C-doku*. As with *Input-output*, the left side contains a complete C program containing definitions of `min` and `main`. There are two differences:

1. In `min`, the statement `return a;` is highlighted, indicating that it is the "target" statement.

2. In `main`, the values for the `min` parameters have been replaced by text fields.

The student is asked to supply values for `a` and `b`, e.g., `1` and `2`, which will cause the target statement to be executed.

Figure 1(c) shows a more complex *Bullseye* example. The `binsearch` function contains four targeted lines. The main function invokes `binsearch` twice, with student-selected values for the search element, `x`. The net effect is that the student must choose two `x` values to achieve 100% statement coverage of `binsearch`.

The third game type, *Liar-liar*, is a variant of *Bullseye*. With *Bullseye*, any C statement can be a target; with *Liar-liar*, each target must be a C assert statement. For each assert statement, the student must supply text field values which will (a) reach the statement and (b) cause the assert to fail.

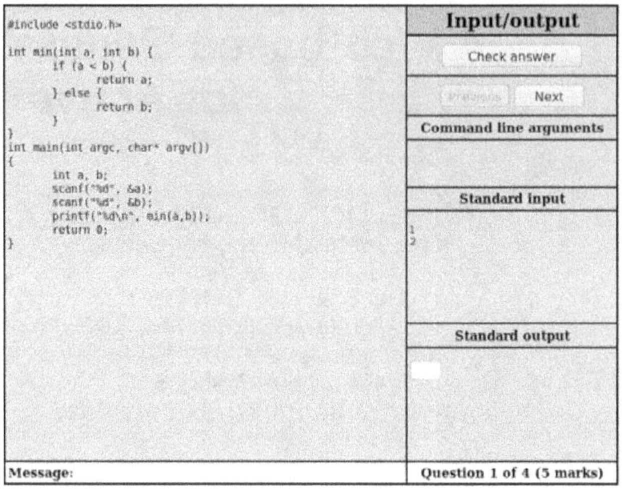

(a) *Input/output*: simple example

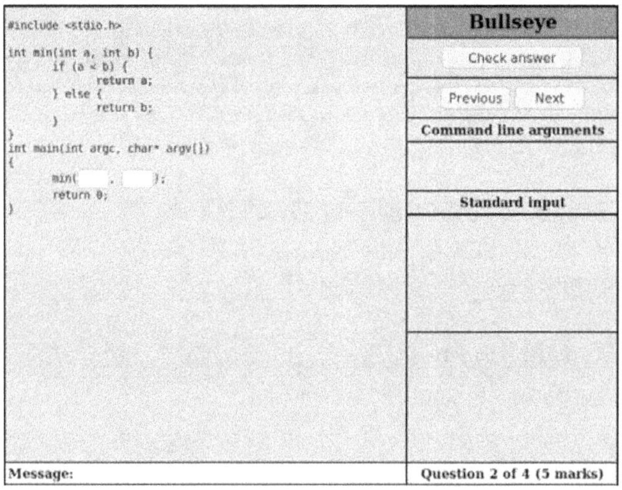

(b) *Bullseye*: simple example

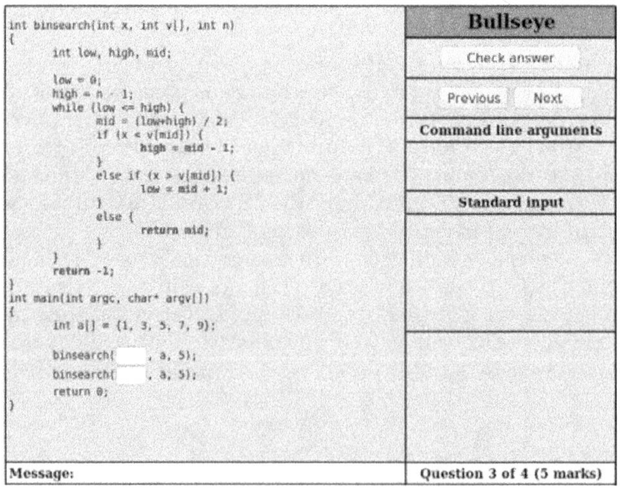

(c) *Bullseye*: typical example

Figure 1: Three *C-doku* examples

The fourth and final game type, *Find-the-failure*, is a variant of *Input-output*. With *Find-the-failure*, the student is given a prose specification of a C function and a purposely faulty implementation. The student must supply failure-revealing text field values, i.e., values which cause the implementation to violate the specification.

In summary, the *C-doku* display contains four main cells: code, command-line, standard input, and standard output (*Input-output* only). Each cell can contain a mixture of fixed text and text fields. The principal difference between the games is the "check answer algorithm". Finally, while the examples in this paper are in C, the code cell can also contain C++, Python or Java.

The tool is designed for two types of quiz: practice and marked.

1. In a practice quiz, the student is informed immediately whether his/her answer is correct. A limit may be placed on the maximum number of attempts for each question. No record is kept of the student's work.

2. In a marked quiz, the student must login before beginning the quiz. No feedback is given on the correctness of his/her answers; there is a time limit for the quiz. The answers to each question are logged; marks are computed automatically from the log.

For reasons of portability and security, the *C-doku* server is implemented in a minimalist fashion. HTML forms [4] are used with no client-side embedded code, e.g., no Javascript. HTML pages are generated on the server side using the web2py [1] framework which provides good support for secure servers. While the students do provide portions of code for later execution, the student-supplied text is limited to string and numeric constants, making *C-doku* immune to code insertion attacks.

4. TOOL FEATURES: GENERATION

Because the effectiveness of *C-doku* depends on a large library of questions, efficient question authoring is a central issue. Computer Science instructors typically have access to a large collection of demonstration code, taken from lecture and textbook examples. We would like to be able take such an example and quickly convert it for C-doku use; we call this process "activating the code." Two problems arise:

1. Each *C-doku* question requires two slightly different versions of the code: one for display by the client and one for execution by the server. For example, in a *Bullseye* question, the executable code must contain a bit of extra code to track coverage of the target statements. It would be tedious and error-prone to maintain the display and executable versions of each question manually.

2. To achive cheat-proof quizzes, we need a number of trivial variations of each question: the variations must be pedagogically equivalent, but with different correct answers. Again, it would be tedious and error-prone to develop and maintain the variations manually.

To avoid these two problems, *C-doku* supports automated question generation from templates and quiz specification based on random selection from sets of equivalent questions.

Global code
```
#include <stdio.h>
int min(int a, int b) {
    if (a < b) {
        return a;
    } else {
        return b;
    }
}
```

Main code
```
int a,b;
scanf("%d",&a);
scanf("%d",&b);
printf("%d\n", min(a,b));
```

Command-line arguments

Standard input
```
$x1
$x2
```

Standard output
```
$y0
```

Tuple list
```
[1,2,None]
[2,1,None]
[1,1,None]
[None,None,2]
[None,None,20]
[None,None,-2]
```

Figure 2: Question template for *Input-output*

4.1 Question generation from templates

A question template mimics the *C-doku* display layout. For example, the question shown in Figure 1(a) was generated from the template shown in Figure 2. Generation is implemented in Python; in actual use, the values shown in Figure 2 are assigned to Python variables. For all question types, the C code is separated into global code and main code to make it easier to generate the extra code needed, e.g., for monitoring coverage in *Bullseye*. Following the code templates are templates for command-line arguments, standard input and standard output. Each of the five templates can contain a mixture of plain text and markers for "hot spots": locations which might contain a text field in a delivered question. In Figure 2, the markers `$x0`, `$x1`, and `$y0` are used; a marker can be any string which does not already occur in the code.

The list of tuples at the bottom of Figure 2 specifies how the hot spots are to be filled in: with a string or numeric constant, or with `None`, indicating that the hot spot should appear as a text field. Since there are six entries in the tuple list, this template will generate six questions. The question in Figure 1(a) was generated from the tuple `[1,2,None]`. The question in Figure 3 was generated from `[None,None,1]`.

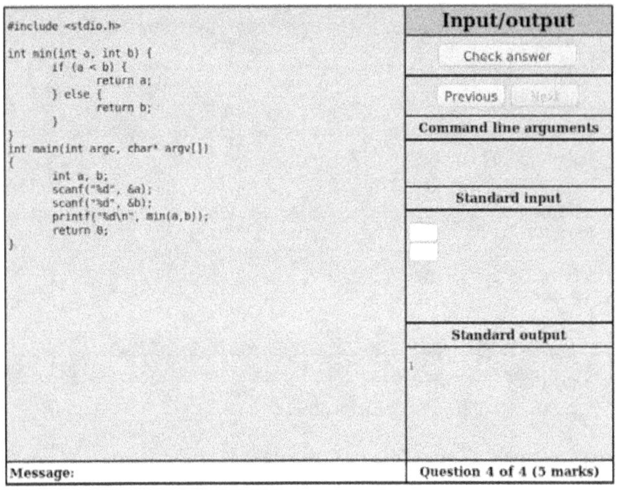

Figure 3: A simple *Input/output* example

4.2 Quiz specification with random selection

Support is also provided for packaging questions in quizzes. The author can simply provide a list of question files, along with a mark for each; each student sees the same quiz.

Given a sufficient collection of templates, however, it is easy to create a "cheat-proof" quiz, where copying from a neighbor is no help at all. To accomplish this, the author specifies a list of question groups. Each group consists of a set of pedagogically equivalent questions and a number N, indicating the number of questions to be randomly sampled from the group. Each time the quiz is begun by a student, the sampling is done again.

Consider a quiz constructed from the six questions generated from the template in Figure 2. Suppose that the author decides that the three "forward" questions are pedagogically equivalent, and that the three "backward" questions are as well. A two-question quiz could be constructed by selecting one question from each of the two groups. Each time a student begins the quiz, he or she will receive one of the nine possible quizzes.

The *C-doku* tool automatically collects data on student performance. Each answer to each question is logged, along with the time spent on the question.

5. EXPERIENCE

5.1 Qualitative

The *C-doku* tool is currently in use in a second-year software engineering course. The course covers the fundamentals of software engineering, using C and Python. There were 56 students in the January–April 2010 offering. Five quizzes were developed and delivered. In each quiz, there were 20 questions, each selected randomly from a question group with 3–6 questions. The same delivery scheme was used for each quiz. The quiz was made available for practice on Monday. Students took the quiz as many times as they liked. In the lab on Thursday, the quiz was taken for a mark, with a 30-minute time limit.

The topics for the five quizzes were:

1. *Loops.* The first quiz is a tune-up, covering `for`, `while`, `break`, and `continue`.

2. *Parameter passing.* Many of the students have a Java background, where the language forces call-by-reference for objects and call-by-value for primitives. Consequently, they struggle with the use of `*` and `&`.

3. *Pointers and arrays.* Even for experienced programmers, there are misunderstandings on these topics.

4. *String libraries.* This quiz covers the use and the implementations of the main functions: `strlen`, `strcpy`, `strcat`, `strcmp`, and `strcasecmp`.

5. *Linked lists.* The standard insertion, deletion, and search algorithms are covered, including passing pointers by reference, along with the use of `malloc` and `free`.

From the instructor's point of view, the quizzes work well. We get fast feedback about the students' strengths and weaknesses in language features and programming techniques. When lecture questions or exam results indicate a weakness, we add questions to the next quiz in that area.

The students like to play *C-doku* and play a lot: typically well over 60 minutes of practice for a 30-minute quiz. We received many e-mail complaints when the occasional server crash occurred. They perform well on the marked quizzes and on hardcopy exam questions which use the *C-doku* format. Anecdotally, they seem to encounter fewer problems on programming assignments using the material covered by previous *C-doku* quizzes.

We have begun to examine the relationships between marks on the *C-doku* quizzes, and marks on exams and C programming assignments.

5.2 Data

In our examination of the data collected we calculated correlations, tested two hypotheses and conducted a series of multiple regression analyses. The data considered included the results from the five C-doku quizzes ($qz1$, $qz2$, $qz3$, $qz4$, $qz5$) as the independent/predictor variables, and two C programming exercises ($ce1$, $ce2$) and three related course exams ($ex1$, $ex2$, $ex3$) as the dependent/criterion variables.

41 of the 56 students enrolled in the course consented to participate (some students were not present at the time that the permission was sought). Because the exams were dissimilar to the quizzes in presentation format, practice opportunities and language level, the 4 students that indicated a first language other than English were removed. Another 10 student records were trimmed because they missed one (5) or more (5) assessments and finally, 2 records were trimmed because they were outliers. This left us with a marginal sample size of 25 students.

It should also be noted that there was a substantial ceiling effect in the C-doku quiz results because they were administered individually once a student became confident that they had mastered the relevant content (proportion of 100% scores: $qz1$: 60%, $qz2$: 28%, $qz3$: 36%, $qz4$: 60%, $qz5$: 28%).

Although some exploratory efforts were made to impute missing data and ceiling data these extreme efforts were difficult to justify and abandoned after only modest improvements were realized (one R^2 value was improved by 0.04).

	$qz1$	$qz2$	$qz3$	$qz4$	$qz5$
$qz2$	0.31				
$qz3$	0.31	0.46*			
$qz4$	−0.08	−0.10	0.15		
$qz5$	0.02	0.44*	0.35	0.62**	
$ce1$	−0.10	0.30	0.50*	0.43*	0.55**
$ce2$	0.13	0.19	0.37	0.30	0.38
$ex1$	0.34	0.71**	0.72**	0.00	0.40*
$ex2$	0.34	0.28	0.51**	0.41*	0.39
$ex3$	0.25	0.36	0.53**	0.15	0.32

* $p \leq 0.05$ ** $p \leq 0.01$

Table 1: Correlations between variables

5.3 Analysis

We began by examining the correlations between variables (see Table 1) and found that many more significant correlations were present between the independent and dependent variables than would be expected by chance.

With knowledge of the content of the quizzes, assignments and tests, we hypothesized that two particular correlations would be significant and tested them explicitly:

H_1: success in $qz3$ (pointers and arrays) was expected to be related to $ce1$ (writing/debugging linked list code) and we found a solid correlation between them ($r = 0.50$, $p = 0.012$).

H_2: success in $qz4$ (string libraries) was expected to be related to $ex2$ (strings) and indeed we found a significant correlation ($r = 0.41$, $p = 0.044$) despite an extremely high ceiling effect (60% in $qz4$).

In addition to these expected relationships we found that success in $qz2$ was predictive of $ex1$, that $qz3$ was highly correlated with all of the exams, that $qz4$ and $qz5$ were also correlated with $ce1$ and that $qz5$ was predictive of $ex1$. It is interesting to note that despite extremely high ceiling effects (60%) in $qz1$, modest correlations ($r = 0.34$, $p = 0.092$) were still found between $qz1$ and both $ex1$ and $ex2$. It is also interesting to note the lack of any correlation between $qz4$ and $ex1$ results, which is appropriate given that $ex1$ doesn't cover content related to $qz4$.

Finally we conducted separate multiple regression analyses searching for maximum R^2_{adj} in conjunction with significant (or close to) positive contributions from independent variables (assuming that each is a valid contributing assessment score). With all significant results we also confirmed by inspection of plots that the residuals were approximately normally distributed and that the independent variables were plausibly linearly related to the dependent variables. Although the limited sample size and ceiling effects preclude the assertion of a normal distribution for some predictor variables, and the reliabilities of the assessments are low we expect that the primary effects of these deviations from the analysis assumptions will be to underestimate significant results [12].

$$ce1 = -0.443 + \underset{(p=0.061)}{0.205 \times qz3} + \underset{(p=0.021)}{0.237 \times qz5} \quad (p=0.003,\ R^2_{adj}=0.357)$$

$$ce2 = 27.60 + 0.186 \times qz5 \quad (p=0.060,\ R^2_{adj}=0.109)$$

$$ex1 = -1.127 + \underset{(p=0.001)}{0.350 \times qz2} + \underset{(p=0.001)}{0.182 \times qz3} \quad (p<0.0001,\ R^2_{adj}=0.679)$$

$$ex2 = 0.291 + \underset{(p=0.013)}{0.241 \times qz3} + \underset{(p=0.062)}{0.238 \times qz4} \quad (p=0.006,\ R^2_{adj}=0.316)$$

$$ex3 = 11.44 + 0.299 \times qz3 \quad (p=0.006,\ R^2_{adj}=0.254)$$

Even with the small sample size, these models suggest that student performances on most of the *C-doku* quizzes are predictive of performances in assignments and exams. We see that the model for Exam 1 ($ex1$) significantly and substantially predicts student performance based on $qz2$ and $qz3$, with approximately 68% of the variance accounted for. We also note that $qz3$ figures prominently in 4 of the 5 regression models, which suggests that most of the assignments and exams shared some commonality with that particular quiz and further study is warranted.

The primary result of this analysis is the large proportion of the variance in $ex1$ that can be linked to student performance in $qz2$ and $qz3$, suggesting that successful practice with *C-doku* may support the learning goals assessed by $ex1$. It is expected that, with a substantially larger sample size in a follow-up study, the nature of additional observed relationships will become clearer.

6. GUIDING PRINCIPLES

The previous sections have described the features and use of the *C-doku* tool. Here, we summarize the four principles on which this tool is based:

- *Active code reading.* Our goal is to evaluate and improve skill in code reading using an active, question-based approach. Unlike slicing tools [3], for example, the *C-doku* tool is not intended to support review of arbitrary code. Instead, *C-doku* is essentially a "playback engine" for carefully constructed exercises.

- *Template-based.* With *C-doku*, the code can vary a great deal but the question formats are few and simple. This allows the students to master the question rules early on and thereafter focus on the question content.

- *Automated oracle. C-doku* depends heavily on an automated oracle: a slightly modified version of the displayed code. Students need the immediate feedback for learning. Instructors need a way to provide that feedback without the effort required to maintain a large database of correct answers.

- *Strong authoring support.* Because the success of *C-doku* depends on a large library of questions, good authoring support is crucial. Instructors today have access to many complete programs of 10-50 lines. All of these are candidates for "activation" under *C-doku*. An author can take such a program, mark it for "hot spots" and quickly generate 10 or so concrete questions. Because quiz questions can be selected randomly from a pool of pedagogically equivalent questions, the questions can be reused with minimal risk of overexposure. Further, quizzes are "cheat-proof" in that copying from your neighbour is no help at all: his/her answers will not be correct for your questions.

7. CONCLUSIONS AND FUTURE WORK

Learning to write computer software is difficult. While it is widely believed that students would write better code if they spent more time reading code, it is often difficult to encourage them to take code reading seriously. We have presented a web-based application intended to support evaluation and improvement of code reading skills.

The initial results are positive. Students like *C-doku* and use it. With *C-doku*, an instructor can motivate students to focus on selected aspects of a selected piece of code. Question generation and random selection allow questions to be reused.

Without question, *C-doku* practice increases *C-doku* skill. We have some support for the claim that *C-doku* practice improves code-writing skill. We have come to believe that, given a language feature or programming technique, we can write a *C-doku* quiz with the following property: if a student passes the quiz, then they understand the code well.

8. ACKNOWLEDGMENTS

The authors would like to thank H. Wang and H. Lien for help with authoring *C-doku* questions, S. Wagner for technical support for game login, and the students of SEng 265 for their patience with bugs in the *C-doku* server.

9. REFERENCES

[1] The official web2py book, 2010. http://www.web2py.com/book.

[2] Problets: the home page, 2010. http://www.problets.org.

[3] P. Anderson, T. Reps, , and T. Teitelbaum. Design and implementation of a fine-grained software inspection tool. *IEEE Trans. Soft. Eng.*, 29(8):721–733, Aug. 2003.

[4] P. Carey. *New Perspectives on HTML, XHTML, and Dynamic HTML*. Cengage Learning, 4th edition, 2010.

[5] P. Denny, B. Hanks, and B. Simon. Peerwise: replication study of a student-collaborative self-testing web service in a U.S. setting. In *SIGCSE '10: Proc. of the 41st ACM technical symposium on Computer Science education*, pages 421–425, 2010.

[6] M. Eagle and T. Barnes. Experimental evaluation of an educational game for improved learning in introductory computing. *SIGCSE Bull.*, 41(1):321–325, 2009.

[7] D. Hoffman and M. Lu. A web tool for active code reading. In *Proc. FECS 2010*, 2010.

[8] E. Jaffe. Will that be on the test? *Assoc. Psych. Science*, 21(10):18–21, 2008.

[9] A. N. Kumar. Data space animation for learning the semantics of C++ pointers. *SIGCSE Bull.*, 41(1):499–503, 2009.

[10] Z. Liu. Is paper-based work sheet out of date for CSII? In *Proc. FECS 2009*, 2009.

[11] J. McConnell. Active learning and its use in Computer Science. In *Proc. SIGCSE/SIGCUE Conf. on Integrating Technology into Computer Science Education*, 1996.

[12] J. Osborne and E. Waters. Four assumptions of multiple regression that researchers should always test. *Practical Assessment, Research and Evaluation*, 8(2), 2002.

[13] R. P. Pargas and S. Bryfczynski. Using ink to expose students' thought processes in CS2/CS7. *SIGCSE Bull.*, 41(1):168–172, 2009.

[14] D. Parnas and D. Weiss. Active design reviews. In *Proc. of the Intl. Conf. on Software Engineering*, 1985.

[15] B. Simon, M. Kohanfars, L. Michael, J. Lee, K. Tamayo, and Q. Cutts. Experience report: peer instruction in introductory computing. In *SIGCSE '10: Proc. of the 41st ACM technical symposium on Computer science education*, pages 341–345. ACM, 2010.

[16] J. Whittington. Increasing student retention and satisfaction in IT introductory programming courses using active learning. In *Proc. 2006 Informing Science and IT Education Joint Conf.*, 2006.

Scratching the Subject Surface: Infusing Computing into K-12 Curriculum

Ursula Wolz (moderator)
Comp. Sci. & Interactive Multimedia
The College of New Jersey
Ewing, NJ
wolz@tcnj.edu

Youwen Ouyang
Comp. Sci. & Information Systems
California State University
San Marcos, CA
ouyang@csusm.edu

Scott Leutenegger
Comp. Sci. & Game Development
University of Denver
Denver, CO
leut@du.edu

Categories and Subject Descriptors
K.3.2 [**Computing Milieux**]: Computers and Education – Computer and Information Science Education

General Terms
Design, Human Factors, Languages.

Keywords
Scratch, K-12, computing foundations, computational thinking

1. SUMMARY
As the computing education community grapples with integrating computing into K-12 curriculum, the focus remains primarily on identifying appropriate grade level content and skills[3]. Two problems articulated by Margolis et al.[5], are (1) how to bring computing into an already over-burdened curriculum, (2) how to provide substantive professional development for teachers. We need to look beyond teaching computing concepts as isolated from other disciplines. The power of computing lies in its broad applicability to facilitate creativity in other domains.

The panelists will report on using Scratch (http://scratch.mit.edu) in language arts, science and social studies curricula. Our programs demonstrate to middle and high school students and teachers how computational thinking, computing concepts and programming are essential to their course of study. We emphasize active learning where computing is a tool for creativity. We demonstrate how learning 21st century computing skills in the classroom can be fun.

This panel will present three perspectives on using Scratch for humane games, scientific modeling and interactive storytelling. There will be significant time for the audience to participate in discussion of broad applicability of our approaches and whether this pedagogy can work at the undergraduate level.

2. URSULA WOLZ
The *Broadening Participation in Computing via Community Journalism*[8,9] project at The College of New Jersey created a model summer/afterschool program. Middle school teacher-editors and students-journalists run a 21st century, media rich newsroom. Our approach relies on the isomorphism between the processes of interactive storytelling [7] and programming.

The journalism program attracted language arts teachers and students who consider themselves good writers, not necessarily good at math. Via Internet research, videography, and Scratch programming, they create news stories that are posted on the web.

A secondary goal was to inspire middle school teachers to integrate Scratch into their classroom curriculum. With minimal formal professional development, participating language arts teachers created curricular modules where Scratch is used as a mode of creative expression. Example curriculum modules and student work will be presented during the panel.

The student body of 900 is divided into teams; 3 teams for grades 6 through 9. The teachers, one 7th, one 8th, each reach approximately 100 students per year, providing approximately 3 weeks of Scratch project work. Thus without formal mandate, curricular overhaul, extensive professional development or deletion of other content from the curriculum, 2/9ths of the students per year are programming with a personal purpose.

Survey responses show that both the teachers and students believe they can be competent programmers, and that it does not take special math, art or writing talent to programm. They believe that programming is fun. These results suggest that mere exposure to creative expression via programming in the mainstream classroom may increase participation in the computing disciplines. Further, we are not explicitly teaching computer science, but are exposing students to it to empower them to make it their own. Within this framework the teachers slowly develop computing expertise on an "as needed" basis, with informal support from expert Scratchers.

We are now studying the code attributes of the student projects, identifying programming constructs Scratchers favor for interactive storytelling. This may give insight into both how Scratch can be used to inspire students to program, and how the computing education community defines essential skills and concepts for K-12 computing.

3. SCOTT LEUTENEGGER
A recent Pew Internet Research survey reported that over 99% of boys and 94% of girls aged 12 - 17 play videogames. *The Pixels, Play, Programming & Pedagogy* (http://P4games.org) project [1] at the University of Denver uses the *creation* of games to engage students in computational thinking with a goal of increasing participation in STEM disciplines. P4games targets middle and high school students and teachers predominantly serving under-represented populations. The project has provided 2-4 week professional development courses to 50 teachers, 1-2 week game camps to 200 students, piloted a service learning afterschool project, and indirectly impacted thousands of students in middle and high school courses. Teachers came from art, math, technology, language arts, literature, Japanese, and social studies.

SIGCSE '11, March 9–12, 2012, Dallas, Texas, USA.
ACM 978-1-4503-0500-6/11/03.

Most students are intrigued with the idea of making their own game and become engaged through a series of simple game design exercises. Students become invested in their game ideas and want to realize them in an actual computer game. This provides a "need to know" opportunity requiring learning programming as a tool and thus leading them towards the computing disciplines. Our approach is to initially alternate time spent on game design and programming. Once students have a good design and have mastered novice programming fundamentals, students develop their games in a workshop setting.

We model, and require teachers to write Humane Games [2] which include: 1) Games for Change; 2) Games for Health; and 3) Games for Education. Games for Change are games that advocate for or raise awareness of a cause. Games for change can easily be integrated into social studies classes. Past students have created games about gender inequity, criminal justice (or lack of justice), the election process, anti-abortion, recycling, and anti-war games.

Our overall approach is not wedded to any programming environment or language. We have used Flash/Actionscript, Greenfoot/Java, and Scratch in different settings. It has been our experience that the greatest success in empowering the largest number of teachers and students across grades 6 - 10 has come from using Scratch, although, we also have had excellent success using Java with math and technology teachers who have used our game approach in semester long programming electives.

4. YOUWEN OUYANG

The *investigations for Quality Understanding and Engagement for Students and Teachers* (iQUEST) project targets 7th and 8th grade science classrooms that serve high percentages of Hispanic students and low socioeconomic populations. It is designed to deliver learning modules that are rich in both computing and science content. Through student summer camps, iQUEST has successfully demonstrated the potential of technology intensive science investigations to promote deeper understanding and appreciation of computing and science concepts and careers [6].

The main focus of iQUEST is professional development for 7th and 8th grade science teachers to change how science is taught in target schools. Teachers attend summer academies and bi-monthly workshops during the school year to enhance their own technology skills and understanding of fundamental computing concepts. The project supports teachers in building a collaborative community through the lesson study model [4] where teachers work together during the school year to brainstorm, design, deliver and reflect upon technology enhanced classroom science learning activities. These activities not only expose students to a wide spectrum of computing applications in scientific discovery but also engage students as creators of digital content that reflects deeper understanding of science concepts.

The design of iQUEST professional development is based on respect for the culture and priorities of partner schools. It acknowledges the challenges faced by teachers in their day-to-day classrooms. Ouyang will share how iQUEST introduced Scratch as a modeling tool for key 8th grade physical science concepts. Sample animations created by computer science students will be presented to illustrate how iQUEST won over teachers' trust in Scratch's ability to probe students' deeper understanding of science concepts. The simplicity of Scratch programming in these animations was an important persuading factor for teachers to allow Scratch activities to take up their hard-to-get computer time. Through further collaboration, teachers were able to take ownership in designing the context and scope of their Scratch projects. Panel audience will hear teachers' reflection of their own experience and teachers' observation of their students' experience. Analyses of student background and complexity of students' Scratch projects will also be presented.

5. ACKNOWLEDGMENTS

The panelists' works are partly supported by the National Science Foundation through CNS-0739173 (Wolz), ESI-0624767 (Leutenegger), and DRL-0833753 (Ouyang). The opinions expressed are those of the panelists and do not represent the views of the National Science Foundation.

6. REFERENCES

[1] Al-Bow et. al., 2009, Using Game Creation for Teaching Computer Programming to High School Students and Teachers, *Proc. of Innovation and Technology in Computer Science Education*, Paris, July 2009.

[2] Argent, L., Depper, W., Fajardo, R., Gjertson, S., Leutenegger, S.T., Lopeez, M.A., Rutenbeck, J., 2006, Building A Game Development Program, *IEEE Computer*, June, 2006, pp.452-60.

[3] Computer Science Teacher Association (CSTA) 2003, *A Model Curriculum for K-12 Computer Science: Final Report by the ACM K-12 Task Force Curriculum Committee*, 2nd ed.

[4] Lewis, C. *Lesson Study: A Handbook for Teacher-Led Improvement of Instruction*, 2002 Philadelphia: Research for Better Schools

[5] Margolis, J., Estrella, R., Goode, J., Holme, J. J., Nao, K. 2008, *Stuck in the Shallow End: Education, Race, and Computing*, The MIT Press, Cambridge, MA.

[6] Ouyang, Y. and Hayden, K. 2010 "A Technology Infused Science Summer Camp to Prepare Student Leaders in 8th Grade Classrooms" *Proceedings of the 41st technical symposium on computer science education,* March 10 – 13, 2010, pp 229 – 233

[7] Pearson, K. and U. Wolz, 2007, " Multi-threaded Interactive Storytelling for Literary Journalism ", *The New Media Consortium Summer Conference 2007*, pp 38 – 45

[8] Wolz, U., Stone, M., Pulimood, M., Pearson, K. 2010, Computational Thinking via Interactive Journalism in Middle School *Proceedings of the 41st technical symposium on computer science education*, March 10 – 13, 2010, pp 239 – 243

[9] Wolz, U., K. Pearson, S.M. Pulimood, M. Stone, M. Switzer 2011, Computational Thinking and Expository Writing in the Middle School: A novel approach to broadening participation in computing", to appear in the *Transactions on Computing Education*, anticipated June 2011.

Nifty Assignments

Nick Parlante, Julie Zelenski
(moderators)
Stanford University
nick.parlante@cs.stanford.edu
zelenski@cs.stanford.edu

Michelle Craig
University of Toronto
mcraig@cs.toronto.edu

Dave Feinberg
Carnegie Mellon University
fberg@cs.cmu.edu

Stuart Hansen
University of Wisconsin-Parkside
hansen@uwp.edu

David J. Malan
Harvard University
dmalan@harvard.edu

Michael Scott
University of Texas at Austin
scottm@cs.utexas.edu

Keith Schwarz
Stanford University
htiek@cs.stanford.edu

Categories and Subject Descriptors
K.3.0 [**Computers and Education**]: General.

General Terms: Algorithms, Design, Languages.

Keywords
Education, assignments, homeworks, examples, repository, library, nifty, pedagogy.

Introduction
I worry over topics for the syllabus, fretting over demos and presentations. And yet, I always come back to the fact that most of what my students learn and remember from my course comes from the assignments. Great assignments are hard to dream up and time-consuming to develop. With that in mind, the Nifty Assignments session is all about promoting and sharing the ideas and concrete materials of successful assignments.

Each presenter will introduce their assignment, give a quick demo, and describe its niche in the curriculum and its strengths and weaknesses. The presentations (and the descriptions below) merely introduce each assignment. A key part of Nifty Assignments is the mundane but vital role of distributing the materials – handouts, data files, starter code – that make each assignment ready to adopt. The Nifty Assignments home page, **http://nifty.stanford.edu**, gathers all the assignments and makes them and their support materials freely available.

If you have an assignment that works well and would be of interest to the CSE community, please consider applying to present at Nifty Assignments. See the nifty.stanford.edu home page for more information.

Nick's standing ACM editorial: a large part of the value of Nifty Assignments is that all the material are on the internet for anyone to see without screening people (or search engines!) out by some affiliation or login. In keeping with the ACM's mission to promote the study of Computer Science, the ACM, must find a way to make its materials freely available on the internet. The ACM should raise funds in some other way, such as charging authors.

SIGCSE'11, March 9–12, 2011, Dallas, Texas, USA.
ACM 978-1-4503-0500-6/11/03.

Image Puzzle (CS0-CS1) - David J Malan, Nick Parlante
A puzzle based on an image makes a neat form of Media Computation assignment. The following small assignments all require students to write image-manipulation code to solve or reveal something. Depending on the level of scaffolding, the code can be quite short.

Red Puzzle (Malan). Odds are, if your childhood was like ours, you pulled a secret message out of a cereal box at one point that could only be revealed by holding a red sheet of plastic over it. For this puzzle, students are challenged to implement that red sheet of plastic in order to solve a murder mystery! The puzzle allows students to experiment with loops, conditions, and file I/O, and it introduces them to steganography more generally.

BMP Puzzle (Malan). Perhaps the simplest way to represent an image is with a grid of pixels, each of which can be of a different color. For this puzzle, students are challenged to resize BMPs, which store images in precisely that manner. Exposes students to file I/O, hexadecimal, and graphics more generally.

Red Puzzle (Parlante). The Red Puzzle "pattern" also works well in CS0 where the I/O etc. is abstracted and the students just play with the 8 lines or so that manipulates the red channel. The computation can be made quite simple, but the puzzle still has an engaging result and the students get to write the key part of the solution code. This assignment pattern is so nifty and versatile, it should be in every teacher's repertoire.

Blue Puzzle (Parlante). Another CS0 variant on the Red Puzzle, designed to require use of an if-logic. The trick is that the true image is hidden in, say, the blue channel, but only in the values which are in the range 0..16, with all other values being garbage.

Generic Scrolling Game (CS1) - Dave Feinberg
This assignment proves that a programming project can be very structured without imposing a particular theme/story, allowing students to draw on their creativity to personalize their work. It's perfect for the CS1 teacher who wants to give students an open-ended project, but lacks the manpower to support students facing a variety of coding challenges. Although each student develops a personalized arcade game with their own theme, story, objectives, twists, etc., all students ultimately complete the same methods with essentially similar code, making it easy for the course staff to support and grade.

In the game, the user controls an image on the left edge of the screen, that can be moved up and down. Images are created on the right edge of the screen, and these scroll toward the user's image on the left edge. There are some images that the user tries to get, and there are other images that the user tries to avoid. The user earns a score, and the game ends when some condition is reached. It is up to the students to develop the game's theme/story, by choosing the title, images, distribution of images, game speed, scoring function, game-over condition, and any additional twists.

Personalized Book Recommendations (CS1) - Michelle Craig

Virtually every student has had an online experience where a website makes personalized recommendations in hopes of future sales or ongoing traffic. Amazon.com tells you "Customers Who Bought This Item Also Bought", YouTube makes suggestions for other videos to watch, and NetFlix ran a contest with a million dollar prize for an algorithm that would improve their movie recommendations. In this assignment, students write a program that makes personalized book recommendations using algorithms with increasing levels of sophistication.

After reading a pre-collected set of ratings for a list of books, the program makes recommendations for a particular reader based on a small set of sample ratings from that reader and the preferences of other readers in the community. The assignment was inspired by current machine learning research and provides the opportunity to talk about many other CS ideas including weighted averages, comparing non-trivial objects, designing distance measures between objects and writing comparators, and sparse data.

The assignment is appropriate for the middle of CS1. It uses arrays and reading from files. The solution requires at least a one-dimensional array of strings and either a 2D array of integers or a 1D array of objects.

Students are inspired by the fact that the NetFlix contest offered significant money for the real-life version of this problem. They find it fun to see their programs make personalized predictions for themselves and their friends.

Wa-Tor World: Predator Prey Simulation (CS1-CS2) - Mike Scott

A. K. Dewdney described Wa-Tor world in a 1984 Scientific American article. The world is a toroid covered entirely by water. The inhabitants of the world are plankton, fish, and sharks. The fish eat the plankton and the sharks eat the fish. Sharks and fish follow a simple set of rules that produces surprisingly complex behavior. The populations of fish and sharks over time approximate the predicted results of the Lotka-Volterra, or Predator-Prey equations.

I use this assignment in a graphics class for non Computer Science majors. The programming proficiency of the students is similar to students in a CS2 course. I give the students the simulator, based on the APCS GridWorld case study, and they implement a GUI to display the world with fish and sharks, plots of the population of each species over time, and controls to alter various parameters such as how often fish breed and how long can sharks survive without eating. The resulting program output is vibrant and complex. When completed, students and the instructor, tweak the parameters of the simulation and observe the changes.

The assignment could be altered to emphasize different concepts. A CS1 version of the assignment would give students the GUI and the GridWorld code and require them to implement classes for the world, fish, and sharks. A CS2 version of the assignment could require students to create all of the necessary classes necessary for the simulation.

Hamming Codes (CS2) - Stuart Hansen

Hamming codes are error-correcting codes. They require $O(lg(n))$ parity bits for n data bits. Each parity bit checks some (but not all) of the data bits. If an error occurs in a data bit, all the parity bits that checked it will show the error, allowing us to uniquely determine where the error occurred and correct it. If two errors occur in the same data block, Hamming codes can detect the errors, but not correct them.

We have used our Hamming code assignment in CS2, but variations can be done in CS1 or a more advanced Data Structures course. Students think the Hamming code assignment is nifty for a variety of reasons. CS Students still like to know how things work at a low level. They find manipulating data at the bit level cool. The assignment integrates matrix multiplication with binary representations of data, two topics typically covered early in a CS curriculum, but often not with an associated programming project. Students also find alternative data representations intriguing. This assignment is in the same spirit as Huffman Trees or LZW compression in that you create an alternative encoding for information. It stretches students' brains into different ways of thinking about encoding data and they like it.

Evil Hangman (CS2) - Keith Schwarz

Considering all the effort we computer scientists have spent teaching computers to play games, it's surprising that so little energy has been invested designing software that excels at cheating. Why spend all the effort trying to teach a computer the nuances of strategy when you can simply write a program that plays dirty and wins handily all the time? In this assignment, students build a mischievous program that bends the rules of "Hangman," repeatedly trouncing its human opponent.

The game Hangman follows simple rules. The computer picks a word, blanks out the letters, and invites the human to guess letters. Whenever the human guesses a letter, the computer then reveals the places in the word where that letter exists. In this "Evil Hangman" variant, the computer does not commit to a single word, but rather maintains a list of every word in the English language of a given length. As the human guesses, the computer pares down this word list, dodging the player's guesses. Once the human has run out of guesses, the computer then picks some arbitrary word from its remaining word list and reveals it as the word it had picked all along. The beauty of this approach is that the human can never prove that the computer was cheating; it just looks like it picked an obscure word and stuck with it the whole way through.

One part of this assignment I especially like is that it has a high ratio of coolness to difficulty. The particular algorithm I suggest to students is straightforward – it can be explained in just a few hours – but it is surprisingly good at trouncing unsuspecting humans. Students often prank their roommates with the program, and I've had several students tell me how they sent the program back to Mom and Dad to show off what they were learning.

This assignment is designed for use early in a CS2 curriculum and gives students a chance to play around with abstract data types such as lists and associative arrays. I have been using Evil Hangman in a CS2-level C++ programming course to help students play around with the STL, though it could easily be adapted for use in Python, C, or Java.

Experience Report: Getting Novice Programmers to THINK about Improving their Software Development Process

Tamara Caruso, Natalie Hill,
Tammy VanDeGrift
Education, EECS
University of Portland
Portland, OR 97203
+1 503 943-7256
{caruso11, hilln11, vandegri}@up.edu

Beth Simon
Computer Science and Engr. Dept.
University of California, San Diego
La Jolla, CA 92093
+1 858 534-5419
bsimon@cs.ucsd.edu

ABSTRACT

Expertise is developed through both a) self-reflection and b) making useful plans for improvement [3, 10]. Traditional novice-level programming assignments require neither of these skills to be used. Could we get students to think about improving their software development processes? What areas would they identify as needing improvement? Could they write effective plans for themselves? In this experience report, we analyze the results of an intervention with 236 CS1.5 students asking them to do these activities. We find that they most commonly make improvements in planning, compared to coding and testing. Additionally, over half of the plans they make are so vague as to be of little use in helping students identify if they have, in fact, improved. Finally, we asked students at the end of the term to reflect on how their experiences with programming assignments changed over the term. We discuss our results in light of how instructors can focus instruction to help students become more meta-cognitive about their own software development processes.

Categories and Subject Descriptors

K.3.2 [**Computer and Information Science Education**]

General Terms

Design

Keywords

Novice, programming, software quality, metacognition.

1. INTRODUCTION

Students' struggles with programming assignments are well documented [8]. However, in addition to programming-related cognitive or conceptual challenges, students working on programming assignments in the context of a university course face additional burdens. Kinnunen et al. [6] have reported on the emotional toll of CS1 students when doing programming assignments. They find external factors which distinguish "just programming" from "programming assignments". These may stem, for example, from factors external to programming concepts or constructs including course-specific issues (e.g., deadlines, course load) or personal maturity (problems with time-management).

After CS1, as students begin to work on more realistic problems, their experiences with programming assignments begin to shift from primarily "programming" concerns to incorporate at least some "software development" concerns. It is the students' experiences with, beliefs about, and self-reflection on these software development issues that this paper explores.

This report analyzes students who in their second 10 weeks of programming instruction were asked to

- Identify improvements needed in their software development skills. This was instantiated by asking students to "Write down at least one SPECIFIC plan that you can implement to improve your software development process in <the next programming assignment>". Students were encouraged to write down more than one plan, and were prompted to provide improvement plans related to different parts of software development (planning, coding, and testing).
- Reflect at the end of the term by telling "the story of how your "experience" doing programming assignments changed from the beginning of the term to now?" Students were prompted to think of what they did during the first assignment, compared to at the end of the term.

These questions were asked as part of a larger intervention in a CS1.5 (second ten weeks of Java) course at a large research-intensive university in the western US. Overall, the instructor was concerned by the number of students who experienced extreme distress in completing the first 2-week programming assignment. For many, the challenges of 2-week long assignments seemed to linger during the entire term. Previously, exhortations made regarding the need to start early, to "sleep on" problems, and specifically to NOT start on the day the assignment was due seemed to have little impact. Even providing actual words of advice from previous students seemed to make little difference. We believed that, perhaps, some students did not think about their programming assignment experiences – at the process level. And even if they did, it was unclear if they reflected on their process in a manner which could help them improve.

Schön reports that experts in their craft reflect upon their process to assist in solving new problems [10]. Ericsson has shown that expertise is developed through the use of deliberate practice [1, 3]. That is, the transformation from novice to expert is enabled by reflection on previous success (or, usually, failure), identification of specific issues for improvement, and then followed by deliberate and conscious practice where those issues are addressed. Examples abound in the arena of sports. Top athletes engage in continuous, highly-scrutinized training plans where specific performance issues are targeted for improvement. Our current programming assignments did nothing to support expertise development in this

SIGCSE'11, March 9–12, 2011, Dallas, Texas, USA.

way. Could we help students move beyond "getting a program to work" to identifying what they could do to "improve their game"?

Our approach was lightweight in structure – asking students to complete a "software development" reflection through a series of open-ended and multiple choice questions, delivered via an online survey after most assignments. The multiple choice questions asked students to identify if they had made any improvements in a given process area (planning, coding, and testing) after their second programming assignment. Students reported making more improvements in the area of planning than coding or testing. When asked to develop up to 6 specific plans to use in improving their software development processes for the next assignment, students produced an average of 4.1 per student, with many of them referring to the planning stage and coding activities. Most of these plans were implementable activities, but stated so vaguely as to be challenging to assess. This is an important component of deliberate practice. If a person sets an improvement goal which cannot be objectively evaluated, it is unlikely to be effective in helping him/her make an improvement (e.g., "I'll get in shape this fall" versus "I'll go to the gym T/Th and do 30 minutes on the treadmill"). Finally, at the end of the term, students were asked to describe in their own words the transformation of their software development experiences as applied to programming assignments across the 10 weeks of the course. Just 5% of students reported transformations in testing and 20% in coding. More transformations came in the planning stage (40%) and better time management (32%).

2. RELATED WORK

Though this work draws primarily on general research on development of expertise [3, 10], there has also been work looking at students' reflections in introductory computing. In [4] they describe different techniques to encourage reflection in computing courses. They stated that "evidence suggests that reflection actually enhances the technical master achieved". Hanks et al. [5] also gathered students' reflections by asking them to provide advice to fellow students in introductory programming courses. They found categories of general, programming-specific, and attitudinal advice – which was impacted by an intervention to get students to adopt a growth-mindset. Our approach is more specifically targeted on the software development process -- requiring students to submit bi-weekly planning sheets and diaries that reflect on their previous programming assignment experiences and reflect on specific, measurable plans to improve.

Although the core of this paper reports on students' development of meta-cognitive skills, this is studied within the context of novices' software development processes. Others have reported in this area. Edwards et al. [2] show results from 5 years of data that, compared to their classmates, A and B earning students start and finish their assignments earlier, wrote more code, but did not necessarily spend more time. Kolikant [7] examined students' definition of correctness especially as it relates to testing. She found that students believe an adequate testing strategy includes testing all the examples he or she can think of – a strategy instructors find incomplete. Porter and Calder [9] describe a study exploring the use of patterns in beginning programming classes found that requiring students to plan a solution before coding was important in getting students to use patterns.

3. METHODS

3.1 Course and Student Information

The data for this study was collected at a large public research-intensive university located on the west coast. The study took place in a 10-week undergraduate CS 1.5 course covering Java and object-oriented programming. Data was collected in two sections of the course (Winter 2010 and Spring 2010) with 163 students enrolled in winter and 73 students enrolled in spring. Eighty percent of the students in winter were CS majors; however, only 45% of the students in spring were CS majors. The course requires 5 two-week long programming assignments, and follows a CS1 course which uses pair programming for 9 1-week long programming assignments.

3.2 Data Collection

Students completed homework (via online surveys) that asked about creating plans for creating their programming assignments, students' perceptions of things they could improve on, the effectiveness of improvement plans, and a reflection on their development as programmers during the term. Slightly varying polls were given in Winter and Spring, but we report here only on questions identical in both terms. Questions varied: some were closed-form (check boxes, radio buttons); others were open-ended questions (text boxes). Students had the option to not respond to some questions, and not all enrolled students completed every survey. Table 1 summarizes the data collection.

Table 1: Number of respondents to each survey

Survey ID (given after which assignment of 5)	Number of Responses in Winter and Spring
S1: Survey1 (after 2nd)	W=109 S=64
S2: Survey 2 (after 3rd)	W=111 S=67
PT: Post Term Survey	W=113 S=73

3.3 Data Analysis

The answers to each question were analyzed independently. Closed-form and open-ended questions were analyzed differently, as described below.

Closed-form questions: students chose from a set of pre-formed answers that best fit their experience and the chosen answers were tallied. Examples include whether they thought a plan was effective or not, how useful a plan was, or how long they spent on a programming exercise.

Open-ended questions: students responded to prompts which asked for their advice, their strategies, what worked for them, and their stories of development over the term. Three authors analyzed the open-ended responses and classified them into emergent categories, with some responses fitting into more than one category. Then the broad categories were condensed and the answers were analyzed further.

Though a number of other related questions were asked in these surveys, this paper only reports on the subset which informs the following research questions:

- How did students believe they improved their software development process?
- How many and what kind of improvement plans did students create?

- What self-identified transformations did beginning programmers report occurred over the term?

4. RESULTS

4.1 How Did They Believe They Improved?

Students were asked to respond to questions about strategies they used to improve their programming experience in the second assignment (S1). This was done by asking separately about the tasks of planning, coding, and testing. For each task students completed one "select all that apply" question providing a list of things they might have improved upon. The first option on each list was "I didn't improve on any <task> activities." The options presented in each process stage were generated by the instructor based on anecdotal evidence regarding students' struggles with the assignments. Immediately following, students were asked in an open-ended question to give a specific description of what they did to make that improvement. This allows us to better understand how students interpreted the available options in the first question.

4.1.1 Planning

The select-all question asked students to check if they improved any of the following when planning. The numbers for each improvement appear in the table below.

Table 2: Self-identified improvements in planning

Improvement in planning	Number (Winter, Spring)
Practicing/understanding fundamentals before starting	37 (33.9%), 29 (45.3%)
Reading the textbook more	34 (31.2%), 13 (20.3%)
Understanding the specification	63 (57.8%), 27 (42.2%)
Planning a solution	41 (37.6%), 13 (20.3%)
Other (most were started earlier)	10 (9.2%), 0 (0.0%)
I didn't do any better planning	27 (24.8%), 19 (29.7%)

The average number of improvements reported by students, including those that reported no improvement, was 1.69 in winter and 1.29 in spring (out of 4). There were 46 students over both terms who selected that they did not do any better at planning on the second assignment.

The most frequent open-ended responses about recommendations to improve planning were:

1. Read specification carefully (28 winter, 27 spring)
2. Start earlier (28 winter, 11 spring)
3. Read textbook (22 winter, 13 spring)
4. Make outline, plan solution (14 winter, 13 spring)

Students talking about understanding the specification almost always indicated that they would recommend reading the specification more carefully. For example, one student commented that he/she would improve planning by: "Read the specification very carefully and know what you're ultimately trying to do with a method when you write it."

4.1.2 Coding

Students answered identical closed-form and open-ended questions about their coding tasks. The average number of improvements reported per student, including those who did not have improvements, was 2.42 in winter and 1.62 in spring (out of 6). There were 28 students who reported making no improvements in coding.

Table 3: Self-identified improvements in coding

Improvement in coding	Number (Winter, Spring)
I organized my code better	52 (47.8%), 20 (31.3%)
I compiled more often	74 (67.9%), 26 (40.6%)
I was better at compile-time debugging	47 (43.1%), 19 (29.7%)
I was better at run-time debugging	30 (27.5%), 11 (17.2%)
I ran into fewer roadblocks	25 (22.9%), 12 (18.8%)
I asked for help more effectively	33 (30.3%), 15 (23.4%)
Other	3 (2.8%), 1 (1.6%)
I didn't do any better on coding activities	10 (9.2%), 18 (28.1%)

The top open-ended responses about recommendations to improve coding were:

1. Compile often (34 winter, 11 spring)
2. Plan before writing code (15 winter, 8 spring)
3. Ask for help from tutors and TAs (16 winter, 2 spring)

Here are some example recommendations made by students from each of three categories above:

1. "compiling more often can help your debugging as it allows you to see your mistake as you make it"
2. "i commented on each method before doing anything else. then after all that i started programming."
3. "When you are stuck in not knowing how to code something, ask a TA for help, but make sure you know exactly what you wanna [sic] do."

4.1.3 Testing

Students were also asked what testing strategies they found effective for producing quality code. The average number of improvements reported per students was .72 in winter and .67 in spring. There were 89 students who reported making no improvements in testing.

Table 4: Self-identified improvements in testing

Improvement in testing	Number (Winter, Spring)
I brainstormed ahead of time possible erroneous situations	33 (30.3%), 16 (25.0%)
I developed test cases	27 (24.8%), 13 (20.3%)
I more robustly tested my code	17 (15.6%), 14 (21.9%)
Other	1 (0.9%), 0 (0.0%)
I didn't do any better on testing activities	55 (50.5%), 34 (53.1%)

Here are the top open-ended student-generated strategies for improving testing:

1. Test each method/class individually (9 winter, 12 spring)
2. Predict errors and try to make errors/break program (10 winter, 9 spring)
3. Create test cases (16 winter, 2 spring)
4. Do nothing different (11 winter, 0 spring)
5. Test early (0 winter, 8 spring)

Here are some examples of students' specific strategies for improving testing:

- "I created a test main method to use on all my methods to make sure they worked properly and implemented what I wanted them to do"
- "Try finding ways to make your code fail and then fix those holes."
- "i made a test sample of the data and practiced my methods on that sample in the interactions panel"

4.2 Plans for Improvement

After being asked to reflect on things they had done, students were encouraged to develop plans for what they could improve for the next assignment (3rd). They were asked:

Write down at least one SPECIFIC plan that you can implement to improve your software development process in <the next assignment>. The more plans you make and the more specific you are, the more likely they will help you.

They were provided with multiple textboxes to fill in with plans: 2 for planning tasks, 3 for coding, 1 for testing, and an "Other" plan. Students were required to fill in at least one plan to complete the survey.

The average student identified 1.75/1.69 improvement plans for the planning stage, 1.65/1.52 for the coding stage, and .70/.66 for the testing stage. The grand majority of plans fell in the planning and coding stages.

Table 5: Student Planning Goals.

	Planning	Coding	Testing
Percent of students creating at least one plan for this stage	95% W 92% S	96% W 67% S	62% W 59% S
Percent of those plans "clearly quantifiable"	45% W 35% S	45% W 42% S	62% W 49% S

But were these goals actually useful to students? A primary goal of this activity was to help students focus on deliberate practice – part of which involves setting a clear, measurable goal for themselves. If you have a vague goal it is hard to say whether you met it, which leads to challenges in identifying whether any change you observed in your performance was attributable to that change in plan. Before being asked to write their plans, students were shown this motivation, which is based off the discussion in [1]:

As every good sports coach will tell you, people with non-specific plans for "improving their game" don't do very well in actually improving. Kobe Bryant doesn't just go out and shoot baskets each day. Serena Williams doesn't "just" hit balls. They have a specific training regimen and identify specific measurable goals for improvement and track their progress in attaining them. Learn from Kobe and Serena -- improve your software development processes.

Students' plans were coded as being either "clearly quantifiable activities," or "vague activities" – which was anything else.

Examples of clearly quantifiable activities include:

- Read the Spec and highlight important key items (planning)
- Compile at each minute (coding)
- Write out a rough framework of the code on paper then attempt to transfer this framework to the compiler with comments about what and how I intend to code it. (coding)
- Test each method as I write them (testing)
- Apply system.out to make sure that everyone works as intended (testing)

Examples of "vague" activities include those that clearly indicate doing something (differently) but are vague enough that one can imagine a student, after the fact, not being able to prove that they had been successful at implementing this plan

- Spend more time brainstorming possible coding to use for certain tasks in the PSA (It's unlikely the student knows how much time they spent previously).
- Read the spec farther in advance to have more time to think about it (What day will you have read it by?)
- Map out a course of action before you start coding (What is in this map? Which calls what? The purpose of each method in English?)
- Use the interactions pane more to test whether a function works. (Close maybe, can you describe how?)
- Write main as soon as possible to make sure methods work (How soon is that? Can't you do it first?)
- Comment the codes before i move on (quite close, indicate level of granularity of commenting)
- Create more effective, less time consuming test classes/methods (what is the metric for effective? Time consuming?)
- Start early so i have time to test it out (what day?)

Words that frequently accompanied "vague" plans include: understand, think about, plan out, organize, check, and make sure. Comparators also were seen in vague plans: more, earlier, and often among them. These are all terms one can imagine a student being able to "fudge" about, when reviewing their plan after the fact.

It should be noted that specificity alone does not determine the potential usefulness of a plan in improving students' experiences. For example, "Read the spec before beginning coding" is clearly quantifiable – a student can answer "yes I did that" or "no I did not do that". However, an instructor can use such an example to help students develop expertise on the content of plans which are possibly more helpful. But getting students to be able to write specific plans is a critical, hopefully easier, first step.

4.3 Transformations Over the Term

At the end of the term (after the last assignment was due) students were asked the following:

Can you tell us the story of how your "experience" doing programming assignments changed from the beginning of the term to now? You might want to describe your typical approach to a programming assignment back in week 1 and now.

These stories were coded into emergent categories. Some stories contained more than one change, so each change was coded separately. For example, a student may have stated that she started assignments earlier and read the specification more carefully – which was coded as two separate transformations. In total, there were 143 transformations in Winter (N = 113) and 98 separate transformations in Spring (N = 73). Table 6 lists the transformations and the aggregate number of students who reported a transformation in that category.

Table 6: Self-reported transformations for students in both Winter and Spring terms

Transformation	# of students (%)
Better time management	60 (32.2%)
Planning	43 (23.1%)
Coding and debugging	37 (19.9%)
Using help resources (tutor, online)	35 (18.8%)
Reading spec more carefully	34 (18.3%)
Testing	10 (5.4%)
Internal change (confidence, independence)	9 (4.8%)
Other	6 (3.2%)
No change	7 (3.8%)

One can see that, collectively, students made transformations throughout the software development process, from the planning stages through the testing stages. Not surprisingly, as the assignments became more difficult, almost a third of the students felt the need to start assignments earlier and become better at managing their time. Several students also realized the importance of planning and documented this change in behavior in their stories.

> *"In the beginning of this term, I wasn't so good at managing my time. Last term, my programming partner always set up times to meet up to work on the PSAs. However, this term, being on my own, I would often leave much of the work to be done on the day that the PSA was due. And, this was also a bad habit because the PSAs this term were more complex, not to mention longer and more in depth, especially since we only did 5 this term. After making the mistake of procrastinating on the first two PSAs, I eventually learned to make sure to set aside adequate time to code, debug, test, etc."*

Some students became more comfortable using resources to get help, either from the tutors or from online information.

> *Now, instead of just trying to complete the assignments so I can get the points I need to pass this class, I make sure that I completely understand the code by getting help from tutors and discussing every detail with them, even if it means that I am using more of my time.*

Some students also noted the importance of carefully reading the entire specification.

> *However, as the quarter went by, I realized that I should read the entire specifications before I dive into the PSA. This helped alot in planning what I was going to do before I started to write the code.*

The strategies offered regarding coding and debugging included frequent compilation, using print statements, and commenting first.

> *A big change that occurred throughout the quarter was when I commented my code. In the beginning I would wait to comment until the very end but now I start commenting in the beginning before I write my code. This helps me maintain an idea of how I should approach the assignment. Also, whenever I came upon a problem like my code not compiling or getting a run time error I would usually depend on asking a tutor but then I started to tracing my code and using print statements to figure out the problem myself. This is a valuable skill that I began to develop. Lastly, after I finished my PSA I would return and review how I approached the assignment in order to have a better understanding of the concepts.*

A few students noted more internal transformations, reporting that they had more confidence in programming and they felt more independent.

> *I feel like I have improved significantly in terms of how independently I program. I felt like I really needed the tutor's help at the beginning and did not understand how crucial it was to start early. For my last PSA I started the day after it was posted and did it completely by myself.*

> *The most significant change has been my confidence in creating programs with little instruction. At the time I am writing this, I feel that I have done so many programming assignments, and usually done so much extra work on them, that all the elements of programming we learned in this class are fixed securely in my mental toolbox.*

5. DISCUSSION

Overall, students in CS1.5 seem highly focused on improving their software development skills in the area of planning (compared to coding or testing). A high percentage of plans for improvement they make are in the planning arena. However, these are also "easy" areas to describe improvements in – involving starting earlier, reading more carefully, etc. Developing specific plans regarding the coding process may be more intimidating as they have less experience with and possibly "control" during that part of the programming process. Perhaps instructors should provide more specific advice or scenarios for students to follow in building better coding skills. Compile after every line or two – perhaps this is something students can grok. Are there better "plans" we can help them adopt?

What about the original motivation of trying to exhort students to pay more attention to process, or at least to start early on their assignments? While students may not take this advice at the beginning of the term, their reflections on their growth show that they have gotten the picture loud and clear by the end, with a third of students identifying this as something that changed in their programming "experience". Maybe this is simply a growth process that students must experience for themselves. Some can even tell us poignantly what they know they must do:

> *With the first assignment, I waited until nearly the last minute, figuring it would be easy, since it was the first assignment. I was wrong, and the extension offered until Sunday saved me, even if my grade for the assignment took a hit. Since then, I vowed not to save my assignments for the last minute, let alone the second week. So assignment two came along, and though I promised myself I would get started on it when I was supposed to, the last minute came, and I only finished about half of the assignment. I again promised myself to start on time for the next one. And though I completed assignment three on time, the same couldn't be said for four and five. I don't have an excuse for why I didn't do the work, and I can't really say I've learned, at least in practice, how to approach the assignments. I know what must be done, I just didn't do it. All I can say I learned is that I need to change all of my habits if I'm going to see any improvement in the future.*

Which hints at the last concern -- that students' abilities to develop appropriate, truly measurable plans for improvements are notably lacking. They may have the right ideas, but could use greater direction in incorporating that key specificity of "what I will do differently" that has been shown to be necessary for engendering deliberate practice. A series of examples may be enough, but likely we need to require our students to incorporate effective reflective practice activities as part and parcel of their programming assignments. We are not just trying to teach them "Java" – and we will not always be there to help them further hone their software development skills. We need to instill the meta-cognitive skills that will allow students to learn new languages and continue the development of their expertise throughout their professional careers. We encourage future work examining more specifically the deliberate practices we should be coaching our students in applying.

6. CONCLUSION

This study used survey instruments to encourage self-reflection skills regarding students' software development processes. Self-reflection is an important component in metacognition, a practice experts use when solving problems [10]. Most introductory computing courses teach the fundamentals of a programming language and rely on teaching software process in a later course. However, we took the approach of incorporating reflection on process during the second ten weeks of learning programming. Even though we targeted a CS1.5 course, these reflection activities could easily be incorporated into the latter half of a CS1 course. Our results showed that most students self-identify improvements in planning, coding, and testing; however most of their improvements come in the planning and coding stages. Over half reported no improvement in testing practices. Perhaps CS1.5 students do not have enough experience to focus improvements in the testing stage or they do not spend much time on this stage; this result may indicate that students and teachers value planning/coding activities more than testing. Most students could create improvement plans; however, over half of these plans were too vague to be assessable quantitatively. Although not reported on here, most of the students who remembered their plans from the previous assignment stated the plans were effective for improving their process and easing frustration on the next assignment. Other instructors may want to incorporate deliberate planning exercises in their introductory courses to encourage reflective behavior. Novice students need scaffolding not only with learning how to program, but also in developing planning and reflection skills.

ACKNOWLEDGMENTS

Our thanks to the students enrolled in the CS1.5 course for generously providing survey responses for data analysis. We also thank Dr. James Male for providing funding for undergraduate students to engage in this research project.

7. REFERENCES

[1] Colvin, G. 2006. What is takes to be great. *Fortune Magazine*. October 19, 2006.

[2] Edwards, S. H., Snyder, J., Perez-Quinones, M. A., Allevato, A., Kim, D., Tretola, B. 2004. Comparing Effective and Ineffective Behaviors of Student Programmers. In *Proceedings of the ACM SIGCSE Symposium.*

[3] Ericsson, K. A. 2006. The influence of experience and deliberate practice on the development of superior expert performance. In *Cambridge handbook of expertise and expert performance* (pp. 685-706). Cambridge, UK.

[4] Fekete, A., Kay, J., Kingston, J. and Wimalaratne, K. 2000. Supporting Reflection in Introductory Computer Science. In *Proceedings of the ACM SIGCSE Symposium.*

[5] Hanks, B., Murphy, L., Simon, B., McCauley, R., Zander, C. 2009. CS1 Students Speak: Advice for Students by Students. In *Proceedings of the ACM SIGCSE Symposium.*

[6] Kinnunen, P. and Malmi, L. 2006. Why students drop out CS1 course? In *Proceedings of the ACM International Computing Education Research Workshop (ICER).*

[7] Kolikant, Y. B.-D. 2005. Students' Alternative Standards for Correctness. In *Proceedings of the ACM International Computing Education Research Workshop (ICER).*

[8] McCracken, M. et al. 2001. A multi-national, multi-institutional study of assessment of programming skills of first-year CS students. *ACM SIGCSE Bulletin.*

[9] Porter, R. and Calder, P. 2004. Patterns in Learning to Program – An Experiment? In *Proceedings of the Australasian Computing Education Conference (ACE).*

[10] Schön, D. A. 1983. The Reflective Practitioner: How Professionals Think in Action. Basic Books.

Measuring the Effectiveness of Error Messages Designed for Novice Programmers

Guillaume Marceau
WPI
100 Institute Road
Worcester, MA, USA
+1 (508) 831-5357
gmarceau@wpi.edu

Kathi Fisler
WPI
100 Institute Road
Worcester, MA, USA
+1 (508) 831-5357
kfisler@cs.wpi.edu

Shriram Krishnamurthi
Brown University
115 Waterman St
Providence, RI, USA
+1 (401) 863-7600
sk@cs.brown.edu

ABSTRACT

Good error messages are critical for novice programmers. Recognizing this, the DrRacket programming environment provides a series of pedagogically-inspired language subsets with error messages customized to each subset. We apply human-factors research methods to explore the effectiveness of these messages. Unlike existing work in this area, we study messages at a fine-grained level by analyzing the edits students make in response to various classes of errors. We present a rubric (which is not language specific) to evaluate student responses, apply it to a course-worth of student lab work, and describe what we have learned about using the rubric effectively. We also discuss some concrete observations on the effectiveness of these messages.

Categories and Subject Descriptors K.3.2 [Computer and Education]: Computer and Information Science Education—Computer science education; H.5.2 [User Interfaces]: Evaluation/Methodology

General Terms Experimentation, Human Factors

Keywords Error messages, Novice programmers, User-studies

1. INTRODUCTION

In a compiler or programming environment, error messages are one of the most important points of contact between the system and the programmer. This is all the more critical in tools for novice programmers, who lack the experience to decipher complicated or poorly-constructed feedback. Thus, many research efforts have sought to make professional compilers more suitable for teaching by rewriting their error messages [10] or supplementing them with hints and explanations [3]. Such efforts complement more general research on improving error messages by means such as error recovery during parsing.

DrRacket[1] [5] goes farther. It defines several sublanguages around what students have learned at different stages [9]. Each sublanguage provides only (versions of) those constructs that make sense at that point, and similarly customizes error messages. The levels and messages have evolved over a decade of observation in lab, class, and office settings.

Despite this care, we still see novices struggle to work effectively with the messages. To understand why, we logged students' edits in response to errors over an entire college-level introductory course and coded whether the edits reflected understanding of the error message. Our work is novel in using fine-grained data about edits to assess the effectiveness of individual classes of error messages. Our coding rubric for assessing the performance of error messages through edits is a key contribution of this work. Our observations about how to use the coding results to reflect on our course is another. Finally, we also present some concrete observations on how students respond to these messages.

2. RESPONSES TO ERROR MESSAGES

We begin by showing a few examples of student responses to error messages during Lab #1. When Lab #1 begins, most students have not had any contact with programming beyond four hours of course lectures given in the days before and two short homeworks due the day before and evening after the lab.

Figure 1 (a) shows one function (excerpted from a larger program) submitted for execution 40 minutes after the start of the lab. The student is defining a function `label`, with one argument `name`. Most likely the student is missing a closing parenthesis after `name`, and another one after `"conservative"`. The nesting suggests that the student is struggling to remember how to combine two Boolean tests into one using the `or` operator. DrRacket provides a textual message (lower pane) and highlights (pink in upper pane) a code fragment that triggered the error.

Figure 1 (b) shows the student's next edit. The student inserted `name` as an argument to the function call to `string=?`. An ambiguity in the error message might have prompted this mistake: the word "function" in the fragment "for the function's second argument" can refer to either the function being defined (`label`) or the function being called (`string=?`). DrRacket means the former, but the student seems to have inferred the latter (perhaps influenced by the highlighting). Our dataset illustrates several situations in which the association of the highlight to the error text is underspecified.

As another example, Figure 2 shows a sequence of programs that each triggered the same error message. The topmost program was submitted first; what follows are the student's first four attempts to correct the problem. The student never identifies the actual problem, which is a missing open parenthesis before the `cond`. The entire sequence lasts 10 minutes, until the end of the lab ses-

[1] Formerly known as DrScheme. **`www.drracket.org`**

SIGCSE'11, March 9–12, 2011, Dallas, Texas, USA.

(a)

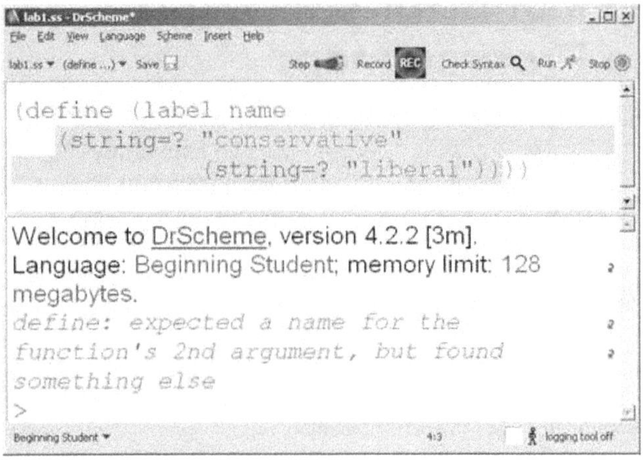

(b)

```
(define (label name
   (string=? name "conservative"
             (string=? name "liberal"))))
```

Figure 1. (a) A student's program and its error message, (b) The student's response to the error message

sion. A few weeks later, when the student participated in an interview, he mentioned how frustrating the experience had been.

Even with our years of experience teaching with DrRacket, the state of the programs we collected was often surprising, if not humbling. Students manage to create quite mangled functions, which the error messages must attempt to help them sort out.

3. METHODOLOGY

In the spring of 2010, we ran a study in WPI's introductory programming course. We configured DrRacket to save a copy of each program each student tried to run, as well as the error message received (if any) plus any keystrokes that the student pressed in response to the error message, up to their next attempt at running the program. We collected data during the course's normal lab sessions, which ran for 50 minutes per week for six weeks (undergrad courses at WPI are 28 hour-long lectures over seven weeks, so the data cover the entire course). During labs, students worked on exercises covering recent lecture material.

Of the 140 students in the course, 64 agreed to participate in this data collection and 53 actually submitted data. We did not ask participants for demographics such as intended majors, but more than a third of the overall course population listed majors other than computer science. Student participation dropped to 24 students by the final week as a result of students changing lab seats and not reinitializing the software at their new stations; no students withdrew from the study.

4. THE DESIGN OF A CODING RUBRIC

There are many ways one might study the effectiveness of error messages. A common approach in the literature (as reviewed in Section 7) is to change the messages or their presentation and compare the impact on student grades at the end of the course. We are interested in a more fine-grained analysis that determines which error messages are effective and in what ways. There is no

```
(define (string-one-of? check-for-match stringOne stringTwo stringThree)
   cond [(and (string=? check-for-match stringOne))]
        [(and (string=? check-for-match stringTwo))]])
```

define: expected only one expression for the function body, but found at least one extra part

```
(define (string-one-of? check-for-match stringOne stringTwo stringThree)
   cond [(string=? check-for-match stringOne)]
        [(and (string=? check-for-match stringTwo))]
        [(and (string=? check-for-match stringThree))]])

(define (string-one-of? check-for-match stringOne stringTwo stringThree)
   cond [and ((string=? check-for-match stringOne))]
        [(and (string=? check-for-match stringTwo))]
        [(and (string=? check-for-match stringThree))]])

(define (string-one-of? check-for-match stringOne stringTwo stringThree)
   cond [(string=? check-for-match stringOne)]
        [(string=? check-for-match stringTwo)]
        [(string=? check-for-match stringThree)]])

(define (string-one-of? check-for-match stringOne stringTwo stringThree)
   cond [(string=? check-for-match)]
        [(string=? check-for-match stringTwo)]
        [(string=? check-for-match stringThree)]])
```

Figure 2. A sequence of responses to an error message

single metric for "effectiveness" of an error message. Possible metrics include whether students demonstrate learning after working with messages or whether the messages help novice programmers emulate experts. We have chosen a narrower metric: does the student make a reasonable edit, as judged by an experienced instructor, in response to the error message?

To gain confidence that our metric and its application to our data were valid, we developed a formal rubric for assessing edits and subjected it to a test of *inter-coder reliability* [2] (where "coder" is the standard term for one who applies a rubric to data).[1] Inter-coder reliability tests whether a rubric can be applied objectively: multiple coders independently apply it to data, measure their consistency, then revise the rubric until sufficient consistency is achieved. After describing how our rubric evolved, we present the standard measurement of inter-coder reliability that we used.

Our rubric attempts to distinguish ways in which error messages succeed or fail. Our design starts from a conceptual model of how error messages intend to help students: if an error message is effective, it is because a student reads it, can understand its meaning, and can then use the information to formulate a useful course of action. This is a three step sequence:

Read ▸ Understand ▸ Formulate

Students can get stuck at any of these steps. One interesting question is whether students get stuck earlier in the sequence with particular kinds of errors. To explore this, we would ideally like a rubric that identifies how far a student successfully went in the sequence when responding to a given error message. This would suggest a rubric with at least four categories: failure-on-read, failure-on-understand, failure-on-formulate, and fixed-the-error. Our initial attempts to distinguish failure-on-read from failure-on-understand were not successful (in that we could not achieve inter-coder reliability). Our recordings of student editing sessions lack attention-based data (such as eye-tracking) that indicate where a student looked or reacted when an error occurred; such data might have helped distinguish between read- and understand-failures. We concluded that a more realistic rubric would com-

[1] This paper uses "coder" exclusively as a social-science term; in particular, "coder" never refers to programmers.

[DEL]	Deletes the problematic code wholesale.
[UNR]	Unrelated to the error message, and does not help.
[DIFF]	Unrelated to the error message, but it correctly addresses a different error or makes progress in some other way.
[PART]	Evidence that the student has understood the error message (though perhaps not wholly) and is trying to take an appropriate action (though perhaps not well).
[FIX]	Fixes the proximate error (though other cringing errors might remain).

Figure 3. Rubric for responses to error messages

bine failure-on-read and failure-on-understand into a single category separate from failure-on-formulate.

Figure 3 presents our final rubric for assessing students' edits. The [UNR] and [PART] codes capture failure-on-read/understand and failure-on-formulate, respectively. All the responses in the sequence shown in Figure 2 were coded [UNR], for example, since none of the edits tried to change the number of parts in the function body position of the `define`, and nothing else suggested that the student had read or understood the message.

Earlier versions of our rubric attempted to discern two nuances of failure-on-understand: failure to understand the text as separate from failure to understand what the message *really* means in terms of the code. An error message can use simple words and simple grammar but still be hard to understand because the underlying problem is difficult or because the message inadequately describes the problem. Responding to these error messages requires students to read beyond the words and understand that "when DrRacket says X, it really means Y". Figure 4 shows an example. On its face, the message contradicts the text of the code: there definitely is a parenthesis before the `and`. To understand the message, one has to realize that the parenthesis before the `and` has been attributed to the `cond`; in the parser's view, the `and` stands on its own without a parenthesis. Predictably, the student failed to formulate a useful response to that message (they deleted the parenthesis before the `and`). Early versions of the rubric tried to capture how often students failed to formulate a response according to the deep meaning of the message (what an expert would understand from the message) because they were being misled by its literal meaning. However, coders were not sufficiently reliable when making these distinctions, and so the final rubric has only one code corresponding to a failure to formulate, namely [PART].

For the remaining codes in Figure 3, [DEL] captures cases when students simply deleted error-inducing code rather than attempting to fix it, [DIFF] captures edits that were useful but unrelated to the reported error (such as fixing a different error or adding more code or test cases), and [FIX] captures successful completion of the read/understand/formulate sequence. These codes and their precise wordings reflect several design decisions that arose while developing the rubric:

The rubric should assess the performance of the error messages, not the students. Consider a situation in which a student's edit corrects a problem that had nothing to do with the original error message. While this is a positive outcome, it does not address our primary concern of how effective error messages are at guiding students through the read/understand/formulate sequence. Similarly, students may experience difficulties with problem solving or program design that should not be attributed to shortcomings of the error messages. To keep our coding focused on the error messages, we include the [DIFF] code for reasonable edits unrelated to the proximate error. Unreasonable edits unrelated to the proximate error are coded [UNR]. Our first rubric design had unified [DIFF] and [UNR]; we split them after considering when the error message could be held accountable. Sometimes, students simply avoid the proximate error by deleting their code (for example, deleting a test case that yields an error). To avoid judging the error message (as [UNR] might), we introduced the separate [DEL] code for such cases. When deletion is the appropriate action (e.g., when removing an extra function argument) and it is performed on a reasonable code fragment, we code it as [PART] or [FIX] as appropriate. Together, [DIFF] and [DEL] characterize situations in which the student's action provides no information about the quality of the error message.

Coding decisions have to be made narrowly, strictly in relation to the proximate error described in the message. DrRacket reports only one error at a time. Fixing the problem mentioned in the message sometimes makes the overall code worse (for example, a student might delete an extra expression rather than add an operator to combine it with the rest of the code). Frequently, an edit fixes the error mentioned but leaves other glaring errors in surrounding code untouched. We nevertheless code such edits as [FIX]. [FIX] implies neither mastery on the part of the student nor oracular accuracy on the part of the message. It simply means that the student formulated a reasonable response to the problem mentioned in the message. The text "though other cringing errors might remain" reminds coders to take this narrow interpretation. In practice, our coders needed the explicit reminder to be self-consistent in applying [FIX].

Coding needs a holistic view of multi-faceted error messages. DrRacket's error messages have two components: text and a highlight. In assessing whether a student had "read" or "understood" an error message, we had to decide whether editing within the highlighted expression sufficed (even if the edit showed no evidence of understanding the text). Some students glance first at the highlight for a quick overview of the error; this should be a credit to the error message, even though we have a bias towards the text when assessing "understanding". At the same time, students often made random edits in the highlighted code that were arguably unrelated to the proximate error. We ultimately decided that location was not sufficient justification for ascribing [PART] or [FIX].

We accepted liberally any evidence that the student read and understood something from the message. In some cases, making this determination required human judgment or teaching experience, as was the case with the "expect a name" example in Figure 1. Because we decided that the student probably got the idea of inserting "name" from having read the words "expected a name" in the message, we coded that response [PART] rather than [UNR]. We found such subjective decisions surprisingly consistent across the coders.

```
(define (label-near? name bias word1 word2 word3)
  (cond
    (and (cond [(string=? name word1) "Name Located"]
               [(string=? bias word1) "Bias Located"])
         (cond [(string=? name word2) "Name Located"]
               [(string=? bias word2) "Bias Located"])
  "Mark")
))
```

and: found a use of `and' that does not follow an open parenthesis

Figure 4. A counterfactual error message

During the design process, we also ruled out ideas that failed to survive inter-coder reliability tests or our own evaluation:

- *Distinguishing [FIX] codes based on elapsed time*: we considered factoring in students' response time by having separate codes for "fixed with hesitation" and "fixed without hesitation" (we have timestamp data on all edits, and can replay editing sessions at their original pace). In theory, errors to which students respond more slowly might be harder for students to process. We ultimately ruled this out for two main reasons. First, response time could be affected by corrupting interferences (such as a student taking a bathroom break or differences in working styles across students). Second, we lacked a good metric for the expected difficulty of each error message; without that, we would not be able to identify messages that were performing worse than expected.
- *Considering whether the edit yielded a new error message as a criterion for [FIX]:* this is a corollary to our observation about coding narrowly. In practice, we found cases in which the student really did fix the error, but had code of such a form that the same error applied after the edit. We chose to ignore this criterion in final coding.

The rubric as shown in Figure 3 meets standards of inter-coder reliability on the data from Lab #1. We used the standard metric of inter-coder reliability [2], κ, which is defined as

$$\kappa = \frac{\text{Agreement} - \text{Expected Agreement}}{1 - \text{Expected Agreement}}$$

κ compares the agreement of the human coders to the agreement that would be expected by chance according to the marginal probabilities. Because of this, it is a more demanding metric than the simple proportions of the number of times the coders agreed. Values of κ usually lie within 1.0 (meaning perfect agreement) and 0.0 (meaning agreement exactly as good as would be expected by chance), but values of κ can be negative if the human coders perform worse than chance. We executed this test of inter-coder reliability on each version of the rubric. The final version of the rubric (the one shown in Figure 3) was the first version which met the $\kappa > 0.8$ standard, with $\kappa = 0.84$ on 18 different responses.

5. APPLYING THE RUBRIC

Our rubric is designed to identify error messages that students respond to poorly. Given that multiple error messages can reflect the same underlying problem, we group messages into nine thematically-related categories, such as "parenthesis matching", "syntax of define", and "runtime type". For each lab, we sampled 15 edits per category (a sufficient size for statistical validity) and coded each against the rubric in Figure 3. We used Köksal, et al.'s edit-replay software [14] to replay programs during coding.

Table 1 shows the results of coding for the 9 most common error categories (the categories not shown occurred very rarely.) The top row shows the number of errors an average student received during each lab (${}^{\#}E_l$). The sub-table for each lab shows the percentage of the error messages presented during that lab that were of the given category (${}^{\%}P_{l,c}$); the percentage of error messages in the category that were badly responded to according to our coding (${}^{\%}B_{l,c}$); and an estimate of the number of errors in that category that each student responded to poorly during the lab. This estimate is the product of the preceding three values:

$$^{\#}B_{l,c} = {}^{\#}E_l \cdot {}^{\%}P_{l,c} \cdot {}^{\%}B_{l,c}$$

When computing each variable for the table, we average across students to avoid due influence by the few students who compile much more frequently than the average. For instance, we compute ${}^{\%}B_{l,c}$ by first taking the ratio of [UNR] + [PART] against the denominator [UNR] + [PART] + [FIX] per individual student. Specifically, for student *s*, lab, *l*, and category *c*, we compute:

$$^{\%}B_{s,l,c} = ([\text{UNR}] + [\text{PART}])/([\text{UNR}] + [\text{PART}] + [\text{FIX}])$$

Then we take the unweighted average across the n students who are represented in the selected samples:

$$^{\%}B_{l,c} = \left(\sum {}^{\%}B_{s,l,c}\right)/\text{n}$$

The bar to the right of #bad in each cell indicates the relative magnitude of #bad values within that lab. The ten lab/error-class combinations with the highest number of poor responses appear in boxes. The sum of the #bad estimates within each lab (under the table) indicates the total estimated number of errors that a student would make in that lab. By this measure, we expect a student to respond poorly to 3.16 errors in Lab #1 and 5.51 errors in Lab #2. While these may seem small out of context, 5.51 errors in 50 minutes translates to a poorly-handled error message every 10 minutes. Worse, this is an average, so the frequency is much higher for some students.

In interpreting the data, we are interested in the cells with boxes (suggesting the highest likelihood of recurrence in a general population) and the cells with the highest %bad values (suggesting errors which were highly problematic for perhaps a small number of students).

We are particularly interested in interventions that might help students at the very beginning of the course (when students form their first impressions of programming and may elect to drop the course). Within Lab #1, syntax errors (including "paren matching") dominate the problematic cases. Based on other data (from interviews with students and a vocabulary quiz), we have good reason to suspect problems with the highlights and the vocabulary. Due to space constraints, we defer discussion of these findings to follow-up papers that report on interventions.

Lab #2 contains four of the ten boxes; students struggled most with the messages in this lab. This might be expected, as students confront many new syntactic constructs and concepts in the preceding week. However, the boxes occur in somewhat surprising

Lab number	#1			#2			#3			#4			#5			#6		
# of errors a student received during this lab (on average)	8.5			16.3			14.4			9.0			9.8			9.8		
	% error	% bad	# bad	% error	% bad	# bad	% error	% bad	# bad	% error	% bad	# bad	% error	% bad	# bad	% error	% bad	# bad
arg. count	5%	48%	0.22	17%	27%	**0.74**	14%	17%	0.33	13%	20%	0.24	35%	21%	**0.74**	12%	31%	0.36
parens matching	28%	24%	0.58	12%	14%	0.27	17%	0%	0.00	14%	0%	0.00	13%	0%	0.00	10%	15%	0.15
runtime cond	3%	0%	0.00	3%	100%	0.49	4%	20%	0.12	6%	72%	0.40	8%	78%	**0.62**	1%	100%	0.06
runtime type	2%	100%	0.15	8%	73%	**0.91**	16%	40%	**0.93**	8%	22%	0.17	6%	44%	0.26	3%	38%	0.13
syntax cond	14%	51%	0.59	4%	50%	0.31	6%	26%	0.24	10%	28%	0.25	9%	20%	0.17	11%	11%	0.12
syntax define	16%	50%	**0.68**	14%	50%	**1.14**	6%	15%	0.14	7%	24%	0.14	2%	17%	0.03	3%	38%	0.10
syntax func. call	14%	64%	**0.74**	14%	17%	0.37	12%	14%	0.26	23%	27%	0.55	4%	29%	0.12	13%	38%	0.48
syntax struct	0%	0%	0.00	8%	32%	0.43	5%	92%	**0.73**	0%	0%	0.00	1%	0%	0.00	0%	0%	0.00
unbound id.	16%	16%	0.21	13%	40%	**0.85**	16%	14%	0.32	16%	0%	0.00	20%	7%	0.14	34%	13%	0.44
Total:			3.16			5.51			3.07			1.75			2.07			1.84

Table 1. Coding results.

categories (e.g., argument count and unbound identifier); manual inspection of the data for those cells might point to the problems.

Most of the boxes occur in the first three weeks. This would be consistent with students improving at error handling. However, curricular aspects of the labs also affect error patterns across cells. For example, the "arg(ument) count" errors in Lab #5 trace to mistakes students made while defining *n*-ary tree data. Constructing *n*-ary trees requires nesting lists inside of structures; students often close expressions for multiple branches incorrectly while nesting calls to the constructors. Understanding the context in which a class of errors becomes problematic is critical to designing good interventions based on this data.

It is tempting to interpret these graphs as indicating students' *conceptual* difficulties in the course. This interpretation is invalid because the error *message* that a student sees is often not a direct indicator of the underlying *error*. For instance, Lab #6 had numerous "unbound-id" errors, but a careful manual analysis revealed that many of them were from students improperly using structures (e.g., using field reference operators incorrectly in various ways), not merely being bad typists. To further confound matters, the precise error that is shown is a function of parsing strategies, because many invalid expressions can be flagged in multiple ways. Therefore, an additional manual analysis is necessary to understand what actual errors students were making.

6. PERSPECTIVE

Fine-grained analysis of student edits has given us detailed insight into student performance both with DrRacket and in our course overall. The data obtained from our rubric identifies errors that students find challenging at different points in the course; refining this with manual inspection of the edit files suggests concrete tasks (such as working with nested data structures) that pose hurdles for students. This information is much harder to identify from looking at the results of homeworks and exams, since these represent a final—rather than ongoing—snapshot of student work.

Effectively, this paper proposes assessing IDE and curricular changes not just on *student achievement* (e.g, course or assignment grades) but to also include assessment based on *error effectiveness*. While our work measures error effectiveness using student actions (edits), we grade the errors, not the students. This has several advantages. Interpreting the success of an action requires a benchmark against which to measure it. When measuring an edit, the benchmark of "made progress" is less subjective and easier to recognize than, say, benchmarking student behaviors against models of behaviors of domain experts.

Our approach does require additional data analysis to identify the conceptual problems underlying the edit message performance. Additional studies are required to determine which problems are best solved by changes to the IDE or curriculum, respectively.

Although our work studies edits to Racket/Scheme programs, our rubric is not language-specific. Our read-understand-formulate model of processing errors is general, as are the categories of edits that appear in the rubric. We have not checked inter-coder reliability of the rubric against edits in other languages, but we hypothesize that the rubric could apply more broadly.

7. COMPARISON TO RELATED WORK

Due to space constraints, we omit citations to efforts to improve error feedback that lack user-oriented evaluation. Early work on the pedagogy of programming sought to classify the errors novice programmers make when using assembly [1] or Pascal [24]. More recent work along the same lines studies BlueJ [12, 22], Java [11], Eiffel [19], and Helium [8]. Others have studied novices' behavior during debugging sessions [18]. These observational studies depend on ad hoc methodologies which impair their reproducibility and makes drawing general conclusions difficult. Our work differs in not studying the students' mistakes broadly and qualitatively; rather, we constructed a quantitative evaluation of the influence of error messages on students' behavior which (we hope) will invite reproduction.

There are still relatively few efforts to evaluate the learning impact of pedagogic IDEs [21]. Gross and Powers survey recent efforts [6], including, notably, those on Lego Mindstorms [4], and on Jeliot 2000 [16], though neither works found a statistically significant improvement. Jadud [13] found a weak relationship between the errors students' received and their final course grade. These studies suffer from having too many confounding factors underneath their dependent variable (the course grades). In contrast, we attempted to tease out the effect of error messages alone.

Other groups have proposed subjective rubrics to study students' development process [14], or to evaluate students' success during individual programming sessions [3, 15]. Coull further added explanatory notes to the error messages of the standard Java compiler based on their observations. These notes made experimental subjects significantly more likely to complete successfully short exercises.

Researchers have interviewed students about the error messages in each of Alice [17] and BlueJ [7]; the difficulty of interpreting the error messages fared amongst the students' primary complaints [23]. One evaluation of BlueJ asked students whether they found the messages useful [25]. Most did, but it is unclear what this means since the evaluation did not gather any comparative data against which to calibrate the students' remarks.

Nienaltowski et al. [20] compared the impact of adding long-form explanation to an error message, and of adding a highlight on three different error messages, in a short web-based experiment. They found that the former has no impact, while the later impairs performance slightly. Unfortunately, the experiment's design has many threats to validity, some of which the paper acknowledged.

8. ACKNOWLEDGMENTS

Fatih Köksal generously provided his software. Ryan S. de Baker, Nate Krach, and Janice Gobert offered extensive advice on social science methodology. We thank the students who participated in our study and Glynis Hamel for enabling it. Tamara Munzner discussed study design and provided useful references. Matthias Felleisen offered valuable discussion and comments on an early draft. This work is partially supported by the US National Science Foundation and Google.

9. REFERENCES

[1] Chabert, J.M. and Higginbotham, T.F. An Investigation of Novice Programmer Errors in IBM 370 (OS) Assembly Language. In *Proceedings of the ACM Southeast Regional Conference*, pages 319-323. 1976.

[2] Cohen, J. A coefficient of agreement for nominal scales. *Educational and Psychological Measurement*, 20(1):37–46, 1960.

[3] Coull, N.J. *SNOOPIE: Development Of A Learning Support Tool For Novice Programmers Within A Conceptual Framework*. PhD Thesis, School of Computer Science, University Of St. Andrews, 2008.

[4] Fagin, B.S. and Merkle, L. Quantitative analysis of the effects of robots on introductory Computer Science education. *Journal on Educational Resources in Computing*, 2(4):1-18, 2002.

[5] Findler, R.B., Clements, J., Flanagan, C., Flatt, M., Krishnamurthi, S., Steckler, P., and Felleisen, M. DrScheme: A programming environment for Scheme. *Journal of Functional Programming*, 12(02):159–182, 2002.

[6] Gross, P. and Powers, K. Evaluating assessments of novice programming environments. In *Proceedings of the International Workshop on Computing Education Research*, pages 99-110. 2005.

[7] Hagan, D. and Markham, S. Teaching Java with the BlueJ environment. In *Proceedings of Australasian Society for Computers in Learning in Tertiary Education Conference*. 2000.

[8] Hage, J. and Keeken, P.V. Mining Helium programs with Neon. *Technical Report, Department of Information and Computing Sciences, Utrecht University*, 2007.

[9] Holt, R.C., Wortman, D.B., Barnard, D.T., and Cordy, J.R. SP/k: a system for teaching computer programming. *Communications of the ACM*, 20(5):301–309, 1977.

[10] Hristova, M., Misra, A., Rutter, M., and Mercuri, R. Identifying and correcting Java programming errors for introductory computer science students. In *Proceedings of the Symposium on Computer Science Education*, pages 153–156. 2003.

[11] Jackson, J., Cobb, M., and Carver, C. Identifying Top Java Errors for Novice Programmers. In *Proceedings of the Frontiers in Education Conference*, pages T4C–24. 2005.

[12] Jadud, M.C. A First Look at Novice Compilation Behaviour Using BlueJ. *Computer Science Education*, 15(1):25–40, 2005.

[13] Jadud, M.C. Methods and tools for exploring novice compilation behaviour. In *Proceedings of the International Workshop on Computing Education Research*, pages 73–84. 2006.

[14] Köksal, M.F., Başar, R.E., and Üsküdarlı, S. Screen-Replay: A Session Recording and Analysis Tool for DrScheme. *Proceedings of the Scheme and Functional Programming Workshop, Technical Report, California Polytechnic State University, CPSLO-CSC-09-03*, :103-110, 2009.

[15] Lane, H.C. and VanLehn, K. Intention-based scoring: An approach to measuring success at solving the composition problem. In *Proceedings of the Symposium on Computer Science Education*, pages 373-377. 2005.

[16] Levy, R.B., Ben-Ari, M., and Uronen, P.A. The Jeliot 2000 program animation system. *Computers & Education*, 40(1):1-15, 2003.

[17] Moskal, B., Lurie, D., and Cooper, S. Evaluating the effectiveness of a new instructional approach. In *Proceedings of the Symposium on Computer Science Education*, pages 75-79. 2004.

[18] Murphy, L., Lewandowski, G., McCauley, R., Simon, B., Thomas, L., and Zander, C. Debugging: the good, the bad, and the quirky — a qualitative analysis of novices' strategies. In *Proceedings of the Symposium on Computer Science Education*, pages 163-167. 2008.

[19] Ng Cheong Vee, M., Mannock, K., and Meyer, B. Empirical study of novice errors and error paths in object-oriented programming. In *Proceedings of the Conference of the Higher Education Academy, Subject Centre for Information and Computer Sciences*, pages 54-58. 2006.

[20] Nienaltowski, M., Pedroni, M., and Meyer, B. Compiler Error Messages: What Can Help Novices? In *Proceedings of the Technical Symposium on Computer Science Education*, pages 168-172. 2008.

[21] Pears, A., Seidman, S., Malmi, L., Mannila, L., Adams, E., Bennedsen, J., Devlin, M., and Paterson, J. A survey of literature on the teaching of introductory programming. *ACM SIGCSE Bulletin*, 39(4):204-223, 2007.

[22] Ragonis, N. and Ben-Ari, M. On understanding the statics and dynamics of object-oriented programs. *ACM SIGCSE Bulletin*, 37(1):226-230, 2005.

[23] Rey, J.S. *From Alice To BlueJ: A Transition To Java*. Master's thesis, School of Computing, Robert Gordon University, 2009.

[24] Spohrer, J.C. and Soloway, E. Novice mistakes: are the folk wisdoms correct? *Communications of the ACM*, 29(7)1986.

[25] Van Haaster, K. and Hagan, D. Teaching and Learning with BlueJ: an Evaluation of a Pedagogical Tool. *Issues in Informing Science and Information Technology*, 1:455-470, 2004.

Which Aspects of Novice Programmers' Usage of an IDE Predict Learning Outcomes?

Gregory Dyke
Ecole des Mines de Saint-Etienne,
France
158, Cours Fauriel
42023 Saint-Etienne CEDEX
+33 6 50 56 30 99
gregdyke@gmail.com

ABSTRACT

We present the preliminary analysis of a study whose long term aim is to track IDE usage to identify novice-programmers in need of support. Our analysis focused on the activity of 24 dyads on a 3 week assignment. We correlated frequencies of events such as use of code generation and of the debugger with assignment grades, final exam grades, and the difference in rankings within dyad on the final exam. Our results show several significant correlations. In particular, code generation and debugging are correlated with the final grade, and running in non-debug mode is correlated with differences in ranking. These results are encouraging as they show that it is possible to predict learning outcomes with simple frequency data and suggest more complex indicators could achieve robust prediction.

Categories and Subject Descriptors

K.3.2 [**Computers and education**]: Computer and information Science Education

General Terms

Measurement, Experimentation, Human Factors.

Keywords

Log data, Novice programmers, IDE usage

1. INTRODUCTION

Within the field of the Learning Sciences and for Technology Enhanced Learning in particular, the role of the tutor and their ability to monitor student activity has been considered crucial [16]. Several approaches have looked at ways of constructing high-level interaction indicators from low-level log data in order to assist such tutor monitoring [4,12]. For the teaching of programming, several studies have tracked programming activity at various levels in order to correlate it with learning outcomes and thus to suggest best practices to students or to identify "at-risk" students [7,10,11].

In these studies, however, metrics have been mostly limited to compiling activity, resulting errors and standard software metrics such as lines of code, code complexity, amount of time spent, etc. and not to other more fine-grained activities, particularly those afforded by IDEs such as code-completion and generation. Furthermore, while there is a general consensus as to the benefits of pair programming [3,8,13] studies investigating such practices have not looked in detail at the programming activity itself.

The field of Educational Data Mining has shown that it is possible to detect many behaviors from tracking data, such as gaming the system, off-task behavior and guessing in intelligent tutoring systems [2]. Such techniques have also been used to detect affect (boredom, frustration, etc.) through analysis of compilation behaviour. Other studies encourage us to think that low-level data [15] can be used in many instances to predict higher-level outcomes.

In this paper, we examine novice programmers' usage of the Eclipse IDE whilst working in pairs, and the relationship between this usage and learning outcomes as measured by their grades. We first explain how our educational context led us to conduct such a study and describe the data we chose to collect and the hypotheses we had concerning how this data might help to predict learning outcomes. We then present and discuss the results of a preliminary analysis which indicate: that several indicators related to use of the full possibilities of the IDE correlate significantly with learning outcomes; that the frequency indicators we calculated are a better predictor of the final exam grade than of the grade of the assignment the students were working on during the data collection; and that similar indicators both positively correlate with the final exam grade and with the within-dyad difference between grades on the final exam in spite of these two outcomes having a very low degree of correlation with each other.

2. STUDY DESCRIPTION AND METHODOLOGY

2.1 Context

This study was conducted on a class of 124 first year students at a French engineering school (a 3-year graduate-level school whose entry exam is usually prepared during the two years after high-school). The salient features of this population are that they are extremely high achievers who are used to working hard but who are mostly not interested in computer science and programming. Unfortunately for them, a significant number of entry-level jobs obtained by graduates from this school feature programming responsibilities. Furthermore grades in Computer Science courses are not expected to be a discriminating factor in students' overall pass rate and, in contrast to the problems reported by many introductory programming courses for non CS majors, the dropout rate is very low (<1%). However, in our department, we are concerned over students' lack of willingness to seek out help during lab work (with many TAs present) – making it difficult for us to help out the students who are in difficulty – and our difficulty in fostering the habit of regularly running the written code, in order to make sure that it works. We are also curious as to whether there are situations where our forcing students to work in pairs (due to lack of available hardware) has a negative impact on their individual learning.

During the *Object-Oriented Programming in Java and UML modeling* course, students have four 90mn lab sessions (small assignments) and three 3h lab sessions (during which they work on a larger assignment) over the course of seven weeks. In all these sessions, students work in pairs, owing to constraints in the number of available workstations. They are encouraged to continue working on their assignment outside of the lab. This is the students' second programming course and their first contact with the Java programming language. It is also their first experience with using the Eclipse IDE (as opposed to the previous course where they edited with a text editor and compiled on the command line).

Students are evaluated via a grade on the assignment, which they must turn in a week after the final lab session (same grade for both members of the pair), and via a grade on a final exam which tests knowledge about object-oriented programming in general, UML modeling and the java language. These grades are given out of 20 with 20 being the best grade and 10 being the pass grade. Half points may be awarded. Although grades on this scale may follow a normal distribution, it is customary to make the first 5-8 points relatively easy to acquire, ramping up the difficulty slightly to reach a pass grade. The last 5 points are particularly hard to achieve (i.e. anything above 15 is considered an excellent grade).

2.2 Indicators of Success in Programming

Use of best practices such as PSP (Personal Software Process [9]) during programming courses has been shown to drastically improve the quality of code produced [11]. The metrics used to evaluate these practices are based on low-level indicators which describe the amount of effort invested in a program, its size and its shortcomings. Effort can be evaluated through the amount of time spent on each file coding and/or browsing.

The prescriptive approach of PSP can be contrasted with various descriptive approaches, in particular in the observation of novice programmers (which may be more appropriate in this case as we can hardly expect novice programmers to better understand programming simply by encouraging them to copy the best practices of expert programmers). Several studies have shown that the persistence of compilation errors from one compilation instance to the next can be positively correlated with failure [10] and with poor scores on midterms [18].

Further work has confirmed these results and indicates that working in short multiple sessions is also beneficial to the final grade [7]. It also adds that time spent on a task is not correlated with the grade: students can spend little time through boredom or because the task is too easy; students can spend a lot of time because of perfectionism or because of multiple successive failures. They further note that students overestimate their compilation frequency, the quality of testing which their code has undergone and the proper breaking up of their code into modules. Other studies have confirmed these findings and show that beginning work early is also a strong predictor of assignment grade [6].

2.3 Further hypothetical indicators

We can complete these indicators by further hypothetical indicators from our own teaching experience which we expect to be correlated with grades: respect of naming conventions, using the capabilities afforded by the IDE (browsing, automatic indentation, refactoring, suggestions for correcting compilation errors), and frequency of execution (i.e. testing). As compiling is automatic in the Eclipse IDE, the EQ (Error Quotient) metric described by [10] cannot be reproduced but may be simulated by the amount of time taken to fix a compilation error.

As one of our long-term goals would be to automatically detect "at risk" dyads, we chose to forego collecting the kinds of verbal and gesture data used in other studies (e.g [14,17]). However, some studies [15] have shown encouraging results with regard to analyzing quality of collaboration based on low-level data (eye-tracking and presence/absence of speech over time). These results suggest that we might get some indication of the nature of the within-dyad collaboration through mouse activity (which can be used for deictic gestures) along with moving from one tab to another (changing source file), which could indicate potential losses of alignment and agreement [1] within the dyad (in spite of having no indication as to which member of the dyad is the author of this activity).

2.4 Data Collection and Preparation

Several tools have been proposed to collect data on programming activity [7,11]. We chose HackyStat [11] because of its integration with the Eclipse IDE and the possibility of extending it with new captors. We added functionality to capture some mouse activity, testing activity (adding capture of run mode to the existing debug mode), use of code generation functionalities (auto-complete, error correction), and use of the information about errors (quick fix, which gives additional info about compile errors and suggests ways to correct them).

This resulted in the following event types and subtypes being captured:

- File edition
    - Open
    - Close
    - Save
    - Edit (triggered by a pause in editing)
    - Code generation (auto-complete, etc.)
    - Program unit creation (when a new class or method is defined)
- Appearance of a new compilation error
- Use of the quick fixes interface to see suggestions
- Testing and debugging
    - Run

- Run in debug mode
- Set/unset breakpoint
- Reach breakpoint
- Step over/into

- Hover (the mouse is pointed long enough for an information tool-tip to appear)

Data and consent forms were collected for 60 student dyads, one monad and one triad. For each group, we also associated the grade on the assignment and the grades of the individuals making up the group.

Surprisingly (based on the experience of previous years), a large proportion of students used their laptops rather than the computers provided in the labs, mainly because of confusion over how to move projects between computers in Eclipse (in spite of explanations). For the first week of the assignment, we have data for nearly all dyads. Over the course of the assignment this number decreases. Because we had not provided the Hackystat plugin for installation on personal laptops, we only have a complete data set (data collected over all 3 weeks) for 28 groups. While this is not necessarily a problem (as we do not intend to provide universal indicators for novice programmers but to identify indicators which are reusable for us in similar conditions in subsequent years), for reasons of data homogeneity and ease of analysis, we restricted the analysis presented in this paper to those 28 groups. Of these, several groups worked in parallel on a laptop and on the lab computers, actually using the lab computers very little. We identified 3 groups whose editing activity was two standard deviations lower than that of the next least-active group. Their data was also not considered for this analysis, again for reasons of homogeneity as many statistical methods are not robust against outliers.

Before proceeding further with the analysis, we compared the grades of the 25 remaining groups (24 dyads and 1 monad) against the grades of all 62 groups, summarized in Table 1. We can see that groups who did their lab work on the lab computers scored 1.6 points fewer on average on the assignment. The students who worked partly/entirely on their own computers during labs have a slightly wider spread on the exam grades, but these grades do not differ significantly.

Table 1. Comparison of grades between the whole population and those for whom we have a complete data set

		128 students / 62 groups	**49 students / 25 groups**
Assignment grade (dyad)	Mean	13.56	11.98
	Std dev.	3.35	3.97
Exam grade (individual)	Mean	10.35	10.21
	Std dev.	3.28	2.97

For each of these 25 groups, frequencies for each sub-type (or type in absence of subtype) were computed. These frequencies were correlated with the average, lower and higher exam grade for each group (Average Grade, Min Grade and Max Grade), with the Assignment Grade for each group, and, where applicable, with the difference in within-dyad grade on the exam.

We were unable to easily compute values regarding persistence of compilation errors over time as the captor only provides the appearance of compilation errors and does not (as we had assumed) record their resolution.

3. RESULTS

Because normality cannot be assumed, either for the frequencies, or for the grades, the Spearman Rank Correlation test was used. For the same reason, the difference in grades on the exam was measured by the difference in rank. Because of ties, the p-values for the test are not the exact values, but are estimated. In Table 2, we report the main results for correlation with between frequencies and grade outcomes, showing only significant values (*$p<0.05$, **$p<0.01$, ***$p<0.001$).

Table 2. Correlation between frequencies and grade outcomes (non-significant values are not reported)

	Assignment grade	Average grade	Max grade	Min grade	Rank difference
Save			0.517**		0.434*
Edit			0.435*		0.465*
Code Generation		0.623**	0.79***	0.44*	0.448*
Change Tab	0.486*		0.45*		
Normal Run			0.443*		0.6**
Debug Run			0.47*		
Reach Breakpoint		0.45*	0.519**		

No significant correlations were found for the other event types, with the highest correlations for Mouse Hover and use of Quick Fixes being with Max grade at around $\rho=0.3$ ($0.20<p<0.25$) and the lowest being with Rank difference at around $\rho=0.1$ ($p>0.75$). The various debug events followed their Normal and Debug run counterparts with slight correlations ($0.1<p<0.2$) with the exam grade values and the Rank difference. Open, Close, Compilation Errors and Program Unit Creation provided universally low correlations ($p>0.5$). The number of compilation errors has particularly low correlation

4. DISCUSSION

4.1 Average grade

The highest levels of significance are found in the correlations with exam grades. This would seem to indicate that certain uses of the IDE, in particular use of code generation and having breakpoints placed in such a way that they get triggered, are either indicators of good understanding or lead to an improved understanding of programming concepts. This is most easily explained for breakpoints, since placing them well is both the easiest way to follow unexpected code execution and a strong sign that students understand where the problems in their code arise.

The correlation with code generation might perhaps be best explained as an indication that students understand the situations in which Eclipse knows to generate code and thus that they have sufficient understanding of the Java programming language to trust in the code generated by Eclipse.

4.2 Assignment grade

It seems almost paradoxical that data collected on fulfilling a given assignment should be better correlated with the grade on a subsequent exam than on the grade of the assignment itself. This is less surprising when we consider that a perfectly correct program might not have the functionality required for a good assignment grade. Furthermore, as the students had a week after the final lab to turn in their assignment, it may be that we are missing the data of the "sprint" to bring the assignment up to full functionality.

Transitioning from one tab to another is the only factor which correlates with the assignment grade. This may be explained by two hypotheses: first, the assignment suggests that students should proceed by related functionalities, performing changes through the call tree, frequently moving from one Java class to another; second, a frequent behavior of TAs, when assisting students, is to move through all the files (and their parent tabs) to assess the current state of the program.

4.3 Max and Min grades and Rank difference

The hypothesis that, under certain conditions, one member of the dyad might benefit more than the other seems to hold out as several other activities associated with "normal" use of the IDE (saving, editing, testing the program) are correlated with the grade of the better performing student of the dyad and with the difference in rank on the exam.

As we do not give any instructions on how work should be distributed within the dyads, a likely hypothesis to explain this is that one student is a more frequent "typist" and that all these activities lead to loss of alignment [1], i.e. their respective understandings of the problem and its solution do not evolve jointly, as one student speeds ahead before the other can understand what he is doing. Again, the causation could go either way (or both): students with a good understanding may use the IDE more and students who use the IDE a lot may gain better understanding.

A similar hypothesis would explain why running the application in debug mode and reaching breakpoints are associated with a higher maximum grade, but not with difference in rank, whilst running the application in non-debug mode is associated with both: debugging slows things down, allowing alignment to be maintained or re-established. Indeed, testing the program in non-debug mode is the most significant predictor for rank difference and the pairing is the third most significant correlation overall.

Only code generation is significantly correlated with average, maximum *and* minimum grade. Surprisingly, however, it is also correlated with rank difference. Our first hypothesis to explain this was that high grades (min, max and average) would correlate with rank difference and thus that factors associated with one would necessarily be associated with the other. While this is slightly the case for the min ($p=0.06$) and the max ($p=0.17$) – a self fulfilling result as dyads where one student has an extreme grade are more likely to see a high rank difference, assuming a distribution centered around the mean – it is emphatically not the case for the average ($\rho=0.09$, $p=0.7$). While we cannot rule out this hypothesis, it seems likely that, given the variety of kinds of code generation (automatic brackets, imports, refactoring, error correction, auto-completion, etc.), a closer look might reveal some kinds of code generation to be correlated with high grades and others with high rank differences. In particular, some kinds of code generation allow "silent" insertion of code of "minor" importance to understanding, such as imports, and could contribute to preservation of alignment.

Another surprising result is that, although we had expected tab changes to cause loss of alignment, they are in fact correlated with maximum grade, but *not* with rank difference. Maybe further investigation into the data will help us explain this – possibly, as suggested above, this is related to TA activity.

Some of the effects found on the maximum grade (particularly those related to debugging) were also present on average and minimum grades, but at non-significant levels of correlation, indicating that, under certain conditions such as pairing students by ability [3] or following a "change role every 15mn" protocol [13], a) the difference in rank might be diminished and b) using the full functionality of an IDE in pairs for learning to program might be beneficial and lead to an increase in understanding for both students.

4.4 Other event types

Several of the events we collected showed no significant correlation with the final grades.

It is hardly surprising that opening and closing files showed no correlation: indeed, it would be hard to explain why this would be true.

Mouse activity was the most far fetched of our indicators. Although the chosen hover activity did not produce any meaningful results, the fact that others hope that mouse activity may be an indicator of affect [17] suggests that we should not give up straight away on this type of event.

As a surprise to us, the number of compilation errors is very poorly correlated with grades. Our unexpected inability to measure how soon errors are corrected has prevented us from exploring the matter further and finding the results the state of the art lead us to expect.

The poor correlations for the use of quick fixes is disappointing, but this metric and mouse hover are among the strongest differentiators between differences in rank and grades and might thus be associated with other events (e.g compile error, quick fix, code generation, in rapid succession) to create robust predictors of poor grades or high within-dyad differences.

5. FURTHER WORK

The analysis presented in this paper is a first step towards our goal of being able to identify "at risk" students as early as possible, based on their activity. We plan to construct robust indicators based on these encouraging preliminary results and to test them on the data for week one (which has data for nearly all the groups).

As shown in Figure 1, it might be possible to construct predictors based on the statistics we currently have alone. Indeed, placing a threshold on the code generation metric at 350 events would yield 58% recall/100% precision and a threshold at 460 events would yield 100% recall/75% precision. However, we believe that examining how events unfold over time and establishing a more detailed hierarchy of event categories will produce even better results.

We therefore plan to use exploratory sequential data analysis tools such as Tatiana [5] to discover the patterns in dyads identified as being typical (e.g. particularly successful groups, particularly unsuccessful groups or groups for which the indicators we have established so far are particularly poor).

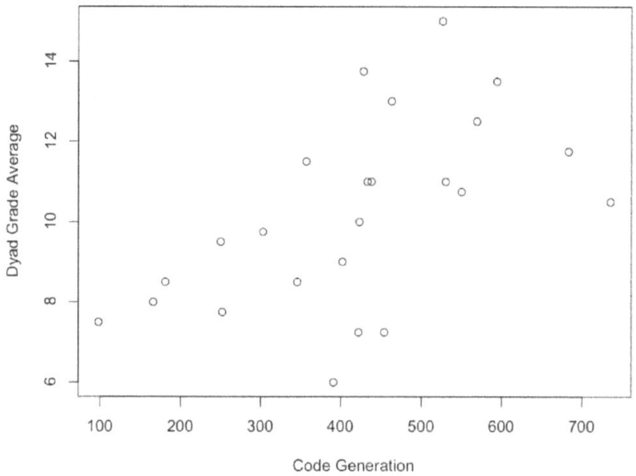

Figure 1. Plot of number of instances of code generation against average grade for each dyad.

For the purposes of detection of "at risk" students, causation is not an issue. However, the question arises with regard to how best to intervene in order to help these students. Aside from extra instruction or explanations, it may be possible that encouraging students to follow certain potential best practices (debugging, following the call tree when writing code, etc.) would be beneficial. Further studies must be carried out to validate whether our findings do in fact give hints as to best practices for using an IDE in a learning situation and whether following these practices leads to better learning.

Finally, correlation between these indicators and detailed grading information, both on the assignment and the final exam, may allow us to predict more precisely which competencies students lack.

6. CONCLUSION

In this paper, we presented the results of preliminary analysis on a study designed to correlate novice-programmer pair-programming activities using the Eclipse IDE with their grades on the assignment, in the final exam and with the within-dyad difference in rank on the final exam. Our long term goal is to use such data to identify and assist "at risk" students. Our results show that the use of code generation functionalities and coming across breakpoints while debugging are both significantly correlated with the final grade. Frequencies of editing, saving, code generation and testing the program in non-debug mode are significantly correlated with within-dyad rank differences on the final exam. Only the frequency of transition from one tab to another proved to be significantly correlated with the grade on the assignment the students were working on when the data was collected.

These results are highly encouraging as they suggest that it will be possible to develop robust indicators of students who are likely to perform poorly and of dyads who are likely to have large differences in rank on the final exam. They also show the value of collecting data in more detail than information about compiling, particularly as our results are strong predictors of performance on the exam, indicating that they may help us access student understanding.

Further avenues for study include a look at the sequentiality of events in order to identify patterns which increase the distinguishing power of the already identified predictors, determining how little data is necessary to predict learning outcomes (earlier detection leads to earlier intervention), answering the question of how best to support "at risk" students, and determining whether the factors we have identified so far could form the basis of best practices for learning to program with an IDE.

7. ACKNOWLEDGMENTS

Our thanks to Gauthier Picard for allowing this study to be run in his class and sharing detailed data regarding the grading, Adrien Hery for assistance with data collection, and to all the students who agreed to take part in this study.

8. REFERENCES

[1] Baker, M. 2002. Forms of cooperation in dyadic problem-solving. In P. Salembier & T. H. Benchekron (Eds.), *Cooperation and complexity in sociotechnical systems* (Vol. 16, pp. 587–620).

[2] Baker, R. S., Corbett, A. T., Koedinger, K. R., and Wagner, A. Z. 2004. Off-task behavior in the cognitive tutor classroom: when students "game the system". In *Proceedings of the SIGCHI Conference on Human Factors in Computing Systems* (Vienna, Austria, April 24 - 29, 2004). CHI '04. ACM, New York, NY, 383-390. DOI= http://doi.acm.org/10.1145/985692.985741

[3] Braught, G., MacCormick, J., and Wahls, T. 2010. The benefits of pairing by ability. In *Proceedings of the 41st ACM Technical Symposium on Computer Science Education* (Milwaukee, Wisconsin, USA, March 10 - 13, 2010). SIGCSE '10. ACM, New York, NY, 249-253. DOI= http://doi.acm.org/10.1145/1734263.1734348

[4] De Laat, M. F., M, C., and Wegerif, R. 2008. Facilitate the Facilitator: Awareness Tools to Support the Moderator to Facilitate Online Discussions for Networked Learning. *In Proceedings of the 6th International Conference on Networked Learning* (pp. 80–86). Halkidiki, Greece.

[5] Dyke, G., Lund, K., and Girardot, J.-J. 2009. Tatiana : an environment to support the CSCL analysis process. *CSCL 2009*. Rhodes, Greece, 58–67.

[6] Edwards, S.H., Snyder, J., Pérez-Quiñones, M.A., Allevato, A., Kim D., and Tretola, B., 2009. Comparing Effective and Ineffective Behaviors of Student Programmers. *ICER '09*, August 10–11, 2009, Berkeley, California, USA.

[7] Fenwick, J. B., Norris, C., Barry, F. E., Rountree, J., Spicer, C. J., and Cheek, S. D. 2009. Another look at the behaviors of novice programmers. SIGCSE '09. ACM, New York, NY, 296–300.

[8] Hanks, B., McDowell, C., Draper, D., and Krnjajic, M. 2004. Program quality with pair programming in CS1. In *Proceedings of the 9th Annual SIGCSE Conference on Innovation and Technology in Computer Science Education* (Leeds, UK, June 28-30, 2004). ITiCSE '04. ACM Press, New York, NY, 176-180.

[9] Humphrey, W. S. 1995. *A Discipline for Software Engineering*. Addison-Wesley.

[10] Jadud, M. 2005. A first look at novice compilation behaviour using BlueJ. *Computer Science Education*, 15(1):25–40.

[11] Johnson, P. M., Kou, H., Agustin, J., Chan, C., Moore, C., Miglani, J., Zhen, S., and Doane, W. E. 2003. Beyond the Personal Software Process: metrics collection and analysis for the differently disciplined. In *Proceedings of the 25th international Conference on Software Engineering*. IEEE Computer Society, Washington, DC, 641–646.

[12] May, M., George, S., and Prévôt, P. 2008. A closer look at tracking human and computer interactions in web-based communications. International Journal of Interactive *Technology and Smart Education*, 5(3): 170–188.

[13] McDowell, C., Werner, L., Bullock, H., and Fernald, J. 2002. The effects of pair-programming on performance in an introductory programming course. In *Proceedings of the 33rd SIGCSE Technical Symposium on Computer Science* Education (Cincinnati, Kentucky, February 27 - March 03, 2002). SIGCSE '02. ACM, New York, NY, 38-42. DOI= http://doi.acm.org/10.1145/563340.563353

[14] Murphy, L., Fitzgerald, S., Hanks, B., and McCauley, R. 2010. Pair debugging: a transactive discourse analysis. In *Proceedings of the Sixth international Workshop on Computing Education Research* (Aarhus, Denmark, August 09 - 10, 2010). ICER '10. ACM, New York, NY, 51-58. DOI= http://doi.acm.org/10.1145/1839594.1839604

[15] Nüssli, M.-A., Jermann, P., Sangin, M,. and Dillenbourg, P. 2009. Collaboration and abstract representations: towards predictive models based on raw speech and eye-tracking data. *CSCL 2009*. Rhodes.

[16] Petrou, A. and Dimitrakopoulou, A. 2003. Is synchronous computer mediated collaborative problem-solving "justified" only when by distance? Teachers' point of views and interventions with co-located groups, during every day class activities. In *Proceedings of the International Conference on Computer Support for Collaborative Learning 2003*.1-10.

[17] Rodrigo, M. T., Baker, R. S., Jadud, M. C., Amarra, A. M., Dy, T., et al. 2009. Affective and behavioral predictors of novice programmer achievement. *ITiCSE '09*. Paris, France. 156-160.

[18] Tabanao, E., Rodrigo, M. M. T. and Jadud, M. 2008. Identifying at-risk novice programmers through the analysis of online protocols. *Philippine Computing Society Congress 2008*, (UP Diliman, Quezon City, February 23-24, 2008).

The Novice Programmer's "Device to Think With"

Dermot Shinners-Kennedy
Dept. of Computer Science and Information Systems
University of Limerick
Limerick, Ireland
dermot.shinners-kennedy@ul.ie

David J. Barnes
School of Computing
University of Kent, Canterbury
Kent CT2 7NF, UK
d.j.barnes@kent.ac.uk

ABSTRACT
We present some ideas for course material for the introductory teaching of programming that are based on the principle of allowing the students to be the domain experts. The idea is that the students' familiarity with the domain of discourse will make course material more motivating, and that it will be more likely that they will be able to model the concepts and artifacts being discussed. This approach thereby seeks to scaffold the students' understanding of programming-related concepts. For reasons discussed in the paper, we have chosen mobile phone technology for this discussion, but there is no reason why the same principles should not be applied to other culturally-accessible domains.

Categories and Subject Descriptors
K.3.2 [Computer and Information Science Education]: Computer science education.

General Terms
Algorithms, Human Factors, Languages.

Keywords
CS1, curriculum ideas, mobile phones, student-centered learning.

1. INTRODUCTION
Our discipline suffers an interesting paradox. It is widely accepted that the development of a knowledge economy is hugely dependent on information technology and yet student enrolments and retention levels on courses are almost universally low. The discipline also has a serious gender imbalance. One of the reasons for these problems is that existing pedagogies and materials can be inaccessible or alienating and haven't always kept pace with cultural changes. Our pedagogy has to develop and embrace new educational thinking and practice if it is to meet the demands made of it. This is one of the reasons why we have witnessed, in recent years, manifold initiatives to make introductory programming attractive and accessible: the development of a plethora of introductory programming environments such as Alice, BlueJ, DrScheme, Greenfoot, Scratch, etc.; initiatives with robotics; advocacy of different pedagogical approaches (objects-first, functions-first, procedures-first, etc.) and curriculum ideas. Yet, for all this effort, there remain no definitive research results or consensus among the education community to identify a clear winner. At present, it seems that the most likely success factor in the initial teaching of programming remains the commitment and enthusiasm of the teacher – which, at least, is reassuring for those of us who are passionate about teaching!

2. MOTIVATING STUDENTS
Teachers are always looking for approaches and examples that will be interesting to their students. At the whole-course level, this is one of the main reasons why we see robotics, for instance, being used in various ways. The same principle is also often applied at the level of individual topics within a course. For instance, recently there was a discussion on the SIGCSE mailing list [10] about the motivational appeal of traditional recursive examples. There was some consensus that exemplars such as Towers of Hanoi and the computation of factorial or Fibonacci values lack appeal. Wirth's example of parking cars [11] was one suggestion offered to provide "some real-world characteristics" in a problem with a good recursive solution. However, the central issue is whether students will be able to understand the problem being addressed, and whether they will also see a rationale for addressing it.

Aristotle once observed that, "It is the customary that is intelligible" [1]. There is a remarkable simplicity and logic to the notion that if someone has a deep interest in puzzles and games, for example, then efforts to stimulate intellectual curiosity and inquisitiveness using puzzles and games are likely to be highly successful. For someone with no interest in puzzles and games the outcomes are likely to be less successful. This is a classic dilemma for teachers – in the context of a diverse set of interests what 'things' can be used to engage the intellectual curiosity of the students?

Results from the international Relevance of Science Education (ROSE) project [9], show that the interest profiles of boys and girls follow typical gender-related differences. For example, girls tend to be more interested in human biology, health issues, reproduction and cosmetics; boys are more interested in explosive chemicals, spectacular phenomena like earthquakes and hurricanes, weapons, engines and other everyday mechanical equipment. However, there are exceptions. Both girls and boys are interested in how mobile phones, CDs and DVDs work. Ironically, none of these key twenty-first century devices appear to receive significant widespread attention in science – including computing science – curricula.

All of the concepts introduced in a typical programming course are within the conceptual competence of a young child. Children can make choices between alternatives, repeat a task until it is complete, search a list for something, and so on. Yet, despite the fundamental simplicity of basic computer operations, traditional approaches are loaded with attempts to develop new skills in students via the medium of unfamiliar and inaccessible scenarios. The ideas we explore here seek to build on the apparently gender-neutral area of familiar technology that the ROSE project highlights, both to scaffold and motivate the learning of introductory programming. Our view is that we should try to develop curriculum ideas around those things that are both familiar and interesting to our students. The problem for us as teachers is that Aristotle's words apply equally well to us as to our students: we are most comfortable with the things that we grew up with, learned about as undergraduates, or are excited about now; but that does not mean that they will be equally accessible or appealing to our students.

3. A DEVICE TO THINK WITH

When, nearly thirty years ago, Seymour Papert published his view of, "how computers may affect the way people think and learn" [7] he described, "[a] computer rich future, a future where a computer will be a significant part of every child's life." We are clearly now in that future. Mobile phones have more computing power than the first Apollo spacecraft that landed on the moon [3], and *virtually every child and student has one*. That computing power represents what Papert identified as an object-to-think-with, "[an object] in which there is an intersection of cultural presence, embedded knowledge, and the possibility for personal identification."

Our approach is to take the students' familiarity with (and acceptance of) the mobile phone as an ordinary everyday object, and use the seemingly limitless potential it offers to explore the world of programming. However, it is important to appreciate that this is not about teaching students to program real mobile phones; rather it is about using the familiar features of a mobile phone to enable students to understand programming concepts, and hence develop traditional programming skills within a bounded, tailored environment. The ideas discussed here are built around a software simulation of a basic mobile phone, to which the students add enhancements that serve to illustrate programming concepts.

Central to this approach is the inversion of the relationship between teaching and learning. By situating the student activities in a scenario (the mobile phone) that they are not only comfortable with but in which they are experts, the teaching and learning dynamic is fundamentally altered. Instead of the tutor introducing material and providing examples, the students explore and investigate concepts and ideas that they are already familiar with. The tutor simply provides the conditions in which the students can learn. In our view, mobile phones epitomize the type of object-to-think-with that Papert envisioned. This approach articulates a pedagogy that exploits students' familiarity with mobile phone technology to scaffold their learning of programming.

Ausubel succinctly summarized the basic idea when he wrote, "If I had to reduce all educational psychology to just one principle, I would say this: The most important single factor influencing learning is what the learner already knows. Ascertain this and teach him accordingly." [2]

There is an interesting parallel to our approach to be found in the nineteenth century. In a series of six lectures he delivered to young people at the Royal Institution in London in 1861, the renowned experimental scientist Michael Faraday chose a candle, a simple, everyday object, to explain the fundamental principles of chemistry. Faraday chose a candle because, he explained, "There is not a law under which this universe is governed which does not come into play and is not touched upon in these phenomena." [5] In a similar vein we would suggest the utility of using a mobile phone for the same purposes within the field of computing. To paraphrase Faraday, we would dare to suggest that, "There is not a law under which computing is governed which does not come into play and is not touched upon in mobile phones!"

4. CURRICULUM IDEAS

In this section, we provide a small sample of the many ideas that can be drawn from the scenario to provide material for various stages of both CS1 and later courses. While our focus is primarily object-based, the domain of the mobile phone is clearly not tied purely to an object-oriented approach. It also offers scenarios for many of the procedural and algorithmic elements we wish to teach.

4.1 Fundamentals of classes and objects

Successful introduction of object-orientation requires the establishment in students' minds of a clear understanding of the nature of classes and objects: class as a type and objects as independent instantiations of that type; objects maintaining state variables that require initialization, may be inspected and might be modified. Classes that relate to concrete artifacts from a student's experience stand the best chance of communicating these facets. An example we might use is that of a text message. We can talk about text messages in general terms: they contain characters that make up the message; they are sent to someone; they have a date and time of sending; they have a sender. All of these are familiar ideas and relate to the notion of class or type. But we can also talk about specific text messages: the one I sent to Helen this morning about meeting up after class; or the one Tim sent me yesterday asking to borrow my notes. These are the individual instantiations of the general idea of a text message. Every text message has the same components (structure) at the class level, but every individual text has its own settings for those components at the object level. Little, if anything, of the scenario needs explaining to the students, because they know this already, and from that understanding we can easily link to the new (programming) terminology we wish to use. From there we can introduce some simple code to implement those ideas.

The class in Figure 11 contains just the essential elements to represent a basic text message: fields to store the configurable items, a constructor to initialize the fields, and accessor methods to inspect the values of the fields. Since text messages are essentially immutable, we can omit mutator methods at this stage. Within an environment such as BlueJ [6] a complete project containing just this class could be defined, and instances created and investigated via its object bench – giving physical reinforcement to the ideas of instance multiplicity, identity of structure, yet individual expression.

In order to illustrate that we are not suggesting that the mobile-phone scenario offers just one route through a course, but a rich source of ideas that can be adjusted to fit the needs of both students and course material, we offer an alternative introduction to these class fundamentals. This route might be used with students who have existing programming experience, for instance, or who require a more sophisticated approach.

```
public class Text
{
    // Components of a text message.
    private String from, to, message;

    // Constructor/initializer
    public Text(String whoFrom, String whoTo,
                String mess)
    {
        from = whoFrom;
        to = whoTo;
        message = mess;
    }

    // Field/property accessor
    public String getFrom()
    {
        return from;
    }
    ...
}
```

Figure 1: Elements of a text-message class

The level at which we pitch the notion of class is completely flexible, and is simply a reflection of the degree of abstraction we wish to work with at any particular time. For instance, we might wish to focus on the phone's physical aspects and look at the whole phone as an object; or we might wish to consider its individual components as objects – the keypad, the screen, the battery, and so on. The notion of abstraction is obviously a particularly important one in the world of object-orientation, and one that will be touched on repeatedly at different times in a course. For some students, being able to relate the concepts of class and object to physical things may be easier than virtual things like text messages. With this in mind, we might define a class to model the battery of a mobile phone. A battery has a very simple state description – its level of charge – that will need to be monitored via an accessor method. We will want to modify the state via charging, and the charge level will be reduced through use of the phone. Exactly how realistically we want to try to model charge depletion and restoration is up to us – sending a text or receiving one might incur a charge cost, for instance. In one simple implementation we have used a small thread associated with a battery object that periodically reduces the level. This means that we can create a fairly realistic scenario in which a number of battery objects can be created and individually queried for their levels, which obviously vary independently. A battery would probably not have a visualization at this stage, because that is not an inherent part of its functionality but an artifact of presentation.

While the scenario is clearly more sophisticated than the one using Text objects, the lessons are still the same: the Battery class defines a regular structure that all battery objects share; the class has a field for storing a battery's level, which can be queried; and each instance maintains its state independently of every other. What both examples have in common is that students get to work with stand-alone elements that they can explore, develop and test independently, and that will later be integrated with other components to build more complex systems. That provides a further important practical illustration of the value of writing cohesive classes that don't try to do too much – sophistication is achieved through composition.

4.2 Collections

Collections are pivotal structures in programming systems. As a source of examples the mobile phone is almost unrivalled. A mobile phone is essentially a collection of collections! For example, a typical mobile phone has a contacts list that is usually alphabetically ordered (ascending); a speed dial list that is ordered on the basis of personal preference (ranking); an incoming message list ordered by time of arrival (last-in first-out); recently-used number lists that reorder dynamically; text prediction and other word lists ordered on frequency of use (self-organizing); and so on. Where audio or image files are supported, the phone allows the user to create their own collections and populate them as they please. For example, most users arrange their audio files into 'playlists' which can be played sequentially or in random order. Similarly, image files can be arranged into 'slide shows.'

Mark Twain once observed that, "It ain't what you don't know that gets you into trouble. It's what you know for sure that just ain't so!" When asked, most students will claim not to have encountered a self-organizing list, a list that uses a last-in first-out mechanism, or a list that could be empty. However, a little prompting helps them to realize that the text prediction feature in some phones initially displays word suggestions based on general usage but, over time, prefers the words that have appeared frequently in the text they have typed. How the phone handles incoming messages by placing the most recent as the first reveals the stack-based nature of the incoming message list. The possibility of an empty 'to-do' or 'missed call' list seems obvious once it has been brought to your attention but invariably evades cognition in a free recall scenario.

This type of inert knowledge is notoriously difficult to utilize and led Perkins to label it as 'troublesome knowledge' because it, "sits in the mind's attic, unpacked only when specifically called for by a quiz or a direct prompt but otherwise gathering dust." [8] Unknown to them, mobile phone users have been exposed to virtually every collection operation that would be included in a typical data structures course. They have experience of collection creation, maintenance and removal. They are aware of the benefits of having a variety of access strategies for collection elements (e.g., browsing, search, random selection, iteration in specified sequences). In addition, the idea of using two different 'keys' to locate entries in a single collection is not a novelty. For example, when they receive a call the phone software searches their contacts list for the number and, if found, displays the associated name on the screen. This useful feature allows them to decide whether to answer the call (i.e., it's a friend calling) or not (i.e., it's a parent calling). Conversely, when they are making a call they can search the contacts list for a particular name and have the software dial the number of the chosen entry.

As the earlier enumeration of different possible organizations highlighted, collections are a rich source of conceptual exemplars ranging from the very simple to the very sophisticated. They also encapsulate a wide variety of simple but significant algorithms that the typical programmer uses and reuses in the course of developing a system. Many of these algorithms are provided in libraries and other support tools but their exposition to novice programmers can help them perfect their design and implementation strategies and skills. Figure 22 is an example of using a list structure that many phone owners will have used unconsciously in a variety of contexts, such as randomly playing tracks in a playlist or randomly displaying images captured with their phone. From examples such as this, parallels can easily be drawn beyond the basic scenario.

```
void playShuffled(ArrayList<Track> playList)
{
    int toPlay = playList.size();
    while(toPlay > 0) {
        int chosen = random.nextInt(toPlay);
        Track track = playList.get(chosen);
        play(track);
        toPlay--;
        // Swap the chosen track with the
        // last one left to play.
        playList.set(chosen,
                     playList.get(toPlay));
        playList.set(toPlay, track);
    }
}
```

Figure 2: Method to play tracks in a playlist randomly

As Figure 3 shows, with minor alterations the algorithm can be used to randomly choose n unique numbers in the range `1..max`. (For the sake of variation we have used an array this time rather than a list.) This is another algorithm the equivalent of which many will have exploited, again unconsciously, if they are in the habit of playing the lottery.

```
void chooseLotteryNumbers(int n, int max)
{
    // Create the set of possible numbers.
    int numbers = new int[max];
    for(int i = 0; i < max; i++) {
        numbers[i] = i+1;
    }
    // Select and print n from the set.
    int remaining = max ;
    for(int i = 0; i < n; i++) {
        int chosen = random.nextInt(remaining);
        int selectedNumber = numbers[chosen];
        System.out.println(selectedNumber);
        remaining--;
        // Swap the chosen number with the
        // last one left available.
        numbers[chosen] = numbers[remaining];
        numbers[remaining] = selectedNumber;
    }
}
```

Figure 3: Method to select n unique values from 1 .. max

4.3 Exception Handling

Most mobile phone users have had the experience of their battery going 'dead' or 'flat' during a call. Similarly, phone users operating on 'pay as you go' or 'top-up' schemes have tried to make a call or send a message only to discover that their credit balance is insufficient to cover the cost or runs out during the call. These experiences will have made them aware of the fact that the severity of the problem will influence both the amount of thought given to its likely occurrence and the effort required to resolve it if it does occur. For example, they know that if they are unable to receive messages because their message box is full the problem can be resolved quite easily by deleting some messages. The problem is a trivial one, as is the solution. A flat battery is more significant. Resolving that problem requires possession of a phone charger and access to a power source. In the absence of either or both of those resources the problem appears unsolvable, unless you are a creative mobile phone user who understands that convincing someone to let you put your SIM-card in their phone keeps you 'online'. In the same vein, running out of credit is a very difficult problem to solve if you have no money. While friends may allow you to run down their battery, they may not be quite so willing to let you run down their bank balance! If you have no credit and no access to funds you are 'offline' – period.

Simple problems can usually be handled easily. For example, putting the same name and number in your contacts list may be a nuisance but nothing more significant. Harder problems may require more work and cooperation with other entities, or objects. Serious problems need to be checked out and acted upon otherwise the system may be compromised. Some problems cannot be resolved and oblige us to stop using the phone.

The fact that the foregoing appears painfully obvious is precisely why it is pedagogically attractive to tutors. Phone scenarios provide a considerable range of contexts for exploring the nuances of exception handling. The following example is but one of very many candidate examples.

Mobile phone companies measure numbers of text messages handled in billions per month and it is not uncommon for young mobile phone users to send *several hundred* text messages a day! As a consequence they are very familiar with the types of difficulties that can arise and those difficulties (literally) need no introduction. For those of us lacking that expertise the difficulties can include:

- unknown number (i.e., recipient);
- a weak or non-existent signal;
- insufficient credit;
- recipient cannot be reached at the moment because of their signal level;
- network difficulties (i.e., the provider's infrastructure is not fully operational).

The outline of a possible message-sending method is shown in Figure 4. It is passed the recipient's number and the message text. It uses the Text class of Figure 11 to encapsulate the details required by the provider transmitting the message. The provider attempts to transmit the message. Success produces a confirmation message on the phone screen. Failure results in an exception being thrown by the provider.

The method handles only those exceptions it is competent to deal with. Cases involving an unknown number or poor signal are propagated up the method-call stack and left to be handled at the appropriate level. For example, the code used to choose a number, or allow one to be entered, can catch the unknown-number exception and provide the user with an option to supply another number. It may even impose a limit on the number of attempts the user can have. Handling exceptions involving poor or no signal may include an option to move the phone before trying to resend.

```
void sendMessage(String whoTo, String msg)
  throws ...
{
    try {
        Text txt = new Text(number, whoTo, msg);
        provider.sendText(txt);
        screen.setStatusBar("Message sent.");
    }
    catch(InsufficientCreditException e) {
        // Put txt in DRAFTS ...
    }
    catch(UnreachableException e) {
        // Handle exception ...
    }
    catch(NetworkProblemException e) {
        // Handle exception ...
    }
}
```

Figure 4: Sending a text-message with exception handling

Readers will, of course, note that many additional features could be added to the scenario and that, in many respects, it is a simplistic exemplar of what is actually required to handle the possibilities that arise. Fortunately the same observations will be made by most experienced mobile users. While the notation may be unfamiliar to them, most phone users can, without prompting, quickly spot deficiencies in the scenario and, more importantly, offer suggestions as to how it might be improved. Students trade their inadequate knowledge of the mechanism used to specify how to achieve something for their expert knowledge of the things that need to be achieved. Their status as collaborators allows them to focus on acquiring what they don't know (i.e., exception handling mechanics and the associated notation) and contributing what they do.

The typical mobile phone user is fully aware that the exceptions enumerated in this example are not unique to the task of sending text messages. In those circumstances the idea of developing a classes of error conditions that would be beneficial for all operations associated with the phone is quite sensible.

One of the key attractions of discussing exception handling in the context of a mobile phone is that you cannot afford to ignore them, or avoid them occurring. Maintaining the integrity of the system by correctly handling exceptions is a critical aspect of a phone's operation. This feature is rarely the case in most example scenarios used to teach students about exception handling. Having the software in your phone 'crash' simply because you mistyped a recipient's number would be completely unacceptable. Broader discussions about software features such as quality, robustness and safety are facilitated by the students' own evaluations of their mobile phone implementations. The centrality of good design is readily identifiable.

5. A CONCEPTUAL MISCELLANY

In its role as a 'device to think' with the range of concepts encapsulated within the mobile phone is truly extraordinary. In the preceding section we considered three examples at some length. In this section we offer a further series of conceptual 'snapshots' as a sample to highlight the diverse nature of the possibilities.

If at your first meeting with a class of novice computing students you ask them if they have ever undertaken a user interface evaluation their initial response will usually be, "A what?" followed quickly by a unanimous, "No." Further investigation will probably reveal that some of the class use 'text prediction' on their mobile phones and some of them don't. Asking each group to explain why they do or don't provides an initial list of pros and cons of text prediction systems. Putting it to them that clearly they had previously undertaken a user interface evaluation, albeit in a superficial and unsystematic fashion, not only establishes the credibility of their experiences but also encourages them to reflect more deeply on activities they are about to engage in.

For most of us "RUK4DD82MWB" is an unintelligible jumble of letters and numbers. (Aside: It rarely occurs to programming tutors that their early examples may have the same status!) That it might be a meaningful representation of something is disconcerting. Yet introducing some minor formatting features may make it a little more comprehensible. For example, simply introducing some white space can make it look like "R U K 4 D D8 2M WB." The knowledge that D8 is an abbreviation for DATE, 2M an abbreviation for TOMORROW and WB for WRITE BACK might allow us to decipher the message as "Are you OK for the date tomorrow? Write back."

While the original message is perfectly understandable to a text-messaging zealot, they often complain about its 'style.' Many, especially those who use text prediction, would insist that the message be typed without abbreviations. Others find the cryptic nature of the abbreviations quite acceptable and even laudable! For a programming language tutor it is quite useful to allow differing views on the stylistic properties of text messages to be voiced because it is a topic that has to be addressed in the context of programming languages as well. Of course, the same issues will surface but the benefits of consensus in the application of stylistic conventions will appear self-evident in light of the prior exposure to the text messaging discussion.

After a number of experiences of the type just outlined, students acquire a slightly different disposition when responding to what appear to be the tutor's innocuous questions and prompts. For example, when invited to state if they have ever used a WORM (i.e., Write Once Read Many) device they tend to pause a little while longer before answering. Their altered disposition is a sign of their maturing ability to reason. They have abandoned their knee-jerk response approach and substituted in its stead a more considered evaluation of the question or problem posed. This is a desirable quality in a graduate of computing!

The WORM question may evoke an association with DVDs, CDs, credit cards, security badges and similar devices or objects. Success with this type of association has a significant impact on the student's confidence and self-belief. This type of affective outcome can be as important as any achievements associated with the acquisition of technical expertise.

The everydayness of WORM-style objects can make the concept of immutable objects seem almost mundane. The fact that, for example, in some programming languages a string can be created but not altered is viewed as a feature of strings not a flaw in the language. Immutable objects have a place in the world and by extension must have a place in any model of that world that we choose build.

Modelling the world of mobile phones invariably draws us into the management of phone charges and billing. At its simplest this affords the opportunity to explore issues of database design, information retrieval and update. In a broader context it provides an opportunity to explore the elicitation of organisation knowledge and rules, the design and specification of systems to operationalize the findings and the implementation of a system to realize the design.

As features are added to the software implementation of a mobile phone, or design decisions made about exactly how those features will be implemented, the sense emerges that we will want to have phones with variations – in the real world, not all phones are the same. Nevertheless, students can probably identify a core of functionality that is shared among all phones, while not resulting in a complete phone. The concept of abstract classes emerges from this analysis, along with concrete subclasses. There is also a technical progression observed in the phone world: manufacturer M adds special feature F to their phone, and other manufacturers quickly follow in order to keep up; the process repeats. When thinking about this in software terms, feature F might start as a subclass feature but, for the sake of utility and good structure, eventually gets refactored from the subclass to the superclass.

Finally, how one interacts with the phone services and facilities provides plenty of opportunities to consider the challenges associated with the development of a GUI for a mobile phone.

6. EXPERIENCE

This approach has been used successfully via a pilot run in 2008 and a more developed version in 2009. We are continuing to expand the ideas further in the current academic year and ultimately plan to make the materials available to the academic community. A number of students have reported that they cannot use their mobile phones now without thinking about what is going on inside. What is particularly powerful about this outcome is that it is reinforced every day because the students use their phones every day.

As indicated in the introduction, it would be naive to suggest that the ideas outlined in this paper necessarily offer a guarantee of success. However, we do believe the mobile phone scenario has the potential to support the type of 'spiral curriculum' approach advocated by Bruner, "A metamorphic spiral in which at some simple level a set of ideas or operations were introduced in a rather intuitive way and, once mastered in that spirit, were then revisited and reconstrued in a more formal or operational way, then being connected with other knowledge, the mastery at this stage then being carried one step higher to a new level of formal or operational rigour and to a broader level of abstraction and comprehensiveness. The end state of this process was eventual mastery of the connexity and structure of a large body of knowledge." [4]

7. CONCLUSION

We have presented a sample of ideas for course material for the introductory teaching of programming that are based on the principle of allowing the students to be the domain experts. Having chosen a subject domain known to have wide appeal across both cultures and genders – the mobile phone – we make use of students' existing interest and expertise to explore a phone's features via software development. This idea mimics an approach taken by Faraday to explore the world of chemistry via the medium of a candle. However, just as a candle would be of little use for this purpose today, it is inevitable that at some point in the future the utility of the mobile phone as we have illustrated it is likely to be surpassed by some other near ubiquitous device. The essential message of this paper, therefore, is to encourage teachers to maximize the opportunity for broad engagement with their students through making use of those things that are familiar to and interesting for the students.

8. ACKNOWLEDGMENTS

This work is supported in part by a SIGCSE Special Projects Grant. The views expressed are those of the authors.

9. REFERENCES

[1] Aristotle 350 BCE. *Metaphysics*.

[2] Ausubel, David 1998. In *Learning, Creating, and Using Knowledge: Concept Maps as Facilitative Tools in Schools and Corporations*, Joseph D. Novak. L. Erlbaum Associates, Mahwah, N.J.

[3] Ben-Ari, M. 2005. The concorde doesn't fly anymore. In *Proceedings of the 36th SIGCSE Technical Symposium on Computer Science Education* (St. Louis, Missouri, USA, February 23 - 27, 2005). SIGCSE '05. ACM, New York, NY, 196-196. DOI= http://doi.acm.org/10.1145/1047344.1047354.

[4] Bruner, J.S. 1960. *The Process of Education*, Harvard University Press, Cambridge, MA.

[5] Faraday, Michael 1978. *The Chemical History of a Candle*, Cherokee Publishing Company, ISBN 978-0877972099.

[6] Kölling, Michael, et al 2010. *BlueJ – the interactive Java environment*, http://www.bluej.org/ Accessed 2010.09.01.

[7] Papert, Seymour 1993. *Mindstorms: Children, Computers and Powerful Ideas*, 2nd edition. Basic Books, ISBN 9780465046744.

[8] Perkins, David 1999. The many faces of constructivism. *Educational Leadership* 57, 3 (Nov 1999), 6-11

[9] ROSE, *The Relevance of Science Education.* http://www.ils.uio.no/english/rose/ Accessed 2010.09.01.

[10] Topham, Dave 2010. *CS1 Functions First*. sigcse-members mailing list discussion initiated 11th July 2010.

[11] Wirth, M. 2008. Introducing recursion by parking cars. *SIGCSE Bull.* 40, 4 (Nov. 2008), 52-55. DOI= http://doi.acm.org/10.1145/1473195.1473219.

Ideas for Adding Soft Skills Education to Service Learning and Capstone Courses for Computer Science Students

Lori Carter
Point Loma Nazarene University
Department of Mathematical,
Information, and Computer Sciences
San Diego, CA 92106
LoriCarter@pointloma.edu

ABSTRACT

Soft skills such as communication, teamwork, and organization are important to students' future success in the working world. Faculty members know it, students know it, and employers are explicitly asking for these skills. Are computer science departments responsible to teach these skills? If so, where in the curriculum should they be covered? This paper explores the soft skills that employers want, and possible places to include the teaching of those skills in the curriculum. It then shows how an extensive set of soft skills were incorporated into a service learning course for the students in the Mathematical, Information and Computer Sciences department at Point Loma Nazarene University. Finally, it makes suggestions as to how other service learning or capstone courses could be altered to afford more opportunity for soft skill education.

Categories and Subject Descriptors

K.3.2 [Computers and Education]: Computer & Information Science Education; K.4.2 [Computers and Society]: Social Issues

General Terms

Management, Design, Human Factors

Keywords

Service Learning in Computer Science, Soft Skills, Communication

1. INTRODUCTION

Fred is a top notch software engineer working at a small engineering firm. As demand for the firm's product grows, additional software engineers are hired to lighten Fred's load. Unfortunately, Fred has not kept written documentation of the conceptual design of his program, nor is he good at explaining what he has done, or how the new-hires can help him. Fred still has an overload of work, and the new-hires are frustrated. Given what we hear from engineering firms, this is lack of soft skills is a far too common problem costing companies time and money.

A significant amount of recent research in computer science and engineering education has been focused on determining the importance of soft skills to potential employers [6,7,8,10,14]. One recent study polled 68 employers on the specific skills that they would like to see in future employees [6]. The skills on the survey fell into two categories: technical skills and general skills. The technical skills were things like programming languages, operating system and network management, database development, web-based technologies, and software engineering. The general (soft) skills included problem solving, self-motivation, leadership skills, communication skills, interpersonal skills and enthusiasm.

The respondents were asked to rank the importance of these skills on a scale of 1-5, 5 being most important. The average rating for all technical skills was 3.3, but the average ranking for general skills was 4.5. While the lower ranking of the technical skills could reflect that they are job-dependent, the high ranking of the general skills indicates that they are important across the board.

Another report points out the importance of soft skills by noting that the deficiency of soft skills has been a significant contributor to negligence claims [9]. Poor communication or lack of integrity could lead to serious misunderstandings, or even a faulty product.

The U.S. Bureau of Labor Statistics Occupational Outlook Handbook for Software Engineers and Computer Programmers notes that the demand for software engineers will continue to increase in the United States while the demand for computer programmers will decrease slightly [14]. In the report, software engineers are differentiated from computer programmers as follows: computer programmers write programs after software engineers have analyzed the end users' needs and designed the programs. The software engineers are expected to have the soft skills necessary to communicate with the client, analyze the problem, and create a solution. Because communication skills aren't as essential to computer programming, tasks that fall under this category are more easily out-sourced.

For a variety of reasons our students need to be educated in the soft skills as well as the hard technical skills. But what exactly are the soft skills that employers want? How and where should this education happen?

Section 2 explores the soft skills most requested by employers based on past research, and validated by new research. It compares these results to the assumptions that faculty and students make as to what employers want. Section 3 considers the possible venues in which the necessary soft skills can be taught. Section 4 provides an overview of the places where soft skills are taught in a year-long service learning course at PLNU and makes suggestions as to how other service learning or capstone courses can be adapted to offer opportunities for soft skill education.

2. WHICH SOFT SKILLS ARE DESIRED?

2.1 According to Employers

Many have provided opinions as to the soft skills that employers want. The Occupational Outlook Handbook indicates that prospective software engineers should cultivate skills such as problem-solving, creativity, communication, and attention to detail [14]. Hissey supports the need for communication skills, but suggests that marketing and business skills should not be overlooked [8]. A study based in Europe also mentions communication, including communication in multiple languages. In addition, this same report lists teamwork, responsibility, flexibility, and the ability to learn among the top skills sought by employers [10].

With the goal of gaining a current understanding of what employers are looking for, employment ads for software engineers from the website Monster.com for software engineers in the United States on June 6, 2010 were examined. Job descriptions from 50 distinct companies were perused to determine which, if any, soft skills were explicitly listed as qualifications for the position. The results are displayed in figure 1.

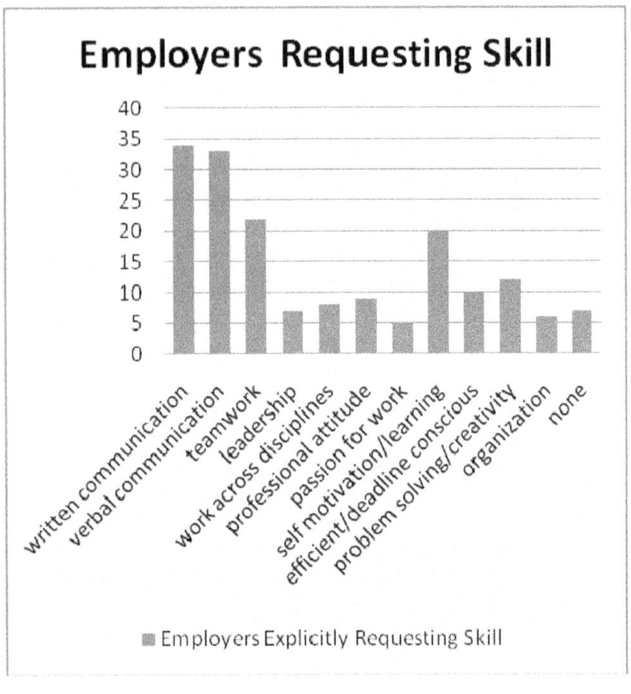

Figure 1. Number of employers requesting soft skill

Only seven of the 50 companies failed to list any soft skills. Forty-three of the companies explicitly listed skills that could be categorized into those shown in figure 1. The top four skills desired were written communication, verbal communication, ability work in a team, and self motivation and learning. To clarify, the category of professional attitude included attributes like the ability to take constructive criticism, the ability to deal with conflict, responsibility, and seeking help when necessary.

These results correlate fairly closely with a similar survey conducted in Europe [10]. In this study, with data gathered from monster.at and jobpilot.at and targeting the Vienna area, the top four desired soft skills were language skills, teamwork, communication and organization/responsibility.

2.2 According to Students

If students are going to be open to learning soft skills, they need to see them as important. What soft skills do students see as valuable for future employment? In an effort to determine this, Kabicher facilitated a group dialog among computer science students [10]. This discussion yielded the information that students, too, see the importance of oral and written communication skills in future employment success.

A more formal survey was offered to students in the Mathematical, Information and Computer Sciences department at PLNU. They were asked to rank the importance of 10 different soft skills to future employers on a scale of 1-5, with 5 being most important. The average responses are presented in figure 2.

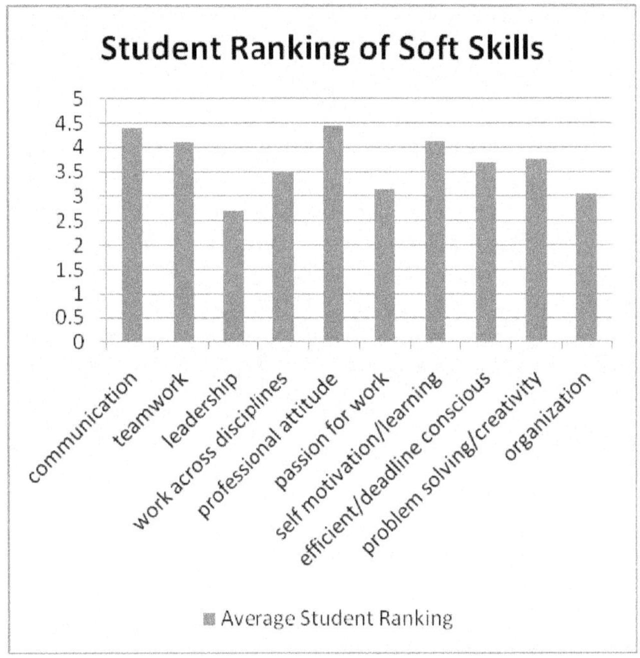

Figure 2. Student ranking of importance to employers

With 27 of 67 students (40%) responding, the students seemed to understand that employers value communication, teamwork, and self-motivation and learning. They also assume that a professional attitude is important.

2.3 According to Faculty

Do faculty members have a clear picture of what skills employers are looking for? In the study referenced in the end of section 2.1, the authors collected data from a job fair in Austria on the perceived importance of 25 different technical and soft skills. Computer science faculty members were given the same survey at a later date. According to Kabicher, faculty saw soft skills as less important than did employers:

"In comparison to employers, instructors rated basic general knowledge and research skills with higher importance. Vice versa, employers rated the capacity for organization and

planning, oral and written communication, the ability to deal with new technology, flexibility, creativity, problem solving and interpersonal skills as more important."[10]

A smaller study interviewed 6 faculty members regarding the skills that they believed students needed in order to be successful engineers [11]. The study revealed 6 categories of skills that they believed students should be proficient in. The authors of this study concluded that faculty members recognized the importance of communication and self-teaching. The additional skills of teamwork, work ethic and social responsibility were also identified, but appeared to be of minor importance.

With employers explicitly asking for soft skills, and students aware that they are important, perhaps faculty members need to find a place for them in the curriculum.

3. WHERE TO TEACH THESE SKILLS?

Communication appears to be the number one desired skill across the board, but employers explicitly ask for employment-ready computer science and engineering students to have other skills as well. Where do we teach these skills? A variety of solutions have been offered.

3.1 GE Classes and Modeled behaviors

Some programs expect that soft skills will be taught in other general education courses [11]. Writing should be taught in Freshman Composition, and presentation skills should be taught in a speech class. Research skills might be taught in a science course, and teamwork can be taught in a social sciences course. The problem is that computer science students need to learn to communicate technical concepts, and present technical concepts to a variety of audiences. That doesn't happen in generic composition and speech classes. Our students need to be able to work in a team of technical people, some of whom might be cross-discipline. That doesn't happen in a social science course.

Another possibility is that students learn through observation [11]. One professor suggested that she tries to model the kind of behavior that assures students that asking questions is OK. She encourages them to be inquisitive and to learn things on their own. Another example of learning through observation is classroom presentations. As professors present material the student learns presentation skills.

3.2 Dedicated Soft Skill Courses

Other computing programs have created special modules for the express purpose of learning the soft skills [12, 13]. The content for the presentations or writing assignments is computer science based. However, these have proven to be extremely unpopular with both students and professors alike. The students feel that they are being presented with information that they already know. They are not necessarily recognizing the different context. Computing professors find these courses more difficult to teach, and feel that these classes are a waste of their talents.

Some computer science and engineering departments encourage their students to take advantage of the Leadership Certificate courses that are being offered by other departments at their universities [5]. Although not technically oriented, they offer courses such as self leadership, group leadership, communication, cultural competency, and ethics and integrity, designed to prepare students for the work place. Once again, the benefit of these courses may be limited by the lack of a technical context.

3.3 Capstone or Service Learning Course

An alternative method of teaching soft skills is to intentionally incorporate things like writing, presenting, and teamwork in a capstone or service learning course. A frequent goal of both kinds of courses is to have the students complete large projects, often for an outside client or stakeholder. These projects are generally completed in teams, require communication with the client, and can easily incorporate presentations or written reports.

Brown reports on a capstone game design course where students work in teams with students from multiple disciplines, and requires design and writing assignments [2]. At Furman University, two experiential courses were offered to students, both of which required teamwork and interaction with a client [1]. In one, the students received explicit instruction in project management. They were required to complete a project plan, gather information from the customer, write project status reports, and present the project deliverables.

The EPICS model of service learning is used in many computer science and engineering departments, particularly in large universities [4]. The model divides students into teams, often multi-disciplinary in composition. Students may or may not be part of the team from design through implementation depending on the length of the project. However, at whatever point they are involved, they learn communication, organizational, and interpersonal skills in dealing with their client and group members.

There are many other good examples of successful service learning and capstone classes that incorporate communication, teamwork and similar soft skills.

Over the past four years, the Mathematical, Information and Computer Sciences department at Point Loma Nazarene University has developed a year-long service learning course that is modeled after a business. Because of this model, opportunities for teaching soft skills beyond what is the norm for capstone and service learning courses have surfaced. These opportunities are discussed in the next section.

4. SOFT SKILLS IN SERVICE LEARNING AT PLNU

4.1 The Service Learning Class

The year-long service learning course in the MICS department at PLNU is run as a business with the professor as the CEO. At the start of the year, potential clients speak to the class about projects they would like a group from the class to complete. Students create resumes and cover letters or proposals for the jobs they would like, and project groups are formed. Over the years, the clients have come from both on and off of the campus community. Projects undertaken include, but are not limited to, statistical analysis and data mining, network implementation, database creation, and curriculum design.

In addition to the projects that are worked on as a group, each individual also has a task to perform for the good of the "business." Some of the students are project managers. Some of the students will research and present to the class a skill (such as the use of a particular statistical or data mining package) that will be required for a job. One student sets up the class wiki where each class member with record his or her progress weekly. A more complete description of the early implementation of the class can be found at [3].

The class is constantly evolving based on feedback from students and clients. This past year, the students complained that their clients kept adding additional requirements to their already completed projects. They recognized the need for written summaries of project requirements that both the students and the clients review to which they formally agree.

Because of the number and variety of the projects each year, coupled with the fact that there is a single professor acting as advisor, the groups work fairly autonomously. However, over the years, we have determined that things run more smoothly if we explicitly talk about some of the soft skills that cause the students to act in a more professional manner.

We have found that some students don't know how to promote themselves in their cover letters without sounding arrogant and disrespectful. They don't know how to make good use of their time when waiting for an answer from a client who might not be available for a meeting at the exact time that the students need an answer. They may not know how to break a project down into steps so they have a feel for how much they need to get done each week to stay on track. They do not think about how to prepare for a meeting with a busy client so as to get the most of out of their limited time during the appointment. They do not understand how to write a concise and professional summary of a meeting to keep an email paper-trail so that expectations are well-understood. They do not know how to present a technical topic in a manner that a lay person can understand.

These skills that apply to all students are discussed in appropriate weeks throughout the year. The students have been interested in them because they have a need to know. They apply directly and immediately to the project on which they are working. Other soft skills such as dealing with group conflict, taking constructive criticism well, or finding information on their particular project are skills that are learned through the actual experience of completing the project.

Table 1 presents the soft skills that employers have said that they explicitly desire, along with the way in which they are learned in our program. As suggested previously, some of these skills are regularly incorporated into many service learning and capstone courses. The next section points out some of the less common opportunities that our design allows.

4.2 Unusual opportunities for soft skill education

4.2.1 Written communication/ Professionalism

Because our course is a year-long commitment, students have the time to complete a meaningful project, along with the documentation that makes it useful to the client. Tools created are delivered with manuals written for the lay person. Statistical reports are written to include not only the statistics, but the bottom-line interpretation of the statistics.

To avoid confusion as to what the client expects, students must write concise and professional summaries of all conversations that must be verified by the clients. This practice also improves the students' ability to listen.

When applying for a particular project, students must complete a professional resume and cover letter, or a formal proposal.

Table 1 Soft Skill Learning Opportunities

Soft skill	**Learning opportunity**
Written communication	• Reflections • Post-client meeting status reports • Manuals (for using tools developed) • Data analysis reports
Verbal communication	• Individual skill presentations • Client communication • Employee-CEO reviews • Poster presentations and small talk at semester dinner • Critiquing other's presentations
Teamwork	• Project groups
Professionalism	• Resume and cover letter or proposal • Discussions on paper trails, preparing for client meetings, how to make a meeting request and how to behave during the meeting, making the most of their time when their clients are unavailable • Periodic progress reviews from CEO where constructive criticism is given
Self motivation and learning	• Researching the information and skills needed for their particular project • Researching the individual skill that they must teach the rest of the class
Leadership	• Project managers • Semester dinner organizer
Work across disciplines	• Clients have been from secondary and elementary schools, fund raising, nursing, IT, and churches. • Project groups are made up of students from math, information systems and computer science majors.
Problem solving and creativity	• Breaking project into sequential and parallel pieces • Finding creative ways to implement features that clients want
Efficiency and meeting deadlines	• Milestone charts • Grade based on meeting deadlines • Conversations on time-management
Organization	• Milestone charts • Wiki entries
Passion for project	• Students spend a year learning about their client and the importance of their project

4.2.2 Verbal communication

At the semester mark, faculty members, administration, and clients are invited to a dinner that is organized by the students. Each project creates a poster showing their progress so far, and each member of the team must take a turn explaining the work to the guests in a one-on-one forum. In addition, the students have the experience of making "small talk" with the attendees during the dinner.

Because so many of our projects involve skills (statistical and data mining packages, wikis, database design), that are not taught to all students regularly in coursework, students have an opportunity to share their knowledge with others. This is accomplished through formal PowerPoint presentations.

4.2.3 *Self-learning/ working across disciplines*

Because most clients are from a different discipline, students must become familiar with that discipline. The class advisor often has no more knowledge than the student does, so could not help even if he or she wanted to. In addition, the client often asks for features on tools that neither the professor nor student knows how to implement.

4.2.4 *Organization and efficiency*

Students must report weekly on their accomplishments for the past week, and plans for the coming week via the class wiki. Students learn to create timelines to layout macro plans. In addition, students prepare periodic reviews to be presented to the CEO to demonstrate their progress.

5. CONCLUSIONS

It is important to teach soft skills to our students as most future employers value them as much as the technical skills. While there are many places these skills could be taught, capstone courses and service learning courses appear to provide many opportunities. The opportunities for experiences with teamwork and communication in these courses could be expanded to include experience with other soft skills by adding such things as a class wiki, a mid-project dinner and poster presentation, student-taught skills, and formal proposals prior to project assignments. Intentional discussions on such things as time-management and meeting planning can be interspersed throughout the course on a need-to-know basis.

6. ACKNOWLEDGMENTS

I am greatly indebted to my forty-six-to-date Service Learning students who have embarked on this adventure with me. I am also indebted to our department chair, Maria Zack, for her vision and support as well as to the community partners who have welcomed the experience.

7. REFERENCES

[1] Abernethy, K. and Treu, K. 2009. Teaching computing soft skills: an experiential approach. *J. Comput. Small Coll.* 25, 2 (Dec. 2009), 178-186.

[2] Brown, Q., Lee, F., and Alejandre, S. 2009. Emphasizing soft skills and team development in an educational digital game design course. In *Proceedings of the 4th international Conference on Foundations of Digital Games* (Orlando, Florida, April 26 - 30, 2009). FDG '09. ACM, New York, NY, 240-247. DOI= http://doi.acm.org/10.1145/1536513.1536557

[3] Carter, L. 2009. The business of service learning. In *Proceedings of the 39th IEEE international Conference on Frontiers in Education Conference* (San Antonio, Texas, USA, October 18 - 21, 2009). IEEE Press, Piscataway, NJ

[4] EPICS at Purdue University, http://epics.ecn.purdue.edu/

[5] Epstein, J. 2010. Teaching a leader. http://www.insidehighered.com/news/2010/06/15/leadership accessed 6/15/2010.

[6] Fernandez, J. D. and Tedford, P. 2006. Evaluating computing education programs against real world needs. *J. Comput. Small Coll.* 21, 4 (Apr. 2006), 259-265.

[7] Greene, M. 2006. Career report: computer science. *The Black Collegian Magazine*. http://www.black-collegian.com/issues/1stsem06/greene_computer_science.htm

[8] Hissey, T.W. 2000. Enhanced skills for engineers. *Proceedings of the IEEE,* Vol. 88, No. 8, (August 2000)

[9] Johnston, S and McGregor, H. Recognising and Supporting a Scholarship of Practice: Soft Skills Are Hard! In *Creating Flexible Learning Environments: Proceedings of the 15th Australasian Conference for the Australasian Association for Engineering Education and the 10th Australasian Women in Engineering Forum. Toowoomba, Qld: Australasian Association for Engineering Education*, 2004: 68-77.

[10] Kabicher, S., Motschnig-Pitrik, R., and Figl, K. 2009. What competences do employers, staff and students expect from a computer science graduate?. In *Proceedings of the 39th IEEE international Conference on Frontiers in Education Conference* (San Antonio, Texas, USA, October 18 - 21, 2009). IEEE Press, Piscataway, NJ, 1260-1265.

[11] Matusovich, H., Streveler, R., and Miller, R. 2009. We are teaching engineering students what they need to know, aren't we?. In *Proceedings of the 39th IEEE international Conference on Frontiers in Education Conference* (San Antonio, Texas, USA, October 18 - 21, 2009). IEEE Press, Piscataway, NJ, 1254-1259.

[12] Pulko, S. H and Parikh, S.2003. Teaching "soft" skills to engineers. *International Journal of Electrical Engineering Education*, Oct 2003.

[13] Spokane Community College: Computer Information Systems webpage. http://cis.scc.spokane.edu/?cissoftdev accessed 6/12/10.

[14] U.S. Bureau of Labor Statistics, Computer Software Engineers and Computer Programmers. *Occupational Outlook Handbook, 2010-11 Edition*

Interdisciplinary Teaching: Introductory Programming Via Creative Writing

Mary Elizabeth "M.E." Jones
Immaculata University
1145 King Road
Immaculata, PA 19345
610 – 647 – 4400 x3254
mjones@immaculata.edu

Melanie Kisthardt
Immaculata University
1145 King Road
Immaculata, PA 19345
610 – 647 – 4400 x3165
mkisthardt@immaculata.edu

Marie A. Cooper
Immaculata University
1145 King Road
Immaculata, PA 19345
610 – 647 – 4400 x3020
mcooper@immaculata.edu

ABSTRACT

Seizing and retaining student interest in programming is a difficult task. Many students find programming to be a dry and tedious task doable only by students gifted with strong analytical skills. Teaching *introductory programming* via *creative writing* begins by connecting the planning, organizing, and detailing of writing a story to the programming process. Creative concepts are taught first and then connected to an equivalent programming concept. Group-oriented activities using art, "Mad-Libs™", "Potato Heads™", and "Legos™" allow students to actively make the connections among the creative concepts, analytical concepts, and programming skills. Students work in pairs. Student pairings are assigned by matching a student with analytical tendencies with a student majoring in one of the humanities disciplines. The pairs apply the concepts and skills by creating stories, designing an animation, and implementing the animation using the Alice programming system. This research recognizes the creative nature of programming, invites students who would not consider studying programming to potentially identify an unrecognized talent, and attempts to develop a new approach for teaching introductory programming. This research and teaching is sponsored by a NSF Grant [11].

Categories and Subject Descriptors

K.3.2 [**Computers and Information Science Education**]: Computer Science Education, Curriculum

General Terms

Design, Experimentation, Languages

Keywords

Alice Programming, Collaboration, Creative Writing, Interdisciplinary Teaching, Introductory Programming, National Science Foundation, Pair Programming, Pedagogy

1. INTRODUCTION

In Frederick P. Brooks, Jr.'s, essay *The Tar Pit*, he delineates the "joys and woes" [4] of the computing profession. Brooks explains that computer scientists are creative problem solvers who especially enjoy identifying the components of a problem and assembling those components in an orderly manner. To Brooks, a computer program is a "tractable medium" [4], providing computer scientists the flexibility to mold their creations (or applications). So the joy stems from designing and creating useful and usable applications. The woes of the task become obvious when implementing the design into a working application. Implementation can be frustrating as computer languages demand the user to be exact in the language syntax, grammar, and logic. Once the application is implemented, seemingly endless hours are spent testing and correcting errors. The message from Fred Brooks is clear. Computing professionals must have an imaginative and creative view as well as a technical and disciplined approach for problem solving.

Approximately a decade ago, much interest was generated regarding the concept of pair programming. The concept is simple – it's based on the adage "two heads are better than one." When collaborative and pair programming was introduced, the initial results were very good [10, 14]. Since that first introduction, further studies [6, 8, 9, 13, 16] have confirmed the benefits of collaborative and pair programming. Studies showed benefits in "increased retention rates, better performance on programming tasks, increased confidence, and decreased frustration" [13]. This approach mirrors the collaborative learning styles educators have long employed in their classrooms. Therefore, it makes sense that pair programming is an effective tool for teaching and learning programming.

Given the difficulty in motivating, encouraging, and retaining computer science students [5], the purpose of this project was designing an interdisciplinary course integrating creative writing and pair programming within an introductory programming course. In addition, the teaching approach responded to the desire to move away from a style "organized according to language constructs" [2].

The course intertwines the processes used for developing software applications and for creating a story with pair programming. Programming is a dynamic and recursive process resulting in a set of precisely sequenced instructions. Similarly, creating stories or narratives requires an attention to the audience's reception/perception as well as a linear sequencing [12].

This paper is organized as follows: Section 2 presents the background and motivation, section 3 presents the research purpose and questions, section 4 provides an overview of the course and its design, section 5 provides the research results, and section 6 presents the conclusion and future work.

SIGCSE'11, March 9–12, 2011, Dallas, Texas, USA.

2. COURSE BACKGROUND AND MOTIVATION

There are 3 factors influencing the development of this interdisciplinary introductory programming course: 1) the university philosophy and environment, 2) student uncertainty regarding their major program of study, and 3) lack of student academic exposure to computer programming.

Immaculata University is a comprehensive, co-educational Catholic university with an educational tradition rooted in the liberal arts. Immaculata also has a tradition of faculty collaboration and inter-disciplinary teaching. Given the difficulties in recruiting and retaining information technology and mathematics-computer science majors, the design and development of an interdisciplinary introductory programming course was encouraged and supported by the faculty and administration.

Many students begin their undergraduate studies without declaring a major. Those students are searching for a discipline that ignites a deep internal interest and passion while suitable to their academic abilities. Students are also trying to determine a minor course of study. Due to the accessibility of this course, students with a preference to either left-brained thinking or right-brained activities can be equally successful. This interdisciplinary course develops problem solving skills as well as logical thinking in a creative framework while enabling students to identify if they have an interest in and/or ability for programming.

Typically students are not exposed to computer programming since many students do not take a high school programming course [5]. Therefore this course teaches core programming fundamentals assuming no prior programming experience. This approach allows the course to be taken by all students – regardless of major plan of study. However it is required for information technology and mathematics-computer science majors.

3. RESEARCH PURPOSE & QUESTIONS

The idea for an interdisciplinary introductory programming course emerged from four years (2005 – 2008) of teaching introductory programming via the Alice programming system. Over the years, non-majors enrolled in the course as an elective. The non-majors performed very well and were surprised by their success. In a few instances, those students decided to major or minor in information technology. Also, after completing this course, information technology majors and mathematics-computer science majors were better prepared for intermediate and advanced programming courses.

Brainstorming about an interdisciplinary introductory programming course and investigating a National Science Foundation (NSF) grant ("CreativeIT") promoting the development of creative interdisciplinary approaches toward the teaching of computer science and information technology fueled the design of the course [11].

The NSF "CreativeIT" program is summarized as follows: "The CreativeIT Program solicits proposals for projects that explore synergistic cross disciplinary research in creativity and computer science and information technology. Information technology is playing an increasing role in extending the capability of human creative thinking and problem solving. The study of creativity and computing as a way to advance computer science and information technology, cognitive science, engineering, education, or science can lead to new models of creative computational processes, innovative approaches to education that encourage creativity, innovative modes of research that include creative professionals, and new technology to support human creativity" [11].

Under the 2-year "CreativeIT' grant award (June 2009 – June 2011) that funded this pilot interdisciplinary course, the researchers considered the questions: 1) Can an introductory computer programming course intertwine basic programming skills and creativity in order to demonstrate how this combination can enhance application development? and 2) Can an integrated teaching approach assist in reforming and enhancing the methods used in the teaching of introductory programming courses?

4. COURSE OVERVIEW AND DESIGN

The course is co-taught by a professor of English and professor of Mathematics-Computer Science. The teaching approach assumes the students have no prior programming knowledge. The Alice programming system is used to teach programming concepts, design, and implementation. The 14-week semester course meets twice a week for 75 minutes. The course is composed of information technology and mathematics-computer science majors as well as students who take the course as a free elective.

The end product of the course is a written story created collaboratively by pairs of students and designed and implemented as an animation using Alice. Where possible, an information technology or mathematics-computer science major is paired with a student of another major.

Students organize their story into chapters and decide who is responsible for animating the specific chapters. Therefore, each student is responsible for animating his/her part of the story using accepted design and coding practices. However, the students do collaborate on the design and determine opportunities for reusing software.

The course design is based on the concept of "creativity first, programming second." During the course, students participate in 2 types of activities: 1) Activities that stimulate creative thought via intuitive, random, holistic, and subjective approaches as well as 2) Activities that teach basic programming design and implementation principles via logical, sequential, rational, and analytical approaches. Most classes begin with a creative writing prompt or activity that is linked to an analytical or programming concept. Since students are familiar and more comfortable with writing, the creative prompts or activities become the mental model with which the students can associate design and programming concepts.

4.1 Intertwining Creativity and Programming

The first example of the "creativity first, programming second" approach is introducing the Alice programming environment. By mapping the similarities between story components to Alice components (Table 1), students recall components of the Alice programming environment quickly and with less trepidation.

Table 1. Similarities between the story components & Alice components

Story Components	Alice Components
Characters	Classes and Objects
Location	World template and scene construction
Plot, action, events (external or psychological)	Properties, Methods, or Events
Passage of time (change)	Code to effect transitions between scenes
Trajectory (shape of the story)	Change in the world template and scene through properties and camera work

The second example of the "creativity first, programming second" approach is mapping the English grammar and structure used when writing to a computer program (Table 2).

Table 2. Similarities between the English grammar and structure and a computer program

Story	Program
Noun: person, place or thing	Classes and Objects
Verb	Class Method
Adjective	Property
Sentence	Instruction
Choice of words	Choice of instructions
Order of Sentences	Order of Instructions
Paragraph	World Method
Order of paragraphs	Order of methods
Connection/Transition between Paragraphs	Relationship between methods
Grammar: syntax and punctuation	Programming language syntax and punctuation

These mappings provide the framework for introducing the software design approaches, programming concepts, and the Alice programming environment. The mapping is introduced at the start of the course and is re-visited as programming concepts are taught and detailed during the semester.

4.2 Creative Perspective and Activities

In order to encourage students to create original stories, students participate in activities that challenge them to consider the very process of creative storytelling. Using Bloom's cognitive taxonomy [3], the focus is on the stages of development that engage the students through the levels of cognition. The **Knowledge** level focuses on what they already know; the **Comprehension** stage asks them to discuss; **Application** requires them to demonstrate; **Analysis** compels them to question; in the **Synthesis** stage they organize material; and finally, their critical thinking is required for the **Evaluation** phase. In creative writing, this paradigm translates thus: Tell a story the class is likely to know; discuss the possibilities for alternative plot or character, show what this revision may "look" like; challenge the possibilities for character and plot; decide how to order the story (linear, spatial, causal, etc.); assess the outcome based on the initial vision and on the audience feedback. [1]

Students reconsider a standard the fairytale "Goldilocks" through Bloom's taxonomy. The results, offered with some hesitation, are frequently amusing and surprising to the students and professors, since the students' personalities impact their revisions of the standard tale. This exercise opens possibilities for creativity and helps students to realize that a linear pattern is not the only possibility for storytelling. More importantly, this exercise immerses students in a narrative point of view, a crucial perspective from which stories are told and from which they achieve their credibility or readers' "willing suspension of disbelief" (Samuel Taylor Coleridge).

To help students understand the importance of setting and character in the story's emotional impact, they view still images —paintings that are ambiguous or that compel the viewers' engagement in discerning meaning. Elements like color, perspective, and connotation are examined through group discussion and individual responses. This activity is designed to help them pause when choosing hues, landscapes, and characters from Alice.

Perhaps the most compelling aspect of the Alice program for creative writing is the immediacy of 3-dimensional picturing text. Students experiment with different characters and settings, but unlike the written story, in Alice, they can visualize the story. When they incorporate action, the program compels them to consider the plot and emotional impact and how to make design/code it. Thus, they must think about the next step and simultaneously edit and re-create.

4.3 Understanding Programming Using Creative Activities

Some students may find programming concepts abstract and difficult to understand their use. However, if the concepts are motivated and described within the context of a need, students tend to demonstrate a persistent and 'no fear' attitude toward implementing the concepts. Since the students desire to create realistic animations, they are motivated to inquire about and attempt a variety of programming concepts. In addition, they tend to be persistent in the use and perfection of programming concepts in order to implement the desired creative actions or effects.

However before students advance to the 'no fear' attitude, common activities are used to demonstrate known knowledge and its relationships to programming concepts. Students participate in graphic novel, Lego™, Mad Lib™, and Potato Head™ activities designed to assist in evolving their written story into an animated form using software design and implementation principles.

Graphic novels are used to teach students a method for beginning the initial design phase of the software development process by transitioning and partitioning their written story into scenes. Each scene sketch (or pane of a graphic novel) limits the environment, props, characters, text, sound, and actions that implement that part of the story. From a software design perspective, students are indentifying, planning, organizing, and partitioning the initial components required for implementation.

Teaching detailed design is facilitated and motivated by a Lego™ activity using 3-in-1 kits. Lego™ 3-in-1 kits provide instruction for assembling 3 different objects from the same kit. Three teams of students are each given an identical 3-in-1 kit. Each of the 3 teams is assigned the task of assembling one of the three objects. Once all the teams have completed the object assembly, the professors facilitate a class discussion reflecting on how this activity relates to software design and implementation. Students connect a Lego™ piece to an Alice class method. Alice methods can be used and sequenced in a variety of ways in order to implement many unique tasks or actions just as the Lego pieces can be assembled in a variety of ways to create multiple unique objects. From a software design perspective, this activity is designed to motivate the design and implementation of single purpose methods. It also introduces the concept and potential of software reusability.

Some students struggle with the concept of a parameter. Introducing parameters via Mad Libs™ connects the concept of a Mad Lib™ fill-in-the-blank with a specific type of word (noun, verb, adjective, adverb, pronoun, etc.) to a value defined by a specific data type. Students are given a Mad Lib™ and create their version of the story by 'filling in the blanks' with the specific word type. After completing the Mad Lib™, students read their stories to the class. Each student's story is unique due to the choice of words. An immediate connection is made to parameters by demonstrating an Alice animation that uses parameters. Students observe how the animation is changed by using different parameters.

To address problems with implementing the personality of their characters, a student recommended use of Potato Heads™. The personality of the Potato Head™ is established by the selection of objects/parts added to the Potato Head™.

Students work in teams and are given a descriptive word or phrase. They use the parts provided in the kit to create a Potato Head™ that represents their given word or phrase. Once completed, the students show their Potato Head™ to the class, and the other students must determine/guess what the descriptive word or phrase the Potato Head™ represents.

This activity helps students understand working with the provided components within Alice. In some cases, what they want to implement may not be readily available or easy to implement. It is a lesson in working within the constraints of the system. It also challenges the students to use creative solutions to solve difficult problems.

4.4 Pedagogical Theory and Support

How can teaching programming using this approach facilitate learning? Part of the answer may lie with studies in cognitive science.

Pair programming is a strategy for efficacious learning of programming. Many cognitive researchers, among them Judy Willis [15], encourage paired note taking, paired problem solving, paired writing and other dyad strategies. The interaction fosters reflection and refinement, critical elements in effective learning. She also notes that personal goals tend to strengthen memory. The semester-long goal of producing a coherent, cohesive, and attractive animation helps collaborating students to internalize and strategically employ programming elements.

James Zull [17, 18] stresses that the power and persistence of learning is proportional to the number of neocortical regions engaged in the learning process. He lists 4 'pillars' of strong and long-lasting learning: 1) gathering data, 2) reflection, 3)creating, and 4) testing. The sensory input of the activities and the analysis of the classes, objects, methods, instructions, and reusabililty serve the first pillar, strengthened by the explicit connection to their creative counterparts. Collaborative and individual reflection on the constructs and strategies form the second pillar. Exploration of the Alice tools and the effort to produce programs strengthens the reflection. Planning and development of the animation foster deliberate connections and careful ordering of instructions. Testing and refinement boost the students' work to the level of cognitive apprenticeship, multiplying the number of mental connections made. Finally, though the course requires serious, sustained work, it also generates a playful and positive emotional environment that further supports effective learning [7, 15].

5. INITIAL RESEARCH RESULTS

The 2 research questions under consideration are: 1) Can an introductory computer programming course intertwine basic programming skills and creativity in order to demonstrate how the combination of logical thinking and creativity can enhance application development? and 2) Can an integrated teaching approach assist in reforming and enhancing the methods used in the teaching of introductory programming courses?

As a pilot project, the first question concerns the ability to integrate creative and analytical thought in an introductory programming course. A successful integration may be important in identifying students who have programming ability, but are unaware of their talent. Students tend to classify themselves as having analytical abilities or not; therefore, a course that integrates the creative with the analytical may be inviting to students who might not otherwise consider studying programming. In addition, this approach could assist in retaining information technology and mathematics-computer science majors.

Evaluating the success of this project, involves gathering data regarding student perception of the course and student performance as assessed by the professors.

A student pre-survey and post-survey are used to assess student perceptions regarding their collaboration, listening, and problem solving skills, as well as the importance of and connection between creative processes and analytical processes. There are also two reflective surveys. The first consists of open-ended questions administered after the stories are created. This survey is used to assess: 1) how the students approached the development of their story, 2) difficulties they encountered while creating their stories, 3) how their ideas evolved and/or changed and 4) how the students managed differences of opinion when developing their story. The second survey is administered approximately 75% through the semester. Its purpose is to understand how student stories changed due to design or implementation issues.

Lastly, the completed animations are evaluated/graded by the professors based on use of software design principles, appropriate use of software implementation techniques as well as effective use of the technology to evoke feeling and emotion.

Thus far, 32 students have completed the course – 20 in the fall 2009 semester and 12 in the spring 2010 semester. Nineteen are presently taking the course (fall 2010 semester). The following results are from the course offered in Fall 2009 semester and compare the pre-survey results to the post-survey results.

5.1 Pre-Post Survey Results

All questions used a Likert (1 – 5) scale with 1 being the lowest score, 3 being neutral and 5 being the highest score.

In summarizing the results, it seems the students: 1) deepened their belief in the importance of collaboration, 2) increased their willingness to listen to other ideas, 3) believed that they improved their ability to problem solve with a team member, 4) remained status quo with regard to creating a solution by combining ideas with others, 5) recognized a deeper connection between creative and analytical processes, 6) increased their belief in the importance of creativity throughout their studies, 7) increased their belief in the importance of analytical thinking throughout their studies, 8) increased their belief in the connection between the liberal arts and technology, and 9) split their belief as to whether creative processes or analytical processes were most important or both were equally important,. The details follow.

Students rated the importance of collaborating with a team member approach problem solving from a perspective different than their own. A response of *not important (1)* remained at 0%, *somewhat important (2)* decreased from 32% to 25%, a response of *N/A (3)* decreased from 5% to 0% while a response of *very important (4)* increased from 53% to 56% and a response of *extremely important (5)* increased from 11% to 19%.

Students rated their willingness to listen to other ideas. A response of *not willing (1)* remained at 0%, *somewhat willing (2)* decreased from 26% to 6%, a response of *N/A (3)* remained at 0%, while a response of *very willing (4)* increased from 42% to 69% and a response of *extremely willing (5)* decreased from 32% to 25%.

Students rated their ability to problem solve with a team member. A response of *no ability (1)* remained at 0%, *some ability (2)* increased from 5% to 6%, a response of *N/A (3)* decreased from 5% to 0%, while a response of *good ability (4)* increased from 53% to 69% and a response of *excellent ability (5)* decreased from 37% to 25%.

Students rated their ability to create a solution by combining ideas with the ideas from others. A response of *no ability (1)* remained at 0%, *some ability (2)* increased from 5% to 6%, a response of *N/A (3)* remained at 0%, while a response of *good ability (4)* increased from 68% to 69% and a response of *excellent ability (5)* decreased from 26% to 25%.

Students rated the connection between the creative processes and the analytical processes. A response of *not connected (1)* remained at 0%, *somewhat connected (2)* decreased from 42% to 38%, a response of *N/A (3)* decreased from 11% to 0%, while a response of *very connected (4)* increased from 32% to 50% and a response of *tightly connected (5)* decreased from 16% to 13%.

Students rated the importance of creativity throughout their studies. A response of *not important (1)* remained at 0%, *somewhat important (2)* decreased from 16% to 13%, a response of *N/A (3)* decreased from 5% to 0% while a response of *very important (4)* decreased from 53% to 50% and a response of *extremely important (5)* increased from 26% to 38%.

Students rated the importance of analytical thinking throughout their studies. A response of *not important (1)* remained at 0%, *somewhat important (2)* decreased from 16% to 13%, a response of *N/A (3)* decreased from 5% to 0% while a response of *very important (4)* decreased from 53% to 50% and a response of *extremely important (5)* increased from 26% to 38%.

Students rated the connection between the liberal arts and technology. A response of *not connected (1)* remained at 0%, *somewhat connected (2)* increased from 26% to 31%, a response of *N/A (3)* decreased from 21% to 6%, while a response of *very connected (4)* increased from 42% to 56% and a response of *tightly connected (5)* decreased from 11% to 6%.

Students rated the relationship between creative and analytical processes. A response of *creative processes are most important* increased from 11% to 29%, *analytical processes are most important* increased from 5% to 21%, a response of *creative processes and analytical processes are equally important* decreased from 84% to 50%.

5.2 Reflective Survey Results

This survey is made up of the following 6 open-ended questions asking the students to evaluate the creative process used during the course. The following statements are a few of the most interesting student thoughts.

Question 1: Describe the approach you used to create your story. One student responded: "We started by looking at all the objects and characters in ALICE. We talked and discussed what kinds of movies and special effects we like to watch. From there, we thought about how the different objects and characters could fit into our own story that relates to the movies we like."

Question 2: Describe any difficulties you encountered while writing your story. One student responded: "The hardest parts for us were trying to come up with a plot that was clear and organized and not just random events thrown together."

Question 3: Describe any aspects of creating your story that were straight forward or relatively problem free. One student responded: "Our story was straight forward; it is just the coding in ALICE that brings problems."

Question 4: As the ideas for your story evolved, describe how you recognized that you needed or wanted your story to change. One student responded: "As we became more advanced programmers in ALICE I realized that could make the story more elaborate because I could animate my ideas."

Question 5: Did you and your team member have differences regarding the story concept – if yes, what were the differences? None of the students expressed problems or difference regarding their story concept. However, one student responded: "No, but we were not always on the same page as far as meeting the project deadlines were concerned."

Question 6: Describe how you approached, discussed, and resolved creative ideas that differed between you and your team member. One student said: "We discussed and resolved creative problems by talking about both the creative and technical sides. Once we did that we decided whether that certain idea would work well in the plot or not."

5.3 Design/Implementation Survey Results

This survey is designed to capture data regarding how the students designed and implemented their animations.

In summary, 66% of the students relied on the objects available in Alice to determine the idea for their story. The stories developed due to collaboration for 72% of the students. Only 61% of the students reported that some of the actions were too complicated to implement. Seventy-eight percent of the students stated that their animation partially changed as a result of programming. The details for each question follow.

Students were asked if the idea for their story was determined by the specific objects available in Alice. The survey response was 11% for *totally*, 44% for *mostly*, 22% for *about half*, 17% for *partially*, and 6% for *not at all.*

Students were asked if their story developed through collaboration with their partner. The survey response was 50% for *totally*, 22% for *mostly*, 22% for *about half*, 6% for *partially*, and 0% for *not at all.*

Students were asked if the actions for their stories were too complicated to implement. The survey response was 0% for *all*, 17% for *most*, 22% for *about half*, 61% for *some*, and 0% for *none*.

Students were asked if based on programming, their story changed. The survey response was 6% for *totally*, 0% for *mostly*, 11% for *about half*, 78% for *partially*, and 6% for *not at all.*

6. CONCLUSION AND FUTURE WORK

In this paper, we presented our approach for teaching an interdisciplinary introductory programming course. Co-taught by English and Mathematics-Computer Science professors, we employ a "creativity first, programming second" style using creative activities to show how creativity positively affects the design and implementation of a program.

It is early to make a definitive statement on the outcomes, but indicators are positive. Projects produced by the interdisciplinary pairs were well designed and more broadly creative than those of earlier, more traditional offerings of the course. Students were generally more confident, more reflective, and more articulate with respect to the elements of the course and the concepts they had learned.

At the writing of this article, the second year of this pilot project is underway. In terms of outreach, a cyber high school has expressed interest in creating an on-line course using this approach.

7. ACKNOWLEDGMENTS

Our thanks to the National Science Foundation as this pilot project is funded by the NSF – IIS CreativeIT program [NSF 08-572], award number 0855870. We are also grateful to the Immaculata University administration, faculty, and students for their support and participation.

8. REFERENCES

[1] Angelo T and K.P. 1984. *Classroom Assessment Techniques.* San Francisco: Jossey Bass.

[2] Bennedsen, Jens and Caspersen, Michael E., 2005. Revealing the Programming Process. In *Proceedings of the 36th SIGCSE technical symposium on Computer science education* (St. Louis, Missouri February 23 – 27, 2005). ACM, New York, NY 186 – 190 DOI = http://doi.acm.org/10.1145/1047344.1047413

[3] Bloom, Benjamin. 1984. *Taxonomy of Educational Objectives.* Boston: Allyn and Bacon.

[4] Brooks, Fredrick P. 1995. *The Mythical Man Month.* Reading: Addison Wesley Longman, Inc.

[5] Carter, Lori. 2006. Why Students with an Apparent Aptitude for Computer Science Don't Choose to major in Computer Science. In *Proceedings of the 37th SIGCSE technical symposium on Computer science education* (Houston, Texas March 01 - 05, 2006). ACM, New York, NY, 27 - 31. DOI= http://doi.acm.org/10.1145/1121341.1121352.

[6] Flood, Raymond and Lockhart, Bob. Teaching Programming Collaboratively, In *Proceedings of the 10th annual SIGCSE conference on Innovation and technology in computer science education* (Monte de Caparica Portugal June 27 – 29, 2005) ITiCSE '05, ACM, New York, NY, 321 - 324. DOI: http://doi.acm.org/10.1145/1067445.1067533

[7] Jernstedt, G. Christian. 2010. *Creating Active Pathways to Student Learning, a SEPCHE Learning to Learn Project.* Grant Funded by the Teagle Foundation.

[8] Lahtinen, Essi; Ala-Mutka, Kristi; Jarvinen, Hannu-Matti, 2005. A Study of the Difficulties of Novice Programmers. In *Proceedings of the 10th annual SIGCSE conference on Innovation and technology in computer science education* (Monte de Caparica Portugal June 27 – 29, 2005) ITiCSE '05, ACM, New York, NY, 14 - 18. DOI: http://doi.acm.org/10.1145/1067445.1067453

[9] McDowell, Charlie; Hanks, Brian, and Werner, Linda, 2003. Experimenting with Pair Programming in the Classroom. In *Proceedings of the 8th annual conference on Innovation and technology in computer science education* (Thessaloniki, Greece June 30 – July 2, 2003). ITiCSE '03. ACM, New York, NY, 60 – 64. DOI: http://doi.acm.org/10.1145/961511.961531

[10] Nosek, John, 1998. The Case for Collaborative Programming. *Communications of the ACM* Vol. 41, Issue 3 (March 1998), 105 – 108. DOI = http://doi.acm.org/10.1145/272287.272333

[11] NSF 08-572 - Program Solicitation (CreativeIT) - Award Number: 0855870 http://www.nsf.gov/pubs/2008/nsf08572/nsf08572.htm?org=NSF

[12] The Council of Writing Program Administrators http://www.wpacouncil.org

[13] VandeGrift, Tammy. Coupling Pair Programming and Writing: Learning about Students Perceptions and Processes, In *Proceedings of the 35th SIGCSE technical symposium on Computer science education* (Norfolk, Virginia March 3 – 7, 2004) SIGCSE '04, ACM: New York, NY, 2 – 6. DOI: http://doi.acm.org/10.1145/971300.971306

[14] Williams, Laurie A, Kessler, Robert R, 2000. All I Really Need to Know About Programming I Learned in Kindergarten. *Communications of the ACM* Vol. 43, Issue 5 (May 2000), 108 – 114. DOI = http://doi.acm.org/10.1145/332833.332848.

[15] Willis, Judy, M.D., M.Ed. 2008. *How Your Child Learns Best.* Naperville, Illinois: Sourcebooks, Inc.

[16] Wilson, Judith; Hoskin, Nathan; and Nosek, John T, 1993. The Benefits of Collaboration for Student Programmers, In *Proceedings of the twenty-fourth SIGCSE technical symposium on Computer Science Education* (Indianapolis, Indiana) SIGCSE '93, ACM, New York, NY, 160 – 164. DOI: http://doi.acm.org/10.1145/169070.169383

[17] Zull, James, Ph.D. 2006. *Key Aspects of How the Brain Learns, from New Directions in Adult and Continuing Education.* Wiley InterScience, Wiley Periodicals, Inc.

[18] Zull, James, Ph.D. 2002. *The Art of Changing the Brain.* Sterling, Virginia: Stylus.

Gumshoe: A Model for Undergraduate Computational Journalism Education

Sarah Monisha Pulimood
Dept. of Computer Science
The College of New Jersey
Ewing, NJ 08628
+1 609 771 2788
pulimood@tcnj.edu

Donna Shaw
Dept. of English
The College of New Jersey
Ewing, NJ 08628
+1 609 771 2793
shaw@tcnj.edu

Emilie Lounsberry
Dept. of English
The College of New Jersey
Ewing, NJ 08628
+1 609 771 2506
lounsber@tcnj.ed

ABSTRACT

This paper describes a collaboration between computer science and journalism students and professors at our small, primarily undergraduate college, and a large metropolitan newspaper. Our students' work was a catalyst for a hard-hitting series of investigative stories, with far-reaching consequences. The Gumshoe project is a model for computational journalism at an undergraduate institution. The project demonstrates that when computer scientists and journalists reach out across disciplinary boundaries, computational thinking and collaboration can solve a real problem, and have a substantive impact on society.

Categories and Subject Descriptors

K.3.2 [**Computing Milieux**] Computer and Information Science Education

K. 4.0 Computers and Society

General Terms

Human Factors

Keywords

Computer science education, computational thinking, journalism education, computer aided reporting (CAR), database systems, interdisciplinary collaboration.

1. INTRODUCTION

For crime-weary citizens of Philadelphia, it may have come as little surprise when, in December 2009, the Philadelphia Inquirer published a four-part series, "Justice: Delayed, Dismissed, Denied," which concluded that most suspects arrested for illegal gun possession in the city never faced trial. Philadelphia's criminal justice system, the newspaper concluded, was seriously out of control, warped by faulty prosecutions, inept court procedures, and savvy defense lawyers and defendants who had learned to "play" the system [11]. As detailed by the newspaper, the enormous number of mishandled cases and the flimsy reasons for their dismissals by city judges led to loud and immediate outcry from readers and politicians alike, with a number of city, state and federal officials stepping in to investigate and promising to find remedies. Those efforts, including interventions by the Pennsylvania Supreme Court and U.S. Senator Arlen Specter, are ongoing as we write this paper. The series also has received recognition by state and national press organizations. What readers of The Inquirer do not know is that the series has its roots in a computer assisted reporting (CAR) project, Gumshoe, conducted in 2007 by undergraduate computer science and journalism students and their professors at our small, primarily undergraduate liberal arts college.

In this paper, we describe the collaboration between students and faculty in our computer science and journalism programs, and the large metropolitan newspaper that found in our students' work a starting point for what ultimately became a hard-hitting series of investigative stories, with far-reaching consequences.

2. BACKGROUND

Computer science educators recognize that rapid advances in technology and paradigm shifts in the global economy are giving rise to new models for how information is gathered, disseminated and used, and that it is essential to expose students from all disciplines to the ideas of computational thinking [1, 18]. While there is as yet no uniform definition, there is general agreement that computational thinking includes a broad range of mental tools and concepts from computer science that help people solve problems, design systems, understand human behavior, and engage computers to assist in automating a wide range of intellectual processes [1]. A recent report from the Committee for the Workshops on Computational Thinking convened by the National Research Council at the National Academies describes computational thinking as a group phenomenon as well as an individual one and this capability can assist specialists in other disciplines to more effectively adopt, use, and develop computational tools [1]. In a world now dominated by Google, Facebook and Twitter, it is imperative that all students, not just computer science majors, understand how information propagation is influenced by databases. Almost every facet of our lives is touched by data that we must analyze in some form to make informed decisions. The natural implication of this trend is the increase in dependence on the credibility and validity of electronic information. As complexity of data increases, it is no longer sufficient to store the data in flat file structures, like spreadsheets; we must be able to retrieve data in interesting ways conducive to deeper analysis.

Computing technologies such as databases, geographic information systems, statistical analysis programs and the Internet have radically changed the way journalists investigate and deliver news to the public. In its 2010 report on the state of the news media, the Pew Project for Excellence in Journalism estimated that 5,900 full-time newsroom jobs were lost in 2009, in addition to a similar number in 2008 with resulting in the loss of almost a third of the workforce in American newspapers since 2001 [10]. Since 2001, newsrooms across the United States have lost more than 25 percent of staffers, bringing the total number of reporters, editors and other staffers employed in daily journalism down to 41,500 – the lowest number since the 1970s, according to the American Society of Newspaper Editors[1]. While much of the staff reductions can be attributed to the dim economy, the drop is also due to lost revenue stemming from the increase in the public's shift to free online news. This underscores the reality that 21st century journalists, like many other professionals in computing-dependent fields, increasingly require a strong computing background [5, 8, 9]. Journalists are departing from traditional story-centric journalism and moving toward the use of information that is structured and compiled by computers to enable more comprehensive and analytical investigations [5], improving the efficiency, accuracy, structuring and quality of the targeted journalistic endeavor over traditional methods and tools.

Both computer scientists and journalists must be able to apply foundational principles of information access and dissemination, fact analysis, process description and decision-making for developing software artifacts and news items respectively. Although there is still some disagreement about how these goals can be accomplished, there is growing recognition among industry leaders that journalists must become technologically literate, and that technological innovation is essential to the fulfillment of the ethical and economic imperatives of the industry [8, 9].

Computer assisted reporting (CAR) has been used in newsrooms for decades. However, "computational journalism" requires a more sophisticated approach to applying algorithms and principles from computer science and the social sciences to gather, evaluate, organize and present news and information [6]. Reporters and editors need quicker access to information that will help them provide more in-depth reports, complete with history, context and the most recent supporting data. An example is the investigation performed by New York Times reporter Jo Craven McGinty. Using a database obtained from the New York Police Department Hate Crimes Task Force, McGinty comprehensively mapped numerous hate crimes in New York City based on type, location, frequency and targeted ethnicity. McGinty concluded that Jews are the targets of most NYC hate crimes and that most of them occur in Brooklyn [7].

Economic reality is forcing colleges and universities to reexamine how to educate young journalists, how to help find a sustainable business model for online news and to figure out what computer skills will be most helpful in newsgathering. Many journalists and journalism professors who once eschewed the idea that reporters and editors would need computer programming skills now realize that such skills are important, perhaps even essential, to the future of professional newsgathering. As former Washington Post top editor Leonard Downie Jr. and Columbia journalism professor Michael Schudson concluded in their report, 'The Reconstruction of American Journalism', sophisticated journalism is increasingly dependent on "reliable, downloadable, and searchable databases" [3]. The report suggests that universities should develop "innovations in news reporting and dissemination for the digital era," and since they are among the nation's largest nonprofit institutions, universities "should play significant roles in the reconstruction of American journalism."

Computational journalism is emerging as a discipline in its own right, gaining traction in higher education. For example, Georgia Tech[2] offers a course on computational journalism and Columbia University recently announced a new dual Master of Science program in Computer Science and Journalism[3]. At Duke University, researchers and professors at the DeWitt Wallace Center for Media & Democracy are examining computational journalism, and journalists and computer scientists are working together to create software tools intended to help reporters move more quickly to produce in-depth, authoritative stories[4]. The Medill School of Journalism at Northwestern University is offering scholarships to lure programmers and web developers to their journalism master's degree program[5].

Models similar to our collaboration are being used elsewhere: Journalism students from the Medill Innocence Project at Northwestern University have helped uncover evidence that so far has freed 11 men from prison[6]. Former '60 Minutes' investigative producer Lowell Bergman, now a professor at the University of California at Berkeley Graduate School of Journalism, has forged an alliance between the New York Times and the PBS documentary program, "Frontline," using his graduate students to assist in stories on corruption in Mexico, the East Africa bombings and the California energy crisis and the role of Enron[7]. The Los Angeles Times and the University of Southern California's (USC) Annenberg School for Communication & Journalism are collaborating to produce stories for the Times' Homicide Report blog. Under this partnership, USC students write dispatches for the Homicide Report, providing more content for the blog and more crime-reporting experience for students[8]. The New York Times announced that New York University students in a new class, "The Hyperlocal Newsroom," would staff the "East Village Local," starting in fall 2010[9], and in a partnership with the Boston Globe, students from Northeastern University have written 11 Page One stories in 20 months[10].

The Gumshoe project described here is a perfect example of how computer scientists and journalists, even at an undergraduate institution, can use computational thinking to collaborate and solve a real problem making a real impact on society.

---

[1] http://asne.org/annual_conference/conference_news/articleid/763/decline-in-newsroom-jobs-slows-763.aspx

[2] http://www.computation-and-journalism.com/main/

[3] http://www.wired.com/epicenter/2010/04/will-columbia-trained-code-savvy-journalists-bridge-the-mediatech-divide/

[4] http://dewitt.sanford.duke.edu/index.php/about/area-of-research/computational_journalism

[5] http://www.medill.northwestern.edu/admissions/page.aspx?id=58645 .

[6] http://www.medillinnocenceproject.org/

[7] http://journalism.berkeley.edu/faculty/bergman/

[8] http://annenberg.usc.edu/News%20and%20Events/News/100127LATimesPartnership.aspx

[9] http://phx.corporate-ir.net/phoenix.zhtml?c=105317&p=irol-pressArticle&ID=1393695&highlight

[10] http://www.nieman.harvard.edu/reportsitem.aspx?id=100934

3. THE COLLABORATION

Our role in the gun crime project began in early 2007 as a discussion among colleagues at our institution. One of the co-authors is a computer science professor who teaches a course on database systems. An important goal of this course is for students to collaborate with other students to solve problems by integrating concepts from computer science, particularly databases, and other disciplines. Students are required to work in teams to design and implement a database system to address a real-world need in order to gain a deeper understanding of and internalize database modeling concepts such as data modeling, queries, normalization, transaction and concurrency control, as well as issues of privacy and security of data. By working with people or "clients" from other disciplines, students also better understand the techniques and process for effectively eliciting requirements for a system outside their familiar domain [14]. Another co-author is a journalism professor who, through an independent study course, sought to provide journalism students with the opportunity for and experience of a painstaking computer assisted reporting (CAR) project that is essential yet frequently too time-consuming and expensive for a newspaper, given the diminishing newsroom resources. In light of market realities, we have sought more opportunities to pair professional journalists with our students not only to train the next generation, but also to fill the investigative reporting gaps created by buyouts and layoffs in our region's print media. What followed was a semester-long collaboration between the nine computer science students in the database systems class and the nine journalism students in the independent study group. We chose to address violent gun crimes because they were prominent in the news and involved one of our areas of journalistic expertise. For the journalism independent study group the project was the sole deliverable for the course. The students worked on the project in class for at least three hours per week throughout the semester.

Initially, an Excel spreadsheet was created that listed demographic data for each person arrested for violating 18 Pa. C.S.A. § 6106, carrying a firearm without a license, in a sample period of January-February 2006. That violation was chosen because almost everyone accused of a gun-related crime would be charged with at least that count. The only exceptions would be a handful of people with licenses to carry weapons. That resulted in a list of 699 people. Of that number, 613 defendants were tracked, since the rest involved juveniles whose cases went almost immediately to Family Court, or defendants whose records were expunged, or those whose charges were not in the defined timeframe. Using Pennsylvania's online court dockets, the journalism students painstakingly created and populated several more columns of data, for example felony charges like murder, manslaughter, aggravated assault, rape, etc. while in possession of a firearm that, under Pennsylvania law, theoretically should result in a convicted gun offender receiving a mandatory minimum prison sentence of five years. We quickly discovered that determining who should receive a mandatory sentence would be almost impossible, in large part because the dockets did not list the degree of the charges, even though there was space provided on the forms for that information. Instead, we tracked each case from the initial arrest, through preliminary hearing, to ultimate disposition (trial and sentencing, if any), to identify where the system was failing. Some questions we wanted to ask were:

- What happens to defendants arrested for gun-related crimes?
- How many people serve prison time for committing violent felonies with guns?
- Are cases regularly being dismissed or bargained down?
- In how many cases do civilian witnesses and/or victims fail to appear in court to testify?

However, as the data grew, effective data management and analysis became more challenging. Excel, like other file-based approaches, has a number of limitations such as isolation of data, duplication of data, incompatible file formats, and fixed query proliferation [2, 4]. It was clear that a well-designed database system would go a long way in helping to analyze the data and find meaningful patterns and information. Moreover, it would eliminate data redundancy, improve data integrity, improve data accessibility, and enforce data consistency.

The students in the Database Systems class were divided into two teams, and each was charged with the task of designing a version of the system, in a series of pre-defined stages. The goal of the project was defined as developing a CAR system to store, manage, track, and query data on gun crime in the Philadelphia region. Throughout the semester, as concepts were covered in class, they were applied to the next stage of the project. The project contributed to 25% of the final grade. However, as we discuss below, exploration and internalization of important concepts contributed indirectly to other aspects such as the assignment grade (20%) and overall understanding of material. Periodically, representatives from each computer science team met with the journalism team to clarify their own understanding and to confirm that their design was progressing in a way that continued to meet the journalistic needs. This was particularly essential as they designed the queries that would retrieve in the data in ways that would be useful and enlightening for the journalists. The computer science professor closely monitored and guided the progress to ensure that pedagogical and system goals were being met. Both versions of the project were completed successfully and presented to the journalism professor. Feedback from the journalism professor indicated that there were useful and compelling features in each of the projects. Elements from each version were integrated into a final system, Gumshoe, in the following semester by one of the computer science students who undertook the task as part of a mentored research project under the guidance of the computer science professor.

4. SYSTEM DESIGN

4.1 Data querying and organization

A number of data querying and organization methodologies were analyzed to determine which would be most effective for the CAR system. One methodology entails organizing data by the specific entity types pertinent to the investigation and tailoring search and sort algorithms to only these entities. This gives the journalist the ability to analyze all the attributes and information about a category of objects within the system, thus enabling focused analysis of a specific entity [2, 4]. Various entity categories concerning gun crimes and criminals such as arrest, defendants, and courts were identified and algorithms that search and organize all objects by the identified entity types were designed. Another methodology entails implementing the ability to search for a specific entity either by value or attribute within the collective data set [2, 4]. This is a contrast to the macro level data organization of the previous method because it focuses on a specific object and the attributes associated with that object. This is a desirable feature for CAR because it allows the journalist to search for a very specific entity or criteria on a micro level. It is also a powerful tool that enables the journalist to narrow down the analysis and precisely examine a more specific investigative query rather than general patterns. An example would be searching for an identification number of a specific criminal to view his or her record. A third methodology enables searching by the characteristics of an object type and comparing the results to other object types. Thus, the search attributes of one object can be compared to the search attributes of a different object in the system. The searching of characteristics or attributes of an object is a middle ground between macro level and micro level searches because it is based on more criteria shared by objects but does not analyze a single record. Most important, this methodology represents a fundamental analytical process common to many journalistic investigations: drawing conclusions by comparing events to similar cases. As an example, one could compare the verdicts decided by one judge to the verdicts of another judge. One technique is to design the database schema or underlying platform of the application to be data neutral with a generic representation of the data to be analyzed. This is a powerful concept because it enables the importing, expansion, and analysis of other data sets in the system for subsequent investigations. Yet another method is to allow data in the system to be exported outside the system boundary. This is important because it gives the journalist greater investigative flexibility by allowing for analysis in other software. For example, Gumshoe allows data to be exported to files that can be opened in Microsoft Excel for graph generation and statistical analysis, abilities not native to Gumshoe's functional scope.

4.2 Database design

The conceptual design of a database focused on constructing a model of the data, i.e. the entities and their relationships, independent of all physical considerations, such as operating systems, database management systems, computer platforms, and other hardware [2, 4]. The resulting entity-relationship diagram (ER diagram) is shown in Figure 1.

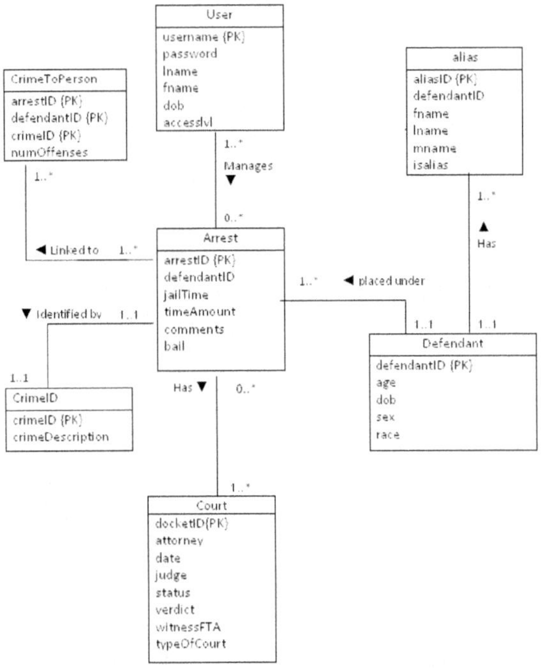

Figure 1: ER Diagram for Gumshoe

As the class considered the data to be stored, such as demographics for the User entity, important concepts of security and issues of privacy of data were examined in class. For example, we examined the necessity and appropriateness of storing the social security number for a defendant, and if we did, which types of users should be allowed to access it. This raised interesting questions about the legal rights of defendants with regard to privacy of their data. Such discussions are more engaging for students when there are real individuals to be considered rather than in the context of some imaginary system. A satisfying outcome of these discussions was that a number of security measures were implemented in both the database as well as the application that interfaced with it.

Two aspects of security were analyzed: system security and data security. System security refers to the access and use of the database at a system level, such as using a username and password while data security refers to access and use of database objects and the associated actions available on each object [15]. Design issues such as connection traps [2, 4], which are design flaws that can lead to misinterpretation among data relationships, were identified and corrected. We opted to use the PostgreSQL database management system (DBMS) since it is open source with a large, active community of developers. This assured us of long-term stability of the DBMS. More important is the fact that PostgreSQL has a number of sophisticated enterprise features [13], missing from many other open source DBMSs, but essential for a secure and robust environment. A number of queries, including several fairly complex ones, were designed to enable retrieval and presentation of data in meaningful ways. This process was particularly powerful pedagogically since the students were obligated not only to gain a good understanding of the journalistic needs but also to seriously consider how the data could best be presented so that it would be compelling for the journalists and their audience. It was clearly this aspect of the system that was most valuable to the journalists and eventually contributed to convincing the editors of the Philadelphia Inquirer.

Access to the database was provided through a web-based application that utilized a number of web technologies and programming languages such as PHP, HTML, CSS, and JavaScript. PHP [12] was especially suitable for this project because it has a number of built in libraries tailored to web programming, including those for addressing web security issues [16] such as SQL injection, cross-site scripting, and session hijacking [17]. Additionally, there is native support for the object-oriented paradigm and its ability to interface with PostgreSQL. The application exposed interface functionality such as helpful display messages, drop down menus, radio button selects, form validation, and clean layout, all designed to help the journalists conduct their investigation effectively. A sample screenshot of Gumshoe is shown in Figure 2.

Being aware of the severe newsroom cutbacks in our region, we decided the time was right to approach potential newspaper partners and propose the use of our students' analysis in a major journalistic endeavor. While we considered approaching at least three different newspapers in our region, we settled on The Philadelphia Inquirer because of our connections there (two of the authors of this paper are former Inquirer reporters) and because, unlike in our state of New Jersey, Pennsylvania's court dockets are online, making them more easily accessible.

Figure 2: Screenshot of Gumshoe

5. ANALYSIS

At the end of the semester, we presented the data and results of our analysis to The Inquirer. Based on 859 dockets in a two-month sample, some of the conclusions we reached were:

1. 392 (45%) cases were withdrawn by the district attorney or discharged by the judge at the preliminary hearing level. At least 55 cases (6%) were nolle prossed in Common Pleas Court. Overall, this meant that at least half of all these prosecutions were dropped or discharged.
2. In nearly four cases out of 10, civilian witnesses and/or victims failed to appear one or more times at court hearings.
3. Only 18 (2%) resulted in convictions on all charges.
4. 162 (19%) resulted in prison time. So, in our sample, the chance of going to jail after being arrested for possession of an illegal firearm and/or violent felonies was less than one in five. The vast majority of defendants received jail time only if they committed violent felonies in addition to gun possession.
5. Among the 162 cases, few received the so-called mandatory minimum of five years in prison for committing a violent felony with a gun. In part, that was because the more serious F1 felonies frequently were reduced to lesser degrees, dropped or plea bargained away. In fact, among those 162 cases, only 60 (37%) resulted in minimum sentences of at least five years. That represented less than 7 percent of the total dockets.
6. In examining the 60 dockets in which there were sentences of five years or more, we found that they involved 38 defendants. (For many incidents there were multiple dockets.) Thus 6 percent of the defendants received jail sentences of five years or more.

While our analysis convinced the editor of the Philadelphia Inquirer that this issue needed to be exposed, he was skeptical about the abilities of an undergraduate cohort. The newspaper conducted its own, more sophisticated and broader computer analysis of some of the same data compiled by our students, but ultimately reached nearly identical conclusions. In December 2009, the Philadelphia Inquirer published a four-part series that documented the widespread failure of violent-crime prosecutions in the Philadelphia court system [11].

Taking a broad look at the crimes of murder, rape, robbery and aggravated assault, the newspaper revealed a dysfunctional system in which defendants had a better than 50-50 chance of walking free, with dismissal or withdrawal of all charges. The series showed that Philadelphia had the nation's lowest felony conviction rate even as law-enforcement authorities struggled with crime rates above the national average. They also identified other problems, extensive witness intimidation, thousands of fugitives with unresolved cases, and approximately $1 billion in uncollected bail [11]. The reporters (including one of the authors of this paper, who at the time was working at the Inquirer while teaching at our institution) sought to show the depth of the dysfunction in Philadelphia's overloaded criminal courts by focusing on violent crimes committed with guns. In nearly two-thirds of violent-crime cases, the reporters found, the defendants walked free, and only 20 percent ended with felony convictions [11]. Most of the cases died in Municipal Court, despite the fact that prosecutors must present only probable cause that a defendant committed a crime to allow a case to proceed to trial in the Court of Common Pleas. The newspaper examined 31,000 criminal cases that involved more than 250,000 individual charges – a targeted analysis of the more than five million records obtained in a huge data run from the state Administrative Office of Pennsylvania Courts, which compiles statewide court records. With a history and experience of publishing major investigative series about problems in the Philadelphia courts, the Inquirer decided, as had we, to examine the current state of the system by looking at how serious cases involving guns, which have become astonishingly available in many neighborhoods of the city, were handled in the city court system. The Inquirer found that prosecutors were most successful in murder cases involving guns, with 83 percent of defendants convicted of at least one charge. But the guilty verdicts plummeted for three other crimes in which guns were used – rape, robbery and aggravated assault. The most stunning conclusions involved robberies and assaults committed with guns. In robbery cases, just 35 percent of defendants were found guilty of any charge and only 19 percent were convicted of robbery and a gun charge. In aggravated assault cases, 35 percent were found guilty of any charge and 10 percent were found guilty of aggravated assault and a gun charge [11].

6. OUTCOMES AND CONCLUSIONS

The student and Inquirer projects, while carried out independently of one another, followed similar paths and, more important, reached virtually identical conclusions. This demonstrates that collaboration between carefully supervised students and veteran journalists in the field can be effective. In fact, the students reached their conclusions well in advance of The Inquirer because two of the staff writers had to put aside the project to cover a five-month trial in late 2008 and early 2009.

The Gumshoe project provided a compelling avenue to teach database design concepts as well as issues relating to privacy and security. Having a real "client" the students could interact with to obtain requirements and get feedback from, as well as the notion of civic engagement, motivated them to keep on task and to be more thoughtful in the design and development not only of the database but also the user interface and application. In doing so, they gained a deeper understanding of and internalized database concepts such as data modeling, queries, normalization, transaction and concurrency control, as well as issues of privacy and security of data. By working with students or "clients" from another discipline, students better understood the techniques and process for effectively eliciting requirements for a system outside their familiar domain as well as for working together as a team to complete a project on schedule. The journalism and computer science students also participated in professional discourse on issues of privacy and security related to the storage and use of private information of the alleged criminals. The investigative series in the Philadelphia Inquirer [11] is resulting in an overhaul of the justice system in that region.

Comments we received from some of the students who participated in this project (now all graduated) include:

- "The gun project was the best lesson I got in the value of public records and how they can be used to unlock stories. It made me realize that any time you have access to a collection of public records, you're sitting on a potential gold mine."
- "I found this gun project a superb thing to be part of. For one, it improved my news gathering and research skills. Now, I do not just read other news reports for story ideas but make sure to look at data and figures. It is something I am using now as I write my MA dissertation. I am always asking myself: what do the figures say about this particular human rights issue?"
- "I'm ecstatic that Gumshoe was used to uncover key defects in the prosecution system and publish these findings to the world. It's always wonderful to hear how your work is benefiting others!"

Gumshoe is a model not only for collaboration with a professional news organization, but also for how students at a small, primarily undergraduate liberal arts institution can make a substantial contribution toward an important but endangered kind of journalism: investigative reporting. Students came away from this project with enhanced analytical skills and a deeper appreciation for the type of computational thinking that is so critical as the United States seeks to preserve its competitive edge in the global market. At a time when the economic crisis in the news industry threatens the ability of news organizations to conduct time-consuming, detail-oriented analyses, it is especially important to continue exploring such models of collaboration.

7. FUTURE STEPS

Our journalism and computer science programs intend the Gumshoe collaboration to be the first of many such projects involving local newspapers, most of which have suffered newsroom budget and personnel cuts. When practicable, we intend to incorporate these projects into our regular journalism classes. We did not do this with Gumshoe, choosing instead the independent-study route, because it would have required far too much class time. Today, as the notion of outside collaborators is becoming more acceptable in newsrooms throughout the country, we are formulating plans to approach additional newspapers with the intent of establishing partnerships.

8. ACKNOWLEDGMENTS

This project would not have been possible without the dedication and efforts of our students in the Database Systems and Computer Assisted Reporting independent study classes.

9. REFERENCES

[1] Committee for the Workshops on Computational Thinking, National Research Council. 2010. Report of a Workshop on the Scope and Nature of Computational Thinking. The National Academies Press.

[2] Connolly, T., and Begg, C. 2005. Database Systems: A Practical Approach to Design, Implementation, and Management. 4th Ed. Harlow, England: Addison-Wesley.

[3] Downie, L., and Schudson, M. 2009. The Reconstruction of American Journalism. The Journalism School, Columbia University, New York NY.

[4] Elmasri, R. and Navathe, S.B. 2007. Fundamentals of Database Systems, 5th edition. Addison-Wesley.

[5] Holovaty, A. 2006. "A fundamental way newspaper sites need to change." http://holovaty.com/blog/archive/2006/09/06/0307/?highlight=structured%2520data. Accessed March 31, 2010.

[6] Mecklin, J. 2009. Deep Throat Meets Data Mining. Miller-McClune Jan/Feb 2009, 1, pp 8-13.

[7] McGinty, J. C. 2005. "Breaking Down Hate Crime." The New York Times July 24 2005. http://query.nytimes.com/gst/fullpage.html?res=9C03EFDC153FF937A15754C0A9639C8B63&scp=1&sq=Breaking+Down+Hate+Crime&st=nyt. Accessed March 31, 2010.

[8] Murray, J. H. 1997. Hamlet on the Holodeck, The Future of Narrative in Cyberspace, MIT Press, Cambridge MA.

[9] Niles, R. 2006. The Journalist as Programmer: Q & A with Adrian Holovaty. Online Journalism Review June 5, 2006. http://www.ojr.org/ojr/stories/060605niles/index.cfm. Accessed March 31, 2010.

[10] Pew Project for Excellence in Journalism. 2010. The State of the News Media: An Annual Report on American Journalism. http://www.stateofthemedia.org/2010/index.php. Accessed March 30, 2010.

[11] Philadelphia Inquirer, The. 2009. Justice: Delayed, Dismissed, Denied. http://www.philly.com/philly/news/special_packages/79211302.html. Accessed March 30, 2010.

[12] PHP Manual. 2010. http://www.php.net. Accessed March 31, 2010.

[13] PostgreSQL. 2010. "PostgreSQL: The world's most advanced open source database. PostgreSQL Global Development Group. http://www.postgresql.org/. Accessed March 31, 2010.

[14] Pulimood, S. M. and Wolz, U. 2008. Problem Solving in Community: A Necessary Shift in CS Pedagogy. In Proceedings of the 39th Technical Symposium on Computer Science Education (ACM SIGCSE), Portland, Oregon, March 12 – 15, 2008.

[15] Schach, S. R. (2007). Object-Oriented Classical Software Engineering. 7th ed. New York, NJ: McGraw-Hill.

[16] Shiflett, C. (2005). Essential PHP Security. Sebastopol, CA: O'Reilly Media.

[17] Welling, L. and Thompson, L. (2005). PHP and MySQL Web Development. 3rd ed. Indianapolis: Sams Publishing.

[18] Wing, J. M. 2006. Computational thinking. Commun. ACM 49, 3 (Mar. 2006), 33-35.

An Engineering Approach to Teaching Writing

Joe Miro Julia
Dept. Matematiques i Informatica
U. de les Illes Balears
07122 Palma de Mallorca, Spain
joe.miro@uib.es

ABSTRACT

Being able to write correctly is a valuable asset for future CS professionals and an important learning tool, but teaching to write is difficult both for professors and students. Part of this difficulty is that writing is taught using unverifiable concepts such as style, and is significantly based on intuition. In this paper we present an engineering approach to writing, in which engineering principles are used to teach and assess writing. The results are as good, and much better in some cases, and teaching and learning become easier.

Categories and Subject Descriptors

K.3 [**Computers and education**]: Computer and Information Science Education

General Terms

Human factors

Keywords

Writing, engineering, principles, verification

1. CLARITY AND STYLE ARE NOT ENGINEERING TERMS

Communication and writing are valued skills in the workplace [8] and an effective learning tool [14] and therefore important in the teaching of Computer Science. It is being taught within the curriculum and across the curriculum in many universities [4] and has received plenty of attention in CS Education symposia. There are papers that focus on how to improve students' motivation [12], the use of communication to promote active learning [11], course organization and assessment [1, 4], or the difficulty of teaching it [6]. Despite the large number of papers dedicated to so many aspects of writing, I have found none on *which* writing skills (from sentence structure to argumentation) should be taught, or *how* they should be taught. This, it seems, is left exclusively to books on writing.

But these books are generic books, not written for scientists or engineers. It is true that they are not written for any specific discipline, but their approach and vocabulary is closer to liberal arts students than to CS ones. In my experience this is one of the reasons why writing is difficult, specially to some students, as it is seen as an elusive, foreign type of knowledge, hard to understand. Central concepts, such as clarity and style, seem arcane as they have no objective, verifiable meaning. This is illustrated with conversations such as the following, of which I have had many:

- This is not clear.
- I think it is.
- No, you see, it is too hard to understand.
- But I understand it perfectly!
- Of course, you are the writer, but a reader will find this step of your argument hard to follow
- What do you mean? It's obvious!

and so on... These conversations, where professors unsuccessfully try to explain a writing concept to a student who *wants* to understand it, are utterly frustrating. They end up realizing that for some students "clarity" has no meaning and "style" is something personal and subjective, almost arbitrary. They almost believe that it is impossible to teach some students how to write competently.

Also, many professors acknowledge that students should write better but do not know what to do about it. They say they do not know what they should explain, how to explain it, how to provide feedback. They provide opportunities to write, but believe there is very little that can actually be taught as they consider it a personal skill that must grow from within.

It is interesting to note that this view of writing as personal and somewhat arbitrary, as arcane and unteachable, goes beyond science and engineering. One of the main points stressed in current writing books is that writing can be taught to *everybody* [9, 15]. These books make an effort to show that it is feasible to learn writing, but still present the matter with many references to the unverifiable clarity and the personal style. They follow, with improvements, the usual approach to teaching writing, that relies significantly on the emergence of a writing intuition. We can call this the *intuition approach*.

This approach makes teaching writing an achievable goal, but still more difficult than it should be for both professors and students. It does not eliminate the *writing anxiety* that pushes students to avoid writing [6]. This is particularly worrisome as when they graduate they will spend most time around non-technical matters [2], mostly communicating through reports, memos, e-mails, or in meetings with clients and coworkers [10]. Not being able to write effectively greatly reduces their future professional value.

I have been teaching writing to CS, engineering, and math students for over 15 years in both 'normal' and technical writing courses in lower- and upper- division courses, with class sizes ranging from a dozen to 60 students. The more I taught writing, the more similarities I found between writing documents, writing programs, and engineering thinking in general. I discovered that although writing quality cannot be measured, it can be verified, and therefore it is possible to teach writing through an engineering approach. This approach uses practically the same knowledge of the best writing books, but repackaged into a method with procedures, objective principles, and verifiable criteria.

Using this approach writing becomes a task that produces effective documents in the same way that any engineering endeavor, with an established process, sound principles, and thorough verification produces consistent and adequate products. Teaching and learning to write is easier and more palatable for both professors and students. Specially those students for which clarity is an unclear goal profit greatly.

In this paper we will explore the basic tenets of the engineering approach, provide examples of how it can be taught and assessed, and show the results obtained.

2. THE ENGINEERING APPROACH

An engineering approach to writing requires a procedure to produce the written document and a set of verifiable principles to check the quality of the product. Given that the procedure (Researching, Drafting, Revising) is well known and has been thoroughly and clearly described [5], we will concentrate here on the principles and verification.

The principles on which the approach is based are not new. They can be found in *Style, Through Clarity and Grace* by Williams [15], *The Craft of Research* by Booth and others [5], *The Oxford Guide to Plain English* [7], and many other books. What we show here is how repackaging this knowledge into units called *writing crafts* makes writing an engineering-like process, easier to teach and assess, and easier to learn and use.

2.1 Writing crafts

A writing craft is a basic writing skill that is needed to produce a competently written document. It is formed by a *principle*, that provides specific guidance on how to write; a *rationale*, that explains why the principle aids good writing; and a *check* that allows the student to unambiguously diagnose if the principle is followed or violated.

As a simple example let us consider the structure of a sentence. A common advice, even written in some books, is to make sure the sentence begins well and to avoid poor endings that make the sentence "fall flat". This advice can be stated, but cannot be taught as it is impossible to assess: "beginning well" and "falling flat" are not verifiable terms. Better advice, that may be considered a principle, is to put the known information at the beginning to aid the flow and put the new and important information at the end of the sentence to finish it strongly. This is much easier to teach as students understand what "known information" and "new information" is, although the concepts "flow" and "strong ending" are vague and cause trouble to some.

This principle is not arbitrary, nor the creation of a judge of taste, an *arbiter elegantiarum*. Its rationale is based on how readers understand what they read. People pay most attention to the beginning and end of things, and less to what is in the middle. Therefore the beginning and end of a sentence are its most important parts. Also people learn better when going from known to unknown information. Therefore putting known information at the beginning of the sentence helps the readers link what is coming to what they know. Putting the new, important information at the end, where the reader pays most attention, highlights it, making it easier to remember. This type of reasoning is not unique to sentences: all important writing principles are supported by similar cognitive rationale.

To convert this principle into a writing craft we package the principle, the rationale and the check. In this case the principle is "Put known information at the beginning of a sentence and new, important information at the end". The rationale is the one explained above. The check can be formulated in many ways. Practiced writers check it on the fly, even subconsciously, but when teaching the craft it is adequate to use a simple systematic approach such as the following. Underline five or six words at the beginning and end of each sentence. The underlined section at the beginning should contain known information. The one at the end, the most important new information. If they do, the principle is followed, if they do not, it is violated. This check, as is usually the case, is not razor-sharp, but is clear-cut enough to be easy to assess.

Not all principles are verifiable. Williams' first principle for concision is: "Usually, compress what you mean into the fewest words."[15, Ch. 7]. This cannot be checked. It is still a sound principle and we must stress its importance to our students, but it cannot become a craft. Fortunately, as we will see later, this does not constitute a problem.

Writing crafts are a good teaching tool. The principles are clear, the rationale show that the principles are not personal or arbitrary and help students apply them. Not having to explain what "falling flat" or "flow" is make them easier to explain and understand. Finally the checks allow the students to evaluate their own writing, help professors give valuable feedback, and facilitate assessment.

2.2 Examples of crafts

The correct structure of a sentence is a very simple craft. Let us illustrate the strength of the engineering approach with more complex ones. We will do so with two very different crafts. One is about writing technique: the correct structure of paragraphs. The other is one that would not seem subjected to principles and verification: the statement of the thesis of a paper. Below we present these crafts in a way that are easy to teach, require no vague concepts, and can be simply and systematically verified.

These crafts have been simplified, as even paragraphs are quite complex entities: one of the books mentioned [15] needs *two* chapters to explain them in detail. The rationale and principle stated here for all three crafts are shorter and simpler than would be used in a course. The checks, on the other hand, are almost complete.

2.2.1 Paragraphs

A sentence is the minimum part of discourse that states an idea while a paragraph is the minimum unit of discourse that *explains* an idea. Explaining requires stating, therefore a correctly crafted paragraph consists of two parts. Following Williams [15] we will call the first part, in which the idea is stated, the issue. It is often, but not necessarily, one sentence long. The second, lengthier, part is called the *discussion*. Here the idea is further explored and developed.

A paragraph is a unit, and therefore must have a common purpose that derives from the development of a single main concept. This main concept is the one located at the end of the last sentence of the issue. For instance, if the issue of a paragraph is "When a task cannot be partitioned the application of more effort has no effect on schedule", the effects on scheduling should be the only concept developed in the discussion section.

Two common errors in student papers are paragraphs with only the issue section and paragraphs without a unity of concept. In issue-only paragraphs students state the issues but do not discuss them. Fragments full of issue-only paragraphs are dry, with a dogmatic tinge, as the claims stated are not discussed and thus expect the reader to accept them in faith.

As for the unity of concept, the most frequent error is to introduce a second concept during discussion. This makes the paragraph seem disperse as it develops two concepts. Also, as readers do not look for information in the middle of units, it is easy for them to miss important information altogether, and feel disoriented when the second concept comes up again later.

Thus we can state the *principle* for constructing paragraphs. A paragraph is the minimum logical unit that explains an idea. It has two parts: the issue, at most a few sentences long, that states the idea to be discussed; and the discussion, that explains the idea stated in the issue. The explanation is centered on only one main concept: the one that appears at the end of the last sentence of the issue.

The *check* for the correctness of paragraphs consists of several steps. Checking for issue-only paragraphs is very simple: these are paragraphs with only one or two sentences, so all that needs to be done is count the sentences of each paragraph. To check for the unity of concept there is a well known technique we all use, called 'speedy reading' or 'diagonal reading': reading just the issues of a section or fragment we should get the same gist as if we read the whole fragment. We should be reading all the issues, the whole reasoning, but without the details, the discussion. For teaching purposes this can be done systematically. Cutting the issues of every paragraph and pasting them to another file creates a new text that should follow the main reasoning of the original text. 'Plot holes' or 'reasoning gaps', signalling some paragraphs are incorrect, are spotted easily once the jungle created by discussions is removed. Once the incorrect paragraphs are identified, all that is needed is to check the end of the last sentence of the issue and make sure that the concept that appears here is the only one discussed in the paragraph.

2.2.2 Thesis

Any document more than a few lines long must have a claim that articulates the purpose of the whole document. This is called a *thesis* or a *main point*. If there is no thesis at all the paper becomes an aimless rambling. Coming up with a thesis is a task that belongs to the discipline the paper is about and is not a writing craft, but stating it correctly is. A nice additional facet is that stating the thesis correctly allows the student to assess its relevance, helping them discard trivial ideas and improve promising ones.

The two most important aspects of the craft of writing a thesis are (1) the thesis must be a relevant claim written in the paper, and (2) it must be located where it better helps the reader understand and assess the whole document.

The thesis should never be implied. For instance the thesis of Dijkstra's Go To Statement Considered Harmful is loud and clear: "The go to statement should be abolished from all 'higher level' programming languages". This claim focusses the reader for the remainder of the paper. An implied thesis, on the other hand, makes the document much harder to understand as each new piece of information must be linked to a vague frame and assessed respect to an indeterminate claim. Therefore the thesis must be written. It also must be relevant.

A claim is relevant if it encourages discussion. Relevant theses are those that are not obviously true and are therefore subject to debate. Clearly, Dijkstra's thesis is highly relevant as many rebuttals were written claiming that go to's should not be abolished. We would also like a claim to be interesting, but that is something that cannot be checked —people differ in what they deem interesting—, so it is left out of the craft.

Two typical types of irrelevant claims students write are the *declaration of intention* ("I am going to talk about Operating Systems") and the *fact* ("Capacity of hard drives have increased over the last years"). They are not relevant because they provide us with no information —the first case— or is a fact that simply can be checked looking at data and therefore fosters no debate. Non-relevant claims, when negated, become either trivial ("I am not going to talk about Operating Systems") or false ("Capacity of hard drives have not increased over the last years").

As for the location of the thesis, it can be either at the beginning or at the end of the document. The beginning is the preferred location as the thesis will give perspective to the readers, simplify their understanding of the reasoning, and allow them to assess better the information provided. Dijkstra's thesis is in the second sentence of his letter. In a short paper the thesis can also be located at the end, as the reader can store in memory the main points of the whole paper and assess the complete argument when the thesis arrives.

The *principle* therefore is that the main thesis is a relevant claim that must be specifically written in the document, preferably at the beginning, although in short papers it might be placed at the end.

The *check* consists in looking at the end of the introductory part of a long document, or at the first few and last paragraphs of a shorter one, and identifying the thesis. If it is not there, look for it in the rest of the document. If it exists, it should be moved to an adequate location. If it does not, it must be stated.

3. CRAFT IS ENOUGH

Writing crafts simplify the professor's and students' tasks. It makes teaching, assessing, giving feedback easier. It helps students to understand better the concepts involved in writing, and to diagnose and correct their errors. But it might

Fundamentals: There are no spelling or punctuation errors. The paper follows the set edition rules.
Vocabulary and grammar: There are no serious grammar errors. Pronouns and ellipsis are used to avoid unnecessary word repetitions. There are no words or figures of speech that appear in the *List of Forbidden Words.* The words are used consistently with their dictionary definition. Overused words (such as *thing*) are used sparingly. In very long sentences the subject is short and the predicate has a simple structure.
Definitions and descriptions: The definitions expose the generic and differentiating traits of the object described. Descriptions are clearly ordered in time, in space or by function. In the latter, the description is ordered from the generic to the specific or from the important to the incidental. In complex descriptions, they are hierarchically subdivided to avoid having more than four or five elements at the same description level.
Paragraphs: All paragraphs have an issue section, a discussion section and a point. Only exceptionally the paragraphs will be less than three sentences long. If you read only the issues and points you obtain an adequate summary of the whole document.
Thesis: The thesis is written in the text and is a relevant statement. It is written towards the end of the introduction. The main concepts that will be developed in the paper are part of the thesis and appear towards the end of the statement.
Arguments: The argument is based on relevant statements, reasoning that is logical and easy to follow and is founded on relevant evidence. If at all possible, the evidence is data.
Story: The paper uses few main characters and few concept families. The characters and concepts are adequately introduced in the introduction section. At least one main character and concept appears prominently in each section.
Cohesion: Sentences begin and end well: the concept is located towards the beginning of the sentence and is known matter; the end of the sentence contains the most important information you want to convey. Each sentence exposes only one idea.

Figure 1: Actual checklist for a term-paper on an upper-level course. This is the concise version. Students also have a complete version with detailed check descriptions.

seem that it does all this at the cost of obtaining simplistic, thoughtless, impersonal papers. Results show this is not so. Let us see why.

As shown above, focusing on crafts does not mean establishing a set of strict rules that students should mindlessly follow[1]. A craft is not just a simple command but a principle that stems from the way readers understand text, and therefore, when followed, creates understandable writing. The same way programming and software engineering principles do not excuse students from thinking when creating an application, writing principles aid the students, but do not write for them.

A good set of crafts must (1) assure competent writing and (2) be manageable[2]. There are crafts to choose adequate words, structure sentences, produce reasonings that can be followed, generate good definitions, write clear and organized descriptions, construct sound arguments over a relevant thesis, and many others. There clearly are enough crafts to assure adequate writing quality, although we might not need all of them. The actual set used depends on the type of writing —short answers to questions require less writing crafts than term papers— and the writing level we want our students to have.

Also, the set is of manageable size. Figure 1 shows a concise version of the complete checklist used for term-papers in an upper-level course. One fact that helps maintain a reasonable amount of crafts is that it is not necessary to have a principle for everything. Correctly writing some parts of the discourse forces the student to correctly craft the rest. It is like a jigsaw puzzle: if you have set enough pieces correctly, the rest will fall on their own. One case is concision: using precise vocabulary, simple grammar, and correct paragraphs forces writing to be brief.

One might think that focussing on crafts, on mechanics, will produce writing that is robotic and constrained, while the intuition approach might be more difficult to master, but will produce refreshing, creative documents. Actually, if anything, it is the opposite. Following clear principles enhances creativity (as artists say, "form is liberating"). Also, once the students dominate the craft they have a sound guideline and can concentrate on the much more enjoyable task of writing something they like, in their own style. On the other hand, the intuition approach usually forces on the students decisions that should be personal and that *does* stifle creativity: teaching a standard impersonal style will produce standard boring papers [13].

[1]I did this many years ago and students obliged: they wrote thoughtless papers that blindly followed the rules to painful results.

[2]The set of crafts I have compiled can be found at `http://bioinfo.uib.es/~joemiro/destrezas/`

4. OTHER ISSUES

As said in Section 1 there are many papers written through the years on how to introduce writing in Computer Science. They describe different forms of writings, student motivation, and many other aspects of course organization. But there are some issues that are either particular to the engineering approach or must be dealt with differently. This is specially true when dealing with high-stakes writing, such as term papers. We cover these issues here.

4.1 Teaching the craft

Your students probably have been taught some of the writing crafts you intend them to master. Others will be new. The known ones require restating the principle and rationale in packaged form. This does not even require lecture time and can be done through course materials the students should read on their own. New crafts can be taught in a similar way to any engineering task: stating the principle and rationale, followed by examples, frequent pitfalls to avoid, exercises.

But in both cases the checks require a mindset change from the students and therefore need to be given special attention. Even if the basics of the checks have been shown through an intuition approach, they are presented there as a list of interesting things that can be done during revision. In the engineering approach they become a systematic set of activities that verify that the writing is of adequate quality. The change from "let's work hard and hope for the best" to "I can assure this paper is good" is new to many. This takes time and must be practiced.

One way of provoking the change is through a series of short preparatory papers. These papers, or at least the first ones, must be personally and thoroughly discussed. During these discussions all craft errors are pointed out against the checklist. After this craft check, style issues might appear. Students learn that they must pay special attention to craft and that they can verify their paper is correct before handing it in. These two aspects are most important to this teaching approach.

Students report that these papers are the hardest to write, and the ones that take most time. As the course progresses writing becomes easier and faster. Interestingly, this ease and speed is accompanied by a quality increase.

4.2 Exposing for style

Craft is not all: style adds personality to a paper and is an important part of making it enjoyable. To help students develop good designing taste and principles in computer architecture, Blaauw and Brooks [3] resorted to a "computer architecture zoo" of excellent exemplars. For writing that becomes a set of excellent literature.

A way to expose the students to style is to have them read every week a short fragment of an excellent document. Some are famous CS papers (Dijkstra, Knuth, Hamming, Hoare are all superb writers), other are short excerpts from literature, theater, or even poetry. Just reading is too passive, so to help them cultivate their style they must select a 100 word fragment that they consider particularly interesting, copy it verbatim, and write a short commentary explaining why they have selected that particular piece. In this way they are exposed to excellent writing, they must "take it in" through the copying, and reflect on it through their comments.

Style is also discussed with students when giving them feedback on their work. Although, as explained above, feedback focuses on the crafts, it is a good moment to talk about style. Awkward pieces are pointed out, alternatives are discussed, but always having in mind that style should not be taught: it is personal and must evolve.

4.3 Grading

Grading intensifies writing anxiety [6], so much so that some authors advocate stepping outside of grading [9, Ch. 19]. Grading only the crafts, with its objective checklist, is a less radical approach that helps reduce anxiety and frustration both for students and professors. Using crafts, grading is faster, easier, and aids learning.

In the case of a term paper, the students have the checklist (Figure 1) before writing it. For a paper to be good it must pass *all* the checks of the list, so a passing grade is only awarded to papers with at most a few minor violations. Students know —or should know— beforehand if they have passed or not, and even have a good estimate of their final grade. This is very helpful in reducing the anxiety in the most productive way: producing better papers and *knowing* they are good.

Grading the papers is a very simple task: all that has to be done is to read them with the checklist in mind, and mark any violations. Major violations are quick and easy to spot and should mean a non-passing grade. If there are no major violations and only a few minor ones they should get a low passing grade. If there are no violations the score should be moderate to high, depending mainly on whether the paper complies with other issues that were discussed in class but are not on the list. An informal, but thorough study, shows that the writing crafts provide a fair grading in the sense that no good paper gets low scores and no bad paper receives good scores.

5. RESULTS

Let us analyze the benefits of the engineering approach in three aspects: writing quality, ease of teaching, and students' attitude towards writing.

A complete assessment of the engineering approach is difficult as it was developed very gradually over many years. To compare the benefits in these three aspects we must compare data from what happened ten or more years ago to current data. This has been possible for the quality of the writing as I do keep many students' documents from back then. It is much more difficult for the other two aspects as I do not keep old students' comments and I did not even write down my comments. For these two cases I will rely on specific happenings that, although incomplete, do shed some light.

The quality of the best papers for both approaches is very similar. The average quality has improved slightly. The main improvement is that the horrible, awful papers written by the students for whom clear writing seemed an impossible task have disappeared. This suggests that most students, those that have a knack for writing or that easily conceive an intuition for writing, will learn almost equally with both approaches. But students that simply cannot understand what clarity and style are or mean will benefit greatly with the engineering approach.

Teaching has become easier. The worst memories when teaching with the intuition approach are those of students, normally while requesting feedback, asking about concepts such as clarity or rhythm and not being able to understand them. Explanations, examples, analogies... nothing worked. No matter how much we all tried the students could not understand what was wrong. It was utter frustration for all. These moments are gone. Being able to explain writing through concepts everybody understands, to give useful feedback, to grade in a manner the students recognize is objective, makes me more confident and sure-footed. Revising, giving feedback and grading take much less time. This is clearly personal, but I am sure that many engineering professors would feel the same way.

For the reasons stated, I cannot say much about how students' attitudes towards writing have changed, but the useless, frustrating conversations have disappeared. For some students this has to be a huge difference. Knowing what to check and being able to assess their own writing is an empowering situation for all students. This seems supported by the fact that the checklist is liked and considered helpful.

Summarizing, the engineering approach produces results at least as good as the standard one, and for some students, much better. Teaching tasks, specially giving feedback and grading, has become simpler and take less time. Students probably feel more empowered and less reluctant towards writing.

Finally, there is a phenomenon that I would like to comment on. Since I began introducing writing in my teaching I have often received comments from grateful students in which they stated that learning to write had been very useful to them. Up until a few years ago they were always general comments: "I've had to write a lot. Taking your course was very useful." Now I receive one or two accounts a year of specific instances in which writing has been useful to former students, be it in other courses or in their jobs. These accounts all focus on how they applied the crafts to solve specific writing problems. It seems that with the engineering approach writing is more than something "generally good;" it is specific knowledge that can be applied when needed. This is significant because one usual complaint on generic writing courses is that the knowledge the students acquire does not transfer easily to other settings [16]. It seems that crafts transfer to other writing much better than intuition.

6. CONCLUSIONS

The engineering approach, with its writing crafts, is a method to teach writing that is closer and more palatable to the engineering community. Students, specially those for which which the world of writing is alien, understand communication better, sense that they can control the quality of what they write, and become capable of writing adequate papers. Professors can explain, give feedback and grade in a simpler manner and using less time. The mindset of writing with this approach is closer to other engineering activities, and should make it easier to integrate writing into other engineering disciplines. Also, professors should feel less reluctant to introduce writing activities in their teaching.

Comparing teaching approaches and attitudes of students and professors is notably difficult. Although we all know what "good writing" is, comparing writing results is problematic. Is the engineering approach a demonstrably better method for teaching writing? Is it useful outside of science and engineering? Answering this would require a multi-year, multi-college effort. If you are interested, let me know.

7. REFERENCES

[1] C. Bauer, K. Figl, M. Derntl, P. P. Beran, and S. Kabicher. The student view on online peer reviews. In *ITiCSE '09: 14th ACM conference on Innovation and Technology in Computer Science Education*, pages 26–30, Paris, France, 2009.

[2] A. Begel and B. Simon. Struggles of new college graduates in their first software development job. In *SIGCSE '08: 39th ACM technical symposium on Computer Science Education*, pages 180–184, Portland, Oregon, USA, 2008.

[3] G. A. Blaauw and F. Brooks, Jr. *Computer Architecture: Concepts and Evolution.* Addison-Wesley, 1997.

[4] L. Blume, R. Baecker, C. Collins, and A. Donohue. A "communication skills for computer scientists" course. In *ITiCSE '09: 14th ACM conference on Innovation and Technology in Computer Science Education*, pages 65–69, Paris, France, 2009.

[5] W. C. Booth, G. G. Colomb, and J. M. Williams. *The Craft of Research.* The University of Chicago Press, 3rd edition, 2008.

[6] S. J. Cunningham and G. Holmes. Writing anxiety in computer science students. Technical Report Working Paper 95/25, Department of Computer Science. university of Waikato, August 1995. Available at http://www.cs.waikato.ac.nz/pubs/wp/1995/uow-cs-wp-1995-25.pdf.

[7] M. Cutts. *Oxford Guide to Plain English.* Oxford University Press, 2nd edition, 2004.

[8] E. Dept. of Education and W. R. of Australia. Employability skills for the future. http://www.skillsinfo.gov.au/skills/SkillsIssues/EmployabilitySkills/. Last access, January 12, 2010.

[9] P. Elbow. *Everyone Can Write.* Oxford University Press, 2000.

[10] R. M. Felder. Sermons for grumpy campers. *Chemical Engineering Education*, 41(3):183 – 184, 2007.

[11] A. Gunawardena, A. Tan, and D. Kaufer. Encouraging reading and collaboration using classroom salon. In *ITiCSE '10: 15th ACM conference on Innovation and Technology in Computer Science Education*, pages 254–258, Bilkent, Ankara, Turkey, 2010.

[12] J. Mertz and S. McElfresh. Teaching communication, leadership, and the social context of computing via a consulting course. In *SIGCSE '10: 41st ACM technical symposium on Computer Science Education*, pages 77–81, Milwaukee, Wisconsin, USA, 2010.

[13] K. Sand-Jensen. How to write consistently boring scientific literature. *Oikos*, 116:723 – 727, 2007.

[14] M. D. Svinicki and W. J. McKeachie. *McKeachie's Teaching Tips: Strategies, Research, and Theory for College and University Teachers.* Wadsworth Publishing, international edition, 2010.

[15] J. M. Williams. *Style: Toward Clarity and Grace.* University Of Chicago Press, 1995.

[16] A. Young. *Teaching Writing Across the Curriculum.* Prentice Hall, 3rd edition, 1997. Available at http://wac.colostate.edu/books/young_teaching/young_teaching.pdf.

Teaching Computer Science Majors about Teaching Computer Science

Tim Bell
Department of Computer Science and Software Engineering
University of Canterbury
New Zealand
+64 3 363-2987
tim.bell@canterbury.ac.nz

Lynn Lambert
Physics, Computer Science and Engineering
Christopher Newport University
Newport News, VA
+1 757 594-7826
llambert@cnu.edu

ABSTRACT
This paper describes the design, implementation, and evaluation of a course teaching Computer Science majors about teaching Computer Science. The course was designed to address the need for teachers and resources to support rapid changes in topics being taught in high schools. It also helped prepare students for research in Computer Science Education, and for careers involving computing and education. The course is described in detail, and is evaluated based on student feedback and the outcomes from the course.

Categories and Subject Descriptors
K.3.2 [**Computer and Information Science Education**]: Computer Science Education

General Terms
Design, Economics.

Keywords
Computer Science Education, K-12.

1. INTRODUCTION
A number of countries currently have initiatives to improve K-12 Computer Science education. For such initiatives to be successful, there needs to be a good supply of people able to teach Computer Science in K-12 schools. At the same time, we need to develop resources suitable for use in the K-12 environment, since the new curricula being developed don't have a canon of textbooks and teaching resources that more traditional subjects have to build on.

This paper reports on a course for CS major students that addresses both the issue of preparing teachers and the challenge of developing new resources. The course covers CS education at all levels, but focused particularly on high school as this is the area with the greatest change in New Zealand at present.

Table 1 shows four sources of new K-12 CS teachers based on their existing background. Each of the groups have relative advantages in terms of availability and preparedness, and all four groups should be considered for growing the teacher population. Teachers in New Zealand come through all four of these paths, although relatively few of the current computing teachers have a formal CS background. This paper discusses the design, implementation, and evaluation of a course that focuses on a group of students in the top right quadrant: existing senior CS students.

Table 1: Sources of potential K-12 Computer Science teachers

	Qualified to teach	**Not qualified to teach**
Has CS background	Ready to teach CS courses	Need to learn about teaching
No CS background	Need professional development in CS	Need both teaching and CS

We developed and taught a course on Computer Science education for honors students in their fourth year of a Computer Science major. The class does not qualify them to teach, but it gives them a taste of teaching and enables them to explore issues in Computer Science education, including the very education they are receiving at the time!

There are several reasons for a student to take such a class, even if they are not preparing to be a teacher:

- it helps them to understand their own education by understanding the pedagogical theory and CS-related issues that their own professors must deal with,
- they are able to create educational resources that can be used by qualified teachers,
- during a career in industry they may be involved in outreach and mentoring to schools or provide policy input to educational organizations, and it provides a good base for this,
- it may be a stepping stone for some to become teachers or professors, and
- it provides a foundation if they are interested in becoming CS Education researchers.

SIGCSE'11, March 9–12, 2011, Dallas, Texas, USA.

The course outline explained the course to students as follows:

> *"Computer Science Education has received a lot of attention recently, as governments seek to boost the competitiveness of their country in the face of falling rolls in universities. A lot of innovation and research over the last few years has changed the kind of resources that are available, and there are a rich range of materials available (e.g. alice.org, cs4fn.org, csta.acm.org). There has also been a lot of debate about related issues such as which programming languages are best for beginners, and how best to get more women involved in CS.*
>
> *In New Zealand, the computing topics taught in schools have been revised in 2009, with the major changes appearing in NCEA [the national qualification taken by most students in their final three years of high school] from 2011. This has raised many new research questions about which topics can and should be taught at high school, and the best way to deliver them.*
>
> *In this course we will look at the many issues surrounding CS education. There will be a major project where students will develop new educational materials and/or evaluate them. As much as possible, the project will be done in conjunction with students from a computing class at the College of Education, who will be able to provide a stronger educational background to complement the CS background of our own students.*
>
> *The course is aimed at people who may be interested in being CS educators (teachers or lecturers), as well as participating in outreach programs (such as industry-sponsored events and school visits), and those who may be involved in educational research and policy. It will assume that you have a broad 3-year background in Computer Science, but no previous background in education is required."*

A course focused on CS education, rather than education in general, is able to tackle the many topics specific to CS education, such as the surges and declines in student interest, gender imbalance, and the choice of a first programming language. We found that there was no shortage of topics to include in the course!

The remainder of this paper gives more detail about the goals of the course (section 2), its structure and assessment (section 3), and a required student project to develop educational resources (section 4). We evaluate the course in section 5, and draw some conclusions in section 6.

2. GOALS OF THE COURSE

The stated goal of the course was to produce students who are well-informed about the wide-ranging issues surrounding Computer Science education, are able to provide balanced and sound advice to existing computing teachers who have a weak background in Computer Science, and are able to develop and use effective resources themselves.

Because a key motivation for this course was to address the issues raised by new topics being introduced into senior high school computing classes in New Zealand [3], the course had a focus on these issues and students were encouraged to develop resources and engage with teachers from this sector. The new topics for high schools, to be introduced in NZ in 2011, contain an optional component called "Programming and Computer Science" that gives senior students an introduction to programming as well as an overview of the breadth of topics in Computer Science. The goal of these topics is to spark interest in the field in the face of low student enrolments in Computer Science. For new courses like this to be successful, NZ teachers will need more resources and professional development (PD) in Computer Science to deliver the new material.

The United States has similar concerns with its high school curriculum. Many would like to modify how Computer Science is taught in high schools, to increase interest in Computer Science, to improve diversity, and to give a more accurate picture of Computer Science. There has been recent focus on the Advanced Placement Computer Science course. The AP CS exam, one measure of high school Computer Science enrolment, has seen a 2% decline in the number of students taking the test from 2000 to 2010, while the number of total number of students taking AP exams has risen by 61% [2]. CRA enrolment tracking in colleges and universities [4] reflects similar trends. An important component of addressing the high school pipeline is to change how colleges train Computer Science teachers, and to improve the resources that Computer Science teachers have. Some are attempting to create a new AP course more focused on Computer Science concepts and less on programming. One goal of this new course would be to increase participation in Computer Science, especially among women. In order to do that, the US will need to recruit more teachers [6]. Computing Education for Computer Science majors would help provide both new teachers and resources for these new courses.

There have been some successes revising high school curricula and preparing teachers to teach Computer Science in the high schools [7, 8]. These have made a point of providing teachers with (a) good professional development and (b) resources for them to use. Teaching a course about teaching Computer Science to CS majors is a less direct approach, but is more easily implemented by CS departments. It may produce a few teachers who are well-prepared to teach Computer Science and may create some new Computer Science education researchers, but importantly, it will also contribute to educational resources, will help students understand their own education, and will provide education-aware professionals who can interact with students and teachers effectively. This means that those who end up working in commercial companies or some other career outside of K-12 education are better prepared to engage in school outreach and support, ultimately improving the relationship between industry and schools.

3. COURSE STRUCTURE AND ASSESSMENT

The course was run over one semester (15 weeks including a three-week break from lectures) in the Computer Science and Software Engineering department at the University of Canterbury. The topics covered were based around the following formal outline, although we also explored topics of interest to students as discussions arose in class.

- Curricula (school and university, New Zealand and international, CSTA/ACM guidelines, ISTE NETS, AP exams)
- Pedagogy (learning models e.g. student centered, instructional design, high-order thinking, Bloom's taxonomy, learning styles; socio-cultural theory e.g. Vygotsky, constructivist approach, Piaget; teaching and learning tools e.g. Learning Management Systems, distance learning, e-learning)
- K-12 Computer Science education and outreach (curricula, programming languages, robotics, kinesthetics, camps, clubs and events)

- Choosing a first programming language (issues such as OO-first, Initial Learning Environments)
- Programming environments for children/learners (Scratch, Alice, Greenfoot)
- Visualization and algorithm animation
- Gender, diversity, disability, and equity issues
- Educational games for CS
- Robotics for K-12

The course was taught by two instructors and several guest lecturers. Three of the guests were from our College of Education, but we also had one school teacher and two CS Education research students speak to the class. Student assessment consisted of a final exam (worth 40% of the final grade) that covered the content of these lectures, and a substantial project (60%), to create a resource for high school Computer Science teachers.

The course enrolled 10 Computer Science majors who had essentially no background studying education, but who were strong in Computer Science (they already had a 3-year Bachelor's degree, and this was a postgraduate class). This was a typical class size at this level. Some of the students had a passion for education and improving the state of K-12 education in NZ, motivated by the lack of CS courses available when they went through high school — generally high school courses in NZ have been focused on user skills, and students in our class were enthusiastic about the discipline of computing, not simply using computers as a tool. Although such students have been part of an educational system for many years, this does not mean that they understand pedagogy, and depending on exactly where they were taught, their model for pedagogy might be based on weak examples that they instinctively emulate, so there was also some "un-learning" to be done.

The class met for two hours of lectures each week, for about 10 weeks of the semester. A lot of the course revolved around the major project, which is described in the next section. Early in the course we had a small online quiz reviewing the lecture topic each week, and students volunteered to write questions. Writing questions for such a quiz is a great exercise for students, and their peers could give them feedback on the quality of the quiz questions. However, their motivation to develop quizzes petered out, apparently as the project became more important later in the course.

Some of the lecture topics were easy for the students to pick up (e.g. introductory programming languages), while other topics were unfamiliar. Few of the students were aware of the various curricula despite their own courses being set in the ACM/IEEE curriculum frameworks. The material on pedagogy was also largely unfamiliar, and ideas like higher-order thinking and constructivist teaching helped them to understand some of the techniques used in their own education. Where possible, examples were given to relate these ideas to Computer Science (for example, examples of exercises from various levels of Bloom's taxonomy).

4. STUDENT PROJECTS

A central part of the course was that students were required to work on a major project to develop an educational resource. This had the dual benefit of having them apply the pedagogical ideas they had learnt, and also generated new resources for CS education. We encouraged students to focus on high school level material, since there was an immediate need for new resources in this area. The "resources" could be anything that could be deployed by an educator, for example:

- lesson plans (including guidance for teachers and sample assessment)
- programming exercises that use CS concepts (such as Scratch, Alice and Greenfoot activities that involve more than animation and games)
- an interactive website, game or visualization
- a set of classroom posters
- creative work such as videos or cartoons that convey CS concepts
- kinesthetic activities or role plays that teach concepts
- material for teaching teachers
- multimedia presentations on topics using systems such as Flash or PowerPoint, with detailed notes that teachers can use in class for introducing topics

The students were given specific examples of a range of existing quality resources to illustrate the variety of approaches that could be taken.

The requirements for the project were reasonably flexible, although each student was expected to have the following structure in their report:

- A choice of a topic from CS that they would create the resource for;
- An evaluation of existing approaches (if any) for teaching that topic (and their strengths and weaknesses for high school teaching);
- An explanation of the target audience and the design choices for the resource (in terms of pedagogical theory), including choices that were considered and rejected;
- An evaluation of the resource – they needed to provide evidence that it works, or at least give ideas on how to improve it based on experience with it. The resource could be evaluated by trying it on students (and since it probably contains feedback/assessment material, that could be used to evaluate what they learned.) The resource could also be evaluated by showing it to teachers or other experts, and asking them questions about how they could use it. On-line resources could have automated feedback, such as comments on YouTube, the number of hits, time spent on each page, or tracking the parts of the resource that people used.

We suggested a list of topics from the new NZ school curriculum for which there was a lack of resources and so would particularly benefit from resources being created, and about a half of the projects produced material that was related to these ideas. The other half were more focused on a student's interest or perception of what they would have liked more help with when they studied the topic.

Students were encouraged to look through CS education research papers from organizations such as SIGCSE and ITiCSE for relevant background material, and as models of what CS Education researchers do. They were expected to look for existing material that taught their topic from places like text books, on-line

CS activity collections, videos (e.g. on YouTube), online games, Wikipedia entries, online tutorials, and papers and ideas from SIGCSE and ITiCSE. They had to critically review these existing resources for their topic and explain why their one was likely to be an improvement.

The students regularly shared their projects with each other through small class presentations and discussions, and posting material online. This enabled them to exercise the critical view of educational material that we wanted them to develop, and help them get constructive feedback for their projects from their peers and lecturers. Towards the end of the course we arranged a meeting at a local school where students could present their projects to teachers, who provided the feedback that was required for their projects. Four of the 10 students took this opportunity; others received feedback from online communities, or friends who were teachers.

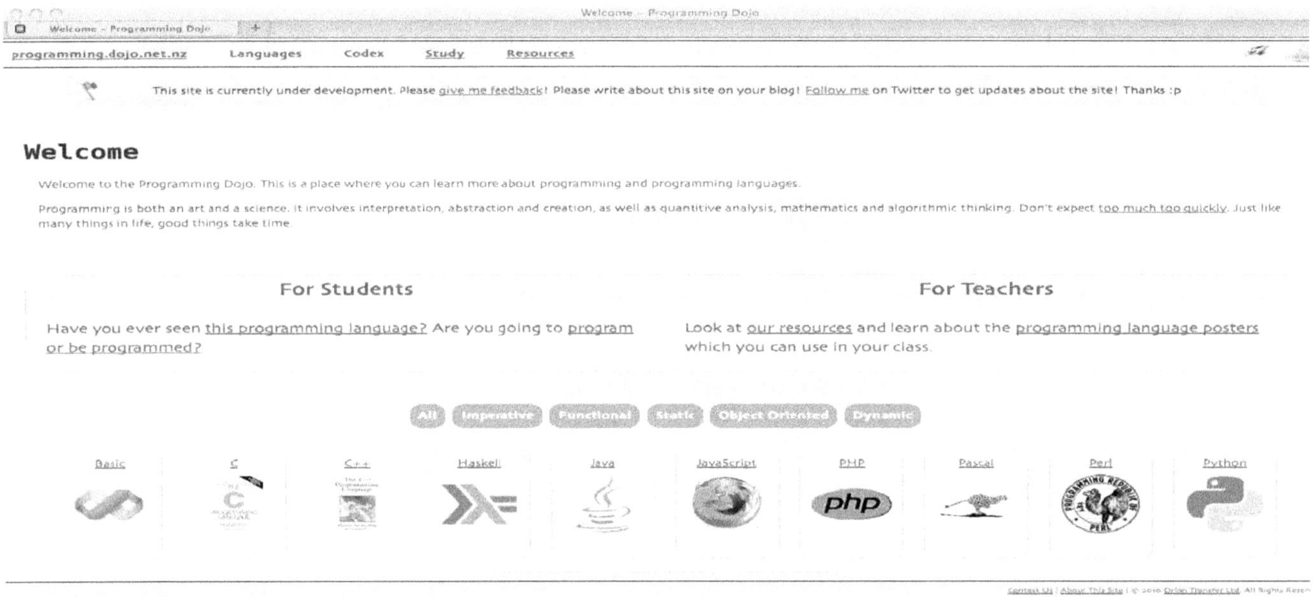

Figure 1: Screenshot from http://programming.dojo.net.nz/

Here is a sample of the projects that the students chose:

- "Programming Dojo" (http://programming.dojo.net.nz/). This web site, created by one of the students (and later blogged by CSTA [5]), contains an extensive overview of programming languages from an educational point of view (some of the home page is shown in Figure 1; not visible in the screenshot are links for Ruby, Scheme and Smalltalk). The site has taken on a life of its own beyond the course; for example C# and Scratch are being added due to interest from teachers. The site also reviews the strengths of different languages for teaching programming by answering 16 questions about each one, such as "Is there a compiler/interpreter available at no cost?", "Are people in education already familiar with the language and environment?", and "Are there good learning resources available for use in education?" It also contains downloadable posters showing the same problem being programmed in many different languages. This website has received considerable attention from teachers. For the evaluation the student posted the site to various programming language forums, and received a very strong response as people defended the appropriateness of their preferred language for teaching programming, and provided answers for the questions used to evaluate the languages! The site itself had over 6000 hits in the first two weeks, and the posters were downloaded hundreds of times. Needless to say, this was considered a very successful project, and exceeded expectations.
- The Traveling Salesman problem with Google maps. This online system was aimed at illustrating tractability, which is a proposed topic for Year 12 students (second to last year of high school in NZ). It had information about the TSP and its associated computational issues, and then showed various TSP problems being solved on a page where students could interact with a Google map; the impossibility of trying all possible routes for large numbers of cities becomes very obvious as students have to wait for exponentially increasing amounts of time to get a result. The resource included notes for teachers.
- Posters promoting Computer Science. This student researched and designed four posters. Three of them featured Turing, Hopper and Dijkstra respectively, and showed a mixture of both humorous and thought-provoking quotes from those people, as well as giving a short but intriguing biography. The fourth poster illustrates how ray tracing works.
- Formal languages. This project was essentially an outline of a lesson plan that enabled teachers who know little about regular expressions or grammars to teach some simple concepts based on games and puzzles. It drew on several existing published resources, and added some new material. The plan was aimed at addressing a new assessment standard in the New Zealand system where students were required to appreciate the nature of formal languages.
- "Java arrays for kids". This resource was aimed at younger students (despite the title, the resource is reasonably

language-independent). It provides some off-line kinesthetic activity ideas based on placing items in small plastic containers, and an on-line game that culminated in trying to sort an "array" of numbers where the only operation possible is to move numbers between two chosen locations in the array.

5. RESULTS

The students were surveyed at the end of the course. Exact statistics for the responses cannot be published to protect the privacy of the students, but we note the following trends in the responses.

Students felt strongly that they had a broad view of Computer Science education around the world after taking the course, and that it helped them think about Computer Science in new ways. They were also positive about having a better understanding of Computer Science after taking this course. Participation in the course made some stronger advocates for Computer Science, especially how it is taught in secondary schools. Some became more interested in teaching high school and/or university Computer Science after taking the course.

Positive comments included "The paper is great. It is creative and useful." Negative comments included "too much stuff to read," "would have been great to work with education students" (the planned collaboration with an education class fell through due to unavailability of the education students, although two education students ended up becoming involved after our course had completed), and several comments about wanting more time and guidance on their projects.

Some of the difficulties the students encountered were a result of the inevitable differences in culture between Education and Computer Science. The Education lecturers did provide a lot of reading material which CS majors aren't so used to dealing with. This could be improved by focusing the material on directly relevant material, as the key material covered only made up a small part of the reading that was handed out.

In general, the two primary lecturers were satisfied with the course, the projects, and the students. The project was loosely structured, which allowed creativity, but also made it difficult for students to narrow their focus, and it required them to shift gear from the large programming projects typically required in senior courses, to complete a working project that relied on external input in only one semester.

The instructors felt that there were several factors that influenced the success of the students. Students from other cultures who were used to different pedagogical styles, and those whose own education included a great deal of rote learning and "sage on the stage" style teaching had a difficult time developing interactive projects that would require higher-order thinking rather than rote memorization.

The multiple guest lecturers from around the university and local schools meant that students heard from experts in multiple areas, including education. That would not have been possible if taught solely by Computer Science professors. It did mean that there was less control in terms of content, delivery and interest to the students, and some of the reading on educational theory was a different style than the students were used to. Having guest professors had the benefit of providing another point of dialog between educationalists and Computer Scientists, and we reciprocated with our College of Education by giving guest lectures in some education classes. Such interdisciplinary relationships can take a lot of effort to develop, and having a common interest in this class gave a concrete goal to work on together.

One of the challenges that came up was that students with web-based projects needed to place it in a publicly visible on-line location so that they could get feedback on it. It was difficult to find a host site that would be suitable if the material became very successful, but not too embarrassing if the material wasn't so good (and since it was initially posted for early evaluation, it needed to be clear that it wasn't a university-endorsed final product). Some of the resources needed PHP and related backend support for their web pages, so it wasn't just a matter of finding somewhere to put static pages. In the end, a variety of sites were used depending on the type of resource and intended audience, but this had the unfortunately consequence that most of the projects are no longer easily accessed online.

The requirement for our students to evaluate their resources was valuable, but for them to get direct feedback from school students would require ethics approval, which typically takes several weeks to obtain. Because the ethics application requires the "experiment" to be fully designed, this made it effectively impossible for students to undertake such evaluations in the timeframe of the course, and thus the feedback had to be based on the opinion of professionals (teachers) and people making public posts on-line. A longer timeframe for the assessment would be required if school students were to be used in the evaluation.

6. CONCLUSION

Teaching a course on CS education to advanced CS students has a number of benefits as well as challenges. The benefits included having students who could work with depth and breadth in CS topics, and produce new resources that can be used for younger students. The students were more informed about pedagogy, and especially issues surrounding CS education.

The main difficulties revolved around students being used to more technical courses, and also not having a strong background in education — possibly not even having had a good experience in their own education.

Next time we would try to find a way to link this group directly with a class of education students, and ideally run joint projects to combine their respective CS and education expertise.

A course teaching Computer Science students about teaching may not develop a large number of Computer Science teachers, but it will enrich the students' undergraduate experience, provide resources to existing teachers, and enlighten soon-to-be professionals about computing education. It also encourages engagement between Computer Science and Education departments, providing a base for other initiatives.

7. REFERENCES

[1] Computing Curricula 2001 Computer Science, Association for Computing Machinery, http://www.acm.org/education/education/education/curric_vols/cc2001.pdf. Accessed September 8, 2010.

[2] College Board, " AP Examination Volume Changes (2000-2010)", February, 2010. Accessed at http://professionals.collegeboard.com/profdownload/Exam-Volume-Change-2010.pdf , December 4, 2010.

[3] Tim Bell, Peter Andreae and Lynn Lambert. "Computer Science in New Zealand High Schools," Proceedings of ACE-2010 (Australasian Computing Education Conference).

[4] Peter Harsha, "Computer Science Majors Increase at Most Significant Rate Since Dot Com Boom", Computer Research Policy Blog, March 16, 2009, http://www.cra.org/govaffairs/blog/2009/03/computer science-majors-increase-at-most-significant-rate-since-dot-com-boom. Accessed September 1, 2010.

[5] "Programming Dojo", by Samuel Williams, May 22, 2010http://blog.acm.org/archives/csta/2010/05/programming_doj.html. Accessed September 1, 2010.

[6] Jan Cuny & Chris Stephenson. "What's Going On With AP CS: The CS 10,000 Teachers Project", at The Computer Science and Information Technology Symposium, http://www.csta.acm.org/ProfessionalDevelopment/sub/CSIT10Presentations/Stephenson_Cuny.pdf, July 13, 2010. Accessed September 6, 2010.

[7] "A Model for Improving Secondary CS Education," *Proceedings of SIGCSE-2005*, St. Louis, pages 332-336.

[8] *Stuck in the Shallow End,* MIT Press, April 30, 2010.

Implementing a Computer Science Endorsement Program for Secondary School Teachers

Christopher Whitehead, Lydia Ray, Shamim Khan, Wayne Summers, Rodrigo Obando
Columbus State University
{Whitehead_christopher, ray_lydia, khan_shamim, summers_wayne, obando_rodrigo}@colstate.edu

ABSTRACT

Computer Science and technology have been driving scientific innovations, expanding the Information Technology sector and increasing productivity in all economic sectors for the last few decades, thus contributing significantly to the economic output of the U.S. Each sector of this country, ranging from national security to everyday life, is enormously impacted by computing technology. Clearly, future economic growth and prosperity of this country heavily rely on the strength and skills of the IT and computing workforce that will be able to expand and maintain the nationwide IT infrastructure. Unfortunately, the decline in students interested in Computer Science over the last several decades may threaten the United States' capability to expand and maintain the nationwide IT infrastructure. One solution that may slow and possibly even reverse this decline is to increase the awareness of Computer Science in the secondary school system and to increase the knowledge of Computer Science, the ability to teach Computer Science, and the Computer Science professionalism of teachers in that system. In this paper, the authors describe one technique for realizing this solution—implementing a Computer Science endorsement program for secondary school teachers.

Categories and Subject Descriptors: K.3.2 [Computers and Education]: Computer Science and Education - Computer Science Education

General Terms: Human Factors.

Keywords: Computer science endorsement, teacher certification, Computer Science education, secondary level.

1. INTRODUCTION

Computer Science and technology have been driving scientific innovations, expanding the Information Technology sector and increasing productivity in all economic sectors for the last few decades, thus contributing significantly to the economic output of the U.S. Each sector of this country, ranging from national security to everyday life, is enormously impacted by computing technology. Clearly, future economic growth and prosperity of this country rely heavily on the strength and skills of the IT and computing workforce that will be able to expand and maintain the nationwide IT infrastructure. The Bureau of Labor Statistics predicts that from 2008 through 2018 more than 1,500,000 high salary computing jobs will be created in the U.S., thereby making computing technology one of the fastest growing occupational fields [1]. However, to date, there is a huge discrepancy between the demand for workers in Computer Science fields and the supply of qualified candidates produced by the educational system. Educators and Computer Science professionals believe that students in high school lack the opportunity to become well prepared to pursue an expertise in this area at the college level, thus contributing to the shortage of workforce. Bill Gates, Chairman of Microsoft Corporation, stated that "Computer Science employment is growing by nearly 100,000 jobs annually. But, at the same time studies show that there is a dramatic decline in the number of students graduating with Computer Science degrees"[5].

As a solution to the problem, the CISE (Computer & Information Science & Engineering) Directorate of the National Science Foundation (NSF) has proposed the CS/10K Project to revitalize high school computing education [2, 3]. The goal of the CS/10K Project is to develop an effective high school curriculum that will be taught by 10,000 well-prepared teachers in 10,000 high schools by 2015. The biggest challenge of the CS/10K Project is to produce these 10,000 well-trained effective CS teachers since few of the current high school teachers have a formal CS background. The NSF envisions launching and supporting high quality teacher preparation programs which will train and certify both in-service and pre-service teachers in various fields of Computer Science.

According to a study conducted by the CSTA (Computer Science Teachers Association) there are about 20 states in the U.S. that neither require nor grant teacher's certification for teaching Computer Science [4]. It is evident that there is an urgent need for developing teacher preparation standards for Computer Science. This necessity motivated a regional university in Georgia to develop the first teacher's endorsement program in Computer Science with support from a National Science Foundation Broadening Participation in Computing (BPC) grant. This program, first offered in Fall 2010, is designed to prepare highly skilled CS teachers for secondary schools in the U.S. This paper describes the process followed in implementing this endorsement program. The paper is organized as follows – section 2 describes the background and motivation for this project, section 3 presents details of the implementation process, and section 4 concludes the paper.

2. BACKGROUND AND MOTIVATION

A 1997 report from the Information Technology Association of America found that 190,000 jobs in the IT industry remained

SIGCSE'11, March 9–12, 2011, Dallas, Texas, USA.

unfilled because of a shortage of qualified workers [6]. After interviewing 441 CEOs of the fastest growing U.S. companies, Coopers & Lybrand reported that 66 percent viewed the shortage of qualified workers to be their greatest concern [7]. Other studies—including a detailed analysis issued by the Computing Research Association (CRA) [8] and two reports from the Office of Technology policy in the U.S. Department of Commerce [9, 10]—provide additional evidence to support the existence of an IT worker shortage.

The main contributing factor to this IT workforce shortage is the fact that the U.S. education system fails to attract and retain adequate number of Computer Science students at the college level. While Computer Science is an established discipline of study at undergraduate and graduate college levels, rates of enrollment and graduation are gradually diminishing in this area, much to the concern of educators and Computer Science professionals [3]. HERI data shows that the percentage of incoming freshmen intending to major in CS has decreased by more than 70% since year 2000. The decrease for women is close to 80%. In 2008, intended majors in CS dropped to a 25 year low [2]. Investigations by CS educators reveal that high school students lack the opportunity to become well prepared to pursue studies in this area at the college level [3]. High schools in the U.S. often fail to teach rigorous, academic computing. IT courses are offered in many schools only as Career and Technical Education, and are limited to very basic IT literacy. While Advanced Placement (AP) CS courses do prepare high school students for college-level CS education, these courses are taught in less than10% of U.S. high schools. Even in those schools, AP CS is programming-oriented and does not focus on fundamental concepts of computing. Also, being extremely programming-oriented, AP CS is taken by very few students [4]. As a consequence, only 15,537 students took the AP CS test in 2008, compared to 222,835 students who took Calculus AB, or 108,284 who took Statistics [4]. Clearly, a reform in high school Computer Science curriculum is absolutely necessary. To address this problem, the National Science Foundation has proposed the CS/10K Project, which aims at developing "an effective new high school curriculum for Computing, taught in 10,000 high schools by 10,000 well-qualified teachers by 2015." [2]

The immediate motivation for the work described in this paper came from the study conducted by the Computer Science Teachers Association (CSTA) to gather information on the current state certification requirements for K-12 teachers of Computer Science, and compare it across states [4]. According to this study, Georgia is one of the 20 states in the U.S. that do not grant a Computer Science endorsement for teachers. The state of Georgia is also among 20 states that do not require a CS endorsement at any level of teaching [4].

3. PROCESS OF IMPLEMENTING THE COMPUTER SCIENCE TEACHERS ENDORSEMENT PROGRAM

Implementation of the Computer Science endorsement program was guided by the requirements for teacher endorsements established by the Georgia Professional Standards Commission (PSC). The following steps were undertaken in order to meet the standards set forth by the PSC:

- Ensuring the programs aligned with the teacher preparation unit's Conceptual Framework
- Developing of the curriculum, including the specific courses within that curriculum
- Developing programs of study that detailed the recommended sequence of courses
- Developing transition points that could be used to assess student progress in the program
- Developing and/or identifying opportunities for student field experiences and clinical practice
- Developing and/or identifying assessments that would be used to measure student progress and provide evidence of meeting the PSC standards
- Soliciting professionals to serve on the advisory board
- Gathering faculty background information including vitas
- Participating in the program review

3.1 Conceptual Framework

Initial preparation for the program review required that the endorsement program be aligned with the teacher preparation unit's Conceptual Framework, which focuses on excellence in teaching, scholarship and professionalism. These three qualities encompass the highest standards represented in the ten principles outlined by the Interstate New Teacher Assessment and Support Consortium (INTASC) and the five core assumptions of accomplished teaching of the National Board of Professional Teaching Standards (NBPTS). As such, development of the program focused on the inclusion of best practices in the preparation of teachers as a means of improving student learning (teaching), on coursework that combines knowledge with practical applications (scholarship), and on providing prospective and in-service teachers with the opportunity to develop an in-depth knowledge in the area of Computer Science (professionalism).

3.2 Curriculum Development

Both the undergraduate and graduate programs were built around existing Computer Science courses, with additional courses added as needed to meet the PSC standards. The undergraduate program was designed for students already enrolled in the teacher education program, or who plan to enroll in the teacher education program. The graduate program, on the other hand, was designed for candidates who already have a bachelor's degree in a teacher education field, or a teaching certificate, or are currently enrolled in a Master of Art in Teaching program. Both programs were centered around effective pedagogical strategies such as the use of lecture/discussion, problem solving, reflective activities, Computer Science laboratory experiences, and field placements in Computer Science classrooms in grades 6-12. Through these experiences, it was felt that candidates would develop a deeper understanding of the content that they would be responsible for teaching in the Computer Science classroom setting. These strategies would also give candidates opportunities to broaden and enhance their repertoire of instructional strategies for addressing the needs of diverse learners as they participate in a community of learners beyond that of their own schools or preparation programs. The following details the specific curriculum implemented as part of each program.

Undergraduate

The initial framework for the undergraduate curriculum was based on five first and second year Computer Science courses and two upper division Computer Science courses currently offered:

- Introduction to Information Technology

- Computer Science 1 and Lab
- Computer Science 2
- Computer Organization
- Data Structures
- Programming Languages
- Computer Networks

In addition, two teacher preparation courses were developed to fill the gaps required for the curriculum to meet the PSC standards:

- Methods of Teaching Computer Science
- Practicum in Computer Science

This curriculum was designed to emphasize fundamental programming and Computer Science concepts including data structures, programming languages and networking while incorporating a course in how to teach Computer Science and a practicum that will allow students to demonstrate their teaching abilities.

Graduate

The endorsement curriculum for graduate students with little or no previous Computer Science academic experience was based on six courses--four existing Computer Science courses and two teacher preparation courses:

- Fundamental Principles of Computer Science
- Fundamentals of Computer Programming and Data Structures
- Programming Languages
- Computer Networks
- Methods of Teaching Computer Science
- Practicum in Computer Science

3.3 Programs of Study

The undergraduate program of study, as shown in Table 1, was developed based on a fall semester entry and a typical four-year undergraduate program, taking into account the typical scheduling of the courses, and the fact that the upper division courses are not offered every semester.

Table 1 Undergraduate Program of Study

	Fall	Spring	Summer
1st Year:	Introduction to Information Technology	Computer Science 1 Computer Science 1 Lab	
2nd Year:	Computer Science 2	Data Structures	
3rd Year:	Computer Organization Internet Programming	Programming Languages	Computer Networks
4th Year:	Methods of Teaching Computer Science Practicum in Computer Science		

The graduate program of study is a two year program for candidates without a Computer Science undergraduate degree. Candidates can be admitted into the program in either the fall or spring. The recommended course of study is shown in Table 2 for those students who enter the program in the fall, and in Table 3 for those students who enter the program in the spring. These programs of study are based in part on when the courses are typically offered. These programs of study could, of course, be modified if the student has already completed equivalent coursework.

Table 2 Graduate Program of Study, Fall Entry

	Fall	Spring	Summer
1st Year:	Fundamental Principles of Computer Science Fundamentals of Computer Programming and Data Structures	Programming Languages	Computer Networks
2nd Year:	Methods of Teaching Computer Science Practicum in Computer Science		

Table 3 Graduate Program of Study, Spring Entry

	Fall	Spring	Summer
1st Year:		Fundamental Principles of Computer Science Fundamentals of Computer Programming and Data Structures	Computer Networks
2nd Year:	Methods of Teaching Computer Science Practicum in Computer Science	Programming Languages	

3.1.1 Transition Points

Transition points serve as opportunities to assess student progress in the program and to recommend changes as necessary. The following describes the transition points that were developed for both the undergraduate and the graduate endorsement programs.

As part of the undergraduate program, the following four transition points were developed:

- Admission to Teacher Education Program
- Entry into Student Teaching
- Exit from Program
- Induction

These transition points will be administered as part of the teacher preparation program. Admission to the teacher education program and into student teaching will be based on satisfactory completion of certain undergraduate core courses, a minimum GPA of 2.5 and completion of a background check. The "Exit from Program" transition will include the following:

- Minimum 2.5 GPA calculated on all undergraduate coursework
- Grades of C or better in all courses related to major

- Satisfactory ratings on all components of the Model of Appropriate Practice (MAP) Evaluation (see section 3.5.3 for a description)
- Satisfactory ratings on all components of the Dispositions Evaluation
- Satisfactory completion of portfolio

The "Induction" transition point evaluates student progress one to two years after completing the program. This evaluation will survey students and obtain their evaluations of their preparation as teachers. At the same time, these students' employers will be surveyed and asked to evaluate the students as teachers.

As part of the graduate program, three transition points were developed:

- Program entry
- Program exit
- Induction

To enter the graduate program, the following requirements were established:

- possess an undergraduate degree from an accredited institution
- maintain a minimum GPA of 2.75 on all attempted coursework
- hold a clear, renewable teaching certificate or be admitted to a Master of Arts in Teaching (M.A.T.) degree program

The decision was made to allow candidates to be admitted provisionally provided they maintained a minimum GPA of 2.5. If admitted provisionally, candidates must complete nine hours of graduate coursework with grades of B or better in each course for admission status to be changed to regular.

To exit the program, the following criteria were established for graduate students:

- Minimum 3.0 GPA calculated on all graduate coursework required in endorsement program
- Grades of B or better in Fundamental Principles of Computer Science and Fundamentals of Computer Programming and Data Structures and grades of C or better in all other required coursework; no more than two (2) grades of "C" or below in graduate courses
- Satisfactory ratings on all components of the Field Experience Evaluation
- Satisfactory ratings on all components of the Dispositions Evaluation
- Satisfactory completion of portfolio

The "Induction" transition point for the graduate program is the same as that for the undergraduate program.

Once the transition points were identified, the field experiences, assessments and additional artifacts used in evaluating student progress at the transition points needed to be identified. These transition point evaluation tools and techniques are discussed in more detail below.

3.4 Field Experiences and Clinical Practice

Field experiences are a required part of the endorsement program in order to provide the teacher candidate with practical experience as a teacher teaching Computer Science. These experiences will also serve as opportunities to evaluate the candidate's teaching abilities and to recommend improvements where necessary. Both undergraduate and graduate students are required to complete 60 hours of field experiences as part of the program in order to ensure the quality of learning.

During the 60 hours of field experience, candidates are required to be engaged in a variety of teaching-related activities that include observing Computer Science classes in grades 6-8 or 9-12, assisting other Computer Science teachers in coordinating classroom activities, working with individual students or small groups, and planning and teaching lessons and units. Candidates will be required to keep a field experience log where they will record their observations and activities as well as their own reflections on different issues. They will have this log signed by the cooperating classroom teacher and include it in their professional portfolio. In addition, each candidate's teaching will be evaluated by the cooperating teacher and/or a university supervisor using a Field Experience Evaluation instrument. Cooperating teachers and supervisors will also evaluate candidates' dispositions using a Dispositions Evaluation instrument.

In addition to more formal field experiences in a middle or high school Computer Science classroom, student candidates will be allowed to satisfy the 60 hour requirement by participating in Computer Science summer camps and/or evening classes (for example, teaching basic programming languages such as Alice to middle or high school students).

In addition to the field experiences requirement, student candidates in the undergraduate endorsement program will be required to complete a 15-week student teaching experience in which they will be required to take over all classroom responsibilities for a period of at least four consecutive weeks.

3.5 Assessments and Evidence for Meeting Standards

To evaluate success in meeting the program requirements and teacher preparation standards and for providing evidence that candidates were meeting the program standards, five primary assessment tools were proposed:

- Content GPA (content knowledge)
- Professional Portfolio (Field Experiences and Clinical Practice)
- Field Experience Evaluation
- Dispositions Evaluation
- Graduate and Employer Surveys

3.5.1 Content GPA

Undergraduate

Candidates' progress will be monitored each semester by their advisors in the teacher preparation unit. Candidates must earn a C or higher in all courses that are part of the program. Those who do not earn a C or higher in these courses may retake them; otherwise, they will not be able to continue in the program. To exit the program, candidates must have a minimum 2.5 GPA calculated on all undergraduate work attempted and grades of C or better in all required program coursework.

Graduate

Candidates' progress will be monitored each semester by their advisors in the teacher preparation unit. Candidates must earn a B or higher in the foundational courses, Fundamental Principles of Computer Science and Fundamentals of Computer Programming and Data Structures. Those who do not earn a B or higher in these courses may retake them; otherwise, they will not be able to continue in the program. In the other courses in the program, candidates must earn a C or higher. Those who do not earn a C or higher may retake the courses; otherwise, they will not be able to continue in the program.

To exit the program, candidates must have a minimum 3.0 GPA calculated on all required graduate coursework in the program. Grades of B or better are required in Fundamental Principles of Computer Science and Fundamentals of Computer Programming and Data Structures and grades of C or better in all other required coursework. Candidates may have no more than two (2) grades of "C" or below in required graduate courses.

3.5.2 Professional Portfolio

The professional portfolio will be used to assess candidates' knowledge of the program objectives and standards. It will contain a collection of artifacts representing all program standards, and may include the candidate's philosophy of professional practice, work samples, lesson and/or unit plans, field experience and clinical practice logs, and evaluations. Candidates will provide written reflection statements for each artifact. The portfolio will be initiated at the beginning of the candidate's program and artifacts will be added throughout the entire program in specific courses. Students will be required to organize their portfolios according to program standards.

3.5.3 Field Experience Evaluation

Undergraduate

The tool that will be used to evaluate the undergraduate field experiences is the Model of Appropriate Practice (MAP). This tool is based on Charlotte Danielson's framework for teaching (http://www.danielsongroup.org/theframeteach.htm) and was created for initial teacher candidates. It puts into practice the principles of the Conceptual Framework underlying the endorsement program. It acknowledges that, with guidance of faculty, teacher candidates must undertake and manage the process of developing an understanding about teaching and learning for themselves. Through their coursework and field experiences, teacher candidates should gain competence in engaging students in constructing important knowledge.

Graduate

The tool that will be used to evaluate the graduate field experiences is the Graduate Model of Appropriate Practice (GMAP). The GMAP was based on the NBPTS Core Propositions and was developed for evaluating candidates in advanced teacher preparation programs.

3.5.4 Dispositions Evaluation

The Teacher Candidate Disposition Evaluation is an instrument used to assess teacher candidates' dispositions. The Graduate Dispositions Evaluation instrument is used during the field experience to assess in-service candidates' dispositions. Corresponding rubrics are used as guides to evaluating candidates' dispositions. Both undergraduate and graduate candidates' dispositions will be assessed in the methods and practicum courses by university faculty and cooperating teachers. Program advisors will counsel with any candidates who have unacceptable ratings on any component, and develop remediation plans as needed. Results of dispositions assessments will be shared with Computer Science program faculty and the advisory board members for analysis. Data collected from these evaluations will be used to make decisions regarding candidate performance, program quality, and unit operations.

3.5.5 Graduate and Employer Surveys

Graduates of the Computer Science Endorsement program will be contacted and asked to complete a brief, Web-based survey designed to elicit candidates' perceptions of their preparation as teachers. Employers of the graduates will also be contacted and asked to complete a brief Web-based survey for each graduate they supervise. The survey will ask employers to rate candidates on job performance. Program coordinators, department chairs, faculty, and staff will use data from the Graduate and Employer Surveys to make decisions regarding candidate performance, program quality, and unit operations.

3.6 Advisory Board

An advisory board for this program was instituted in order to provide feedback on the program and to make recommendations for improving the curriculum. Several middle and high school teachers together with the director of the Career and Technical Education for the local school district were solicited and agreed to serve on the board. This board will meet two or three times each year to discuss the program and to make recommendations for improving it.

3.7 Program Review

During February 14-17, 2010, a three-member team representing the Professional Standards Commission conducted an electronic review of the undergraduate and graduate endorsement programs to determine if the proposed programs met or exceeded the following Georgia standards:

- Candidate knowledge skills and dispositions
  - Content Knowledge for Teacher Candidates
  - Pedagogical Content Knowledge for Teachers
  - Pedagogical and Professional Knowledge and Skills for Teachers
  - Student Learning for Teachers
  - Professional Knowledge for Other School Professionals
  - Student Learning for Other School Professionals
  - Professional Dispositions
- Assessment system and unit evaluation
  - Assessment System
  - Data Collection, Analysis, & Evaluation
  - Use of Data for Program Improvement
- Field experiences and clinical practices
- Diversity
- Faculty qualification, performance and development

- Unit governance and resources
- Standards specific in Rule 505-3-01
- Program content standards

The program received "Developmental Approval" by the Professional Standards Commission on May 13, 2010.

4. CONCLUSION

The decline in students interested in Computer Science over the last several decades may threaten the United States' capability to compete in a world built around an ever increasing need for information technology and computing professionals. In this paper, the authors have described an effort aimed at arresting and possibly reversing this trend by implementing a Computer Science endorsement program for secondary school teachers. The process involved a careful review of teacher preparation standards, development of both an undergraduate and a graduate curriculum, programs of study and transition points. Field experiences, clinical practice, assessments for measuring student progress as well as an advisory board to assist in improving the program have been put in place. After a careful review by the Georgia Professional Standards Commission, both the undergraduate and graduate Computer Science endorsement programs for secondary school teachers were approved. Steps are currently underway to market the program and to make it as widely available to prospective and in-service teachers as possible. Implementation of this online program will no doubt play a significant role in improving the standard of Computer Science teaching at schools for the foreseeable future.

5. ACKNOWLEDGEMENT

This work was supported by Broadening Participation in Computing grant from National Science Foundation (award number: 0940495, PI: Wayne Summers).

6. REFERENCES

[1] Advancing Computing as a Science & Profession, *Association for Computing Machinery, ACM,* July 30, 2010, http://www.acm.org/press-room/news-releases/2010/cs-ed-act

[2] Transforming High School Computer Science: CS /10K Project, *ACM-Ed-Week*, http://www.csedweek.org/wp-content/uploads/2009/12/ACM-Ed-Week-CS10K.pdf

[3] Stephenson, C. and Cuny, J. 2010. What's Going on with AP CS: The 10,000 Teachers Project. DOI= http://www.csta.acm.org/ProfessionalDevelopment/sub/CSIT10Presentations/Stephenson_Cuny.pdf

[4] Ghada, Khoury. 2007. Computer Science State Certification Requirements: CSTA Certification Committee Report. http://csta.acm.org/ComputerScienceTeacherCertification/sub/TeachCertRept07New.pdf

[5] Gates, Bill. 2007. How to Keep America Competitive. *Washington Post.* February 25, 2007. http://www.washingtonpost.com/wp-dyn/content/article/2007/02/23/AR2007022301697.html

[6] Roberts, E. Computing Education and the Information Technology Workforce. *ACM SIGCSE Bulletin,* (32:2), 2000, pp. 83-90.

[7] Coopers & Lybrand. High-tech growth firms scale back 12-month growth outlook to match current pace: Worker shortage stifles growth. *Trendsetter Barometer.* January 7, 1998. http://www.colybrand.com/eas/trendset/170.html

[8] Peter F. and William A. The supply of information technology workers in the United States. Washington, DC: *Computing Research Association*, July 1999.http://www.cra.org/reports/wits/it_worker_shortage_book.pdf.

[9] Office of Technology Policy. America's New Deficit: The Shortage of Information Technology Workers. U.S. *Department of Commerce*, January 1998. http://www.ta.doc.gov/reports/itsw/itsw.pdf.

[10] Office of Technology Policy. The Digital Work Force: Building Infotech Skills at the Speed of Innovation. *U.S. Department of Commerce*, June 1999. http://www.ta.doc.gov/reports/itsw/Digital.pdf

Building a Community to Support HS CS Teachers: the Disciplinary Commons for Computing Educators

Lijun Ni & Mark Guzdial
School of Interactive Computing
Georgia Institute of Technology
85 5th Street NW
Atlanta, GA, 30332-0760
{lijun, guzdial}@cc.gatech.edu

Allison Elliott Tew
Department of Computer Science
University of British Columbia
Vancouver, BC V6T 1Z4
Canada
aetew@cs.ubc.ca

Briana Morrison
School of Computing & Software Engineering
Southern Polytechnic State University
1100 S. Marietta Parkway
Marietta, GA 30060
bmorriso@spsu.edu

Ria Galanos
Centennial High School
9310 Scott Road
Roswell, GA 30076
galanos@fultonschools.org

ABSTRACT
In this paper, we describe our experience in supporting high school CS teachers by building a local community through the Disciplinary Commons for Computing Educators (DCCE) project. The DCCE project is an effort to explore ways of supporting these CS teachers through the creation of a local community and by promoting teacher reflection. DCCE achieved this goal through an academic-year-long program where a cohort of CS teachers engaged in collaborative portfolio creation and peer observation of classroom teaching. We describe the design of the DCCE activities and present preliminary results from initial evaluations. Our short-term evaluations indicate that this project was successful in creating a supportive community, promoting teacher reflection, and advancing change in teaching practices among a group of computing educators.

Categories and Subject Descriptors
K.3.2 [**Computers and Education**]: Computer and Information Science Education–*computer science education.*

General Terms
Design, Experimentation, Theory.

Keywords
CS Teacher, Community, Reflection.

1. INTRODUCTION
Computer science education is important in both secondary and post-secondary systems, because it can contribute to the intellectual development of students, the innovation potential of other scientific disciplines, as well as the economic well being of countries [5, 15]. However, computer science (CS) is a relatively new and small discipline in K-12 education. We are facing many challenges in growing high school computing education, including issues related to teacher development. The Computer Science Teachers Association (CSTA) National Secondary Computer Science Survey reports the top three greatest challenges in teaching secondary CS as rapidly changing technology, lack of staff support, and lack of curriculum resources [3]. All three of these challenges in sum point to the need for learning opportunities and continual support for current CS teachers.

Most current efforts aimed at growing high school (HS) or secondary school CS teachers in the United States focus on preparing new teachers through workshops and similar short-term professional development [4, 6, 8], which are important for creating enough new teachers with the appropriate skills to teach CS courses. However, teacher turnover rate is high, and beginning teacher attrition is a serious problem in secondary education [10, 11]. To grow secondary school computing education, we need to support those trained teachers so that they stay and develop into high-quality CS teachers.

As there are still very few HS CS teachers, these in-service teachers are especially isolated. Often there are no other CS teachers in their schools to whom they can ask for CS teaching support. HS CS teachers are often heard saying: "I'm the only [CS] teacher in my school." This suggests that in-service CS teachers are in great need of a community for continual support and professional development opportunities.

The teacher education literature [2, 9, 13] suggests that there are many ways of supporting teacher learning, and offering continued collegial opportunities to develop a professional community is a key to teacher development and teacher retention. The CSTA National Secondary Computer Science Survey results point out that the top two most effective methods identified for delivering professional development to CS teachers are workshops/seminars and networking with others [3]. The current isolation of HS CS teachers further indicates the need for supporting these teachers in making connections with other CS teachers to learn from and to support each other.

This paper describes our experience in providing longer-term support for in-service HS CS teachers by creating a local community of CS teachers and promoting teacher learning through reflection on teaching practices. We ran a cohort of teachers currently teaching introductory computing through the Disciplinary Commons for Computing Educators (DCCE) project over the past year. Although our focus is on supporting the HS teachers, who were teaching the Advanced Placement (AP) course, we invited college computing faculty to join this community. Since few HS CS teachers have taken collegiate level CS courses, the college faculty offered insights about undergraduate CS courses and how to best prepare students for college. In our cohort of HS and undergraduate teachers, we adopted three main strategies from the Disciplinary Commons project [7, 16]: collaborative course portfolio creation, peer-observation of classroom teaching and focusing on a specific discipline (CS). These strategies are used to promote teacher reflection and build a community of peer CS teachers. Our initial evaluations for the DCCE project show that this type of long term outreach effort is effective in supporting a sense of community among HS CS teachers and promotes reflection on their teaching practices.

2. DCCE: CREATING A COMMUNITY OF CS TEACHERS

2.1 DCCE Design

To address the issue of teacher isolation and the need for peer support, our DCCE project was intended to create a supportive local community, where HS CS teachers were comfortable in exchanging resources and ideas, as well as to provide emotional support among peer CS teachers. More importantly, this teacher cohort was intended to provide professional development for HS CS teachers, where they were motivated to improve their own teaching and acquire skills to develop into more effective teachers. Promoting teacher reflection is critical for fostering good teachers, who can continue learning and become better teachers through reflective practices [14].

2.1.1 The Disciplinary Commons

Fincher and Tenenberg [7, 16] created the Disciplinary Commons project[1], which invites a group of computing educators within the same discipline to meet monthly during an academic year in order to share, reflect upon, and document their teaching. Participants in the Disciplinary Commons project prepare a course portfolio that describes their own teaching of a particular course, critique each other's portfolios, and visit each other's classrooms. The course portfolio typically includes a course's learning objectives, contents and structure, rationales for course design, the course's role in a larger context, evaluations of student work and the type and quantity of feedback the students are receiving. Further, its focus on student work can lead to insights into how this course might be taught differently in the future [7, 16]. As identified in the Disciplinary Commons project, the course portfolio can serve a number of purposes, such as providing a structure for the meetings and keeping individual reflection and group discussion grounded in teachers' teaching experiences [16].

The Disciplinary Commons project has been repeated in several institutions internationally[1]. Through participation and reification within a community of practice [17], the college faculty participants in the past Disciplinary Commons projects found values in the project including opportunities to systematically reflect on teaching practices and learn skills that apply directly to their teaching practices [16]. The Disciplinary Commons project offers a model of "building a community of scholars who can engage with and support each others' practice" [16]. Our project, the DCCE, adopted the course portfolio model including its peer-review and peer-observation mechanism to structure our meetings around teacher reflection and community building.

2.1.2 Bringing CS Faculty into the HS CS Teacher Community

The DCCE project invited college faculty who were teaching introductory CS to join with high school AP CS teachers. These teachers naturally shared a common interest in both the knowledge of and approaches to teaching introductory computing concepts and skills. Our approach of combining college and HS teachers is similar to the idea of teachers' vertical teaming used in K-12 education [12], and is unique among the Disciplinary Commons efforts. Related work on vertical teaming shows that, in addition to enhancing communication on curriculum standards and how different teachers interpret and teach the standards at each grade level, the collaboration and networking in a vertical team provides a support system that reduces teachers' feelings of isolation and promotes greater enthusiasm for their teaching [1, 12]. In the DCCE project, we attempted to offer cross-level communication opportunities with computing faculty to help HS teachers further their understanding of the computing field and computing education. In this paper, we are focusing our analysis on the impact the DCCE project had on the HS teachers, and explicit analysis of the interactions between college and high school faculty will be left for future work.

2.2 DCCE Agenda

We had eight teachers in the 2009-2010 cohort: four HS AP CS teachers and four college computing faculty participating in nine monthly sessions over one year. These eight teachers came from different institutions in Georgia. Meanwhile, we invited one HS teacher and one college faculty from the first year pilot DCCE to work as peer leaders to help plan and run the meetings.

Table 1 DCCE Meeting Agenda

Dates	Topics
Oct 24, 2009	Building the Commons Institutional Context
Nov 14	Course Context
Dec 12	Course Content
Jan 16, 2010	Teaching Methods Introducing Peer-observation
Feb 20	Teaching Philosophy
Mar 6	Evidence of Student Learning (Assessment)
Apr 24	Course Delivery: Debriefing Peer Observations
May 15	Feedback to Students
June12	Portfolio Presentations
Dec, 2010	Reunion

In the 2009-2010 teacher cohort, each of the teachers created a course portfolio for the introductory CS course they were

[1] http://www.disciplinarycommons.org/.

teaching. The portfolios were individually written and peer-reviewed. The participants all conducted a peer observation, visiting another participant's classroom. The meetings were organized around the elements of the course portfolio as showed in Table 1, which were modeled after the Disciplinary Commons project. We merged and adjusted the order of the topics based on our participants' needs.

3. OUTCOMES

3.1 Data Sources

We conducted both formative and summative evaluation of the DCCE activities. These evaluations were conducted by both an external evaluator on the project and the internal research team.

For formative evaluation, the external evaluator of this project gathered feedback after each meeting to ensure the quality of the meetings. For the summative evaluation, the external evaluator administered a post-DCCE Survey to gather information about the participants' experience in this project. The survey included a set of Likert scale questions and open-ended questions. This survey was administered at the conclusion of the last meeting session. In total, seven (four high school teachers and three college faculty) of the eight participants completed this survey. In addition, the first author conducted interviews with the four HS teacher participants to collect further information about their participation experience and the impact the DCCE project had on them. While a small sample, the in-depth interviews provided a detailed view of the DCCE project which permits an investigation and understanding of the issues that matter to the HS CS teachers. Transcripts from the interviews were coded using thematic analysis, noting ideas mentioned by at least two participants. These common ideas clustered into three themes: creating a local community, promoting teacher reflection, and promoting change in teaching practices.

In the next section, we summarize the results from the formative survey evaluations and the post-DCCE survey (Section 3.2). We then discuss the three major outcomes of the DCCE project identified as repeated themes by the HS teacher participants (Sections 3.3-3.5).

3.2 Overall Outcomes

The overall feedback from the evaluation surveys gathered at the end of each meeting on the effectiveness of the meeting's events was positive. The participants were asked to rate (on a scale from 1 (low) to 4 (high)) how informative, engaging, and useful they found each agenda item was. The overall average rating for all meetings was 3.5 on a 4 point scale, indicating that the participants were satisfied with the overall quality of the meetings. Each meeting had specific, defined learning objectives, and the participants also evaluated the degree to which they perceived these learning objectives were met for each meeting. As with the agenda items, we asked each participant to rate the degree to which the meeting addressed each learning objective on a semantic differential scale from 1 (Not at all) to 4 (To a great extent). Overall, the feedback was positive, with an overall average rating of 3.5 for all meetings.

While the feedback collected after each meeting was focused on the effectiveness of the meetings, the post-DCCE survey measured participants' experiences over the course of all the meetings. Among the seven responses of the post-DCCE survey, all participants reported that they enjoyed the DCCE experience. They all believed that the decision to take part in the DCCE was a good one and that their participation was a good use of time. The participants rated the overall organization of the DCCE was either "good" (1 of 7), "Very Good" (5 of 7), or "Excellent" (1 of 7). However, three participants recommended that there needed to be greater organization around the peer review process outside of the meetings. One participant reported that, although he benefited from reading others' portfolios, he did not always receive timely feedback from others on his portfolio.

All participants reported that they came to a better understanding about their teaching philosophy and saw connections between their teaching philosophy and teaching practices. Moreover, all of them agreed that they had a better understanding of why they taught their course the way they did.

Through open-ended questions, the participants reported they saw the primary benefit of the course portfolios as aiding in reflection. Furthermore, in terms of how often they would engage in reflecting on their teaching practices in the coming year, all the participants indicated they would reflect either several times (3 of 7) or many times (4 of 7) during each term. In addition based upon their reflective practices, all of them expected to try a new teaching practice.

Overall, participants reported that they gained new ideas for teaching, and they adopted teaching practices from other participants. Furthermore, most participants (6 of 7) reported that they had made definite plans to change their teaching the next time they taught the same course.

In terms of creating a local community of CS teachers, the participants rated small group discussion and peer observation as the most valuable interactions with other community members. Also, they all agreed that they were better able to provide feedback to colleagues on their teaching after attending the DCCE meetings. All the survey respondents planned on staying in touch with their DCCE colleagues. They also reported they would contact members of the DCCE cohort in the future for three main purposes: sharing resources, collaboration (e.g., for unit design), and gaining motivation and inspiration from their peers.

In the next section, we discuss the reported outcomes from the interviews with the HS teachers, through three main themes: creating a local community of CS teachers, promoting teacher reflection, and change in teaching practices.

3.3 Creating a Local Community

One of the main goals of the DCCE project was to create a local community of CS teachers to support the HS CS teachers who were often isolated. After attending the DCCE project over the past year, the HS CS teachers reported that they were able to build a sense of belonging to a community of CS teachers. Participation in a variety of community activities helped to validate what they already did well and built confidence in themselves as HS CS teachers. The participants also saw the values of a local community specifically for CS teachers.

3.3.1 Belonging to a Community of CS Teachers

All the HS teacher participants reported that attending the DCCE teacher cohort helped them to find a community to join, which did not exist for them before their participation in the DCCE project. For example, all the HS teacher participants made comments like this one:

> [P2]: "I felt like I didn't belong to a community at all of CS teachers until DCCE. But now I have a lot of teachers that I would feel fine about either calling up or emailing. That did not exist before. That's one reason I think it's so important that we have things like DCCE, because CS teachers are usually pretty isolated in high schools. That has now been changed because now I know a lot of people that do what I do."

The participants further pointed out the value of this community and its activities with its disciplinary focus on Computer Science.

> [P1]: "It's nice to go into a classroom and watch somebody teach what you teach, because you don't get that in CS. I can go into 13 different people's rooms and watch a Math classroom, but I can't go into anybody's classroom and watch what I do three periods a day. So, it's nice to go in and it's reassuring to go in and say, 'Hey, you know what? This does kind of look like my classroom.'"

3.3.2 Feeling Confident and Affirmed in Teaching CS

The HS CS teachers reported that participating in a CS specific community allowed them to see the similarities of their teaching, which helps them to feel more confident as CS teachers.

> [P1]: I think we all have a lot of things that are similar. When I watched [another teacher], I think he and I had some similar styles, similar ways to approach things. It's reassuring to watch him because it makes me feel like, 'Yeah. I'm doing it right.' I'm more confident hearing other people are doing it similarly. That gives you confidence when you don't teach it in a vacuum."

Another participant further identified that some of the community activities (e.g., peer observation and peer review) as enabling the members to validate what they already did well and to incorporate what they learned from other members.

> [P4]: "I guess I was very surprised at how excited [another teacher] was about his observation of my class. I didn't feel it was that exceptional a job. But somehow the questioning process and brainstorming discussions seemed to really be inspiring to him. I realized it's something I need to focus on more than I already do, because it has a potential. I guess I felt affirmed in a way I had never felt before. I felt that there's a place for my approach and I could incorporate some of those strengths that other teachers were bringing. I felt affirmed for having some of the ideas I had. So, I did leave with more confidence than when I came in."

3.3.3 Seeing the Value of Sustained Community with Other CS Teachers

After their participation in DCCE over the past year, the participants were able to see the values of having regular communication with other CS teachers.

> [P4]: "The other thing I learned that needs to be done is having a sustained professional dialogue with other teachers of CS. So, that's directly from DCCE, even though it's something we've always known. You know, our Deans of academics tell us, 'You need to go talk to the other teachers. You need to work together in the school more.' This is the first experience that really has underscored how fruitful it could be."

Furthermore, one of the participants reported that her DCCE experience motivated her to join the local CSTA chapter and even became a leader of it, as an extension of her participation in the local community of CS teachers—DCCE.

> [P1]: "I joined CSTA and became a leader because of the DCCE. I don't want to lose contact. I want to be able to still have a purpose to meet every couple of months, and to learn new things, and learn from each other. What the DCCE gave us was the ability to talk with other people and to see how they're doing things. That's what we're hoping CSTA kind of continues to do is to facilitate a community of people teaching the same thing."

3.4 Promoting Reflection

After the year-long project, our HS teacher participants were able to see the primary benefit of the portfolios in aiding reflection on their own teaching. They found that the portfolios served a useful forcing function for reflection and provided a structure for guiding reflection. Teachers reported that completing the portfolio also enabled self-reflection after the DCCE project.

First, the process of producing course portfolios provided a venue that forced teachers to reflect on their own teaching.

> [P2]: "I think all of these things [pieces of portfolios] just help teachers think more about what they do when they teach, and why they teach. I think that's something a lot of teachers don't really have the time to do unless they're forced to."

Furthermore, the course portfolio also provided a structure for guiding reflection. The structure of the course portfolio with well-designed guiding questions allowed teachers to see the structure of their course and examine the rationales and ways of improving the teaching of that course.

> [P1]: "[What I Learned] through creating the course portfolio is reflection on my teaching. I learned a ton. It helped me to examine my own structure of the course. It made me question the order that I teach things in when I looked at the order that other people taught things in, my instructional presentation of it. I mean, it's just kind of nice to be reflective and to put those kinds of things on paper and to say, 'Okay. This really is truly how I do it.' Then to kind of ask yourself, 'Is it working the way that I do it, or is something that somebody else is doing working better?' So, I love those processes where they get you thinking about what you're doing and how you can improve."

Similar to what was reported in the post-DCCE survey, the HS teachers pointed out that their experience of creating a course portfolio enabled them to conduct self-reflection after the DCCE project.

> [P3]: "As future plans for professional growth, I think [I would] just take time to sit down and reflect on what I've done, which DCCE has helped me do."

3.5 Promoting Pull Transfer and Change in Teaching Practices

Pull transfer is a phrase used to describe a bottom-up model of teacher change, where teachers change their practices, adopting ideas and materials from direct, personal contact with other practitioners as and when they need [7]. In pull transfer, the transfer of ideas or practices is achieved directly from practitioner to practitioner rather than pushed from researcher to practitioner. Previously, the Disciplinary Commons project showed that pull transfer happened among their participants [7, 16]. Although we did not explicitly design the DCCE to facilitate pull transfer, we did observe some plans for changes in teaching practices among the HS teacher participants.

3.5.1 Motivation to Change

In the post-DCCE survey, all respondents reported that they would continue applying what they learned from their DCCE experience. In the interviews, the HS teachers reported their DCCE experience motivated them to make changes, in particular, through seeing and learning what other teachers did in their teaching practices.

> [P2]: "After seeing [another teacher] teach, I realized that there were definitely a lot of things I could do in my own teaching to improve. It really inspired me a lot and made me realize I've got a lot of room for improvement... I definitely have a lot of plans of how I will do things differently. I think a lot of them are a direct result of [the DCCE]. A lot of them directly come from conversations I had with teachers at DCCE."

3.5.2 Changes and Plans to Change

Through interactions with other participants, the HS teachers identified ways of improving their teaching by changing what they were currently doing. One participant had already made some changes during his participation in the DCCE cohort and planned to extend those changes in the future.

> [P2]: "As far as the sessions go, I'll probably give students a lot more free responses, and I'll use rubrics that [the HS teacher leader] wanted to. ...That actually affected this past year of teaching. I created about eight rubrics. .... So, I will use those for next year, and I plan on creating more of them that are simulated to look just like the AP exam graders, how they grade their AP exams."

Participants also reported different ideas to improve their teaching next year, such changing their pedagogy to have more focus on problem-solving, to implement more discovery learning, and to introduce an IDE earlier.

> [P1]: "There are a lot of ideas that were shared that I will implement next year, you know, doing more hands-on things, some more discovery things like [one participant] had mentioned, doing tests more like GridWorld[2] test that [another participant] had shared. He shared a great one that's just less multiple-choice and more short answer. Then [I] have to do more problem-solving that way."

> [P3]: "I definitely would make changes the next year for two reasons. One, going through it the first time. But number two, listening and reflecting back, you know, on things...GridWorld is being taught because it's an application we can dump into this class. It's done. It's proven. And I can teach them about how to declare an object, and how to give some methods to it, and how to, therefore, extend a class. This application can do that for us. So, as a tool, let's introduce early. So, that's a change definitely that I will make."

4. SUMMARY AND DISCUSSION

4.1 Reflection on Outcomes

By the current evaluations conducted, we believe that the DCCE project has achieved its main goal: to support HS CS teachers by building a local community of CS teachers, where teachers can share, reflect on and improve their own teaching. Our initial evaluations indicate that the participation in this discipline-specific teacher cohort led to an increased sense of community and increased teacher reflection for high school teachers. These outcomes also led to reported plans for changing teaching practices.

First, working with teachers who were passionate about teaching and were teaching the same level of course enabled the HS CS teachers to see the common ground in their developing community. The interaction with other teachers helped them identify the similarities in the course and practices which helped them build a sense of belonging as a group of CS teachers. Now the often isolated HS CS teachers could connect with and support each other. Our participants reported they valued this community and felt a sense of belonging to it. They also felt more confident about themselves as CS teachers.

Second, the collaborative process of portfolio creation offered opportunities that forced the HS CS teachers to reflect on their practices. It also provided a structure to guide them in effective reflection on their own teaching. The portfolio thereby led teachers to better understand their own teaching and identify ways to improve. Our HS teacher participants even reported reflecting in a similar way on their practices after leaving the DCCE project.

Third, the peer review and peer observation activities allowed these HS teachers to understand and learn from each other's teaching. These activities provided opportunities for them to validate what they were already doing well and to identify places where innovation and change were desirable.

In summary, three major strategies enabled the project to achieve the outcomes of an increased sense of community and teacher reflection and pull transfer to enable changes in teaching practices for HS teachers: course portfolio creation, peer-observation of classroom teaching and focusing on a specific domain, introductory computing.

---

[2] GridWorld is a component of the current AP CS course.

4.2 Teacher Leaders and Scaffolding

In addition to the three strategies we adopted in this project, we also recognize the important roles the two teacher leaders played in achieving our goals of this project.

First of all, our experience working with the two teacher leaders was very valuable. The leaders volunteered to help the project researchers organize the meetings based on their own experience with us in a pilot DCCE cohort in 2008-2009. They brought enormous insights to this project with their passion for teaching CS and for connecting with other teachers. They offered first-hand experience in organizing the DCCE activities and communicated with the other CS teachers in "teacher language." The leaders and researchers met weekly to plan meetings, review feedback reports from each meeting, discuss issues identified, and brainstorm ways of improving the meetings. In particular, the leaders developed a set of structured guidelines for creating and reviewing portfolios, peer-observing classroom teaching, as well as reflecting on the teaching of specific concepts for the participants. As peer teachers, the leaders understood many teachers were not familiar with course portfolio creation and peer review, nor were they in the habit of reflecting on their teaching. These activities proved to be powerful tools for teacher learning, but their effective implementation required scaffolding provided by our teacher leaders.

Moreover, the leaders' work as facilitators was greatly appreciated by the participants. All the participants rated the facilitators' contributions to the DCCE as good. The leaders were perceived as open and inviting. Moreover, the HS teacher participants also commented on the many roles of leaders played, such as moderating discussions, guiding portfolio writing, suggesting additional resources, and providing insights.

4.3 Future Plans

Our initial evaluations indicate that the DCCE teacher cohort was a rewarding experience for the participants and successfully achieved its goal of creating a support community for HS CS teachers. However, a longitudinal evaluation will be needed to determine the extent to which the project is ultimately successful. We are currently organizing follow-up meetings with participants to share changes in their teaching practices and planning additional evaluations. We plan to conduct follow-up interviews with the participants to track their status and analyze the development of the sense of community through a social network analysis. Given the on-going process of evaluation, the results reported in this paper should be regarded as preliminary. In addition, we also plan to offer a HS CS teacher cohort in the 2010-2011 academic year, incorporating our findings and expanding our efforts to new participants.

5. ACKNOWLEDGMENTS

We would like to thank all the participants in the *Disciplinary Commons for Computing Educators*. Our thanks also to Tom McKlin who compiled the survey information for the DCCE project evaluation. This work is supported by the National Science Foundation CPATH program under Grant No. 0829601. Any opinions, findings, and conclusions or recommendations expressed in this material are those of the author(s) and do not necessarily reflect the views of the National Science Foundation.

6. REFERENCES

[1] Bertrand, L., Roberts, R. and Buchanan, R. Striving for success: Teacher perspectives of a vertical team initiative. National Forum of Teacher Education Journal, 16 (2006).

[2] Borko, H. Professional development and teacher learning: Mapping the terrain. Educational Researcher, 33, 8 (2004), 3-15.

[3] CSTA. CSTA National Secondary Computer Science Survey: Comparison of 2005, 2007 and 2009 Survey Results. Retrieved August 10, 2010 from http://www.csta.acm.org/Research/sub/Projects/ResearchFiles/CSTASurvey05-07_09Comp.pdf, 2009.

[4] Cuny, J. Finding 10,000 teachers: Transforming high school computer science. The CSTA Voice, 5, 6 (2010), 1-2.

[5] Ericson, B., Armoni, M., Gal-Ezer, J., Seehorn, D., Stephenson, C. and Trees, F. Ensuring Exemplary Teaching in an Essential Discipline: Addressing the Crisis in Computer Science Teacher Certification: Final report of the CSTA Teacher Certification Task Force, CSTA, 2008.

[6] Ericson, B., Guzdial, M. and Biggers, M. Improving secondary CS education: Progress and problems. In Proceedings of the 38th SIGCSE Symposium. Covington, Kentucky, USA, 2007.

[7] Fincher, S. and Tenenberg, J. Warren's question. In Proceedings of the Third International Computing Education Research Workshop (ICER). Atlanta, GA, USA, 2007.

[8] Goode, J. If you build teachers, will students come? Professional development for broadening computer science learning for urban youth. Journal of Educational Computing Research, 36, 1 (2007), 65-88.

[9] Guskey, T. Professional development and teacher change. Teachers and Teaching: Theory and Practice, 8, 3/4 (2002), 381-391.

[10] Ingersoll, R. M. Teacher turnover and teacher shortages: An organizational analysis. American Educational Research Journal, 38, 3 (2001), 499-534.

[11] Ingersoll, R. M. The teacher shortage: A case of wrong diagnosis and wrong prescription. NASSP Bulletin, 86, 631 (2002), 16-31.

[12] Kowal, P. Vertical teaming: Making connections across levels. Middle Ground, 6, 1 (2002), 20-22.

[13] NCTAF. Unraveling the "teacher shortage" problem: Teacher retention is the key. National Commission on Teaching and America's Future (NCTAF), 2002.

[14] Schön, D. A. Educating the Reflective Practitioner: Teaching Artistry through Reflection-in-action. Jossey-Bass, 1987.

[15] Shackelford, R. Why can't smart people figure out what to do about Computing Education? In Proceedings of the CS and IT Symposium. St. Louis, Missouri, U.S.A, 2005.

[16] Tenenberg, J. and Fincher, S. Opening the door of the computer science classroom: The Disciplinary Commons. In Proceedings of the 38th SIGCSE Symposium. 2007.

[17] Wenger, E. Communities of Practice. Cambridge University Press, 1998.

A Study on Attitudes and Emphases in Computer Science Teacher Preparation

Noa Ragonis
School of Education - Computer Science Department
Beit Berl College, Israel
and Department of Education in Technology and Science
Technion – IIT
noarag@beitberl.ac.il

Orit Hazzan
Department of Education in Technology and Science
Technion – Israel Institute of Technology
oritha@tx.technion.ac.il

Judith Gal-Ezer
Computer Science Department
The Open University of Israel
galezer@cs.openu.ac.il

ABSTRACT

This paper focuses on the development and implementation of computer science (CS) teacher preparation programs, which are two of the main educational and pedagogical challenges faced by those involved in CS education. Specifically, the paper presents the second stage of a study, the first stage of which focused on the accumulative knowledge gained in Israel over the past twenty years on CS teacher preparation. The first stage of the study, presented in SIGCSE 2010, emphasized the obvious: *CS deserves designated CS teacher preparation programs*. The second stage of the study, presented in this paper, is based on a deeper analysis of the data gathered in the first stage. Specifically, we approached a wider community of CS teacher educators (from Israel, Europe, and the USA) and explored its perspective on one element of teacher preparation programs – the Methods of Teaching CS (MTCS) course. The conclusions from this stage can be viewed as a comprehensive framework for the design of an MTCS course, both in terms of topics to be included in the course as well as the relative weight (in time) that is to be dedicated to each topic.

Categories and Subject Descriptors

K.3.2 [**Computers and Education**]: Computer and Information Science Education – *Computer science education, Curriculum*.

General Terms: Management, Performance, Human Factors.

Keywords: Computer science education, computer science teacher preparation, Methods of Teaching Computer Science course, K-12 instruction.

1. INTRODUCTION

The dynamic development of computer science (CS) poses a variety of pedagogical and educational challenges, including those related to high school CS teacher preparation, which are the focus of this paper. The importance of high school CS teacher preparation emerges from the observation that although it is addressed extensively by the international community of CS educators, designated CS teacher preparation frameworks do not exist in many countries [1,4,7].

SIGCSE'11, March 9–12, 2011, Dallas, Texas, USA.

In [11] we presented the findings of the first stage of a survey, conducted among Israeli heads of CS teacher preparation programs and instructors of the Methods of Teaching Computer Science (MTCS) course that investigated the rationale and implementation of CS teacher preparation programs. One of the main observations that emerged from the survey was that *the characteristics of the field of CS have a significant impact on the design of the surveyed CS teacher preparation programs* and, therefore, that *CS deserves designated CS teacher preparation programs*. In this paper we present the second stage of the survey, which was distributed to a wider community of CS teacher educators from Israel, Europe, and the USA.

The second stage of the survey focused on the content of the MTCS course from two perspectives: First, the importance the surveyed participants attributed to the inclusion in the MTCS course of 48 different topics in 8 categories; and second, the relative time allocated in the MTCS course to each of the 8 categories, as proposed by the survey participants.

Three differences exist between the two stages of the survey:

- **Survey focus.** The first stage focused mainly on common aspects of teacher preparation programs; the second stage concentrated on the MTCS course.
- **Participant population**. All participants in the first stage were Israeli; participants in the second stage were from the international community of CS educators.
- **Survey question type**. Questions in the first stage of the survey were mostly open; questions in the second stage were mostly closed.

We propose that the conclusions of the second stage of the survey be viewed as a comprehensive framework for the design of an MTCS course, in terms of both topics to be included in the course and the relative weight (time) to be dedicated to each topic.

Before we delve into the details of the second stage of the survey, we note that the material presented here does not refer to any specific high school CS curriculum and can therefore be applied to a variety of high school CS curricula implemented in different countries. Furthermore, based on the accumulative knowledge and experience exhibited by the survey participants, we suggest that each institution can tailor its own CS teacher preparation program, and MTCS course in particular, according to its specific prospective CS teacher population.

2. SURVEY BACKGROUND

2.1 CS Teacher Preparation[1]

The rapid changes and developments in the field of CS pose a huge challenge for designers of high school CS curricula and, consequently, for designers of teacher preparation programs [2,6,8,9,10,12]. This fact is amplified by the fact that in many countries no CS teacher preparation programs are offered [1,3,4,7], and further, no requirements for CS teaching certificates are defined. This lack of designated CS teacher preparation programs can, subsequently, explain why CS is taught in many high schools by mathematics teachers or teachers of other scientific disciplines [5,15]. The CS education community has expressed its awareness of the need for special teacher CS preparation programs by establishing professional organizations such as the Computer Science Teachers Association (CSTA) [14,15].

Our literature review revealed that descriptions of CS teacher preparation programs in the international literature are rare, thought recently, awareness of the topic has increased. We also found that much of the literature on CS teacher preparation is based on the Israeli experience, where the first stage of the survey presented in this paper took place [11].

2.2 The Methods of Teaching Computer Science Course[2]

Since the second stage of the survey presented in this paper focused on the MTCS course, we first elaborate on the place and role of the MTCS course in CS teacher preparation programs.

Teacher preparation programs are usually based on general pedagogical knowledge, subject matter knowledge, pedagogical content knowledge (PCK), and practicum in real classes. PCK is one category of Shulman's Teacher Knowledge Base Model [13] and it refers to what a teacher is required to know in order to teach a certain subject matter: how to make it understandable, learners' preconceptions and misconceptions, and strategies for coping with learners' misconceptions [13].

From this perspective, the MTCS course aims to broaden students' PCK and sets the basis for their in-school training, which takes place after the course. Based on the working assumption that the prospective CS teachers learn the discipline of CS and general pedagogy topics in other courses, the MTCS course focuses on the uniqueness of teaching CS. The main objective of the MTCS course is, therefore, to prepare the students for their future fieldwork as CS teachers. These objectives can be achieved by facilitating various activities, discussions, reflective-thinking processes and other tasks.

Course participants are either prospective or in-service CS teachers who wish to broaden their knowledge on CS education in the high school. The course's academic pre-requisites are relevant CS courses and some of the general education and teaching studies.

3. SURVEY DESCRIPTION

3.1 Survey Objective

The objective of the second stage of the survey was to characterize the value, attributed by CS teacher educators, to the inclusion of different topics in the MTCS course in terms of importance and time allocation.

3.2 Survey Participants

Twenty five CS teacher educators responded to the survey and were categorized into two groups: Group A – 11 educators who participated also in the first stage of the survey, and Group B – 14 educators who did not participate in the first stage of the survey. Table 1 presents the country composition of the survey participants.

Table 1. Participants in the second stage of the research

Group	#	Characteristics
A	11	Israeli CS teacher educators who participated in the first stage of the survey
B	14	CS teacher educators who did *not* participate in the first stage of the survey: - 6 from Israel; - 4 from Europe: Austria, Lithuania, Poland, Switzerland; - 4 from the USA: Indiana, New York (2), Oregon.

We decided to divide the participants into these two groups since the questions in the second stage of the survey were formulated based on answers given by the participants in first stage, that is, Group A members. The contents of the second stage of the survey were, therefore, new for the Group B participants. As we shall see later in the Survey Finding section, this categorization enabled us to explain the survey participants' perspectives with respect to the importance and relevance of different topics addressed in the MTCS course.

Here are several additional details about the 25 participants:

- The participants represent 20 different institutes (12 in Israel, 4 in Europe, 4 in the USA);
- Sixteen of the 20 institutes offer a CS teacher preparation program, either as a main study track or combined with a mathematics or sciences education track (11 in Israel, 4 in Europe, 1 in the USA);
- The number of years the participants have been involved in pre-service or in-service CS teacher preparation:
  1-5 years - 5 participants;
  6-15 years - 8 participants;
  Over 15 years - 12 participants.

Please note that in the context of our topic, namely CS teacher preparation, which boasts a relatively small community of practitioners, a sample of 25 experienced participants is quite considerable. We did, however, consider this number carefully when choosing the data analysis methods.

3.3 Survey Structure

The second stage of the survey included three parts:

I. Details on the CS teacher preparation program offered by the CS teacher educator's institute (if such exists) and the participant's experience in CS teacher preparation[3];
II. The importance of including different topics in the MTCS;
III. Time allocation for the different topics in the MTCS course.

[1] For additional details, see [11].

[2] For additional details, see [9].

[3] Only Group B participants completed part I of the survey; these details were gathered from Group A participants in the first stage of the survey. Only partial data gathered in this part of the survey is presented in this paper (see the above demographic details).

Part II and III of the survey were constructed based on the analysis of the data gathered in the first stage of the survey (partially presented in [11]). Specifically, we identified a list of 48 topics that the participants in the first stage of the survey (Group A) thought should be included in the MTCS course. These 48 topics were grouped into the following 8 categories:

1. National high school CS curriculum
2. Discipline of CS
3. Didactics of CS education
4. Research in CS education
5. General didactics
6. Practicum in the high school
7. Web ethics
8. The role of the CS teacher in the school

Since the participants in the first stage of the survey addressed Category 3 (Didactics of CS education) extensively, it was further divided into four sub-categories, namely: core topics, teaching methods, evaluation methods, and additional aspects.

Parts II and III included closed questions. In part II, which investigated the importance of including different topics in the MTCS course, participants were asked to rank each of the 48 topics on a Likert 0-3 scale according to the importance he or she attributes to the inclusion of the said topic in the MTCS course (rankings are presented in the Findings section)[4].

In Part III, the participants were asked to indicate a relative time allocation for each of the eight categories. Since the course extent in each institute is different, the participants were asked to refer as the course extent is of 100 hours (as to 100%) and to divide the hours between the course topics as to enable achieving the course objectives, as they perceive them. The participants were also asked to add any topics that in their opinion were missing from the list but should be addressed in the MTCS course[5]. Due to the extensive attention given to Category 3 (Didactics of CS education), the participants were asked to further refine the time allocation for this specific category and to indicate the time allocation for each of its sub-categories.

Although Parts II and III are somewhat related, they highlight different, though complementary, aspects, namely importance and relevance. For example, a survey participant may perceive a specific topic as being very important for inclusion in the MTCS course, but at the same time, may think that only a relatively small number of hours is sufficient for its discussion in the course.

4. SURVEY FINDINGS

In this section, we present and analyze the survey findings with respect to a) the importance the participants attributed to the topics included in each of the eight categories, and b) the participants' suggestions for time allocation of each category in the MTCS course. Due to space limitations, we limit the details presented here and will further elaborate on them at the conference.

4.1 Topic Importance

Tables 2-10 present the importance attributed by the survey participants to the 48 topics (in 8 categories) presented in Part II of the survey. The data for each topic includes the average ranking by each group, the average ranking by the entire population, and the frequency at which the category was ranked by 2 or 3 ("important" and "very important").[6]

Table 2. Importance of Category 1 topics: The national high school CS curriculum

Topic	A	B	All	2-3 Frq.
1. Acquaintance with the national high school CS curriculum	2.91	2.64	2.78	24
2. Understanding past changes in the high school CS curriculum	1.73	1.57	1.65	14
3. Acquaintance with the planning and implementation of the high school CS curriculum in your country: the government's role, professional curriculum committees, the supervision of high school CS education, etc.	1.73	1.86	1.79	17
4. Acquaintance with study material for high school CS pupils and teachers	2.82	2.71	2.77	25
5. Acquaintance with different online information resources for CS teachers	2.64	2.29	2.46	24
6. Acquaintance with information technology standards	1.55	1.64	1.59	15
7. Acquaintance with the national computing program (if such exists)	1.64	1.77	1.70	13

As can be seen in Table 2, the two groups exhibited a similar perspective on the topics included in this category, attributing greater importance to topics that deal with the actual high school CS curriculum (Topics 1,4,5) than to peripheral topics (Topics 2,3,6,7).

Table 3. Importance of Category 2 topics: The discipline of CS

Topic	A	B	All	2-3 Frq.
8. Historical overview of the development of the discipline of CS	2.09	2.14	2.12	19
9. Discussion: Is CS a science?	1.70	2.00	1.85	16

The greater importance attributed by Group B participants to the discussion of aspects related to the discipline of CS (as reflected in Table 3) is further supported in Part III of the survey and is part of a more global observation of this survey. According to this global observation, since Group A participants are more involved in actual CS teacher preparation programs, they tend to emphasize, in the MTCS course, the didactics of CS over the discussion about the nature of the discipline of CS.

[4] The following instructions were presented in Part II:
The following table presents topics taught in the Methods of Teaching Computer Science course as suggested by the participants of the first stage of the research conducted in Israel. Please rank each topic in terms of the importance you attribute to its inclusion in the Methods of Teaching Computer Science course.Use the following scale: 0 - not at all important; 1 - slightly important; 2 - important; 3 - very important.

[5] The following instructions were presented in Part III:
Assume that you have 100 hours, representing 100% of the scope of the MTCS course. Please suggest time allocations for the different topics so that the course objectives, as you perceive them, are achieved in the best way possible.

[6] In general, it is interesting to note the relative high ranking given by Group A participants to most of the topics. Since the topics were formulated based on Group A's open answers in the first stage of the survey, these ranks actually also indicate the reliability of the data analysis performed in the first stage of the survey.

Table 4. Importance of Category 3a topics: The didactics of computer science education - Core topics

Topic	A	B	All	2-3 Frq.
10. Learners' difficulties, typical mistakes and misconceptions related to different topics in the curriculum	2.91	2.86	2.88	25
11. Problem-solving heuristics: abstraction, bottom-up and top-down design, stepwise refinement, generalization, analogy	2.55	2.86	2.70	24
12. Teaching by patterns	2.09	2.36	2.22	20
13. Learning from mistakes	2.64	2.50	2.57	25
14. Reflective processes in problem-solving processes	2.45	2.43	2.44	24
15. Argumentation and convincing presentation (of the rationale of a solution to a given problem and of the solution itself)	2.00	2.29	2.14	19
16. Teaching debugging	2.64	2.00	2.32	21
17. Acquiring experience in the design of exercises, exams, matriculation-format exams	2.91	2.50	2.70	25
18. Acquiring pedagogical tools and skills related to learners' diversity	2.36	2.71	2.54	24
19. Acquiring pedagogical tools to create a research-based learning environment	2.18	1.93	2.06	18
20. Teaching programming paradigms – emphases and principles, and how they are expressed in the curriculum	2.45	2.29	2.37	23
21. Teaching soft ideas of CS (such as recursion and abstraction)	2.45	2.57	2.51	23
22. Preparation of the first CS lesson	2.09	2.43	2.26	22

Most of the rankings in this category (Table 4) are relatively high, as is the frequency of the 2-3 ranks given. This is not surprising since this category comprises the essence of CS teaching.

Table 5. Importance of Category 3b topics: The didactics of computer science education - Teaching methods

Topic	A	B	All	2-3 Frq.
23. Presentation and examination of a variety of CS teaching methods	2.64	2.71	2.68	25
24. Integration of educational games into CS education	2.09	1.64	1.87	17
25. Projects in CS education and mentoring projects	2.09	2.36	2.22	21
26. Integrating the Web into the teaching of CS and acquaintance with computational pedagogical models	1.91	1.86	1.88	16
27. Integrating the computer lab into CS education	2.64	2.43	2.53	24
28. Acquaintance with animation- and visualization-based environments for teaching different concepts included in the high school CS curriculum	2.09	2.00	2.05	21

As can be seen in Table 5, Topics 24 – Integration of educational games into CS education – and 26 – Integrating the Web into the teaching of CS – are considered to be as relatively less important by members of both groups; this phenomenon, we suggest, warrants further examination. Nevertheless, the difference between the two groups reflected in their ranking of Topic 24 – Integration of educational games into CS education – may be explained by the greater awareness of Group A members to the importance of diversifying teaching methods in CS education.

Table 6. Importance of Category 3c topics: The didactics of computer science education - Evaluation methods

Topic	A	B	All	2-3 Frq.
29. Evaluation of programming exercises	2.45	2.43	2.44	23
30. Construction and evaluation of CS tests	2.73	2.50	2.61	23
31. Alternative evaluation methods of student achievements	2.18	2.43	2.31	21
32. Evaluation as a tool for the promotion of learning	2.36	2.29	2.32	21
33. Acquaintance with the requirements, structure, and evaluation methods of the matriculation exams	2.55	2.14	2.34	21

As can be seen in Table 6, both groups attribute high importance to evaluation methods in CS education. This may indicate the participants' awareness to known challenges involved in the evaluation of CS learners' knowledge. The difference between Groups A and B with respect to Topic 33 - Acquaintance with the requirements, structure, and evaluation methods of the matriculation exams – apparently stems from the fact that some of the participants in group B are from countries that have no national exams.

Table 7. Importance of Category 3d topics: The didactics of computer science education - Additional aspects

Topic	A	B	All	2-3 Frq.
34. Increasing the motivation to study CS	2.09	2.57	2.33	22
35. Ethics in CS education	1.91	2.43	2.17	20
36. Gender and minorities in CS	1.45	1.79	1.62	14

As can be seen in Table 7, Group B participants attribute greater importance to social aspects of CS: motivation, ethics, and diversity. Although this observation still requires further exploration, it can be related to the relatively higher importance that Group B members attribute to the discussion of the nature of the discipline of CS (Table 3). It is also relevant to note the low number of participants (14) who ranked Topic 36 – Gender and minorities in CS – either 2 or 3, relative to the ranking of other topics and in contrast to the significant attention this topic receives, for example, at CS education conferences.

Table 8. Importance of Category 4 topics: Research in CS education

Topic	A	B	All	2-3 Frq.
37. Research in science education – basic concepts, research tools, gaining research experience, how to conduct research while teaching	1.82	1.93	1.87	17
38. Review of appropriate resources and journals as sources for papers to support the construction of lesson plans	2.18	2.14	2.16	22
39. Preparation and presentation of a research paper that deals with CS education or with the integration of computers into the school	1.55	1.64	1.59	14
40. Conducting a mini-research and writing a final report on it	2.00	1.64	1.82	17

The rankings presented in Table 8 indicate the relatively low importance attributed to most of the topics in this category

(37,39,40) compared with most of the preceding topics. Specifically, approximately 40% of the survey participants are not convinced that it is essential to deepen and experience educational research in CS education. At the same time, however, almost all participants (22 of 25) are convinced that Topic 38 as highly important, and they see the benefits gained by prospective CS teachers' reviewing appropriate resources and journals to select papers that support their construction of lesson plans.

Table 9. Importance of Category 5 topics: General didactics

Topic	A	B	All	2-3 Frq.
41. Acquiring tools and skills for the construction of a collaborative learning environment	1.82	2.07	1.94	18
42. Acquiring tools and skills for the design and development of learning units	2.09	2.21	2.15	20
43. Acquiring class management skills	2.55	1.86	2.20	17
44. Preparation of lessons and teaching them to fellow course participants	2.27	2.29	2.28	20
45. Creating of a pool of learning materials for novice teachers to use during their first years as teachers	2.18	2.21	2.20	21

With respect to Category 5 topics (Table 9), we wish to highlight the difference between the two groups in the importance they attribute to Topic 43 – Acquiring class management skills. We speculate that this difference results from the different teaching experience of participants in the two groups in high school classes, but this speculation requires further examination.

Table 10. Importance of Categories 6-8 topics

Category	Topic	A	B	All	2-3 Frq.
6. Practicum in the high school	46. Analysis of observations made during CS lessons in the school	2.00	2.43	2.21	21
7. Web ethics	47. Exposure to the dangers of the Web and acquaintance with values, ethical norms and Web-based intellectual properties laws	1.73	2.21	1.97	17
8. The CS teacher in the school	48. The role of the CS teacher in school (for example, the CS teacher as the computing and technical coordinator)	1.45	1.64	1.55	14

With respect to Categories 6, 7 and 8 (Table 10), we note the fact that, once again, like in Table 7, Group B participants attribute greater importance to ethical issues (Topic 47) and that both groups attribute low importance to Topic 48 – The role of the CS teacher in school .

4.2 Time Allocation

Table 11 presents the time allocation suggested by the survey participants for the main categories included in Part B of the survey with a total of 100 hours (100% of a real course time allocation). The table presents the average number of hours allocated by each group (A and B), the average number of hours allocated by all participants, and the minimum and maximum values given for each category.

We first address the wide range of values given to each category and sub-category, which may be explained either, by the participants' different perspective on the course or by different interpretations that different participants gave to each category (as some of them communicated to us following their participation in the survey).

Table 11. Participants' time allocation for the main categories (Part III of the survey)

No	Category	A	B	All	Range Min	Range Max
1	The national high school CS curriculum	8.00	7.07	7.54	1	25
2	The discipline of CS	5.27	14.50	9.89	0	55
3	Didactics of CS education	54.00	50.86	52.43	20	92
4	Research in CS education	8.27	5.50	6.89	0	20
5	General didactics	11.18	7.64	9.41	0	25
6	Discussing the practicum in the high school	7.73	8.36	8.04	0	28
7	Web ethics	2.18	2.93	2.56	0	5
8	The role of the CS teacher in the school	1.82	2.36	2.09	0	8
	Didactics of CS education – Internal division	**A**	**B**	**Avg**	**Range Min**	**Range Max**
3 a	Core topics	23.91	19.42	21.66	0	54
3 b	Teaching methods	15.18	18.08	16.63	5	46
3 c	Evaluation methods	11.64	13.50	12.57	3	46
3 d	Additional aspects	3.27	5.00	4.14	0	10

Despite the wide range of values obtained, Table 11 indicates that the average number of hours allocated to each category is similar among the two groups. This similar perspective is reflected also visually in Figure 1. Two differences between the two groups, as described below, support some findings of Part II of the survey; further exploration is needed to establish them.

The two main visual[7] differences with respect to Categories 2 – The discipline of CS – and 3 – Didactics of CS education are: (a) Group A participants allocated a greater portion of the course to the Didactics of CS education category than did Group B members; and (b) Group B participants allocated more hours in the MTCS course to the Discipline of CS category than did Group A members (see also Table 3). This difference can be explained by the fact that the participants in the first stage of the survey (Group A) were heads of CS teacher preparation programs and instructors of the MTCS course (most with over 10 years of experience), whose involvement in CS teacher preparation was higher compared with Group B participants. Therefore, they might regard the didactics of CS as a more important topic to be addressed in the course. This interpretation is supported by the time allocation for Category 5 – General didactics: here too, Group A members assigned more hours than did Group B. Both groups, however, agreed that Category 3 – Didactics of CS

[7] Due to the relatively small number of participants, we did not base this conclusion on a statistical test.

education – is the main category to be addressed in the MTCS course.

Another difference between the two groups is seen with respect to Category 4 - Research in computer science education (see also Table 8). This difference should further be explored together with the other findings related to the inclusion of CS education research in the MTCS course.

Figure 1. Time allocation for the eight categories presented in Table 11

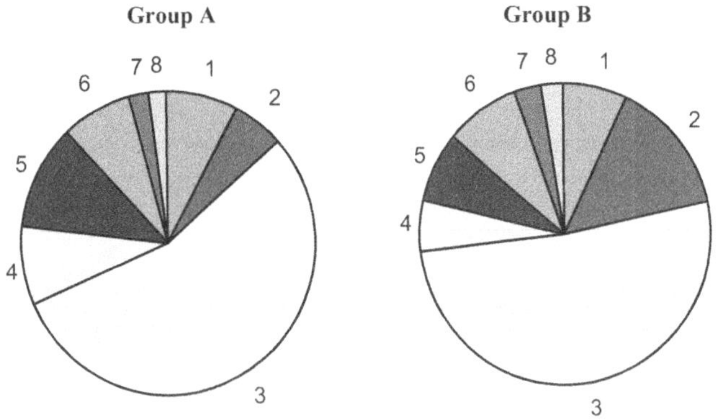

5. DISCUSSION

The first stage of the survey presented in [11] delivered a clear message: *Since CS has unique characteristics, designated CS teacher preparation programs should be offered.* In this paper, we focused on one component of such programs – the Methods of Teaching CS course. For a wider discussion, see [8], which deals with the establishment of CS teacher preparation programs.

Our conclusions from the two stages of the survey are:

- The list of categories and topics (constructed based on the data analysis in the first stage of the survey), together with the data on their importance and relevance (gathered in the second stage of the survey), can serve as a basis for an MTCS course design. Each instructor can choose from this list those topics that are especially relevant for his or her particular population of prospective CS teachers and design the course accordingly. Indeed, since different opinions were expressed about the course emphases, it seems reasonable to tailor the MTCS course to each specific national curriculum and prospective CS teacher population.
  The completeness of the list of topics can be further strengthened by the fact that even though the participants in the second stage of the survey had the opportunity to add topics to the list presented to them, only two of them added a topic (two different topics) and assigned them small number of hours.
- Beyond the mere list of topics, CS teacher educators can use the time allocation recommended for each topic in the MTCS course. Once again, although different opinions were expressed about specific time allocations, it seems that, from the survey participants' perspective, these recommendations give a valuable picture of the recommended time allocation.

ACKNOWLEDGMENTS

We would like to thank all of the survey participants who dedicated time and responded to our questionnaires. Their contribution is highly appreciated. We also wish to thank Beit Berl College for its partial funding of this research.

5. REFERENCES

[1] Armoni, M. (in preparation): Looking at Secondary Teacher Preparation through the Lenses of Computer Science – a Literature Survey.

[2] Blum, L. and Cortina, T. J. (2007). CS4HS: an outreach program for high school CS teachers. *ACM SIGCSE Bulletin*, 39(1), 19-23.

[3] CSTA (2007). Computer Science State Certification Requirements - CSTA Certification Committee Report, http://www.csta.acm.org/ComputerScienceTeacherCertification/sub/TeachCertRept07New.pdf [2009, July]

[4] CSTA (2008). Ensuring Exemplary Teaching in an Essential Discipline: Addressing the Crisis in Computer Science Teacher Certification, *Final Report of the CSTA Teacher Certification Task Force*.http://www.csta.acm.org/Communications/sub/DocsPresentationFiles/CertificationFinal.pdf [2009, July]

[5] Deek, F. P. and Kimmel, H. (1999). Status of computer science education in secondary schools: One state's perspective. *Computer Science Education* 9(2), 89-113.

[6] Eurydice (2004). Key Data on Information and Communication Technology in Schools in Europe. *Eurydice, The information network on education in Europe*, Belgium. http://www.eurydice.org/ressources/eurydice/pdf/0_integral/048EN.pdf [2009, July]

[7] Gal-Ezer, J. (1995). Computer science teachers' certification program. *Computers and Education*, 25(3), 163-168.

[8] Hazzan, O., Gal-Ezer, J. and Ragonis, N. (2010). How to establish a Computer Science teacher preparation program at your university? – The ECSTPP Workshop, *ACM Inroads magazine* **1**(1), pp. 35-39.

[9] Kavander, T. and Salakoski, T. (2004). Where have all the flowers gone? — Computer Science education in general upper secondary schools. Proceedings of the Fourth Finnish/Baltic Sea Conference on Computer Science Education 2004, Koli, Helsinki University,Finland,112-115.

[10] Ragonis, N. and Hazzan, O. (2009). Integrating a tutoring model into the training of prospective Computer Science teachers. *Journal of Computers in Mathematics and Science Teaching* 28(3), 309-339.

[11] Ragonis, N., Hazzan, O. and Gal-Ezer, J. (2010). A survey of Computer Science teacher preparation programs in Israel tells us: Computer Science deserves a designated high school teacher preparation!, *Proceedings of SIGCSE 2010 - The 41st ACM Technical Symposium on Computer Science Education*, Milwaukee, WI, USA, pp. 401-405.

[12] Stephenson, C., Gal-Ezer, J., Haberman, B. and Verno, A. (2005). The new educational imperative: Improving high school computer science education. Final report of the CSTA Curriculum Improvement Task Force http://csta.acm.org/Communications/sub/DocsPresentationFiles/TCEAPres07.pdf [2009, September].

[13] Shulman, L. S. (1986). Those who understand: Knowledge growth in teaching. *Educational Teacher,* 15(2), 4-14.

[14] Tucker, A., Deek, F., Jones, J., McCowan, D., Stephenson, C. and Verno, A. (2004). A Model Curriculum for K-12 Computer Science. The ACM K-12 Education Task Force http://www.csta.acm.org/Curriculum/sub/ACMK12CSModel.html [2009, September]

[15] White, J. (2004). Computer science teachers association report for ACM's sigs, http://www.acm.org/sigs/sgb/minutes/agenda100304_3_2.ppt [2009, September]

The Images of Computing: Engaging Undergraduates in the Broad Issues of Computer Science

Carol Frieze
Carnegie Mellon University
School of Computer Science
5000 Forbes Avenue
Pittsburgh, Pa 15213
412-268-9071
cfrieze@cs.cmu.edu

ABSTRACT

In this paper we describe a new course designed to give undergraduate students, including those who will be tomorrow's computer science professionals, the opportunity to think beyond the classroom, to reach out and examine some of the broader issues surrounding computing. This "research and action" based course – "Understanding and Broadening the Images of Computing" – explores the images, the realities and the (mis)perceptions of computing that influence public understanding and participation in the field. Students have the opportunity to reflect on some issues often taken for granted e.g. *What do we mean by computer science and how does it differ from computing? How do cultural images, attitudes and access to resources impact participation in computing? Are our attitudes to computing generalizable or culturally specific?* By engaging students in cultural analysis the course aims to prepare them to be critical thinkers, and better informed professionals, in the fields they have chosen to enter.

Categories and Subject Descriptors

K.3.2. [**Computers and Education**]: Computer and Information Science Education – *computer science education.*

General Terms

Human Factors, Experimentation

Keywords

Images of computing, culture, perceptions, broadening participation, outreach, global perspective

1. INTRODUCTION

In 2000 an ItiCSE working group made the following observation: "Students in today's university programs will be the CIT professionals of tomorrow. Industry and workplace professionals realize that skills beyond the technical are vital to the success of the students ..... Cultural issues are becoming more important as the world moves towards increased communication and globalization." [7]

In this paper we describe the design and implementation of a new course, a 7 week elective hosted by the computer science (CS) department at Carnegie Mellon University (CMU) and first offered in spring 2008. The course is designed to give undergraduate students the opportunity to think beyond the classroom and examine the broader issues surrounding computing. This research and action based course – "Understanding and Broadening the Images of Computing" – explores the images, the realities and the (mis)perceptions of computing that influence public understanding and participation in the field. In this sense exploring the *images* of computing provides a vehicle for exploring the broader issues and the cultural context of the discipline. Though specifically cultural in focus, and much lighter in CS concepts, we might place this course among others which also require students to examine the broader issues of computing. Fisk University, for example, offers "Exploring Computer Science – A Freshman Orientation and Exploratory Course"[1] and Duke has "CompSci 82",[2] both of which have been around for some time. Also, we see and welcome the development of a new AP Computer Science Principles[3] course in which students "learn to analyze, critique, and discuss the ethical, legal and social implications of computing."

The CS curriculum at CMU provides a solid foundation in computer science and aims to prepare "students to be industry and academic leaders who can apply technology and computer science principles across a wide variety of fields"[4]. Students are also required to take arts and humanities classes and to complete a minor in a second subject to gain depth in another area. Thus the CS program recognizes that gaining other skills in addition to their technical expertise will help broaden and strengthen their contribution as future computer scientists and citizens. At the same time the department offers non-CS majors the opportunity to explore the field through such courses as "Principles of Computation"[5] in which students with no prior background in

SIGCSE'11, March 9–12, 2011, Dallas, Texas, USA.

[1] See http://www.cs.duke.edu/csed/fyi/egarievwe.pdf
[2] See http://www.cs.duke.edu/courses/fall08/cps082
[3] See http://csprinciples.org/
[4] See Carnegie Mellon's School of Computer Science web site http://www.cs.cmu.edu/about/index.html
[5] This course provides an alternative to an introductory programming class and satisfies the computing requirement for non-CS majors at CMU.

computing study the key concepts of the discipline. It is within this rich educational framework that the course – "Understanding and Broadening the Images of Computing" – fits and meets the school's aims and philosophy. By engaging students in cultural analysis the course aims to prepare them to be critical thinkers, and better informed professionals, in the fields they have chosen to enter.

2. COURSE OBJECTIVES

"Understanding and Broadening the Images of Computing" asks students to challenge their own assumptions about computing and computer science and to examine public perceptions of the field in the USA and globally. Students learn that in an image-based culture knowledge is often shaped by the images that surround us. [8] At the same time, as future professionals, students can be actively involved in re-shaping and re-presenting the field.

The objectives of this course are for students:

- To self-reflect on their own attitudes towards, and understanding of, computing and computer science.
- To research images of computing in the public media to identify images which might have broad appeal and images which might not.
- To understand the role of images in determining and perpetuating public (mis)understanding of computing.
- To examine how computing and computer science are defined and envisioned by CMU, by students and by experts in the field, and how this plays out in representations of computing in popular media in the USA.
- To gain understanding from a global perspective of how access to computing resources, attitudes to computing, and participation in the field are subject to cultural factors including how the field is represented.
- To practice and experience teamwork, collaboration and teaching, and to engage in cross-disciplinary debate.
- To design and implement an outreach presentation aimed at broadening the images of computing.

Ultimately, the course also aims to engage students in the following questions: a) by understanding and broadening the images of computing can we help broaden participation? and b) why might this be beneficial to the field of computing and the nation as a whole?

3. COURSE PARTICIPANTS

This 6 unit elective[6] is open to undergraduates from all levels and all majors, although as one might expect most students are from the CS major. That said students from most schools across campus have participated including Humanities and Social Sciences, Engineering, Art, Science and Mathematics. We have found that the course works best with a mixture and balance of CS and non-CS majors. In this environment a range of perspectives and pre-conceived ideas about the field emerge to make discussions particularly interesting. The public perception of CS is often best articulated by non-CS majors, while CS majors do a good job of describing their field and of challenging and changing the perceptions of CS to non-CS students.

Each class runs for one hour and twenty minutes and meets twice a week over a 7 week period. The syllabus includes many in-class team/panel presentations and individual presentations. With this in mind it is not surprising that a small class size (16-18 students) appears to work best. As with any discussion-based course a small class size can also mean that all students get a chance to participate, to improve their public speaking skills and to feel included. This is particularly important if a student's class participation is included in their final grade.

The course has become increasingly popular and the waitlist has grown longer each year. Many students sign up out of strong interest and/or curiosity while some students are simply looking to fill course units for the second half of the semester. In 2009 the class size (even though still relatively small at 22 students) proved too unwieldy for the number of required presentations. At the same time class discussions were dominated by CS students who made up almost 70% of the class. By 2010 we limited the class size to 16 and, as in 2008, we were able to engineer a much better balance of CS and non-CS students. This situation meets the initial vision for the class structure and objectives.

The class has attracted students from all years but primarily sophomores through seniors. For the most part the class has had good gender balance with 29% women in the 2008 class, 36% women in the 2009 class and 44% women in the 2010 class. The class has also consistently attracted a good number of non-US born students from among the many international students that we have at CMU. Discussions in such a diverse atmosphere have proved favorable for developing students' understanding of what we mean by culture and different cultural values and expectations – concepts which are fundamental to the course.

4. COURSE DESCRIPTION

Figure 1. Image from "Take on Orbitz " T.V. Ad (2005)[7]

In this research and action based course we use the term "images" to refer to almost any text which carries meaning related to computing (however loosely or deliberately) and which can impact perceptions both of the field and those who work in it. Using images of computing as a focal point provides an ideal vehicle for examining the broader issues surrounding the field and for showing that images of computing can contribute to how the field is understood. CS is often crudely represented in the public domain and poorly understood outside of the CS community and even there CS professionals struggle to define this ubiquitous discipline. Limited understanding and exposure to the realities of CS leave the field open to the perpetuation of stereotypes and

[6] The majority of undergraduate full-semester courses at CMU are worth 12 units while most minis earn 6 units -- one unit being equivalent to one work hour, in class and homework.

[7] See http://pressroom.orbitz.com/index.php?s=43&item=236

misunderstanding. This is epitomized in an old "Take on Orbitz" commercial (see Figure 1.) which featured two male opponents, one a busy but clearly loving, friendly father complete with several happy, active kids, the other a single computer scientist. They were paired off in a "humorous" sketch to see who could get the best vacation package in the shortest time. The busy well-rounded father won. By using Orbitz.com, or so the message goes, using the computer becomes quick and simple for any user, regardless of distractions. On one hand the viewer sees a progressive/young image in the father-plus-happy-children representation. At the other extreme, we see the stereotypical image of the computer scientist as an isolated, nerdy looking, somewhat incompetent figure. At the same time the notion that the computer scientist should be set up as an expert at searching the web suggests a very odd and limited view of CS. All in all, the advertisement takes advantage of, and perpetuates, the negative stereotypes and lack of understanding that surround the field and the people in it. The irony, of course, is that Orbitz is a product of modern computer science.

So we see that misleading images of computing apply not only to the familiar geeky images but also to the field itself. One of the fundamental misconceptions is that CS equals programming and/or office applications. The content of many advanced CS courses in high school could easily suggest that CS *is* programming. Alternatively, many K-12 students in the USA are simply denied exposure to any CS courses – CS not being on the standardized national curriculum. This situation has become increasingly critical, indeed the ACM recently announced the introduction of the *Computer Science Education Act,* a new measure to address the crisis in K-12 computer science education.[8] Thus, many smart high school students are either missing out or may not be excited by a future in programming. [3]

Figure 2. Images of computers and computing have "evolved" into humorous graphics on t-shirts.[9]

We use academic papers, web sites, media texts, videos, personal testimony, group discussion and interviews to examine the above mentioned issues trying to understand how cultural images, attitudes and access to resources can impact participation in computing. We use our findings to build an action component in which student teams develop and implement a public presentation aimed at broadening understanding of computing. Students' own understanding of these issues is further enhanced by the section on computing in other cultures.

[8] For more on this see ACM's news release: http://www.acm.org/press-room/news-releases/2010/cs-ed-act

[9] Image at www.scs.sk.ca/cyber/blog/evolutio.jpg

4.1 Introduction and Overview, Issues and Definitions

Figure 3. Gamer as portrayed in TV's Southpark show[10]

We begin this 4 part course by exploring the meaning of culture, the role of images in determining the public understanding of computing, and definitions of computing and computer science. We look to cultural studies and Raymond Williams in particular, for useful definitions of culture. [18] For an understanding of how meaning is produced through the interplay of images and viewers we look to the work of philosopher Roland Barthes. [2] We also examine how the "same" image can produce different messages. Students describe their own definitions of computer science and also hear definitions from past CS seniors at CMU. We use both terms – computing and computer science – throughout the course and students are encouraged to think about their different and/or similar meanings and how they would explain them to various audiences. We turn to the Computing Curricular Reports for expert definitions of the 5 disciplines that make up the field of computing including computer science. [13] The ultimate aim of this discussion is *not* to define computer science but rather to expose students to the ongoing debate on *what is computer science?,* a debate which has engaged the SIGCSE community for several years. Discussions on broadening participation in CS in the USA are prompted after reading the perspectives of CS faculty Sanjeev Arora, Bernard Chazelle, Richard Ladner and Peter Lee. [1, 10, 11]

4.2 Participation in Computer Science and Images of the field (USA)

We examine and analyze images of computing throughout the entire course. Many researchers have concluded that stereotypical images, like the gamer from T.V.'s Southpark shown in Figure 3, frequently appear among the list of factors that deter some students from seeing themselves in the field[11]. Thus, in part two we pay close attention to the issue of participation in CS by asking if, and why, this matters and how this relates to images of the field.

We read and discuss arguments from different perspectives (the equity case, the academic case and the business case) that have been made to support broadening participation in CS. We look at data on participation in CS at the undergraduate level and at the

[10] http://blogs.courierpostonline.com/worldofwarcraft/files/2008/12/southpark_wow2.jpg

[11] Such researchers include (but are not limited to) Aspray, Blum, Borg, Camp, Cohoon, Cuny, Fisher, Frieze, Greening, Gurer, Keisler, Kuhn, Margolis, Schmidt, Spertus, Sproull, and Townsend.

K-12 level and compare projected CS Bachelors' production with projected jobs in the USA. [6, 14] And while the 2010 Taulbee survey notes a welcome upturn in applications to the CS major in the USA it is not yet clear if women and minorities are included in the good news. What the survey does tell us is that women represent only 11.3% of CS bachelor's recipients, African-Americans 3.4% and Hispanics 5.8% [6], at a time when they comprise 50.7%, 12.8% and 15.4% of the US population respectively. [17]

Data clearly indicate the low representation of women and minorities in CS and discussion centers around reasons why this might be. Students are encouraged to explore cultural factors and in particular to see factors *outside of gender* as contributing to participation in CS. While images are the primary focus throughout the course, we also discuss other cultural factors that would affect participation, such as different experiences, opportunities, mentors, expectations and levels of encouragement.

In this section we also look at myths and stereotypes and include readings and discussions of the work of Claude Steel and Margaret Shih on stereotype threat. [15, 16] We pay particular attention to how images of computing rely on myths and stereotypes – for better or worse – and how such images might work to include or exclude women and minorities and those men who might not see themselves as fitting the field.

4.3 Outreach and Broadening Understanding

Part three is the action component of the course. Students examine and discuss some current outreach efforts and assess their potential for providing new images of computing and for broadening understanding of CS. In particular students are exposed to the ideas presented in CSUnplugged [5] and cs4fn [4] which provide interesting material to ilustrate the concepts of computational thinking for young audiences. Discussions focus on creativity, on ideas and preparation for their own outreach efforts. Students are assigned to work in teams and are encouraged to choose a specific audience and venue for their outreach presentations.
Students are given the following guidelines:

- What is your goal?
- Who is your target audience?
- How will you make the presentation interactive?
- What materials/equipment will you use?
- How long should the presentation be?
- How will you measure impact?

Where time allows teams practice in class and receive feedback from their fellow classmates. They are all required to do at least one practice presentation with the course instructor.

4.4 A Global Perspective

In this final section students read and discuss a selection of research papers focusing on computing around the globe. Papers range from a study of women's participation in CS in Armenia, to CS education in China, to the representation of computing in Indian cinema. [9, 19, 12] In particular, by looking internationally at the different levels of participation of women in the field we can establish that the image of computing in some cultures is not as gendered as it is in the USA. We explore the different perceptions of CS in different cultures and countries. For example we can see how in some cultures CS is perceived as being closely related to math while in other cultures CS is perceived as being closely related to engineering. We discuss the implications of such different cultural perceptions. We also examine the relationship between computing, technology and developing nations where the images of computing can range from positive and aspirational to paternalistic and damaging.

5. ASSIGNMENTS AND GRADING

Students are graded primarily on the quality of their performance in 3 assignments – 2 individual assignments and one team assignment. The assignments constitute 80% (25%, 25%, and 30% each) of the final grade. Students are also expected to do a considerable amount of reading and to lead the discussions of particular research papers. In most cases this takes the form of a panel in which student teams initiate a debate on the paper. This component along with attendance and participation accounts for the rest of the grade, i.e. 20%.

Assignment 1: This assignment has taken two formats: a) interviews and b) researching images. In the former a) (given in 2008 and 2009) students were required to interview a CS faculty, or industry researcher/engineer, to find out firsthand about their self-image, their day-to day work, and general computing company/department culture. Each interview transcript was accompanied by a report comparing expectations with interview findings along with comments on ways in which findings challenge and/or support popular images of computing professionals. In 2010 this first assignment was changed to researching images of computing in the USA in popular media: e.g. online sites, television, games, books, journals and magazines, etc. The goal is to identify an image which could have broad appeal and one which might not. The assignment also includes a short paper and a "show and tell" presentation on the chosen images.

Figure 4. Students Present at Take Your Child To Work Day

Assignment 2: For this assignment students work in small (mixed gender) teams on an outreach component in which each team prepares and implements a presentation at a local venue, or on campus, with the goal of showing the breadth of computing and the potential for diversity. For example, students use introductions of themselves to show that computer science students have a range of backgrounds and interests. Where team members are not all CS majors they reach the same goal by asking audiences to guess their majors. Other outreach activities include robotics, cryptography, "magic" tricks, and algorithmic style problems and puzzles to encourage interaction and audience participation.

Assignment 3: For the final assignment students are required to write a 3-5 page research paper exploring attitudes to, and participation in, computing in a specific country, culture, or micro-culture. This assignment carries most weight because there is such a paucity of international data. Students are also given tips on writing a good research paper.

6. OUTCOME AND STUDENT FEEDBACK

Students have responded well to this course. Anonymous feedback from *informal* end-of-course surveys and the school's *formal* anonymous faculty course evaluations (FCEs) have been very positive. Many students have said how much they value the opportunities for teamwork and for improving their presentation and public speaking skills. FCE's ranged from "Interesting course, but it does squeeze a lot into a mini which can get a little confusing at times as the class structure jumps around a lot from writing papers, reading articles, presenting, etc." to "great experience with outreach. Excellent practice for presentations and stimulating class discussions" and "a lot of hands-on work made it very enjoyable and informative".

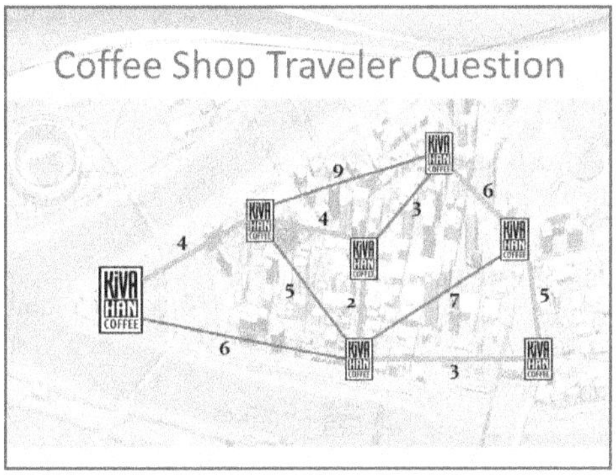

Figure 5. Slide from Student Outreach Presentation

Early in the course, during a class which focused on definitions, two CS seniors mentioned that this was the first time in the CS major that they had actually thought about what computer science means. This was echoed in this student's feedback response to the question *what new ideas did you learn in this class?:* "This was the first class after 3 years as a CS major that tried to define CS! THANK YOU!"

Students had very little idea about the ups and downs of CS enrollments. Most appeared to have a good sense of how CS and computing professionals were narrowly perceived by the general public but it was often left to the non-CS students to describe just how poorly understood the field is generally.

The gender gap in CS enrollments was also a new issue for most students. However, students raised in countries where women are well represented in CS were quick to bring this fact to the attention of the class promoting the point that the level of women's participation in CS is largely a cultural issue. Arguments for gender differences (in characteristics, attitudes and abilities) as a cause for the low participation of women in CS in the USA have generally been argued as *untenable* since from their experiences at CMU students have seen both men and women fitting the field.

Students were quick to recognize a possible connection between participation in CS and how the field is represented in the popular media. They soon discovered that images of computing were for the most part either absent or negative. Some students had difficulty in discerning whether or not an image had broad appeal, thus recognizing that many images are not easily categorized. By the time they were reading about the global situation students seemed comfortable in doing basic cultural analysis. However, each year this final section has been the weakest section of the course largely due to poor time management. Not surprisingly writing the final papers was noted as the *least* favorite part of the course and students have often ended up using online blogs and news sites as sources rather than research papers.

In 2010 time management was still an issue even though attempts were made to find more space for the global studies section. The first assignment, for example, was changed from having students conduct interviews to researching images of computing. While the interviews turned out to be very interesting the time spent on them, along with having to meet IRB requirements, proved too demanding for a mini course, although this assignment would work well in a full 12 unit course. Researching images proved to be a very successful change and it was surprising to see few duplications in the images chosen and discussed by individual students. Most images came from TV advertising of computing related products. Figure 6, for example, is from a series of Intel television commercials – these provoked disagreement among students in terms of whether or not the images had broad appeal. Other images came from movies featuring gamers or geeky characters. Students overwhelmingly agreed that it was much harder to find images with broad appeal than to find images which presented a narrow view of computing. This research activity showed a very real need for changing the images of computing to encourage broader representations of the field.

Figure 6. 'Our Jokes Aren't Like Your Jokes' Intel Commercial[12]

The outreach assignments were particularly well done and clearly the students enjoyed presenting the field in a fun and exciting way to their audiences. It seemed clear, however, that they could use more guidance in how to work in teams. The most popular strategy involved each student individually contributing several slides which were then put into one final presentation. But even students who were fairly reticent in class showed a flair for presenting CS to young audiences. Most presentations were designed and implemented for K-12 audiences taking advantage of Take Your Child to Work Day on campus and an after school technology program for middle school girls. Other audiences consisted of high school students who had been accepted in CS at

[12] 'Our Jokes Aren't Like Your Jokes' – 2010 Intel Sponsors of Tomorrow http://www.youtube.com/watch?v=e0FULHGwPkw

CMU, undergraduates from a variety of CMU majors, and even the random clientele of a local coffee shop.

All students said they would recommend the class to other students. Almost all said they would recommend the course to CS majors and about half said they would recommend the course to non-CS majors noting that "Other students would understand CS better after taking this course". Almost all students said that they felt comfortable expressing their views in class. For the majority of students the outreach presentation was their favorite part of the course even though it was time intensive. Several students said they thought the class should be a full length course. Most students indicated that the course had met its goals i.e. it challenged them to re-think their ideas about the images of computer science, what we mean by computer science, the reasons for participation in the field, and what we mean by culture and cultural assumptions. One student summed up the course in this way: "How to think about how other people think about CS".

7. SUMMARY

The predictions of the ItiCSE working group have played out over the past ten years as the fields of computing have been immersed in issues of national and international concern, ranging from the fear of jobs being outsourced and declining enrollments (especially among women and minorities), to the future and safety of the internet. The course described in this paper, "Understanding and Broadening the Images of Computing", uses the images of computing as a thought provoking vehicle for engaging students in the broader issues that surround the field. The course has been well received by undergraduates and the numbers of students interested in taking the class has increased quite dramatically. Revisions of the course will be ongoing as new material comes to light and time management improves.

For both CS and non-CS majors the opportunity to explore what we mean by computing and computer science and how the discipline is perceived and represented helps develop their critical thinking skills and broadens their own understanding. This computer science major noted: "I felt that this course helped me understand a lot about my major from an entirely new angle – how computer science is perceived from a cultural perspective". By coupling this new understanding with the task of designing and implementing an outreach presentation reinforces what they have learned and helps them imagine the field outside of the classroom. One student said the course helped her "to break down the complex language of CS and present it to a non-CS related audience". This is a challenge for us all; indeed, ongoing discussions on the SIGCSE d-list indicate the need to pay attention to what we mean by computer science and computing and to how the field is understood within and beyond the CS community. If computer science is to be a highly valued discipline contributing to the future of the nation we need to pay attention to how the field is represented and perceived. In an image based culture understanding and broadening the images of computing is no trivial matter.

More information about this course can be found at http://www.cs.cmu.edu/~cfrieze/courses/index.html

8. REFERENCES

[1] S. Arora and B. Chazelle. 2005. Is the Thrill Gone? In Communications of the ACM 48, 31-33.

[2] Roland Barthes. 1977. Selections from Rhetoric of the Image. In *Image, music, text.* Hill and Wang.

[3] L. Blum, C. Frieze, O. Hazzan and M.B. Dias. 2007. A Cultural Perspective on Gender Diversity in Computing. In *Reconfiguring the Firewall: Recruiting Women to Information Technology across Cultures and Continents* eds. Carol J. Burger, Elizabeth G. Creamer, and Peggy S. Meszaros, AK Peters, Ltd.

[4] Computer Science for Fun Cs4fn http://www.cs4fn.org/

[5] Computer Science Unplugged http://csunplugged.org/

[6] CRA Taulbee Surveys: http://www.cra.org/resources/taulbee/

[7] J. Currie Little, M. Granger, E. S. Adams, J. Holvikivi, S. Lippert, H. M. Walker and A. Young. 2001. Integrating Cultural Issues into the Computer and Information Technology Curriculum. In Proceedings of the ITiCSE-WGR '00 Working group reports from ITiCSE on Innovation and technology in computer science education. ACM

[8] C. Frieze and E. Treat. 2006. Diversifying the Images of Computer Science: Carnegie Mellon Students Take on the Challenge! In Proceedings of the 2006 WEPAN conference

[9] H. Gharibyan and S. Gunsaulus. 2006. Gender Gap in Computer Science Does Not Exist in One Former Soviet Republic: Results of a Study. ITiCSE'06, ACM June 26–28.

[10] Richard Ladner. 2009. Broadening Participation. In Communications of the ACM, Vol.52, No. 12.

[11] Peter Lee. 2004. Shrinking Pipeline. blog. http://www.cs.cmu.edu/~cfrieze/courses/Lee_ShrinkingPipeline.pdf

[12] Joyojeet Pal. 2010. Of mouse and men: Computers and geeks as cinematic icons in the age of ICTD. In iConference 2010 Conference Proceedings.

[13] The Joint Task Force for Computing Curricula. 2005. Selections from: Computing Curricular Report. ACM and IEEE

[14] The Computing Community Consortium. 2010. Where the jobs are. CCC Blog.

[15] Claude Steele. 1997. A Threat in the Air: How Stereotypes Shape Intellectual Identity and Performance. In *American Psychologist.* Volume: 52. Issue: 6. Page Number: 613.

[16] M. Shih, T. Pettinsky and A. Trahan. 2005. Domain Specific Effects of Stereotypes on Performance. In Faculty Research Working Papers Series, Harvard School of Government.

[17] US Census Bureau Quick Facts http://quickfacts.census.gov/qfd/states/00000.html

[18] Raymond Williams. 1958. Culture is Ordinary, originally published in N. McKenzie (ed.), *Convictions.*

[19] M. Zhang and V.M. Lo. 2010. Undergraduate Computer Science Education in China. In Proceedings of SIGCSE'10, ACM.

On the Design of an Educational Infrastructure for the Blind and Visually Impaired in Computer Science

Andreas Stefik
Department of Computer Science
Southern Illinois University Edwardsville
Edwardsville, IL 62026-1656
stefika@gmail.com

Christopher Hundhausen
School of Electrical Engineering and Computer Science
Washington State University
Pullman, WA 99164-2752
hundhaus@wsu.edu

Derrick Smith
Department of Education
University of Alabama in Huntsville
Huntsville, AL 35899
derrick.smith@uah.edu

ABSTRACT

The blind and visually impaired community is significantly underrepresented in computer science. Students who wish to enter the discipline must overcome significant technological and educational barriers to succeed. In an attempt to help this population, we are engaged in a three-year research project to build an educational infrastructure for blind and visually impaired middle and high school students. Our primary research goal is to begin forging a multi-sensory educational infrastructure for the blind across the United States. We present here two preliminary results from this research: 1) a new auditory programming environment called Sodbeans, a programming language called Hop, and a multi-sensory (sound and touch) curriculum, and 2) an empirical study of our first summer workshop with the blind students. Results show that students reported a significant increase in programming self-efficacy after participating in our camp.

Categories and Subject Descriptors

K.3.2 [**Computer and Information Science Education**]; K.4.2 [**Social Issues**]: Assistive Technologies for persons with disabilities

General Terms

Design, Human Factors, Experimentation

Keywords

Accessibility, Visual Impairments, Auditory Debugging, Assistive Technology

1. INTRODUCTION

Blind and visually impaired students have few pathways for entering the computing profession. Successful students and professionals in this community are predominately self taught and have often overcome significant technical and practical barriers. While much work has been dedicated to helping the blind use various computer technologies, more research is needed on finding ways to make it easier for blind users to obtain high-paying and meaningful careers. While computing is potentially appealing as a career option due to its rich sound and tactile facilities, no standardized educational infrastructure exists to help these students succeed. Indeed, with 61% of working adults (aged 16 to 64) with vision loss out of the work force [1], and with households that include a blind member having a significantly higher rate of poverty [16], creating more opportunities for this group of individuals is sorely needed.

Our research attempts to address a broad research challenge: to build a multi-sensory educational infrastructure for the blind and visually impaired across the United States, and to broaden participation from this community in the computing discipline. This is particularly challenging for at least two reasons. First, modern programming environments are quite inaccessibile to the the blind and visually impaired. For example, when the screen reader JAWS® 11 is coupled with Visual Studio® 2010, no sound is generated when the user switches between tabs; a graphical window appears, but JAWS®does not speak. Further, the debugger in Visual Studio®outputs only the key pressed while stepping into or over (e.g., "F11, F11, F11, F11."). To address this problem, we have collaborated with developers at Oracle to develop Sodbeans, a computer programming environment built into NetBeans 6.9. Sodbeans includes a custom screen reader, talking debugger (e.g., "a to 5"), and programming language called Hop. Elements of our tools have been iteratively refined in formal empirical studies for nearly five years [15]. Second, existing programming curricula were not written with the blind and visually impaired in mind, relying heavily upon visual representations to teach key concepts. In contrast, we have opted to build a curriculum tailored to this population's unique needs. As is commonly done in schools for the blind and visually impaired, we have developed learning activities that make extensive use of tactile manipulative objects to teach computing concepts.

This paper presents two primary contributions toward the broad challenge of building an educational infrastructure for the blind and visually impaired. First, we introduce a new auditory programming environment called Sodbeans, a programming language called Hop, and multi-sensory (sound and touch) curriculum that will be used at five schools for

SIGCSE'11, March 9–12, 2011, Dallas, Texas, USA.

the blind over the next three years. Second, we present the results of an empirical study of our first summer programming camp, which introduced computer programming to blind high school students over a three-day period. Results from this preliminary study show that students reported a significant increase in programming self-efficacy through participating in the camp. Our research project constitutes the first large-scale attempt to develop an educational pipeline specifically designed for blind and visually impaired users to enter the computing discipline.

The remainder of this paper is organized as follows. We begin with related work in Section 2 and discuss our educational infrastructure in more detail in Section 3. After presenting an empirical study of our first workshop in Section 4, we present our summary and future work.

2. RELATED WORK

While there is a rich legacy of work in auditory display (using sound to convey information), and an extensive literature regarding how to make programming easier for novices, there is relatively little work on programming blind or with audio. In this section, we present related research on the following topics: 1) programming blind, 2) auditory display, and 3) novice and end-user programming. Perhaps the most well known work on programming blind was conducted by Smith et al. [13]. In this work, Smith noticed that blind students tended to have difficulty in courses like data structures, which often rely extensively on visual representations. Moreover, this work provided some pertinent observations on how blind students program. Notably, Smith coined the "Where am I?" problem, the idea that when programming blind, the need to determine one's location (e.g., in an editor, during an execution, general context of use), is crucial.

More recently, Bigham et al. used instant messaging chatbots to inspire blind individuals to enter computer science as part of the National Federation for the Blind's Youth Slam program [3]. Students used off-the-shelf-technologies (The JAWS screen reader and TextPad 4.73), which works well for basic text editing. In contrast, while our tools are compatible with JAWS and other screen readers, we have built our own programming language, compiler, debugger, and supporting auditory technologies, which aurally narrate programming sessions. Our tools are publicly available on sourceforge.net (search for Sodbeans).

Sánchez and Flores [12] created a custom programming language called APL (auditory programming language), which was designed for the blind. APL was tested with the blind population, but supplied a limited set of commands for a blind person to use, making it difficult to scale such tools to a general programming curriculum such as the one we are developing. Since our tools are based on NetBeans, students have a rich set of programming environments and tools they can use in our program (e.g., Java, PHP, Ruby), although our talking debugger is only available for our language: Hop.

The use of auditory technologies in programming is not new. Boardman [4] created LISTEN to explore mappings between source code and sound. Similarly to LISTEN, our tools use a code-to-audio mapping architecture, which is integrated with our compiler, debugger, and virtual machine. However, LISTEN focused on facilitating code-to-audio mappings, not on the design of specific applications, like blind programming environments. Brown and Hershberger [5] augmented algorithm animations in their Zeus system with "algorithm auralizations." Their musical auditory displays mapped higher-pitched tones to larger magnitude data in the algorithms being auralized. Brown and Hershberger claimed that their auditory displays assisted in the comprehension of the algorithms; however, they did not carry out any empirical evaluations to test these claims.

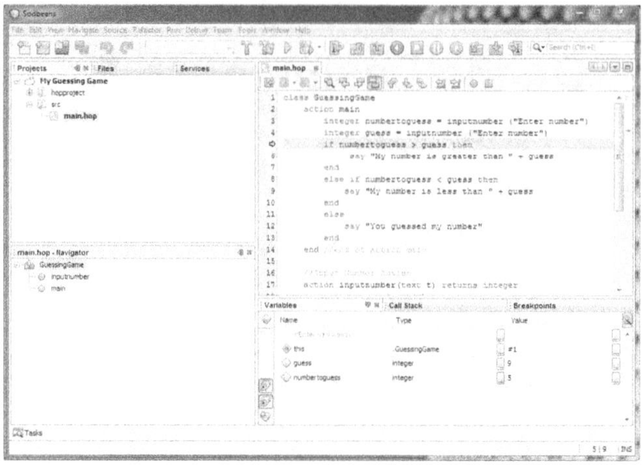

Figure 1: Snapshot of Sodbeans.

Several authors have promoted the specific use of *musical* cues as auditory representations of computer source code. Vickers [17], for example, built a program auralization system called CAITLIN, which used musical auditory cues to represent the execution of computer programs written in Pascal. In experimental studies, Vickers failed to show that participants could find more bugs with musical cues, although he claimed to have found that the effectiveness of the musical cues increased with the cyclomatic complexity of the source code. Subsequent work has shown that musical auditory cues are, in fact, difficult to learn [10].

Finally, there is a rich legacy of research into novice programming environments (see Kelleher and Pausch [7] for an excellent overview). Within this large body of work, some of the themes that resonate with our work are studying programming practices of novices using traditional languages [14], trying to find "natural" ways of programming [9], and the use of multimedia and graphics in programming [6]. Our work is similar in the sense that we have conducted formal studies on our environment as a multimedia novice environment and have completed formal studies on the efficacy of the words chosen in our programming language [15], to try to make the language easier to understand.

3. EDUCATIONAL INFRASTRUCTURE

We are working toward a *broad research challenge*: to *create* a multi-sensory educational infrastructure for the blind and visually impaired and to implement it widely, so as to *broaden* the participation of this community in the computing discipline. Our preliminary approach toward this challenge has three primary components: 1) Technology creation, 2) curriculum development, and 3) infrastructure.

3.1 Technology Creation

We are developing a programming environment for the blind called Sodbeans, shown in Figure 1. Recognizing the difficulty of describing auditory user interfaces in written

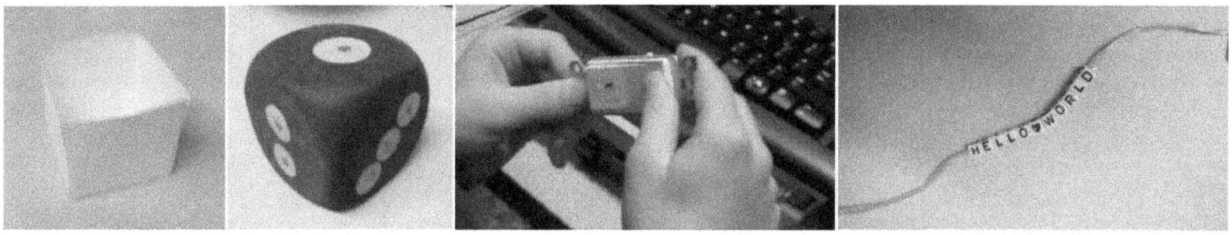

Figure 2: Manipulatives for teaching programming concepts, representing (a) a variable as a box; (b) a numeric value as a die; (c) a Boolean value as a light switch; (d) a string value as a string of beads.

prose, a blind user interacts with our environment similarly to how they would using a screen reader, with the exception that we "take over" the screen reader, on occasion, to supplement or replace the information that it provides. For example, if a user installs Sodbeans on Windows, and that user has JAWS®installed, we ask JAWS®to speak additional words and phrases designed for our language (e.g., information about the execution of a program in the debugger or text editor). If, however, a blind user does not own a screen reader, Sodbeans has an optional, and free, drop-in screen reader replacement that starts up automatically.

In contrast to modern screen readers, this "take over" process works through what we call a *push* accessibility model. For example, when JAWS®attempts to read the screen, it *pulls* information from an accessibility API (if one exists), for that environment and attempts to aurally present information to the user. Unfortunately, such APIs are often poorly maintained by corporations, as they are not particularly flashy or profitable. In our approach, we integrate deeply into the listener architecture in NetBeans, allowing us to *push* appropriate information to a screen reader, without reliance upon such APIs. This gives us significant freedom in how we approach accessibility internally, and has made it much easier to build tools like talking debuggers.

Sodbeans includes a custom virtual machine, compiler, and debugger for the Hop programming language. To give an example of how this works, suppose the Hop auditory debugger executes the line of code `integer a = a + 1`. In this case, the debugger would say "a to 5" (or another value). Similarly, if the user executes an `if` statement, like `if a < b then end` (the `then` and `end` statements serve as a block in Hop), the debugger would say either "if true" or "if false." The auditory cues we are using, and the syntax and semantics in Hop, have been carefully selected and chosen in formal empirical studies. For example, we use the word `repeat` over `for` and `while`, or `cycle` (see e.g., Sánchez and Flores [12]), because a recent study showed that the word `repeat` represents the concept of iteration significantly better than these words [15]. The full documentation for our language and environment is available in our online wiki at `https://sourceforge.net/apps/trac/sodbeans/`.

Our previous work on the design of auditory cues includes complex statistical analysis and formal studies [15]. We offer here a condensed overview of the results of our empirical observations related to how we design our auditory cues. Generally, we think that *good* auditory cues follow a pattern similar to the following: 1) they are short, 2) they are "browsable," and 3) the most important information comes first. First, auditory users rarely want to listen to lengthy cues, and we would encourage cue designers to remove extraneous words. Second, users interacting with our auditory debugger have a tendency to press the debugger keys (e.g., step over, step into) rapidly, which means that users often hear only the first few milliseconds of an auditory cue before moving on to the next. As such, an auditory cue like "variable a set to 5" is inferior to "a to 5," as a user browsing with the former could hear "va, va, va, va, va (the first part of the word variable)," which has little meaning for browsing. We *suspect* such cues make it more difficult for users to answer Smith et al. [13]'s classic question: "Where am I?"

Finally, sometimes an auditory cue must accommodate complex information, an example of which is in the use of "meta-auditory cues." A meta-auditory cue supplements another cue. For example, NetBeans 6.9 uses visual display information called *editor hints*, which try to help a user determine information about their code (e.g., a yellow lightbulb on the left gutter of an editor, a red underline for a compiler error). This kind of information can potentially be embedded into auditory cues as well, but we have observed that such information can get in the way if presented first. For example, a cue like "integer a = 5x; compiler error" appears to be more usable in practice than "compiler error, integer a = 5x;" as the former is more browsable and gives the most pertinent information immediately, allowing a user to easily skip over the meta-auditory cue.

3.2 Computer Programming Curriculum

We are developing a custom computer programming curriculum specifically tailored for the blind and visually-impaired. In order to provide an empirical foundation for this curriculum, we conducted a field study at the Washington State School for the Blind in the summer of 2010. While there, we interviewed two instructors and observed several classes. Our observations and interviews yielded three key and unexpected requirements for a programming curriculum to be used at a school for the blind: 1) introduce concepts, whenever possible, through the use of manipulative objects that students can touch, 2) favor hands-on activities and projects over lecturing, which is virtually non-existent, and 3) since students work at varied paces and most teaching is done one-on-one, provide a rich array of projects and activities that students can work on at their own pace.

In order to address (1), we have created a suite of manipulative objects to help students learn programming concepts. For example, Figure 2 presents examples of manipulatives we have prototyped for teaching variables and variable values. In order to address (2) and (3), our curriculum stresses hands-on activities, programming projects, and discussions over lectures. A typical class might begin with a hands-on activity involving manipulatives, in order to help students initially explore the concept being taught. Following that, students might open up Sodbeans, load some starter code, and modify it to meet a set of specifications. As students do this, one or more teachers circulates, helping students as needed. Students who work at a faster pace could move on to more advanced projects when they were ready. As students finished projects, they would be given the opportunity to "play" them to the class for feedback and discussion. At our summer 2010 programming camp (see Section 4), we piloted this style of curriculum, with encouraging results.

3.3 Infrastructure

Blind and visually impaired students at schools for the blind generally have few avenues for learning programming. While schools for the blind have expertise in working with blind children, expertise in computer programming is rare. Of our five partner schools for the blind in Washington, Texas, Indiana, Tennessee, and Massachusetts, none reports having a state-approved curriculum for blind students to learn to program, and most teach a curriculum more akin to basic computer skills (e.g., screen reader or keyboarding skills). A state-approved curriculum for middle and high school blind students to learn to program is sorely needed.

We are working with partners to build up an infrastructure for blind children to learn computing. This includes obtaining government approval in our partner states, training teachers from each school on how to program (blind), and creating a support network for all stakeholders involved. Our support network includes the use of 1) our community driven Sodbeans documentation, 2) mailing lists for the project for teachers, students, and developers, 3) a Sodbeans web portal with information on the project and how to get in touch with our team, and 4) a concerted effort to foster a community of like-minded individuals interested in improving the educational infrastructure for the blind. We encourage any group interested in this population to freely use our materials and tools or to work with us to establish an infrastructure for blind students in your local area.

4. EMPIRICAL STUDY

We conducted an empirical study as part of our first annual summer camp, which had the goal of introducing blind students to computer programming. Our empirical study associated with this camp had two research goals: RG1) to obtain insight into student interests and motivations in coming to and participating in a programming workshop, RG2) to determine whether the students felt confident about their ability to engage in computer programming (programming self-efficacy) and to determine whether our workshop might help improve students' programming self-efficacy. While the results in this section should be considered preliminary, we hope the data will provide some insight into how blind children view and consider topics like computer programming.

4.1 Participants

We recruited twelve legally blind students for our first workshop from Washington and Oregon. Students ranged from 13 to 18 years old (M=15.75). Of these students, six reported total blindness, while six reported low visual acuity. Of those with residual vision, the student with the highest visual acuity was rated at 20/300, while the lowest was approximately 20/2200-2400. Students who attended the conference were required to have previously taken at least pre-algebra, although in practice all but one had taken algebra I or higher. The student with the highest previous math experience had taken trigonometry. All students had taken courses in computing, but two students had taken courses in web site design and one had taken a course in computer programming, self reporting some experience in both python and C.

To help determine the experience level each student had with various technologies, we asked participants a series of questions regarding technological usage and experience. Students self-reported on a 1-7 Likert scale high experience with screen readers (M=5.58, SD=1.68), low experience with screen magnifiers (M = 2.833, SD=2.17), moderate experience with embossers (M = 3.875, SD = 2.02), very high experience with personal digital assistants like BrailleNotes designed for the blind (M = 6.33, SD = .99), moderate/high experience with talking books (M = 4.91, SD = 2.5), and high experience with the Perkins Brailler (M = 5.67, SD = 2.27). Students also rated themselves in the use of the Internet (M = 5.375, SD = 1.4) word processing applications (M = 5.33, SD = .89), spreadsheets (M = 2.75 ,SD = 1.49), presentations (M = 3.58, SD = 1.78), online games (M = 3.125, SD= 2.05), web design (M = 2, SD = 1.13), and computer programming (M = 1.875, SD = 1.13).

4.2 Materials and Tasks

We examined whether students with blindness or visual impairments (N =12) ratings on a measure of self-efficacy by Askar and Davenport [2] would change after exposure to a three-day camp in which students used Sodbeans. In addition, we used a scale by Pintrich et al. [11] to measure students' perceptions of 1) Task Value, 2) Self-Efficacy, 3) Critical Thinking, 4) Peer Learning, 5) Task Goal Orientation, 6) Performance—Approach, 7) Performance—Avoidance, 8) Connectedness, and 9) Learning. Students completed all of these 1- 7 point Likert scales at the beginning and conclusion of the workshop. For the Askar and Davenport scale, which was originally designed to test programming self-efficacy in Java, we adapted it for use in our language, Hop. The adaptation was trivial, in that we literally replaced the word "Java" with the word "Hop" throughout. All surveys have been validated previously using standard factor analysis procedures (see e.g., Kline [8] for an introduction).

4.3 Procedure

Students arrived at the Washington State School for the blind on July 13th, 2010 in the afternoon. On arrival, students were first welcomed and parents or students signed appropriate informed consent forms. Once forms were signed, a member of our research group guided a student to a room where they were interviewed and given our surveys aurally. On the last day of the workshop, we repeated the procedure, interviewing and surveying the students a second time.

During our workshop, students participated in a series of activities. On day one, our teachers taught programming in two 1.5 hour sessions. Students in these sessions learned some of the syntax of the Hop programming language, how to use the auditory debugger, and how to write code that connects to their screen reader (e.g., a complete program in Hop to connect to a screen reader would be `say "Hello, World!"`). After our two programming sessions were complete, and students had been given lunch, they were brought back to listen to one of several guest speakers. Over the course of the workshop, we brought in 1) an auditory GPS and tactile maps researcher, 2) mechanical braille researchers, and 3) two professional blind programmers to talk to the students about obtaining a career in the computing industry. In sum, we attempted to *engage* students in programming activities, to *inspire* them to consider programming, and to *encourage* them that computer programming is possible as a blind or visually impaired person.

4.4 Results

To begin our analysis, we first used an omnibus repeated measures analysis of variance (ANOVA) with Trial (i.e., pre-test scale scores and post-test scale scores) and Scale (Task Value, Pintrich Self-Efficacy, Critical Thinking, Peer Learning, Task Goal Orientation, Performance —Approach, Performance —Avoidance, Connectedness, and Learning) as the two within-subjects factors. This test tells us whether there existed statistically significant differences in our data set as a whole. This analysis revealed statistically signifiant differences in the main effects for Trial, $F(1, 11) = 4.85, p = .05, \eta_p^2 = .306$, and Scale, $F(8, 88) = 6.66, p = .001, \eta_p^2 = .377$. These main effects were qualified by a statistically significant $Trial \times Scale$ interaction, $F(8, 88) = 3.24, p = .003, \eta_p^2 = .306$. Thus, some of our metrics showed a significant change in the beginning of our workshop compared to the end, but that others did not.

In order to explore differences with respect to specific attitudinal metrics, we performed follow-up repeated-measures ANOVAs. The means for each metric appear in Table 1, divided as a function of Trial (i.e., Pre-Workshop, Post-Workshop). Note that participants' ratings showed a non-significant (unreliable) decrease across time for all scales except Connectedness, which showed an equally unreliable increase. However, the Performance —Approach and Performance —Avoidance scales showed a significant decrease. We ran a separate repeated measures ANOVA for the the Askar and Davenport self-efficacy scale, which showed a significant positive difference with a large effect size, $F(1, 11) = 35.56, p = .001, \eta_p^2 = .764$. Finally, our results continue to hold even if a Bonferroni correction is applied, with the exception of Performance—Approach (it needed to reach $p < .005$ using this correction). In English, for those of our results that showed significant differences, they can be considered reliable even by very conservative estimates.

4.5 Discussion

Our observations suggest three primary results of participation in our workshop: students self reported a 1) significant increase in the Askar-Davenport self-efficacy scale, 2) significant decrease in performance—approach (e.g., I want to do better than other students in my class), and 3) a significant decrease in performance avoidance (e.g., An important reason I do my school work is so that I don't embarrass myself). We generally consider these results to be positive, as they appear to imply that students reported both a gain in self-confidence with programming and a decrease in worrying about their performance in comparison to their peers.

Notice, however, that our two self-efficacy ratings, both of which have been validated in the literature did not achieve the same result. The Pintrich scales shows a small non-significant drop in self-efficacy, while the Askar and Davenport scale shows a positive, significant, result, with an effect size that explains nearly 76.4% of the variance in the sample—an extremely large effect. How should we interpret such results? We speculate that these metrics are measuring different attributes. Consider for example, that the questions in the Pintrich self-efficacy scale are very general (e.g., I'm confident I can understand the basic concepts taught in this course), whereas the Askar self-efficacy scale is more focused on programming skills (e.g., I could write syntactically correct Hop statements), which is of more interest in our case, since we are focused on programming and computer science. We think that future designers of self-efficacy surveys should focus their attention on the external validity of such measures, as this would give the community a better idea of the real-world applicability of each.

5. SUMMARY AND FUTURE WORK

We are engaged in the first large-scale attempt to create a multi-sensory educational infrastructure for blind and visually impaired middle high schools students, starting with five schools for the blind throughout the U.S. We have made two primary contributions in this work: 1) an environment (Sodbeans), which includes auditory debuggers, a programming language (Hop), and a multi-sensory educational curriculum using tactile manipulatives, and 2) an empirical study of our first summer workshop working with the blind and visually impaired students at the Washington State School for the Blind. We are our encouraged that, despite a small sample size and only a few days with our population, we were able to show a significant increase in programming self-efficacy, which, perhaps, could help inspire students from this community to consider learning more about computing. Over the next three years, we are expanding our program to include more schools for the blind, are making regular upgrades and expansions to our software, and are working with local and state governments to approve a multi-sensory curriculum that can be put into practice.

6. ACKNOWLEDGMENTS

We would like to thank the contributors to the Sodbeans project for their help with creating our technology, including Melissa Stefik, Neelima Samsani, Andrew Hauck, Susanna Siebert, Kim Slattery, and Sina Bahram. Sarah Hawkinson and Jason Neufeld contributed to the design of the programming curriculum. We would also like to thank the Washington State School for the Blind, especially Dean Stenehjam and Sherry Haun. This work would also not have been possible without the extraordinary technical expertise of Tim Boudreau (Oracle) and Tom Wheeler (A NetBeans Platform expert). This work was funded by the National Science Foundation under grant no. (CNS-0940521).

7. REFERENCES

[1] American Foundation for the Blind. Interpreting BLS Employment Data. retrieved august 31, 2010, from `http://www.afb.org/Section.asp?SectionID=15&SubTopicID=177`, 2010.

[2] P. Askar and D. Davenport. An investigation of factors related to self efficacy for java programming among engineering students. *The Turkish Journal of Educational Technology*, 8(1):26–32, 2009.

[3] J. P. Bigham, M. B. Aller, J. T. Brudvik, J. O. Leung, L. A. Yazzolino, and R. E. Ladner. Inspiring blind high school students to pursue computer science with

Test	Example Item	pre	post	F	p	η_p^2
Task Value	I think I will be able to use what I learn in this course in other courses.	5.81 (1.08)	5.54 (1.23)	0.83	.38	0.70
Pintrich - Self-Efficacy	I'm confident I can understand the basic concepts taught in this course.	5.54 (.896)	5.42 (1.15)	0.27	0.61	0.102
Critical Thinking	I treat the course material as a starting point and try to develop my own ideas about it.	5.18 (1.05)	4.83 (1.29)	1.25	0.29	0.102
Peer Learning	When studying for this course, I often try to explain the material to a classmate or a friend.	4.56 (1.35)	4.33 (1.41)	0.53	0.48	0.46
Task Goals	I like school work that I'll learn from even if I make a lot of mistakes.	5.68 (.876)	5.57 (1.23)	0.46	0.51	0.40
Performance Approach	I want to do better than other students in my class.	4.50 (1.11)	3.57 (1.44)	11.09	0.007	0.502**
Performance Avoidance	An important reason I do my school work is so that I don't embarrass myself.	4.15 (1.30)	3.06 (1.44)	15.85	0.002	0.590**
Connectedness	I feel connected to others in this course.	4.86 (1.15)	5.08 (1.22)	0.66	0.44	0.056
Learning	I feel that I am encouraged to ask questions.	5.38 (.486)	5.30 (.689)	0.11	0.75	0.010
Askar - Self-Efficacy	I could write syntactically correct Hop statements.	3.178 (1.10)	4.04 (.884)	35.56	< 0.001	0.764 ***

Table 1: Summary table of the statistical results. All but the last metrics are from the Pintrich scale [11], with one example question for each factor. The last row gives an example question from the Askar-Davenport self-efficacy scale [2]. In the columns labeled pre and post, the first number is the mean and the second is the standard deviation. * = $p < .05$, ** = $p < .01$, *** = $p < .001$

instant messaging chatbots. In *SIGCSE '08: Proceedings of the 39th SIGCSE technical symposium on Computer science education*, pages 449–453, New York, NY, USA, 2008. ACM.

[4] D. B. Boardman, G. Greene, V. Khandelwal, and A. P. Mathur. Listen: A tool to investigate the use of sound for the analysis of program behavior. In *Computer Software and Applications Conference, 1995. COMPSAC 95. Proceedings., Nineteenth Annual International*, pages 184–189, Dallas, TX, 1995.

[5] M. H. Brown and J. Hershberger. Colour and sound in algorithm animation. In *Proceedings of the IEEE Workshop on Visual Languages*, pages 10–17, Los Alamitos, CA, 1991. IEEE Computer Society Press.

[6] C. D. Hundhausen, S. F. Farley, and J. L. Brown. Can direct manipulation lower the barriers to computer programming and promote transfer of training?: An experimental study. *ACM Trans. Comput.-Hum. Interact.*, 16(3):1–40, 2009.

[7] C. Kelleher and R. Pausch. Lowering the barriers to programming: A taxonomy of programming environments and languages for novice programmers. *ACM Comput. Surv.*, 37(2):83–137, 2005.

[8] P. Kline. *An Easy Guide to Factor Analysis.* Routledge, New York, NY, 2002.

[9] B. A. Myers, A. J. Ko, S. Y. Park, J. Stylos, T. D. LaToza, and J. Beaton. More natural end-user software engineering. In *WEUSE '08: Proceedings of the 4th international workshop on End-user software engineering*, pages 30–34, New York, NY, USA, 2008. ACM.

[10] D. K. Palladino and B. N. Walker. Learning rates for auditory menus enhanced with spearcons versus earcons. In *Proceedings of the 13th International Conference on Auditory Display*, pages 274–279, Montréal, Canada, june 2007.

[11] D. Pintrich, D. Smith, T. Garcia, and W. McKeachie. A manual for the use of the motivated strategies for learning questionnaire (technical report no. ncriptal-91-b-004). Technical report, National Center for Research to Improve Postsecondary Teaching and Learning, Ann Arbor, MI, 1991. Retrieved from `http://eric.ed.gov/ERICDocs/data/ericdocs2sql/content_storage_01/0000019b/80/23/3c/44.pdf`.

[12] J. Sánchez and F. Aguayo. Blind learners programming through audio. In *CHI '05: CHI '05 extended abstracts on Human factors in computing systems*, pages 1769–1772, New York, NY, USA, 2005. ACM.

[13] A. C. Smith, J. S. Cook, J. M. Francioni, A. Hossain, M. Anwar, and M. F. Rahman. Nonvisual tool for navigating hierarchical structures. In *The Tenth International ACM SIGACCESS Conference on Computers and Accessibility*, number 77-78, pages 133–139, New York, NY, 2004. ACM Press.

[14] E. Soloway, J. Bonar, and K. Ehrlich. Cognitive strategies and looping constructs: an empirical study. *Communications of the ACM*, 26(11):853–860, 1983.

[15] A. Stefik and E. Gellenbeck. Empirical studies on programming language stimuli. *Software Quality Journal*, In Print. Currently available in Online First format., 2010.

[16] U.S. Census Bureau. Disability and American Families: 2000. retrieved may 4, 2009, from `http://www.census.gov/prod/2005pubs/censr-23.pdf`, july 2005.

[17] P. Vickers and J. L. Alty. When bugs sing. *Interacting with Computers*, 14(6):793–819, 2002.

Enhancing Participation and Education in CS through Guided Research Projects in Underserved Communities

Yonina Cooper
Carnegie Mellon University in Qatar
P.O. Box 24866
Doha, Qatar
+974-4454-8641
yonina@cs.cmu.edu

M. Bernardine Dias
Carnegie Mellon University
5000 Forbes Avenue
Pittsburgh, PA 15213 USA
+1-412-268-9365
mbdias@cs.cmu.edu

Ermine A. Teves
Carnegie Mellon University
5000 Forbes Avenue
Pittsburgh, PA 15213 USA
+1-412-268-1289
eteves@cs.cmu.edu

Sarah Belousov
Carnegie Mellon University
5000 Forbes Avenue
Pittsburgh, PA 15213 USA
+1-412-268-7147
sarahtbw@ri.cmu.edu

M. Freddie Dias
Carnegie Mellon University
5000 Forbes Avenue
Pittsburgh, PA 15213 USA
+1-412-268-1289
mfdias@ri.cmu.edu

ABSTRACT
While the needs and applications for computing technology have been growing, the enrollment and interest in Computer Science (CS) at the university level has not been growing in proportion. Moreover, the increasing prevalence of globalization requires a new set of skills for future technology leaders. These skills include the ability to work well in multidisciplinary and globally distributed teams, cross cultural boundaries with ease, create innovative solutions for problems that arise in unfamiliar settings, and think outside the box to solve a variety of problems while building effectively upon related work in the literature. These changes are also reflected in the growing interest among youth in global issues and how we can make a difference in underserved communities. This paper reports on our experience in designing and deploying an innovative internship that addresses these issues and seeks to enhance participation and education in CS through guided research projects in underserved communities.

Categories and Subject Descriptors
K.3.2 [**Computers and Education**]: Computer and Information Science Education – *computer science education.*

General Terms: Design, Experimentation, Human Factors.

Keywords: Guided research, globally distributed team, interdisciplinary research, internship education, multidisciplinary team.

1. INTRODUCTION
The increasing prevalence of globalization in today's corporate culture demands a new set of skills for future leaders in technology. Students looking to pursue a career in the technology field now need to be able to work well in globally distributed teams that are diverse in cultural and professional backgrounds. In 2008, the TechBridgeWorld research group began designing and deploying an innovative internship that seeks to enhance participation and education in CS through guided research projects in underserved communities. The concept for this internship program developed from student interest in summer opportunities which combined research with impact in developing community settings. Students also desire global experiences which enhance their teamwork skills, provide them with ways to work with people from a variety of cultural, academic, and professional backgrounds, and prepare them for real-world problem-solving. Students seek such experiences to build relevant work skills particularly generally-useful skills for this age of globalization. These are the kind of experiences that future technology leaders seek when pursuing an education in CS and considering jobs post-graduation.

1.1 Related Work
The benefits of working in a research group, such as students developing domain expertise, gaining an understanding and appreciation of the research process and its practice, and acquiring team, communication, problem-solving, and higher-level thinking skills, are accepted within the university community and have been extensively reported in technical education conferences (e.g. [6], [9], [4]). Additionally research experiences enhance recruitment and retention of students in computer science ([3], [8], [2]). Interdisciplinary research ([4], [9]) and real-world problem research [1] have been reported for these purposes as well. Wenderholm [11] and Ward [10] have examined strategies for success in undertaking or building undergraduate research projects. Not only are these goals of the iSTEP program but also the larger task of introducing students to working in multidisciplinary and globally distributed teams to find innovative solutions to real-world problems. The value of

SIGCSE'11, March 9–12, 2011, Dallas, Texas, USA.

using such guided research (in physics) as a teaching methodology is presented in [5].

No literature was found that specifically addresses designing guided field research to be carried out by multidisciplinary, globally distribute teams. However the changing needs of industry due to globalization require technologists who have these additional skills to work across cultural and disciplinary boundaries and create innovative solutions that address a variety of real-world problems.

1.2 Contributions

The contributions of this paper are our internship model, deployment experience, and lessons learned. We first describe the components of the internship model created by TechBridgeWorld faculty and staff, followed by aspects of student preparation, needs assessment, technology, dissemination and team experience outcomes, and lessons learned from the first two years of the program. We conclude with a summary of the key points of the paper and a brief exploration of future work.

2. INTERNSHIP MODEL

In the summer of 2009, the TechBridgeWorld research group (http://www.techbridgeworld.org) in the School of Computer Science at Carnegie Mellon University launched a new internship program: iSTEP (innovative Student Technology ExPerience). iSTEP (www.techbridgeworld.org/istep). iSTEP provides Carnegie Mellon students and recent graduates from both the Pittsburgh and Doha campuses with an opportunity to work in a multidisciplinary and globally distributed team to develop needs-based computing solutions in collaboration with underserved communities. TechBridgeWorld's primary hypothesis is that the iSTEP internship will provide a unique educational opportunity that enhances the research, teamwork, creativity, and leadership skills of talented and motivated students while introducing them to the different ways in which technology can impact underserved communities. The iSTEP internship model is composed of several key elements designed to provide the interns with a rewarding experience while also positively impacting partner communities. The first important component is the active participation of the TechBridgeWorld team (faculty and staff) who identify partners, work with the partners to identify projects, select interns, invite relevant advisors, and work with the interns and partners to execute the projects. The community partners are the primary motivators for the projects, and the projects determine the required skills for the team of interns. We also select a group of advisors with expertise relevant to the projects and location. The interns are paid a stipend for their participation in the program. We feel this is important in order to attract the caliber of student needed for the projects.

2.1 Intern Selection Process

The selection process for the interns is another crucial component of the internship model. Partnerships and potential projects for the internship need to be identified almost a year before the internship starts and the interns have to be selected early enough so that there is time to prepare them prior to the internship. Information sessions are conducted for both graduate and undergraduate students to encourage applications to the program. The application process along with the requirements and selection criteria for the internship, the program application timeline, and information regarding the location, partners, projects and team roles are also posted on the iSTEP internship program website. The application consists of a series of questions that ask about the student's interest in and expectations of the program, about any relevant experiences they have had to contribute to the team's work, about the strengths they think they would bring to the team, and if they have any preferences for their project role or work location. The TechBridgeWorld team reviews all applications for the identified skill sets and identifies a top tier of finalist candidates for the program. These candidates are then individually interviewed by appropriate TechBridgeWorld members. All interviewers follow established interview procedures which include a standard set of questions for the respective positions on the internship team to guide each interview. Students must provide a set of references which are contacted. The culmination of this process is the formation of the iSTEP team for the next summer. Typically the partners and projects are determined in the previous summer, recruiting is conducted in the fall, and the team is chosen by the end of the fall.

The interns are selected to satisfy a diversity of skills. Key criteria for success in all the team roles are the willingness to work together as a team, willingness to work hard and be totally dedicated to the success of the team, ability to adapt to unforeseen and challenging situations, and ability to persevere and work towards success despite many challenges in living and working conditions. Field work in developing communities, especially when it involves technology, can be frustrating, very difficult, and even overwhelming at times, but in the end, the work is extremely rewarding and teaches the interns many important skills that will be useful in their future professional life.

2.2 The Team

The team of interns consists of several necessary roles. Key roles in the team are Technical Leads for each project, Technical Floater(s), a Needs Assessment Lead, and a Documentation Lead. The intern in the Needs Assessment Lead role will plan for and manage on-site relationships with partners as well as tasks such as explaining and obtaining consent forms from research participants and ensuring research compliance procedures are followed appropriately. The Technical Lead roles require the interns to manage and lead the design, implementation, and iterative enhancements to the technology solution for each project as well as participate in the needs assessment and dissemination tasks. The intern in the Documentation Lead role must effectively collaborate with all members of the team to capture the team's experiences and stories through video, photos, and text in a creative and compelling manner, and format this content for distribution to diverse audiences. The interns in the Technical Floater roles focus on technology development (predominantly software development and troubleshooting) under the direction of the Technical Leads. At least one Technical Floater is always stationed at "home base" at our Pittsburgh or Doha campus and thereby ensures that the team has access to all of the infrastructure and resources available on campus.

The iSTEP teams have been multidisciplinary teams consisting of undergraduate and graduate students from the different colleges within Carnegie Mellon. For example, the 2009 iSTEP team included members from the School of Computer Science, the College of Humanities and Social Sciences, and the College of Engineering while the 2010 team hailed from the School of

Business, School of Computer Science, the College of Humanities and Social Sciences, the School of Information Systems and Management, and the School of Public Policy and Management.

2.3 The Partners

Working with a community partner is imperative to selecting projects that are feasible, relevant, and significant to the community as well as sustainable. Extensive interactions – e.g. visits, correspondence, phone calls, and online chats – with potential partners precede finalization of a partnership agreement and identification of project areas. TechBridgeWorld fundraises to cover operational expenses of running the program, the interns' summer stipend and their international airfare and visa expenses. The partner provides local housing, local transportation and work space for the interns. Additionally the partners are instrumental in coordinating multiple other aspects of the partnership, for example assisting with travel visas, research permits, and residency permits, connecting with local organizations as field partners for specific projects, establishing housing and transportation support for interns, and liaising between TechBridgeWorld and any local officials and local students involved with the projects.

Partners are chosen based on their understanding of the local community needs, their leadership in the community, and their capability to sustain the projects locally. The primary partner for iSTEP 2009 in Tanzania was the University Computing Centre (UCC), a limited-liability company owned by the University of Dar es Salaam (UDSM). UCC provides information and communication technology (ICT) products to both the UDSM community and the general public (www.ucc.co.tz). The primary partner for iSTEP 2010 in Bangladesh was the Asian University for Women (AUW) located in Chittagong, Bangladesh (www.asian-university.org). AUW is a leading institution of higher education based on the firm belief that education—especially higher education—provides a critical pathway to leadership development, economic progress, and social and political equality. Both 2009 and 2010 partners were enthusiastic about local university students becoming more involved with technology development and research projects. The local students work as liaisons to the community partners, facilitating communication between stakeholders and translating between the local language and English. They contribute significantly to the needs assessment process and to the design and testing of the technology solutions.

2.4 Research Projects

The projects are chosen jointly by the partners and the TechBridgeWorld team, and determine the required skill sets that in turn influence the recruitment of the interns. The projects often have some overlap with current or past TechBridgeWorld projects so that some of the developed expertise translates to the new projects. In addition, the projects must be scoped to have a significant component that can be completed within a ten-week internship. Examples of projects we have undertaken in the iSTEP program are creating a mobile phone tool for use by para-social workers to track information on services provided to AIDS orphans and vulnerable children, creating culturally-relevant educational technology and games for child literacy, and customizing a low-cost Braille Writing Tutor for visually impaired students. While projects are scoped to a certain degree before the internship begins, the needs assessment process when the interns arrive on site is vital in order to ensure that the final outcomes of each of the projects is relevant and has a positive impact on the community.

2.5 Logistics

Maintaining a good working relationship with the primary partner organization is critical to the success of the internship. As a result, TechBridgeWorld staff meets weekly with the partner to discuss administrative, legal, and financial issues related to the internship. The weekly meetings typically last one hour and are conducted via phone or online chat at a time mutually convenient for both parties. The meetings provide our partner with an opportunity to voice any concerns and provide us with the opportunity to discuss any concerns related to the safety and well-being of the interns.

Equally important is ensuring the professional and personal well-being of the interns. Thus, weekly meetings are held usually via online voice chat with the iSTEP team to discuss work updates and other concerns. Chats with all of the team members, as a group, highlight areas needing better team coordination as well as any potential team tension. Chats with individual team members are also held to address individual concerns.

An important aspect of TechBridgeWorld's research philosophy is that the community partner invests significantly in the endeavor to ensure joint ownership and sustainability of outcomes. The primary investment that the community partners make for this internship model is to provide housing and local transportation for the iSTEP interns at no cost to the interns. For example, during the 2009 iSTEP internship, the interns resided in housing provided by the primary partner, two or three kilometers away from their workplace. Due to safety concerns, the interns were provided with transportation to and from the work location. In contrast, for the 2010 internship, the housing provided for the interns was on the site of the campus where they worked. In both cases, other transportation options were provided by the community partners as needed so that the interns and partners could conduct work at various field locations for the projects.

TechBridgeWorld provides guidance and feedback for every stage throughout the project including needs assessment, technology development, solution demonstrations, and project sustainability. A final presentation summarizing the interns' work is given to the partners along with a final report, which formally documents the experiences and outcomes of the internship. Letters and emails are sent to community partners to thank them for their time, resources, and cooperation and to discuss sustainability options for the projects. The final report is also typically published in the form of a technical report.

3. STUDENT PREPARATION

Since there is no assumption that the interns have relevant prior knowledge, a six-week long preparation course plus some additional preparation sessions have been designed to prepare the interns for their summer work. Specifically, faculty members take the lead on introducing students to good research practices, teamwork skills, and preparation for the project work, and also supervise the projects. Staff members take the lead on logistical, financial, and legal matters pertaining to the internship, and also participate in some of the technical planning and development.

The interns are also provided with an emergency number which they can call at any time of the day and any day of the week. This number forwards any phone calls to a member of TechBridgeWorld who is on call and different members of the team take turns being on call during the internship.

3.1 Preparation Course

All selected interns are required to complete a six-week course designed to teach students the practical skills necessary to conduct field research in the context of an underserved community. The course is taught during the first half of the spring semester, and meets for one hour, twice a week at a time convenient for both the Pittsburgh and Doha campuses. Videoconferencing technology allows iSTEP team members at the different campuses to participate in the course sessions. The course is also open to students who are not participating in the internship and to those who wish to apply to iSTEP in future years. Various speakers are invited to speak to students about topics such as background information on the country and culture of the specific location of that year's internship, challenges of research in low-resource environments, importance of project sustainability, understanding research requirements, and dissemination and marketing techniques. The course requires the interns to complete three significant group assignments: (1) a background research report on the iSTEP location to help the traveling team prepare for their work; (2) a work plan, which outlines the tasks for each of the team roles and for the team as a whole during the internship; and (3) a documentation and media plan. The interns then enroll in a six-week independent study course in the second half of the spring semester. This enables the interns to prepare independently for their specific team role.

3.2 Additional Preparation

In addition to the six-week course, the iSTEP interns participate in several other mandatory sessions. The team members traveling to the international location meets with the Study Abroad Coordinator from Carnegie Mellon's Office of International Education (OIE) to learn how to prepare for their travel. This presentation includes information on administrative procedures, health and safety, culture, and the importance of journaling and self reflection. The TechBridgeWorld team and the iSTEP interns also meet to discuss a variety of issues including travel, health, safety, research compliance procedures, logistics, and partner contacts. A reception is also hosted to provide an opportunity for the interns to meet with advisors. Additionally, the interns are provided with a medical kit to use in the case of illnesses, injuries, accidents, or emergencies.

4. OUTCOMES

Within the ten-week span of the internship, after the initial needs assessment, the iSTEP interns with the TechBridgeWorld team brainstorm possible solutions. At this phase, overextending is a possible pitfall and the team may need assistance in scoping a solution achievable in the ten-week timeframe. Typically the interns spend the first few weeks conducting needs assessment, they then spend a few weeks developing a prototype technology solution to address those needs, and then in the final weeks they run pilot field testing of the projects. The goal is to present the prototype to the partners and constituents in a timely manner so they can receive feedback and make modifications as needed as well as evaluate the solution. Thus far, the iSTEP interns have been able to implement prototype solutions for all projects and obtain initial feedback from the local partners.

Figure 1. Interns and users interacting with technology solutions in iSTEP 2009 and iSTEP 2010.

4.1 Needs Assessment

Although the projects are chosen to address needs identified by the community partners, the iSTEP research interns conduct a more detailed needs assessment to explore the feasibility of these projects and the features needed for each solution, prior to developing prototypes and field testing. As part of the preparatory course they conduct initial research to educate themselves on the challenges that the partner communities face. However, on-the-ground needs assessment remains an important factor for success. This process also teaches the interns valuable soft skills such as initiating, fostering and maintaining a direct line of communication with the various communities based on honesty, mutual respect, and trust. Understanding the needs of the various communities involved also ensures that the solutions created are practical, sustainable, and relevant.

The needs assessment process often involves individual as well as group interviews. These interviews frequently reveal issues that were not manifested in the preparatory research or communications prior to arrival on-site. Failure to address such issues will result in solutions which are not sustainable. Developing solutions that are viewed favorably by the end-users is equally important for sustainability. Guided by results from the initial needs assessment phase, as well as feedback from the partner organizations, the interns begin designing and developing relevant technology solutions.

4.2 Technology Outcomes

The technology outcomes of the internship are largely based on the combination of the project requirements and the skills of the interns. Therefore the outcomes vary depending on the projects and the teams. Two examples of project outcomes are described next for illustrative purposes.

The first example, from iSTEP 2009, is a project where the interns were aiming to improve the efficiency of reporting information from rural social workers to the national database for orphans and vulnerable children (OVC). Based on the needs assessment conducted by the 2009 team, the most cost-effective way to transfer information from the social workers in rural areas to the district level administration was through SMS (text messaging). The interns designed a solution that used a key code style format SMS message similar to that used by the LINKS [7] project which they discovered during their literature review. In this solution scenario, each social worker is given a small card, which contains all of the codes to be used in the SMS message. The social workers use these codes to transmit specific information about the AIDS orphans and vulnerable children (OVC) they are serving via SMS to a central server, where the information is automatically processed into the national database.

A second example, also from iSTEP 2009, was related to improving English literacy education at a primary school in Tanzania. Given the lack of electricity and the challenges of teaching English at this school, the interns chose to implement an English literacy game on a mobile phone platform. The implemented solution consists of two parts: (1) a quiz-based educational game that students can access via mobile phones and (2) an online content authoring tool for teachers to create new content that can be downloaded to the phones.

4.3 Dissemination

Another important aspect of the learning experience through the iSTEP internship is effective dissemination. Throughout the summer the interns document their work and stories from the field, reach out to media to promote the partnerships and projects, and create a final report and presentation. Initial planning and understanding of the purpose of the dissemination aspect of their experiences and outcomes begin in the six-week preparation course. Interns created websites in both years of the iSTEP internship to convey information about the internship, team, projects, and partners (http://istep2009.techbridgeworld.org and http://istep2010.techbridgeworld.org). Given the effectiveness and popularity of social media, the interns have also shared their experiences and outcomes through Facebook, Twitter, Flickr, YouTube, and blogs. TechBridgeWorld also facilitates interviews between interns and local media. The final report provides a more formal documentation of the internship experiences and outcomes and is published as a technical report. Finally, the students prepare and deliver a variety of presentations to disseminate their work. Through these different modalities, the interns learn effective means of dissemination to a variety of audiences.

4.4 Team Experience

A final key element of the internship is the experience of the interns. The multidisciplinary and globally distributed nature of the team allows iSTEP interns to draw on the different strengths of their teammates and take advantage of resources available in different geographic locations. The internship also gives the iSTEP interns the opportunity to positively impact several communities. One intern reflected, "Seldom does one get an internship experience that allows students to conduct research and find their own solutions to problems that positively impact developing communities in the world." Furthermore, iSTEP provides interns with the opportunity to interact directly with the people being impacted by the developed solutions. Another intern states, "Not many internships allow their participants to see how people interact with their work ... It completely changes the purpose of the work, to really know whom you're developing for and to really understand why your work is valuable."

The interns face many challenges and frustrations during the internship, mainly while they learn to deal with new environments and cultures. Furthermore, for most of the interns, this is their first experience conducting field research. "Field research, in my opinion, is a struggle. Field research involving people is even tougher. There are so many unknowns that it is impossible to anticipate everything." However, the interns learn to adapt over the course of the internship and gain new skills and knowledge in problem solving despite the challenges. As one intern recommends, "It's important to expect the unexpected and to react strategically and leverage my resources when those unexpected challenges arose." "Despite the challenges, I still see this field as something I'm passionate about and want to do further work in."

Figure 2. Interns from iSTEP 2009 and iSTEP 2010 interact with local community partners.

The interns also value and appreciate the importance of working closely with the communities. "Regardless of how wonderful and powerful the technology solution is, community involvement is the most important. Technology cannot overcome challenges on its own. Rather, the community and its people are the ones who can transform the technology into a solution."

5. LESSONS LEARNED

In this paper we have described our internship model for providing guided opportunities for students to engage in computing research in real-world settings. The model is successful based on currently obtainable indicators. Next, we highlight some of the important lessons we have learned through the first two years of this program.

- Strong partnerships are vital and the partners' time and effort must be valued and appreciated. Partners with technical expertise can be an asset to sustainability of the work.
- It is important to learn as much as possible about local constraints and operational procedures through partners and other means prior to the start of the internship.
- Preparation is essential. However, interns will not always remember what they learned once they are in the field and need reminders of key lessons throughout the internship.
- Team building is important since the interns will need to adjust to each others' living and working styles.
- Working in a multidisciplinary team can be challenging but these challenges can be mitigated by establishing clearly defined team roles and value for each person's skills.
- Accomplishing needs assessment, technology development, and field testing is challenging in a summer time frame of

roughly ten weeks, but participating with all of these aspects of the research projects is highly valuable for the interns.

- Effective team communication between all involved parties is crucial. The interns working on-site in the community as well as those working remotely must communicate frequently and keep each other informed about progress.
- Documentation and dissemination are important aspects of this work and should be accounted for in planning.
- Structured deliverables help to keep the team on track.

6. CONCLUSIONS AND FUTURE WORK

In this paper we have presented a new model for a computing research internship, sample outcomes and lessons learned from the program's first two years. Feedback from the interns at the end of the internship program has revealed that they found iSTEP to be a positive experience and would recommend the program to their colleagues and friends. The interns' response to a post-internship survey revealed they were also able to improve their research skills, real-world project learning, multidisciplinary team learning, globally-distributed team learning, cross-cultural experience, cultural knowledge of their community partner, creative problem solving skills, image of computing/technology, communication skills, leadership skills, and confidence. Furthermore, the interns felt that having a multidisciplinary team was important for the internship, that they were able to work well together in accomplishing tasks, and that being globally distributed was challenging, but useful to their work. The feedback from the interns each year is considered when organizing the following year's internship so that the internship experience improves each year. For iSTEP 2011 we are planning to partner with organizations in Montevideo, Uruguay. Programmatically, we are reexamining the role composition of the team to make sure there are sufficient people and skills to accomplish the identified projects.

7. ACKNOWLEDGMENTS

We are grateful to the many people and organizations that have made this internship program possible. We especially thank our community partners, research interns, and advisors, in Pittsburgh and Doha who have participated in the planning and implementation of iSTEP. This research was supported in part by Yahoo!, the Qatar Foundation for Education, Science, and Community Development, the Qatar National Research Fund National Priorities Research Program grant #30-6-7-91, Carnegie Mellon University in Qatar, the Holleran Scholars Fund, the University Computing Centre, Ltd. located at the University of Dar es Salaam in Tanzania, the Asian University for Women, and discretionary gifts to TechBridgeWorld. The opinions expressed in this paper are solely those of the authors and do not necessarily represent the views of any of our sponsors.

8. REFERENCES

[1] Bailey, R., Amoussou, G., Barnes, T. Bischof, H. and Naps, T. 2010. Relevant real-world undergraduate research problems: lessons from the nsf-reu trenches, In Proceedings of the 41st ACM Technical Symposium on Computer Science Education (Milwaukee, WI, USA, Mar. 10-13, 2010). SIGCSE '10. ACM, New York, NY, 62-63. DOI= http://doi.acm.org/10.1145/1734263.1734283.

[2] Beck, J., Buckner, B. and Nikolova, O. 2007. Using interdisciplinary bioinformatics undergraduate research to recruit and retain computer science students. In Proceedings of the 38th ACM Technical Symposium on Computer Science Education (Covington, KY, USA, Mar. 07-11, 2007). SIGCSE '07. ACM, New York, NY, 358-361. DOI=http://doi.acm.org/10.1145/1227310.1227436.

[3] Dahlberg, T., Barnes, T. Rorrer, A. Powell, E. and Cairco, L. 2008. Improving retention and graduate recruitment through immersive research experiences for undergraduates. In Proceedings of the 39th ACM Technical Symposium on Computer Science Education (Portland, OR, USA, Mar. 12-15, 2008). SIGCSE '08. ACM, New York, NY, 466-470. DOI=http://doi.acm.org/10.1145/1352135.1352293.

[4] Granger, M. J., Amoussou, A., Labrador, M. A., Perry, S. and Van Busum, K. M. 2006. Research experience for undergraduates: successes and challenges. In Proceedings of the 37th ACM Technical Symposium on Computer Science Education (Houston, TX, USA, Mar. 03-05, 2006). SIGCSE '06. ACM, New York, NY, 358-361. DOI=http://doi.acm.org/10.1145/1121341.1121513.

[5] Guisasola, J., Furió, C. and Ceberio, M. 2008. Science education based on developing guided research. In Thomase, M. V. (ed) Science Education in Focus. Nova Science Publishers, Inc., Hauppauge, NY, 55-85.

[6] Hadfield, S. and Schweitzer, D. 2009. Building an undergraduate computer science research experience. In Proceedings of the 39th IEEE International Conference on Frontiers in Education Conference (San Antonio, Texas, USA, October 18-21, 2009). IEEE Press, Piscataway, NJ, USA, 1193-1198.

[7] Kaitho, R. J., Stuth, J.W. and Jama, A.A., "Application of Information and Communication Technology in Livestock Marketing in the Pastoral Areas of Eastern Africa," The International Archives of the Photogrammetry, Remote Sensing and Spatial Information Sciences, Part XXX, Vol. 34, 2004.

[8] Peckham, J., Stephenson, P. Hervé, J., Hutt, R. and Encarnação. 2007. Increasing student retention in computer science through research programs for undergraduates. In Proceedings of the 38th ACM Technical Symposium on Computer Science Education (Covington, KY, USA, Mar. 07-11, 2007). SIGCSE '07. ACM, New York, NY, 124-128. DOI=http://doi.acm.org/10.1145/1227310.1227354.

[9] Raicu, D. S. and Furst, J. D. 2009. Enhancing undergraduate education: a REU model for interdisciplinary research. In Proceedings of the 40th ACM Technical Symposium on Computer Science Education (Chattanooga, TN, USA, Mar. 04-07, 2009). SIGCSE '09. ACM, New York, NY, 468-472. DOI=http://doi.acm.org/10.1145/1508865.1509027.

[10] Ward, K. 2005. Research with undergraduates: a survey of best practices. J. Computing Sciences in Colleges 21, 1 (Oct. 2005), 169-176, Consortium for Computing Sciences in Colleges, U.S.A.

[11] Wenderholm, E. 2004. Challenges and the elements of success in undergraduate research.ACM SIGCSE Bulletin 36, 4 (Dec.2004), 73-75. DOI=http://doi.acm.org/10.1145/10.1145/1041624.1041661.

Reaching Out to Aid in Retention: Empowering Undergraduate Women

Rebekah Overdorf
Moravian College
1200 Main St.
Bethlehem, Pennsylvania 18018
strjo01@moravian.edu

Matthew Lang
Moravian College
1200 Main St.
Bethlehem, Pennsylvania 18018
lang@cs.moravian.edu

ABSTRACT

Creating programs that engage undergraduate women with the broader community and encourage them to take an active role in changing the underrepresentation of women in computer science can effectively address *both* retention *and* recruitment of women in the discipline.

This paper is an experience report describing the creation and outcomes of an outreach program for K–12 girls run entirely by undergraduate women.

The contributions of this paper are the description of the creation of a successful student-led outreach program and a set of active-learning modules for K–12 students that illustrate advanced topics.

Categories and Subject Descriptors

K.3.2 [**Computers and Education**]: Computer and Information Science Education

General Terms

Human Factors

Keywords

women in computing, K–12 outreach, retention, gender issues

1. INTRODUCTION

The recruitment and retention of women in undergraduate computer science programs are long-standing problems in computer science education. Though the computer science education community has made correcting the underrepresentation of women in our discipline a priority, [14, 6, 18] little has changed over the past 20 years [13].

A frequently used recruiting tool has been for CS educators to run workshops or roadshows for K–12 students. These programs typically have the goal of dispelling misconceptions that young people have about computer science as well as inspiring students to choose computer science as a topic of study [8].

Our approach has been similar. Over the course of 2009–2010, we ran a series of short workshops and lectures for Girl Scout troupes, camps, and K–12 classrooms. However, instead of having these activities be faculty-designed and delivered, we built a program in which undergraduate women were given complete ownership of both the design and delivery of the workshops.

Recent research suggests that environmental cues that align with computer science stereotypes (*e.g.*, science fiction movie posters, comic book imagery, etc.) foster a feeling of not belonging among women considering computer science as a field of study [7]. So, the advantage of such an approach is two-fold: first, by placing undergraduate women in front of audiences of K–12 girls, the girls are presented with a positive and non-stereotypical image of a computer scientist. Second, the undergraduates involved gain a greater appreciation of computer science and a deeper connection to the discipline, which aids in retention.

In July of 2010, the Girl Scouts of Eastern Pennsylvania invited the authors to present at a summer day camp for K–12 girls. The 2.5 hour-long workshop was to be delivered to nearly 50 girls and to be focused on the theme of the camp—criminal justice.

The authors along with a group of undergraduate women designed a series of active-learning activities that served to illustrate fundamental ideas ranging from information theory to the separation between specification and implementation. These activities were received with near-unanimous approval by the girls and led to a dramatic shift in responses to a survey administered before and after the workshop.

Beyond the shift in attitudes among the girls involved, the experience led to a shift in attitude among the undergraduates who designed and administered the workshop. Beginning in April 2010, a group of undergraduate women met regularly with each other and a faculty mentor to design the workshop. Inside and outside of these meetings, the women involved researched a broad range of computer science topics.

Though there exists a wealth of pre-designed activities and lectures for K–12 students, the women chose to design their activities from scratch. Furthermore, despite the availability of programming languages accessible to K–12 students (*e.g.*, LOGO, Scratch, etc. [16, 19]), the women chose to design a series of "unplugged" [11] activities.

In order to align with the theme of the camp, the women researched topics that may have applications in criminal jus-

SIGCSE'11, March 9–12, 2011, Dallas, Texas, USA.

tice. Pursuit-evader games, the art gallery problem, steganography, cryptography, and DNA sequencing were researched and subsequently discussed with a faculty mentor in meetings. In the end, the women chose to illustrate ideas in information theory with an activity related to facial recognition; to discuss abstraction and generality by relating facial and fingerprint recognition to DNA fingerprinting; and to introduce specification, algorithms, and composition with a maze activity.

The activities presented in this paper, along with the observations reported by the undergraduate women involved, complement a long list of related projects and programs at other colleges and universities. Summer camps and programs designed to introduce K–12 girls to computer science concepts are becoming more widespread [15, 10, 4] and computer science faculty have a wealth of activities and presentations available to them that have been prepared, evaluated, and refined by their colleagues [2, 1, 22]. Further efforts to correct the gender imbalance involve comprehensive programs that link colleges and universities with their communities [21, 9, 5].

The structure of this document is as follows. Section 2 describes the workshop and activities in detail. Section 3 details the experiences of the undergraduate women involved in the outreach program and Section 4 details the experiences of the Girl Scouts involved in the workshop. Finally, Section 5 concludes the paper.

2. A COLLECTION OF ACTIVE LEARNING MODULES FOR K–12 STUDENTS

The following activities—designed wholly by undergraduate women—were designed to be components of a single workshop. However, each was designed so that it could be delivered in isolation.

Each of the activities designed for the workshops share one common objective—to present the girls with experiences that introduce to them the concept of "computational thinking" (*i.e.*, thinking abstractly and assertionally) [24] through active experimentation and feedback. Furthermore, each of the activities is unplugged both in the sense that computers are not necessary and in the sense that there is no syntactic barrier (in the form of a formal language) to the activities.

Additionally, each activity has multiple layers of difficulty so that they are truly applicable to K–12 students of all levels. In fact, the group of girls involved in the summer-camp workshop ranged from grades 4–8.

2.1 Guess Who?

In the classic children's board game Guess Who?^{TM}each player is given a board with a set of characters on hinged holders (see Figure 1). Play begins by each player choosing a random character from a deck of cards. This character—the player's "secret character"—is not shown to their opponent. The game proceeds in rounds; in a round, a player asks her opponent a question about the opponent's secret character and eliminates possible characters on her game board based on the other player's response. The game is won when a player determines the other player's secret character.

This activity is a variant of the Guess Who?^{TM}game. However, instead of students playing in rounds and selecting their next questions based on answers to previous questions, the students must select a set of yes/no questions *a priori*

Figure 1: The Guess Who?^{TM}Board Game

Figure 2: Guess Who Game with Characters Grouped by Characteristics

that are able to uniquely identify each possible character. In other words, the students must determine an enumeration from a set of yes/no answers to the set of characters.

The objectives of this activity were to introduce the concepts of representation, information, and optimization; to practice assertional reasoning; and to discuss the concept of reduction.

Students were given game boards containing 16 characters that were chosen such that they could be represented by answers to 4 questions about "obvious" characteristics. In order to accommodate a range of ages, two variations of a game board were produced. In the first (Figure 2), characters are arranged by common characteristics, whereas in the second, characters are placed randomly.

Students were asked to fill out a sheet of questions that permitted them to ask at most 20 questions to their opponent. When students finished writing their questions, they were asked to pair up with another student and exchange their question sheets. A student was to think of a character, answer the question sheet honestly, and return it to her partner.

Students were then asked to revise their questions if they were unsuccessful in creating a set of questions that were able to identify their opponent's character. If their questions were successful, they were asked to try to reduce the amount of questions asked of their opponent. The students then played a second time; however, instead of thinking of a "random" character, they were asked to try to find a character that "broke" their opponent's questions.

All students were ultimately successful in creating questions that enumerated the characters. However, not all students were able to create an optimal number of questions.

This activity lends itself particularly well to lively discussion both during and after the activity. There are a great deal of questions that can be posed to the students, for example:

- Is it necessary to ask more than 16 questions?
- Are there four questions that will work?
- Can there be less than four?
- Does another set of characters exist that requires more than four?
- Does another set of characters exist that could be successfully enumerated with less than four questions?
- What is the relationship between four and sixteen?

In addition, this activity can be done in the context of facial recognition, which can lead a discussion about the similarity between facial recognition, fingerprint recognition, and DNA fingerprinting. In the presentation, this discussion featured the observation that Google Maps^{TM}mapping service and certain methods for DNA sequencing reduce to the shortest path problem.

2.2 Mazes and Robots

The barriers to learning how to program have been lessened by simple, accessible, visually-oriented programming languages like LOGO and Scratch. However, control structures like loops, conditional execution, and the idea of state are difficult concepts for students with no previous exposure.

The women chose to create activities that involved navigating a robot through a maze in order to introduce of the idea of programming as an activity involving the assembly of state-modifying instructions that, as a whole, map an input to an output. These tasks use a familiar model of state (the position of a robot in a maze) and familiar instructions (directional commands).

In the following activities, groups of students are given a floor-mat maze and a set of cards. Each card contains one of three commands: **go forward**, **turn right**, or **turn left**. Students then create a program (*i.e.*, a stack of cards) that, when followed by a student volunteer playing the role of a robot, navigates a maze.

Though the set of available instructions lacks selection or repetition, well-designed mazes can challenge students to use concepts like recursion and abstraction and to think about issues like resource utilization and efficiency. Indeed, these are some of the objectives of these activity.

2.2.1 *Activities for Young Students*

The act of solving a maze off-line and creating a set of instructions that can be followed to navigate the maze can be sufficiently challenging to provoke interesting points for discussion with young students. "Solving a maze" means a pencil-on-paper backtracking exploration to most young students, so the intellectual profile of building a precise set of instructions that guides directly from entrance to exit differs from their past experience.

Furthermore, opportunities arise to discuss other ideas in computer science. For example, mazes with multiple solutions can spur discussion about whether some are "better" than others (efficiency).

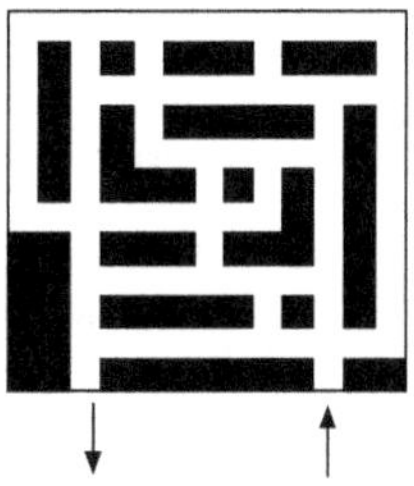

Figure 3: Robert Abbott's No-Left-Turn Maze

The following maze activities provide larger challenges and therefore expose other interesting, and sometimes deep, ideas to students.

2.2.2 *Multi-State Mazes*

Solving a traditional maze holds little challenge for older students. Multi-state mazes [20] on the other hand, use constraints on player movement to create mazes in which a player may be in the same position in the maze, but *not* the same state. For example, consider a maze in which the player cannot make left-hand turns or U-turns. When a player approaches an intersection in such a maze, the direction from which they approach the intersection determines the set of available directions that the player can travel. See, for example, Robert Abbott's no-left-turn maze [3] in Figure 3.

We used such a maze for this activity. A solution strategy that students can be encouraged to adopt is to recursively solve the maze. In other words, to guide the robot to the end of the maze from the start, first find a possible right hand turn that places the robot directly on the path to the exit. Once a suitable intersection is found, the problem has been reduced to guiding the robot to that location from the start. Students quickly adopted this strategy, even with minimal prompting. For example, prompting one group of 7th grade girls with "what does the *last* instruction have to be?" was enough prompting for the group to solve the problem recursively.

2.2.3 *Composition Mazes*

The specification for a set of instructions that solve a maze is obvious: if the player follows the instructions starting from the entrance, the instructions terminate with the player at the exit. In order to introduce the idea of specification and composition, small teams of students were given two maze specifications that, when their solutions were composed, solved a larger maze.

Students were given large mazes with entrances on the top and bottom of the maze and highlighted regions in the center of the maze. One team of students was then instructed to create a program that navigated their robot from the entrance to a highlighted region. Another team of students was to create a program that navigated the robot from a highlighted region to the exit.

To further illustrate the difference between a specification and a program, there were multiple highlighted regions in the center of the maze. The team starting the maze had a weak postcondition: rather than their program terminating with the robot in a specific region, their program simply required the robot to be in *any* of the regions.

The team ending the maze, therefore, had a correspondingly weak precondition: their program was required to guide the robot from any one of three starting positions to the exit of the maze.

Given that students had no instructions that permitted branching execution or loops, the maze contained isomorphic paths (in the sense that a single program could be used to navigate any of the paths) from the highlighted regions to the exit. The isomorphism of the paths was non-obvious, though, so students were forced to think abstractly about what it meant for instructions to solve a maze For example, instructions that correctly solve a maze might have a player make wrong turns and then backtrack, or an instruction—like going straight into a wall—might not affect the state of the robot.

This activity, like the others, contains layers of difficulty. Clearly, the team that must end the maze has a more difficult task than the team that starts the maze. Not only does this allow the activity to accommodate a range of ages, it is by design a source of discussion.

Students see firsthand that the more information they are given and the more freedom they are given, the easier a problem is to solve. Furthermore, if the starting team's postcondition is strengthened, their solution is no longer correct. However, if the ending team's precondition is strengthened, their solution remains correct. Similar to other activities [23], students see the practical application of Hoare's rule of consequence [17].

2.3 Discussion

These three activities form the basis of a 2.5 hour workshop. Though in a workshop, they are given in sequence and tied together through discussion and short talks, each of the activities can be presented separately. All contain elements that require students to think abstractly and assertionally, all illustrate fundamental ideas in the discipline, all contain several layers of difficulty, and all were received positively and enthusiastically when they were presented by the authors.

Section 4 contains the result of pre- and post-workshop surveys administered to a group of 46 girls at a workshop containing these three activities. Though none of the surveys assessed the learning of the girls at the workshop, they did assess the primary objective of the workshop itself: to undermine misconceptions of computer science as a viable field of study.

However, as the next section demonstrates, the students who attended the workshops were not the only beneficiaries of this program.

3. OUTREACH AS A TOOL FOR RETENTION

An outreach program controlled by undergraduate women benefits two groups: the girls that participate in the program's activities and the women themselves. The program founded by the authors grew over the course of months to include not just one undergraduate and faculty mentor, but four undergraduate computer science majors, who together make up the entire female population of the computer science program, as well as two mathematics majors.

Through informal interviews, the women reported three common reasons that participating in the program was a positive experience: a) they felt as though they were making a difference in the girls' lives, b) they learned about topics that they would not have otherwise encountered, and c) they felt more connected to the world outside of campus.

3.1 Changing Lives

> It's important that they interact with people they can relate to and know that they have a future in almost anything. I also enjoyed spending time with the students and being able to convince them computer science is fun and interesting, which in turn convinced me I was in the right field. *– junior computer science major*

> I feel like I am part of the solution to a problem that directly affects me. *– junior computer science major*

A common theme among the women was a sense of empowerment. They uniformly felt that they were making a positive impact on the girls involved by changing their perception of computer science. Furthermore, they reported that being in direct control of the program was an extremely important part of their experience; *they* were responsible for changing the girls' minds. To them, it would not have been as valuable of an experience had they merely been enlisted to help a faculty member.

They also felt that it was important that the girls were presented with non-stereotypical figures and, as young women, they were better able to relate to the girls. They were adamant from the very start of the planning process that they present the problem-solving aspects of the discipline—rather than the technical aspects—to the girls.

3.2 Going Deeper

> I feel more likely to continue in the field of computer science because I greatly enjoyed the activity, and I also learned more about computer science through helping the girls with the activity. *– freshman computer science major*

> To create this activity we had to take an in-depth look into the problem and learn as much as we could about it. While designing the activity, we also had to look at different applications of the problem in the real world. *– junior computer science major*

> It was a good experience for me and I hope in the future we can do more of these projects to teach girls how great computer science really is. *– freshman computer science major*

Running the outreach program also gave the undergraduate women involved the opportunity to research sub-disciplines that they would not have otherwise had the chance to study. This allowed them to study branches of computer science that were interesting to them, but may not be included in the curriculum. Beyond being introduced to new topics, they were also given an opportunity to participate in a research-like experience: they read papers, followed citations, looked for applications of ideas, and created novel work with sound theoretical underpinnings.

An activity the women designed for forty-five minute workshops, but is not included in the paper, involved girls writing strategies for an iterated Prisoners' Dilemma tournament that was presented as a game-show. One participant reported that it was an extremely valuable experience for her to look at the myriad applications of the problem and that it helped her understand the abstraction of the game-theoretic problem.

In order to write their talks, the women had to not only research specific problems and algorithms, but also had to think about computer science itself as a entity. The history of the discipline, the patterns of thought that are woven throughout the discipline, and the commonalities between sub-disciplines are sometimes masked by discrete courses and are sometimes opaque to novices. However, through their broad research, these ideas became parts of their presentations and incorporated into how the women viewed their studies.

3.3 Building Connections

> Participating in this activity gave me the opportunity to look into what computer scientists really do on a day to day basis in their jobs. I learned a lot about how computer scientists are addressing this problem and it made me feel more connected to the broader community of computer scientists. – *junior computer science major*

The women reported that being a part of the efforts to include more women in computer science also helped them to feel a deeper connection to the computer science community outside of the college campus. By reading technical and education research papers and by representing themselves and the college to outside organizations, they realized that there is much more to their field of study than what they are learning from their professors. This, in turn, invoked a sense of curiosity about the different opportunities that their computer science education would present to them.

Finally, the undergraduate women needed to understand precisely why they liked computer science in order to determine how to attract other women to the subject. It has been noted that women are generally attracted to computer science for different reasons than men [12]. Designing activities geared at getting other women involved in computer science forced them to reflect on what initially attracted them to computer science and how they could communicate how their studies are aligned with that attraction.

Finally, each of the women reported that participating in the program gave them a renewed interest in the subject.

4. RESULTS

The goal of the women's outreach program was to change the perception of computer science among K–12 girls and for the girls to consider computer science as a viable field of study. In order to measure the effectiveness of their workshops, the women administered a survey both before and after a 2.5 hour long workshop. The before survey featured two free-response questions and two Likert items:

1. What is the first thing that comes to mind when you hear "computer science?"
2. What do you think computer scientists do?

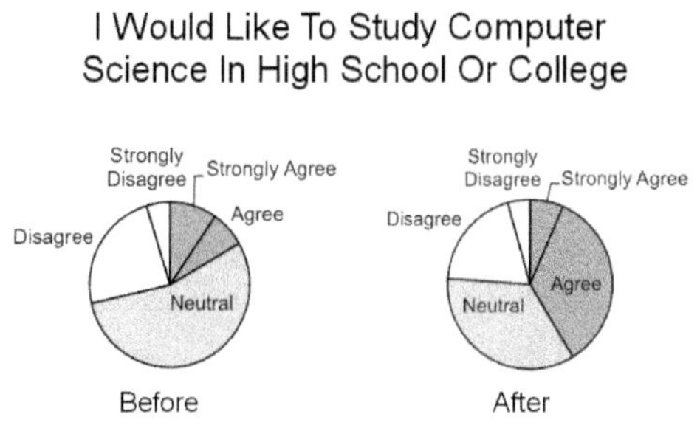

Figure 4: Responses to Question 3: "I would like to study computer science in high school or college."

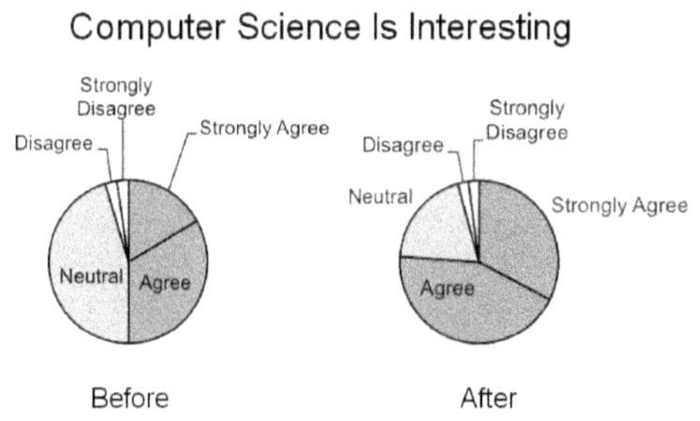

Figure 5: Responses to Question 4: "Computer science is interesting."

3. I would like to study computer science in high school or college. (Likert)
4. I think computer science is interesting. (Likert)

Question one received responses such as, "nerds," and "PowerPoints [sic], to make a website." Many responses to the second question were "study computers" and others such as "I think they learn about computers" or "I think they design microchips inside the computer."

The survey administered at the conclusion of the activity featured the same two Likert items along with a free response question: **"Has your opinion of computer science changed? If so, how?"** To this question, responses spanned a wide range:

- "I don't think it can change."
- "A little, I began to understand more."
- "Yes, I think that computer science is interesting, I might want to study it."

A vast majority of the answers were positive. Many were similar to the following: "I thought computer scientists sat at the computer all day." Another response was: "yes, because at first I thought that it's all about technology, but now I know it's much more."

The responses to the Likert items appear in Figures 4 and 5, respectively.

In the pre-workshop survey, "neutral" received an overwhelming majority of responses. Though the "disagree" and "strongly disagree" responses did not change dramatically in the post-workshop survey, the amount of neutral responses decreased sharply with a corresponding increase in "strongly agree" and "agree" categories.

The results of both the Likert item and free-response questions indicate that the workshop was successful in changing the perception of computer science for many of the participants.

5. CONCLUSION

Many K–12 outreach programs are designed and run by either computer science faculty or industry professionals with undergraduate students playing an assisting role. The authors have taken another tack. The program created by the authors has been successful in not only changing the opinions of K–12 girls about computer science, but also as an exciting opportunity for the young women involved.

Beyond the experience of the women, the activities presented in this paper can be presented without access to computers, either as a sequence of activities in a single long workshop or as the centerpiece activities of short presentations. The Guess Who? activity could even be used with slight modification in CS0 or CS1 classes. Materials needed to recreate the activities in this paper are available at `www.cs.moravian.edu/~lang/ugrad_outreach`.

6. REFERENCES

[1] Cs4fn: Computer science for fun. CS4FN Website. Retrieved November 15, 2010 from `http://www.cs4fn.org`.

[2] Women@scs computer science outreach roadshow. Retrieved November 15, 2010 from `http://women.cs.cmu.edu/What/Outreach/Roadshow/`.

[3] R. Abbott. Logic mazes. Website. Retrieved November 15, 2010 from `http://www.logicmazes.com`.

[4] J. C. Adams. Alice, middle schoolers & the imaginary worlds camps. In *Proceedings of the 38th SIGCSE technical symposium on Computer science education*, SIGCSE '07, pages 307–311, New York, NY, USA, 2007. ACM.

[5] A. Bruckman, M. Biggers, B. Ericson, T. McKlin, J. Dimond, B. DiSalvo, M. Hewner, L. Ni, and S. Yardi. "georgia computes!": improving the computing education pipeline. In *Proceedings of the 40th ACM technical symposium on Computer science education*, SIGCSE '09, pages 86–90, New York, NY, USA, 2009. ACM.

[6] T. Camp. The incredible shrinking pipeline. *Commun. ACM*, 40(10):103–110, 1997.

[7] S. Cheryan, V. C. Plaut, P. G. Davies, and C. M. Steele. Ambient belonging: How stereotypical cues impact gender participation in computer science. *Journal of Personality and Social Psychology*, 97(6):1045 – 1060, 2009.

[8] J. A. Cottam, S. S. Foley, and S. Menzel. Do roadshows work?: examining the effectiveness of just be. In *Proceedings of the 41st ACM technical symposium on Computer science education*, SIGCSE '10, pages 17–21, New York, NY, USA, 2010. ACM.

[9] M. Craig and D. Horton. Gr8 designs for gr8 girls: a middle-school program and its evaluation. In *Proceedings of the 40th ACM technical symposium on Computer science education*, SIGCSE '09, pages 221–225, New York, NY, USA, 2009. ACM.

[10] P. Doerschuk, J. Liu, and J. Mann. Pilot summer camps in computing for middle school girls: from organization through assessment. In *Proceedings of the 12th annual SIGCSE conference on Innovation and technology in computer science education*, ITiCSE '07, pages 4–8, New York, NY, USA, 2007. ACM.

[11] M. Fellows, T. Bell, and I. Witten. Computer science unplugged, 2002. Retrieved November 15, 2010 from `http://www.csunplugged.org`.

[12] A. Fisher and J. Margolis. Unlocking the clubhouse: the carnegie mellon experience. *SIGCSE Bulletin*, 34(2):79–83, 2002.

[13] N. C. for Women & IT. Ncwit scorecard: A report on the status of women in information technology., 2007. Retrieved November 15, 2010 from `http://www.ncwit.org/pdf/2007_Scorecard_Web.pdf`.

[14] K. A. Frenkel. Women and computing. *Commun. ACM*, 33(11):34–46, 1990.

[15] D. P. Groth, H. H. Hu, B. Lauer, and H. Lee. Improving computer science diversity through summer camps. In *Proceedings of the 39th SIGCSE technical symposium on Computer science education*, SIGCSE '08, pages 180–181, New York, NY, USA, 2008. ACM.

[16] B. Harvey. *Computer Science Logo Style: Symbolic Computing*. MIT Press, Cambridge, MA, USA, 1997.

[17] C. A. R. Hoare. An axiomatic basis for computer programming. *Commun. ACM*, 12(10):576–580, 1969.

[18] K. Howell. The experience of women in undergraduate computer science: what does the research say? *SIGCSE Bulletin*, 25(2):1–8, 1993.

[19] D. J. Malan and H. H. Leitner. Scratch for budding computer scientists. In *Proceedings of the 38th SIGCSE technical symposium on Computer science education*, SIGCSE '07, pages 223–227, New York, NY, USA, 2007. ACM.

[20] E. Pegg. Math games: Multi-state mazes. MAA Website, 2003. Retrieved November 15, 2010 from `http://www.maa.org/editorial/mathgames/mathgames_11_24_03.html`.

[21] I. Pivkina, E. Pontelli, R. Jensen, and J. Haebe. Young women in computing: lessons learned from an educational & outreach program. In *Proceedings of the 40th ACM technical symposium on Computer science education*, SIGCSE '09, pages 509–513, New York, NY, USA, 2009. ACM.

[22] S. H. Rodger and E. L. Walker. Activities to attract high school girls to computer science. In *Proceedings of the Twenty-seventh SIGCSE Technical Symposium on Computer Science Education*, SIGCE '96, pages 373–377, 1996.

[23] P. A. G. Sivilotti and S. A. Laugel. Scratching the surface of advanced topics in software engineering: a workshop module for middle school students. In *Proceedings of the 39th SIGCSE technical symposium on Computer science education*, SIGCSE '08, pages 291–295, New York, NY, USA, 2008. ACM.

[24] J. M. Wing. Computational thinking. *Commun. ACM*, 49(3):33–35, 2006.

Teaching Mobile Computing and Developing Software to Support Computer Science Education

James B. Fenwick Jr.
Computer Science Department
Appalachian State University
Boone, NC, USA 28608
828-262-2708
jbf@cs.appstate.edu

Barry L. Kurtz
Computer Science Department
Appalachian State University
Boone, NC, USA 28608
828-262-7008
blk@cs.appstate.edu

Joel Hollingsworth
Computer Science Department
Elon University
Elon, NC, USA 27244
336-278-6241
jhollingsworth@elon.edu

ABSTRACT

Many schools have introduced, or are considering, a programming course targeting mobile devices to satisfy student interest in programming smart phones. In addition, a new class of mobile devices are appearing that combine the functionality of an eBook reader with a web browser, and many of them are based on the same programming frameworks as the smart phones. We report on the successes of mobile device programming courses at two schools. In addition, we report on the accomplishments of students developing software to leverage these newer, multi-function devices in supporting broader computer science education initiatives. In particular, we have developed a service-oriented application that allows students to compile and test programs written in Java and C++ that can be invoked from these devices. We have developed other software allowing these devices to function like Tablet PCs. After describing these important tools, we discuss our current efforts to use these mobile devices in computer science education.

Categories and Subject Descriptors

K.3.1 [**Computing Milieux**]: Computer Uses in Education—*Collaborative Learning, Computer Science Education*

General Terms

Human Factors

Keywords

eBook, mobile computing, Android, microlab

1. INTRODUCTION

Many schools have begun, or are considering, offering courses for programming mobile phones. In addition to our two schools, an Internet search shows college courses on mobile phone programming appearing at a variety of institutions including NYU, Stanford, Maryland, and Austin (TX) Community College. In addition, there are a large number of free, online courses offered such as those at edumobile.org. A search of ACM education publications unfortunately reveals less information to assist educators in their own efforts [7]. We have offered four such courses and several independent study groups over the past two years and report on these experiences as well as recommendations.

The first half of 2010 is marked by the emergence of a new generation of devices that attempt to combine the functionality of an eBook Reader (similar to a Kindle) and a web browser (similar to an iPod Touch). The underlying operating systems for many of these devices are the same as for the smart phones, and this presents an opportunity to broaden the focus to a larger class of multi-function devices. We have a well-published history of using emerging technologies in innovative ways to support and enhance the education experience and are very intrigued with the possibilities offered by these devices. In particular, the authors have reported on using iPod Touch devices and tablet PCs [8].

This paper describes a variety of these emerging devices, details course experiences at our institutions on mobile device programming, and describes our efforts on developing software enhancements that target improving the educational experience for students using these new devices.

2. EBOOK/BROWSER DEVICES

The most talked about device is the Apple iPad [1]; the larger screen on the iPad makes the web browsing experience much quicker and typing much easier than the iPod Touch device. The large screen also makes this a device where one can view books, lecture presentations, and other documents. The screen on the iPad is 9.7" with 1024 x 768 resolution. The iPad does not have any camera or video capabilities. The iPad weighs 1.5 lb. and the base model costs $499.

The Entourage Edge [3] combines two large screens: a 9.7" gray scale e-ink screen with 1200 x 825 resolution and a 10.1" LCD screen with 1024 x 600 resolution. A unique feature of the e-ink screen is that the user can write on it with a stylus. The Edge can record the audio part of lectures and has a video camera that would allow students to communicate with classmates and instructors. The Edge has the size and weight (3 lb.) of a larger netbook and has a comparable price ($499).

We also purchased a dual-screen Alex Reader from Spring

SIGCSE'11, March 9–12, 2011, Dallas, Texas, USA.

Design but found its capabilities to be too limited for our endeavors. There are at least twenty small tablets that are in development or have been released using the Android OS; particularly promising is the Samsung Galaxy Tab, a 7" tablet running Android 2.2 [15].

3. DEVELOPMENT ENVIRONMENTS

3.1 The iPhone OS

The iPhone SDK is freely available from Apple (registration is required). Applications are developed using the XCode development environment, which is a mature and productive tool. User interfaces are developed using the Interface Builder (IB) environment. While these two systems work together for application construction, they are not seamlessly integrated; for example, a common error for novices is forgetting to save the IB work when returning to XCode. Applications are built with Objective-C, which has features of SmallTalk and C. These tools and the SDK only run on a Mac platform; thus, a hardware investment may be necessary. However, we purchased Mac Mini machines and used KVM switches to re-use monitors also connected to lab PCs at 50-60% of the price of a Mac desktop. The SDK comes with a robust device emulator. There are many books and online resources available. Deploying applications to a device requires a developer license with Apple. The University license is free but has (sensible) restrictions on the applications and uses. Personal licenses are about $100 USD and must be renewed annually.

3.2 The Android OS

Android is a free, open source, full featured software platform based on Linux for mobile devices. It supports a number of features including a touch and/or keyboard interface, camera, video, accelerometer, compass, audio, phone, SMS, email, maps, and GPS. Android includes a number of open source libraries such as SQLite, OpenGL ES, and WebKit along with application programming interfaces in Java [4]. Android provides a rich SDK which gives the application programmer full access to the same framework API which is used by the core applications. Applications are run in their own process in order to enforce isolation. Most applications are written in Java and run using Dalvik, a Java VM which has been optimized for mobile devices. Android does allow code to be implemented in C and provides a native interface between Java and C.

3.3 Mobile Web Applications

Both the iPhone and Android SDKs require learning new frameworks. These frameworks are well documented yet remain large and can intimidate some students. Another strategy is to use common web technologies to build web applications that can be run on nearly all mobile devices. Rogers describes how to use HTML5, CSS, and JavaScript to accomplish these goals; specifically building the same application (Note Pad) that is one of the cornerstone Android tutorial applications [13]. This is an attractive option since many students may already possess enough familiarity with these technologies from other courses. In addition, no specific hardware (Mac platform) or software (Eclipse ADT) are required or encouraged. Students can develop in their usual way. Moreover, the application can be run on many different devices without requiring porting any code. Specialized libraries are coming online allowing JavaScript access to underlying phone, location, acceleration, sound, camera, etc. functionalities of the devices.

3.4 Other Software

In considering newer multi-purpose devices like the Entourage Edge, there are additional frameworks to learn. The Edge adds a its own SDK on top of the base Android system. At present, this SDK is not released for developers. A primary feature of these devices is the e-ink screen. Any EPUB formatted document can be displayed on the e-ink screen. The EPUB format is an XML format composed of three open standards developed by the International Digital Publishing Forum [6]. This open standard allows the possibility of developing content that can integrate with the device (e.g., Entourage Edge) SDK to make the dual-screen device a seamless and integrated multi-media content provider. For instance, section 5.3 describes work we have accomplished in having students use the stylus pen on the e-ink screen to answer a question posed by the e-ink text. This response is then sent wirelessly to an instructor station for review and possible classroom discussion. As the device manufacturers release their SDKs even more robust educational interactions will be possible.

4. TEACHING MOBILE COMPUTING

4.1 Experiences at Elon University

A course called Mobile Computing has been taught at Elon University each Spring semester since 2008. The past two iterations of this course have been taught using Android. This required senior-level course has become very popular with the students as it gives them a chance to explore the emerging world of software development for smart phones.

The course was taught using an e-book, as supplemental reading material, along with the Android Developers SDK and Dev Guides available directly from Google [4]. The students developed applications using the Eclipse IDE and the Android Development Tools plugin [2]. The Eclipse ADT plugin gives the students an intuitive development environment along with direct integration with the Android emulator that can be used to test applications before deployment to actual devices. Deployment to Android phones is quite easy and can be done to any Android phone by selecting an option in the phone's settings. Elon purchased eight Android Developer Phones from Google that are made readily available to the students. A number of students used their own Android phones during the course. By the end of the course, students were running applications on six different types of Android phones.

The first half of the course was lecture-based. Lectures were reinforced by a fairly straight forward programming assignment based on the lecture topic. Topics included: XML-based GUI development, using orientation sensors, touch-based input, gesture-based input, using media and the camera, and a number of general software development topics for mobile computing. Instead of using lecture slides, students were presented application requirements and then were led by the instructor through the development process for the application. This process included discussion of any new topics that might arise. All of the application code developed during the course has been made available at the course website [5].

The hands-on approach mentioned above has worked very well for the past two iterations of the course. The course has been taught in a lab to allow the students to both follow along with the instructor and to try their hand at slight changes to the application. This allows the students to be active during the learning process while also gaining experience in the development environment.

The second half of the course was project-based. The students were required to submit project proposals which outline a mobile application they wished to develop. This was done individually or as a team. The students then orally presented their proposal to their peers and requested feedback. After the project was accepted by the instructor, the students used the remaining course time to implement this application. Student applications in 2010 included: a 2-D animation of fireflies in a lantern, a Mad Libs application which incorporated SMS and email, GPS-enabled application for setting hiking waypoints, and a multi-tool for ROTC cadets. A couple of groups have continued to work on their application in an effort to polish them for upload to the Android Market.

Android has proven to be an exciting environment which can be used to teach both software development and mobile computing topics. Students and instructors at Elon have been pleasantly surprised by the ability to quickly develop interesting applications. We have found Android to be so intuitive, we have incorporated it into both the CS II and CS III course [12].

4.2 Experiences at Appalachian State

A summer course called Mobile Device Programming was offered in Summer 2010 that emphasized Android programming (80%) with enough iPhone programming (20%) to gain some familiarity. This course was an upper-level elective course that filled to capacity easily. The course used the Rogers et.al. O'Reilly text [14] and also frequently consulted the online Android Developers website materials [4]. The students developed applications using the Eclipse IDE and the Android Development Tools plugin [2]. The department provided Entourage Edge devices and a number of students used their own Android phones during the course. The Android SDK provides an emulator that is quite robust, and most work was developed with the emulator primarily and deployed to actual devices as a final step.

The course was run in a programming studio fashion. A new assignment was posted daily and students worked on the assignment in class completing it outside of class. Following the text, the course explored the Android SDK environment, coding, debugging, use of XML configurations, manifests, and publishing applications in the context of a single running application. Then specific features of the mobile device framework were learned, including SQLite databases; location-based services and mapping; a large variety of user interface features (input methods, widgets, etc.); telephone, accelerometer, camera usage. This intensely hands-on approach worked very well. Students formed pairs for a final project that required several of the features mentioned above. A few student final projects included: a bouncing ball pit game with speed, size, number controls as well as highest score database; a graffiti-inspired applications dubbed 'Stash-Mash allowed user to add pre-loaded mustaches to a picture taken with the camera; a mobile application for ticket purchasing for our university's athletics website; a time-management app that is designed to integrate with a popular web-based management application; and lastly, the instructor created a mobile app for a popular, local weather website.

The students enjoyed the course and the studio format. Students largely solved problems they encountered, such as out-of-date text code, undocumented XML configuration items, etc. Two other items of positive feedback, while anecdotal, are valuable indicators. One student developed an application outside the requirements of the course to support an activity of his own interest – rock climbing. The application uses the camera and geo-location subsystems to record coordinates and photo of a good rock climbing spot along with ratings, textual descriptions, and a feature to share with other social networking systems. Another student said that his final project had nearly 1,000 Android Market downloads a month after the class had completed. This entrepreneurial and independent spirit seemed to be missing from our CS students generally, so it was refreshing to witness again.

4.3 Independent Study Experiences

Kurtz is co-PI on an NSF STEP grant where one of the activities is to sponsor Freshman research clusters of four students to explore a topic of their own choice [16]. In Spring 2009 his cluster elected to work on iPhone software development. Despite providing students sole access to a machine for development, no significant progress was made by the end of the semester beyond getting some programs taken directly from reference books up and running. His Spring 2010 research cluster, a different group of four freshmen students, elected to do Android development. They made significant progress by the end of the semester developing a 3D tic-tac-toe game and a program that queried an earthquake web service (earthquake.usgs.gov) to find any large earthquakes in the world in the last 24 hours and then using Google maps to display this information on an Android smart phone. In Fall 2010 this group moved to iPad software development after their experience using Android. They have been much more successful than the original group noted above and have developed three different two person games that can be played using Bluetooth connectivity. Kurtz believes that the Android experience may have eased the learning curve for development using the iPhone/iPad.

The software described in this paper for the Entourage Edge, namely the editor for microlabs and submission software to WAGS (see section 5.2) and the Tablet PC mode of operation (see section 5.3), was developed by two different students completing an independent study. Development of this software went smoothly due to the familiarity with Java and the Android plugin for Eclipse. The only problems dealt with the lack of an SDK for the Edge inhibiting automation of operations between the e-ink screen and the LCD screen, use of Android 1.6 instead 2.1 or 2.2, and lack of Bluetooth support on the Android simulator.

4.4 Teaching Recommendations

Our advice to instructors considering entering this area of mobile device programming is to consider your goals and resources first. iPhone development requires a specific hardware platform so there may be an expense incurred and space may need to be allocated for these machines. If students are not familiar with Objective-C or SmallTalk then iPhone development will likely progress more slowly as the base language is learned.

The Android framework is heavily object-oriented. Students who know Java will be comfortable from their use of Java Collections, etc. A procedurally-motivated C++ programmer may incur a steeper learning curve to assimilate the use of composition, delegation, interfaces, abstract classes, etc. that are mainstays of the framework. The Android SDK itself works on all platforms.As described in section 3.4 above, a web application strategy using HTML5, CSS, and JavaScript can be a good choice for some as it can alleviate the hardware and software dependences of the SDKs.

Hybrids are also possible, covering some of each technology. We have found that the requirement of using a large framework is a good learning experience for students. Moreover, learning how to work with a framework was easier for the second framework. For this reason we tend to suggest starting with the platform which will incur the least effort in learning the base language. We also recommend allowing students flexibility in project selection. They are highly adept consumers of these types of applications and need gentle nudges to begin thinking entrepreneurially, but this truly is "right up their alley."

5. SOFTWARE TOOLS FOR MICROLABS

We developed our microlab approach to active learning as part of NSF grant (0737355) entitled Modern Distributed Computing Education funded under the CCLI program. The use of programming microlabs is reported in [11]. A microlab is a hands-on activity typically lasting 3-20 minutes that is completed by students during lecture. The programming microlabs take the most time and depend on software that makes it possible to compile, run and test programs in Java and C/C++ on eBook/Browsers. Logical microlabs are similar to active learning interactions commonly used with tablet PCs and are of much shorter duration.

Figure 1: Solving a Microlab on the Entourage Edge

5.1 Using Programming Microlabs

To provide a concrete example, we discuss one programming microlab in detail. The Readers-Writers problem involves many processes trying to read a data value and one or more other processes trying to write to the data value. Simultaneous readers are allowed but only one active writer is allowed; all other readers or writers must be blocked. In the microlab students are given a program that compiles and runs but does not function properly; the primary problem is that there are 25 readers and only one writer that is starved from changing the data value. Students have to modify the program to make sure the writer has priority. Specifically students have to: (1) declare the locks and conditions, (2) add the appropriate operations to the startRead, endRead, startWrite and endWrite methods, and (3) run the test program to make sure everything works properly.

5.2 The Web-based Automated Grading System (WAGS)

Our automated grading system is designed to provide students immediate feedback on their solution to a microlab. Clients can submit programs for compilation and execution using Java, C/C++, or MPI (Message Passing Interface). The server machine is typically a multicore machine (we are currently using an eight core machine) so that the advantages of parallelism are evident.

We now present a sequence of screenshots that show how a student uses the WAGS system to complete the Readers-Writers microlab. We use an Entourage Edge in dual screen mode where useful documentation can appear on the e-ink screen and the LCD screen is used to edit the skeleton code and then submit a solution to WAGS. We developed a simple text editor under the Android OS that can open text files, allow editing using the built-in electronic keyboard, and save the modified files to either the SD card or to a jump drive plugged into the USB port. The modifications require declaring a ReentrantLock and then creating two condition variables associated with this lock. The JavaDoc APIs for the Lock Interface and the Condition Interface are vital to completing this exercise; these interfaces are displayed on the e-ink display (see figure 1). The LCD screen shows the skeleton code after the student has made the requested modification.

The program is then copied to WAGS and compiled. If there are no compile errors the testing proceeds automatically. However, as shown in Figure 2 there were compile errors and then logic errors in the submitted code before a successful submission. In this case the compile errors were due to the student not using the proper import statements to make the ReentrantLock and Condition types visible. Once the imports are added to the program, it compiles and is executed. The program prints a sequence of statements that indicate when a reader starts to read and finishes reading and when a writer wants to write, actually starts to write, and then finishes the write. The test program has been set up to detect that the writer will block any new readers and that once all the existing readers are finished the writer can proceed. The most common error is that the request from the writer to write is not given priority and the writer can never proceed because there are many readers always accessing the data.

When the instructor logs into WAGS, she is recognized as having administrative privileges and can examine any or all of the solutions submitted by students in her class. Often the instructor can look at the most recent submissions from a student and provide some helpful advice.

5.3 Using Logical Microlabs

Using Tablet PCs during lecture is a form of active learning that is popular with students; our second major project was to emulate this tablet PC mode of instruction. Here is an example of a logical microlab. After covering the basic concepts of a binary search tree, an instructor may ask students to draw the final tree after inserting the nodes M, A, Z, P, B, T, O, D, Q into an initially empty binary search tree. Students draw their solutions and submit them anonymously to the instructor. The instructor can view all responses and select one or two of the responses for class discussion.

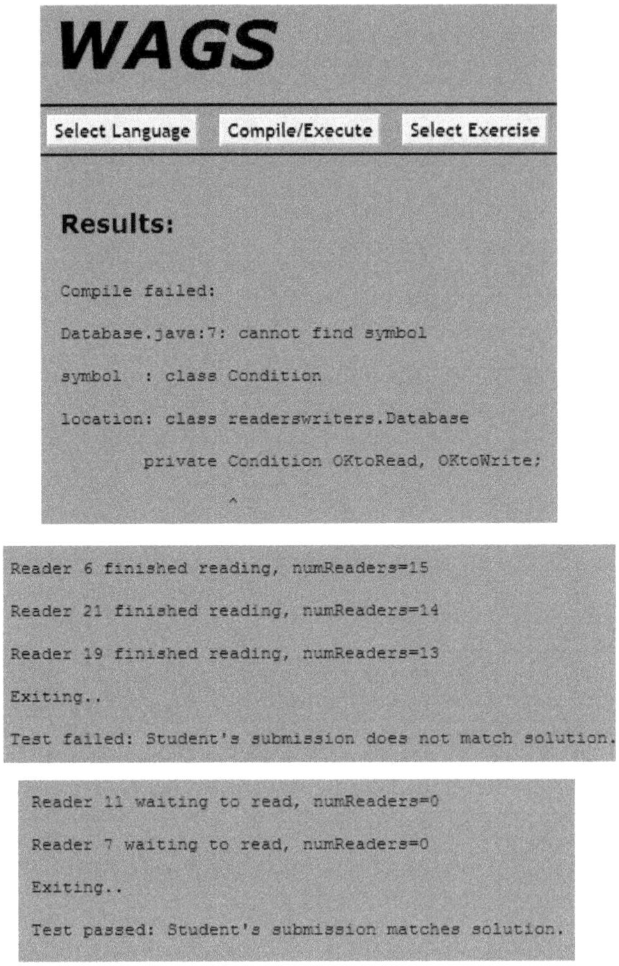

Figure 2: Sample WAGS output: (top) compilation error, (middle) logic error, (bottom) correct behavior.

We implemented our approach on the Entourage Edge since its e-ink screen accepts hand written annotations. The instructor machine is the server and can select either Bluetooth mode or WiFi mode for submission.. After selecting a submission mode the instructor can transfer a pdf file to all the clients by selecting a file from a list. On the client side, after the student has registered as part of the network, the student can elect to either receive a file or send a file to the server machine. In this case, the student receives the binary search tree problem sent by the instructor and, using an Android intent, this pdf is automatically transferred to the e-ink screen. The student enters annotation mode and draws in a proposed solution, such as the one shown in figure 3, which is then exported as a pdf file thereby completing the process by sending the file back to the server machine.

The server program on the instructor machine receives multiple pdf files from students and stores them in a common directory. The instructor can view these responses and select one or more for further discussion. The selected student response is sent back to all client machines and automatically transferred to the e-ink screen. Alternatively, using a USB to VGA graphics adapter it is possible to project the selected response for everyone to see. It is important that solutions be submitted anonymously and that students do not know which of their classmate's solution is being discussed. In practice, often a student will self-acknowledge that it is his/her solution being discussed.

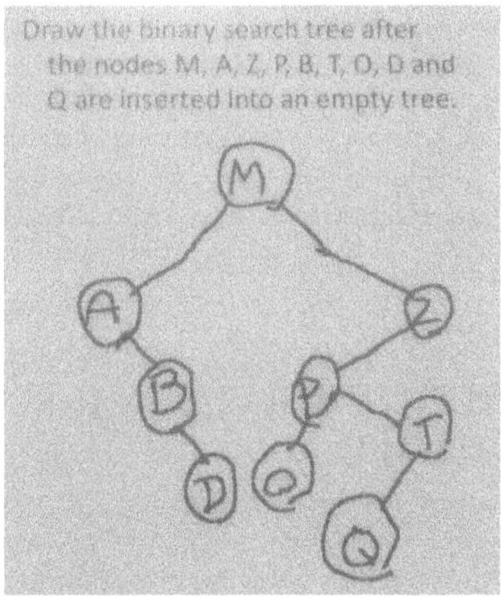

Figure 3: Student response entered on e-ink screen

6. USING NEW CAPABILITIES

These eBook/Browser devices have many built-in capabilities that have immediate application in an educational setting. For example, using the Entourage Edge it is possible to record the audio portion of a lecture or to hand write lecture notes on the e-ink screen.

6.1 Using the Communications Capabilities

The Entourage Edge contains a front facing video camera for online meetings. Synchronous real-time meetings can be used for:

VIRTUAL OFFICE HOURS - The instructor may wish to set up designated times that she would be able to answer questions posed during a live chat session.

PROJECT GROUP MEETINGS - If students are working on a group project, they may find it convenient to meet electronically rather than have to meet physically at the same location.

VIRTUAL CLASS SESSIONS - The instructor might want to offer voluntary virtual class sessions, such as review before a test, to answer student questions.

DISCUSSION GROUPS - Students may be asked to watch some presentation, such as talk on an educational television channel, or review an educational document and then form groups to discuss the presentation or documents.

6.2 Using the Audio/Video capabilities

The audio and video playback capabilities can be used to provide tutorial materials in various forms. Rather than have the instructor give a "talking head" lecture on a topic, we show a student trying to solve a typical problem. We have developed a set of Asynchronous Instruction Patterns that are used to simulate student interaction in a virtual classroom based on the earlier work [9, 10]. Here are some of the more commonly-used patterns:

ANSWER INSTRUCTOR QUESTION - The instructor asks an open ended question in a video clip and the student responds using handwriting, typing, audio or video as appropriate; feedback would be delayed until the instructor or a teaching assistant can review the responses.

EVALUATE CLASSMATE - The student listens to a stored response of a classmate to an instructor question and evaluates the classmate's response.

ANSWER CLASSMATE QUESTION - A virtual classmate asks the instructor a question about the material just covered; the instructor asks the student using the eBook/Browser to answer the classmate question using an appropriate input mode. If immediate feedback is desired, the student could be shown several possible responses and asked to choose the most suitable response.

7. TEACHING PROGRAMMING LANGUAGES

We are currently using the Entourage Edges to teach programming languages. Every student in the course was given an Entourage Edge to keep for the duration of the semester to support instructional activities. We illustrate the tablet PC mode to implement logical microlabs. Prolog was introduced using a family tree of data where facts for gender and parent relations are given. Students have to write rules for mother and father; both are very easy. Writing a rule for sibling is more challenging. The logical microlab shown in Figure 4 helps students focus on a sibling rule. Most student found X = rosa and Y = gregory; others will give the reverse bindings. Some will say both bindings are possible, but very few students notice that this rule allows you to be a sibling to yourself. This leads to an interesting discussion on how the Prolog inference engine discovers solutions. By

List All X,Y Values Satisfying sibling

- Use only this very small database
- parent(douglas,rosa).
- parent(rita,rosa).
- parent(douglas,gregory).
- parent(rita,gregory).
- female(rosa).
- male(gregory)
- sibling(X,Y):- mother(M,X), mother(M,Y),
  father(F,X), father(F,Y).

Figure 4: A Logical Microlab in Prolog

using both programming microlabs and logical microlabs interspersed with lectures students quickly learned to program using a logical programming language (Prolog) and a functional programming language (F#).

8. CONCLUSIONS

Many schools are beginning to offer mobile device programming courses. We have offered such courses at two institutions for 4 terms and report on how these courses are working. Meanwhile, a new generation of devices has emerged that combine the functionality of an eBook reader and a web browser, such as the iPad and Entourage Edge. We report on ways that we are exploring that leverage these new devices to enhance computer science education including automated grading system integration, EPUB textbook hooks to make content come alive, and implementation of a variety of instructional patterns. Because these devices are programmed with the same tools and technologies as many modern mobile phone devices, our own students are able to translate skills from a mobile device programming course into research efforts with the new devices.

9. REFERENCES

[1] Apple. Apple ipad. *www.apple.com/ipad.*

[2] Eclipse. Adt plugin for eclipse. *developer.android.com/sdk/eclipse-adt.html.*

[3] Entourage. Entourage edge. *www.entourageedge.com.*

[4] Google. Android developers. *developer.android.com.*

[5] J. Hollingsworth. Csc 442: Mobile computing. *trumpy.cs.elon.edu/joel/2010/csc442/.*

[6] International Digital Publishing Forum. Epub specification. *www.idpf.org/specs.htm.*

[7] S. Kurkovsky. Engaging students through mobile game development. In *Technical Symposium on Computer Science Education*, March 2009.

[8] B. Kurtz, J. Fenwick, and C. Ellsworth. Using podcasts and tablet pcs in computer science. In *Proceedings of the 45th ACM Southeast Conference*, March 2007.

[9] B. Kurtz, D. Parks, and E. Nicholson. Effective internet education: A progress report. In *Technical Symposium on Computer Science Education*, February 2002.

[10] B. Kurtz, D. Parks, and E. Nicholson. Effective internet education: Strategies and tools. In *International Conference on Frontiers in Education*, November 2002.

[11] B. Kurtz, R. Tashakkori, J. Helfert, and M. Sage. Using microlabs to teach modern distributed computing. In *Technical Symposium on Computer Science Education*, March 2010.

[12] D. Powell and J. Hollingsworth. Integrating mobile computing with android in CS II and CS III. In *International Conference on Frontiers in Education*, July 2009.

[13] R. Rogers. Developing portable mobile web applications. *LinuxJournal*, September 2010.

[14] R. Rogers, J. Lombardo, Z. Mednieks, and B. Meike. *Android Application Development.* O'Reilly, 2009.

[15] Samsung. Samsung galaxy tab. *http://galaxytab.samsungmobile.com/.*

[16] R. Tashakkori, B. Kurtz, J. Fenwick, D. Parks, and A. McRae. Early participation of cs students in research. In *submitted to SIGCSE 2011*, March 2011.

Human Computer Interaction That Reaches Beyond Desktop Applications

Susan Loveland
Department of Computer Science, Adams State College
Alamosa, Colorado, USA
1-719-587-7586
sloveland@adams.edu

ABSTRACT

Recently, several frameworks have been developed for writing mobile and web applications in Java, making the development of web and mobile applications accessible to HCI students with only a CS1 Java background. In this paper we describe using student projects based on the Google Android mobile platform and Google's Web Toolkit to provide students with experience designing and implementing user interfaces for mobile and web applications. Specific examples demonstrate how programming on these platforms reinforces standard HCI topics. As a result of being able to learn mobile device programming in the context of "cool" Google platforms, students expressed increased interest in studying HCI.

Categories and Subject Descriptors

K.3.2 Computer and Information Science Education

General Terms

Human Factors

Keywords

Human Computer Interaction (HCI), mobile, web, Android, Google Web Toolkit (GWT)

1. INTRODUCTION

The percentage of people using web and mobile applications is steadily increasing compared to the percentage of people using more traditional desktop applications. While it is difficult to obtain definitive statistics with regard to this trend, there are numerous examples to support it. For example, the number of people accessing Twitter from web and mobile applications is far greater than those accessing it from a desktop application [27]. Even steadfast desktop applications such as office productivity software are facing competition from completely online versions such as Google Docs [12]. Indeed, Word 2010 [20] has both web and mobile word processing built into it. The rising popularity of mobile and web applications makes them an increasingly important topic of study in HCI classes.

SIGCSE'11, March 9–12, 2011, Dallas, Texas, USA.

Finding an appropriate user-interface programming project for an HCI course can be difficult, since HCI courses are often sophomore level courses with only CS1/CS2 pre-requisites. Because the common CS1/CS2 programming languages are not languages often thought of as web or mobile programming languages a desktop application is the natural choice for a user-interface programming project. However, the recent development of web and mobile application development environments based on popular CS1/CS2 languages such as Java, C++, and Python means that human computer interaction classes can be made more relevant to today's students through the incorporation of mobile and web user-interface projects.

In this paper, we describe an applied HCI course at Adams State College that involves the development of both a web-based and a mobile-based user interface. The web user interface makes use of the Google Web Toolkit (GWT) [11], a Java framework for writing web applications; the mobile user interface makes use of Google's open source Android [2] platform. We give examples of how the projects were used to motivate HCI topics.

2. RELATED WORK

A number of colleges and universities have reported successful efforts integrating mobile application development into the computer science curriculum. For example, mobile game development using Java Micro Edition [15] has been incorporated throughout the computer science curriculum at Central Connecticut State University [16]. An observed benefit includes helping students see applications of computer science to a real-world technology that they use every day, the cell phone. A second reported benefit is that mobile game programming is more accessible to beginning students than more traditional desktop game programming. At the University of Guelph [19], an academic kit has been developed for integrating mobile devices into the CS curriculum. The kit uses a combination of Blackberry [3] and Java ME labs, tutorials, and assignments designed for an introductory course on mobile application development. It also includes teaching modules for software engineering, game design and development, web services, information security, and operating systems. Other educators have demonstrated that mobile application programming is accessible to beginning computer science students by integrating it into the CS1/CS2 beginning programming sequence [18, 21]. There are also student mobile programming projects for non-profit organizations [24, 4] that apply human computer interaction concepts to user interface design and development.

This paper differs from previous work, in that it focuses specifically on the use of student web and mobile user-interface projects to motivate and modernize HCI topics. It also demonstrates how existing student knowledge of Java can be leveraged to write web and mobile user interfaces using the recently developed Google Android and GWT platforms.

3. COURSE OVERVIEW

Human Computer Interaction is a sophomore-level, semester-length, course at Adams State College which meets three hours per week. The course has a CS1 prerequisite where the students learn the fundamentals of programming in Java using the Eclipse [8] development environment. The HCI course covers the topics recommended by the 2008 ACM/IEEE curriculum recommendations [1] by using student projects to motivate lecture topics.

Two student projects were used for the spring 2010 semester: one a web-based and the other a mobile-based user-interface programming project. Students were given weekly programming assignments that involved incremental steps in completing the applications. After each assignment deadline the course instructor graded the submitted assignments and then merged them into a codebase that could be used as the starting point for the next assignment. In this way, students who did not successfully complete an assignment were able to work with minimal handicap on the subsequent assignment. By using comprehensive projects instead of short, unrelated projects, the students were able to experience all aspects of the user-interface development process in a more realistic manner.

4. PROJECT DESCRIPTIONS

This section provides details on the two student projects selected to motivate the classroom topics in the human computer interaction course. The first is a web-based project that involved writing a form-submission system for the university's Curriculum Review Committee (CRC). A mobile scavenger hunt game application was chosen for the second project in the course to give students exposure to a completely different game-based user interface.

4.1 Web CRC Form-Submission System

Web-based forms are ubiquitous in modern society, and this was one of the motivating factors in choosing to implement a form-based document submission system for the CRC committee as an HCI project. CRC serves as a campus oversight committee for adding new courses and making changes to existing courses. The current system for course change submissions involves filling out a Microsoft Word [21] template concerning course and program changes and submitting it to a shared file system. One of the problems with the current system is that the Word template does not provide type checking of the required fields. Many submissions contain missing and incorrect information. A second problem is that once a form is approved, a secretary must enter the information in the form into a database, providing the opportunity for more errors. The web-based prototype for the form-submission system developed by the students provides both data-validation and storage of the forms in a database, eliminating two important sources of errors from the process, so the students in the class made an important first step toward modernizing the current system.

4.2 Mobile Scavenger Hunt

The second course project was to write a mobile scavenger hunt for campus recruitment and orientation activities. The rules for the game were as follows:

- Groups of students would be provided with a cell phone showing a campus map with targets marked. Targets would be generated randomly so some groups of students might have campus targets located close to their starting location whereas other groups might be unlucky and have to travel from one end of campus to the other to reach a target.
- When a group reached their GPS determined target, the cell phone would reveal a question to be answered. Questions could be configured based on the purpose of the activity through an XML file. As soon as a group correctly answered a question, a new campus map would appear showing the next target for the hunt.
- The group finding all of its targets and supplying correct answers to the questions in the least amount of time wins.

5. TECHNOLOGIES

Not only did the projects involve two very different types of user interfaces, they also required the use of different programming technologies. We discuss the mobile and web platforms used to develop the projects in this section.

The criteria used to select technologies for the projects were the following:

1. Easily accessible technology so the course could remain focused on human computer interaction instead of the intricacies of programming in a particular language. This criterion limited the choice of technology to a Java-based language since a background in Java was the only pre-requisite of the course.
2. Technology available as a plug-in for the Eclipse integrated development environment.
3. Open source technology to minimize cost.
4. Student interest in learning the technology.

There are a number of platforms available for mobile application development including Microsoft Windows Mobile [28], Sun's Java Platform Micro Edition (Java ME) [17], Google Android [7], and Qualcomm's Brew [23]. However, only two of these mobile platforms support development in the Java programming language: Android and Java ME. Even more daunting is the number of platforms that have been developed recently that provide a Java environment for writing web applications such as: Sun's JavaFX [14] and JavaServer Faces (JSF) [16], Google's Web Toolkit (GWT) [13], Struts 2 [26], OpenXava [22], and Rife [25]. Of those platforms meeting the first three criteria, we selected Google's GWT and Android platforms, primarily because of the enthusiasm and interest our students display toward all things Google. Below, we provide an overview of the two platforms.

5.1 Google Web Toolkit (GWT)

The GWT was used to implement the web-based CRC form-submission system. GWT contains a standard library of widgets (also very similar in usage to Swing widgets). Applications are written in Java which are then compiled into JavaScript and AJAX [9]. Layout is specified dynamically within the Java code using a style similar to Swing. The appearance of widgets can be customized by the use of a cascading style sheet (CSS) and the ability to add CSS class selectors to the widgets dynamically in the Java code. The Google plug-in for Eclipse comes with a web server for development and testing. Once the application is deployed, it can be viewed and tested on any browser using the computer's loopback address. GWT projects can also be deployed at no cost on Google's web servers.

For more complex web applications, the toolkit supports three different communication mechanisms with a web server: extensible mark-up language (XML), JavaScript Object Notation (JSON) [7], and remote procedural calls. The Google App Engine [10] datastore can be used to provide a database persistence layer.

5.2 Android

The Google Android platform was selected for the implementation of the Scavenger Hunt Project. The Android platform provides a library of pre-built user interface widgets such as radio buttons, text boxes, date pickers, and picture galleries that are very similar in usage to Swing widgets. Standard layouts are also available that mirror many of the layout managers that students are familiar with from Swing. Other features of the framework include:

- Layout is specified in an XML file.
- Strings that are part of the user interface are defined in an XML file that is easily internationalized.
- Code integration with Google Maps [11] including map display and GPS location updates.
- Loose coupling of user-interface elements through a message passing system based on serializing Intent objects.

The framework also provides a nice mobile emulator that can be configured to display a variety of screen sizes and both vertical and horizontal orientations for effective user interface testing. A snapshot of the emulator running the scavenger hunt application is displayed in Figure 1.

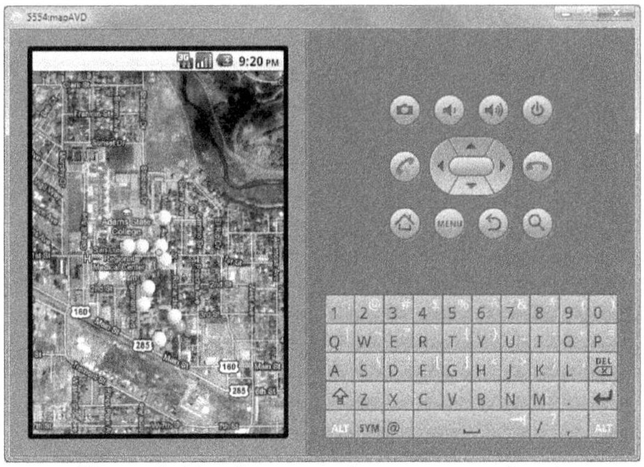

Figure 1: Emulator running scavenger hunt.

6. CURRICULUM ENHANCEMENTS

This section contains examples of how the projects were used to enhance human computer interaction classroom topics such as accessibility, internationalization, widget layout, mobile design, and user-interface testing. In addition, we discuss how the CRC application project extended the traditional context of human computer interaction course to include the typical software developer's task of tying the view layer to a persistence tier in order to store and retrieve user data.

6.1 Accessibility

Creating products that can be used by people with a wide range of abilities is an important aspect of user interface design. This section begins with a discussion of accessibility support on the GWT platform followed by a look at the Android platform. Both subsections include examples of how the projects complimented classroom coverage of accessibility through practical programming experience.

6.1.1 GWT Accessibility

Using JavaScript and AJAX can make a web page difficult for screen readers to interpret since a developer could use a list HTML [29] element on a page and write JavaScript to make it behave like a tree control. The ARIA [5] specification adds a set of DOM [6] properties to HTML elements that can be used by browsers to raise events during user interaction that screen readers can react to. The GWT 1.5 release provides automatic, built-in ARIA support for GWT widgets and the ability to add ARIA to custom widgets. GWT also supports adding attributes to widgets such as "title", "summary", and "alt" that improve the accessibility of the underlying HTML. However, Google's layout mechanisms tend to generate complex HTML and JavaScript code with a heavy reliance on nested HTML tables that can present accessibility problems. Thus, the GWT Toolkit provides an interesting mix of contrasts with regard to accessibility.

One of the weekly HCI assignments involved submitting the baseline CRC Application code to online automated accessibility evaluation tools and then fixing as many accessibility problems as possible. While HCI classes often include a discussion of web accessibility issues and an evaluation of a web site in terms of accessibility, actually implementing accessibility features on a web application strongly reinforced classroom topics.

6.1.2 Android Accessibility

Accessibility was added to the Android mobile platform with the 1.6 release which includes a built-in screen reader and text-to-speech (TTS) engine that makes it possible to use an Android application when not looking at the screen. A number of non-visual forms of feedback are available including speech, auditory (non-speech sounds) and haptic (vibration) feedback. These accessibility features are turned off in applications by default, since they entail a performance hit, but they can be turned on through the Settings menu. The small keyboard available with smart phones can make typing large amounts of text challenging for any user, and the Android platform comes with the ability to integrate speech input into applications.

The Scavenger Hunt application allowed students to explore a number of Android accessibility features. Students implemented speech feedback into the Scavenger Hunt by providing periodic speech updates of "Nearer" or "Farther" depending on whether the group had travelled nearer to or farther away from their target since the last update. In addition, speech input allowed groups to record application comments and provide feedback easily while the game was in progress. The students were particularly fascinated and excited about the powerful speech recognition software available with the platform. They also became more cognizant of the challenges of developing accessible application by porting their code onto a cell phone and testing it with their vision obscured.

6.2 Internationalization

Being able to translate a user interface into another language without software changes that require recompiling is an important aspect of HCI in today's global economy. This section provides a brief overview of how developing projects on the GWT and Android platforms provided students with practical experience internationalizing applications.

To internationalize a GWT application, key-value pairs are defined in a properties file, named based on the language being supported, for example a US properties file might be named strings_en_US.properties. A corresponding interface is defined in the Java code with method names corresponding to property file keys. For example, the property key-value pair,

```
helloWorld=Hello, World
```

corresponds to the interface method declaration:

```
public interface HC extends Constants {
  String helloWorld();
}
```

To use the constants, a class implementing the interface is created using a static method of the GWT class:

```
HC cnst = (HC) GWT.create( HC.class );
cnst.helloWorld();
```

The strengths of this approach to internationalization include compile time checking of the property keys and compiler optimization based on inlining the local strings.

Localization on the Android platform is similar with the key-value property file replaced with an XML file that matches attribute names to text values. Look-up of specific string values in the Java code takes place through a context object that contains locale specific information.

Actually implementing internationalization in a project has much greater impact than just talking about it. Internationalizing a student project can also bring a real sense of diversity to the classroom. Adams State College is a Hispanic Serving Institution, and there are usually Spanish speaking students in the HCI class and occasionally students speaking other languages who can quickly translate a property or XML file. By changing the locale of the browser or the mobile emulator (depending on the platform), the students can see a dramatic demonstration of how good design can lead to a quick transformation of an application to another language.

6.3 Layout

GWT and Android take contrasting approaches to layout of user-interface widgets. GWT uses a Swing-like approach to user-interface construction. There are a number of Layout managers that generate HTML tables and div elements when they are compiled. There is also a full library of View widgets that translate to standard HTML/AJAX input controls such as radio buttons, text fields, and combo boxes upon compilation. View widgets are added dynamically to a layout manager in the Java code.

While it is possible to create widgets and add them to containers dynamically on the Android platform, the more usual approach is to use a static XML file for specifying the layout of view widgets. Some of the advantages of this latter approach include increased flexibility, readability, and separation of responsibilities. Implementing projects using these two different, contrasting styles give HCI students practical experience with the architecture of layout management.

6.4 Mobile Design

While many user-interface design guidelines apply equally well to desktop, mobile, and web applications, there are a number of differences that students discovered when designing mobile applications.

For example, traditional form design for a desktop or web application includes placing a label directly to the left of the form control that it describes. Students took this guideline to heart in implementing their mobile applications only to discover that there is not enough screen real-estate available on cell phones to use this guideline effectively. After analyzing other Android form applications on the market, they realized that a standard form design for mobile applications is to place the input descriptor as initial text inside the form field as illustrated in Figure 2.

Figure 2: Mobile application placement of form labels.

Designing for various screen sizes and resolutions becomes more of an issue for mobile applications because of the huge range of screen sizes available in the mobile device market. The Android emulator provides numerous hardware options for configuring the emulator, including the specification of screen size and density. The architecture allows the developer to specify resources for a variety of screen densities and sizes through folder naming conventions. Students gained experience with the challenges of supporting different screen densities through implementing the scavenger hunt on both HVGA (160 dpi, 3.6" diagonal) and QVGA (120 dpi, 3.3" diagonal) virtual devices.

A standard user design principle is to prefer widgets that offer a fixed set of options to the user over text fields that provide free-form input in order to minimize user work and to minimize the need to provide input validation. However, students in the HCI course became particularly cognizant of the importance of avoiding textual input fields on mobile devices when they experienced first-hand the difficulty of using the small keyboards on cell phone devices. The typing issue was particularly interesting with regard to mobile design guidelines for password fields. Rather than immediately masking password characters as they are typed, the Android password widget displays them briefly before masking them. Because of their small display size, shoulder-surfing for passwords is less feasible for mobile applications, and the brief display of the typed character allows the user to correct typographical errors that are more common on mobile devices due to the small key pads.

One of the big differences between designing for desktop and web applications versus mobile applications is that mobile applications can take advantage of their context to provide targeted information to users. The scavenger hunt application provided the HCI students with the opportunity to see first-hand how context can be effectively used in a user interface. The cell phone's global positioning sensor was used to provide a blinking dot indicating the current position of the cell phone relative to the campus targets. When the application was initially tested, several of the targets were inadvertently located inside buildings where global positioning updates were not available. After the initial user interface testing, students suggested providing contextual feedback to the user in the form of a warning message if the cell phone lost contact with the global positioning service providing updates. This experience added relevance to the classroom discussion on how contextual feedback can be used to provide relevant information to the user.

6.5 Testing

While most HCI classes emphasize the importance of user-interface testing, the web application made realistic user-interface testing more accessible than it might be with a traditional desktop application. The class demonstrated the CRC form-submission system at one of the CRC committee's normally scheduled meetings. There was enough interest in the prototype application after the demonstration, that several committee members asked to try out the application themselves. Google provides a free hosting service for web applications on its App Engine architecture, and the Google plug-in for Eclipse provides a wizard for quickly deploying a web application on the Google site. CRC committee members required only a Google account in order to access the prototype application. By using Google's servers, there were none of the usual hassles of setting up and maintaining a local web server. CRC committee members accessed the application for testing from their offices without any of the installation headaches that a normal desktop application would entail.

In contrast, the Android testing environment added an element of fun to the testing experience and emphasized the importance of testing on an actual device in a realistic environment. Rather than a classroom based testing experience, students deployed their applications onto cell phones and enjoyed a break from the classroom by racing around campus on a simulated outdoor scavenger hunt. Some of the problems that were discovered that were not seen on the emulator included the need for a high contrast display that would be clearly visible in sunlight, the need to support both portrait and landscape layouts when their cell phones quickly switched orientation, and the need to provide a compass device in the application to aid in locating targets (improved user feedback). While all of these issues can be discussed in the classroom, actually discovering them as defects through realistic testing makes the issues more relevant.

6.6 Providing a Development Context

The CRC form submission system used a database for storing submitted institutional syllabi and course change information. The backend for the project was implemented using Google's App Engine datastore as a student project in a database course taught the previous semester. By extending the project across two different courses, students were able to see a connection between two traditionally separate areas of computer science. From a pedagogical point of view, building code on top of an existing persistence tier was a good experience for the students because it is often the case in industry that software developers must work with a pre-existing code base. In particular, it is often the job of the user-interface programmer to retrieve and store user data using an existing interface to a persistence tier.

An anonymous survey administered at the end of the semester indicated that the students felt that it was a useful experience to build a web user interface to interact with an existing server backend. Indeed, three quarters of the students strongly agreed with the statement:

> *Having the database backend to build a user interface on top of made me see how user interface programming and database programming fit together.*

7. RESULTS

Due to time limitations only about half of the CRC form-submission system was implemented. CRC committee members expressed a great deal of interest in seeing the prototype finished and used to replace the current Word template form-submission system. However, completion of the prototype depends on using it as the basis for another student project in a subsequent computer science class. The Android scavenger hunt mobile will be customized and used as an educational team-building activity in our computer literacy course.

While there were only 12 students enrolled in the course, too few students to provide a reliable statistical analysis, student assessments of the course do indicate that students reacted positively to the course. Student evaluations for the course were high with an overall rating of 4.6 out of a possible 5 pts. All students in the course either agreed or strongly agreed with the statement:

> *The inclusion of two student projects using Google platforms for mobile and web application development increased my level of interest in the course.*

Student evaluation comments were positive with the following two comments specifically addressing the use of mobile and web platforms to motivate HCI principles:

> *I found it especially interesting that we developed GUIs for multiple platforms.*

> *It is cool that the course applied the latest technologies in software development to mobile and web design.*

8. FUTURE IMPROVEMENTS

Learning two different platforms as part of the human computer interaction class made the class more challenging than if desktop projects had been chosen that leveraged the student's existing knowledge of Java Swing. Students picked up programming on the Android platform relatively easily, but the GWT toolkit was more challenging partly because the students encountered some bugs with the Google plug-in for Eclipse. Occasionally, the development server would shut down incompletely, leaving some processes running in the background. The students would then either have to completely reboot the computer or track down the background processes that were still running and shut them down from the command line. The compilation process was also very slow, leading many students to comment that it was very frustrating to write GWT code in Eclipse. Next time the course is offered, it will be important to assess competing platforms for writing web applications in Java in an attempt to find something that offers a combination of an easy-learning curve with a more robust development environment.

9. CONCLUSION

The development of Java environments for both web and mobile applications make it feasible to include both web and mobile student projects in Human Computer Interaction courses. The inclusion of such projects modernizes the curriculum and provides students with practical applications of classroom concepts. The use of Google's Android and GWT platforms for mobile and web development increased student interest and enthusiasm for the course by capitalizing on student perceptions of mobile computing and Google, in general, as "cool".

10. REFERENCES

[1] ACM/IEEE Interim Review Task Force on Computing Curricula. "Computing Science Curriculum 2008: An Interim Revision of CS 2001", Final report, *IEEE Computer Society, Association for Computing Machinery*, December 2008.

[2] Android Developers. *Google*. Retrieved November 23, 2010 from http://developer.android.com/index.html.

[3] Blackberry. Retrieved November 23, 2010 from http://na.blackberry.com/eng/.

[4] Bond, A., W. Schone, B. Beez, T Marx, W. Bering, B. Bergemann, R. Kamoua, W. Tang, "Application of Smart Phones with RFID in Museums: A Case Study of Global Engineering Entrepreneurship", *Proceedings of the 2009 International Conference on Frontiers in Education: Computer Science and Computer Engineering*, 2009.

[5] Craig, J. and M. Cooper. 2010. Accessible Rich Internet Applications (WAI-ARIA) 1.0 (W3C Working Draft 16 September 2010. *W3C*. Retrieved November 23, 2010 from http://www.w3.org/TR/wai-aria/.

[6] Document Object Model (DOM). *W3C*. Retrieved November 23, 2010 from http://www.w3.org/DOM/.

[7] ECMAScript Language Specification. *ECMA International*. Retrieved November 23, 2010 from http://www.json.org/.

[8] Eclipse. Retrieved November 23, 2010 from http://www.eclipse.org/.

[9] Garrett, J. 2005. "Ajax: A New Approach to Web Applications", *Adaptive Path*. Retrieved November 23, 2010 from http://www.adaptivepath.com/ideas/essays/archives/000385.php.

[10] Google App Engine. *Google*. Retrieved November 23, 2010 from http://code.google.com/appengine/.

[11] Google APIs Add-On. *Google*. Retrieved November 23, 2010 from http://code.google.com/android/add-ons/google-apis/.

[12] Google Docs. *Google*. Retrieved November 23, 2010 from http://www.google.com/accounts/ServiceLogin?service=writely&passive=1209600&continue=http%3A%2F%2Fdocs.google.com%2F&followup=http%3A%2F%2Fdocs.google.com%2F&ltmpl=homepage.

[13] Google Web Toolkit. *Google*. Retrieved November 23, 2010 from http://code.google.com/webtoolkit/.

[14] JavaFX Technology at a Glance. *Oracle*. Retrieved November 23, 2010 from http://java.sun.com/javafx/.

[15] Java ME at a Glance. *Oracle*. Retrieved November 23, 2010 from http://java.sun.com/javame/index.jsp.

[16] JavaServer Faces Technology. *Oracle*. Retrieved November 23, 2010 from http://java.sun.com/javaee/javaserverfaces/.

[17] Kurkovsky, S., "Engaging StudentsThrough Mobile Game Development", *Proceedings of the 40th SIGCSE Technical Symposium on Computer Science Education*, 2009.

[18] Mahmoud, Q.H., Dyer, A., "Mobile Devices in an Introductory Programming Course", *Computer 41, 6, (Jun. 2008), 106-108.*

[19] Mahmoud, Q.H., T. Ngo, R. Niazi, P. Popowicz, R. Sydoryshyn, M. Wilks, "An Academic Kit for Integrating Mobile Devices into the CS Curriculum", *Proceedings of the 14th SIGCSE Annual Conference on Innovation and Technology in Computer Science Education, 2009.*

[20] Microsoft Office. *Microsoft*. Retrieved November 23, 2010 from http://office.microsoft.com/en-us/word/.

[21] OpenXava. Retrieved November 23, 2010 from http://www.gestion400.com/web/guest/home.

[22] Powell, D. and J. Hollingsworth, "Integrating Mobile Computing with Android in Computer Science II and Computer Science III", *Proceedings of the 2009 International Conference on Frontiers in Education: Computer Science and Computer Engineering*, 2009.

[23] Qualcomm Brew MP. *Qualcomm*. Retrieved November 23, 2010 from http://brew.qualcomm.com/brew/en/.

[24] Reiser, S. and Bruce, R. 2008. Service learning meets mobile computing. In *Proceedings of the 46th Annual Southeast Regional Conference on XX* (Auburn, Alabama, March 28 - 29, 2008). ACM-SE 46. ACM, New York, NY, 108-113.

[25] Rife. Retrieved November 23, 2010 from http://rife.dev.java.net/.

[26] Struts 2. *The Apache Software Foundation*. Retrieved November 23, 2010 from struts.apache.org/2.1.6/index.html.

[27] Twitter Clients. Retrieved June 9, 2010 from http://twitstat.com/twitterclientusers.html.

[28] Windows Mobile. *Microsoft*. Retrieved November 23, 2010 from http://msdn.microsoft.com/en-us/windowsmobile/default.aspx.

[29] XHTML 1.0 The Extensible HyperText Markup Language. *W3C*. Retrieved November 23, 2010 from http://www.w3schools.com/html/default.asp.

App Inventor and Real-World Motivation

David Wolber
Department of Computer Science
University of San Francisco
2130 Fulton Street
San Francisco, CA 94117
wolber@usfca.edu

ABSTRACT

App Inventor is a visual "blocks" language for creating mobile apps. As part of a Google pilot program, App Inventor was taught to university students in a core curriculum course at the University of San Francisco. This paper introduces App Inventor and the course, focusing on how the language facilitated interactions with the world outside of the classroom.

Categories and Subject Descriptors

D.1.7 Visual Programming, K.32 Computer and Information Science Education http://www.acm.org/class/1998/

General Terms: Design, Languages

Keywords

Visual Programming, Blocks Programming, Motivation.

1. INTRODUCTION

The number of computer science majors increased by 14% over the last two years, but enrollments are still nearly 50% below the count of early 2000 [6]. With CS-related fields expected to grow rapidly [4], there is a need for more computer science courses that engage students both in K-12 and the university level [16].

In the Summer of 2009 Google launched a pilot program with ten universities. They gave each university 20 Android phones and accounts to a yet-to-be-released tool, App Inventor for Android. The goal was to explore the use of this new visual language for building mobile apps. Here's an except from the pilot announcement:

"open mobile platforms like Android can bring some of that same change to introductory Computer Science, to make it more about people and their interactions with others and with the world around them. It's a vision where young people—and everyone—can engage the world of mobile services and applications as creators, not just consumers. Through this work, we hope to do the following:

** Make mobile application development accessible to anyone.*

** Enhance introductory learning experiences in computing through the vehicle of Android's open platform.*

SIGCSE'11, March 9–12, 2011, Dallas, Texas, USA.

** Encourage a community of faculty and students to share material and ideas for teaching and exploring."*[1]

I had been teaching a general education course, "Computing, Robots, and the Web" for a few years, using the Lego Mindstorms system [9] and Media computing [8] for the programming component. Programming robots and multi-media motivated student to learn some programming and problem solving, but I felt that most had trouble seeing a direct application to their lives.

Before attending the Google pilot, I was considering Alice [5] and Scratch[11,13], both of which motivate programming through the storytelling metaphor and letting students create multi-media animations in a visual environment. But App Inventor and mobile apps intrigued me because students could create personalized software for their most precious device, the phone, and literally augment their own reality. App Inventor provides high-level components for process incoming SMS texts, interfacing with the GPS location sensor of the phone, scanning barcodes, and communicating with web APIs. The mobile world was exploding and here was this visual language the let beginning students be creative in that world.

I also knew that App Inventor used a similar blocks language to that of Scratch, which had proven successful not only with kids but as an initial module in a university course [11]. Though App Inventor was only partially complete at the initial summer workshop, Hal Abelson, the co-director of the project, stood and said, "Trust us, it's Google." I took Hal's advice and re-designed my course. I figured my students wouldn't be too displeased if the "Robot" in my course title was an Android phone!

My leap of faith was rewarded: teaching App Inventor has been my most satisfying teaching experience in seventeen years. The apps created by my students have been incredible, especially given that they had no prior programming experience and most took the class to fulfill the dreaded math core requirement. One team built "Android Where's My Car", an app that records where you park your car so you can find it after a concert or ballgame. Another team created "Droid Muni", which tells you when your next bus is coming. Others created games, quiz apps, and restaurant guides for the USF area. As you might imagine, such projects were not just about programming but engaged the students with the world outside of the computer lab.

There were three projects that stood out in terms of their real-world impact. One student built "No Text While Driving" and State Farm Insurance released a remarkably similar app a few months later, the goal being to save lives [15]. Another student built an Android version of an SMS broadcast tool that has helped people in developing countries communicate, and a non-profit in Helsinki customized the student's version to organize a thousand-person event. Another pair of students had an idea for an SOS emergency app to help people when they're walking late at night, and the project turned into a startup with a role for one of the students.

The stories exemplify an important aspect of App Inventor: in a manner of weeks, beginners can build apps that are not only fun, but have real-world utility. It allows creative people to transform their ideas into working, interactive apps that can be taken up by large companies, used by non-profit organizations, and turned into startups. In my experience, such real-world impact for student projects is rare, even for upper classmen.

The students were surprised and empowered by what they created. Here are a few excerpts from an end-of-course survey:

"This course helped me see how powerful modern technology really is. Before this class, I never in a million years thought that creating apps for phones was so accessible and simple to create/test. "

"I can actually participate in conversations about Computer Science when before I used to check out and not listen because I figured it was just something I didn't understand."

"I thought we were going to be in a dark room working with these creepy monitors and everything would be code text but it is not. Its hands on, fun and a good challenge."

App Inventor is now publicly available in Google Labs and has matured significantly from the initial pilot phase. Having observed the excitement of my students, I was not surprised at the large user community that quickly materialized [3] or the fact that the New York Times [10] and others saw its potential as much more than simply an educational tool.

I have now based my course on App Inventor for three semesters and have developed course materials [18], tutorials for the App Inventor site [17] and a video breakdown series [19]. In this paper, I'll introduce the environment and how I use it in my class, then share the three examples of student projects with a real-world impact.

2. "Hello World" in Three Languages

A student's initial experience with programming should be both comprehensible and motivating. With *Java*, the prototypical first example is *Hello World:*

```
class HelloWorldApp {
    public static void main(String[] args) {
        System.out.println("HelloWorld!");}}
```

Because of its object-oriented nature, even this simplest Java example has a lot of packaging. Just about every term used in the sample is indecipherable to a beginning student. Beginners are not developmentally ready to learn any of it, and the teacher must wave his hand and move on.

Besides being hard to understand, the Java initial example is hardly motivating: if students can get it to run, "Hello World" is displayed in a terminal screen..

Next, consider the *Whirling Butterfly* introductory tutorial from the *Scratch* site:

Figure 1. An introductory tutorial in Scratch

With Scratch, you drag blocks from the left panel to the middle scripts panel, and immediately see your program run in the right panel. The blocks are understandable and the environment lets you explore their meaning interactively. The result is an engaging tool proven successful with kids and as an initial component of a university course [11].

App Inventor can be thought of as Scratch for mobile phones—the two languages even use the same underlying code library for their blocks [14].

Because App Inventor blocks encapsulate complex technologies like SMS texting and GPS location sensors, even an initial sample can be quite motivating. Consider this one, which I used this past semester on the first day of class:

Figure 2. An Introductory App Inventor app

This sample auto-responds to a text received by the phone, sending back the text, "Sorry, I'm driving, I'll get back to you later." It's a simplified version of the "No Text While Driving" app which will be discussed later. The blocks are understandable, as with the Scratch example. However, the app's effect is not enclosed within a virtual world, but has meaning in the real one. Because of this, students immediately ask questions. "Could you make it so the response sent back could be customized? Can you make it so the texts are spoken aloud? Can you write an app that let's people vote for something by text, like on American Idol?"As a teacher, I know that such inquiries translate into students wanting to learn and driving the learning process.

3. App Inventor and its use in the classroom

App Inventor has two main windows: a component designer for building the user interface and a blocks editor for defining an app's behavior. You can also test your apps live directly on your phone or an emulator.

The Component Designer, shown in Figure 3, is a fairly typical WYSIWYG tool for designing user interfaces: you drag objects into a view, modify component properties like background color and width, and in general specify how the app will look. There are UI components for building form-based apps,

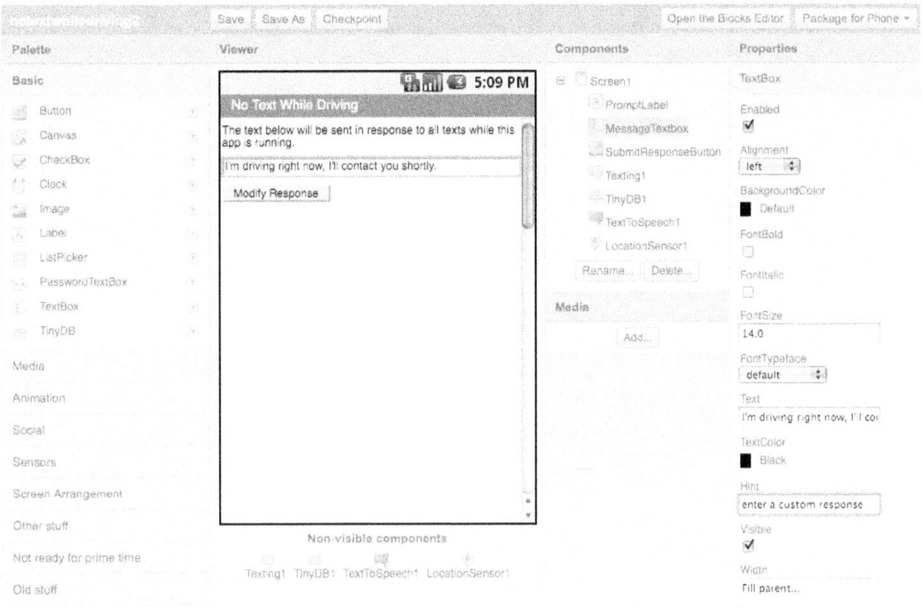

Figure 3. App Inventor Component Designer and *No Text While Driving*

canvas and image sprite components for building graphical, animated apps, and video and sound components for multi-media.

In the Component Designer, you also specify the non-visual components your app needs for accessing the technology available on the Android device. These include components for sending and responding to SMS texts, for interacting with the GPS and orientation sensors, for text-to-speech and speech recognition, for scanning barcodes, for saving data persistently, and for talking to the web.

3.1 Programming Behaviors

Once the components of the app have been specified in the Component Designer, the app's behavior is defined in the Blocks Editor (see Figure 4). The Blocks Editor has two palettes. The first, My Blocks, contains functional blocks for interacting with the components that have been added to the particular app. The second palette contains built-in blocks for standard programming control and functionality including foreach, if-else, list and text manipulation, and logical operators.

The blocks language provides a low-threshold entry to programming. The elimination of most typing dramatically reduces the frustrations beginners have with syntax, the blocks provide visual cues to ease the development task, and only some blocks lock into place, reducing the possibility of errors.

The language also works because you define an app's behavior directly as a set of event-handlers: when event X occurs, do Y (think of the complexities of programming the response to even a button click event in Java). For the app in Figure 4, the programmer has specified three event handlers: Texting.MessageReceived for processing an incoming text, LocationSensor.LocationChanged for tracking the driver's current location, and SubmitResponseButton.click for recording a custom response entered by the user. Within weeks, students can learn enough event-response programming to create simple location-aware apps, SMS processing apps, and games on the order of *Mole Mash* or *Tic Tac Toe.*

Once students become comfortable with event handling and function call blocks, I introduce more complexity and abstraction through a quiz app assignment. Quizzes are fun because students can choose a topic of interest and easily include video and sound with the provided high-level components. Motivation is important because building a quiz requires a significant amount of abstract thinking, logic and traditional programming skills, e.g., using an index variable to walk through a list. When you add in variations such as multiple-choice answers and user-generated quizzes, the task is event more difficult. Fortunately, the students have been "lured in" by this point and are thus sufficiently motivated to make the conceptual leap necessary.

Later in the semester we explore persistent data, accessing APIs, and mutli-user apps using the high-level components provided. The TinyDB and TinyWebDB allow for persistent storage using simple key-value pairs. TinyDB is used to store data directly on the device, while TinyWebDB is used for shared databases and also for accessing web information sources.

The TinyWebDB bridge to the web is important because as students feel more empowered creative, they often want to build apps that access web information. I don't want the response to their creativity to be, "no, that's not possible". Furthermore, I've found that class discussions concerning APIs, mashups, interoperability and cloud computing are much better when the students have had some direct experience.

To allow for web-enabled projects, my teaching assistants and I have created a number of App-Inventor-compliant "wrapper" APIs for student projects, including one that gets event information from the Eventful API and another that accesses San Francisco's MUNI bus schedule. Creating the APIs requires traditional programming knowledge: we wrote them using

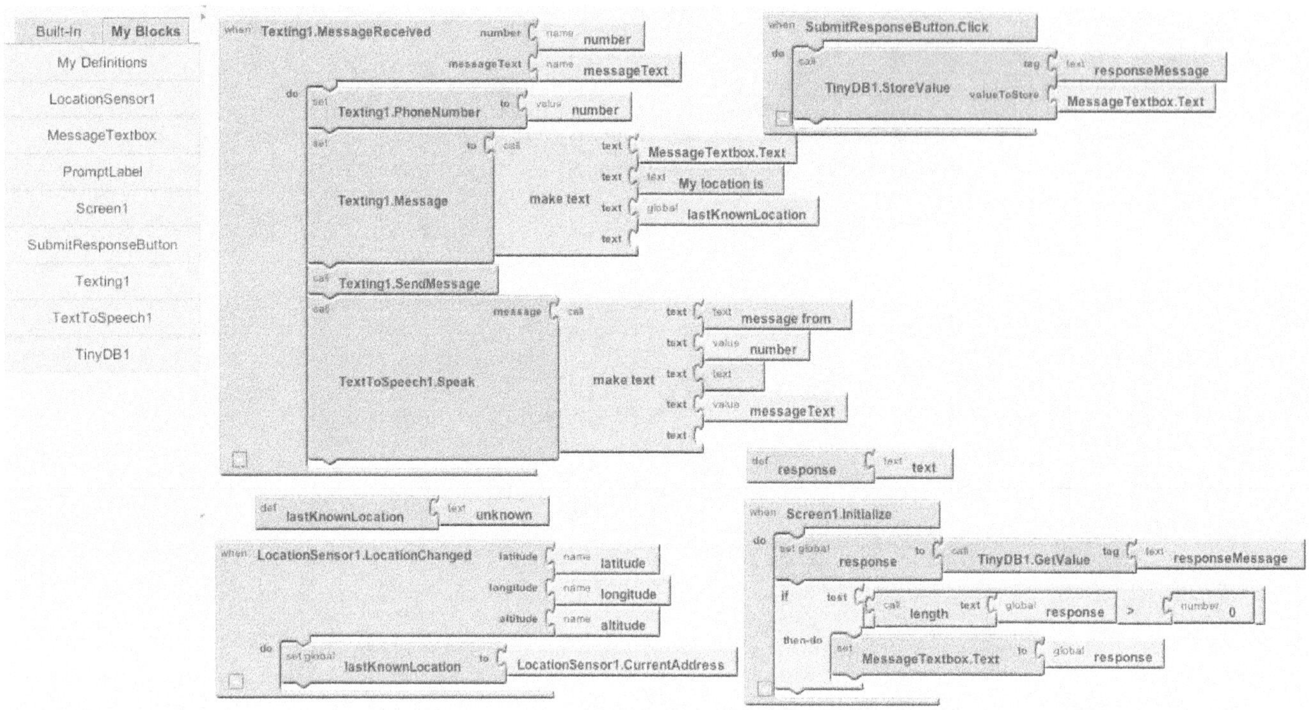

Figure 4. App Inventor Blocks for *No Text While Driving*.

Python and App Engine (see appinventorapi.com for more information). Once created, the students can create client apps in App Inventor using a simple getValue(tag) call to the TinyWebDB component.

3.2 Testing, Deploying, and Sharing

In the summer of 2010, App Inventor added live testing to the environment: you can now plug in a phone during development and interact with the app you are building in real-time without compiling or downloading after modifications.

Live testing helps immensely with user interface refinement: you can modify component properties and immediately see how they'll look on the phone. It also helps with testing behaviors. For example, after plugging in some or all of the blocks in the Texting.MessageReceived event of Figure 4, a student can ask the person next to them to send them a text, and immediately know if the app is responding as it should.

Live testing is also integrated with an Android emulator, so you can develop and test apps even if you do not have a device available. This is especially important for education and settings in which not every student has access to a phone.

Once an app is tested, you can deploy it by packaging it into an Android app (.apk file) or generating a barcode for it. The barcode appears on screen and you can then scan it on to your phone.

Finally, you can generate source code for an app that you want to share. Because the source "blocks" are actually decipherable, App Inventor apps tend to be open-source in practice and not just theory. This sharing will be even further enhanced when App Inventor launches its planned Scratch-like community site.

4. Impact Outside the Classroom

The USF Computer Science Department has a Senior/MS Project course in which the students develop software for a client from industry or academia. At the end of the semester, the students present their work at our CS Night. The course has been successful in giving students real-world experience and helping them get internships and jobs.

Whereas the project course is a capstone for our most advanced students, the App Inventor course is on the other end—beginners with no programming experience from every major in the university *besides* computer science. Despite this, the App Inventor course has provided many of the same benefits as the advanced project class. In fact the students in the course now present alongside the seniors and masters students at our CS Night. This section tells the stories of three App Inventor projects that had a particular "real-world" impact outside of the classroom.

4.1 *No Text While Driving* and State Farm

Daniel Finnegan is a creative writing major who I'm sure spends more time thinking about the human condition than cell phone apps. But he had read about the dangers of texting while driving: incredibly, something like 28% of accidents involve a phone [12]. He came up with an idea for an app to help and built the precursor to the SMS auto-response app shown in Figure 4.

Daniel's app struck a chord with people. The App Inventor team described it on their About page and it was cited in a New York Times article [10]. I had begun writing tutorials for the App Inventor site and created an annotated and refined version of the app. In August 2010, we were excited to see that State Farm Insurance launched "On the Move", an Android app that was quite similar to "No Text While Driving":

"It is our hope that this widget will prevent crashes and save lives," said Laurette Stiles, Strategic Resources vice president at State Farm. "This new service will help drivers manage the temptation to read or respond to text messages when they are behind the wheel. We wanted to make this widget available free-of-charge as just one of the ways we're working to keep our roadways safe for drivers."[15]

The State Farm app may not have been directly inspired by "No Text While Driving", but it's quite possible it was. In pondering this question, I realized the incredible nature of it: an app created in an introductory course, by an English major who had never programmed a computer, possibly helping inspire a mass-produced piece of software! And one that saves lives!

Figure 5. State Farm's "On the Move" app

4.2 *BroadcastHub* in Helsinki

Ken Banks gave a talk in my fall App Inventor course on his FrontlineSMS tool [7]. Ken, one of the leading authorities on mobile technology for the public good, had observed that many people in developing countries have cell phones but no Internet access. Sending texts is expensive, but receiving them is not. So he built FrontlineSMS, a PC-based tool that serves as a broadcast hub for SMS communication. With it, people send an SMS text to the hub to register, then receive broadcasted messages from the group. Amongst other things, FrontlineSMS has been used to monitor election fraud in Afghanistan and help with health care in Malawi.

Carly Kralji, a student in my class, was especially enthused by Ken's work. Her idea was this: because some situations, such as election monitoring, are so volatile, why not make the hub itself run on a mobile Android device (instead of software for a desktop or laptop, as with FrontlineSMS).

Ken Banks and his lead engineer, Alex Anderson, became interested in Carly's project and generously gave their time to help Carly along. One thing Carly learned was that, ideally, the hub would make use of the contact groups on the phone. App Inventor does not yet allow full access to the contact groups, so Carly had to make due with a separate broadcast list in her version. The discussions with Ken and Alex, and the analysis between the ideal and the possible, gave Carly some great experience with real project specification and implementation.

Carly completed her Android version of the broadcast hub and posted it on her course portfolio site as well as the course's "USF Android Market" page. Later that summer, Ken Banks contacted me to say that his group was creating a full-fledged Android version of FrontlineSMS. He very politely pointed out that Carly had named her app Android FrontlineSMS and he thought it would be less confusing if Carly changed the title.

We quickly changed the name to "Broadcast Hub" and I made a note to do a better job monitoring projects. I also realized I had a great example for use in class discussions involving ethics and copyright issues.

As with the "No Text While Driving" example, I was again struck by the fact that Carly, an International Design major in a core-curriculum course, had created something with utility to the world, something that Ken Banks cared about. Because of this, she (and I) had gained some great real-world experience and dealt with issues rarely faced in the classroom.

The story got better. Some weeks later, I created a version of the broadcast hub as a tutorial available on the App Inventor site [17]. Soon thereafter, I was contacted by Myles Byrne of a non-profit group based in Helsinki, Finland:

"My wife and I are respectively a cancer scientist and a bioinformatician who moved from San Francisco to Helsinki last year. We're working extracurricularly with a local arts organization to try to lift a central neighborhood to a more creative and inclusive plane, especially regarding the growing immigrant population. So there is at least some relatedness to the mission of FrontlineSMS.

So we're organizing events from now till 2012, when Helsinki is World Design Capital. The first such event is Saturday, and we're trying to get broadcastHub working...

I was planning to learn App Inventor at leisure. But hours of searching for commercial SMS providers doing what broadcastHub does (for Helsinki users) turned up nothing."

This first email went on to ask about some minor technical issues he was having with App Inventor. I received a second email a few days later:

Dave, our community raising event in Helsinki went off really well. About 1000 people came (see http://www.punajuuri.org/) We needed SMS broadcast capabilty for up to a thousand people over a few days. We looked at FrontlineSMS, Clickatell, and others – nothing had the right fit. Then I got my invitation to App Inventor, looked at the broadcasterHub tutorial, and realized with a shock this was the perfect solution. In a few hours I was able to modify the broadcastHub tutorial app to fit exactly our needs:

Any SMS's sent to my phone number with the app running received an autoreply: "Text 'beatroot' to this number to sign up for our message list." Any numbers sending an SMS to me containing 'beatroot' or 'Beatroot' were added to the broadcast list. But because our event was in Helsinki, the broadcast messages needed to be in Finnish. So instead of writing them myself, I told the app to take any messages sent to me from Heta and Jon, the Finnish organizers of the event, and automatically re-send it to all the numbers on the broadcast list.

It really was incredibly fast and easy to modify the broadcastHub app to do only what we needed. The app worked perfectly and can be easily re-used, modified, and shared. Having the capabilities of an android phone plugged into a graphical programming environment is an amazing experience. You're not just learning logic, you're learning it in the context of the social world connected to your phone.

Thanks David and Google for bringing the next level.

Carly's project had not only given her great experience, it had been customized for a real event! It occurred to me that App Inventor was not only an experiment in motivating beginners, but an experiment in open source software. Plenty of software is theoretically open source, but in practice is only "open" if you have the key: expert programming knowledge and the time to rebuild a project from the source. Myles and his group were able to use the BroadcastHub sample because, unlike most programming code and systems, *App Inventor source is decipherable, even to people who are not expert programmers.*

4.3 SOS Emergency App

Chris Witte and Elena Miguelena were in my first App Inventor class of Fall 2010. The first version of App Inventor began working about a week before the semester began and the bugs were not yet ironed out.

Despite these drawbacks, Chris and Elena came up with a great idea for an app: you're walking home at night, approaching that dark and street that always gives you the creeps. Before you turn onto it, you start the app and press a button. If you don't press the button again within the next minute, an SOS text message is sent to a pre-determined list of numbers.

They built a prototype of the app in class, and Chris showed it to his mother. Late in the semester, his mother mentioned Chris's app to a man sitting next to her at a basketball game. The man happened to be a former executive at Apple, and really liked the idea. He gave Chris's mother his contact information and told her to have Chris call him. Soon Chris was involved with a startup developing the SOS app and applying for a patent on it.

One interesting side note to the story is that Chris is dyslexic. He'd tried programming before and was overwhelmed trying to learn the Java programming language, which is text-based. Chris had much greater success with App Inventor's visual language and its color-coded blocks.

5. Summary

App Inventor combines a low-threshold entry to programming with the ability to create apps that have a real impact. The visual, event-based nature of the language reduces the syntax problems common to beginners and gets them past the first "bump" in learning programming. They can almost immediately build apps with real-world utility, which motivates them to tackle the second "bump": learning how to solve hard logic problems and specify interactive behavior with a static (though visual) language.

6. ACKNOWLEDGMENTS

Thanks to Google for its grant support and the App Inventor team for their support of App Inventor at USF.

7. REFERENCES

[1] Hal Abelson. 2009. App Inventor Pilot Announcement. Retrieved Dec. 6, 2010 from http://googleresearch.blogspot.com/2009/07/app-inventor-for-android.html.

[2] App Inventor Launch Announcement. 2009. Retrieved Dec. 6, 2010 from http://googleblog.blogspot.com/2010/07/app-inventor-for-android.html.

[3] App Inventor User Group. Retrieved Dec. 6, 2010 from http://groups.google.com/group/appinventor.

[4] Bureau of Labor Statistics. 2009. *Employment Projections:2008-2018.* Retrieved Dec. 6, 2010 from http://www.bls.gov/news.release/ecopro.nr0.htm.

[5] Cooper, S., Dann, W., and Pausch, R., Teaching Objects-first in Introductory Computer Science, *Proceedings of the 34th SIGCSE technical symposium on Computer science education*, Reno, NV, 2003.

[6] Computing Research Association. *2008-09 Taulbee Survey.* Retreived Dec. 6, 2010 from http://www.cra.org/resources/taulbee/

[7] FrontlineSMS, Retrieved Dec. 6, 2010 from http://frontlinesms.com.

[8] Guzdial, M. and Forte, A., Design Process for a Non-majors Computing Course, ", in *Proc. of the SIGCSE Technical Symposium on Computer Science Education*, pp. 361-365, St. Louis, Missouri, 2005.

[9] Lego Mindstorms. 2010. Retrieved Dec. 6, 2010 from http://mindstorms.lego.com.

[10] Lohr, S. *Google's Do-It-Yourself App Creation Software*, New York Times, July 12, 2010.

[11] Malan, D. ,Leitner, H., "Scratch for Budding Computer Scientists", *in Proc. of the 38th SIGCSE Technical Symposium on Computer Science Education*, pp. 223-227, Covington, KY, 2007.

[12] National Safety Council Report. 2010. Retrieved Dec. 6, 2010 from http://www.nsc.org/pages/nscestimates16millioncrashescausedbydriversusingcellphonesandtexting.aspx

[13] Resnick, M., et. al., Scratch: programming for all, *Communications of the ACM*, v.52 n.11, November 2009 DOI=http://doi.acm.org/10.1145/1592761.1592779.

[14] Roque, R., 2007. *OpenBlocks : an extendable framework for graphical block programming systems.* Retrieved Dec. 6, 2010 from http://hdl.handle.net/1721.1/41550.

[15] State Farm Press Release, 2010. Retrieved Dec. 6, 2010 fromhttp://www.statefarm.com/aboutus/newsroom/20100819.asp

[16] Wilson, et.al. 2010. *Running on Empty: The Failure to Teach K-12 Comptuer Science in the Digital.* http://www.acm.org/runningonempty/fullreport.pdf, 2010.

[17] Wolber, D. *App Inventor Advanced Tutorials.* 2010. Retrived Dec. 6, 2010 from http://appinventor.googlelabs.com/learn/tutorials

[18] Wolber, D. *Computing, Robots, and the Web.* 2010. Retrieved Dec. 6, 2010 from https://sites.google.com/site/cs107fall2010/, with teaching materials at http://appinventor.org.

[19] Wolber, D., *Creating SMS Texts with App Inventor: O'Reilly Breakdown Series.* 2010. Retrieved Dec. 6, 2010 from http://oreilly.com/catalog/0636920016175/.

Smart Smartphone Development: iOS versus Android

Mark H. Goadrich
Mathematics and Computer Science
Centenary College of Louisiana
Shreveport, LA 71104
mgoadric@centenary.edu

Michael P. Rogers
Computer Science Information Systems
Northwest Missouri State University
Maryville, MO 64468
Michael@nwmissouri.edu

ABSTRACT

In a remarkably short timeframe, developing apps for smartphones has gone from an arcane curiosity to an essential skill set. Employers are scrambling to find developers capable of transforming their ideas into apps. Educators interested in filling that void are likewise trying to keep up, and face difficult decisions in designing a meaningful course. There are a plethora of development platforms, but two stand out because of their popularity and divergent approaches — Apple's iOS, and Google's Android. In this paper, we will compare the two, and address the question: which should faculty teach?

Categories and Subject Descriptors

K.3.2 [**Computer Science Education**]: Computer and Information Science Education – *computer science education*

General Terms

Languages, Performance, Standardization

Keywords

iPhone, Android, iOS, Xcode, Eclipse, Objective-C, Java, Smartphones, Mobile Devices, apps

1. INTRODUCTION

Driven by industry needs, student interest, and the relative maturation of the technologies, more faculty are now in a position to consider including modules or even offer full courses in mobile development [10, 12-15, 22, 23, 26]. There are a plethora of platform possibilities — Apple's iOS, Google's Android, Microsoft's Windows Mobile, Nokia's Symbian OS, RIM's BlackBerry, etc. — and while a survey course might be intriguing, the logistics would be daunting, and the failure to develop expertise on any single platform would likely prove unsatisfying. In short, a choice must be made.

A detailed examination of so many platforms is impractical here, so to assist faculty in their most critical first decision, the authors, too, have had to make a choice: we have elected to contrast development on two of the leading platforms among college students [7], Apple's iOS and Google's Android. We will compare their hardware/operating system requirements, Software Development Kits (tools, frameworks, languages, documentation), instructor resources, and finish up by describing the development of a "Hello, World!" app on both platforms.

SIGCSE'11, March 9–12, 2011, Dallas, Texas, USA.

2. HARDWARE/OS REQUIREMENTS

2.1 iOS

iOS development requires Macintosh computers running Mac OS X 10.6 (Snow Leopard). Since apps tend to be relatively small in size, and run on much slower processors, the computers themselves need not be particularly powerful.

Realistically, hardware may be one of the most irksome impediments to iOS development: while Macintoshes are common on campus, they are less so in Computer Science departments. One solution is to network with colleagues in other departments, or failing that, purchase some low end (but perfectly adequate) Mac Minis, so named for both their dimensions and price.

iOS development can almost be done entirely on the computer, as the simulator that is bundled with the iOS SDK is perfectly acceptable in most situations. The only difficulties arise in usability testing —using the mouse with a simulated touch screen feels unnatural — and apps that require access to particular hardware (GPS, Camera, Accelerometer, Magnetometer) cannot be realistically tested on the simulator. For accurate testing, an actual iPhone, iPad, or iPod Touch (an "iFamily device") is required.

Outfitting an entire class with an iFamily device could be expensive. While an iPhone 3G^s can be purchased for $99, in the United States a minimum 2-year AT&T contract is required, pushing the true cost to over $1000. A more palatable option might be an iPad ($499) or iPod Touch ($199). These lack some of the iPhone's more interesting amenities (built-in GPS, accelerometer, compass, and camera), but those might not be necessary in a beginning class. It would not be necessary to provide a device to each student; either one per team, or just a handful available for checkout would suffice, and perhaps provide an accidental lesson in scheduling algorithms.

2.2 Android

Unlike iOS, which is restricted to Mac OS X, Android can be developed using any of the current major operating systems, Windows (XP or higher), Mac OS X (10.5.8 or higher), and Linux systems (running with kernel 2.6 or higher). This provides great flexibility as almost any modern computer science laboratory should be suitable: no specialized hardware is required.

Developers can create Android Virtual Devices (AVDs), each AVD configured to represent a particular physical mobile device, that run on the Android Emulator [2]. As the name suggests, AVDs allow for extensive testing without the need for an actual phone. An AVD can be instantiated with many different screen resolutions, SD card sizes, and SDK versions to fully test the compatibility of their application over a wide range of Android implementations. GPS readings and phone/SMS interrupt signals can be passed to the emulator through a telnet connection, and accelerometer, orientation and compass readings can be manipulated using OpenIntent's SensorSimulator [21].

As is the case with iOS, testing applications on actual devices is invaluable. Two different development phones can be purchased from Google through an Android Market account, the Nexus One at $529 running SDK 2.2, and Developer Phone 2 at $399 running SDK 1.6. For educational grants, Google also recommends contacting individual hardware manufacturers such as HTC, Motorola and Samsung.

3. SDK

3.1 iOS

iOS apps are written using Xcode, a modern IDE used to code, debug, and lay out the interface. Students familiar with Eclipse, NetBeans or Visual Studio will feel right at home.

For more sophisticated debugging, a separate application called Instruments can be used to detect memory leaks, profile where the app spends most of its time, and ascertain how it utilizes system resources. Both Xcode and Instruments require the hardware described in section 2.1.

Xcode projects can be targeted specifically for iPhones or iPads (the interface is sized appropriately), or written to be universal, running on the iPhone in full-size or on the iPad at a user-selectable resolution.

The iOS SDK is not new. Its origins can be traced to NeXT OS, and while it continues to evolve at a rapid pace to accommodate mobile devices, it has been in widespread use on Mac OS X for over 10 years [11]. This shows in the iOS frameworks, collectively known as Cocoa Touch, which are meticulously designed, exhaustively tested, and thoroughly documented. They provide an excellent example for students to emulate.

Cocoa Touch incorporates numerous unusual, if not unique, design patterns that by themselves are worth studying [5]. For example:

- Interface elements, created visually using a graphical editor, are stored in .xib files, then graphically connected to code via *outlets*.
- Object allocation and initialization take place in distinct steps, which reduces the number of initialization methods (equivalent to Java constructors) that must be defined.
- Instead of subclassing, distinctive behavior is achieved by equipping classes with *delegates*. Delegates are simply references to objects that implement a particular protocol, and consulted whenever an object needs to respond.
- Blocks (equivalent to lambda expressions and closures in other languages), while not unique to iOS 4, are ubiquitous in the SDK, and provide an even simpler alternative to delegation

iOS applications are most commonly written using Objective-C, a superset of ANSI-C that borrows its OO syntax from SmallTalk. Cocoa Touch provides a rich set of collections, so it is possible to do most coding without having to dwell on the arcana of pointers. However, students must deal with memory management themselves — for performance reasons garbage collection is not available — a bonus for those who spend most of their time in Java or C#.

Perhaps one of the most fundamental design patterns is the separation of interface and implementation, and this is embedded into all iOS apps. In the language itself, an Objective-C class is defined in two files. The interface, in a .h file, contains instance variables, method signatures and properties (simplifying the writing of accessors and mutators). The implementation, in a .m file, contains method bodies. In an Xcode project, the interface is specified in a .xib file, and the implementation in an Objective-C class.

3.2 Android

Android OS is considerably newer than iOS. It has been under rapid development, moving from version 1.0, released in May 2007, to version 2.2, released in May 2010. A majority of Android devices now use 2.1 or above, although a significant portion of devices remain at 1.5 or 1.6 due to hardware limitations [3]. In classroom settings, this fragmentation can either be ignored, with students standardizing on one screen size and OS version, or exploited, to create tangible real-life testing scenarios of cross-platform development.

Eclipse is the recommended and most popular development environment for Android. With the use of the Android SDK plugin, developers can employ this powerful IDE to create projects and skeleton code, push apps to the emulator, and sign apps for release in the Android Market. Although it is possible to develop for Android outside of Eclipse, the benefits of having quick access to the SDK, easy deployment to the emulator or phone, and an integrated debugging environment make it an obvious choice.

The GUI layout for an Android app consists of XML files which include Layout and View elements. Views can be placed hierarchically inside Layouts to create the GUI functionality in either a relative or absolute mode. Eclipse includes a simple WYSIWYG editor for creating views and editing their properties, as well as exposing the underlying XML for manual alterations to the code. Another alternative for layout creation is DroidDraw [6], a platform independent application that can export XML for use in Android projects.

The controller and model functionality of an Android app are written in Java, using a subset of the Java 6 SE API, where the swing, awt, and applet classes have been replaced with custom libraries for graphics and mobile development. Instead of running on a Java Virtual Machine, Google developed its own virtual machine environment for mobile devices called Dalvik. Projects are compiled to run on a Dalvik VM, with each application running inside its own VM on the device. Unless they have had experience with the Java GUI framework, students familiar with Java from a CS1 and CS2 sequence will not notice a difference between standard Java and the subset available in Android. They do not require prior GUI programming exposure. Mapping functionality can be added by including a separate SDK and obtaining an API key for Google Maps.

There are two other main avenues for developing for Android. Scripting Language for Android (SL4A) provides quick access to the API through Python, Perl, JRuby, among others. Apps using SL4A can be written directly on the phone and used immediately without the need for compiling and exporting an apk (Android package). And at the time of writing this article, Google is beta testing App Inventor for Android, where apps can be written using a graphical language based on LogoBlocks, the same language that underlies Scratch and StartLogo TNG. While these significantly lower the entry barrier for development and would be suitable for introductory CS1 courses, upper-level courses specifically geared to application development and mobile operating systems will want to use the full SDK.

4. INSTRUCTOR RESOURCES

4.1 iOS

There are no textbooks on iOS per se, but the number of books geared to professionals is growing, and some could be adopted for classroom use [8, 16, 25]. Apple's technical documentation is vast, precise, comprehensive, and free, and much of it could be used to supplement the textbooks (or serve as the main reference for recent changes in the SDK). A plethora of video tutorials are also available, and some universities are putting entire courses online [4, 28].

While the iOS SDK is free to all developers, it only allows testing on the simulator: however universities can join Apple's free iPhone Developer University Program, which among other benefits permits the installation of the iOS SDK on lab machines, and uploading of apps to iFamily devices.

4.2 Android

As with iOS, there are no explicit textbooks for Android development, however many professional introductory texts can easily be used in the classroom [17, 18]. The official tutorials, development guide, and API reference include numerous basic code examples and complete Eclipse projects, and many tricky coding questions are answered in the StackOverflow forums [20, 27]. In addition, a number of courses on Android have been offered with the course materials publicly shared [1, 9, 19].

5. HELLO WORLD EXAMPLE

To compare the two platforms, we narrate the development of a small "Hello, world!" style app called HelloPermute: each time a button is clicked, the characters of the phrase "Hello, world!" will be displayed in a different order.

Readers interested in seeing the creation of HelloPermute in its entirety may wish to view the videos of the process [24].

5.1 iOS

5.1.1 Creating the Project

When creating a new project in Xcode, the user is offered multiple templates. In this case, we choose one of the simplest, a View-based application, targeted for the iPhone. The template provides:

- a single view, stored in a .xib file, on which we graphically lay out the interface elements of the project;
- a view controller, stored as code in a .h (header) and .m (implementation) file, which plays its customary role as an intermediary between the view and model; and
- a .plist (property list) file, in which we define the app's name, and icon, and other items.

The template does not provide a model. It is simple to add one, but in the interests of brevity, and because our model is almost trivial, we will merely incorporate it into the view controller.

5.1.2 Creating the Interface

Double-clicking the .xib file reveals a window consisting of 3 components — a View, which will display our interface elements; the File's Owner, which represents the view controller; and the First Responder, which references the UI element that first receives an event.

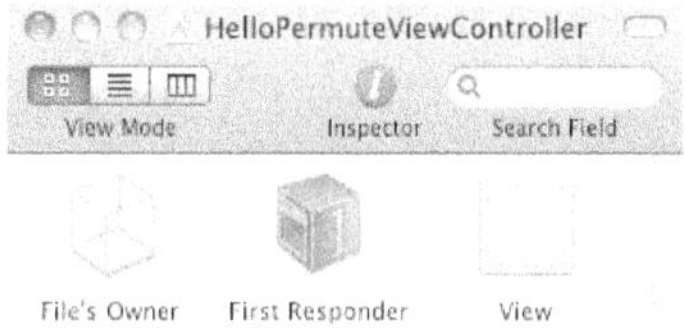

Figure 1: Components of a .xib file

To create our GUI, we drag a UITextField and UIButton from a library console onto the View, center them, and configure them (selecting the font, background, text, etc.).

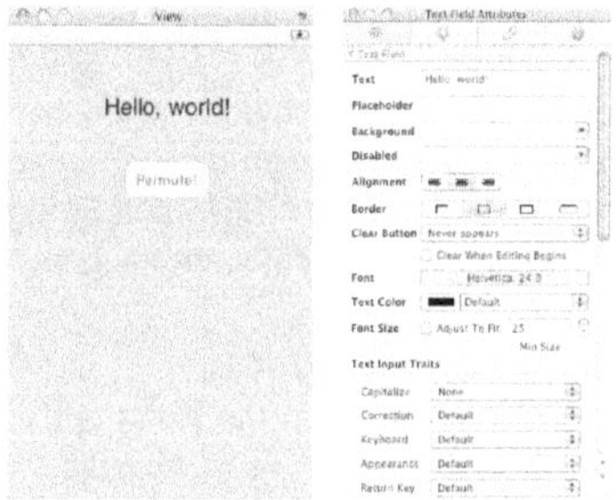

Figure 2: Creating and configuring a GUI

5.1.3 Writing the View Controller

In the view controller class, we must define a method for the UIButton to execute (its *action*), and an instance variable (an *outlet*) so that we can reference the UITextField. Figure 3 shows the interface, HelloPermuteVC.h:

```
// HelloPermuteVC interface, defined in HelloPermuteVC.h
#import <UIKit/UIKit.h>

@interface HelloPermuteVC : UIViewController
{
    IBOutlet UITextField * phraseTF;
}

-(IBAction)permuteWord:(id)sender;

@end
```

Figure 3: The interface of HelloPermuteVC

The syntax may appear daunting at first blush, but it takes just a few minutes in the classroom to explain to students familiar with

OO-ideation. Briefly, the class is called HelloPermuteVC, and it extends the Cocoa Touch class UIViewController. The entire interface is enclosed in an @interface ... @end block (@ prefaces Objective-C keywords). The interface is divided into two parts: instance variables are defined in curly brackets, and method signatures follow. The instance variable, phraseTF, is a pointer to a UITextField. It is adorned with IBOutlet (an empty macro), which makes phraseTF visible when connecting it to the UITextField object placed earlier.

The method permuteWord, is an instance method, as indicated by the leading - sign. It returns void (IBAction is a macro defined as void). It has one parameter, called sender, of type id (a generic type that can store any reference variable).

Figure 4 shows the body of permuteWord, defined in the corresponding .m file, is as follows:

```
-(IBAction)permuteWord:(id)sender {

    int strLength = [phraseTF.text length];
    NSMutableString * permutedPhrase = [NSMutableString stringWithCapacity:strLength];
    [permutedPhrase setString:phraseTF.text]; // put phraseTF's text -> permutedPhrase

    for(int i=0; i < [permutedPhrase length]; i++)
        [permutedPhrase swapCharsAt:random() % strLength and:random() % strLength];

    phraseTF.text = [permutedPhrase description]; // put permutedPhrase -> phraseTF
}
```

Figure 4: The body of permuteWord, in HelloPermuteVC.m

permuteWord demonstrates the use of *categories*, a powerful feature of Objective-C that makes it possible to add functionality to classes without resorting to subclassing. NSMutableString, as supplied by Apple, does not include swapChars:at:and:. The author added it as a category method, and can consequently be invoked like any other "native" NSMutableString method. The actual code is trivial and therefore not shown here.

5.1.4 Completing the Interface

With the controller class finished, the last steps are to bridge the gap between the code and the user interface, specifically, to associate the method permuteWord: with the UIButton, and the variable phraseTF with the UITextField on the view. Both are done graphically. The line labeled 1 in Figure 5 shows the first step: dragging from the UIButton to the File's Owner causes a small pop-up menu to appear, with permuteWord visible. Choosing permuteWord completes the connection. [permuteWord appears because its return type was an IBAction: had we merely labeled it as void, we would not see it].

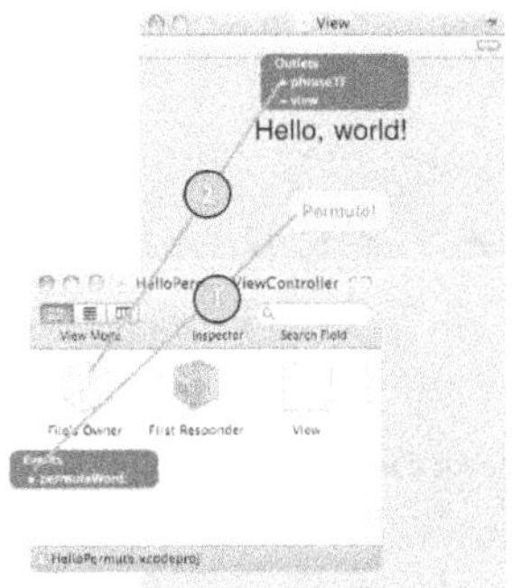

Figure 5: Connecting actions and outlets

The second step, depicted by the line labeled 2 in Figure 5, is almost the same, except dragging occurs in the opposite direction, from the File's Owner to the UITextField.

It is difficult to convey just how quickly and intuitively one can wire together an application using the techniques described above [24], and most developers embrace it. However, there are times when it is necessary to create a user interface dynamically, and some developers feel more comfortable when they are "in control", so to speak. For those situations and persons, it is possible to eschew .xib files and develop the entire interface in code.

5.2 Android

An Android project has three main elements: the Manifest file detailing its internal organization, resources, such as images and files, and the main Activity and associated class files. The directory hierarchy and a basic template for all three elements are created when a new project is begun in Eclipse.

5.2.1 Project Manifest

The AndroidManifest.xml file, akin to the iOS .plist, stores an overall summary of the app, including the name, version, and minimum SDK necessary to run the app. This is created upon initialization of a new Android project within Eclipse. Resources in other files are accessed with @ notation, such as @drawable/icon. Within this file a developer would also place tags for requesting permissions such as Internet Access, GPS location or Vibrate functionality, and a link to any associated background services. This file can be altered graphically within Eclipse as well as through changing the underlying XML.

```
<?xml version="1.0" encoding="utf-8"?>
<manifest
   xmlns:android=
     "http://schemas.android.com/apk/res/android"
   package="edu.sample.hellopermute"
   android:versionCode="1"
   android:versionName="1.0">
   <application android:icon="@drawable/icon"
                android:label="@string/app_name">
      <activity android:name=".HelloPermute"
                android:label="@string/app_name">
         <intent-filter>
            <action android:name=
             "android.intent.action.MAIN" />
            <category android:name=
             "android.intent.category.LAUNCHER" />
         </intent-filter>
      </activity>
   </application>
   <uses-sdk android:minSdkVersion="1" />
</manifest>
```

5.2.2 XML Resources

Standard resources for an Android project include drawables such as any necessary images and the application icon (png format preferred for transparency), GUI layout, and a strings file commonly used for allowing language independence. Shown first is the /res/values/strings.xml, which names the *app_name*, *hello* and *button* strings.

```
<?xml version="1.0" encoding="utf-8"?>
<resources>
  <string name="hello">HelloWorld!</string>
  <string name="app_name">HelloPermute</string>
  <string name="button">Permute</string>
</resources>
```

The GUI layout is stored in in /res/layout/main.xml. The outer container for the whole application is a RelativeLayout, and placed inside are a centered TextView for displaying the current jumble of “HelloWorld!”, centered horizontally, and a Button relatively below the TextView labeled “Permute”.

```
<?xml version="1.0" encoding="utf-8"?>
<RelativeLayout
   android:id="@+id/RelativeLayout01"
   android:layout_width="fill_parent"
   android:layout_height="fill_parent"
   xmlns:android=
     "http://schemas.android.com/apk/res/android">
   <TextView
      android:id="@+id/TextView01"
      android:layout_width="wrap_content"
      android:layout_height="wrap_content"
      android:textSize="30sp"
      android:padding="10sp"
      android:layout_centerHorizontal="true"
      android:text="@string/hello"></TextView>
   <Button
      android:layout_below="@+id/TextView01"
      android:layout_height="wrap_content"
      android:layout_width="wrap_content"
      android:id="@+id/Button01"
      android:layout_centerHorizontal="true"
      android:text="@string/button"></Button>
</RelativeLayout>
```

5.2.3 *Activity*

The HelloPermute Activity file is saved in the source directory as src/edu/sample/hellopermute/HelloPermute.java. The onCreate method takes the place of the usual constructor for an Activity, first initializing the Activity with a call to the super constructor, then inflating the layout from res/layout/main.xml, and finally binding the data member *phrase* to the TextView and *b* to the Button. Unlike iOS's graphical wiring, connections between the GUI view and functionality are linked programmatically. In more complicated applications, an anonymous class is used for the Button's OnClickListener callback detailing the method to be executed. However, since there is only one Button in HelloPermute, we simply implement the onClick method from OnClickListener as part of the Activity, where it grabs the text, shuffles the characters and returns the jumbled String to the TextView. A demonstration of the application running on the Android emulator is shown in Figure 6.

```
package edu.sample.hellopermute;

import android.app.Activity;
import android.os.Bundle;
import android.view.View;
import android.view.View.OnClickListener;
import android.widget.Button;
import android.widget.TextView;

public class HelloPermute
   extends Activity implements OnClickListener {

   private TextView phrase;

   @Override
   public void onCreate(Bundle icicle) {
      super.onCreate(icicle);
      setContentView(R.layout.main);
      phrase = (TextView)
         findViewById(R.id.TextView01);
      Button b = (Button)
         findViewById(R.id.Button01);
      b.setOnClickListener(this);
   }

   @Override
   public void onClick(View arg0) {
      StringBuffer sb = new
          StringBuffer(phrase.getText());
      for (int i=0; i < sb.length()-1; i++) {
         int where = (int)(Math.random() *
                        (sb.length() - i));
         char temp = sb.charAt(i + where);
         sb.setCharAt(i + where,
                        sb.charAt(i));
         sb.setCharAt(i, temp);
      }
      phrase.setText(sb);
   }
}
```

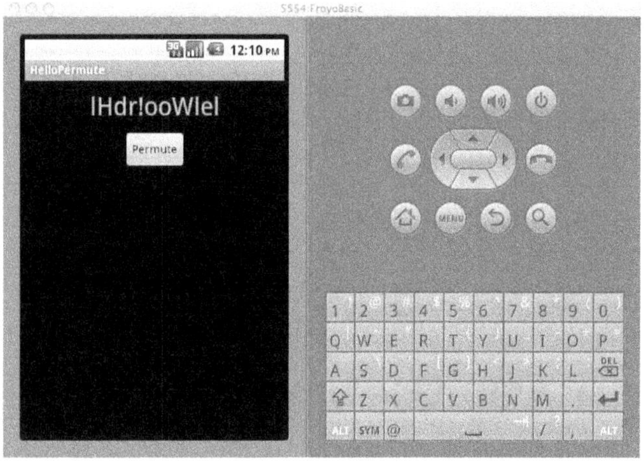

Figure 6: Hello Permute screenshot in Android emulator

6. CONCLUSIONS

Our comparison is summarized in Table 1. Both iOS and Android have their advantages. iOS development requires a specific type of hardware that may be more difficult to obtain — but that might encourage cross-departmental collaboration and expose students to another operating system. The bar for Android is somewhat lower, as development can take place in any modestly equipped computer science laboratory.

Students are much more likely to have seen the combination of Java and Eclipse than Objective-C and Xcode. Again, there is an advantage to exposing students to a relatively novel language and development environment, and a price to pay. Having to confront memory management issues is not necessarily a bad thing, nor is having to work with blocks. But there can be no denying that students studying Android will likely know Java; students studying iOS will very likely *not* know Objective-C. There is, therefore, a modest upfront cost to choosing iOS.

There is easily enough material to devote an entire course to a single environment. However, if curricular constraints make such a course impractical, either could serve well as an intriguing modular programming assignment in an upper-level course. Both are capable of 2D and 3D graphics with OpenGL and database management with SQLite. Students could see practical examples of embedded operating systems and learn to cope with threading, synchronization and locking.

Computing on mobile devices is mushrooming, and regardless of platform choice, a course on the subject will likely be oversubscribed. Either iOS or Android will enable faculty to present the key ideas of mobile computing; strengthen student programming skills that will serve them in good stead regardless of what platform they end up writing on; and make for an exciting classroom experience.

Table 1. Comparison of iOS and Android across multiple dimensions

	iOS	Android
Minumum Development Operating System Requirements	Mac OS X 10.6	Windows XP Linux Mac OS X 10.5.8
Development Device	\$99 iPhone 3G \$199 iPod Touch \$199 iPhone 4 \$499 iPad	\$399 Dev Phone 2 (v1.6) \$529 Nexus One (v2.2)
IDE	Xcode	Eclipse 3.5
GUI Creation	Xcode	XML
Language	Objective-C	Java (Dalvik) Scripting (SL4A) LogoBlocks (AppInventor)
Reference Website	http://developer.apple.com/iphone	http://developer.android.com/

7. ACKNOWLEDGMENTS

Our thanks to various colleagues at our respective institutions and the SIGCSE reviewers for their support and careful reading of this paper.

8. REFERENCES

[1] Abelson, H. *Building Mobile Applications with Android.* 2008. Retrieved from http://people.csail.mit.edu/hal/mobile-apps-spring-08/

[2] Android Developers. Retrieved from http://developer.android.com/guide/developing/tools/emulator.html

[3] Android Developers. Retrieved from http://developer.android.com/resources/dashboard/platform-versions.html

[4] Benson, E. *Introduction to iPhone Application Development.* 2010. Retrieved from http://courses.csail.mit.edu/iphonedev/

[5] Buck, E. 2010. *Cocoa Design Patterns.* Addison-Wesley.

[6] Burns, B. droiddraw. Retrieved from http://www.droiddraw.org/

[7] Digital Media Test Kitchen. 2010. *Smartphone Survey Questions & Results.* Retrieved from http://testkitchen.colorado.edu/projects/reports/smartphone/smartphone-appendix1/#q1b

[8] Dudney, B. 2010. *iPhone SDK Development.* Pragmatic Programmers.

[9] Google Code University. 2010. Retrieved from http://code.google.com/edu/android/index.html

[10] Grissom, S. 2008. iPhone Application Development Across the Curriculum, *The Journal of Computing Sciences in Colleges*, 24, 1 (Oct. 2008) 40-46.

[11] History of Mac OS X. In Wikipedia. Retrieved from http://en.wikipedia.org/wiki/History_of_Mac_OS_X

[12] Kurkovsky, S. 2009. Engaging students through mobile game development. *SIGCSE Bulletin* 41, 1 (Mar. 2009), 44-48. DOI= http://doi.acm.org/10.1145/1539024.1508881

[13] Mahmoud, Q. H. and Dyer, A. 2007. Integrating BlackBerry wireless devices into computer programming and literacy courses. In *Proceedings of the 45th Annual Southeast Regional Conference* (Winston-Salem, North Carolina, March 23 - 24, 2007). ACM-SE 45. ACM, New York, NY, 495-500. DOI= http://doi.acm.org/10.1145/1233341.1233430

[14] Mahmoud, Q. H. and Dyer, A. 2008. Mobile Devices in an Introductory Programming Course. *Computer* 41, 6 (Jun. 2008), 108-107. DOI=http://dx.doi.org/10.1109/MC.2008.200

[15] Mahmoud, Q. H., Ngo, T., Niazi, R., Popowicz, P., Sydoryshyn, R., Wilks, M., and Dietz, D. 2009. An academic kit for integrating mobile devices into the CS curriculum. In Proceedings of the 14th Annual ACM ITiCSE (Paris, France, July 06 - 09, 2009). ACM, New York, NY, 40-44. DOI= http://doi.acm.org/10.1145/1562877.1562896

[16] Mark, D. 2010. *Beginning iPhone 3 Development.* Apress.

[17] Meier, R. 2010. *Professional Android 2 Application Development.* Wrox Press.

[18] Murphy, M. 2010. *Beginning Android 2.* Apress.

[19] Nieh, J. *Mobile Computing with iPhone and Android.* Retrieved from http://www.cs.columbia.edu/~nieh/teaching/e6998/

[20] Nurik, R. 2010. *Hello, Stack Overflow!* Retrieved from http://android-developers.blogspot.com/2009/12/hello-stack-overflow.html

[21] Openintents. Retrieved from http://code.google.com/p/openintents/wiki/SensorSimulator

[22] Rogers, M. P. 2009. It's for you!: an iPhone development primer for the busy college professor. *The Journal of Computing Sciences in Colleges*, 25, 1 (Oct. 2009), 94-101.

[23] Rogers, M. P. 2010. Wrong number: avoiding the hidden perils in iPhone development. *The Journal of Computing Sciences in Colleges*, 25, 5 (May. 2010), 300-305.

[24] Rogers, M. P. iPhone App Demo [Video file]. Retrieved from http://www.youtube.com/watch?v=spOQJ1DRl88

[25] Sadun, E. 2010. *iPhone Development Cookbook.* Addison-Wesley.

[26] Spertus, E., Chang, M. L., Gestwicki, P., and Wolber, D. 2010. Novel approaches to CS 0 with app inventor for android. In *Proceedings of the 41st ACM SIGCSE* (Milwaukee, Wisconsin, USA, March 10 - 13, 2010). ACM, New York, NY, 325-326. DOI= http://doi.acm.org/10.1145/1734263.1734373

[27] Stackoverflow. Tagged Questions. 2010. Retrieved from http://stackoverflow.com/questions/tagged/android

[28] Stanford University. 2010. CS 193P iPhone Application Development. Retrieved from http://www.stanford.edu/class/cs193p/cgi-bin/drupal/downloads-2010-winter

Rediscovering the Passion, Beauty, Joy, and Awe: Making Computing Fun Again, Part 4

Daniel D. Garcia (moderator)
University of California, Berkeley
777 Soda Hall
Berkeley, CA 94720
+1 (510) 517-4041
ddgarcia@cs.berkeley.edu

Michelle Friend Hutton
Stanford University
485 Lasuen Mall
Stanford, CA 94305
+1 (650) 723-2109
mfh@pobox.com

Eugene Lemon
Ralph J. Bunche High School
1240 18th St
Oakland, CA 94607
+1 (510) 879-1730
elemon@pacbell.net

Josh Paley
Henry M. Gunn High School
780 Arastradero Road
Palo Alto, CA 94306
+1 (650) 354-8200
josh.paley@gmail.com

Categories and Subject Descriptors
K.3.2 [**Computer and Information Science Education**]: Computer science education

General Terms: Experimentation

Keywords: Computer science education

1. SUMMARY

In 2006, computing education was suffering from a crisis – enrollments were dropping sharply at universities and colleges across the United States, and interest in computing from high school and middle school students was waning significantly. At the 2007 SIGCSE Symposium, the ACM Education Board organized a special session to explore the underlying causes [7]. In his keynote at the same conference, Grady Booch exhorted us to share the "passion, beauty, joy and awe" (PBJA) of computing [4]. This led to a series of room-packed sessions at the following three SIGCSE symposia to explore that idea from different perspectives [8, 9, 12]. They have provided a forum for sharing:

- **What we've done**: Highlighting successful PBJA initiatives the presenters have undertaken or seen and wish to celebrate.
- **What we should do (curriculum)**: Pointing out where our curriculum is lacking in PBJA, and how to fix it.
- **How we should do it (pedagogy)**: Sharing how a change in attitude / focus / etc. can make strides to improving PBJA.

Fortunately, enrollments have been continually rising, and there are colleges where the numbers are so strong (returning to historic highs), that some claim the crisis is over [10, 13]. Many dispute this, however, citing statistics that indicate under-represented students have not returned, and continuing negative connotations about the field [2]. Also, recent news of limited hiring in the information technology sector could have a damping affect [11]. This PBJA "movement" was born out of this enrollment crisis, but is not tied to it. There is always value in sharing novel best practices and advocating techniques that make computing fun.

In the past, we tried to gather educators who brought a wide variety of perspectives (e.g., in 2010 we heard from international, domestic, high school, university and industrial representatives). This year, we've shifted from that "breadth-first" model to a "depth-first" one, and have invited three K-12 teachers who, collectively, have taught computing at an all-girls middle school, an under-served high school, and an affluent high school. The hope with this panel is to be able to drill down and understand the K-12 space, in terms of extolling the PBJA of computing.

2. MICHELE HUTTON

Middle school students are an extraordinary group, full of contradictions – thoughtful, obnoxious, loud, introspective, self-absorbed, and excited about making the world a better place. Middle school is when children become young adults, able to think deeply and grapple with abstract ideas. Additionally, we are free from the pressure to directly prepare students for college and the workforce. What better time to teach complex computing concepts, helping students find beauty, joy, and awe in what we are passionate about?

The Girls' Middle School computer science program where I taught has engaged hundreds of students in a variety of computer science approaches, from programming to robotics to web design to computational thinking. There are significant advantages to providing a diversity of entry points and opportunities for students to find their own passion and joy in computer science. The notion of "differentiation" means providing work at different levels of challenge and in different areas of strength – including non-technology-based activities.

Middle school is an opportune time to help students discover passion for computer science – while they're still joyful about learning and the sciences, and when they're able to see the beauty in complex concepts.

SIGCSE'11, March 9–12, 2011, Dallas, Texas, USA.
ACM 978-1-4503-0500-6/11/03.

3. EUGENE LEMON

The vast majority of students in my school district are underrepresented ethnic minorities, and even though our district has an exemplary technology infrastructure with a high student-to-computer ratio, the computer science curriculum currently being taught at most of our schools leaves much to be desired (in terms of sharing PBJA).

I've been teaching for eighteen years, and on a few occasions I've been pulled out of my computer science classroom to work as a Teacher on Special Assignment (TSA). On some of my TSA assignments I would be asked to assist the HR office and other departments to design and manipulate PC databases. I would agree to leave the classroom on one condition; the department would have to allow me to bring some of my students to assist me.

Often these were students who were looked upon as outcasts; they were young people who came from dysfunctional homes; group homes; juvenile hall; and some were even homeless. As they worked in the district offices with me, you could really sense their PBJA. They were excited because they were using database software to manipulate information that provided a service to adult staff members who truly appreciated them for the work they were doing. They were "giving back" to these adults, who were sharing their honest appreciation for jobs well done.

In my talk I will discuss how, over the years, I've given my students a sense of self-esteem and joy by enabling them to provide a service that was greatly appreciated by adults who would otherwise have disdain for them. The realization that they could use computing to make a real difference was quite transformative for them, and I contend service-based projects (as in [5]) could have a profound impact for marginalized students.

4. JOSH PALEY

I currently teach four different CS courses: a variant of AP Computer Science AB, Programming Concepts in Scheme, Introduction to Java, and Animation Using Virtual Worlds (using Alice [3] and Scratch [14]). This last class is targeted at students who otherwise would never touch a CS class. The other classes are more demanding, particularly in terms of mathematics.

One of my notions of PBJA is mathematical in nature. I find the elegance of functional programming and the simplicity of a clean abstraction to be wonderful things. One of my favorite examples of this is the *binary mobile* problem [1, ex 2.29], which asks students to write selectors for given constructors for a mobile abstract data type with weights, then use their selectors to calculate the total weight of this recursive structure, and find out whether it is balanced or not. In AP CS, Programming Concepts, and Intro to Java, I work very hard to get students to produce clean programs with powerful results. This past summer, I was able to get *incoming ninth graders* – most of whom had no prior programming experience – to draw a fractal tree in 90 minutes using BYOB based on Scratch [6] on the first day of a programming camp. I accidentally stumbled on the card game *War* as nature's perfect test for AP CS AB students: player hands (queues), wars on the table (stacks), deck of cards (hash set), interesting end-game conditions, the potential for non-terminating programs... and the students loved it!

I would like to see us try to make all of computing as exciting and glorious as these examples. This is why I am excited about seeing PBJA listed explicitly in the learning goals for the new AP curriculum. It has the spirit of all of these things in visually compelling and intellectually stimulating ways.

5. REFERENCES

[1] Abelson, H., Sussman, G. J., and Sussman, J. *Structure and Interpretation of Computer Programs 2/e*. MIT Press, 1996.

[2] ACM, WGBH. Interim report. *New Image for Computing*. April, 2009. `www.acm.org/membership/NIC.pdf`

[3] Alice website. `www.alice.org`

[4] Booch, G. 2007. Readn', writ'n, 'rithmetic… and code'n. *SIGCSE Bull.* 39, 1 (Mar. 2007), 197-197. `doi.acm.org/10.1145/1227504.1227380`

[5] Buckley, M. 2009. Viewpoint. *Commun. ACM* 52, 4 (Apr. 2009), 29-30. `doi.acm.org/10.1145/1498765.1498779`

[6] BYOB based on Scratch website. `BYOB.berkeley.edu`

[7] Cassel, L., McGettrick, A., Guzdial, M., and Roberts, E. 2007. The current crisis in computing: what are the real issues?. In *Proceedings of the 38th SIGCSE Technical Symposium on CS Education* (Covington, KY, USA, March 07-11, 2007). SIGCSE '07. ACM, New York, NY, 329-330. `doi.acm.org/10.1145/1227310.1227426`.

[8] Garcia, D. D., Cutler, R., Dodds, Z., Roberts, E., and Young, A. 2009. Rediscovering the passion, beauty, joy, and awe: making computing fun again, continued. In *Proceedings of the 40th ACM Technical Symposium on CS Education* (Chattanooga, TN, USA, March 04-07, 2009). SIGCSE '09. ACM, New York, NY, 65-66. `doi.acm.org/10.1145/1508865.1508889`

[9] Garcia, D. D., Chapman, G., Hazzan, O., Johnson, M., and Sudol, L. A. 2010. Rediscovering the passion, beauty, joy, and awe: making computing fun again, part 3. In *Proceedings of the 41st ACM Technical Symposium on CS Education* (Milwaukee, WI, USA, March 10 - 13, 2010). SIGCSE '10. ACM, New York, NY, 394-395. `doi.acm.org/10.1145/1734263.1734399`

[10] NY Times. *CS Programs Make a Comeback in Enrollment*. `www.nytimes.com/2009/03/17/science/17comp.html`

[11] NY Times. *Once a Dynamo, the Tech Sector Is Slow to Hire*. `www.nytimes.com/2010/09/07/business/economy/07jobs.html`

[12] McGettrick, A., Roberts, E., Garcia, D. D., and Stevenson, C. 2008. Rediscovering the passion, beauty, joy and awe: making computing fun again. In *Proceedings of the 39th SIGCSE Technical Symposium on Computer Science Education* (Portland, OR, USA, March 12 - 15, 2008). SIGCSE '08. ACM, New York, NY, 217-218. `doi.acm.org/10.1145/1352135.1352213`

[13] Reges, S. Email to SIGCSE-members mailing list. *enrollment crisis over?* 2009-05-21.

[14] Scratch website. `scratch.mit.edu`

Progress in Surfacing Computer Science in STEM

Susan H. Rodger
Duke University
Durham, NC USA
rodger@cs.duke.edu

Mark Stehlik
Carnegie Mellon University
Pittsburgh, PA
mjs@cs.cmu.edu

Chris Stephenson
CSTA Executive Director
Eugene, OR
cstephenson@csta.acm.org

Cameron Wilson
ACM
Washington, DC
wilson_c@hq.acm.org

Categories and Subject Descriptors

K.3.2 [**Computing Milieux**]: Computers and Education-Computer and Information Science Education

General Terms

Standardization, Legal Aspects

Keywords

Computer Science Education, Education Policy, K-12 curriculum

1. SUMMARY

As the Science, Technology, Engineering, and Mathematics (STEM) education reform wave has swept the United States, ACM and CSTA, among other organizations, have worked to push K-12 computer science toward the "core" of a student's education. We are at a critical point for K-12 computer science education - particularly with a potential new AP course called CS Principles [2] being designed and piloted for introduction into secondary schools in the next few years. Significant questions remain as to whether computer science is really at the table when key decisions are made about how schools and states allocate their education resources. Major policy issues still exist for K-12 computer science education. There is deep confusion about computer science teacher certification, courses, gender and diversity gaps in students, and whether computer science courses "count" toward a student's graduation requirements. This special session will present groundbreaking research reflecting how computer science education is treated in each of the 50 states coupled with initiatives to transform the national education policy landscape for K-12 computer science education. It will connect the broad SIGCSE community by giving them new data and a call to action to get involved in a new coalition called "Computing in the Core." This new coalition seeks to ensure computer science is at the core of education for all students.

SIGCSE'11, March 9–12, 2011, Dallas, Texas, USA.
ACM 978-1-4503-0500-6/11/03.

2. OVERALL OBJECTIVES

This special session reports on the recent activities of ACM's Education Policy Committee (EPC)[1] and how the SIGCSE community can connect with new initiatives such as Computing in the Core and Computer Science Education Week. The EPC's purpose is to develop policy positions and educate policy makers on behalf of the ACM, CSTA, and the broader computing community with the goal of improving the opportunities for quality education in computing and computer science. It has worked to ensure that computer science education is identified as a critical component of K-12 education policy in the U.S. at both federal and state levels. The EPC has been working on four major initiatives to help achieve its mission. Since last year's SIGCSE special session, each of the following initiatives has resulted in significant gains:

- Conducted an analysis of computing standards and graduation requirements within the education standards of the 50 states, as compared to the ACM Model Curriculum outcomes
- Developed the framework for the Computer Science Education Act, which was introduced in Congress by Congressman Jared Polis[5]
- Created a new coalition to advocate for K-12 computer science education at the state and federal levels of government called *Computing in the Core* and through the efforts of this coalition introduced the Computer Science Education Act.
- Helped create and support Computer Science Education Week in 2009 and 2010

This session seeks to educate SIGCSE attendees about the major developments for the past year including the release of ACM's and CSTA's state by state report on computer science education presenting new, compelling research on the substantial gaps in the ways in which states treat computer science education in K-12, and the launch of the "Computing in the Core" coalition.

3. OUTLINE

ACM EPC members will discuss how ACM and CSTA engage on policy issues and then will touch the four major initiatives noted above. After each presentation, additional members of the EPC will discuss related issues facing the field as reform moves forward and how the community can become more involved.

The first topic will cover the current components of ACM's education activities, how they fit together, and their intended impact.

The second topic will provide the results of new research on the extent to which 1) the ACM K-12 Computer Science Model Curriculum Standards [3] have been (or have not been) integrated into grade 9-12 math, science, and technology standards across the United States; and 2) computer science courses are or are not mapped into state graduation requirements.

The third topic will be the proposed Computer Science Education Act (CSEA). It will cover the contents and purpose of the act, its intended outcomes, and the potential for greater individual involvement in building community and political support for the act.

The fourth topic will cover the new Computing in the Core initiative and its mission in these related efforts and how it is seeking to strengthen K-12 computer science education through advocacy and education.

After each topic there will be a short question period, and after the fourth topic there will be an extended dialog with the audience.

4. EXPECTATIONS

This session is intended to engage the broad constituency of SIGCSE, that is, computer science educators from K-12 to higher education. As a result of the presentations and the broader discussion, the participants will have a deeper understanding of the current gaps in how computer science fits into the STEM education discussion and reforms that the ACM Education Policy Committee and the Computing in the Core Coalition are supporting. The discussion will also give members of the broader computer science education community an opportunity to provide key feedback regarding these policy initiatives and to consider them in the broader context of providing consistent messages to policy makers with regard to the nature and importance of the discipline.

5. SUITABILITY FOR SPECIAL SESSION

All of the speakers for this Special Session are members of the ACM Education Policy Committee, and one member, Chris Stevenson, is also the CSTA Executive Director. The ACM EPC's mission is to engage policymakers and the public on public policy issues in science and math education relevant to computing and computer science.

There is broad interest within the SIGCSE community about the state of computer science education in K-12 and the need to address the well-known issues [6, 4]. A special session is sought because of the nature of the discussion and the need to update the entire community on significant gains in EPC inititiatives.

6. REFERENCES

[1] ACM. Education Policy Committee resources, last accessed 9/8/2010. www.acm.org/public-policy/education-policy-committee.

[2] CollegeBoard. CS Principles website, last accessed 9/2/2010. csprinciples.org.

[3] CSTA. ACM K-12 CS Model Curriculum, 2nd edition, last accessed 9/8/2010. www.csta.acm.org/Curriculum/sub/ACMK12CSModel.html.

[4] J. Goode. Reprogramming college preparatory computer science. *Communications of the ACM*, 51(11):31–33, 2008.

[5] Polis. The Computer Science Education Act (H.R. 5929), last accessed 9/8/2010. thomas.loc.gov/home/gpoxmlc111/h5929_ih.xml.

[6] C. Stephenson, J. Gal-Ezer, B. Haberman, and A. Verno. *The New Education Imperative: Improving High School Computer Science Education.* ACM/CSTA, 2005.

NSF/IEEE-TCPP Curriculum Initiative on Parallel and Distributed Computing – Core Topics for Undergraduates

Sushil K. Prasad (Coordinator)
Georgia State University
sprasad@gsu.edu
Almadena Chtchelkanova NSF
Sajal Das
University of Texas at Arlington, NSF
Frank Dehne
Carleton University, Canada,
Mohamed Gouda
University of Texas, Austin, NSF
Anshul Gupta
IBM T.J. Watson Research Center
Joseph Jaja
University of Maryland

Krishna Kant
NSF, Intel
Anita La Salle NSF
Richard LeBlanc
Seattle University
Manish Lumsdaine
Indiana University
David Padua
University of Illinois at Urbana-Champaign
Manish Parashar
Rutgers, NSF
Viktor Prasanna
University of Southern California

Yves Robert
INRIA, France
Arnold Rosenberg
Colorado State University
Sartaj Sahni
University of Florida
Behrooz Shirazi
Washington State University
Alan Sussman
University of Maryland
Charles Weems
University of Massachusetts
Jie Wu
Temple University

1. SUMMARY

This special session will be our first formal curriculum committee report. A working group from IEEE Technical Committee on Parallel Processing (TCPP), National Science Foundation (NSF), and the sister communities, including ACM, has taken up proposing curriculum for computer science (CS) and computer engineering (CE) undergraduates on parallel and distributed computing. The goal of this committee has been to propose a core curriculum for CS/CE undergraduates, with the premise that *every* such undergraduate should achieve a specified skill level regarding PDC-related topics as a result of *required* coursework.

The working group has deliberated upon various topics and subtopics, agreed upon their learning outcomes and level of coverage, has identified where in current core courses these could be introduced, and has provided examples of how they might be taught. Limited reviews have been carried out by selected stakeholders. Early adopters in Spring-11 will be employing the proposed curriculum.

In this session, multiple committee members will introduce the community to our curriculum initiative, its year-long activities, our proposed curriculum, and the current and future roadmap. This session is also intended (i) to discuss and collect direct feedback from the community, which would be timely and will influence our subsequent round of revisions and mid-course correction, and (ii) to further develop a community of interest.

Categories and Subject Descriptors: K.3.2 [Computing Milieu]: Computers and Education- Computer and Information System Education [Curriculum, Computer science education]

General Terms: Standardization

SIGCSE'11, March 9–12, 2011, Dallas, Texas, USA.
ACM 978-1-4503-0500-6/11/03.

Keywords: Education, Undergraduate Curriculum, Parallel and Distributed Computing, Bloom's Classification, Learning Outcomes.

2. BACKGROUND

Parallel and Distributed Computing (PDC) now permeates most computing activities. The increasingly ubiquitous deployment of PDC makes it imperative that users be able to depend on the effectiveness, efficiency, and reliability of this technology. The increasing presence of computing devices that contain multiple cores and general-purpose graphics processing units (GPUs) in home and office PCs and laptops is making even common users dependent on advanced computing technology. Certainly, it is no longer sufficient for even basic programmers to acquire only the traditional, conventional sequential programming skills. The preceding trends point to the need for imparting a broad-based skill set in PDC technology at various levels in the educational fabric woven by Computer Science and Computer Engineering programs as well as related computational disciplines. However, the rapid change in computing hardware platforms and devices, languages, supporting programming environments, and research advances, more than ever challenge educators in knowing what to teach in any given semester in a student's program. Students and their employers face similar challenges regarding what constitutes basic expertise.

As background preparation for the development of this curriculum proposal, a planning workshop funded by the NSF was held in February 2010, in Washington, DC; this was followed up by a second workshop in Atlanta, alongside the IPDPS conference in April 2010. These meetings were devoted to exploring the state of existing curricula relating to PDC, assessing needs, and recommending an action plan and mechanisms for addressing the curricular needs in the short and long terms. The planning workshops and their related activities benefited from experts from various stakeholders, including instructors, authors, industry, professional societies, NSF, and the ACM Education Council.

The primary task identified was to propose a set of core topics in parallel and distributed computing for undergraduate curricula for CS and CE students. Further, it was recognized that, to make a timely impact, a sustained effort was warranted. Therefore, a series of weekly tele-meetings was begun in May 2010; the series has continued through December 2010.

In the three PDC sub-areas of Programming, Algorithms, and Architecture, the working group has deliberated upon various topics and subtopics and their level of coverage (Bloom Classification), has identified where in current core courses these could be introduced, and has provided examples of how they might be taught. Selected stakeholders have carried out limited reviews.

One impact of a goal of *universal* competence is that many topics that experts in PDC might consider essential are actually too advanced for inclusion. Early on, our working group's participants realized that the set of PDC-related topics that can be designated *core* in the CS/CE curriculum across a broad range of CS/CE departments is actually quite small, and that any recommendations for inclusion of required topics on PDC would have to be limited to the first two years of coursework. In addition, we recognized that whenever it is proposed that new topics be included in the curriculum, many people automatically assume the implication that something else will need to be taken out. However, for many of the topics we propose, this is not the case. Rather, it is more a matter of changing the approach of teaching traditional topics to encompass the opportunities for thinking in parallel. In a few cases, we are indeed proposing material that will require making choices about what it will replace in existing courses. The resulting reevaluation is an opportunity to review traditional topics, and perhaps shift them to a place historical significance or promote them to more advanced courses.

We are recruiting early adopters of the curriculum for spring, 2011 in order to get a preliminary evaluation of our proposal. These adopters will include (i) instructors of introductory courses in Parallel and Distributed Computing, (ii) instructors, department chairs, and members of department curriculum committees, who are responsible for core CS/CE courses, and (iii) instructors of general CS/CE core curriculum courses.

Our larger vision in proposing this curriculum is to enable students to be fully prepared for their future careers in light of the technological shifts and mass marketing of parallelism through multicores, GPUs, and corresponding software environments, and to make a real impact with respect to all of the stakeholders including employers, authors, and educators. This curricular guidance and its trajectory, along with periodic feedback and other evaluation data on its adoption and use, will also help to steer companies hiring students and interns, hardware and software vendors, and, of course, authors, instructors, and researchers.

The time is ripe for parallel and distributed computing curriculum standards, but we also recognize that any revision of a core curriculum is a long-term community effort. More details and workshop proceedings are available at the initiative's website (sign on to access the draft curriculum documents):

http://www.cs.gsu.edu/~tcpp/curriculum/index.php

3. OVERALL OBJECTIVE OF THE SESSION

The objective of the session is to report on our proposed curriculum for undergraduates and its related activities, and gather community feedback. Some seed level NSF funding is available for selected group of adopters.

Why the proposed session is important? Our vision for our committee is one of stakeholder experts working together and periodically providing guidance on restructuring standard curricula across various courses and modules related to parallel and distributed computing. A primary benefit of the proposed curriculum would be for CS/CE students and their instructors to receive periodic guidelines that identify aspects of PDC that are important to cover, and suggested specific core courses in which their coverage might find an appropriate context. New programs at colleges (nationally and internationally) will receive guidance in setting up courses or integrating parallelism in the Computer Science, Computer Engineering, or Computational Science curriculum. Employers would have a better sense of what they can expect from students in the area of parallel and distributed computing skills. Curriculum guidelines will similarly help inform retraining and certification for existing professionals.

4. OUTLINE OF THE SESSION

The session will be organized as follows:

1) Introduction to the Curriculum Initiative -10 minutes (Sushil Prasad, Georgia State University and Andrew Lumsdaine, Indiana University)
    a) Background Activities and Roadmap
    b) Why a Parallel and Distributed Computing Curriculum now?
    c) What should every (computer science/engineering) student know about computing?
    d) How to Interpret this Curriculum Proposal?
2) Curriculum and Rationale for Architecture Topics – 10 minutes (Chip Weems – University of Massachusetts)
3) Curriculum and Rationale for Programming Topics – 10 minutes (Alan Sussman, University of Maryland)
4) Curriculum and Rationale for Algorithms Topics – 10 minutes (Arnold Rosenberg, Colorado State University)
5) Discussion and Q&A - 35 minutes

5. EXPECTATIONS

The intended audience is a wider group of CS and CE educators and students who are interested in PDC, or teach related courses, or are interested in adopting some of the PDC topics. There has already been good interest in the industry, which are chipmakers and parallel software and tool creators (e.g., Intel, Microsoft and IBM), therefore, some attendees from industry are expected as well. The feedback will be timely, which will influence our revision. This session is expected to draw 30-50 attendees in addition to the part of the committee itself.

6. ACKNOWLEDGMENTS

We acknowledge the support of NSF grants CNS-0950432 and CCF-1048711 for the committee coordinator (Prasad). We also thank about two dozen experts from among the stakeholders for their two sets of reviews of draft curriculum and feedbacks in March and Aug 2011.

Teaching Introductory Programming with Popular Board Games*

Peter Drake
Department of Mathematical Sciences
Lewis & Clark College
Portland, Oregon
drake@lclark.edu

Kelvin Sung
Computing and Software Systems
University of Washington, Bothell
Bothell, Washington
ksung@uw.edu

ABSTRACT

Games assignments are increasingly popular in computer science education [28]. This paper advocates and analyzes the inclusion of board, card, and dice games as programming assignments in introductory programming courses (CS1/2). The simple interface and strategy-based play of these types of games complement the immersive multimedia and agility-based play of video games. The implementation of board, card, and dice games typically demands less background knowledge from the instructor and offers fewer opportunities for extraneous work by the students. The paper lists 32 specific games that are suitable for teaching the major topics in CS1/2 and discusses the implementation of some of these games and their successful use as programming projects.

Categories and Subject Descriptors

K.3.2 [**Computers and Education**]: Computer and Information Science Education – *computer science education*

General Terms

Design, Experimentation

Keywords

CS1/2, Assessment, Games, Assignments, Adaptation

1. INTRODUCTION

Note: In this paper, *games* or *board games* refer to board, card, or dice games that are typically not played on a computer, while *video games* refer to modern interactive graphical games played on computers or gaming consoles.

Games are among the oldest human activities. Their origins are shrouded in the mists of prehistory and entangled with the origins of mathematics, accounting, religion, and science [23]. Game boards dating back over 4,000 years have been found in Egyptian tombs [24].

Board, card, and dice games remain a popular pastime today. Hundreds of millions of players worldwide enjoy classics such as *Chess*, *Checkers* (*Draughts*), *Bridge*, and *Go* [2]. American children grow up with 20th-century inventions such as *Monopoly*, *Scrabble*, and *Risk*. Europe has recently produced an explosion of innovative designs such as *Settlers of Catan*, *Puerto Rico*, and *Agricola*.[1]

Many computer scientists have a natural affinity for board games, which share an important trait with computer programming: a few simple rules give rise to deep and fascinating complexities. Many algorithms are embedded in games, including procedures for taking a turn or determining the winner. As more tractable stand-ins for messier real-world problems, games have a long tradition as subjects of study in artificial intelligence [26].

Taking advantage of these observations, the first author has incorporated games into the second introductory programming course (CS2) at Lewis & Clark College since 2002 [7]. This resulted in the publication of a textbook in 2006 [6]. The course is now entirely project-driven, with eight to ten board game projects covering all of the major concepts in the curriculum. This paper draws on this experience and presents board games as a particularly engaging and relevant topic for programming assignments in introductory programming courses (CS1/2). From this context, the next section of the paper discusses the relevant merits of video and board games. Section 3 covers the choice of appropriate games and lists specific games for important CS1/2 topics. Section 4 addresses implementing board games and turning them into effective programming assignments. This section also introduces the tiny ljing (Learn Java in N Games) library that we have created to make these programs easier to write. In section 5, we describe our experience using this type of assignment in the classroom.

2. GAMES AND CS1/2 CLASSES

There are many types of games that are suitable for teaching Computer Science (CS) subjects, including board games, video games, and games that are based on dedicated devices (e.g., Lego robots [20]). These games have been used in various ways, from conceptual examples (e.g., [31]) to programming assignments (e.g., [30]). It is also important to differentiate between learning about how to build games (e.g., [35]), learning about algorithms used in games (e.g., [32]), and learning about CS concepts using games (e.g., [28]). This paper focuses on using the development of board games as programming assignments to teach typical topics in traditional CS1/2 courses.

*This work was supported in part by the Northwest Distributed Computer Science Department Project funded by the NSF CPATH program award number 0829651. The second author was also supported in part by Microsoft Research under the Computer Gaming Curriculum in CS RFP, award numbers 15871/16531, and a grant from the Teaching & Scholarship Enhancement Project, University of Washington, Bothell

SIGCSE'11, March 9–12, 2011, Dallas, Texas, USA.

[1] http://www.boardgamegeek.com/

2.1 Previous Work on Board Games

Perhaps as a result of overwhelming success of commercial video games, there has been a surprisingly limited amount of research on using board games in CS classes. Huang [12] described approaches to design programming projects for different CS courses based on analysis of strategy games (e.g., *Connect Four* for CS2, *Mancala* for AI). Goschnick and Balbo [8] used the building of board games to teach object-oriented programming concepts to Information Systems students. Lim [18] based the programming assignments of his graph theory class on the *Ticket to Ride* game. Many others discussed board games in the context of interactive graphical video games, e.g., *Minesweeper* [3], general puzzle games [25], or *Othello* [29]. Except for Huang's analysis of strategy games in supporting traditional CS courses [12], the other work seemingly adapted board games in a piecemeal, anecdotal fashion. The work presented in this paper is a comprehensive evaluation of board games across the CS1/2 curriculum that analyzes the challenges of implementing the games and incorporating them into existing courses.

2.2 Board Games vs. Video Games

The work presented in this paper involves programming board games that users can interactively play with. This subsection relates our work to the vast amount of recent work done in teaching CS concepts through programming video games [28]. We first discuss the differences in game play, then in programming, and finally in pedagogy.

The largest difference in game play is that board games are generally turn-based, while video games are generally real-time. In turn-based systems, a game can only be changed by the players acting upon it, as is obviously necessary when playing with inanimate game equipment. In a real-time game, in contrast, things continue to happen even in the absence of player action. Real-time games therefore require some degree of mental or physical agility, which can be exciting for some players but frustrating for others. Additionally, the rules of board games must be simple, comprehensible, and enforceable by average human players. This is contrasted with the potential for complex and often unpredictable game play conditions of modern video games where a player may not have access to the precise rules but must learn by trial and error. This immersive experience can be engaging to some players but overwhelming or distracting for others. As a result of these differences, board games tend to involve deeper strategic decisions than video games.

Programming real-time video games can be considerably more complex than programming board games. Video games typically include Graphical User Interfaces (GUIs); they cannot reasonably be text-based. As events happen while the player is acting, programs are usually multithreaded, a trait that makes debugging much more difficult. Seeking to emulate the major commercial games they have experience playing, students may be disappointed by games that lack sound effects, networking, elaborate graphics, and artificially intelligent opponents.

All of these features require additional and potentially extraneous work on behalf of students programming video games. They also require instructors to be conversant in a number of different fields of programming. Since video game programs are so complex, it is difficult for students to write many games over the course of a term. The instructor may have to use a complex supporting library (e.g., [17, 4]) or assign pieces of games or "game-like" projects, leaving an unsatisfying final product (e.g., [11]). More recently there have been efforts at simplifying the programming environments (e.g., [14, 5]) and work done specifically to assist adoption to teach with video games (e.g., [29]). However, for faculty with no backgrounds in video games, adopting such complex materials remains challenging [16, 21].

A board game project, in contrast, can be simple enough that students can write and understand the entire program and have a complete working game when they are done. Graphics, while useful and compelling, are optional and can be developed after the game logic has been thoroughly tested.

Video games can be effective tools for engaging students and teaching CS concepts [32, 34, 22, 15, 28]. The above discussions do not attempt to argue against video games, rather, the discussions highlight the complementary nature of popular board games, e.g., exciting fast-paced interaction vs. strategic thinking, sophisticated immersive multimedia vs. simplicity. Both approaches are based on the general philosophy of "contextual education" [9] where knowledge is presented in contexts that are relevant to the learners. In this framework, as in any effective teaching methodologies, board games are just one among many powerful educational tools.

3. BOARD GAMES AND CS1/2 TOPICS

This section raises some issues to consider when choosing a game for a programming assignment. A list of specific games for major topics in a typical CS1/2 course is then presented. In Section 5 we present examples of implementing some of these games in our CS2 class.

3.1 The Right Game for the Job

Instructors who are not board game hobbyists may have difficulty coming up with games to teach various topics; the next subsection fills that gap. Instructors who are board game hobbyists, on the other hand, might be overcome by their zeal for their favorite game. The followings are considerations that can guide the choice for appropriate games.

- Custom vs. existing games. It is wise to choose an existing game. Designing a well-balanced, entertaining game with precise and consistent rules can be surprisingly difficult [27].
- Familiarity with the games. There are advantages to using both games with which students are already familiar and new games. Familiar games require less class time to explain and have some emotional resonance. New games can be refreshing to students. Instructors should be aware that some students may not be familiar with even popular, classic games, e.g., foreign students may not be familiar with Western playing cards. Alternately, games from various students' home cultures might enhance inclusivity.
- Complexity of the games. The rules of the game should be simple, though not necessarily trivial. Avoid games with more than one page of rules (e.g. *Star Fleet Battles*), games whose boards form complicated graphs (e.g., *Scotland Yard*), or games that involve many different pieces (e.g., *Roads & Boats*).
- Length of game play. The game should be quick to play, e.g., five to fifteen minutes. It is a good idea to play the game in class before programming. This provides a welcome break and helps tease out subtleties in the game rules. Note that a few games can be scaled down to play

Primitives and Control Structures	
Pig Footsteps (Quo Vadis) Crown & Anchor (isomorphic to Chuck-a-Luck) Guess a Number	cs.gettysburg.edu/~tneller/resources/pig/ www.boardgamegeek.com/boardgame/2634/quo-vadis www.boardgamegeek.com/boardgame/17520/crown-and-anchor en.wikipedia.org/wiki/Binary_search_algorithm#Number_guessing_game
One-dimensional Arrays	
Anagrams Hangman Poker Dice Nim	www.boardgamegeek.com/boardgame/3359/anagrams en.wikipedia.org/wiki/Hangman_(game) www.boardgamegeek.com/boardgame/10502/poker-dice en.wikipedia.org/wiki/Nim
Objects	
Sherlock (Der Plumpsack geht um) Mastermind Shut the Box Beetle (Cootie)	www.boardgamegeek.com/boardgame/3586/sherlock www.boardgamegeek.com/boardgame/2392/mastermind www.boardgamegeek.com/boardgame/9851/shut-the-box www.boardgamegeek.com/boardgame/4378/cootie
Multidimensional Arrays	
Travel Blokus Black Box Domineering (Stop-Gate, Crosscram) Othello (Reversi)	www.boardgamegeek.com/boardgame/16395/travel-blokus www.boardgamegeek.com/boardgame/165/black-box www.boardgamegeek.com/boardgame/7450/stop-gate www.boardgamegeek.com/boardgame/2389/othello
Array-based Linear Structures	
Idiot's Delight No Thanks! Cheeky Monkey Go Fish	www.solitairecentral.com/rules/IdiotsDelight.html www.boardgamegeek.com/boardgame/12942/no-thanks www.boardgamegeek.com/boardgame/29773/cheeky-monkey www.pagat.com/quartet/gofish.html
Linked Linear Structures	
Geography (Word Chain) BuyWord Focus (Domination) Coloretto	en.wikipedia.org/wiki/Word_chain www.boardgamegeek.com/boardgame/8920/buyword www.boardgamegeek.com/boardgame/789/focus www.boardgamegeek.com/boardgame/5782/coloretto
Trees and Recursion	
Questions Connect Four (The Captain's Mistress) 3-D Tic-Tac-Toe (3-D Noughts and Crosses Backgammon	en.wikipedia.org/wiki/Twenty_Questions www.boardgamegeek.com/boardgame/2719/connect-four www.boardgamegeek.com/boardgame/16387/3d-tic-tac-toe www.world-backgammon-association.com/
Graphs	
Hex Go Nine Men's Morris (Mill) Sim	en.wikipedia.org/wiki/Hex_(board_game) www.usgo.org/index.html www.boardgamegeek.com/boardgame/3886/nine-mens-morris www.boardgamegeek.com/boardgame/33153/game-of-sim

Table 1: References to board games.

in less time for demonstration purposes. For example, a full game of *Go* can take an hour or more to play, but the standard 19x19 board can be reduced to 9x9 or even 5x5 to explain the rules.

- Number of players. Games designed for two players are the best. These games mesh well with pair programming. Games with more players may be difficult to test, take a long time to play, or be awkward to play when all players must be seated around the same machine.
- Public information. Hidden information, such as hands of cards not visible to the other players, should be avoided. If a game has hidden information, we must either have one player look away from the screen (awkward), implement networking (difficult), or provide an AI opponent (potentially difficult). Unfortunately, this rules out many card games, such as currently popular *Texas Hold-'em* variant of *Poker*.

A note on proprietary games: the notion of game designer as a profession is a very recent one. Even in the twentieth century, many published games did not credit their designers. More recently, some games has become intellectual property. The exact nature of this property is still unclear; the text of a game's rules might be copyrighted, the design might be patented, or the name might be trademarked. Many computer implementations of games exist on the web. We believe the very simple implementations proposed here for non-profit educational use in the classroom may constitute fair use.

It should be strongly emphasized that neither of the authors are lawyers. We are not qualified to give legal advice.

3.2 Games for CS1/2

Table 1 presents four games each for eight of the topics in CS1/2. In an object-oriented language, the games in the "Primitives and Control Structures" section might be coded in a single, monolithic function/method and those in the "One-dimensional Arrays" section in a single class; beyond this point, multiple classes are in order. Any of these games can be written with a text-only interface, but students used to GUIs may find such an interface awkward for all but the simplest games. The games for array-based and linked linear structures can be interchanged freely.

Of the games mentioned in the table, *Sherlock*, *Travel Blokus*, *No Thanks!*, *Cheeky Monkey*, *BuyWord*, and *Coloretto* are recent, proprietary games. The status of *Mastermind*, *Beetle*, *Black Box*, *Domineering*, *Othello*, and *Focus* is less clear; these games are either based on folk games, have been published in multiple sources, are long out of print, or are so widely implemented on the web that they may have entered the public domain. The remaining games are in the public domain.

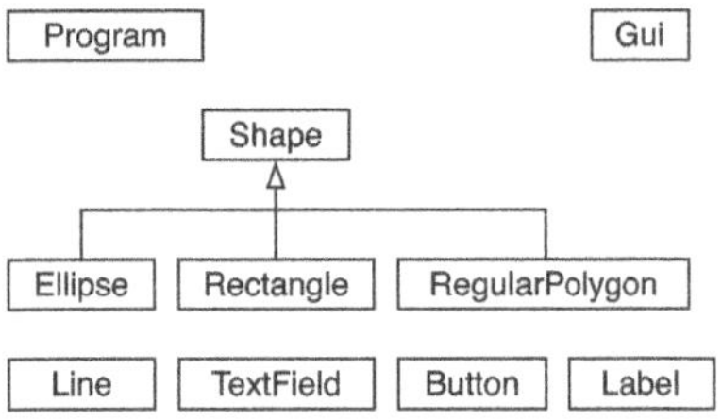

Figure 1: Classes in the ljing Library.

4. DESIGN AND IMPLEMENTATION

This section discusses our implementation of some of the games listed in the previous section and the use of these games as programming assignments. All of these games are programmed to allow play between two or more human players. The board representation, detection of legal moves, and scoring provide sufficient challenges; only more advanced students would attempt to add artificially intelligent opponents.

4.1 Programming the Games

The first author has implemented in Java eight of the games listed in Table 1: *Pig*, *Hangman*, *Sherlock*, *Domineering*, *No Thanks!*, *Focus*, *Questions*, and *Hex*.[2] Each implementation has a text-only interface; all but the first two have optional GUIs that can be added once the text-based program is working correctly. These implementations also include a set of JUnit tests designed to provide instant feedback as the students make progress and to facilitate grading.

A purely text-based interface has a number of advantages. Such programs are easier to write and have clearer control flow. They get students into the habit of writing toString() methods even for complicated objects, which can aid debugging. Finally, such games are more accessible, e.g., to blind students. The first author is working with a blind teaching assistant in the current semester of his CS2 course.

The advantages of text-based interfaces aside, primitive graphics can greatly improve student motivation and understanding [19]. After students have built working text-based programs, they can attach GUIs to them, following the Model-View-Controller pattern. Figures 2 and 3 are screen shots of the GUI implementations for *Sherlock* and *Domineering*. Notice the simplicity of the interface, allowing students to easily focus on the concepts being explored.

4.2 The ljing Library

Figure 1 shows all the classes that are defined in the the ljing (Learn Java in N Games) library. This package was created to shield students from the tedious keyboard input and the vast, intimidating GUI and graphics libraries. It may be viewed as a smaller, simpler alternative to the ACM Java Task Force library [1].

The ljing library supports text-based programs via a single class, *Program*, with less than 100 lines of code, that implements I/O utilities such as *readInt()* and *readLine()*.

To support GUI programming, the ljing library provides the *Gui* class for students' classes to extend. This class allows students to focus on "what do I want to put where, and how should it behave?" rather than arcana such as layout managers, default close operations, or the incantations required to make a Swing window actually appear on the screen.

[2]The code can be obtained by contacting the first author.

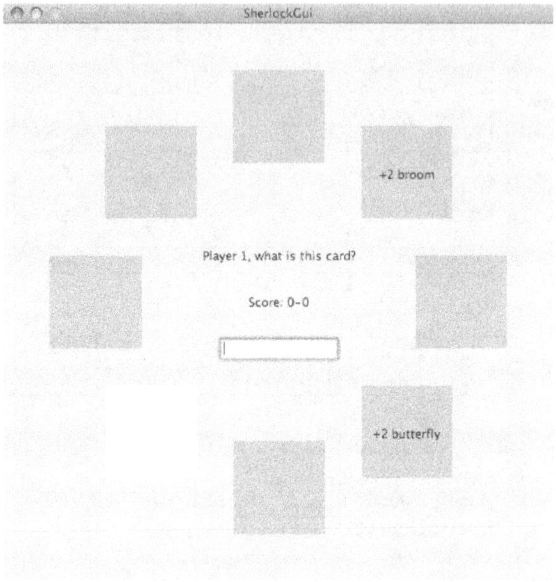

Figure 2: Graphic user interface for the Sherlock game.

To support drawing and user interaction in the GUI environment, ljing provides several simple graphical objects (Ellipse, Rectangle, RegularPolygon, Line, and Label) and interactive components (TextField and Button). Working with ljing GUI objects is as simple as creating instances and specifying the locations where the objects are to be drawn.

4.3 Programming Assignments

Student preparedness and skill varies greatly between and within institutions. The level of challenge offered by the board game programming projects offered here can be adjusted by altering how much of the work the students must do:

- At the most difficult level, students may simply be given the problem specification (i.e., the rules of the game) and asked to implement the entire game.
- For a slightly simpler assignment, students may be advised as to how best to break the program into classes, and/or how to break each class into methods.
- Students may be given JUnit tests. These both provide instant feedback as students make progress and greatly facilitate grading.
- Students may be given some of the classes. One reasonable case is to ask the students to write the text-only game, then give them the GUI.
- Students may be given some classes and parts of the classes they must write, with the bodies of a few methods removed.
- At the simplest level, students may be given all but one method. For example, as a recursion assignment based on the *Questions* game, students might be given all of the game except for the recursive method that prints the tree in outline form. Alternatively, same game can be used to teach about references where students are given everything except the method that modifies the tree to learn from an incorrect guess.

Figure 3: Graphic user interface for Domineering.

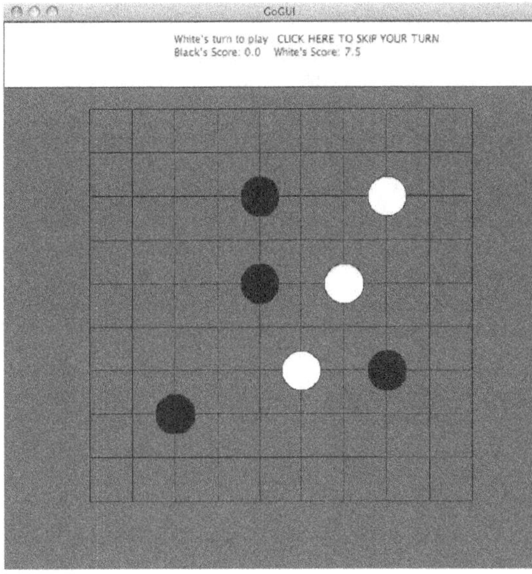

Figure 4: Example Student Project: The Go Game

GUI and graphics may be omitted in any case, again noting that GUIs are more complicated to program but more engaging than text-only interfaces.

5. RESULTS

Lewis & Clark College is a small, liberal arts college in Portland, Oregon. The usual CS2 enrollment is between 10 to 20 students. While the College's student body is approximately 60% female, enrollment in computer science courses is overwhelmingly male. The CS1 course is taught in C, CS2 in Java.

For the current (fall 2010) semester, the first author has assigned the eight games described in Section 4.1. The previous (spring 2010) semester used the same assignment strategy described below, but with different games. This CS2 course is driven by the eight game projects, plus a final project of the student's own choosing (which may or may not be a game). Most of the in-class time is spent working on these projects, with the instructor and a teaching assistant circulating and answering questions.

The first project, *Pig*, is given as a "traditional" assignment: the desired behavior of the program is described, then students are asked to implement it. For the second project, *Hangman*, students are given a skeleton of the program and asked to complete some methods. This makes it easy to provide, e.g., the method that reads the words from the dictionary file, so students don't have to perform file i/o at this early stage. The third project, *Sherlock*, introduces JUnit tests. The students are given a skeleton of the class and a set of JUnit tests. A GUI is also introduced in this assignment, although the students are not asked to write it. If their text-based program is working correctly, the GUI given to them should work. In the remaining projects, students are given JUnit tests and decreasingly complete skeletons of the text-based and gui versions of the program. The skeletons may be omitted completely near the end of the course. Students must write their own JUnit tests for the final project.

The "Learn Java in *N* Games" approach was extremely successful in the spring 2010 semester. Students were engaged with their assignments and in some cases continued to play the games they had built after the assignments. Figure 4 shows the screen shot of an example of students' implementation of the *Go* game.

Comments on student evaluations included:

> *"I will definitely play the games I made like all summer!"*
>
> *"Learned a lot, loved hands-on approach. And now I have a ton of cool games on my [computer]."*
>
> *"The course was a lot of fun, it made it exciting to be programming games."*
>
> *"[the] game based approach to teaching Java is innovative and effective."*
>
> *"I feel that having projects with clear objectives is a good way to learn material, since one has to understand it to be able to use it, and using the material in context improves my ability to retain it."*

6. CONCLUSION

Like video games, board games can be engaging to students and cover the spectrum of topics in CS1/2 classes. The simple rules and strategic thinking game play complement corresponding features of video games. Together with other contextual approaches to teaching CS1/2 courses (e.g., video games[28], media computing [10]), board games can be valuable and powerful tools in the hands of innovative educators.

Many of the characteristics associated with board games discussed in Section 2.1 suggest potentials for attracting and engaging female [13] and other traditionally underrepresented groups [33]. Regrettably, due to our small class sizes and limited diversity, we have not been able to pursue investigations in these areas. We believe these are interesting future work with board games and CS education.

Acknowledgments

This work was supported in part by the National Science Foundation grant 0829651, Microsoft Research award numbers 15871 and 16531, and a grant from the Teaching & Scholarship Enhancement Project, University of Washington, Bothell. All opinions, findings, conclusions, and recommendations in this work are those of the authors and do not necessarily reflect the views of the National Science Foundation, Microsoft Research, or the University of Washington, Bothell. The authors wish to thank the Northwest Distributed Computer Science Department (NWDCSD) Project, especially Rob Bryant, Jenny Orr, and Scott Wallace, for their tireless efforts in creating and maintaining the NWDCSD community. This paper is a direct result of the stimulating discussion from the NWDCSD 2010 Summer workshop.[3]

7. REFERENCES

[1] Acm java task force, 2006. *http://jtf.acm.org/*.

[2] I. M. S. Associatino. World mind sports games, 2008. http://www.usgo.org/IMSA/WMSG2008.pdf.

[3] K. Becker. Teaching with games: the minesweeper and asteroids experience. *J. Comput. Small Coll.*, 17(2):23–33, 2001.

[4] K. Bierre, P. Ventura, A. Phelps, and C. Egert. Motivating oop by blowing things up: an exercise in cooperation and competition in an introductory java programming course. In *SIGCSE '06: Proceedings of the 37th SIGCSE technical symposium on Computer science education*, pages 354–358, New York, NY, USA, 2006. ACM Press.

[5] W. Dann, S. Cooper, and R. Pausch. *Learning to Program with Alice*. Prentice Hall, Upper Saddle River, NJ, 2006.

[6] P. Drake. *Data Structures and Algorithms in Java*. Prentice Hall, Upper Saddle River, NJ, 2006.

[7] P. Drake and N. Kerr. Developing a computer strategy game in an undergraduate course in software development using extreme programming. *J. Comput. Small Coll.*, 22(2):39–45, 2006.

[8] S. Goschnick and S. Balbo. Game-first programming for information systems students. In *IE 2005: Proceedings of the second Australasian conference on Interactive entertainment*, pages 71–74, Sydney, Australia, Australia, 2005. Creativity & Cognition Studios Press.

[9] M. Guzdial. Contextulized computing education. In *Invited Presentation, Microsoft Research Faculty Summit, http://home.cc.gatech.edu/guzdial/169*, July 2008.

[10] M. Guzdial and B. Ericson. *Introduction to Computing and Programming with Java, A Multimedia Approach*. Prentice-Hall, 2007.

[11] C. Hillyard, R. Angotti, M. Panitz, K. Sung, J. Nordlinger, and D. Goldstein. Game-themed programming assignments for faculty: a case study. In *SIGCSE '10: Proceedings of the 41st ACM technical symposium on Computer science education*, pages 270–274, New York, NY, USA, 2010. ACM.

[12] T. Huang. Strategy game programming projects. In *CCSC '01: Proceedings of the sixth annual CCSC northeastern conference on The journal of computing in small colleges*, pages 205–213, , USA, 2001. Consortium for Computing Sciences in Colleges.

[13] J. Jenson, S. de Castell, and S. Fisher. Girls playing games: rethinking stereotypes. In *Future Play '07: Proceedings of the 2007 conference on Future Play*, pages 9–16, New York, NY, USA, 2007. ACM.

[14] M. Kölling and P. Henriksen. Game programming in introductory courses with direct state manipulation. In *ITiCSE '05: Proceedings of the 10th annual SIGCSE conference on Innovation and technology in computer science education*, pages 59–63, New York, NY, USA, 2005. ACM Press.

[15] S. Leutenegger and J. Edgington. A games first approach to teaching introductory programming. In *SIGCSE '07: Proceedings of the 38th SIGCSE technical symposium on Computer science education*, pages 115–118, New York, NY, USA, 2007. ACM Press.

[16] R. B.-B. Levy and M. Ben-Ari. We work so hard and they don't use it: acceptance of software tools by teachers. *SIGCSE Bull.*, 39(3):246–250, 2007.

[17] M. C. Lewis and B. Massingill. Graphical game development in cs2: a flexible infrastructure for a semester long project. In *SIGCSE '06: Proceedings of the 37th SIGCSE technical symposium on Computer science education*, pages 505–509, New York, NY, USA, 2006. ACM Press.

[18] D. Lim. Taking students out for a ride: using a board game to teach graph theory. In *SIGCSE '07: Proceedings of the 38th SIGCSE technical symposium on Computer science education*, pages 367–371, New York, NY, USA, 2007. ACM.

[19] S. Matzko and T. A. Davis. Teaching cs1 with graphics and c. In *ITICSE '06: Proceedings of the 11th annual SIGCSE conference on Innovation and technology in computer science education*, pages 168–172, New York, NY, USA, 2006. ACM Press.

[20] M. McNally, M. Goldweber, B. Fagin, and F. Klassner. Do lego mindstorms robots have a future in cs education? In *SIGCSE '06*, pages 61–62, New York, NY, USA, 2006. ACM Press.

[21] L. Ni. What makes cs teachers change?: factors influencing cs teachers' adoption of curriculum innovations. In *SIGCSE '09*, pages 544–548, New York, NY, USA, 2009. ACM.

[22] I. Parberry, M. B. Kazemzadeh, and T. Roden. The art and science of game programming. In *SIGCSE '06*, pages 510–514, New York, NY, USA, 2006. ACM Press.

[23] D. Parlett. *The Oxford History of Board Games*. Oxford University Press, 1999.

[24] P. A. Piccione. In search of the meaning of senet. *Archaeology*, pages 55–58, 1980.

[25] J. M. Ross. Guiding students through programming puzzles: value and examples of java game assignments. *SIGCSE Bull.*, 34(4):94–98, 2002.

[26] S. Russell and P. Norvig. *Artificial Intelligence: A Modern Approach*. Prentice Hall, third edition, 2010.

[27] J. Schell. *The Art of Game Design: A book of lenses*. Morgan Kaufmann, 2008.

[28] K. Sung. Computer games and traditional computer science courses. *Communications of the ACM*, 52(12):74–78, December 2009. Invited Paper, Peer Reviewed.

[29] K. Sung, M. Panitz, C. Hillyard, R. Angotti, D. Goldstein, and J. Nordlinger. Game-themed programming assignment modules: A pathway for gradual integration of gaming context into existing introductory programming courses. *IEEE Transactions on Education*, 2010. To appear.

[30] K. Sung, M. Panitz, S. Wallace, R. Anderson, and J. Nordlinger. Game-themed programming assignments: the faculty perspective. In *SIGCSE '08: Proceedings of the 39th SIGCSE technical symposium on Computer science education*, pages 300–304, New York, NY, USA, 2008. ACM.

[31] K. Sung, P. Shirley, and R. Reed-Rosenberg. Experiencing aspects of games programming in an introductory computer graphics class. In *SIGCSE '07: Proceedings of the 38th SIGCSE technical symposium on Computer science education*, pages 249–253, New York, NY, USA, 2007. ACM Press.

[32] E. Sweedyk, M. deLaet, M. C. Slattery, and J. Kuffner. Computer games and cs education: why and how. In *SIGCSE '05: Proceedings of the 36th SIGCSE technical symposium on Computer science education*, pages 256–257, New York, NY, USA, 2005. ACM Press.

[33] H. M. Walker. Do computer games have a role in the computing classroom? *SIGCSE Bull.*, 35(4):18–20, 2003.

[34] U. Wolz, T. Barnes, I. Parberry, and M. Wick. Digital gaming as a vehicle for learning. In *SIGCSE '06*, pages 394–395, New York, NY, USA, 2006. ACM Press.

[35] M. Zyda. Guest editor's introduction: Educating the next generation of game developers. *Computer*, 39(6):30–34, 2006.

[3] http://ai.vancouver.wsu.edu/~nwdcsd/wiki/index.php/SummerWorkshop-081310.

A Snapshot of Current Practices in Teaching the Introductory Programming Sequence

Stephen Davies
University of Mary Washington
Department of Computer Science
Fredericksburg, VA 22401
540-654-1317
stephen@umw.edu

Jennifer A. Polack-Wahl
University of Mary Washington
Department of Computer Science
Fredericksburg, VA 22401
540-654-1318
polack@umw.edu

Karen Anewalt
University of Mary Washington
Department of Computer Science
Fredericksburg, VA 22401
540-654-1362
anewalt@umw.edu

ABSTRACT

We present results from a nationwide survey of undergraduate computer science departments regarding languages and techniques taught in CS0, CS1, and CS2. This snapshot of 371 schools provides an intriguing look into the state of computing education today in the U.S., quantifying which practices are actually in common use. Among other things, the study reveals the great variety in CS0 approaches, the relative uniformity of CS1 and CS2 approaches, the dominance of Java as a language for the introductory major sequence, and the tendency for departments to teach CS1 and CS2 in a consistent manner, rather than exposing students to different ideas in each.

Categories and Subject Descriptors

K.3.2 [**Computers and Education**]: Computer and Information Science Education – *computer science education, curriculum.*

General Terms

Languages, Measurement.

Keywords

Survey, Programming Languages, CS0, CS1, CS2.

1. INTRODUCTION

Computing Curricula 2001 provides the most recent comprehensive curricular recommendations for undergraduate programs in Computer Science [10]. This document combined with the 2008 update [9] provides guidelines and suggestions for undergraduate computer science programs and represents joint work done by the two most widely recognized organizations in the computing discipline, the ACM and IEEE. While the recommendations are widely known, much less is known about the state of computing education today. We present results from a nationwide survey of undergraduate computer science departments regarding languages and techniques taught in CS0, CS1, and CS2. We undertook this project in an effort to quantify practices in common use today. Our hope is that through understanding more about current practices the discipline will better be able to contextualize innovations and trends in computer science education.

2. RELATED WORK

Several surveys have been done related to various aspects of computer science education.

In 2001, a group of professors from the University of Southern Queensland, Australia conducted a census on all thirty-nine Australian universities about the language trends in introductory programming courses. The census asked approximately 19,900 students taking an introductory programming course at one of the 37 Australian universities which languages were taught in their courses. The most widely taught language was Java, followed by Visual Basic, although, if C and C++ were combined (as they are often taught interchangeably), then the number of students receiving instruction in C/C++ surpassed the number of students receiving instruction in VB [4]. The census further broke down language in terms of discipline. Students indicated a discipline for which their course was designed; the options were: computer science/information technology (CS/IT), engineering, business, and other. Java was the most widely used language in all of the categories. VB was used frequently in business disciplines, and C++ and Haskell were used in CS/IT and engineering disciplines. Students were further asked about the paradigm used in the course. While 81% of the respondents reported using an object-oriented language in their course, most students reported that they did not use an early objects approach in their course. Instructors were asked to identify reasons for selecting a language for their course and 56% indicated industry relevance of the language. A separate study showed that the languages thought to be relevant by the instructors were actually the most in demand languages by industry [5]. The census project was repeated in 2003 for Australian and New Zealand universities. Again the results showed a dominance of Java in programming courses [6].

In spring of 2004, a survey of 351 faculty members was conducted concerning the content in the first course in computing [2,3]. The survey participants were either faculty who had contacted a medium-sized publisher of Computer Science textbooks or were members of the SIGCSE email list. Survey results showed that Java was used twice as often as C++ with members of the SIGCSE list; however, C++ was used more than Java with the publisher list. Scheme, C, and other languages were available answers but the number of people selecting them was small (5, 7, and 19 respectively). 66.9% of the survey respondents reported using the object-oriented paradigm for at least part of the course [2]. Referencing comments received with the survey, the author observed "Those who were using the object-oriented paradigm seemed to be struggling to find a balance between object oriented concepts and the more traditional constructs that appear in the general programming category [3]."

In 2006 Schulte and Bennedsen conducted a survey concerning what is taught in introductory programming [11]. Because no international list of all instructors who teach programming exists, the online survey was sent to the authors of articles for the 5th Koli conference, 37th SIGCSE, the 11th ITiCSE, two OOPSLA Conferences, the two issues of SIGCSE Bulletin, the members of the Danish Association of Datamatician Educators, the participants of workshops on computer science education in Germany, and recipients of the SIGCSE mailing list. 242 fully completed surveys were received. The results of interest to this research are as follows:

- Object oriented principles were covered by 85% of respondents. Of these respondents, 60% indicated using an objects first approach.
- Java was used by 58.3% of the respondents, followed by C++ 18%, and Pascal 9%. 20% of the respondents indicated that they used a language other than the three receiving the most responses.

Our study adds to these results in part simply by updating them, since the most recently published survey of this kind was four years ago[11]. Also, our survey solicited a broader set of information than most of the works above, covering aspects of the entire CS0-CS1-CS2 sequence. Additionally, we include information about institutional characteristics, so that differences between practices at different types of schools become apparent.

3. PROCEDURES AND METHODS

We sent our online survey to 785 institutions in the USA that have a Computer Science (CS) or Computer Information Systems (CIS) major. The aim was to survey as wide a spectrum of schools as possible with respect to geographical distribution, private versus public institution, and school size, so as to have a measure of the uniformity of languages used within the introductory sequence in computer science. The schools were originally selected from the Carnegie Classification List [1]; every 10th school in alphabetical order that had a CS or CIS program was selected. In order to find every tenth school, we started with the first school in the Carnegie Classification List and did an Internet search on that school to verify that that school had a CS/CIS department. If the school did not have a CS/CIS major the next school in the list was selected and verified that it had a CS/CIS major. After successfully finding a school with a CS/CIS major, we then counted ten schools down and repeated the same process. It became apparent that this procedure was cumbersome and the yield was low since the Carnegie Classification List includes every school within the USA and does not allow the list to be filtered based on major programs offered. Upon further research we found and used the US News University Directory because it listed all the universities in the USA and can generate a list of universities filtered to include only those with a CS/CIS major program [12]. From the list of all universities with a CS/CIS major, we selected every 5th school in alphabetical order. If a selected school was already selected from the Carnegie Classification List then the next school in the search results was selected. The overall result of this procedure is that 785 schools out of the estimated 1350 total institutions with a computing program (see [12]) were solicited. This represents about 58% of the total, and our alphabetical approach prevented any obvious bias towards any particular demographic.

Schools were contacted via email containing a link to an online survey hosted at Survey Monkey (www.surveymonkey.com). The survey contained the following information and questions.

During this survey, please use the following definitions:

- **CS0** – an introductory course with no prerequisites, involving at least some programming, that does not count towards the major
- **CS1** – the first required course in the major programming sequence
- **CS2** – the second required course in the major programming sequence (traditionally called "Data Structures")

1. What is the name of your institution?
2. Does your department regularly offer a CS0 course?
3. What language(s)/environment(s) are covered in your CS0, CS1, CS2 courses? Check all that apply: Alice, C, C++, Greenfoot, Java, Java Applets, JavaScript, Lisp/ Scheme, Python, Ruby, Scratch, Visual Basic, Other
4. Do your students develop programs using a command-line environment, a graphical IDE, or both in CS0, CS1, and CS2? Command-line, Graphical IDE, Both
5. What programming paradigm best describes the programming portion of your CS0, CS1, CS2 courses? Check all that apply: Imperative/procedural, Object-oriented, Functional, Other
6. Do you teach the use of an interactive debugger in at least some sections of any of the following: CS0, CS1, CS2? Yes, No
7. Approximately what percentage of class time do your CS0 courses spend on teaching algorithmic and programming skills? (as opposed to broader, holistic topics about computer science in general?) (If this varies considerably by instructor, semester, or section, try to give a reasonable average.) 0-10%, 10-20%, 30-40%, 40-50%, 50-60%, 70-80%, 80-90%, 90–100%.
8. What degrees do you offer? Associate's CS, Associate's CIS, Associate's SE, Bachelor's CS, Bachelor's CIS, Bachelor's SE, Master's CS, Master's CIS, Master's SE, Ph.D. CS, Ph.D. CIS, Ph.D. SE, Other

4. RESULTS AND ANALYSIS

With one follow-up email request, we received 371 responses from the 785 schools contacted, or 47.2%. Based on the US News University Directory[12] there are 1350 institutions with CS/CIS majors; therefore, this represents 27.5% of these institutions.

For simplicity, we use the most conservative "universal" margin of error in computing the confidence interval for all items, using 0.5 as the sample proportion $\hat{p}$. We apply the finite population correction $\sqrt{(N-n)/(N-1)}$ to the standard margin of error formula $1.96\times\sqrt{\hat{p}\times(1-\hat{p})/n}$, where N is the population size and n is the sample size. In this case, N represents the total number of computer science degree programs in the United States. We estimate this number as 1350 based on [12]. With n=371, then, our (conservative) margin of error for all items on the survey is ± 4.3%.

4.1 CS0

4.1.1 Frequency of offering

The definition of CS0 we provided on the survey was "an introductory course with no prerequisites, involving at least some programming, that does not count towards the major." Only 60.1% of respondents (223 total) indicated that their department regularly offered such a course. This was lower than we expected, and apparently indicates that at over a third of institutions, a student's earliest exposure to programming concepts will be the major sequence.

Note that the Computing Curricula 2001 Task Force endorsed the concept of moving to a three-course introductory sequence in order to make it easier to cover the growing amount of material included in introductory courses and to provide students with more time to assimilate course material[10]. This can be achieved in at least two ways, one of which would be to "front load" the traditional CS1/CS2 sequence with a CS0 course. The other approach would be to "backload" CS1/CS2 with a third course, a strategy which perhaps accounts for the relatively low number of institutions offering CS0.

We hypothesized that larger institutions, with more faculty and resources, would offer CS0 courses more often, but this did not turn out to be the case. The likelihood did depend on graduate degrees offered, however: 75% (±4.3%) of PhD-granting institutions regularly offered CS0, compared with only 57% (±4.3%) of other institutions (by χ^2 this was significant to $\alpha<0.05$.)

Table 1. Number of respondents regularly offering a CS0 course that use certain languages in at least some sections. (Note the percentages do not total to 100% since some schools regularly offer more than one CS0 language.) As with all items on the survey, the margin of error is ± 4.3%.

Language in CS0	# respondents (%)
Ada	1 (0.4%)
Alice	70 (31.4%)
C	13 (5.8%)
C++	17 (7.6%)
C#	5 (2.2%)
Greenfoot	2 (0.9%)
Java	41 (18.4%)
JavaScript	38 (17.0%)
Lisp/Scheme	5 (2.2%)
Python	45 (20.2%)
Ruby	1 (0.4%)
Scratch	3 (1.3%)
Visual Basic	45 (20.2%)
Other	39 (10.5%)

4.1.2 Languages

The programming languages in CS0 vary widely (see Table 1 and Figure 1.) Alice was the most common in our survey (31.4% of respondents), but Python (20.2%), Visual Basic (20.2%), Java (18.4%), and JavaScript (17.0%) appear in almost equal numbers. Alice is by far the most common novice-focused environment in common use: Scratch (1.3%) and Greenfoot (0.9%) are not yet widely adopted. Many other languages – from Lisp to Ruby to C# to ActionScript – were also mentioned, testifying to the great degree of innovation surrounding making programming accessible to non-majors.

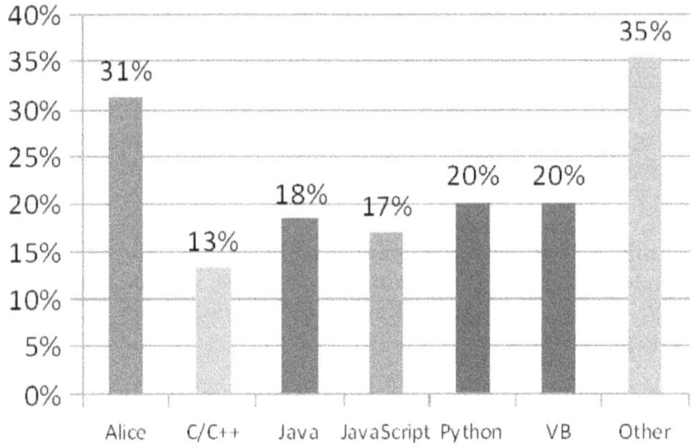

Figure 1. The most popular languages used in CS0 courses. (The "other" bar combines respondents who literally answered "other" with those who chose an item on the survey other than the most popular six.)

4.1.3 Degree of programming content

Also widely varying among CS0 courses is the percentage of time devoted to programming and algorithmic development, as opposed to broader, holistic topics about computer science in general. Respondents were asked to estimate the percentage of overall class time that was spent on programming, in increments of 10% (see Figure 2.) As is apparent, there is no consensus, although the most common strategy is to spend between 80 and 90 percent. Clearly, most educators feel it is important to devote at least some time to breadth-first topics, though the relative emphasis on this is highly variable.

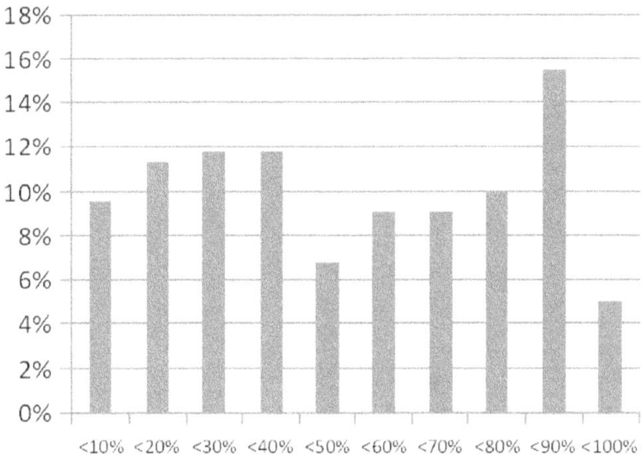

Figure 2. Percentage of CS0 class time spent "teaching algorithmic and programming skills."

4.2 CS1 and CS2

CS1 was defined on our survey as "the first required course in the major programming sequence," and CS2 as "the second required course in the major programming sequence (traditionally called

'Data Structures.')" We concede that there is widespread disagreement among institutions about the precise meanings of these two designations (see, e.g., [8]), and also that many schools spread the programming "core" across three courses. For simplicity and ease of comparison, however, we only surveyed two major courses.

4.2.1 *Language choice*

Table 2 and Figure 3 depict the relative frequencies of language use reported for CS1 and CS2. There is far more consensus here than in CS0, with Java and C++ being the driving factors (reported by a combined 73% (CS1) and 85% (CS2) of all respondents.)

Table 2. Number of respondents offering CS1 and CS2 in various languages. (Note the percentages do not total to 100% since some schools indicated more than one.) The margin of error is ± 4.3%.

Language	CS1: # (%)	CS2: # (%)
Ada	4 (1.1%)	3 (0.8%)
Alice	16 (4.3%)	2 (0.5%)
C	27 (7.3%)	18 (4.9%)
C++	107 (28.8%)	134 (36.1%)
C#	7 (1.9%)	6 (1.6%)
Greenfoot	2 (0.5%)	0 (0.0%)
Java	179 (48.2%)	207 (55.8%)
JavaScript	12 (3.2%)	10 (2.7%)
Lisp/Scheme	7 (1.9%)	1 (0.3%)
Python	48 (12.9%)	12 (3.2%)
Ruby	2 (0.5%)	1 (0.3%)
Scratch	6 (1.6%)	0 (0.0%)
Visual Basic	36 (9.7%)	27 (7.3%)
Other	39 (10.5%)	29 (7.8%)

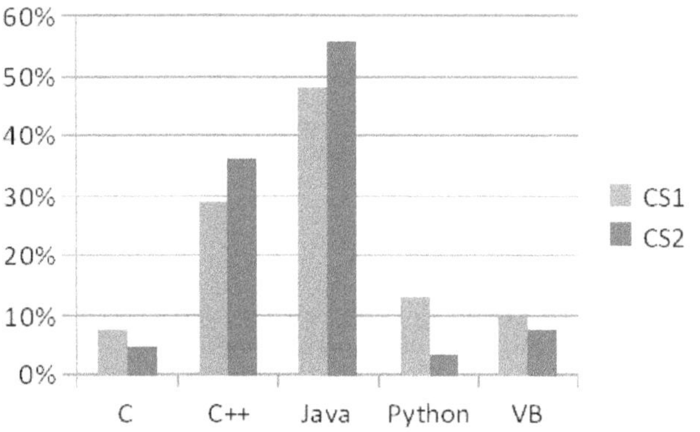

Figure 3. The most popular languages used in CS1 and CS2.

Note that the dominance of Java in our survey responses confirms previous results [2,4,6,11] collected over a span of nearly ten years. Despite what else may be happening in computer science education, the preference of Java as an instructional language is remarkably stable.

It is interesting to examine the correlation between languages used and school ranking. U.S. News and World Report[13] annually ranks institutions within four broad categories – National Universities, Liberal Arts Colleges, Regional Universities, and Regional Colleges – based on the finer-grained Carnegie Basic classification[1]. It then assigns each school to one of four "tiers" in its category, with tier 1 being the highest ranked, and tier 4 the lowest. U.S. News further ranks the schools within the top two tiers more precisely, but for purposes of this comparison we use only the "tier number" for each school.

Java and C++ are of course used broadly across all four tiers. But there is a strong correlation between ranking and certain other languages. Python, for instance, is used far more frequently in the higher-ranked tiers (for CS1, the percentages in each tier are 20.9%, 14.6%, 10.6%, and 1.6%), while Visual Basic is more frequent in tiers 3 and 4 (for CS1: 8.2%, 1.0%, 12.9%, 18.0%.) Both of these results are significant to $\alpha<0.05$. The Visual Basic trend continues in CS2 – tier percentages are 4.5%, 1.0%, 8.2%, and 14.8% – though Python does not, with 87.5% of the Python CS1 schools moving to either Java or C++ for CS2. (See Figures 4 and 5 for a summary of these results.)

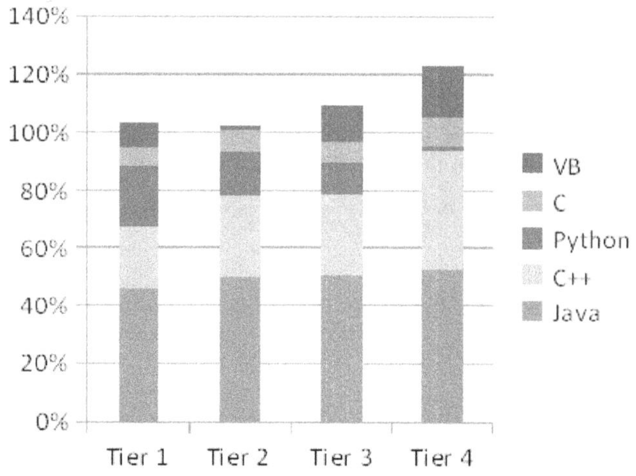

Figure 4. Percentages of schools in each ranking "tier" (as defined by U.S. News) who use each language (in at least some sections) for CS1. (Note the totals do not add to 100% since some schools reported more than one language used.)

Rankings are, of course, not a conclusive indicator of a school's strength, reputation, or anything else. But these trends are worth considering. Perhaps tier 1 and 2 schools choose Python because they feel it is more theoretically sound; perhaps tier 3 and 4 schools choose Visual Basic because they believe it is more vocationally relevant. These are speculations. What is certain is that Java and C++ (in that order) are currently dominant, and that the ways in which institutions differ from the mainstream is somewhat dependent on their type.

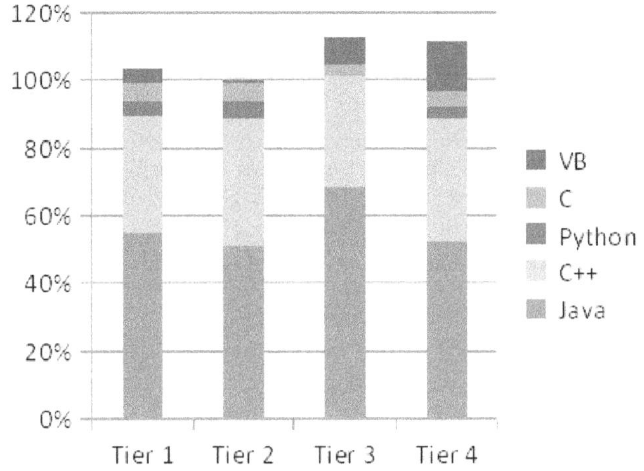

Figure 5. Language use by tier for CS2.

4.2.2 Language continuity

This gives rise to another question: how many schools use a *different* language for CS1 than they do for CS2? There are arguments to be made both for switching languages and for not switching. On the one hand, there may be pedagogical advantages to different languages in the different courses: perhaps Java or Python is seen as easier for novices to learn the basics of programming with, while C++ lends itself to a transparent view of memory usage appropriate to CS2. Too, it is advantageous for students to know more than one language – for diversity of skill set, as well as broader comprehension – and the CS1/2 sequence may be as good a time as any to introduce the second one. (Note that in Computing Curricula 2001, the task force recommends that computer science programs teach students to become competent in languages that make use of at least two programming paradigms[10].) The implications of switching languages received attention a decade ago, for instance in [7].

In any event, the answer to the question is summarized in Table 3. A total of 244 respondents said they use either Java for both courses or C++ for both, and of the "other/other" group 18 used Visual Basic for both. This means that in our survey, at least 70.6% of schools (262/371) teach CS1 and CS2 in the same language.

Table 3. To switch or not to switch? The number of respondents using various combinations of languages in their CS1/CS2 sequence.

CS1	CS2	# respondents (%)
Java	Java	151 (41%)
Java	C++	37 (10%)
Java	other	7 (2%)
C++	Java	26 (7%)
C++	C++	93 (25%)
C++	other	3 (1%)
Other	Java	42 (11%)
Other	C++	18 (5%)
Other	other	30 (8%)

It is worth calling attention to the fact that according to this data, at least half of schools teach only Java and/or Python in the CS1/2 sequence. (We compute this as 184/371=50.0%, since 30 of the "other/Java" responses were for Python/Java and 3 of the "Java/other" responses were for Java/Python.) Note that unlike C and C++, both of these languages use automatic garbage collection and (normally) do not compile natively. While we do not condemn the practice of using them exclusively in the sequence, we note that certain topics traditionally associated with CS2 may be more difficult to illustrate in Python and Java, such as: pointer arithmetic, memory leaks, explicit memory deallocation, and the tradeoffs of passing parameters by value or by reference. Further we note that in Computing Curricula 2008 the topic of "pointers and references" is identified as a core topic in the Programming Fundamentals/Data Structures component [9]. Computing Curricula 2001 also included these topics in the Fundamental Data Structures core area [10]. Both documents also listed "parameterization mechanisms (reference vs. value)" as a core topic for the Programming Languages component. While this topic could be deferred until after the introductory sequence, it seems appropriate to present it at this time.

4.2.3 Other aspects

4.2.3.1 Paradigm

We asked respondents what programming paradigm best described the programming portion of their CS1 and CS2 courses, offering as choices "imperative/procedural," "object-oriented," "functional," and "other." Based on the languages that were specified, we believe there may have been some confusion about the term "functional": it seems many respondents interpreted "functional" to be the same as "imperative/procedural" (presumably because "functions" are employed). Hence, we do not believe the numbers reported for these two categories are meaningful. "Object-oriented," however, resulted in no ambiguity, and these figures are summarized in Table 4.

Table 4. Percentage of respondents who indicated that the "object-oriented programming paradigm" was used.

OO in CS1	OO in CS2	# respondents (%)
Yes	Yes	234 (63%)
Yes	No	9 (2%)
No	Yes	106 (29%)
No	No	22 (6%)

In summary, the object-oriented paradigm is very popular. A strong majority of schools use it for both courses in the intro sequence, with around a third switching from procedural to OO in CS2. Only six percent of schools did not teach OO at all.

4.2.3.2 Tools

Finally, we asked about tools employed: whether students used a command-line environment, an Integrated Development Environment (IDE), or both; and whether they received instruction in using an interactive debugger. The results on the environment question are summarized in Table 5. IDEs clearly carry the day, though a surprising number of schools claim to use both environments within a single course.

Table 5. Types of development environments used.

Environment	CS1	CS2
Command-line	56 (15%)	55 (15%)
Graphical IDE	173 (47%)	149 (40%)
Both	138 (37%)	157 (42%)

Interactive debuggers, too, are popular, but by no means universal. They were reported as being taught in 228 (61.5%) of CS1 courses, and 244 (65.8%) of CS2 courses. Only 70 schools (18.9%) answered this question differently for CS1 and CS2, perhaps indicating that stability is the general rule for tools as well as for languages.

5. CONCLUSIONS

There is a tremendous variety in approaches to CS0. This could be interpreted as a sign of pedagogical innovation, or as a field struggling to identify best practices. Over one-third of schools don't regularly offer a CS0 course at all, and those that do use an enormous variety of languages, and spend a widely differing amount of class time on programming vs. other topics.

CS1 and CS2, by contrast, are far more uniform across schools. Combining several results from the survey, we can say that the most popular approach seems to be an object-oriented pedagogy from start to finish, the Java programming language, and a development environment including IDEs and interactive debuggers. This composite sketch describes perhaps about 2/3rds of schools in the country.

Interestingly, institutions tend to stay with the same approach between CS1 and CS2, rather than introduce a new paradigm, language, or environment. This pedagogical consistency presumably reduces some aspects of cognitive demand, although it means that if students are exposed to variety, it will typically not be in the introductory sequence.

As a final note, we remark that it may be beneficial to the computer science education community to develop a practice of polling institutions about their practices on a regular basis. This would help track trends in what our field is actually implementing in everyday classrooms, and provide a larger context to the noteworthy innovation our leading educators are developing.

6. ACKNOWLEDGMENTS

We are grateful to Debra Hydorn, Megan Martin, and Amy Sams for their help with very time-consuming data processing and analysis.

7. REFERENCES

[1] Carnegie Foundation. 2009. Carnegie Classifications of Institutions of Higher Education. Retrieved December 2, 2009 from http://classifications.carnegiefoundation.org/.

[2] N. Dale. 2005. "Content and emphasis in CS1," *SIGCSE Bulletin*, vol. 37, pp. 69-73.

[3] N. Dale. 2006. "Most difficult topics in CS1: results of an online survey of educators," *SIGCSE Bulletin*, vol. 38, pp. 49-53.

[4] M. De Raadt, R. Watson, and M. Toleman. 2002. "Language Trends in Introductory Programming Courses" *Proceedings of Informing Science and IT Education Conference*.

[5] M. De Raadt, R. Watson, and M. Toleman. 2003. "Language Tug-Of-War: Industry Demand and Academic Choice" *Proceedings of the fifth conference on Australasian computing education*-Volume 30.

[6] M. De Raadt, R. Watson, and M. Toleman. 2004. "Introductory programming: what's happening today and will there be any students to teach tomorrow?," *Proceedings of the sixth conference on Australasian computing education*-Volume 30, p. 282.

[7] A. Dingle and C. Zander. 2000. "Assessing the ripple effect of CS1 language choice," in *Proceedings of the second annual CCSC on Computing in Small Colleges Northwestern conference*, pp. 85–93.

[8] M. Hertz. 2010. "What do CS1 and CS2 mean?: investigating differences in the early courses," in *Proceedings of the 41st ACM technical symposium on Computer science education (SIGCSE 2010)*, pp. 199–203.

[9] Interim Review Task Force. 2008. Computer Science Curriculum 2008: An Interim Revision of CS 2001. Retrieved December 2, 2009 from http://www.acm.org//education/curricula/ComputerScience2008.pdf.

[10] Joint Task Force on Computing Curricula. 2001. Computing Curricula 2001: Curriculum Guidelines for Undergraduate Degree Programs in Computer Science. Retrieved December 2, 2009 from http://www.acm.org/education/education/education/curric_vols/cc2001.pdf.

[11] C. Schulte and J. Bennedsen. 2006. "What do teachers teach in introductory programming?," *Proceedings of the second international workshop on Computing education research*, pp. 17-28.

[12] U.S. News and World Report. 2010. University Directory. Retrieved May 3, 2010 from http://www.usnewsuniversitydirectory.com/.

[13] U.S. News and World Report. 2010. College Rankings. Retrieved June 19, 2010 from http://www.usnews.com/rankings.

Reviewing CS1 Exam Question Content

Andrew Petersen
Dept. of Mathematical and Computational Sciences
University of Toronto Mississauga
andrew.petersen@utoronto.ca

Michelle Craig
Dept. of Computer Science
University of Toronto
mcraig@cs.toronto.edu

Daniel Zingaro
Ontario Institute for Studies in Education
University of Toronto
daniel.zingaro@utoronto.ca

ABSTRACT

Many factors have been cited for poor performance of students in CS1. To investigate how assessment mechanisms may impact student performance, nine experienced CS1 instructors reviewed final examinations from a variety of North American institutions. The majority of the exams reviewed were composed predominantly of high-value, integrative code-writing questions, and the reviewers regularly underestimated the number of CS1 concepts required to answer these questions. An evaluation of the content and cognitive requirements of individual questions suggests that in order to succeed, students must internalize a large amount of CS1 content. This emphasizes the need for focused assessment techniques to provide students with the opportunity to demonstrate their knowledge.

Categories and Subject Descriptors

K.3.2 [**Computers and Education**]: Computer and Information Science Education—*Computer Science Education*

General Terms

Measurement

Keywords

novice programming, exams, CS1

1. INTRODUCTION

The computer science education community has expended considerable energy studying the performance of novice programmers. First programming courses (CS1) suffer from very high attrition, with many students choosing not to complete the course [1]. In extreme cases, grade distributions in CS1 can resemble a bimodal distribution, with many students performing extremely well and many performing extremely poorly. Researchers have postulated that this distribution may result from the combination of two more-conventional normal distributions representing the grades from two disjoint populations — students who can easily learn how to program and those who cannot. For practical reasons, educators want to identify the students at risk of being in the latter population, and researchers have proposed a number of factors that might be used to differentiate the groups including mathematical ability, previous programming experience, spatial visualization and reasoning skill, ability to articulate strategy, study skills, attitudes and approaches, and self-efficacy [21, 26, 16, 4, 6, 13].

Recently, Robins proposed an alternative explanation: learning edge momentum (LEM) [14]. Robins hypothesizes that the set of concepts that a student must master to learn how to program is highly interdependent, with later concepts relying on mastery of earlier concepts. Calling the sections of a programming course "chunks", Robins argues that a student who is unable to master an early chunk has a much lower probability of mastering the next. He further claims that successful mastery of an early chunk increases the likelihood of mastering the later chunk. Inclusion of a momentum term in his mathematical model of this learning process leads to the classic CS1 distribution even when all the students are treated as coming from the same population with the same probability of success on an individual chunk.

We agree with Robins that programming concepts are highly interdependent, but the proposed model relies on several assumptions that do not match typical CS1 courses. Robins' work assumes that chunks are ordered linearly, with each chunk dependent only on previous chunks. However, other researchers have acknowledged that the concepts involved in learning to program are not easily placed in a single linear sequence [12], and teaching introductory CS has followed a long-accepted tradition of a spiral approach [19] where concepts are visited several times in increasing depth throughout the term. In addition, Robins' model of mastery of a chunk is itself bimodal: either a student masters a chunk or she does not. However, with time, learners progress from a fairly fragile understanding of a concept to a more robust one, and even while they are still making this progression, students can build on their limited understanding.

In response to Robins, Lister proposed that skewed CS1 results may stem from poor validity of our assessments [10]. In the context of typical CS1 exams, we believe that the dependencies between concepts in CS1 indeed make it difficult for students to demonstrate what they know. Concepts that are encountered early in CS1 tend to be revisited — and re-evaluated — throughout the course. Over the term, students are expected to commit these concepts to memory, but given the limited time-frame of the course, students may

SIGCSE'11, March 9–12, 2011, Dallas, Texas, USA.

be unable to fully internalize all concepts. Research into cognitive architectures suggests that students will be unable to reason about complex interactions between concepts unless they are all fully internalized, and cognitive load theory assumes that students will be unable to operate on more than two or three chunks of material at a time [22].

For example, a student may be asked to trace a loop containing a conditional statement in the loop body. Even if the student understands how the loop works, an earlier misunderstanding of conditionals can prevent the student from demonstrating her knowledge. Even in the absence of a misunderstanding, the extra burden of reasoning about new and unfamiliar concepts can limit her ability to use them to solve the problem. In Robins' model, a misunderstanding of conditionals may result in a decreased probability of understanding loops. Instead, we argue that her misunderstanding of conditionals decreases the probability that she can *demonstrate* understanding of loops. Furthermore, we claim that most evaluation instruments used in CS1 evaluate far more concepts than intended, and the number of required concepts in each question exceeds the amount of information that students can comfortably handle in working memory.

A number of groups have worked to develop exam questions that more precisely evaluate specific programming topics [3, 11, 5], and other groups have worked to enumerate the concepts included in CS1 courses [8] or in data structure exams [20]. However, to our knowledge, no one has reviewed CS1 exams from a range of schools and attempted to identify the skills and concepts required by each question. To perform this analysis, we employed nine experienced CS educators and evaluated fifteen examinations from fourteen schools. Because of the limited sample, this paper does not provide a thorough statistical analysis of the complete body of CS1 examinations. Instead, we report primarily on the process we used and present observations about the exams we analyzed.

2. THE INITIAL DATA INSTRUMENT

Final exams are a useful proxy for deriving curricular expectations and determining what instructors understand to be important. For example, Simon et al. [20] analyzed hashing and stack questions on CS2 exams to determine whether CS2 was transitioning from a focus on implementation to a focus on interface and application. These authors also explored the cognitive demands on students by developing a list of skills for classifying exam questions. Categorizing the activity involved provides an indication of the mental processes expected of our students, but does not indicate the cognitive demands in terms of conceptual knowledge.

We are interested in measuring the range and depth of understanding required by common CS1 questions, so we considered categorizing exams using several popular taxonomies. The first we considered was Bloom's original cognitive taxonomy, which provides six descriptors (knowledge, comprehension, application, analysis, synthesis, and evaluation) for classifying cognitive requirements of tasks. Researchers have mapped CS-specific tasks onto the Bloom levels [24, 18] to increase agreement when CS educators attempt to make Bloom classifications. Even so, experience suggests that effectively classifying exam questions requires participation in the delivery of the associated course. For example, a question could be classified as *knowledge* if the instructor had given the same example in class but *analysis* or *synthesis* otherwise. Since most of our exams came from institutions with which we had no affiliation, we felt we could not accurately assess questions using Bloom's taxonomy.

To address concerns when classifying using Bloom's taxonomy, Fuller et al. [7] developed a CS-specific taxonomy based on the earlier observation that application informed by synthesis and evaluation involves the deepest cognitive processing [9]. Fuller et al. argue that in order to classify computer science tasks, we must make two classifications: one for the required processing of existing code, and one for the required ability to write new code. This results in a two-dimensional grid into which various skills (e.g. adapt, analyze, debug, implement, model) can be mapped. We found the list of skills useful as an observable characterization of what CS students must be able to do, and we included the list in our instrument, with the aim of identifying skills commonly required on CS1 tests. Those skills could be traced back to their location on the CS-specific taxonomy to gauge the cognitive difficulty of common CS1 questions.

The Structure of the Observed Learning Outcome [2] (SOLO) taxonomy focuses on characteristics of observable student outputs, rather than the cognitive activity required to produce those outputs. For example, if a question elicits a response about a single, coherent idea, the response is termed unistructural, while a response about multiple, unconnected ideas is classified as multistructural. This categorization appears less tightly connected to course delivery than most other taxonomies, so we included SOLO in our data collection instrument and asked the evaluators to evaluate the characteristics of a response to which they would award full marks.

In addition to relating CS1 questions to taxonomies, we aimed to identify concepts instructors believe are important and to examine how they evaluate them. No standard concept inventory for CS1 yet exists, so researchers have used varying methods to derive lists of important concepts. Tew and Guzdial [23] used the contents of textbooks and the ACM's Computing Curricula 2001 to identify ten critical topics. Goldman et al. [8] engaged instructors in the creation of a concept list for three areas of CS using a structured approach for negotiating consensus among experts. For CS1, the result was a list of 64 topics. Schulte and Bennedsen [17] culled 28 topics from the literature and asked instructors to rate the difficulty and relevance of each. While their goal was not to develop an exhaustive concept list, Robins et al. [15] examined the distribution of "help calls" made by students in a lab setting to identify where and why students struggle when learning their first programming language. Each student question was classified according to its most salient concepts: control flow, loops, selection, etc. Their collection instrument contained 21 concepts.

Our instrument drew concepts from two of these CS1 concept inventories [17, 8] and the study of problem distributions [15]. Concepts identified in all three studies were included. In some cases, one study divided a concept identified in the others into more than one category, while in other cases, several related concepts were identified but divided in different ways by the various studies. In these cases, we merged these concepts into a larger category. Table 1 displays the final list of concepts included on our instrument.

program structure	function structure	data flow
trivial syntax	variables	expressions
data types	booleans	if-else
sequential control flow		input/output
definite loops	indefinite loops	nested loops
strings	lists (arrays)	collections
trees	recursion	exceptions
object structure	basic OO	reference types
accessors/mutators	constructors	inheritance
polymorphism	visibility/scope	

Table 1: Concepts on the evaluation instrument

3. GROUP REVIEW

We divided our nine educators into two groups. For each exam, all members of a group individually assessed the skills, concepts, and SOLO level of each question, then negotiated consensus in a group discussion. We collected data from both the individual and group-consensus analyses, training the evaluators and analyzing four exams over two days.

3.1 SOLO Level

Our evaluators had difficulty agreeing on SOLO level, and persuasive arguments could often be made to categorize a question in more than one level. For example, consider an exam question about searching for a value in an array. A student who recalls an identical example from lecture could provide a unistructural response and be awarded full marks. A student from a different class might need to generate a solution from scratch, pulling together content from across his course. Despite SOLO's focus on observable outputs, we found, as others have found with Bloom's model [24], that precise determination of SOLO level requires knowledge of the content covered in class. The group summaries revealed a distinct lack of consensus, so we have not analyzed the SOLO data further.

3.2 Skills

Unfortunately, developing a group consensus on skills is just as difficult as agreeing on Bloom or SOLO level. While some skills from the CS-specific taxonomy (such as *implement* or *debug*) appear to be externally observable, others rely on assumptions about student knowledge. Without information about the course content, evaluators selected different skills based on their conceptions of what students "should" know or have seen. For example, in one exam containing questions about developing code with loop invariants, two reviewers with experience teaching CS1 in a similar way believed the students were *applying* a standard technique, while other reviewers believe the questions were an exercise in *implementation*. As before, group discussion could not eliminate the disagreements. The group summaries revealed a lack of consensus and the need for more information about the content of the course.

3.3 Concepts

For each question, evaluators were requested to independently identify (a) which concepts were being *evaluated* and (b) which additional concepts were *used* in a correct solution. We analyzed the individual and negotiated group results to determine how effectively individuals identified the concepts the group subsequently decided were *evaluated* or *used*. We assumed that the group summaries fully and accurately described the concepts involved in the question and found that individuals were generally able to identify all the *evaluated* concepts but usually did not identify all of the *used* concepts. In the majority of cases (81%), individual group members identified all the concepts that were eventually marked as *evaluated* but sometimes categorized them as *used* instead of *evaluated*. Group discussion was necessary to come to agreement on the full set of *evaluated* concepts.

Furthermore, we found that no individual was reliably able to identify all of the concepts that were *used* by a question. However, while instructors commonly failed to identify concepts that were eventually included in the group summary, very few concepts were identified by individuals and then eliminated from the summary by the group discussion. On average, taking the union of all concepts identified by individuals for a specific question results in a set that is only 14% (.26 concepts per evaluator) larger than the group summary. In conclusion, false negatives (omitted concepts) were common, but false positives (extraneous concepts) were rare. Assuming that the difficulty of a question is related to the number of concepts required to solve it, this implies that instructors generally underestimate the difficulty of their questions.

4. INDIVIDUAL REVIEW

The group review indicated that many questions involved a large number of concepts, but more data was needed to determine if this is true at a wide range of schools. To evaluate additional exams, we performed a second round of analyses using individual reviewers. Since the skills and SOLO components of the instrument were inconclusive, they were removed for this round, but as before, reviewers were asked to identify which concepts were *evaluated* and *used* for each question. Because individuals reliably identify a subset of the concepts identified by a group, the data from the individual reviews should underestimate the number of concepts *evaluated* and *used*.

4.1 Question types

We reviewed a total of fifteen exams from fourteen schools.[1] The selected exams were mostly recent (2006–2010)[2] and came from a range of North American institutions. Table 2 lists the types of schools (using the Carnegie Foundation classification) and languages represented.

Type	Exams	Languages
Very High Research Activity	6	Java, Javascript, PHP, Python
High Research Activity	3	C, Haskell, Python
Masters	1	C++
Arts and Sciences	5	Java, Python

Table 2: Schools and languages of the reviewed exams

The courses reflected a wide variety of CS1 strategies, so some exams contained a significant number of questions that were focused on topics other than programming such as algorithmic complexity or computer organization. Evaluators

[1]One school had recently changed the language of instruction and provided two exams — one from before the change and one from after.

[2]The exception was one 1997 exam, kept due to the difficulty of finding publicly available non-imperative language exams.

identified what type of question was being asked, determining both the question's content (whether or not it is programming related) and its form (multiple-choice, short answer, etc.). The categories for the latter were drawn from the recent study of data structures exams [20].

Distribution of Question Types					
	Question Form				
Content	Multiple choice	Short answer	Writing code	Drawing diagrams	Total
Writing Code	0 (0%)	12 (5%)	83 (54%)	0 (0%)	95 (59%)
Reading Code	21 (3%)	29 (9%)	0 (0%)	2 (2%)	52 (13%)
Prog. Concepts	11 (2%)	17 (8%)	0 (0%)	0 (0%)	28 (10%)
Non-Prog.	8 (3%)	23 (14%)	0 (0%)	2 (1%)	33 (18%)
Total	40 (7%)	81 (36%)	83 (54%)	4 (3%)	208 (100%)

Table 3: The number of questions of each type and, in parentheses, the associated percentage of exam marks.

Table 3 describes the question types encountered in our study. The exams contained a total of 208 questions. 95 (45.7%) involved writing code and another 80 (38.5%) involved code reading or programming concepts. Of those that involved code writing, 12 were short answer questions. Those questions involved writing code within a structure provided on the test, such as filling in the correct stopping condition for a loop. The remaining 83 questions were generally of the form "write this function/method/class/program".

Code writing questions were the most heavily weighted, averaging 59% of exam weight. Other programming questions composed another 23% of exam weight.[3] However, the average weight of the code writing component varied significantly across schools. Four schools had exams composed only of programming-related (i.e. code-reading and code-writing) questions, and of the other 10 schools, two used exams that covered a great deal of non-programming material (80% and 77% non-programming weight, respectively). While many schools offer a traditional programming-focused CS1, some schools offer courses with more breadth.

4.2 Concepts

Table 4 shows the average number of concepts *required* (either *used* or *evaluated*) for each type of question. *Required* represents the number of questions that require an understanding of the concept in order to generate a correct answer. The reported values should be underestimates, since our analysis of the group evaluations showed that individuals were generally unable to identify all of the concepts that were *required*. In each cell, the upper number is the average if each question contributes equally. The parenthesized number is the average if each question is weighted according to the percentage of marks it contributes to its exam. The two examinations that did not specify a marks breakdown are omitted from the weighted average.

Some of the programming concept questions are reported

[3]Two exams did not specify the point value of each question and were omitted from these averages.

Average Number of Concepts Per Question					
	Question Form				
Question Content	Multiple choice	Short answer	Writing code	Drawing diagrams	Total
Writing Code	0 (0)	5.0 (5.0)	7.4 (7.6)	0 (0)	7.1 (7.4)
Reading Code	3.1 (4.0)	6.7 (6.7)	0 (0)	5.2 (1.8)	5.2 (6.0)
Prog. Concepts	0.9 (0.9)	2.3 (2.1)	0 (0)	0 (0)	1.8 (1.9)

Table 4: The average number of concepts per question and, in parentheses, the weighted average where each question contributes according to its exam weight.

to require no concepts. These questions often tested programming concepts that were difficult to categorize or not included in the list in Table 1. For example, several questions asked about numeric representations within the language, and the evaluator chose to indicate this by writing in a new category. We did not count these write-in categories, since they were often language-specific and/or potentially overlapped with an existing category. The counts in the table are already an underestimate, so omitting categories does not detract from the results.

On average, code writing and reading questions each require students to understand 5 to 7 concepts. Furthermore, the weighted averages for these questions tend to be higher, which indicates that questions worth more marks — those that have the largest impact on grades — evaluate more concepts. The Spearman's correlation coefficient between the number of *required* concepts and the weight of each question is 0.38, which is moderate evidence that the more difficult questions (in terms of number of concepts) correspond to those of greatest value.

This means that the questions which impact students' grades most dramatically require them to understand a large fraction of typical CS1 material. If a student has a misconception or doubts about any one of the *required* concepts, the question becomes more difficult to solve. Furthermore, errors caused by underlying concepts can make it difficult for a student to demonstrate his or her understanding of higher-level topics. These high-value, integrative questions are a clear majority of the marks in the exams that we reviewed. For example, the two categories of questions that required more than 6 concepts on average account for 63% of marks on exams.

4.3 Over-representation of Concepts

For each concept, Table 5 reveals the number of times it was identified as *evaluated* or *used*. Since the table is ordered from most to least frequently *required*, basic concepts like syntax and function structure are found at the top, and more advanced concepts like polymorphism and inheritance are found at the bottom.

Several concepts in the table are *used* much more frequently than they are *evaluated*. During the group evaluation, one group argued that these concepts were fundamental and were required in every code writing question. These fundamental concepts are indicated by a star in Table 5 and are undercounted since that group stopped explicitly indicating them, assuming that every question would require them. However, one evaluator strongly objected to omitting these categories since doubts about the syntactic structure

Concept	Used	Evaluated	Required
trivial syntax*	74	44	118
variables*	69	30	99
function structure*	46	28	74
expressions*	36	25	61
if-else	19	39	58
sequential control flow*	39	16	55
collections	8	41	49
strings	11	36	47
data types	17	30	47
definite loops	10	37	47
data flow	15	28	43
object structure	18	20	38
booleans	8	29	37
lists (arrays)	3	27	30
I/O	11	18	29
basic OO	8	19	27
recursion	4	18	22
program structure	14	8	22
indefinite loops	2	17	19
reference types	6	11	17
accessors/mutators	6	7	13
exceptions	2	9	11
nested loops	0	10	10
constructors	2	8	10
inheritance	0	4	4
visibility/scope	0	3	3
trees	1	1	2
polymorphism	0	2	2

Table 5: The number of questions that *require* (either *use* or *evaluate*) each programming concept. Some groups stopped marking the concepts indicated by a star.

of an unfamiliar language made it difficult for her to accurately categorize questions.

We recalculated Table 4, omitting the Table 5 fundamental concepts, and found that questions still require a large number of significant (non-fundamental) concepts. For example, the average number of significant concepts per question required by all "Writing Code" questions only drops from 7.1 to 4.1, and the average number of significant concepts for all "Reading Code" questions becomes 2.7.

Cognitive load theory [22, 25] partially explains the objecting evaluator's difficulty, arguing that concepts which are not fully internalized (committed to long-term memory) must be reasoned about in working memory. The mind is limited in its ability to work with multiple concepts simultaneously, so students uncertain about syntax face an increased cognitive burden. Their working memory is partially occupied and cannot focus on the higher-level design and implementation issues being explicitly evaluated by the question. Since writing code depends on several fundamental concepts, students will find it difficult to demonstrate understanding of significant concepts.

Trivial syntax and function structure are extreme examples, since any student having significant problems with these is likely to face significant problems with higher-level concepts. However, the data includes a number of moderately difficult concepts such as conditionals, collections, and loops, that are frequently used in questions that evaluate high-level concepts like exceptions or recursion. Furthermore, due to the limited time available (less than a full semester in many cases) many students will be unable to fully internalize all of these concepts. Relying on questions that consistently require a large number of concepts nearly guarantees that students will encounter at least one concept that they do not fully understand but which is not the focus of the question.

5. CONCLUSIONS

We have evaluated CS1 examinations from a range of schools across North America, almost all of which focused on evaluating programming concepts and skills. The majority of questions focused on code writing; a smaller number of questions involved code reading or more abstract questions about programming concepts. Together, these questions composed over 80% of the total weight on the tests, reflecting a broad emphasis on programming skill in CS1.

The programming-related questions we saw were quite comprehensive, simultaneously requiring the use of multiple programming concepts. In the most common case, students were required to write significant pieces of code, and on average, these questions required students to demonstrate understanding of more than 7 concepts. We believe that these types of questions are one reason why a significant fraction of CS1 students perform poorly or fail to complete the course. The top students, able to internalize almost all the concepts over the course of the term, will obtain high marks, but most students will frequently encounter concepts that remain underdeveloped. In these situations, students may be unable to demonstrate their understanding of other concepts, conveying the impression that they have made little progress to the instructor and, more importantly, to themselves. Given that mastery and internalization of concepts requires time and practice, this study suggests that programming abilities should be developed over a longer sequence of courses.

We are running a study to support or refute our claim that students may be able to deal with concepts individually but struggle when required to demonstrate mastery of multiple concepts simultaneously. We provide students with exams that contain single- and dual-concept questions in addition to the more-traditional integrative code-writing questions. We have found that restricting the number of concepts per question requires both a change in the proportion of question types used and the introduction of new question types. For example, in the exams we reviewed, both multiple choice format and structured code writing questions generally require fewer concepts but are not widely used. We hope to see more efforts to produce alternate types of questions for CS1 [5] and hope that instructors will consider cognitive load while constructing examinations.

6. ACKNOWLEDGMENTS

Thanks to the faculty whose exams were reviewed and to the lecturers at the University of Toronto who donated their time to evaluate exam questions from other schools.

7. REFERENCES

[1] J. Bennedsen and M. E. Caspersen. Failure rates in introductory programming. *SIGCSE Bull.*, 39(2):32–36, 2007.

[2] J. B. Biggs and K. F. Collis. *Evaluating the quality of learning: The SOLO taxonomy (Structure of the Observed Learning Outcome)*. Academic Press, 1982.

[3] T. Clear, J. Edwards, R. Lister, B. Simon, E. Thompson, and J. Whalley. The teaching of novice computer programmers: bringing the scholarly-research approach to Australia. In *ACE '08: Proceedings of the Tenth Conference on Australasian Computing Education*, pages 63–68, Darlinghurst, Australia, Australia, 2008. Australian Computer Society, Inc.

[4] M. de Raadt, M. Hamilton, R. Lister, J. Tutti, S. Simon, K. Sutton, B. Baker, I. Box, Q. Cutts, J. Hamer, M. Petre, and D. Tolhurst. Approaches to learning in computer programming students, and its effect on success. In *Proceedings of Higher Education in a Changing World, Higher Education Research and Development Society of Australia Conference*, pages 407–414. N/A, 2005.

[5] P. Denny, A. Luxton-Reilly, and B. Simon. Evaluating a new exam question: Parsons problems. In *ICER '08: Proceedings of the Fourth International Workshop on Computing Education Research*, pages 113–124, New York, NY, USA, 2008. ACM.

[6] S. H. Edwards, J. Snyder, M. A. Pérez-Qui nones, A. Allevato, D. Kim, and B. Tretola. Comparing effective and ineffective behaviors of student programmers. In *ICER '09: Proceedings of the Fifth International Workshop on Computing Education Research*, pages 3–14, New York, NY, USA, 2009. ACM.

[7] U. Fuller, C. G. Johnson, T. Ahoniemi, D. Cukierman, I. Hernán-Losada, J. Jackova, E. Lahtinen, T. L. Lewis, D. M. Thompson, C. Riedesel, and E. Thompson. Developing a computer science-specific learning taxonomy. In *ITiCSE-WGR '07: Working group reports on ITiCSE on Innovation and Technology in Computer Science Education*, pages 152–170, New York, NY, USA, 2007. ACM.

[8] K. Goldman, P. Gross, C. Heeren, G. L. Herman, L. Kaczmarczyk, M. C. Loui, and C. Zilles. Setting the scope of concept inventories for introductory computing subjects. *Trans. Comput. Educ.*, 10(2):1–29, 2010.

[9] C. G. Johnson and U. Fuller. Is Bloom's taxonomy appropriate for computer science? In *Baltic Sea '06: Proceedings of the 6th Baltic Sea conference on Computing education research*, pages 120–123, New York, NY, USA, 2006. ACM.

[10] R. Lister. Computing education research: geek genes and bimodal grades. *ACM Inroads*, 1(3):16–17, 2010.

[11] R. Lister, E. S. Adams, S. Fitzgerald, W. Fone, J. Hamer, M. Lindholm, R. McCartney, J. E. Moström, K. Sanders, O. Seppälä, B. Simon, and L. Thomas. A multi-national study of reading and tracing skills in novice programmers. In *ITiCSE-WGR '04: Working group reports from ITiCSE on Innovation and technology in computer science education*, pages 119–150, New York, NY, USA, 2004. ACM.

[12] J. Mead, S. Gray, J. Hamer, R. James, J. Sorva, C. S. Clair, and L. Thomas. A cognitive approach to identifying measurable milestones for programming skill acquisition. In *ITiCSE-WGR '06: Working group reports on ITiCSE on Innovation and technology in computer science education*, pages 182–194, New York, NY, USA, 2006. ACM.

[13] V. Ramalingam, D. LaBelle, and S. Wiedenbeck. Self-efficacy and mental models in learning to program. *SIGCSE Bull.*, 36(3):171–175, 2004.

[14] A. Robins. Learning edge momentum: A new account of outcomes. *Computer Science Education*, 20(1):37–71, 2010.

[15] A. Robins, P. Haden, and S. Garner. Problem distributions in a CS1 course. In *ACE '06: Proceedings of the 8th Australian conference on Computing education*, pages 165–173, Darlinghurst, Australia, Australia, 2006. Australian Computer Society, Inc.

[16] A. Robins, J. Rountree, and N. Rountree. Learning and teaching programming: A review and discussion. *Computer Science Education*, 13:137–172, 2003.

[17] C. Schulte and J. Bennedsen. What do teachers teach in introductory programming? In *ICER '06: Proceedings of the Second International Workshop on Computing Education Research*, pages 17–28, New York, NY, USA, 2006. ACM.

[18] T. Scott. Bloom's taxonomy applied to testing in computer science classes. *J. Comput. Small Coll.*, 19(1):267–274, 2003.

[19] B. Shneiderman. Teaching programming: A spiral approach to syntax and semantics. *Computers & Education*, 1(4):193 – 197, 1977.

[20] B. Simon, M. Clancy, R. McCartney, B. Morrison, B. Richards, and K. Sanders. Making sense of data structures exams. In *ICER '10: Proceedings of the Sixth International Workshop on Computing Education Research*, pages 97–106, New York, NY, USA, 2010. ACM.

[21] B. Simon, S. Fincher, A. Robins, B. Baker, I. Box, Q. Cutts, M. de Raadt, P. Haden, J. Hamer, M. Hamilton, R. Lister, M. Petre, K. Sutton, D. Tolhurst, and J. Tutty. Predictors of success in a first programming course. In *ACE '06: Proceedings of the 8th Austalian conference on Computing education*, pages 189–196, Darlinghurst, Australia, Australia, 2006. Australian Computer Society, Inc.

[22] J. Sweller, J. van MerriÃńboer, and F. Paas. Cognitive architecture and instructional design. *Educational Psychology Review*, 10(3):251–296, 1998.

[23] A. E. Tew and M. Guzdial. Developing a validated assessment of fundamental CS1 concepts. In *SIGCSE '10: Proceedings of the 41st ACM technical symposium on Computer science education*, pages 97–101, New York, NY, USA, 2010. ACM.

[24] E. Thompson, A. Luxton-Reilly, J. L. Whalley, M. Hu, and P. Robbins. Bloom's taxonomy for CS assessment. In *ACE '08: Proceedings of the Tenth Conference on Australasian Computing Education*, pages 155–161, Darlinghurst, Australia, Australia, 2008. Australian Computer Society, Inc.

[25] J. J. van MerriÃńboer and J. Sweller. Cognitive load theory and complex learning: Recent developments and future directions. *Educational Psychology Review*, 17(2):147–177, 2005.

[26] B. C. Wilson and S. Shrock. Contributing to success in an introductory computer science course: a study of twelve factors. *SIGCSE Bull.*, 33(1):184–188, 2001.

Distributed Version Control in the Classroom

Daniel Rocco
Department of Computer Science
University of West Georgia
Carrollton, Georgia 30118-2310
drocco@westga.edu

Will Lloyd
Department of Computer Science
University of West Georgia
Carrollton, Georgia 30118-2310
wlloyd@westga.edu

ABSTRACT

Modern distributed version control systems offer compelling advantages for teaching students professional software development practices and skills. In this paper, we explore the potential for incorporating Mercurial into introductory, intermediate, and advanced computing courses. By incorporating version control into the entire CS curriculum, instructors create unique opportunities to engage students in collaborative, real-world projects and activities, giving them critical early exposure to the expectations and assumptions prevalent in the software development community. Early introduction to version control provides students with an important foundation in both personal and collaborative development excellence, offering them a competitive edge in the marketplace and a superior understanding of software development best practice.

Categories and Subject Descriptors

K.3.2 [**Computing Milieux**]: Computing and Information Sciences Education; D.2.6 [**Software**]: Software Engineering, Programming Environments

General Terms

Management, Education

Keywords

Education, Distributed version control, Mercurial, Software tools, Software development process

1. INTRODUCTION

Software development professionals have long argued that version control is a critical component of software development practice, even claiming that version control can be used as a litmus test to determine whether a software project will succeed [6, 10, 11]. The CC2008 report features version control prominently, noting several times the desire from industry commentators for students with experience in software development processes and management techniques [3]. Given its importance in industry, version control is a vital skill for computing students to master, yet is not taught in the majority of computing curricula or is taught at a superficial level, perhaps in a single course [2, 8, 10]. In considering potential explanations for the lack of version control in many CS classes, several themes emerge in the literature and discussions with CS educators:

- version control systems impose too much administrative overhead to be added to already overloaded CS classes
- version control is viewed as "one tool among many," a peripheral concern rather than an integral part of the software development lifecycle and process
- version control does not foster student learning or enhance CS instruction

In our experience, version control is not a peripheral or optional tool but a vital component in the software development toolkit. Modern distributed version control systems (DVCS) eliminate the administrative overhead of traditional, centralized systems and provide direct, tangible benefits to both students and teachers [4]. Students get experience with a professional software development tool that is easy to use and provides a safety net for developing code. By using distributed version control, students learn software development process and practice working in an iterative, incremental, and intentional development mindset [7]. As the students gain experience, distributed version control scales with them, enabling them to collaborate with their peers, contribute to open source software projects, and eventually transfer their new knowledge to the work environment [3].

In this paper, we present a model for incorporating version control into the entire CS curriculum using a modern distributed version control system, Mercurial. Mercurial is a fast, robust, and scalable distributed version control system noted for its well-balanced command set. It is easy to learn in use, even for beginners with no programming experience, yet scales to serve the needs of very large projects [9], making it an ideal choice for an educational setting. Early introduction of version control establishes and reinforces an iterative software process while facilitating detection of cowboy coding and cheating. Students using Mercurial gain valuable experience using a professional version control tool, which underscores the process-oriented nature of software development. Since distributed version control systems are designed to address the problems associated with collaborative development, they are ideal for group projects of all kinds. The knowledge and experience students gain using Mercurial transfers well to other version control systems such as CVS, Subversion, and Git. Mercurial includes excellent migration tools to help ease the transition to or from another version control system should circumstances warrant.

SIGCSE'11, March 9–12, 2011, Dallas, Texas, USA.

2. PEDAGOGICAL MOTIVATION

The University of West Georgia Computer Science Department offers an ABET-accredited Bachelor's of Science in Computer Science with an emphasis on program construction and software development. Most of our students enter the computing industry as apprentice software developers, working with web and database application development teams for businesses in and around the Atlanta area. Graduates will be expected to collaborate with senior developers and contribute to software development projects using modern development best practices and tools. The Department's software development focus necessitates a strong emphasis on program construction and software engineering topics throughout the curriculum; these topics include iterative, incremental development, object-oriented architecture and design, design patterns, testing, documentation, and the use of professional development tools and techniques. This emphasis begins very early: in CS1, students begin using a simplified software process while being inculcated into good development habits. The entire educational process highlights the intentional nature of software development: by following a process, students begin to understand software not as opaque monolithic artifacts but in terms of systems, modules, packages, and classes that can be designed, implemented, and tested in a methodical way.

Version control is an important component of successful software development projects that supports and encourages good habits and skills. For the individual programmer, version control encourages intentional development by forcing the developer to reflect on what they have just done and summarize it to create a commit comment. On the development team, version control is good hygiene, providing critical concurrency control, coordination, and conflict resolution tools to manage the otherwise chaotic enterprise of building software. And for individuals, teams, and educators, distributed version control systems offer compelling advantages in the form of ease of use, superior semantic models, and richer collaboration mechanisms compared to traditional, centralized version control solutions.

2.1 Introductory Classes

The primary goal of our introductory classes is to teach students the fundamentals of object-oriented software development. From the outset, we teach, demonstrate, and grade for an iterative, incremental, and intentional software construction process. As an iterative approach, we encourage students to work in small development cycles, repeatedly planning, documenting, implementing, and testing the functionality they are currently developing. These small cycles help avoid the last-minute "big bang" and provide structure for incrementally building new features by focusing on one feature at a time. This process is intentional as students must reflect on what has been done and plan what to do next.

Version control directly supports these objectives in addition to providing its benefits of change management and concurrency control. We require students to turn in their revision logs with their assignments, making it easy to see if a student waited until the last minute. These logs also provide an audit trail for determining if a student followed the incremental process, which will be demonstrated by a logical and coherent sequence of commit messages that indicate a methodical progression toward the end goal. At each commit, students must stop and describe their work in a commit comment, which forces reflective pauses and helps promote an intentional attitude toward their work.

2.1.1 DVCS Benefits

Version control must be introduced early in the curriculum if it is to be integrated as a habitual part of students' development process. In the early stages of their educational career, however, most students are simply overwhelmed, trying to assimilate and understand such topics as language syntax, object-oriented concepts and their connections, data types, and software process; even the behavior and usage of unfamiliar software development applications is intimidating. In this environment, version control cannot be viewed as an option; it must be presented as an integral part of the development process and be perceived as such by the students. It must also be simple to set up a new project, since new students spend so much of their time working on small, short-lived assignments. For introductory students, then, a version control system must

- be easy to use, particularly when starting a new project or assignment
- be unobtrusive, both conceptually and mechanically
- provide tangible benefits in relation to its costs, even if those benefits are only dimly perceived at first
- be understood as a mandatory component of the software development process

Given these requirements, a traditional, centralized version control system such as CVS or Subversion might seem to be an appropriate choice for introductory computer science students. Paradoxically, while a distributed version control system's decentralized, replicated-repository model might seem more complicated to use than a centralized system, in practice the opposite is true. Let us consider two of the pedagogically significant differences between centralized and distributed version control systems: project initialization and submission of student work.

Project initialization: Centralized version control systems build upon a client/server architecture and interaction pattern; the assumptions inherent to this architecture pervade these systems, even in instances where the repository is hosted on the local machine. Because of this, most tasks in a centralized system require a depth of understanding beyond the capabilities of many introductory students; this is particularly evident during the creation of a new project. Before they can even begin using a centralized version control system, students must grapple with creating a repository, project, and working directory and with connecting these different locations together correctly. If the repository is hosted remotely, they must additionally worry about connecting the version control client to a centralized server, network connectivity and firewall issues, and credentials and authentication. Setting up a new project requires feeding cryptic arguments to several version control system commands, even after all the network and authentication issues have been handled. These administrative surface features have little to do with software development and distract students from deeper version control learning objectives, while the high cost of establishing a new repository and importing a project makes it unlikely that students will use version control outside of assignments where points are at stake.

In contrast, initializing a new project in Mercurial requires a single command: `hg init`. Repository initialization is instantaneous. This speed and simplicity represents not merely convenience, but a drastic reduction in the technical and cognitive overhead required to use version control. Being able to create a new repository in a matter of seconds makes it more likely that students (and instructors) will use version control. The low cost of using Mercurial makes it easy to motivate, since its students can see the benefits of protecting their work without being distracted by difficult commands.

Assignment submission: Another significant pedagogical benefit of distributed version control systems is the ease with which student work can be handled. As has been noted elsewhere, centralized version control systems pose significant challenges in an educational setting, including the problems of inadvertent repository damage, authorization, and access control. Deploying a traditional centralized version control system in an educational environment requires a significant commitment of administrative, development, and educational resources to be successful. From an administrative perspective, the instructor will require a server to host repositories along with a sysadmin to create user accounts and maintain the server. The sysadmin would need to implement a security protocol to protect student work and prevent cheating while allowing the instructor and TAs access for grading purposes. The administrator would also need to provide technical support for inevitable connectivity issues and damaged repositories.

Using a centralized version control system will also require tool development support. Because of centralized systems' client/server architecture and the associated startup and infrastructure costs, customized administration scripts must be used to support classes at scale. Similarly, submission and grading of assignments will likely require the use of custom scripts and tools. While these tools need not be complicated, like any software they must be designed, created, tested, and debugged.

Mercurial's distributed architecture, by comparison, makes assignment submission straightforward. Each repository in a distributed version control system is fully autonomous, which allows students to simply zip up their entire project and upload it. Since the Mercurial repository is contained in a subfolder of their working directory, their repository is automatically included in their submission without any additional work on their part. Graders see not only the student's submitted work but their entire version control repository including its complete revision history, which provides insight into the student's development process. Assignment grading rubrics can include an assessment of the student's process based upon their project start time, total number of commits, and iterative and incremental development.

2.1.2 *Example Usage Scenario*

The following exercise, given to CS1 students in Fall 2009, is typical of both our introductory courses and any upper-level courses where students did not learn version control in their prior classes. As background, we teach CS1 in Java using BlueJ; our computing environment is Windows preloaded with the TortoiseHg GUI shell interface and other software the students need. Students receive instructions detailing the process of installing the required software on their own machines should they wish to do so.

Early in the semester, students hear a single mini-lecture on version control with Mercurial and do a lab assignment in which they

1. learn the purpose of version control and major version control terminology like working directory, repository, and revision
2. configure their username in Mercurial, which is recorded whenever they commit their work
3. create a new BlueJ project and put it under version control
4. learn how to add files to version control and commit changes
5. practice making changes to their project, committing their work as they go

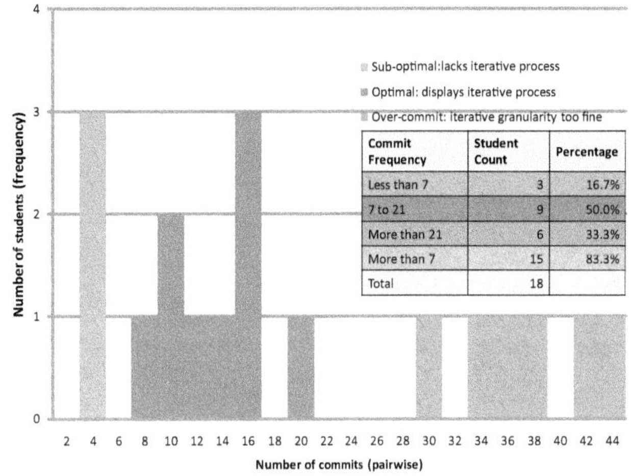

Figure 1: CS1 Project commit frequency, Fall 2009. More than 80% of the students demonstrated their ability to use Mercurial as part of an iterative, incremental software development process. Approximately one third of the students demonstrated effective use of version control but committed too frequently.

6. understand the purpose and basic usage of the revision log, and practice updating to earlier revisions

Students are expected to use version control for all subsequent assignments. The vast majority of students are able to use version control effectively for their individual assignments with little or no assistance after this one lab assignment.

2.1.3 *Evaluation*

CS1: Figure 1 shows student incorporation of version control into their development process by the end of CS1 Fall 2009. The project included 12 classes and required "incremental, iterative development, as documented by a Mercurial repository." Although version control was required, no commit frequency or other constraints were specified, which allowed the students to determine how best to use the repository. Over 80% of the students displayed an understanding of iterative process as measured by commit frequency. 50% of the students used a commit frequency consistent with the scope of the project (i.e. committing initially, for each class and associated code, and for long breaks). Those students with a commit frequency above 21 display incremental development but lack a full understanding of "significant change."

Web Tech: Figures 2 and 3 show two successive assignments from our Fall 2009 Introductory Web Technologies course. The cohort of students was introduced to version control and Mercurial during this course prior to these successive assignments. The assignments were of similar scope and required version control; however, assignment 3 specified a minimum commit frequency while assignment 4 allowed the students to determine how best to use the repository. Over the course of the assignments, students demonstrated their ability to use version control consistently: the vast majority created and used a repository for both assignments, with only 3 of 32 failing to do so. Students met the minimum reasonable commit frequency consistently—75.0% and 81.3% for assignments 3 and 4, respectively—and effectively (average commit frequency increased from 4.8 to 6.3 suggesting a better understanding of iterative development).

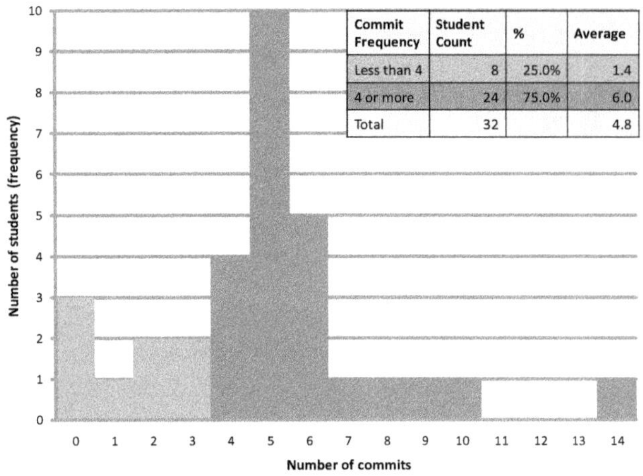

Figure 2: Assignment 3 commit frequency, Web Tech Fall 2009. Version control required by instructions, which specify a 4 commit minimum.

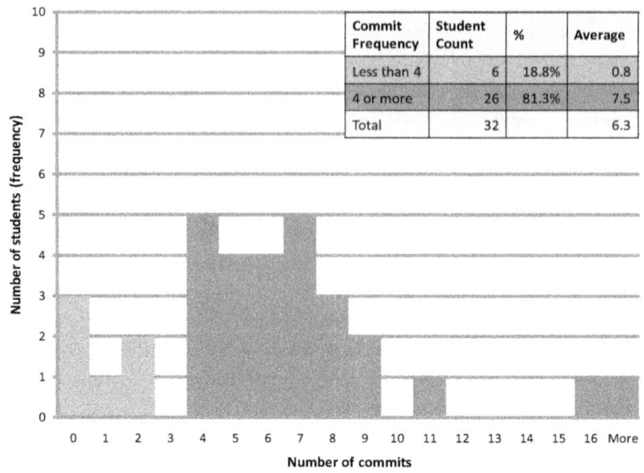

Figure 3: Assignment 4 commit frequency, Web Tech Fall 2009. Version control required by instructions, but no commit frequency was specified.

2.2 Upper-Level Classes

As students progress through the curriculum, Mercurial's rich, balanced feature set supports the expansion of the process-oriented software development model toward more challenging assignments and group work. One of the key advantages of distributed version control systems is their support for both rich collaboration options and iterative, incremental development. In a centralized version control system, the commit command incorporates two distinct operations: save and publish. By committing, a developer both saves the current state of the working directory and simultaneously publishes it to the central repository. This property is common to centralized version control systems and makes it difficult or impossible for individual developers to reap the benefits of version control [1]. It also has a tendency to set up an antagonistic class system among developers between the elite few who have commit access to the repository and the remainder who do not.

Distributed version control systems break the connection between commit and publish, making it easier to explore and work incrementally without the overhead incurred by the assumptions of inflexible coordinated development. Individual developers are free to experiment, to create branches, explore, commit their work, revise, scrap everything and start over, all without affecting anyone else working on the project. By offering robust tools for managing branching, merging, and conflict resolution, distributed version control systems provide excellent support for asynchronous development.

These qualities make distributed version control systems ideal in an educational setting. Mercurial supports several collaboration options including

- push/pull commands that can be used to synchronize changes on a shared disk
- a built-in command to start an internal web server that can be used to synchronize changes
- permanent hosting using CGI scripts or server applications
- project forges that support Mercurial including Google Code, BitBucket, and Assembla

This plethora of flexible working styles and configurations enables Mercurial to scale to the needs and capabilities of each class. For intermediate courses that emphasize pair or small group work on short-lived projects, an informal collaboration setup is appropriate, either through shared disk space or Mercurial's internal server on the local network. More advanced students working on larger projects can benefit from the availability of more powerful collaboration options and discussions of the benefits and tradeoffs of each. As students gain skills and experience, instructors can illustrate advanced commands and different working topologies, giving students more latitude for creative exploration.

We have not settled on formal recommendations for instructors giving group assignments in upper-level courses, although other schools are exploring the self hosting option [5]. Informally, we tend to use online project forges for group assignments and projects as they both minimize our administrative costs and introduce students to a suite of important development tools. These systems are simple to use for both the student and teacher, are freely available, and allow access any time, anywhere there is an Internet connection.

2.3 After Graduation

Mercurial provides students with a solid foundation for personal development work upon graduation. Students leave West Georgia having worked with version control and an explicit software development process for most of their college career. Students will enter the workforce already knowing version control core concepts and terminology, which will prepare them for the process of integrating into the development team by giving them a vocabulary with which to discuss software projects. Mercurial also gives students a solid understanding of version control commands, many of which are analogous to similar commands in other systems like Subversion. Its excellent conversion and integration components allow Mercurial to interact with other version control systems; it can even be used as a front end for centralized systems. Since it does not require any management commitment in a single-user scenario, Mercurial also allows developers to practice good version control habits even in corporate settings that do not have version control as part of their software process.

3. RELATED WORK

Reid and Wilson [10] describe an early attempt to incorporate version control into the curriculum using CVS. They note the importance of collaborative work in student learning and used a course redesign as an opportunity to increase students previously limited introduction to version control. Their approach, while successful, uncovered significant problems with administering version control topics in the curriculum and required significant support resources. Distributed version control systems like Mercurial eliminate much of this complexity, allowing version control to be taught earlier and with fewer resource commitments.

Clifton et. al. [2] used Subversion primarily as a collaboration and administration framework in a CS1 course. The course instructors distributed assignments and feedback through a central repository. The authors note that their tests were run on unusually small sections; given the multiple administrative functions Subversion served and the custom setup required to support these functions, it is difficult to determine if their approach will scale to larger sections or upper-level courses without further testing.

Meneely and Williams [8] describe their experiences with a collaborative development framework, Jazz, which includes its own version control client. Jazz aggregates several development tools into an integrated dashboard that allows students to examine software defects, explore test run results, communicate with other team members, and commit and share changes in the project repository. While Jazz appears to be an interesting and useful tool, it is implemented as an Eclipse plug in, limiting its deployment potential to Java projects using the Eclipse platform.

Distributed version control systems have garnered significant attention in developer communities [4] while attracting relatively little in CS education. Horstmann [5] has explored using Mercurial for intermediate students using a combination of command line tools and NetBeans integration, with a server for hosting student work.

4. CONCLUSIONS & FUTURE WORK

Our initial impressions from using Mercurial and distributed version control has been very positive. We have seen introductory students voluntarily using version control on projects for other classes; one of our intermediate students independently set up an online hosted account for his web project, while another was using online hosting to collaborate on a group project for another class. Introductory students have consistently been able to grasp the basics well enough to complete the version control requirements for their assignments. Students have even asked about advanced topics that were not covered as part of their assignments.

Our ongoing work includes exploring the use of distributed version control in novel ways throughout the curriculum. In particular, we are interested in the application of distributed version control in senior-level courses, including Capstone. Using Mercurial allows us to implement an open, flexible project structure that provides opportunities for meaningful contributions from large, diverse groups of students. Although our experiences with this project structure are very preliminary, we are excited about the possibilities afforded by distributed version control for teaching effective software development habits through large, realistic projects.

5. ACKNOWLEDGMENTS

We would like to thank Dr. Jennifer Rocco for her help constructing the original poster presentation of this work, assistance with the data analysis, and her unflagging support for this project. We would also like to thank the members of the community who have provided thoughtful comments, suggestions, and encouragement.

6. REFERENCES

[1] B. Cannon, S. J. Turnbull, A. Vassalotti, B. Warsaw, and D. Ochtman. Choosing a distributed vcs for the python project. Retrieved September 6, 2010 from http://www.python.org/dev/peps/pep-0374/.

[2] C. Clifton, L. C. Kaczmarczyk, and M. Mrozek. 2007. Subverting the fundamentals sequence: using version control to enhance course management. In *SIGCSE '07: Proceedings of the 38th SIGCSE technical symposium on Computer science education*, pages 86–90, New York, NY, USA. ACM.

[3] Computer science curriculum 2008. Retrieved September 7, 2010 from http://www.acm.org/education/curricula/ComputerScience2008.pdf.

[4] B. de Alwis and J. Sillito. 2009. Why are software projects moving from centralized to decentralized version control systems? In *CHASE '09: Proceedings of the 2009 ICSE Workshop on Cooperative and Human Aspects on Software Engineering*, pages 36–39, Washington, DC, USA. IEEE Computer Society.

[5] C. Horstmann. Mercurial on opensolaris and glassfish. Retrieved April 3, 2010 from http://weblogs.java.net/blog/cayhorstmann/archive/2010/03/28/mercurial-opensolaris-and-glassfish.

[6] A. Hunt and D. Thomas. 2000. *The Pragmatic Programmer*. Addison-Wesley.

[7] R. C. Martin. 2003. *Agile Software Development*. Pearson Education, Inc., Upper Saddle River, NJ, USA.

[8] A. Meneely and L. Williams. 2009. On preparing students for distributed software development with a synchronous, collaborative development platform. In *SIGCSE '09: Proceedings of the 40th ACM technical symposium on Computer science education*, pages 529–533, New York, NY, USA. ACM.

[9] Mozilla developer center mercurial introduction. Retrieved September 6, 2010 from https://developer.mozilla.org/en/Mercurial.

[10] K. L. Reid and G. V. Wilson. 2005. Learning by doing: introducing version control as a way to manage student assignments. In *SIGCSE '05: Proceedings of the 36th SIGCSE technical symposium on Computer science education*, pages 272–276, New York, NY, USA. ACM.

[11] J. Spolsky. 2004. *Joel on Software*. Springer-Verlag, New York, NY, USA.

LIFT: Taking GUI Unit Testing to New Heights

Jason Snyder, Stephen H. Edwards, Manuel A. Pérez-Quiñones
Department of Computer Science
Virginia Tech
Blacksburg, VA 24073
{snyder84, edwards, perez}@cs.vt.edu

ABSTRACT

The Library for Interface Testing (LIFT) supports writing unit tests for Java applications with graphical user interfaces (GUIs). Current frameworks for GUI testing provide the necessary tools, but are complicated and difficult to use for beginners, often requiring a significant amount of time to learn. LIFT takes the approach that unit testing GUIs should be no different than testing any other type of code. By providing a set of frequently used filters for identifying GUI components and a set of operations for acting on those components, LIFT lets programmers quickly and easily test their GUI applications.

Categories and Subject Descriptors

K.3.2 [**Computer and Information Science Education**]: Computer Science Education; D.2.5 [**Sofware Engineering**]: Testing Tools

General Terms

Verification, Design

Keywords

GUI testing, unit testing, Java, JUnit, Swing, Java Task Force, JTF, objectdraw

1. INTRODUCTION

The primary goal of LIFT is to enable programmers, and especially new or student programmers, to write GUI tests for Java applications without having to learn a new, complicated tool set. LIFT does this in several ways. The first is by treating GUI testing as much like traditional testing as possible. The majority of tests written using LIFT follow the simple pattern of retrieving a reference to an object, manipulating the object in some way (usually by calling one or more of its methods), then testing the state of the object to ensure it behaved as expected. Second, LIFT greatly improves upon the typical methods that other frameworks use to retrieve and manipulate graphical interface objects, and does so in a type safe way. Finally, LIFT transparently deals with synchronization between the GUI event thread and the main thread running the tests.

SIGCSE'11, March 9–12, 2011, Dallas, Texas, USA.

2. RELATED WORK

Testing applications has always been an integral part of the software development process. Unit testing is one type of testing where the programmer writes many tests for one unit (usually a class or module), and each one verifies that one aspect of the unit is working correctly and behaving as intended. There are many Java libraries available to do unit testing, with JUnit being the most popular [9]. Unit testing has become very popular, especially with the introduction of Test Driven Development (TDD). In TDD, tests are written before the corresponding application code is written, and tests serve as a specification of the intended behavior. Then the corresponding code is written and refined until all of the tests pass. This is an effective technique, but can be difficult to do with applications that have a GUI. Testing GUIs requires being able to programmatically access the on-screen components along with a way to manipulate those components.

Since version 1.3, the Java language has provided the `java.awt.Robot` class to simulate user input. It allows the user to programmatically manipulate the mouse and keyboard to interact with a running program. Beyond these basic capabilities, `java.awt.Robot` provides little support for testing. In particular, it does not provide a way to access user interface components. In addition, the mouse simulation methods take specific location parameters. If the program's interface changes, the tests would need to be rewritten to reflect the new locations of the components. The brittleness this introduces makes raw tests using only `java.awt.Robot` difficult to write and cumbersome to maintain as the underlying program evolves.

To overcome these challenges, several GUI testing frameworks for Java have already been created. These frameworks tend to fall into one of two categories: those where tests are created by recording user actions (recorders), and those where tests are created by writing code (coders). Marathon [4] is an example of the recorder type. After telling Marathon to start recording, the user performs the actions necessary to test part of his or her program. Marathon converts the actions into a python or ruby script that can then be run later to test the program. While recording can make it easier to define tests, it also necessitates that the test scripts be re-recorded if the program interface changes, just like with `java.awt.Robot`. In addition, because the test scripts are in either Python or Ruby, it requires the programmer to learn at least one language in addition to Java. Finally, because recording interactions requires the program interface to be present, these types of frameworks require that at least the user interface portion of the program be written before testing can start, making TDD more difficult.

UISpec4J [6] and jfcUnit [3] are both examples of the coder type of GUI testing framework. Rather than recording program interactions, when using these frameworks the programmer writes test methods that interact with his or her program. They provide a way to retrieve references to components and a way to manipulate those references or the graphical interface. Unlike recorder frameworks, testing can begin at the start of development, as with Test-driven Development. However, both frameworks are fairly complex, especially for new or student programmers.

Some frameworks combine these two approaches. Abbot [1] is one example, and is arguably the most popular GUI testing framework currently available for Java. Users can use the Abbot libraries to programmatically run their tests, or use Abbot's sister software Costello to record Abbot-compatible tests. Like UISpec4J and JFCUnit though, Abbot is much too complex for new programmers.

LIFT is an example of the coder type of framework. It is based on enhancements made to Abbot for use with the objectdraw [5] student graphics library. Objectdraw is a framework that allows students to create simple graphical applications with geometric shapes on a canvas. Thornton, et. al. added support for testing these graphical applications [10]. After this proved successful, the testing support was then ported to the ACM Java Task Force (JTF) library [2], another popular educational graphics framework. LIFT was created during this porting process when we realized that many of the same techniques used for testing objectdraw and JTF applications could also be used with Swing applications. This would benefit many more people, as objectdraw and JTF are only used in education, while Swing is used by a large portion of the Java community.

3. USING LIFT

In undergraduate courses, many textbooks and instructors using JUnit employ v.3.x-compatible tests, since the 3.x API is simpler for novices to understand and does not require using annotations. Typical JUnit (v.3.x) tests are written by extending the `junit.framework.TestCase` class. This class provides test running infrastructure and several types of assert statements for testing objects. Programmers write methods to test their code, usually along with start up and tear down methods that are run before and after each test method.

LIFT provides the class `GUITestCase`, an extension of `junit.framework.TestCase`, that adds support for GUI testing. By extending `GUITestCase` rather than `TestCase`, the programmer gains access to all of the LIFT methods for use in writing tests.

3.1 Component Retrieval

In Abbot, the standard way to retrieve a GUI component is to create an Abbot `Matcher` that describes the component you are looking for. Figure 1 shows an example of a `Matcher` that finds a `JButton` with the text "OK".

```
button = (JButton)getFinder().find(
  new Matcher() {
    public boolean matches(Component c)
    {
      return c instanceof JButton
          && ((JButton)c).getText()
              .equals("OK");
    }
  });
```

Figure 1: Using an Abbot Matcher.

```
button = getComponent(
    JButton.class, Filter.textIs("OK"));
```

Figure 2: Using the generic version of `getComponent()`.

A `Matcher` like this needs to be written every time a different component needs to be retrieved. Note that defining a new matcher typically requires declaring an anonymous inner class containing an in-line method definition, as well as multiple type casts. This style of programming is common for Swing programmers, but is not covered in most introductory Java courses and can be challenging for programmers who are still learning how to write GUI programs.

Though not all matchers are complex, writing a `Matcher` can be very tedious. LIFT improves upon this by providing a simpler set of `Matcher`-like objects that we call `Filters`. The `Filter` class contains a set of static methods that return custom `Filters`. For example, the `Filter.textIs(String text)` static method returns a `Filter` that will only match components where `getText()` returns the string passed into the method.

Along with `Filters`, LIFT also provides several methods analogous to the Abbott `find()` method that take a `Filter` as a parameter and return one or more components that match the `Filter`. The main one of these is called `getComponent()`—a generic method that takes both a component type and a filter. The Abbot matcher code in Figure 1 can rewritten using LIFT as shown in Figure 2. This templated version is type-safe and guarantees that the returned object is of the right type. Not only does this make the code more robust, it also makes casting the returned object to the correct type unnecessary.

The `getComponent()` method is intended to find a single, unique component determined by the given filter. If no component or multiple components exist that match the `Filter`, an appropriate exception is thrown. LIFT also provides `getFirstComponentMatching()` and `getAllComponentsMatching()` for when there may not be a unique match. The `getFirstComponentMatching()` method returns one (arbitrary) match if multiple components conform to the filter, or null if none are found. The `getAllComponentsMatching()` method returns a (possibly empty) `List` of matching components. Both methods are generic on the type of component being sought.

Along with `textIs(String text)`, LIFT provides many other filters based on commonly used component attributes. Some of these include:

```
b = new JButton(...);
b.setName("OKButton");
```

Figure 3: Setting a component's name.

```
button = getComponent(
    JButton.class, "OKButton");
```

Figure 4: Specialized `getComponent()` for named components.

- `nameIs(String name)`
- `enabledIs(boolean enabled)`
- `widthIs(int width)`
- `parentIs(Component parent)`
- `ancestorIs(Component ancestor)`
- `hasFocusIs(boolean focus)`

When used in conjunction with the `setName(String name)` method shared by all `Component` objects, the `nameIs(String name)` filter can greatly simplify testing. If all of the components that will need to be used during testing are given unique names in the GUI code, the `nameIs(String name)` filter can then be used to retrieve them when necessary. This turns out to be so useful in practice that an overloaded version of `getComponent()` is provided in LIFT that takes a `String` parameter and internally uses the `nameIs(String name)` filter to retrieve the component. Returning to our previous example, if the button had been named as shown in Figure 3, it could then be retrieved with the code in Figure 4.

3.2 A Filter Mini-language

The filter system used by LIFT allows programmers to easily create objects much like Abbot `Matchers`, but without all of the overhead and details usually required by that tool. However, the filters each only test for a single component attribute, and often more specificity is needed. Abbot `Matchers` allow you to make the matching criteria as specific as desired. For example, Figure 5 shows how to create a `Matcher` that returns a button with the text "Next" that is currently not enabled.

```
button = (JButton)getFinder().find(
  new Matcher() {
    public boolean matches(Component c)
    {
      return c instanceof JButton
          && ((JButton)c).getText()
             .equals("Next")
          && c.isEnabled() == false;
    }
  });
```

Figure 5: A more complex Abbot Matcher.

```
button = getComponent(
    JButton.class,
    where.textIs("Next")
        .and.enabledIs(false));
```

Figure 6: A compound LIFT filter.

```
button = getComponent(
    JButton.class,
    where.textIs("Next")
        .and.enabledIs(false)
        .or(where.textIs("Previous")
            .and.hasFocusIs(true)));
```

Figure 7: A somewhat convoluted (though legal) LIFT filter.

To enable creating this type of filter in LIFT, a mini-language of sorts was created. Figure 6 shows how to create a `Filter` that acts like the Abbot `Matcher` in Figure 5.

All "sentences" in this language begin with the keyword `where`, which is a static field that refers to a filter generator object. The name of this field was chosen to provide for more readable expressions, as an alternative to explicitly using the name of the `Filter` class, for example. The `where` field is declared in the base class used for writing GUI tests, called `GUITestCase` (a subclass of JUnit's `TestCase` class).

For this mini-language, objects like `where` that generate filters are instances of a special class called `Operator`—that is, they are *filter operators* used to create and combine filters. The `where` object provides access to the various primitive filter-creating methods, which can be combined using `and`, `or`, and `not` operators. Parentheses can also be used to group filters together if necessary. The example shown in Figure 7, while unlikely to be necessary, is perfectly legal. In this example, LIFT would search for a disabled `JButton` with the text "Next", or a `JButton` that currently has the focus and has the text "Previous".

3.3 GUI Interactions

The first step in testing GUIs is retrieving references to on-screen components. The `getComponent()` method along with the composable filter mini-language provides a convenient mechanism for retrieving such references. Once the components are retrieved, one must then interact with them in some way. This could mean clicking on buttons, typing in text boxes, selecting things from combo boxes, or other GUI interactions. With Abbot, this is accomplished through the use of `Tester` objects. There are different `Testers` for different types of `Components`. The programmer must first create a `Tester` by passing the `Component` they wish to manipulate to the `getTester()` method. He can then call methods like `actionClick()` or `actionSelectItem()` on that tester to manipulate the GUI. This is demonstrated in Figure 8.

LIFT uses the same mechanism conceptually, but does so internally, hiding all of the details from the programmer. Instead, the LIFT `GUITestCase` base class provides methods called `click()`, `doubleClick()`, `mouseMove()`, `mouseDragFrom()`, `mouseDropOn()`, and so on. Once a GUI

```
button = (JButton)getFinder().find(
  new Matcher() {
    public boolean matches(Component c)
    {
      return c instanceof JButton
          && ((JButton)c).getText()
            .equals("OK");
    }
  });

tester = (ButtonTester)ComponentTester
    .getTester(button);
tester.actionClick(button);
```

Figure 8: Creating and using an Abbot Tester.

```
button = getComponent(
    JButton.class, where.textIs("OK"));
click(button);
```

Figure 9: Figure 8 rewritten using LIFT.

component reference has been retrieved, the programmer can simply pass the reference into the appropriate GUI manipulation method. Internally, LIFT will take care of automatically creating (or reusing) an appropriate Abbot `Tester` object to perform the action. Figure 9 shows the previous code example rewritten using LIFT.

3.4 Synchronization Issues

When testing a GUI-based program, there are typically (at least) two different threads running. The first is the main thread itself, which is where the test methods run. The second is a special thread called the event dispatching thread (EDT), which handles all GUI interactions. The EDT is a special background thread that is a standard part of Java AWT and Swing GUIs—it is the sole thread that can update or change the visual appearance of all GUI components. Students rarely see these two threads, since most student-written GUI programs do nothing with the main thread other than to create the application's main window.

Once the GUI is created, all event processing is handled by the EDT. Swing methods are not thread-safe, in fact, and keeping all event processing on the same thread naturally serializes their invocations. Problems can arise if the programmer does not know how to deal with the two separate threads. For example, if one is testing a button that increments a counter, the code might looking something that in Figure 10.

In this case, any listener attached to the button will be executed in the EDT, while the assert statement will be executed by the main thread as part of the test method. If the button's listener(s) takes a long time to execute, the assert statement may be called before the button code has a chance to update the label, resulting in a failed assertion even if the label does eventually get updated correctly. In order to prevent this, all LIFT methods use Abbot methods internally so all GUI interactions are executed on the EDT. In effect, LIFT interaction methods like `click()` post the necessary interaction event(s) for the GUI components to receive, and then block, waiting for those events to be completely processed. Even if a listener responding to one event triggers additional events, Abbott's internals wait until the EDT's queue of GUI events has emptied, indicating that the GUI has once again become idle. Only then does the LIFT method return back to the test, allowing the next statement in the test method to be executed.

```
button = getComponent(
    JButton.class, "addButton");
label = getComponent(JLabel.class, "count");
click(button);
assertEqual(label.getText(), "1");
```

Figure 10: Testing a button and label.

This "post and wait" strategy ensures that the main thread (executing the test) and the EDT (processing GUI events) are transparently synchronized in most cases. Performing this synchronization prevents race conditions between interaction events in test cases and other object manipulation or inspection actions carried out on the main thread as part of each test. In effect, students can safely use a 'naive, single-threaded mental model when writing their tests, and typically do not need to take the EDT into account when writing their tests.

However, there are still some situations where the "post and wait" strategy alone is insufficient. Several Swing modal dialog components provide helper methods that block the calling thread while the dialog is presented, the user interacts with it, and a selection is made. This is a natural way to use a modal dialog, since no other part of the application should be accessible to the user while the modal dialog is visible. When modal dialogs like this are created from the EDT in response to GUI interactions, the "post and wait" strategy works perfectly. However, problems arise if such a modal dialog helper method is invoked directly on the main thread as part of a test case.

For example, suppose a student is testing a `Player` class with a `makeAMove()` method. In some situations, perhaps no legal moves are available, and the student has written `makeAMove()` to use a `JOptionPane` to present an error message in this case. One test for this method might consist of one or more method calls to alter the program state so that no moves are possible, a call to `makeAMove()`, a confirmation that a JOptionPane appeared, and finally a click on the "OK" button of the error message. Figure 11 shows such a test method.

```
player.makeAMove();   // no moves possible

// confirm the JOptionPane opened
assertNotNull(
    getComponent(JOptionPane.class));

// click the OK button
click(getComponent(
    JButton.class, where.textIs("OK")));
```

Figure 11: Incorrectly testing a method producing a JOptionPane.

```
// no moves possible
callGUIIOMethod(player,
    "makeAMove");

// confirm the JOptionPane opened
assertNotNull(
    getComponent(JOptionPane.class));

// click the OK button
click(getComponent(
    JButton.class, where.textIs("OK")));
```

Figure 12: Correctly testing a method producing a JOptionPane.

Unfortunately, showing a `JOptionPane` inside `makeAMove()` is a *blocking* action, so that `makeAMove()` will not return to its caller *until the dialog has been closed.* Because of the way modal dialogs work in Swing, if the call to `makeAMove()` is placed directly in the test code (which is executed on the main thread), this will block the main thread until the modal dialog is closed. However, that means that no statements following the `makeAMove()` call in the test method will be able to execute, and the test method would never terminate (unless a person intervened and clicked the button on the screen manually).

For situations like this, LIFT provides a method named `callGUIIOMethod()`. This generic method takes an object, a method name, and a list of parameters. It then calls the named method on the object with the specified parameters using reflection, but does so from the EDT rather than the main thread, using the "post and wait" strategy to allow the GUI to process any pending events before it returns back to the test method. `callGUIIOMethod()` must be used for methods on student-written classes that indirectly cause GUI events. This allows modal dialogs like `JOptionPane` to be handled correctly, and also ensures that any other Swing actions are carried out on the EDT. Figure 12 shows the `makeAMove()` example rewritten using `callGUIIOMethod()`, which now works correctly. The EDT waits for the modal dialog to complete, while the remainder of the test method continues to run in the main thread.

4. CLASSROOM USAGE

While LIFT can be used by anyone who needs to test a Swing GUI, it was created for use in the classroom. One use is to have students write tests for their programs. Studies have shown that students who write tests for their programs are "more likely to complete assignments, are less likely to turn assignments in late, and receive higher grades" [7].

We have successfully used LIFT in the classroom in this way for two semesters, and have used its predecessor for many more. Students quickly pick up how to set names on their interface components, and how to use `getComponent()` to retrieve interface objects in test cases. Clicking the mouse, moving, dragging, pressing buttons, and other basic actions are all simple method calls that students understand without difficulty. Because all of the other issues that make GUI testing more complex have been abstracted away and hidden, writing GUI tests is very similar to writing tests on plain (non-GUI) Java classes.

Similarly, LIFT benefits instructors as well. Many instructors who use simple Swing assignments in their courses are unfamiliar with the professional-level tools available for testing such GUIs, and may find the learning curve for such tools a steep investment. Because the simplified model in LIFT makes this learning curve much smaller for students, it also makes it much smaller for instructors who wish to write automated tests for student-written GUI programs.

While many instructors feel that students benefit from writing their own tests, not all instructors are ready to add this to their courses. Nevertheless, instructors still can make use of LIFT in the classroom. Whether or not students have to write their own tests, the instructor can write a set of reference tests to evaluate student solutions. This can simplify grading and evaluation since the instructor can simply run the reference tests against the student solutions. As long as the reference tests exercise all necessary program behaviors, a successful run with no failures would then indicate that the student implemented all of the required behaviors correctly. Any failures would indicate errors or improper behaviors. The instructor can then spend his or her time providing feedback on software design and other issues. When used in combination with a system such as Web-CAT [8], this portion of the grading process can be automated.

5. EVALUATION

At this point, no formal evaluation of LIFT has been conducted. However, a formal study of the objectdraw-based predecessor to LIFT was performed and the results are summarized here. Thornton et al. provide further information [10].

Three semesters of data were analyzed in the study. Students in the first semester wrote and tested non-GUI programs. Students in the second semester wrote GUI programs using the objectdraw library, but did not have to test the GUI portion of their programs. Students in the third semester wrote GUI programs using objectdraw along with a complete set of tests, including tests for their GUIs. The first finding was that GUI assignments require writing slightly more code than non-GUI assignments. However, more code does not necessarily mean more work. GUI tests usually required more lines of code than their non-GUI counterparts, but are often conceptually easier to grasp. "In a GUI assignment, students have an instant visualization of what is happening, which results in faster development of the program and the test cases." The study also revealed that students working on GUI assignments typically start and finish earlier, despite spending more time overall than on non-GUI assigments. Finally, the study found that those students who did not have to test their code (the first semester) did progressively worse as the semester went on, while the performance of those who were testing from the start (the third semester) improved throughout the semester.

Along with a quantitative analysis, the study also included student survey results about their experiences testing GUIs. The survey results indicate that students thought the graphical assignments were more interesting and fun, and that the testing helped them find more bugs. Lastly the students agreed that testing their GUIs was beneficial.

Our classroom experiences with LIFT in a CS2-level course where students learn the basics of Swing GUI programming are promising. The simplicity of the LIFT test methods does simplify the process of writing test cases and students understand them as easily as other library methods. Assignments ranging from simple panels containing buttons all the way up to full blown 2D-shape editing/drawing programs have used LIFT successfully. When students follow model-view-controller (MVC) design principles carefully, they find that testing their model separate from the GUI is easy, and then writing unit tests for the GUI is simplified because of the separation of concerns and responsibilities the design pattern imposes.

Also, having the capability of automatically running unit tests on GUIs has been a major help in assignment grading. Course staff no longer have to manually download and run each student's work. Further, by using Web-CAT, students can get immediate feedback on the quality of their solution and thoroughness of their testing right away, which often reveals hidden bugs. As an example, we have used a 2D-shape-based graphical editor as an assignment in our CS2 course, both with and without LIFT. Without using automated tests (or requiring students to write their own test cases), many students would fail to consider the different possibilities when using the mouse to drag a rubberbanded shape outline to define a shape's position and size. Students nearly always handled the typical case of an initial click on the upper left corner of a shape's final location, followed by a drag down and to the right. However, many students failed to consider an initial click followed by a drag up and to the left, and others implemented their logic incorrectly. However, without explicit tests, these bugs often went undiscovered until grading, and some no doubt slipped through then as well. However, when LIFT was used in the class, students received feedback on these failures before the assignment deadline because they had to test their own code, and all submissions were exercised to the same degree of rigor before course staff manually graded the assignment. Anecdotally, course staff felt that this reduced the number of latent defects in student solutions, because many more errors were detected and reported back to students through the use of LIFT tests.

At the same time however, there have been some negatives to using LIFT in the classroom. Three notable issues arose, all of which center around student perceptions. In our CS2 course, students were required to write their own LIFT-based tests, and their submissions were also checked against instructor-written LIFT tests. First, we found that some students reacted negatively to being required to thoroughly test their own code. Such students typically complained that they "knew" their code was correct, and viewed writing detailed tests (say, to cover all the possibilities for dragging out rubber-banded shapes) as unnecessary effort—a perception that is contrary to the empirical evidence. Other students felt that writing tests for GUI interfaces was more tedious that writing tests for text-based programs because there were more details to check, an observation reported elsewhere [10]. Finally, GUI tests run close to "human" speed because the interface and all of its changes are fully rendered on the screen and all mouse interactions are faithfully simulated. As a result, running GUI tests can take longer. For students who perceived one or more of these issues, their perception of the value of GUI testing—and, by extension, the value of the LIFT library—was somewhat reduced.

6. FUTURE WORK

So far, LIFT has been used successfully in our introductory Java courses. Though no formal evaluation has been performed on the current generation of LIFT for Swing interfaces, students found the LIFT API to be straightforward and easy to use. Future work will include a more formal evaluation to determine what impact LIFT has on student work, including final score, amount of code testing coverage, and time spent writing code. In addition, we plan to survey students to determine which features in LIFT they liked and did not like, along with possible areas for improvement.

7. ACKNOWLEDGEMENTS

This work is supported in part by the National Science Foundation under grant numbers DUE-0618663 and DUE-0633594. Any opinions, findings, conclusions, or recommendations expressed in this material are those of the authors and do not necessarily reflect the views of the National Science Foundation.

8. REFERENCES

[1] Abbot home page. `http://abbot.sourceforge.net/`.

[2] Java Task Force home page. `http://jtf.acm.org/`.

[3] jfcUnit user documentation. `http://jfcunit.sourceforge.net`.

[4] Marathon. `http://www.marathontesting.com/Home.html`.

[5] The objectdraw library. `http://eventfuljava.cs.williams.edu/library/`.

[6] UISpec4J: Java/Swing GUI testing made simple! `http://www.uispec4j.org/`.

[7] S. Edwards. Rethinking computer science education from a test-first perspective. In *Companion of the 18th Annual ACM SIGPLAN Conference on Object-Oriented Programming, Systems, Languages, and Applications*, pages 148–155, New York, New York, 2003. ACM.

[8] S. Edwards and M. A. Perez-Quinones. Web-CAT: automatically grading programming assignments. In *Proceedings of the 39th SIGCSE Technical Symposium on Computer Science Education*, pages 328–338, New York, New York, 2008. ACM.

[9] P. Tahchiev, F. Leme, V. Massol, and G. Gregory. *JUnit in Action*, volume 2. Manning Publications, 2010.

[10] M. Thornton, S. Edwards, R. P. Tan, and M. A. Perez-Quinones. Supporting student-written tests of GUI programs. In *Proceedings of the 39th SIGCSE Technical Symposium on Computer Science Education (Portland, OR, USA, March 12 - 15, 2008)*, pages 537–541, New York, New York, 2008. ACM.

Promoting Creativity in the Computer Science Design Studio

Katherine Cennamo
Learning Sciences and Technologies
Virginia Tech
Blacksburg, VA
cennamo@vt.edu

Sarah A. Douglas
Computer Science
University of Oregon
Eugene, OR
douglas@cs.uoregon.edu

Mitzi Vernon
Industrial Design
Virginia Tech
Blacksburg, VA
vernon@vt.edu

Carol Brandt & Brigitte Scott
Teaching and Learning
Virginia Tech
Blacksburg, VA
cbbrandt@vt.edu & brigit2@vt.edu

Yolanda Reimer
Computer Science
University of Montana
Missoula, MT
reimer@cs.umt.edu

Margarita McGrath
Architecture
Virginia Tech
Blacksburg, VA
mmcgrath@vt.edu

ABSTRACT

Revolutionary advances in technologies will require computer science professionals who are able to develop innovative software solutions. In order to identify techniques that can lead students to creative insights in their work, we have conducted an ethnographic study of the studio method as enacted in architecture, industrial design (ID), and human-computer interaction (HCI) classes. Our analysis of the activities conducted during studio critiques revealed that while the ID and architecture studios had a primary focus on experimentation, the primary emphasis of the HCI studios was on idea refinement. In this paper, we describe four barriers to creative thought observed in the HCI classrooms and identify ways that the architecture and ID instructors helped students to overcome similar challenges.

Categories and Subject Descriptors

D.2.2 [**Software Engineering**]: Design Tools and Techniques
H.5.3 [**User Interface**]: User-centered Design

General Terms

Design

Keywords

Design, studio, creativity, computer science education research

1. INTRODUCTION

> "Designers put things together and bring new things into being, dealing in the process with many variables and constraints, some initially known and some discovered through designing." [15 p. 42]

Design is prevalent in many areas within computer science. For example, application areas such as graphics and visual programming, artificial intelligence, information systems, and human computer interaction all may require the design of algorithms, interfaces, interactions, programs, specifications, simulations, and/or systems. Many years ago Herbert Simon [17] described design as an instance of problem solving, moving from the current problem situation progressively closer to the desired goal situation. Problem solving was simply a matter of finding a workable solution to a designated problem. In contrast, Frederick Brooks [1] argues that the Simon rational model is not sufficient to describe real-world design activity. Based on his experience as a software engineer, Brooks believes the hardest part of design is deciding what to design. The development of innovative hardware and software solutions often requires designers to solve problems that are "at least in part, uncertain, ill-defined, complex, and incoherent" [18, p. 42]. Although we need software designers who can follow rules when presented with technical and rational problems, we also need designers who can make good sense out of those problems that are not technical or rational: that is, designers who are aware of multiple possibilities for solutions, who can make good choices, and who can reflect on the choices they make to determine if their goals have been met.

During the past 20 years, the goals of a human-computer interaction (HCI) curriculum have changed from primarily teaching the psychological foundations and surveys of human-computer interaction technologies to teaching competence in designing interactive objects. As early as 1990, Professor Terry Winograd of Stanford University in a CHI conference plenary entitled "What can we teach about Human-Computer Interaction" urged the participants to embrace HCI design education and explore the studio as a teaching concept [22]. Since then, several innovative computer science programs have incorporated the studio approach within their curricula (e.g. [4, 7, 8. 14]) Although the logistics and procedures of the design studio have been described for HCI education [8, 14]—project-based assignments, supplemented with public critiques and individual student-teacher conferences—little is known about the instructional methods and processes through which students can learn to develop innovative design solutions.

As indicated in the National Science Foundation's Science of Design call for proposals "Revolutionary advances in hardware, networking, and human interface technologies will require entirely new ways of thinking about how software systems are conceptualized, built, understood, and evaluated. ... To these ends, importing and adapting ideas from other design fields (engineering, biology, architecture, economics, and the arts, for example) are encouraged" [12, p.2].

The central goal of this project was to examine studio-based courses as they are enacted in the traditional design disciplines of architecture and industrial design (ID), as well as in HCI, to discover ways in which students learn to develop innovative design solutions. To achieve this goal, we are engaged in a 3-year research and education project involving 6 faculty across 3 universities representing HCI, ID, architecture, learning sciences, and qualitative research methods. In this paper, we focus our analysis on how studio-based activities guide students to creative insights in their work.

1.1 What is Studio?

In the traditional design studio, students work in an environment where they are provided with dedicated workspace available to them at all times. Studio classes usually meet three times a week for several-hour sessions, but students are encouraged to work in the studio rather than at home during off-hours.

The specific teaching methods vary by program and university, but typically, students are presented with a design problem that is grounded in the realities of professional practice. Although periodic lectures on some aspect of the design problem may be delivered as needed, students are expected to work independently or in groups to learn various skills from each other. Faculty and peer interactions stimulate student reflection on, and discovery of, their developing knowledge. At various points in the class, students present their work to faculty, peers, and occasionally guests for critiques that complement and extend informal reviews. The project critique, or "crit", can take many forms including desk crits, pin-ups, juries, reviews, and open houses [3].

As enacted in computer science education, the design crit is the cornerstone of the studio method [8]. In her examination of the role of dialogue in a design studio, Dannels [3] supports the prominence of the design crit and argues that the oral genre of the crit is the site for learning disciplinary conventions and for developing a sense of oneself as a professional.

1.2 What is Creativity?

In some fields, "creativity" is valued through aesthetic expression. However, creative thought is also of value in domains focused on problem solving, such as HCI. Whether the goal is to develop an aesthetically pleasing product or to solve a challenging problem that requires thinking in new ways, the literature on creativity and innovation reveals that development of creative solutions is an iterative process, involving a cycle of idea generation and refinement.

The ability to generate a wide variety of potential solution ideas is generally accepted as a key precursor to creative design outcomes. In fact, most measures of creative thought assess creativity in terms of how many possible solutions are generated to a given prompt, as well as the originality of the solution in terms of how different the solutions are from one another (e.g. [9, 20]).

Researchers in the area of creativity (e.g. [2, 12, 18]) have identified several techniques that contribute to the generation of multiple original ideas. Creative thinkers are able to examine ideas from various perspectives, often exploring a challenge using a variety of raw materials, stimuli, and experiences to provide alternative perspectives on a challenge. As they explore ideas from various perspectives, they observe carefully, make inferences, and elaborate on their thinking. In addition, creative thinkers use analogies or metaphors to think through novel problems, reasoning from examples or similar situations to consider multiple possible courses of action.

Although many measures of creativity focus on the fluency and originality of ideas generated in response to a problem or prompt, the development of creative products also requires reflective judgment to select the best ideas to move forward. Reflective judgment requires analysis, synthesis, and evaluation skills [2]. The studio crit is, to a great extent, intended to develop such skills. Students present their work to faculty and other students. In order to do so, they organize and summarize their work in a way that communicates their ideas to others. They interpret their work and respond to questioning. And during this process, they learn to evaluate their work and the work of others through making judgments about the value, worth and logic of the product as well as its applicability to the problem situation.

However, it must be recognized that this is an iterative process. Creative thinkers do not simply generate a variety of ideas, and then select the best one to move forward. Instead they cycle through the process multiple times—generating ideas, judging those ideas, using the outcomes of their reflective judgment to generate more and different ideas, and so forth until a desired solution is reached.

2.0 METHODOLOGY

The purpose of this analysis was to examine the studio method, as enacted in architecture, ID and HCI classes, to identify how the creative design process unfolds and techniques used to encourage creative thought. This research uses ethnographic case study methodology as described by Merriam [11, p. xiii], in which a case is defined as "an intensive, holistic description and analysis of a bounded phenomenon such as a program, an institution, a person, a process, or a social unit."

The present study did not involve a purposefully designed intervention, but rather focused on the everyday practices of the studio-classroom community. Data have been collected and analyzed from one semester long course in architecture, one semester long course in ID, two semester-long courses in HCI, and one quarter-long class in HCI.

2.1 Context of Investigation

The architecture and ID studio classes met for 4-hour blocks of time, 3 days per week. In addition, each student had a dedicated workspace in the studio accessible 24 hours a day, 7 days a week, 365 days a year, and students were encouraged to work in the studio space outside of scheduled class time. Students were presented with a series of assignments that they were expected to submit individually; however, they were encouraged to use additional resources, including their peers, as needed to complete the assignment. Project-based assignments were supplemented by frequent public critiques where students presented their design ideas to faculty, peers, and occasional guests. Students in both courses were in the first semester of their second year of professional study and had participated in a two-semester studio experience the prior year.

The three HCI courses that are the subject of our investigation were selected because of the prior experience of the two course instructors in implementing the studio method into HCI instruction. These instructors have used a "modified studio approach" based on their observations of an architecture studio [14] for at least ten years. A modified studio approach was necessary because the typical course structure of computer science departments made it difficult for all of the features present in architecture or ID studios to be implemented easily. As is typical in studio classes, the HCI courses incorporated a series of project-based assignments followed by design crits where students publicly presented their concepts to their peers and professors. Approximately half of the class time was devoted to lectures, with the course assignments and associated crits providing an opportunity for the students to apply the principles that were introduced in the lectures. Class projects were completed in teams. These courses did not provide dedicated studio space for students, nor was the studio scheduled for the extended hours that are common in architecture and ID studio courses. Instead, students met in a typical classroom for approximately three hours per week, as they would for a standard lecture-based course. The courses were each elective, enrolling students who were at the senior or graduate level. Thus, a key aspect of our work was to identify ways to facilitate creative design thinking within the constraints of the computer science academic environments.

2.2 Role of Researchers

The authors of this paper represent the two educational researchers, the research assistant, and the instructors of each of the courses. Data were analyzed by the educational researchers and assistant while the course instructors, as key informants, reviewed the cases to provide domain-specific insight on the educational researchers' interpretations of the data.

2.3 Data Collection and Analysis

In all the classes, key classroom interactions, as identified by the instructor of each course, were videotaped for analysis. In addition, we collected all student and instructor-generated artifacts produced for each class as well as instructor reflections on the course activities. The bulk of our data was captured through video which included: project crits, discussions among students in project groups, and discussions between faculty and students (at "roundtables" or "desk crits").

Each of the five courses served as one case study [11]. Each case was analyzed within case for elements essential to the studio approach. Constructing the cases for each studio course relied upon qualitative data analysis in which the researcher undertakes a continual process of looking for patterns in themes and categories within the data. LeCompte [9] describes this method of qualitative analysis as a series of step-wise activities. This technique also is partially derived from the tradition of constant comparative analysis as described by Glaser and Strauss [6].

To understand the cultural practices and construction of knowledge in the design studio, we developed tools to track and analyze the process of learning over the course of a university term (semester/quarter). Each video was viewed in full at least two times, with sections of the video watched multiple times for a more detailed analysis of dialogues and action. While watching the video, the analyst composed a written narrative marked frequently with time stamps. This written narrative provides a detailed description of the action in the video by topics, speakers, objects, and contexts.

The construction of the cases began by first organizing the video narratives and other diverse types of data for each course into a case. In order to organize our data, we relied on the coding categories of surface features, pedagogy, and epistemology, derived from Shaffer's [16] analysis an architecture studio at MIT. After several readings of the data, and several drafts of each case, we developed a tentative version of each case for instructor review.

Lincoln and Guba [10] coined the term "trustworthiness" to talk about reliability and validity in qualitative research. Our attempts at trustworthiness focused on gathering a wide range of data that has assisted us in being able to see alternative explanations and other dimensions to the analysis and construction of the research text. We collected a range of different types of data over an extended period of time (an entire semester or quarter) that included videotapes of interactions in the studio, artifacts (student assignments and final projects), syllabi, project briefs, instructor journals, and student surveys. These various kinds of data "triangulated" or corroborated our initial conjectures. We brought our final narratives of each case back to the instructors for member checking. In some situations, we went back to the video or primary data to double-check those places in the case narrative highlighted by the instructors.

Once the cases were finalized, the individual cases were reviewed and coded for factors that have been shown in the literature to facilitate creative thought and innovative outcomes [3]. Excerpts from the cases were coded as to whether they focused on idea generation or idea refinement, and within those broad categories, the researcher further coded the instances using categories derived from the literature. In addition, the five cases were analyzed to discern patterns within and across studio classrooms. The findings we report were informed by multiple data sources and were observed, in one form or another, on multiple occasions and in multiple classrooms.

3.0 FINDINGS

One key difference between the Architecture and ID studios we observed and the HCI studios observed was the focus on idea generation relative to idea refinement. While the ID and architecture studios have a primary focus on experimentation and innovative thought, the primary focus of the HCI studio activities is on idea refinement.

Our discussion of the findings will be organized by four primary challenges to creative thought that we observed in the HCI classrooms and techniques used by the ID course instructor to push students to generate new and different ways of approaching the design problem. Although we use excepts from one ID course and one HCI course to illustrate our findings in order to streamline the discussion, the trends observed in the HCI course we describe were observed in the other two HCI courses and the trends observed in the ID course were evident in some form or another in the architecture course as well.

3.1 Understanding the Place of the User's Experience

In all the studios we observed, the faculty encouraged students to see a design problem from the perspective of the user. For example, HCI students were asked to perform a walkthrough of a user interacting with a peer's design and ID students were asked to imagine the user's experience. However, in most cases, these activities were in the service of different goals. For example, the second exercise in an HCI class required students to put themselves in the situation of actually trying to use the software the students designed while blindfolded. Students were either "blindfolded testers" or observers. The activity in which students attempted to work with an interface while blindfolded was intended to help students see the problem from a different perspective, but still, within the context of evaluating a proposed solution.

In contrast, the ID instructor used a focus on the user's experience to push students to move beyond obvious solutions in the initial stages of idea generation. For example, when refining designs for a medical hand dispenser and "brainstorming" with the students, the instructor created a narrative in which she was a doctor or nurse going about her day and thinking out loud the various ways in which she might use this dispenser, how the dispenser could be used for various tools, and how easy or difficult it would be. By thinking and surmising out loud, she drew the students into the project on a deeper level, expanding their perspectives, and engaging them in the problem of the design.

3.2 Breaking Beyond the Familiar

Students often relied on familiar templates for their designs. One group of HCI students, for example, borrowed models from iTunes to design their user interface. In her critique of their final project, the instructor encouraged students to expand their design options: "One of the problems of using an analogy like iTunes is that it's so well-developed that you can't get your head outside of it. And you want to try and burst through that". But despite the instructor's exhortation, students seemed unsure how to begin to design a novel HCI interface.

Students in ID also relied on familiar ideas in their initial designs. As students were refining their designs for the medical hand dispenser, one student was trying to develop a non-threatening alternative to a syringe for children's vaccinations. The student developed a series of toy-like sheaths that could be fitted over a syringe, which generated much discussion among his classmates. At this point, the instructor stepped in to actively model the process of thinking beyond obvious solutions.

> The instructor responded: "This goes back to my point from the very beginning. I'd like to see you depart from, big time.
>
> Just go to an extreme from that. Forget about the sheathing, and start thinking about actually redesigning the syringe. And just see. It may be, not, you know, the better path to take. But I want you to think that way. I mean, what if it were a pancake instead of a cylinder. Maybe it's just something I slap on the arm, and the doctor does that. And something about that activity lets me see as a doctor what I'm doing..."
>
> The instructor continues: "But I would really start looking at, what are five completely ridiculous, different forms? You know, a bladder you just slap on the arm..., that's one idea. Maybe you have a long tube and you stand at a distance from the kid. I mean I don't know. You see what I'm saying, I'm trying to go really wild..."
>
> The student chimes in: "A dart!"
>
> Instructor: "A dart! Great! There are no bad ideas in the beginning!"

Afterward "the dart" becomes a metaphor for creative designs that come from what might be thought of as an absurd, impractical idea or pushing the boundaries of what is a feasible design. Later in the semester, the metaphor was used repeatedly. During a subsequent assignment, for example, the instructor encourages students to: "Be very dart-like. Be very edgy." One student asked the instructor what she is talking about, and then she reminded him how the student used the dart as one of his ideas for vaccinating kids. She's told them to be "wild and crazy" in their generation of ideas. In this case, the "dart" metaphor reflected the underlying beliefs of how the design process should operate within the ID studio and provided a short hand reference by both instructors and students to communicate a more complex idea.

3.3 Overcoming Limits

When generating ideas, the students in HCI often limited their solutions to what they could program. An example of how skills and experience with programming served to limit students' designs occurred early in the semester during the second project crit. Students were presenting a sprinkler system, and a volunteer user was attempting to set up the system. The volunteer became confused because the program did not contain a pop-up window that the group knew needed to be there but that they could not program:

> Student 1: I have taken a mental note. That was actually a part of our heuristic evaluation, was that we needed a better. .
>
> Student 2: (interrupting) It was in the primary design that we would use the pop-up window, but I couldn't make it in html.
>
> Instructor: But again, I want to stress, right, in these early designs you should not be limited in terms of what you show us based on what you can program . . . . We're not even talking about implementation. These could just as well be a hand-drawn sketch. So if there's something that happens, you could just put up a little hand-drawn pop-up to give us some feedback. But I don't want your designs to be limited at this point by what you can or cannot program.

Despite the instructor's encouragement to avoid such limitations, students' awareness that they would eventually have to build their design created a tension between innovation and what they could build.

In order to overcome students' tendencies to focus on a narrow set of achievable solutions, the ID instructor often required students to generate multiple ideas that would then be winnowed down through a public discussion. The ID instructor noted in her journal that: "So, I decided to use a method of iteration that I had used before with juniors as a way of giving structure and a deadline, which is often so much more valuable than time. We asked the students to develop 10 different concepts for their dispensers on 10 different pieces of paper...We spent much of last week going through these pin-ups on the wall." Pinning up all the designs next to each other permitted students to view the design problem from alternative perspectives. This process helped students to make decisions, but also demanded that they begin the design process by generating a broad range of ideas, some of which pushed the boundaries of being practical. This emphasis on innovation permitted students to have the freedom to think broadly and to experiment with their ideas.

3.4 Need for Low-fidelity Work

We also observed that the HCI students' willingness to modify their designs was influenced by the materials used to develop and present their ideas. As designers of computer programs, the use of computer technology, often PowerPoint, was a dominant way of communicating their ideas in the project crits. Students created annotated screen shots and detailed digital mock-ups of interfaces, as well as presenting the typical bullet points and scanned drawings. However, the media through which students executed their initial ideas influenced their willingness to modify their designs. The instructor encouraged students to avoid a polished creation in the early stages of the design process saying: "Detail here is not critical. This is the whole reason I urge people to take poster paper and just rip it up. As soon as we make it really beautiful and put it on PowerPoint slides, you become very invested in this design and it becomes very difficult to throw it away". Yet students appeared to be at a loss as to how to communicate their designs through other media.

In the third exercise, the HCI instructor asked one of the groups to draw their design on the white board, rather than relying on PowerPoint, or in this particular case, very small index cards. As the student drew the display and then the controls, it created an interactive situation: students were asking the presenter questions as he was creating a context for his project, as well as clarifying what the actual drawings were. At this point in the crit, the instructor stepped back and students guided the discussion.

After this crit, the groups began to use the white board and function as a team where one person would narrative key design features while the other team members would sketch design features on the white board. When students presented their original ideas in a polished form, they were less open to change. When the same students made hand drawn representations, the discussion was richer and fostered more interaction among classmates.

In the ID studios, multiple modes of conceptualization were encouraged constantly. We observed that not all students work well in every form. Exploring design ideas using a mix of tools such as computer-aided devices (software, scanners, 3D printers, digital photography) and analog methods (3D physical hand-built modeling, hand sketching, workshop construction) elicited fluency, originality, and iteration, hence affording a greater probability of reaching the best resolution.

4.0 DISCUSSION

As an ethnographic study, we do not propose that our findings are necessarily true for other HCI, ID, or architecture studio classes. Yet, we believe we have gained a deeper understanding of ways to develop creative thought through our analyses.

It is obvious that studio critiques are useful in developing reflective judgment in HCI students--a very important skill. But in order to develop creative thinkers and innovative products, students of HCI need to also learn to develop fluency and originality in idea generation. One key difference between the ID studio and the HCI studios we observed was in the relative emphasis on experimentation and idea refinement.

It could be argued that our conclusions may be an artifact of the data we collected. By collecting data of the project crits, were we indeed focusing on idea refinement rather than generation? Yet the project crits provided ample evidence of the encouragement of divergent thinking within the ID and architecture studio courses.

There may be many reasons for this obvious difference, not the least of which is the differences in the time available for studio work. Whereas the ID studio had 172 hours of time dedicated to formal studio activities, the HCI classes formally met for only 37 hours in the semester-long classes and for only 24 hours in the quarter-long class. The severe constraints of time within the HCI studio were evident throughout our observations; students and faculty constantly struggled with the time restrictions.

Yet even in the most time-limited HCI course we observed, the instructor was able to make changes in her course activities that positively affected students' openness to new and different ways of seeing, once she became aware of the need to focus on experimentation and ideation, as well as evaluation and refinement. Based on her review and reflection on our studio case studies, she made several simple changes that had a positive impact. An analysis of videotaped data collected during the formative evaluation of her modified course revealed the impact of one of these changes.

The seemingly simple requirement that students may not use PowerPoint as a mode of presentation during project crits made notable changes to the HCI classroom environment. In the prior data collected in this HCI classroom, PowerPoint served to be a severe limitation to students' willingness to modify their design ideas. As the instructor mentioned to her class, taking the time to put together a Power Point presentation only serves to make students feel highly attached to their designs—and less likely to be open or amenable to critiques and suggestions that would necessitate design changes. The instructor insisted from the outset that students present their projects using hand-drawn illustrations, whether on paper or on the white board. The impact of this simple change was powerful in comparison to previous HCI courses for which we have data.

In lieu of performing project crits using PowerPoint, students instead either drew their interfaces on the white board in the classroom while they talked (often manipulating, erasing, redrawing, drawing arrows, and so forth), or taped hand-drawn, usually poster-sized paper illustrations to the white board while presenting. As students physically engaged with a static, imperfect drawing, they seemed to naturally present their work as "in process," talking and making additional drawings as they went along, in order to narrate their thinking. As Tufte [21] has noted, PowerPoint tended to encourage students to linearly narrate their designs—from start to finish. The difference between narrating "thinking" and narrating "designs" was also a function of placing emphasis, respectively, on process and product. The conversations these drawings produced seemed, in comparison to previous data collected, to be quite additive, meaningful, and productive. The students presenting their designs were very receptive to their peers' comments, and likewise, the students seemed very comfortable and free to provide a critique knowing that the presenters, by way of their presentations, were soliciting comments to help move their designs forward.

Whether designing algorithms, interfaces, interactions, programs, specifications, simulations, and/or systems, students can be encouraged to generate multiple design ideas before winnowing their ideas down to the one that will be implemented. At least in the initial stages of idea generation, computer science instructors may want to separate design from implementation, possibly by loosening the requirement that all—or even most—designs eventually get implemented. In the HCI classes we observed, one very effective technique for evaluating designs involved students putting themselves into the role of the user in order to switch perspectives and experience how their own designs might be interpreted and experienced from different viewpoints. Students can use this technique during the initial generation of design ideas as well; carefully considering the design problem from multiple perspectives can effectively open up new possibilities for productive solutions. Furthermore, the role of the instructor in modeling how they would go about generating multiple innovative design solutions is of critical importance in teaching students how to go beyond the limits of their own programming skills and in thinking beyond familiar designs.

5.0 CONCLUSIONS

The studio method is gradually becoming an accepted method of teaching design skills to computer science students. However, if we want future computer science professionals that are able to think beyond the obvious solutions to develop innovative products, we need to use assignments and design critiques for more than idea refinement. Students learn to value the things we emphasize in our courses through activities and project assessments. If we want our computer science students to become innovative problem solvers who go beyond the obvious to develop creative solutions to novel problems, we need to find ways to value novel solutions in our course activities. From our analyses, we see that projects and associated critiques can be used to encourage students to think broadly and engage in divergent as well as convergent thought, so that, as designers, they are able to creatively "put things together and bring new things into being" [15, p. 42].

ACKNOWLEDGMENTS

This work is supported by the National Science Foundation (NSF) Grant No. 0725290. Opinions expressed are those of the authors and do not necessarily reflect the views of the NSF.

REFERENCES

[1] Brooks, F.P. 2010. The design of design: Essays from a computer scientist. Boston: Addison-Wesley.

[2] Combs, L. B., Cennamo, K. S. & Newbill, P. L. 2009. Developing critical and creative thinkers: Toward a conceptual model of creative and critical thinking processes. *Educ. Technol.*, 49, 5 (September-October. 2009), 3-14.

[3] Dannels, D. P. 2005. Performing tribal rituals: A genre analysis of "crits" in design studios. *Commun. Educ.*, 54, 2, 136-160.

[4] Docherty, M., Sutton, P., Brereton, M. & Kaplan, S. 2001. An innovative design and studio-based CS degree. *ACM SIGCSE Bulletin, Proceedings of the 32nd SIGCSE Technical Symposium on Computer Science Education, 33(1)*, 233-237.

[5] Guilford, J.P., Christensen, P.R., Merrifield, P.R., & Wilson, R.C. 1978. *Alternate Uses: Manual of instructions and interpretations*. Orange, CA: Sheridan Psychological Services.

[6] Glaser, B. G., & Strauss, A. L. 1967. *The discovery of grounded theory*. Chicago: Aldine.

[7] Hendrix, D., Myneni, L., Narayanan, H., and Ross, M. (2010). Implementing studio-based learning in CS2. In *Proceedings of the 41st ACM Technical Symposium on Computer Science Education (SIGCSE 2010)*, March 10-13, 2010, Milwaukee, WI.

[8] Hundhausen, C.D., Narayanan, N. H., & Crosby, M. E. (2008). Exploring studio-based instructional models for computing education. *Proceedings of the SIGCSE Technical Symposium on Computer Science Education*, ACM Press, 392-396.

[9] LeCompte, M. D. 2000. Analyzing qualitative data. *Theor. Pract.*, 49, 3, 146-154.

[10] Lincoln, Y. S., & Guba, E. G. (1985). *Naturalistic inquiry*. Beverly Hills, CA: Sage.

[11] Merriam, S. B. 1998. *Qualitative research and case study applications in education*. Revised and expanded. San Francisco: Jossey-Bass.

[12] National Science Foundation 2006. Science of Design (SoD) Software-Intensive Systems, Program Solicitation. Retrieved November 13, 2006 from http://www.nsf.gov/pubs/2007/nsf07505/nsf07505.htm?org=CCF.

[13] Raths, L. E., Wasserman, S., Jonas, A., & Rothstein, A. (1986). *Teaching for thinking: Theory, strategies, & activities for the classroom*. New York: Teachers College.

[14] Reimer, Y. J. and Douglas, S.A. 2003. Teaching HCI design with the studio approach. *Computer Science Education Journal*, 13, 3, 191-205.

[15] Schon, D.A. 1987. *Educating the reflective practitioner*. London: Jossey-Bass.

[16] Shaffer, D. W. 2007. Learning in design. In R. A. Lesh, J. J. Kaput & E. Hamilton (Eds.), *Foundations for the future in mathematics education* (pp. 99-126). Mahweh, NJ: Erlbaum.

[17] Simon, H. A. 1981. *The sciences of the artificial* (2nd ed.). Cambridge, MS: MIT.

[18] Starko, A. J. 2005. *Creativity in the classroom: Schools of curious delight* (3rd ed.). Mahwah, NJ: Erlbaum.

[19] Sternberg, R. J., & Spear-Swerling, L. (1996). *Teaching for thinking*. Washington, DC: American Psychological Association.

[20] Torrance, E.P. 1974. *Torrance tests of creative thinking*. Bensenville, IL: Scholastic Testing Service.

[21] Tufte, E. R. 2003. *The cognitive style of PowerPoint*. Cheshire, CT: Graphics Press.

[22] Winograd, T. 1990. What can we teach about human-computer interaction? *Proceedings of the Conference on Human Factors in Computing Systems*, 443-449. New York: ACM.

Investigating the Effective Implementation of Pair Programming: An Empirical Investigation

Alex Radermacher
North Dakota State University
IACC Bldg., Room 258
Fargo, ND 58108
701-231-8562
alex.radermacher@ndsu.edu

Gursimran S. Walia
North Dakota State University
IACC Bldg., Room 258-A14
Fargo, ND 58108
701-231-8185
gursimran.walia@ndsu.edu

ABSTRACT

Pair programming is a programming technique where two programmers work together on the same programming task. Previous research has shown that it is effective for improving the learning effectiveness, efficiency, and enjoyment of students in introductory programming courses. Much research has also been dedicated to determining effective strategies for forming pairs. This paper discuss two different empirical studies conducted at North Dakota State University to a) test the feasibility of using pair programming in introductory computer science courses and b) determine whether or not major-based pairing produces effective pairs. The results of these studies provide support for implementing pair programming in introductory computer science courses and show that pairing of computer science and non-computer science students may produce pairs which are less compatible than other pairing methods.

Categories and Subject Descriptors

K.3.2 [**Computer and Information Science Education**]: Computer Science Education.

General Terms

Measurement, Performance, Experimentation, Human Factors.

Keywords

Pair Programming.

1. INTRODUCTION

Pair programming has been shown to have multiple positive benefits. Previous research has empirically demonstrated that using pair programming in introductory computer science courses leads to an improvement in the quality of student work, an increase in student retention in computer science programs, and an increase in the student's level of enjoyment of learning [4, 7, 8, 9]. At North Dakota State University (NDSU), it was noticed that the student retention among first year students was low and that the instructors of these first-year courses were experiencing low class attendance in addition to several students dropping those courses. To investigate the use of pair programming as a potential solution for these issues, multiple empirical studies (each with a different research goal) was planned and conducted in introductory computer science courses at NDSU near the end of the spring 2010 semester. This paper presents findings from two of those studies.

The first study evaluated the feasibility of implementing pair programming in introductory computer science courses at NDSU. Prior research indicates that pair programming is effective when used in introductory computer science courses, so this study served as a study replicated to verify the results from previous studies [6, 9, 10, 12]. The results from this study provided increased support that the pair programming is more effective in improving student's learning of programming concepts as compared to individual learning.

Researchers have also investigated the effect of the factors (e.g., student's skill levels) on the pair performance of students. In order to understand how pair programming can be most effectively implemented in an introductory computer science course, the second study explored a major-based pairing strategy. In this study, the subjects were arranged into pairs based on declared major to determine if any particular pairing arrangements were more effective than the others. It was thought that it would be most effective in terms of student learning and enjoyment to pair students such that one of those students had a computer science major and the other student had some other major. The results from this study indicate that the pairing a computer science student with a non-computer science student may produce a less compatible pair than other pairing methods.

The remainder of this paper is organized as follows: Section 2 provides a general background of pair programming and discusses previous empirical studies of pair programming related to our research. Section 3 details the design of two experiments conducted as part of our research of pair programming. Section 4 presents an analysis of the results of the two experiments. Section 5 lists threats to validity that were identified. Section 6 gives a summary and short discussion of the results. Section 7 concludes the paper and discusses future work that is being conducted as part of ongoing research into pair programming at NDSU.

2. BACKGROUND AND RELATED WORK

Pair programming as a term was first coined by Kent Beck and his colleagues in *Extreme Programming Explained: Embrace Change* [1], but the concept of collaborative programming had been

SIGCSE'11, March 9-12, 2011, Dallas, Texas, USA.

studied previously. Pair programming was introduced as a part of Beck's Extreme Programming (XP) as a programming technique where two individuals collaborate on a programming task by taking on the roles of a driver (i.e. the person who controls the keyboard and types in the program) and a navigator (i.e. the person who writes the code) and by frequently exchanging these roles. After the publication of this book, a large number of researchers began to actively investigate pair programming through controlled experiments to gain empirical evidence of the effectiveness of pair programming for student learning.

An early empirical study of pair programming conducted at Temple University studied fifteen full-time systems programmers employed at a program trading firm [9]. Results from this study indicated that programmers who worked as a pair were able to produce higher quality code, both in terms of readability and functionality. Additionally, the programmers that used pair programming reported a greater amount of confidence in their work and a higher level of enjoyment than programmers who worked individually. A study conducted at the University of Utah that used students in the university's Senior Software Engineering course found similar results [12]. Researchers additionally found that pair programmers were able to produce solutions significantly faster than individuals and found that in the best case, the pair programming teams only required 15% more programmer hours than an individual required to complete a programming exercise.

Studies have also been conducted to find effective methods for pairing and examining other factors which may impact the effectiveness of pair programming. Chaparoo et al., performed a study on student perceptions of pair programming where they found that the difficulty of the programming task and the skill level of individual students played a major role in the effectiveness of pair programming [5]. They found that the students preferred to work with a partner with a similar skill level so that they can contribute equally to the pair. Students also felt that the pair programming was less useful if the programming exercises were trivial or could easily be completed by a single person Williams et al., performed a comprehensive study of the effects of student ability, learning style, personality type, and other factors on pair programming [13]. The results showed that the perceived technical competence (as opposed to the actual skill level) plays a role in determining pair compatibility, and that the personality type did not play a large role in pair compatibility.

Researchers have also shown that pair programming can help improve student retention in computer science. McDowell et al., reported that students who used pair programming in an introductory computer courses were more likely to remain enrolled three quarters after the study was conducted and were more likely to have a declared computer science major than students who had worked individually [7, 8]. A similar study at Mississippi State University found that the use of pair programming in an introductory computer science course lead to a higher rate of retention among computer science, software engineering, and computer engineering students after one year [4].

3. EXPERIMENT DESIGN

The major objectives of this research were to:

- Evaluate the impact of pair programming on student learning effectiveness, efficiency, and enjoyment of programming compared to individual learning.
- Investigate the effects of major-based pairing strategies on student learning effectiveness and enjoyment of using pair programming.

Study 1 examined the effects of pair programming on students' learning and performance in a highly controlled setting and serves as a baseline with which to compare the results from the previous studies. One group of subjects worked with pairs and used pair-programming to complete a programming assignment whereas the other group of subjects worked individually to complete the same assignment.

Study 2 examined effects on pair performance when students are paired based on their declared majors. Three different pairing archetypes were created and evaluated for their effect on the pair programming. These archetypes are explained in section 4.3.2. All subjects used pair programming to complete the same assignment.

3.1 Study Goals and Hypotheses

Using the Goal Question Metric (GQM) approach, the following five goals and hypotheses were created.

Goal 1: Analyze pair based learning and individual learning for the purpose of their evaluation with respect to the students' preferences of learning method.

> ***Hypothesis 1***: Students prefer working in pairs rather than working individually.

Goal 2: Analyze pair based learning and individual learning for the purpose of their evaluation with respect to students' perception of the effectiveness of learning methods.

> ***Hypothesis 2***: Students perceive working in pairs as being a more effective learning method when compared with working individually.

Goal 3: Analyze pair based learning and individual learning for the purpose of their evaluation with respect to the effectiveness of students' actual learning of programming concepts.

> ***Hypothesis 3***: Students working in pairs are more effective (when examining the correctness of their work.) than the students who work individually.

Goal 4: Analyze major-based pairing methods for the purpose of understanding the effects on pair performance with respect to students' effectiveness and enjoyment.

> ***Hypothesis 4***: Pairing a computer science student and a non-computer science student will be more effective in improving their learning and their level of enjoyment than other major-based pair types when using the pair programming.

Goal 5: Analyze pair programming pairs and individuals for the purpose of evaluating their efficiency with respect to the time taken to complete a given programming task.

> ***Hypothesis 5***: Students working in pairs are more efficient (able to complete a programming task more quickly) than students working individually.

3.2 Independent and Dependent Variables

The experiments manipulated following independent variables:

- *Time Limit*: the amount of time given to complete the programming exercise.
- *Subject's major*: the declared major of a subject.

We also measured the following dependent variables:

- *Effectiveness*: measures the correctness of a subject's implementation of a programming exercise.
- *Efficiency*: measures the amount of time taken by a subject to complete a programming exercise.
- *Enjoyment*: measures the student's preference for using pair programming rather than working individually.

3.3 Participating Subjects

Study 1: The subjects were thirty-five undergraduate students enrolled in the CS1 course at NDSU during the spring 2010 semester. The subjects were randomly divided into either an experimental group, which included eighteen students, or a control group, which included seventeen subjects. Eight subjects dropped out of study, chose not to participate, or did not attend class on the day of the experiment run, leaving sixteen students in the experiment group and eleven students in the control group.

Study 2: The subjects were sixty-four undergraduate students enrolled in two sections of the CS2 course at NDSU during the spring 2010 semester. Twenty-five subjects chose not to participate in the study, did not attend class on the initial day of the study, or were removed from the analysis because they did not complete the assignment as a pair. Table 1 provides a list of the remaining thirty-nine participating subjects' majors.

Table 1: List of Subject Majors

Declared Major	*Number of Subjects*
Computer Science	20
Computer Engineering	6
Electrical Engineering	4
Undecided/Non-Degree	4
Mechanical Engineering	1
Mathematics	1
English	1
Biotechnology	1
Statistics	1

3.4 Experiment Procedure

Study 1: This study used a control group experiment design with students in the CS1 course randomly assigned into either the experimental group (in which they used pair programming), or a control group (in which they worked individually). Experimental group pairs were formed by selecting subjects with similar grades, as previous research has suggested that this is an effective method of pairing students [2, 3, 4].

On the day prior to beginning the programming exercise, subjects were shown a ten minute video in class that described how to use pair programming effectively on their programming assignment [11]. The next day during their lab session, subjects in both groups worked on a programming exercise that was specifically designed by the instructor such that it should not take more than one lab period (fifty minutes) to complete.

Finally, the subjects were asked to complete a short post-study survey that was used to provide feedback about their pair programming experience, their perception of their learning of programming concepts, and their preferences for using pair programming. Two different sets of surveys were used for the subjects in the experiment and control group. The experiment steps and training lectures are illustrated in Figure 1.

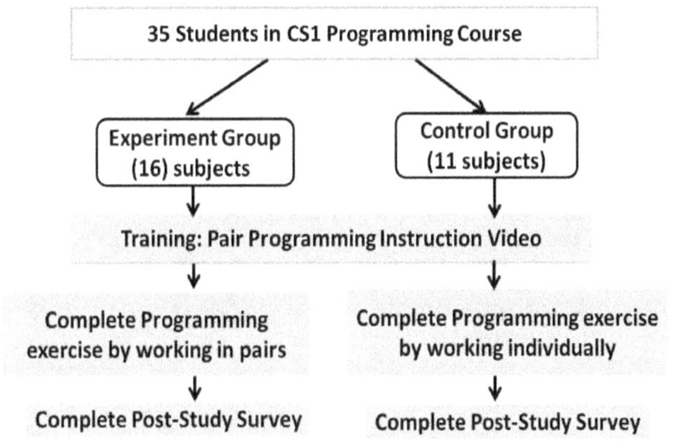

Figure 1: Experiment Design for Study 1

Study 2: This study used a repeated measures design (without a control group) in the CS2 course. Thirty-nine participating subjects were randomly assigned into one of three groups:

- ***CSE/CSE group***: pairs were comprised of two subjects, each with a declared major in computer science or computer engineering.
- ***CSE/non-CSE group***: pairs were comprised of one subject with a declared major in computer science or computer engineering, and one subject with a declared major other than computer science or computer engineering (e.g. Math, English, Psychology, etc.).
- ***Non-CSE/Non-CSE group***: pairs were comprised of subjects, each with a declared major other than computer science or computer engineering.

Similar to the Study 1, pairing within all groups was done by pairing subjects with the closest grades together. The subjects in this study were shown the same instructional video from Study 1.

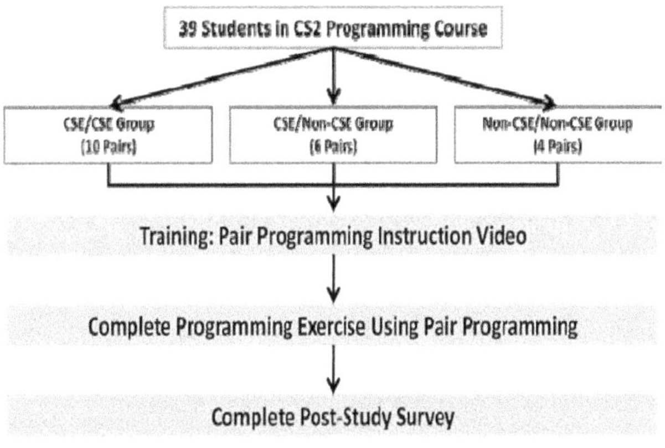

Figure 2: Experiment Design for Study 2

Subjects were given a programming exercise related to the topics that were being covered in class that week and were given two lab periods (with each lasting fifty minutes) and three days of out-of-class time to complete the programming exercise. Subjects were only monitored while working on the exercise during the designated lab periods. Subjects worked with their assigned partner to complete the programming exercise.

After completing the exercise, subjects were asked to complete a short post-study survey. The survey used in this study was the same eleven question survey that was used by subjects in the experimental group in Study 1. The experiment steps, and training lectures in this study are shown in Figure 2.

4. ANALYSIS AND RESULTS

This section provides an analysis of qualitative data and quantitative data collected during the Study 1 and Study 2. The data analyzed includes the subject's responses to post-study survey questions, the grade received on the programming exercise, and the time taken to complete the programming exercise. Survey questions were based on a five-point Likert scale ranging from a strong agreement response to a strong disagreement response. A full list of the survey questions is available in the technical report for these studies [10]. This section is organized around the hypotheses presented in Section 3.1. An alpha value of 0.05 was used for all statistical tests and an r^2 value of 0.30 was used for correlations.

4.1 Hypothesis 1: Analysis of Student's Preference of Learning Method

Subjects rated their level of preference of using pair programming on the following 5-point scale: 1- strongly prefer to work in pairs, 2- prefer to work in pairs, 3- no preference, 4- prefer to work individually, 5- strongly prefer to work individually.

As shown in Table 2, the results from Study 1 showed that the experimental group expressed a strong opinion for using pair programming, but the control group did not show any preference for using pair programming or working individually. The results from Study 2 showed that the subjects belonging to the CSE/CSE group and non-CSE/non-CSE group expressed a strong preference for using pair programming rather than working individually.

Table 2: Preference for using Pair Programming

	Study 1		Study 2		
Group	Exp.	Control	CSE / CSE	CSE / non-CSE	non-CSE / non-CSE
p-value	0.002	0.572	0.001	0.125	0.016

Table 2 also shows the p-values for a non-parametric binomial test used to determine whether the mean response of subjects in studies 1 and 2 was significantly less than the midpoint of the scale. Significantly positive characteristics are shaded in Table 2.

Based on these results, hypothesis 1 can be accepted as the majority of students, who used pair programming, show a significantly strong preference for using pair programming.

4.2 Hypothesis 2: Analysis of Students' Perception of Learning Improvements

Subjects who used the pair programming in both studies rated their perception of how pair programming affected their learning by answering three survey questions. The three questions asked: 1) Whether or not students felt pair programming impacted their understanding of the concepts present in the programming exercise, 2) Whether or not they felt they learned more though using pair programming, and 3) Whether or not they believed that pair programming would have improved their understanding of the entire course if it had been used for the entire semester. A similar five-point scale was used for all questions ranging from strong disagreement to strong agreement. For analyzing the subject's response to each of the three questions, a non-parametric binomial test was used to determine whether the mean response of subjects is significantly less than the midpoint of the scale.

Analysis of the subject's response to the first question (as shown in Table 3) shows that, in all three groups from Study 2, subjects strongly agreed that pair programming improved their understanding of the programming concepts present in the programming exercise. Subjects from the experimental group in Study 1 also strong agreed with that assessment. Table 3 also shows the p-values from a non-parametric binomial test. Significantly positive characteristics are shaded.

Table 3: Impact of Pair Programming on Concept Learning

	Study 1	Study 2		
Group	Experimental	CSE / CSE	CSE / non-CSE	non-CSE / non-CSE
p-value	0.000	0.000	0.003	0.002

Table 4 shows the p-values for a non-parametric binomial test performed on responses to the second question. Two of the three groups in study 2 strongly agreed that they learned more through using pair programming on this programming exercise than they would have if they had worked individually on it. The exception in this case was the CSE / non-CSE group from Study 2. Also, subjects in the both the experimental and control groups of Study 1 felt as though pair programming would have improved their learning of the programming concepts present in the programming exercise.

Table 4: Learning Individually vs. Pair Programming

	Study 1		Study 2		
Group	Exp.	Control	CSE / CSE	CSE / non-CSE	non-CSE / non-CSE
p-value	0.000	0.003	0.001	0.056	0.002

Analysis of the subject's response to the third question shows that, two out of three groups in Study 2 strongly agreed that pair programming would have improved their learning of the course content if pair programming had been used for the entire semester

Table 5: Learning with a Full Semester of Pair Programming

	Study 1		Study 2		
Group	Exp.	Control	CSE / CSE	CSE / non-CSE	non-CSE / non-CSE
p-value	0.000	0.044	0.102	0.009	0.016

(as shown in Table 5). Subjects in the CSE / CSE group from Study 2 were the exception in this case. Both experiment and control group subjects also strongly agreed with this assessment.

Based on these above results, hypothesis 2 can be accepted. A majority of students perceive pair programming as being a more effective learning method than working individually.

4.3 Hypothesis 3: Analysis of Students' Actual Learning Improvements

To measure student effectiveness, their grades from previous laboratory assignments were compared against the grade received on the programming exercise used as part of the study. None of the groups from either study showed a statistically significant increase in their grades.

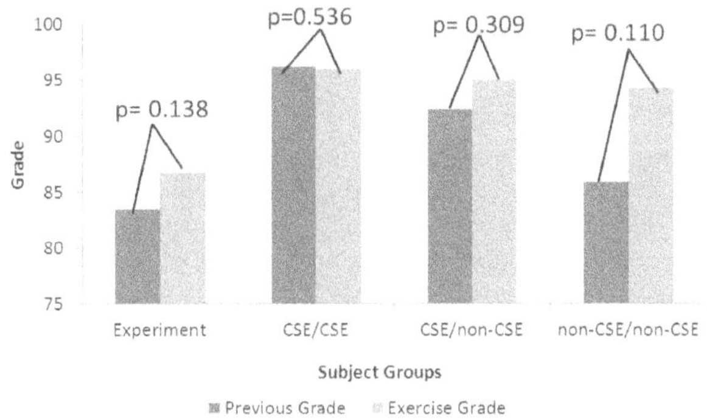

Figure 3: Comparison of Previous and Exercise Grades

Figure 3 shows the mean grade for previous course programming assignments, mean grade for the programming exercise completed as part of the study, and p-value from a paired t-test used to determine whether there was a significant difference between the grades. A comparison was also made between the exercise grades of the experimental and control groups subjects in Study 1. The average grade for the experimental group subjects was 86.80 and the average grade for the control group subjects was 76.40. A two-sample t-test was used to compare the results and yielded a p-value of 0.074, which was not statistically significant

In both experiments, many of the subjects who participated had previous course grades above 90%, which leaves marginal room for improvement. When examining only subjects who had previous course grades below 90%, there was a statistically significant increase in the grades of subjects from Study 2 as shown in Table 6.

Table 6: Comparison of Grades for Subjects Below 90%

	Study 1	Study 2
Previous Grade	77.20	75.14
Exercise Grade	81.00	93.89
p-value	0.224	0.008

In Study 1 there was a strong inverse correlation (r^2 = .468) between the amount of time taken to complete the programming exercise and the previous course grade of the subjects. This suggests that those subjects who were not doing as well in the course may not have had sufficient time to complete the programming exercise within the allotted fifty-minute time limit. This may be a possible explanation of why subjects in Study 1 with previous course grades below 90% did not perform significantly better on the pair programming exercise.

Based on these results, hypothesis 3 can be accepted. However, it may be difficult to measure improvements among students who are already doing well in the course. It is also possible that pair programming is most effective for students who would otherwise struggle with the course. Future work will investigate this issue.

4.4 Hypothesis 4: Analysis of Pair Effectiveness on Students' Learning

As seen from Tables 2, 4, and 5, there are some differences in students' perceptions of pair programming when different forms of major-based pairing are used. Subjects in the CSE / non-CSE group did not have a strong perception that pair programming can improve their learning or a strong preference for using pair programming in the future.

A non-parametric binomial test was used on survey question that asked subjects how well they got along with their partner. The mean response for all groups was lower than the midpoint of the scale indicating that subjects agreed that they got along with their partner. This suggests that general conflict between group members was not a cause. One other potential explanation may be that members of the CSE / non-CSE pairs reported a greater perceived skill disparity between each other than other groups. This was interesting as there was little disparity between the actual grades of each pair member. Previous research has shown that perceived similarities in skill are actually more important than actual similarity in skill for pair compatibility [13]. This may explain the differences in results between the different groups, but does not the cause of those differences.

Based on these results, hypothesis 4 can be rejected. There are differences that arise as the result of using different major-based pairing strategies. However, it is not evident that major-based pairing is the cause of these differences. Also, the initial assumption that pairing computer science students with non-computer science students may produce pairs which are less compatible than pairs created using other methods.

4.5 Hypothesis 5: Evaluating the Efficiency of Students using Pair-Programming

In Study 1 the amount of time taken to complete the programming exercise was measured for subjects in both groups.. Subjects in the experimental group completed that exercise in a mean time of 39.13 minutes and subjects in the control group completed it in a mean time of 43.54 minutes. A two-sample t-test used to compare the times from each group showed that the difference in completion times was statistically significant (p-value = 0.016).

Based on these results, hypothesis 5 can be accepted. Students who use pair programming are able to complete a programming exercise in less time than students who work individually.

5. THREATS TO VALIDITY

Study 1: As mentioned in the analysis of hypothesis 3, subjects may have scored lower on the programming exercise used during the study due to the strict, fifty-minute time limit. It may have also had an impact on the students' perceptions of pair programming as well. The training video, which was shown to students prior to completing the programming exercise, included multiple statements and testimonials about how pair programming was more fun and would provide a better education experience than working individually. This may have biased the students' perception of the benefits of using pair programming.

Study 2: was conducted shortly after the drop date for the course. Many students who were struggling with the course had either dropped the course or had stopped coming to class. This may have led to the inflation in student grades as seen in the analysis of hypothesis 3. This also means that it may not be possible to generalize the results of this study. Some pairs did not complete the assignment together. These results were removed from analysis and it is believed that all such cases were correctly identified. However it is possible that one instance was missed and may have affected the results.

6. SUMMARY OF RESULTS

Results from both studies show that students perceive pair programming as being beneficial and all of the subjects who used pair programming indicated that they would prefer using it again in the future as opposed to working individually. It also shows that pair programming is beneficial to student performance among students who may be struggling with the course. Additionally, the results indicate that pair programming allows a student pair to complete a given amount of work more quickly than individuals.

Major based pairing has also been shown to have an impact on student perceptions of pair programming. However, it is not clear exactly what causes these differences. Previous research has shown that personality does not have a major impact on pair compatibility so it is unlikely that this was the cause [13]. It is also unknown what caused a large perceived difference in skill between subjects in the CSE / non-CSE group, even when grades from previous course exercises indicated that there was little difference in actual skill.

7. CONCLUSION AND FUTURE WORK

Because it is likely that there are remaining unknown factors which contribute to the differences identified between pairs using different major-based pairing strategies, further research is necessary to determine what causes these differences and if these factors can be manipulated to produce more effective pairs.

It is suspected that while a student's declared major is not the cause of these results, it may be correlated to other factors which do have a causal effect on the student effectiveness and enjoyment when using pair programming. Ongoing research at NDSU is being conducted to evaluate other factors that may determine pair effectiveness. The current studies at NDSU are being run over the course of an entire semester and the impact of pair programming on student retention will be monitored.

8. ACKNOWLEDGMENTS

Our thanks to Sameer Abufardeh and Oksana Myronovych for their assistance in conducting these studies.

9. REFERENCES

[1] Beck, K. Extreme Programming Explained: Embrace Change. Addison-Wesley, Reading, Massachusetts, 2000.

[2] Bevan, J., Werner, L., and McDowell, C. Guidelines for the use of pair programming in a freshman programming class. In Proceedings of the 15th Conference on Software Engineering Education and Training, Washington, DC, USA, 2002. IEEE Computer Society.

[3] Braught, G., MacCormick, J., and Wahls, T. The benefits of pairing by ability. In SIGCSE '10: Proceedings of the 41st ACM technical symposium on Computer science education, pages 249-253, New York, NY, USA, 2010.

[4] Carver, J., Henderson, L., He, L., Hodges, J., and Reese, D. Increased retention of early computer science and software engineering students using pair programming. In Proceedings of the 20th Conference on Software Engineering Education & Training, p. 115-122, Washington, DC, USA, 2007. IEEE Computer Society.

[5] Chaparro, E., Yuksel, A., Romero, P., and Bryant, S. Factors affecting the perceived effectiveness of pair programming in higher education. In Psychology of Programming Interest Group 17th Workshop, pages 5-18, 2005.

[6] McDowell, C., Werner, L., Bullock, H., and Fernald, J. The effects of pair-programming on performance in an introductory programming course. SIGCSE Bull., 34(1):38-42, 2002.

[7] McDowell, C., Werner, L., Bullock, H., and Fernald, J. The impact of pair programming on student performance, perception and persistence. In Proceedings of the 25th International Conference on Software Engineering, pages 602-607, Washington, DC, USA, 2003. IEEE Computer Society.

[8] McDowell, C., Werner, L., Bullock, H., and Fernald, J.. Pair programming improves student retention, confidence, and program quality. Commun. ACM, 49(8):90-95, 2006.

[9] Nosek, J. The case for collaborative programming. Commun. ACM, 41(3):105-108, 1998.

[10] Radermacher, A., Walia, G., Myronovych, O., Abufardeh, S., and Rummelt, R. "Investigating the Use of Pair Programming at North Dakota State University: A Family of Empirical Studies," Technical Report, The Department of Computer Science, North Dakota State University, 2010, http://cs.ndsu. edu/ research/reports.

[11] Williams, L. Introduction to pair programming, version 2. http://www.youtube.com/watch?v=rG_U12uqRhE

[12] Williams, L., Kessler, R., Cunningham, W., and Jeffries, R. Strengthening the case for pair programming. IEEE Softw., 17(4):19-25, 2000.

[13] Williams, L., Layman, L., Osborne, J., and Katira, N. Examining the compatibility of student pair programmers. In Proceedings of the conference on AGILE 2006, pages 411-420, Washington, DC, USA, 2006. IEEE Computer Society.

Beyond Clickers: Using ClassQue for Multidimensional Electronic Classroom Interaction

Steven Robbins
Department of Computer Science
University of Texas at San Antonio
srobbins@cs.utsa.edu

ABSTRACT

ClassQue is a classroom response system that goes beyond clickers to allow a wide selection of classroom interactions: teacher to individual student, teacher to all students, student to teacher and student to student. Questions are not restricted to multiple choice, and multiple questions can be pending at one time. One student can anonymously comment on another student's answer. After the class, students and teachers can receive reports of the classroom interactions. The current version of ClassQue is available for use in an environment in which each student is seated at a computer.

Categories and Subject Descriptors

K.3.2 [**Computers & Education**]: Computer & Information Science Education—*Computer Science Education*

General Terms

Management

Keywords

Classroom Response System, Clickers, Curriculum

1. INTRODUCTION

Much has been written about how the traditional teacher-student interaction through lectures has failed to keep student's attention [4]. Producing an environment in which students are willing to interact with the teacher and classmates can be difficult, especially in a large class or in a class in which the students feel unsure of their abilities. Clickers [1, 2, 3] have been used for several years to allow teachers to pose questions to students and get real-time response information. Responses can drive or motivate classroom discussion and pique student interest. Others have used graphing calculators [9] or tablet PCs [7].

In a typical clicker application, a teacher asks a multiple choice question, usually by posting it using an overhead projector. The students then have a fixed amount of time to answer. When the time expires, the teacher displays a summary of the results and discusses the question. The teacher must allow enough time for the slowest students in the class to answer the question. Meanwhile, there is dead time in which students who have answered the question must wait quietly for the full time to expire.

The dead time problem is addressed by Informa [5, 6], an extensible system written in Java that has students use standard computers in place of clickers. An Informa plugin includes both a question type and an aggregate visualization for displaying solutions. Informa has been used to teach introductory Java programming, with an enhanced set of question types. Informa addresses the issue of dead time by allowing students to evaluate other's answers. In the Informa terminology, each question has three phases: solve, evaluate, reveal. In the solve phase, a question is posed and students work on the solution. During the evaluate phase, students who have solved the problem evaluate the solutions of other students. In the reveal phase the teacher displays solutions and discusses the results.

ClassQue, which also uses computers in place of standard clickers, provides a wide selection of question types that are applicable to many teaching situations. ClassQue fills the dead time with student reviews, allowing multiple questions to be pending, and allowing questions with open-ended answers. After answering a question, a student can look at and comment on other students answers to that question, or look at reviews to his/her answers. Teachers can also review or grade student answers.

An important aspect of clicker responses is the impression of anonymity they give. This allows students to answer freely without fear of scorn or intimidation from classmates. Having responses mandatory (in the sense that a lack of response can have a negative impact on the student's grade) is also useful in encouraging students to respond. In ClassQue, students do not know which students they are reviewing or which students have reviewed their answers.

During the discussion phase, teachers can display all of the answers given by the students in several formats including anonymous summaries and can also show reviews given to the answers.

ClassQue has support for students requesting help from the teacher or a remote teaching assistant without disturbing the rest of the class. It also supports group communication among students.

ClassQue requires the teachers and students to have a network-connected computer capable of running a recent version of Java. It is best used in an environment in which the teacher can display a computer screen using an overhead projector. The ClassQue system is available for download [8].

The rest of the paper is organized as follows. Section 2 discusses the basic ClassQue interface from the student and teacher viewpoint. Section 3 describes additional ClassQue features. Section 4 discusses a utility for creating questions for use by ClassQue. Section 5 goes into the details of setting up ClassQue and Section 6 presents some conclusions.

2. CLASSQUE BASICS

When students enter the classroom they sign into ClassQue which then displays an initial window. Figure 1 shows a student window after a simple query has been issued.

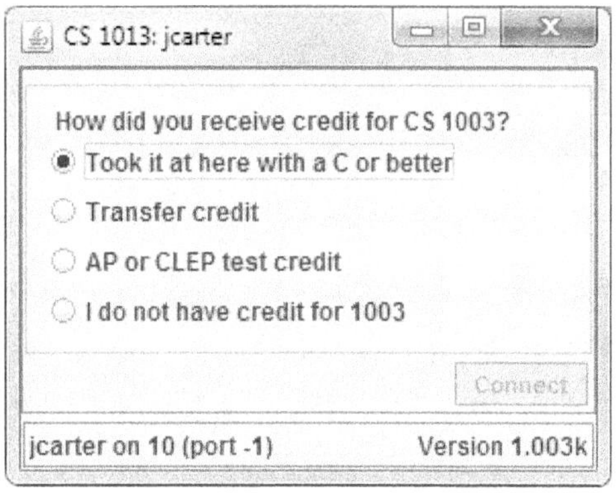

Figure 1: A student query window.

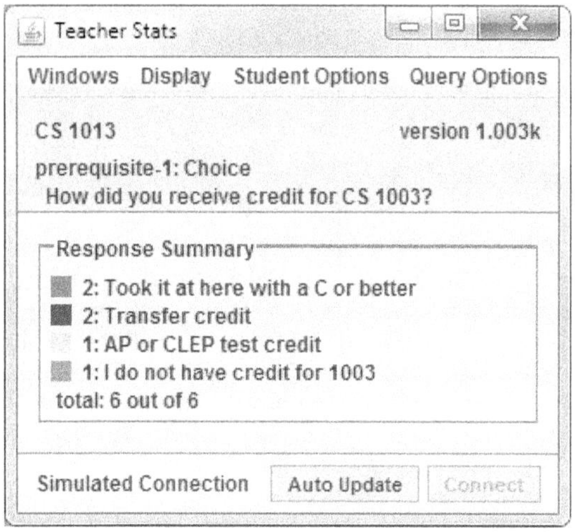

Figure 2: A teacher summary window.

ClassQue supports five basic types of queries. **Choice** queries allow students to choose one of a predetermined selection of answers. **Checkbox** queries are similar, but students can choose more than one answer. **Integer** queries allow students to enter a single integer as a response. **Freeform** queries allow students to make arbitrary text responses ranging in size from a few words to many paragraphs, possibly pasted from another document. **Code** queries allow students to type in program code as a response, displayed with a fixed width font and preserving indentation and spacing.

Figure 2 shows an example of a response summary for the multiple choice query of Figure 1. This display, which is similar to those of clicker systems, is one of the many possible teacher display formats. The **Responses by Student** view of Figure 3 displays a list of the students who have answered the query along with the answer given. The **Responses by Answer** view gives a list by answer, with the count of the number of students giving that answer. The underlined values in the responses shown in Figure 3 are links. Clicking on a **Review** link brings up a review window (described in Section 3.2). Clicking on a name or numbered answer link shows or hides the reviews for that answer.

Figure 4 shows a detailed view of the answers to a freeform query. In this figure the answer for each student is shown in the order that the answers were given, and the teacher has chosen to hide the names of the students, with the name replaced by a number in square brackets.

Figure 5 shows two views of the answers to a query with an integer answer. The **Responses by Student** view shows the response of each student. The teacher has the option of hiding the name of the student giving the answer, so that this window can be shown to the class for discussion. The **Responses by Answer** view is organized by answer. The value after the colon is the number of students giving the answer that appears below.

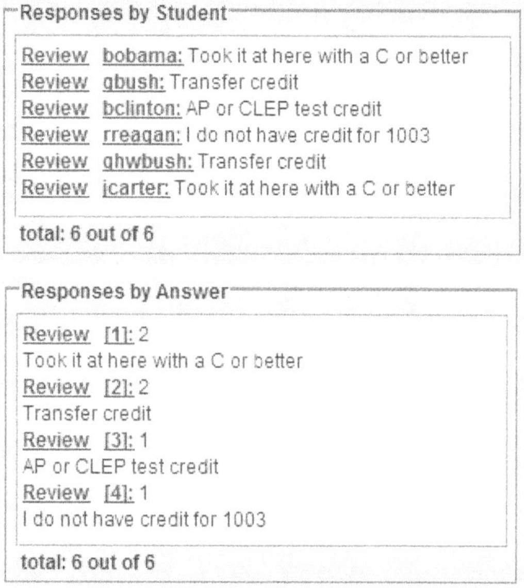

Figure 3: Two additional teacher views for a query with a choice answer.

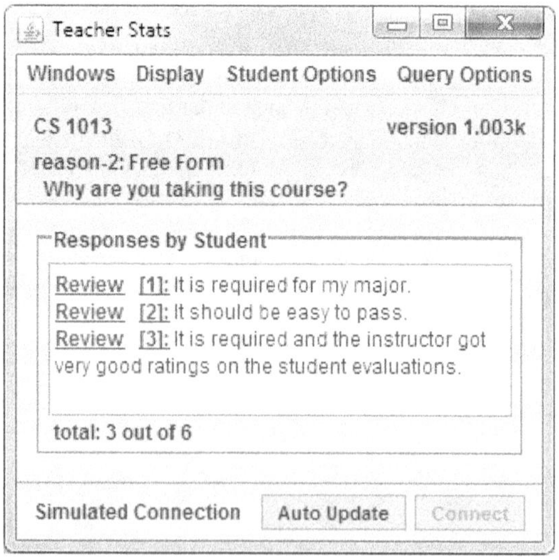

Figure 4: A teacher window for a query with a freeform answer.

Clicker technology requires students to work in lock-step with the slowest members of the class. Students who answer quickly are left with nothing to do until the answer time has completed.

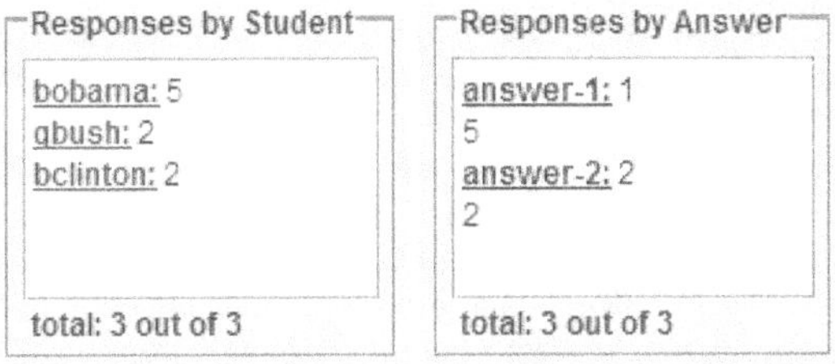

Figure 5: Two teacher views for a query with an integer answer.

ClassQue handles this problem in two ways. First, ClassQue supports the use of surveys. A survey is a collection of queries that students can answer at their own pace. The queries do not have to be answered in order. Some of the queries can be optional, or have open-ended answers, allowing the faster students to answer more queries or give more in-depth answers.

ClassQue also gives students something to do after they have answered all of the pending queries. If the teacher allows it, students can look at individual (anonymous) answers that other students have given and comment on those answers. These comments (referred to as student reviews) are also sent to the student that gave that answer. Students can see these comments, again anonymously, and have the option of adjusting their own answers. These revised answers can also be reviewed.

While waiting for responses, the teacher can also review student answers. Teacher reviews are marked, so students can see that these reviews are authoritative. Teaching assistants can also review answers. Teaching assistants do not need to be physically in the same classroom, but can log into a ClassQue assistant console from any machine on the network.

The teacher can also use the wait time to decide which of the student responses to use as a basis for classroom discussion. During the discussion, the teacher can display a window similar to Figure 6 and scroll through all of the answers, asking for comments or quickly describing what is right or wrong with each answer. The teacher can hide the names of the students to avoid embarrassing students who have given incorrect answers. This is important for encouraging student to submit answers.

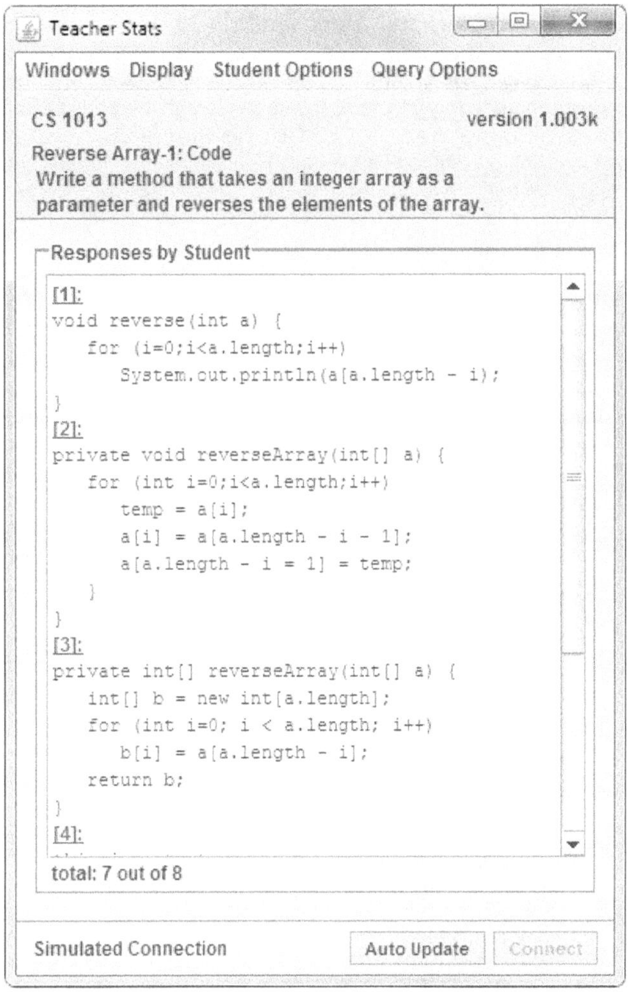

Figure 6: A teacher window showing many solutions to the same problem.

3. CLASSQUE FEATURES

The ClassQue system consists of a suite of Java programs. During class, students and teachers communicate with a server. Typically, the server program starts automatically before each class (e.g., as a cron job on a Linux system) and the server terminates after the class is over. While the server is up, students, teachers, and assistants can sign in. The server keeps track of all queries, answers, and reviews, logging them to a file on the server host. After the class is over, reporting programs automatically process and email reports to the teacher and the students. Teachers can also receive attendance summaries.

3.1 Seating Chart

Figure 7 shows two teacher's seating chart views. ClassQue supports seating diagrams consisting of one or two rectangular arrays of seats. This seating chart view is useful for quickly picking out which students have answered the current query. The left diagram in Figure 7 shows answers for a **Choice** query. The color of the box indicates which answer was given. Color codes correspond to the colors in Figure 2. The right diagram shows answers for a **Checkbox** query. If more than one answer is selected, the box is divided into regions. For example, in the right diagram of Figure 7, the student in seat 1 selected two answers (red and blue) and the student in seat 26 selected three answers. In all cases, a light gray box indicates that the student is signed in but has not yet answered the query.

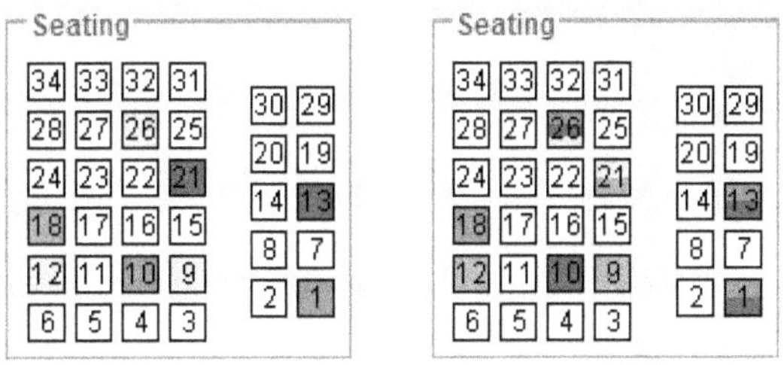

Figure 7: Seating charts for choice and checkbox queries.

3.2 Reviews

ClassQue allows students or teachers to comment on (review) the answers given by students. A teacher can review an answer by clicking on the **Review** link optionally displayed in the Responses window shown in Figure 4. This brings up a review window containing the query and the student answer along with an area for commenting on the answer given.

Teachers can also allow students to review the answers of other students on questions they have already answered. When a student requests an answer to review, ClassQue anonymously chooses a response using a method that attempts to maximize the number of answers that are reviewed by students. A student can see the reviews of his/her answers. Teacher reviews are marked, and student reviews are anonymous. After seeing a review, students can revise answers and resubmit.

If a query is of type choice, checkbox, or integer, it is likely that several students will give the same answer. In this case a review is associated with the answer, so that once an answer is reviewed, all students who gave that answer can see the review.

Teachers can also display **Correct**, **Incorrect**, and **Grade** links in the **Response** area to quickly mark answers as right or wrong, or assign a numeric grade.

Figure 8 shows a portion of the teacher's response window in which some reviews are shown. Student reviews are anonymous, but reviews by the teacher or assistant are marked as such so that students can pay careful attention to these.

Figure 8: A part of a teacher window showing reviews.

3.3 Shares

Shares allow groups of students to share information and communicate. Suppose the teacher asks the students to collaborate on developing a method with a given specification. Each student in the group will have a *common window* for typing in. All students belonging to the share see the same contents in the common window and can contribute.

The share also has a chat area that allows students to post comments that other members can see. While the contents of the common window are unattributed, the chat area shows a history of the attributed comments made by each member of the share. When the students agree that the solution is complete, a member of the group can submit the contents of the common window. This saves a permanent copy of the contents of the window, which the teacher can later grade. Students can move the contents of the shared window into another program using cut and paste.

Figure 9 shows the student view of a share with the common window near the top and the chat session below. The students are writing a method to reverse the elements of an array. The figure shows the share for **bclinton**. Other members of the share are **gbush** and **bobama**. Most of the writing was done by **bclinton** but the other two members made contributions as shown in the chat area.

A teacher can join any share. As with any other member of the share, the teacher can add comments to the chat area or modify the common window. The teacher can also add or remove members of the share or submit all shares.

ClassQue allows students to create their own shares and invite students to join that share. ClassQue allows teachers to easily divide the students into groups, either by explicit choice or by random selection and to create a share for each group. Each share has a leader who has priority in writing to the shared window.

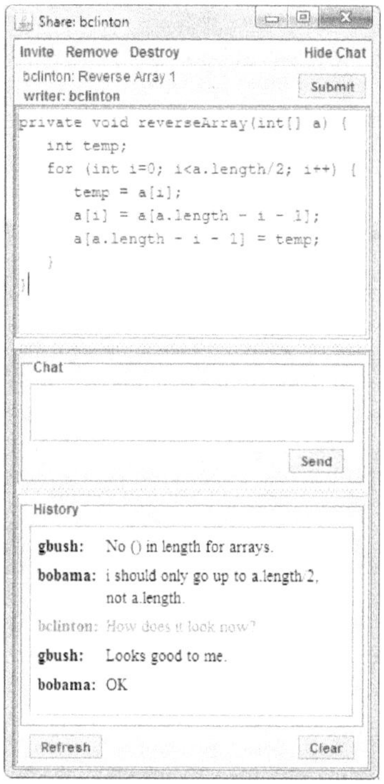

Figure 9: A student share window (reduced in size).

3.4 Messages

A teacher can send a message to an individual student or to a group of students. Figure 10 shows the window that a teacher can use to send a message to students. ClassQue allows two types of messages, those that require a response and those that do not. The figure shows a message sent to three students, two of whom have replied. The teacher can display the reply by hovering the mouse pointer over a student name.

Messages immediately appear in the student console window if the student is signed in. Otherwise they are queued until the student signs in, allowing the teacher to send messages before the class starts. I have used these messages to congratulate students who have done particularly well on an assignment or have put in an extra effort, and these have evoked positive responses from the students. Messages are also useful to obtain clarifications on assignment solutions that students have turned in.

3.5 Passwords

ClassQue can be set up to require a password from the teacher.

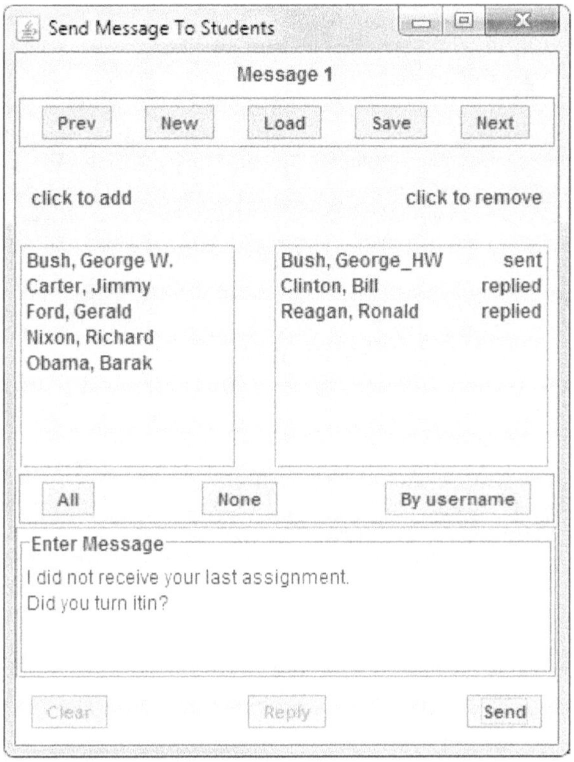

Figure 10: A window for creating messages.

Without passwords, anyone with a copy of the teacher program can run as a teacher and possibly disrupt the ClassQue system by injecting extraneous queries or sending messages to students. We ran the ClassQue system for a year without passwords and never had an problem with this. However, the public release of ClassQue will make it easier for hackers to disrupt a class if passwords are not used.

Students who sign in using the ClassQue student application do not have to enter a password, but they are identified by their host machine. ClassQue can be set up to allow only students from a specified collection of IP addresses to discourage hackers from disrupting the system. Students who log in using the browser interface are required to enter a username and password.

3.6 Other Features

Student List: The teacher can display a list showing where students are or should be sitting and whether they have signed into ClassQue. A teacher can also use this feature to sign students out of ClassQue, for example, disconnecting students who post inappropriate answers.

Pictures: If student pictures are available, ClassQue can display pictures of the students in a chart corresponding to where the students are sitting. This feature is useful for learning the names of the students in the class.

Help: Teachers can activate a student **Request Help** button. Students use this button to notify the teacher or an assistant that they need help. This feature is useful when the class is working on a classroom exercise. The teacher or an assistant can view a list of students who have requested help and provide assistance. The student does not have to wait for teacher attention with his/her hand raised.

The Assistant: ClassQue can be set up with two types of passwords for the teacher. The *teacher password* gives the user full teacher privileges. The *assistant password* marks the user as an assistant with restricted privileges. An assistant can sign in from one of the computers in the classroom and be available to offer physical assistance to students who request help or be signed in remotely and offer assistance using ClassQue messages (Section 3.4). In either case, assistants can review student answers. Reviews given by the assistant are marked as such, but are still distinguished from student reviews.

Annotations: A teacher can add annotations to the queries. An annotation can be attached to the query (the prompt) or to an individual answer of a choice or checkbox query. Annotations are not seen by the student when the queries are asked, but can be seen by the teacher. Annotations can be used to indicate the correct answer to a query, or to provide additional feedback to students in the reports they receive.

Start Discussion: When the teacher pushes the **Start Discussion** button, the time is logged. This marker indicates that the teacher has started discussion of the current query, so that answers given after this time can be ignored by the reporting system or treated as additional notes.

Greeting: The teacher can set up a file with a message, allowing instructors to insert instructions at the beginning of the student reports. Instructions might include the assignment for the following class or a reminder of due dates.

Simulator: The simulator is a standalone program that allows instructors to run the full system on a single machine. The simulator, which includes a server, teacher windows, and student windows, can be used for training of instructors, testing questions and verifying the seating chart. Teachers can use the simulator to read in log files from a previous class to recreate the state of the ClassQue system from any point in that class. This capability allows instructors to perform additional operations such as reviews after the class has ended or to send a student an individual message that will appear in the student's report.

4. THE QUERY CREATOR

Queries can be generated on the fly during class, but the usual way is to have a prepared set of queries in a file. Normally, the teacher loads this file when he/she signs into ClassQue at the start of class. In order to allow students to start answering queries before the class starts and before the teacher arrives, ClassQue provides a mechanism for starting a teacher client on a remote machine in such a way that it will wait until the server starts up and then send the queries.

The file format used for ClassQue queries is a user-readable ASCII text query file, but the structure is fairly complex, and it would be difficult to create one of these files manually. ClassQue comes with a **Query Creator** program for creating and editing these files. The Query Creator is menu driven, allowing the user to create a query by choosing the query type, entering the prompt, and if appropriate, the choices for the answers. The Query Creator also allows for entering annotations.

ClassQue supports queries formatted in HTML to allow for colors, font changes, and even tables. The ClassQue Query Creator provides an interactive environment for creating, editing, combining and previewing query files.

5. SETTING UP CLASSQUE

Download ClassQue [8] and unzip the file. Among the files included will be jar files for the server, teacher, student, query creator and report generators as well as a user's guide.

Each course that uses ClassQue has two port numbers dedicated to it. The ClassQue server is a Java program that can run on any system that supports Java 6. The server hardware and operating system needs to be able to handle multiple connections in a timely manner. A three-year-old mid-level Linux desktop can easily handle a couple of classes of 40 or more students simultaneously, without noticeable delay.

A copy of the ClassQue server is started before each class, and it uses one port to communicate with the teachers and one to communicate with the students. The server terminates after running for a specified length of time. For example, if a class meets MWF from 9:00 am to 9:50 am, the server might be started at 8:50 am every MWF by a cron job on a Linux machine. A configuration file provides the port numbers for this copy of the server as well as specifying how long the server runs before termination. For the above class, the duration might be set to 70 minutes, which will allow it to run until 10:00. All communication among teachers, assistants, and students flows through the server.

In addition to handling communication, the server logs sufficient information to recreate the ClassQue state at any time. One of the log files generated is an XML file that logs all teacher queries and student answers, as well as reviews and submitted shares. After the server terminates, another cron job can start a report generator that analyzes the XML log file and sends reports to the teacher and the students.

The teacher and student programs are clients of the server. They can be run on any system that supports Java 5 or later. Alternatively, the student console can be run from a browser. If run as an application, the student console attempts to determine the username and seat number from the host machine. If running from a browser, the student logs in, giving his/her username and seat number. In either case, a given student may run only one copy of the program at a time.

The teacher may have any number of sessions running. Multiple sessions on the same machine allow for several views of the student information. Additional teacher client programs can be run on other hosts. A special type of teacher, called an assistant, behaves like a teacher, but with restricted privileges. This can be used by a teaching assistant to interact with the students. The assistant does not need to be in the classroom.

6. CONCLUSIONS

ClassQue has been used for three semesters by 6 different instructors. It has been used in courses in MATLAB programming, Java programming, computer organization and operating systems.

While no comparison was made between courses using and not using ClassQue, ClassQue was well-received by the students and instructors. Students found it particularly useful in the operating systems class in which a survey was given at the beginning of class to evaluate the comprehension of the previous class. These results were mainly used as formative feedback, highlighting parts of the course material that needed further explanation. The instructor posted the queries (with answers) on the web, and students found this helpful in reviewing for exams. In some cases the use of ClassQue seems to have had a positive effect on the student evaluations of the course.

We teach our beginning programming courses using a development system such as Eclipse. Some faculty members believe that it is better for students to develop programs on paper without the assistance of a system that automatically finds and corrects syntax errors. Programming on paper forces students to think carefully about the programs they write, rather than to program using trial and error. We have used ClassQue shares (Section 3.3) to force students to first write their programs in a non-development environment and then paste them into Eclipse for debugging.

We have also used ClassQue in modified pair programming exercises, which I call barrier pair programming. Using traditional pair programming in a classroom situation suffers from a number of technical difficulties: including dividing the class into pairs, moving students around, making sure that a stronger student does not dominate a weaker one. For short problems, the overhead of setting up this environment makes it impractical to use in a 50-minute class period.

Barrier pair programming handles the logistics as follows. We design a problem with fixed milestones and use ClassQue to randomly divide the class into groups of size 2. Each student in the class works on the problem independently. When a student reaches a milestone, that student may not proceed (the barrier) until the paired student has also reached that milestone. The student who gets there first must help his/her partner (using the ClassQue share). A ClassQue checkbox question with the milestones as choices can help the teacher monitor the progress of the class.

ClassQue is available [8] for download. The single zip file contains jar files for the server, student, teacher, query creator, and report generators. It also includes a user's guide.

7. ACKNOWLEDGMENTS

Kay Robbins has written the report feature of ClassQue and has provided numerous useful suggestions.

8. REFERENCES

[1] A. L. Abrahamson. 1998. "An Overview of Teaching and Learning Research with Classroom Communication Systems," *International Conference on Teaching of Mathematics*, (1998), Village of Pythagorion, Samos, Greece.

[2] S. Draper, J. Cargill, and Q. Cutts. 2002. "Electronically Enhanced Classroom Interaction," *Australian Journal of Educational Technology*, (2002), pp. 13–23.

[3] C. Fies and M. Jill. 2006. "Classroom Responses Systems: A Review of the Literature," *Journal of Science Education and Technology*, (2006), 101–09.

[4] R. R. Hake. 1998. "Interactive-engagement vs. traditional methods: A six-thousand-student survey of mechanics test data for introductory physics courses," *American Journal of Physics*, vol. 66, (1998) pp. 64–74.

[5] M. Hauswirth and A. Adamoli. 2008. 'Informa: An extensible framework for group response systems." *Proceedings of the 4th International Conference on Collaborative Computing*, (2008).

[6] M. Hauswirth and A. Adamoli. 2009. "Solve & Evaluate with Informa: A Java-based Classroom Response System for Teaching Java," *Principles and Practice of Programming in Java*, (2009).

[7] K. Koile and D. Singer. 2006. "Development of a Tablet-PC-based System to Increase Instructor-Student Interactions and Student Learning," *Workshop on the Impact of Pen-based Technology on Education*, April 2006.

[8] S. Robbins. 2010. ClassQue. Retrieved November 30, 2010 from http://vip.cs.utsa.edu/classque

[9] J. Roschelle, P. Vahey, D. Tatar, J. Kaput, and S. Hegedus. 2003. "Five key considerations for networking in a hand-held-based mathematics classroom." *Proceedings of the 27th Conference of the International Group for Psychology of Mathematics Education*, (2003).

Overcoming Barriers among Israeli and Palestinian Students via Computer Science

Shiri Azenkot
Computer Science and Engineering
DUB Group
University of Washington
Seattle, WA
shiri@cs.washington.edu

Theodore Golfinopoulos
Electrical Engineering
and Computer Science
Massachusetts Institute
of Technology
Cambridge, MA
golfit@mit.edu

Adam Marcus
Computer Science and Artificial
Intelligence Lab
Massachusetts Institute of
Technology
Cambridge, MA
marcua@csail.mit.edu

Alessondra Springmann
Earth, Atmospheric, and
Planetary Science
Massachusetts Institute of
Technology
Cambridge, MA
sondy@sondy.com

Jonathan S. Varsanik
Electrical Engineering and
Computer Science
Massachusetts Institute of
Technology
Cambridge, MA
jon@meet.mit.edu

ABSTRACT
The Middle East Education Through Technology (MEET) program is a non-profit organization based in Jerusalem, that aims to empower future Israeli and Palestinian leaders by teaching them computer science and business. From the perspective of MEET's instructors, this paper describes how MEET uses computer science education to foster professional and personal contact among Israeli and Palestinian high school students, two groups who otherwise would have little or no interaction with each other. MEET's primary method of overcoming the barrier is teamwork: students are divided into groups that include both Israelis and Palestinians and are assigned software engineering tasks. We believe that the techniques used by MEET can serve as examples for other computer science programs that overcome barriers between groups in the United States and other countries.

Categories and Subject Descriptors
J.4. Social and behavioral sciences: Psychology. K.4.3 Computers and Society: Organizational Impacts: Computer-supported collaborative work.

General Terms
Design, Human Factors.

Keywords
Ethnic conflict, Israeli-Palestinian relations, computer science education.

1. INTRODUCTION
Israeli and Palestinian relations in the Middle East are strained and segregated. The movement of Palestinians from the West Bank into the State of Israel is highly controlled and restricted [10]. Also Palestinians who reside within the State of Israel live in separate Palestinian communities and have little interaction with Israeli Jews [5]. Palestinian and Israeli youth attend separate schools throughout K-12 and have little or no contact with each other [5]. This paper describes how MEET, Middle East Education Through Technology, uses computer science education to bridge the barriers between Israeli and Palestinian high school students by promoting interpersonal contact and professional collaboration.

Students enrolled in MEET attend sessions for three summers over two years in Jerusalem where Palestinian and Israeli high school students learn computer science and business, working together on software engineering projects. MEET aims to dispel misconceptions and foster understanding between Israelis and Palestinians. It selects top students who show leadership potential and instructors affiliated with the Massachusetts Institute of Technology (M.I.T) to teach them computer science and business.

The MEET model for overcoming the barrier between Israelis and Palestinians follows two widely studied principles from social psychology: the *Contact Hypothesis* [1] and *recategorization* [4]. The Contact Hypothesis states that interpersonal contact under specific conditions can reduce prejudice, stereotyping, and discrimination between groups in conflict [8]. Recategorization suggests that forming superordinate groups that consist of members from both conflicting groups improves intergroup relations.

We explore the specific ways in which MEET follows the Contact Hypothesis and recategorization, showing how well computer science education lends itself to improving intergroup relations. We describe equalizers that remove various disparities among the students, the incorporation of teamwork and pair programming, building an international team of trusted instructors, and ways to continually unite students of both groups outside the classroom as well. We conclude by discussing the lessons learned and providing an informal assessment of the success of these techniques. The views presented are those of the instructors and not necessarily of the MEET organization.

The authors hope that MEET can serve as an example for other computer science programs that aim to bridge barriers across different ethnic, gender, race, and socio-economic divisions in the United States as well as other regions in the world.

2. OVERVIEW OF MEET

MEET is a non-profit organization based in Jerusalem. Its mission is to educate and empower promising Palestinian and Israeli leaders to prepare them to take on the social, economic, and political challenges of their region. MEET selects Israeli and Palestinian high school students who have excelled on a set of academic and leadership exams from Jerusalem (East and West), the West Bank cities of Bethlehem and Ramallah, and the Israeli cities of Mevasseret and Bet Shemesh. Students study computer science and business with a focus on software engineering with instructors recruited at M.I.T. MEET is affiliated with M.I.T's Computer Science and Artificial Intelligence Laboratory (CSAIL).

2.1 Program Structure

MEET is a two-year program with three intensive summer sessions. Students enter the program during the summer after 9th grade and continue through the summer before 12th grade, their final year in high school. Students are divided into their year in the program, and referred to as "Y1," "Y2," and "Y3" students.

During the summer sessions, MEET students spend over eight hours a day for four or five weeks (depending on available funding) with instructors. Students of each year attend lectures and work on labs and large projects. Between summer sessions, students participate in the "year-long" program. The year-long involves weekly meetings of lecture and labs with a local instructor. The summer sessions remain the crux of the program.

2.2 Curriculum

The MEET curriculum teaches computer science, software engineering, and business as it fosters teamwork. Students work with increasing independence on progressively larger projects as they advance in the program while instructors assume the roles of mentors rather than teachers.

The Y1 curriculum provides an introduction to programming in Java. Using an objects-first approach, students learn control structures, basic data structures, inheritance, and object-oriented program development. Initially, students work on short assignments individually and in pairs, but towards the end of the summer they work on a week-long final project in small groups.

Y2 students learn about proper program design and testing. At least two weeks of the summer are spent developing projects in teams. The topics of lectures and labs are driven by the needs of the projects, which often involve playing and recording multimedia, database access, and web development. In 2010, for example, students developed multimedia plug-ins for an instant messaging chat client. Students gain experience using libraries and toolkits such as Java's Swing.

During the third summer, students work on a single project for the entire summer. Projects are usually web-based and commissioned and specified by an internal or external client (such as a software company like HP). The students are given much of the leadership of the project—from designing the project to interacting with the client. The curriculum includes several lectures covering topics such as web application technologies like Java servlets, databases, web UI design, and client-side scripting.

During Y2 and Y3, business is incorporated into the curriculum. Students attend two or three weekly business workshops and are assigned business tasks, including writing a business plan for their software engineering projects.

3. RELATED WORK: THEORIES FOR OVERCOMING INTERGROUP CONFLICT

3.1 The Contact Hypothesis

Allport [1] introduced the Contact Hypothesis for improving relations among groups in conflict. It has been shown that interpersonal contact between members of a majority and minority group can reduce stereotyping, prejudice and discrimination when Allport's conditions are met [8]. The conditions are as follows:

- **Equal status** – members of both groups must experience equal status within the situation.
- **Common goals** – there must be an active, goal-oriented effort.
- **Intergroup cooperation** – the effort toward the common goal must involve intergroup cooperation and interdependence; it should avoid intergroup competition.
- **Support of authorities, law or customs** – there must be support for a common authority with explicit rules or sanctions.

Table 1 summarizes the ways in which MEET fulfills each of Allport's conditions. Section 4 discusses the techniques used by MEET in detail and shows how interpersonal contact between Israelis and Palestinians is promoted.

Table 1. A summary of how MEET satisfies Allport's conditions for the Contact Hypothesis.

Allport's Contact Hypothesis Conditions in MEET
Equal status - Students must wear uniforms, MEET is free to everyone, students must all speak English, and students are recruited who have diverse and balanced technical backgrounds.
Common goals – Programming, software development, and business tasks, competitions among teams.
Intergroup cooperation - Students in a team have roles (*e.g.* Project Manager, Business Manager) that require them to depend on one another to complete all tasks in their project.
Support of authorities, law, or customs - M.I.T-affiliated instructors who are "experts" in computer science or business.

3.2 Recategorization

Recategorization is the idea that dividing members of "ingroups" and "outgroups" into superordinate, or higher-level, categories improves relations between the original groups. Research has shown that members of a group based on a superordinate category, which may be arbitrary, experience positive feelings towards group members regardless of their original group divisions. MEET's focus on teamwork involves constant recategorization into superordinate groups that include both Israelis and Palestinians. Table 2 summarizes the superordinate groups that MEET students belong to.

Table 2. MEET students are recategorized into groups that usually include equal numbers of Israelis and Palestinians.

Superordinate groups in MEET
Year in MEET, Y1, Y2, or Y3 (about 45 students or less)
Large project team (6-8 students)
Recitation group for Y1 and Y2 (6-8 students)
Lab pair (2 students)

4. TECHNIQUES FOR OVERCOMING INTERGROUP BARRIERS IN MEET

4.1 Equalizers

The following are policies MEET uses to reduce disparity among the students that may arise because of ethnicity, academic background, or socio-economic status. These policies induce *equal status*, Allport's first condition for the Contact Hypothesis.

Uniforms. During the summer session, all MEET students must wear their MEET T-shirts.

Program cost. MEET is free for all students. Meals and snacks, MEET T-shirts, transportation to and from the program, and supplies are included in the program at no cost.

English language. MEET enforces the "English Rule," which requires all students to speak English at all times during the program. Generally, Israelis in the region speak Hebrew as their native language while Palestinians speak Arabic. Few Palestinians in MEET are fluent in Hebrew and few Israelis are fluent in Arabic. The English Rule ensures that no students or instructors are excluded from conversation. Repeated offenses to the English Rule result in expulsion from the program.

Technical background. The program selects students with varying technical backgrounds among both Israeli and Palestinian students. MEET uses Linux, which the vast majority of students are not familiar with. Students with access to computers outside of MEET will have less of an advantage over their peers since all students must learn how to use an unfamiliar operating system.

4.2 Teamwork

Teamwork is a critical part of MEET. Students are constantly being "recategorized" into diverse groups. Teaching computer science facilitates teamwork by enabling students to develop multi-faceted software engineering projects. This follows Allport's [1] conditions of *intergroup cooperation*, where Palestinian and Israeli students within a team are dependent on each other, and *common goals*, where students of each team must complete a single task.

Throughout MEET, students are divided into teams when reviewing and applying programming concepts. During Y1 and Y2, students are split into groups of six to eight students for recitation sessions and a final programming project. Students work on their final projects for several hours a day during the last week or two of the summer session. In Y3, students work within the same teams throughout the summer on their summer-long project. Team members sit at adjacent seats in the computer lab and work on a single program from one codebase (using version control).

Students within a team are often given specific roles such as "project manager," "business manager," and "quality assurance manager." Each role has distinct responsibilities, requiring students to manage and depend on each other for completing the various organizational, engineering, and business tasks involved in their project. This fulfills Allport's condition for *intergroup cooperation* (between Israelis and Palestinians within a team).

Figure 1. A pair of Y3 students demonstrates their lab assignment to their classmates.

The business curriculum also affords opportunities for teamwork. In Y2, students propose a plan to further the goals of a local business in an activity called "The Apprentice," modeled after Donald Trump's reality television show. When creating a website in Y3, each project team wrote vision and mission statements for the website and competed to determine which vision and mission statements would be used for the final presentation.

Competition among teams is common in the computer science curriculum as well as the business curriculum. In the summer of 2010, Y1 recitation groups competed to earn points awarded for good behavior throughout the summer. Also, final project teams, who implemented the card game Set, competed for best project quality. Small prizes are often awarded to winning teams. Competitions and prizes serve as effective incentives, especially for the younger students, since grades are not given in MEET.

Dividing students into teams is a constant challenge. To ensure diversity within each team, students are grouped by a staff member who knows the students well outside the classroom, possibly with the help of the head of instructors. The top priority when creating a team is to achieve a balance of Israeli and Palestinian students. The next priorities are to achieve an equal male to female ratio, diverse technical abilities within each group, and finally to avoid personal conflicts among the students in the team.

Project contents and the clients who commission them often reinforce MEET's values. For example, in Summer 2010, Y3 students created a website that provided a forum for intercultural discussion through user-posted questions and answers. The students designed the user experience, developed both the frontend and backend from a skeleton provided by the instructors, and wrote a business plan to promote the website. The students named the project Okolico, which means "neighborhood" in Slovenian; it can be accessed at http://www.okolico.com. Another project example is a web portal developed by Y3 in the summer of 2007 for a non-governmental organization called the Palestinian Media Development Institute. The web portal supported female Palestinian business owners.

Figure 2. Y3 MEET students pair program while working on their summer-long software engineering project.

4.3 Pair Programming

In addition to working in teams, MEET employs pair programming by assigning two students, usually a Palestinian and an Israeli, to one workstation. The students tackle a single task such as writing a program together, using one keyboard, monitor and mouse. Pair programming promotes interpersonal contact in close physical space, while once again recategorizing students into (albeit small) superordinate groups.

Pair programming is used throughout the three years in MEET during labs and projects. Labs are several-hour exercises that review and apply the students' understanding of computer science topics covered during a lecture. When students are working on projects in teams, instructors will often give them tasks to complete with another team member on a single workstation.

Instructors usually assign the student pairs, especially for the younger students. As with creating teams, the top priority is to pair an Israeli and a Palestinian followed by pairing a male with a female. Other considerations may be pairing a weaker student with a stronger student or simply pairing two students with similar interests.

Pair programming has been shown to improve technical skills [3] and, more importantly in the context of MEET, to increase communication between team members [3]. However, it is a continuous challenge for instructors to ensure that both students in the pair are equally engaged in the task.

4.4 Neutral Instructor Platform

MEET recruits M.I.T-affiliated computer science and business instructors for its summer session who represent neutral authority figures for the students.

MEET aims to build a team of instructors with a broad background in both teaching and their specialized subject. Instructor recruitment is done on the M.I.T campus through posters and word-of-mouth. As a result, instructors are generally M.I.T undergraduate or graduate students or alumni. The instructor team is composed of 12 computer science instructors, two business instructors, and a head of instructors who has usually worked as an instructor in the past.

Though mostly American nationals, MEET instructors have included people of various backgrounds and nationalities, including China, Canada, Turkey, Spain, Mexico, and Israel. The Israeli instructors (including two authors of this paper) spent many years living in the United States, and do not associate their Israeli background with their role as instructors.

During the year-long program, MEET strives to have equal numbers of Palestinian and Israeli instructors work with the Y1 and Y2 students as mentors for the computer science curriculum. This is challenging, however, because Palestinian instructors are more difficult to find.

A significant portion of MEET instructor training is dedicated to the classroom environment. Instructors are discouraged from discussing political issues with their students during lectures and lab time. The students understand that their instructors from M.I.T are experts in either computer science or business, and are not there to lecture about peace or the importance of conflict resolution. The instructors are common trusted authorities for the students (following Allport's [1] *support of authority, law or customs* condition for the Contact Hypothesis). M.I.T's reputation as being an excellent university for mathematics, science, and engineering underscores for the students that their instructors have a strong computer science background.

Political and identity issues are discussed during the summer in a session called "Deeper Understanding." This group conversation, lead by the Student Relations Manger (a member of MEET's local staff), provides students with a structured forum for discussion of close-to-home issues in a respectful and educational (rather than combative) environment.

By bringing in an international team of instructors as well as having mentors from both Israeli and Palestinian backgrounds, MEET emphasizes professionalism, teamwork and excellence in computer science and business rather than conflict resolution.

4.5 Overcoming Barriers Outside the Classroom

Instructors are expected by MEET to be a constant "bridge" between the Palestinian and Israeli students. This is achieved in a variety of ways outside the classroom.

Instructors are expected to bring students together during break times (snack and lunch) by mingling with them. By being a part of students' conversations, instructors can remind students of the importance of MEET's English Rule without overtly focusing on rule enforcement. Instructors also play games with students, ranging from catch with footballs and Frisbees to card games such as Set.

Each year of students participates in an "Outdoor Training" activity, where students and instructors spend a day working on teambuilding skills and problem solving. Held at different outdoor settings for each year, the students are separated into groups different from their recitation or project teams and assigned a different instructor for the duration of the day. Outdoor Training gives students whose strengths do not necessarily lie in computer science or business an opportunity to demonstrate leadership skills outside of the classroom, as well as for the entire year of students to work as part of a different team to accomplish a non-academic common goal.

MEET students also established a student council that organizes events during the year-long program and provides feedback to the MEET staff and board. Student council elections are organized such that an equal number of Palestinian and Israeli males and females are elected to the council.

Although MEET is focused on academics, students are recategorized and encouraged to work together on common goals in non-academic settings as well. The academic instructors are expected to facilitate and encourage this.

5. LESSONS LEARNED

As instructors in MEET, we learned several lessons about the benefits and challenges of the techniques outlined in this paper.

The combination of the English Rule, instructor neutrality, and instructor involvement outside the classroom was most effective for fostering friendships among students. Students commonly formed separate Israeli and Palestinian cliques during breaks, speaking their native languages. Simply reminding them of the English Rule was not enough to merge the cliques. However, when instructors actively participated in social activities, students from both backgrounds came together, eager to get involved. Speaking English throughout the program was difficult for many students, but they wanted to interact with instructors on a personal level. This improved their English and enabled them to socialize with other students through the instructors. Since instructors usually did not speak Hebrew or Arabic, students felt that they should speak English out of respect; this was a far more powerful incentive than the negative consequences imposed by not following the rule.

Continual instructor engagement is challenging and may require some training. It was difficult for some instructors to join student social activities, especially after a grueling day of teaching. Discussing strategies was helpful; the most effective strategies were playing card and ball games. Also, we found it helpful to sit at an empty lunch table at the beginning of the lunch period and encourage various students to join our table as they get their food.

Uniforms and teamwork were effective ways to steer the competitive nature of the students toward nonpolitical goals. The MEET T-shirts had the students' year in the program printed on them. The program drew very competitive students who were energized by the competition among years and teams.

The focus on pair programming prevented some students from receiving sufficient coding experience. Students who were shy or less confident in their technical skills often deferred all coding to their programming partner. Since there are no homework or strictly individual assignments in MEET, some students would never get a chance to catch up to their peers. Even during the final summer of the program, some students struggled with basic programming tasks such as reversing for-loops.

Choosing projects that reflected MEET values was a less effective tool for increasing interaction than expected. While these project themes are good for the organization itself, students often didn't appreciate the blatant conflict resolution efforts.

6. ASSESSMENT: ISRAELI-PALESTINIAN INTERACTIONS WITHIN MEET

We describe the interactions between Israeli and Palestinian students in MEET as an informal assessment of the techniques discussed in the paper. This section is based on the experiences of instructors as well as interviews with students in the press.

Although the initial draw to the program is usually academic enrichment, both Israeli and Palestinian students are excited to get to know their Palestinian and Israeli counterparts. Students acknowledge that this "great opportunity" is rare; their school friends don't know people from the other group [6].

Palestinian and Israeli students collaborate effectively and in a friendly and respectful manner on academic projects and assignments. Assigning teams and pairs that include an equal ratio of Palestinians and Israelis is important, however, because when choosing teams and sitting in class students tend to associate with students of their ethnic group.

During snack and lunch times, instructors must sometimes instigate Israeli-Palestinian social interactions. Students tend to divide into cliques of their ethnic group and speak their native language. However, with a bit of help from instructors or an organized activity, many Israeli-Palestinian friendships become evident. Students play sports, card games, listen to music, and chat. These friendships are manifested on Facebook, which is heavily used by MEET students. Both Israelis and Palestinians are "friends" with dozens of students from the other ethnic group on the site.

The students say that they feel comfortable with one another. One Israeli student says it feels like there is "no fence" between the Israeli and Palestinian students in the program [9]. Another Palestinian student explains students in MEET discuss various issues and there is "no discrimination" [9]. Students describe each other as "partners" and "friends" [9].

There have been no incidents of violence between an Israeli and a Palestinian since MEET's inception in 2004. There have been heated arguments, however, during "Deeper Understanding" sessions. These resulted in noticeable tension among students. Instructors do not attend these sessions to maintain a neutral position, however, so we have no first-hand experience with the arguments that arise.

Interactions between Palestinians and Israelis in MEET have been positive on the whole. The fact that Israeli and Palestinian students are interacting in a social and academic context throughout two years including three intensive summers is rare and remarkable. We believe MEET provides a model wherein an academic discipline, in this case computer science, provides the common ground upon which intercultural dialog flourishes and prejudice withers.

7. ACKNOWLEDGMENTS

The authors thank Anat Binur, Abeer Hazboun, Jacob O. Wobbrock, Batya Friedman, and Max Goldman. We also thank Clare Bayley for permitting us to use her photos in the paper.

8. REFERENCES

[1] Allport, G. W. 1954. *The nature of prejudice*. Perseus BooksDing, Cambridge, MA.

[2] Amit, Y. 1969. Contact Hypoethsis in Ethnic Relations. In *Psychological Bulletin* 71, 319-342.

[3] Cockburn, A. and Williams, L. 2001. The costs and benefits of pair programming. In *Extreme Programming Examined*, G. Succi and M. Marchesi, Eds. The XP Series. Addison-Wesley Longman Publishing Co., Boston, MA, 223-243.

[4] Gaertner, S, Dovidio, J. F., Anastasio, P. A., Bachman, B. A., and Rust, M. C. 1993. The Common Ingroup Identity Model: Recategorization and the Reduction of Intergroup Bias. In *European Review of Social Psychology*. 4:1-26.

[5] Halabi, R. 2004. *Israeli and Palestinian Identities in Dialog*. Rutgers University Press, New Brunswick, NJ.

[6] The Media Line Staff. Israeli and Palestinian Teens Mix at MEET. *All Health News*. July 29, 2010. Available at: http://www.allheadlinenews.com/articles/7019431924?Israeli%20and%20Palestinian%20Teens%20Mix%20at%20MEET

[7] MEET: Middle East Education Through Technology. Available at http://meet.mit.edu.

[8] Pettigrew, T. 1998. Intergroup Contact Theory. In *Annual Review of Psychology* 49, 65-89.

[9] Shapiro, L. Unleavened Media: Can Technology Bring Peace in the Middle East? *Jerusalem Post*. July 18, 2010. Available at: http://cgis.jpost.com/Blogs/unleavenedmedia/entry/can_technology_bring_peace_to

[10] World Bank Report, 2010. West Bank and Gaza Checkpoints and Barriers: Searching for Livelihoods. Report No. 49699.

Case Study: Faculty Professional Development Workshops for Innovation Diffusion

Beth Simon, Elizabeth Bales, William G. Griswold
Computer Science and Engineering Dept.
University of California, San Diego
La Jolla, CA USA 92093-0404
{bsimon, ebales, wgg}@cs.ucsd.edu

Stephen Cooper
Computer Science Dept.
Stanford University
Stanford, CA USA 94035
coopers@cs.stanford.edu

ABSTRACT

Part of computer science education research focuses on the design of new technologies and techniques for improving educational experiences. However, for these systems and techniques to be truly impactful, their use must be disseminated to the larger instructor population. Single-instance workshops, where instructors are brought together to learn about a new technique or system so that they can possibly adopt it, are a common dissemination method. Unfortunately, rarely do we see reports regarding their effectiveness. In this case study, we report on two NSF-funded single-instance workshops designed to support adoption of the Ubiquitous Presenter (UP) active learning classroom presentation system. Though only 44% of workshop attendees used the system in their classrooms, 65% of those used the system repeatedly. Overall this impacted 1570 students. Additionally, 60% of our attendees used the active learning features of UP – a much higher usage rate than in the general UP user population. We reflect on the aspects of the workshops which seemed to promote, and hinder, instructor adoption and, finally, suggest some metrics for evaluating innovation dissemination workshops in general.

Categories and Subject Descriptors
K.3.1 [**Computers and Education**]: Computer use in Education.

General Terms: Human Factors

Keywords
Tablet PC, Ubiquitous Presenter, Instructor adoption, Faculty development workshop.

1. INTRODUCTION

It was Chairman Mao who created the Hundred Flowers movement (百花運動), which advocated "[l]etting a hundred flowers blossom and a hundred schools of thought contend is the policy for promoting progress in the arts and the sciences...." [12] Indeed, this approach of allowing many ideas from many sources to flourish has been replicated elsewhere, such as through the US National Science Foundation's (NSF) Transforming Undergraduate Education in Science, Technology, Engineering and Mathematics program [13]. While Mao may have used this movement to trap his intellectual opponents, the intent of NSF and other such groups is to encourage many innovative approaches towards improving undergraduate STEM education, with the hopes that the best approaches should rise to the top, and be adopted by others.

SIGCSE'11, March 9–12, 2011, Dallas, Texas, USA.

And yet, it is not clear how to foster such adoption in the educational arena. Two of the most well-known books in innovation adoption are Diffusion of Innovation [10] and Crossing the Chasm [7], which are staples of many business programs. But, the challenge of diffusing innovation and crossing chasms with respect to educational interventions remains. Popular approaches to such adoption include making materials available on websites (and in digital libraries), publishing information about the intervention and its impact on student learning in journals and at conferences, publishing textbooks, and running professional development workshops, among many others., However, the relative effectiveness of these various dissemination strategies in computing education is unknown. Some research, such as [8] have suggested reasons for the non-adoption of computing inventions in specific areas, but the relative effectiveness of various dissemination approaches was not examined. [6] argued for specific technical aspects of tools to make them more instructor-friendly, as well as for the use of professional development workshops, without exploring why or what aspects of professional development workshops are likely to be most effective. This paper provides a case study of the effectiveness of one such workshop and, based on that study, discusses useful metrics for future work in studying dissemination effectiveness.

In this paper we look at two workshops designed to introduce instructors to the Ubiquitous Presenter (UP) program. UP is a web based presentation system designed to facilitate student engagement in the classroom through a combination of digital, web-based student submissions and inkable instructor slides via a Tablet PC [11]. In our analysis we consider the following questions:

- What impact did these workshops really have? What was the rate of adoption among workshop attendees? What barriers did they face?
- What did the workshop organizers do to address perceived problems in the second deployment of the workshop?

- How do adopters via professional development workshops (costly adoption) differ from lower cost, over-the-web adopters?
- How did metrics regarding the success of this workshop compare to others recently reported and what metrics do we recommend be considered in the future?

2. RELATED WORK

Most comparable to this work is that by Ni [9] looking at what issues influence computing instructor change. She studies one year of workshops promoting use of a media computation context in CS0/CS1, and we compare with her results.

There is also literature on the broader issue of technology adoption among instructors at higher education institutions. In [5] they report on university-instructor technology adoption by studying the impact of job relevance and perceived relevance on user acceptance of new technologies. They show the importance of motivating relevance when introducing a new technology to a potential adopter.

Harris studied technology adoption by focusing on internal barriers to instructor technology adoption [3]. While not focusing on the workshop scenario itself, it does classify adoption barriers which should be taken into account when designing technology dissemination workshops. These barriers range from low level of perceived usefulness to user self-confidence when interacting with technological systems, and are important to keep in mind when recruiting workshop attendees and designing workshop curriculum.

Henderson and Dancy's study of active learning in physics also informs our research, as it highlights the differences between the instructor's perceptions of how they teach and how an unbiased observer would classify the same teaching methods [4]. This study shows the importance of using quantitative data of instructor usage to back up self-reported data, since instructors may perceive their adoption rate as higher than it truly is.

3. BACKGROUND

3.1 Ubiquitous Presenter (UP)

UP is an extension of the University of Washington's Classroom Presenter (UWCP) Tablet PC presentation system [1]. The UP system seeks to bring the spontaneity of dynamic instructor "ink" to static, digitally prepared materials. It also supports anonymous, electronically-enabled active learning in the classroom, by allowing students to "submit" work via a web-based application and easing the sharing (e.g., digital projection) of that work in the classroom.

UP differs from UWCP in that it is both web-enabled and supports both pen-based and typing-based student submissions [11]. Web support provides student access and control: Should the instructor so choose, nearly any computing device can view the instructor's replayable inked slides, in any order, at any time, in the classroom or out. Student submissions permit students to author solutions to in-class active learning exercises and submit them anonymously to the instructor. Both pen and keyboard inputs are available – supporting students with normal laptops or Tablets. Students can make submissions in a variety of formats including multiple choice, typed text, drawn, or screen shot. The instructor can display student submissions and multiple-choice bar graphs for discussion, and students can peruse them on their own.

3.2 The UP Workshops

The 2-day UP workshops studied were held for two consecutive years at UC San Diego – though numerous other UP workshops had been held in the Tablet PC education community. The UP workshops were funded by an NSF CCLI Phase 2 grant which sought to train STEM faculty to engage UP's technology-based active learning system to enhance or enable active learning experiences in their classrooms. The 2007 workshop had 25 attendees (64 applicants), and the 2008 workshop had 20 attendees (44 applicants). Most attendees received a grant of \$1600 to cover most of the cost of a Tablet PC. This decision was among a number made specifically to try to increase the likelihood of an attendee's personal and institutional buy-in.

3.2.1 Practices to encourage adoption

Each year the workshop organizers designed activities specifically to engender user adoption – while also fulfilling our goal to disseminate broadly and diversely.

Applications. Applications were encouraged from institutional teams of two faculty (from different departments), with the goal of providing "partners" for instructors. Applicants were selected from diverse STEM disciplines and university characteristics (students served, class size, department size, under-represented group representation, etc.). We also asked about the import of research for tenure-track faculty -- to get an impression as to whether participants would be supported not only in adopting UP technology, but in assessing and reporting on its use. Applicants also answered two short answer questions on their definition of active learning and why they valued it in their classrooms. In the first year applicants were asked to describe how they would benefit from the workshop and what skills or strengths they brought to it.

Finally, we attempted to communicate both the expectations and value of the workshop through a series of statements applicants were asked to agree (or disagree) with, such as, "I intend to teach at least 2 courses next year using active learning as the primary classroom pedagogy." Others asked whether students would have access to required technology, whether the applicant's department would support them in their use of the technology, whether they would agree to obtain IRB approval to study student use of UP, and commitment to pre-workshop meetings.

The primary goal of our detailed application was to indicate the "high bar" we were placing on participation – we felt the appeal of a free Tablet PC would be high and wanted to make clear our expectations for system adoption in at least 2 classrooms.

Pre-Workshop Communication. Pre-workshop contact was minimal in the first year with no required communication. We advised regarding Tablet PC purchases and asked participants to install UP client software before the workshop, though few did so.

Workshop Activities. Workshop activities were designed both to engage instructors with each other in discussion of active learning and how UP might support them in their classes (especially across their disciplines), the workshop format itself employed an active learning format with numerous planned individual and group activities, and time was dedicated to getting instructors set up technically.

Post-Workshop Communication. Post workshop communication involved emails from the leaders to the participants offering assistance and requests for attendees to complete on-line surveys regarding their UP use.

Second Year. Table 2 summarizes changes made in the second year to increase adoption. Overall these changes sought to better prepare people technically and give them greater ownership over (and hopefully commitment to) workshop activities. By putting workshop activities more in the lens of group research activities we hoped to increase engagement during the academic year through research's natural position within academia.

Table 1. Workshop Changes To Support Adoption.

Application: Asked more about applicant support/reward by dept/university for making and studying innovation Asked about specific pedagogical or instructional assessment activities/experience Exactly which 2 classes will you use UP in, and what is the motivation for using it in those classes? How many hours per week could you spend on implementing and assessing, what is teaching load?
Pre-meeting: Strongly encouraged conference calls (75% attended), required pre-installation of UP (75% complied)
Workshop: Added time for technical help(both providing setup and use training) Had participants brainstorm their own research questions/studies and then form interest groups (on day 1), which they continued to work in. Provided much more time (with structured development activities) for the groups to outline what they would do, including filling in and presenting to the group their plan for continuing work after the meeting – including a specific "next meeting" **post-workshop** conference call date.

4. RESULTS

Here we consider both server log information and surveys to give a more explanatory picture of the adoption patterns of these NSF-funded workshop participants. We also compare workshop attendee data to general UP user data.

In general, we can postulate a number of ways in which the NSF workshop participants may differ from other UP users. First, the workshop participants were selected to cover a broad and balanced range of STEM disciplines, in contrast we find that 39% of UP classrooms target computing-related material. Concerns might arise that workshop participants possess less technological expertise than the general UP user. However, our workshop users self-reported a high level of technological self confidence with 100% of participants reporting they felt "mostly" or "very" confident in using technology, and 92% reporting that they felt mostly/very confident in their ability to use technology in the classroom. It is important to note that only 62% of our workshop participants responded to our survey, which biases the results.

The next difference we might expect between workshop participants and general users is in the level of motivation. Usage data taken from the entire set of UP users reports on those instructors who came to use UP "on their own". Some may have found the system on the internet, read about it in a conference or lay publication, or possibly attended a short (1-2 hour) introductory workshop. People who sought out UP of their own volition might be more persistent in dealing with technology-related barriers or concerns that arise in using UP. The motivation of our workshop attendees may have varied. It seems likely that they had some motivation, as they were willing to give up three days of their summer to travel to and attend a workshop.

In the recruiting process we expressed preference for interdisciplinary teams of two from each institution, so it is possible that up to half of our attendees were somewhat less interested in UP than their partner colleague from their institution. Additionally, workshop attendees were awarded a grant covering the majority (or all) of the cost of purchasing a Tablet PC so that they could use the UP system. Perhaps some participants were more interested in having a Tablet PC than using UP, specifically. Another possibility is that general users (finding UP on their own) may have likely already had access to a Tablet PC (and were looking for a lecturing system to take advantage of it) and that this meant that their technical skills and comfort in using a Tablet PC were higher than those of the workshop attendees (who were, on the whole, not already Tablet PC users).

Next we present data from the general UP server logs of all users to provide a better context for workshop data.

4.1 General UP usage

We have previously characterized adoption rates and differences of UP system users since 2006, based on server usage logs [2]. Here we replicate that, but separate out workshop participants to assess the impact of the workshops compared against overall UP use. We look at usage through the lens of classrooms created, instructors and their use, and student impact (students who "enroll" to view course materials online and who engage by "submitting" via the active learning supports).

Those results showed that UP has been used by 520 instructors affecting 8,348 students in 969 classrooms around the world. Of the 969 classrooms, about 20% regularly use UP in a classroom setting (at least 5 lectures with at least 5 students enrolled on UP for that class). Additionally, 44% of those classrooms make use of the active learning supports of UP (with an average of 5 submissions or more per student).

19% of instructors who registered a login on UP have gone on to actively use UP in at least one classroom (using it for at least 5 lectures, and having at least 5 students register on UP for the course). Of instructors who used UP in a real classroom environment 50% used active learning features such as student submissions (with at least an average of 5 submissions per student). Of the 8,348 students enrolled 3,246 engaged in active learning creating a total of 82,162 submissions. This UP general usage data will serve as a backdrop as we take a closer look at the 2007 and 2008 workshop participants.

4.2 Workshop Server Results

There were notable differences between 2007 and 2008 workshop attendees which are highlighted in Table 2. While the 2007 workshop had 5 more participants than the 2008 group, we see much higher engagement numbers across a range of metrics for the 2008 instructors.

The first thing an instructor needs to do is create a classroom. Many classrooms are created by users who are testing the system and are never used live in a classroom. There were a total of 130 classrooms created by workshop attendees 58 by the 2007 group and 72 by the 2008 group. Through human inspection we found that 16 (28%), of the 2007 classrooms and 48 (67%) of the 2008 classrooms were used "live", with real students in the classroom. Additionally, 12 of the 16 classrooms created by the 2007 instructors, and 39 of the 48 classrooms created by the 2008 instructors made significant use of student submissions.

It is also important to look at individual instructor success when determining the success rate of the workshops. We found that of the 25 instructors from 2007 only 6 succeeded in using UP live in the classroom, while in 2008, 14 of 20 instructors succeeded. Also, of those combined 20 instructors using UP in the classroom, 13 chose to use UP in a second class. This is interesting to note since while only 44% of instructors adopted the technology for classroom use, 65% of those who succeeded at using UP in one classroom decided to use UP in future classes.

Another notable difference between the two workshop groups is the number of students impacted, with 521 student enrolled in classrooms created by 2007 instructors and twice that many students in the 2008 instructor classrooms.

Table 2. 2007 and 2008 workshop usage statistics compared with general UP usage.

	2007	2008	All Users
Classrooms created	58	72	969
Non-test classrooms[1] (% of total)	16 (28%)	48 (67%)	192 (20%)
Active learning classrooms (%)	12 (75%)	39 (81%)	84 (43%)
Instructors	25	20	520
Instructors using UP in the classroom	6 (24%)	14 (70%)	100 (19%)
Instructors using active learning in classroom	3 (50%)	9 (64%)	50 (50%)
Students enrolled	521	1,049	8,348
Students engaged in active learning (submitting)	445 (85%)	619 (59%)	3,246 (39%)
Number active learning exercise answers (submissions by students)	1,317	10,647	82,162
Average Submissions per student	3	17	28

4.2.1 If at first you don't succeed

It is also important to look more closely at those instructors who never succeeded in using UP in their classrooms. They invested varying levels of effort regarding how long they tried before they gave up. We call each of the unused classrooms created by a user a "try" (often test classrooms made to explore system use). Figures 1 shows the differences in use across the years (note that "successful" instructors are included).

In 2007, 7 attendees never made a classroom while in 2008 that number was only 2. The 2007 group invested much less effort before discontinuing use with 10 giving up after one try (classroom creation), 2 giving up after 2 tries and one giving up after 3 tries. It should be noted that all participants should have (but didn't necessarily) make a classroom before or at the workshop. The 2008 group was more resilient, with only one participant giving up after a single try, and 6 after two or more tries.

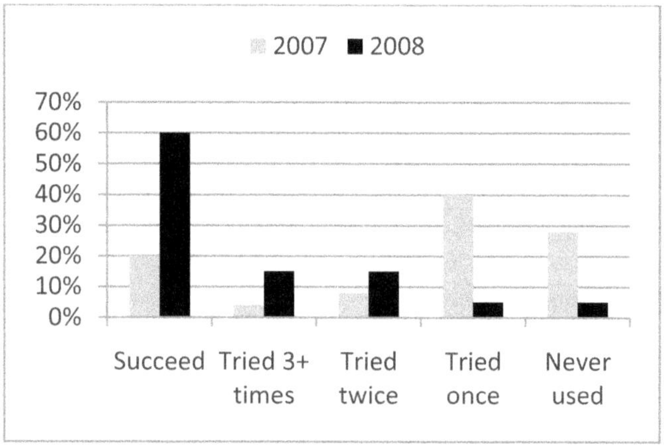

Figure 1. Workshop Adoption Rates

4.3 Workshop Survey Results

In addition to the data collected via server logs we also requested that attendees from both years participate in online surveys to help our understanding of why they chose to use or not use the system. Of the 45 total instructors that attended the workshops 28 (62%) participated in the online surveys. From these we identified 4 common barriers to adoption and 2 common circumstances that encouraged adoption.

4.3.1 Barriers

Barriers to adoption are critical to identify because when left unadressed their presence can result in an otherwise well designed workshop having minimal impact.

Technological Support. Lack of technological support was by far the most cited reason for not using UP in the classroom. This is despite the fact that all survey participants self-identified as "mostly" or "very" confident in their own technological ability. Many cited technological barriers that were outside their range of control such as "[Our] classroom environment [has] limited access or no access to Internet" and "none of my students have tablets, and many (most) don't bring laptops to class". These comments are interesting since those specific factors were asked about in the application process (where they were indicated not to be a problem). Surprisingly, 54% of survey participants indicated that it was difficult to get classes scheduled in technologically appropriate rooms. These barriers exist at the institution level and are hard for instructors to change.

Lack of Institutional Support. Some institutional support was intended to be built into the workshops in that institutional pairs

[1] For workshop attendees we manually determined non-test classrooms. To get the usage numbers for all users we selected classrooms with at least 5 students and 5 lectures.

of attendees were recommended. Still, many felt alone in trying to use UP in the classroom. Respondents stated they would have used UP more "if other faculty around me were more supportive of technology use in the classroom." They also said "lack of supportive environment within faculty at my home institution" discouraged use. 57% said they had not met with another UP-using faculty member at their institution, and 46% expected they would have used UP more if someone else in the department was using it too.

Perceived Time Commitment. 29% of survey respondents said the perceived time commitment of UP moderately or significantly deterred them from using the system. Specifics mentioned include "time to update slides was prohibitive to using UP in the classroom" and "time to prepare for uploading [and] editing."

Other Technology. Four study participants used other active learning teaching technologies adopted by their university (which resulted in them not using the UP system). This is not a barrier in terms of supporting student engagement with active learning, but it is a barrier to specific tool dissemination and reinforces the importance of institutional support.

4.3.2 *Positive Influences*

There were also influences positively affecting instructor adoption reported in the surveys.

Good Technology Support. Instructors who reported that they had good technology support at their home institution felt more confident about using UP in the classroom. One instructor credited their success to their IT person, saying they didn't have technological problems "in large part because my colleagues and [IT person], were very familiar with it". This level of technological support can be critical and may indicate that workshops should additionally focus on IT personnel who will be supporting instructors.

Community. "I worked in the team of other faculty who attended the workshop. Together we were helping each other." This respondent reflected our original goal of having pairs of participants support each other, but only one response of this type was noted.

4.3.3 *Suggestions*

In addition to asking participants to reflect on their own UP usage, we also asked them what suggestions they had for future workshops. A common suggestion was to devote more time to the introduction of the UP system. Of the participants who responded to the survey 90% had never used UP before and over 50% had never used a Tablet PC before. Both workshops included a session on learning to use UP, but respondents requested more time devoted to basic training at the expense of sessions on more general topics such as integrating active learning in the classroom. Several respondents suggested including practice presentations where they could practice using UP in front of each other (though at least one such opportunity was offered each workshop, not everyone managed to accomplish this). There were also requests for more follow up after the workshop with instructors to see how well they were doing at using the technology in the classroom and to offer advice when instructors had trouble.

5. DISCUSSION

Were these workshops successful? Is a 44% adoption rate a reasonable expectation for a project of this scope? What about a 22% adoption rate (which reflects those instructors who actively used UP for active learning – the stated workshop goal)? Is it still reasonable considering the investment per instructor, which included typical workshop costs plus $1600 towards a Tablet PC purchase? Ni reports one workshop-based effort to get teachers to adopt new curriculum [9]. They surveyed 36 summer workshop participants, 24 (67%) responded. Of respondents, 63% reported adopting or adapting workshop curricular materials. Making the most pessimistic assumption of non-respondents, the adoption rate would be similar to ours -- 42%. We hope to see more reports of adoption rates so that as a community we can develop a better understanding of what methods are successful in diffusing innovations.

Workshop Specific Recommendations. There are several observations we make concerning increasing the potential positive impact of faculty professional development workshops:

1) "Pre-meetings" can be an effective means to help get participants ready for a workshop – serving both to ensure they have done necessary technical and educational set-up, as well as helping them to get excited about the workshop to follow.

2) In order to increase response rates of participants concerning post-workshop work, it is important to repeatedly e-mail reminders to participants to complete surveys as well as following up with phone calls. Understanding regarding these commitments should be outlined at the time of application.

3) It is important for potential workshop organizers to realize the difference between a "one and done" workshop versus continual support. Clearly the latter is more effective (and helps more to build community among participants), but can be significantly more expensive (in terms of money and personnel) to implement. Future grant proposers should be aware of the differences.

4) Having institutional "partners" for closer institutional support still seems valuable, but perhaps within department pairs would be better or groups (2-5?) of faculty with a support IT person.

5) When considering participants from research-intensive institutions (who, in this case were quite likely to have greater benefit from the use of UP), it is important to know if such an activity will count towards promotion/tenure for the faculty member in terms of teaching and/or research (reporting on the effectiveness of the intervention).

6) Offering desirable "free stuff" can lead to faculty applying to attend a workshop for other reasons than improving student learning. In our case, it was necessary to offer faculty Tablet PCs, but this can be a problem.

7) It is essential to make clear what technology is needed, and to ensure that workshop attendees do have sufficient technology in the classrooms in which they'll be teaching and are comfortable using it.

8) It is hard to differentiate potential workshop attendees who are "innovators" (using Moore's [7] terminology) and who will overcome all technological hurdles at their home institution from those who are "early adopters", who won't. Workshop developers should be clear which group they are seeking to target.

Metrics for Measuring Diffusion. In a sense, measuring adoption of an innovation like the UP system is relatively easy. Because all use was logged on our server, we could effectively get data from all attendees, whether they elected to respond to us (via survey) or not. But the variation in use we saw emphasizes that innovation adoption is not a binary event. Variations on use, use in restricted forms, use of features (be they key or not) – are all important to recognize and assess. As we consider more global innovation diffusion metrics and data which would help describe the impact of various types of innovation diffusion techniques, we urge the community to consider:

- Define adoption (in various forms). How many courses did it impact? Was adoption maintained? Were there any 2nd-order adoption effects (e.g. others the adopters inspired)? Do you have a reliable source for measuring adoption?
- What kinds of adopters is your diffusion method targeting? Innovators (who are always trying the next thing), early adopters (who are looking to make lasting change using something new)? Is there support for 2nd order effect adopters – which could be a result of a train the trainers model or simply local diffusion enabled by an adopter.
- What were the goals of your recruitment methods? How well were they met? Did your recruitment attract the appropriate adopters? How did your recruitment affect diversity?
- How many students were impacted, and what was the "depth" of the impact? How many "learning hours" did this affect? Did variation in use among adopters affect the impact on students and how can that be used to guide adoption practices in the future?
- What are the barriers to adoption? Can you give both quantitative and qualitative descriptions of these barriers and their importance? What recommendations can you make for overcoming them?
- What was the cost of your method? What was the monetary cost per adopter? What was the cost in terms of required time commitment of adopter, both in "training" and in "deployment"? What was the cost to the trainer/disseminator?

6. CONCLUSIONS

This case study of two single-instance workshops found that the rate of instructor adoption can vary greatly depending on recruiting methods and workshop design (including pre-workshop events). We found that encouraging participants to make commitments in the application process increased the chances that the participant would later use the technology in the classroom.

We found that the workshops increased instructor usage by 20% and had a stronger increase in use of active learning features (in terms of instructors using active learning) when compared with the adoption rates of general users. However, we also found that non-workshop users who used active learning, used it more pervasively, with non-workshop active learning courses averaging 28 submissions per student over the course. This is in contrast to an average of 3 submissions per student in the 2007 courses, and 17 submissions per student in the 2008 courses.

Though pervasive active learning use was lower, overall general adoption rate by participants in the workshop was 44%, comparable to the rate reported by Ni [9]. We would encourage others disseminating through workshops or other forms to report on their successes and contribute to a more robust body of knowledge in this area.

7. ACKNOWLEDGMENTS

We thank our workshop participants for their patience, allowing us to report on their activities, and their time in responding to surveys. This work was funded, in part, by NSF DUE 0618511 and by the HP Technology for Teaching program.

8. REFERENCES

[1] Anderson, R. Anderson, R., Simon, B., Wolfman, S. VanDeGrift, R. and Yasuhara, K. Experiences with a Tablet PC Based Lecture Presentation System in Computer Science Courses. *SIGCSE 2004.*

[2] Bales, E., Griswold, W.G., Simon, B., Hieber, A., Kelly, M.J., Lintern, J., and Ouyang, D. USE OF UBIQUITOUS PRESENTER: 2006-2009. In *Workshop on the Impact of Pen-based Technology on Education* (2009).

[3] Harris, R.W. Teaching, Learning and Information Technology: Attitudes Towards Computers Among Hong Kong's Faculty. *Journal of Computing in Higher Education*, 9, 2 (1997), 89-114.

[4] Henderson, C. and Dancy, M.H. Barriers to the use of research-based instructional strategies: The influence of both individual and situational characteristics. *Physical Review Special Topics - Physics Education Research*, 3, 1 (2007), 020102-1-14.

[5] Hu, P., Clark, T., and Ma, W. Examining technology acceptance by school teachers: a longitudinal study. *Information and Management*, 41, 2 (December 2003), 227-241.

[6] Levy, R. B. and Ben-Ari, M. 2008. Perceived behavior control and its influence on the adoption of software tools. *ITiCSE 2008.*

[7] Moore, G. A. (2002) Crossing the chasm: Marketing and selling high-tech products to mainstream customers. Harper Collins Publishers, Inc., NY.

[8] Naps, T., Cooper, S., Koldehofe, B., Leska, C., Rößling, G., Dann, W., Korhonen, A., Malmi, L., Rantakokko, J., Ross, R. J., Anderson, J., Fleischer, R., Kuittinen, M., and McNally, M. 2003. Evaluating the educational impact of visualization. In Working Group Reports From ITiCSE 2003. D. Finkel, Ed. ITiCSE-WGR 2003. ACM, New York, NY, 124-136.

[9] Ni, L. What Makes CS Teachers Change? Factors Influencing CS Teachers' Adoption of Curriculum Innovations. *SIGCSE 2009.*

[10] Rogers, E. M. (2003) Diffusion of innovations, 5th ed. The Free Press, NY, NY.

[11] Wilkerson, M., Griswold, B., and Simon, B. Ubiquitous Presenter: Increasing Student Access and Control in an Digital Lecturing Environment. *SIGCSE 2005.*

[12] http://www.phrases.org.uk/meanings/226950.html

[13] http://www.nsf.gov/pubs/2010/nsf10544/nsf10544.htm

Analysis of Undergraduate Teaching Evaluations in Computer Science

Joshua T. Guerin and Daniel Michler
University of Kentucky
Department of Computer Science
773 F. Paul Anderson Tower
Lexington, KY 40506-0046
{jtguer2, dmmich2}@uky.edu

ABSTRACT

Undergraduate teaching evaluations are widely believed to be biased. We analyzed the evaluations from our department for all classes from 2000 through 2008, looking for specific biases. We looked for correlations between evaluation numbers and whether the course was required; how much time students spent on the course; student classification (freshman, sophomore, etc.), and expected grades. While all of these show correlations with teaching evaluation responses, the effect of each factor is not consistent over all questions and varied strongly depending on the evaluation question and the course level.

Categories and Subject Descriptors

K.3.2 [**Computing Milieux**]: COMPUTERS AND EDUCATION—*Computer and Information Science Education*

General Terms

Measurement, Performance

Keywords

Course Evaluation, Teaching Evaluation, Evaluation Bias, Linear Models

1. MOTIVATION

Many institutions use teaching evaluations as a primary tool for evaluating faculty teaching. Despite biases which may be inherent in these evaluations, they are often important factors in major departmental decisions including of tenure and promotion. In some instances these numbers are referenced directly, with little or no effort to control or correct for these biases.

This can lead to scenarios where high-quality instructors are resistant to teaching certain courses, understanding that difficult-to-control factors may have an unfair and negative impact on their evaluations. Introductory-level computer science courses provide a conspicuous example of this. Early courses in CS are not only required by computing related majors, but in many institutions are either required by other majors or are non-optional general requirements. Further, these courses introduce students to ideas and problem solving skills which may seem foreign, adding to both conceptual difficulty and time required to complete assignments. Lower scores in such courses may otherwise be comparable to seemingly higher scores in other courses.

In this paper we investigate potential sources of statistical biases in evaluations within our own department. We show that linear models developed directly from evaluation data provide a good model for the data, and can be used to identify and correct for some biases.

2. RELATED WORK

The efficacy and appropriate application of teaching and instructor evaluations have been a topic of much discussion in the higher education community. Many believe that there are varied biases in teaching evaluations based on teaching and grading style, course-specific attributes (course level, requiredness, material difficulty), and inherent attributes of the instructor (gender, age, race). Others are likely to disagree with one or more of these asserted sources of bias. Moreover, the question of evaluating teachers has moved beyond academic circles, gaining more mainstream interest [5].

Intuitions regarding evaluation biases have been the focus of detailed study over the years, and several sources of biases have been confirmed. For example, researchers have noted a correlation between grades obtained and scores on teaching evaluations [6, 7]. Larsson et al. showed that even grades achieved early in the semester may be correlated with course evaluations at the end of the semester [8]. Similarly, relative course difficulty and workload have also been shown to have an effect on course evaluations [4]. Numerous studies have been conducted regarding evaluation biases, but conclusions are not always consistent. Additionally, evaluation biases may not be consistent across universities [2]. For a review on the study of evaluation biases see [1].

Studies of course evaluation bias have been conducted in a number of university departments, however studies examining evaluation biases in the field of computer science remain conspicuously sparse. One of the few studies that does concern bias in CS course evaluations is "What impacts course evaluation?" by Larsson et al. [8]. Their research differs from our study in both primary focus and methodology.

SIGCSE'11, March 9–12, 2011, Dallas, Texas, USA.

They asked questions related to how evaluations changed as a function of time (both between semesters and as a semester progressed) and medium (web based vs. paper evaluations). Their methodology included direct comparison of course evaluations administered at four points throughout the semester as well as evaluations from past semesters.

Instead, we are asking about how factors related to the specific course (required/elective, hours students spent on the course), the student's classification (freshmen, sophomore, etc.), and the student's perception of the course (belief about grade obtained) influence their ratings. Using these factors we learn linear models for several questions related to instructor quality (e.g. OVERALL QUALITY OF TEACHING) and course utility (e.g. OVERALL VALUE OF THE COURSE).

These models serve as a more neutral metrics for individual evaluation questions because they account for variance within course evaluations with respect to multiple biases. In this study we used end of semester evaluation data spanning multiple years for all courses in our department. We do not have access to intermediate measurements (beginning or mid-semester measurements). Because of this we seek to detect biases inherent in course evaluations which can be accounted for by data contained in the evaluations.

3. TEACHING EVALUATIONS AT OUR UNIVERSITY

3.1 Content

Teaching evaluations at our university are divided into sections based on question content. In this study we evaluated five primary categories: information about the student, course items, instructor items, learning outcomes, and summary items. Student information includes classification of the student (freshman to graduate student, professional, other), expected grade (A to E/Fail, Incomplete, Pass or Audit), reason for taking course (Required by University Studies Program, Required by major, Other (e.g., elective)) and hours spent per week on the course (1 or less, 2, 3, 4–5, 6–7, 8+).

Course items include questions regarding the textbook, examinations, the grading for the course, and the initial outline of course material and grading procedures by the instructor. Many of these are also relevant to the instructor as well as the course, but aren't directly relevant to the teaching. Instructor items focus on teaching of the primary instructor. Questions include how effectively material was presented, the instructor's knowledge of the subject, and how well interest was stimulated in the subject. Learning outcomes focus on the success of the course/instructor at teaching general items, such as respecting different viewpoints, analyzing information, and concepts in the field of study. Summary questions ask the student to provide a single rating for an entire course or instructor. There are two summary questions: RATE THE OVERALL VALUE OF THIS COURSE and RATE THE OVERALL QUALITY OF TEACHING BY THE PRIMARY INSTRUCTOR OF THE THIS COURSE.

Possible answers to questions are consistent across broader categories of questions, and are provided by the student using fill-in bubbles. Available answers are an ordered set of Likert-style responses. Students are explicitly instructed to mark only one response per question. For course items, instructor items, and learning outcomes, possible responds to questions are: STRONGLY DISAGREE, DISAGREE, AGREE, STRONGLY AGREE, or NOT APPLICABLE. For the two summary items, possible responses are: POOR, FAIR, GOOD, and EXCELLENT.

Table 1: Evaluation Data Totals.

Level	Total	100	200	300	400	500	600
Evaluations	1,216	628	153	77	98	130	130
Responses	16,091	6,987	1,872	1,600	1,903	2,180	1,549
Avg Resp	13.23	11.13	12.24	20.78	19.42	16.77	11.92

3.2 Evaluation Totals

Our data includes a total of 1,216 section evaluations for 60 different computer science courses. Each section evaluation consists of the aggregate ratings of the students who filled out the evaluation form. This information was parsed from publicly available data provided by the university.[1] The first row of Table 1 shows how these evaluations are distributed by course level.

Our courses are typically categorized by their most significant digit (of three). The 100-level courses are typically for freshman and 400-level courses are typically senior undergraduate courses. We also consider 500-level courses, which are open to advanced undergraduates and new graduate students, and 600-level courses which are are almost exclusively graduate courses. Our data consists of all available computer science course evaluations from the academic years of 2000 through 2008 at our university.

It is important to note that these numbers represent the total number of course sections accounted for, and that they are irrespective of either course enrollment (which was not recorded in the evaluation data) or participation in the evaluation procedure. Because students may not fill out all survey sections, or may make different decisions regarding the applicability of questions or entire sections, it is difficult to get concrete numbers regarding how many students these totals represent. We found that in many instances this inconsistency included student information (classification, expected grade, etc.).

In order to get an approximation of how many students these totals represent we calculated totals based on the number of students that responded to the summary item RATE THE OVERALL VALUE OF THIS COURSE. The overall total calculated in this manner is 16,091 students, or an average of approximately 13 responses per course evaluation. The results of this calculation by course level are reported in the second row of Table 1.

As expected from a large undergraduate institution, we find a greater total number of students enrolling in low level courses, therefore more course sections are needed at the 100 level. In our case this is largely because at least one introductory level computer science course is required for majors of all engineering disciplines. Total responses by course decrease as course level increases, ranging from 4888 responses in CS 101 (Intro to Computers) to as low as 2 responses for CS 673 (a graduate course in Error Correcting Codes).

The average number of responses per section are recorded in the third row of Table 1. Despite the large enrollment for introductory courses in our major, highest responses per

[1] A public link to this data can be provided by either author upon request.

section are recorded for mid and upper level undergraduate courses (300 and 400 level).

4. METHODS

Potential sources of bias we tested are: student's expected grades, student classification, hours spent per week on the course, and requiredness of the course (required by major, university studies, etc). Each of these possible sources of bias are treated as predicting dependent variables, or factors, in our model. For each question we ran a linear regression with each factor as a predicting variable and the corresponding question answers as the dependant variable. This creates a line by minimizing the sum of the squares of the distance between the line and the data points in a multidimensional space.

To run linear regression on Likert scales we first adjusted the scale to a continuous distribution. There are known issues with this sort of conversion. For instance, the resulting distribution may not be a normal distribution. It is possible that this could detrimentally effect our metrics of performance (the adjusted r^2 value), however it should not invalidate the model or the significance of the factors [3].

We modeled how each of these questions is affected by each factor, from which we can infer where and how biases affect evaluation questions. For example, if we find that requiredness is strongly negatively correlated with view of the teacher we infer that teachers get worse evaluations when they teach required courses rather than electives.

For each factor we looked at multiple measures to determine their importance and effects on the questions. For each model we looked at adjusted r^2 value, the coefficient of determination, which describes the percent of the data's total variance which the model accounts for. For each individual factor we examined p values, which are the probabilities of a false positives (considering a factor significant when it is not). For our model we chose to accept values of p where $p < .05$ as significant. We will refer to this as our significance threshold.

For each question we generated seven linear models. The first of which is a full model, constructed using evaluations from all CS courses. Because student demographic varies greatly with the course level in our department, we also constructed individual models for each course level up to 600. While the first model gives us a big-picture view of how biases affect evaluations from the entire department, the additional models give us indications about how the effects of biases may change with respect to course level.

5. RESULTS

Results of our analysis are provided in Tables 2–9.[2] Tables 2–8 detail the significance of each factor (p) for a given question. Table 9 provides the adjusted r^2 value for each model generated. "Strike-through" style text identifies instances where the p value for an entire model did not meet our significance threshold. Additionally, p values in Tables 2–8 that meet our threshold of .05 are in boldface.

[2]In order to conserve space, evaluation questions are condensed in a way which preserves the question's meaning. For instance, the question RATE THE OVERALL QUALITY OF TEACHING BY THE PRIMARY INSTRUCTOR IN THIS COURSE. appears as OVERALL QUALITY OF TEACHING BY INSTRUCTOR in tables displaying results.

As shown in Table 1, it is important to note that stronger conclusions should be drawn from models over all courses as well as 100 level courses due to the availability of more data points. Because of the greater availability of data for full models (labeled "All" in tables), these models will be the primary focus of our analysis. In Section 5.1 we discuss factor significance and variance for models generated over all course levels. In section 5.2 we discuss some of the trends seen when modeling by course level.

5.1 Modeling over all CS courses

We found that p values were typically lowest when models are constructed using all computer science courses. This may be due in part to the large sample size available when modeling the entire department, which would allow trends to emerge that are not available at individual course levels. For these models all values are significant at $p < .01$.

We find that both expected grade and hours spent per week were significant in all models, with $p < 2 * 10^{-16}$ in more than half of the models.

The student classification and course requiredness both met the significance threshold in more than half of the full models, with student classification being significant in six and student classification being significant in five of the seven questions tested.

In all questions tested we were able to account for at least 26% of the total variance for full models across the board, with the highest variance accounted for being 43.87%. Of the questions evaluated we accounted for the largest amount of variance for summary items and items related to learning outcomes (all >32% of variance as seen in Table 9), indicating that they are most influenced by the four factors.

For the summary question OVERALL QUALITY OF TEACHING BY THE INSTRUCTOR we were able to account for over 32% of the total variance. For summary question OVERALL VALUE OF THE COURSE we were able to account for over 40% of total variance in the data. For the learning outcome related question THE COURSE STIMULATED ME TO READ FURTHER we accounted for over 43% of the variance (the highest value of r^2 that we found) and for THE INSTRUCTOR STIMULATED MY INTEREST IN THE SUBJECT we accounted for over 40% of the variance.

5.2 Modeling by course level

Despite lower volumes of data available for models generated by course level, we find evidence of some interesting trends (or discrepancies depending on your perspective) that emerge when looking at courses by level. At the graduate level (600) none of the factors are deemed significant for 5 of the questions examined. The models for 600 level courses also poorly account for variance within the data as seen in Table 9. Additionally, over the seven 600 level models generated, six failed to meet our significance threshold.

Discrepancies at the 600 level may be partially due to limited evaluations available, however as shown in Table 1, totals for 600 level courses are comparable to those at other levels. While there is not enough evidence to support the claim that graduate level courses may be less biased in general, this evidence indicates that the biases tested have less of an effect on graduate level courses at our university.

Courses at the 200 level may appear to share modeling similarities to those at the 600 level. However, at the 200 level the majority of models meet the significance threshold,

Table 2: Factor significance (p) for "Overall quality of teaching by instructor".

	All	100	200	300	400	500	~~600~~
Expected Grade	**<2e-16**	**1.24E-06**	**0.00644**	**0.000135**	**0.000841**	**1.34E-10**	~~0.114~~
Requiredness	**0.00429**	0.07846	0.27361	0.121843	0.095432	0.143568	~~0.457~~
Hours/week	**<2e-16**	**3.27E-08**	0.97167	0.228574	0.056315	**0.025121**	~~0.857~~
Student Classification	**0.00192**	**0.00124**	0.15137	0.584178	0.526633	0.461251	~~0.49~~

Table 3: Factor significance (p) for "Overall value of course".

	All	100	200	300	400	500	~~600~~
Expected Grade	**<2e-16**	**2.13E-08**	**0.00016**	**3.65E-08**	**0.000237**	**3.49E-12**	~~0.283~~
Requiredness	**0.000517**	0.18738	0.084938	0.682	0.076	0.18389	~~0.846~~
Hours/week	**<2e-16**	**5.58E-16**	0.568035	**0.0021**	**0.013767**	**0.00624**	~~0.444~~
Student Classification	0.054175	**0.000576**	0.829094	0.1104	0.49605	0.97415	~~0.335~~

Table 4: Factor significance (p) for "Material was presented in an effective manner".

	All	100	200	300	400	500	~~600~~
Expected Grade	**<2e-16**	**7.91E-06**	**0.000864**	**0.000107**	**0.015**	**3.36E-08**	~~0.124~~
Requiredness	**0.00122**	0.13627	0.510186	**0.017597**	0.1282	0.0886	~~0.281~~
Hours/week	**<2e-16**	**3.23E-06**	0.97412	0.199502	0.1571	**0.0107**	~~0.567~~
Student Classification	**0.00832**	**0.00137**	0.150507	0.870019	0.5045	0.8475	~~0.684~~

Table 5: Factor significance (p) for "Instructor had a good knowledge of subject".

	All	100	~~200~~	300	~~400~~	500	~~600~~
Expected Grade	**0.000687**	**0.0274**	~~0.0534~~	0.235	~~0.20635~~	**0.0099**	~~0.082~~
Requiredness	0.133357	0.6299	~~0.9097~~	**0.0408**	~~0.066529~~	0.2157	~~0.891~~
Hours/week	**<2e-16**	**7.10E-05**	~~0.3713~~	**0.0401**	~~0.587313~~	**0.0496**	~~0.4221~~
Student Classification	**4.88E-08**	0.1404	~~0.1996~~	0.0852	~~0.695043~~	**0.0473**	~~0.1924~~

Table 6: Factor significance (p) for "The course stimulated me to read further".

	All	100	200	300	400	500	~~600~~
Expected Grade	**<2e-16**	**6.75E-06**	**0.000873**	**8.28E-06**	**1.25E-05**	**8.24E-16**	~~0.109~~
Requiredness	**1.68E-07**	**0.0199**	0.306635	**0.04024**	**0.0253**	0.0824	~~0.918~~
Hours/week	**<2e-16**	**6.02E-10**	0.057486	**0.00284**	0.5315	**9.38E-06**	~~0.781~~
Student Classification	**0.0096**	**0.0021**	0.855987	**0.01635**	0.3063	0.0974	~~0.946~~

Table 7: Factor significance (p) for "The instructor stimulated my interest in the subject".

	All	100	200	300	400	500	~~600~~
Expected Grade	**<2e-16**	**8.49E-07**	**0.000218**	**9.89E-06**	**0.00151**	**2.21E-12**	~~**0.0292**~~
Requiredness	**1.14E-05**	0.10626	0.263293	0.7781	**0.04064**	**0.01986**	~~0.5976~~
Hours/week	**<2e-16**	**1.64E-09**	0.304724	**0.0344**	0.38441	**0.00141**	~~0.8242~~
Student Classification	**0.000275**	**0.00205**	0.14186	0.1284	0.41762	0.70857	~~0.6693~~

Table 8: Factor significance (p) for "Grading in the course was fair and consistent".

	All	100	200	300	400	500	600
Expected Grade	**<2e-16**	**6.97E-08**	**5.46E-05**	**1.08E-06**	**2.81E-07**	**1.26E-09**	**0.000901**
Requiredness	0.15687	0.53	0.7023	0.996	0.075339	0.368	0.447425
Hours/week	**9.74E-08**	**0.039**	0.9073	0.632	0.087219	0.951	**0.018935**
Student Classification	**0.000657**	0.398	0.0931	0.422	0.57531	0.763	0.789576

Table 9: **Percent of variance accounted for by model.**

Question	Adjusted r^2						
	All	100	200	300	400	500	600
Overall quality of teaching by instructor	0.3271	0.1182	0.1071	0.1903	0.1967	0.3135	~~-0.0004681~~
Overall value of course	0.4099	0.1995	0.1785	0.4123	0.2555	0.3519	~~-0.01486~~
Material was presented in an effective manner	0.29	0.09362	0.133	0.2124	0.1032	0.2466	~~-0.004994~~
Instructor had a good knowledge of subject	0.2629	0.042	~~0.03478~~	0.1201	~~0.01399~~	0.09165	~~0.02471~~
The course stimulated me to read further	0.4387	0.1336	0.1514	0.3901	0.258	0.4608	~~-0.002755~~
The instructor stimulated my interest in the subject	0.4097	0.1288	0.1878	0.288	0.1563	0.3751	0.01398
Grading in the course was fair and consistent	0.29	0.06956	0.1721	0.3337	0.3471	0.28	~~0.1061~~

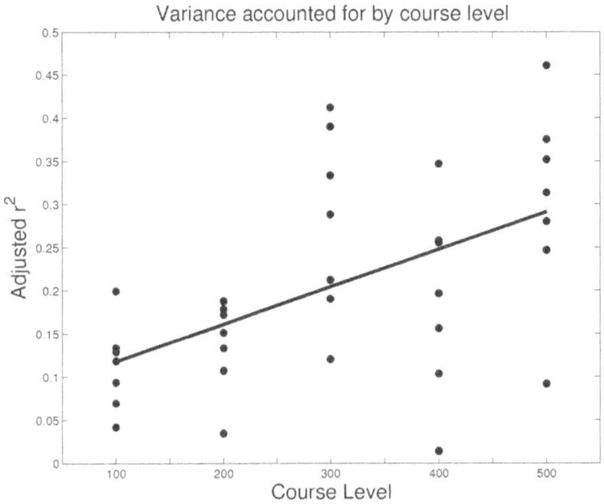

Figure 1: Variance accounted for by course level.

and in all accepted models expected grade met our significance threshold. Further, total variance accounted for by accepted models at the 200 level accounted for significantly more variance than models at the 600 level.

With the exception of 600 level courses, average total variance accounted for by models increases as a function of course level. The scatter plot in Figure 1 the percent of variance accounted for by course level, for levels 100–500. The positive slope of the line indicates that the effects these biases grow stronger as course level increases.

6. CONCLUSION

In this paper we analyzed course evaluations from our computer science department, using linear modeling techniques to discover inherent biases. We tested seven evaluation questions related to the quality of instructor and the value of the course. We tested the following evaluation biases: expected grade, course requiredness, the number of hours a student spent per week on assignments, and the student's classification (freshman, sophomore, etc.). We discovered not only that these variables correlated with teaching evaluations, but that the significance of the effects of these biases varies strongly with the both questions being asked and approximate course level.

We have demonstrated that despite these bias variations, informative models can be generated from the evaluation data of all courses in a department. Some specific trends we observed were:

- students' expected grade and the number of hours that a student spent per week had a significant effect on all questions tested,
- student classification and requiredness had a significant effect on the majority of questions tested,
- graduate-level course evaluations appear largely unaffected by the biases tested,
- with the exception of graduate level courses, the effects of these biases appears to increase as a function of course level.

Linear models indicated where biases exist in our computer science course evaluations, and provide a rough indication of the strength of each bias.

We believe that straight numeric values from teaching evaluations are not, by themselves, good indicators of the value of classes and teaching. Rather, departments should run similar analyses, and should pay attention to the operative biases for each category of course when using teaching evaluations.

7. ACKNOWLEDGMENTS

The authors would like to thank University Statistical Consultant Adam Lindstrom from the SSTARS lab for answering numerous question regarding statistical analysis and validation. We would also like to thank Dr. Judy Goldsmith for her input, and the Department of Computer Science, University of Kentucky for partial support of this research.

8. REFERENCES

[1] L. M. Aleamoni and P. Z. Hexner. A review of the research on student evaluation and a report on the effect of different sets of instructions on student course and instructor evaluation. Instructional Science, 19:67–84, 1980.

[2] N. A. Bowling. Does the relationship between student ratings of course easiness and course quality vary across schools? the role of school academic rankings. Assessment and Evaluation in Higher Education, 33(4):455–464, August 2008.

[3] J. Carifio and P. J. Rocco. Ten common misunderstandings, misconceptions, persistent myths and urban legends about likert scales and likert response formats and their antidotes. Journal of Social Sciences, 3(3):106–116, 2007.

[4] J. A. Centra. Will teachers receive higher student evaluations by giving higher grades and less course work? Research in Higher Education, 44(5):495–518, 2003.

[5] S. Dillon. Formula to grade teachers' skill gains acceptance, and critics. `http://www.nytimes.com/2010/09/01/education/01teacher.html`, August 2010. Last accessed September 8, 2010.

[6] L. C. Hamilton. Grades, class size, and faculty status predict teaching evaluations. Teaching Sociology, 8(1):47–62, 1980.

[7] A. C. Krautmann and W. Sander. Grades and student evaluations of teachers. Economics of Education Review, 18(1):59 – 63, 1999.

[8] E. Larsson, M. Amirijoo, D. Karlsson, and P. Eles. What impacts course evaluation? SIGCSE Bull., 39(3):333–333, 2007.

The Use of Evidence in the Change Making Process of Computer Science Educators

Davide Fossati
Computer Science Department
Carnegie Mellon University
dfossati@cmu.edu

Mark Guzdial
College of Computing
Georgia Institute of Technology
guzdial@cc.gatech.edu

ABSTRACT

This paper explores the issue of what kind of evidence triggers changes in the teaching practice of Computer Science educators, and how educators evaluate the effectiveness of those changes. We interviewed 14 Computer Science instructors from three different institutions. Our study indicates that changes are mostly initiated from instructors' intuition, informal discussion with students, and anecdotal evidence.

Categories and Subject Descriptors

K.3.2 [**Computer and Information Science Education**]: Computer science education

General Terms

Human Factors

1. INTRODUCTION

This paper investigates the question of what kind of evidence triggers and informs changes in the everyday teaching practice of Computer Science educators. As educators, we want to be constantly improving our practice. Success depends on identifying the opportunities or need for improvement, implementing appropriate changes, and then (iteratively) evaluating whether the change met the need.

Our community is productive in providing tools for implementing change. A number of innovative approaches for teaching introductory Computer Science have been designed, such as Beyond LEGOs [3], Media Computation [14], and TeachScheme [9]. Many software systems to support new teaching approaches have been developed, such as Scratch [23] and Alice [6], as well as tools such as algorithm visualization systems [25] and intelligent tutoring systems for Computer Science topics [20, 12].

Researchers are studying the factors that influence adoption of these teaching innovations [21, 22, 16, 8]: What leads a teacher to choose one kind of implementation versus another? These studies explore both catalysts and barriers to change. For example, Ni [22] reports external pressure, limited time, poor background of students, and conflicting views on desired learning outcomes as barriers to change. She also highlights that perceived benefits for students, well-defined pedagogical recommendations, and successful first-hand experience with new approaches are catalysts to innovation adoption. Thus, we know a good bit about innovative approaches, and what leads to their adoption.

In this study, we would like to understand the factors that influence teachers' decisions at a more microscopic level. The teacher has to make decisions about where there is a need for change, and whether the change is effective at meeting the need. For example, why would a teacher change a specific example, a homework assignment, or the format of a group project? Once a change is made, how does a teacher decide whether the change addressed the concern that initiated the change? If those decisions are not made well (e.g., a change is made to something that wasn't really broken, or a change is actually ineffective when judged successful), we are not actually improving practice when we make change.

Specifically, we are interested in understanding the role of *evidence* in the decision making process of instructors. Researchers have spent some effort in understanding and affirming the important role of evidence in higher-level educational policy and practice [5]. The use of formal evidence is also an essential component of accreditation programs such as ABET [1]. Less attention has been devoted to the use of evidence in the the design decisions in classroom.

Our study aims to provide an initial understanding of this issue in the context of Computer Science education. We interviewed 14 Computer Science instructors from three higher education institutions in the United States, and we extracted the recurring themes in the interviewees' answers. These answers suggest the predominance of instructors' intuition, informal discussion with students, and anecdotal reports as the primary evidence used to inform practical decisions.

2. METHODOLOGY

We interviewed 14 Computer Science instructors, most of them teaching in large research institutions in the Midwest. The background and range of expertise of the interviewees spanned across the majority of sub-disciplines in Computer Science. Some of the instructors were full-time lecturers, whereas others were mostly dedicated to research. The range of classes taught by these instructors also ranged from introductory CS courses for undergraduate students to advanced elective classes taken mostly by graduate students. All the interviews were audio recorded.

We asked the instructors to recall episodes in which they implemented a change in their instructional practice. In particular, we asked for examples in which the change worked well, and cases in which the change did not work as expected. Then, we asked them to speculate on why those changes worked well, or did not work as expected. Then, we asked what triggered the change, and what kind of evidence was used to determine that a change was needed. A detailed script of the interview questions can be found at *http://www.fossati.us/papers/cschange-interview.pdf*. All the instructors felt comfortable answering these questions, and provided detailed and insightful answers.

The audio recordings of the interviews were fully transcribed by a professional transcription service. The transcripts were analyzed by a single annotator (one of the authors of this paper) who iterated through the answers extracting, summarizing, aggregating, and counting the recurring themes. These themes were not specified in advance, and emerged entirely from the data. Because the analysis was carried out by only one annotator, we cannot report any measure of inter-coder reliability.

3. RESULTS

3.1 Inventory of changes

Each instructor reported at least one example of successful change and one instance of failure. The episodes ranged from the simple change of a textbook to the introduction of more sophisticated pedagogical strategies, such as peer-supported interaction. They are summarized in Tables 1 and 2. We report some of these episodes, as voiced by the instructors, in the following subsections.

Table 1: Success stories

Teacher	Description
T01	Increased the number of examples in class
T02	Introduced short quizzes in class
T03	Introduced peer-share interactions between students
T04	Had students work with a real database system
T05	Presented more actual code in class
T06	Changed paper presentations in classroom into critical analysis of the papers
T07	Introduced a new class in software engineering
T08	Asked students to write a short evaluation essay after every homework assignment
T09	Introduced the JFLAP animator of finite state automata in a theory course
T10	Introduced short bursts of collaborative work in class
T11	Kept a consistent picture making links between two courses in the same sequence
T12	Switched to programming languages with better tools
T13	Started doing in-class design exercises, using props like cards to get students out of the seats and talk to each other, thinking up design ideas.
T14	Gave lab exercises to practice the programming constructs just explained

Table 2: Failures

Teacher	Description
T01	Wanted students to give presentations on various topics
T02	Asked for a teaching evaluation in the middle of the semester
T03	Developed a complicated example that students found boring
T04	Had students write term papers
T05	Reduced the number of quizzes
T06	Moved from open projects to constrained projects
T07	Removed Smalltalk from an object-oriented programming class
T08	Introduced audio-recordings of the lectures
T09	Changed the textbook
T10	Had students give project presentations
T11	Used both Fortran and Matlab in the same course
T12	Used Java in a course where you needed a language that requires the programmer to take care of more details
T13	Tried stepping through code in a very detailed way using PowerPoint in class
T14	Tried some peer-programming by letting students work on projects together

3.1.1 *Success stories*

One of the instructors implemented peer-sharing activities in class after being exposed to this methodology himself in a workshop. In this quote, we see both the instructor's decision to implement an innovation, and how the instructor judged the innovation to be successful.

> T03: The person at the seminar was talking about pedagogy, ways that we teach. Typically, in a class, you know, the lecturer might ask a question to get the audience to participate, but this person did something different. He called it "Peer-share." He said, "I want you to turn to the person next to you, and I want you to ask them this question." I don't even remember what the topic was. But the exercise of peer-share really struck me because all of us got to vocalize. Then after that, he had a few people talk, but everybody got to participate. So, that really struck me.
>
> So, then I started doing that in my classes, and that's been very effective. [...] I think it worked from a practical sense that people were able to participate, speak out loud. So, they were interacting with the material with a different mode of interaction, rather than listening passively. Socially, it also helps because often students in Introductory Programming class have questions, but they're afraid to ask because they might appear ignorant. So, by asking the person

> next to them if that person also doesn't understand, then they feel confident that it's a good question to ask the entire class.

The following example is an alternative implementation on the same line of enabling peer interaction. In both of these cases, the teacher is identifying a need for increased collaboration as a desired change, implemented a methodology designed to enable collaboration, and then evaluated whether the methodology succeeded.

> T10: One of the changes that I implemented, and it really worked well, and then carried it through all my classes is little bursts, like five-minute collaborative work in class. So, I after I explain something, I typically pose a question which is just a tiny extension of the concept that was just explained or a variation. I let the students sort of turn to a neighbor, shake his or her hand, and do five minutes of brainstorming.
>
> [...] In general, my teaching style is very interactive. So, I ask questions and actually expect answers from a class, even if it's a 50-people class. But the problem with asking questions of 50 people is that only one or two ever sort of engage and give answers, and I want the whole class to be engaged. I want the whole class to actually think for a second about the concept that's just been explained, and internalize it. The only way I see of doing it is if they actually have to work with somebody else, and they have to either explain or ask questions of somebody else.

A different motivation from collaboration was a desire for greater authenticity. Generally, instructors believe that greater authenticity leads to greater motivation. Another instructor reflected on the need to provide students with hands-on experience with real systems.:

> T04: When I was first handed a database textbook and told to go teach it, we were using Date, which is a very well-written book, but we didn't have an actual system for people to work with. Once we got one, people were more interested, more motivated then trying to make things really work. That was effective. That's something that I guess happens in every Computer Science classroom. People really need practical examples to understand what it is they're doing effectively at a certain time.
>
> Then I started dividing the course up into groups and having groups of people construct actual databases for real applications. That also turned out to be an improvement. It turned out not to be sustainable as the class got to be 50 or 60 people. So, I had to give it up. But I kept those applications so that people could at least work with a variety of applications. [...]
>
> I think it worked well because the students got greater understanding from hands-on usage, but also because I think the groups worked well because the people involved had to explain things to each other and argue with each other, and consider alternative implementations.

Sometimes the motivations for change are external to the instructor. The following instructor successfully integrated students' feedback on previous homework assignments in his design of the homework assignments in the same course in the next iteration:

> T08: The one significant change I did after my first offering in class was that after every programming homework, I expect students to submit an essay, you know of ten lines, telling me the highs and lows of the homework. So, I make them reflect on the homework and give it a difficulty rating between zero and ten. Then what were the parts they found difficult? Were there any problems in the homework handout description, and all kinds of things. So, I made them sit and reflect on the homework after they have finished it for some time.
>
> Then I collect all the essays and I read them. Then if there was some problem with the homework, the way things are worded and so on, I made the changes to the homework so that next time around —I can't go back and change it for that class— but next time around I can at least make that experience better. So, over time, I see that there's a little bit better description of homeworks. I also know where the problem areas in homeworks are, and try to address that in my lecture.

3.1.2 Failures

Sometimes things don't work as expected. A common factor, like in the success stories, is the desire to generate increased motivation among the students. The following story shows how even a well-thought example in class might prove boring to the students:

> T03: I developed this long example that I thought was interesting. But as I presented it to this class, very smart kids in the top high school here, I realized that it was boring to them. I realized that they were just doing the exercise just to get the answer and they didn't connect it to things that were more meaningful. It was not good. [...]
>
> It didn't work because there were no follow on questions. It didn't make them excited. It didn't make them want to do it again. It didn't make them want to keep it, and do it at home with their friends or their brothers or sisters. I think good pedagogy, and good training, good examples lead you to more, rather than being closed-ended.

A teacher might decide that an idea is good, but the particular implementation is flawed. In this example, the teacher was also responding to student requests, but felt that the result was a failure due to the technical implementation of what seemed to be a good idea:

> T08: So, there was a time when I was trying to experiment with audio recordings for my lectures. Basically, you know, people wanted it. I, therefore, recorded my lectures and tried to put

Table 3: Reasons for success of instructional changes

Reason	Frequency
Motivation	8 (57%)
Practice, hands-on	3 (21%)
Environment and tools	3 (21%)

> it online. But without the proper context, you know, where I was in the slides and so on, it just didn't work. [...]
>
> It did not work because I was not screen-casting. I think what's important there is to do the screen-casting, you know, where you record both the screen and the voice.

Teaching is highly contextualized. The same idea may fail with a different course, set of students, or specific teacher. In this example, the teacher has decided that the idea of "peer-programming" (or pair-programming [19]), which has been highly successful in the literature, failed in hes course because of the context of her students:

> T14: I did at one point try to do a little bit of peer-programming. This was at my other job. So, I'd let people work on projects together. What wound up happening is one person would do the project, and the other person wouldn't be involved at all. So, I don't think that worked particularly well in that situation.
>
> I'm doing the same thing in my current job though, and I think it works better just because the traditional students in there are around and they're able to work together, where I had adults that just weren't able to do that.
>
> [...] That's why I think it didn't work is that they just weren't able to spend time working together.

3.2 Reasons for success and failure

In the previous section, we already saw some examples of how the instructors explained their success and failure stories. Overall, a fairly structured pattern emerged from the teachers' reflections on the causes of success or failure of their interventions (Tables 3 and 4). The responses were not mutually exclusive, so the percentages reported in the tables do not necessarily sum up to 100%.

The majority of instructors credited the success of the change to motivational factors such as improved student participation and interaction; positive support for creativity and confidence; variety; and more appeal to the students. Another success factor mentioned by some of the instructors is the increased engagement of students in hands-on activities, such as programming assignments or projects dealing with interesting real-world problems. Other teachers mentioned environmental factors such as better programming environments, useful tools, and effective visualizations, as reasons for success.

Blame was attributed to the background of students; motivational issues; organization or presentation of the information; and technical or logistical issues.

Table 4: Reasons for failure of instructional changes

Reason	Frequency
Background of students	4 (29%)
Motivation, appeal to students	3 (21%)
Presentation, organization of the material	3 (21%)
Technical, logistical issues	2 (14%)

Table 5: Evidence that triggered the change

Response	Frequency
Informal discussions with students; anecdotal reports; reaction of students	9 (64%)
Reflections of the instructor; feeling, perception, intuition	9 (64%)
Bad student performance; test results	4 (29%)
Perceived a need for constant change	3 (21%)
Teaching evaluation from students	2 (14%)
Opinion of the department, other teachers	2 (14%)
Research results, literature	2 (14%)

3.3 Triggers of change

When asked about what triggered the change and what kind of evidence was used to determine that a change was needed, the instructors elaborated on several reasons, summarized in Table 5. The responses were not mutually exclusive, so the percentages do not sum up to 100%. Overall,, the answers revealed that some kind of informal evidence was used, such as informal discussion with some students — maybe just the top students, as one instructor explicitly commented, implying a particular focus or value from the instructor:

> T12: Oftentimes, there's a set of the top students in there. You know, you build up a rapport and you start talking to them about different stuff. In this, they give you kind of a feedback. They'll say, "Well, you know, I just didn't understand why we covered this. It seemed like a waste of time." It's like, okay.

Some instructors verbalized the conflict between a perceived —or requested— need for formal evidence, and the real driving factors:

> T13: Well, I would love to say that I was carefully monitoring the students the whole time, and once a certain percentage became bored, I switched over. But really it was just the dictates of the curriculum. I mean, I could tell, you know, that the lectures weren't the best thing to use.

> T12: But it almost always seems that you feel the need is there. Then it's almost with the ABET stuff that you almost have to go about and, "Okay. We feel the need. We want to make this change. Oh, look! Here's a statistic that we can use to prove this." Okay. We're just pulling that statistic in just to, "Okay. Good. We can check off the ABET box and said we did it in there."

Sometimes it was a combination of anecdotal evidence, teaching evaluations, and general observation of student performance, with informal evidence being the main reason:

> T05: It's really anecdotal mostly, I guess. But student performance seemed to degrade a little bit, a few comments from evaluations that indicated that there was a feeling that the structure wasn't as strong. Of course, these weren't students that had taken it in the other form, but this is my inference. But it's a little anecdotal.

Some instructors felt that there is an explicit need for constant change in teaching Computer Science:

> T07: Well, in Computer Science you always think about change. Things change all the time. So, you cannot teach the same course, except for certain materials.

Sometimes external forces, such as pressure from the Department, played a role into the instructors' decisions:

> T11: That one was based upon my opinion. Part of it was from the Department saying, "Hey, we want more MATLAB," and part of it was I thought my experience was that these other disciplines, the syntax of any one language is not the problem.

Only a few instructors mentioned test scores and student performance as their primary source of evidence. But even when evidence was cited, it was not often used to target a particular need to change:

> T14: My first exam. They did not do very well. So, that's self-explanatory.

4. DISCUSSION

Education is a designed activity, and can be studied like any other design activity [24]. When they make decisions, teachers are engaging in a design process, specifically, an instructional design process [13]. Specifically, some researchers have talked about creating a science of studying educational design decisions [7]. To interpret and understand the data presented in this paper, we propose to think about an ideal decision-making design process of instructors as composed of three parts:

1. Making a determination that a change is needed.
2. Either finding existing solutions or creating new interventions to address the desired change.
3. Evaluating the effectiveness of the solution and deciding whether to retain it or not.

To date, mostly the second step of this process benefits from abundant research in Computer Science Education, as it is shown by the number of good papers appearing in professional meetings such as the ACM SIGCSE. More and more resources are becoming available to Computer Science educators, such as in the Computing and Information Technology Interactive Digital Educational Library (CITIDEL) [15] and the Ensemble project [4].

However, we argue that taking into account the first and the third step of the design pipeline is essential if we want to ensure that teaching innovations are adopted by practitioners in a sustainable way. As in any serious science and engineering design task, we don't just want good components: we also want good decisions grounded in evidence, and good evaluation and quality control. Without a careful determination of needs and requirements (step 1), we may end up "fixing the wrong thing," implementing changes that are not really needed, and overlooking areas that would need real improvement. Without a careful quality control (step 3), we may attribute the outcome of an intervention to the wrong causes, or fail to recognize the influence of the implementation context to the specific interventions.

The *Disciplinary Commons* [26, 11] is an approach that addresses the first step of the pipeline. In this model, the practice of Computer Science teachers is documented and shared among peers, making this information public and available for future use. By reflecting on their practice, and comparing their practice to others, the teachers engage in a process of review that can highlight areas in need of change in their practice. A Disciplinary Commons approach can be effective, but is expensive (in terms of teacher time). Empirical measures may be more useful for the individual teacher working on his or her own.

For the third step of the design pipeline, we note that Multi-Institutional, Multi-National (MIMN) studies [18, 17, 10] offer a way of comparing results across institutions, and thus, creating benchmarks that inform our decisions about effective practice. If students do better in my class than on problems from these studies, I have effectively compared them to all those institutions. The MIMN studies themselves are teachers working collaboratively to pool data to facilitate analysis and provide greater insight. It is still not common practice, however, for regular instructors to "scale down" this process to their own classrooms. Further, the scale of MIMN studies prevents teachers from using them for informing microscopic decisions. How do I decide that *that* particular homework assignment worked, or didn't?

Within the limitations of size and scope of this study, our results suggest that Computer Science instructors rely mostly on intuition and anecdotal evidence to make decisions about changes in their daily teaching practice. We are not arguing that the teachers' decisions are bad ones. In fact, our interviews show several examples of (what seemed to us to be) good decisions. All we know is that instructors used little empirical data for deciding to make a change, and for deciding whether a change was successful or a failure.

Why aren't instructors using more empirical evidence? We can formulate two alternative hypotheses. On the one hand, instructors may not want to use this kind of evidence. Basing day-to-day decisions on empirical evidence might take too much time to be practical. At this level, some decisions should be made rather quickly, and the overhead required by a formal data analysis might paralyze the decision-making process. Additionally, some forms of data analysis would require methods and skills outside the expertise and interests of most instructors.

On the other hand, data may simply not be available, or it may be difficult to access. Available data may have been collected for different purposes, and it might not contain the exact information needed to make meaningful decisions. For example, exams and homework assignments are usually graded in a way that facilitates summative evaluation of student performance, and just the bare grades are usually not detailed enough to inform specific teaching interventions.

A promising way to alleviate this problem is the development of technology that can automate the analysis of educational data collected during regular classroom practice, and support the decision-making process of instructors by extracting actionable information from such data. Researchers in the emerging field of Educational Data Mining [2] are actively working on such techniques and applications.

5. ACKNOWLEDGMENTS

This work is supported by the Computing Research Association (Computing Innovation Fellowship CIF–186 under NSF Grant 0937060), and the National Science Foundation (Broadening Participation in Computing Award 0940394).

6. REFERENCES

[1] ABET: Leadership and quality assurance in applied science, computing, engineering, and technology education. http://www.abet.org/.

[2] R. Baker and K. Yacef. The state of educational data mining in 2009: A review and future visions. *Journal of Educational Data Mining*, 1(1):3–17, October 2009.

[3] D. Blank, L. Meeden, and D. Kumar. Python robotics: an environment for exploring robotics beyond legos. In *SIGCSE '03: Proceedings of the 34th SIGCSE technical symposium on Computer science education*, pages 317–321, New York, NY, USA, 2003. ACM.

[4] L. Cassel, H. Gregory, and B. Nadella. Ensemble: Enriching communities and collections to support education in computing. In *ITiCSE 2009, 14th Annual Conference on Innovation and Technology in Computer Science Education*, page 355, Paris, 2009.

[5] A. Cooper, B. Levin, and C. Campbell. The growing (but still limited) importance of evidence in education policy and practice. *Journal of Educational Change*, 10(2–3):159–171, May 2009.

[6] W. P. Dann, S. Cooper, and R. Pausch. *Learning to Program with Alice.* Prentice Hall, 2005.

[7] A. Disessa, M. Gardner, J. G. Greeno, F. Reif, A. H. Schoenfeld, and E. Stage. *Toward a Scientific Practice of Science Education.* Lawrence Erlbaum Associates, Hillsdale, NJ, 1990.

[8] R. Donnelly. Exploring lecturers' self-perception of change in teaching practice. *Teaching in Higher Education*, 11(2):203–217, 2006.

[9] M. Felleisen, R. B. Findler, M. Flatt, and S. Krishnamurthi. *How to Design Programs: An Introduction to Computing and Programming.* The MIT Press, 2001.

[10] S. Fincher, R. Lister, T. Clear, A. Robins, J. Tenenberg, and M. Petre. Multi-institutional, multi-national studies in CSEd research: some design considerations and trade-offs. In *ICER 2005, First International Workshop on Computing Education Research*, pages 111–121, Seattle, WA, 2005.

[11] S. Fincher and J. Tenenberg. Warren's question. In *ICER 2007, Third International Computing Education Research Workshop*, pages 51–60, September 2007.

[12] D. Fossati, B. Di Eugenio, C. Brown, S. Ohlsson, D. Cosejo, and L. Chen. Supporting computer science curriculum: Exploring and learning linked lists with iList. *IEEE Transactions on Learning Technologies, Special Issue on Real-World Applications of Intelligent Tutoring Systems*, 2(2):107–120, May 2009.

[13] R. M. Gagné, L. J. Briggs, W. W. Wagner, K. Golas, and J. M. Keller. *Principles of Instructional Design.* Wadsworth, 5th edition, 2004.

[14] M. Guzdial and B. Ericson. *Introduction to Computing and Programming with Java: A Multimedia Approach.* Prentice Hall, 2006.

[15] D. Knox. Citidel: Making resources available. In *ITiCSE 2002, 7th Annual Conference on Innovation and Technology in Computer Science Education*, page 225, Aarhus, Denmark, 2002.

[16] R. B.-B. Levy and M. Ben-Ari. We work so hard and they don't use it: Acceptance of software tools by teachers. In *ACM SIGCSE Bulletin*, volume 39, pages 246–250, 2007.

[17] R. Lister, E. S. Adams, S. Fitzgerald, W. Fone, J. Hamer, M. Lindholm, R. McCartney, J. E. Moström, K. Sanders, O. Seppälä, B. Simon, and L. Thomas. A multi-national study of reading and tracing skills in novice programmers. In *ITiCSE-WGR '04: Working group reports from ITiCSE on Innovation and technology in computer science education*, pages 119–150, 2004.

[18] M. McCracken, V. Almstrum, D. Diaz, M. Guzdial, D. Hagan, Y. B.-D. Kolikant, C. Laxer, L. Thomas, I. Utting, and T. Wilusz. A multi-national, multi-institutional study of assessment of programming skills of first-year CS students. *SIGCSE Bulletin*, 33(4):125–180, 2001.

[19] C. McDowell, L. Werner, H. E. Bullock, and J. Fernald. Pair programming improves student retention, confidence, and program quality. *Communications of the ACM*, 49(8):90–95, 2006.

[20] A. Mitrović, P. Suraweera, B. Martin, and A. Weerasinghe. DB-suite: Experiences with three intelligent, web-based database tutors. *Journal of Interactive Learning Research*, 15(4):409–432, 2004.

[21] L. Ni. What makes CS teachers change? factors influencing CS teachers' adoption of curriculum innovations. In *SIGCSE 09, The 40th ACM technical symposium on Computer science education*, pages 544–548, Chattanooga, TN, 2009.

[22] L. Ni, T. McKlin, and M. Guzdial. How do computing faculty adopt curriculum innovations? the story from instructors. In *SIGCSE 10, the 41st ACM technical symposium on Computer science education*, pages 544–548, Milwaukee, WI, 2010.

[23] M. Resnick, J. Maloney, A. Monroy-Hernández, N. Rusk, E. Eastmond, K. Brennan, A. Millner, E. Rosenbaum, J. Silver, B. Silverman, and Y. Kafai. Scratch: Programming for all. *Communications of the ACM*, 52(11):60–67, 2009.

[24] H. A. Simon. *Sciences of the Artificial.* MIT Press, Cambridge, MA, 1996.

[25] J. T. Stasko and C. D. Hundhausen. Algorithm visualization. In S. Fincher and M. Petre, editors, *Computer Science Education Research*, chapter 6, pages 199–228. Routledge, London, 2004.

[26] J. Tenenberg and S. Fincher. Opening the door of the computer science classroom: The disciplinary commons. In *SIGCSE 2007, 38th SIGCSE technical symposium on Computer Science Education*, pages 514–518, Covington, KY, 2007.

Keynote Talk

Three Human Computation Projects

Luis von Ahn
Computer Science Department
Carnegie Mellon University
biglou@cs.cmu.edu

Abstract

At the height of its construction, 44,733 people worked on the Panama Canal. The Great Pyramid of Giza required 50,000 workers and the Apollo Project 400,000. No matter what you put on this list, humanity's largest achievements have been accomplished with less than a few hundred thousand workers because it has been impossible to assemble (let alone pay!) more people to work together --- until now. With the Internet, we can coordinate the efforts of billions of humans. If 400,000 people put a man on the moon, what can we do with 100 million? My research aims to develop theories and build computer systems that enable massive collaborations between humans and computers for the benefit of humanity. I am working to develop a new area of computer science called human computation, which studies how to harness the combined power of humans and computers to solve problems that would be impossible for either to solve alone.

In this talk I will discuss several examples of my work in human computation, including reCAPTCHA, The ESP Game, and Duolingo. I have used these projects in many of my courses to illustrate state of the art concepts in computer science.

Categories & Subject Descriptors: K.3.2 [Computers and Education]: Computer and Information Science Education – computer science education

General Terms: Human Factors

Bio

Professor Luis von Ahn works in the Computer Science Department at Carnegie Mellon University. He also works for Google after the acquisition of his company reCAPTCHA. His current research interests include encouraging people to do work for free, as well as catching and thwarting cheaters in online environments. He is the recipient of a MacArthur Fellowship, a Packard Fellowship, a Microsoft New Faculty Fellowship, and a Sloan Research Fellowship. He has been named one of the 50 Best Minds in Science by Discover Magazine, one of the 100 Most Creative People in Business of 2010 by Fast Company Magazine, one of the "Brilliant 10" scientists of 2006 by Popular Science Magazine, one of the 50 most influential people in technology by Silicon.com, and one of the Top Innovators in the Arts and Sciences by Smithsonian Magazine.

SIGCSE'11, March 9–12, 2011, Dallas, Texas, USA.
ACM 978-1-4503-0500-6/11/03.

SIGCSE 2011 Workshops

Wednesday Workshops, 7:00 p.m. to 10:00 p.m.

1. Advanced Scratch: Computer Science Through Storytelling and Games

Ursula Wolz, *The College of New Jersey*
John Maloney, *Massachusetts Institute of Technology*
Christopher Dunne, *Self-employed*

A set of Scratch storytelling and game project starters are presented to those with some Scratch experience. Each project demonstrates good media design, intermediate/advanced programming and core computing concepts. Initially developed to integrate Scratch into middle school language arts curriculum, the projects are now used in a CS 0 course, a one semester CS1/CS 2 course, and a course in game design. Computing concepts include modular design via game engine architecture, data management and communication via sprite interaction, and algorithm efficiency via sound production and sprite animation. Participants will have ample time to extend the project starters and discuss the ramifications for computing curriculum. See http://www.tcnj.edu/~wolz/AdvScratch **Laptop required**.

2. Developing an Effective Assessment Program for Student Educational Outcomes

Donald Sanderson, *East Tennessee State University*

New requirements, especially among ABET accredited programs, require measuring the performance of graduates against a set of program level student outcomes. This workshop is aimed at those new to this approach, and focuses on the techniques needed to move from high level student outcome statements to specific methods to collect, aggregate and evaluate the needed data. Participants can choose to use example materials, or bring their own outcomes and related course syllabi. They will leave with the tools needed to create evaluable performance indicators for student outcomes, develop appropriate direct and indirect measures of performance, integrate measurement into existing classroom activities, and aggregate the collected data into useful information. **Laptop recommended.**

3. Pedagogical Progressions for Teaching Object-Oriented Design

Carl Alphonce, *University at Buffalo, SUNY*
Michael Caspersen, *Aarhus University*
Dale Skrien, *Colby College*

This workshop is intended for anyone teaching object-oriented programming who has an interest in developing the pedagogy used to teach students sound object-oriented design. Both beginning and experienced instructors of object-oriented design are welcome. The workshop presenters will sketch lessons learned from eight years' worth of workshops held at OOPSLA, discuss techniques to effectively engage students in determining good vs. poor design, and provide ample opportunity for workshop participants to develop, present, and discuss OO concepts/design patterns in an interactive segment of the workshop. **Laptop optional.**

4. Explore, Customize, and Create: Getting Your Hands Dirty with UC Berkeley's Lab-Centric Curricula

Michael Clancy, *University of California, Berkeley*
Daniel Garcia, *University of California, Berkeley*
Nathaniel Titterton, *University of California, Berkeley*

At UC Berkeley, we have refined lab-centric instruction, an innovative pedagogical approach that integrates many research-based practices with a variety of hands-on activities (see our article in Computer Science Education, June 2010). We have developed a wide range of curricula using a variety of programming languages (including Scratch, Java, C, and Scheme), used by students ranging from junior high to college. This workshop will first introduce our experiences and approach. Next, we'll help instructors integrate our customizable curricular modules and relevant technology, such as our customized Moodle, into their classes. We'll end with a look at our online community site, designed to support instructors as they adopt the lab-centric approach in their classroom. **Laptop required.**

5. Open Source and Freeware Tools for 3D Game Development Courses

Victor M. Larios, *University of Guadalajara CUCEA*
Kelvin Sung, *University of Washington Bothell*

3D game development is a complex and labor intensive process that involves the creation, management, and integration of multimedia resources from diverse domains involving drastically different tools. A 3D game development class should touch upon all of these aspects of game development process. This workshop is design specifically for interested faculty members new to the field, where it can be overwhelming to identify the required software tools and to work with the potential overburdening budget. Based on experience teaching 3D game development courses, this workshop will: 1) Introduce a streamlined 3D game production pipeline, 2) Demonstrate simple, free, and compatible tools for each stage of the pipeline and 3) Describe our strategies for managing the resources.

6. Web Development with Python and Django

Ariel Ortiz, *Tecnológico de Monterrey, Campus Estado de México*

Many instructors have already discovered the joy of teaching programming using Python. Now it's time to take Python to the next level. This workshop will introduce Django, an open source Python web framework that saves you time and makes web development fun. It's aimed at CS instructors who want to teach how to build elegant web applications with minimal fuss. Django is Python's equivalent to the popular Ruby on Rails framework. Topics that will be covered include: setup and configuration, template language, and database integration through object-relational mapping. Participants should have some familiarity with Python, HTML and SQL. Please check the following link to get more information: http://django.arielortiz.com/ **Laptop required.**

7. How to Use Algorithm Visualizations in Your Class

Cliff Shaffer, *Virginia Tech*
Tom Naps, *University of Wisconsin, Oshkosh*
Susan Rodger, *Duke University*
Stephen Edwards, *Virginia Tech*

Students and instructors say overwhelmingly that they love algorithm visualizations, but most instructors rarely incorporate them into their classes. Instructors tell us that two things get in their way: (1) difficulty in finding good AVs and information about how they can be used effectively and (2) difficulty in making changes to the class that are needed to introduce this new approach. We will guide you past the real-life pitfalls that get in the way of using AVs in the classroom. We show you how to find the resources that you need, and present case studies of successful classroom deployments. This workshop is about helping you to make the changes you have said for years that you want to make. You will get time to try out some recommended AVs during the workshop. **Laptop recommended.**

8. Making Mathematical Reasoning Fun: Tool-Assisted, Collaborative Techniques

Jason Hallstrom, *School of Computing, Clemson University*
Joe Hollingsworth, *Computer Science, Indiana University Southeast*
Joan Krone, *Mathematics and Computer Science, Denison University*
Murali Sitaraman, *School of Computing, Clemson University*

Is it possible to excite students about learning the mathematical principles that underlie high-quality software? Can we teach them to apply these principles using modern software tools? Can this be accomplished without displacing existing content? Yes! But it takes the right set of pedagogical principles, teaching tools, and classroom exercises. This hands-on laboratory will introduce a set of principles, tools, and exercises that work. Participants will be better prepared to teach students to reason rigorously about the software they develop and maintain. Funding is available to cover registration for some attendees; please contact the workshop organizers for details. **Laptop required.**

9. General Purpose Computing using GPUs: Developing a Hands-On Undergraduate Course on CUDA Programming

Barry Wilkinson, *University of North Carolina Charlotte*
Yaohang Li, *Old Dominion University*

GPUs (graphical processing units) with large numbers of cores are radically altering how high performance computing is conducted. With the introduction of CUDA for general-purpose GPU programming, we can now program GPUs for computational tasks and achieve orders of magnitude improvement in performance over using the CPU alone. With CUDA-enabled GPUs, any desktop or laptop computer can become a very high performance computer. Some HPC clusters now incorporate large numbers of GPUs, which now impact how clusters are programmed. The purpose of this workshop is to provide CS educators with the fundamental knowledge and hands-on skills to teach CUDA materials at the undergraduate level. A **laptop is required**, which does not need to be CUDA-enabled as remote GPU servers will be provided.

10. Writing Effective NSF Proposals

Sue Fitzgerald, *National Science Foundation*
Scott Grissom, *National Science Foundation*
Victor Piotrowski, *National Science Foundation*

This workshop will focus on writing effective education NSF proposals. It will cover writing goals, objectives and outcomes; constructing a convincing rationale; preparing a responsive evaluation plan; crafting a useful and believable dissemination plan; and dealing with the realities of the review process. The workshop will use a guided-interactive methodology to introduce topics and related issues, engage participants in group exercises, and provide "expert" opinions on these issues. The intended audience is faculty at two-year and four-year colleges and universities who are seeking NSF funding in support of undergraduate education. Participants will include novice proposal writers as well as those who seek to improve their proposal writing. **Laptop Optional.**

11. Audacious Android Application Programming

Frank McCown, *Harding University*

As smartphones and mobile devices become ubiquitous, many CS departments are adding mobile computing electives to their curriculum. Google's Android OS is a freely available and popular smartphone platform with applications programmed in Java. Workshop participants will be introduced to mobile app development and the Android SDK. We will write some simple Android apps with Eclipse and run them on an emulator. For those interested in teaching an upper-level Android course, reusable programming labs and projects will be distributed, and we will discuss some teaching strategies. Participants should be capable of writing Java programs in Eclipse and should bring their own laptop preloaded with Eclipse and the Android SDK. http://www.harding.edu/fmccown/android/workshop.html **Laptop recommended.**

12. Using Map-Reduce to Teach Parallel Programming Concepts Across the CS Curriculum

Richard Brown, *St. Olaf College*
Elizabeth Shoop, *Macalester College*
Patrick Garrity, *St. Olaf College*
Timothy Yates, *St. Olaf College*

Map-reduce, the cornerstone of Google- and Yahoo!-style computing, has star appeal to draw students to the study of parallelism. Workshop participants will carry out exercises that introduce data-parallel processing concepts, using the open-source Hadoop map-reduce programming environment. The exercises are designed for the CS1, intermediate, and advanced curricular levels. CS1 exercises use a simplified interface developed by the presenters for Hadoop programming by introductory students, using Java, Python, Scheme, or C++. Intermediate and advanced exercises use standard Hadoop programming in Java or C++. Expository materials and portable software infrastructure provided to participants. Intended audience: CS instructors. **Laptop required** (Windows, Mac, Linux).

Friday Workshops, 7:00 p.m. to 10:00 p.m.

13. Developing an Android Mobile Application for the Google App Engine Cloud

Joel Hollingsworth, *Elon University*
David Powell, *Elon University*

The web is the dominant computing platform of our time. Google has led the rapid development of technologies to create mobile and cloud computing applications and has freely provided them to the world. This workshop provides hands on exposure using Eclipse plugins from Google to develop a mobile application with both stand alone and cloud based services for data persistence. In the first of three sessions, the Android plugin will be used to develop a fully functional Android application. In the second session, the App Engine plugin will be used to develop cloud based services using Java Servlets and JPA. In the third session, participants will extend the stand alone mobile application to support cloud based services. For more information: http://www.cs.elon.edu/sigcse2011. **Laptop required.**

14. Computer Science Unplugged and Outreach Activities

Tim Bell, *University of Canterbury*
Bengt Aspvall, *Blekinge Institute of Technology*
Daniela Marghitu, *Auburn University*
Lynn Lambert, *Christopher Newport University*

You've been asked to talk to an elementary or high school class about Computer Science, but how can you ensure that the talk is engaging? Or perhaps you're trying to introduce a concept from Computer Science to a school group, but you want a fun way to get the class engaged. This workshop introduces CS Unplugged (www.csunplugged.org), a widely used set of kinesthetic, fun activities that cover many core areas of computer science without using high technology. We will explore how to use the activities in a variety of situations (including with special needs students), show some novel applications, and discuss ways that they can be combined with "plugged-in" activities. Attendees will receive a copy of a handbook for teachers and a collection of video files demonstrating the activities.

15. Basic 2D Graphics and Animation Concepts for iPhone/iPad Games

Jonathan Lartigue, *Auburn University*
Russell Thackston, *Auburn University*
Prateek Hejmady, *Auburn University*

iOS and Android devices and their respective app stores have revived the individual- and small-publisher game industry. App downloads in Apple's iTunes store - mostly games - now exceed song downloads. Developers are learning or refreshing game development skills to capitalize on this trend. A first step is understanding simple, 2D game design. We start at the beginning - presenting basic 2D graphics, animation, and game development on the iPhone platform. We introduce concepts such as basic sprites; versatile sprite class design; drawing, transforming, and animating sprites; and simple game engines. Hands-on activities apply these concepts to create a simple but functional prototype. Although we focus on the iPhone/iPad, concepts apply to any platform. No experience required.

16. Making the Most of Undergraduate Research

Andrea Danyluk, *Williams College*
Susan Rodger, *Duke University*
Lori Pollock, *University of Delaware*
Margaret Martonosi, *Princeton University*
Kathryn McKinley, *The University of Texas at Austin*

Involving undergraduates in CS research has many benefits. It's an exciting way for students to gain knowledge and independent problem solving skills. It exposes them to interesting projects and the research process, thereby keeping them in CS, even encouraging them to go to graduate school. And especially in primarily teaching institutions, it's a rewarding way for faculty to remain engaged in their own research. In this workshop we will (1) present proven mentoring strategies for undergraduate research, (2) equip participants with materials to run mentoring workshops for undergraduates, and (3) further develop (1) and (2) by brainstorming with attendees. This workshop is intended for all college-level CS educators. For more, see: www.cs.williams.edu/~andrea/SIGCSE11 **Laptop Optional.**

17. 2D Game Design and Development 101

Scott Leutenegger, *University of Denver*
Rafael Fajardo, *University of Denver*

You have attended or heard about the game talks at SIGCSE over the past few years. You know inside that there is something there, your students want to make games, but, you have no clue how to go about designing and creating a game. You can write/teach the code to move objects around and detect collisions between objects, but how the heck do you design the game? In this workshop we will teach participants how to create a simple 2D game using their ideas and then transition to a rapid development exercise using Scratch. This workshop is intended for any CS instructor wishing to use game creation as an assignment but who is uncomfortable and/or unknowledgeable about how to design and create a simple game.

18. Listening to Linked Lists: Using Multimedia to Learn Data Structures

Mark Guzdial, *Georgia Institute of Technology*
Barbara Ericson, *Georgia Institute of Technology*

Everybody teaches linked lists, with homework like implementing duplicate, weave, and reverse. When those nodes contain strings or numbers, these are pretty boring assignments. When these nodes contain music (MIDI), these operations are composing music, which can then be played. This workshop shows how to use music, images, and sounds to teach the basic data structures, including linked lists, circular linked lists, stacks, queues, and trees. These pieces are then tied together through the use of simulations to generate animated movies. We will be using Java, though many of the methods can also be used in Python. **Laptop recommended**, if you want to play along.

19. Multithreading (Pretty) Early for Everyone: Parallelism and Concurrency in Second-Year Data-Structures

Dan Grossman, *University of Washington*

There is wide interest in introducing students to threads earlier, but how? This workshop gives an answer: a 3-week unit in data structures. It should appeal to data-structure instructors and those tasked with curriculum revision. A key approach is to distinguish parallelism (using more resources to solve problems faster) and concurrency (managing shared access to resources). The material is taught via core data-structure topics (asymptotic complexity, sorting, queues, etc.) and using Java and its Fork/Join Framework. Participants will write parallel programs, find concurrency errors, and discuss how to use/adapt the material developed by the presenter and already used by others. Those with or without knowledge of threads and fork-join are welcome. **Laptop required.**

20. Reinvigorating CS1 with Creative Web 2.0 Programming

Stephen Edwards, *Virginia Tech*
Godmar Back, *Virginia Tech*
Michael Woods, *Virginia Tech*

Improving recruitment and retention depends on linking activities to real-world contexts that illustrate the social and societal impact of computer science. The sleek interaction and underlying technologies that define Web 2.0 applications offer a unique opportunity to teach CS concepts in a real-world context. Learn how students can create engaging Web 2.0 applications using simple Java programming and basic XHTML, without learning JavaScript or AJAX. See a full set of CS1 assignments leveraging this strategy. See how students can write a personal "Facebook-lite" they can show to friends. Play with live demos yourself. Leave with new assignment ideas. **No laptop required.**

21. Computational Art and Creative Coding: Teaching CS1 with Processing

Ira Greenberg, *Southern Methodist University*
Deepak Kumar, *Bryn Mawr College*
Dianna Xu, *Bryn Mawr College*
Ursula Wolz, *The College of New Jersey*

This workshop showcases a new approach to teaching CS1 using computational and generative art as a context. Participants will be introduced to the Processing programming language and environment, designed for the construction of 2D and 3D visual forms. Its IDE is light-weight, but well-suited for the kind of rapid proto-typing needed for dynamic visual work. We hope to bring the excitement, creativity, and innovation fostered by Processing into the computer science education community. Instructors of all experience levels - including none - are welcome. At least one-half of the workshop will be hands-on: participants will be able to learn and explore Processing and create a variety of visual effects on the fly. **All participants will need to bring their own laptop computers.**

22. Build Your Own Blocks: A Scratch Extension for CS Courses for Non-Majors

Brian Harvey, *University of California, Berkeley*
Daniel Garcia, *University of California, Berkeley*
Colleen Lewis, *University of California, Berkeley*
Luke Segars, *University of California, Berkeley*
Josh Paley, *Henry M. Gunn High School, Palo Alto*

This workshop is for high school and college teachers of general-interest ("CS 0") CS courses. It presents the programming environment used in one of the five "AP CS Principles" pilot courses. BYOB (Build Your Own Blocks) is a graphical, drag-and-drop programming language based on Scratch. Originally designed for 8-14 year olds, Scratch is unthreatening, object-oriented, and multithreaded. But a Scratch program is written as "scripts" without names, arguments, or return values. BYOB supports older learners by adding named procedures (thus recursion), procedures as data (thus higher order functions), and structured lists. Participants will learn BYOB through discussion, programming exercises, and exploration. See http://byob.berkeley.edu for details and software. **Laptop required.**

23. Broadening Participation in Computer Science with Scratch, Jeroo, and GridWorld

Stacey Armstrong, *Cypress Woods High School*
Judy Hromcik, *Arlington ISD*
Robert Martin, *Dallas School for Talented and Gifted*

This workshop is intended for all Computer Science teachers, especially those looking for strategies to broaden participation. Examples and approaches will be provided using Scratch, Jeroo, and GridWorld to teach fundamental Computer Science concepts in a relevant and engaging way, including iteration, decision-making, procedural abstraction, and inheritance. Tool differences and limitations will be covered as well as ways to use each tool to teach a particular topic more effectively. Examples will be relevant and engaging for a diverse audience of learners. The workshop will be hands-on and no prior experience will be required. Java 6.0 pre-installation is required and pre-loading Jeroo, Scratch, and GridWorld is strongly recommended. **Laptop Required.**

24. Greenfoot: Introducing Java with Games and Simulations

Michael Kölling, *University of Kent*

Greenfoot is a programming environment, from the creators of BlueJ, that allows teaching of object-oriented programming concepts – using Java – in a highly motivating context. Built to be interactive and graphical, Greenfoot offers a more engaging experience than previous systems. Building widely differing scenarios, such a simulations or games, is easy and quick. This workshop is aimed at teachers of introductory Java programming courses (high schools and universities) who have no or little experience with Greenfoot. Laptop recommended for hands-on exercises. Participants without laptops will be paired with laptop owners. The workshop is practically oriented and allows participants to use Greenfoot in their classroom immediately. More information at www.greenfoot.org. **Laptop Recommended.**

25. Using the FIRST (robotics) Experience to Reach Pre-College Students via Near-Peer Mentors

Stephanie Ludi, *Rochester Institute of Technology*

This workshop introduces participants to using FIRST (For Inspiration and Recognition of Science and Technology) robotics challenges and technologies as a means of conducting outreach with middle and high school students. The use of FIRST goes beyond programming providing linkages to various domains in a manner that promotes teamwork and research. Participants will learn about how to conduct a FIRST team, using university students as near-peer mentors. The workshop is divided into outreach strategies, managing a FIRST team, and practicing robot design and programming using a sample FIRST challenge. You can learn more about FIRST at: http://www.usfirst.org

Saturday Workshops, 3:00 p.m. to 6:00 p.m.

26. Making Music With Scratch

Jesse M. Heines, *Univ. of Massachusetts Lowell*
John Maloney, *MIT Media Laboratory*

This workshop introduces playing and generating music with Scratch, a media-rich visual programming system (scratch.mit.edu). It is based on lessons learned using Scratch to teach both music and computer science in an interdisciplinary GenEd course. As students write programs that make music, they learn control flow, user interaction, synchronization, real-time programming, and data structures. Participants will use their own laptops to explore progressively complex musical Scratch programs (see www.scratchmusic.org). They will also write their own programs and use external sensor devices to make custom musical instruments. Samples and an extensive handout will be provided. The workshop will culminate in a concert of participant-created music. **Headphones and laptop required.**

27. Hands-On Teaching Modules for Secure Web Application Development

Li-Chiou Chen, *Pace University*
Lixin Tao, *Pace University*

This workshop will discuss security issues in web application development and demonstrate a set of teaching modules in this area through hands-on exercises, developed by a NSF-funded project called SWEET (Secure WEb dEvelopment Teaching). The workshop will guide the participants to run through a couple of web security hands-on exercises, such as web server threat assessment, security testing, and secure web transactions. The workshop will also discuss examples of incorporating these teaching modules in computing curriculum. To facilitate the exercises, the workshop will provide every participant a lab DVD, which contains the teaching materials and software needed. Further information is available at http://csis.pace.edu/~lchen/sweet/. **Laptop Required.**

28. Storytelling in CS Education: Examples from Programming and Software Engineering Courses

Henrik Baerbak Christensen, *Computer Science, Aarhus University*
Michael E. Caspersen, *Computer Science, Aarhus University*

Storytelling is a viable technique to structure courses and exercises to improve student motivation and learning: a realistic story is constructed such that new learning topics are introduced and revisited as demanded by the story, typically of a software product that evolves in response to customers' new requirements. We will exemplify storytelling as used in an advanced programming course, discuss pitfalls, and shortly relate it to cognitive learning theories. Next, the organizers will coach participants in developing stories for their own courses. Finally, a plenary discussion will sum up ideas, tips and tricks. Visit www.daimi.au.dk/~hbc/story. **Laptop Optional.**

29. Agility Training

Brian Ladd, *SUNY Potsdam*

Whether it is called Scrum, eXtreme Programming, Kanban, or something newer and shinier, the use of Agile methodologies in industry is growing. This workshop examines how computer science students can be supported in learning to apply these methodologies in software engineering classes and across the curriculum. The focus is on the use of open-source tools that assist students in following an Agile approach. The workshop follows the introduction of Scrum into a senior-level SE course with the use of wiki documentation, an online product backlog, Git version control, Ant, JUnit, and Maven for building, testing, and integrating projects. The use of individual tools in other courses is discussed with an eye toward easing the learning curve in software engineering.

30. Testing Graphical User Interfaces in the Classroom

Stephen Edwards, *Virginia Tech*
Manuel Pérez-Quiñones, *Virginia Tech*
Jason Snyder, *Virginia Tech*

Software testing has become popular in introductory courses. But many introductory courses use graphical user interfaces (GUIs) as an "attention grabber" for students and as a metaphor for teaching object-oriented programming. Unfortunately, developing software tests for programs that have significant GUIs is beyond the abilities of typical students (and, for that matter, many educators). This workshop introduces participants to LIFT, the Library for InterFace Testing. LIFT works with the ACM Java Task Force library, Java GUIs using Swing, and Objectdraw. LIFT was developed at Virginia Tech by the Web-CAT team. Participants will learn how to use LIFT, including how to write simple, student-friendly tests for GUIs used in typical CS1/CS2 courses as well as more complex user interfaces.

31. Teaching a Consulting Course to Develop Communication and Leadership Skills

Scott McElfresh, *Wake Forest University*
Joseph Mertz, *Carnegie Mellon University*

The daunting logistics of managing service projects and the difficulty of defining their academic benefits tempers interest in service learning. Our approach is to teach students consulting skills as they work each week as consultants for non-profit organizations (http://cmu.edu/tcinc). Students learn to lead a consulting project, communicate effectively in oral and written forms, and engage in a systematic inquiry into the social and organizational context of technology. Workshop participants will receive sample materials for implementing such a course. All participants will share ideas for addressing the problems associated with developing and managing relationships with community partners and ideas for promoting new proposals for community engagement to their peers and administrators.

32. Reaching Out Internationally with Programs to Promote Computing to High and Middle School Students

Catherine Lang, *Swinburne University of Technology*
Annemieke Craig, *Deakin University*
Reyyan Ayfer, *Bilkent University*
Mary Anne Egan, *Siena College*
Jane Chu Prey, *Microsoft*

Computing workshops for high school/middle school students are often used as avenues to create interest in ICT. We will explore several established workshops with a view of sharing resources and ideas. We will begin a conversation with university and high school faculty to build a future strategy to determine if current workshops do enough to engender student desire to act by committing to a higher degree in ICT. We will present information on existing programs in different countries, such as the Digital Divas program (Australia), the Digigirlz program (various countries), Project IMPACT (US) and an ACM-W Student Chapter in Turkey. Current trends indicate that we need to act now to encourage more women into ICT to meet future employment and creativity demands. **Laptop Optional.**

33. Teaching with Greenfoot: From Development of Material to Delivery in the Classroom

Michael Kölling, *University of Kent*
Frances P. Trees, *Drew University*
Stephanie Hoeppner, *Clermont Northeastern Schools*
Daniel Green, *Oracle Corporation*

Greenfoot is an introductory Java programming environment that gives teachers a high level of control over the nature and context of teaching examples. This workshop is aimed at teachers of introductory programming courses (high school/university) who have seen Greenfoot and want to learn how to use it more effectively in their teaching. Participants will develop their own teaching project for use in their classroom under consideration of pedagogical and technical aspects. Other topics discussed include educational strategies for programming, advanced Greenfoot programming techniques, transition from/to other systems (Scratch, Alice, BlueJ) and integration of media. Laptop recommended for hands-on exercises. Participants without laptops will be paired with laptop owners. **Laptop Recommended.**

34. Exploring Wonderland: Teaching with Alice and Media Computation

Barbara Ericson, *Georgia Tech*
Wanda Dann, *Carnegie Mellon University*
Stephen Cooper, *Stanford University*

This workshop is designed for instructors who are interested in teaching a course combining Alice and Media Computation in Java. The goal of this approach is to provide a complete CS1 experience that uses Alice to reduce syntax frustration while beginners are learning computing concepts, and then uses Media Computation to reinforce the same concepts in Java. We will introduce the approach and show some sample work. Participants will do hands-on Alice and Media Computation projects. For example, they will use chroma key to change the background of an Alice movie. We will leave 15 minutes at the end of the workshop to answer questions. **Laptop Required.**

35. Short Mobile Game Development Projects for CS1/2

Stan Kurkovsky, *Central Connecticut State University*
Delvin Defoe, *Rose-Hulman Institute of Technology*

Game development and mobile computing have been successfully used to increase student motivation. However, instructors with no background in mobile computing, computer graphics, and/or game development may find it difficult to develop or adopt course materials on these topics. This workshop is designed to address these concerns. Using Java Micro Edition, we have developed several project-based course modules focused on mobile game development and designed to study fundamental programming principles (e.g. loops) while also exposing students to more advanced concepts (e.g. databases). Using a mobile phone emulator, participants will test-drive one of our modules and develop a simple game, which can then be transferred to and played on a mobile device. **A Windows or Mac laptop is recommended.**

SIGCSE 2011 Birds of a Feather

The following Birds-of-a-Feather sessions were organized for attendees of the SIGCSE 2011 symposium.

AP CS A: Sharing Teaching Strategies and Curricular Ideas

Paul Tymann, *Rochester Institute of Technology*
Karen Donathan, *George Washington High School*

This BOF will provide an opportunity for high school and college faculty to discuss the AP CS A curriculum and to explore possibilities for collaborations and outreach activities between high schools and colleges.

Assessing Interdisciplinary CS Initiatives

Leen-Kiat Soh, *University of Nebraska*
Jesse Heines, *University of Massachusetts Lowell*

With the revitalization of computational thinking and increasing recognition of the potential impact of interdisciplinary CS curricula in attracting students of both genders to CS and broadening participation in computing in other disciplines, we have seen a number of initiatives anchored with interdisciplinary CS curricula, accompanied with program evaluation and student assessment mechanisms. However, due to the often-convoluted multiple purposes of such initiatives, it is not entirely clear how best to assess such initiatives. This BOF aims at exploring this issue as a platform for a more comprehensive, future treatment of the subject.

Attention and Learning in the Computer Science Classroom

Durga Suresh, *Wentworth Institute of Technology*
Karina Assiter, *Wentworth Institute of Technology*

In the modern connected classroom, where each student has a laptop (or iPad/ iTouch/iPhone), faculty in the Computer Science programs must consider how much attention students are able to pay to instructor directed activities; how are students able to learn in such a distracting environment? For this reason, faculty are increasingly searching for (and collaborating on) techniques and tools for holding students' attention and enhancing learning in the CS classroom. The discussion that we hope will ensue should provide a scaffold to this cohort of students who classify themselves as the net generation. We recognize that there is not one set of strategies that work for all educators, so our intention is to provide a forum for computer science instructors to share their own best practices.

Capstone Projects in CS and SE: How do you Reach Out?

Carsten Kleiner, *University of Applied Sciences & Arts Hannover*
Dean Knudson, *North Dakota State University*

The goal of this birds-of-a-feather session is to bring together instructors in computer science and software engineering that teach capstone courses and who have interest in doing outreach within these courses. Most importantly, it is meant as a forum to gather ideas and experiences on how to do outreach in such classes. There will also be the opportunity to discuss possibilities on how to set up an electronic platform for the exchange of future experiences with reaching out in capstone projects. This platform might also be used as a marketplace for instructors interested in offering inter-organizational and/or international experiences.

Computer Science: Small Department Initiative

James Jerkofsky, *Walsh University*

Faculty in small departments (perhaps 3 FTE, perhaps only 1 or 2,…) face special situations – both challenges and strengths. In this BOF, members will have a chance to talk about both. Challenges include maintaining a well-rounded curriculum and attracting students. Strengths include a close relationship with other members of the department and majors. These and other topics are open for discussion; the specific topics will be based upon the composition and interests of the group assembled.

Computing Education that Supports Research: Connecting with the Committee of Education of the Computing Research Association (CRA-E)

Edward Fox, *Virginia Tech*
Jane Prey, *Microsoft*
Richard DeMillo, *Georgia Tech*

Few US students move into computing research. CRA-E seeks to address this challenge by supporting community-wide activities. NSF CISE and DUE, as well as other agencies/foundations, have new and continuing programs that fund undergraduate students interested in research, e.g., individual or site REU awards. Nevertheless, there are few umbrella mechanisms to collect and disseminate effective practices regarding how best to attract students to engage in research, nor many on how to expand and improve the pipeline guiding such students to research activities/studies/careers. We seek to engage SIGCSE attendees involved or interested in better understanding and supporting future computing research. This must involve those in R1 universities, 4-year colleges, 2-year colleges, and K-12 education.

Connecting Biomedical and Health Informatics with Computer Science

Bonnie MacKellar, *St. John's University*

There is currently a lot of interest among students in applications of computer science to the biological and medical fields. This session is aimed at faculty who are teaching, developing, or interested in developing courses that tie together computer science and biology, medicine, or health care. We will share our expertise and experience on such questions as choosing software and textbooks, developing case studies and projects, and developing links with biologists and clinicians. We will also discuss how best to continue the conversation, perhaps via electronic mailing list or blog.

Creating a Game Development Course for Pre-Collegiate Schools

Alfred Thompson, *Microsoft*
Patricia Philips, *Microsoft*

Game development computer science courses are gaining in interest as a means to increase excitement and enrollment in computer science. What are the tools, topics and curriculum modules that actually work in high schools and middle schools? This BOF will give teachers who have created game development courses and teachers who are considering creating them a chance to share ideas, solutions and concerns.

Designing Open Source Labs for Distance Education

Daniel Sanford, *Ivy Tech Community College South Bend*
Michael Rivera, *Ivy Tech Community College South Bend*

Teaching students through distance education methods often leads to new difficulties. When teaching new operating systems to students this can be especially pronounced. Commercial online "labs" are often limited in their flexibility to be tailored to the curriculum. Especially with open-source software there is a greater degree of flexibility. This birds-of-a-feather session will provide a platform to discuss how to use open-source software to allow for the creation of online lab solutions that can be more easily tailored to curriculum needs than traditional commercial solutions by publishers.

Education, Computers and Society

Joseph Oldham, *Centre College*
Florence Appel, *Saint Xavier University*

This session is organized by ACM SIGCAS (Computers and Society) for those interested in addressing the social and ethical consequences of computing within their curricula. We will emphasize sharing resources and ideas, and strengthening our network. Discussion typically includes best practices and approaches to teaching computer ethics and social impact, developing programs for recruitment and retention of under-represented populations, and implementing service learning course components. We offer an update on happenings in SIGCAS and encourage discussion of ways in which SIGCAS and SIGCSE can collaborate, including organizing a future pre-SIGCSE conference dedicated to computers and society issues.

Enhancing Undergraduate Education through the ACM Distinguished Speakers Program

Barrett Bryant, *University of Alabama at Birmingham*

As indicated on the ACM Distinguished Speaker (DSP) website (http://www.dsp.acm.org), a core mission of the DSP is to provide students with access to computing professionals by facilitating personal visits by DSP speakers to ACM Student Chapter meetings. DSP speakers come from all areas of computer science and from throughout the world and include Turing Award winners. The opportunity to have such a distinguished speaker visit is a highlight for ACM Student Chapters. Yet the program is currently underutilized. This session will provide an overview of the program along with discussion of how to use it to enhance undergraduate education, for both universities which have and do not have active ACM Student Chapters.

Exploring Computer Science: Fostering Computational Thinking through Engaging and Relevant Curriculum

Gail Chapman, *University of California, Los Angeles*

Computer science teachers are always looking for new projects to use with their students that are engaging and relevant while providing an opportunity for computational thinking at a high level. The Exploring Computer Science curriculum is based on projects of this type. This BOF will provide a platform for the discussion of what teachers are currently doing in ECS classrooms and provide teachers who are not teaching ECS an opportunity to learn more about the kinds of projects that have been successful.

Introducing Software Engineering Principles in the First Two Years of Computer Science Education

Jacqueline Hundley, *Auburn University*

Guidelines are needed to successfully produce a software product of high-quality. The principles of software engineering provide a solid approach to software development. Most introductory level computer science courses focus on the programming, or coding, phase of the software lifecycle. Courses that teach software engineering principles tend to be near the end of the undergraduate curriculum. Introducing software engineering principles early would allow the maturing of students' knowledge through the application of the principles in their advanced courses. Time and resource limitations can prevent additional courses to teach software engineering principles. What software engineering principles can be introduced in the first two years of the computer science curriculum?

An iOS BOF

Michael Rogers, *Northwest Missouri State University*

More and more instructors are teaching iOS (iPhone, iPad and iPod Touch) Development in the classroom. The primary purpose of this Birds of Feather session is to enable practitioners to share their experiences — what works and what does not — and discuss techniques, textbooks, and strategies. For those contemplating offering either a course or module on the subject, this will serve as an opportunity to learn from the experiences of their colleagues on the vanguard.

Lifesavers! Favorite Online Tools and Resources for Teaching CS1

Ria Galanos, *Centennial High School*
Jill Pala, *Girls Preparatory School*

Do you ever wish there was a "one stop shop" to find all of the cool online resources for teaching introductory CS? Do you wish you could read reviews from teachers who use these resources? If so, then this is the BOF for you! Some of the best gems for teaching CS1 remain hidden to many teachers. This BOF will allow attendees to share their favorite online tools/resources and discuss how they use them to introduce or reinforce computer science topics. These lifesavers include: online practice tools, multiple-choice practice question generators, web-based IDEs, code visualization tools, automatic grading programs, and great teacher websites. Attendees will be given an annotated list of resources at the beginning of the BOF; the hope is for the list to grow with contributions from the group.

Logisim and Circuit Simulation: Future Directions

Carl Burch, *Hendrix College*

Logisim is an open-source, cross-platform tool that provides a graphical environment for designing and simulating circuits. It is used widely for classes such as introductory surveys of computing, sophomore-level computing systems courses, and upper-division computer organization and architecture. The software is in the midst of heavy development; revision should be complete by Summer 2011, with intermediate versions released along the way. In this BOF led by Logisim's primary developer, attendees will have the opportunity to discuss how they use circuit simulation in their courses (if at all), to provide feedback on recent developments, and to discuss openly directions for Logisim's near-term future.

Mathematical (and Other) Reasoning in Computer Science Education

Doug Baldwin, *SUNY Geneseo*

This birds-of-a-feather session explores the relationships between mathematical and other kinds of reasoning typical of computer science, and the implications of those relationships for computing education. For example, is mathematical thinking a foundation for learning other forms of thinking? Or are other forms of thinking a necessary context for computing students to appreciate mathematics? All points of view are welcome.

Media Computation

Mark Guzdial, *School of Interactive Computing, Georgia Tech*
Barbara Ericson, *College of Computing, Georgia Tech*

Media Computation is an approach to teaching computing (introductory and data structures, in Python and Java) in which students learn through manipulation of digital media: images, sounds, text, video, and animations. Research on Media Computation has demonstrated effectiveness at increasing retention, especially among women and members of under-represented minorities. At Media Computation BOFs, faculty share their favorite Media Computation inventions and assignments, presented with samples of some of their students' productions.

A Neglected Pipeline? How Faculty Teach, Advise, and Mentor Transfer Students

Mihaela Sabin, *University of New Hampshire*
Susan Miertschin, *University of Houston*

Two-year community colleges are critical entry points to postsecondary education for low-socioeconomic status students. Record numbers of students enroll in Information Technology programs at community colleges. Many of these students transfer into bachelor's IT programs, which reside in CS departments and/or have overlapping curricula with CS programs whose faculty teach and advise both CS and IT students. Articulation agreements between two- and four-year computing programs facilitate student transfer. However, these agreements do not spell out support structures that help transfer students succeed in a bachelor's program. The goal of this session is to examine the role of faculty in contributing to an effective transfer culture across computing programs.

Outreach and Reaching Out in K12: An International Perspective

Margot Phillipps, *CSTA*
Chris Stephenson, *CSTA*
Judith Gal-Ezer, *Open University*

CSTA's international mandate includes a commitment to sharing knowledge and expertise with educators around the world who want to build CSTA-like organizations. As CSTA has grown to represent members more than 100 countries, many of these countries, including Armenia, England, France, India, New Zealand and Nigeria have approached CSTA for information and assistance. The problems we face are universal — lack of understanding or respect for CS, teacher isolation, teacher training in content and pedagogy, and volunteer effort from overworked teachers. The session will solicit the experiences of audience members with regard to the benefits, challenges, and best practices for building our community, in a manner which both values K12 teachers and assists, without dominating.

Parallelism and Concurrency in the Curriculum

Daniel Ernst, *University of Wisconsin - Eau Claire*
Jens Mache, *Lewis and Clark College*
David Bunde, *Knox College*
Matthew Wolf, *Georgia Institute of Technology*
Libby Shoop, *Macalester College*
Richard Brown, *St. Olaf College*
Michael Wrinn, *Intel Corporation*

Multicore, multiprocessor, and clustered platforms have become the standard computing platforms available for executing programs. Thus, Computer Science education increasingly entails teaching programming in parallel environments. This BOF is designed to gather colleagues to exchange ideas and discuss questions such as the following: 1) What fundamental ideas of concurrency and parallelism should every CS graduate know? 2) How should concurrency and parallelism be integrated in the curriculum? At what levels and depths? If broad integration is appropriate, what resources and initiatives are needed to educate the educators? 3) What are some good/proven practices and platforms for teaching this material to undergraduates in these various contexts?

Program by Design: TeachScheme/ReachJava

Viera Proulx, *Northeastern University*

Program by Design is a new name for the comprehensive introduction to programming at all levels that began with TeachScheme/ReachJava. This unconventional introductory computing curriculum covers both functional and the object-oriented program design in a systematic design-based style, enforcing test-first design from the beginning. The Bootstrap curriculum makes programming and algebra exciting for children ages 11-15. Special libraries support the design of interactive graphics-based games, musical explorations, client-server and mobile computing. We invite you to come and meet those who have used the curriculum, learn about new additions, libraries, bring in your experiences with the curriculum, show your projects, or ask questions about how it works and how you can use it.

Report of Findings: ACM Summit on Computing Education at Community Colleges

Elizabeth Hawthorne, *Union County College*
Robert Campbell, *CUNY Graduate Center*
Karl Klee, *Alfred State College*
Anita Wright, *Camden County College*

At the request of and funded by the National Science Foundation, the ACM Two-Year College Education Committee (TYCEC) conducted a Strategic Summit on the Computing Education Challenges at Community Colleges. A distinguished group of academicians and employers, accomplished in their various fields, were assembled not to identify solutions to challenges, but to ferret out and articulate the nature and scope of the challenges confronting computing programs in community colleges. At this session, the TYCEC will facilitate a dialogue about these challenges and associated opportunities. Attendees should come away from the session with ideas for crafting funding proposals and other initiatives. Many of the findings are applicable at and beyond the scope of the community college environment.

SIGCSE and the International Community

Alison Young, *Christchurch Polytechnic Institute of Technology*

ACM are very clear about their focus, they include the word "world" in their introductory statement. "ACM is an Educational and scientific society uniting the world's computing educators, researchers and professionals to inspire dialogue, share resources and address the field's challenges." SIGCSE has over 2600 members from 63 countries. There are many opportunities for international members; however, it has become apparent that not many of the international members are aware of these opportunities. This session is to help the international community to become more involved in SIGCSE activities, to promote the current opportunities and to feed back to the Board ideas for the international community to become more involved.

Sustainability and Computing Education

Alison Young, *Christchurch Polytechnic Institute of technology*

Following the two very successful Working Groups at ITiCSE in 2008 and 2009 the SIGCSE Community now has a framework to include sustainability in computing education. This session will bring together participants with an interest in incorporating sustainability into their curriculum. It will provide an opportunity for those who have already done this to share their experiences and describe how it can be done. It will also provide an opportunity to create an ongoing list of faculty with similar interests.

Teaching and Learning with Scratch

Karen Brennan, *MIT Media Lab*
John Maloney, *MIT Media Lab*
Ricarose Roque, *MIT Media Lab*

Do you use Scratch as part of your teaching practice? Would you like to? Join members of the MIT Scratch Team for a discussion about how Scratch is being used in a variety of educational settings and learning environments. You will have an opportunity to share your experiences and resources and to find out about what others are doing. For those who are new to Scratch, we will provide a brief introduction to the Scratch authoring environment and to ScratchEd, an online community for Scratch educators, where more than 2300 educators have joined – sharing stories, contributing resources, participating in discussions, and connecting to other educators.

Teaching Open Source (Software)

Sebastian Dziallas, *Franklin W. Olin College of Engineering*
Heidi Ellis, *Western New England College*
Mel Chua, *Red Hat*

Many instructors are turning to Free and Open Source Software (FOSS) to provide students with experience in real-world projects at no cost. FOSS projects offer opportunities for students with a wide range of backgrounds to participate in the creation of a real-world project. Student contributions can range from the simple (e.g., writing user instructions), to the complex (e.g., coding an enhancement or new feature). Would you like to involve students in FOSS? This BOF, run by members of the Teaching Open Source http://teachingopensource.org) community, will host discussion on the process of turning students into FOSS contributors.

Teaching Secure Programming

Blair Taylor, *Towson University*
Diana Burley, *George Washington University*
Bill Chu, *University of North Carolina, Charlotte*
Steve Cooper, *Stanford University*
Ron Dodge, *United States Military Academy at West Point*
Trish Gregory, *Anne Arundel Community College*
Siddharth Kaza, *Towson University*

There is growing concern among educators that secure programming is inadequately addressed in the curriculum. In order to better prepare our graduates to address tomorrow's security challenges, we wish to examine the following questions: What do CS students need to know about secure software development? Are we teaching secure programming in CS1 and CS2? How can we encourage a security mindset among faculty? What steps are needed to include secure coding in the curriculum? How can we teach secure programming across different schools – community colleges, universities, high schools?

Teaming up to Change K-12 CS Education, One State-at-a-Time

Mark Guzdial, *Georgia Tech*
Susan Rodger, *Duke University*
Barbara Boucher Owens, *Southwestern University*
Chris Stephenson, *CSTA*

The CSTA has established a Leadership Cohort: Two K-12 teachers in each state who are supported and charged with improving CS education in their state. The SIGCSE Board recognizes that the cohort is even stronger if it approaches state-level education leaders with post-secondary faculty as part of the team. The goal of this BOF is to identify and connect SIGCSE members with CSTA Leadership Cohort members.

Technology Available to Educators: How Does Access to Next-Generation Hardware Impact Students?

Lauren Dankiewicz, *Intel Corporation*
Mike Pearce, *Intel Corporation*
Tom Murphy, *Contra Costa College*
Skylar Thompson, *University of Washington*

This BOF will explore opportunities for CS students to gain hands-on experience using state of the art hardware and software in the classroom. Options include cloud service providers, university hosted cloud solutions, and the Intel® Manycore Testing Lab—a remotely accessible, 32-core, 64-thread server that teachers and students can access at no charge. Audience members will share ideas and collaborate on actionable solutions that will directly impact their students. Discussion points will cover: What resources are available for students to learn parallel programming? Can parallelism be taught effectively without state of the art hardware? What are the minimum hardware requirements to teach parallelism? How can teachers provide students with a consistent environment and tool set?

Technology that Educators of Computing Hail (TECH) Site in the Ensemble Computing Portal

Daniel Garcia, *UC Berkeley*
Sally Fincher, *University of Kent*
Don Bailes, *East Tennessee State University*

The judicious use of technology in computing education (in and out of the classroom) can be empowering and transformative. However, it is very difficult to discover what tools are available and how effective they have been. The ACM Education Council Technology and Tools task force has been developing a website, "Technology that Educators of Computing Hail (TECH)", that hopes to provide a central, organized collection of links to teaching technology resources. It will feature search, rating, tagging and commentary. We're delighted to announce that we have moved our site into the Ensemble Computing Portal. The goal of this BOF is to demonstrate the site, gather feedback, and collect "experience reports" from educators who have used technology for teaching computing – with success or not!

A Town Meeting: SIGCSE Committee on Expanding the Women-in-Computing Community

Gloria Childress Townsend, *DePauw University*

In January 2004, we organized the second SIGCSE Committee ("Expanding the Women-in-Computing Community"). Our annual Town Meeting provides dissemination of information concerning successful gender issues projects, along with group discussion and brainstorming, in order to create committee goals for the coming year. We select projects to highlight through listserv communication and through our connections with NCWIT, ABI, ACM-W, etc. This year we will highlight the new NSF Broadening Participation in Computing grant – a grant that encompasses projects we presented in previous BOFs and a grant that builds on an alliance among ACM-W, ABI and NCWIT.

Undergraduate Information Security Curriculum Development

Michael Locasto, *University of Calgary*
Richard Weiss, *Evergreen State College*

Incorporating information security into the undergraduate curriculum has been a topic of ongoing interest to SIGCSE attendees for quite some time. The purpose of this BOF is to help sustain the existing community of educators and researchers interested in bringing ethical hacking skills and an understanding of security into the classroom and relating these topics to the foundations of Computer Science. We plan to facilitate communication with BOF attendees to ask questions, suggest curriculum approaches, and share their own experiences. We also plan to briefly discuss our ongoing efforts and programs (e.g., infosec curriculum modules, the expansion of the SISMAT (Secure Information Systems Mentoring and Training) course, dissemination of infosec laboratory exercises).

Using Game Development to Teach Parallelism: Where Can I Find Resources to Get Started?

Robert Chesebrough, *Intel Corporation*
Tom Murphy, *Contra Costa College*
Joel Adams, *Calvin College*

What resources are available for students to learn parallel programming? Can parallel programming be taught effectively using game codes? Isn't game programming difficult and parallel programming more so? What advantage is there in teaching parallelism through games development? This BOF will discuss opportunities for computer science students and their instructors to access pre-coded games codes, such as Ticker Tape, Destroy the Castle, or Smoke and use them as base to which they add significant performance through parallelism. Audience members will be able to interact with others that have used game development as a vehicle for teaching concepts in parallelism.

Web Programming

Marty Stepp, *University of Washington*
Jessica Miller, *University of Washington*

For the last three years we have held BOF sessions about teaching web programming at the college level. Our feedback indicates that the most valuable aspect of the past sessions was to get everyone together for an exchange of ideas and information. We'd like to bring together two groups of instructors: Newcomers who have not yet taught this material before (or are just starting), and veterans who may have insights to share with the group. Newcomers can ask questions about materials, languages and technologies to use, what works, and so on. Veterans can share tips from the classroom and helpful resources. We can also discuss the latest web technologies such as HTML 5, ECMAScript 5, Flash, iPhone, Android, Rails, Zend, Django, and .NET.

What Makes a Good Scratch Program? Examining Structure and Style in Scratch Programs

Ursula Wolz, *The College of New Jersey*
Karen Brennan, *Massachusetts Institute of Technology*
John Maloney, *Massachusetts Institute of Technology*
Ricarose Roque, *Massachusetts Institute of Technology*

The increasing popularity of Scratch as an introduction to computer programming raises questions for educators and researchers alike. Can we tell what students are learning by studying their programs? Do some problem domains result in richer learning experiences for students than others? What makes a "good" Scratch program? What programming structures and coding styles do we hope to see as students gain experience and understanding? This BOF is an opportunity to explore these questions together. As a way to start the discussion, the organizers will show an experimental visualization tool that may shed light on some of these questions. They will also share a few things they have learned from studying student Scratch programs.

SIGCSE 2011 Poster Sessions

Posters present work-in-progress and other topics for which dialog with Symposium attendees is particularly appropriate. Posters are on display Friday morning and afternoon, and authors will be available for discussion during these sessions.

Session I: Friday, March 11, 10:00 a.m. – 12:00 p.m., Lone Star Preconvene

Incorporating Application Domains in Software Engineering Education

Sriram Mohan, *Rose-Hulman Institute of Technology*

dLife: A Java Library for Robotics, AI and Computer Vision

Grant Braught, *Dickinson College*

Recruiting via a First-Year Seminar: Storytelling Through Computer Animation

Mark LeBlanc, *Wheaton College*

A Java Ray Tracer for Introductory Computer Graphics Courses

Helen Hu, *Westminster College*

Building and Managing Paths of Web-based Computer Science Content

Richard Furuta, *Texas A&M University*
Frank Shipman, *Texas A&M University*

Pacific Rim Summer School in Global Distributed Software Development

Virginia (Ginnie) Lo, *University of Oregon*
Andrzej Proskurowski, *University of Oregon*
Arthur Farley, *University of Oregon*
Stuart Faulk, *University of Oregon*
Lian Yu, *School of Software and Microelectronics, Peking University*
Kathleen Freeman-Hennessy, *University of Oregon*

Building a Generator-Based Cyber Platform for Automating Production of PPT-Based Algorithm Visualization Teaching Materials

Sen Zhang, *SUNY College at Oneonta*
James Ryder, *SUNY College at Oneonta*

Scrape: A Tool for Visualizing the Code of Scratch Programs

Ursula Wolz, *The College of New Jersey*
Christopher Hallberg, *The College of New Jersey*
Brett Taylor, *The College of New Jersey*

Lego NXT Mindstorms Robot Simulator

Richard James, *Rollins College*
R. Taylor Hanson, *Rollins College (class of 2011)*
Addison Sims, *Rollins College (class of 2011)*

Computer Science for the Liberal Arts: Reaching More Students

Madeleine Schep, *Columbia College*
Nieves McNulty, *Columbia College*

SPLICE: Self-Paced Learning in an Inverted Classroom Environment

Matthew Boutell, *Rose-Hulman Institute of Technology*
Curtis Clifton, *Rose-Hulman Institute of Technology*

Empirical Evaluation of Success Factors for Capstones in Software Engineering and their Interdependencies

Carsten Kleiner, *University of Applied Sciences & Arts Hannover*
Arne Koschel, *University of Applied Sciences & Arts Hannover*

Engaging Female Students in Computer Science Using Role Models

Jonathan Black, *Queen Mary University of London*
Paul Curzon, *Queen Mary University of London*
Chrystie Myketiak, *Queen Mary University of London*
Peter McOwan, *Queen Mary University of London*

Developing and Supporting Communities of Computing Educators

Lillian Cassel, *Villanova University*

Google Forms as a Classroom Response System in Programming Classes

Edward Gehringer, *North Carolina State University*

Early Successes and Failures of a Comprehensive Student Service Retention Plan for Computing and Digital Media Programs

Amber Settle, *DePaul University*
John Glatz, *DePaul University*

Scala for CS1 and CS2: A Statically Typed Alternative to Python

Mark Lewis, *Trinity University*

Inspire-CT: Vertically Integrated Student Teams

Gregory Hislop, *Drexel University*
Massood Towhidnejad, *Embry-Riddle Aeronautical University*
Joseph Urban, *Texas Tech University*

Revitalizing Labs: Lessons from 2.5 Years of Iterative Development and Assessment of Digital Logic Labs

Elizabeth Patitsas, *University of British Columbia*
Steven Wolfman, *University of British Columbia*
Meghan Allen, *University of British Columbia*

Increasing Security Awareness: The Next Level

Helen Schneider, *The University of Findlay*
Mary Jo Geise, *The University of Findlay*
Loren Wagner, *The University of Findlay*

An Inter-Disciplinary Workshop Based On Social Robotics

Nick Webb, *University at Albany, SUNY*
Jennifer Goodall, *University at Albany, SUNY*
Michael Ferguson, *University at Albany, SUNY*
Kathryn DeCorah, *University at Albany, SUNY*
Kristen Kielbasa, *University at Albany, SUNY*

Project Expression: A Cloud Computing & Multimedia-based Java Course that Helps Solve the Empathy Crisis

Joseph Shanahan, *Auburn University*
Daniella Marghitu, *Auburn University*

Curricular-Wide Problem Based Learning for Computer Science and Programming Education

Amanda Holland-Minkley, *Washington & Jefferson College*
Samuel Fee, *Washington & Jefferson College*
James Gralka, *Washington & Jefferson College*

The Virtual Studio: Implementing Studio-Based Learning Techniques in an Online Introductory Programming Course to Address Common Programming Errors

Blanca Polo, *Leeward Community College*

Session II: Friday, March 11, 3:00 p.m. – 5:00 p.m., Lone Star Preconvene

The Beaver Contest on Informatics and Computer Fluency – Attracting Youngsters to Study Computer Science

Bruria Haberman, *Holon Inst. of Technology and Davidson Inst. of Science Education*
Avi Cohen, *The Ministry of Education, Israel*
Valentina Dagiene, *Institute of Mathematics and Informatics, Vilnius*

Integrating "Soft Skills" into a Computing Degree

Alison Young, *Christchurch Polytechnic Institute of Technology*

SKA for RBTs: An Algorithm Visualization System to Support Red-black Trees

Kadian Davis, *The University of the West Indies, Mona, Jamaica*
Ashley Hamilton-Taylor, *The University of the West Indies, Mona, Jamaica*

Reaching Out to Many Majors: A Database Approach

Suzanne Dietrich, *Arizona State University*
Don Goelman, *Villanova University*

GUIGraph – Editing Live Object Diagrams for GUI Generation Enables New Pedagogy in CS1/2

Duane Buck, *Otterbein University*

Introduction to Programming with Alice: Bringing a College Course to High Schools in Memphis

Juan Carlos Olabe, *Christian Brothers University*
Laine Agee, *White Station High School*

Deconstruction Kits in Scratch: Designing Scratch Debugems for Learning Core Programming Concepts

Jean Griffin, *University of Pennsylvania*
Eliot Kaplan, *University of Pennsylvania*
Quinn Burke, *University of Pennsylvania*
Yasmin Kafai, *University of Pennsylvania*

The Laptop Instrument

Kristin Raudonis, *Villanova University*

Getting CS Undergraduates to Communicate Effectively

Andreas Karatsolis, *Carnegie Mellon University Qatar*
Iliano Cervesato, *Carnegie Mellon University Qatar*
Yonina Cooper, *Carnegie Mellon University Qatar*
Khaled Harras, *Carnegie Mellon University Qatar*
Kemal Oflazer, *Carnegie Mellon University Qatar*
Nael Abu-Ghazaleh, *Carnegie Mellon University Qatar*
Thierry Sans, *Carnegie Mellon University Qatar*

What Today's College Students Know About Technology and What They Don't

Mary Jo Geise, *The University of Findlay*
Helen Schneider, *The University of Findlay*

Student-Authored Wiki Textbooks in Computer Science

Edward Gehringer, *North Carolina State University*

Impact of Direct Tutoring that Utilizes Visual Learning and Translations for Deaf Students

Brian Trager, *National Technical Institute for the Deaf*
Raja Kushalnagar, *National Technical Institute for the Deaf*

Programming By Voice with Scratch

Jeff Gray, *University of Alabama*
Ramaraju Rudraraju, *University of Alabama*
Srinivasa Datla, *University of Alabama*
Avishek Banerjee, *University of Alabama*
Mandar Sudame, *University of Alabama*

Analyzing the Similarity of Scratch Programs to Detect Plagiarism

Jeff Gray, *University of Alabama*
Brittany Stewart, *University of Alabama*
Joel Tully, *University of Alabama*
Joshua Swank, *University of Alabama*
Barrett Bryant, *University of Alabama*

VIBES: Visual Interpreter of Bytecodes for Educating Students

Cory Sheeley, *William Penn University*
Caitlyn Pickens, *Lake Forest College*
William Clements, *University of Wisconsin - Oshkosh*

Teaching Computer Science Concepts Using Computer Science Unplugged and Kodu

Daniela Marghitu, *Auburn University*
Taha Ben Brahim, *Auburn University*
Yasmeen Rawajfih, *Auburn University*

Major Challenges Facing Computing Programs at Community Colleges

Elizabeth Hawthorne, *Union County College*
Robert Campbell, *CUNY Graduate Center*
Karl Klee, *Alfred State College*
Anita Wright, *Camden County College*

Students Believe Live Coding Helps Them Learn

Kristin Vadas Marsicano, *Georgia Institute of Technology*
Jay Summet, *Georgia Institute of Technology*

A Deconstruction Kit for the LilyPad Arduino: Designing Debugging Sets for Learning about Circuitry & Programming for High School Students

Eliot Kaplan, *University of Pennsylvania*
Jean Griffin, *University of Pennsylvania*
Yasmin Kafai, *University of Pennsylvania*
Quinn Burke, *University of Pennsylvania*

Introducing Case Study Based Teaching in Computing Curricula

Salamah Salamah, *Embry Riddle Aeronautical University*
Massood Towhidnejad, *Embry Riddle Aeronautical University*
Thomas Hilburn, *Embry Riddle Aeronautical University*

Engaging Participants in the Ensemble Computing Pathway

Luke Segars, *University of California, Berkeley*
Dan Garcia, *University of California, Berkeley*

Graph Algorithms Using Highway Mapping Data and the Google Maps API

James Teresco, *Siena College*

Universal Design for Learning in CS1

Suzanne Rivoire, *Sonoma State University*

A Grounded Embodied Approach to the Instruction of Computational Thinking

Cameron Fadjo, *Teachers College, Columbia University*
John Black, *Teachers College, Columbia University*

SIGCSE 2011 Video Exhibition Abstracts

Speaking in Code

Andreas Stefik, Kim Slattery, Susanna Siebert, *Southern Illinois University Edwardsville*

The blind and visually impaired community must overcome significant technical and practical barriers in order to succeed in the computer science discipline. In collaboration with five schools for the blind across the United States, we are trying to help by creating a national educational infrastructure for teaching computer programming to blind and visually impaired students. In this video, we highlight our first blind programming workshop at the Washington State School for the Blind, where students and their teachers learned about computer science, the challenges of programming with limited or no vision, and our auditory integrated development environment: Sodbeans.

Reaching Out (Binary Codes)

Tim Bell, *University of Canterbury*
Michael Bell, *Orange Studio (NZ)*

This may look like a video that teaches about binary numbers, but it also contains steganographic codes (hidden messages). The lyrics explain how the main code works, but there are actually over 20 hidden messages in the video using various musical and visual encodings (drums, horns, dance moves, background colors etc.). The codes only use binary numbers, and the video is intended as an extended exercise in working in binary. Some simple warm-up songs and more information are provided at csunplugged.org/modem to ease students into the exercise. The main message is coded in the tune of the song using the same idea as a modem – a high tone is a one, and a low tone is a zero. The title of the song is from the theme of the 2010 SIGCSE conference.

Santa's Dirty Socks (Divide and Conquer)

Tim Bell, *University of Canterbury*
Michael Bell, *Orange Studio (NZ)*
Victor Chicha, *Ecole des Mines de Nantes, France*

This original story introduces the idea of a divide-and-conquer algorithm using a narrated picture-book verse about the serious problem of finding a pair of dirty socks that have been accidentally wrapped with a child's present. This story can be played or read to students, and used as the basis of a follow-up discussion. A set of discussion starter questions is available (csunplugged.org/DivideAndConquer) to encourage students to engage in computational thinking and think about algorithm analysis – in the story 1024 presents are searched in 10 steps, and students can be asked to extend this to other cases, and generally think about the implications of having an algorithm with logarithmic complexity (but not necessarily using any of that terminology!)

Introducing Scrape, A Visualization Tool for the Analysis of Scratch Code

Ursula Wolz, Brett Taylor, Christopher Hallberg
Computer Science and Interactive Multimedia, *The College of New Jersey*

Scrape is a visualization tool for analyzing the quality of Scratch (mit.scratch.edu) code. Scrape enables users to discern whether code is using traditional computational forms or perhaps inventing new ones. Scrape generates a visual representation of code for a fresh perspective on the quantifiable characteristics of any Scratch program. This video demonstrates the core functionalities of Scrape and then provides a rationale for this sort of analysis. By abstracting and visualizing code statistics, it is easy to draw conclusions about programs, categorize programs based on analyst-defined criteria, and find patterns in code from similar or dissimilar sources. The benefits of taking a step back and studying code structure and contents is shown. Find more information at happyanalyzing.com.

The Recursive Case

Lucas Starrett, David Zinn, *Purdue ROCS*

Recursion is an almost magical method of solving problems — a function that, when having not yet found the answer to a given problem, simply calls itself again! Recursion can be a difficult concept to grasp, but hopefully made simpler by experiencing Private Investigator Ruby's search for 5 factorial in "The Recursive Case."

Intel(R) Manycore Testing Lab: A Hands-On Approach to Integrating Parallelism in Today's Classrooms

Jennifer Teal Levine, *Intel Academic Community, Intel*

How will students gain the parallel programming experience that they need — and that employers require — if they don't have access to modern multi-core hardware? The Intel® Manycore Testing Lab provides free remote access to state-of-the art, 32-core software development environments for academics worldwide. Learn how you can engage students with hands-on manycore testing, demonstrate software scaling up to 32 cores / 64 threads, and even conduct research to support parallelism and scalability in the classroom. Prepare your students to compete in today's job market as parallel programming and manycore processors reshape the computing industry. Extend your college hardware and software budgets with remote access to a wide range of industry-leading software tools and resources.

How Much Is That Hole?

Madalene Spezialetti, *Trinity College*

The We Dig Holes Company digs holes…and they dig neat holes. But how do they determine how much to charge for a hole? It's an art they say, based on years of experience and dealing with the many surprises found in holes. But can computing help this hole-digging family determine hole costs and pricing? The owners talk about (and the viewers observe) the wide-ranging factors that can effect hole pricing, as well as the varied and vague measurements the proprietors use to determine the price of a well-dug hole. The viewer is challenged to devise ways in which computing tools can help turn the art of hole pricing into a science … and help the We Dig Holes company answer the question "How much is that hole?"

SIGCSE 2011 SRC Graduate Student Research Abstracts

Automatic Semantics Discovery for Adaptive Web-based Educational Courses

Marian Simko, *Slovak University of Technology*

In order to make the learning process more effective, educational systems tailor learning material to user goals, needs and characteristics. Adequate adaptation requires a domain description enabling adaptation engines to make at least basic reasoning. State-of-the-art approaches rely mostly on domain experts or teachers, who supply an adaptive system with necessary semantic descriptions. In our work we aim at automatic semantics acquisition for adaptive courses. We proposed a method for automatic domain relationship discovery based on content processing leveraging graph algorithms. We evaluated our approach in a domain of learning programming by utilizing the automatically generated domain model to support course navigation with recommendation of learning objects.

Augmenting Educational Tools through Conversion to Games

Acey Boyce, *University of North Carolina at Charlotte*

Video games have been shown to have great potential for use as educational tools. Their combination of internal motivation, challenge, and replayability make them ideal designs for effective educational software. Many successful educational tools currently do not feature these three key elements. Through our work on BeadLoom Game we have shown that by augmenting educational tools with game elements we can increase the enjoyment, engagement, and learning gains resulting from use of the tool. Therefore our research is focused on analyzing BeadLoom Game to determine which game elements contribute to its success and developing a simple system for the conversion of educational tools into more successful educational games. Such a system would make a strong contribution to both the educational software and educational game communities and would allow us to bring out the full potential of all educational tools.

Adaptive Peer-Review in Computer Science Education

I-Han Hsiao, *University of Pittsburgh*

The value of peer review in the context of education has already been exploited and widely applied to real world classrooms. However, most of the peer-review related work focuses on writing-intensive courses and disciplines. In this paper, we propose an adaptive support for peer review by matching authors' and reviewers' knowledge levels. A peer review based collaborative quiz authoring system is designed, which integrates assessment, authoring, peer reviewing, and improving stages for creating Java programming quizzes. A synthesis summary of system design and study results is reported.

SIGCSE 2011 SRC Undergraduate Student Research Abstracts

Hiding In Images

Justin Babey, *Central Connecticut State University*

This project implements a steganographic technique that embeds secret information into the low order bits of the colors of a bitmap image. The algorithm employs a secret passphrase that both sender and receiver must know to communicate. Without this passphrase, an eavesdropper will be unable to read or even detect the secret message. The implementation embeds the hidden information into an image and automatically uploads it to a web server where it can be retrieved by the intended receiver. The information is embedded in such a way that there is very little statistical or perceivable abnormalities, so the medium does not arouse suspicion. The implementation has a simple user interface that provides a solid foundation for expansion into a full information security software package.

Investigating Computational Methods for Evaluating Putative Substrate Conformations in Cytochrome P450s

Zachary Zappala, *The College of New Jersey*

In biological systems, the chemical activities of cells are carried out by enzymes that carry out their work by binding to molecules known as substrates. A great challenge in the field of biology is to figure out which substrates bind to which enzymes. This research aims to automatically categorize computationally generated putative substrate conformations into one of seven different categories that represent different substrate orientations within the enzyme's active site; the individual parts of the program make this final goal possible.

TheCave: Using GPUs and Classical Philosophy to Data-Mine Images

Charles Stolper, *Furman University*

In The Republic, Plato's Cave Allegory describes how all instances of an object merely share the properties of an 'ideal form' of that object. Data-mining of images is crucial to numerous applications and a large subset of these applications require determining first what the contents of the image are before any interpretation can take place. The goal of TheCave was to create an extendable hardware/software architecture to perform an 'ideal form'-based content identification in order to facilitate data-mining.

A Computational Clustering Approach to Studying Metagenomics

Shanti Bramhacharya, *Hiram College*

Clustering genomic sequences can be very time consuming depending on the size and complexity of the sequences. The clustering algorithm I designed uses a greedy incremental approach using a banded global alignment and sorting clusters as optimization factors. All the data after clustering is made available to the user in a graphical interface along with analysis tools such as BLAST, the Ribosomal Database Project, abundance graphs, cluster summary and alignment. The program was designed to be a research and educational tool for biologists and their students.

Looking for Novel Subgroups in Mammography Data using a Modified Distance Metric for Clustering

Elizabeth Ellis, *Hiram College*

Mammography research has helped doctors identify potentially dangerous lesions in the breasts. We hope to take that research further by examining recorded mammogram data and the outcomes (malignant/benign) to find clusters that are different from the data as a whole yet are successfully classified by a classification model. To do this, we started by finding clusters that were different from each other and still strongly correlated to the classification feature. We tested two clustering algorithms (K-Means and Hierarchical) and developed a new distance metric to test against a simple Euclidean distance metric (to validate its use in our research).

Metaphor: A Declarative Approach to Computational Art

Shrutarshi Basu, *Lafayette College*

In recent years the use of computational tools has greatly increased in the art communities. Though popular computational tools provide powerful utilities and make possible brilliant works of art, they either (1) require the artist to become competent in programming, particularly procedural programming or (2) do not provide help in creating patterns. The Metaphor system takes a different approach -- its interaction model is based on declarative programming and it allows the artist to specify complex, beautiful patterns that will be generated using Lindenmayer systems. Artists describe relationships between image components without having to specify how those relationships are implemented. Furthermore the image generation component is replaceable allowing artists to use different rendering engines.

Implementing Ruppert's Algorithm for Generic Curves in 2D

Matthew Flatau, *Southwestern University*

Mesh generation involves dividing a generic domain (a shape) into many simpler regions (here, triangles). Scientific simulations require meshes for computation, but generating meshes for complex domains is often quite time-consuming. The two competing goals of mesh generation are to produce a mesh with: (1) well-shaped triangles and (2) as few triangles as possible. Ruppert's algorithm is widely used and guaranteed to accomplish both goals for inputs whose boundaries are straight lines. Naturally many shapes people would like to mesh have boundaries with curved portions that cannot be well-approximated by straight lines. While theoreticians have developed provable strategies for curved inputs, no full-featured code available is guaranteed to work on curved inputs. We provide a software package that handles a variety of smooth inputs in 2D, based on a minimal modification of Ruppert's algorithm.

Dance Tool: Creation of a New Culturally Situated Educational Game

Shaun Pickford, *University of North Carolina at Charlotte*

Use of Culturally Situated Design Tools (CSDTs) has been shown to be an effective method of teaching basic mathematical and Computer Science related concepts (Eglash, Bennett, O'Donnell, Jennings, & Cintorino, 2006). Converting these tools into games can improve learning gains and interest among players (Boyce & Barnes, 2010). Our project, Dance Tool, is a new culturally situated game that seeks to leverage dance and pop culture in order to teach grade school students introductory level Computer Science concepts.

Author Index

www.ingramcontent.com/pod-product-compliance
Lightning Source LLC
LaVergne TN
LVHW080108011026
849160LV00013B/1052
9781450305006